Beginnings
and
Beyond

FOUNDATIONS IN
EARLY CHILDHOOD
EDUCATION

7TH EDITION

Beginnings and Beyond

FOUNDATIONS IN EARLY CHILDHOOD EDUCATION

7TH EDITION

Ann Miles GORDON
Consultant
Sonoma, CA

Kathryn Williams BROWNE
Faculty, Early Childhood Education
Skyline College
San Bruno, CA

Voices of Experience
Josué Cruz, Jr.
Peter Mangione
Thelma Harms
Diane Trister Dodge
Sharon Lynn Kagan

THOMSON

DELMAR LEARNING   Australia   Brazil   Canada   Mexico   Singapore   Spain   United Kingdom   United States

THOMSON

DELMAR LEARNING

Beginnings & Beyond: Foundations in Early Childhood Education, Seventh Edition
Ann Miles Gordon & Kathryn Williams Browne

Vice President, Career Education SBU:
Dawn Gerrain

Director of Learning Solutions:
John Fedor

Managing Editor:
Robert L. Serenka, Jr.

Senior Acquisitions Editor:
Erin O'Connor

Editorial Assistant:
Alison Archambault

Director of Production:
Wendy A. Troeger

Production Manager:
Mark Bernard

Senior Content Project Manager:
Betty L. Dickson

Art Director:
Joy Kocsis

Director of Marketing:
Wendy E. Mapstone

Channel Manager:
Kristin McNary

Marketing Coordinator:
Scott A. Chrysler

Cover Design:
TDB Publishing Services

Library of Congress Cataloging-in-Publication Data

Gordon, Ann Miles.
  Beginnings & beyond : foundations in early childhood education / Ann Miles Gordon, Kathryn Williams Browne; voices of experience, Josué Cruz, Jr. . . . [et al.].—7th ed.
    p. cm.
  Includes bibliographical references and index.
  ISBN-13: 978-1-4180-4865-5
  ISBN-10: 1-4180-4865-8
  1. Early childhood education. 2. Early childhood education—Curricula. 3. Child development. I. Browne, Kathryn Williams. II. Cruz, Josué, 1946– III. Title. IV. Title: Beginnings and beyond. V. Title: Foundations in early childhood education.
  LB1139.23.G663   2007
  372.21—dc22
                                    2006038117

NOTICE TO THE READER

DEDICATION

To my wonderful granddaughter, Megan Lynn Miles. May you grow up with a discerning heart, a spirited intellect, and a life of grace and love.
—AMG

For Scott—A respected colleague, a fellow author, and the best brother a sister could be blessed to have.
—KWB

Contents

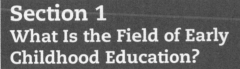

Section 1
What Is the Field of Early Childhood Education? 1

VOICE OF EXPERIENCE: CHALLENGES FACED BY TEACHERS OF EARLY CHILDHOOD EDUCATION by Josué Cruz, Jr., M.S., Ph.D. ✳ 2

CHAPTER 1
History of Early Childhood Education ✳ 5

CHAPTER 2
Types of Programs ✳ 47

Section 2
Who Is the Young Child? 93

VOICE OF EXPERIENCE: GROWING YOUR BRAIN: THE FIRST THREE YEARS ARE SPECIAL by Peter L. Mangione ✳ 94

CHAPTER 3
Defining the Young Child ✳ 97

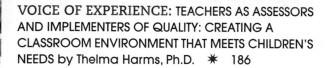

Section 3
Who Are the Teachers?   185

VOICE OF EXPERIENCE: TEACHERS AS ASSESSORS
AND IMPLEMENTERS OF QUALITY: CREATING A
CLASSROOM ENVIRONMENT THAT MEETS CHILDREN'S
NEEDS by Thelma Harms, Ph.D. * 186

Section 4
What Is Being Taught?   379

Section 5
How Do We Teach for Tomorrow?   585

VOICE OF EXPERIENCE: HOW DO WE TEACH
FOR TOMORROW? by Sharon L. Kagan,
M.A., Ed.D ✳ 586

Foreword

By Carol Brunson Day, Ph.D.

Carol Brunson Day is president of the National Black Child Development Institute and former president/CEO of the Council for Professional Recognition, Child Development Associate National Credentialing Program in Washington, DC. Dr. Day received her bachelor of arts degree in psychology from the University of Wisconsin, her master's in Early Childhood Education from Erikson Institute in Chicago, and her doctorate from Claremont Graduate School. Dr. Day has been involved in the profession of early childhood education since 1970. For many years she was a member of the Human Development Faculty at Pacific Oaks College in Pasadena and is a national expert on cultural influences on child development.

Many authors of child development texts have taken on the challenge to be sensitive and respectful of diversity, particularly cultural diversity. They often pursue that challenge by making mention of cultural differences in random places in their texts, or in some cases, devoting a chapter to the topic. What we read in *Beginnings & Beyond: Foundations in Early Childhood Education* is quite different. Throughout this seventh edition, Ann Gordon and Kate Browne respond to issues involving *human development diversity*.

Human development diversity involves thinking beyond the superficial approaches that stem from the desire to "respect" culture and cultural differences. For example, rather than just learning to reserve judgment about cultural habits, promoting human diversity means breaking the habit of thinking about children of African American, Hispanic, or Asian/Pacific Rim ancestry as having cultural qualities. To make genuine progress in how we address human diversity, we need to fundamentally change our subconscious responses, so that Western Eurocentric values no longer serve as the standard against which everything is judged or measured. In the pages of this text, we learn to see Western values as only one among many cultural takes on the world.

This kind of shift in perspective is transformational. It could free us to create the kind of new knowledge in human development that our science strives for— knowledge upon which to craft program practices that are liberating for children's growth and development in ways we never thought possible.

This edition provides experiences to assist us in this change process. By being asked to think about specific issues, we can be engaged in the work it will take to get Western Europe out of the center of our *thought* universe. As readers, we are cast in the role of change agents. Each of us can become active in reconstructing what we know about children and families. Toward this end, the seventh edition of *Beginnings & Beyond* offers the following strategies:

- **New facts must be added to our child development database to expand the limits of traditional care.**

  This text presents the fact that the history of early childhood goes back to a time before European thinkers, to the Nile Valley civilization. We are also pointed to sources of information and introduced to researchers and theorists from a wide variety of cultural backgrounds whose views are often neglected elsewhere. Through the practice of juxtaposing new material against the traditional, an important message comes through—our perspective on human development is dynamic and changing, and what we do "know" today is limited, incomplete, unfinished work.

- **We must be reminded of our ethnocentrism and helped to be reflective about it.**

  Up-front and straightforward statements punctuating this theme can be found throughout this text—statements such as "these things are true for one cultural group but not another." Messages such as these situate English-speaking white children of Western European ancestry as part of just one cultural group, one that does not represent all children. Since the earliest theories were based on observations of males or white subjects, we are admonished to not use one standard for "normal," and we are encouraged to question the generalizations of our knowledge. Thus, we are challenged to become and remain conscious of the risk of distortion in how we view developing children and their families.

- **We must consciously shift our goal from an emphasis on multiculturalism to an emphasis on pluralism.**

  As a melting pot/tossed salad debate is unveiled in the book, the opposing and contrasting views among various ethnic and cultural groups are presented. Important developmental topics such as group identity and bicultural development are posed and effectively discussed without falling in the traps of the either/or mentality to which the traditional melting pot of multiculturalism can succumb. A new frontier looms as an ideal, where the preservation of home culture is an important developmental goal for all children and their families.

- **Bias must be identified as a contributor to underdevelopment and discussed in its broadest sense.**

  Topics such as biracial identity development and homophobia are discussed here in the search for ways to make practices appropriate to development. We are given permission to address such topics as a matter of course and a vocabulary to use when addressing them. Bringing these topics to the discussion table adds to our ability to directly address bias and stereotypes—what teachers and other adults ought to do to prevent them from being obstacles to development.

- **We must promote activism among child development professionals in direct and indirect ways.**

  As this text tells us, eliminating inequality in our society will require a national reform agenda. Topics such as children's rights and strategies for social action must be discussed in our child development courses, and we must give students an abundance of examples to guide their thinking to new places. To this endeavor, the examples in this text come from the best voices of experience in the field—Peter Mangione, Diane Trister Dodge, and Sharon Lynn Kagan, among others.

It is very encouraging to have as a view of our field one that expects it to do better than it already has done. And it is empowering to know that the change requires each of us to participate. This seventh edition of *Beginnings & Beyond: Foundations in Early Childhood Education* is full of the action and energy one would expect in the place where change happens. It only awaits you to jump in and get busy.

Preface

Looking back on the last 25 years of writing *Beginnings & Beyond,* we see gradual but critical changes in early childhood education that affect our programs, policies, philosophies, and practices. A steady momentum and a strong commitment on the part of national and local early childhood leaders have transformed the field into today's dynamic profession. Through textbooks and teaching, today's students are more attuned to the influences of the schools of Reggio Emilia, the effects of anti-bias education, the implications of a career ladder, the significance of developmentally appropriate practices, the importance of social and cultural diversity, and the pressures of standards, among other things.

Throughout these 25 years, *Beginnings & Beyond: Foundations in Early Childhood Education* has expressed a viewpoint about quality early education and what practices ensure excellence. Particularly in the area of cultural sensitivity and multicultural relationships, we promote a "both/and" attitude, following the National Association for the Education of Young Children (NAEYC) guidelines for Developmentally Appropriate Practices. Readers will find the "both/and" influence throughout the text, but especially in the areas of early literacy, spiritual development, discipline, diversity and anti-bias strategies, and where cultural sensitivity is discussed. It is particularly emphasized in school and family relationships where cultural differences and distinctions are always at play.

Demographic issues continue to drive the direction of early childhood programs and the text reflects that fact. *Beginnings & Beyond* maintains the emphasis that every child and family is unique and that they deserve the respect and affirmation of their cultural identity. The seventh edition, therefore, persists with a multicultural approach to teaching and learning in order to help prospective teachers and caregivers increase their sensitivity to different cultural practices and values. We still weave a strong multicultural perspective and consciousness throughout the text, and this feature has become one of the book's strongest points.

The original purpose of the book remains "to promote the competence and effectiveness of new teachers through a presentation of basic knowledge, skills, attitudes, and philosophies, based on the premise that new teachers must have opportunities to learn fundamental skills as they begin their teaching experience." The overall organization of the book takes the reader from the history of early childhood education to current and future trends. Five basic questions set the tone for each section by asking the reader to reflect on the wide-ranging nature of early childhood education. The book's flexibility allows instructors to begin with any section that seems appropriate to meet the needs of their classes. In each of the sections, the topic question is expanded within the chapters.

- *What Is the Field?* In Section 1, early childhood history and types of programs provide a basis for understanding the complexity of the field in Chapters 1 and 2, respectively.

- *Who Is the Young Child?* In Section 2, a discussion of the young child's developmental growth in Chapter 3 provides students with an understanding of the nature of the children they will teach. This is followed in Chapter 4 by an exploration of the major theories and developmental topics on which sound early childhood principles and practices are based.

- *Who Are the Teachers?* The many functions of a teacher are explained in Section 3, beginning with the teacher's role defined in Chapter 5, followed by a discussion of the teacher's responsibility in observing and assessing the child in Chapter 6. Since guidance and behavior are a critical factor in the life of a classroom teacher, Chapter 7 helps the teacher learn strategies and practices that promote learning and self-discipline. Creating a partnership between families and teachers as explored in Chapter 8 offers the student a perspective on this all-important collaboration. Chapter 9 defines the environment as a child's teacher and makes the point that a teacher's deliberate use of the environment serves as a teaching strategy for appropriate behavior and learning to take place.

- *What Is Being Taught?* Curriculum areas are the focus of Section 4, beginning with an overview of early childhood curriculum basics in Chapter 10. Physical development (Chapter 11), cognitive development (Chapter 12), language development (Chapter 13), and affective development—emotional, social, creative, and spiritual growth (Chapter 14) follow. Each chapter explores the growth and development of the young child and looks at the teacher's role in relation to each, and provides curriculum plans in the environment, with materials and activities.

- *How Do We Teach for Tomorrow?* Section 5 helps the student take a broad look at the field today. It also serves as a bookend to the first chapter. As the significant issues in the field of early childhood education are explored, students become more aware of the comprehensive nature of working in the early childhood field today.

ANCILLARY MATERIALS

Instructor's Manual

Available with the seventh edition is an updated instructor's manual, which is a chapter-by-chapter plan for organizing a course using *Beginnings & Beyond*. In addition to chapter overviews, outlines, key terms, resource lists, and teaching tips, this manual will include a complete list of PowerPoint masters, arranged by chapter in the E-Resource. Instructions for using the E-Resource are also part of the manual.

 ### Online Companion™

You'll spot the Online Companion icon next to web references throughout the text, indicating where additional information or activities on that topic can be found in the online resource. The Online Companion also contains critical-thinking questions and activities for each "Insights" found in the text, and questions relevant to chapter learning objectives, which are presented for individual or group consideration. Web links and other resources are also included. The Online Companion can be found at www.earlychilded.delmar.com.

Professional Enhancement Series

Introduced with the sixth edition, an additional supplement to accompany the seventh edition is the Introduction to Early Childhood Education Professional Enhancement resource for students. This resource, which is part of Thomson Delmar Learning's Early Childhood Education Professional Enhancement series, focuses on key topics of interest to future early childhood teachers, directors, and caregivers. Some of the tools provided are:

- tips to getting off to a great start in your new environment.
- suggestions for materials that promote development for children from infancy through primary grades.

- tools to assist in observing children and gathering data to help set appropriate goals for individual children.
- case studies of relevant, realistic situations and best practices for successfully navigating them.
- insight into issues and trends facing early childhood educators today.

WebTUTOR

WebCT and Blackboard courseware, designed to help instructors create an online teaching and learning environment, is available for the seventh edition of *Beginnings & Beyond*. The courseware offers an easy-to-use, common interface with integrated tools and content for online course creation. Instructors can customize the course as much or as little as they wish, as there is a pre-built and class-ready course requiring minimal or no modification. Components of the courseware include:

- *Course Information Section*—Course Description, Required Materials, Course Objectives, Recommended Materials, Policies, Testing, Attendance, Grading.
- *Contents Section* with chapters organized according to core text.
- *Communication*—Chat, E-Mail, Calendar, White Board, and Discussion Area.
- *Tools*—Calendar, Search, Content Compile, Change Password, White Board options.
- *Student Progress Section*—My Records and Progress.
- *Resources*—Glossary of Terms, Web-link Resources.

ALL NEW ANCILLARY MATERIALS FOR THE 7TH EDITION

Front-of-Book CDs

The CDs contained in the front of this text include video clips of infants and toddlers, preschoolers, and school-age children in a variety of early childhood settings and at different developmental stages. Disc one contains video clips of infants and toddlers and preschool-age children; disc two contains video clips of school-age children. Please note that disc two contains the pre-school competencies: Professional; Program Management; and Social Development. Designed to integrate technology and early childhood education, this invaluable resource provides instructors and students with ample opportunities for reflection and personal and professional development. The Video View Point boxes found in each chapter can be used to connect the material presented in the text to the segments contained on the CDs. To view the video clips, place the appropriate CD in your computer; then select the age range (infants and toddlers, preschool, or school-age); then select the competency from the list that corresponds to the Video View Point for that chapter.

E-Resource

A special new accompaniment to this edition of *Beginnings & Beyond* is our E-Resource, which integrates Internet technology and early childhood education. The E-Resource includes an electronic copy of the Instructor's Manual, PowerPoint Masters, and the Computerized Test Bank (CTB).

The updated computerized test bank allows instructors to create student exams composed of multiple choice, true/false, short answer, and completion questions for each chapter. The CTB provides approximately 1,000 questions in addition to the following features:

- Multiple methods of question selection.
- Multiple outputs (print, ASCII, and Rich Text Format).
- Graphic support.
- Random questioning output.
- Special character support.

ABOUT THE AUTHORS

Ann Gordon has been in the field of early childhood for more than 40 years as a teacher of young children, a teacher of parents, and a teacher of college students. She has taught in laboratory schools, church-related centers, and private and public preschool and kindergarten programs. Ann taught at the Bing Nursery School, the laboratory school for Stanford University's Department of Psychology, for 11 years and was a lecturer in the Psychology Department. For 10 years she also served as an adjunct faculty member in four colleges, teaching the full gamut of early childhood courses. Ann served as executive director of the National Association of Episcopal Schools for 14 years, where more than 1,100 early childhood programs were a part of her network. She is now consulting in the areas of early childhood curriculum, governance, and professional development. Ann is the mother of two grown children, and a doting grandmother. She brings an enhanced perspective on infants and toddlers to *Beginnings & Beyond*, as well as up-to-date experience with center-based child care. She is delighted that her granddaughter Megan is enrolled in an NAEYC-accredited center. Semi-retired, Ann is currently working with Kate on three other textbooks.

Kathryn Williams Browne has been a teacher most of her adult life: a teacher of young children for nearly 20 years, a parent educator for 15, and a mentor for teachers and an instructor of college students for more than 20 years. Her work with children includes nursery school, parent cooperatives, full-day child care, pre-kindergarten and bilingual preschools, and kindergarten and first grade. Kate's background in child development research led her to choose early childhood education, for to truly understand child development one needs to *be* with children. While a head teacher at Bing Nursery School and a lecturer with Stanford University, Kate developed a professional relationship with Ann, which blossomed into working together in teacher and parent education. Moreover, *Beginnings & Beyond* has been influenced by Kate's role as a parent; her two children were born during the first two editions, so the book grew along with them. Work as a consultant and public elementary school board trustee offered Kate new perspectives into schools, reform, and collaboration. Perhaps most important, Kate has been teaching in California community colleges, which offer the richness of a diverse student population coupled with the

challenges of access and privilege that parallel those in the early education field itself. Working closely with her students, she has been given constructive insights that inform this text in every revision. The balance of career and family, of work *with* children and *for* children, and of the special challenges of diversity and professionalism of early childhood education guide her work.

Ann and Kate are also co-authors of *Guiding Young Children in a Diverse Society* (Allyn & Bacon, 1996), and *Beginning Essentials in Early Childhood Education* (Delmar, 2007).

UNIQUE FEATURES

- *What Do You Think?*, a boxed question in each chapter brings attention to a relevant topic and invites the student to reflect on the concept in relation to his or her own life and learning.

- Each *Voice of Experience* lends other professional voices to the test. Nationally renowned leaders in the field of early childhood education address important issues as an introduction to each section of the text. Representing a broad range of influences, backgrounds, and experiences, this edition is enhanced by the contributions of Josué Cruz, Peter Mangione, Thelma Harms, Diane Trister Dodge, and Sharon Lynn Kagan.

- *Insights* continue to be a popular staple of each chapter. In order to engage the reader more effectively, the authors have made the Insights more student-centered, focusing on the practical application that illustrates a fundamental part of the chapter. Insight contributors to this edition are Scott Williams, the late Edith Dowley, Francis Wardle, Rosalind Charlesworth, Barbara Biglan, Karen Wiggins-Dowler, Elizabeth Crary, Libby Miles, Louise Cadwell, Marjorie Kostelnik, Rae Pica, Arleen Prarie, Wilma de Meléndez, and Sue Warford. They add a useful and relevant opinion to every chapter.

- *Our Diverse World*, a footnote at the bottom of a page, provides additional information to enrich the student's understanding of cultural pluralism and inclusion. A primary function of Our Diverse World is to help students learn that the children they teach will have to interact in new and different ways with others in a world grown small.

- Culturally and Developmentally Appropriate Practice (DAP) is clearly the subtheme of *Beginnings & Beyond*. In the creation of this book we emphasized the importance of creating programs and building curriculum based on an understanding of the nature of the child and the factors affecting a child's growth and development. We have maintained the feature Word Pictures in Chapter 3, which describe the major charac-

teristics of children from infancy through age eight. Under each photo of the children of various ages, there are questions prompting the student to use the Word Pictures to plan age-appropriate activities and responses. This helps students become familiar with expected behaviors in young children as a frame of reference in creating programs and planning curriculum that responds to the children's interests as well as their abilities and needs. At the same time, it is imperative that the student realize the deep and crucial contributions that children's family, culture, and language make to development. NAEYC's years of experience in the definition and application of developmentally appropriate practice has given us further insights, which are reflected throughout the book, but especially in Chapters 2, 3, 4, 6, 7, 9, 10, and 11 through 14. The Voices of Experience and Insight articles complement and demonstrate DAP as well.

- The use of technology. A unique feature of this text is the Video View Points section that allows students and instructors to relate important chapter content to video clips provided on the CD at the back of the book. Critical thinking questions that tie to both the concepts presented in the book and the clips on the CD provide students with ample opportunities for reflection and to promote their development as future early childhood professionals.

ACKNOWLEDGMENTS

We owe a great deal to the colleagues who contributed their thoughts and support and we thank them for adding their thoughts and ideas to this edition. Carol, your kind words in the preface launch our newest edition; Josué, Peter, Thelma, Diane, and Lynn, your voices add depth and meaning to the five sections you introduce. Scott, (the late) Edith, Francis, Roz, Karen, Barb, Betsy, Libby, Louise, Marjorie, Rae, Arleen, Wilma, and Sue, your insights make each chapter come alive. Thanks also to Louise Boyd Cadwell for furnishing pictures of the St. Louis-Reggio Collaborative class-rooms; to Robin Reed, developmental editor, for her positive enthusiasm and gentle nudging; and to Barb Tucker, our project editor, for being such a good sport as we moved through the production process.

Our reviewers, whose valuable gift of time and energy enhances the book's use-fulness, have been superb with their insights and suggestions. We want to thank:

Audrey Beard
Albany State University

Mary Cordell
Navarro College

Leann Curry
Midwestern State University

Marsha Grace
Texas A&M–Corpus Christi

Jennifer Jones
Baker College of Muskegon

Sheri Leafgren
Kent State University

Trish Saccomano
University of Utah

Patricia Weaver
Fayetteville Technical College

Alan Weber
Suffolk County Community College

Gloria Tansits Wenze
University of Scranton

Stacey York
Minneapolis Community and
    Technical College

Section 1

What Is the Field of Early Childhood Education?

VOICE OF EXPERIENCE

CHALLENGES FACED BY TEACHERS OF EARLY CHILDHOOD EDUCATION

Josué Cruz, Jr., M.S., Ph.D.

In the last decade and a half, the boundaries of the profession have changed rather dramatically for teachers. As we have become a more complex and diverse society, the roles traditionally ascribed to teachers have taken new meaning and significance. In the case of teachers of young children, their role has expanded to encompass many, heretofore, duties and responsibilities that were often considered to be part of the home.

Young children, for all intents and purposes, have become a social and political commodity. The welfare and education of children have become fair game for those seeking to win votes or sympathy for a particular cause. Consequently, teachers are finding themselves in the midst of a social revolution between forces competing for the hearts and minds of parents and their children. On the one side are those that advocate for custodial care and on the other those that promote learning. Both sides have caused sufficient upheaval in the profession such that what teachers of young children should know and be able to do has taken new meaning.

Early childhood educators face insurmountable challenges in meeting their professional obligations. Aside from the traditional roles that teachers have assumed, they are now expected to serve as curriculum specialists, diagnosticians, health care providers, family counselors, adult educators, program managers, child development experts, child advocates, mental health specialists, nutrition specialists, and many others too numerous to list. At the same time, the teaching profession is confronting new notions of pedagogy and more intense scrutiny by professional groups. With the focus on standards, readiness intiatives, assessment, and other forms of accountability, the field of early education is truly being reinvented.

Because the early years have now become a *cause célèbre* for many people and groups, there is no shortage of self-described experts ready to promote their opinions and solutions for the care and education of young children. Unfortunately, such entities often lack the preparation and the grounding in the various bodies of knowledge that comprise the field of early care and education. For example, all

too often the curriculum is misunderstood and looked upon as something that teachers do *to* children and not as something that teachers do *with* children. Parents are frequently considered a part of the physical landscape and not as the child's first teacher or partner in the teaching and learning enterprise. Here teachers are relegated to assembly line roles and pressured to keep to a certain instructional time schedule under the guise of teaching and children learning. This approach to the care and education of young children will surely undermine the current mantra of "no child left behind." In this highly politicized environment of schools and child care, early educators are faced with the challenge of defining what to teach, when to teach it, and why it is important to teach it, all against enormous barriers.

The challenges are, indeed, daunting. But it is important for us as a profession to be able to assure the public that we know what children should know and when they should know it. As professionals, early educators must take ownership of the challenges and provide the leadership to make it happen. The early childhood profession is not for the faint of heart or the passive individual. We are an active, demanding, and complex profession and we must be willing to step forward and assume the leadership of our field. Our ability to communicate with others around the world and share our knowledge about teaching and learning is an opportunity that will allow our voices to be heard and to improve our services to all children and families.

Early educators are the first line of defense in the teaching and learning of young children. The impact we have today will be felt tomorrow and for generations to come. Hence, our legacy will be revealed.

JOSUÉ CRUZ, JR.

JOSUÉ CRUZ, JR., has an M.S. in Early Childhood Education from the University of Wisconsin, Milwaukee, and a Ph.D. in Education from the University of Wisconsin, Madison.

CHAPTER 1

History of Early Childhood Education

QUESTIONS FOR THOUGHT

What distinguishes early childhood education from other levels of education?

Why is it important to know about the history of early childhood education?

How has our field been influenced from abroad?

What are nontraditional perspectives that we include in our thinking?

What are the major American influences to our field?

What other fields have influenced the development of the early childhood philosophy? What has been their impact?

What have been the basic themes in early childhood education throughout history?

How do current events—political, social, and economic—affect the direction of education?

Please refer to Figure 1-2, A Timeline for Early Childhood Education, as you read this chapter.

INTRODUCTION TO THE FIELD

Early childhood education has a rich and exciting history. In this chapter, the story of its development is also the chronicle of courageous people who took steps toward improving children's lives. Critical events have had a hand in shaping the history of early childhood education. As the images of the child change through the centuries, so, too, does the education of the young child and the educators themselves.

For the moment, imagine yourself as a time traveler. As you go back in time, you span the centuries and meet the people whose vision helped to shape our profession. You learn how Froebel's own unhappy childhood inspired a new way of teaching called the kindergarten. You see the passion and struggle of Montessori as she convinces the world that "slum children" can learn and succeed. In the 1960s, you witness the dedication of America to create a program for preschoolers known as "Head Start."

New models are forged through necessity and innovation, thus changing what we know about children and their care and education. The energies of so many on behalf of children have produced bold ideas, creative models, even contrary beliefs and practices. Across the globe and through the centuries, the education of young children has evolved.

Why History?

Most early childhood students and many educators know little about the origins of their chosen profession. The names of Rousseau, Froebel, Montessori, and Dewey may not seem to have much significance at this time (although many teachers are familiar with some of their techniques), but knowing something about the roots of this profession is important. Every time period has social and political events that influenced the reaction of people at the time, which then influenced how children were raised and educated. Further, most of these individuals were crusaders for education. Their thinking was revolutionary, often going against the mainstream of the time, and always offering insights that changed our ways of educating children. Let their voices be heard, so you can develop your own.

What do YOU Think?

Do you currently work in a center or family child-care setting? What is its history? Which people or ideas inform the school's approach? Who of the historical figures in this chapter influences you as you arrange the environment? Plan the curriculum? Interact with children and their families?

First, there is a sense of *support* that comes from knowing that history. Contemporary education has its roots in the past; finding a suitable beginning point for that past helps provide an educator with perspective. New insights blend with ideas from past traditions, as the history of early childhood education is truly a history of rediscovery.

Think about this, then: The "education" of the 21st century actually stems from children's schooling thousands of years ago.

For instance, works of Socrates, Plato, and Aristotle are part of the philosophical foundation on which our educational practices are built. Schools in ancient Greece and Rome taught literature, the arts, and science. These subjects are part of schools across the country today. One can see how traditional early childhood practices reflect and reinforce the European values and beliefs.[1]

However, in order to recognize and respect all cultures of our children, we need to look beyond the dominant culture. Unfortunately, most common historical documents are works of Western Europe and European-American only. A search for historical records from diverse cultures would be beneficial to understanding the full "American" educational experience. For instance, both oral and written records exist describing education in Africa, particularly about those cultures found in the Nile Valley (Hilliard, 1997). In more current terms, teachers must educate themselves about the culturally diverse roots of early educational practices.

Knowing that early childhood *philosophy* has deep roots can be an *inspiration* and helps teachers develop *professional expression*. As early

1 To honor diversity, all perspectives deserve a place in our history. Educators can focus on many cultures, thus broadening everyone's viewpoints.

Video VIEW Point 1-1

COMPETENCY: Professionalism

AGE GROUP: Preschool

CRITICAL THINKING QUESTIONS:

1. List the characteristics of professions that describe the work of an early childhood teacher, and then add a component from your work or your knowledge of early childhood in your community.

2. What stage of professional development best describes you? What activities will help you grow professionally?

childhood educators, we must learn to express our ideas, finding our own voice. **Professionalism** in education "relates to doing things well, at the right time, and for the right reason" (Spodek, Saracho, & Peters, 1988). The past as well as the present and future must be considered when developing sound educational programs for young children. The *tenets* expressed by past educators help develop better methods of teaching. Looking at history gives an overview of how various ages looked at children and their learning, based on the religious, political, and economic pressures of the time. Reviewing the professional record demonstrates how the needs of society affect education. Perhaps some of the mistakes of the past can be avoided if history is remembered.

Drawing upon knowledge of the past creates an awareness and understanding of changes in education. Into the fabric of early childhood education are woven many threads of influence that are responsible for current philosophies. By understanding and telling the story of the past, we are better equipped to interpret our own history, to have a sense of mission and purpose. "Doing history" is a good idea for early childhood educators, for Spodek tells us:

When we [become] early childhood educators, each of us accepts as our own, either deliberately or implicitly, the mission that is central to our field: We are committed to enhancing the education, development, and well-being of young children. Our saga helps renew our sense of identity and commitment to our profession. (Spodek in Bauch, 1988)

We also get in touch with our own early childhood and education (see "Insights" by Scott Williams at the end of this chapter), thus connecting us to the children of long ago, ourselves, and those we care for every day.

All professions have a canon of beliefs and practices. As you acquire this knowledge, you begin to develop your own *philosophy of teaching* (based, in part, on information gathered this chapter). As you do, be sure to constantly rethink your practices. Every professional should reexamine itself on a regular basis, and each professional teacher must do the same. For while understanding historical records makes sense for professional development, recognizing that they are a reflection of certain cultural norms is also crucial. Remember that the voices you hear in these chapters aren't from on high. Learn to be particularly suspect of the current proclaimed universal American practices that have to do with

- early attainment of individuality and independence;
- the necessity of early and free exploration;
- the critical importance of the early stimulation of intellect and language.

These are the three areas that previous research has seen as universal, which cross-cultural research has shown not to be. The first reflects a priority of many Western European cultures, but is not a common practice in societies that promote group harmony and interdependence. Second, many indigenous groups hold their very young children close, carrying them along while they work; there is no data that indicate these children develop poorly. Third, while American educational systems of early 21st century are being built on increasing academic and intellectual standards, there is no universal mandate for an exclusive focus on this developmental domain in the early years. Figure 1-1 offers other traditional educational practices, their historical context, and alternatives to consider as you create your own educational philosophy.

As authors, we strive to offer a broader view of our field, including its history. We recognize, for instance, that schools of the past were overwhelmingly created for boys and young men. This gender bias added to the underdevelopment of girls and women, and prevails today in some parts of the world. By understanding the concept of institutional as well as individual oppression, teachers can begin to examine their own notions and become "critical consumers" of information, both from the past and present.

Reflecting on Practices: Building Your Philosophy of Teaching

Educational Practice	Historical Context and ECE Trend/Practice	Think Again . . .
Same-age grouping	K–12 schools in the United States since 1850s target curriculum goals.	• Learning takes place with "guided collaboration," which often occurs with an older "expert."
		• Children learn when challenged to accommodate to higher level thinking, likely to occur with a mixed-age range.
		• Developing values of caring and responsibility happen best when children practice helping and protecting younger children.
		• Reduced family size indicates that multi-age experiences should happen in schooling.
		• Diversity (gender, culture, exceptionality, etc.) makes strict target goals unrealistic.
Daily schedules	Routines are the framework for programs, offering security and predictability.	• Children's sense of time is unlike that of adults, so rigid schedules do not correspond to their development.
		• Brain research indicates a need for stimulation, change, and challenge rather than the same structure constantly.
Curriculum is at the center of good programs	A plan for learning should be driven by specific outcomes in order to be assured that children are learning.	• Not following an adult-planned and driven curriculum worked well for geniuses such as Einstein, Erikson, and Bill Gates.
		• Educators as diverse as Dewey and Steiner promoted curricula based on children's interests or innate spirit.
		• Children appear to learn well through a curriculum that emerges, following their interests and timetable.

FIGURE 1-1 As you develop a philosophy of teaching, be sure to examine common beliefs and practices of the profession.

However, educational programs that included girls and the role of people of color in the early childhood movement are documented, if not always in the dominant literature of the time (see nontraditional perspectives later in this chapter and the footnotes on Our Diverse World throughout the book).

Every culture has had and still does have the task of socializing and educating their young. So although the written record may document a part of educational philosophy and teaching, there is no single monopoly on ideas about raising and educating children. Educational changes of a more recent nature follow. The impact of other disciplines, such as medicine and psychology, and the recurrent themes of early childhood education are also explored.

Defining the Terms

The term **early childhood education** refers to group settings deliberately intended to effect developmental changes in children from birth to eight years of age. In school terms, it includes group settings for infants through the primary years of elementary school, kindergarten through third grade. In programmatic terms, the education of young children includes formal and informal group settings regardless of their initial purpose. For instance, after-school programs for elementary ages are included, as are their formal academic sessions.

Early childhood educators thus build bridges between a child's two worlds, school (or group experience) and home. It is during these years that the foundation for future learning is set; these are the **building block years**, during which a child learns to walk, talk, establish an identity, print, and count. In later years, that same child builds on these skills to be able to climb mountains, speak a second language, learn to express and negotiate, write in cursive, and understand multiplication.

INFLUENCES FROM ABROAD

When did early childhood education first begin? Refer to Figure 1-2, *A Timeline for Early Childhood Education*, as you read this chapter. Getting a visual sense of when and where things happened can help you make sense of the various threads in our tapestry of early childhood educational history. It is impossible to pinpoint the origins of humankind because there are few records from millions of years ago. Some preparation for adult life was done informally, mostly through imitation. As language developed, communication occurred. Children learned dances, rituals, and ceremonies, and both boys and girls were taught skills for their respective roles in the tribe. Ancient historical documents seem to indicate that child-rearing practices were somewhat crude; DeMause (1974) even suggests that the further one goes back in history, the more likely the case of abandonment and brutality.

In Ancient Times

The definition of childhood has varied greatly throughout history. For example, in ancient times children were considered adults by age seven. A society's definition of childhood influences how it educates its children.

Many of our own practices are founded on those developed in Greece and Rome. Greek education—and virtually all classical European schooling—was provided for the boys of wealthy families, while girls and working-class children received training for domestic work or a trade.[1,2]

Education began by age six or seven, although Plato and Aristotle both spoke of the need to educate the younger child. Some ancient Romans felt that education should begin at home as soon as a child began to talk, and highlighted the use of rewards and ineffectiveness of corporal punishment (Hewes, 1993).

Probably the first education in schools outside the home or homelike apprenticeship was in ancient Greek and Roman times. Plato (427 B.C.), Aristotle (384–323 B.C.), Cicero (143–106 B.C.), and Polybius (222–204 B.C.) founded schools, with the model of small-group tutoring, teaching wealthy boys thinking skills, governing, military strategy, and managing commerce. Our word educate comes from a Latin verb *educare*, through a French verb *educere*, to draw forth or to lead.

As the Roman Empire deteriorated and society fell apart (400–1200 A.D.), childhood lasted barely past infancy. Although education was the responsibility of parents, most were busy fighting for survival. Childhood was not seen as a separate time of life, and children were used as a labor force. People left villages and towns for the safety of a local baron or king, and schools ceased to exist. Few members of the ruling class could read or write their names, and the monastery schools were for priests and religious instruction only.

The education of children was fairly simple before the 15th century; there was no educational system, and the way of life was uncomplicated as well. The church control of school in the medieval period meant that education projected a view of children as basically evil in their natural state. The value of education was in preparation for an afterlife. Children learned mostly through their parents or by apprenticeship outside the family. The child was expected and encouraged to move into adulthood as fast as possible. Survival was the primary goal in life. Because the common religious belief was that people were naturally evil, children had to be directed, punished, and corrected constantly.

What little we know of systematic learning developed during the Dark Ages through the policies of Charlemagne—who proclaimed that

---

1   Early childhood professionals need to keep in mind the heavy influence of Western European thought in the philosophy that dictates our teaching practice, especially when working with children from families of non-Western European cultures.

2   Keep in mind how much of the research and history in our field has a race, class, and gender bias (i.e., the tendency to be based on the experiences of, writings about, and research on white, middle-upper-class males).

Authors' Note: A debt of gratitude is owed to D. Keith Osborn for his outstanding historical research and to James L. Hymes, Jr., for his generous time and perspective.

5th–3rd centuries BC to AD 1400s Few records exist concerning child-rearing practices; the development of cities gives rise to schooling on a larger scale.

1423 & 1439 The invention of printing and movable type allows knowledge to spread rapidly; ideas and techniques become available to large numbers of people; printing is credited with bringing about the end of the Middle Ages and the beginning of the Renaissance.

1592–1670 Johann Amos Comenius

1657 *Orbis Pictus*, by Comenius, is the first children's book with pictures.

1632–1714 John Locke
English philosopher, considered the founder of educational philosophy, who postulated that children are born with a *tabula rasa*, or clean slate, on which all experiences are written.

1712–1788 Jean Jacques Rousseau

1762 *Emile*, by Rousseau, proclaims the child's natural goodness.

1746–1826 Johann Heinrich Pestalozzi

1801 *How Gertrude Teaches Her Children*, by Pestalozzi, emphasizes home education.

1740–1860s Sabbath Schools and Clandestine Schools are established as facilities to educate African Americans in the United States.

1782–1852 Friedrich Wilhelm Froebel

1826 *Education of Man*, by Froebel, describes the first system of kindergarten education as a "child's garden," with activities known as "gifts from God."

1837 Froebel opens the first kindergarten in Blankenburgh, Germany.

1861 Robert Owen sets up infant school in New Lanark, England, as an instrument of social reform for children of parent workers in his mills.

1873 The Butler School at Hampton Institute is opened as a free school for black children, including kindergarten curriculum for five-year-olds.

1837 Horace Mann, known as the "Father of the Common Schools" because of his contributions in setting up the U.S. elementary school system, becomes Secretary of Massachusetts State Board of Education.

1856 Margarethe Schurz opens the first American kindergarten, a German-speaking class in her home in Watertown, Wisconsin.

1804–1894 Elizabeth Peabody

1860 Elizabeth Peabody opens the first English-speaking kindergarten in Boston.

1843–1916 Susan Blow

1873 First public school kindergarten, supported by Superintendent William Harris, is directed by Susan Blow in St. Louis, Missouri, who becomes the leading proponent of Froebel in America. The first public kindergarten in North America opens in 1871 in Ontario, Canada.

1856–1939 Sigmund Freud (see Chapter 4)

1892 Freud cites the importance of early experiences to later mental illness, ushering in the beginning of psychoanalysis and the emphasis on the importance of the first five years.

1858–1952 John Dewey

1896 John Dewey establishes a laboratory school at the University of Chicago and develops a pragmatic approach to education, becoming the father of the Progressive Movement in American education.

1897 *My Pedagogic Creed* is published, detailing the opposition to rote learning and the philosophy of educating "the whole child."

1860–1931 Margaret McMillan

1911 Deptford School, an open-air school in the slums of London, is opened by Margaret McMillan. The school emphasizes health and play, thus coining the phrase "nursery school."

1868–1946 Patty Smith Hill

1893 Patty Smith Hill becomes director of the Louisville Free Kindergarten Society, augmenting her original Froebelian training with her work in scientific psychology (G. Stanley Hall) and progressive education (John Dewey). She goes on to found the National Association of Nursery Education (now known as NAEYC) in 1926.

1870–1952 Maria Montessori (see Chapters 1 and 2)

1907 Casa di Bambini (Children's House) is opened by Maria Montessori in a slum district in Rome, Italy. She later develops an educational philosophy and program to guide children's growth through the senses and practical life experiences.

FIGURE 1-2 A Timeline for Early Childhood Education.

1874–1949 Edward Thorndike, behavioral psychologist (see Chapter 4)

1878–1958 John B. Watson, behavioral psychologist (see Chapter 4)

1878–1967 Lucy Sprague Mitchell

1916 The Bureau of Educational Experiments, which becomes Bank Street College of Education (and laboratory school) in 1922, is founded by L. S. Mitchell, who is a leading proponent of progressive education at the early childhood level.

1879 The first psychological laboratory is established in Germany to train psychologists in the systematic study of human beings.

1880 First teacher-training program for kindergartners, Oshkosh Normal School, Pennsylvania.

1880–1961 Arnold Gesell (see Chapter 4)

1923 Gesell, originally a student of G. Stanley Hall, publishes *The Preschool Child*, which emphasizes the importance of the early years.

1926 Gesell establishes the Clinic of Child Development at Yale University and studies norms of child growth and behavior, founding the maturation theory of development (see Chapters 1 and 4).

1885–1948 Susan Isaacs

1929 Susan Isaacs publishes *The Nursery Years*, which contradicts the more scientific psychological view of behavior shaping and emphasizes the child's viewpoint and the value of play.

1892–1992 Abigail Eliot

1922 Dr. Eliot opens Ruggles Street Nursery School and Training Center.

1892 International Kindergarten Union founded.

1895 G. Stanley Hall runs a child development seminar with kindergarten teachers, explaining the "scientific/new psychology" approach to education. While most leave, Anny Bryan and Patty Smith Hill go on to incorporate such techniques and to see early childhood education as a more multidisciplinary effort.

1896–1980 Jean Jacques Piaget (see Chapter 4)

1926 *The Language and Thought of the Child*, one of a multitude of writings on the development of children's thought, is published by Jean Piaget, who becomes one of the largest forces in child development in the twentieth century.

1952 Piaget's *Origins of Intelligence* in children is published in English.

1896–1934 Lev Vygotsky (see Chapter 4)

1978 *Mind in Society: The Development of Higher Psychological Processes*, the seminal work of Vygotsky's sociocultural theory, is first published in English.

1897–1905 Alfred Binet develops a test for the French government to determine feeblemindedness in children. Known as the Binet-Simon test (and tested by Jean Piaget, among others), it is now known as the Stanford-Binet IQ test.

1902–1994 Erik Erikson (see Chapter 4)

1950 *Childhood and Society*, which details Erikson's Eight Stages of Man, is published, thus adding a psychoanalytic influence to early childhood education.

1903–1998 Benjamin Spock

1946 Dr. Spock's *Baby and Child Care* is published. It advocates a more permissive attitude toward children's behavior and encourages exploratory behavior.

1903 The Committee of Nineteen, a splinter group of the International Kindergarten Union, forms to report various philosophical concepts. Members include Patty Smith Hill, Lucy Wheelock, and Susan Blow.

1904–1988 B. F. Skinner (see Chapter 4)

1938 *The Behavior of Organisms*, by B. F. Skinner, is published, advocating the concepts of "radical behaviorism" in psychology.

1906 Josephine Yates publishes an article in the *Colored American Magazine*, which advocates play in the kindergarten and helps translate Froebel's concepts into Black kindergartens of the day.

1908–1984 Sylvia Ashton Warner

1963 *Teacher*, published by this New Zealand kindergarten teacher, develops the concepts of "organic vocabulary" and "key vocabulary."

1909 First White House Conference on Children is held by Theodore Roosevelt, leading to the establishment of the Children's Bureau in 1912.

1915 First U.S. Montessori school opens in New York City.

1916 First Cooperative Nursery School opens at the University of Chicago.

1918 First public nursery schools are opened in England.

1918– T. Berry Brazelton

(*continues*)

1969   *Infants and Mothers*, along with several other books and numerous articles, is published by this pediatrician, advocating a sensible and intimate relationship between parents and children.

1980s   Dr. Brazelton is one of the founders of "Parent Action," a federal lobby to advocate for the needs of parents and children, particularly for a national policy granting parental leave from work to care for newborns or newly adopted children.

1919   Harriet Johnson starts the Nursery School of the Bureau of Educational Experiments, which later becomes Bank Street School.

1920–1994   Loris Malaguzzi theorizes about good programs and relationships for children, emphasizing the child's individual creative expression; starts school of Reggio Emilia, Italy, in 1946.

1921   Patty Smith Hill opens Columbia Teacher's College Laboratory School.

1921   A. S. Neill founds Summerhill school in England, which becomes a model for the "free school" movement (the book entitled *Summerhill* is published in 1960).

1922   Edna Nobel White directs the Merrill-Palmer School of Motherhood and Home Training, which later becomes the Merrill-Palmer Institute Nursery School.

1925–1926   The National Committee on Nursery Schools is founded by Patty Smith Hill; it becomes NANE and eventually NAEYC.

1925–   Albert Bandura, psychologist in social learning theory (see Chapter 4)

1926–1927   Research facilities are founded at several American universities and colleges (e.g., Smith College, Vassar College, Yale University, Mills College).

1927   Dorothy Howard establishes the first Black Nursery School in Washington, DC, and operates it for over 50 years.

1928   John B. Watson publishes *Psychological Care of Infant and Child*, applying his theories of conditioning to child-rearing (see Chapter 4).

1929   Lois Meeks Stolz (1891–1984) becomes the first President of the National Association for Nursery Education (later to become National Association for the Education of Young Children) and joins the Teachers College (Columbia University) faculty to start the laboratory school and Child Development

Instituto. Stolz later becomes the Director of the Kaiser Child Service Centers during World War II.

1929–1931   Hampton Institute, Spellman College, and Bennett College open Black laboratory nursery schools, emphasizing child development principles as in other lab schools and serving as training centers.

1930   International Kindergarten Union, founded in 1892, becomes the Association for Childhood Education, increasing its scope to include elementary education.

1933   WPA (Works Projects Association) opens emergency nurseries for Depression relief of unemployed teachers. Enrolling over 4000 teachers in 3000 schools, they also help children of unemployed parents and operate under the guidance of people such as Edna Noble White, Abigail Eliot, and Lois Meeks Stolz until World War II.

1935   First toy lending library, Toy Loan, begins in Los Angeles.

1936   The first commercial telecast is shown in New York City, starring Felix the Cat. The pervasiveness of television sets and children's viewing habits become a source of concern for educators and parents in the latter half of the twentieth century.

1943–1945   Kaiser Shipyard Child Care Center, run by Lois Meeks Stolz, James Hymes, and Edith Dowley, operates 24-hour care in Portland, Oregon.

1944   *Young Children* is first published.

1946   Stanford University laboratory school is founded by Edith Dowley.

1948   USNC OMEP, the United States National Committee of the World Organization for Early Childhood Education, is founded to promote the education of children internationally and begins to consult with UNICEF and UNESCO in the United Nations. It starts publishing a journal, *The International Journal of Early Childhood*, in 1969.

1956   *La Leche League* is established to provide mothers with information on breast-feeding, childbirth, infants, and child care.

1957   *Sputnik*, a Soviet satellite, is successfully launched, sparking a renewed interest in—and criticism of—American education.

1960   Katherine Whiteside Taylor founds the American Council of Parent Cooperatives, which later

(continues)

FIGURE 1-2

becomes the Parent Cooperative Pre-schools International.

1960 Nancy McCormick Rambusch (1927–1994) founds the American Montessori movement, splitting from her European counterparts to try to shape Montessori education as a viable American public school alternative and to establish teacher training programs at both early childhood and elementary levels.

1962 Perry Preschool Project, directed by David Weikart, opens in Ypsilanti, Michigan, and conducts longitudinal study to measure the effects of preschool education on later school and life (see Chapter 2).

1963 & 1966 Lawrence Kohlberg publishes child development works on the development of gender and sex roles and on moral development (see Chapter 4).

1964–1965 The Economic Opportunity Act of 1964 passes, becoming the foundation of Head Start Programs in the United States, as part of a federal "War on Poverty."

1966 The Bureau of Education for the Handicapped is established.

1966 NANE becomes National Association for the Education of Young Children (NAEYC).

1967 Plowden Report from England details the British Infant School system.
The Follow Through Program extends Head Start into the primary grades of the elementary system.

1969 John Bowlby publishes the first of his major works on *Attachment* (see Chapter 4).
The Ford Foundation, Carnegie Corporation, and Department of Health, Education, and Welfare subsidize the Children's Television Workshop, which develops *Sesame Street*.

1971 Stride-Rite Corporation of Boston opens a children's program on site, becoming a vanguard for employer-supported child care.

1972 The Child Development Associate Consortium, headed by Dr. Edward Ziegler, is established to develop a professional training program. Now known as CDA, its administration moves to NAEYC in 1985.

1974 Eleanor Maccoby publishes *The Development of Sex Differences* (see Chapter 4).

1975 P.L. 94-142, the Education for All Handicapped Children bill, passes, mandating appropriate education for special needs children in the "least restrictive environment" possible, thus defining the concepts of "mainstreaming" and "full inclusion."

1975 Mary Ainsworth publishes developmental research on mother–child interaction and follows up with work on patterns of attachment (see Chapter 4).

1979 Nancy Eisenberg publishes the theory of the development of prosocial development in children (see Chapter 4).
The United Nations declares an International Year of the Child.

1980 The Department of Health, Education, and Welfare is changed to that of Health and Human Services, and a separate Department of Education is established.

1982 Carol Gilligan publishes *In a Different Voice*, challenging accepted psychological theory on moral development (see Chapter 4).

1982– Marion Wright Edelman establishes the Children's Defense Fund, a Washington-based lobby on behalf of children, and particularly children of poverty and color.

1983 Howard Gardner publishes *Frames of Mind*, which outlines the concept of multiple intelligences (see Chapters 4 and 13).

1984 NAEYC publishes a report entitled "Developmentally Appropriate Practices," which outlines what is meant by "quality" work with young children from infancy through age eight.

1985 NAEYC establishes a National Academy and a voluntary accreditation system for centers, in an effort to improve the quality of children's lives, and confers its first accreditation the next year.

1986 U.S. Department of Education declares the Year of the Elementary School.
P.L. 99-457, amending 94-142, establishes a national policy on early intervention for children as young as infants.

1988–1990 The Alliance for Better Child Care, a coalition of groups advocating on behalf of young children, sponsors the ABC bill in an effort to get federal support for children and families. It fails to be signed in 1989, but is passed in 1990 and establishes the Child Care Development Block Grant to improve the quality, availability, and affordability of child care programs.

1988 The National Association of State Boards of Education issues *Right from the Start*, a report that calls for a new vision of early childhood education with the establishment of separate public school early childhood units.

(continues)

1988	The National Education Goals are adopted by President Bush and the nation's governors. Goal One states that all children will come to school ready to learn.
1990	U.N. Children's World Summit includes the following goals to be reached by the year 2000: (1) to reduce child mortality below age five by one third; (2) to provide universal access to basic education; and (3) to protect children in dangerous situations. The Americans with Disabilities Act (ADA) is passed, requiring programs of all sizes to care for and accommodate the needs of children with disabilities whenever they are reasonably able to do so.
1991	"Ready to Learn/America 2000," part of the U.S. government's educational strategy for reforming American public schools, is published.
1991	The first Worthy Wage Day, organized by the Child Care Employee Project, is held on April 9, drawing attention to the inadequate compensation of early childhood workers and how this affects the retention of a skilled and stable work force.
1993	The Family and Medical Leave Act (FMLA) is passed, providing new parents with 12 weeks of unpaid, job-protected leave.
1996	The first "Stand For Children" demonstration is held in Washington, DC, drawing 200,000 participants. *Rethinking the Brain*, published by the Family and Work Institute, summarizes the new research on children's brain development, shows the decisive impact of early experiences, and considers policy and program implications of these findings.
1997	The Child Development Permit Matrix is adopted by the California Commission on Teacher Credentialing, introducing the career ladder concept into early childhood public education.
1998	The 100,000th CDA Credential is awarded by Carol Brunson Phillips, Executive Director of the Council for Early Childhood Professional Recognition, at NAEYC Annual Conference in Toronto, Ontario, Canada.
2000	In California and other states, public elementary and secondary school systems implement stringent academic and performance standards, with substantial assessment requirements.
2002	In the U.S., the "Leave No Child Behind" legislation is passed.
2003	Universal preschool is considered as a next step in providing equal access to quality early educational experiences for all children under five years of age.

FIGURE 1-2 *(continued)*

the nobility should know their letters—and from those monastery schools that maintained libraries. A new social class in the form of craft guilds began to grow as apprenticeships expanded. Although education was sparse, the seeds of learning were planted, including the introduction of the concepts of equality and brotherhood, a continuing concern of educators today.

European Renaissance and Reformation

The European Renaissance and Reformation (1400–1600) brought more ease and freedom for the common person. The first humanist educators began to advocate for basic education, including for the poor and girls. Children were seen as pure and good. The printing press, invented by Johannes Gutenberg in 1439, made books more available to the common person rather than exclusively the domain of monks and church-sponsored schools. Martin Luther (1482–1546) urged parents to educate their children by teaching them morals and catechism.

The first humanist educators began to advocate a basic education for all children, including girls and the poor. The call for a *universal education* and *literacy* are two fundamental effects of this period on education as we know it today. Concern for the common man was on the rise, as skilled craftsmen formed a kind of middle class. By the 1500s, schools that taught subjects such as reading, writing, arithmetic, and bookkeeping were fairly common throughout Europe.

The German school system was established at this time and would continue to influence education in all parts of Europe. People changed the way they looked at children and their education. Towns grew and expanded, and there was an opportunity to move to new lands. Living conditions improved and infant mortality waned. Children were living longer. The acquisition of knowledge and skills at an earlier age became important. If educated, children could be expected to help their family improve its situation. Parents found they needed help in teaching their children.

Into Modern Times

Comenius

John Amos Comenius (1592–1670), a Czech educator, wrote the first picture book for children. Called *Orbis Pictus (The World of Pictures, 1658),* it was a guide for teachers that included training of the senses and the study of nature. Comenius fostered the belief that education should follow the natural order of things. His ideas included the "school of the mother's lap," where children's development follows a timetable of its own and their education should reflect that fact. Comenius advocated approaching learning based on the principles of nature. He believed that "in all the operations of nature, development is from within," so children should be allowed to learn at their own pace. He also proposed that teachers should work with children's own inclinations, for "what is natural takes place without compulsion." Teachers must observe

Cornix cornicatur, à à	**A a**
The *Crow* crieth.	
Agnus balat, b è è è	**B b**
The *Lamb* blaiteth.	
Cicàda stridet, cì cì	**C c**
The *Grasshopper* chirpeth.	
Upupa dicit, du du	**D d**
The *Whooppoo* saith.	
Infans ejulat, è è è	**E e**
The *Infant* crieth.	
Ventus flat, fi fi	**F f**
The *Wind* bloweth.	
Anser gingrit, ga ga	**G g**
The *Goose* gagleth.	
Os halat, hà'h hà'h	**H h**
The *Mouth* breatheth out.	
Mus mintrit, ì ì ì	**I i**
The *Mouse* chirpeth.	
Anas tetrinnit, kha, kha	**K k**
The *Duck* quaketh.	
Lupus ululat, lu ulu	**L**
The *Wolf* howleth.	
[mum	
Ursus murmurat, mum-	**M m**
The *Bear* grumbleth.	

Orbis Pictus, by John Comenius, is considered the first picture book written for children.

and work with this natural order, the timetable, to ensure successful learning. This idea was later reflected in Montessori's sensitive periods and Piaget's stages of development. Today it is recognized as the issue of school **readiness**.

Comenius also stressed a basic concept that is now taken for granted: learning by doing. He encouraged parents to let their children play with other children of the same age. Rather than pushing a standard curriculum, Comenius said that "the desire to know and to learn should be excited . . . in every possible manner" (Keatinge, 1896). He also reflected the growing social reform that would educate the poor as well as the rich. In summary, probably the three most significant contributions of Comenius are *books with illustrations,* an emphasis on *education with the senses,* and the *social reform* potential of education.

Locke

An English philosopher of the 1600s, John Locke (1632–1714) is considered to be the founder of modern educational philosophy. He based his theory of education on the scientific method and the study of the mind and learning. Locke theorized the concept of **tabula rasa**, the belief that the child is born neutral, rather than evil, and is a "clean slate" on which the experiences of parents, society, education, and the world are written. He based his theory on the scientific method and approached a child as a doctor would examine a patient. He was one of the first European educators to discuss the idea of individual differences gleaned from observing one child rather than simply teaching a group. Education needed to take the individual learner into account.

The purpose of education, he claimed, is to make man a reasoning creature. A working knowledge of the Bible and a counting ability sufficient to conduct business was the fundamental education required of adults, so children were taught those basics. Locke suggested that such instruction should be pleasant, with playful activities as well as drills. Locke's influence on education was not felt strongly at the time. Later, however, his best ideas were popularized by Rousseau, such as the notion that the teacher must work through the senses to help children reach understanding. Today, teachers still emphasize a sensory approach to learning.

In summary, Locke's contribution is felt most in our acceptance of *individual differences,* in *giving children reasons* as the basis for helping children to learn, and in his *theory of a "clean slate"* that points to the effect of the environment on learning.

Rousseau

After Comenius, new thoughts were everywhere in Europe. Locke offered some educational challenges, and Darwin brought a change to science. The time was ripe for new ideas about childhood. Jean Jacques Rousseau (1712–1778), a writer and philosopher of the middle 1700s, brought forth the idea that children were not inherently evil, but naturally good. He is best known for his book *Emile* (1761) in which he raised a hypothetical child to adulthood. He reasoned that education should reflect this goodness and allow spontaneous interests and activities of the children. "Let us lay it down as an incontrovertible rule that the first impulses of nature are always right; there is no original sin in the human heart . . . the only natural passion is self-love or selfishness taken in a wider sense."

Rousseau's ideas on education in and of themselves were nothing short of revolutionary for the times. They include the following:

● The true object of education should not be primarily a vocational one.

● Children only really learn from firsthand information.

● Children's view of the external world is quite different from that of adults.

● There are distinct phases of development of a child's mind and these should coincide with the various stages of education.

● Teachers must be aware of these phases and coordinate their instruction appropriately (Boyd, 1997).

Although he was not an educator, Rousseau suggested that school atmosphere should be less restrained and more flexible to meet the needs of the children. He insisted on using concrete teaching materials, leaving the abstract and symbolism for later years. His call to *naturalism* transformed education in such a way that led educators to eventually focus more on the early years. For instance, he extolled others to "sacrifice a little time in early childhood, and it will be repaid to you with usury when your scholar is older" (*Emile*, 1761). Pestalozzi, Froebel, and Montessori were greatly influenced by him. The theories of developmental stages, such as of Jean Piaget and Arnold Gesell (see Chapter 4), support Rousseau's idea of natural development.

In Europe, his ideas had a ripple effect that sent waves across the Atlantic Ocean.

Rousseau's ideas are still followed today in early childhood classes. *Free play* is based on Rousseau's belief in *children's inherent goodness* and ability to choose what they need to learn. Environments that stress autonomy and self-regulation have their roots in Rousseau's philosophy. Using *concrete rather than abstract materials* for young children is still one of the cornerstones of developmentally appropriate curriculum in the early years.

Pestalozzi

Johann Heinrich Pestalozzi (1746–1827) was a Swiss educator whose theories on education and caring have formed the basis of many common teaching practices of early childhood education. Like Rousseau, he used nature study as part of the curriculum and believed that good education meant the development of the senses. Rather than simply glorify nature, however, Pestalozzi became more pragmatic, including principles on how to teach basic skills and the idea of "caring" as well as "educating" the child. Pestalozzi stressed the idea of the **integrated curriculum** that would develop the whole child. He wanted education to be of the hand, the head, and the heart of the child. Teachers were to guide self-activity through intuition, exercise, and the senses. Along with intellectual content, he proposed that practical skills be taught in the schools. He differed from Rousseau in that he proposed teaching children in groups rather than using a tutor with an individual child. Pestalozzi's works *How Gertrude Teaches Her Children* and *Book for Mothers* detailed some procedures for mothers to use at home with their children. Probably his greatest contribution is the blending of Rousseau's strong romantic ideals with his own egalitarian attitude that built skills and independence in a school atmosphere that paralleled that of a firm and loving home.

In summary, Pestalozzi's contributions are strongest around the *integration of the curriculum* and *group teaching*.

Froebel

Friedrich Wilhelm Froebel (1782–1852) is one of the major contributors to early childhood education, particularly in his organization of educational thought and ideas about learning, curriculum, and teacher training. He is known to us as the "Father of the Kindergarten," not only for giving it a name, but for devoting his

A Froebelian kindergarten at the end of the nineteenth century. (Copyright 2006 Scott Bultman, used with permission.)

life to the development of a system of education for young children. The German word **kindergarten** means "**children's garden**," and that is what Froebel felt best expressed what he wanted for children under six years of age. Because his own childhood had been unhappy, he resolved that early education should be pleasant. He advocated the radical thought that children should be able to play, to have toys, and to be with trained teachers, so he started the first training school. Early childhood historian Dorothy Hewes (1993) notes:

> Froebel started his kindergarten in 1836, for children aged about two to six, after he had studied with Pestalozzi in Switzerland and had read the philosophy promoted by Comenius two hundred years earlier. His system was centered around self-activity and the development of children's self-esteem and self-confidence. In his *Education of Man,* he wrote that "Play is the highest phase of child development— the representation of the inner necessity and impulse." He had the radical idea that both men and women should teach young children and that they should be friendly facilitators rather than stern disciplinarians.

Over 100 years ago, Froebel's kindergartens included blocks, pets, and fingerplays. Froebel observed children and came to understand how they learned and what they liked to do. He developed the first educational toys, which he termed "gifts."

Angeline Brooks (1886), a teacher in an American Froebelian kindergarten in the late 1800s, described the gifts this way:

Froebel regarded the whole of life as a school, and the whole world as a school-room for the education of the [human] race. The external things of nature he regarded as a means to making the race acquainted with the invisible things of the minds, as God's *gifts* for use in accomplishing the purpose of this temporal life. Regarding the child as the race in miniature, he selected a few objects which should epitomize the world of matter in its most salient attributes and arranged them in an order which should assist the child's development at successive stages of growth.

Some of his theories about children and their education later influenced Montessori and were reflected in the educational materials she developed.

When the children are just making friends with the teacher and with each other, it is very interesting and profitable for them to formulate their mite of knowledge into a sentence, each one holding his ball high in the air with the right hand and saying:

My ball is red like a cherry.
My ball is yellow like a lemon.
My ball is blue like the sky.
My ball is orange like a marigold.
My ball is green like the grass.
My ball is violet like a plum.

When introducing the gifts, a teacher in Froebelian settings would teach children rhymes and fingerplays.

...ery day, teachers in centers and homes ... the country practice the Froebelian ... that a child's first educational experiences ...ould be a garden: full of pleasant discoveries and delightful adventure, where the adults' role is to plant ideas and materials for children to use as they grow at their own pace.

Montessori

At the turn of the century, Maria Montessori (1870–1952) became the first female physician in Italy. She worked in the slums of Rome with poor children and with mentally retarded children. Sensing that what they lacked was proper motivation and environment, she opened a preschool, *Casa di Bambini*, in 1907. Her first class was 50 children from two to five years of age. The children were at the center all day while their parents worked. They were fed two meals a day, given a bath, and provided with medical attention. Montessori designed materials, classrooms, and a teaching procedure that proved her point to the astonishment of people all over Europe and America.

Before her, no one with medical or psychiatric training had articulated so clearly the needs of the growing child. Her medical background added credibility to her findings and helped her ideas gain recognition in this country. The Montessori concept is both a philosophy of child development and a plan for guiding growth, believing that education begins at birth and the early years are of the utmost importance. During this time, children pass through "sensitive periods," in which their curiosity makes them ready for acquiring certain skills and knowledge.

Dr. Montessori was an especially observant person and used her observations to develop her program and philosophy. For instance, the manipulative materials she used were expensive, so they were always kept in a locked cabinet. One day the cabinet was left unlocked, and the children took out the materials themselves and worked with them quietly and carefully. Afterward, Montessori removed the cabinet and replaced it with low, open shelves. She noticed that children liked to sit on the floor so she bought little rugs to define the work areas. She designed the school around the size of the children. Through her enlightenment, child-sized furniture and materials are now used in classrooms.

By focusing on the *sequential steps of learning*, Montessori developed a set of learning

Maria Montessori designed materials, classrooms, and learning methods for young children. (Photo courtesy of the Archives of the Association Montessori Internationale.)

materials still used widely today. One of her most valuable contributions was a theory of how children learn. She believed that any task could be reduced to a series of small steps. By using this process, children could learn to sweep a floor, dress themselves, or multiply numbers.

Montessori materials are graded in difficulty and emphasize her interest in self-help skills. To foster this, she developed frames with buttons and laces so children could learn to be responsible for themselves when dressing. The layout of the room and the distribution and presentation of materials furthered this concept. Montessori placed great emphasis on the environment—the "prepared environment," as she called it. A sense of order, a place for everything, and a clear rationale are hallmarks of the Montessori influence.

Her procedures as well as her materials contain **self-correcting** features. Nesting cylinders, for example, fit together only one way and are to be used that way. Montessori supported earlier educational ideas of sensory developments; she felt that cognitive abilities stem from sensory discrimination. Thus, most of her equipment was tactile and enhanced the senses as well as the mind. In the Montessori method, the role of the teacher is primarily one of observer and facilitator. Teachers demonstrate proper use of materials and communicate as needed, avoiding any acts that might cause a child to become dependent on them for help or approval. At the same time, Montessori saw the goal of education as the formation of the child and development of character.

After Montessori was introduced in the United States in 1909, her methods received poor reception and were often misunderstood. Chattin-McNichols (1993) notes that "adaptation of her methods in a variety of ways, a focus on academics by demanding middle-class parents, and a flood of 'trainers' and authors eager to capitalize on Montessori contributed to a rapid downfall of Montessori schools in the U.S. by 1925 or so." A second American Montessori movement began in the late 1950s and early 1960s. Differences between Europeans and Americans generated the American Montessori Society, founded by Dr. Nancy McCormick Rambusch. According to Chattin-McNichols (1993):

> Today with a much wider range of children than ever before, the majority of Montessori schools are private preschools and child care centers, serving 3- to 6-year-old children. But there are many which also serve elementary students, and a small (but growing) number of programs for infants, toddlers, and middle-school students. . . . The word *Montessori*, however, remains in the public domain, so that Montessori in the name of a school or teacher education program does not guarantee any adherence to Montessori's original ideas.

To summarize, Montessori's contributions were substantial to all we do in early childhood programs today. A *prepared environment, self-correcting and sequential materials*, teaching based on *observation*, and a trust in *children's innate drive to learn* all stem from her work. For more information on Montessori programs, see Chapter 2.

Steiner

Rudolf Steiner (1861–1925) was an Austrian philosopher, scientist, and artist whose lectures for the German factories of Waldorf-Astoria led to the establishment of a school now known as Waldorf Schools. This system has influenced mainstream education in Europe, and its international reputation is felt in North America today. Steiner theorized that childhood is a phase of life important in its own right, and the environment must be carefully planned to protect and nurture the child (see Figure 1-3).

Steiner's philosophy emphasized the children's spiritual development, imagination, and creative gifts. As did Froebel and Montessori, Steiner emphasized the whole child and believed that different areas of development and learning were connected into a kind of unity. The role of the teacher is that of a mother figure, and her goal is to allow the child's innate self-motivation to predominate. The teacher is to understand the temperament of each child, and to go with it; thus, play has a large place in Waldorf classrooms.

Self-discipline will emerge from the child's natural willingness to learn and initiate, and the classroom needs to support this self-regulation process. Yet, while the child's inner life is deeply valued by Steiner, experiences in early childhood must be carefully selected. For instance, fairy stories help children acquire time-honored wisdom; modern Waldorf followers insist that television be eliminated.

In summary, for Steiner, the people with whom the child interacts are of central importance. Waldorf schools are discussed later in this chapter and in Chapter 2.

Steiner's Ages of Childhood

Age	Span	Child Learns by . . .	Emphasis
The Will	0–7	Imitation	Role models and beautiful environment
The Heart	7–14	Authority	Consistency with enthusiasm and feeling
The Head	14+	Challenge	Intellectual study for real mastery

FIGURE 1-3 Rudolf Steiner created a system of education in the early 1900s that was based on educational goals for the whole child and the transformation of the spirit/soul.

NONTRADITIONAL PERSPECTIVES

You can likely notice how traditional early childhood educational practices reinforce European-American values and beliefs. Education is often built from the knowledge base of its teachers; curriculum usually draws from the system [cultural, economic, political] most familiar. If teachers are trained on European writings and the ideas of university-educated Americans, then their own teachings would likely reflect those philosophies.

But there have always been other influences on our child-rearing and educational practices, especially those of our own upbringing or of the communities whose children and families we teach. We know that there is more than one "right way" to care for and educate children.[1] What nontraditional perspectives influenced early childhood education? As mentioned before, information about non-Western early childhood history is not easily accessible; see "Additional Resources" for a reading list. Gonzalez-Mena (2001) summarizes some of these perspectives in this way:

> Historically, attitudes toward childhood in China and Japan were influenced by Confucius' writings (551–479 B.C.), which stressed harmony. Children were seen as good and worthy of respect, a view not held in Europe until more recently.
>
> Native-American writings show close ties and interconnectedness, not only among families and within tribes but also between people and nature. Teaching children about relationships and interconnectedness are historical themes of early education among many indigenous peoples.
>
> Strong kinship networks are themes among both Africans and African Americans; people bond together and pool resources for the common good. Whether these contemporary tendencies come from ancient roots, historic, and modern oppression, or all three remains unclear.

Latin American and Hispanic cultures value children highly, and emphasize the importance of coorperation as well as a sensitivity to authority figures. Families from the Pacific Islands stress the connection to family as well as the importance of respecting one's elders.

Early education practices have been influenced by many of these perspectives. For instance, understanding and accepting each child's family and cultural perspectives includes a working knowledge of the variations in attitudes and child-rearing practices (see Our Diverse World footnotes throughout the book). Learning about nontraditional cultures and behaviors has become critical for professional teachers, to honor diversity both in the classroom and in the larger societal context (see Chapters 9–14). Chapter 3 expands on these ideas with definitions of the young child, and Chapter 15 elaborates on these issues in today's early childhood programs.

AMERICAN INFLUENCES

Colonial Days

The American educational system began in the colonies. When thinking of Colonial America, people often envision the one-room schoolhouse. Indeed, this was the mainstay of education in the New England colonies. Although home teaching of the Bible was common, children were sent to school primarily for religious reasons. Everyone needed to be able to read the Bible, the Puritan fathers reasoned. All children were sent to study, though historically boys were educated before girls.[2] Not only was the Bible used in school, however; new materials like the New England Primer and the Horn Book were also used.

Early life in the New England colonies was difficult, and estimates run as high as 60 percent to 70 percent of children under age four dying in colonial towns during the "starving season." Discipline was harsh, and children were expected to obey immediately and without question. Parents may have loved their children, but Puritan families showed little overt affection. Children were important as economic tools, and they worked the land and were apprenticed into trades early.

In the South, it was a different story. Plantation owners imported tutors from

1 We must be careful in our assumptions of what we think is good or right for our young children. A wider view of history reveals that there are many right ways, and much that is "good" comes from sharing our diverse viewpoints.

2 History can provide us with reminders of the strides that have been made in American society in providing equal educational experiences for both boys and girls—the challenge continues.

England or opened small private schools to teach just their sons to read and write.[1] Although the reasons were different, the results were similar: a very high percentage of adult readers. From these came the leaders of the American Revolution and the new nation.

The Revolutionary War brought the establishment of both the Union and religious freedom. By affirming fundamental principles of democratic liberty, the Founding Fathers paved the way for a system of free, common, public school systems, the first the world had seen (Cubberly, 1920). However, after the Revolutionary War, there were no significant advances in education until the late 1800s. Leaders such as Thomas Jefferson felt that knowledge ought to be available to all, but that opinion was not widely shared. Most of the post-Revolutionary period focused on growing crops and pioneering the frontier, not teaching and educating children. Even by the 1820s, education for the common man was not readily available. Industrialization in both the North and South did little to encourage reading and writing skills. Manual labor and machine-operating skills were more important. Although public schools were accepted in principle, in reality no tax basis was established to support them.

Children in Enslavement

The first African Americans were not slaves but indentured servants, whose debts repaid by their labor would buy them their freedom. However, by 1620 Africans were being brought to the New World as slaves. In many states, children of slaves were not seen as human beings but rather as property of the owner. During the Revolutionary War, many Americans turned against slavery because of the principles of the natural rights of the individual, as embodied in the Declaration of Independence and the U.S. Constitution. By the early 1800s, most northern owners had freed their slaves, although living conditions for them were generally poor.

Because of the high economic value of children as future laborers, there was a certain level of care given to pregnant women and babies. Osborn (1991) tells of a nursery on a

South Carolina plantation (around 18 which

> infants and small children were left in a small cabin while the mothers worked in the fields nearby. An older woman was left in charge and assisted by several girls 8–10 years of age. The infants, for the most part, lay on the cabin floor or the porch—and once or twice daily, the mother would come in from the field to nurse the baby. Children of toddler age played on the porch or in the yard and, at times, the older girls might lead the group in singing and dancing.

Prior to the Civil War, education was severely limited for African Americans. Formal schools were scarce, and most education came through the establishment of "Sabbath schools." As part of religious instruction, slaves were often provided literary training. However, many plantation owners found these schools threatening, and banned them by making laws prohibiting the teaching of slaves. Another facility then developed, that of the clandestine, or midnight, school. Because of its necessary secretive existence, few records are available, although it is reasonable to conclude that the curriculum was similar to that of the prohibited Sabbath schools.

After the Civil War, private and public schools were opened for African Americans.[2] Major colleges and universities were founded by the end of the 1800s. Booker T. Washington, born into slavery, founded the Tuskegee Normal & Industrial Institute in Alabama in 1881, and emphasized practical education and intercultural understanding between the two races as a path to liberation. Many former slaves and graduates established schools for younger children. Of integrated schools, Osborn (1991) reports:

> Generally, however, if the schools accepted Blacks at all, it was on a strictly quota basis . . . Blacks were often excluded from kindergartens. Thus, as the early childhood education movement began to grow and expand in the years following the Civil War, it grew along separate color lines.

Hampton Institute of Virginia established a laboratory kindergarten for African Americans in 1873, and by 1893 the Institute offered a

---

1   We need to remember that the challenge of equity in education for girls and boys remains; early childhood educators must stay alert to the biases that still exist in society and are replayed in the classroom.

2   Although great strides have been made in providing public education for all children in America, remember that inequities based on color, linguistic ability, and social class continue to exist.

school and courses in ...aduates of Hampton ...achers at the laboratory ...e words of its principal ...e children and the influ- ...m.... Their people are ...hing. They furnish what ...issing link between me and the parents (......ant, 1992).

John Dewey

By the end of the 1800s, however, a nationwide reform movement had begun. In education, the *Progressive Movement*, as it was called, received its direction primarily through one individual, John Dewey (1858–1952).

Dewey was the first real American influence on American education. Raised in Vermont, he became a professor of philosophy at both the University of Chicago and Columbia University. In the years that followed, Dewey would be responsible for one of the greatest impacts on American education of all time.

Dewey believed that children were valuable and that childhood was an important part of their lives. Like Froebel, he felt that education should be integrated with life and should provide a training ground for cooperative living. As did Pestalozzi and Rousseau, Dewey felt that schools should focus on the nature of the child. Until this time, children were considered of little consequence. Childhood was rushed. Children as young as seven were a regular part of the work force—on the farms, in the mines, and in the factories. Dewey's beliefs about children and learning are summarized in Figure 1-4.

Dewey's ideas of schooling emerged from his own childhood and his family life as a parent. Jane Dewey, his sixth child, offered that "his own schooling had bored John; he'd disliked the rigid, passive way of learning forced on children by the pervasive lecture-recitation method of that time" (Walker, 1997). Furthermore, the Deweys' parenting style caused a stir among friends and neighbors; the children were allowed to play actively in the same room as adult guests, to ignore wearing shoes and stockings, and even to "stand by during the birth [of brother Morris] while Mrs. Dewey explained the process" (Walker, 1997). His passionate belief in the innate goodness of children, and encouragement of their experimentation, shaped John Dewey's ideals.

My Pedagogic Creed—John Dewey	What It Means Today
1. "... I believe that only true education comes through the stimulation of the child's powers by the demands of the social situations in which he finds himself."	This tells us that children learn to manage themselves in groups, to make and share friendship, to solve problems, and to cooperate.
2. "... The child's own instinct and powers furnish the material and give the starting point for all education."	We need to create a place that is child-centered, a place that values the skills and interests of each child and each group.
3. "... I believe that education, therefore, is a process of living and not a preparation for future living."	Prepare children for what is to come by enriching and interpreting the present to them. Find educational implications in everyday experiences.
4. "... I believe that ... the school life should grow gradually out of the home life ... it is the business of the school to deepen and extend ... the child's sense of the values bound up in his home life."	This sets the rationale for a relationship between teachers and parents. Values established and created in the home should be enhanced by teaching in the schools.
5. "... I believe, finally, that the teacher is engaged, not simply in the training of individuals, but in the formation of a proper social life. I believe that every teacher should realize the dignity of his calling.	This says that the work teachers do is important and valuable. They teach more than academic content; they teach how to live.

FIGURE 1-4 John Dewey expressed his ideas about education in an important document entitled *My Pedagogic Creed* (Washington, DC: The Progressive Education Association, 1897).

1 It would be worth investigating whether all the laboratory schools for African Americans copied European models, as did those of most American universities, or reflected some African influences.

A new kind of school emerged from these ideals. Even the buildings began to take on a different look. Movable furniture replaced rows of benches. Children's projects, some still under construction, were found everywhere. The curriculum of the school began to focus on all of the basics, not just a few of the academics. If a group of six-year-olds decided to make a woodworking table, they would first have to learn to read to understand the directions. After calculating the cost, they would purchase the materials. In building the table, geometry, physics, and math were learned along the way. This was a group effort that encouraged children to work together in teams, so school became a society in miniature. Children's social skills were developed along with reading, science, and math. The teacher's role in the process was one of ongoing support, involvement, and encouragement.

The contribution of John Dewey to American education cannot be underestimated. As described in Figure 1-3, Dewey's ideas are part of today's classrooms in several ways. His child-oriented schools are a model of child care centers and family child care homes, as learning and living are inseparable. As the following sections on kindergarten and nursery schools illustrate, John Dewey had a vision that is still alive today.

The Field Expands: Kindergarten

The word *kindergarten*—German for "children's garden"—is a delightful term. It brings to mind the image of young seedlings on the verge of blossoming. The similarity between caring for young plants and young children is not accidental. Froebel, the man who coined the word *kindergarten*, meant for that association to be made. As a flower opens from a bud, so too does a child go through a natural unfolding process. This idea—and ideal—are part of the kindergarten story.

The first kindergarten was a German school started by Froebel in 1837. Nearly 20 years later, in 1856, Margaretha Schurz, a student of Froebel, opened the first kindergarten in the United States. It was for German-speaking children and held in her home in Wisconsin. Schurz inspired Elizabeth Peabody (1804–1894) of Boston, who opened the first English-speaking kindergarten there in 1860. Peabody, in turn, after studying kindergartens in Germany, influenced William Harris, superintendent of schools in St. Louis, Missouri. In 1873, Harris allowed Susan Blow (1843–1916) to open the first kindergarten in the United States that was associated with the public schools. By the 1880s kindergarten teachers such as Eudora Hailmann were hard at work inventing wooden beads,

Music time at Hampton Institute kindergarten. (Courtesy of Hampton University Archives.)

Traditional nursery and kindergarten included circle time. (Reprinted with permission of the Golden Gate Kindergarten Association.)

paper weaving mats, and songbooks to use with active five-year-old children.

Look at kindergarten in a historical perspective to trace the various purposes of this specialized educational experience. At first, Froebel's philosophy (see section on Froebel earlier in this chapter) was the mainstay of kindergarten education. At the same time, kindergartens began to become an instrument of social reform. Many of the kindergartens started in the late 1800s were established by churches and other agencies that worked with the poor and were called charity kindergartens. For instance, "in the early kindergartens, teachers conducted a morning class for about 15 children

and made social calls on families during the afternoon. The children were taught to address the teachers as "Auntie" to emphasize her sisterly relationship with their mothers" (Hewes, 1993).

Moreover, by early 1900 traditional kindergarten ideas had come under the scrutiny of G. Stanley Hall and others, who were interested in a scientific approach to education. Dewey advocated a community-like (rather than garden-style) classroom. A classic clash of ideals developed between followers of Froebel (conservatives) and those of Dewey's new educational viewpoint (progressives). For those who saw kindergartens as a social service in an era of rising social conscience, the reasons for helping the less fortunate were similar to the rationale that led to the creation of Head Start 60 years later.

The emphasis in a Froebelian kindergarten was on teacher-directed learning. Dewey's followers preferred a more **child-centered approach**, with teachers serving as facilitators of children's learning. This is the same tension that exists today between the "back to basics," movement and the supporters of child-centered education. The progressives found fault with the "gifts" of Froebel's curriculum. Those who followed Dewey believed that "real objects and real situations within the child's own social setting" should be used (Read & Patterson, 1980). Froebel

John Dewey's lab school involved children in activities of a practical, real-life nature, such as weaving small rugs to use in the classroom. (Reprinted with permission from Special Collections Research Center, Morris Library, Southern Illinois University Carbondale.)

was viewed as too structured and too symbolic; Dewey was perceived as child-oriented and child-involved. Even the processes they used were different. Froebel believed in allowing the unfolding of the child's mind and learning, whereas Dewey stressed adult intervention in social interaction.

The reform of kindergarten education led to the creation of the modern American kindergarten. By the 1970s, the trend was a focus on the intellectual development of the child; thus, there was an emphasis on academic goals for five-year-olds. By the late 1990s, the concept of developmentally appropriate practices advocated a shift toward more holistic, broad planning for kindergarten. Today, only 14 states require age-eligible children to attend kindergarten, although 98 percent of American children attend at least half-day. Chapter 2 will discuss the issue of programs, as we continue to decide "how the best ideas of the past can be integrated with the best practices of today and transformed into the best programs for the future" (Bauch, 1988).

Patty Smith Hill

Patty Smith Hill (1868–1946) of Teacher's College, Columbia University, was an outstanding innovator of the time and one of the Progressive Movement's most able leaders. It was she who wrote the song "Happy Birthday" and founded the National Association for Nursery Education (NANE). The largest association of early childhood educators, it is known today as the National Association for the Education of Young Children (NAEYC). Trained originally in the Froebelian tradition, she worked closely with G. Stanley Hall and later with John Dewey. Thus, her philosophy of classroom teaching was a blended one. She believed strongly in basing curricula and programs on the nature and needs of the children, and she was one of the major education experimenters of her day. She was

> . . . guided by principles of democracy and respect for individuals. She argued for freedom and initiative for children, as well as a curriculum relevant to children's lives. It was she who originated large-muscle equipment and materials suitable for climbing and construction, a departure from the prescribed small-muscle activities of the Froebelians. Patty Hill also urged unification of kindergarten and first-grade work, but her objective was not to start 5 year olds on first-grade work, as we today might readily

assume. Rather, emphasis was on giving six year olds the opportunity for independent, creative activities before embarking on the three R's. (Cohen & Randolph, 1977)

These ideas became the backbone of kindergarten practice. Moreover, Hill did not work for kindergarten alone. In fact, during the 1920s Hill rekindled Froebel's early ideas to promote nursery schools for children too young to attend kindergarten. Regardless of controversy within, kindergartens were still on the fringes of the educational establishments as a whole. In fact, Hill (1941) herself commented that "adjustment to public-school conditions came slowly . . . [and] until this happy adjustment took place, the promotion of the self-active kindergarten children into the grades has made it possible for the poorest and most formal first-grade teacher to criticize and condemn the work of the best kindergarten teacher as well as the kindergarten cause, because of the wide gap that existed between kindergarten and primary ideals at that time. . . ."

As Hill and others prevailed and made continual improvements in teaching methods, materials, guidance, and curriculum, the interests of kindergarten and primary education could be seen as more unified.

Nursery Schools

Establishment in America

The very phrase "nursery school" conjures up images of a child's nursery, of a carefully tended garden, of a gentle place of play and growing. In fact, the name was coined to describe a place where children were nurtured (see the section later in this chapter on the McMillan sisters). Nursery schools have always been a place of "care," of physical needs, intellectual stimulation, and the socioemotional aspects of young children's lives.

Early childhood educators took Dewey's philosophy to heart. Their schools reflected the principles of a child-centered approach, active learning, and social cooperation. By the 1920s and 1930s, early childhood education had reached a professional status in the United States. Nursery schools and day nurseries went beyond custodial health care. They fostered the child's total development. The children were enrolled from middle- and upper-class homes as well as from working families. However,

American nursery schools, from the turn of the century through the present day, have included time for the group to be together. (Reprinted with permission of Golden Gate Kindergarten Association.)

until the 1960s, nursery schools served few poor families.[1]

Parent education was acknowledged as a vital function of the school and led to the establishment of **parent cooperative schools**. Brook Farm, a utopian cooperative community in the 1840s, had "the equivalent of an on-site child care center 'for the use of parents doing industrial work' or for mothers to use 'as a kindly relief to themselves when fatigued by the care of children'" (Hewes, 1993). The first of these parent participation schools was developed in 1915 at the University of Chicago. A group of faculty wives started the Chicago Cooperative Nursery School. Chapter 2 describes the parent cooperative model in detail.

Research centers and child development laboratories were started in many colleges and universities from about 1915 to 1930. These laboratory schools were active in expanding the knowledge of how important a child's early years are. As Stolz (1978) describes it, "the [preschool] movement from the beginning was integrated with the movement for child development research. The purpose . . . was to improve nursery schools, and, therefore, we brought in the people who were studying children, who were learning more about them, so we could do a better job." It is noteworthy that professionals such as Hill, Stolz, Dowley, and others encouraged researchers to share their findings with classroom teachers to integrate these discoveries right into the daily programs of children.

These schools followed one of two basic models. One model, patterned after the first psychological laboratory in Leipzig, Germany, in 1879, was formed to train psychologists in the systematic training of child study. This model adopted a scientific approach to the study of human beings, as the field of psychology itself attempted to become more like the biologic sciences. The second approach, like the Butler School of Hampton Institute and later Spelman College, was established primarily for training teachers. The latter model took its influence almost exclusively from educational leaders. The nursery school laboratory schools attempted a multidisciplinary approach, blending the voices from psychology and education with those of home economics, nursing, social work, and medicine. By 1950, when Katherine Read (Baker) first published *The Nursery School: A Human Relationships Laboratory* (now in its ninth printing and in seven languages), the emphasis of the nursery school was on understanding human behavior, and then building programs, guidance techniques, and relationships accordingly. In her estimate (1950),

> . . . the nursery school is a place where young children learn as they play and as they share experiences with other children. . . . It is also a place where adults learn about child development and human relationships as they observe and participate in the program of the school. . . . Anyone working in an educational program for children,

even the most experienced person, needs to be learning as well as teaching. The two processes, learning and teaching, are inseparable.

Lucy Sprague Mitchell

Early childhood education in the United States grew out of John Dewey's progressive movement largely because of Lucy Sprague Mitchell (1878–1967) and her contemporaries. Raised in an environment of educational and social reform, Mitchell developed the idea of schools as community centers as well as places for children to learn to think. As Greenberg (1987) explained, she gathered together, in a democratic, cooperative venture, many talented people to brainstorm, mastermind, and sponsor:

● A remarkable Bureau of Educational Experiments

● A school to implement and experiment with these principles

● A laboratory to record and analyze how and why they function as she knew they did (and as we know they do!)

● A teachers' college to promote them

● A workshop for writers of children's literature (a new genre—a number of currently famous authors of juvenile books attended)

● A bulletin to disseminate it all, as well as disseminating what a plethora of progressive educators were up to elsewhere, *beginning in 1916!*

Strongly influenced by John Dewey, she became a major contributor to the idea of "educational experiments," that is, trying to plan with teachers the curriculum experiences that would then be observed and analyzed "for children's reactions to the various learning situations [and] the new teaching techniques" (Mitchell, 1951). For instance, Mitchell suggested that teachers expand on what they knew of children's "here-and-now" thinking by making

> trips with kindergarteners to see how work was done—work that was closely tied up with their personal lives. . . . the growth in thinking and attitudes of the teachers had moved far . . . toward the conception of their role as a guide as differentiated from a dispenser of information.

By establishing Bank Street College of Education (and its laboratory school), Lucy Sprague Mitchell emphasized the link between theory and practice, namely, that the education of young children and the study of how children learn are intrinsically tied together.

Abigail Eliot

The nursery school movement was pioneered by Abigail Eliot (1892–1992). A graduate of Radcliffe College and Harvard University, Eliot had worked with the McMillan sisters (see section in this chapter) in the slums of London. A social worker by training, she became interested in children and their relationships with their parents. Eliot had a lively and clear view of what good schools for children could be. She is generally credited with bringing the nursery school movement to the United States. She founded the Ruggles Street Nursery School in the Roxbury section of Boston, teaching children and providing teacher training, and was its director from 1922 to 1952, when it was incorporated into Tufts University and today is alive as the Eliot-Pearson Department of Child Study.

Eliot became the first woman to receive a doctoral degree from Harvard University's Graduate School of Education, and after retiring from Tufts moved to California, where she helped establish Pacific Oaks College. In all her work, she integrated Froebel's gifts, Montessori's equipment, McMillans' fresh air, as well as her own ideas. As she put it (Hymes, 1978):

> . . . the new idea—was program. I had visited many day nurseries in Boston as a social worker. I can remember them even now: dull green walls, no light colors, nothing pretty—spotlessly clean places, with rows of white-faced listless little children sitting, doing nothing. In the new nursery school, the children were active, alive, choosing.

Midcentury Developments

While the economic crisis of the Depression and the political turmoil of World War II diverted attention from children's needs, both gave focus to adult needs for work. Out of this necessity came the Works Progress Administration (WPA) nurseries of the 1930s and the Lanham Act nurseries of the 1940s. The most renowned program of the midcentury was the Kaiser Child Care Centers.

Kaiser Child Care Centers

During World War II, funds were provided to deal with the common situation of mothers working in war-related industries. Further support came from industry during World War II. An excellent model for child care operated from 1943 to 1945 in Portland, Oregon. It was the Kaiser Child Care Centers. Kaiser became the world's largest such center and functioned "'round the clock" all year long. A number of services were made available on-site. An infirmary was located nearby for both mothers and children. Hot meals were made available for mothers to take home when they picked up their children. Lois Meek Stolz was the director of the centers, and James L. Hymes, Jr. was the manager. They describe the centers this way:

> . . . The centers were to have three distinctive qualities. One, they were to be located not out in the community but right at the entrance to the two shipyards, convenient to mothers on their way to and from work. They were to be industry-based, not neighborhood-centered. Two, the centers were to be operated by the shipyards, not by the public schools and not by community agencies. They were to be industrial child care centers, with the cost borne by the Kaiser company and by parents using the service. Three, they were to be large centers, big enough to meet the need. In the original plan each center was to serve a thousand preschool children on three shifts. (Hymes, 1978)

These centers served 3,811 children. As Hymes points out, they provided 249,268 child care days. They had freed 1,931,827 woman work-hours.

Once the war had ended, though, the workers left. Child care was no longer needed, and the centers closed. The Kaiser experience has never been equaled, either in the universal quality of care or in the variety of services. However, it left us a legacy, which Hymes has stressed ever since (in Dickerson, 1992):

> It is no great trick to have an excellent child care program. It only requires a lot of money with most of it spent on *trained* staff.

The model they provided for child care remains exemplary.

Chances to Learn

The Depression was a particularly difficult time for African Americans, as the living standards for those Americans in poverty plummeted. Roosevelt's administration and the emerging industrial union movement gave impetus to blacks looking for both employment and political change. World War II continued the process of transformation for many adults, but for children the situation was still bleak. As DuBois (1903) wrote:

> the majority of Negro children in the United States, from 6 to 18, do not have the opportunity to read and write. . . . even in the towns and cities of the South, the Negro schools are so crowded and ill-equipped that no thorough teaching is possible.

In fact, the legal challenge to segregation offered new focus, struggle, and ultimately improvement for black children. As Weinberg (1977) states:

> Midcentury marked a turning point in the history of black America. The movement for equality came under black leadership, embraced unprecedented numbers of Negroes, and became national in scope. A persistent black initiative forced a reformulation of public policies in education.

The attack against the segregation system had begun. As seen in the historic cases of *McLaurin* (1950) and *Brown v. Board of Education* of Topeka (1954 [see Weinberg, 1977]), the concept of "separate but equal" was overturned. Furthermore, the Civil Rights Act of 1964 continued the struggle for equality of opportunity and education, one that persists today in our schools and society.

"Free School"

A. S. Neill (1883–1973) was the most famous proponent of the "free/natural school" movement of the midcentury. His book *Summerhill* describes 40 years of that educational program, of which he was headmaster. Neill claimed that most education was defective because it arose from the model of original sin. Assuming children were inherently evil caused educators to force children into doing what was contrary to their nature. Neill shared Rousseau's belief in noninterference, as he states: "I believe that a child is innately wise and realistic. If left to himself without adult suggestion of any kind, he will develop as far as he is capable of developing" (Neill, 1960).

Neill's belief in freedom was practiced in his school, where children governed themselves and worked toward equal rights with adults. The benefits from such liberties were touted as highly therapeutic and natural, an escape from repression and guilt. Several influences are clear in these educational programs: Rousseau's belief in the *child's innate goodness*, Freud's idea of the *dangerous effects of guilt*, and some of the *social idealism* of Dewey and the Progressives.

Head Start

After the war, few innovations took place until a small piece of metal made its worldwide debut. Sputnik, the Soviet satellite, was successfully launched in 1957 and caused an upheaval in educational circles. Two questions were uppermost in the minds of most Americans: Why weren't we first in space? What is wrong with our schools? The emphasis in education quickly settled on engineering, science, and math in the hope of catching up with Soviet technology.

The civil rights struggle in the early 1960s soon followed. In pointing out the plight of the poor, education was highlighted as a major stumbling block toward equality of all people. It was time to act, and Project Head Start was conceived as education's place to fight the "war on poverty." The same goals of Froebel and Montessori formed the basis of Head Start: helping disadvantaged preschool children. This was a revolution in American education, not seen since the short-lived child care programming during World War II. This project was the first large-scale effort by the government to focus on children of poverty.

Project Head Start began in 1965 as a demonstration program aimed at providing educational, social, medical, dental, nutritional, and mental health services to preschool children from a diverse population of low-income families. In 1972, it was transformed into a predominantly part-day, full-year program. Key features included offering health services, small groups, parent-teacher collaboration, and the thrill of communities getting involved with children in new ways. Osborn (1965) tells us:

> I wish I knew how to tell this part of the story . . . the bus driver in West Virginia who took time off from his regular job and went to the Center to have juice and crackers with "his" children because they asked him to. . . . The farmer who lived near an Indian Reservation and who each morning saddled his horse, forded a river and picked up an Indian child—who would not have attended a Center otherwise. . . . they represent the true flavor of Head Start.

Over the years, Head Start has provided comprehensive developmental services to more than 10 million children and their families.

This was an exciting time—a national recognition of the needs of young children and a hope for a better quality of life. Three major points included in the Head Start program are noteworthy:

- *Compensatory education*—programs that compensate for inadequate early life experiences.
- *Parental involvement*—inclusion of parents in planning, teaching, and decision making.
- *Community control*—local support and participation.

These three objectives combined to reinforce the goals of the program in real and concrete ways. Head Start was an attempt to make amends, to compensate poor children by preparing them for school and educational experiences. Parents, by being required to participate at all levels, were educated along with their children. The purpose of the community-based governing boards was to allow the program to reflect local values and concerns. Concurrently, underprivileged, poor people were being encouraged to take part in solving some of their own problems.

The spirit of Head Start was infectious. As a result of community interest in Head Start, there was a burst of enthusiasm for many programs for the young child. Because of Head Start's publicity, there has been an expanding enrollment in nursery school, kindergarten, and day care programs. Thanks to Head Start, there is national attention to the need for providing good care and educational experiences for young children. The Head Start program is

Head Start is the largest publicly funded education program for young children in the United States.

alive and well today and is nationally recognized as an effective means of providing comprehensive services to children and families, serving as a model for the development of the ABC Child Care Act of 1990. We will discuss it further in Chapter 2.

Early Child Care for the Very Young

Some people say we are in the midst of a second child care revolution for young children, as two parents, single parents, and step-parents all leave the home to work in greater numbers than ever before. Parents must rely on educators to teach their children from a very young age, including infants. While many European industrialized nations have addressed these issues, the United States has not completely faced this reality or risen to the challenge.

The American public is unclear about what is the best way to raise our very young children, especially those under three. Women, by and large, are working outside of the home and are not available around the clock to care for infants and toddlers; men are not, by and large, electing to stay home or raise their children full time. There are not nearly enough properly funded centers or family child care homes for very small children, and the patchwork system of parents, extended family, and neighborhood adults fragments the care.

We need to look carefully at child care for infants and toddlers, questioning the relationship between child care and children's development. Once, when America was mobilized around a world war, children's care was addressed so as to enable mothers to work while fathers were in the armed forces. During the last thirty years both parents have once again focused on work outside the home.[1] Care for children by extended family, family child care homes, and centers is on the rise.

INTERDISCIPLINARY INFLUENCES

Several professions enrich the heritage of early childhood. This diversity was apparent from the beginning; the first nursery schools drew from six different professions: social work, home economics, nursing, psychology, education, and medicine. Three of the most consistent and influential of those disciplines were medicine, education, and child psychology.

Medicine

The medical field has contributed to the study of child growth through the work of several physicians. These doctors became interested in child development and extended their knowledge to the areas of child rearing and education.

Maria Montessori

Maria Montessori (1870–1952) was the first woman in Italy ever granted a medical degree. She began studying children's diseases, and through her work with mentally defective children found education more appealing. Her philosophy is discussed earlier in this chapter and will be part of Chapter 2 on educational programs.

Sigmund Freud

Sigmund Freud (1856–1939) made important contributions to all modern thinking. The father of personality theory, he drastically changed how we look at childhood. Freud reinforced two specific ideas: (1) a person is influenced by his early life in fundamental and dramatic ways; and (2) early experiences shape the way people live and behave as adults. Thus, psychoanalytic theory is mostly about personality development and emotional problems. Freud's work set into motion one of the three major strands of psychological theory that influence the developmental and learning theories of early childhood today. Although the impact of psychoanalysis on child psychology is not as great as it was 25 years ago, it still contributes significantly to the study of early childhood. Though he was not involved directly in education, Freud influenced its development. Freud and psychoanalytic theory influenced education greatly. Chapter 4 will enlarge on the theory and its application in early childhood education.

Arnold Gesell

Arnold Gesell (1880–1961) was a physician who was concerned with growth from a medical point of view. Gesell began studying child development when he was a student of G. Stanley

1   The women's movement of the 20th century has brought attention to deeply help beliefs about child-rearing and early childhood practices. Be alert to adult attitudes as they voice interest in and concern for young children, their schooling, and the people who care for them.

Hall, an early advocate of child study. He later established the Clinic of Child Development at Yale University, where the data he collected with his colleagues became the basis of the recognized norms of how children grow and develop. He was also instrumental in encouraging Abigail Eliot to study with the McMillan sisters in England.

Gesell's greatest contribution was in the area of child growth. He saw maturation as an innate and powerful force in development. "The total plan of growth," he said, "is beyond your control. It is too complex and mysterious to be altogether entrusted to human hands. So nature takes over most of the task, and simply invites your assistance" (Gesell, Ames, & Ilg, 1977).

Through the Gesell Institute, guides were published using this theory. With such experts as Dr. Frances Ilg and Dr. Louise Bates Ames, Gesell wrote articles that realistically portrayed the child's growth from birth to adolescence. These guides have sharp critics regarding their overuse and inappropriate application to children of cultures other than those studied.[1] Moreover, their approach can be limiting, particularly as we think of developmentally appropriate practices and the importance of both individual variation and family and cultural diversity. Still, the "ages and stages" material is used widely as a yardstick of normal development. Gesell's maturation theory is discussed in Chapter 4.

Benjamin Spock

Benjamin Spock's book *Baby and Child Care* was a mainstay for parents in the 1940s and 1950s. In a detailed "how-to" format Dr. Spock (1903–1998) preached a common-sense approach that helped shape the childhood of many of today's adults. By his death in 1998, the book had sold almost 50 million copies around the world and had been translated into 42 languages.

Spock saw himself as giving practical application to the theories of John Dewey (see this chapter) and Sigmund Freud (see Chapters 1 and 4), particularly in the ideas that children can learn to direct themselves, rather than needing to be constantly disciplined.

Spock suggested that mothers use the playpen less and allow children freedom to explore the world firsthand. To that end, he asked parents to "child proof" their homes—a radical thought at the time. The word *permissiveness*, as it relates to child-rearing, became associated with Dr. Spock's methods, although Spock himself described his advice as relaxed and sensible, while still advocating for firm parental leadership.

Dr. Spock became an outspoken advocate for causes that extend his ideas. He was an active critic of those forces—economic, social, or political—that destroy healthy development. Dr. Spock noted:

> Child care and home care, if well done, can be more creative, make a greater contribution to the world, bring more pleasure to family members, than 9 out of 10 outside jobs. It is only our mixed-up, materialistic values that make so many of us think the other way around. (Spock, 1976)

T. Berry Brazelton

Dr. T. Berry Brazelton (1918–) is a well-known pediatrician who supports and understands the development of infants and toddlers. He developed an evaluation tool called the Neonatal Behavioral Assessment Scale (also known as "the Brazelton") to assess newborns. Cofounder of the Children's Hospital Unit in Boston and professor emeritus of pediatrics at Harvard Medical School, he is also a well-known author. His pediatric guides for parents deal with both physical and emotional growth. His writings speak to the parents' side of child raising, such as setting limits, listening to what children say, and observing what they do, as in the following discussion:

> I think many working parents have a very tough time thinking about limits. They find it difficult to say no, to set behavior standards. . . . Parents tell me, "I can't stand to be away all day and then come home and be the disciplinarian." We have to realize how hard it is for parents to discipline these days. They need a lot of reinforcement to understand how important reasonable discipline is to the child. Teachers can be very important here, helping parents see the need to expect more adequate behavior. (2001)

More recently Brazelton has advocated a national parental leave standard and is involved

 1 This is another reminder of the importance of being able to notice the sociocultural bias in the research in our field, keeping the information that is supportive to sound practice, and expanding or disregarding what does not support good practice with children in a multicultural society.

in a federal lobbying group known as "Parent Action." He is also a popular TV personality, hosting the nationally syndicated show entitled *What Every Baby Knows*. He is co-founder of Touchpoints, an educational training center helping professionals engage and communicate with parents and their infants or toddlers.

Education

Early childhood is one part of the larger professional field known as education. This includes elementary, secondary, and college or postsecondary schools. Along with John Dewey and Abigail Eliot, several other influences from this field bear attention.

The McMillan Sisters

In the first three decades of this century, these two sisters pioneered in early education. Nursery schools in Britain and America probably were developed because of the drive and dedication of the McMillan sisters.

Both women had broad international backgrounds. They grew up in North America and Scotland. Margaret studied music and language

Margaret McMillan, along with her sister Rachel, developed the "open-air" nursery school and training schools in England. (From *Margaret McMillan: Portrait of a Pioneer*, © 1989 Routledge. Reproduced by permission of Taylor & Francis Books UK.)

in Europe. She was well read in philosophy, politics, and medicine. Rachel studied to become a health inspector in England.

Health studies of 1908–1910 showed that 80 percent of children were born in good health, but that by the time they entered school only 20 percent could be classified that way. Noticing the deplorable conditions for children under age five, the McMillan sisters began a crusade for the slum children in England. Their concern extended beyond education to medical and dental care for young children. In 1910 they set up a clinic in Deptford, a London slum area, which became an open-air nursery a year later. The McMillans called it a "nurture school." Later, a training college nearby was named for Rachel. With no private financial resources, these two women faced tremendous hardships in keeping their school open. It is to their credit that Deptford still exists today.

The McMillan theory of fresh air, sleep, and bathing proved successful. "When over seven hundred children between one and five died of measles, there was not one fatal case at Deptford School" (Deasey, 1978). From the school's inception, a primary function was to research the effects of poverty on children.

Of the two sisters, Margaret had the greatest influence at the school at Deptford. In fact, it was Margaret who continued to champion early education issues beyond Deptford. "Her clinics, night camps, camp school, baby camp, open-air nursery school, and training college all reflected her conviction that health was the handmaiden of education" (Bradburn, 2000). Abigail Eliot writes of her:

> Miss McMillan invented the name [nursery school]. She paid great attention to health: a daily inspection, the outdoor program, play, good food—what she called "nurture." But she saw that an educational problem was also involved and she set to work to establish her own method of education for young children. This was why she called it a "school." (Hymes, 1978)

Susan Isaacs

Susan Isaacs (1885–1948) was an educator of the early 20th century whose influence on nursery and progressive schools of the day was substantial. In 1929 she published *The Nursery Years*, which emphasized a different point of view than that of the behaviorist psychologists of the times. She interpreted Freudian theory for teachers and provided guidance for how schools could apply this new knowledge of the unconscious to the education of children. She proposed:

> the opportunity for free unhindered imaginative play not only as a means to discover the world but also as a way to reach the psychic equilibrium, in working through wishes, fears, and fantasies so as to integrate them into a living personality. (Biber, 1984)

The teacher's role was different from that of a therapist, she asserted, in that teachers were "to attract mainly the forces of love, to be the good but regulating parent, to give opportunity to express aggression but in modified form, and not to attract herself to the negative explosive reactions of hatred and oppression" (Biber, 1984).

Isaacs's influence is felt today in schools whose philosophy emphasizes the child's point of view and the notion of play as the child's work.

The Progressive Education Movement

As indicated earlier in the sections on John Dewey and Patty Smith Hill, it was the Progressive Movement of the late 1800s and first half of the 20th century that changed the course of education in both elementary and nursery schools in America. Coinciding with the political progressivism in this country, this philosophy emphasized a child-centered approach that gained advocates from both the scientific viewpoint, such as G. Stanley Hall and John Dewey, and those of a psychoanalytic bent, such as Susan Isaacs and Patty Smith Hill.

Some of the major features of the educational progressive philosophy were:

1. We must recognize individual needs and individual differences in children.
2. Teachers [must be] more attentive to the needs of children.
3. Children learn best when they are highly motivated and have a genuine interest in the material.
4. Learning via rote memory is useless to children.
5. The teacher should be aware of the child's total development—social, physical, intellectual, and emotional.
6. Children learn best when they have direct contact with the material (Osborn, 1991).

These beliefs were instrumental in changing the old traditional schools from a strict and

subject-based curriculum to one that centered on children's interests as the foundation for curriculum development. Creating mass education during the Progressive Era was a struggle between the values of efficiency and those of individual development. The Progressives, under the leadership of Dewey and others, believed that public school should nurture individual differences, while at the same time encourage problem solving and teamwork. They wanted educators to work on "how a school could become a cooperative community while developing in individuals their own capacities and satisfying their own needs" (Dewey, 1916). Although Dewey and others did not reject the teaching of basic skills, the shift was away from such subject matter education. Therefore, it is no surprise that progressive education had many critics among those interested in schooling for academic preparation. Still, most early childhood centers can thank the progressives for much of their philosophy and techniques for developing curriculum for their children today.

The Waldorf School

The first Waldorf School was established in Stuttgart, Germany, in 1919, by Rudolf Steiner, who is described earlier in this chapter. Patterned after his educational philosophy and personal beliefs, it was based on the premise that education's aim is to help all people find their right place in life and thus fulfill their destiny. There is close personal attention to the child's developing temperament, and self-directed activity is valued. Children must be protected as they develop, so the teacher and parents must adhere to specific actions to protect the child from the noise of the modern world and technology.

Steiner agreed with Froebel and others that education should begin where the learner is. Whatever the child brings to the educational experience is to be worked with, not against. The curriculum of Waldorf schools is, therefore, both interdisciplinary and multisensory, with an emphasis on the arts, on tales of wisdom, and the concepts of community and respect for a person's individual needs. Often a teacher stays with the same group of children for eight years.

Although this movement is essentially an elementary and secondary one, it is noteworthy as one of the largest nonsectarian, independent school movements in the world. Waldorf has about 870 schools in 60 countries (http://www.waldorfanswers.org, 2004); moreover, it is the model of choice for the changing Soviet and Eastern European school systems (Caniff, 1990). With its foundations similar to Froebelian tradition, and with elements of both Montessori and progressive education, Waldorf School has contributed to the educational philosophy of responsiveness to children and their phase of development. Waldorf Schools as a program model are discussed and analyzed in Chapter 2.

The Child Study Movement

A survey of education influences is incomplete without mentioning the child study movement in the 1920s and 1930s. It was through the child study movement that education and psychology began to have a common focus on children. Besides the Gesell Institute, many research centers and child development laboratories were established at colleges and universities around the country. Their inception reflects the interest of several disciplines in the growth of the young child. Schools of psychology looked for children to observe and study; schools of education wanted demonstration schools for their teachers-in-training and for student-teacher placement. Schools of home economics wanted their students to have firsthand experiences with children. These on-campus schools provided a place to gather information about child development and child psychology.

This period of educational experiments and child study led to an impressive collection of normative data by which we still measure ranges of ordinary development. Broman (1978) sums up the influence of the movement this way:

> From the beginning of the child study movement in the 1920s . . . early childhood was not a major emphasis in education until after the War on Poverty and the establishment of Head Start in 1965. The child study movement, however, was the impetus that began the search for the most appropriate means of educating young children.

The British Infant School

Developed by Robert Owen in the early 19th century, the British infant schools had a strong commitment to social reform. Owen was a self-made businessman whose philosophy extended to the creation of an ideal community. Like Rousseau, he believed that people were naturally good but were corrupted by harsh environment and poor treatment. He took his ideas to the British House of Commons, speaking against the common practice of child labor. He established instruction and exercise for children until ten, although it was common for children as young as five to work in the mills. He then immigrated to the United States and founded the community of New Harmony.

In England, the term *infant school* refers to the kindergarten and primary grades. In 1967, the Plowden Report proposed a series of reforms for the schools. These changes paralleled those of Owen and mainstream American early education. As a result, many American teachers in both the preschool and primary grades adapted the British infant school approach to their own classrooms.

Three aspects of this **open school** style that received the most attention were:

1. *Vertical, or family, groupings.* Children from five to eight years of age are placed in the same classroom. Several teachers may combine their classes and work together in teaching teams. Children may be taught by the same teachers for two or three years.

2. ***Integrated day.*** The classroom is organized into various centers, for math, science, and the arts. The teacher moves from one child

The history of early childhood education includes contributions from many ethnic groups. San Francisco's Golden Gate Kindergarten Association has provided nursery education for the city's various neighborhoods from the turn of the century to the present. (Reprinted with permission of Golden Gate Kindergarten Association.)

or center to another as needed. Play is often the central activity, with an emphasis on follow-through with children's ideas and interests as they arise.

3. *Underlying concept.* There is a fundamental belief that the process of thinking takes precedence over the accumulation of facts. Learning how to think rather than stockpiling data is encouraged. How to identify and solve problems is valued more than having a finished product. Teachers focus on the child's current learning rather than on the future.

Just as Owen's ideas took hold in America in the 19th century, so, too, did the 20th-century version of the infant school fire the imaginations of teachers in the United States. Their tenets of open education are developmentally appropriate for both preschool and primary schools.

Reggio Emilia

In the last part of this century, yet another educator and educational system have influenced early childhood thinking. Loris Malaguzzi (1920–1994) developed his theory of early childhood education from his work with infants, toddlers, and preschoolers while working as the founder and director of Early Education in the town of Reggio Emilia, Italy. His philosophy includes creating "an amiable school" (Malaguzzi, 1993) that welcomes families and the community and invites relationships among teachers, children, and parents to intensify and deepen to strengthen a child's sense of identity. Malaguzzi continually asked teachers to question their own practices and listen to the children, as we can hear in his letter (Gandini, 1994) excerpted below:

> My thesis is that if we do not learn to listen to children, it will be difficult to learn the art of staying and conversing with them. . . . It will also be difficult, perhaps impossible, to understand how and why children think and speak; to understand what they do, ask, plan, theorize or desire. . . . Furthermore, what are the consequences of not listening? . . . We adults lose the capacity to marvel, to be surprised, to reflect, to be merry, and to take pleasure in children's words and actions.

Reggio Emilia has attracted the attention and interest of American educators because of its respect for children's work and creativity, its project approach, and its total community support. Reggio Emilia serves as a model of early childhood practices. This high quality program is also discussed in Chapters 2, 9, 11, and 14.

Psychology

The roots of early childhood education are wonderfully diverse, but one taproot is especially deep: the connection with the field of psychology. In this century particularly, the study of people and their behavior is linked with the study of children and their growth.

Initially, child development was mostly confined to the study of trends and descriptions of changes. Then the scope and definition of child development began to change. Developmental psychologists now study the processes associated with those changes. Specifically, child development focuses on language acquisition, the effect of early experiences on intellectual development, and the process of attachment to others. Such is the world of early childhood—it is no wonder that we are so closely tied to the world of psychology.

There is no one theory or name that encompasses all of developmental psychology. Indeed, there are many. The major theories of the psychodynamic, behaviorist, cognitive schools of thought, along with sociocultural and multiple intelligences theories, join with maturation and humanist viewpoints. Most recently, brain-based research is included to describe these important influences in early education. Their creators and influence will be discussed in depth in Chapter 4.

THEMES IN EARLY CHILDHOOD EDUCATION

When we review the colorful and rich history of early childhood education, four major themes emerge. Each is reflected in the ensuing thought and theory of each age.

Ethic of Social Reform

The first theme, the ethic of **social reform**, expects that schooling for young children will lead to social change and improvement. Montessori, the McMillans, Patty Smith Hill, Abigail Eliot, and Head Start all tried to improve children's health and physical well-being by attending first to the physical and social welfare aspects of children's lives. Other more recent examples illustrate how important

CDF: Child Advocacy as Social Reform

1979	Blocked attempts to eliminate $200 million for Social Services
1980	Supported Adoption Assistance & Child Welfare Act
1982	Helped forward the Children's Mental Health Program
1990	Supported Act for Better Child Care (Child Care & Development Block Grant)
1994	Reauthorized Head Start with Quality Improvements
1997	Promoted Children's Health Insurance Program (CHIP)
2001	Expanded Child Care Tax Credit
2002	Preserved CHIP funding to all states

FIGURE 1-5 Children's Defense Fund, led by Marian Wright Edelman, has successfully advocated for children with research and persistence for more than three decades.

this theme is to our work. Marian Wright Edelman is an outstanding children's advocate. A graduate of Spelman College and Yale Law School, Edelman began her career as a civil rights lawyer (the first black woman to be admitted to the Mississippi state bar). By the 1960s she had dedicated herself to the battle against poverty, moving to Washington, DC, and founding a public interest law firm that eventually became the Children's Defense Fund (CDF). CDF has become the United States' strongest voice for children and families (see Figure 1-5).

The author of several books, including *Families in Peril, The Measure of Our Success*, and *Guide My Feet*, Edelman advocates for equity in social reform:

> [We] seek to ensure that no child is left behind and that every child has a Healthy Start, a Head Start, a Fair Start, a Safe Start, and a Moral Start in life with the support of caring families and communities (Edelman, 2006). This reform work is being carried on by her son, Jonah, who now organizes the annual Washington, DC, rally "Stand for Children."

Dr. Louise Derman Sparks, in collaboration with Betty Jones and colleagues from Pacific Oaks College, published *Anti-Bias Curriculum: Tools for Empowering Young Children* (1989). This book outlined several areas in which children's behavior was influenced by biases in our society and suggested a host of ways that teachers (and parents) could begin addressing these issues.[1] These professionals have added an important dimension to the notion of social reform, for they focus our attention on ourselves, the school environment, children's interactions, and the community of parents and colleagues in educational settings.

Finally, social reform in the last 20 years has been championed by educators and citizens beyond early childhood education. Robert Coles, a psychiatrist and educator, has written and lectured extensively about his observations and work with children of poverty and is best known for *Children of Crisis: A Study of Courage and Fear* (1971). Additionally, Jonothan Kozol has spoken extensively about segregation in the schools, most notably in his book *Savage Inequalities: Children in America's Schools* (1991), where he writes:

> Surely there is enough for everyone in this country. It is a tragedy that these good things are not more widely shared. All our children ought to be allowed a stake in the enormous richness of America. Whether they were born to poor white Appalachians or to wealthy Texans, to poor black people in the Bronx or to rich people in Manhasset or Winnetka, they are all quite wonderful and innocent when they are small. We soil them needlessly.

Educators today still assert that tired, undernourished children are not ready to learn or to be educated. Social reform can go a step further, such as with Universal Preschool (see Chapter 15), improving access to quality early childhood programs and involving the community in its efforts.

Importance of Childhood

The second theme is the **importance and uniqueness of childhood**. In fact, the entire notion of the importance of childhood rests on the concept of the child as a special part of human existence and, therefore, a valuable part of the life cycle. Before 1700 or so, Western society showed little concern for children. Infanticide was pervasive, if not actually accepted. Once families and society began to value children, life changed dramatically for the young.

1 It is critical that today's teachers learn to integrate cultural awareness and the effects of bias on children's behavior into their daily practices.

The saying "As the twig is bent, so grows the tree" could apply to all children and their early childhood learning experiences as well as to an individual child. When people accepted the importance of childhood, they began to take responsibility for a quality life for children. From Comenius, Rousseau, and Froebel of earlier centuries to Neill, Russell, and the Child Study Movement of the 1900s, society has begun to provide for the health and physical welfare of children and come to understand the necessity to care for their minds.

We believe the early years form the foundation for later development, physically, intellectually, socially, and emotionally. This viewpoint takes a holistic approach; that is, all developmental areas of a child matter and blend together to form a complete child. Teachers may "sort out" the various aspects of development to concentrate their focus. For instance, a teacher may profile the child's motor skills or level of language development. Even so, we must take into account the whole child, for each part influences the whole. A current trend in our field to address the preservation of childhood is NAEYC's developmentally appropriate practices (DAP) and the Accreditation movement.

Childhood is a special time of life.

Chapters 2 and 9 expand on DAP and program quality, and Chapter 4 elaborates on developmental issues. Moreover, we must take the child in context. Children come to us with a genetic history and from, as Gonzalez Mena (2001) puts it, "a family that is part of a racial, ethnic, cultural, language, and socioeconomic group. We welcome not only the individual child into our classroom but also his or her family." Chapter 8 develops this aspect further.

Believing that childhood is a special time of life brings with it a commitment to honor what children do during this time. Play is extremely important to children, but this importance is not widely understood. We introduce both our environment and curriculum development chapters (Chapters 9 and 10) with this theme.

One trend that is of increasing concern to childhood advocates is the "pushing" of children toward adulthood too fast and away from childhood too quickly. David Elkind wrote in the 1980s of a "hurried child" syndrome, in which children were pushed unnecessarily out of a relaxed childhood by a fast-paced society whose pressure to succeed and move fast put children of all ages at risk. As he put it (1982):

> We should appreciate the value of childhood with its special joys, sorrows, worries, and concerns. Valuing childhood does not mean seeing it as a happy, innocent period but rather as an important period of life to which children are entitled. They have a right to be children, to enjoy the pleasures and to suffer the trials of childhood that are infringed upon by hurrying. Childhood is the most basic human right of children.

Children need special attention during these years. Childhood is fundamentally different from adulthood; it needs to be understood and respected as such. Children's styles of learning, of letting the child "learn by doing" and "learn by discovery" are part of the essential respect for children and childhood. Public recognition of that need has created a wealth of programs for the young not dreamed of at any other time in history.

Transmitting Values

The third recurrent theme in our educational heritage is that of **transmitting values**. What children should ultimately *do* and *be* is at the core of all child-rearing practices, whether in the home or the school. Values—be they social, cultural, moral, or religious—have been the essence of education for centuries. For example, the Puritan fathers valued biblical theology. Therefore,

Early educational experiences transmit society's values to children.

schools of their time taught children to read in order to learn the Bible. Rousseau and Froebel valued childhood, so they created special places for children to express their innate goodness and uniqueness. The works of Montessori, Dewey, and Steiner reflected a belief in the worth and dignity of childhood. They transmitted these values into the educational practices we have inherited. Finally, the initiators of Head Start (see Chapter 2) and the Anti-bias Curriculum (see Chapter 9) realized that the child's self-worth would be enhanced by valuing one's culture or origin. An awareness and an appreciation of ethnic heritage is becoming an integral part of the early childhood curriculum.[1]

Many issues clamor for our attention; we live in a world of information overload and are barraged constantly by different social, political, economic, and media issues. Especially in the United States, where advertising and consumerism reign, we get distracted and have difficulty focusing on our values. "People are so overwhelmed," write Brazelton and Greenspan (2001). "While they're whirling around, they don't have time to stop and think, 'What are my values? Do my children really come first? Am I making time for them in my life?'" Many young

families today are aware of this situation and are looking for spiritual and moral direction for themselves and their children. Look at "What do you think?" for an outline of issues that indicate priority areas.

We know that children learn what they live. Valuing and connecting home cultural knowledge with an early childhood program is challenging. Successful teaching practices must reflect teaching practices at home in substantial ways; blending basic life skills, ethics, culture, and traditions build substance in our children and in our society. This teamwork is possible if (and this is a big *if*) adults can find a way to honor diversity and still form a cohesive culture. "An ability to reach unity in diversity will be the beauty and test of our civilization," said Mahatma Gandhi. It is our ethical responsibility to articulate our values as educators and to include those of the families we teach.

Teaching children to live in a democratic society has always been valued in the United States. In the curriculum from early education through college, this belief is reflected as we educate our children for citizenship.[2] It is how we define these values and how we teach them that are the critical issues in education.

1 Informed early childhood educators really are leading the way in educational practice in terms of *celebrating* the diversity of the families!

2 The early childhood profession provides the opportunity for one to be an agent for social change—to actually translate the values of democracy into practice.

What do YOU Think?

What are your values for young children? What do you think are priorities in your program? Compare your list with this one, by Brazelton and Greenspan (2001).

1. Ongoing nurturing relationships
2. Physical protection, safety, and regulation
3. Experiences tailored to individual differences
4. Developmentally appropriate experiences
5. Limit-setting, structure, and expectations
6. Stable, supportive communities and cultural continuity

Professionalism

"If you are thinking about working with young children as a career, perhaps you are wondering how early childhood education compares in prestige and importance with elementary or secondary education," wrote Stanford's Edith Dowley (1985). As one of the original head teachers of the Kaiser Child Care Centers, Dowley had seen many changes in her nearly half-century in

Video VIEW PoinT 1-2

COMPETENCY: Professionalism

AGE GROUP: Preschool

CRITICAL THINKING QUESTIONS:

1. Locate the Position Statements from NAEYC and select one that interests you. Offer your interpretations and comments, and what it means to you or your early childhood program.

2. Since membership in a professional organization supports individual growth, find out about the local NAEYC affiliate in your community, its activities and meetings, and how you can join.

the field: "Is it truly a profession for growth and change? Can a student preparing to work with young children today look forward to a challenging, intellectually stimulating, and rewarding future in an early childhood profession?"

If you have read this chapter, then you already know the answer. The early years are a special time of life, and those who work with young children can openly declare their calling. There are four aspects of this sense of professionalism.

These are:

- *Sense of identity.* Early childhood professionals see themselves as caregivers who strive to educate the whole child, taking into consideration the body, the mind, and the heart and soul. Chapter 3 explains this holistic focus.

- *Purpose to engage in developmentally appropriate practices (DAP).* What constitutes quality care and education calls for blending three knowledge bases:

  1. child development and learning.
  2. the strengths, interests, and needs of each child.
  3. The social and cultural contexts in which children live. Chapter 2 further defines DAP, and Chapters 9 through 14 demonstrate how to teach in this way.

- *Commitment to ethical teaching and to child advocacy.* Being a professional means behaving with a child's best interests in mind, keeping confidentiality when discussing issues in the classroom and about families, upholding a code of ethics, and taking themselves and their work seriously. Chapter 5 elaborates on a teacher's role and includes our Code of Ethical Conduct.

- *Participation in the work as a legitimate livelihood.* Early childhood education is more than glorified babysitting; the people who provide care and education to young children deserve wages and working conditions that are worthy of their efforts. Chapter 15 underscores the importance of compensation.

"Ours is a profession that is constantly growing, branching out in many directions and ready to meet emerging challenges in flexible, innovative ways," continues Edith Dowley. We have professional organizations to guide us. The National Association for the Education of Young Children (NAEYC), formerly the National Association of Nursery Educators, is the largest, best known organization. The Association for Childhood Education International (ACEI)

Guides to Early Childhood Professionalism

Document	Goal	Source/Access
Code of Ethical Conduct	Provide a moral compass for early childhood educators	Feeney & Freeman (1999) Appendix A
Developmentally Appropriate Practices	Provide guidance about current understandings, values, and goals for working with children in group settings	Bredekamp & Copple (1998) Chapters 2 and 9
Program Accreditation Criteria & Procedures	Establish recommended standards for practice, serving as benchmarks	NAEYC Academy (2006) Chapters 2 and 15
Early Childhood Professional Preparation	Guidelines for teacher education Advancing careers in child development	Hyson (2003) Sharpe (2002)

FIGURE 1-6 Documents that promote professionalism in early childhood education.

began with kindergarten and then expanded to include both preschool and elementary school. Children's Defense Fund (CDF) advocates for children, particularly addressing the needs of poor and minority children and those with disabilities. These organizations have made improvements in the status of children, and they have begun to outline standards and practices for the people who call themselves "early childhood professionals." (See Figure 1-6.)

These four themes have been at the center of early education for centuries. Occasionally one theme dominates, as it did in the 1960s when the desire for social reform led to the creation of Head Start. At other times they seem indistinguishable from one another. Together, they have shaped the direction of early childhood education as we know it today. As we learn more about children, society, and ourselves, the 21st century will be a time to reconsider and redefine our aims and directions. It is a formidable challenge—and a worthy one.

SUMMARY

The history of early childhood education is like a tapestry—woven of many influences. A broad field such as medicine is a thread in this cloth, as is the passion of a Patty Smith Hill or a Lucy Sprague Mitchell. The history forms the theory on which we base our teaching. Every child, every class, and every experience translates our history into educational practice and makes another thread in this grand cloth.

Events of history have had a hand in shaping early childhood education. Forces such as war (which produced the Kaiser Shipyards project), political movements (such as progressivism), and the state of the economy (which brought the War on Poverty and Head Start) bring about change and development in how children are cared for in this country. The ingredients that early childhood educators consider essential today—that care and education are inseparable, that teaching practices are developmentally appropriate, and that adequate funding is critical for success—all stem from historical events and people.

Several fields of study and a number of professions have added to our knowledge of children and thus have affected educational theory. From the professions of education, medicine, and psychology, early childhood education has developed ideas of what is best for children. Medicine offered a view of childhood that is both maturational and environmental. Psychology confirmed this blending of nature and nurture and offered observational study as a basis for educational practice. As a result, early childhood theory includes both an attention to physical growth and developmental stages and a respect for personal experience in learning. The field of education brought to early childhood theory the components of a holistic approach to child and family, variable grouping of children and activities, and a sensitivity to the social and reform possibilities of educating our young. These influences will be described at length in Chapter 4.

The individuals who created our history have had a profound effect on early childhood theory and practices. Their strong and passionate beliefs have captured our imaginations and fueled our commitment to enhancing the well-being of children. What John Comenius, Maria Montessori, and Marian Wright Edelman all had in common was a drive to extend themselves on behalf of young children. Thus, early childhood theory has a *personal* component, an emotional investment that gives each of you a sense of belonging to a larger cause. The work that has gone before goes on through us and extends beyond us—to children of all ages and any era.

Each historical figure posed questions about the nature of childhood, of children, and of teaching. The answers have influenced educational philosophy and practice, and, in turn, have been affected by the social, political, religious, and economic forces of the day. Early childhood education itself is an interdisciplinary field, with important contributions from medicine, education, and psychology. From a child's garden to the child care model, each innovation has added to our "story." The four themes—the ethic of social reform, the importance of childhood, transmitting values, and professionalism—shape our ideas of ourselves in our work.

The contributions of many pioneers leave us dreams for the young children of our society. This can give meaning to our lives as teachers as we continue to create a climate for the child who will make history tomorrow.

A DELIGHTFUL STORY

by
Scott M. Williams, M.S.

The field of Early Child Education eagerly awaits, with hopeful expectation, your special contribution. "What could I possibly have to offer?" you ask. Your own history, or life story, is your greatest asset. Tucked away in your own early years are special experiences that can shape the lives of small children.

Your background is vitally important to the lives of others. The strengths and weaknesses of your life add a richness and diversity to the ever-growing tapestry of early child education. Your cultural heritage and life experiences enable you to touch children in a unique and powerful way.

A troubled childhood does not make you exempt from being a contributor. Remember Friedrich Froebel, the founder of kindergarten who was inspired to make a difference *because* of his unhappy childhood. The difficulties of our background can create an understanding and sensitivity to the challenges others face. If you were fortunate to be raised in a family with an abundance of love and resources, then children are waiting for you to share your gift with them.

Writing Your Own Story

A reflective search into your own early childhood can reveal these treasures. Writing is a powerful medium to accomplish this. Questions follow that will stimulate your thinking. For many of us, we may not have clear memories of these early stages of life. Therefore, draw upon the stories and memories that have been offered by your family and others who knew you then. If you find that you cannot answer a question, simply move onto the next, then plan on asking a family member who may be able to offer insight into your answer. We encourage you to write and save your answers for future reference. Addressing these questions later in your professional journey may provide fresh insights.

When finished with these questions, you may want to continue writing your story by responding to the phrase: *When I was a toddler . . .* or *When I was six . . .*

Regarding your early years:

1. What expectations does your culture have for young children? (*Consider what messages society sends to families about the activities these children should participate in.*)

2. In which activities did you participate as a child less than eight years old? (*Remember the toys with which you may have played or activities your family said you liked.*)

3. Did you participate in preschool? If so, what was the setting? Was it in your home, the home of others, a neighborhood child care facility, or a larger group center? (*You might consider how it was physically organized and the people involved.*)

4. Were your contacts with others ethnically diverse or localized to one cultural group? (*Cultural identity can be defined in many ways such as geographical, religious, racial, and so forth. Many of our identities include many cultures; that is, they are multicultural.*)

5. What did you gain from those early years that will help you as an early childhood educator? (*Look for a way this can be passed to others.*)

6. Describe one way you would like to improve the early childhood education you received. (*By rethinking what you did not receive, you can change this in the lives of those you are involved with.*)

Your personal story and love of children can be your greatest motivators in this field. Return often to your story to find fresh treasures to share with those young people you serve.

Scott M. Williams is on the faculty of California State University at Northridge in the Human Development department and is in private practice as a marriage, family, and child counselor.

For more activities and information, visit our Web site at
http://www.EarlyChildEd.delmar.com

KEY TERMS

professionalism

early childhood education

building block years

readiness

tabula rasa

integrated curriculum

kindergarten/children's garden

self-correcting

child-centered approach

parent cooperative schools

compensatory education

open school

integrated day

social reform

importance of childhood

transmitting values

REVIEW QUESTIONS

1. Identify and describe five key people who influenced the field of early childhood education. With whom would you like to have studied or worked? Why?

2. Match the name with the appropriate phrase. Put them in the order that best matches your own theory of early childhood education. State your reasons.

Rousseau	"prepared environment"
Montessori	"nurture" school
Froebel	children are naturally good
Malaguzzi	father of kindergarten
Dewey	common-sense approach
Spock	first picture book for children
McMillan sisters	Progressive Movement
Comenius	Reggio Emilia

3. Define early childhood education in your own words. Include age ranges and what you believe to be its purpose. Contrast this to the text definition and defend your position.

4. Name three institutions or living persons who are influencing the history of early childhood today. Describe your reactions to each and how they have influenced your educational philosophy.

5. Read the list below of some nontraditional and mainstream perspectives as described in the chapter. After each, trace its original root and put at least one example of how this perspective could be practiced in an early childhood classroom today.

Perspective	Roots in Early Childhood Practice
Harmony	
Kinship networks	
Close ties to nature	
Respect for elders	
Cooperative work	
Expressiveness	

6. Maria Montessori made several contributions to education. What are some of her theories, and how did she adapt them for classroom use? How are Montessori materials or teaching methods used in your classroom?

7. Name the four themes that have guided early childhood education throughout its history.

LEARNING ACTIVITIES

1. Find out when and by whom the school or center in which you are teaching was started. What were some of the social, economic, and political issues of those times? How might they have affected the philosophy of the school?

2. Write your own pedagogic creed. List five of what you consider to be the most important beliefs you hold about educating young children. How do you see those beliefs expressed in school today?

3. Make a list of the values you think are important to teach children. In an adjoining column, add the ways in which you would help children learn those values. In other words, list the materials and curriculum you would use.

4. Consider an informal interview with the director. What philosophies are important? Ask to look at any old photos, handbooks, or newspaper clippings. Do you think starting a history of your program would be useful?

REFERENCES

Aries, P. (1962). *Centuries of childhood*. New York: Knopf.

Bain, W. E. (1967). *75 years of concern for children*. Washington, DC: Association for Childhood Education International.

Bauch, J. P. (Ed.). (1988). *Early childhood education in the schools*. Washington, DC: National Education Association.

Biber, B. (1984). *Early education and psychological development*. New Haven, CT: Yale University Press.

Boyd, D. (1997). *Jean Jacques Rousseau*. Unpublished paper. Redwood City, CA: Cañada College.

Bradburn, E. (2000). "Margaret MacMillan: 1860–1933." In A. Gordon & K. W. Browne (Eds.), *Beginnings and beyond* (5th ed.). Clifton Park, NY: Thomson Delmar Learning.

Brazelton, T. B., & Greenspan, S. (2001, March). The irreducible needs of children, *Young Children*, 56 (2).

Bredekamp, S., & Copple, C. (Ed.). (1998). *Developmentally appropriate practice in early childhood programs*. Washington, DC: NAEYC.

Broman, B. L. (1978). *The early years in childhood education*. Chicago: Rand McNally College Publishing.

Brooks, A. (1886). *Four active workers*. Springfield, MA: Milton Bradley.

Caniff, D. I. (1990, November 28). Why the 'Waldorf' movement is thriving in Eastern Europe. *Education Week*, X(13).

Chattin-McNichols, J. (1993). In A. Gordon & K. W. Browne (Eds.), *Beginnings and beyond* (3rd ed.). Clifton Park, NY: Thomson Delmar Learning.

Cohen, D. H., & Randolph, M. (1977). *Kindergarten and early schooling*. Englewood Cliffs, NJ: Prentice-Hall.

Coles, R. (1971). *Children of crisis: A study of courage and fear*. New York, NY: Houghton Mifflin.

Comenius, (1658). *Orbis Pictus (The World of Pictures)*.

Cubberly, E. P. (1920). *A brief history of education*. Boston: Houghton Mifflin.

Deasey, D. (1978). *Education under six*. New York: St. Martin's Press.

DeMause, L. (1974). *The history of childhood*. New York: Psychohistory Press.

Derman Sparks, L. (1988). *The Anti-Bias Curriculum*. Washington, DC: NAEYC.

Dewey, J. (1897, 1916). *My pedagogic creed*. Washington, DC: The Progressive Education Association and Democracy and Education.

Dickerson, M. (1992, Spring). James L. Hymes, Jr.: Advocate for young children. *Childhood Education*.

Dowley, E. (1985). "Early childhood education in the shipyards." In A. Gordon & K. W. Browne, *Beginnings and beyond* (1st ed.). Clifton Park, NY: Thomson Delmar Learning.

DuBois, W. E. B. (1995). The talented tenth. Published in *The Negro Problem* (1903), excerpted in F. Schultz (Ed.), *Sources: Notable selection in education*. Guilford, CT: Dushkin.

Edelman, M. W. (2006). *The state of America's children*. Washington, DC: Children's Defense Fund.

Elkind, D. (1982). *The hurried child*. Reading, MA: Addison-Wesley.

Feeney, S., & Freeman, N. K. (1999). *Ethics and the early childhood educator: Using the NAEYC Code*. Washington, DC: NAEYC.

Froebel, F. (1887). *The education of man* (M. W. Hailman, Trans.). New York: D. Appleton.

Gandini, L. (1994, July). Tribute to Loris Malaguzzi. *Young Children*, 49(5).

Gesell, A. L., Ames, L. A., & Ilg, F. L. (1977). *The child from five to ten*. New York: Harper & Row.

Gonzalez-Mena, J. (2001). *Foundations: Early childhood education in a diverse society*. Mountain View, CA: Mayfield.

Greenberg, P. (1987, July). Lucy Sprague Mitchell: A major missing link between early childhood education in the 1980s and progressive education in the 1890s–1930s. *Young Children*, 42(5).

Hewes, D. (1993). On doing history. In A. Gordon & K. W. Browne (Eds.), *Beginnings and beyond* (3rd ed.). Clifton Park, NY: Thomson Delmar Learning.

Hill, P. S. (1996). Kindergarten. From the *American Educator Encyclopedia* (1941). In Paciorek & Munro. *Sources: Notable selections in early childhood education*. Guildford, CT: Dushkin.

Hilliard, A. G., III. (1997, September). Teacher education from an African American perspective. In J. Irvine

(Ed.), *Critical knowledge for diverse teachers and learners.* Washington, DC: AACTE.

Hymes, J. L., Jr. (1978–79). *Living history interviews* (Books 1–3). Carmel, CA: Hacienda Press.

Hyson, M. (Ed.) (2003). *Preparing early childhood professionals: NAEYC's standards for programs.* Washington, DC: NAEYC.

Keatinge, M. W. (1896). *The great didactic of John Amos Comenius* (Trans. and with introductions). London: Adams and Charles Black.

Kozol, J. (1991). *Savage inequalities: Children in America's schools.* New York: Crown Publishers.

Malaguzzi, L. (1993, November). For an education based on relationships. *Young Children.*

McMillan, M. (1919). *The nursery school.* London and Toronto: J. M. Dent & Sons; New York: E. P. Dutton.

Mitchell, L. S. (1951). *Our children and our schools.* New York: Simon & Schuster.

Montessori, M. (1967). *The Montessori method* (Trans. A. E. George). Cambridge, MA.

National Academy. (2006). *Accreditation criteria & procedures (Revised).* Washington, DC: NAEYC.

Neill, A. S. (1960). *Summerhill: A radical approach to child rearing.* New York: Hart.

Osborn, D. K. (1991). *Early childhood education in historical perspective* (3rd ed.). Athens, GA: Education Associates.

Pleasant, M. B. B. (1992). *Hampton University: Our home by the sea.* Virginia Beach, VA: Donning.

Read, K. B. (1950). *The nursery school: A human relationships laboratory.* New York: Saunders.

Read, K., & Patterson, J. (1980). *The Nursery School & Kindergarten: Relationships and Learning* (7th ed.). New York: Holt, Rinehart, & Winston.

Rousseau, J. J. (1761). *Emile* (Trans. by B. Foxley). London and Toronto: J. M. Dent & Sons.

Sharpe, C. (2002) *Advancing careers in child development in California.* Pasadena, CA: Pacific Oaks College & Children's School.

Sparks, L. D. (1989). *Anti-bias curriculum: Tools for empowering young children.* Washington DC: National Association for the Education of Young Children.

Spock, B. (1947). *The common sense book of baby and child care.* New York: Duell, Sloan & Pierce.

Spock, B. (1976, April). Taking care of a child and a home: An honorable profession for men and women. *Redbook Magazine.*

Spodek, B., Saracho, O. N., & Peters, D. L. (Eds.). (1988). *Professionalism and the early childhood practitioner.* New York: Teachers College Press.

Steiner, R. (1926). *The essentials of education.* London: Anthroposophical Publishing.

Stolz, L. M. (1978). In Hymes, J. *Living history interviews.* Carmel, CA: Hacienda Press.

Walker, L. R. (1997, Fall). John Dewey at Michigan. *Michigan Today.*

Weinberg, M. (1977). *A chance to learn: The history of race and education in the United States.* Cambridge, MA: Cambridge University Press.

HELPFUL WEB SITES

American Federation of Teachers Educational Foundation	http://www.aft.org/teachers/jft/grants.htm
Association for Childhood Education International	http://www.acei.org
Center for the Child Care Workforce	http://www.ccw.cleverspin.com
Child Care Information Exchange	http://www.childcareexchange.com
The Children's Defense Fund	http://www.childrensdefense.org
National Association for the Education of Young Children	http://www.naeyc.org
Southern Poverty Law Center	http://www.teachingtolerance.org

 For more activities and information, visit our Web site at http://www.EarlyChildEd.delmar.com

CHAPTER 2

Types of Programs

QUESTIONS FOR THOUGHT

What are some of the different types of early childhood programs and why are they important?

What are the indicators of quality in group programs for young children?

What is meant by "developmentally appropriate practices" (DAP)?

What is the range of early childhood programs, and how do they differ?

What are the major issues facing kindergartens today?

How does the role of the teacher differ in each of the early childhood settings?

How are programs structured to meet specific needs of children and families?

How does Head Start differ from other early childhood programs?

How do infant/toddler programs differ from preschool programs, and how do they differ from one another?

How can evaluating programs help children and teachers?

DIVERSITY OF PROGRAMS

From the types available, to the numbers of children who attend these schools, the name of the game in early childhood programs is diversity. The range can encompass a morning nursery school for toddlers, a primary school classroom, an infant–parent stimulation program, or a full child care service for three- to six-year-olds. Some programs run for only a half-day; others are open from 6:00 a.m. until 7:00 p.m. Still other centers, such as hospitals, accept children on a drop-in basis or for 24-hour care. Child care arrangements can range from informal home-based care to more formal school or center settings. Churches, school districts, community-action groups, parents, governments, private social agencies, and businesses may run schools. Figure 2-1 shows some of the factors that determine different types of early childhood programs.

Serving Many Needs

Programs for young children exist to serve a number of needs, which often overlap. Some of these are:

- Caring for children while parents work (e.g., family child care homes or child care centers)
- Enrichment programs for children (e.g., half-day nursery school or laboratory school)
- Educational programs for parent and child (e.g., parent cooperatives, parent–child public school programs, or high school parent classes)
- An activity arena for children (e.g., most early childhood programs)
- Academic instruction (e.g., kindergarten or many early childhood programs)
- Culturally or religiously specific programs (e.g., a school setting with a definitive African American focus or a church-related school that teaches religious dogma).

These programs generally reflect the needs of society as a whole. Millions of mothers of children under age six are in the labor force as never before. Early childhood schools provide a wide range of services for children from infancy through eight years of age to meet the demands of today's working mothers. The U.S. Bureau of Labor Statistics (2002) notes that nearly 60 percent of mothers in married-couple families were employed in 2001, and nearly 68 percent of mothers in families maintained by women were employed as well.

In the human life cycle, early childhood is a period of maximum dependency. The various programs available reflect this in a number of ways. The teacher–child ratio varies in relation to the child's age; infants, at the higher end of the dependency scale, require more teachers per child in a classroom than do six-year-olds. The program itself reflects the age group it serves. The size of the group, the length of the program, and the equipment used are related to the enrolled children's capabilities and needs. Even the daily schedule mirrors the dependent relationship between the child and the teacher. Bathrooming, snack and meal routines, as well as clothing needs, call for longer periods of time in a toddler group than in a class of four-year-olds.

Diversity is apparent, too, in the philosophy expressed by the specific program.[1] Some schools, such as Montessori programs, follow a very clear, precise outline based on a philosophical approach developed by Maria Montessori nearly 100 years ago. Other schools are more eclectic; they draw from a number of theories, choosing those methods and ideas that best suit their needs, some of which may be culturally or theologically based (see Figure 2-1).

SPECIAL FEATURES

Mixed-Age Groupings

One factor that may cut across program considerations is that of placing children of several age levels, generally separated by a year, into the same classroom. In these classes, younger children learn from older children and older children learn by teaching younger children. This practice is often referred to as family, heterogeneous, vertical, or ungraded grouping (Katz, Evangelou, & Hartman, 1990) and, though

[1] In observing programs for young children, consider the influences on the teachers' philosophy and practice; in many cases it is eclectic, a little bit of this and a little bit of that. It is another indication of how practice is influenced by life in a democratic and multicultural society.

Factors That Determine Types of Early Childhood Education Programs

Many factors determine exactly what type of program will best serve young children. Some of these variables are:

- age of the children served

- philosophical, theoretical, or theological approach

- goals of the program

- purpose for which the program was established

- requirements of a sponsoring agency

- quality and training of teaching staff

- shape, size, and location of physical environment

- cultural, ethnic, economic, and social makeup of community

- financial stability

FIGURE 2-1 Programs in early childhood settings are defined by these elements, and each factor has to be taken into consideration regarding its impact on the program. Any given program is a combination of these ingredients.

Differences in age can enrich the learning environment.

not a new idea, is emerging as an area of considerable interest to early childhood educators.

The age range among children in **mixed-age groups** is usually larger than one year, in anticipation that the differences among the children provide a greater depth of intellectual and social advantages. The intention is to capitalize on the difference in age, experience, knowledge, and abilities of the children (Katz, 1995). Mixed-age groupings have been a practice in Montessori programs, in the schools of Reggio Emilia, and in one-room schoolhouses for many years. Advocates of mixed-age groups point to a number of developmental advantages when children interact with peers above and below their age level:

- The child's own developmental level and pace are accommodated, allowing children to advance as they are ready.

- Age and competition are deemphasized, as cooperative learning is enhanced.

- Caring and helping behaviors toward younger children and a sense of responsibility toward one another are fostered.

- Diverse learning styles and multiple intelligences are appreciated.

- A variety and number of different models for learning and for friendships are available.

- Children grow in independence in their work and in socialization.

Katz (1995) further asserts that teachers and children alike tolerate a wider range of individual differences and behaviors in a mixed-age group, and cooperation, sharing, and giving help to one another are more frequent. Younger children participate in and contribute to more complex projects and activities than they would otherwise. Older children seem to spontaneously help and assist the younger ones (Chase & Doan, 1994).

There are risks associated with mixed-age groupings. The potential for older children to take over and/or overwhelm the younger ones is real, as is the possibility that younger children will pester the older children. This requires monitoring by the teaching staff, and the Reggio Emilia schools offer a good model here. In these Italian programs, older children have the responsibility to work with the younger children, explaining things and helping them find appropriate roles to take in their projects.

The academic and social advantages of mixed-age grouping cannot occur without a variety of activities from which children may freely choose and the opportunity for small groups of children to work together. Teachers must be intentional about encouraging children to work with others who have skills and knowledge they do not yet possess. Other considerations are the optimal age range, the proportion of older to younger children, the amount of time spent in mixed-age groups, and the implementation of a project-oriented curriculum (Katz, Evangelou, & Hartman, 1990).

It is easy to see how mixed-age groupings reflect the principles of Dewey, Piaget, Gardner, and Vygotsky, whose "zone of proximal development" is made more available through the interactions of peers as well as adults. The practice of mixed-age grouping has much to commend it and must be seriously addressed as an issue in programs for young children.

Looping

The practice of keeping a group of children and their teacher together in the same class for at least two years is called **looping**. Like multi-aged grouping, it is an old idea revisited. Today, looping is customary in the Waldorf Schools and Reggio Emilia programs, and it has emerged in other programs for a number of reasons. Proponents of looping suggest that it:

- Offers stability and emotional security to children.

- Gives teachers a greater opportunity to get to know children and therefore be able to individualize the program for them.

- Provides more instructional time without time being spent at the beginning of the school year on routines of procedures and familiarization.

- Fosters better social interactions among children.

- Enhances a sense of family and community within the classroom (Bellis, 1999; Chapman, 1999).

In the schools in Reggio Emilia infants and toddlers are kept in the same class with the same teachers for three years to provide a family-like environment. Looping is often paired with multi-aged classrooms, which further extends the natural, family-like atmosphere.

Critics of looping cite the need for experienced teachers who enjoy teaching across the age levels and who can work with the same children over an extended period of time. Looping does not fit all teachers and all children, and it could be offered as an option for parents and teachers to meet the needs of those who believe its advantages are worthwhile (Bellis, 1999; Chapman, 1999).

Indicators of Quality

Early childhood programs vary greatly in their educational goals and practices, their methods of instruction, and even in the kind of social "mood" or atmosphere they create. Yet, varied as they are, most early childhood programs share some common principles. The quality of these programs is based on three essential factors:

1. the teacher-child ratio; that is, the number of children cared for by each staff member;

2. the total size of the group or class; and

3. the education, experience, and training of the staff. The importance of these three factors cannot be underestimated, and they underline each of the principles that follow.

The National Association for the Education of Young Children (NAEYC), the largest professional organization for early childhood educators and caregivers, has established a list of criteria for high-quality early childhood programs, based on a consensus of thousands of early childhood professionals (NAEYC, 2005). Earlier, NAEYC defined "high quality" as a program that "meets the needs of and promotes the physical, social, emotional, and cognitive development of the children and adults—parents, staff, and administrators—who are involved in the program."

Figure 2-2 indicates the 10 criteria that serve as a standard of excellence for any group program for young children. After each one is a reference to the chapter(s) in this text where the topic is more fully developed.

Developmentally Appropriate Practice (DAP)

Throughout this text and whenever NAEYC principles are discussed, we use the term *developmentally appropriate practice*. What exactly is **developmentally appropriate practice**, or DAP, as it is more familiarly known?

In the late 1980s, NAEYC published a position paper, which articulated standards for high-quality care and education for young children. The guidelines were a response to the need for a set of unified standards for accreditation through NAEYC's newly established National Academy of Early Childhood. They had great impact and influence in the early childhood field, and "DAP" became common terminology in early childhood circles.

A DAP approach stressed the need for programs based on what we know about children through years of child development research

NAEYC Criteria for High Quality Programs

1. *Relationships.* Positive relationships help children develop personal responsibility, self-regulation, constructive interactions, and academic mastery. Warm, sensitive, and responsive relationships help children feel secure, develop a positive sense of self, respect for others, and the ability to cooperate. (Chapters 3, 5, 7, 8, and 14)

2. *Curriculum.* The curriculum draws on research for concepts, skills, and methodology that fosters children's learning and creates experiences that enhance growth across a broad range of development and content areas. The daily planning maximizes learning through time and materials and provides learning opportunities for children individually and in groups. (Chapters 4, 10, 11, 12, 13, and 14)

3. *Teaching.* Developmentally, linguistically, and culturally appropriate teaching practices enhance children's learning, as does multiple instructional methods, including teacher-directed, child-directed, and structured and unstructured learning opportunities. Teachers reflect the children's backgrounds, needs, interests, and capabilities in their instructional approaches. Where more than one teacher is in the classroom, a team teaching approach is used. (Chapters 5, 8, and 10)

4. *Assessment of Child Progress.* Appropriate and systematic assessment measures, which are culturally sensitive, inform the decisions made about children, teaching, and program improvement. Curricula are then tailored to specific children's needs. Assessments aid in identifying children who need additional instruction and/or intervention and further assessment. (Chapters 3, 6, and 10)

5. *Health.* A healthy state of well-being enhances a child's ability to learn. Adults help protect children from illness and injury and help them make healthy choices for themselves. (Chapters 9 and 15)

6. *Teachers.* The teaching staff is educationally qualified, knowledgeable, and professionally committed to support children's learning and development, as well as families' diverse needs and interests. The teachers who have specific preparation in child development and early childhood education are more likely to have warm, positive interactions with children, promote richer language experiences, and create a higher quality learning environment. Ongoing professional development ensures that they will reflect current research and best practices. (Chapters 2, 5, 9, and 10)

7. *Families.* Good family relationships are a collaboration between home and school and reflect family composition, language, and culture. They are based on mutual trust and respect in recognition of the primacy of the family in the life of the child. (Chapters 8 and 15)

8. *Community Relationships.* The program establishes relationships with and uses the resources of the community to realize program goals. By helping to connect families with a variety of resources, the children's health and development is enhanced. (Chapters 2, 3, 9, and 15)

9. *Physical Environment.* A safe, healthy, and accessible environment and well-maintained indoor and outdoor areas fosters learning, health, and safety for young children. The design of the facilities and the activities support a high-quality program. (Chapters 2, 9, 10, and 11)

10. *Leadership and Management.* The program effectively administers policies, procedures and systems that support a stable staff, strong personnel, fiscal, and program management. Effective governance and structure, program accountability, positive community relations and supportive workplace create a high-quality environment for all. (Chapters 2, 5, and 15)

FIGURE 2-2 These are the 10 essential components on which a program is judged for accreditation through NAEYC's Academy of Early Childhood Programs. (Adapted from the National Association for the Education of Young Children (NAEYC), NAEYC Early Childhood Program Standards and Accreditation Criteria: The Mark of Quality in Early Childhood Education (Washington, DC: NAEYC, 2005), 9–12. The 10 NAEYC Early Childhood Program Standards are available online at http:// www.naeyc.org/accreditationstandards.)

and what we observe of their interests, abilities, and needs, and called for an activity-based learning environment. These guidelines provided a necessary antidote to the more teacher-directed, academic preparation and skills-teaching approach, which was encroaching on many early childhood programs.

DAP was not without controversy. Many felt that NAEYC's position was too rigid, did not apply to all children at all times, and did not consider family background or the cultural context of children's lives.[1] There was concern that "good" practice meant only one definition of "good," rather than "many best ways" to support

 1 Many thought that the developmental norms reflected primary Euro-American culture.

a child's growth and development (Hynn, 1998). Further, some critics felt that the definitions of DAP did not leave enough leeway for teachers to make decisions that were culturally congruent and developmentally appropriate (Bredekamp, in Bredekamp & Copple, 1997). Others considered the age-appropriate expectations questionable because they are usually based on data from the majority culture (Bredekamp, in Bredekamp & Copple, 1997). The position paper was revised and adopted by NAEYC in 1996, following an extensive review by early childhood professionals.

Three Criteria

That position statement of "Developmentally Appropriate Practice in Early Childhood Programs Serving Children from Birth through Age 8" (NAEYC, 1997) now cites three criteria on which teachers and caregivers should base their decisions about young children's growth and development:

1. *What is known about child development and learning*—knowledge of age-related characteristics that permit general predictions within an age range about what activities, materials, interactions, or experiences will be safe, healthy, interesting, achievable, and also challenging to children.
2. *What is known about the strengths, interests, and needs of each individual child*—to be able to adapt and respond to individual variation?
3. *Knowledge of the social and cultural contexts in which children live*—to ensure that learning experiences are meaningful, relevant, and respectful for the children and their families (NAEYC, 1997).

What does this mean to an early childhood professional who wants to develop a program and curriculum that is developmentally appropriate? The key element in the DAP philosophy is a solid grounding in child development knowledge and theory. That is the core around which the idea of "developmentally appropriate" is built and provides the base for learning environments where children's abilities are matched to the developmental tasks they need to learn. Programs are designed *for* young children based on what is known *about* young children (Bredekamp & Copple, 1997).

To that mix, we add what we know about the individual children and their families. This collective knowledge is applied to each decision

that is made about the program. What are children like? How do they learn? When should they learn it? How should they be taught? How do we know they are learning? Gestwicki (2007) reminds us that finding a balance between the teacher's knowledge and understanding of the child and the family's desires and expectations is an important component of DAP. This can be particularly sensitive when cultural values are at stake. The following are examples of developmentally appropriate planning. Figure 2-3 describes it in another way.

DAP Principles in Action

Developmentally appropriate principles are reflected when:

- Programs and curriculum respond to the children's interests as well as their needs.
  Example: While digging in the sand pit, four children uncover water. Others rush to see it. The teacher sees their interest and asks them about the bridges and tunnels they are starting to build. A project in the making: children research, experiment, build, and learn.
- Children are actively involved in their own learning, choosing from a variety of materials and equipment.
  Example: Some children search the yard for materials that would bridge the water. Others go inside to find the big book on bridges. Still others dig in other areas of the sandpit to find more water. One child finds a walnut shell and floats it on the water. The teacher encourages and supports each child's involvement.
- Play is the primary context in which young children learn and grow.
  Example: Each day, the children rush outside to see their bridges and tunnels. The teacher has helped them find materials that will act as a cover over the bridge. Inside several children are making dolls from twigs and fabric scraps to use in the project.
- Teachers apply what they know about each child and use a variety of strategies, materials, and learning experiences to be responsive to individual children.
  Example: Josephina is drawing a picture of the bridge and is having trouble with the arches. Knowing that Josephina is somewhat shy and uneasy in large groups, the teacher asks Aldo (who is easygoing and loves to draw) to look at Josephina's picture to see if he might help her. The two children focus on the drawing, each making observations that help Josephina take the next

step. Teachers consider widely held expectations about each age group and temper that with challenging yet achievable learning goals.

Example: In preparation for a field trip to see two bridges that are near the school, the teacher sets out her expectations (walk with a buddy, stay together, stay on the sidewalk, don't run, etc.). Because this is their first field trip of the school year, the teacher rehearses the children for several days prior to the trip. Music and rhythm accompany them as they practice walking with a friend and play number games of "two-by-two" during group times.

- Teachers understand that any activity has the potential for different children to realize different learning from the same experience.

  Example: After the field trip, Josephina draws a different type of arch for her bridges. Selena, Gracie, and Sam take over the block corner to build bridges and tunnels; three others join them. Maddie finds a book on flowers. They look like some of the flowers she saw on the way to the bridges. Reilly wants to play London Bridge at group time.

- All aspects of development—physical, social/emotional, cognitive, and language—are integrated in the activities and opportunities of the program.

  Example: The bridge project promoted physical (walking, digging), social-emotional (pairing up two-by-two), cognitive (learning how bridges and tunnels are built, researching in books), and language (construction terms, such as piers, spans, suspension).

The early childhood professional should address all three principles of DAP when designing programs for young children, keeping in mind that each is connected to the other two in significant ways. How does this work? Figure 2-3 shows what might happen when planning programs for a toddler group and a class of four-year-olds.

How Children Benefit

According to NAEYC (2005), developmentally appropriate principles benefit children in many ways:

1. Children construct their own understanding of concepts and benefit from instruction by more competent peers and adults.

2. Children benefit from opportunities to see connections across disciplines through integration of curriculum and from opportunities to engage in in-depth study.

3. Children benefit from predictable structure and routine in the learning environment

and from the teacher's flexibility and spontaneity in responding to their emerging ideas, needs, and interests.

4. Children benefit from making meaningful choices about what they will do.

5. Children benefit from situations that challenge them to work at the edge of their capacities and from ample opportunities to practice newly acquired skills.

6. Children benefit from opportunities to collaborate with their peers and acquire a sense of community.

7. Children need to develop a positive sense of their own self-identity and respect for other people, whose perspectives and experience may be different from their own.

8. Children have enormous curiosity and capacities to learn and have recognized age-related limits on their intellectual and linguistic capacity.

9. Children benefit from engaging in self-initiated, spontaneous play and from teacher-planned structured activities, projects, and experiences.

As you observe in classrooms and read further chapters on the teacher's role, behavior, environments, and curriculum, reflect on these benefits. Do they match your own understanding of early childhood development?

DAP is integrated into other sections of the text. The Word Pictures in Chapter 3 offer a view of some general characteristics of children at various age levels, which can inform a teacher's decision-making process about developmentally appropriate practices. In Chapter 6, observations that focus on individual children are discussed and related to DAP. Chapter 9 outlines DAP daily schedules and environments for young children. Chapter 3 discusses developmentally appropriate evaluation of children, and, in Chapter 10, curriculum approaches that meet DAP criteria are discussed. A reading of NAEYC's position paper (see Appendix B) provides a more in-depth rationale for the various components of DAP, its philosophical foundation, and examples of appropriate practice for infants and children through age eight.

Developmentally and Culturally Appropriate Practice (DCAP)

Culturally appropriate practice is the ability to go beyond one's own sociocultural background to ensure equal and fair teaching and learning experiences for all. This concept, developed by

What does child development tell us about toddlers? We know that they want to do everything by themselves, usually more than they can actually achieve. We know they like to feel independent and learn quickly if given a little help and then encouraged to do what they can for themselves.

What do we know about each individual child in the group? Many of these toddlers rely on their parents to do things for them, such as helping them put on coats or shoes, feeding them, or putting their toys away. Others are being encouraged to try these activities by themselves, and some of them are being taught step by step at home. Most children come to a teacher for assistance, and a few call for help. On the other hand, one child will stay at a dressing task for nearly five minutes, while another will throw shoes across the floor if they don't slip on easily the first time she tries.

What do we know about the social and cultural context of their homes? Most of the children in this group come from homes where help is readily available through siblings and extended family members. The dominant cultural values and child-rearing practices reinforce dependence and community, although there is a smaller group of families that want their children to become independent as soon as possible.

By looking at all three criteria in conjunction with one another, we have some decisions to make about how or whether to go forward in setting goals for the toddlers, which would help them achieve greater independence. Respecting cultural diversity means we begin by talking to parents, perhaps at a parent meeting, where families are invited to share their child-rearing practices from their cultural viewpoints. Once we have an understanding of what families expect and want, we have an opportunity to work together to find a solution that would be good for the toddler and good for the parents as well.[1] This is what Hyun (1998) refers to as "'negotiable curriculum,' where teachers are no longer the ultimate power holders in any decision making." According to Hyun, the diverse voices of children and their parents are the "main agent in teacher's appropriate approach," creating a sense of shared power.

What does child development tell us about four- and five-year-olds? We know that they are great talkers; they like to play with language, making up stories, songs, and poems. They love being read to, and they enjoy dictating stories of their experiences and ideas. We know that children this age need increasing experiences in using oral language to connect those experiences with words and letters to begin to understand the use of the written word in their daily lives. We know that children learn to read by spending time reading and writing about what interests them.

What do we know about each individual child in the group? We have observed that a few of the children are creating more elaborate stories, complete with drawings. At the same time, there are several children who rarely participate in any of the art or story activities.

What do we know about the social and cultural context of their homes? We know that all of the parents have expressed interest, if not concern, that their children learn to read to do well when they get to kindergarten. Many of the children come from homes where reading is highly valued and where all members of the family enjoy books. Many come from family backgrounds where storytelling is a primary method of transmitting culture, history, and values. Most of the children are encouraged by their families to draw "stories" about their experiences.

There appears to be a common interest among the parents about reinforcing the concept of reading. The task becomes one of helping parents understand the meaning of literacy in the early years and developing an activity area that engages the preschoolers in meaningful activities that support the program's goals for literacy development. The daily schedule is adjusted to allow for small group times when the children tell stories to one another or dictate them to a teacher. Areas of the classroom are modified for literacy-rich experiences: picture books about building are added to the block corner; children are encouraged to write or draw notes to one another, recipes with drawings instead of words are used in cooking activities; paper and crayons are placed in the dramatic play area to encourage the writing of grocery lists and telephone numbers. Long-term projects involving children writing stories together or writing stories of their lives can be integrated into the planning as well.

FIGURE 2-3 Programs that are developmentally appropriate take many factors into consideration that reflect the children, their families, and the teacher's understanding and knowledge of child development. That's DAP!

Hyun, expands DAP to address cultural influences that emphasize the adult's ability to develop a "multiple/multiethnic perspective" (Hyun, 1998).

Preparing teachers and caregivers for multiculturalism is not just about becoming sensitive to race, gender, ethnicity, religion, socioeconomic status, or sexual orientation, according to Hyun. It is also related to an understanding of the way individual histories, families of origin, and ethnic family cultures make us similar to and yet different from others. Through such

1 Although DAP stresses importance of self-help skills, this may need to be examined as a culturally sensitive teaching practice for all children.

DAP in Action—Respect for Cultural Diversity

Using NAEYC's criteria for cultural diversity, these examples demonstrate how DAP supports greater consistency between home and school cultures when you:

- Build a sense of the group as a community, bringing each child's home culture and language into the shared culture of the school so each child feels accepted and gains a sense of belonging

- Provide books, materials, images, and experiences that reflect diverse cultures that children may not likely see, as well as those that represent their family life and cultural group

- Initiate discussions and activities to teach respect and appreciation for similarities and differences among people

- Talk positively about each child's physical characteristics, family, and cultural heritage

- Avoid stereotyping of any group through materials, objects, language

- Invite families' participation in all aspects of the program

- Take trips to museums and cultural resources of the community

- Infuse all curriculum topics with diverse cultural perspectives, avoiding a "tourist" approach

(NAEYC, 1998)

FIGURE 2-4 All children and their families deserve to be in programs where their lives are respected and where they can be proud of their cultural heritage.

insights, teachers will be able to respond positively to the individual child's unique expressions of growth, change, learning styles, culture, language, problem-solving skills, feelings, and communication styles (Hyun, 1998).

Hyun stresses the need for "cultural congruency"[1] between a child's home and school experience and suggests the following questions as a way to begin addressing the issue:

1. What relationships do children see between the activity and work they do in class and the lives they lead outside of school?

2. Is it possible to incorporate aspects of children's culture into the work of schooling without simply confirming what they already know?

3. Can this incorporation be practiced without devaluing the objects or relationships important to the children?

4. Can this practice succeed without ignoring particular groups of people as "other" within a "dominant" culture? (Hyun, 1998)

A consistency between home and school would "allow for children to express and show the importance of their own family culture and identity" by "using children's personal experience, family culture, and diverse language expressions as important sources of learning and teaching" (Hyun, 1998).

A culturally congruent approach to DAP would respect the variances in children's perceiving and understanding, and teaching practices would be based on children's different decision-making styles and social interaction abilities (Hyun, 1998). NAEYC's criteria for respecting cultural diversity (see Figure 2-4) provide examples of ways in which to connect a child's sense of cultural continuity between home and school.

THE CORE OF PROGRAMS OF EARLY CHILDHOOD EDUCATION

What do programs for the young child look like? How are the similarities and differences expressed in school settings? What marks a program as unique? The answers to these questions can be found by looking at some of the most common programs in early childhood education.

1 Children's growth and development can be understood only within their cultural context.

The Traditional Nursery School

The **traditional nursery school** (often called pre-school) exemplifies a developmental approach to learning in which children actively explore materials and where activity or learning centers are organized to meet the developing skills and interests of the child. Most of these programs serve children from two-and-a-half to five years of age.

The philosophy of these schools is best described by Katherine Read Baker in her now classic book *The Nursery School: A Human Relationships Laboratory* (1955). First published over fifty years ago, this book serves as an encyclopedia of the traditional nursery school, its methods, and its philosophy, reflecting the influence of Comenius, Locke, Rousseau, Pestalozzi, Froebel, and Montessori.

The idea of a school as a place of human activity mirrors the thoughts of Dewey, Piaget, Erikson, and others. Baker develops this philosophy fully with an educational model that emphasizes the human needs, growth patterns, and relationships in a young child's life.

Developmentally, a traditional nursery school focuses on social competence and emotional well-being. The curriculum encourages self-expression through language, creativity, intellectual skill, and physical activity. The basic underlying belief is the importance of interpersonal connections children make with themselves, each other, and adults.

The daily schedule (see Figure 2-5) reflects these beliefs. Large blocks of time are devoted to free play, a time when children are free to initiate their own activities and become deeply involved without interruptions, emphasizing the importance of play. In this way,

Video VIEW PoinT 2-1

"A consistent structure for the day helps preschoolers develop a sense of security."

COMPETENCY: Program Management

AGE GROUP: Preschool

CRITICAL THINKING QUESTIONS:

1. How does the daily schedule reflect a sense of security?

2. What changes would you make in a preschool program where you have observed or worked to enhance a child's feeling of security?

children learn to make their own choices, select their own playmates, and work on their interests and issues at their own rate. A dominant belief is that children learn best in an atmosphere free from excessive restraint and direction.[1]

Typically, there is a balance of activities (indoors and out, free choice, and teacher-directed times) and a wide variety of activities (large- and small-muscle games, intellectual choices, creative arts, social play opportunities).

The Role of the Teacher

The role of the teacher and methods of teaching are important. Nursery schools assume that young children need individual attention and should have personal, warm relationships with important adults. Therefore, the groups of children are generally small, often fewer than 20 in a class. The teacher–child ratio is low, as few as six to ten children for each teacher. Teachers learn about children's development and needs by observation and direct interaction, rather than from formalized testing. They work with children individually and in small groups and often teach through conversation and materials. Always, the teacher encourages the children to express themselves, their feelings, and their thinking. Such rapport between teacher and pupil fosters self-confidence, security, and belonging. Proponents of the traditional nursery school believe that these feelings promote

9:00	Children arrive at school
9:00–9:45	Free play (indoors)
9:45	Cleanup
10:00	Singing time (large group)
10:15–10:30	Toileting/snack time (small group)
10:30–11:30	Free play (outdoors)
11:30	Cleanup
11:45	Story time
12:00	Children leave for home

FIGURE 2-5 A sample schedule for traditional half-day nursery schools is the core of early education programs.

1 This is not true for all cultures.

Individual attention and warm relationships are essential components of every program.

positive self-image, healthy relationships, and an encouraging learning environment.

Universal Preschools

A growing number of school districts offer prekindergarten programs for four-year-olds, although some include three-year-olds as well. Depending on their goal, these programs fall somewhere between traditional nursery schools and not quite full-day care. For some, the focus is on school readiness; others give priority to children at risk for school failure, children who come from families where English is not spoken, or low-income families. In states where early education has achieved a level of support, all four-year-olds are eligible for enrollment, regardless of income. Currently, nearly forty states plus the District of Columbia have prekindergarten initiatives (Children's Defense Fund, 2005). See Chapter 15 for further discussion.

Laboratory Schools

The college and university **laboratory schools** were among the first preschools established in the United States. They focus on teacher training, research, and innovative education.

As part of the child study movement, laboratory schools gathered information previously unknown about children and child development. Early ones include Hampton Institute in 1873, the University of Chicago founded by John Dewey in 1896, Bank Street School in 1919, begun by Harriet Johnson, and the laboratory nursery school at Columbia University's Teachers College, started in 1921 by Patty Smith Hill. In the late 1920s, Vassar, Smith, and Mills colleges all opened laboratory schools. Shortly after World War II, the Bing Nursery School at Stanford University opened. More recently, community college campuses have followed the lead of these pioneers. Campus **child care centers** have begun to combine child care services with the laboratory function of teacher training in one setting. The types and roles of the schools vary, depending on the educational philosophy and needs of the college and its students.

Regardless of their specific purposes, laboratory schools enlarge our understanding of children. They are often excellent places for beginning teachers to learn good teaching practices. They encourage the joining of psychology, medicine, and other related fields to early education, and they serve as professional models for the public at large for what is good in child care and education.

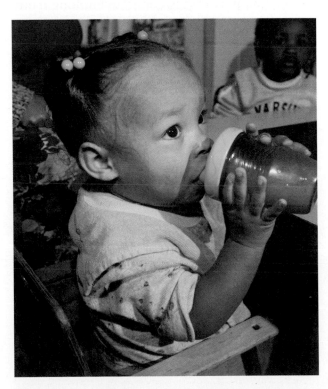

Routines, such as feeding, provide a balance to an active and busy day at the child care center.

Parent Cooperatives

Parent cooperative schools are organized and run by parents. This type of early childhood setting offers a unique opportunity for parents to be involved in the education of their child. Faculty wives at the University of Chicago started the first parent cooperative, the Chicago Cooperative Nursery School.

Parent cooperative schools may offer half-day or full-day child care programs and are usually nonprofit organizations. They are similar to other nursery schools, with two notable exceptions. First, parents organize and maintain the school: they hire the teachers, buy supplies and equipment, recruit members, raise funds, influence school philosophy, and manage the budget.

Second, parents or their substitutes were required to participate in the classroom on a regular basis. In light of current family work patterns and the unavailability of many parents, this requirement has been modified in some programs. Professional teachers are hired, or other parents who are available are paid to substitute for parents who cannot work at the center.

Cooperative schools work well for many reasons. Popular with young families, they have low operating costs, the appeal of being with parents in similar circumstances, and the mutual support that is generated among members of a co-op. Friendships grow among parents who share child rearing as participants in their own and in their child's education. But what a co-op does not cost in dollars, it may cost in time. By their very nature, cooperatives can exclude working parents unless another adult is able to substitute for them in classroom participation. Maintenance is very much the parents' responsibility; they must regularly schedule work parties to refurbish the facility.

Depending on the size of the school, parents hire one or more professional teachers. These teachers must be able to work well with adults, have curriculum-building skills, and model good guidance and discipline techniques. Because many parent cooperatives require a weekly or monthly parent meeting, the teaching staff must also be competent in parent education. Child development and child-rearing topics are part of almost any cooperative nursery school discussion and require a practiced teacher to lead. The role of the teacher in this setting, then, is twofold: to provide for a sound educational experience for young children and to guide and direct parents in their own learning.

FULL-DAY CHILD CARE PROGRAMS

Quality Is the Issue

Child care in the United States used to be primarily custodial, providing basic health and physical care. But times have changed. Full-day care is an American way of life, providing enriched programs for total development. Each day, close to 20 million children spend time in early care and education settings (National Center for Education Statistics, 2000). As of 2000, 67 percent of mothers are in the workforce (U.S. Bureau of Labor Statistics, 2002).

Quality early care and education contribute to the healthy cognitive, social, and emotional development of all children but particularly those from low-income families[1] (Cost, Quality, and Child Outcomes Study Team, 1995). Yet data from the Children's Defense Fund (2005) paint a bleak picture for those who might benefit the most. The cost of child care, which may range from $4,000 to $10,000 a year, is disproportionately high for poor parents. Child care costs can equal as much as one-third of an average poor family's income (Smith, 2000).

Good, affordable, accessible child care that will meet the increasing needs of American families is one of today's most crucial issues. The distinction between child care (stressing the protective, custodial services) and early education (emphasizing schooling) has appropriately blurred. Today, child care professionals recognize the concept of child care inherent in all programs for young children and the concept of education as an integral part of caring for young children.

Three Studies on Quality

Every day, scores of parents search for affordable programs and reliable providers. A Carnegie Corporation study (1996) confirmed that the quality of child care has a lasting impact on children's well-being and ability to learn and that too many three- to five-year olds are in substandard programs. They also reported that children in poor-quality child care have

---

 1 There is a critical need for early childhood advocates to be the voice for poor and minority children.

been found to be delayed in language and reading skills and display more aggression.

Highlights from three other studies underscore the quality issue:

1. The Carolina Abecedarian Project (1999), conducted by the Frank Porter Graham Child Development Center in Chapel Hill, NC, is the first study to track participants from infancy to age 21. The children were considered at risk for potential school failure. The study showed the strong influence of high-quality child care when comparing those who were enrolled full time in a quality early childhood program from infancy to age five versus those who did not attend a preschool program, although all attended comparable public schools from kindergarten on.

Important factors in determining quality were in place to ensure success: staff experience and education, little or no staff turnover, small teacher/student ratios, group size, and parent participation. Significant benefits for the children enrolled in the program included the likelihood of attending a four-year college and delaying parenthood until after high school. Moreover:

- At age 21, 65 percent of the child care graduates either had a good job or were in college, compared to 40 percent of the non-child-care subjects.

- By age 15, twice as many of the children who did not receive intervention services had been placed in special education programs than those who had been in child care.

- Only 30 percent of the child care children had to repeat a grade in school compared with 56 percent of the others

2. The Cost, Quality, and Child Outcomes Study (CQCOS, 1995) found that the average child care is mediocre in quality and that some were of such poor quality that they threatened children's emotional and intellectual development.[1] Infants and toddlers were most likely to be at risk for poor care in these centers; nearly half of their settings failed to meet basic health and safety needs.

A follow-up study, The Children of the Cost, Quality, and Outcomes Study Go to School (Whitebook, Sakai, Gerber, & Howes,

2001), tracked the children through second grade. The findings noted that:

- Children who receive good, quality child care had better social and cognitive skills in kindergarten and beyond.

- Children who were at risk gained the most from positive child care experiences and sustained these gains through second grade.

- Children who had closer relationships with their child care teachers had better behavior and social skills through second grade.

3. A study by the RAND Corporation (Karoly & Bigelow, 2005) for the first time reported the economic returns of one state's (California) investment in quality preschools for all four-year-old children. The study projected that for every dollar invested in a quality universal program, society would get between $2 and $4 back. The benefits include:

- Major increase in lifetime earnings ($2.7 billion per class year of children served);

- Improved K–12 schools (19 percent reduction in grade repetition per class year; 15 percent fewer special education years; 15 percent reduction in high school dropouts);

- Significant reductions in violent juvenile offenses, arrests, and incarceration.

Related Issues

The focus of the child care issues centers on a few core problems that threaten the *quality* of child care throughout the country. A few statistics highlight these issues:

- The annual turnover rate for child care staff is over 30 percent (Whitebook, Sakai, Gerber, & Howes, 2001).

- Thirty-two states do not require prior training to teach in child care centers, and 39 and the District of Columbia do not require training of family child care providers (Children's Defense Fund, 2005).

- A study of child–staff ratios (Snow, Teleki, & Reguero-de-Atiles, 1996) found that fewer states met NAEYC-recommended standards for four-year-olds in 1995 than in 1981. Snow and coworkers (1996) also found that only 18 states met the NAEYC recommendations for group size for infants.

Quality programs are being undermined. Children benefit emotionally, socially, and

1 Eliminating inequalities such as this requires a national agenda for children.

cognitively when child care centers have a high staff-child ratio, small group sizes, low staff turnover, and higher levels of staff compensation and training.

A Trilemma

Bredekamp and Glowacki (1996) succinctly summarize the primary issues in child care today: "The economics of child care continue to create a trilemma—quality for children, affordability for families, and adequate compensation for staff." Even though the past decade has brought about greater awareness of what quality means and what it costs, the solutions remain elusive.

The average annual salary for a child care worker is approximately $17,610 (U.S. Bureau of Labor Statistics, 2005). Fees for parents have remained relatively unchanged over the last 15 years, however. Child care costs for families seem unevenly distributed. According to the Urban Institute (Giannarelli & Barsimantov, 2000), child care expenses reflect this disparity:

- Two-parent families pay 7 percent of their earnings for child care.
- Single parents pay 16 percent.
- Poverty-level families pay 23 percent.

Despite these threats to quality child care, there are a few encouraging signs. The Child Care Center Licensing Study (The Children's Foundation, 2002) found a 24 percent increase

in licensed centers from 1991 to 2002. The National Academy of Early Childhood Programs reports that as of April, 2005, more than 10,000 early childhood programs have been accredited

Child Care Quality and Poverty

The Child Care and Development Block Grant Act which has been in effect since 1990 is a federal child care program of importance because it includes direct aid to lower-income parents through child care certificates that can be used to purchase services from child care providers. Yet only one out of seven children eligible under this law receive child care assistance. Across the country, there are not enough legislated funds to provide services to those who may need it the most.

Work in child care is long and intense and coupled with undesirable wages. This creates high staff turnover and low morale. Occasionally, a center will cut corners to keep tuition reasonable, but these shortcuts are usually detrimental to children.

The issues can be reduced to their core: how to expand affordable quality child care and at the same time address the lack of salary compensation and benefits so urgently due the early childhood professionals who subsidize the enterprise. Chapter 15 discusses this issue in greater depth. Figure 2-6 shows the choices parents make when looking at child care.

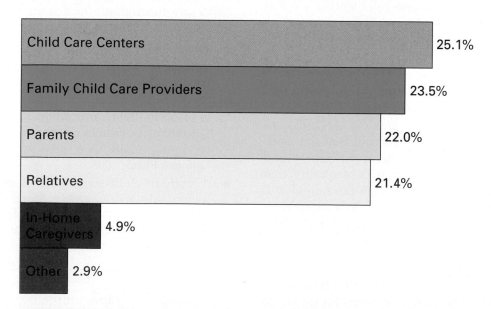

FIGURE 2-6 Child care options: What parents choose. (Data from Smith, Kristin. *Who's Minding the Kids? Childcare Arrangements.* Bureau of the Census. Current Populations Report, p. 70. (2000).)

Child Care Centers

Full-day child care is not a modern phenomenon. Some of the first nursery schools in England operated from 8:00 a.m. until 4:00 or 5:00 p.m. At the end of this chapter, an Insights article by the late Edith Dowley tells the fascinating story of the child care centers established in the Kaiser Shipyards in Portland, Oregon, during World War II. It is a prime example of the kind of business and political support that is needed to support children and their families today. By definition, a child care center is a place for children who need care for a greater portion of the day than what the traditional nursery school offers. The school schedule is extended to fit the hours of working parents. See Figure 2-7 for an example of a full-day schedule. A longer day means that ordinary routines such as meals and naps are part of the schedule. These full-day options are also educational settings, echoing the curriculum of a half-day program.

Child care centers often serve infants and toddlers, as well as two-and-a-half to five-year-olds. Many offer kindergarten and an after-school option as well.

Scheduling

Compare the nursery school schedule (Figure 2-5) with the child care schedule (Figure 2-7).

7:00-8:30	Arrival/breakfast; limited indoor play
8:30	Large group meeting
8:45–9:45	Free play (inside)
9:45	Cleanup/toileting
10:00	Snack time (small groups)
10:15–11:30	Free play (outside)
11:30	Cleanup/hand-washing
12:00	Lunch
12:30	Toothbrushing/toileting
1:00–2:00	Nap time
2:00–3:00	Free play (outside)
3:00	Group time
3:15	Snack time (small groups)
3:30–5:00	Inside and outside free play/library hour
5:00	Cleanup
5:15–5:30	Departure

FIGURE 2-7 A typical full-day care schedule. Most child care programs combine education and caring for basic needs.

The morning starts slowly. Children arrive early because their parents must go to work. The center may supply breakfast, midmorning and midafternoon snacks, and a noon lunch. A nap period for one to two hours for all the children gives a needed rest and balances their active, social day with quiet, solitary time. The program also includes extended experiences outside the school—field trips, library story hour, or swimming lessons—because children spend the major portion of their waking hours on-site. As the day draws to a close, children gather together quietly, with less energy and activity.

Licensing

Licensing is the process of fulfilling the legal requirements, standards, and regulations for operating child care facilities. There are no national standards or policies regarding licensing of child care facilities in the United States. Many local and state governments require licensing of child care centers and family child care homes, but there is not a central licensing agency in each state. Depending on the state, a license may be issued by the Department of Health, Department of Education, or Department of Social Welfare. Certification of child care workers is again left to local options.

Early childhood professional groups are calling for increased standardization of licensing procedures to ensure that children are receiving the best possible care in safe and healthy environments. The primary concern is to establish effective licensing policies that are reinforced and will ensure that all programs will provide adequate care to meet the basic developmental needs of children. The same minimum standards will apply to adult–child ratios, suitable safety precautions, health and nutrition needs, and the amount of training and preparation required of caregivers.

The need for standards arises out of recent changes in early childhood. The number of children in out-of-home care settings has increased. Many are infants and toddlers. Children are spending longer hours in child care, and there are more programs sponsored by a variety of agencies such as churches, public schools, and private for-profit firms. With this diverse mix, a common set of standards for licensing is imperative to ensure the best possible care for all children who need these services.

In 1997, NAEYC issued a position statement in support of licensing and regulation of early care and education programs by the states (NAEYC, 1998a). Some of their recommendations for an effective regulatory system, including the provisos that:

- All programs providing care and education for two or more unrelated families should be regulated and that there be no exception or exemptions from this requirement.
- All centers or schools serving 10 or more children that provide services to the public should be licensed.
- States should establish licenses for individuals, such as teachers, caregivers, and program administrators.
- Licensing regulations should address health and safety, group size, adult–child ratios, and preservice and inservice standards.

Staffing

The staff in a full-day setting is often called on to deal with the parenting side of teaching. Children in full-day care may need more nurturing and clearer consistency in behavioral limits. At the same time, they need individual flexibility and understanding and regular private time with caring adults.

Parents' needs also may be greater and require more of the teachers' time. Teachers should communicate with and support parents effectively. Parents want to trust their children's teachers and be relaxed with them. Child care parents may require extra effort; they have full-time jobs as well as child-rearing responsibilities draining their energies. It takes a strong team effort on the part of the teacher and the parent to make sure the lines of communication stay open.

The teaching staff undoubtedly has staggered schedules, perhaps a morning and an afternoon shift. Administration of this type of program is therefore more complex. An effort must be made to ensure that all teachers get together on a regular basis to share the information and details about the children in their

care. Both shifts must be aware of what happens when they are not on-site to run the program consistently. See Chapter 15 for further discussion on child care issues.

Family Child Care

In Family Child Care, the provider takes care of a small numbers of children in a family residence. The group size can range from two to 12, but most homes keep a low adult–child ratio, enrolling fewer than 6 children. It is reminiscent of an extended family grouping.

One of the most popular options, nearly 25 percent of working mothers with children under five select **family child care** (Smith, 2000). The home setting, sometimes right within the child's own neighborhood, offers an intimate, flexible, and convenient service for working parents. There are one million family child care providers in the United States today (National Association for Family Child Care, 2002), and they make up nearly one-half of all child care workers (U.S. Bureau of Labor Statistics, 2002). Children in a family child care home can range from infants to school-age children who are cared for after regular school hours.

Trawick-Smith and Lambert (1995) have noted four distinct differences between family child care providers and those who work in child care centers. Because they often care for infants, preschoolers, and after-schoolers, the developmental ranges that family child care providers must meet may span up to twelve years. That poses a challenge to develop experiences and activities for a mixed-age group of children. Family child care providers work and live in the same environment posing logistical problems of storage, space definition, and activity space. Often, family child care providers care for their own children within their programs, leading to problems with separation and autonomy of their children and providing enough time to the child as a parent. Family child care providers are administrators and managers as well as teachers and caregivers, faced with budgets and fee collections.

Advantages

Family child care is especially good for children who do well in small groups or whose parents prefer them in a family-style setting. This is especially true for infants and toddlers. Family child care homes often schedule flexible hours to meet the needs of parents who work. The wide age range can be advantageous as well. Consistency and stability from a single

What do YOU Think?

Are statistics about child care issues important? What story do they tell you? How can you make use of them in your understanding of the early childhood field today? Which statistics are the most surprising? Why?

The family child care provider runs a small business in her home. She is flexible enough to adapt to changing work schedules and children's needs.

caregiver throughout the child's early years and a family grouping of children provide a home-like atmosphere that is especially appropriate for infants and toddlers.

Family child care providers own and operate their own small business in their homes. Providing child care is a way for women who want to remain at home with their children to contribute to the family income. Meeting the requirements for licensing, fulfilling all the administrative tasks of a business and an educational program, and keeping current with the local, state, and federal tax requirements are part of the professionalism required for this type of child care arrangement.

Challenges

Many homes are unregulated; that is, they are not under any sponsorship or agency that enforces quality care, and many are exempt from state licensing.

Accountability to a licensing agency and training in child development are the two major factors affecting the quality of family child care programs. A study by The Children's Foundation

(2001) found that licensing of family child care homes increased 37 percent between 1990 and 2001. Training on an annual basis is mandated for family child care providers in only 13 states (Children's Defense Fund, 2001).

Family child care providers can feel isolated from others in the child care field. A hopeful sign, however, is that more articles on family child care are being included in professional publications, and early childhood conferences and workshops are now including issues related to the family child care provider. The National Association for Family Child Care, a network of family child care providers, has been established and publishes a quarterly publication of interest to its members.

The "Study of Children in Family Child Care and Relative Care" conducted by the Families and Work Institute (Galinsky, Howes, Kontos, & Shinn, 1994) made a number of important observations regarding in-home care. They found that:

● Families select providers who are similar to themselves in race and income.

● Ethnic background and economics aside, parents and providers agreed that the following were characteristics of quality care: (1) the child's safety; (2) communication between parent and provider about the child; and (3) warm and attentive relationships between provider and child.

● Characteristics of providers that affect the quality of child care were: (1) they had a commitment to taking care of children and felt the work was important; (2) they took part in family child care training and sought to learn more about child development and planned experiences for the children in their care; (3) they networked with other providers and participated in their state's regulation process; (4) they cared for slightly larger groups and had higher adult-child ratios; and (5) they charged higher rates and followed standard business and safety practices.

The study also identified concerns, most notably that only half the children they observed in homes were securely attached to their providers and that only 9 percent of the homes studied were of good quality. They also found that children from low-income families are in lower quality care than children from higher income families and that children from minority families are in somewhat lower quality care than nonminority children.[1] These last

 1 Responsibility for meeting the child care needs of all families should be shared more equitably by employers and governments as well as families.

two issues may be related to the fact that child care centers for low-income families have historically been subsidized by the government but those funds are not yet available for in-home providers.

This type of care could be a star in the galaxy of child care options. Small and personalized, it offers parents an appealing choice of home-based care. It is obvious, though, that further regulation of standards, availability of training for providers, and an awareness of the advantages of family child care need to be addressed. For those who need child care, this should be a viable alternative; for those who want to work at home, this type of career should be given serious consideration.

Employer-Sponsored Child Care

Employer-sponsored child care refers to child care facilities on or near the job site and supported by the business or industry. Hospitals, factories, colleges, and military bases often provide this service.

The number of women working outside the home and the increase in single-parent families encourage us to look at the workplace as a logical solution for child care needs. Employers who have implemented child care claim that the benefits are increased employee morale and better recruitment and retention of employees. For parents, there is the added appeal of having their children close by and being part of their educational process.

Industry has begun to respond to the need to create a supportive structure for women who combine work and family. Child care has become a corporate issue, with both large and small corporations participating. In 1990, 64 percent of private employers with more than 2,000 employees offered some form of child care assistance. By 1995, that number had risen to 85 percent (Neugebauer, 1998).

Government agencies are among the largest employers offering child care options. The federal government has over 1,000 centers and sponsors nearly 10,000 family child care providers for use by military personnel (Neugebauer, 1998).

More companies are hiring management organizations to operate their child care facilities rather than maintaining them themselves. Employers are also insisting on quality, and centers are being accredited through NAEYC. The Cost, Quality, and Child Outcomes Study (1995) revealed that work-site centers receiving

More and more corporations and businesses, including hospitals, help parents by offering on-the-job child care facilities.

employer subsidies ranked among the highest in quality.

Benefits to employees may include the option for one or more of the following: parental leave, flexible hours, corporate group discounts at local centers or family child care homes, resource and referral services, pretax salary reductions for child care, vouchers to purchase child care, reserved spaces in specific child care settings supported by the company. Companies located near each other may collaborate on the costs of these benefits.

These signs of growth are positive and likely to continue, especially in light of the new tax credit bill for work-site child care. Employers may provide a 25 percent tax credit for costs associated with providing child care and a 10 percent tax credit for child care resource and referral (Neugebauer, 2001).

Workplace Schools

A recent spinoff of employer-supported child care has emerged in an unusual collaboration between businesses and public school districts. In Florida and Minnesota, kindergartens have been established in rent-free corporate space while the school district supplies the staff and materials. Children ride to work with their parents, attend school, and stay on for a child care program until their parents are ready to go home. This innovative program, which is open to employees of other local businesses, hopes to include first and other elementary grades in the future and is a way for businesses to become more sensitive to families. It is a movement that bears watching.

For-Profit Child Care

Sometimes called "proprietary child care," the for-profit establishments comprise over one-third of all child care centers. A number of national chains of child care centers developed rapidly over the last 20 years, with some controlling anywhere from 10 to 1,200 centers. For-profit child care was seen as a good investment opportunity, so businesses flourished and grew. A few very large companies dominate the scene, creating child care chains across the country, primarily as managers of employer-sponsored programs or franchisers of centers.

For-profit centers offer a variety of programs to meet parents' needs. Infant and toddler programs, preschools, kindergartens, before-school and after-school care, and summer sessions accommodate working parents. Many programs are expanding into kindergarten and primary grades, and some are opening charter schools (Neugebauer, 1998). Originally criticized for minimal salaries, lack of benefits, and a less educated staff (Meisels & Sternberg, 1989), the quality of for-profit child care has improved; yet the major concern of 80 percent of the chief executives of the nation's for-profit child care organizations is the shortage of qualified teachers (Neugebauer, 1997, 1998).

Many for-profit owners are providing on-site child care in industrial parks or focusing on employer-based child care. Future directions for the for-profit child care sector may lie in the area of elder care[1] and may provide the growth opportunity for child care organizations in the near future (Neugebauer, 1997).

Nannies

Nannies are professional in-home child care providers. Originating in England, the nanny movement became popular during the 1980s as a child care option for parents who could afford to have child care in their homes.

The International Nanny Association emphasizes training and professionalism and provides training and mentoring programs, publications, and a Nanny Credential exam. Nanny training programs can be found in community colleges and vocational schools where their training may include child development, nutrition, and family relationships. Living arrangements vary; nannies may or may not live in the child's home and they may or may not be responsible for housekeeping or meal preparation.

Au pairs differ from nannies in that they are allowed to spend only one year in the United States and do not receive any special training for their child care role.

Programs in Religious Facilities

As one of the largest single providers of child care in the United States, church/synagogue-based centers provide a variety of early childhood programs. Twenty-five percent of all child care centers are housed in a religious facility (Neugebauer, 2000) and their numbers are increasing. From 1997 to 1999, the number of child care facilities in churches and synagogues increased by over 26 percent, compared to a

Church-housed programs are the largest single provider of child care in the United States.

1 Many facilities already exist where an intergenerational approach to child care includes young children and senior citizens.

19 percent rise within the field in general (Neugebauer, 2000).

Each center is owned or operated by an individual congregation or other recognized religious organization. Many different denominations house a variety of educational and child care programs. A program can be under the jurisdiction of an individual congregation or a nonprofit ministry of the congregation, or be operated by tenants in a religious facility.

According to the Ecumenical Child Care Network (Hampton, 2002), there are four purposes for these program to exist:

1. *Pastoral Care*—as a service to families within the congregation.

2. *Community Service*—as a service to families within the local community.

3. *Education/Enculturation*—to teach religious beliefs.

4. *Social Justice*—as outreach to low-income families or those with special needs.

Hampton also defines three distinct types of operations in religious facilities:

1. *Direct Operation*—the individual congregation has full financial and programmatic control over the center.

2. *Indirect Operation*—the congregation incorporates the center as a separate, nonprofit entity, but maintains representation on the governing board.

3. *Independent Operation*—the congregation rents out space to an independent group, such as a secular, nonprofit center.

Throughout this nation's history, churches have demonstrated their concern for the welfare of children and their families. It was the churches that established many of the early schools, advocating the education of children. At the turn of the last century, church day nurseries and settlement houses cared for children of immigrants and poor working mothers. Later, hospitals and orphanages were founded, and churches spoke out for children's rights and the creation of child labor laws. In each era, depending on social and economic conditions, the churches have responded to the needs of children.

Role in Child Care

Toddler groups, full- and part-time nursery classes, all-day care, and after-school care are typical offerings. Some religious congregations sponsor programs for children with special needs and children of migrant farm workers. They serve the community at large and rarely restrict participation to their own congregations or denominations. [1]

Religious or spiritual development is not the explicit aim of the majority of programs for preschoolers. Religious-housed programs are committed to caring for children of working parents, providing a warm and loving environment to help children develop positive self-esteem (Lindner, Mattis, Rogers, 1983). The teaching of religious values to children in this age group is not common practice in most child care settings. The policy will vary, however, with each individual setting.

Religious institutional support of child care programs is primarily in the use of space. Known as "benign landlords" (Lindner, et al., 1983), these programs typically offer free or reduced-cost rent and may subsidize utilities, maintenance services, repairs, and some insurance. Their nonprofit tax-exempt status is usually applied to child care programs that exist as part of the congregation's ministry. Programs housed in churches, however, suffer the same indignities as other child care facilities, such as low staff wages and poor or nonexistent benefits.

Common problems that arise in religious facilities include sharing space with other congregational programs, frequent changes in leadership in the congregation's governing body, unclear policies and procedures regarding

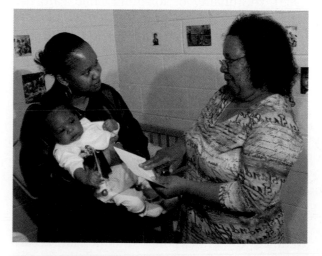

There are similarities among all programs, but the relationship among parents, children, and caregiver is the universal consideration.

1 Churches and synagogues have been forerunners in providing comprehensive early care and education to the underserved populations of children and families in the United States, adding to the diversity of program options for all families.

decision-making groups within the congregation, and inappropriate governance structures regulating the operation of the child care program.

For those families who seek alternative education in a religious context, religious-based schools fill the need. Many denominations serve children from early childhood through high school. The relationship with the individual religious organizations and the academic philosophy will vary from setting to setting.

Most religious groups support the need for regulations and abide by licensing procedures even if their state exempts them. Early childhood professionals, joined by many religious leaders, are deeply concerned that exemption from even the most minimal standards not only undermines the national effort to create uniform standards for child care but also threatens the safety and welfare of children.

EXTENDING SERVICES TO FAMILIES

To serve the scope of human needs today, some early childhood programs focus on caring for children and families in a very specific context.

Head Start: A Program with a Message

Beginnings

In 1965, the federal government created the largest publicly funded education program for young children ever. Head Start began as part of this country's social action in the "war on poverty," and the implications of the program were clear: If at-risk poverty-stricken children could be exposed to a program that enhanced their schooling, their intellectual functions might increase, and these gains would help break the poverty cycle.

Over the last 40 years, Head Start has served more than 20 million children and their families (Head Start, 2002). The success of Head Start can be attributed to its guiding objectives and principles, most notably expressed through:

- *Its comprehensive nature.* The child was seen as a whole, requiring medical, dental, and nutritional assessment, as well as intellectual growth. Extensive health, education, and social services were offered to children and their families. Today, Head Start is "the leading health care system for low-income children in the country" (Greenberg, 1990), providing health and medical screening and treatment for thousands of youngsters.

- *Parent participation and involvement.* Head Start expected parents to serve as active participants and get involved in the program at all levels: in the classroom as teacher aides, on governing boards making decisions about the program, and as bus drivers and cooks. The success of that approach is apparent. By 2000 Head Start reported that nearly 30 percent of the staff were parents of current or former Head Start students (HHS News, 2002).

- *Services to families.* Many of the comprehensive services offered to children were extended to parents as well to assist them in their fight against poverty. Paid jobs in the program, continuing education, job training, and health care are some of the support services families received.

- *Community collaboration.* Interest and support from the local community helped Head Start respond to the needs of the children and families it served. Public schools, religious institutions, libraries, service clubs, and local industry and businesses helped to foster responsible attitudes toward society and provided opportunities for the poor to work with members of the community in solving problems.

- *Multicultural/multiracial education.* Since its inception, Head Start has sought to provide a curriculum that reflects the culture, language, and values of the children in the program.[1] Head Start efforts in this regard have been the models for other early childhood programs.

- *Inclusion of children with special needs.* Since 1972, Head Start has pioneered the inclusion of children with disabilities in its classrooms.[2] Head Start has the distinction of being the first and largest federally funded program for children with special needs (Greenberg, 1990).

- *Ecology of the family.* Head Start programs looked at children within the context of the family in which they lived and viewed the family in the context of the neighborhood and community. This concept of taking the

1, 2 See footnote 1 on p. 70 Head start created a model for providing services that are inclusive (i.e., race, ethnicity, language, and physical ability of all children).

Early Head Start has a successful history serving infants and toddlers.

many forces that work against low-income families and viewing them as interrelated was a key factor in Head Start's success. (See also Chapter 15.)

The success of Head Start led to the creation of three specific programs that furthered the goals of Head Start: Parent and Child Centers, which serve infants and toddlers and their families; the Child and Family Resource Programs, which provide family support services; and the Child Development Associate credential, which provides early childhood training and education for Head Start teachers.

It should be noted that at the beginning, one aim of Head Start was to change the language and behavior patterns of the low-income children served, many of whom came from minority groups, and to resocialize them into cultural patterns and values of the mainstream, middle class. Head Start was a "compensatory" program, and the implications were that children from poor or minority families were unprepared for the demands of school in terms of language and cognitive skills, achievement, and motivation. This widely held perspective of the 1960s was known as the "cultural disadvantage" model, which suggests that any language,

cognitive, or relational style that differs from the Anglo, mainstream, middle-class style is necessarily detrimental rather than supportive to the educational process.

Contrast this view with the more recent, pluralistic perspective, called the "cultural difference" model, which affirms that no one way of "behaving and believing" should be required for successful participation in school or society. Current "multicultural policies" of Head Start reflect this pluralistic view. Figure 2-8 summarizes today's Head Start programs.

Early Head Start

Early Head Start was established in 1994 as part of the Head Start Reauthorization Act. This program serves low-income families with infants and toddlers and pregnant women and is based on Head Start's four cornerstones: child development, family development, staff development, and community development.

A seven-year national study of Early Head Start conducted by the Department of Health and Human Services (HHS News, 2002) shows positive results for the three-year-old children who completed the program.

Children in the program

- performed better in cognitive and language development than did those not participating in the program;

A Picture of Head Start	
Enrollment	
906,993 children	
Ages enrolled	
5-year-olds:	4%
4-year-olds:	52%
3-year-olds:	34%
Under 3:	10%
Race/ethnic composition	
Native American:	5.2%
Hispanic/Latino:	32.9%
African American:	31.3%
White:	35%
Asian/Pacific Islander:	1.9%
Biracial/Multiracial:	7.4%
Other:	18.6%
Children with disabilities	13%

FIGURE 2-8 Head Start continues to be a vital program that serves the needs of a diverse population. This information is for the fiscal year 2005. (U.S. Department of Health and Human Services, 2006)

- may need fewer special learning interventions later on;
- developed behavior patterns that prepared them for school success, such as engaging in tasks, paying attention, and showing less aggression.

Parents in the program

- showed more positive parenting behavior;
- reported less physical punishment of their children;
- were more likely to read to their children;
- were more emotionally supportive.

African American families and families that enrolled during pregnancy were most positively affected. A positive impact was noted especially for teen parents.

Head Start Today

Head Start has had a rocky history, its contributions notwithstanding. Struggling against budget cuts and controversy over its effectiveness, Head Start has undergone program improvements and expansions.

The original vision of Head Start was improved and expanded for the 1990s as a model that challenges the effects of poverty and promotes physically and mentally healthy families. Head Start has a formidable challenge ahead as it protects the high quality of its original charter while expanding and increasing services.

Head Start and Multiculturalism

Head Start Program Performance Standards (1998) reflect a strong commitment to multicultural principles, with explicit references to the importance of respecting cultural diversity, language differences, and cultural backgrounds.

The Performance Standard guidelines define diversity as "a key element to consider in organizing and planning the use of materials," in designing space, the aesthetic environment, and teaching styles, and they state that environments "reflect the community and the culture, language, and ethnicity of the children and families" (Head Start Program and Performance Standards, 1998). The Performance Standards define an "environment of respect" as provided by adults who:

- Demonstrate through actions a genuine respect for each child's family, culture, and lifestyle.
- Provide an environment that reflects the cultures of all children in the program in an integrated, natural way.
- Foster children's primary language while supporting the continued development of English.
- Avoid activities and materials that stereotype or limit children according to their gender, age, disability, race, ethnicity, or family composition.
- Model respect and help children demonstrate appreciation of others (Head Start Program Performance Standards, 1998).

Evaluating Head Start's Effectiveness

Two studies have helped highlight Head Start's impact over the years. One, the Consortium for Longitudinal Studies, pooled data from a number of smaller studies in the hopes that clear trends regarding early intervention could be identified. Brown (1985) noted two significant findings: (1) that Head Start children were less likely to be placed in special education classes, and (2) that early intervention programs were associated with a significant increase in IQ and school achievement.

The second study, the High/Scope Perry Preschool Project, was not of a Head Start program but had an enormous impact on policy makers and government officials and affected Head Start funding in significant ways.

The High/Scope Perry Preschool Study.

This project presented the most convincing evidence to date of the effectiveness of early intervention programs for low-income children. Begun in the 1960s, it is the first longitudinal study to measure the effects of preschool education and to track the children from preschool years through age 27.

Children from one randomly assigned group were placed in high-quality early childhood programs at age three, the other group did not attend preschool. The results showed great differences between the children who had the advantage of a high-quality program and those who did not. Low-income children who had attended preschool significantly outperformed those who had not.

The children attending the preschool program were better educated, spent fewer than half as many years in special education programs, had higher earnings, were less likely to receive welfare, and were five times less likely to be arrested (Schweinhart & Weikart, 1993).

Gender differences were also noted: preschool program girls had a significantly higher rate of graduation than did the girls who did not attend preschool, whereas, in comparison, preschool program boys completed slightly less schooling than nonpreschool boys (Cohen, 1993b).

Not only does this study underscore the need for high-quality preschool programs for children who live in poverty, but it also demonstrates the potential impact that Head Start has on the country's future. It is the first study of its kind to suggest the economic impact of early intervention. Because most of the children in the high-quality early childhood program required less remedial education, had better earning prospects, and were less costly to the welfare and justice systems, early intervention in education was shown to be cost-effective.

Other Programs

Teen Parent Programs

Many high schools now have on-campus child care programs. Some serve as laboratory facilities to introduce adolescents to child care principles and practices before they become parents. Others are part of a growing trend to provide support services to teenage parents. Young parents are encouraged to complete their high school education by returning to campus with their children. In addition to their regular academic classes, parents are required to participate in parent education classes, where they discuss child-rearing policies and parenting concerns. They also spend time in the children's classroom, applying their skills under the supervision of professional child care workers.

The aim of these programs is to help meet the long-term needs of adolescent parents by providing educational skills necessary to secure a job. At the same time, valuable support and training for parenthood help teenagers deal with the reality of the young children in their lives.

Early Intervention and Special Education Programs

 Programs for children with special needs[1] offer a combination of educational, medical, and therapeutic services. Early Childhood Special Education (ECSE) is a relatively new field and includes programs for early intervention for infants and toddlers through age two, and preschool special education for three- to five-year-old children with disabilities or developmental delays. A team of professionals, including early childhood special educators, social workers, and physical, language, and occupational therapists, work together with parents to enhance each child's progress.

Any inclusive early childhood program may be an appropriate setting for children with disabilities as long as there is adequate planning and support (Allen & Cowdery, 2005). Further discussion of children with special needs follows in Chapter 3.

Hospital Settings

Hospitals may provide group settings for children who are confined for a period of time. Many hospitals provide on-site child care for their employees as well.

Migrant Children's Programs

Early childhood programs serve the needs of migrant farm families and rural poor families. Often migrant farm worker mothers are employed to work alongside the early childhood professionals. The focus of these programs is often on improving the child's primary language skills and developing a second language, job training, and access to health care and social services.

Meeting the Needs of Homeless Children

The plight of homeless children raises questions about program needs for this new and tragic phenomenon. Families with children now represent more than one-third of the homeless population (Children's Defense Fund, 2001). These children may attend schools closest to the shelter in which they stay for a brief time, and then change schools when their parents move to another shelter. Many times these are children who already experience problems and failures in school. State and federal legislation is now being enacted to ensure full and equal educational opportunities for homeless children.[2]

---

1 In the study of child development one needs to be aware of the full range of development and not focus on only typically developing children. Many programs are attempting to integrate 75 percent typically developing children along with 25 percent children who have been recognized as having a special need.

2 Early childhood educators should advocate for consistent and quality care and education for all children whether their challenge is economic, social, or physical.

Note: A discussion of children at risk from abuse and neglect is found in Chapter 15 under "Endangered Childhood." A discussion of children with special needs and programmatic implications follows in Chapter 3.

HOMESCHOOLING

The homeschool movement began in the 1950s as an alternative to public education. It was illegal in many states until the last ten to twenty years (Cloud & Morse, 2001) and is now legal in all 50 states and the District of Columbia. In the 1980s, groups of conservative Christians rallied support for homeschooling. Today, approximately 850,000 students are homeschooled, reflecting a diverse range of participants. About 75 percent are non-Hispanic whites in contrast to 65 percent in public schools. Nearly 4 percent are African American and another 4 percent are Hispanic (Bieleck, Chandler, & Broughman, 2001).[1]

The primary reasons parents give for this fast-growing movement have been documented in the first comprehensive study by the federal government to research homeschooling in the United States (Bieleck, Chandler, & Broughman, 2001). Nearly half of the parents cite the potential for a better education as their first reason. Thirty-eight percent say that religious philosophy is their motivation, and one-quarter of the parents cite poor learning environments in public schools as their grounds.

The study unearthed other little-known facts regarding this movement:

- About 62 percent of the families involved in homeschooling have three or more children, compared to 44 percent of those in schools.
- In over half of the families with two parents, only one was in the labor force, a dramatic difference in contrast to the 19 percent for those in schools.
- The number of boys and girls being homeschooled is essentially equal.

Educational Philosophies

The educational philosophies and methods are widely diverse and range from prepackaged curriculum, which parents buy, to "relaxed home schooling" and "unschooling" (Cloud & Morse, 2001). The "relaxed" or "natural" homeschooling method involves real-life projects as teaching opportunities, such as taking care of the farm animals or building a table. *Using* real life's teachable moments, the education is often tailored to the child's interests and abilities. About 7 percent of homeschoolers use no curriculum plans, and children pursue their own interests in the method called "unschooling" (Cloud & Morse, 2001). If some of this seems familiar, you might want to look back at Chapter 1 and review the various educational philosophies on which early childhood programs are based.

Concerns

There are a number of concerns expressed by educators regarding homeschool educational programs, particularly the lack of:

- *Regulations,* which vary widely throughout the United States regarding teaching qualifications, evaluation of student work, and accountability. Both the National Association of Elementary School Principals and the National Education Association have criticized homeschooling in part because of the lack of quality control.

- *Socialization opportunities,* which have to be addressed along with the academic aspects of homeschooling. To promote interaction with peers, some homeschoolers take some classes in their local public schools or participate in field days and science fairs with groups of other homeschooled students.

- *Sports opportunities, the arts, and other extracurricular activities,* which may not be available unless parents utilize other resources, such as local school programs, which may be open to homeschoolers. Cloud and Morse (2001) note that one in five of every homeschool students takes advantage of these opportunities.

- *Accountability,* regulations, unstructured curriculum, and policies that surround this movement.

- *Experiences* with others who differ from themselves may cause students to become insulated from the issues of society.[2]

- *Support* and loss of revenue for public education exists.

1 One parent started Heritage Home Schoolers, a support group for minorities, after finding that other organizations included few African American families (Cloud & Morse, 2001).

2 A homeschool support group in Maryland includes parents who are gay and heterosexual, African American, white, Asian American, and other biracial families (Cloud & Morse, 2001).

The time commitment demanded of parents is extreme and requires dedication and stamina. The majority of homeschool students have one parent who stays at home to teach. A number of parent support networks have emerged as well as a broader number of resources to support the homeschool parent.

As this movement progresses it will be interesting to watch how these criticisms are addressed and how more effective educational programs are developed through homeschooling.

Out-of-School-Time Care

Before-school and after-school programs are designed for children before they start or after they finish their regular academic day. This type of care is usually available for children from ages six to 16, with the vast majority (83 percent) in the kindergarten to third-grade age group (Neugebauer, 1996). Over two million children attend programs in child care centers, public and private schools, churches and synagogues, family child care homes, community centers, work sites, and recreation and youth programs (NAEYC, 1999). Over two-thirds of all school-age programs provide services both before and after school hours (Neugebauer, 1996).

Staff for after-school programs come from a variety of backgrounds, most of which include some experience with children, such as teachers, recreation specialists, or specialists within the arts. As with most child care programs, however, high turnover and low wages affect the quality of the service.

Two national organizations, the National School-Age Care Alliance and the School-Age Child Care Project (now called the National Institute on Out-of-School Time) joined forces to create an accreditation system for after-school care. Their goals are to set professional standards, accredit high quality programs, and support program improvement.

There is a critical need for safe, recreational programs for after-school care. According to one source, nearly seven million school-age children between the ages of five and 14 of employed mothers were self-care children, a term that replaces latchkey (Children's Defense Fund, 2001).

What happens to these children after school? For the kindergartener, school may be over at noon. From 1:30 to 3:00 p.m., first-, second-, and third-graders are released from their school day. Too often these children are sent home

After school programs provide opportunities to make new friends and try new skills.

with a house key around their neck or in their pocket. They are instructed to look after themselves and possibly a younger sibling until the parent (or parents) comes home from work. These self-care children are a young and vulnerable population.

Recent studies (Seligson, 1997) indicate that children unsupervised during out-of-school time are likely to engage in risky behaviors, receive poor grades, be truant, and abuse substances. According to Seligson (2001), more recent studies indicate that attendance in an after-school program is associated with better academic achievement and social adjustment when compared to more informal after-school arrangements, such as babysitting and self-care. The prevention of violence and crime is also linked to children attending after-school programs. Vandell and Pierce (1999) noted in their research that children in after-school programs had better school attendance, better conflict-management strategies, and better work habits at school than did their peers who did not attend such programs.

The essentials of out-of-school care are: flexible hours, reasonable tuition rates, and clear lines of communication. To ensure continual care, scheduling must take into consideration the elementary school calendar.

Holidays, conference times, and minimum-day schedules of schools must be considered. Opportunities to extend the after-school program can originate from the use of community resources such as library story hours, swimming facilities, and parks.

Out-of-school care is not intended to be an extension of a regular school day. Ideally, the program should supplement and support the regular school program. The teaching staff is usually different from the regular school faculty and should be specially trained in how to operate extended programs for young children. They must know how to create a homey, relaxed, and accepting atmosphere in an environment that supports large blocks of time for free play, where children can be self-directed and self-paced, where there are many opportunities for creative expression, where cooperation is emphasized and competition is limited, and where children may form small groups or find private spaces and places to play.

Children need the safety, the creative opportunity, and the emotionally supportive relationships that out-of-school care can provide. These programs are natural extensions of responsible child care and are essential services to children and their families.

EXTENDING THE AGE RANGE

Infant/Toddler Programs

The inclusion of group care for infants and toddlers was affected by the rising number of women in the work force over the past 20 years, and by the increasing number of single-parent families in which the parent must work. Gonzalez-Mena and Eyer (1993) define the infant/toddler age group: infancy is from babyhood until the child learns to walk. Then he or she is called a toddler until almost three years old.

Infant/toddler programs may be full-day centers or they may be part-time. They may be more educational, with parent involvement programs. Most are a combination of physical care coupled with intellectual simulation and development.

Parent relationships are an especially important part of any program for babies and toddlers. The general intention of these centers

The need for early child care has increased as thousands of mothers enter the workforce.

is to provide care that is supplemental to family life and that supports the child's family structure. To do that, the caregiver at an infant/toddler center involves the parents in the everyday decisions about the care of their child, provides them with information about the child's day, and strengthens the child's sense of belonging to that particular family.[1]

Video VIEW PoinT 2-2

"Routine caregiving skills are needed to meet children's need on a daily basis."

COMPETENCY: Program Management

AGE GROUP: Infants and Toddlers

CRITICAL THINKING QUESTIONS:

1. How would you describe the caregiving skills needed for infants as compared with those for preschoolers?

2. What routine could you use to provide a high level of interaction with an infant or toddler?

 1 The early childhood educator should respond to the child and parent as individuals in a unique family context and foster healthy family relationships.

ilosophy of
Infant/Toddler Care

Through the insights of Piaget and Erikson (see Chapter 4), we have come to view the infant more and more as an involved person, one who experiences a wide range of intellectual and emotional abilities. Although they may appear to be helpless beings, babies are in fact persons with feelings, rights, and an individual nature. The caregiver in a quality infant/toddler center understands that feeding, diapering, and playing are the curriculum of this age group.

Caregiving routines are at the heart of the infant/toddler program. The challenge for the caregiver is to find ways to use these daily routines to interact, develop trust and security, and provide educational opportunities. In many cases, the caregiver's role extends to helping parents use these same common occurrences to promote the optimal development of their child.[1]

Magda Gerber has been a pioneer in infant care and coined the term **educaring** to describe the relationship between an infant and an adult. Observing, listening, and reading babies' cues are key elements in educaring.

Gerber's philosophy is based on a respect for babies and the use of responsive and reciprocal interactions in which baby and caregiver learn about each other. Communicating through caregiving routines (diapering, feeding) in one-to-one intense and focused interactions is a foundation of Gerber's approach to caring for infants and toddlers (Gerber, 1979).

Active involvement with people and objects helps infants and toddlers develop feelings of self-identity, curiosity, and creativity.

Program Differences

Infant and toddler programs differ from preschool programs in a number of ways. There is a need for:

- More one-to-one physical care.
- Immediate response from adults.
- More follow-up to experiences and activities.
- Use of ordinary routines as learning opportunities.
- Skills that go beyond teaching: mothering, being a playmate.
- Intentional rather than discovery learning.
- Keener attunement to interpreting need and distress signals in young children.

The distinction between programs for infants and those for toddlers is also important. Just as a scaled-down version of preschool is not a toddler program, neither is a scaled-down version of a good day for toddlers an appropriate model for infants. The mobility of the toddler, for instance, requires different amounts of space and time in the schedule than are required for infants. Babies sleep more their first year of life; their rhythm of eating, sleeping, and playing must be met. They thrive when someone responds to their smiles and developing skills. Common routines provide the caregivers time to talk with the babies about what they are doing and what is happening to them. They get babies to focus on themselves through gentle, extensively personal involvement. Good programs for babies recognize their capacities and the extent of their awareness of themselves and others in their environment.

Routines are also the focus of the toddler's day but in a somewhat different way. Mealtimes and toileting provide daily opportunities for toddlers to explore and to express their emerging sense of self. Hand-washing—even eating—becomes a time to fill, to taste, to dump, to pick up. Again, the curriculum emerges from a developmental need toddlers have of "Me! Mine!" To foster that independence, that wanting to "do it myself," routines that allow for experimentation, mistakes, and messes make a good toddler curriculum. Good programs for infants and toddlers, then, are distinctly arranged for them and are not simply modified versions of what works well in a program for three-year-olds.

 1 The caregiver must be culturally sensitive to the parent's background. There are many cultural differences in caring for infants, such as the amount of vocalizations, how and when babies are held, and sleep routines.

What Is Good Quality Infant/Toddler Care?

The high level of dependency on adults, the rapid growth changes from birth to age three, and the interrelationship among developmental areas (see Chapter 3) call for certain elements to ensure high-quality infant and toddler programs. Honig (1985) calling infant/toddler caregiving "the scarcest commodity in the world of child care," lists key elements for quality programs:

- The quality of the caregiver and the stability of the staff.
- The expensive staff–infant or staff–toddler ratio of at least one to four.
- The need for a rich language experience integrated into daily routines.
- The need to build a prosocial curriculum that promotes children to care for and about one another.
- The necessity for caregivers to devote individual attention for both learning and caregiving, balancing between the group and the individual child.
- The need to support and renew staff so they in turn will be supportive to parents and serve as appropriate resources.
- The need to promote a sense of choice and control to young children throughout the curriculum and routines of caregiving.
- The critical need for ongoing training for caregivers.

Issues. Critics of child care—any child care—raise questions about the negative effects on family life and the harmful aspects of group care for the very young. The most critical question is in regard to infant attachment (see Chapter 4 for an in-depth discussion on attachment). Some studies (Belsky & Braungart, 1991) concerning children who are placed in child care outside the home before the age of one, have raised questions about the higher level of insecurity attachment they show compared with infants who were raised at home. Berk (1994), who suggests that this small number of children is at risk for attachment insecurity because of poor-quality child care, calls for high-quality child care and parent education in infant emotional development.

The task for the early childhood professional seems clear. Learn what the issues are, defend policies that reflect high standards, and be prepared to further influence group care for infants and toddlers that is of the highest quality.

Kindergarten

The kindergarten year is one of transition from early childhood programs into a more formal school setting. While some kindergartens extend the "learning through play" philosophy found in developmental preschool programs, others become more focused on the academic skills of five-year-olds and less developmentally appropriate.

Kindergarten programs are universally available throughout the United States. They are found in elementary public and private schools, religious institutions, and as part of preschool child care centers. As of 1999, 93 percent of all five-year-olds were enrolled in a kindergarten program (National Center for Education Statistics, 2001). Every state provides some funding for kindergartens, and 41 of the states require kindergarten programs. 19 states have a set of standard expectations for kindergarten education (Doherty, 2002). Kindergarten teachers are primarily white, well-educated females (Digest of Education Statistics, 2001).

Length of Day

The length of kindergarten programs is under debate in many states and schools districts. Some offer whole-day options; others offer only half-day kindergarten. Only eight states require offering a full-day program.

Too often the arguments regarding the costs of such programs overshadow a more basic question: What are the best and most appropriate kindergarten programs, teaching methods, and curricula, regardless of the length of day? The following should be considered in response to this question:

- *The purpose of the kindergarten program.* How will the kindergarten program foster the goals in appropriate curricula and adapt to the needs of children? The goal should begin with the child and build the program to fit the child's needs, skills, and developing abilities.
- *The effects of a full day on children.* Many children have already been in a child care setting for up to 10 hours a day and have shown they thrive in programs that are suited to their ages, development styles, and needs. There is no question that most children can handle a full-day kindergarten program, providing it is adapted to their age, interests, and abilities.
- *The needs and concerns of families.* Some families may want a full-day program because they work and need a safe and nurturing place for

Kindergarteners are able to enjoy close friendships.

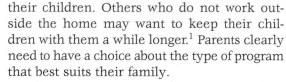

their children. Others who do not work outside the home may want to keep their children with them a while longer.[1] Parents clearly need to have a choice about the type of program that best suits their family.

- *The effect on teachers.* A full-day kindergarten means that class is extended for a longer period of time, providing opportunities to improve the quality of the program by individualizing the curriculum. Teachers in half-day kindergartens often teach one class in the morning and one in the afternoon. The negative effects on planning, continuity, parent relationships, and individualizing curriculum are obvious, not to mention teacher burnout.

- *The concerns of the administration.* The cost effectiveness of extending a kindergarten program all day will undoubtedly require more staff, more supplies and equipment, and greater food-service costs. The policy makers in any school setting must take these into account along with the other issues, but one would hope they would not be limited by them.

- *The nature and quality of the extended-day program.* Often, in programs in which children

are in half-day kindergarten, the quality of the extended-care part of their day is not equal to their school experience. In many extended-day programs, the staff is untrained, has a high turnover rate, and does not reflect the same program goals for the kindergartener.

School Entry Age

Every state establishes an arbitrary date (e.g., December 1) by which children must be a

What do YOU Think?

Do you think that all kindergartens should be full day? Why? Should half-day kindergartens be retained? Why? Are "transitional" or "developmental" kindergartens useful? How? What do you think about the use of more testing as a way to assess kindergartners' success in school?

1 This may or may not be culturally related.

certain age to enter kindergarten. In the United States, compulsory age for kindergarten ranges from five to eight. A few of the states have a cutoff date of August 15, ensuring that all of the children are five years old as they enter kindergarten (Kagan & Kauerz, 2006).

Several trends are adding to the discussions about kindergarten. Lowering and raising the age for beginning school is debated periodically. Parents hold children out of kindergarten for one year and enroll them when they are six; teachers retain many children each year in kindergarten; and administrators have created an array of kindergarten-substitute programs such as "developmental," "extra-year," or "transitional" kindergartens. By the time they finally reach kindergarten, children are now in class with late-four-year-olds, fives, and sixes—a vast developmental span under one roof. These questionable practices are called by various names: "academic redshirting" (Katz, 2000), the "birthday effect" (Peck, McCaig, & Sapp, 1988), or the "graying of kindergarten" (Suro, 1992).

The National Center for Education Statistics (NCES, 2001) notes that approximately 9 percent of eligible kindergarteners are held back each year and that most are males who were born in the months between July and December. White, non-Hispanic children are more than twice as likely as black, non-Hispanic children to be delayed in kindergarten entrance (West, Meek, & Hurst, 2000).[1]

Some of the methods used to create more homogeneous kindergarten classrooms, or to raise expectations for kindergarten admittance are

- Inappropriate uses of screening and readiness tests.
- Discouragement and/or denial of entrance for eligible children.
- Creation of transitional classes for those who are considered not ready for kindergarten.
- An increasing use of retention (NAECS/NAEYC, 2001).

Katz (2000) notes that research does not yet provide a clear direction for retaining children in kindergarten or denying them entrance. Along with NAECS/NAEYC, Katz supports the issue of tailoring programs to fit children rather than requiring that children fit the prescribed kindergarten format.

Curriculum: Developmental or Academic?

Critical issues such as school-entry age and length of school day are deeply related to kindergarten curriculum issues. Kindergarten programs range from relatively traditional classes to highly structured, academically oriented classes. Over the last 20 years, the push to teach separate skills, such as reading, writing, and math, has created more and more academically focused kindergartens where worksheets and teacher-directed lessons are the norm. As kindergartens have changed, there is greater pressure on teachers to accelerate children's learning. Hatch (2005) cites three specific changes that have altered the course of kindergarten programs:

1. Children today experience very different childhoods than even a decade ago;
2. Knowledge of how children learn and develop has expanded;
3. The standards-based reform movement has changed expectations for kindergarteners by imposing arbitrary standards of performance. This increases the academic expectations on them and the pressure on teachers to comply with regulations.

Hatch recommends a more balanced approach to kindergarten teaching that would merge the traditional and emerging knowledge and understanding of what children are like and what they need to meet the challenges of the accountability movement.

It is clear that some of Froebel's "children's garden," has wandered far from its child development roots. Curricula in which play is not respected as a vehicle for learning, reading is taught as a separate skill, and attempts are made to accelerate children's learning are at odds with kindergarten history. Revisit Chapter 1 and read again about Froebel, Dewey, Piaget, Patty Smith Hill, Susan Isaacs, and other pioneers and their approach to learning. Educating the whole child is very much in evidence in their work, as is their basic connection to child development theory and research.

Historically developed curricula, based on interaction and involvement of children in their own learning, with methods and materials to match the child's age level, are at the core of developmentally appropriate practice. The

---

 1 Poverty puts children at a greater risk of falling behind in school than does living in a single-parent home or being born to teenage parents (Children's Defense Fund, 2005).

current system of labeling children "immature," "slow," or "not ready" means that the program is not ready for the children; yet we know that young children are ready to learn and grow.[1] It is time to fix the program, not the children.

For further discussion on the negative effects of early academics, see Chapter 3 for developmental ranges and Word Pictures for appropriate expectations. In Chapter 6, the related questions of standardized testing and screening are discussed. In Chapters 10 and 15, related issues are explored.

Kagan and Kauerz (Gullo, 2006) provide four reflections on what kindergartens can and should be in the future. They integrate concerns about the developmentally appropriate integrity of kindergartens and the domination of imposed standards and testing.

1. Kindergarten must remain "special," that unique year where play is a legitimate medium for establishing children's learning patterns, and where curriculum, standards, and assessments are in sync with preschool and first grade.

2. Kindergarten must keep the child front and center, even with the new emphasis on content. Curriculum must address the full range of developmental domains (social, emotional, cognitive, physical) to prepare children for more formally taught content. Children's curiosity, enthusiasm, initiative, and willingness to learn must be nurtured to enhance their overall ability to learn.

3. Kindergarten must acknowledge and support differences in the needs of children and their families. Different learning styles in children must be addressed as well as family needs for flexibility in the structure, such as full- or half-day sessions.

4. Kindergarten must foster positive relationships between the children and their teachers, between families and the school, and between the school and the community. The success of these relationships can help establish trust and respect that lasts throughout the child's school years.

Primary Grades

Early childhood is defined as children from birth through age eight. Often overlooked as part of a **comprehensive** view of young children are grades one, two, and three, serving children who range from six to eight years old. Primary grades, in both public and private schools, focus on the basic academic skills of reading, writing, math, science, social studies, art and drama, health and safety, and physical education. They are usually part of a larger school with grades up to six or eight.

A report from the Carnegie Corporation (1996) noted that by the fourth grade, most primary school students did not meet the basic achievement levels in reading and math. According to the report, the reasons that primary children nationwide achieve far below their potential are related to ineffective teaching strategies, poorly trained teachers, outmoded curricula, and inadequate home–school partnerships. Linking success in the primary years with good early childhood education and high-quality child care programs prior to kindergarten, the study suggests reforms that promote children's learning in families and communities, expansion of high-quality early learning opportunities, and the creation of a comprehensive, coordinated education system (Jacobson, 1996a).

As the NAEYC position statement on developmentally appropriate practice states, "too many schools . . . adopt instructional approaches that are incompatible with . . . how young children learn and develop . . . emphasizing rote learning of academic skills rather than active, experiential learning in a meaningful context," with the result that children "are not learning to apply those skills to problems . . . and they are not developing more complex thinking skills" (Bredekamp & Copple, 1997). Fortunately, this seems to be changing in the primary grades. Collaborative learning, an integrated curriculum (see Chapter 10), an emphasis on literacy, and promoting critical thinking skills is now on the agenda of many elementary schools.

Bredekamp and Copple (1997) underscore the necessity to integrate teaching practices for children from birth through age eight:

> Along with the home, church, and community,[2] primary-grade schools and school-age care programs are among the key settings in which children's character is shaped. Therefore, the primary-grade

---

1 If programs are to be based on democratic and inclusive values, then perhaps school should be thought of as being ready for all children.

2 This presents a broad, ecological view of the child's socialization in the family and community context.

years are an important time not only to support children's intellectual development but also to help them develop the ability to work collaboratively with peers; express tolerance, empathy, and caring for other people; function responsibly; and gain positive dispositions toward learning, such as curiosity, initiative, persistence, risk taking, and self-regulation.

Class Size

A U.S. Department of Education report, "Reducing Class Size: What Do We Know?" (1998), concluded that reducing class size to below 20 students leads to higher student achievement. Critics of the proposal cite the high cost of lowering student–teacher ratios and the objectivity of the research data. If the initiative were successful, class size would be more in keeping with NAEYC standards for staff–child ratios in primary programs. Optimal group size for first-, second-, and third-grade classes are 15 to 18 children with one adult or 25 children with a second adult (Bredekamp & Copple, 1997).

Evaluations are part of everyday life in an early childhood setting. How are these children learning to listen? To relate to the teacher?

EVALUATING PROGRAMS FOR QUALITY

Evaluation Is a Process

As educators, we are constantly evaluating, judging, and rating, such as:

- *Curriculum.* Will this language game help develop the listening skills of three-year-olds?

- *Materials and equipment.* If we order the terrarium, will there be enough money for the math lab?

- *The environment.* Should the children begin school with free play or a group time? Where can we store the nap cots? Do the cubbies create a hazard out in the hallway?

- *Children's behavior.* Evan and Francie interrupt each other too much. Should they be placed in separate work groups?

- *Teacher effectiveness.* Yolanda still finds it difficult to lead a group time. How can she be supportively challenged?

As a process, **evaluation** is at once a definition, an assessment, and a plan. Evaluation involves making decisions, choices, and selections. In its simplest form, it is a process of appraisal. A good one encourages positive change. It is easy to continue the same program, the same teaching techniques year after year when a school is operating smoothly. Sometimes it is not clear

what—or how—improvements could be made. A regular evaluation process keeps a system alive and growing.

Evaluations help give meaning and perspective to children, teachers, and programs. An assessment that helps clarify issues and ideas brings renewed dedication and inspiration.

Programs may be evaluated by taking an inventory of a school's curriculum and educational materials. Program evaluation involves analyzing children, teachers, parents, and administrations to see how they all work together to meet the goals of the program.

Video VIEW PoinT 2-3

"Quality school-age programs build on opportunities in the local community."

COMPETENCY: Family Interactions, School, and Community

AGE GROUP: School-age

CRITICAL THINKING QUESTIONS:

1. What programs in your community would enhance a child's understanding of the larger society in which he or she lives?

2. Why is it important to give students opportunities to explore their community?

Evaluation Essentials

1. *Setting goals.* Without evaluation, goals are meaningless. Evaluation helps shape a goal into a meaningful plan of action. To be useful, an evaluation must include suggestions for improving the performance or behavior. The assessment tool that only describes a situation is an unfinished evaluation; goals for improvement must be established.

2. *Expectations.* In every early childhood setting, more than one set of expectations is at work. The director has job expectations of all the teachers. Teachers have standards of performance for themselves, the children, and parents. Parents have some expectations about what their children will do in school and about the role of the teachers. Children develop expectations regarding themselves, their parents, teachers, and the school.

3. *The degree to which expectations are met.* A good evaluation tool outlines clearly and specifically how expectations have been met in a system of mutual accountability. Evaluation is a way to look at where and how improvements can be made, to challenge methods, assumptions, and purposes. Total programs are evaluated to see if they accomplish their objectives. Evaluations provide information by which to rate performance, define areas of difficulty, look for possible solutions, and plan for the future.

4. *The degree of inclusivity.* A good evaluation instrument should be culturally appropriate and recognize the many ways that a program can be multicultural and anti-biased in its operations. Figure 2-9 expresses a number of points designed to assess the diverse and inclusive nature of an early childhood program.

Why Evaluate?

To Gain an Overview

Evaluating a program gives an overview of how all the various components function together. The fundamental questions are, "Is this a good place for children? Would you want your child to be here? What is a high-quality program for young children?"

Looking at children, teachers, and the total environment, a program evaluation reveals the environment as an integrated whole. These assessments add an awareness of how one area

Identifying Inclusive Programs

The program and environment should:

1. Foster the development of positive gender, racial, class, cultural, and individual identities.

2. Promote the ability to identify, empathize, and relate with individuals from other groups.

3. Demonstrate respect and appreciation for the ways in which other people live.

4. Encourage a concern for and interest in others, a willingness to include others, and a desire to cooperate.

5. Express a realistic awareness of contemporary society, a sense of social responsibility, and an active concern for people outside of their immediate environment.

6. Cultivate in the staff the autonomy to become critical analysts and activists in their social environment.

7. Support the staff in the development of educational skills and social knowledge that will enable them to become full participants in all aspects of society.

8. Uphold effective and reciprocal relationships between homes and schools.

FIGURE 2-9 These basic points help determine if an early childhood program is diverse and inclusive. (Reprinted with permission from Ramsey, P. (1987). *Teaching and Learning in a Diverse World: Multicultural Education for Young Children.* New York: Teachers College Press.)

is related to another and how the parts mesh in a particular setting. Such evaluations, then, are the standards of quality and include:

- Children's progress
- Teacher performance
- Curriculum development
- The financial structure
- Parents' involvement
- The community at large
- The governing organization of the school

In program evaluations, each of these is assessed for how it functions alone and how each works in concert with the others.

To Establish Accountability

A program evaluation establishes **accountability**. This refers to a program's being answerable to a controlling group or agency, for instance, the school board or the government office or to parents and the community in which you work.

Evaluations in programs with a wide age range may need to be individualized to adequately record children's skills.

These groups want to know how their funds are being spent and how their philosophy is being expressed through the overall program.

To Make Improvements

Program evaluations are an opportunity to take an objective look at how the goals of the school are being met. A good evaluation will support the strengths of the existing program and suggest where changes might improve overall effectiveness. An in-depth assessment increases the likelihood that program goals and visions will be realized. The evaluation helps determine the direction the program may take in the future.

To Acquire Accreditation

Evaluations are a necessary step for some schools that wish to be approved for certification or accreditation by various organizations or government agencies. Such groups require that a school meet certain evaluation standards before the necessary permits are issued or membership is granted. Agencies, such as a state department of social services or department of education, often license family day care homes, and private schools may need to follow certain criteria to be affiliated with a larger organization (such as the American Montessori Society).

One system established by early childhood professionals is noteworthy. The National Academy of Early Childhood Programs, a division of NAEYC, has established an accreditation system for improving the quality of life for young children and their families. Attempting to define a high-quality early childhood program, the accreditation system articulates what promotes the physical, social, emotional, and cognitive development of children in group care. The

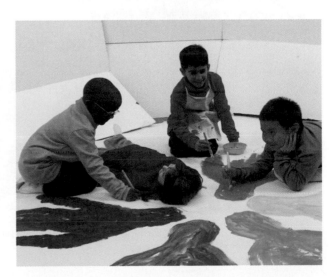

Program evaluations should represent the diversity of the field of early childhood education, from family day care for infants, to after-school programs for primary schoolchildren.

academy established goals for schools around ten criteria, which are outlined in Figure 2-2.

How to Evaluate a Program

Defining the Objectives

A program evaluation begins with a definition of the program's objectives. Knowing why a program is to be evaluated indicates how to tailor the procedure to the needs and characteristics of an individual school. With the objectives defined, the choice of evaluation instrument becomes clear. If, for example, a program objective is to provide a healthy environment for children, the evaluation tool used must address the issues of health, safety, and nutrition.

Choosing an Evaluation Instrument

Evaluation instruments vary with the purpose of the program evaluation. NAEYC's accreditation

guidelines are suitable, as is the *Early Childhood Environmental Rating Scale–Revised (ECERS-R)* (Harms, Clifford, and Cryer, 1998) for most preschools. Instruments for program evaluation are woven together to give a more comprehensive look at the total program.[1] These instruments will include many, if not all of the areas noted in Figure 2-10. They may be self-administered or be used by an outside evaluator.

Implementing the Findings

The evaluation process is complete when the results are tabulated and goals are set to meet the recommendations of the evaluation. Program administrators meet with the teaching staff to discuss the challenges highlighted by the evaluation. A process is put into place for addressing the issues, a calendar is established to create a timeline for improvement, the appropriate staff members are assigned the responsibility for

A program evaluation can determine how the class includes parents. The presence of parent volunteers shows the school welcomes parent involvement.

1 Principles of quality care in a diverse society must include building on the cultures of families and promoting respect (Chang et al. 1996).

The Physical Environment

____ Are the facilities clean, comfortable, safe?

____ Are room arrangements orderly and attractive?

____ Are materials and equipment in good repair and maintained?

____ Is there a variety of materials, appropriate to age levels?

____ Are activity areas well-defined?

____ Are cleanup and room restoration a part of the daily schedule?

____ Are samples of children's work on display?

____ Is play space adequate, both inside and out?

____ Is personal space (e.g., cubby) provided for each child?

The Staff

____ Are there enough teachers for the number of children? How is this determined?

____ Are the teachers qualified? What criteria are used?

____ Is the staff evaluated periodically? By whom and how?

____ Does the school provide/encourage in-service training and continuing education?

____ Do the teachers encourage the children to be independent and self-sufficient?

____ Are the teachers genuinely interested in children?

____ Are teachers aware of children's individual abilities and limitations?

____ What guidance and disciplinary techniques are used?

____ Do teachers observe, record, and write reports on children's progress?

____ Are teachers skilled in working with individual children, small groups, and large groups?

____ Does the teaching staff give the children a feeling of stability and belonging?

____ Do teachers provide curriculum that is age-appropriate and challenging?

____ How would you describe the teachers' relationships with other adults in the setting? Who does this include, and how?

____ Can the teaching staff articulate good early education principles and relate them to their teaching?

Parent Relationships

____ How does the classroom include parents?

____ Are parents welcome to observe, discuss policies, make suggestions, help in the class?

____ Are different needs of parents taken into account?

____ Where and how do parents have a voice in the school?

____ Are parent-teacher conferences scheduled?

____ Does the school attempt to use community resources and social service agencies in meeting parents' needs?

The Organization and Administration

____ Does the school maintain and keep records?

____ Are scholarships or subsidies available?

____ What socioeconomic, cultural, and religious groups does the school serve?

____ What is the funding agency, and what role does it play?

____ Is there a school board, and how is it chosen?

____ Does the school serve children with special needs or handicaps?

____ Is the classroom group homo- or heterogeneous?

____ What hours is the school open?

____ What age range is served?

____ Are there both full- and part-day options?

____ Is after-school care available?

____ Does the school conduct research or train teachers?

____ What is the teacher-child ratio?

The Overall Program

____ Does the school have a written, stated educational philosophy?

____ Are there developmental goals for the children's physical, social, intellectual, and emotional growth?

____ Are the children evaluated periodically?

____ Is the program capable of being individualized to fit the needs of all the children?

____ Does the program include time for a variety of free, spontaneous activities?

____ Is the curriculum varied to include music, art, science, nature, math, language, social studies, motor skills, etc.?

____ Are there ample opportunities to learn through a variety of media and types of equipment and materials?

____ Is there ample outdoor activity?

____ Is there a daily provision for routines: eating, sleeping, toileting, play?

____ Is the major emphasis in activities on concrete experiences?

____ Are the materials and equipment capable of stimulating and sustaining interest?

____ Are field trips offered?

____ Do children have a chance to be alone? In small groups? In large groups?

Cultural Responsiveness

____ Are multicultural perspectives already incorporated throughout the school, classroom curriculum, and classroom environment?

____ Do my attitudes (and those of all staff) indicate a willingness to accept and respect cultural diversity? How is this demonstrated?

____ Do classroom materials recognize the value of cultural diversity, gender, and social class equity?

____ Do curricular activities and methods provide children opportunities to work and play together cooperatively? In mixed groups of their choice or at teacher direction?

____ Do schoolwide activities reflect cultural diversity? How is this noticed?

____ Does the program planning reflect the reality (views and opinions) of families and the community?

____ Does the curriculum include planning for language diversity? For full inclusion? (Adapted from Baruth and Manning, 1992, and de Melendez and Ostertag, 1997.)

FIGURE 2-10 Checklist for areas of program evaluation.

making the changes, and the process begins anew. Evaluations are only as useful as the implementation plan. They can help identify specific concerns, determine the areas of growth and potential development, and be a blueprint for the future.

SUMMARY

Educational facilities for young children reach a broad population. They serve children from infancy through elementary-school age. An array of programs is available; each varies for philosophical reasons as well as because of the ages of children enrolled. Early childhood teachers have a wide range of programs from which to choose—as do parents.

The traditional nursery school and its sister programs of child care, laboratory schools, and parent cooperatives form the core of early childhood programs. Many different agencies and people sponsor early childhood programs, including employers, churches, universities, and hospitals. Some are located in family homes as a business. The intervention models of the 1960s and 1970s—Head Start and Follow-Through—are variations on the theme. They are specific attempts to provide early education and intervention to children caught in poverty's cycle.

Reflecting the needs of society, extended day programs have been created. Not only are children being cared for in group situations before and after school hours; they are also being placed in the group settings at an earlier age. Infant/toddler programs are common, and out-of-school care is a service that meets the demands for good, safe, and challenging programs for children who need care on either side of their school day. As varied as they are, there is also a certain similarity among all programs for young children.

Consideration must be given to a number of factors when reviewing the needs of young children and their families. Some of these elements are the ages of the children the program will serve, the qualifications and experience of the teaching staff, the funding base and financial support available, and the goals of the program to meet the needs of all children and their families. With so many choices, those who desire child care will find options that suit their specific needs.

A good evaluation process includes a clear purpose, knowing who and what will be evaluated, and what use will be made of the results. Any program designed to meet the needs of children must be evaluated on a regular basis. Teachers, children, and the program must be assessed individually and then evaluated as a whole. Each supports and depends upon the other; an evaluation is a way to look at how these relationships are working. The result is a program of greater quality.

EARLY CHILDHOOD EDUCATION IN THE SHIPYARDS

by
Edith M. Dowley

This editorial is about an unforgettable experience I had with young children in a period of national crisis. It occurred during World War II, in an innovative project that not only was a remarkable solution to a problem for those times, but that also has special relevance and appropriateness, I believe, for the 21st century.

In early 1943, the Kaiser Shipbuilding Corporation was faced with the necessity of employing more women to meet the stepped-up schedule for producing warships in their two shipyards in Portland, Oregon. Of the 12,000 women already employed, one-third of them were mothers who had no place to leave their preschool children while they worked. Absenteeism among women was running 50 percent higher than among men and was contributing to slow-downs in production that seriously affected the war effort. The reasons most women gave for being late or for missing work were that the babysitter did not show up or a child was ill and could not be left at home until seen by a doctor. Henry Kaiser, reportedly in typical fashion, responded to the dilemma by saying that if mothers were worried about leaving their children, he would provide them with nurseries. He resolved to build the finest child care centers in the country.

Within a few weeks, architects were drawing plans for two child service centers to be placed at the entrances to the shipyards—one at Swan Island and the other at Oregon Yard. Paid for by the United States Maritime Commission and absorbed as part of the cost of building ships, these centers turned out to be not only very fine centers, but also the largest child care centers in the world.

Dr. Lois Meek Stolz, a well-known leader in the fields of child development and early childhood education, was chosen by Edgar Kaiser to direct the two child service centers. She planned the entire children's program and made provisions for staffing the centers. She brought James L. Hymes, Jr., former editor of *Progressive Education*, to the program as Manager of the Child Service Centers, and she recruited Dr. Miriam Lowenberg, a well-known nutritionist, to be responsible for the children's nutritional needs.

The Staff

Each center had a supervisor who was responsible for the total operation over all three shifts—day, swing, and graveyard. There were group supervisors, head teachers, assistant teachers, dieticians, and nurses under her direction. In addition, each center had a social worker who served as a liaison between the teachers in the centers and the parents in the shipyard. All of the staff members were recruited from nursery school training centers throughout the United States. All of the teachers had college degrees, and the supervisors and most of the head teachers had master's degrees and years of experience with children. They were young, energetic women "chosen for their comfortable qualities as well as for their scientific knowledge" (Jean Muir, from an article she wrote for the *Oregon Journal*, Sunday, December 12, 1943).

The Setting

The teaching staff began arriving in late October as the finishing touches were being made on the buildings. They found, to their delight, that the centers, although temporary, were beautifully and functionally designed. Each center was built around a large, octagonally shaped courtyard with four wading pools where children could play away from the hazards of traffic. The courtyard itself was grass-covered, with a hard-surfaced area designed for wheel toys that extended around the perimeter. Because of the long rainy season in Portland, covered porches, equipped with jungle gyms, climbing boxes, slides, and large, hollow blocks, connected the interior rooms to the grassy areas. Children could thus enjoy vigorous outdoor play every day of the year, regardless of the weather.

A cog-wheel plan of architecture provided for 15 rectangular playrooms (26′ by 49′) extending out from a central circular corridor. Between and opposite every two playrooms were smaller rooms for teachers' meetings, special play, or story times. Each of the 15 playrooms had windows on two sides to provide light and interesting views of the outside world. Window seats, low enough for children to sit on, were built so that the children could curl up on them and watch the ships, cars, trucks, and cranes in the busy shipyard below where their parents were working. This proved to be a special delight as darkness came and the yards were lighted, showing the outlines of the ships and their reflections in the water.

The interior colors were soft pastel shades of blue, yellow, and apricot, depending on the exposure of the individual room. Adult-height counterspace covered the expansive shelving where children could readily reach the many unit blocks, toys, games, books, and puzzles that were neatly and meaningfully stored there. Children's lockers, arranged like a dressing room unit, provided hooks for coats and jackets, a shelf for caps, mittens, and art work to take home, and a place for safekeeping of special possessions. Each room had its own toilet room with toilets and wash basins scaled to child size. Wash cloths and towels provided by the center were hung on hooks within the children's reach and marked with individual symbols matching the ones on their lockers.

There was a large room in each center, separated from the playrooms, where children could be cared for when they were ill. Comfortable cribs, like those used in children's hospitals, were placed in glass-sided cubicles that allowed children quiet places to sleep, eat, or sit up and play while recovering from colds, coughs, earaches, or upset tummies. A registered nurse was on duty at all times in the infirmary, and teachers planned and provided the play materials and projects for both the bed patients and those who were up and about.

Each center had a fully equipped, large, modern kitchen that was adequate for serving meals and snacks, over a 24-hour day, to some 400 children and their teachers. Large, heated rolling carts were available to deliver the china, silverware, and food to each room, where children were served at small, low tables. Usually, five children and a teacher dined together each day as a "family."

The architects thoughtfully included one additional feature: several large, square bathtubs raised two steps above the floor. These tubs allowed teachers, when necessary or desirable, to bathe a child without bending over. These tubs also provided safe places for children to "swim" and splash and engage in relaxing water play.

Opening Days

Oregon Center, where I was a group supervisor, opened its doors on November 8, 1943, to children, age 18 months to six years, of parents working on the day and swing shifts. On that day, a total of 67 children came to the center. We were, of course, very disappointed in this turnout. We realized, however, that the majority of people in the area had never even heard of a nursery school and were not able to imagine a children's center that would stay open twelve months a year, six days a week, and twenty-four hours a day! So we planned "open house" on Sundays and invited the public to tour the centers. We went down into the shipyards to talk to the workers about the child services available. Feature articles with many photographs appeared in the local newspapers. Gradually, more children were enrolled. By Christmas of that year, there were over 100 children being cared for in the center. In January, the graveyard shift was started, as was a Saturday and after-school program for older children. By August 27th, when Oregon Shipyard went on a seven-day work week, the Center was operating seven days a week, with an average daily attendance of 370 children.

Everything possible was done to keep workers on the job of building ships. Parents paid only nominal fees for child service: 75 cents a day for one child in a family and 50 cents for each additional child, paid by the week. If a child came seven days a week, parents were only charged for six days.

The Children

Mothers or fathers brought the children to their rooms at the Center each day before their shifts began, and picked them up after the shift ended. Day-shift children often spent nine or more hours in the Center as that was the longest shift. Day-shift parents were always in a hurry, it seemed, and were less able to spend time helping their children make the transition from home to school. Separating from their mothers and fathers was painful for some children at first.

After working out in the cold and rain for long hours at a stretch, day-shift parents were very tired and in a hurry at the end of the day when they came to pick up their children. Some were cross and impatient as they hurried their preschoolers to avoid missing the bus or car-pool ride. There was no time to talk over their child's day with the teacher. So, teachers communicated with parents about their children by writing brief comments next to a child's name on a chart hung outside the playroom door. These comments had to be worded with great tact, we discovered. Even such comments as "John didn't finish his lunch" or "Betsy didn't take a nap today" could result in angry scolding or slapping of the child. We tried to emphasize the positive behaviors in our messages in order to make each child appear more lovable and interesting to parents.

For the children on the swing shift, life was quite different. They usually arrived early after a leisurely day at home or out shopping with their parents. Mothers and fathers on their way to work often stayed for a while at the center, reading stories or looking at toys or interesting things the children described to them the night before. There was a more relaxed atmosphere in the playrooms during the swing shift than during the day shift. This was evident in the conversations between children, and especially in their dramatic play.

Swing-shift children were served supper as a group, after which they had time to play, listen to stories, enjoy music and play games, paint pictures and, in summertime, play outside until dark. They then undressed and went to bed. The children were then awakened and dressed before their tired parents arrived.

Additional Services

The Center also tried to provide time-saving services to parents that might relieve some of the stresses under which they worked. Home Service Foods began in January of 1944. Precooked meals, planned by Dr. Lowenberg, were prepared in the centers' kitchens. Priced at fifty cents each, one order was ample for a working man or woman, and a single portion would serve two preschool children. These ready-packaged meals were ordered two or more days in advance and contained the main course and dessert, the foods that usually required the most preparation time. Directions were included for heating and serving, and suggestions for additional foods to round out the meal were offered.

In time, other services were added, such as mending children's clothes, buying their shoelaces, and haircutting. In February, a program of immunizations was begun. Children whose parents had not been able to arrange for the necessary shots required for nursery school attendance were able to receive their shots at the Center. Teachers, in the absence of parents, brought children in turn to the Center's physician, holding them on their laps to reassure and comfort them while they got their shots.

Parent–Teacher Interactions

Parent–teacher conferences were usually difficult to arrange. We found ways to talk briefly with a mother by walking with her to a waiting bus or car. Teachers invited parents into the playrooms to see the artwork of their children or to view special block buildings preserved for their admiration.

Parent meetings took place occasionally when dinner was served to the mothers and fathers in one room while their children had dinner in another. Group supervisors went down into the shipyard to talk to a parent when it seemed necessary. On these occasions, I found myself surrounded by fathers and mothers who eagerly asked "What was my child doing when you left?" As parents realized how much teachers knew and cared about their children, they made time for interviews and shared their problems and pleasures with them.

Program Results

Many good things happened in the Child Service Centers in the Kaiser Shipyards—for children, for parents, for the industry, for all of us. We all had a part in winning the war as "champion shipbuilders," as we were told, and for that we were proud. The head of the Maritime Commission told the teachers that, without their help, it would have been impossible to keep the shipyards in production seven days a week. Parents told us that when they were tired and tempted to sleep late on Sunday morning, their children would awaken them, saying "Get up, get up. If you don't go to work, we don't get to go to school." When the centers were closed in 1945 at the end of the war, records showed that "3,811 children were taken care of—a total of 250,000 child care days—which freed almost 2 million working hours for the women" (Stanford University Campus Report, Interview with Lois Stolz, March 30, 1983).

But I think the most remarkable, the best thing that happened was that, in a time of war, when mothers of preschool children worked eight and nine hours a day, six or seven days a week, the lives of almost 4,000 children were made happy, healthy, and in some ways, better than they ever were before. This could only happen as a combination of skillful professional planning, strong professional leadership, and some of the best teachers the nursery school profession has ever prepared. I believe that all children deserve to benefit from that combination, especially in their early years.

We must wonder if, in the future, there will be enough professionally prepared specialists in the field to provide leadership. Will there be enough teachers who are knowledgeable about the nature and development of infants and young children and sensitive to their individual needs? Will there be enough enlightened and caring personnel to license and monitor (with in-service education) facilities and programs for an entire nation's children? You—and those who follow in your footsteps—hold the answers to these questions.

Edith M. Dowley was involved in early childhood education for fifty years. She was a group supervisor in the Kaiser Child Service Centers, and later became the first director of Stanford University's Bing Nursery School, a position she retained until 1975. She served as a national consultant to Project Head Start from 1965 to 1968, and from 1971 to 1972 she was a member of the California Task Force on Early Childhood Education. The late Dr. Dowley was most recently Professor Emerita of Psychology and Education at Stanford University.

For more activities and information, visit our Web site at http://www.EarlyChildEd.delmar.com

KEY TERMS

mixed-age groups
looping
developmentally appropriate
practice (DAP)
traditional nursery school

laboratory schools
child care center
parent cooperative schools
family child care
employer-sponsored child care

educaring
comprehensive
evaluation
accountability

REVIEW QUESTIONS

1. What are the three most important factors that determine the quality of an early childhood program?

2. Match the type of program with the appropriate description:

   Infant/toddler   Staggered staff schedules
   Full-day child care   Comprehensive programs
   Church-based   Teacher training
   Head Start   In home
   Employer-sponsored   Key experiences
   Proprietary   Benign landlord
   High/scope   For profit
   Laboratory schools   Educaring
   Family child care   Fringe benefit

3. Why are some early childhood programs called "intervention" schools?

4. Are there differences between preschool and kindergarten programs? Between infant and toddler programs? What are they? Should there be a difference? Why?

5. What are some of the features that affect all children's programs?

6. What has been the unique contribution of the Perry Preschool Project, and how do you see this affecting legislation and program development in early childhood?

7. Describe the influence of Piaget, Gardner, and Vygotsky on three types of early childhood programs.

8. What are the three premises on which evaluation of programs are based?

9. What are the reasons for evaluating early childhood programs? Which do you think would be the most difficult?

10. What is NAEYC's National Academy's accreditation, and how does it attempt to enhance program quality?

LEARNING ACTIVITIES

1. Choose one program and describe why you would like to teach in it. What are the most attractive elements of the program? What are some of the challenges you would have working in such a program?

2. Visit a family child care home. Look at the home as if you were a prospective parent. What did you like most? Least? Is the home licensed? If so, for how many children? After talking with the family child care provider, what do you think are the disadvantages of this type of program? What do you think are possible solutions to these problems?

3. What are the licensing regulations for child care in your area? Describe the steps necessary in your town to open a nursery school, child care center, and a family child care home.

4. Which government agencies are involved in the licensing procedure?

5. Visit a Head Start program and a local kindergarten. Compare their programs in terms of appropriate or inappropriate curriculum. What are the major concerns of the teaching staff in each type of setting? What are the controversies about each of these programs in your community?

6. Does your own setting have an evaluation plan? Analyze the goals of your process and note where the implementation meets (or does not meet) the goals.

7. Visit an NAEYC accredited program. Discuss the following with the director or supervisor: How did the staff respond to the process? What were some of the most difficult issues to address? What was the role of parents in the process? What have been the benefits of accreditation?

REFERENCES

Allen, K. E., & Cowdery, G. (2005). *The exceptional child: Inclusion in early childhood education.* Clifton Park, NY: Delmar Learning.

Baker, K. R. (1955). *The nursery school.* Philadelphia, PA: Saunders.

Bellis, M. (1999, May). Look before you loop. *Young Children,* pp. 70–72.

Belsky, J., & Braungart, J. M. (1991). Are insecure-avoidant infants with extensive day-care experience less stressed by and more independent in the strange situation? *Child Development 62,* 567–571.

Berk, L. E. (1994). *Infants and children.* Boston: Allyn & Bacon.

Bieleck, S., Chandler, K., & Broughman, S. (2001). Homeschooling in the United States: 1999. *Education Statistics Quarterly* (NCES 2001-033). U.S. Department of Education, Washington, DC.

Bredekamp, S., & Copple, C. (Eds.). (1997). *Developmentally appropriate practice in early childhood programs.* Washington, DC: National Association for the Education of Young Children.

Bredekamp, S., & Glowacki, S. (1996). The first decade of NAEYC accreditation: Growth and impact on the field. In S. Bredkamp & B. A. Willer (Eds.), *NAEYC accreditation: A decade of learning and the years ahead.* Washington, DC: National Association for the Education of Young Children.

Brown, B. (1985, July). Head Start—How research changed public policy. *Young Children,* 9–13.

Carnegie Corporation. (1996). *Years of promise: A comprehensive learning strategy for America's children.* New York: Author.

(The) Carolina Abecedarian Project. (1999). The Frank Porter Graham Child Development Institute. The University of North Carolina at Chapel Hill: Author.

Chang, H. M., Muckelroy, A., Pudilo-Tobiassen, D., Dowell, C., & Edwards, J. O. (1996). *Looking in, looking out: Refining child care in a diverse society.* San Fransisco: California Tomorrow.

Chapman, J. (1999, May). A looping journey. *Young Children,* pp. 80–83.

Chase, P., & Doan, J. (Eds.). (1994). *Full circle: A new look at multi-age education.* Portsmouth, NH: Heineman Publishers.

Children's Defense Fund. (2001). *The state of America's children, yearbook 2001.* Washington, DC: Author.

Children's Defense Fund (2005). *The state of American's children, yearbook 2005.*

Cloud, J., & Morse, J. (August 27, 2001). Home sweet school. *Time,* pp. 47–54.

Cohen, D. L. (1993b, April 21). Perry preschool graduates show dramatic new social gains at 27. *Education Week,* p. 1.

Cost, Quality, and Child Outcomes Study Team (1995). *Cost, quality and child outcomes in child care centers.* Denver: Department of Economics, University of Colorado at Denver.

Digest of Education Statistics. (2001). *Chapter 2: Elementary and secondary education.* National Center for Education Statistics, Washington, DC: Author.

Doherty, K. M. (Jan. 10, 2002). Early learning. *Education Week.*

Galinsky, E., Howes, C., Kontos, S., & Shinn, M. (1994). *The study of children in family child care and relative care: Highlights of findings.* New York: Families and Work Institute.

Gerber, M. (1979). Respecting infants: The Loczy model of infant care. In E. Jones (Ed.), *Supporting the growth of infants, toddlers, and parents.* Pasadena, CA: Pacific Oaks.

Gestwicki, C. (2007). *Developmentally appropriate practice: Curriculum & development in early education.* Clifton Park, NY: Thomson Delmar Learning.

Giannarelli, L., & Barsimantov, J. (2000 December). *Child care expenses of America's families.* Urban Institute 1997 National Survey of America's Families. Washington, DC.

Gonzalez-Mena, J., & Eyer, D. W. (1989, 1993). *Infants, toddlers, and caregivers.* Mountain View, CA: Mayfield.

Greenberg, P. (1990, September). Before the beginning: A participant's view. *Young Children,* pp. 41–52.

Gullo, DF. (ED.) 2006. *Teaching and learning in the kindergarten year.* Washington, DC: National Association for the Education of Young Children.

Hampton, D. (April 2002). Executive Director, Ecumenical Child Care Network. Speech delivered to Delaware Valley Child Care Council, Philadelphia, PA.

Harms, T., Clifford, R. M., & Cryer, D. (1998). *Early Childhood Environmental Rating Scale* (Rev. ed.). New York: Teachers College Press.

Hatch, J. A. (2005). *Teaching in the new kindergarten.* Clifton Park, NY: Thomson Delmar Learning.

Head Start (2002). *2002 Head Start fact sheet.* Washington, DC: Head Start Bureau, Department of Health and Human Services.

Head Start Program Performance Standards and Other Regulations. (1998). Head Start Bureau, Administration on Children, Youth and Families, Administration for Children and Families, United States Department of Health and Human Services. Washington, DC: U.S. Government Printing Office.

HHS News (2002, June). *Study shows positive results from early head start program.* U.S. Department of Health and Human Services, Washington, DC (1).

Honig, A. S. (1985, November). High quality infant/toddler care: Issues and dilemmas. *Young Children,* pp. 40–46.

Hyun, E. (1998). *Making sense of developmentally and culturally appropriate practice (DCAP) in early childhood education.* New York: Peter Lang.

Jacobson, L. (1996a, September 18). Carnegie offers reform strategy for ages 3 to 10. *Education Week,* p. 1.

Kagan. S. L., & Kauerz, K. (2006). Making the most of kindergarten: Trends and policy issues. In D. F. Gullo (Ed.) *Teaching and learning in the kindergarten year.* Washington, DC: National Association for the Education of Young Children.

Karoly, L. A., & Bigelow, J. H. (2005). *The economics of investing in universal preschool education in California.* Santa Monica, CA: RAND (Research and Development Corporation).

Katz, L. (1995, May). The benefits of mixed-age grouping. *ERIC Digest.* (EDO-PS-95-8)

Katz, L. (2000, August). Academic redshirting and young children. *ERIC Digest.* (EDO-PS-00-13)

Katz, L. G., Evangelou, D., & Hartman, J. A. (1990). *The case for mixed-age groupings in early education.* Washington, DC: National Association for the Education of Young Children.

Lindner, E., Mattis, M. C., & Rogers, J. (1983). *When churches mind the children.* Ypsilanti, MI: High/Scope Press.

Meisels, S. J., & Sternberg, L. S. (1989, June). Quality sacrificed in proprietary child care. *Education Week,* p. 36.

National Association for Family Child Care. (2002). *NAFCC an accreditation and professional family child care.* Salt Lake City, UT: Author.

National Association for the Education of Young Children Position Statement. (1997). Developmentally appropriate practice in early childhood programs serving children from birth through age 8. In S. Bredekamp & C. Copple (Eds.), *Developmentally appropriate practice in early childhood programs.* Washington, DC: National Association for the Education of Young Children.

National Association for the Education of Young Children. (1998a, January). NAEYC position statement on licensing and public regulation of early childhood programs. *Young Children,* pp. 43–50.

National Association for the Education of Young Children. (1998b). *Accreditation criteria and procedures of the National Academy of Early Childhood Programs.* Washington, DC: Author.

National Association for the Education of Young Children. (1999, July). NAEYC position statement on developing and implementing effective public policies to promote early childhood and school-age care program accreditation. *Young Children,* 36–40.

National Association for the Education of Young Children. (2005). *NAEYC early childhood program standards & accreditation criteria.* Washington, DC: National Association for the Education of Young Children.

National Association of Early Childhood Specialists in State Departments of Education and the National Association of Education for Young Children. (2001, September). Still unacceptable trends in kindergarten entry and placement. *Young Children,* pp. 59–62.

National Center for Education Statistics (2000). Preprimary enrollment/various years. Washington, DC: U.S. Department of Education.

National Center for Education Statistics (2001). *Digest of education statistics, 2001: Chapter 2, Elementary and secondary education.* Washington, DC: Author.

National Center for Education Statistics. (n.d.). *Digest of education statistics: 2000.* Washington, DC: U.S. Government Printing Office.

Neugebauer, R. (1996, July). Promising development and new directions in school-age care. *Child Care Information Exchange,* pp. 7–13.

Neugebauer, R. (1997, May/June). How's business? Status report #10 on for-profit child care. *Child Care Information Exchange,* pp. 65–69.

Neugebauer, R. (1998, January/February). Sesame Street meets Wall Street. Eleventh annual status report on for-profit child care. *Child Care Information Exchange,* pp. 12–16.

Neugebauer, R. (2000, March). Non-profit child care: A powerful worldwide movement. Child Care Information Exchange, pp. 6–12.

Neugebauer, R. (2001, September). Employer child care growth and consolidation issues. *Child Care Information Exchange,* pp. 14–17.

Peck, J. T., McCaig, G., & M. E. Sapp (1988). *Kindergarten policies—What is best for children?* Washington, DC: National Association for the Education of Young Children.

Ramsey, P. (1987). *Teaching and learning in a diverse world: Multicultural education for young children.* New York: Teachers College Press.

Schweinhart, L. J., & Weikart, D. P. (1993, November). Success by empowerment: The High/Scope Perrry preschool study through age 27. *Young Children,* pp. 54–58.

Seligson, M. (1997). School-age child care comes of age. *Child Care ActioNews,* 14(1).

Seligson, M. (2001, January). School-age child care today. Young Children, pp. 90–94.

Smith, K. (2000). *Who's minding the kids? Child care arrangements: Fall, 1995.* Current Population Reports Series P 70-70 (Table 14). Washington, DC: U.S. Government Printing Office.

Snow, C. W., Teleki, J. K., & Reguero-de-Atiles, J. T. (1996, September). Child care center licensing standards in the United States: 1981 to 1995. *Young Children,* pp. 36–41.

Suro, R. (1992, January 5). Holding back to get ahead. *The New York Times,* 4A, pp. 30–32.

The Children's Foundation. (2001). *Family child care licensing summary data.*

The Children's Foundation. (2002). *Child care center licensing study summary data.*

Trawick-Smith, J., & Lambert, L. (1995, March). The unique challenges of the family child care provider: Implications for professional development. *Young Children,* pp. 25–32.

United States Bureau of Labor Statistics (1999). Childcare workers. *Occupational Outlook Handbook.* Washington, DC: U.S. Department of Labor.

United States Bureau of Labor Statistics (2002). *Families with own children: Employment status of parent, child and family type, 2000–01 annual averages.* (Table 4.) Washington, DC: U.S. Department of Labor.

United States Bureau of Labor Statistics (2005). Childcare workers. *Occupational Outlook Handbook.* Washington, DC: U.S. Department of Labor.

United States Bureau of the Census. Current Population Survey. Supplements 1970–2000. (2002 March). Washington, DC: U.S. Bureau of the Census: Author.

United States Department of Education (1998). *Reducing class size: What do we know?* Washington, DC: U.S. Government Printing Office.

Vandell, D. L., & Pierce, K. M. (1999). *Can after-school programs benefit children who live in high crime neighborhoods?* N. L. Marshall, Chair, Children's out-of-school time: The next generation of research. Poster symposium conducted at the Society of Research in Child Development.

West, J., Meek, A., & Hurst, D. (2000). *Children who enter kindergarten late or repeat kindergarten: Their characteristics and later school performance.* National Center for Education Statistics No. 2000-039. Washington, DC: U.S. Department of Education.

Whitebook, M., Sakai, L., Gerber, E., & Howes, C. (2001). *Then and now: Changes in child care staffing, 1994–2000.* Washington, DC: Center for the Child Care Workforce.

HELPFUL WEB SITES

Bureau of Labor Statistics	http://www.stats.bls.gov
U.S. Department of Education	http://www.dhhs.gov
Families and Work Institute	http://www.familiesandwork.org
National Institute on Out-of-School Time	http://www.niost.org
National Network for Child Care	http://www.nncc.org
National Association for Family Child Care	http://www.nafcc.org
Child Care Information Exchange	http://www.ccie.com
National Center for Education Statistics	http://www.nces.ed.gov
Culturally and Linguistically Appropriate Services	http://www.clas.uiuc.edu
Ecumenical Child Care Network	http://www.eccn.org
Center for Child Care Workforce	http://www.ccw.cleverspin.com
International Nanny's Association	http://www.nanny.org
Head Start/Early Head Start	http://www.acf.dhhs.gov/programs/hsb
ChildStats	http://www.childstats.gov
U.S. Census Bureau	http://www.census.gov
Children's Defense Fund	http://www.childrensdefense.org
About Homeschooling	http://www.homeschooling.about.com
National Association for the Education of Young Children	http://www.naeyc.org

 For more activities and information, visit our Web site at http://www.EarlyChildEd.delmar.com

Section 2

Who Is the Young Child?

GROWING YOUR BRAIN: THE FIRST THREE YEARS ARE SPECIAL

Peter L. Mangione

As with all other times of life, the infant and toddler years are unique. Research on early brain development shows that a child's brain is not fully formed at birth. The brain develops throughout childhood, but the foundation is laid in the first three years. Because basic structures of the brain must still develop, nature sets the course for that development to proceed. In every domain, infants are programmed to follow developmental sequences. It is as if infants and toddlers have their own agenda or curriculum for development and learning. But to pursue their curriculum, they need the support of adults. The way in which adults nurture infants and toddlers has a profound impact on the quality of children's early development and learning.

The content of early development and learning. All children are internally driven to learn. What sets infancy apart from other age periods is the specific content they actively seek to learn. Infants and toddlers are genetically programmed to build knowledge about people and things, and to learn language. For example, they will spontaneously fiddle with objects to search for causal mechanisms and constantly explore how things fit and move in space. Likewise, children begin communicating with us right from the start of life, imitating our sounds, gestures, and eventually words and sentences.

Adults do not have to create lessons on, for example, cause and effect or language. In fact, in countless hours of observing parents communicate with infants and toddlers, Hart and Risley (1995) did not observe instances when adults intentionally tried to teach language (Risley, 2005). Generally speaking, the most effective strategy to foster early learning is to be responsive to children. By sensitively following the children's lead, adults can discover ways to enrich the learning experiences that infants and toddlers are genetically programmed to pursue.

The holistic nature of learning. Infants take in information almost seamlessly, making discoveries in the physical, emotional, social, intellectual, and language domains at the same time. From their actions, interactions, and observations, they simultaneously build knowledge and skills in all areas of development. Of particular importance is the emotional quality of every learning experience (Siegel, 1999). A positive emotional tone will motivate infants to continue to engage in learning and want to revisit the experience. In contrast, they are likely to withdraw from a highly stressful or negative learning situation. Because infants learn holistically, adults need to take a much more organic approach to facilitating early learning. The learning environments adults create and their responses to infants should reflect an awareness of the impact that every experience has on all the domains of learning and development, including intellectual and language development (Mangione, 1995; PITC, 1998).

Movement through major developmental periods. During the first six to eight months of life, most infants organize their attention and behavior around developing a sense of security. Their explorations and their growing knowledge of themselves as individuals with separate identities are played out on the stage of seeking security. They need adults who consistently read their cues and respond predictably. As children grow a little older, their focus turns to exploring with their ever-increasing gross and fine motor skills. The developmental organization of children in the next period (from about six months to sixteen to eighteen months of age) shifts. Still needing security, these children spend less time giving engagement cues to their trusted caregiver. Now, captivated by the exciting world around them, they want to use their developing skills to move out and explore. They occasionally check in with their caregiver for emotional refueling or to look together at things such as a book and communicate. Their sense of identity changes as they see themselves as active explorers no longer physically bound to the trusted adult, but on their own for brief periods. Children prosper in this stage of infancy when free to explore in a safe and secure environment, and use the caregiver both as a base of security and as someone with whom to share attention and meaning.

As children enter the third period of infancy—around 16, 17 or 18 months of age—their focus changes again. For the rest of infancy, children attend to issues of me and mine, and notions of good and not so good. Interactions and negotiations with others lead to learning about themselves as independent, dependent, and interdependent beings. Their explorations and feelings of security are interpreted through this new identity lens. To be responsive, the adult provides security by setting boundaries to help older toddlers learn the rules of social behavior. The adult also should be responsive to the older toddlers' emerging interest in the world of ideas. These children thrive in environments that support their interest in creating things, in engaging in pretend play, in solving increasingly complex problems, and in using language to communicate about ideas with their caregivers and their peers.

Relationships are at the heart of early learning. Children's first and most prominent concern in life is to form relationships with the adults who nurture them. In the intellectual and language development domains, learning is rooted in relationships. During the first months of life, reciprocal interactions provide opportunities for children to learn from adults. For example, adults' responsiveness to cues helps infants make connections between actions such as crying and having their needs met. Young infants also learn about the rhythm and flow of communication, which is an important foundation for language development. As infants grow older, they use secure relationships as a base for exploring their environment and solving problems. They also rely on familiarity in close relationships to begin communicating with language and sharing meaning. In the older period of infancy, children depend on trusting relationships for guidance, for help in understanding social rules and the way things work, and for support during stressful moments.

The years from birth to three are marked by genetic programming, holistic learning, rapid developmental changes, and relationship-centered learning. Taken together, these factors make this time of life distinct from all other age periods. In light of the uniqueness of the first three years, adults need to relate to infants and toddlers differently from older children.

- Because infants are wired for specific learning, the adult's role in supporting learning is to be respectful and responsive to each child's learning focus, rather than generating lessons for the child.

- Because early learning is holistic, adults need to attend to the whole learning experience, in particular the emotional tone that the environment and their style of interacting convey.

- Because infants' focus on security, exploration, and identity formation shifts as they grow, adults should respond to these needs in a way that fits with each child's rapidly changing developmental focus.

- Because relationships are at the heart of all development and learning during infancy, the top priority for adults is to establish responsive, nurturing relationships with infants and toddlers.

Above all, through close, emotionally supportive relationships adults can offer to infants and toddlers rich experiences that optimally facilitate early development and learning.

BIBLIOGRAPHY

Hart, B., & Risley, T. R. (1995). *Meaningful differences in the everyday experience of young American children.* Baltimore: Brooks.

Mangione, P. L. (Ed.). (1995). *Infant/Toddler caregiving: A guide to cognitive development and learning.* Sacramento: CDE Press.

PITC (Program for Infant/Toddler Care). (1998). *Early messages: Facilitating language development and communication* (Video). Sacramento: CDE Press.

Risley, T. (2005). http://www.childrenofthecode.org/interviews/risley.htm.

Siegel, D. J. (1999). *The developing mind.* New York, NY: Guilford.

PETER L. MANGIONE

PETER L. MANGIONE, Ph.D., is the co-director of WestEd's Center for Child & Family Studies. With his colleague Ron Lally, he has played a leading role in the development of the Program for Infant/Toddler Care, a comprehensive, multimedia training system for early care and education professionals.

CHAPTER 3

Defining the Young Child

QUESTIONS FOR THOUGHT

What is meant by "the whole child"?

How are age-level charts (Word Pictures) useful?

What are the implications for teaching children of varying levels of development?

Who are children with special needs?

What are some of the common types of disabilities found in young children?

What is an inclusive classroom?

THE WHOLE CHILD

The concept of "the whole child" is based on the accepted principle that all areas of human growth and development are integrated. It is only for the purpose of studying one area or another in depth that such categories are created. The five developmental areas labeled in the Word Pictures in Figure 3-1 help us focus on certain aspects of a child's normal development. In reality, all areas of growth are "intertwined and mutually supportive" (Allen & Marotz, 2003).

Each Child Is Unique

There are several reasons to consolidate the different developmental areas when looking at children. The first is the uniqueness of each child. Each one is a sum total of a multitude of parts and, as such, is different from anyone else. Individual natures and learning styles affect the way teachers will teach any two children of the same age in the same class.

We often begin to define children by their physical characteristics. Initially, their differences are most obvious by the way they look.

> Eric is a tall blond. He is much larger than his just-three age would indicate. He has long slender fingers and arms to match. His movements are fluid; he lopes across the room toward the easel.

> Lamar's short stocky build and constant swagger lend the impression that he is a pretty tough character at age six. His twinkling eyes and infectious smile offset that image.

> Natalie at four is a study in perpetual motion. Green eyes flashing, arms and legs waving, she ignores the bulk of her diaper as she propels herself down the slide. There is little indication that the mild case of spina bifida she has inhibits her motor activities. It certainly hasn't affected her daring.

Nothing will heighten an awareness of the individuality of each child more than working in the classroom. Teachers quickly learn what makes each child special and accumulate a great deal of information. We learn what children look like as children move their bodies, change expressions, and assume a posture. A teacher can sense whether Sonja is happy, hurt, or hurried by the way she moves and how she looks. Rodrigo's face mirrors his distress or his delight. The observant teacher learns to read children for evidence of their social, emotional, physical, and intellectual growth. Children quite naturally express these characteristics with their whole body and each child's response is unique.

Children: alike, yet different.

Growth Is Interrelated

One area of development affects the other. One way for teachers to look at this concept of development is to plot the relationships visually. Think of each area of development as a circle. There are five of them: physical-motor, language, intellectual, social-emotional, and creative. See Figure 3-1.

Think how each area might affect or interact with the others.

- Physical development affects how children feel about themselves. Children who appreciate their body and its power feel confident in what they can do (social-emotional).
- Intellectual skills interact with language development and creativity. When children have mastered their primary language, they can then clarify some of their thought processes.
- The kindergartner who masters using scissors (physical) is ready to try printing. The fine-motor skills enhance the cognitive task of learning the alphabet.
- A child with a hearing loss is likely to have language delay as well; thus, the physical development affects the language part of growth.
- The child who has trouble making friends (social) is likely to exhibit his unhappiness (emotional) in the school yard (physical) and in the math period (intellectual).

Valuing Wholeness

The concept of the whole child strongly suggests the uniqueness of the person. Although they are often discussed separately, the areas of development (social-emotional, physical, language, cultural awareness, intellectual, and creativity) cannot be isolated from one another. They each make a valuable contribution to the total child.

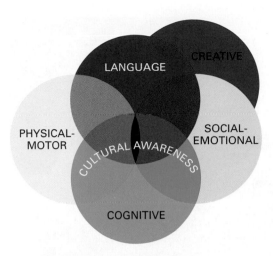

FIGURE 3-1 How areas of growth are interrelated: each area of growth is affected by and influences every other area of development.

COMMON CHARACTERISTICS

How Children Are Alike

The similarities of the many children in a class are striking. Teachers can see the differences—wide differences—yet there are common characteristics within the age group itself. Six toddlers working on an art project exhibit six different personal styles, yet typically, they all become distracted and leave their projects half finished.

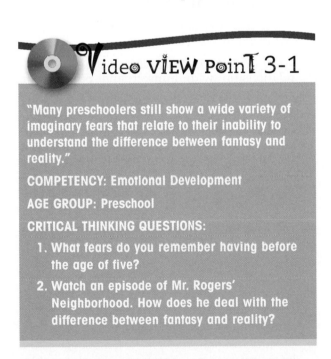

ideo VIEW Point 3-1

"Many preschoolers still show a wide variety of imaginary fears that relate to their inability to understand the difference between fantasy and reality."

COMPETENCY: Emotional Development

AGE GROUP: Preschool

CRITICAL THINKING QUESTIONS:

1. What fears do you remember having before the age of five?

2. Watch an episode of Mr. Rogers' Neighborhood. How does he deal with the difference between fantasy and reality?

Observation of children—how they look and how they act—helps a teacher see each child as an individual. There is enough standard behavior appropriate to certain age levels that allows for some generalizations about children's behavior.

Caldwell (1993) cites three universal characteristics that unite children of the world. Each child is like every other in that (1) they all have the same needs, the most important of which are food, shelter, and care; (2) they all go through the same developmental stages; and (3) they all have the same developmental goals, although the timing and the cultural influences will differ.[1]

WORD PICTURES

Each developmental phase has characteristic traits. In the following pages some of the classic normative data collected by Gesell and Ilg (1943) are combined with theories of Piaget, Elkind, Erikson, and Vygotsky (see Chapter 4) to demonstrate what children have in common at various ages. Despite the wide range of individual differences at all ages, common behaviors lend a perspective to help teachers prescribe programs, plan activities, and create curricula.

The Value of Word Pictures in Behavior and Guidance

Guidance and discipline are based on an awareness of the expected behaviors common to a given age range. Many so-called problem behaviors are normal behaviors of the age at which they occur: for example, the difficulty some toddlers and two-year-olds have with sharing their toys. This does not imply a passive approach; teachers and parents do not ignore undesirable behavior because the child is "going through a stage." Instead adults seek to guide and direct children in ways that enhance their overall growth. Four-year-olds test limits and are resistant to controls. The wise teacher accepts the testing of power and individuality, yet still maintains necessary limits to behavior.

Word Pictures of a child, taken from age-level charts, help teachers know what to expect and when to expect it. By using the charts as a reference, teachers lessen the risk of expecting too much or too little of children at any given age. If, for instance, four-year-olds typically "tell tall tales," teachers' responses to their stories reflect an awareness of that tendency. The fun of

1 Children are sometimes more alike than they are different.

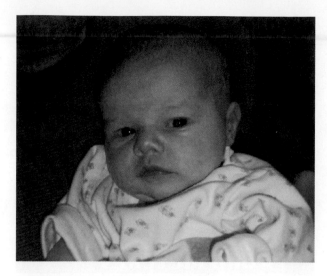

Adults see children through many filters. What is it like to look through children's eyes?

making up a story and the use of imagination are acknowledged, but there is not a concern that the child is lying. **Age-level characteristics** give a frame of reference with which to handle daily situations and a basis for planning appropriate guidance measures.

In Curricula

Word Pictures can be used to tailor curriculum planning to an individual child or a particular class or group on the basis of known developmental standards. A group cooking experience, for instance, allows children to choose their level of comfort and involvement. As an early reader at age four, Darragh loves to read the recipe to others. Lourdes's favorite activity is to mix the ingredients together, refining her small motor skills. Von, who loves to play with mud and clay, spreads the cookie sheet with oil while Felicity helps the teacher adjust the oven temperature. When planning an activity, the teacher takes into account what she knows about each child's development. Cooking is always a fun activity but serves a greater purpose when planned with individual children in mind. See Figure 3-2 for guidelines on using the Word Pictures as tools for planning. Chapter 10 has more practical applications and examples for planning curriculum.

Cultural Awareness and Identity

Derman-Sparks (1989) points out that children become aware of and form attitudes about racial and cultural differences at a very early age. Their experiences with their bodies, social environment, and cognitive development combine to help them form their own identity and attitudes. As they develop cognitively, children become aware of differences and similarities in people. These cultural milestones are included in the Word Pictures to indicate how, as children come to a sense of themselves as individuals, their attitudes and behaviors towards others can be influenced.

USING WORD PICTURES

Six Developmental Areas

Six basic developmental areas are included in the Word Pictures:

- *Social-Emotional Development.* Includes a child's relationship with himself and others, self-concept, self-esteem, and the ability to express feelings.
- *Language Development.* Includes children's utterances, pronunciation, vocabulary, sentence length, and the ability to express ideas, needs, and feelings. It includes receptive language (do they understand what they hear?) and verbal levels (what do they say?).
- *Physical-Motor Development.* Includes gross motor, fine motor, and perceptual motor.
- *Cognitive Development.* This includes curiosity, the ability to perceive and think, memory, attention span, general knowledge, problem solving, analytical thinking, beginning reading, computing skills, and other cognitive processes.
- *Cultural Identity Development.* This suggests the interconnections between developmental stages and a growing awareness of one's attitudes toward others of differing cultures.

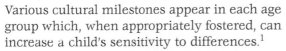

Guidelines for Using Word Pictures

Balance your impressions of the Word Pictures with classroom experience. Observe children to add a measure of reality as you interpret these phrases.

Example: Toddlers are always on the move and seem to prefer standing and squatting to sitting in a chair. Observe a toddler story-time to see how many children are sitting on the floor, how many are standing, and how many are squatting on their haunches. What do they do if the story lasts too long?

Make a profile of the whole child, and resist the tendency to categorize him or her.

Example: "The terrible twos" is an unfortunate label that has defined this age group for years. Yet seeing them at play, you get another picture of their emerging development: they enjoy singing parts of the songs they know; they are intrigued by sensory activities; they watch and imitate other children; and they are excited about their own capabilities. They enjoy the attention when adults interact with them and, with proper encouragement, they learn how to control their impulses

Get perspective on the range of developmental norms a child exhibits over several of the chronological age groupings.

Example: Look at the Word Pictures for the group just below and just above the age level of the child. Children will exhibit some of the behaviors appropriate to all three groups. Darius, who is five, lacks the coordination of most children his age, yet his interest in using symbols and devising codes is that of a six-year-old and his bossiness echoes that of some four-year-olds. This picture shows his unique development across the age span. Teachers will want to support him in each of these areas of development and respect his pace of growth.

Remember that these norms of development refer to average or typical behavior. They cannot be applied too literally.

Example: In a class of seven-year-olds, maybe half of the children would fit the majority of the description in the Word Picture for that age. Some would not yet have reached this development level, and others would show characteristics common to the eight-year-old. There may even be characteristics that some of the children will never exhibit. Sabina, for instance, seems typically seven. She is feeling peer pressure for the first time, loves jokes and guessing games, but she does not limit her friendship to girls nor does she enjoy physical activity. Yet Sabina is all of seven years old and needs to be appreciated for her unique self.

Keep in mind that children probably go through most of the stages described and in the same sequence, but they will do so at their own rates of growth.

Example: Individual differences occur as development follows its own orderly, predictable sequence. Teachers need to create programs that allow children the time and space to acquire the abilities and skills that are necessary to succeed in the following stages. Pushing children to read or write when they do not yet have the physical and developmental skills to do so is ignoring one of the key elements in a developmentally appropriate program: applying your knowledge about child development in planning programs.

Focus on what the child can do rather than on what he or she cannot do. Use the characteristics to compare the child's own rate of growth.

Example: Word Pictures are not meant to compare one child to another. In observing Dwayne, it is important to know where he is in relation to most eight-year-olds, but it is more important where he is six months from now, a year from now, and what he was like a year ago. A clear picture of his rate of growth emerges.

FIGURE 3-2 Use age level charts with discretion. Follow the Guidelines and the Word Pictures can be a valuable teaching tool.

 Various cultural milestones appear in each age group which, when appropriately fostered, can increase a child's sensitivity to differences.[1]

- *Creative Development.* This includes creative activities such as movement, dance, music, and painting, as well as originality, imagination, divergent thinking, and problem solving.

How Word Pictures Help Teachers

The following Word Pictures are designed to help classroom teachers. They focus on the critical issues that teachers address when planning for a group of children. These are:

- Behaviors most common to the age group.
- Those that have implications for children in group settings.
- Those that suggest guidance and disciplinary measures.
- Those that have implications for planning a developmentally appropriate curriculum.
- Those that are cultural milestones, which are highlighted to suggest the interaction of children's development and their awareness of attitudes toward race and culture.[2]

In Chapter 4, students will come to appreciate the importance of research and significant theories from which these Word Pictures are drawn.

1 Very early in the course of normal development, children develop attitudes about differences in people.

2 In order to build attitudes that go beyond mere tolerance, we must help children gain more accurate pictures of persons and cultures different from their own.

INFANT

Social-Emotional

0–1 month: cries to express emotions; bonding
                  begins
4–10 weeks: social smiles
2 months: begins social games
3 months: distinguishes familiar faces*
                turns head toward human voice
                smiles in response to a smile
                kicks, smiles, waves in response
                cries when left alone
                recognizes parent
4 months: genuine laugh
                smiles when spoken to
                loves attention
5 months to 1 year: stranger anxiety*
6 months: distinguishes between voices
                smiles, babbles at strangers
                develops attachment
                begins to play imitation games
                plays peek-a-boo
                sensitive to parental moods
8 months: laughs out loud
9 months: screams to get own way
Play is activity only for present moment.
Fears unfamiliar: people, places, things.*
Beginning sense of separate self.*

Language

0–1 month: turns head in response to voices
                  cries to express needs
6–8 weeks: coos
Gestures to communicate:
    pushes objects away, squirms,
    reaches out to people,* pouts,
    smacks lips, shrieks, points
2 months: voluntary vocal sounds
3 months: babbles
6–12 months: imitation sound games
Responds to variety of sounds*
Makes vowel sounds
Acquires receptive language*
Cries to communicate
12 months: first words

Physical-Motor

By 1 year: grows 10 to 12 inches, triples birth weight,
                  lengthens by 40%, doubles brain size, grows
                  full head of hair
Bounces in crib
Uses whole-body motions
4 months: sees, grasps objects
5 months: examines fingers
                sits when propped
6 months: rolls over
                discovers feet
                teething begins
7 months: crawls
8 months: sits up unaided
                pulls to standing position
                pincer grasp established
9 months: creeps
10 months: feeds self with spoon
11 months: stands alone, cruises
12 months: first steps
Late infancy: can move hands in rotation to turn knobs
Newborn motor activity is mostly reflexes.

Creative

Discovers and explores hands and feet
Expresses and discovers emotion
Talks by babbling, cooing, and gurgling
Plays Peek-a-Boo
Responds to facial expressions

Cognitive

0–1 month: responds to mother's voice:
                  senses function, especially pain, touch*
10 weeks: memory is evident*
4 months: smiles of recognition
7–10 months: solves simple problems (knocks over
                  box to get toy)
8 months: begins to believe in permanence of objects;
                  follows a simple instruction
8–12 months: intentionality in acts
11 months: begins trial-error experimentation
12 months: plays drop/retrieve games, pat-a-cake
Explores with hands and fingers
Smiles, vocalizes at image in mirror*

*Key characteristics of cultural awareness or identity.

TODDLER

Social-Emotional

Almost totally egocentric
Likes to be noticed; loves an audience
Lacks inhibitions
Insists on own way, assertive
Likes doing things by self
Independent, has self-identity*
Adapts easily
Plays by self in playpen
Refers to self by name
Laughs loudly at peek-at-boo
Cries when left alone
Curious*
Relates to adults better than children
Active, eager
Talks mostly to self
Usually friendly
Strong sense of ownership
Mimics adult behavior*
Experiences and shows shame*

Language

Some two-word phrases
Enjoys vocalizing to self
Babbles in own jargon
Uses "eh-eh" or "uh-uh" with gestures
Names closest relatives*
Repeats adults' words*
Points to communicate needs, wants
Shakes head "no" to respond*
Responds to directions to fetch, point
Obeys verbal requests
Asks "What's that?" or "Whassat?"*
Understands simple phrases
Uses 5 to 50 words

Physical-Motor

Awkward coordination; chubby body
Tottering stance

Creeps when in a hurry
Walks with increasing confidence
Walks with feet wide apart, arms out, head forward
Finds it difficult to turn corners
Goes up and down stairs holding on
Backs into chair to sit down
Can squat for long periods of time
Motor-minded: constant motion
Loves to pull/push objects
Runs with stiff, flat gait
Uses whole-arm movements
Carry and dump becomes a favorite activity
Scribbles
Turns pages two or three at a time
Zips/unzips large zipper
Likes holding objects in both hands

Creative

Responds to mood of music
Develops ways to move across space
Freely examines every object
Sings phrases of nursery rhymes
Loves to fingerpaint and explore texture
Stares; takes it all in
"The age of exploration"
Makes up nonsense syllables

Cognitive

Points to objects in a book
Matches similar objects
Fits round block in round hole
Loves opposites: up/down, yes/no*
Imitates simple tasks
Interest shifts quickly
Short attention span
Follows one direction
Gives up easily but easily engaged*
Conclusions are important: closes doors, shuts books
Thinks with feet; action-oriented
Builds tower of three or four small blocks

*Key characteristics of cultural awareness or identity.

TWO-YEAR-OLD

Social-Emotional

Self-centered
Unable to share, possessive
Clings to familiar; resistant to change*
Ritualistic; insists on routines*
Dependent
Likes one adult at a time*
Quits readily; easily frustrated
Goes to extremes
Impulsive; shifts activities suddenly
Easily distracted
Pushes, shoves
Finicky, fussy eater, some food jags
Refers to self by given name*
Treats people as inanimate objects*
Dawdles; slow-geared
Plays parallel
Watches others*
Likes people*
Excited about own capabilities

Language

Uses two- or three-word sentences
Telegraphic sentences: "Throw ball"
Has difficulty in pronunciation
"Me," "Mine" most prominent pronouns*
Spontaneous language; rhythmic, repetitive
Constant talking; interested in sound
Sings phrases of song, not on pitch
Can't articulate feelings
Frustrated when not understood
May stutter
Asks "Whassat?" about pictures*
Can match words with objects
Repeats words and phrases
Uses 50 to 300 words

Physical-Motor

Uses whole-body action
Pushes, pulls, pokes
Climbs into things
Leans forward while running

Climbs stairs one by one
Dependent on adults for dressing
Can help undress
Has reached one-half potential height
Bladder/bowel control begins
Feeds self
Thumb-forefinger opposition complete
Grasps cup with two hands
Awkward with small objects
Lugs, tumbles, topples; unsteady
Alternates hands; preference developing
Can rotate to fit objects
Expresses emotions bodily*
Sensory-oriented
Cuts last teeth
Has difficulty relaxing

Creative

Imitates other children
Combines parallel play and fantasy play
Plays with sounds; repeats syllables over and
   over
Enjoys simple finger plays
Can follow simple melodies
Learns to scribble
Uses art for sensory pleasure

Cognitive

Recognizes, explores physical characteristics*
Investigates with touch and taste
Intrigued by water, washing
Likes to fill and empty things
Has limited attention span
Lives in present
Understands familiar concepts*
Can tell difference between black and white*
Needs own name used
Likes simple make-believe
Does one thing at a time
Remembers orders of routines
Recalls where toys are left
Classifies people by gender*
Names familiar objects in books

*Key characteristics of cultural awareness or identity.

THREE-YEAR-OLD

Social-Emotional

Highly imitative of adults*
Wants to please adults; conforms*
Responds to verbal suggestions
Easily prompted, redirected
Can be bargained with, reasoned with
Begins to share, take turns, wait
Avid "me-too"-er*
Exuberant, talkative, humorous
Has imaginary companions
Has nightmares, animal phobias
Plays consciously, cooperatively with others*
Plays spontaneously in groups
Demonstrates fears
Goes after desires; fights for them
Asserts independence often
Often stymied, frustrated, jealous
Sympathizes*
Strong sex-role stereotypes*

Language

Talkative with or without a listener
Can listen to learn*
Likes new words*
Increases use of pronouns, prepositions
Uses "s" to indicate plural nouns
Uses "ed" to indicate past tense
Uses sentences of three or more words
Says "Is that all right?" a lot
Talks about nonpresent situations
Puts words into action
Moves and talks at the same time
Substitutes letters in speech: "w" for "r"
Intrigued by whispering
Uses 300 to 1000 words

Physical-Motor

Has well-balanced body lines
Walks erect; nimble on feet
Gallops in wide, high steps
Alternates feet in stair climbing
Suddenly starts, stops
Turns corners rapidly
Swings arms when walking
Jumps up and down with ease
Uses toilet alone

Loses baby fat
Achieves bladder control
Rides a tricycle
Puts on, takes off wraps with help
Unbuttons buttons
Has some finger control with small objects
Grasp with thumb and index finger
Holds cup in one hand
Pours easily from small pitcher
Washes hands unassisted
Can carry liquids
Has activity with drive and purpose
Can balance on one foot

Creative

Dramatizes play
Enjoys slap-stick humor
Laughs at the ridiculous
Experiments with silly language
Imaginary companion may appear
Tricycle becomes many objects in dramatic play
Acts out own version of favorite story
Enjoys simple poems
Learns color concepts

Cognitive

Matches people according to physical
    characteristics*
Estimates "how many"
Enjoys making simple choices
Alert, excited, curious
Asks "why?" constantly*
Understands "It's time to . . ."
Understands "Let's pretend . . ."
Enjoys guessing games, riddles
Has lively imagination*
Often overgeneralizes*
Has short attention span
Carries out two to four directions in sequence
Often colors pages one color
Can't combine two activities
Names and matches simple colors
Has number concepts of one and two
Sees vague cause-and-effect relationships*
Can recognize simple melodies
Distinguishes between night and day
Understands size and shape comparisons

*Key characteristics of cultural awareness or identity.

INFANT

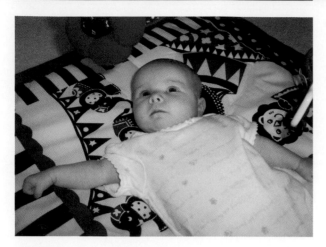

FIGURE 3-3a *Look. Read. Apply.* How do the Word Pictures for Infants inform you about the infant's creative and cognitive abilities that help you choose the appropriate toys and materials to further her small motor development?

TODDLER

FIGURE 3-3b *Look. Read. Apply.* What characteristics in the Word Pictures for Toddlers help you plan appropriate challenges for developing new skills in movement?

TWO-YEAR-OLD

FIGURE 3-3c *Look. Read. Apply.* What do the Word Pictures say about a two-year-old's ability to become distracted and how does that impact your planning a group time for two-year-olds?

THREE-YEAR-OLD

FIGURE 3-3d *Look. Read. Apply.* How would you use the language and creativity characteristics in the Word Pictures for Three-Year-Olds to encourage this boy to tell a story about this painting?

FOUR-YEAR-OLD

Social-Emotional

Mood changes rapidly
Tries out feelings of power
Dominates; is bossy, boastful, belligerent
Assertive, argumentative
Shows off; is cocky, noisy
Can fight own battles
Hits, grabs, insists on desires
Explosive, destructive
Easily overstimulated; excitable
Impatient in large groups*
Cooperates in groups of two or three*
Develops "special" friends* but shifts loyalties often
In-group develops; excludes others*
Resistant; tests limits
Exaggerates, tells tall tales
Alibis frequently
Teases, outwits; has terrific humor
May have scary dreams
Tattles frequently
Has food jags, food strikes

Language

Has more words than knowledge
A great talker, questioner
Likes words, plays with them
Has high interest in poetry
Able to talk to solve conflicts*
Responds to verbal directions
Enjoys taking turns to sing along
Interested in dramatizing songs, stories
Exaggerates, practices words
Uses voice control, pitch, rhythm
Asks "when?" "why?" "how?"*
Joins sentences together
Loves being read to

Physical-Motor

Longer, leaner body build
Vigorous, dynamic, acrobatic
Active until exhausted
"Works": builds, drives, pilots
Can jump own height and land upright
Hops, skips
Throws large ball, kicks accurately
Hops and stands on one foot
Jumps over objects
Walks in a straight line

Races up and down stairs
Turns somersaults
Walks backward toe-heel
Accurate, rash body movements
Copies a cross, square
Can draw a stick figure
Holds paint brush in adult manner, pencil in fisted grasp
Can lace shoes
Dresses self except back buttons, ties
Has sureness and control in finger activities
Alternates feet going down stairs

Creative

Is adventurous
Shows vivid imagination
Displays great interest in violence in imaginary play
Loves anything new
Demonstrates more elaborate dramatic play
Makes up new words, sounds, and stories
Enjoys complexity in book illustrations
Exaggerates and goes to extreme
Likes funny poetry
Tells spontaneous story with artwork
Can put on elaborate plays with puppets
Finds ways to solve problems
Combines words and ideas

Cognitive

Does some naming and representative art
Gives art products personal value
Can work for a goal*
Questions constantly*
Interested in how things work
Interested in life-death concepts
Has an extended attention span
Can do two things at once
Dramatic play is closer to reality*
Judges which of two objects is larger
Has concept of three; can name more
Has accurate sense of time
Full of ideas
Begins to generalize; often faulty*
Likes a variety of materials
Calls people names*
Has dynamic intellectual drive*
Has imaginary playmates
Recognizes several printed words

*Key characteristics of cultural awareness or identity.

FIVE-YEAR-OLD

Social-Emotional

Poised, self-confident, self-contained
Sensitive to ridicule*
Has to be right; persistent
Has sense of self-identity*
May get silly, high, wild
Enjoys pointless riddles, jokes
Enjoys group play, competitive games*
Aware of rules, defines them for others*
Chooses own friends; is sociable*
Gets involved with group decisions*
Insists on fair play*
Likes adult companionship*
Accepts, respects authority*
Asks permission
Remains calm in emergencies

Language

Uses big words and complete sentences
Can define some words
Spells out simple words
Takes turn in conversation
Has clear ideas and articulates them*
Uses words to give, receive information
Insists "I already know that"
Asks questions to learn answers*
Makes up songs
Enjoys dictating stories
Uses 1500 words
Tells a familiar story
Defines simple words
Answers telephone, takes a message
Thinks out loud*

Physical-Motor

Completely coordinated
Has adultlike posture
Has tremendous physical drive
Likes to use fine-motor skills
Learns how to tie bow knot
Has accuracy, skill with simple tools
Draws a recognizable person*

Handedness is evident
Dresses self completely
Cuts on a line with scissors
Begins to color within the lines
Catches ball from 3 feet away
Skips using alternate feet
Enjoys jumping, running, doing stunts
Rides a two-wheeler
Balances on a balance beam
Jumps rope, skips
Runs lightly on toes
Likes to dance; is graceful, rhythmic
Sometimes roughhouses, fights

Creative

Explores variety of art processes
Becomes engrossed in details of painting, blocks
Fantasy is more active, less verbal
Thinks out loud
Likes to copy
Has ideas; loves to talk about them
Can learn simple dance routine
Enjoys making patterns, designs
Puts on simple plays
Has idea of what to draw—wants to make something
   recognizable

Cognitive

Curious about everything*
Wants to know "how?" "why?"*
Likes to display new knowledge, skills
Somewhat conscious of ignorance*
Attention span increases noticeably
Knows tomorrow, yesterday
Can count 10 objects, rote counts to 20
Sorts objects by single characteristic*
Knows name, address, town
Makes a plan, follows it, centers on task
Sorts objects by color, shape
Concepts of smallest, less than, one-half
May tell time accurately, on the hour
Knows what a calendar is used for
Seldom sees things from another's point of view

*Key characteristics of cultural awareness or identity.

SIX- AND SEVEN-YEAR-OLDS

Social-Emotional

Six-year-old

Likes to work, yet often does so in spurts
Does not show persistence
Tends to be a know-it-all
Free with opinions and advice
Brings home evidence of good schoolwork
Observes family rules*
Gender-role stereotypes are rigid*
Friends easily gained, easily lost*
Tests and measures self against peers*
Makes social connections through play*
Friends are of same sex*
Believes in rules except for self*
Active, outgoing
Charming
Proud of accomplishments
Shows aggression through insults, name-calling*

Seven-year-old

More serious
Sensitive to others' reactions*
Eager for home responsibilities
Complaining, pensive, impatient
Shame is common emotion*
Leaves rather than face criticism, ridicule, disapproval*
Complains of unfair treatment, not being liked*
Shows politeness and consideration for adults*
Enjoys solitary activities
First peer pressure: needs to be "in"*
Wants to be one of the gang*
Relates physical competence to self-concept*
Self-absorbed; self-conscious

Language

Six- and seven-year-olds

Enjoy putting language skill to paper
Talk with adults rather than to them*
Chatter incessantly
Dominate conversations
Speech irregularities still common
Learning to print/write
Acquisition of new words tapers off
Bilingual capacities nearly complete* if English is second
    language
Ability to learn new language still present*

Physical-Motor

Six- and seven-year-olds

Basic skills develop; need refinement
Like to test limits of own body
Value physical competence*
Work at self-imposed tasks
Need daily legitimate channels for high energy
Learn to ride two-wheeler, skate, ski
Motor development is tool for socializing
Boisterous, enjoy stunts and roughhousing
Susceptible to fatigue
Visual acuity reaches normal
Hungry at short intervals, like sweets
Chew pencils, fingernails, hair

Creative

Six-year-old

Tries out artistic exploration seriously for the first time
Industrious
Greater interest in process, not product
Eager, curious, enthusiastic
Loves jokes and guessing games
Loves to color, paint
Understands cause and effect
Likes cooperative projects, activities, tasks
Interested in skill and technique

Seven-year-old

Likes to be alone listening to music
Wants work to look good
The age for starting music lessons
Driven by curiosity, desire to discover and invent
Intensely interested in how things work; takes apart,
    puts back together
Uses symbols in both writing and drawing
Interested in all sorts of codes
Likes to select and sort

Cognitive

Six- and seven-year-olds

Work in spurts, not persistent
Letter and word reversal common
Learn to read, beginning math skills (see Figure 3.2c)
Can consider others' point of view*
Use logic, systematic thinking*
Can plan ahead
Enjoy collecting: sorting, classifying
Can sequence events and retell stories
Concepts of winning and losing are difficult*
Like games with simple rules*
May cheat or change rules*
Want "real" things: watches and cameras that work
Sift and sort information*
Can conceptualize situations*
Enjoy exploring culture of classmates*

*Key characteristics of cultural awareness or identity.

EIGHT-YEAR-OLD

Social-Emotional

Outgoing, enthusiastic
Enormously curious about people and things*
Socially expansive*
Judgmental and critical of self and others*
Ambivalent about growing up
Often hostile but attracted to opposite sex
Growing self-confidence
Learns about self through others: peers, parents*
Is aware of and sensitive to differences from other
    children*
Begins to evaluate self and others through clothing,
    physical attraction, social status*
Likes to meet new people, go new places*
Has emerging sensitivity to personality traits of others*
Eager for peer approval and acceptance*
Growing sense of moral responsibility
Joins clubs
Chooses same-sex playmates
Struggles with feelings of inferiority
Likes to work cooperatively
Responds to studies of other cultures*
Has growing interest in fairness and justice
    issues*

Language

Talks with adults
Attentive and responsive to adult communication*
Teases members of opposite sex
Talks about "self"*
Talkative, exaggerates
Likes to explain ideas
Imitates language of peers
Enjoys story telling and writing short stories

Physical-Motor

Beginning to engage in team sports*
Often a growth-spurt year

Speedy, works fast
Restless, energetic, needs physical release
Plays hard, exhausts self
Eye–hand coordination matures; learning cursive
    handwriting
Enjoys competitive sports*
Hearty appetite, few food dislikes
Repeatedly practices new skills to perfect them

Creative

Has great imagination
Enjoys riddles, limericks, knock-knock jokes
Likes to explain ideas
Visual acuity and fine motor skills come together
Is most productive in groups
Shows interest in process and product

Cognitive

Criticizes abilities in all academic areas
Seeks new experiences*
Likes to barter, bargain, trade
Enjoys creating collections of things
Interested in how children from other countries
    live*
Thinks beyond the here-and-now boundaries of time
    and space
Enjoys role-playing character parts*
Tests out parents to learn more about them
Needs direction, focus
Enjoys all types of humor
Full of ideas, plans
Gaining competence in basic skills
Concrete operations are solidifying*
Industrious, but overestimates abilities
Interested in process as well as product of schoolwork
Growing interest in logic and the way things
    work
Takes responsibility seriously*

---

*Key characteristics of cultural awareness or identity.

FOUR-YEAR-OLD

FIGURE 3-4a **Look. Read. Apply.** Based on the characteristics in the Word Pictures of a Four-Year-Old, what skills do four-year-olds have for solving conflicts and maintaining friendships? What characteristics might need teacher support to solve conflicts?

FIVE-YEAR-OLD

FIGURE 3-4b **Look. Read. Apply.** What characteristics of Word Pictures for Five-Year-Olds and Six-Year-Olds would help you create a challenging outdoor environment for these girls?

SIX- AND SEVEN-YEAR-OLDS

FIGURE 3-4c **Look. Read. Apply.** How might the ability to read affect a seven-year-old's social interactions and a six-year-old's creative ability? What activities would you provide for each?

EIGHT-YEAR-OLD

FIGURE 3-4d **Look. Read. Apply.** In the Word Pictures for an Eight-Year-Old, what implications are there for this boy's language and creative skills in working on group projects?

Video VIEW PoinT 3-2

"Children's self-esteem and confidence rise when they are able to learn new skills and to practice their independence."

COMPETENCY: Program Management

AGE GROUP: Infants and Toddlers

CRITICAL THINKING QUESTIONS:

1. How would you foster independence in a toddler?

2. How can you teach toddlers to be able to participate in their own self-care?

HOW CHILDREN DIFFER

Watching and working with children exposes how very different each child is. What makes children differ so, especially when they have so many features in common? Megan gives the tire swing a big push. Ariel shrieks with delight, but Hans bursts into tears and screams to get off. What accounts for the wide range of behaviors?[1]

Developmental Differences

You are aware by now that children grow and develop at different rates. Each child has an inner timetable that is unique, which means that each child is ready to learn according his or her maturation process. This readiness factor is to be respected and may or may not coincide with the rest of the children in the class. This is what makes teaching exciting and challenging!

We do know, however, that development follows a sequence. It is fairly predictable for all children, even those who are disabled. Physical development, for instance, tends to be from the head downward. Have you ever noticed how small a baby's head is in comparison to the rest of the body? Young children gain control over arm movements before mastering finger control because growth is from the center of the body outward.

When used appropriately, the Word Pictures demonstrate how growth is predictable, yet

unique to each child. They help identify typical behaviors at a given age and to remind us to take a long-range view regarding children's growth and development.

Other Factors

Genetic Makeup. Each child has a unique combination of genes that determine eye and hair color, height, body shape, personality traits, and intelligence (Bee, 1999). Certain diseases, such as Tay Sachs, cystic fibrosis, and sickle cell anemia, are linked through heredity (Berk, 2002).

Environment. Genetics (nature) may account for some of the differences among children but not all. The environment (nurture) has great impact throughout development. From conception, the brain is affected by environmental conditions. An individual child's rate and sequence of development reflects "an ongoing dialogue between the brain, the body, and the physical and social environment" (Berk, 2002).

The attitudes with which children are raised, their culture, their socioeconomic status, the kinds of caregiving they experience, and their community combine in countless ways to affect growth.[2] In Chapter 15, this subject is more thoroughly discussed as the "ecology of the family." Nutrition, safety, play space, adult

Video VIEW PoinT 3-3

"Developmentally, school-age children are keen to forge relationships with their peers and with adults. Their curiosity about the world is at its peak."

COMPETENCY: Learning Environment

AGE GROUP: School Age

CRITICAL THINKING QUESTIONS:

1. What were you most curious about when you were six to nine years old?

2. How would you use your relationship with a seven-year-old to extend her curiosity and learning?

1 In considering developmentally appropriate practice, think of both the universal and individual characteristics of children. Be aware of observing and honoring (not judging) children's individual characteristics.

2 This interaction also results in an ever-growing understanding of the world.

relationships, neighborhood, and family stability affect individual development. Whether a child lives in relative poverty or riches, environmental factors interact with genes to create a single, individual person.

Gender and Race Differences. Girls and boys differ in both the rate and the pattern of growth, especially in adolescence. Ethnic variations in growth are common. African American and Asian American children seem to mature faster than do North American Caucasian children (Berk, 2002). Growth "norms" should be used with caution and with respect to ethnic differences.

Implications for Teaching

Differences in children's development must be accounted for when planning a program for a group. Teachers consider all these factors as they meet the needs of the individual child while addressing the concerns and interests of the total group.

Learning Styles

As you observe young children, you will notice they exhibit a number of different approaches to learning. Some are quiet; others move around and talk, while others seem never to listen. While on a field trip to the farm, these children demonstrate three common learning styles:

- Lorenzo watches, looks around, and visually absorbs the environment. He calls to others, "See the goat!" and "Look at that." Lorenzo is a visual learner.

- Olivia is a talker and chatters away to her friends as they enter the barnyard. "Listen to all the noise the sheep are making." "Hear the horses?" While she enjoys listening to what others have to say, Olivia has difficulty waiting for her turn to talk. Olivia is an auditory learner.

- Anna gestures as she talks and does not listen well to others. As she runs ahead of the other children, Anna calls out, "Get over here so we can touch them!" Looking up at the teacher, she begs, "Take me closer. I want to feel the sheep." Anna is a tactile learner.

Each of the children will remember and reflect upon their experience at the farm in a way that supports their individual learning style. Lorenzo will likely interpret the field trip in pictures, by drawing pictures or painting what he saw. Olivia will repeat stories from her experience over and over again as she integrates her experience at

What do YOU Think?

What is your preferred learning style? How do you learn best? Think about your favorite teachers. How did they take individual learning styles into account? What different modes of symbolic representation were offered to you as a child? How do you think this affected your ability to learn?

the farm. Anna may play out her farm experience by making clay animals or dancing an "animal dance."

See Figure 3-5 for tips on how to plan for developmental differences and learning styles. Also see Chapter 10 for further discussion about learning preferences and how to accommodate them when planning curriculum.

Grouping of children by rigid age levels seems contrary to our understanding of

In our diverse world, teachers should be sensitive to the influence of sex, race, and individual patterns of development.

Program Planning for Developmental Differences and Learning Styles

- Plan individual and group activities according to the age level of the class, considering the behavior patterns and learning styles that exist. Make sure the materials and activities are in a variety of formats so that children can choose the ones that support their style of learning. *For example:* storytelling and books, blocks, puzzles, writing and drawing equipment, music and dance accessories provide a wide range of materials through which a child can explore math.

- Plan for all age levels with understanding and appreciation of the variations within a one-year age span. *For example:* a gardening project will provide many opportunities for involvement by children with different learning styles. Some will want to do the physical work of digging; others will want to plan out the flowerbeds with their friends; still others will want to draw pictures to label what is growing in the garden.

- Know the individual children, their strengths, and their challenges. Observations are one of the best ways for teachers to get a picture of each child's developmental progress (see Chapter 6). Families bring further knowledge of each individual child and that is added to the mix when assessing children's progress. *For example:* Sherlyne is a quiet six-year-old who spends most of her time alone in reading and writing activities and rarely participates in any messy art work or outside play. Her parents told the teacher that Sherlynne has a snake collection at home and wants to show it to her classmates. Taking this information into account, the teacher begins to plan science activities that will encourage the rest of the class to explore and discover the world of snakes and reptiles, culminating in a visit by a few of Sherlynne's snakes. It is this kind of planning that helps Sherlynne grow in social skills and adds richness to learning science that will benefit the rest of the class.

- Plan around the known similarities, the developmental tasks, and age-appropriate behavior common to that group of children, including planning for children with special needs.[1] The needs, interests, abilities, and unique characteristics of all the children in the class must be considered. *For example:* Music, movement, and dance are a staple of early childhood curriculum. Yet Margie gets upset when the music is too loud, Aaron gets too over stimulated, and Carlo, who is in a wheelchair, cannot dance. Each of these children's needs can be accommodated in the planning. Dancing with scarves to soft music might help Margie and Aaron participate more eagerly. Asking children to dance with their hands and arms adds a new movement experience and allows Carlo to participate without making an unnecessary point about it.

- Set group and individual goals based on the general characteristics of the age group but changes the goals as needed. *For example:* A teacher of four-year-olds may have a goal that her class will have good listening skills and are able to participate in group discussions before they go to kindergarten. Throughout the year, the teacher will assess each child's capacity for sitting and listening, and then plan strategies to help them expand these activities. For the children who need more time to develop, small groups are created to allow for differences in development and the ability to concentrate. Group and discussion times will incorporate opportunities for children to move, sing, draw, and observe so that each child may find a source of learning that is satisfying.

- Modify activities to make them more accessible or appropriate for children with special needs. *For example:* tables can be made higher or lower for wheelchair access; or a teacher may spend extra time in the dramatic play area to help individual children learn social skills.

FIGURE 3-5 When teachers are aware of the range of developmental differences and learning styles of the children in the class, they can incorporate those variations into the planning process.

individual learning styles, rates of growth, readiness factors, and wide ranges of abilities. It is a convenient, though arbitrary, system of teaching children. The implication for teachers, however, is clear: programs are planned to meet the needs and challenges of the whole group. Individual differences are incorporated into the planning. Activities are selected to allow for a variety of responses from children at different stages of development and learning styles.

See Chapter 5 for specific suggestions on how teachers plan to accommodate the individuality of children, particularly these sections: Self-awareness, Attitudes and Biases, Ten Essentials to Successful Teaching, and A Student Teacher's Guidelines for Beginning. The curriculum chapters, 10 through 15, demonstrate other examples of planning for a wide range of skills. It might be useful, too, to read Chapter 9, particularly the self-help environment and the anti-bias curriculum.

1 Planning for children with special needs always begins by looking at typical development.

Teachers of Young Children May Encounter a Variety of Disabilities

- *Speech and language:* hearing impairment, stuttering, articulation problems, cleft palate, chronic voice disorders, learning disabilities.

- *Physical-motor:* visual impairment, blindness, perceptual motor deficits, orthopedic disabilities such as cerebral palsy, spina bifida, loss of limbs, muscular dystrophy.

- *Intellectual:* cognitive delays, brain injury, brain dysfunction, dyslexia, and learning disabilities.

- *Social-emotional:* self-destructive behavior, severe withdrawal, dangerous aggression toward self and others, noncommunicativeness, moodiness, tantrums, attention-deficit hyperactivity disorder, severe anxiety, depression, phobias, psychosis, autism.

- *Health impairments:* severe asthma, epilepsy, hemophilia, congenital heart defects, severe anemia, malnutrition, diabetes, tuberculosis, cystic fibrosis, Down's syndrome, sickle cell anemia, Tay-Sachs disease, AIDS.

- *Specific learning disabilities:* difficulties with language use and acquisition, spoken and written language affected, perceptual handicaps, brain injury, minimal brain dysfunction, dyslexia, developmental aphasia.

FIGURE 3-6 These disorders may range from mild to severe, and children will exhibit a wide variety of abilities and needs even if they are diagnosed with the same condition. For further information concerning a specific one, the student will want to consult a special education textbook.

CHILDREN WITH SPECIAL NEEDS

Approximately 15 to 20 percent of all children in the United States will exhibit some form of atypical development and need special services (Bee, 1999). These are children who did not develop according to normal standards. They exhibit a wide range of atypical disorders ranging from short-term behavior problems to long-term physical, mental, and emotional disabilities.[1]

Two types of children come under the category of children with special needs: children who are disabled and children who are gifted. They extend the definition of "Who is the child?"[2] and are discussed separately in this section.

Children Who Are Disabled

- Five-year-old Pete, blind from birth, has been in nursery school for three years.

- Chrissy, a four-year-old with multiple disabilities, has her daily program in a special school supplemented by attending the child care center three afternoons each week.

- Travis is a child with **Down syndrome**, and this is his first experience in a school not restricted to atypical children.

These children have some obvious characteristics that qualify them for special-needs status. Other children with less apparent disabilities also fall into this category. The term **special needs** includes a great many conditions that may or may not be noticeable. Allen and Cowdery (2005) suggest three conditions under which a child is considered disabled. To be so designated, a child's normal growth and development is (1) delayed; (2) distorted, atypical, or abnormal; or (3) severely or negatively affected. This definition includes the physical, mental, emotional, and social areas of development. Figure 3-6 highlights many of the disabilities a teacher may encounter.

In the course of normal development, any one area of a child's growth is affected by the development of the whole child and this holds true for children who are disabled. The disability may lead to multihandicapping:

- A child with a profound hearing loss is often delayed in speech production or language abilities and suffers social isolation due to the inability to hear and speak with peers.

- A child with a speech impairment or cleft palate may have the intellectual capacity to put simple puzzles together but may not yet have the language to engage verbally in songs and finger play.

---

1 More and more early care and education programs are reflecting diversity by creating groups of children exhibiting a wide range of developmental abilities.

2 Our picture of what to consider while thinking about diversity continues to expand—race, gender, ethnicity, social class, and physical and cognitive ability.

- A child with Down syndrome may have congenital heart defects, intellectual impairments, eye abnormalities, or poor physical coordination.

- Children who have cerebral palsy, a central nervous system disorder, often have other disabling conditions such as intellectual delays, epilepsy, and hearing, visual, and speech problems (Kiernan et al., n.d.).

Learning Disabilities

Children with learning disabilities are found in almost every classroom; they have no discernable disability condition but nevertheless are having problems with one or more basic skills or learning.[1] According to Berk (2003), five to ten percent of school-age children have some kind of learning disability. They may have, among other things, poor memory skills, difficulty in following directions, eye–hand coordination problems, and trouble discriminating between letters, numbers, and sounds, which keep them from storing, processing, and producing information.

Dyslexia, the most common specific learning disability, occurs when children have difficulty in learning to read. They may reverse letters (such as *d* and *b*) or words (such as *was* and *saw*), although many children do this who are not dyslexic. A child with a learning disability may have strength in one area, such as math, and yet have a disability in another area, such as language. A learning disability does not mean that a child is intellectually impaired or delayed.

Learning disorders are usually not a singular dysfunction. Children who exhibit problems with reading and writing will often have difficulties with spatial relationships and body coordination. Observations of these behaviors can give teachers some of the first warning signs of learning disorders.

There is continuing controversy on how to define and identify these children; a broad use of the term learning disorder is commonplace, sometimes to qualify for special education funding. Although some experts consider minimal brain damage to be the cause of learning disabilities, there is not consensus yet on why children have these problems.

According to Bee (1999), a child with a learning disorder develops normally in other respects and has no obvious brain damage, but the task of reading seems to highlight several areas of difficulty: problems of visual perception, inability to integrate visual and auditory information, impaired memory, problems with language, and difficulty distinguishing the separate sounds in words. This wide range of symptoms, the number of potential causes, and the varying degrees to which children exhibit the symptoms make learning disorders difficult to diagnose.

Allen and Cowdery (2005) caution against early diagnosis of a young child as "learning disabled." As noted earlier in this chapter, young children differ in their individual rate of growth, and many differences and delays are still within the normal range of development.

Attention-Deficit/Hyperactivity Disorder (ADHD)

Do you remember a classmate who could never sit still—one who was constantly on the move, talked excessively, and disrupted classroom activities? You may have also seen a preschool counterpart in the form of a child who couldn't finish a puzzle, take a nap, or wait for a turn. These children are typical of children with a condition known as **attention-deficit hyperactivity disorder (ADHD)**, which affects up to 3 to 5 percent of all school-age children (Berk, 2003).

ADHD (previously called hyperactivity) is a condition affecting children and adults and appears to be hereditary. According to Berk (2003), a child diagnosed with ADHD has normal intelligence and seems to have no serious emotional disturbances. Figure 3-7 describes the three subtypes of ADHD that are common today.

Children with ADHD are difficult to manage, both at home and in the classroom. They are prone to restlessness, anxiety, short attention spans, and impulsiveness. They have difficulty remaining seated, they are in constant motion, do not listen well, may talk excessively, are easily distracted, and have difficulty with social relationships. This constellation of behaviors may apply at some level to many children, but teachers must be cautious about labeling the normally active, somewhat disruptive child as having ADHD. The child with ADHD exhibits these behaviors in extreme, usually before age seven.

Medication is a common treatment for children with ADHD, but because its effects are short term and its side effects can be serious, it is controversial. The most effective approach appears to be a combination of medication and

---

[1] Children with special needs cut across social, economic, and cultural lines.

Three Subtypes of Attention-Deficit/Hyperactivity Disorder

ADHD predominantly inattentive type (ADHD-I)

- Makes careless mistakes

- Does not pay close attention to details

- Easily distracted; hard to maintain attention

- Does not appear to listen; seems forgetful

- Has trouble with follow-through

- Loses things; has difficulty with organization

- Might avoid tasks that take prolonged intellectual effort

ADHD predominantly hyperactive-impulsive type (ADHD-HI)

- Fidgets, squirms

- Has trouble staying seated, runs about

- Talks excessively; difficulty with being quiet during activities

- Blurts out answers; interrupts; intrudes on others

- Has difficulty waiting to take turns

ADHD combined type (ADHD-C)

- Child or adult meets criteria from both categories listed above)

FIGURE 3-7 A list of symptoms define each of the three categories of ADHD. Typically, these symptoms appear in early childhood and some may continue into adulthood. (Adapted from National Resource Center on ADHD, 2006.)

individual behavior management strategies (Allen & Cowdery, 2005). There is no easy solution for dealing with children who have ADHD; further research into the cause of this disability and development of safe effective treatments are clearly needed.

Figure 3-8 outlines guidance techniques that are good for children with ADHD.

Asperger Syndrome

Asperger syndrome (AS) is a developmental disorder linked to autism and characterized by a lack of social skills, poor concentration, self-absorption, and limited interests (Allen & Cowdery, 2005). The difference between autism and AS is the level of mental functioning. Those with autism will have a lower than average intelligence while the children with AS will have average or above mental capabilities (Berger, 2000).

Gallagher and Gallagher (2002) explain the four separate categories of AS as defined by the American Psychological Association:

1. Impaired social functioning: inability to make friends or show empathy, avoids eye contact.

2. Restricted and stereotyped behaviors and interests; overly intense interest in one area; repetitive hand movements, and compulsive repetition, often long passages memorized from television or the movies.

3. Average or above average language development; normal use of vocabulary yet may use language in such a complex manner that it makes no sense. They lack the language of social communication with others.

Effective Guidance Strategies for Children with ADHD

- Maintain regular and consistent routines and rules: "Remember, Sitara, we always wash hands before eating snacks."

- Have realistic expectations: "I know it is hard for you to wait for a turn, Eddie. While you are waiting, why don't you collect all the colors you will need."

- Make eye contact when giving directions, using clear and simple requests: "Look at me, Toby, so that I know you are listening. Good. Now let's go over the homework assignment together."

- Allow time for transitions by giving a plan for the next step: "In three minutes it will be time to get ready to go home. When the other children begin to leave, I want you to get your coat and come back here to sit with us."

- Select jobs in which the child can be successful: "Connie, please pass out the napkins to this table today. Thanks."

- Recognize accomplishments: "Good work, Connie. You gave everyone a napkin and then sat down with one for yourself."

FIGURE 3-8 Guidance techniques that work well with children who have ADHD are also successful with children who have a variety of behavior problems, proving again that children are more alike than they are different.

4. Average or above average cognitive development: ranges anywhere from average to highly gifted.

Many children with AS attend schools with children who do not have disabilities. Their behaviors may seem odd to their peers and disruptive to the class. Allen and Cowdery (2005) suggest the following strategies for working with children with AS:

● Simple and direct communication.

● Combine objects and actions: show the child the book and demonstrate where it goes in the shelf.

● Provide peer interactions with other children who are disabled and have similar levels of language and social development.

● Establish a predictable routine and environment; minimize distractions.

● Improve communication skills by having the child ask for something rather than point.

● Encourage frequent communication with the family.

Teachers and Families Working Together

Parents are usually the first to notice that their child is not developing according to the norms. They may ask the child's teacher to watch for signs of hearing impairments, lack of necessary motor skills, or language imperfections. Because early diagnosis and intervention are important, teachers will want to assess the child's overall skills.[1] They can then plan appropriate follow-through with the family. This may include a consultation with a physician for further developmental screening and testing. If both the family and the teachers feel there is a potential problem, the task is to help identify it and secure the services needed.

The teacher's role is to observe the child and provide current information, to support the family through their concern, to help them find appropriate resources (such as social service agencies, public health offices, private and public schools), to assist with future placement for child care, and to be available for consultation with others who are working in the best interests of the child. The early childhood professional is not an expert in diagnosing learning

disabilities but can be effective in helping families secure proper referrals and treatment.

Public Recognition

Since the mid-1960s there has been significant public recognition of and the advent of public funding for the education programs for disabled persons. Prior to that, public—and private—attitudes seemed to be ones of shame and segregation. Past generations hid adults and children with disabilities in their homes or secluded them in institutions. Keeping special populations out of sight gave way to providing separate opportunities for them. Schools, classes, and recreational programs were started exclusively for people with special needs. Public consciousness is now sufficient to understand that not all people with special needs are necessarily mentally impaired. The current practice of integrating children with disabilities into ongoing programs in schools—the mainstream of American life—is not only more humane, but practical as well. The story over the past 35 years:

● Over the years a small number of schools had routinely accepted children with special needs. The idea gained national attention in 1972 when Head Start required that a minimum of 10 percent of its enrollment be reserved for children with disabilities. Head Start led the way toward large-scale inclusion.

● In 1975, Public Law 94-142, the Education for All Handicapped Children Act, was passed. This so-called Bill of Rights for the Handicapped guarantees free public education to disabled persons from three to 21 years of age "in the least restrictive environment." An individualized program (IEP) for each person is mandatory, to be worked out in concert with the child's family. This provides a more family-centered approach where the strengths and the needs of the family are taken into consideration. The success of P.L. 94-142 means that thousands of children who are disabled who would have been denied any educational opportunities are now in school with their nondisabled peers.[2]

● P.L. 99-457, the Education of the Handicapped Amendments Act of 1986, has had an even more profound impact for early childhood educators. Sections of this law provide funding

---

1 Early childhood professionals need to be skilled at carefully observing and documenting the growth and development of individual children.

2 We need to remember that inclusion refers to abilities and gender as well as race and culture.

for children who were not included in the previous law: infants, toddlers, and three- to five-year-olds. This law also allows for the inclusion of "developmentally delayed" youngsters and leaves local agencies the opportunity to include "at risk" children in that definition. The vague definitions give local agencies the right to define disabling conditions in terms of local needs.

- In 1990, Congress reauthorized P.L. 94-142 and renamed it the Individuals with Disabilities Education Act (IDEA) (P.L. 101-576). Two new categories, autism and traumatic brain injury, were included, and children from birth to age five years were now eligible to receive services.

- Many programs may be affected by another piece of legislation, P.L. 101-336, the American with Disabilities Act (ADA), which was passed in 1990. This civil rights act makes it unlawful to discriminate against people with disabilities because of their disability and requires that people with disabilities have equal access to public and private services, as well as reasonable accommodations.[1] This law has had an impact on hiring practices in early childhood centers and family child care homes and may require adaptations to facilities and work environments to make them more accessible to individuals with disabilities. Although not specifically an education law, ADA is another step toward respecting the dignity and worth of all individuals.

Legislation makes strong demands on the family to be intimately involved with their child's program. Family involvement greatly improves the child's chances for success (Allen & Marotz, 2003). Teachers and families work together on a planned, consistent set of expectations. The child's confidence is reinforced at home and at school for the same achievements. Families of children with disabilities find support from other parents since they share common child-rearing concerns. Teachers learn a great deal about disabilities from the families of the children who have special needs. This helps them become more effective teachers and be aware of the special needs of the child.

The importance of all of this legislation cannot be underestimated by those in and entering the field of early childhood. The integration and transition of children with disabilities into early childhood programs require knowledgeable teachers. Early childhood educators would be

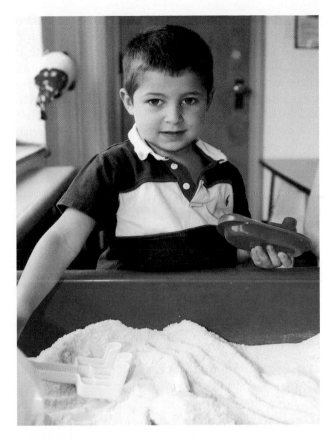

The inclusive classroom fosters children's interactions with sensory material.

wise to avail themselves of special education courses now to meet this challenge. Many states require such course work before certification; others will surely follow to fulfill these mandates.

Inclusion of Children with Special Needs

Allen and Cowdery (2005) differentiate between the terms **inclusion** and **mainstreaming**. In the past, children with special needs were integrated into classrooms only after they had met certain standards and expectations. Often they were assigned to separate special education classes. When ready, they were mainstreamed into classrooms with typically developing children. Inclusion means that a child with a disability is a full-time member of a regular classroom, a more natural environment, with children who do, as well as those who do not, have special needs.

More than a word definition is at stake, however. Allen and Cowdery (2005) go on to point out that inclusion is about belonging,

 1 Each person's needs are assessed on an individual basis.

having worth, and having choices. An inclusive classroom is about "accepting and valuing human diversity and providing support so that all children and families can participate in the program of their choice." Teachers are a key factor in the successful integration of children with disabilities. Their attitude is critical; they must be committed to teaching all children with equal caring and concern, regardless of their intelligence or skill levels. Promoting inclusion means that all teachers:

- foster interactions between children who are disabled and children who are not disabled that promote healthy social relationships.

- recognize that every child with special needs has strengths as well as deficits and build on those strengths.

- receive training and guidance in the critical task of working with children who have special needs and are developmentally disabled in their classes.

- work with families to plan and implement the child's individualized program.

- see that children with disabilities are actively involved and accepted in the total program.

- help children with special needs to take advantage of, to the fullest extent of their capabilities, all the activities the school has to offer.

- consider children's individual disabilities are addressed in program planning and that procedures and curriculum are adapted to fit the children with special needs.

Inclusion is an important concept for all children. For the children without disabilities it is an opportunity to learn to accept differences in people.[1] In the early education center much of the curriculum is directed toward fostering the child's self-esteem and self-worth. Teaching is dedicated to helping youngsters see themselves and others as important and valuable. Inclusion presents an opportunity to extend that principle to the full range of human characteristics.

For the child with disabilities, the large numbers of typically developing children who serve as age-appropriate behavior models is important. Many children have not had an opportunity to

What do YOU Think?

What would be your biggest challenge when working in a classroom with children who are disabled as well as children who are not? Have you ever had friends, relatives, or neighbors who are disabled? How would that experience inform your attitude about working in an inclusive classroom?

hear the language of their normal peer group. They may not know how to play with another child or how to communicate in socially acceptable ways. In the inclusive classroom, with sensitive and knowledgeable teachers, children with disabilities are helped to realize their potential as growing and learning children.

Fortunately, the preschool teacher rarely needs to face the task of inclusiveness alone. Many early childhood centers have access to a team of professionals who can provide the child, the family, and the teaching staff with effective therapeutic activities. Their combined knowledge helps teachers understand the specific disability and plan an appropriate curriculum for each child. Together, teachers, clinicians, and parents work out a well-rounded program. This is called an interdisciplinary approach to teaching.

In 1993, NAEYC endorsed a Position on Inclusion, written by the Division of Early Childhood of the Council for Exceptional Children. This statement, which follows, offers guidelines for implementation.

Position on Inclusion
Division for Early Childhood (DEC) of the
Council for Exceptional Children
Adopted April 1993
(Endorsed by NAEYC November 1993)[2]

Inclusion, as a value, supports the right of all children, regardless of their diverse abilities, to participate actively in natural settings within their

---

1 One needs to see creating diverse learning situations as a benefit to everyone—everyone has something to learn. It is not a one-way street—those born with more abilities are not simply helping "others" (e.g., in an inclusive classroom of three-year-olds, the "special needs child" having had numerous hospitalizations may easily separate from a parent, while the "typically developing" child may still be clinging to his mother's leg at the doorway and could gain support from the special needs child").

2 *Position on Inclusion,* from Division for Early Childhood (DEC), April 1993. Reprinted with permission of Division for Early Childhood of the Council for Exceptional Children.

communities. A natural setting is one in which the child would spend time had he or she not had a disability. Such settings include but are not limited to home and family, playgroups, childcare, nursery schools, Head Start programs, kindergartens, and neighborhood school classrooms.

DEC believes in and supports full and successful access to health, social service, education, and other supports and services for young children and their families that promote full participation in community life. DEC values the diversity of families and supports a family-guided process for determining services that are based on the needs and preferences of individual families and children.[1]

To implement inclusive practices, DEC supports (a) the continued development, evaluation, and dissemination of full inclusion supports, services, and systems so that the options for inclusion are of high quality; (b) the development of preservice and inservice training programs that prepare families, administrators, and service providers to develop and work within inclusive settings; (c) collaboration among all key stakeholders to implement flexible fiscal and administrative procedures in support of inclusion; (d) research that contributes to our knowledge of state-of-the-art services; and (e) the restructuring and unification of social, education, health, and intervention supports and services to make them more responsive to the needs of all children.

Allen and Cowdery (2005) make a significant point about teaching young children with diverse behaviors and the labels or categories that define their disability. "It is not how a child is classified," they say, "but how the child is cared for and taught as an individual, that is the most important issue in addressing behavior and learning problems in young children."

Children Who Are Gifted and Talented

Who Are the Gifted and Talented?

Gifted children are those who demonstrate an intellectual and creative potential superior to that of most children in the same age range and may exhibit an exceptional in-depth knowledge or skill of one or more specific areas (Bee, 1999;

Allen & Cowdery, 2005; Berk, 2002). Traditionally, children have been identified as gifted if they score between 130 and 150 on standard IQ tests. Today, the definition for children who are gifted includes those who exhibit exceptional talent in other than just intellectual superiority—children who are gifted in music, art, and athletics, math, science, and leadership. Today's definition must include children with disabilities as well because a child who is gifted may have *dual exceptionalities*, that is, be hearing-impaired and gifted or learning-disabled and gifted, or ADHD and gifted.

Children who are gifted come from all social, economic, and cultural groups. There is increasing concern, however, that children from low-income populations, children who are ethnically and culturally in the minority, children who have disabilities, and children who are bilingual are underrepresented in the gifted category.[2]

Early childhood teachers should be aware of some traits children who are gifted display so they can recognize potentially gifted children in their care. These are listed in Figure 3-9.

Teaching Children Who Are Gifted and Talented

The teacher's role with children who are gifted is that of providing challenge and stimulation. In some cases the children who are gifted may be advanced to an older group, moving on to kindergarten or first grade, or spend part of the day in special classes. A more common approach in early childhood has been in the area of curriculum enrichment. In this way the child remains with age-level peers to develop social skills.

Curriculum areas are developed in more complex ways. The child is ready to learn in greater depth; the teachers provide added materials and activities that will probe the extent of their interests. All the children in the classroom benefit from this enrichment; each responds according to his or her abilities and a rich curriculum benefits the whole class.

This brings to mind Gardner's multiple intelligences (MI) (Gardner, 1993). The eight different kinds of knowing that Gardner developed seem appropriate for teaching children who are

---

1 The child's family helps determine what program best suits the needs of their child, ensuring that their cultural beliefs will be noted.

2 This information provides another opportunity to examine the impact of bias in thinking about children (i.e., do the existing instruments for identifying giftedness identify only particular strengths for a particular segment of the population?).

Characteristic Traits of Children Who Are Gifted and Talented

- *Language:* advanced verbal skills and vocabulary; experiments with words; expresses ideas easily; inventive with songs and stories

- *Intellectually:* long attention span and ability to concentrate; learns rapidly and has a strong memory; imaginative and original; plans and organizes well; problem-solves; questions; understands abstract concepts; creative thinker; advanced sense of humor

- *Socially:* independent and content to be alone in purposeful activity; heightened awareness of people and environments, especially changes; social relationships sometimes difficult

- *Overall:* exceptional gift or talent is evident in at least one area of development

FIGURE 3-9 Children who are gifted and talented exhibit a wide range of exceptional behaviors. (Allen & Cowdery, 2005; Berk, 2002.)

gifted and talented. (See Multiple Intelligences in Chapters 4 and 10, especially Figures 4-12 and 10-5). A variety of meaningful activities across the MI spectrum helps children learn according to their strengths and primary intelligence, and suggests curriculum that will help develop new skills and knowledge. Concepts, knowledge, and information are presented in multiple ways so that each child will succeed in learning through the most meaningful method.

Families of children who are gifted will need support and encouragement as well as guidance in dealing with their child's exceptionality. Together, teachers and parents can explore what will best suit each individual child so that this giftedness may be nurtured and challenged at home and at school.

Dealing with Bias and Stereotypes

Vincent is a husky five-year-old boy whose physical skills match those of his classmates. When Vincent was born he was diagnosed with spina bifida, a spinal cord injury, which left him with no bladder or bowel control. As a result, he wears diapers. Noah watched Vincent changing his diapers and later refused to let Vincent join him at the art table. Noah taunted: "I don't like him. He's a baby. He's not like us big guys. He wears diapers. He can't sit here. I'm not gonna play with no babies." Vincent looked both surprised and hurt. (Gordon & Browne, 1996)

One of the greatest needs a child with disabilities has is to be accepted. Rejection by their peers who are not disabled may occur. Young children are known for their forthrightness in commenting on and asking questions about what confuses and frightens them. They may be anxious about what another child's disability means to them. Although this is a common reaction and age appropriate, we cannot allow an individual to be rejected on the basis of a disability. Derman-Sparks and colleagues' (1989) suggestions follow, along with examples of supportive and sensitive teacher interactions (Gordon & Browne, 1996).

- The rejection must be handled immediately, with support and assurance given to the child who was rejected that this type of behavior will not be permitted. *Example:* The teacher put her arm around Vincent, and said, "Noah, what you said about Vincent is very hurtful. Tell me more about what you meant." Noah began to deny that he had said anything, and then admitted that Vincent looked funny in diapers because he was so big. The teacher asked Vincent if he would like to tell Noah why he wore diapers. Vincent agreed and responded, "When I was born there was something wrong with my spine so I don't feel it when I have to go to the bathroom. I wear diapers so that I don't wet my pants." "Does it hurt?" asked Noah. "No way," answered Vincent. "I just have to remember to change so I don't get a rash." The teacher then said to Noah, "It's okay for you to ask questions about why Vincent wears diapers, but you can't tell him he can't sit at the table with you. In our class, everybody gets to play and work together."

- It is important to help children recognize how they are different and how they are alike. *Example:* "Noah, both you and Vincent have to go to the bathroom during the day. Your body tells you when it is time to go and since Vincent's doesn't, he has to wear protection. You are both good at drawing dinosaurs, too."

- Children need to have their fears about disabilities taken seriously and to have adults understand their concerns. *Example:* Noah was approached by the teacher in a way that allowed him to admit part of his concern. The teacher understood his unstated fear: "Noah, what happened to Vincent took place before he was born. It can't happen to you."

- Questions must be answered promptly, truthfully, and simply. Use the children's own natural curiosity, and let the child with disabilities answer for himself whenever possible. *Example:* Before leaving the art table, the teacher spoke to Noah, "Are there any more questions you have for Vincent?"

All children benefit when adults are willing to confront bias and deal with children's prejudice and misconceptions.[1] This example could have been about girls rejecting boys or one child being rejected because of skin color. When we provide opportunities for children to interact with people who look and act differently than they do, we actively foster acceptance and respect for the individual. More gender diversity issues are found in Chapter 15.

CULTURAL, RACIAL, AND ETHNIC CONSIDERATIONS

The answer to "Who is the young child?" takes on a powerful new meaning as we look at the ethnic mix of American life. A multicultural explosion has swept across the nation, filling early childhood programs with children from many different cultural backgrounds. Some indicators of the population changes are:[2]

- In the 2000 U.S. Census, for the first time Americans were able to identify themselves as belonging to more than one race (U.S. Census Bureau).

- By 2015, in New York, Texas, New Mexico, Arizona, and California the school-age population will be more than 50 percent minority. Nationally, that is likely to happen by 2040 (U.S. Census Bureau).

- Nearly 40 percent of Californians over the age of five speak a language other than English at home; in New Mexico it is 35 percent, and in Texas, 32 percent (Ness, 2001).

For a teacher of young children, these statistics have important implications. There will be more students in the classroom who are culturally and linguistically different. Unless teachers are informed and educated about these differences, they may misinterpret a child's abilities, learning, and needs. Too often, language barriers between a teacher and a child lead to the conclusion that the child is a slow learner or has a disability.

Working with families will become more challenging to a teacher's ingenuity and communication skills. Many families are unfamiliar with school culture in the United States and the expectations schools have about family involvement and participation. Some parents are illiterate in their own language. An informed and supportive teacher can help family's help their children succeed under these circumstances. (See Chapter 8, Needs of Immigrant Parents.)

A lack of understanding about the culture, history, beliefs, and values of the children is harmful to their self-concept (see Derman-Sparks et al., 1989, and other references in this book). When there are no assessment tools or instructional materials in the language of the children or depict their native heritage, they are placed at a distinct disadvantage. Minorities have argued for years that testing instruments that determine IQ and placement in special programs for children who are gifted or disabled are biased because they are not written in the predominant culture of the child being tested. As a result, minority children are underrepresented in programs for children who are gifted. Yet they are over-represented in programs for children with disabilities, a fact that some relate to a lack of sensitivity to a child's cultural and linguistic heritage.

Cultural Sensitivity

Cultural and linguistic sensitivity means that each child's heritage is honored, that it is understood as unique from other cultures, and that it is respected. It means that teachers must become familiar with the cultural norms of the children in their classes and build bridges for

1 Children need correct information, appropriate language, brief answers, and adults who are comfortable answering their questions and talking about their fears.

2 Early childhood educators need to move from an ethnocentric orientation (based on their own or the dominant culture experience) and move toward a more multicultural approach. Examination of terms such as *minority* and *majority* is needed.

children and their families into the more dominant culture.

The culturally sensitive teacher will get to know each of the families as a separate entity and become familiar with their individual expressions of culture and values. Today's teacher will recognize that one family does not represent the totality of the culture (which would be stereotyping) and will be careful not to overgeneralize from one example. The effective teacher will be called on to integrate these insights into curriculum planning as well as in their relationships with the children's families.

SUMMARY

The child in early childhood programs ranges from the dependent infant to the outgoing eight-year-old. In those few short years teachers witness tremendous physical, intellectual, social, and emotional gains. The child learns to crawl, walk, run, climb, throw a ball, write with a pencil, use scissors, hold a spoon, and manipulate toys. Both large and small muscles are called into play throughout each stage of development.

Language development is equally impressive. The babbling infant becomes fluent, sometimes in more than one language. Intellectual gains coincide as children become able to express thoughts, solve problems, and exhibit growth in their reasoning powers.

Socially, the child learns to relate to family members, schoolmates, teachers, and other adults. Every range of human emotion is developed during these early years as children learn appropriate ways to express and release their feelings.

Teachers notice that children share many common characteristics while displaying wide individual differences. Profile charts—Word Pictures—describing normal development help teachers understand when a particular behavior is likely to occur. With advance notice, then, teachers can plan activities and curricula that appeal to children at every age level; disciplinary and guidance measures can match the child's specific level of development.

Yet it is obvious that growth and development do not proceed normally for all children. Two groups of children have special needs within the early childhood classroom. Children with disabilities require particular attention to their particular disability and teachers need special skills to teach them. Children who are gifted also require attention; their exceptional abilities must be challenged and stimulated within the regular early childhood program.

The changing demographics that bring more and more culturally and linguistically diverse children into early childhood settings require that teachers become familiar with the specific cultural norms represented in America today. This will call for new teaching strategies, culturally appropriate curriculum, and special efforts to work with parents from a multicultural perspective.

CHILDREN OF MIXED HERITAGE

by
Francis Wardle, M.S., Ph.D.

Trell's first-grade teacher asked him to research the life of one of his grandparents for a Black History Month project. Trell enthusiastically collected photographs, old letters, and newspaper clippings of his favorite grandfather. He asked his parents for anecdotal information; he also remembered his favorite times with his grandfather. He spent hours preparing.

Before the important day, Trell went over the report with his teacher. He knew she would be as excited as he was about his grandfather, who had been a famous politician in his day. Much to Trell's disappointment, his teacher rejected his report. Trell, a biracial boy, had chosen to tell about his white/Carib grandfather. The teacher wanted only black people presented. Trell was devastated.

Anti-bias, multicultural education has found a permanent place in our early childhood programs. Psychologists have recognized that a crucial part of children's self-esteem is contingent on a postivie view of their racial and ethnic heritage and that children with high self-esteem do better in school. So programs now provide materials, books, dools, activities, content, and discussion to help support the ethnic and racial identity of their children.

Multicultural approaches place children within five distinctive groups: African American, Hispanic/Latino, Native American, Asian American, and white. Progams then respond to children on the basis of the group to which they belong. For children like Trell, whose parents represent more than one of these categories, this does not work. And teachers who work with the growing number of multiracial and multiethnic students find themselves without tools to support these children. Where do they fit in?

Children of mixed heritage—multiracial and multiethnic—have a racial and cultural heritage that includes both biological parents' complete backgrounds. Educators must carefully help these children develop a pride and positive self-esteem in their *total* multiracial heritage, culture, and identity.

There are no multiracial holidays, no heroes, no puzzles of multiracial families, very few books, no posters, and no curriculum activities. Here are a few suggestions to help teachers begin to fill this void:

- Use interracial and interethnic families in your program to help with information, photographs, holidays, stories, histories, and curriculum resources.

- Create your own posters, materials, and books that show interracial families (including foster, adoptive, and blended families).

- Pressure companies that provide books and curriculum materials to include multiracial and multiethnic materials in their selections.

- Provide an immediate response to any language or behavior that in any way negates a multiethnic or multiracial child's identity, heritage, or pride. This includes comments implying that the child cannot embrace his full multiracial identity.

- Research multiracial and multiethnic heroes (e.g., composer Gottschalk, ornithologist Audubon) and present material to your class.

- Never celebrate acitivty that requires a child to select only part of his heritage. If you celebrate cultural days, such as Cinco de Mayo and Martin Luther King Day, present them in a way all children can benefit. Make sure a multiracial child is comfortable identifying both with Cinco de Mayo and Martin Luther King Day, if the child has those combined heritages.

- Contact a local multiracial support group to get ideas, information, and advice.

- Do not teach about race, ethnicity, and culture in a way that excludes children and people. We should teach about culture and heritage to be inclusive, and as a way to give individuals strength, traditions, and values, not to group and exclude people.

Francis Wardle, M.S., Ph.D., is Executive Director of the Center for the Study of Biracial Children. He has written extensively on this topic, including Proposal: An Anti-Bias and Ecological Model for Multicultural Education, *an article that presents a multicultural model inclusive of children with multiracial and multiethnic heritages, and* Meeting the Needs of Multiethnic & Multiracial Children in Schools, *a 2004 Allyn & Bacon publication written with Maria Cruz-Janzen.*

For more activities and information, visit our Web site at
http://www.EarlyChildEd.delmar.com

KEY TERMS

Word Pictures

age-level characteristics

Down syndrome

special-needs children

attention-deficit/hyperactivity
disorder (ADHD)

Asperger syndrome

inclusion

mainstreaming

gifted children

REVIEW QUESTIONS

1. Match the word picture to the age group in which it belongs:

Observes family rules	toddlers
Plays peek-a-boo	fives
Has dynamic intellectual drive	sixes and sevens
Is intrigued by whispering	infants
Needs to be "in"	twos
"Mine" most prominent pronoun	fours
Backs into chair to sit down	sixes
Likes to be alone listening to music	sevens
Can balance on one foot	threes
Letter, word reversal common	fours
Mood changes rapidly	sevens

2. Name one way children are alike and one way they differ from one another. Describe the curriculum planning implications for the teacher of these children.

3. One area of development affects another. List two ways that social or emotional problems can affect other areas of growth.

4. What are some of the reasons for using the concept of the whole child in early education?

5. What are some of the advantages of including children with special needs? What are some of the difficulties that must be overcome for successful integration of children with special needs?

6. Why is it important for teachers to know about attention-deficit/hyperactivity disorder (ADHD)?

7. How important is it to know and understand the cultures of children we teach?

8. How are inclusion and mainstreaming different?

LEARNING ACTIVITIES

1. Select two children who are approximately the same age. Compare their physical and social development. How are they alike? How are they different? What do you think accounts for these differences?

2. Look at the Word Picture for a three-year-old. Compare it with a three-year-old you know. What behavior do you observe in the real three-year-old that falls within the range of the chart? What is different? Are there cultural differences?

3. Observe a class of children with special needs in an inclusive classroom. What would you do to foster interactions between the children who are disabled and the children who are not? What verbalizations are used about a child's handicapping condition, and do the nondisabled children seem to understand how their friends are similar to them as well as different?

4. Using the Word Pictures, how would you design an appropriate art activity for children who are 18 months old? What kind of playground experience would you provide for a three-year-old? How would you schedule a day for a six-year-old you were babysitting? Justify your answers by citing specific developmental references.

REFERENCES

Allen, K. E., & Cowdery, G. (2005). *The exceptional child: Inclusion in early childhood education.* Clifton Park, NY: Delmar Learning.

Allen, K. E., & Marotz, L. (2003). *Developmental profiles: Birth to eight.* Clifton Park, NY: Delmar Learning.

Bee, H. (1999). *The developing child.* Menlo Park, CA: Addison-Wesley.

Berger, K. S. (2000). *The developing person.* New York, NY: Worth.

Berk, L. E. (2002). *Infants and children.* Boston: Allyn & Bacon.

Berk, L. E. (2003). *Child development.* Boston: Allyn & Bacon.

Caldwell, B. M. (1993). One world of children. In A. Gordon & K. W. Browne (Eds.), *Beginnings and beyond: Foundations in early childhood education* (3rd ed.). Clifton Park, NY: Thomson Delmar Learning.

Derman-Sparks, L., & the ABC Task Force. (1989). *Anti-bias curriculum: Tools for empowering young children.* Washington, DC: National Association for the Education of Young Children.

Gallagher, S. A., & Gallagher, J. J. (2002). *Understanding our gifted,* 42 (2), Winter 2002. Boulder, CO: Open Space Communications.

Gardner, H. (1993). *Frames of mind: The theory of multiple intelligences.* New York: Basic Books.

Gesell, A., & Ilg, F. L. (1943). *Infant and child in the culture of today.* New York: Harper Brothers.

Gordon, A. M., & Browne, K. W. (1996). *Guiding young children in a diverse society.* Boston: Allyn & Bacon.

Kiernan, S., et al. (n.d.). *Mainstreaming preschoolers: Children with orthopedic handicaps.* Washington, DC: U.S. Department of Health, Education, and Welfare.

National Resource Center on ADHD. (2006). *The disorder named ADHD.* What We Know Series K1. Chadd Web site.

Ness, C. 100-year high in California's percentage of foreign-born. (2001, August 6). *San Francisco Chronicle,* page 1.

U.S. Bureau of the Census. (1997).

U.S. Bureau of the Census. (1997). *A population projection by age, sex, race, and Hispanic origin for 1995–2025.*

HELPFUL WEB SITES

Children and Adults with ADHD	http://www.chadd.org
National Dissemination Center for Children with Disabilities (NICHCY)	http://www.nichcy.org
ERIC Documents	http://www.eric.ed.gov
American Academy of Pediatrics	http://www.aap.org
Individuals with Disabilities Education Act	http://www.ideapractices.org
Council for Exceptional Children	http://www.cec.sped.org/
The Division of Early Childhood for Exceptional Children	http://www.dec-sped.org/
The ARC (formerly National Association of Retarded Citizens)	http://www.thearc.org/
Circle of Inclusion	http://www.circleofinclusion.org/

 For more activities and information, visit our Web site at http://www.EarlyChildEd.delmar.com

Developmental and Learning Theories

QUESTIONS FOR THOUGHT

What are the basic questions of developmental and learning theories?

What are the psychosocial stages of early childhood?

What are the tenets of behaviorist theory?

How does a cognitive/constructivist theory explain children's thinking processes?

How does sociocultural theory affect early childhood practices?

Does ecological theory further our understanding of young children's development?

What is the theory of multiple intelligences?

How can humanist theory apply to education?

How does maturation theory describe growth?

What is the role of ethnicity and culture in development and learning?

How can attachment theory explain child–adult relationships?

How do children learn through play?

What are gender differences, and how do they explain behavior?

Does children's moral development grow in stages?

How does brain-based research increase our knowledge of child development?

How can development and learning theories be applied to the classroom and work with young children?

INTRODUCTION

> While taking a routine report at an elementary school, a police officer was interrupted by a girl of about six years old. Looking the officer up and down, she asked, "Are you a cop?" "Yes," said the woman, and continued writing the report. "My mother said if I ever needed help I should ask the police. Is that right?" "Yes, again," replied the officer. "Well, then," she said as she extended her foot forward, "would you please tie my shoe?"

What was this child thinking? Can you see how she took in information from her mother and then applied it to her own life? How do children do that? What is the process of listening, thinking, and then doing?

> While working for an organization that delivers lunches to elderly shut-ins, a mother used to take her preschool son on the afternoon rounds. He was always intrigued by the various appliances there, particularly the canes, walkers, and wheelchairs. One day she saw him staring at a pair of false teeth soaking in a glass. He turned to her and whispered, "The tooth fairy will never believe this!"

Look how this child applied his fantasy world to what he encountered. During the years from birth to middle childhood, how do young children come to understand the world? How do they make sense of what they see, touch, and experience?

> The father of six-month-old Michiko puts one end of a toy monkey in his mouth and dangles it in front of her. Michiko gazes intently, getting still and wide-eyed, finally reaching up tentatively to touch the doll. Yet when Keith's nanny tries the same thing with him, the nine-month-old smiles and laughs as he grabs it and tries to shove it back into her mouth.

How is it that two children can respond so differently? Is this simply a few months' age difference? Is it because of their gender or ethnic differences? Or has one child played this game before and not the other?

So many remarkable transformations take place in the early years. Development, the orderly set of changes in the life span, occurs as individuals move from conception to death. So much changes over time, and those of us curious about children want to know the nature of these changes and the reasons why things happen. What are the theories? What has research told us?

Yet why do we need to know anything about theory or research? Isn't direct experience with children enough to plan good programs? Certainly the practical aspects of teaching young children are important. However, only with a genuine understanding of why a practice is conducted may early educators successfully plan and achieve meaningful and effective intervention. If the processes involved in development are not random, then we must try to know them. As complex as the system of children's growth, thinking, feeling, and behaving may be, we cannot consider ourselves responsible professionals until we understand the theory behind the practice.

Early childhood education draws from several fields of study. The connection with the field of psychology is particularly strong. Much of what we know about children today comes from child development and child psychology research. As educators, we apply those findings in the classroom. Our knowledge base comes directly from psychological studies.

- How do children develop?
- What do they learn, and in what order?
- What do people need to be ready to learn?
- What affects learning?
- Do all people develop in the same ways?
- What are the similarities and differences in growth and development?

To begin to answer these questions, we need some way to look for information and then choose and organize the facts so that we can understand what we see. In other words, we need a **theory**. Psychologists and educators have been doing just that for years, and in the 20th century a great deal has been discovered about these issues. Theories are especially useful in providing a broad and consistent view of the complexity of human development. They allow us to make an educated guess (called **hypothesis**) about children's behavior and development. Because these theories are based on experience, their validity can be checked by teachers as they observe children every day. Thus, the basic quest for sound theories about development and knowledge, for systematic statements about behavior and development, has given educators much to consider in bringing forth their own ideas about children (see Figure 4-1).

The Nature of Development

A child is a blend of so many parts that interrelate in different ways and change with growth over time. Such complexity and dynamic

FIGURE 4-1 We use images, such as this rainbow, to developmental areas, to capture the concept of the whole child as a sum of many parts.

change is difficult to describe, much less predict. In order to simplify the study of development, we try to consider separately the three aspects that make up the whole of development (Figure 4-1). We can then better understand the major processes of development that parallel these developmental areas.

- Biological processes describe changes in the body.
- Cognitive processes are those changes in one's thought, intelligence, and language.
- Socioemotional processes reflect changes in an individual's relationships with other people, emotions, and personality.

Major issues are raised in the study of development:

Is children's development due more to maturation or experience? The changes we see in children over time may be due to internal or external influences. Some theories claim children change because of innate, biologic, or genetic patterns built into the human being; others claim that they are shaped by the environment and experiences (such as parents, materials, TV, school, and so on) of life. This argument is often referred to as the **nature/nurture controversy**, also known as the problem of heredity versus environment. As you

will remember from Chapter 1, this issue has been discussed for centuries. On the "nature" side, Rousseau argued that the child is born with natural, or innate, goodness. Locke, however, asserted that it was "nurture" that mattered. He contended that children entered the world with a tabula rasa, or clean slate, on which all experience and learning was then written. Today, most psychologists and educators agree that the patterns of development and learning are complex and not so simply explained. Modern theories are not set in such black-and-white terms but rather focus on variations that emphasize one or the other (see Figure 4-2).

Is growth smooth and continuous or more stage-like? Some theories emphasize a gradual, cumulative kind of growth, more like "from an acorn, a giant oak will grow." This continuity of development is usually the viewpoint of theories that emphasize experience (nurture). Others see children growing in stages that are clearly marked by distinct changes. "This view sees each of us as passing through a sequence of stages in which change is qualitative rather than quantitative. As an oak moves from seedling to giant tree, it becomes more oak-like and its development is continuous. As a caterpillar changes into a butterfly, it does not become more caterpillar, but,

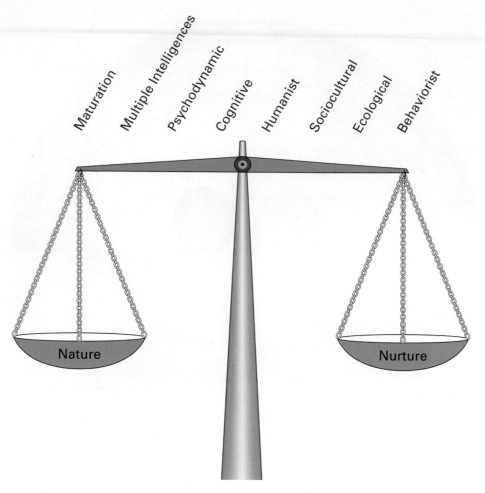

FIGURE 4-2 Development is a combination of the forces of nature (heredity and prenatal conditions) and nurture (environmental and life experiences). Every theory focuses on various areas of development and emphasizes a different proportion of these two forces.

instead, becomes a different kind of organism" (Santrock, 2001). This viewpoint emphasizes the innate nature of development. Figure 4-2 shows the relative orientations of each theory presented in the chapter.

What can theory and research do for early childhood educators? Science has opened our eyes to the amazing complexity of the mind and the wondrous path of growth in the body. This was not always so. In previous generations, little scientific information was available by which parents (and teachers) could assess the validity of theories. Many beliefs were espoused by adults about children, such as "You'll spoil the baby if you respond to his demands too quickly," or "Children who suffer early neglect and deprivation will not realize their normal potential." These statements can be powerful, particularly as they are passed on to you by your family and culture. However, some ideas are rooted in myth rather than reality. Child

development researchers and theorists have accumulated a rich store of knowledge, based on scientific hypothesis that is then tested with evidence. They can help sort fact from fiction.

Initially, the study of child development was mostly confined to the study of trends and descriptions of age changes. As the 20th century progressed, the scope and definition of child development changed radically. Developmental psychologists now study how psychological processes begin, change, and develop. Child development now focuses on language acquisition, various early effects on later intellectual development, the process of attachment to others, and the social and cultural contexts of development.

Early childhood teachers should know how children develop and how they learn. Knowing how children develop is critical in making the daily decisions about curriculum, the classroom setting, and children. To be effective with children, teachers need a thoughtful philosophy and approach that is based on what we know about how children develop and what works to help them learn and understand. The teacher who is well versed in theory has invaluable tools to work with parents, advise the family of the range of typical behavior, and talk to parents about concerns that are beyond the norms. Therefore, it is important to have a background in both developmental psychology and learning theories.

No one set of principles encompasses all developmental and learning theories. We have chosen eight theories. They are commonly known as (1) psychodynamic theory, (2) behaviorist theory, (3) cognitive theory, (4) sociocultural theory, (5) ecological theory, (6) multiple intelligences theory, (7) maturation theory, and (8) humanistic theory.

In addition, there are several special topics for educators in the study of child development. The chapter ends with a discussion of ethnicity and culture, attachment, learning through play, gender differences, moral development, and brain-based research. It includes an "Insights" article by Roz Charlesworth about the intersection between child development and developmentally appropriate practices (DAP).

> The children were playing "school" in the dramatic play area. Noemi insisted on wearing pretend glasses, as her favorite teacher did. "No!" cried Venecia. "They will make you mad and crabby!" (In fact, her teacher only wore the glasses when she was too tired to wear contact lenses.) "Yes, I will," replied Noemi. "She wears them cuz they makes her smarty-pants." (Another viewpoint, and a kind of myth about intelligence and eyewear.) "You're both wrong," called out Charly. "Everybody knows you have to wear glasses and hoop earrings to be a teacher." (As a matter of fact, both teachers did look like this.) Everyone looked puzzled, and then the play resumed.

Just like the children, not all the experts agree or even think alike. Because the field of child development is broad, encompassing a wide variety of opinion and fact, there is no one theory that describes everything. Moreover, these theories arose at different time periods, in various countries. Each theory will describe children and their processes in a different way. It is up to you, the educator, to decide which ones best describe children and their growth. Read carefully, and then compare your experiences with the theories and concepts you read here.

As a teacher you have a diversity of thought on which to establish a professional philosophy.

PSYCHODYNAMIC THEORY

Psychodynamic theory is about personality development and emotional problems. **Psychodynamic,** or psychoanalytic, theories look at development in terms of internal drives that are often **unconscious,** or hidden from our awareness. These motives are the underlying forces that influence human thinking and behavior and provide the foundation for universal stages of development. In psychoanalytic terms, children's behavior can be interpreted by knowing the various stages and tasks within those stages.

Sigmund Freud

Sigmund Freud began his career as a medical doctor and became interested in the irrational side of human behavior as he treated "hysterics." His technique, asking people to recline on a couch and talk about everything, was ridiculed by the medical establishment as the "talking cure." Then, as patients revealed their thoughts, fantasies, and problems, he began to see patterns. According to Freud, people possess three basic drives: the sexual drive, survival instincts, and a drive for destructiveness. Of the first, childhood sexuality, Freud outlined development in terms of psychosexual stages, each characterized by a particular part of the body (see Figure 4-3). In each stage, the sensual satisfaction associated with each body part is linked to major challenges of that age. For instance, think about how some of the issues of toddlers, such as biting or thumb sucking, and the preschool concerns with "doctor play," masturbation, or gender identification in the dress-up corner might be seen in a psychosexual context. Each stage also has its own conflicts between child and parent, and how the child experiences those conflicts will determine basic personality and behavior patterns.

Freud put forth this theory (Freud, 1968), and his ideas were expanded on by Anna Freud (his daughter), Carl Jung, Karen Horney, and others. Although Freud's interest was abnormal adult behavior and its causes, his conclusions have had a major effect on our conception of childhood and its place in the life span.

To Freud, the personality was the most important aspect of development, more central to human growth than language, perception, or

Stage	Age	Description/Major Area
Oral	Birth to 2	Mouth (sucking, biting) source of pleasure Eating and teething
Anal	2–3	Bowel movements source of pleasure Toilet learning
Phallic	3–6	Genitals source of pleasure Sex role identification and conscience development
Latency	6–12	Sexual forces dormant Energy put into schoolwork and sports
Genital	12–18	Genitals source of pleasure Stimulation and satisfaction from relationships

FIGURE 4-3 Freud's psychoanalytic theory of childhood sexuality. Freud's stage theory contends that each stage has its own area of pleasure and crisis between the child and parent of society.

cognition. Personality was defined by three structures:

1. Id—the instinctive part that drives a person to seek satisfaction
2. Ego—the rational structure that forms a person's sense of self
3. Superego—the moral side that informs the person of right and wrong.

He thought that the personality developed in a fixed pattern of stages that emerged as the body matured naturally. But even though the sequence of the stages might be firm, how children were treated while going through those stages determined whether they developed healthy or abnormal personalities. In particular, the mother–child relationship was important in each stage. Thus, the interaction between the child's wishes and needs and how these were treated (by the mother or other adults) was a focal point for proper development.

All psychoanalytic explanations of human development emphasize the critical importance of relationships with people and the sequence, or stages, of personality development. The psychoanalyst Erik Erikson expanded and refined Freud's theory of development. It is Erikson whose ideas have most affected early childhood education.

Erik Erikson and His Theory of Human Development

Erik Homberg Erikson is perhaps the most influential psychoanalyst of the modern era, certainly a key figure in the study of children and development. His interests in children and education included a teaching background in progressive and Montessori schools in Europe. After clinical training in psychoanalysis, he remained interested in the connections between psychotherapy and education. Erikson became the first child analyst in the Boston area and worked for years in several universities in the United States.

Erikson's theory of human development, like those of Freud and Piaget, states that life is a series of stages through which each person passes, with each stage growing from the previous ones. He proposes eight stages of **psychosocial** development, each representing a critical period for the development of an important strength. Positive growth allows the individual to integrate his or her physical and biologic development with the challenges that the social institutions and culture present. Each stage is characterized by an emotional challenge. Erikson gave us the term *identity crisis* to describe how people struggle with a pair of contrasting issues at each stage (see Figure 4-4) as they try to answer, "Who am I?"

A second key point of Erikson's theory is balance. Essential in Erikson's framework, balancing a child's wishes and the demands of the environment with a mentally healthy dose of each emotion is essential for personality strength.

In other words, every growing organism passes through certain developmental stages. A stage is a period during which certain changes occur. What one achieves in each stage is based on the developments of the previous stages, and

FIGURE 4-4 An Eriksonian crisis in a young child's life. The child who has successfully mastered the first of Erikson's psychosocial conflicts will then be able to cope with future challenges. In this instance, the child who takes initiative (grabbing a toy) can also feel guilt (returning it).

each stage presents the child with certain kinds of problems to be solved. When children succeed, they go on to attack new problems and grow through solving them.

Erikson differed from Freud in some fundamental ways. First, he emphasized the drive for identity and meaning in a social context rather than the Freudian notion of sexual and aggressive drives. Second, development occurs throughout the life span, in contrast with the notion that personality is shaped only in childhood. Finally, the developmental struggles that occur during one's life can be overcome later. You can go back; while it is true that the first four stages play a key role in developing ego identity, problems of childhood can be dealt with in later stages so the adult can achieve vitality.

Everyone has certain biologic, social, and psychological needs that must be satisfied to grow in a healthy manner. Medicine has learned much about physical needs—diet, rest, exercise. Basic intellectual, social, and emotional needs also must be met for an organism to be healthy. Eriksonian theory speaks to these needs. Whether these needs are met or unfulfilled will affect development.

Erikson's stage theory is expanded here because of its importance to the field of early childhood education. (See Figure 4-5.)

Stage 1: Trust versus Mistrust (Birth to One Year)

Erikson's first stage is roughly the first year of life and parallels Freud's oral–sensory stage. Attitudes important to development are the capacity to trust—or mistrust—inner and outer experiences. By providing consistent care, parents help an infant develop a basic sense of trust in self and an ability to trust other people. They give affection and emotional security as well as provide for physical needs. Inconsistent or inadequate care creates mistrust. In extreme cases, as shown by Spitz's classic studies on infant deprivation (Spitz & Wolf, 1946), lack of care can actually lead to infant death. A less extreme case might form isolation or distrust of others. Recent studies suggest a strong hereditary element in this disorder rather than environmental (Myers et al., 1984). Given a solid base in early trust, though, the typical infant develops the virtue, or strength, of hope.

Babies must learn trust at two levels: "external (belief that significant adults will be present to meet the baby's needs) and internal (belief in her own power to effect changes and

Stage	Description	Challenge	Strength
Stage One	Newborns	Trust vs. Mistrust	Hope
Stage Two	Toddlers	Autonomy vs. Shame and Doubt	Willpower
Stage Three	Childhood	Initiative vs. Guilt	Purpose
Stage Four	School	Competence (or industry) vs. Inferiority	Competence
Stage Five	Adolescence	Search for identity vs. Role confusion	Fidelity
Stage Six	Young adulthood	Intimacy (love and friendship) vs. Isolation (loneliness)	Love
Stage Seven	Grown-ups	Generativity (caring for the next generation) vs. Stagnation	Care
Stage Eight	Old age	Integrity vs. Despair	Wisdom

FIGURE 4-5 Erikson's theory of psychosocial development centers on basic crises that people face from birth to old age. This stage theory of development proposes that these conflicts are part of the life process and that successful handling of these issues can give a person the "ego strength" to face life positively.

cope with a variety of circumstances" (Mooney, 2000). As adults engage with infants, they encourage attachment (see "Developmental Topics" at the end of this chapter). Caregivers and families teach in two ways:

● Holding babies close with warm physical contact with them while being fed.

● Responding right away to their distress when they cry (Mooney, 2000).

When working with infants and toddlers, teachers must take special care to provide a predictable environment and consistent caregiving. Babies are totally dependent on adults to meet their needs; they are particularly vulnerable to difficulties because they have few skills for coping with discomfort and stress. It is critical, therefore, that they be cared for by warm, positive adults who are sensitive and respond affectionately to an infant's needs as soon as they arise. In this way, the very young develop the trust in the world that will support their growth into the next stage.

Stage 2: Autonomy versus Doubt (Two to Three Years)

The second stage, corresponding to the second and third years of life, parallels the muscular-anal period in Freudian theory. The child learns to manage and control impulses and to use both motor and mental skills. To help a child develop a healthy balance between **autonomy** and doubt, parents should consider how to handle their toddlers' toilet training and growing curiosity to explore. Restrictive or compulsive parents may give the child a feeling of shame and doubt, causing a sense of insecurity. Successful growth in this stage gives a child strength of will. "This stage, therefore, becomes decisive for the ratio of love and hate, cooperation and willfulness, freedom of self-expression and its suppression. From a sense of self-control without loss of self-esteem comes a lasting sense of good will and pride; from a sense of loss of self-control and of foreign overcontrol comes a lasting propensity for doubt and shame" (Erikson, 1963).

Encouraging a sense of autonomy while teaching limits without shaming is a delicate balance. Adults foster independence in toddlers by (Mooney, 2000):

giving children simple choices	"Milk or juice today?"
not giving false choices	"Do you want to get in your car seat?"
setting clear, consistent, reasonable limits	"People are not for hiting,"
accepting children's swings between independence and dependence	"Sometimes you want to play by yourself, and sometimes near me; both are ok."

Chapter 7 elaborates on how to help guide children using positive discipline.

Budding curiosity means high energy, so the daily schedule should include plenty of time for active movement and flexibility to deal with fluctuating energy and mood. Toileting is a learned behavior just as dressing, painting, and singing are; a relaxed attitude about this area helps the child gain mastery without shame. Allowing for plenty of "two steps forward, one back" acknowledges the child's natural doubts and the balancing that happens in this stage.

Stage 3: Initiative versus Guilt (Three to Five or Six Years)

The third stage of Eriksonian theory corresponds to the preschool and kindergarten years and parallels Freud's phallic stage of development. The developmental task is to develop a sense of purpose. Out of autonomy comes initiative, and from healthy doubt can come a conscience. The preschooler who grabs another's toy may also hide when the crying begins; gently leading the child to give it back allows the regret to be expressed through taking charge. Children are ready to plan and carry out ideas, so teachers can encourage their natural curiosity by allowing them to choose and then execute activities that are constructive and cooperative. An overly restrictive adult may raise a child who is easily discouraged and inhibited. On the other hand, parents or teachers giving no restraints signal to the child no clear idea of what is socially acceptable and what is not. The key strength that grows out of this stage is purpose.

Teaching children of this age is both exhilarating and exasperating. Many find this stage easier than the previous two but more challenging socially. It is a time when children move in two opposing directions: accomplishment or destruction. To support children's development of initiative with reasonable expectations, teachers can:

● encourage children to be as independent as possible.

● focus on gains as children practice new skills, not on the mistakes they make along the way.

- set expectations that are in line with children's individual abilities.
- focus curriculum on real things and on doing (Mooney, 2000).

Section 4 of this book concentrates on environmental and curricular issues.

Remember, the child who takes initiative is ready to meet the world head-on and wants to do it "all by myself." This may include both putting on a jacket and hitting someone who has said something unkind. An environment that can respond to a child's interests, both in theme and at the moment, will be interesting and successful. At the same time, teachers must be prepared with a small set of logical limits (or "rules") and the means to follow through kindly and firmly when those limits are tested. Socializing at this age is the very point of the emotional states of initiative and guilt; children must have enough freedom to develop their own ways to deal with one another and still develop a sense of fairness and conscience. Chapter 7 offers strategies for setting and maintaining limits at this age.

Stage 4: Industry versus Inferiority (Six to 12 Years)

Erikson's fourth stage, beginning with the primary school years and ending with puberty, parallels Freud's latency period. The major theme in this stage is mastery of life, primarily by adapting to laws of society (people, laws and rules, relationships) and objects (tools, machines, the physical world). This is the child's most enthusiastic time for learning. The stage is "the end of early childhood's period of expansive imagination. The danger in the elementary school years is the development of a sense of inferiority—of feeling incompetent and unproductive" (Santrock, 2001). It is also a time of great adventure. The child begins to think of being big and to identify with people whose work or whose personality he can understand and admire.

- Finding a place in one's own school: line leader on the way to the cafeteria, the goalie on the soccer field, or the secretary at a scout meeting.
- Applying themselves to skills/tasks: systematic instruction in the culture, as in how to organize and serve snack at the after-school center.
- Handling the "tools of the tribe": learn to use pencils, read aloud, fill out forms, run the computer, check out and use balls and bats.

Problems arise if the child feels inadequate and inferior to such tasks. A parent or teacher who overemphasizes children's mistakes could make them despair of ever learning, for instance, the multiplication tables or cursive handwriting. At the same time, adults must encourage children to work toward mastery. Adults should "mildly but firmly coerce children into the adventure of finding out that one can learn to accomplish things which one would never have thought possible by oneself" (Erikson, 1963). Parents must not let their children restrict their own horizons by doing only what they already know. Particularly in social situations, it is essential for children to learn to do things with others, as difficult and unfair as this may sometimes be.

Applying Erikson's Theory to Work with Children

First, Erikson has a clear message about the importance of play. Second, the theory helps shape guidelines for the role of adults in children's lives.

Play is a critical part of children's total development. Most schools for children under age six have periods of time allotted for play called "choice time" or "free play." Erikson supports these ideas explicitly by stating that the senses of autonomy and of initiative are developed mainly through social and fantasy play. He suggests that child's play is "the infantile form of the human ability to deal with experiences by creating model situations and to master reality by experiment and planning. . . . To 'play it out' in play is the most natural self-healing measure childhood affords" (Erikson, 1964).

The adult is primarily an emotional base and a social mediator for the child. Teachers become interpreters of feelings, actions, reasons, and solutions. We help children understand situations and motives so that they can solve their own problems. Look at each child's emotional makeup and monitor their progress through developmental crises; each crisis is a turning point of increased vulnerability and also enhanced potential. Allow the child, in Erikson's words:

. . . to experience over and over again that he is a person who is permitted to make choices. He has to have the right to choose, for example, whether to sit or whether to stand, whether to approach a visitor or to lean against his mother's knee . . . whether to use the toilet or to wet his pants. At the same time he must learn some of the boundaries of self-determination.

In Erikson's theory the adult serves as a social mediator for the child.

> He inevitably finds that there are some walls he cannot climb, that there are objects out of reach, that, above all, there are innumerable commands enforced by powerful adults. (Erikson, 1969)

In preschool and kindergarten, a teacher allows children to take initiative and does not interfere with the results of those actions. At the same time, teachers and parents provide clear limits so that the children can learn what behaviors are unacceptable to society.

The issues of early childhood, from Erikson's theory, are really our own issues. While the remnants of these stages stay with us all our lives, teachers who are aware of their own processes can fully appreciate the struggles of children.

BEHAVIORIST THEORY

Behaviorism is the most pragmatic and functional of the modern psychological ideologies. Behaviorist theories describe both development and learning. Developed during the 1920s and continually modified today, behaviorism is "the most distinctively American contribution to psychology" (Suransky, 1982). Countless developmental psychologists and researchers have defined and expanded on this idea, several of whom are mentioned later in this chapter. To summarize the behaviorist theory, we have chosen five theorists: John Watson, Edward Thorndike, Ivan Pavlov, B. F. Skinner, and Albert Bandura.

The Behaviorists

What is known today as "behaviorism" begins with the notion that a child is born with a "clean slate," a "tabula rasa" in Locke's words, on which events are written throughout life. The condition of those events cause all important human behavior. Behaviorists often insist that only what can actually be observed will be accepted as fact. Only behavior can be treated, they say, not feelings or internal states. This contrasts to the psychodynamic approach, which insists that behavior is just an indirect clue to the "real" self, that of inner feelings and thoughts.

Ivan Pavlov, a Russian physiologist, was working in a laboratory, studying how animals digest food. He noticed that the dogs in his laboratory would anticipate their meals when they heard or saw their attendants making preparations. Instead of starting to salivate just when food was set in front of them, the dogs would salivate to a number of stimuli associated with food. He identified this simple form of learning as respondent conditioning. The association of involuntary reflexes with other environmental conditions became known as classical conditioning, a cornerstone of behaviorist theory.

John B. Watson was an American theorist who studied the animal experiments of Russian scientist Ivan Pavlov. He then translated those ideas of conditioning into human terms. In the first quarter of the 20th century, Watson made sweeping claims about the powers of this classical conditioning. He declared that he could shape a person's entire life by controlling exactly the events of an infant's first year. One of his ideas was to discourage emotional ties between parents and children because they interfered with the child's direct learning from the environment (though he later modified this). Nonetheless, he gave scientific validity to the idea that teachers should set conditions for learning and reward proper responses.

Edward L. Thorndike also studied the conditions of learning. Known as the "godfather of standardized testing," Thorndike helped develop scales to measure student achievement and usher in the era of standardized educational testing (see Chapter 6). He set forth the famous **stimulus–response** technique. A stimulus will recall a response in a person; this forms learned habits. Therefore, it is wise to pay close attention to the consequences of behavior and to the various kinds of **reinforcement**.

B. F. Skinner took the idea of tabula rasa one step further to create the doctrine of the "empty organism." That is, a person is like a vessel to be filled by carefully designed experiences. All behavior is under the control of one or more aspects of the environment. Furthermore, Skinner maintained that there is no behavior that cannot be modified. Some people argue that Skinnerian concepts tend to depersonalize the learning process and treat people as puppets. Others say that behaviorist psychology has made us develop new ways to help people learn and cope effectively with the world.

Albert Bandura has developed another type of learning theory, called social learning. As behaviorists began to accept that what people said about their feelings and internal state was valid, they looked at how children became socialized. **Socialization** is the process of learning to conform to social rules. Social-learning theorists watch how children learn these rules and use them in groups. They study the patterns of reinforcement and reward in socially appropriate and unacceptable behavior. According to Bandura:

> Children acquire most of their social concepts—the rules by which they live—from models whom they observe in the course of daily life, particularly parents, caregivers, teachers, and peers. Social learning theory [suggests] the models most likely to be imitated are individuals who are nurturant—warm, rewarding, and affectionate. Attachment also affects the process: the most significant or influential models are people to whom the child is emotionally tied. (Fong & Resnick, 1986)

From this arose a new concept known as **modeling**. This is what used to be known as learning and teaching by example. For instance, children who see their parents smoking will likely smoke themselves. In fact, Bandura's studies provided "strong evidence that exposure to filmed aggression heightens aggressive reactions in children. Subjects who viewed the aggressive human and cartoon models on film exhibited nearly twice as much aggression than did subjects in the control group who were not exposed to the aggressive film content" (Bandura, 1963). This work suggests that pictorial mass media—television, video games, and computer activities—serve as important sources of social behavior. Any behavior can be learned by watching it, from language (listening to others talk) to fighting (watching violence on television).

Bandura's theory has expanded into a more social-cognitive model, theorizing that children think hard about what they see and feel. Thus personal and cognitive factors influence behavior, as does the environment, and, in turn, children's behavior can effect the environment around them. Adding the factors of observation and thinking to behaviorist theory links it to Piaget's cognitive theory (next in this chapter).

Theory of Behaviorism and Learning

What is behavior, or learning, theory all about? Learning occurs when an organism interacts with the environment. Through experience, behavior is modified or changed. In the behaviorist's eyes, three types of learning occur: (1) classical conditioning; (2) operant conditioning; and (3) observational learning or modeling. The first two are based on the idea that learning is mostly the development of habit. What people learn is a series of associations, forming a connection between a stimulus and response that did not exist before. The third is based on a social approach. Figure 4-6 summarizes these three types of behaviorist learning processes.

Classical Conditioning

Classical conditioning can be explained by reviewing Pavlov's original experiments. A dog normally salivates at the sight of food but not when

	Classical Conditioning	Operant Conditioning	Observational Learning
Kind of behavior	Reflexive	Voluntary	Voluntary
Type of learning	Learning through association	Learning through reinforcement	Learning through observation and imitation
Role of learner	Passive	Active or Passive	Active

FIGURE 4-6 Behaviorist learning processes. Classical conditioning, operant conditioning, and observational learning are three ways to develop learned behavior. Each describes how certain kinds of behavior will be learned and what role the learner will take in the process.

he hears a bell. When the sound of a bell is paired with the sight of food, the dog "learns" to salivate when he hears the bell, whether or not food is nearby. Thus, the dog has been conditioned to salivate (give the response) for both the food (unconditioned stimulus) and the bell (conditioned stimulus). Similarly, when the school bell rings in the afternoon, children begin to gather their papers into backpacks to go home. They have been conditioned to the sound of the bell; ask any teacher who has had to deal with a broken bell system how strong this conditioning is. Classical conditioning can also account for the development of phobias. Watson used a young boy in a laboratory to test this theory. He showed the boy a white rat, then sounded a loud noise. After only seven pairings, the boy would cringe at the sight of the rat without the bell sounding at all. Only a few painful visits to a childhood dentist can teach a lifetime fear of dental health professionals.

Operant Conditioning

Operant conditioning is slightly different from classical conditioning in that it focuses on the response rather than the stimulus. In operant conditioning, the process that makes it more likely that a behavior will recur is called reinforcement. A stimulus that increases the likelihood of repeated behavior is called a reinforcer. Most people are likely to increase what gives them pleasure (be it food or attention) and decrease what gives them displeasure (such as punishment, pain, or the withdrawal of food or attention). The behaviorist tries to influence the organism by controlling these kinds of reinforcement.

A positive **reinforcer** is something that the learner views as desirable:

"social reinforcers"	attention, praise, smiles or hugs
"nonsocial reinforcers"	tokens, toys, food, stickers

For example, you would like Claire to begin to use a spoon instead of her hands to eat. Before conditioning, you talk to her whenever she eats. During the conditioning period, you can give attention (a positive reinforcer) each time she picks up a spoon during feeding times and ignore her when she uses her hands. Afterward, she is more likely to use a spoon, and less often her hands. This is an example of a positive reinforcer, something that increases the likelihood of the desired response.

The reinforcers can be either positive or negative. A negative reinforcer is removal of an unpleasant stimulus as a result of some particular behavior. Circle time is Jimmy's favorite activity at school. Yet he has difficulty controlling his behavior and consistently disrupts the group. Before conditioning, he is told that if he talks to his neighbors and shouts responses at the teacher, he will be asked to leave the circle. During the conditioning period, Jimmy is praised whenever he pays attention, sings songs, and does not bother those around him (positive reinforcement). When he begins to shout, he is told to leave and return when he can sing without shouting (negative reinforcement). A negative reinforcer is used to stop children from behaving in a particular way by arranging for them to end a mildly aversive situation immediately (in this case, the boy has to leave the group) by improving their behavior. Jimmy, by controlling his own behavior, could end his isolation from the group.

Punishment is different from negative reinforcement. Punishment is an unpleasant event that makes the behavior less likely to be repeated; that is, if Jimmy were spanked every time he shouted, then his shouting would be the punished behavior and it is likely he would begin to shout less. However, when leaving the group is the reinforcer for shouting, he tries to stop shouting to increase the likelihood of being able to stay, and not being taken away from the group. Negative reinforcement thus increases the likelihood that the desired behavior will be repeated (staying in the group) and removes attention from the less desirable behavior (the shouting). The "time-out" chair, for instance, could be viewed as either a punishment or a negative reinforcer. If used as exclusion from the group or a withdrawal of playing privileges, a child would find the time-out as a punishment. If, on the other hand, a child could leave the time-out more quickly if she exhibited certain behaviors (instead of the "bad" behavior), it might be seen as a negative reinforcer.

Reinforcement, both positive and negative, is a powerful tool. It is important for adults to realize that it can be misused. It is wise to be careful, particularly in the case of negative reinforcement. An adult may not be gentle with a negative reinforcer when angry with a child's inappropriate behavior. Educators and parents should be aware of the possibilities and check their own responses.

Modeling

The third kind of conditioning is called *observational learning* or *modeling*. Social behavior

Modeling is a special kind of observational learning; children learn from a teacher how to use materials and behave in group settings.

is particularly noteworthy to early childhood professionals, as most work with children in groups and thus witness social behavior constantly. Any behavior that involves more than one person can be considered social. One of the most negative social behaviors is aggression. It is this type that Albert Bandura researched, finding that much of it is learned by watching others.

Aggression is a complex issue, involving various definitions and behaviors. To illustrate social learning theory, Bandura defines aggression as behavior intended to inflict harm or discomfort to another person or object. Bandura showed a short film of aggressive behavior to young children. The original mid-1960s studies are summarized below:

> Each child in Bandura's experiment viewed one of three films. In all three films, an adult hit, kicked, and verbally abused an inflated Bobo doll in ways that young children are unlikely to do spontaneously. The films differed in what happened to the model after the aggressive sequence. In one film the model was lavishly rewarded with praise and foods that appealed to preschoolers, such as candy and caramel popcorn. In another film the model was punished in a dramatic way, including severe scolding and a spanking. The third film simply ended after the model's aggressive behavior, with no consequences following the aggression. After viewing one film, each child in the experiment was allowed to play in a room with a Bobo doll, all the toys used in the aggression film, and a variety of other toys.

The results are most impressive, especially to those working with young children. The level of aggression expressed by each child was directly related to what the children saw as the consequences in the film. When offered prizes, they imitated almost exactly what their model had done. Also, children appeared more likely to attack one another after viewing the attacks on the Bobo doll in film. Further studies have shown that children's level of aggression is higher right after viewing the film but less so when shown it again six months later (Berger, 2005). Regardless of the controversy that may surround any study of children's aggression, or the effects of watching filmed violence on youngsters, the social-learning theory deserves serious consideration. The effect of television watching on children is discussed in Chapter 15.

Applying Behaviorist Theory to Work with Children

Behaviorist theories make a strong case for how the environment influences our behavior.

- Physical environment: A teacher arranges the room so that positive learning is enhanced.
- Daily schedule: Routines and sequence of events are planned to encourage habits.
- Teacher/child interaction: Teachers respond carefully to children to shape their behavior.

Adults are powerful reinforcers and models for children. A learning situation comprises many cues; it is up to adults to know what those cues are and how to control them. Teachers who use behavior modification techniques know both what children are to do and how they will be reinforced for their behavior. The ethics and usefulness of using this kind of control concern everyone (see "What Do You Think?"). Each teacher and program must consider the impact of this theory and how to apply it to classroom and client. Chapter 7 has examples of behavior modification techniques.

What children learn is shaped by the circumstances surrounding the learning.

Experiences that are enjoyable are reinforcing. From the peek-a-boo game with an infant to a seven-year-old's first ride on a skateboard, an experience is more likely to be repeated and learned if it is pleasant. Social learning is particularly powerful in the lives of young children. Adults must be mindful of their own behavior; watching children as young as two years old play "family" or "school" will convince the most skeptical critic that any behavior is learnable and can become part of children's behavioral repertoire.

COGNITIVE THEORY

Adult: What does it mean to be alive?

Child: It means you can move about, play—that you can do all kinds of things.

Adult: Is a mountain alive?

Child: Yes, because it has grown by itself.

Adult: Is a cloud alive?

Child: Yes, because it sends water.

Adult: Is wind alive?

Child: Yes, because it pushes things.

How do children learn to think, and what do they think about? Cognitive theory describes the structure and development of human thought processes and how those processes affect the way a person understands and perceives the world. Piaget's theory of cognition forms a cornerstone of early childhood educational concepts about children; others have developed this theory further into a constructivist theory of learning.

Jean Jacques Piaget

Jean Jacques Piaget (1896–1980) was one of the most exciting research theorists in child development. A major force in child psychology, he studied both thought processes and how they change with age. Piaget's ideas serve as our guide to the cognitive theory because of the thoroughness of his work. He had great influence on child psychology, theories of learning, intellectual development, and even philosophy. He became the foremost expert on the development of knowledge from birth to adulthood.

How did Piaget find out about such matters? A short review of his life and ideas reveals a staggering volume of work and a wide scope of interests. Born at the turn of the century, Piaget built on his childhood curiosity in science and philosophy by working with Dr. Simon at the Binet Laboratory (Simon and Binet devised the first intelligence test). While recording children's abilities to answer questions correctly, he

What do YOU Think?

Alfie Kohn, nationally known educator and author, is a strong critic of behaviorism. He cites research showing that rewards decrease motivation; in fact, the more rewards are used, the more they seem to be needed. Punishment and negative reinforcement produce short-term compliance only, and often disregard feelings, needs, and intentions. "Skinnerian thinking—caring only about behaviors—has narrowed our understanding of children and warped the way we deal with them . . . In a nutshell, it's the child who engages in the behavior, not the behavior itself, that matters (Kohn, 2005)."

1. Do you think children end up being "punished by rewards"?

2. How do you shape children's behavior?

3. How much of what we do with children can be explained by behaviorism?

became fascinated with children's incorrect responses. He noticed that children tended to give similar kinds of wrong answers at certain ages.

Thus, Piaget launched into a lifelong study of intelligence. He believed that children think in fundamentally different ways from adults. He also developed a new method for studying thought processes. Rather than using a standardized test, he adapted the psychiatric method of question and response. Called the methode clinique, it is a technique in which the adult asks questions, then adapts her teaching and further inquiries based on children's answers. This method of observation and assessment, which focuses on children's natural ways of thinking, is discussed in detail in Chapter 6.

Piaget then began studying children's thought processes. With his wife, one of his former students, he observed his own children. He also began to look closely at how actively children engage in their own development. Prolific his entire life, Piaget gave us a complex theory of intelligence and child development. He recorded, in a systematic way, how children learn, when they learn, and what they learn (Elkind & Flavell, 1996).

Piaget's Theory of Cognitive Development

While others thought that the development of thinking was either intrinsic (nature) or extrinsic (nurture), Piaget thought that neither position offered a full explanation for a child's amazing and complex behaviors.

His theory relies on both maturational and environmental factors. It is called maturational because it sets out a sequence of cognitive (thinking) stages that is governed by heredity. For example, heredity affects our learning by (1) how the body is structured biologically and (2) automatic, or instinctive, behavior, such as an infant's sucking at birth. It is an environmental theory because the experiences children have will directly influence how they develop. Piaget claimed that children build their own knowledge; that "construction is superior to instruction" (Santrock, 2001).

Thinking and learning is a process of interaction between a person and the environment. Piaget also believed that all species inherit a basic tendency to organize their lives and adapt to the world around them. This is known as a constructivist theory; that is, children actively construct knowledge on an ongoing basis. They are developing and constantly revising their own knowledge. As they experience the world, they take in new information and either absorb it into what they already know (**assimilation**) or create a new place for it (**accommodation**), thus returning to a sense of balance (**equilibration**). In doing so, all organisms "figure out" what the world is all about and then work toward surviving in that world. Piaget believed children learn best when they are actually doing the work (or play) themselves, rather than being told, shown, or explained to, which were the dominant teaching methods of the day. Having studied Montessori methods, Piaget concluded that teachers could prepare a stimulating environment and also interact with the children to enhance their thinking.

Regardless of their age, all people develop **schemas**, or mental concepts, as a general way of thinking about, or interacting with, ideas and objects in the environment. Very young children learn perceptual schemas as they taste and feel; preschool children use language and pretend play to create their understanding; older children develop more abstract ones, such as morality schemas that help them determine how to act.

Throughout, we use three basic processes to think: these are known as the adaptive processes of assimilation and accommodation and the balancing process of equilibration. Figure 4-7 demonstrates how these work.

Piaget theorized that thinking develops in a certain general pattern in all human beings. These stages of thinking are the psychological structures that go along with adapting to the environment. Piaget identified four major stages of cognitive development:

Sensorimotor stage	0 to 2 years
Preoperational stage	2 to 6 or 7 years
Concrete operational stage	6 to 12 years
Formal operational stage	12 years to adulthood

Each person of normal intelligence will go through these stages in this order, although the rate will change depending on the individual and his or her experiences. Each stage of development has critical lessons for the child to learn in order to think and make sense of the world. Figures 4-8 and 4-9 illustrate key experiences at each stage of cognitive development in the early years. Piaget's work has been a major influence in early childhood programs for 40 years.[1]

---

 1 Piaget's stages have been validated in cross-cultural studies (Dasen & Heron, 1981; Mali & Howe, 1980; Voyat, 1982).

Piaget's Adaptive Process

Assimilation: Taking new information and organizing it in such a way that it fits with what the person already knows.

Example: Juanita sees an airplane while walking outside with her father. She knows that birds fly. So, never having seen this flying thing before, she calls it a "bird (pájaro)." This is what we call *assimilation*. She is taking in this new information and making it fit into what she already knows. Children assimilate what they are taught into their own worlds when they play. This happens when children play "taking turns" or "school" and "house" with their dolls and toy figures. Another way to see assimilation at work is during carpentry, as children hammer and nail triangles and squares after being shown shape books and puzzles by their teacher.

Accommodation: Taking new information and changing what is already thought to fit the new information.

Example: Aaron is at the grocery store with his mother and newborn baby. He calls the woman in the line ahead of them "pregnant" although she is simply overweight. After being corrected, he asks the next person he sees, "Are you pregnant or just fat?" This is what we call *accommodation*. Having learned that not all people with large bellies are pregnant, he changes his knowledge base to include new information. Children accommodate to the world as they are taught to use a spoon, the toilet, a computer.

Equilibration: A mental process to achieve a mental balance, whereby a person takes new information and continually attempts to make sense of the experiences and perceptions.

Example: Colby, age seven, gets two glasses from the cupboard for his friend Ajit and himself. After putting apple juice into his short, wide glass he decides he'd rather have milk, so he pours it into Ajit's tall, thin glass. "Look, now I have more than you!" says his friend. This puzzles Colby, who is distressed (in "disequilibrium"): How could it be more when he just poured it out of his glass? He thinks about the inconsistency (and pours the juice several times back and forth) and begins to get the notion that pouring liquid into different containers does not change the amount (the conservation liquids). "No, it isn't," he says, "it's just a different shape!" Thus, Colby learns to make sense of it in a new way and achieve equilibrium in his thinking. Children do this whenever they get new information that asks them to change the actual schemas, making new ones to fit new experiences.

FIGURE 4-7 In Piagetian theory, the processes of assimilation, accommodation, and equilibration are basic to how all people organize their thoughts and, therefore, to all cognitive development.

Piaget's theories revolutionized our thinking about children's thinking and challenged psychologists and educators to focus less on *what* children know than the *ways* they come to know (see Figures 4-8 and 4-9). But was Piaget right? Researchers have been exploring and debating the ideas of cognitive theory for many years, often engaging in what Piaget himself called "the American question"; can you speed up the rate in which children pass through these intellectual stages of development?

Now, developmental psychologists believe that Piaget's theory of distinct stages is not correct, but the idea of a sequence in thinking is. Furthermore, current research on the brain supports Piagetian theory. Brain maturation, as reflected in **myelination**, a process that speeds transmission of nerve impulses between neurons, seems to follow a sequence that parallels the various thinking stages of development. Figure 4-10 illustrates some of the research results from an outstanding cognitive psychologists, Dr. John Flavell. Brain-based research and

its implications for early childhood teachers are discussed at the end of this chapter.

What we do know is that children progress from one stage to the next, changing their thinking depending on their level of maturation and experience with the environment. Certain physical skills, such as fine-motor coordination, determine how much a child is capable of doing. Certain environmental factors, such as the kinds of experiences the world and adults provide, influence the rate of growth. Yet throughout the process, children take in new knowledge and decide how it fits with what they already know. As new information comes in, the child learns and grows.

Constructivist Theory

For more than a century there has been regular debate about how children learn and concerning the best methods of teaching. Traditional methods of teaching, particularly for school-age children, are based on behaviorist views of

Stage	Age	What Happens
Sensorimotor	Birth to 18 months to 2 years	Intial use in inherent reflexes (sucking, crying) at birth. Out of sight, out of mind, at the beginning; object permanence is learned by experience by around one year. Movements from accidental and random to more deliberate and intentional—throughout stage. Learn to coordinate perceptual and motor functions (such as seeing object and then grabbing it). Learns relationship between means and ends (pushes aside barrier to get a toy). Beginning forms of symbolic behavior (opens and closes mouth when doing same to a jar).
Preoperational	2 to 6 or 7 years	Gradual acquisition of language (new words, such as "yummed it up," or "my ponytail was keeping me in bothers"). Symbolic (play doll as baby, stick as sword). Egocentric (not aware of another point of view, only one's own). Physical characteristics, such as size, judged by appearance only (a ball of play dough looks bigger when made into a long roll, so therefore it is bigger). "Conservation" develops slowly; ability to reserve operations is not understood (the milk cannot be visualized as being poured back into the first glass). Inability to think of the whole and its parts at the same time (given a set of blue and red wooden beads, the child will say that the blue beads will make a longer necklace than the wooden ones).
Concrete operational	6 to 12 years	Begins to "conserve" (can see that quantity, size, length and volume remain the same no matter how they are arranged). Can handle several ideas at the same time (given an array of objects of various colors and shapes, can find all the "red, square, small ones"). Starts to remove contradictions (can understand and follow rules and make up own). Can understand other points of view, although needs to be in real situations, rather than abstract ones.

FIGURE 4-8 In their early childhood, children will pass through the sensorimotor and preoperational stages and enter the stage of concrete operations.

What do YOU Think?

There are two main criticisms of Piaget's theory: the age and the stage.

1. *The Age:* He seems to have been wrong about just how early many cognitive skills develop. For example, virtually all the achievements of the concrete operational period are present in at least rudimentary or fragmentary form in the preschool years. This might simply mean that Piaget just had the ages wrong—that the concrete operations stage really begins at age three or four.

2. *The Stage:* Research on expertise now shows that specific knowledge makes a huge difference. Children and adults who know a lot about some subject or some set of materials (dinosaurs, baseball cards, mathematics, or whatever) not only categorize information in that topic area in more complex and hierarchical ways; they are also better at remembering new information on that topic and better at applying more advanced forms of logic to material in that area.

3. So, was Piaget right? And about what?

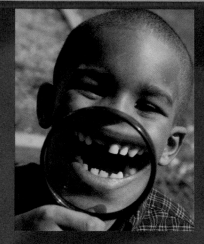

As a baby

Sensorimotor Period

Key concept

Object permanence

Definition

—the understanding that
   objects continue to exist even
   when they are out of sight.
—essential to understanding
   the physical world.

Explanation

—birth to four months, infants
   respond to objects, but stop
   tracking them if they are covered.
—four to eight months, infants
   will reach for an object if it is
   partially covered.
—by eight to twelve months,
   infants will search for hidden
   objects randomly, anywhere.
—by 12 to 18 months, toddlers
   will search for an object where
   they last saw it.
—by 18 to 24 months, toddlers
   will search for hidden objects
   in systematic way.

As a preschooler

Preoperational

Key concept

Symbolic play and language

Definition

—the use of ideas, images, sounds,
   or symbols to stand for objects and
   events = symbolic play.
—the use of an abstract, rule-
   governed system of symbols that
   can be combined to communicate
   information = language.
—essential to developing the
   capacity to think.

Explanation

—from 14 to 19 months,
   representational ability emerges.
—by 24 months, most can use
   substitute objects in pretend play.
—nine to twelve months, infants
   begin to use conventional social
   gestures.
—around one year, first words
   emerge.
—18 to 24 months, first sentences
   appear.

As a primary child

Concrete Operational

Key concept

Reasoning

Definition

—actions can be carried out mentally.
—logical reasoning replaces
   intuitive thinking in concrete
   situations.
—classification skills develop.
—essential to ability to think
   logically.

Explanation

—can coordinate several
   characteristics rather than a
   single property.
—reversibility emerges; can see
   the same problem from several
   perspectives.
—can divide things into sets and
   reason about their relationships.
—conservation skills emerge; an
   amount of liquid remains the same,
   no matter the container.

FIGURE 4-9 In cognitive theory, children's thinking develops in stages, with critical learning occurring at each stage (see Chapters 12 and 13). The formal period is not a part of early childhood.

learning. Articulated by Thorndike and Skinner (see the behaviorist section in this chapter), these methods emphasize learning by association and in a stimulus–response manner. With this **transmission model** of teaching, the teacher possesses the knowledge and transmits it directly to the children.

In contrast, a method called **constructivism** has emerged. Based on ideas from Dewey and Piaget and supported by sociocultural theory,

FIGURE 4-10 Children have different ways in which they mentally represent the same things. The older child recognizes that, although the contents of the box are only one thing out in the world, they can be represented in people's heads in more than one way—a possibility that escapes the younger child. (Special thanks to John Flavell for the example and the research. Reprinted by permission of John Flavell.)

this **transactional model** of teaching actively engages a child in tasks designed to create personal meaning. Learning is an active process, based on the belief that knowledge is constructed by the learner rather than transferred from the teacher to the child.

"Constructivism is a theory of learning which states that individuals learn through adaptation. What they learn or adapt to is directly influenced by the people, materials and situations with which they come into contact" (Meade-Roberts & Spitz, 1998). People build on preexisting knowledge, be it intellectual, social, or moral. One of its basic tenets is that "knowledge is subjective; that is, everyone creates his own meaning of any particular experience, including what he hears or reads" (Heuwinkel, 1996). Another fundamental idea is that children learn by taking new ideas and integrating them into their existing knowledge base. This is exactly in line with Piaget's processes of assimilation and accommodation.

The teacher's role is to build an environment that is stimulating and conducive to the process of constructing meaning and knowledge. The preprimary schools of Reggio Emilia (see Chapters 2, 9, 10, 14) encourage children to create their own material representations of their understanding by using many types of media (drawing, sculpture, stories, puppets, paper). At kindergarten and school-age levels, learning literacy and mathematics is considered a developmental process that the teacher "facilitates by providing modeling, authentic experiences, mini-lessons on specific topics and frequent opportunities for students to consult with and learn from each other" (Heuwinkel, 1996). Many constructivist classrooms work on creating community through rule-creating; in fact, those teachers would tell us that "the only way to help students become ethical people, as opposed to people who merely do what they are told, is to have them construct moral meaning" (Kohn, 1993).

Constructivist classrooms look diverse because the style and cultures of the teacher and children will prevail. Furthermore, a constructivist class is often noisy. Children will have choices and make decisions on significant parts of their learning. There may be more "arguments" about how children are to play and build, with children leading discussions and many participating in solutions. The teacher is a facilitator and does less talking while the learners do more, and provides more guidance and written observations rather than enforcing rules or giving tests.

Although there may still be some direct instruction and demonstrations as there are in classes based on behaviorist views, a constructivist program has fundamental differences about teaching and learning, about how children learn best, who and how they should be taught, and who has the answers. Constructivist classrooms may do a better job promoting children's social, cognitive, and moral development than do more teacher-centered programs (DeVries & Kohlberg, 1990). It is a theory used extensively in "emerging curriculum" programs (see Chapters 10–14).

Applying Cognitive Theory to Work with Children

What can teachers learn from the complicated cognitive theory? Piaget's writings do not apply directly to classroom methods or subject matter per se, and therefore careful interpretation is required. In fact, he never claimed to be an educator. However, Piaget's theories provide a framework, or philosophy, about children's thinking. Piagetian theory has some implications for both environment and interactions.

Materials

Children need many objects to explore, so that they can later incorporate these into their symbolic thinking. Such materials need to be balanced among open-ended ones (such as sand and water activities, basic art and construction materials), guided ones (cooking with recipes, conducting experiments, classification and seriated materials), and self-correcting ones (puzzles, matching games, such as some of the Montessori materials). It is important to remember that young children need to be involved with concrete objects and to explore and use them in their own ways, which include both sensorimotor and beginning symbolic play.

Scheduling

Children need lots of time to explore their own reality, especially through the use of play. A Piagetian classroom would have large periods of time for children to "act out" their own ideas. Also, time should be scheduled for imitation of adult-given ideas (songs, fingerplays, and stories).

Teachers

Children need teachers who understand and agree with a developmental point of view. The teacher who knows the stages and levels of thinking of the children will be one who can guide that class into new and challenging opportunities to learn and grow.

What are the implications for early childhood teachers and parents? In working with children under age five, we must remember that, because they do not understand mental representations very well, they will have trouble recognizing that another person may view or interpret things differently than they do. This **egocentric** viewpoint is both natural and normal but must be factored into teachers' thoughts as they work with children. For instance, you may be able to ask a six- or seven-year-old "How would you feel if you were in that situation?" For a younger child the question is incomprehensible. For the same reason, the younger child may have trouble distinguishing how things seem or appear from how they really are. As Flavell puts it,

> For them, if something seems dangerous (the menacing-looking shadow in their unlit bedroom), it is dangerous, and if it seems nondangerous (the friendly acting stranger) it is nondangerous. We often think of young children as naive, credulous, gullible, trusting, and the like. Their inadequate understanding that things may not be as they appear might be partly responsible for this impression. (Flavell, Green, & Flavell, 1989)

To encourage thinking and learning, teachers should refrain from telling children exactly how to solve a problem. Rather, the teacher should ask questions that encourage children to observe and pay attention to their own ideas. Teachers should:

- Use or create situations that are personally meaningful to children.
- Provide opportunities for them to make decisions.
- Provide opportunities for them to exchange viewpoints with their peers.

Awareness

Perhaps more important is the awareness on the part of all adults that all children have the capability to reason and be thinkers if they are given appropriate materials for their stage of development. Teachers must remember that young children:

1. Think differently from adults.
2. Need many materials to explore and describe.

3. Think in a concrete manner and often cannot think out things in their heads.

4. Come to conclusions and decisions based on what they see, rather than on what is sensible and adult-logical.

5. Need challenging questions and the time to make their own decisions and find their own answers.

The thoughts and ideas of Jean Piaget are impressive, both in quantity and quality. The collective works of this man are extremely complex, often difficult to understand. Yet they have given us a valuable blueprint. Clearly, Jean Piaget has provided unique and important insights into the development of intelligence and children.

> It is Piaget's genius for empathy with children, together with true intellectual genius, that has made him the outstanding child psychologist in the world today and one destined to stand beside Freud with respect to his contributions to psychology, education, and related disciplines. Just as Freud's discoveries of unconscious motivation, infantile sexuality, and the stages of psychosexual growth changed our ways of thinking about human personality, so Piaget's discoveries of children's implicit philosophies, the construction of reality by the infant, and the stages of mental development have altered our ways of thinking about human intelligence. (Elkind, 1977)

SOCIOCULTURAL THEORY

In the last decade, many American early educators have turned their attention to another theorist. Because of the interest in the programs at Reggio Emilia, Italy, we now look closer at the works of Vygotsky. His sociocultural theory focuses on the child as a whole and incorporates ideas of culture and values into child development, particularly the areas of language and self-identity. In his view, children's development was more than just a response to personal experience. Rather, children are influenced in fundamental ways by their family, community, and socioeconomic status. Vygotsky also emphasized the deep role of culture in learning. This theoretical framework and the ecological theory [the next section] have shifted mainstream thinking to encompass more than a child's individual experiences. Work by Janice Hale (see Chapter 3)

has identified and applied sociocultural theory to the development of the African American child. Ramirez and Castaneda (1974) have identified particular cognitive and language patterns among young children in selected Hispanic populations. In both cases, these patterns are linked to family and cultural styles of relating and problem solving.

Lev Vygotsky

Born in 1896 in Byelorussia, Lev Vygotsky graduated from Moscow University with a degree in literature in 1917. For the next six years he taught literature and psychology and directed adult theater as well as founding a literary journal. In 1924 he began work at the Institute of Psychology in Moscow, where he focused on the problems of educational practice, particularly those of handicapped children. Toward that end, he gathered a group of young scientists during the late 1920s and early 1930s to look more closely at psychology and mental abnormality, including medical connections. Unfortunately, his career was cut short by tuberculosis; he died in 1934 at age 38. Yet in that short time, he studied the works of Freud, Piaget, and Montessori. His theory is also rooted in experimental psychology, the American philosopher William James, and contemporaries Pavlov and Watson (see the behaviorist theory section of this chapter).

Vygotsky's Sociocultural Theory

Vygotsky's work is called **sociocultural** because it focuses on how values, beliefs, skills and traditions are transmitted to the next generation. Like Erikson, Vygotsky believed in the connection between culture and development, particularly the interpersonal connection between the child and other important people. Like Maslow (see later in this chapter), he considered the child as a whole, taking a humanistic, more qualitative approach to studying children. And though he understood the primary behaviorists of his day, he differed from them in that he emphasized family, social interaction, and play as primary influences in children's lives, rather than the stimulus–response and schedules of reinforcement that were becoming so popular in his day.

Vygotsky believed that the child is embedded in the family and culture of his community and that much of a child's development is culturally specific. Rather than moving through certain stages or sequences (as Piaget proposed), children's mastery and interaction differ from culture to culture.[1] Adults, Vygotsky noted, teach socially valued skills at a very early age; children's learning is, therefore, quite influenced by what their social world values.

Like Piaget, Vygotsky asserted that much of children's learning takes place during play. This is because language and development build upon each other, and the best way to develop competency is through interaction with others in a special way. According to Vygotsky, children learn through guided participation with others, especially in a kind of apprenticeship whereby a tutor supports the novice not only by instruction but also by doing.

Social interactions between a teacher and a learner not only impart skills but they also give the learner the context and the cultural values of that skill, and they teach relationship building and language at the same time. Engaging together matters.

When a mentor senses that the learner is ready for a new challenge—or simply wants the learner to come along—he or she draws the novice into a **zone of proximal development** (ZPD), which is the range of learning that would be beyond what the novice could learn alone but could grasp with help. For example, Sergio can ride a tricycle alone, and has hopped onto his sister's two-wheeler. Surely he will fall. But if his uncle runs alongside and helps him get balanced, he can do more. Of course, it will take many attempts, but with assistance, Sergio can increase his ZPD and eventually ride on his own.

Who can be part of a child's ZPD, sharing experiences and developing a cooperative dialogue with the child? Initially, of course, it is the family. For instance, a young girl is carried even as a toddler to the open market with her mother. There she watches and is guided toward learning how to touch cloth, smell herbs, taste food, and weigh and compare amounts. Is it any wonder she learns advanced math skills and the language of bargaining early on?

The reciprocal relationships in the child's ZPD can also include the teacher. Think about your role, for example, in helping a child in your program learn problem-solving skills in completing a puzzle, putting on mittens, or resolving a conflict. Finally, other children— older ones who have more expertise or peers who may have superior skills or simply offer help—can be part of a child's learning in this sociocultural theory. "Cooperative learning, in which small groups of peers at varying levels of competence work toward a common goal, also fosters more advanced thinking," writes Berk (2000). "In a Vygotskian classroom, learning is highly interactive and simultaneously considers where children are and what they are capable of becoming."

Effectively, then, other people create a kind of **scaffolding**, or helpful structure, to support the child in learning. Although not originally used by Vygotsky, the term helps define the most important components of tutoring. Just as a physical scaffold surrounds a building so that it might be worked on, so does the child get hints, advice, and structure in order to master a skill or activity. This can be seen in children's developing speech, in guidance, and in ordinary tasks, as learning to ride a bike. Adults can arouse interest in a task, simplify it—scaffold it—so that it is within the child's ability, and teach enthusiasm by helping the task get accomplished (Rogoff, 1990).

Sociocultural theory dictates that learning is active and constructed, as does cognitive theory. Vygotsky differs from Piaget, however, in the nature and importance of interaction. Piaget insisted that while children needed to interact with people and objects to learn, the stages of thinking were still bound by maturation. Vygotsky claimed that interaction and direct teaching were critical aspects of a child's cognitive development and that a child's level of thinking could be advanced by just such interaction.

Vygotsky believed that language, even in its earliest forms, was socially based. Rather than egocentric or immature, children's speech and language development during the years of three to seven is merged and tied to what children are thinking. During these transitions years, the child talks aloud to herself; after a while, this "self-talk" becomes internalized so that the child can act without talking aloud. Vygotsky contended that children speak to themselves for self-guidance and self-direction and that this private speech helps children think about their behavior and plan for action. With age, **private (inner) speech** (once called "egocentric speech"), which goes from out loud to whispers to lip movement, is critical to a child's self-regulation.

---

1 Vygotsky understood the importance of diversity nearly 100 years ago.

Applying Sociocultural Theory to Work with Children

Sociocultural theory has five implications for the classroom teacher.

1. *A child's family and culture need to be incorporated into a child's schooling.* Teachers must genuinely embrace (rather than give lip service) to the concept that the child's first teacher is the family. Each family may emphasize certain skills (vocabulary development, cooperation with siblings, self-care, and independence). These family and cultural practices serve as the sociocultural context for learning.[1] This is also a growing specialty in psychology, with several minority scholars at the forefront. Many teachers and researchers have observed that children of color in this society are socialized to operate in "two worlds," and thus must achieve a kind of **"bicognitive development,"** along with bicultural and bilingual skills. Such work led the way for the popular "learning styles" movement of the 1970s and 1980s. Research done with different cultural groups has reinforced the importance of looking at culture as part of the context in which the child lives and learns (see "Our Diverse World").

2. *Teacher/child relationships are key.* The teacher and learner adjust to one another; teachers use what they know about children to guide their teaching and plan their curriculum. Sociocultural theory supports both "emergent curriculum" and spontaneous, teachable moments of the anti-bias curriculum (see Chapters 9 and 10). Of course, young children need adults to help create curriculum and set an environmental stage for learning. But they also need teachers to mediate social relationships and conflicts, to ask questions and know where a child is headed. Adults help children learn by seeing the challenge, giving assistance when needed, and noticing when the task is mastered and the child is ready for a new challenge.

3. *Pay close attention to the psychological "tools" used to learn.* For example, some American children are taught to tie a string around their fingers as a memory device whereas in Russia they tie a knot in their handkerchief. Tunes can aid learning (like the alphabet song); the higher mental functions need the help of a person who knows the tools of the society to learn.

4. *Play is valuable.* It is in play that the child can practice operating the symbols and tools of the culture. Vygotsky (1978) puts it this way:

   Action in the imaginative sphere, in an imaginary situation, the creation of voluntary intentions, the formation of real-life plans and volitional motives—all appear in play and make it the highest level of preschool development. The child moves forward essentially through play activity. Only in this sense can play be considered a leading activity that determines the child's development.

   For instance, children might build a structure with blocks; the teacher encourages them to draw the building and then map the entire block corner as a village or neighborhood. The adult serves an important role as an intellectual mediator, continually shifting to another set of symbols to give children a different way of looking at the same thing.

5. *Individual differences are important.* In a Vygotskian classroom there will be activity and an awareness of individual differences.

Video VIEW Point 4-1

"The interconnection of all processes of development becomes more apparent as the school-age child becomes older."

COMPETENCY: Cognitive Development

AGE GROUP: School-age

CRITICAL THINKING QUESTIONS:

1. How could Erikson's theory of psychosocial development help with the cognitive problem of a child saying his schoolwork is too hard?

2. What does Vygotsky's theory of sociocultural development suggest the teacher do?

---

1 The whole area of racial/ethnic identity development is a growing field; works by B. D. Tatum (1995) and Stacey York (2005) are of interest here.

Plan activities that encourage assisted and cooperative learning. Observe for opportunities to increase an individual's ZPD by planning experiences for extending the upper limit. Classrooms work best with multi-aged grouping, or at least with plenty of opportunity for older "buddies" to lead and younger ones to help.

ECOLOGICAL THEORY

As with sociocultural theory, the ecological theory is based on the premise that development is greatly influenced by forces outside the child. Urie Bronfenbrenner applied a general systems theory to human development in the 1970s, as the ecology movement began in America and Europe. Development, in his view, is "a joint function of person and environment (Bronfenbrenner, 2000), and human ecosystems include both physical factors (climate, space, home, and school) and the social environment (family, culture, and the larger society).

Bronfenbrenner's model describes four systems that influence human development, nested within each other like a circle of rings. With the child at the center, these four are the settings in which a child spends a significant period of time, the relationships of those settings, the societal structures, and then the larger contexts in which these systems operate. Figure 4-11 illustrates these systems. The influences between and within these systems is critical to acknowledge: Just as in nature, activity in one part will affect all the other parts. A sudden income drop will affect the family in many ways: The parents may be preoccupied and unavailable to the child, who may then need more attention from the caregivers at school, who in turn may ask for more resources from the community for the family.

Moreover, the values of the community (the exosystem) can influence social conditions (the macrosystem) and, in turn, be influenced by the individual family or program (microsystem). For example, think of an area where several families with young children move into the neighborhood. The community priorities shift to incorporate more family interests; parents get everyone involved in creating a neighborhood playground. In doing so, the city council lobbies the state legislature to adopt more "family-friendly" political policies. The many systems in those children's worlds thus have a profound effect, both directly and indirectly, on their development. Imagine a situation in which the

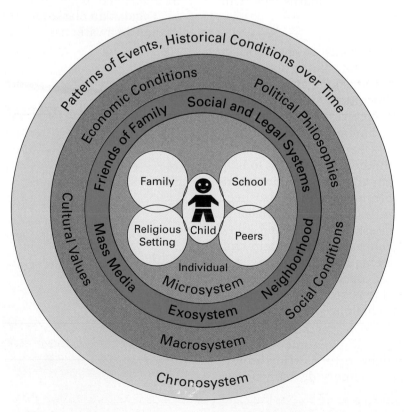

FIGURE 4-11 Ecological theory shows how many influences in a child's life can affect development.

In Vygotsky's sociocultural theory, the child's development is inseparable from social and cultural activities.

parents had very little voice in their community, or the town council was unresponsive to their needs. The playground would never have been built, the children would have little visibility in the neighborhood except to be troublesome, and the families would feel like outsiders in the community. The ecological theory surely underscores the need to have a working partnership between early childhood programs, the families they serve, and the structures children need to grow.

MULTIPLE INTELLIGENCES THEORY

Howard Gardner

Howard Gardner, a professor of human development at the Harvard Graduate School of Education, has been very influential in the ongoing debate about the nature of intelligence. Born in Pennsylvania, he earned both bachelor's and doctorate degrees at Harvard University. Influenced by the works of Piaget and Bruner, Gardner's ideas are best read in his books *Frames of Mind: The Theory of Multiple Intelligences* (1983) and *Multiple Intelligences: The Theory in Practice* (1993).

Gardner's Theory of Multiple Intelligences

The century-old argument that Gardner presents is whether intelligence is a single, broad ability (as measured by an IQ test) or is a set of specific abilities (more than one intelligence). His theory of **multiple intelligences** asserts that there is strong evidence, both from the brain-based research (see discussion in this chapter) and from the study of genius, that there are at least eight basic different intelligences.

Gardner's view of the mind (1993) claims that:

> human cognitive competence is better described in terms of sets of abilities, talents, or mental skills, which we call "intelligences." All normal individuals possess each of these skills to some extent; individuals differ in the degree of skill and the nature of their combination. . . . Multiple intelligences theory pluralizes the traditional concept.

Intelligence becomes the ability to solve a problem or to create a product that is in a culture. This is a key point that needs an explanation.

Solving a problem includes the ability to do so in a particular cultural setting or community.

Thus, the skill needed and developed depends very much on the context in which the child lives. For example, we all know now that certain parts of the brain are designated for perception, bodily movement, language, or spatial processing. Everyone who has a functional brain will be able to demonstrate some skill in these areas. But the child who has special "musical intelligence," for instance, will hear a concert and insist on a violin (as did Yehudi Menuhin).

Or the child whose culture depends on running for its daily living (as do some people of Kenya) is more likely to have children well developed in that area of intelligence. Gardner writes of Anne Sullivan, teacher of blind and deaf Helen Keller, as an example of interpersonal intelligence, for she could understand what Helen needed in a way no one else could.

Gardner's descriptions of the various intelligences are described in Figure 4-12.

How Are You Smart?

Area	Definition
Musical Intelligence	is the capacity to think in music, to be able to hear patterns, recognize, and then remember them. Certain parts of the brain help in the perception and production of music. Gardner cites as evidence of this as an intelligence the importance of music in cultures worldwide, as well as its role in Stone Age societies.
Bodily-Kinesthetic Intelligence	is the capacity to use parts or all of your body to solve a problem or make something. As bodily movements became specialized over time, it was an obvious advantage to the species. We can see this in a person's ability in sport (to play a game), in dance (to express a feeling, music or rhythm), in acting, or in making a product.
Logical-Mathematical Intelligence	is the capacity to think in a logical, often linear, pattern and to understand principles of a system. Scientists and mathematicians often think this way. Gardner asserts that there are two essential facts of the logical-mathematical intelligence. First, in the gifted individual, the process of problem-solving is often remarkably rapid, and the second is the often nonverbal nature of the intelligence (the familiar "Aha!" phenomenon).
Linguistic Intelligence	is the capacity to use language to express your thoughts, ideas, feelings, and the ability to understand other people and their words. The gift of language is universal, as evidenced by poets and writers as well as speakers and lawyers. The spoken language constant across cultures, and the development of graphic language is one of the hallmarks of human activity.
Spatial Intelligence	is the capacity to represent the world internally in spatial terms. Spatial problem-solving is required for navigation, in the use of maps, and relying on drawings to build something. Playing games such as chess and all the visual arts—painting, sculpting, drawing—use spatial intelligence, and sciences such as anatomy, architecture, and engineering emphasize this intelligence.
Interpersonal Intelligence	is the capacity to understand other people. Master players in a nursery school notice how others are playing before entering; some children seem to be born leaders; teachers, therapists, religious or political leaders, and many parents seem to have the capacity to notice distinctions among others. This intelligence can focus on contrasts in moods, temperaments, motivations, and intentions.
Intrapersonal Intelligence	is the capacity to understand yourself, knowing who you are and how you react. Intrapersonal intelligence is a knowledge of the internal aspects of one's self. These people have access to their own feeling life, a range of emotions they can draw on as a means of understanding and guiding their own behavior. Children who seem to have an innate sense of what they can and cannot do often know when they need help.
Naturalist Intelligence	is the capacity to discriminate among living things (plants, animals) as well as a sensitivity to other features of the natural world (clouds, rock configurations). This intelligence is clearly of value in our roles as hunters, gatherers, and farmers and is important to those who are botanists or chefs.

FIGURE 4-12 Gardner's multiple intelligences theory describes a new way of looking at intelligence that has serious implications for teaching.

Applying Multiple Intelligences Theory to Work with Children

Gardner's theory of multiple intelligences has had a big impact on schools, transforming curricula and teaching methods from preschool to high school (Gardner, 2000). Even Sesame Street has taken to applying the theory to developing its programs. Teachers in early childhood use the theory daily as they individualize their environments, curricula, and approaches. The child whose facility with puzzles excels that of his classmates is given a chance to try more complex ones. The children who thrive in dramatic play are offered a time to put on a puppet show for the class. The child whose mind works especially musically, or logically, or interpersonally is encouraged to develop those special gifts.

At the same time, there is no one right way to implement multiple intelligences. The theory is both culture and context specific, so that, in a similar way to a constructivist classroom, "multiple intelligence classes" would have teachers developing their own strategies, developing curricula and assessment methods based on both their own and their children's culture and priorities and on the individual children's intelligences. Chapters 12 and 13 will give examples of the multiple intelligences curriculum.

MATURATION THEORY

Arnold Gesell

As noted in Chapter 1, Arnold Gesell (Gesell, 1940) was a physician intrigued with the notion that children's internal clock seemed to govern their growth and behavior. In the 1940s and 1950s, Gesell established norms for several areas of growth and the behaviors that accompany such development.

The Gesell Institute, which fosters the work of Dr. Louise Bates Ames (1979) and others, continues to provide guidelines for how children mature from birth to puberty. The word pictures in Chapter 3 are an excellent example of the information maturational theory and research have provided.

Theory of Maturation

Maturation, by definition, is the process of physical and mental growth that is determined by heredity. The maturation sequence occurs in relatively stable and orderly ways. Maturation theory holds that much growth is genetically determined from conception. This theory differs from behaviorism, which asserts that growth is determined by environmental conditions and experiences, and cognitive theory, which states that growth and behavior are a reflection of both maturation and learning.

Maturation and growth are interrelated and occur together. Maturation describes the quality of growth; that is, while a child grows in inches and pounds, the nature (or quality) of that growth changes. Maturation is qualitative, describing the way a baby moves into walking, rather than simply the age at which the baby took the first step. Growth is *what* happens; maturation is *how* it happens.

Studies have established that the maturation sequence is the same for all children, regardless of culture, country of origin, or learning environment. But there are two vital points to remember:

- Although maturation determines the sequence of development, the precise age is *approximate*.[1] The sequence of developmental stages may be universal, but the rate at which a child moves through the stages varies tremendously.

- Growth is *uneven*. Children grow in spurts. Motor development may be slow in some stages, fast in others. For instance, a baby may gain an ounce a day for two months, then only half a pound in an entire month. Usually there is a growth spurt at puberty, with some children at 13 nearly their adult height, others not yet five feet tall. This unpredictability brings, again, much individual variation.

Applying Maturation Theory to Work with Children

Maturation theory is most useful in describing children's growth and typical behavior. In Chapter 3, these normative data are used to develop word pictures that describe common characteristics of children at different ages. Such charts will help adults understand behavior better and will keep them from expecting too much or too little. Remember that there is great individual variation and uneven growth. Be cautious in overgeneralizing from these normative charts. Gesell's initial data were focused on a narrow portion of the population and were derived from American children only. Further

 1 There are so many ways in which children differ; their maturation is one aspect of their development that is universal.

work in the last two decades has adjusted the ranges with succeeding generations of children and an ever-larger and more diverse population. Maturation theory has inspired developmental norms that help parents, teachers, and physicians alike determine whether a child's growth is *within* the normal range.

HUMANISTIC THEORY

The Humanists

As the field of psychology began to develop, various schools of thought arose. By the middle of this century, two "camps" dominated the American psychological circles. The first, known as psychodynamic, included the Freudians and is best known to us through the works of Erik Erikson. The second, called behaviorism, began with Watson and Thorndike and was later expanded by Skinner and Bandura.

In 1954, Abraham Maslow published a book that articulated another set of ideas. He called it the Third Force (or Humanistic Psychology), which focused on what motivated people to be well, successful, and mentally healthy.

This humanist theory has a place in early childhood education because it attempts to explain how people are motivated. Specifically, humanistic theory is centered on people's needs, goals, and successes. This was a change from the study of mental illness, as in psychotherapy, or the study of animal behavior, in the case of much behaviorist research. Instead, Dr. Maslow studied exceptionally mature and successful people. Others, such as Carl Rogers, Fritz Perls, Alan Watts, and Erich Fromm added to what was known about healthy personalities. The humanists developed a comprehensive theory of human behavior based on mental health. Maslow's theory of human needs is clearly a "Western" philosophy, although it is often presented as a universal set of ideas. In fact, other cultures would see life differently. An African worldview might see the good of the community as the essential goal of being fully human. Cultures with more of a "collective" orientation, rather than an emphasis on the individual or self, would see serving the family or group as the ultimate goal of humanity. Humanistic psychology can also be seen as being at odds with cultures and religions that seek ultimate reliance on a supreme deity, putting "God" rather than "self" at the top of the hierarchy.[1]

Maslow's Theory of Human Needs

Maslow's theory of **self-actualization** is a set of ideas about what people need to become and stay healthy. He asserts that every human being is motivated by a number of basic needs, regardless of age, gender, race, culture, or geographic location. According to Maslow (1954), a basic need is something:

- Whose absence breeds illness.
- Whose presence prevents illness.
- Whose restoration cures illness.
- Preferred by the deprived person over other satisfactions, under certain conditions (such as very complex, free-choice instances).
- Found to be inactive, at a low ebb, or functionally absent in the healthy person.

These needs, not to be denied, form a theory of human motivation. It is a hierarchy, or pyramid, because there is a certain way these needs are interrelated, and because the most critical needs form the foundation from which the other needs can be met.

Applying Humanistic Theory to Work with Children

The basic needs are sometimes called deficiency needs because they are critical for a person's survival, and a deficiency can cause a person to die. Until those are met, no other significant growth can take place. How well a teacher knows that a hungry child will ignore a lesson, or simply be unable to concentrate. A tired child often pushes aside learning materials and experiences until rested. The child who is deprived of basic physiologic needs may be able to think of those needs only; in fact, "such a man can fairly be said to live by bread alone" (Maslow, 1954). The humanists would strongly advocate a school breakfast or lunch program and would support regular rest and nap times in programs with long hours.

Once the physiologic needs are satisfied, the need for safety and security will emerge. Maslow points at insecure and neurotic people

---

 1 One must always question the underlying values of a theory.

Young children need materials and time to explore the world on their own.

as examples of what happens when these needs are left unfulfilled. These people act as if a disaster is about to occur, as if a spanking is on the way. Given an unpredictable home or school, a child cannot find any sense of consistency, and so is preoccupied with worrying and anxiety. Maslow would advise teachers to give freedom within limits, rather than either total neglect or permissiveness.

Growth needs can emerge when the basic needs have been met. Higher needs are dependent on those primary ones. They are what we strive for to become more satisfied and healthy people.

The need for love and belonging is often expressed directly and clearly by the young children in our care. A lack of love and sense of belonging stifles growth. To learn to give love later in life, one has to learn about love by receiving it as a child. This means learning early about the responsibilities of giving as well as receiving love.

The *need for esteem* can be divided into two categories: self-respect and esteem from others. "Self-esteem includes such needs as a desire for confidence, competence, mastery, adequacy,

achievement, independence, and freedom. Respect from others includes such concepts as prestige, recognition, acceptance, attention, status, reputation, and appreciation" (Goble, 1970).

Self-actualization is what gives a person satisfaction in life. From the desire to know and understand the world and people around us comes a renewal of self-knowledge. For the early childhood educator, these needs are expressed in the enthusiasm, curiosity, and natural "drive" to learn and try. In meeting these needs, a person finds meaning for life, an eagerness to live, and a willingness to do so. Figure 4-13 describes both basic and growth needs in detail.

Children must have their physical and basic emotional needs met before these requirements of higher cognitive learning can be fulfilled. Moreover, the child who seems stuck in a particular "needs area" will likely stay there until that basic need is satisfied. A hungry, insecure, or hurt child is a poor learner. Teachers must continually advocate better physical and social conditions for all children.

Maslow's theory has important implications for child care. Children's basic needs are

SELF-ACTUALIZATION

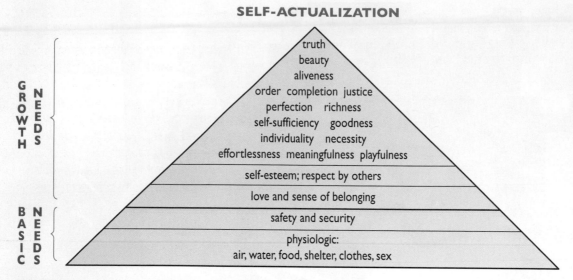

FIGURE 4-13 Abraham Maslow studied healthy personalities and theorized that what people need for growth is a hierarchy of basic and growth needs. (Adapted from Abraham Maslow, 1954.)

teachers' first concern: Teachers must ensure that children are properly clothed, fed, and rested as well as safe and secure. Only then are they ready to address curriculum and skill development.

DEVELOPMENTAL TOPICS

To complete the chapter on developmental and learning theories, we need to expand our knowledge of child development to include several important topics. The teacher well versed in these developmental topics will be able to make better decisions concerning classrooms and curricula. Moreover, they will be able to connect with families around those points and those people most important to them: the children.

Ethnicity and Cultural Diversity

"Human nature is a cultural process. As a biological species, humans are defined in terms of our cultural participation. We are prepared by both our cultural and biological heritage to use language and other cultural tools, and to learn from each other" (Rogoff, 2003). Development can be fully understood only when it is viewed in the larger cultural context. We can readily see the importance of culture in child rearing and family interaction, yet we often overlook its effect on education. We must know about children in their own setting, their own context, to understand them well enough to teach

them. The ecology of a child's life must be acknowledged and brought into our work. These international examples show the influence of cultural orientation (Rodd, 1996):

> The primary curricular emphasis in England is upon children's social development until age three, after which academic competence is emphasized. Swedish educators focus on developmental issues, particularly socio-emotional development. . . . In Asian countries where children's physical well-being and primary health care have improved to the point where they are no longer issues, the focus is upon academic achievement and excellence. While academic achievement is not stressed in the Czech Republic, young children are taught the value and importance of work and aesthetics, and they participate in cultural programs by the time they are three.

Let us turn to the United States. "[I]nterpersonal episodes [are] absolutely saturated with cultural assumptions about the right way to think, feel and behave. And there are some real cultural differences about how to be a good parent and how to be a good child," states Stanford University's Hazel Markus (2005).

- A mom leaned over a stroller, handed a silent three-year-old a juice drink and announced "It's hot. You must be thirsty."
- A seven-year-old ran up to his mother and grandmother and tried to get the younger woman's attention. She said, "I don't care how excited you are—don't interrupt your grandmother when she's speaking."

● A dad, sounding exasperated, told his 18-month-son, "Okay, now, you have a choice: either you wear this hat or we put on sunscreen. Which do you want?" The child replied, "I want juice."

These conversations reflect values—middle-class Euro-American, Latino, or East Asian. Ethnicity and cultural identity clearly play an important role in child development. Culturally competent teachers understand different patterns of ideas and practices. One important issue for teachers is the fact that "large numbers of children are members of one cultural group while being taught or cared for by members of other cultural groups. Although this need not create problems, research shows that special problems can arise in many cross-cultural teaching settings" (Hilliard & Vaughn-Scott, 1982). In fact, Lightfoot (1978) has documented four problems that tend to develop:

1. There are problems when the *language* that is spoken by the child is not understood by caregivers from another culture.

2. There are problems when caregivers have low *expectations* for children based largely on the children's membership in a low-status cultural group, rather than on the actual abilities of the children.

3. There are problems when caregivers are unprepared to deal with children whose general behavioral *style* is different from that of the caregivers.

4. There are problems when standard *testing* and *assessment* techniques are applied to certain cultural groups with insufficient recognition of, or respect for, the cultural patterns of the group.

Next, most early theories were based on observations of male or white subjects. We encourage you to read studies of development that include other ethnic populations, such as Rogoff (2003), Garcia Coll (2003, 2005), Ramirez and Castaneda (1974), Gura (1994), and York (2005).

Third, ethnic minority children have been ignored in research or viewed as variations from the norm. Often the group studied is given an ethnic label (such as Latino) that assumes the group is homogeneous and glosses over critical differences among the people in the group. Also, when ethnic groups are studied, often the focus is on children's problems (Santrock, 2001). The range of existing differences makes more research—and also more teacher interest in individual family cultures—essential.

Finally, Nakahata (Hironaka Cowee, 2001) states:

> In the critical early childhood years, children begin to develop a sense of self as families hand down beliefs, attitudes, and behaviors. Much of what is handed down is unspoken and is acquired through social interactions. In this way adults pass on their culture and shape children's understandings of themselves, their world, and their place in it. As children are forming their identity and self-worth, they often struggle with conflicting messages from home, media, school, and peers about who they are and what they are worth.

Child development and learning theories have limits. They can foster a global outlook about children in general, but these theories must be viewed in light of both cultural diversity and a respect for individuality. Certain universals hold for all children.

> There is a great deal of knowledge in Child Development of what seems to be universal and what seems to be culture specific. Let's talk about language: All children, unless there is something really wrong in their environments or in their biology, learn how to speak. What language they speak; how much they use language to communicate, how large is their vocabulary in said languages is more context specific. (Garcia Coll, 2003)

Knowing what child development information to use across cultures and what varies over

Video VIEW PoinT 4-2

"Child care providers are dependent upon regular communication with parents in order to care adequately for infants and toddlers."

COMPETENCY: Family Interactions, School and Community

AGE GROUP: Infants and Toddlers

CRITICAL THINKING QUESTIONS:

1. What strategies might be used to communicate with parents if the family's language differs from that of the teachers?

2. How can child care providers deal with potential differences in values of families from many cultures?

All children are affected by the socializing experiences they have early in life.

cultures helps teachers apply theories (see Figure 4-14). Chapter 3 helps you identify these universals. While reading all these theories, try to look beyond any one model, and define a set of principles that are fundamental to good practice and that can incorporate varied cultural patterns and values.

Attachment

Attachment is a term used particularly in the works of John Bowlby and Mary Ainsworth, and a concept used in Burton White's descriptive work and Magda Gerber's Resources for Infant Educarers (RIE) programs for infants and toddlers. Attachment is the emotional connection, an "affectional tie that one person or animal forms between himself and another specific one—a tie that binds them together in space and endures over time" (Ainsworth, 1979). The child or adult who is attached to another uses that person as a "safe base" from which to venture out into the world, a source of comfort when distressed or stressed, and a support for encouragement. Attachment behaviors are anything that allows a person to get and stay attached, such as smiling, eye contact, talking, touching, even clinging and crying.

Children: All, Some, One

All children are alike . . .

- have the same needs and rights
- go through the same developmental stages
- have the same developmental goals

Some children are alike . . .

- similar cultural and social expectations will create commonalities
- rate of vocabulary increase is similar within groups with priority of language expression
- children show similar helping behaviors from families who value harmony

Each child is unique . . .

- genetic makeup
- temperament
- sensory sensitivity
- interests
- motivation

FIGURE 4-14 Caldwell (1983) offers examples for teachers to make child development theories useful without overgeneralizing.

"It is an essential part of the ground plan of the human species—as well as that of many other species—for an infant to become attached to a mother figure. This figure need not be the natural mother but can be anyone who plays the role of the principal caregiver" (Ainsworth, 1979). Freud believed infants became attached to those who fed them. Erikson asserted that the first year of life was critical for attachment, in the stage of trust versus mistrust.

Research does show that human and animal babies do indeed send signals to their mothers very early on. Infants begin the social smile at six weeks and positive reactions to familiar people by three months. The human infant's early signals include crying and gazing, both of which are powerful to adults, and a kind of rhythmic sucking that appears to keep the mother engaged. Soon after appears the synchrony, a coordinated interaction between an infant and caring adult, that connects the two. Becoming more frequent and elaborate as time goes on, it helps the infant express their feelings and the sensitive adult to respond.

Developmentally, children develop an initial bond, then proceed to develop real mutuality—that is, to learn and practice almost a "dance" between themselves and their favored loved one. Ainsworth found that, although virtually all infants develop attachments, including to multiple caregivers, they differ in how secure they are in those attachments. Furthermore, attachment can be measured in the infant and toddler, as seen in children's response to a stranger both in and out of the parent's presence (see Figure 4-15).

Not all developmental psychologists believe that attachment is so important to later competence and identity. Kagan (1987) believes infants are resilient and that children can grow

	Exploratory Behavior Before Separation	Behavior During Separation	Reunion Behavior	Behavior with Stranger
Secure	Separates to explore toys; shares play with mother; friendly toward stranger when mother is present, touches "home base" periodically.	May cry; play is subdued for a while; usually recovers and is able to play.	If distressed during separation, contact ends distress; if not distressed, greets mother warmly; initiates interaction.	Somewhat friendly; may play with stranger after initial distress reaction.
Anxious/ambivalent (resistant)	Has difficulty separating to explore toys even when mother is present; wary of novel situations and people; stays close to mother and away from stranger.	Very distressed; hysterical crying does not quickly diminish.	Seeks comfort and rejects it, continues to cry or fuss; may be passive—no greeting made.	Wary of stranger; rejects stranger's offers to play.
Anxious/avoidant	Readily separates to explore toys; does not share play with parent; shows little preference for parent versus stranger.	Does not show distress; continues to play; interacts with the stranger.	Ignores mother—turns or moves away; avoidance is more extreme at the second reunion.	No avoidance of stranger.

SOURCE: Compiled from Ainsworth, M. D. S., & Wittig, B. A. (1969). "Attachment and Exploratory Behavior of One-Year-Olds in a Strange Situation." In B. M. Foss (Ed.), *Determinants of Infant Behavior* (Vol. 4) London: Methuen.

FIGURE 4-15 Patterns of attachment in 12- to 18-month olds in Ainsworth's "Strange Situation" show how critical the interpersonal environment is for young children. (From *Understanding Children*, by Judith Schickendanz, © 1993 by Mayfield Publishing Company. Reprinted with permission of McGraw-Hill Companies.)

Learning through play.

positively within wide variations of parenting. Researchers have found cultural variations in attachment. German babies are more likely than American babies to be categorized as avoidant, but this might be because the culture encourages early independence. Japanese babies are more likely to be seen as avoidant, but this could also be a factor of the method used to record it, which calls for children to be left in a room without the mother, a situation that rarely occurs for most Japanese infants.

Another criticism of attachment theory is that it ignores the context and diversity of how children are socialized, and by whom. "I believe that European Americans are obsessed with attachment because we hold our babies less than almost any other cultural group in the world," writes a colleague (Saxton, 2001). "Attachment does not seem to be an issue, much less a concept, in cultures in which children are carried, held, or sleep with their parents for the better part of the first three years." Attachment to a primary caregiver is another example of the dual nature of development: "Unless something is really wrong in their environment or their biology, all children get attached to a primary caregiver. In most cases it is the mother, but cultures differ in if it is the father, or it is multiple caregivers, grandparents, etc., who is part of the daily life of the child (Garcia Coll, 2005).

Play: the essence of childhood.

Researchers have found that a majority of American infants tested in the stranger situation demonstrated secure attachment. Still, when attachment fails, children are placed at tremendous risk. Failure of attachment can come from:

- parents who did not have secure attachments as children
- neglectful conditions, such as depression, abject poverty
- abusive parents that discourage bonding
- premature infants with underdeveloped systems
- blind infants who cannot engage in gazing

Intervention can help unattached persons learn the skills to connect, teaching specific interactive techniques with ongoing supports such as crisis hotlines and personal counseling.

Also, parents and researchers have asked careful questions about full-day child care, particularly for infants, wondering if such care undermines children's attachment to their parents. The debate has spurred research into both parent–child attachment and child care programs. Whether concerns about infant child care prove valid or not, as of this date we can conclude that children are not at any higher risk in high-quality child care. This highlights the need for such programs, as will be addressed further in Chapters 9 and 15.

Learning through Play

Play! What a wonderful word! It calls up images from the past, those childhood years when playing was the focus of our waking hours. "Will you play with me?" is one of the most expressive, expectant questions known. It carries with it hope and anticipation about a world of fun and make-believe, a world of adventure and exploration, a world of the young child.

City streets, parks and fields, tenements, huts, empty rooms, and backyards are all settings for play. Play is a way of life for children; it is their natural response. It is what children do and it is serious business to them. Any activity children choose to engage in is play; it is never ending.

Play is the essence of creativity in children throughout the world. Play is universal and knows "no national or cultural boundaries" (Frost & Sunderlin, 1985).[1] Educators and psychologists have called play a reflection of the

child's growth, the essence of the child's life, a window into the child's world. It is a self-satisfying activity through which children gain control and come to understand life. Play teaches children about themselves; they learn how tall—or short—they are, what words to use to get a turn on the swing, and where to put their hands when climbing a ladder. Through play, children learn about the world: what the color purple is, how to make matzoh balls, and how to be a friend. Play helps children define who they are.

Play takes many forms. Children play when they sing, dig in the mud, build a block tower, or dress up. Play can be purely physical (running, climbing, ball throwing) or highly intellectual (solving an intricate puzzle, remembering the words to a song). Play is creative when crayons, clay, and fingerpaint are used. Its emotional form is expressed when children pretend to be mommies, daddies, or babies. Skipping rope with a friend, playing jacks, and sharing a book are examples of the social side of play.

Types of Play

There is a general sequence to the development of social play. Babies and toddlers have a clearly defined social self. Infant play begins with patterns established at birth: babies gaze, smile, and make sociable sounds in response to the quality and frequency of attention from a parent or caregiver. Socialization of infants occurs through interaction. By the end of their first year, infants smile at and touch one another and vocalize in a sociable effort (Berk, 1996). Toddlers play well on their own (*solitary play*) or with adults. They begin solitary pretend play around 1 year of age. They still watch others (*onlooker*). During the toddler years, as children become more aware of one another, they begin to play side by side, without interacting (*parallel play*). They are aware of and pleased about, but not directly involved with the other person. It is during this second year that toddlers begin some form of *coordinated play*, doing something with another child. This is similar to the preschooler's associative play. The preschool years bring many changes for children in relation to social development. The number and quality of relationships outside the home increase as does the ability to play with other children. At first, this is accomplished just by a

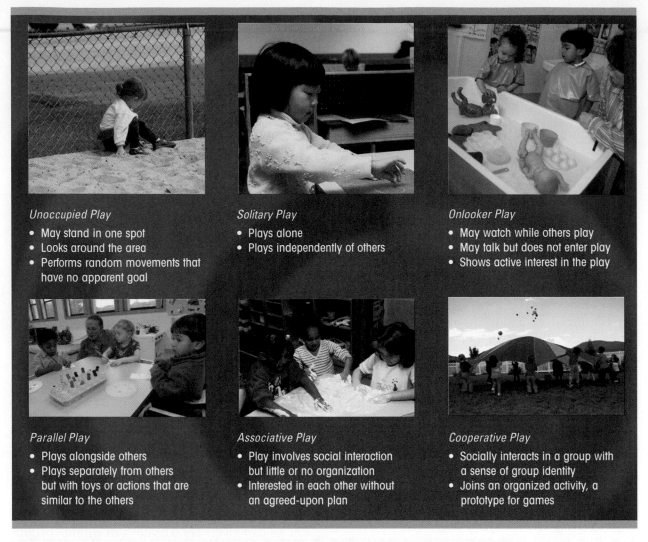

Unoccupied Play
- May stand in one spot
- Looks around the area
- Performs random movements that have no apparent goal

Solitary Play
- Plays alone
- Plays independently of others

Onlooker Play
- May watch while others play
- May talk but does not enter play
- Shows active interest in the play

Parallel Play
- Plays alongside others
- Plays separately from others but with toys or actions that are similar to the others

Associative Play
- Play involves social interaction but little or no organization
- Interested in each other without an agreed-upon plan

Cooperative Play
- Socially interacts in a group with a sense of group identity
- Joins an organized activity, a prototype for games

FIGURE 4-16 Parten's play categories were developed observing free play in a nursery school.

child's presence in a group: playing at the water table with four other children or joining a circle for fingerplays (*associative play*). When children join forces with one another in an active way, when they verbalize, plan, and carry out play, group play is established (*cooperative play*). This is the most common type of peer interaction during these preschool years. Figure 4-16 shows Parten's classic 1932 study of children's play patterns, also described in Chapter 6.

Yet developmentally and culturally appropriate practice would remind us that our understanding and knowledge about play have been based on Euro-American cultural patterns.[1] The way in which we interpret children's development through play differs from culture to culture. Children's play always portrays their own social values and family ethnic practices (Hyun, 1998), and wise early childhood practitioners will incorporate this perspective into their work with children.

Most play is unstructured and happens naturally when the curriculum is designed for play. Spontaneous play is the unplanned, self-selected activity in which children freely participate. Children's natural inclinations are toward play materials and experiences that are developmentally appropriate. Therefore, when they are allowed to make choices in a free play situation, children will choose activities that express their individual interests, needs, and readiness levels.

Dramatic play—or imaginative or pretend play—is a common form of spontaneous play.

 1 Children's play is culturally grounded.

Three- and four-year-olds are at the peak of their interest in this type of activity. In dramatic play, children assume the roles of different characters, both animate and inanimate. Children identify themselves with another person or thing, playing out situations that interest or frighten them. Dramatic play reveals children's attitudes and concepts toward people and things in their environment. Much of the play is wishful thinking, pretending great strength and deeds. This is the way children cope with their smallness or lack of strength.

Two types of dramatic play are noteworthy. Dramatic play provides the means for children to work out their difficulties by themselves. By doing so, they become free to pursue other tasks and more formal learning. For all these reasons, play is invaluable for young children.

Superhero play is appealing to children because it so readily addresses their sense of helplessness and inferiority. Pretending to be Wonder Woman makes it easier to understand and accept the limitations of the real world. It helps children learn about power and friendship, allows them a way to test their physical limits and explore feelings, and answer the "big questions about the world, such as 'what is right and wrong, what is good and bad, what is fair and unfair, what is life and death, what is a boy and a girl, and what is real and fantasy'." (Hoffman, 2004)

At the same time, this kind of play gets many adults uncomfortable, since the children's play is often loud, disruptive, full of conflict and problems solved with violence. Children sometimes end up in stereotypical, repetitive play that seems to ignore other learning. Chapters 14 and 15 address how to set the stage and support superhero play in ways that foster positive growth.

Sociodramatic play happens when at least two children cooperate in dramatic play. Both types of play involve two basic elements: imitation and make-believe (Smilansky, 1990).

> Pretending to be a firefighter, Sherry grabs a piece of rope and runs toward the playhouse, saying "shhshhshshshshsh" while pretending to squirt water on the fire. She shouts to her playmates, "Over here! Come over here! The fire is on this side."

Sherry's make-believe scenario and her ability to follow the rules of behavior common to firefighters (grabbing hoses, calling for help) are the two critical factors from Vygotsky's point of view: that firefighting scene supports his theory that cognitive skills develop through social interactions. Sherry examplifies a child moving from concrete to abstract thought because she did not require realistic objects (a hose and water) but imagined them with a rope and her ability to create the sound of water. This ability to separate thoughts from actions and objects will stand Sherry in good stead when she studies math concepts. Rules that children follow in make-believe play teach them to make choices, to think and plan about what they will do, and to show a willingness toward self-restraint, as children learn to follow the social rules of pretend play.[1] This is important preparation for real-life situations. Vygotsky, more than anyone else, has made that critical connection between social and intellectual development.

Gender Differences in Play

Teachers and parents, as well as researchers, have observed that boys and girls seem to show distinct differences in their play choices, play behavior, and toy selection from an early age. In fact, gender differences are first noticeable in children around one year of age and quite obvious by the later preschool years, and are discussed later in this chapter. Although biology certainly plays a part, it would seem that parents and society exert powerful influences[2] (Frost, 1996). The toys parents and teachers choose (dolls for girls, trucks for boys), the predominance of females in early childhood settings, television shows and advertising, and toy store displays combine to communicate a very strong reinforcement of traditional sex-role expectations.

Values of Play

For the first half of the 20th century, interest in children's play focused on emotional causes and effects (Bowman, 1990). The main theme was the emotional release play provided children. Psychodynamic theory recommended play as a suitable outlet for expressing negative

---

 1 Curriculum should foster children's decision-making abilities and their social participation skills. Effective interpersonal skills are necessary for interactions across cultures, gender, and abilities.

2 Early childhood educators need to be constantly vigilant in noticing their personal gender biases, along with staying current about research in gender differences.

feelings, hostility, and aggression. Clay can be pounded, balls can be kicked and thrown, dolls can be spanked. Young children give free expression to a wide range of emotions, playing them out and releasing tension.

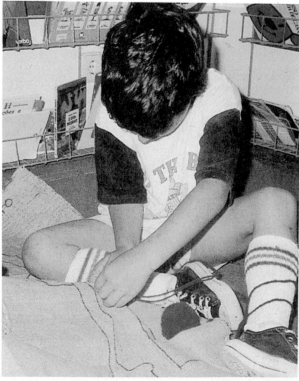

With encouragement, boys can learn to enjoy activities, such as drawing and sewing, that are often associated with girls. (Courtesy of Centro Infantil & de Reabilitacao de A-Da-Beja, Lisbon, Portugal.)

But play is more than an avenue for emotional release. Rubin, Fein, and Vandenberg (1983) cite three common factors that emerge from the many definitions of play:

● children's feelings and motivations,
● how children behave when they play, and
● the environment that supports play and where play occurs.

Why do children play? Why is play so universal to childhood experiences? One answer may be that play is intrinsically motivated; that is, it is naturally satisfying to children. Rubin and associates suggest other reasons as well:

● Play is relatively free of rules except for what children will impose themselves.
● Play is controlled and dominated by the children.
● Play is carried out as if the activity were real life.
● Play focuses on the activity—the doing—rather than on the end result or product.
● Play requires the interaction and involvement of the children.

Play promotes learning for the whole child as well. A wide range of learning opportunities is inherent in any single play activity. All play activity holds this potential for growth and learning.

Play as a Cornerstone of Learning

Outside of child development circles, there has been little appreciation in the U.S. culture for the value and importance of play for young children. "In an age of rising expectations and tougher academic standards, educators are more likely to pay attention that seem to be more closely related to school readiness" (Bodrova & Leong, 2003). Early childhood educators continually search for ways to answer, "Don't they do anything but play?" In many settings, parental pressure and teacher uncertainty have led to curricula with more table tasks and less active play periods in the daily schedule.

Jones (2000) states the case aptly: "But if children are just playing, how will they learn? Each child learns by asking his or her own next questions and trying out the answers. Often both the questions and the answers take the form of actions rather than words. Children learn by doing." In summing up, Jones adds, "In play, children are autonomous; they're independent. They make decisions, solve the problems, deal with the consequences." Early

Play is fun, and play is serious work.

childhood specialists must become adept at speaking out on the value of play and its relationship to what children learn.

Play, Work, and Learning

Play is viewed by some as the opposite of work; play does not mean learning. Play is often trivialized by sayings like "That is mere child's play" or "He is only playing" as if to say play is unimportant. (Klein, Wirth, & Linas, 2003)

To reclaim play as a special activity crucial to children's development and growth, we should look at play and work as equally important developmentally appropriate activities for young children.

Play is the cornerstone of learning, the foundation from which children venture forth to investigate, to test out. Curriculum takes on expression through play; teachers plan curriculum that uses play as the medium for learning. As they mature, children integrate and assimilate their play experiences. What started out as play—the sheer fun of it—is transformed into learning experiences. Curiosity about magnets at age five nourishes a scientific attitude for the later years, as well as a foundation for studying gravity, planetary movements, and the like. Feeling free to sing out at group time at age three can prepare a child to be an active participant in the kindergarten classroom at age six.

Teachers want children to learn about themselves, to learn about the world around them, and to learn how to solve problems. A childhood filled with play opportunities should culminate in these three types of learning.

1. *Learning about themselves* includes developing a positive self-image and a sense of competence. Children should know and feel good about themselves as learners. They should develop a sense of independence, a measure of self-discipline, and knowledge based on full use of their sensory skills.

2. *To learn about others and the world around them* means developing an awareness of other people. Teachers want children to perfect their communication and social skills so that they will be more sensitive participants in the world in which they live. This means that children learn and appreciate the values of their parents, the community, and society at large. When children become aware of the demands of living in today's society, that awareness can help them become more responsible citizens. The emphasis on social interaction and group relationships in the early childhood setting underscores this goal.

3. *To learn to solve problems,* children need to be accomplished in observation and investigation. When exploring a puzzle, for example, children need to know how to manipulate it, take it apart, and put it back together, to see how other people solve puzzles, and to know how to get help when the pieces just do not seem to fit together. They should know how to predict and experiment. What will happen, wonders a kindergartner, when a glass is placed over a glowing candle? How will that change if the glass is large or small? What is the effect if the glass is left over the candle for a long time or for a second? Young children also need to learn how to negotiate,

discuss, compromise, and stand their ground, particularly when they encounter and solve problems socially. "I want the red cart and someone already has it," thinks the preschooler. "Now what? How can I get it? What if the other person says no? Will the plan that works with my best friend work with someone else? When do I ask for help? Will crying make a difference?" To be effective problem solvers, children must know and experience themselves and others.

Gender Identity

Are girls and boys different in terms of development and learning? What are these differences, and how do they occur? What differences are caused by "nature" and which ones by "nurture"? Should we treat our girls and boys the same or differently? The realities and the myths surrounding sex differences and their effect on behavior from infancy to adulthood is the subject of interest, controversy, and research. Definitions. **Sex differences** are the biological differences between males and females; *gender differences* are culturally imposed distinctions in the roles and behaviors. While boys and girls are about the same size and shape in childhood, gender differences and adult distinctions are more significant.

There are two aspects of gender development that are particularly important in the early years: *gender identity* (the sense of being female or male, which most children acquire by three years), and gender role (the set of expectations that define how a male or female should behave, think, and feel). Gender has been important to some developmental and learning theories.

Freud asserted that behavior was directly related to reproductive processes. His stages of psychosexual development reflect the belief that gender and sexual behavior are instinctual. Erikson also claimed that anatomy was destiny: males were more intrusive because of genital structure, and females were more inclusive. He later modified his view, saying that women were overcoming their biological heritage. These identification theories come from the view that the preschool child will find the opposite-sex parent attractive but will steer away from this by identifying with the same-sex parent.

Bandura and Piaget emphasize that children learn through observation and imitation, and that through reinforcement children learn gender-appropriate behavior. Proponents of this view point to how parents encourage girls and boys to engage in certain activities and types of play. Certainly the media communicates sexist messages; this theory would claim that such stereotyping influences the development of gender roles. The work of Eleanor Maccoby (1998) and others have provided both hard data and an open forum for discussions about how people grow and the complex interaction between heredity and environment that makes child development so fascinating. By age two, children name themselves as girl or boy and can identify adult strangers as daddies or mommies. By age four, children will label toys (dolls, trucks) and some roles (soldier, nurse) appropriate for one gender and not the other (Bauer, Liebl, & Stennes, 1998).

They develop gender stability (the understanding of staying the same sex throughout life) by age four and gender constancy (a person keeps the same gender regardless of appearance) by about five or six. Sex-typed behavior begins to appear at two or three, when children tend to choose same-sex playmates and sex-typed toy preferences, and children become more selective and exclusive as they mature (Martin & Fabes, 2001).

By elementary school, the playground is like a "gender school," with children showing a clear preference for same-sex peers (Maccoby, 1998).

What are the real differences between girls and boys? Physically, males grow to be 10 percent taller than females, and girls are less likely to develop physical or mental disorders than are boys. Boys are also more active than girls. However, there are fewer differences in verbal aggression, although males do show less self-regulation than females (Eisenberg, Martin, & Fabes, 1996). There are no significant differences between girls and boys in intelligence or reasoning behavior. Some cognitive functioning and personality differences do exist, but overall the differences are small and there is no overall pattern.

To break through the restrictiveness of gender stereotyping, teachers need to pay careful attention to the messages they give children.[1] One challenge we face is the female culture of early childhood programs. Women dominate the early childhood education workforce, so

---

 1 Working with young children and their families invites early childhood educators to carefully examine their own upbringing, values, beliefs, and biases, especially about gender roles.

children are often only exposed to women's interaction styles (Wardle, 2004). If boys struggle in our programs, we must be alert to the activities and schedules we establish, behaviors we may reward or punish, the "goodness of fit" for both boys and girls in our programs. In the environments we prepare for them, the materials they use, and the examples we model, children create their own ideas and learn behavior that works for them in the world.

Moral Development

People used to assume that young children needed to be taught exactly what was "right" and "wrong" and that was enough. In the last 20 years, research has shown that moral development is a more complex process with both a cognitive and an emotional side to it. Several theorists and researchers have proposed how to think about children's moral development. Jean Piaget, Lawrence Kohlberg, Nancy Eisenberg, and Carol Gilligan are discussed here.

Piaget investigated children's moral reasoning by presenting children with pairs of stories and asking them which child was "naughtier." From this, he discovered that children under age six base their judgment on the amount of damage done, not the child's intentions. By middle childhood, children are beginning to take intent into account, so that one can begin to see a shift in moral reasoning toward the end of the early childhood period from objective judgments, based on physical results and concrete amounts, to more subjective considerations (such as the purpose of the perpetrator or psychological factors). The connections to children's cognitive stage of development is interesting, and adults might consider that a child's protests over wrongdoing ("I didn't mean to do it!") may very well signal a new level of reasoning, with the realization that one's intentions do matter.

Lawrence Kohlberg (1981) is best known as a theorist in social development, addressing educational practice and gender constancy as well. Building on Piagetian dimensions, Kohlberg's theory of moral development involves both social growth and intellectual reasoning. People move from stage to stage as a result of their own reasoning power and they see for themselves the contradictions in their own beliefs. As with Erikson and Piaget, Kohlberg's stages are hierarchical—a person moves forward one by one, and no stage can be skipped. On the basis of children's responses to moral

Moral Reasoning: Cultural Implications

Disagreement: Brahman children think it is right; American children think it is wrong:

—Hitting an errant child with a cane
—Eating with one's hands
—Father opening a son's letter

Disagreement: Brahman children think it is wrong; American children think it is right:

—Addressing one's father by his first name
—Eating beef
—Cutting one's hair and eating chicken after father's death

Agreement: Brahman and American children think it is wrong:

—Ignoring a beggar
—Destroying another's picture
—Kicking a harmless animal
—Stealing flowers

Agreement: Brahman and American children think it is right:

—Men holding hands.

FIGURE 4-17 Children's moral reasoning has a cultural aspect, as shown by comparing children in the United States and India. (From *Child Development*, 9th ed., by J. W. Santrock, © 2001 McGraw-Hill Companies. Reprinted with permission of McGraw-Hill Companies.)

dilemmas similar to those of Piaget, Kohlberg identified three levels of moral development, as illustrated in Figure 4-17. For early childhood educators, research shows that preconventional reasoning (stages 1 and 2) is dominant into elementary school.

Kohlberg's theory has been criticized for placing too much emphasis on moral thought and not enough of moral behavior. Further, many point out that his view is culturally biased and the stories asked are not applicable to all children. Western moral doctrine emphasizes individual rights; other cultures focus on a greater respect for traditional codes and practices. (See Figure 4-18 for an example of such differences.)

Most of the stories, or dilemmas, that Piaget and Kohlberg used were about stealing, lying, disobeying rules, and the like. Researcher and theorist Nancy Eisenberg (1983) has explored the kinds of reasoning children use to justify good (prosocial) behavior. She asks children what they would do in situations with a

I. Preconventional Morality

Stage 1:   Punishment and obedience orientation
            Might makes right; obey authority and avoid punishment.

Stage 2:   Individualism and relativist orientation
            Look out for number one; be nice to others so they will be nice to you.

II. Conventional Morality

Stage 3:   Mutual interpersonal expectations
            "Good girl, nice boy;" approval more important than any reward.

Stage 4:   Social system and conscience
            "Law and order;" contributing to society's good is important.

III. Postconventional Morality

Stage 5:   Social contract
            Rules are to benefit all, by mutual agreement; may be changed same way; the greatest good for the greatest number.

Stage 6:   Universal ethical principles
            Values established by individual reflection, may contradict other laws.

FIGURE 4-18 Kohlberg's Stages of Moral Development. Fairly broad cross-cultural data and extensive American research indicate a persuasive universality and a strong sequence of stage development in children's moral development.

moral dilemma. One of her stories involves a child on the way to a friend's birthday party. The child encounters someone who has fallen and is hurt. What should the child do: help the hurt child and miss cake and ice cream, or leave the child and go on to the party?

Such questions brought to light several levels of prosocial reasoning. In the early childhood years, children seem to be engaged in level 1 (*hedonistic reasoning*), in which the individual's own needs are put first. In the case mentioned earlier, the child would leave the hurt person and go to the party ("I won't help because I have to go to the party.") As children move through middle childhood, they tend to move to level 2, in which the needs of another begin to be considered and increase in importance. Answers to the story would begin to shift toward including others ("I'd help because they'd help me next time."). Eisenberg's stages roughly parallel Kohlberg's and help broaden these concepts without contradicting the fundamental arguments.

Carol Gilligan (1982) challenges Kohlberg's strong emphasis on justice and fairness and his omission of caring for others. In her book *In a Different Voice* (1982), Gilligan points out that mostly males were studied for such work, and that, because girls and boys are socialized dif-

ferently, their moral judgments will be quite different. For instance, boys may be raised with the idea that justice and fairness are the key moral basis, whereas girls may be taught that caring and responsibility to others are central.[1] Buzzelli (1992) has also worked extensively on young children's moral understanding and has applied recent research to children's development of peer relationships. Although this claim of different moral ideas based on gender differences has yet to be fully researched, it is an important thought to keep in mind, particularly when teaching and raising young children.

Moral development is often deleted from the curriculum in American schools. Yet even John Dewey called moral education the "hidden curriculum" conveyed through the atmosphere of every program. Elementary schools occasionally have some kind of teaching for "character education," or a values clarification class. Nonetheless, most caregivers will tell you that how children notice and care for each other is part of everyday experiences.

Secondly, one aspect of moral development that has been studied very little is that of children's spirituality and faith. Because of the separation of church and state in American public schools, many educators shy away from discussions of anything that might be considered

 1 These characteristics may not be *gender specific* (i.e., "only girls do this and only boys do that"), but may be *gender related* (i.e., "many girls often . . . and some boys may do the same"). What is important to remember in our diverse world is that one way is *not necessarily* better than another way, just *different*.

"religious." In doing so, educational programs also find themselves staying out of anything that helps children understand who they are and the greater questions of life and its meaning. Dr. Ruth Saxton addresses this issue in the "Insights" article at the end of the chapter.

Brain-Based Research

Some of the most exciting research discoveries in the last two decades have been in the area of brain-based research. Neuroscience research has developed sophisticated technologies, such as ultrasound, magnetic resonance imaging (MRI), position emission tomography (PET), and effective, noninvasive ways to study brain chemistry (such as the steroid hormone cortisol). Brain scans and other technologies have made it possible to investigate the intricate circuitry of the brain.

What have we learned? The brain seems to operate on a "use it or lose it" principle. At birth, one has about 100 billion brain cells and 50 trillion connections among them. With use, these cells grow branches (**dendrites**), that reach out to make connections with other cells. With impoverishments, you may lose the dendrites. By age two, most pruning of dendrites has already occurred, and the brain weighs 75 percent as much as the adult brain.

As children move from toddlers to preschool, brain functions are developed. Myelination speeds transmission of nerve impulses between neurons, which enables children to think and react faster. Fast and complex communication can now occur.

New information on brain development suggest that the system of acquiring cultural knowledge is more open in the early stages of life than later. So we know that the best time to learn a second language is before seven years of age. We know that babies lose their ability to discriminate some phonetic distinctions as a function of the language they are exposed to by twelve months of age! So culture-language, communication, social interactions are ingrained very early on. (Garcia Coll, 2003)

By age seven, the brain has grown to its adult size, and the basic areas of sensory and motor cortexes are functioning. Now is the time to add experiences that encourage the dendrites to reach out to neurons. The brain's two hemispheres are connecting, and the brain can now become more efficient in its functions. As Galinsky (1997) tells us, "the connections that have been reinforced by repeated experience tend to remain while those that are not are discarded. Thus, a child's early experiences—both positive and negative—help shape the brain, affecting to some degree how he thinks, feels, and relates to others throughout his life." Figure 4-19 summarizes these research findings.

Key Finding	Implications for Educators
1. "Human development hinges on the interplay between nature and nurture."	Remember the nature/nurture controversy described in Chapter 1 and this chapter? Think, too, about the contributions of Piaget, the constructivists, and sociocultural theorists in regard to the dynamic interplay between the environmental and learning. We now know that the brain is affected by all kinds of environmental and interactive conditions. The impact is both specific and dramatic, influencing both the general direction and the actual circuitry of the brain.
2. "Early care has a decisive and long-lasting impact on how people develop, their ability to learn, and their capacity to regulate their own emotions."	This finding confirms the work on attachment (see this chapter) and underscores the importance of warm and responsive care. It is in the daily interaction with nurturing adults that children develop the network of brain cells that help them learn to regulate and calm themselves, which actually helps the brain turn off a stress-sensitive response quickly and efficiently.
3. "The human brain has a remarkable capacity to change, but timing is crucial."	Sound familiar? Montessori's sensitive periods and Steiner's belief in a seven-year cycle of growth (see Chapter 1) both stress the notion of timing. Brain research is helping us pinpoint those periods. Experiments have proven that there are certain "windows of opportunity" for the proper development of vision and language, and studies show certain effective times in the learning of music. There are limits to the brain's ability to create itself, and researchers have found that these limitations have some time periods to them that we ought not to ignore.

FIGURE 4-19 Decades of brain-based research is summarized here from the 1996 Conference of Brain Development in Young Children, sponsored by the Families and Work Institute (Shore, 1997).

Early stress. Every environment has opportunities for interaction with a variety of objects, people, and circumstances that can stimulate brain growth. Conversely, any environment can be impoverished. This is less about toys than it is about interactions and the atmosphere. Repeated exposure to extreme **stress** kills some neurons and prevents others from developing properly (Sanchez, Ladd, & Plotsky, 2001). When the brain perceives a threat or stress, the body reacts. Stress can trigger a flood of hormones, particularly **cortisol**, that may create an overreaction. Or, as in some abused children, a blunted stress response may occur (Gunnar & Vasquez, 2001). Since brain circuits are formed especially in infancy and toddlerhood, early mistreatment can cause damage. In later childhood, the chronic threat of emotional embarrassment, social disrespect, or simply hurried, restrictive time settings can all trigger stress responses.

Applications to the classroom. Applying brain research to the early childhood classroom is a challenge. Early in life, neural connections form rapidly in the brain and tail off during adolescence—but why? Does anything we do make much of a difference, when this pattern has presumably taken place over eons of time? "Neuroscientists know very little about how learning, particularly school learning, affects the brain at the synaptic level," claims Bruer (1998). "We should be skeptical of any claims that suggest they do." Thirty years of research has shown that critical periods are quite complex. Again, Bruer: "For humans, even in an early developing system like vision, these periods can last until early childhood. For language, the critical period for learning to speak without an accent ends in early childhood, but the critical period for learning language's grammar does not end until around age 16." Moreover, the brain can reorganize itself throughout our lifetimes, so we do not yet understand what brain-based research might mean for education. For now, this framework for action gives us some general advice:

- *First, do no harm.* Let us do everything to help parents and caregivers form strong, secure attachments. At the same time, we need to provide parent education and information about what does help their children's brain and well-being to grow. Finally, we must educate ourselves so the quality of child care and early education is ensured.

- *Second, prevention is best, but when a child needs help, intervene quickly and intensively.*

The brain is a work in progress, and children can recover from serious stress. But the list of preventable conditions is clear, and it is everyone's job to work toward eliminating the unnecessary traumas.

- *Third, promote the healthy development and learning of every child.* "Risk is not destiny," reminds Shore (1997), "The medical, psychological, and educational literatures contain a sufficient number of examples of people who develop or recover significant capacities after critical periods have passed to sustain hope for every individual." Figure 4-20 gives 12 key principles for teachers in early childhood classrooms.

USING DEVELOPMENTAL AND LEARNING THEORIES

As a teacher, you must think about what you believe about children, development, and learning. This chapter gives much food for thought in this regard, and students are often overwhelmed. Two critical questions arise: (1) Why do contradictions exist among the theories, and (2) How can I decide which is the "right" one? To answer the first question, remember that each theory addresses a particular aspect of development. For instance, psychodynamic theory focuses on the development of personality, behaviorist on the conditions of learning, cognitive on how children think and learn, maturation on how development progresses, and humanist on the conditions for overall health. Each has its avid proponents with a body of research that supports it. Because every theory has its own focus and advocates, each viewpoint is rather subjective and somewhat narrow. In other words, no one theory tells us everything . . . and that is the answer to the second question. Thoughtful teachers develop their own viewpoints. Begin to decide what you believe about children, learning, and education. Try to avoid the pitfall of taking sides. Instead, integrate theory into your teaching practices by comparing the major developmental and learning theories with your own daily experiences with young children. Figure 4-21 reviews the highlights of each theory.

Most early childhood educators are eclectic in their theoretical biases. That is, they have developed their own philosophies of education based on a little of each theory. Each teacher has an obligation to develop a clear set of ideas of how children grow and learn. We are fortunate to have choices. Most educators

Principles of Brain-Based Learning

1. Each brain is unique. It develops on different timetables; normal brains can be as much as three years apart in developmental stages. We should not hold each age- or grade-level learner to the same standards.

2. Stress and threat impact the brain in many ways. They reduce capacity for understanding, meaning, and memory. They reduce higher order thinking skills. Learners are threatened by loss of approval, helplessness, lack of resources, and unmeetable deadlines.

3. Emotions run the brain. Bad ones flavor all attempts at learning. Good ones create an excitement and love of learning. More importantly, we believe something and give it meaning only when we feel strongly about it.

4. The neocortex is strongly run by patterns, not facts; we learn best with themes, patterns, and whole experiences. The patterns of information provide the understanding learners seek.

5. We learn in a multipath, simultaneous style that is visual, auditory, kinesthetic, conscious, and nonconscious. We do most poorly when we "piecemeal" learning into linear, sequential math facts and other out-of-context information lists.

6. Our memory is very poor in rote, semantic situations. It is best in contextual, episodic, event-oriented situations.

7. All learning is mind–body. Physiology states posture, and breathing affect learning. Teachers should learn how to better manage students' states as well as teach students how to manage their own states.

8. Feed the brain. Our brains are stimulated by challenge, novelty, and feedback in our learning environments. Creating more of these conditions is critical to brain growth.

9. Ritual is a way for the reptilian brain to have a productive expression. More positive and productive rituals can lower perceived stress and threat.

10. The brain is poorly designed for formal instruction. It is designed to learn what it needs to learn to survive. It can usually learn what it wants to learn. By focusing on learning, not instruction or teaching, we can allow the brain to learn more.

11. Cycles and rhythms. Our brain is designed for ups and downs, not constant attention. The terms "on" or "off task" are irrelevant to the brain.

12. Assessment. Most of what is critical to the brain and learning cannot be assessed. The best learning is often the creation of biases, themes, models, and patterns of deep understanding.

FIGURE 4-20 All early childhood teachers can benefit from the knowledge of the brain and how it works (Jensen, 1995).

agree on some basic tenets based, in part, on theories of development and learning.

1. Children's basic physiologic needs and their needs for physical and psychological safety must be met satisfactorily before they can experience and respond to "growth motives." [Maslow and brain-based research]

2. Children develop unevenly and not in a linear fashion as they grow toward psychosocial maturity and psychological well-being. A wide variety of factors in children's lives, as well as the manner in which they interpret their own experiences, will have a bearing on the pattern and rate of progress toward greater social and emotional maturity. [Erikson, Vygotsky, the behaviorists, maturationists]

3. Developmental crises that occur in the normal process of growing up may offer maximum opportunities for psychological growth, but these crises are also full of possibilities for regression or even negative adaptation. [Erikson]

4. Children strive for mastery over their own private inner worlds as well as for mastery of the world outside of them. [Erikson, Piaget]

5. The child's interactions with significant persons in his life play a major part in his development. [Erikson, the behaviorists, Vygotsky, and Maslow]

Developmental Research Conclusions

Results

Research, and the information it yields, must serve the needs of the practitioner to be useful. Teachers can combine researchers' systematic data with personal observations and experiences,

Theory	Major Theorists	Important Facts
Psychosocial	Erik Erikson	Maturational emphasis Stage theory of social and emotional development Crises at each level Teacher: Emotional base, social mediator
Behaviorist	John Watson Edward Thorndike B. F. Skinner Albert Bandura	Environmental emphasis Stimulus–response Conditioning (classical and operant) Reinforcement (positive and negative) Modeling Teacher: Arranger of environment and reinforcer of behavior
Cognitive	Jean Piaget	Maturational and environmental emphasis Assimilation and accommodation Stage theory of cognitive development Teacher: Provider of materials and time and supporter of children's unique ways of thinking
Sociocultural	Lev Vygotsky	Zone of proximal development Private speech Collaborative/assisted learning
Multiple intelligences	Howard Gardner	Many kinds of intelligence Problem-solving and product-creating
Maturation	Arnold Gesell	Emphasis on heredity Normative data Teacher: Guider of behavior based on what is typical and normal
Humanist	Abraham Maslow	Environmental emphasis Mental health model Hierarchy of human needs Teacher: Provider of basic and growth needs
Others	Mary Ainsworth John Bowlby Nancy Eisenberg Carol Gilligan Lawrence Kohlberg Eleanor Maccoby	Attachment and categories research Attachment theory Expands moral development to prosocial Questions categories of moral development Moral, cognitive, and sex-role development Sex differences research
Brain-based research	Neuroscientists	New insights into early development "Use it or lose it" principle Warm and responsive care matters

FIGURE 4-21 The major theories of and research on development and learning describe children and their growth in different ways.

including the significance of relationships, language and thinking, biologic factors, and special needs (see also Chapters 6 and 12–14). To keep in mind the real child underneath all these theories, teachers apply developmental research to their own classroom settings. Figure 4-22 consolidates what developmental research has found and how it can be put into practical use with young children.

There is so much information now about children and their development. It is easy to feel overwhelmed, and easier still to believe what we read. Santrock (2001) advises us:

- Be cautious about what is reported in the popular media.
- Don't assume that group research applies to an individual.

- Don't generalize about a small or clinical sample.
- Don't take a single study as the defining word.
- Don't accept causal conclusions from correlational studies.
- Always consider the source of the information and evaluate its credibility.

Conditions for Learning

Caring for children means providing for total growth, creating optimal conditions for learning in the best possible environment. Developmental theory helps define conditions that enhance learning and from which positive learning environments are created. Research on all theories extends the knowledge of children and learning. Coupled with practical application, both theory and research have helped all to recognize that:

1. *Learning must be real.* We teach about the children's bodies, their families, their neigborhoods, and their school. We start with who children are and expand this to include the world, in their terms. We give them the words, the ideas, the ways to question and figure things out for themselves.

2. *Learning must be rewarding.* Practice makes better, but only if it is all right to practice, to stumble and try again. We include the time to do all this by providing an atmosphere of acceptance and of immediate feedback as to what was accomplished (even what boundary was just overstepped). Also, practice can make a good experience even better, as it reminds children in their terms of what they can do.

3. *Learning must build on children's lives.* We help connect the family to the child and the teacher. We realize that children learn about culture from family and knowledgeable members of the community, such as teachers, librarians, grocers, and the like. We know important family events and help the family support happenings at school. For children, learning goes on wherever they may be, awake and asleep. Parents can learn to value learning and help it happen for their child.

4. *Learning needs a good stage.* Healthy bodies make for alert minds, so good education means caring for children's health. This includes physical health, and emotional and mental health, too. Psychological safety and well-being are theoretical terms for the insight, availability, and awareness teachers bring to their classrooms. On the lookout for each child's successes, we prevent distractions in the way furniture is arranged, how noisy it is, how many strangers are around. Mental health is both emotional and intellectual. We try to have a variety of materials and experiences, and a flexible schedule, when someone is pursuing an idea, building a project, finishing a disagreement. As long as we care for children, we will have our hands full. With the theoretical underpinnings presented here, we have the tools with which to make our own way into the world of children and of early childhood education.

SUMMARY

Developmental and learning theories form the cornerstone of our knowledge about children. What we know about how children grow, learn, and adapt to the world around them is critical in our quest for understanding.

Our field is greater for the contributions of several schools of study. Freud reminds us of the importance of early experiences. Erikson's theory of psychosocial development gives us insight into children's feelings and how their emotional and social lives affect their learning. The behaviorists, a distinctively American group of psychologists, demonstrate how much we can learn of human affairs by applying the methods of science. Piaget, a "giant in the nursery school" (Elkind, 1977), opens our eyes to a stage theory of growth and shows us how active children are in their own learning. Vygotsky reminds us of how values, beliefs, skills, and traditions are transmitted to the next generation within a "zone of proximal development" based on relationships with other people. The ecological theory is very useful in highlighting the complex influences on children's development. Gardner suggests multiple kinds of intelligence, rather than seeing the mind as a static "black box" or empty vessel. Gesell offers us developmental norms. Maslow, a humanistic psychologist, establishes a hierarchy of needs, reminding us that the basic physical and psychological needs must be met before higher learning can take place. The developmental topic of ethnicity and culture reverberates through the study of attachment, play, gender differences, and moral development. The brain-based research opens doors to new vistas of possibility and better teaching and learning.

Developmental Research Tells Us	Teachers Can
1. Growth occurs in a sequence.	Think about the steps children will take when planning projects. Know the sequence of growth in their children's age group.
2. Children in any age group will behave similarly in certain ways.	Plan for activities in relation to age range of children. Know the characteristics of their children's age group.
3. Children grow through certain stages.	Know the stages of growth in their class. Identify to family any behavior inconsistent with general stages of development.
4. Growth occurs in four interrelated areas.	Understand that a person's work in one area can help in another. Plan for language growth, while children use their bodies.
5. Intellectual growth: Children learn through their senses. Children learn by doing: Adults learn in abstract ways while children need concrete learning. Cognitive growth in four areas:	Have activities in looking, smelling, tasting, hearing, and touching. Realize that talking is abstract; have children touch.
Perception (visual, auditory, etc.)	Provide materials and activities in matching, finding same/different, putting a picture with a sound, taste, or with a symbol.
Language	Provide opportunities to find and label things, talk with grown-ups, friends, tell what it "looks like," smells like, etc.
Memory	Know that memory is helped by seeing, holding objects, and people.
Reasoning	Recognize that reasoning ability is just beginning, so children judge on what they see rather than what they reason they should see. Be sure adult explanations aid in understanding reasons. Practice finding "answers" to open-ended questions such as "How can you tell when you are tired?"
6. Social growth: The world is only from the child's viewpoint.	Expect that children will know their own ideas only. Be aware that the rights of others are minimal to them.
Seeing is believing.	Remember that if they cannot see the situation, they may not be able to talk about it.
Group play is developing.	Provide free-play sessions, with places to play socially. Understand that group play in structured situations is difficult, because of "self" orientation.
Independence increases as competence grows.	Know that children test to see how far they can go. Realize that children will vary from independent to dependent (both among the group and within one child).
People are born not knowing when it is safe to go on. Adult attention is very important. Young children are not born with an internal mechanism that says "slow down."	Understand that children will need to learn by trial and error. Know the children individually. Move into a situation before children lose control.
7. Emotional growth: Self-image is developing.	Watch for what each person's self-image is becoming. Give praise to enhance good feelings about oneself. Know that giving children responsibilities helps self-image. Talk to children at eye level. Children learn by example. Model appropriate behavior by doing yourself what you want the children to do.
8. Physical growth: Muscle development is not complete. Muscles cannot stay still for long. Large muscles are better developed than small ones.	Do not expect perfection, in either small- or large-muscle activity. Plan short times for children to sit. Give lots of chances to move about; be gentle with expectations for hand work.
Hand preference is being established.	Watch to see how children decide their handedness. Let children trade hands in their play.
A skill must be done several times before it is internalized.	Have materials available to be used often. Plan projects to use the same skill over and over.
Bowel and bladder control is not completely internalized.	Be understanding of "accidents." If possible, have toilet facilities available always, and keep them attractive.

FIGURE 4-22 Developmental research tests theories of growth and learning to find out about children and childhood.

In learning about these theories, we are more able to formulate our own philosophy of education. By consistently applying the insights from research and theory, we show our willingness to make a commitment to children. What we know about growth and development helps us fight for our most important resource—our children.

What do YOU Think?

Decision making in teaching can be difficult. Can theory help us?

It is 10 a.m. at the infant-toddler center. Fifteen-month-olds Kenya and Peter are crying and fussy this morning. Neither has eaten since breakfast. They have been indoors all morning.

Theory: *Maturation theory.* Children's physical developmental needs affect their emotional states.

Plan: Schedule regular times for active movement. Be sure to offer food and watch for signs of hunger.

Mario and Therese, both in wheelchairs, joined the first grade last month, but their parents report that neither wants to come to school. Their academic work is at grade level but they participate very little. They seem familiar with their teacher.

Theory: *Sociocultural theory.* Children need to feel part of the class culture in order to learn well.

Psychosocial theory. The children can identify with the teacher and become successful, but may feel incompetent with unfriendly or indifferent classmates.

Cognitive theory. They can understand other points of view as long as it is in real situations.

Plan: Put each child in a small group to design and build wheel toys for pets. Building upon the newcomers' expertise in a cooperative activity gives all the children the scaffolding needed to be successful and helps the new children become accepted into the class.

Preschoolers Jared and Panya have been arguing about who has brought the "best" toy to child care. Others have heard the ruckus and have stopped to watch the two start a fight.

Theory: *Cognitive theory.* Their egocentric thinking prevents them from seeing any view other than their own. Also, they are unable to hold two ideas at the same time, so cannot see that both toys are "good."

Behaviorist theory. The children can learn from watching others and applying other's example to their own behavior.

Plan: The teacher engages the children in a conflict resolution method that gets all children to express their own ideas, both about the problem and for some solutions, so they can practice hearing another's ideas while still holding their own. The teacher models praising each child's positive characteristics in the other's presence, showing other ways to behave appropriately and how the children and their toys can play together.

DEVELOPMENTAL THEORY: THE FOUNDATION OF DEVELOPMENTALLY APPROPRIATE PRACTICE

by
Rosalind Charlesworth

Developmental theory serves as a guide for developmentally appropriate practice (DAP). Age appropriateness and individual appropriateness were the original basic dimensions for DAP (Bredekamp, 1987). Age appropriateness is based on "what is known about child development and learning" and individual appropriateness on "what is known about the strengths, interests, and needs of each individual child." Developmental theories can provide clues as to where individuals or groups of children may be developmentally. Cultural appropriateness is a third critical dimension that was included in the 1997 revision edited by Bredekamp and Copple. Cultural appropriateness is based on "knowledge of the social and cultural contexts in which children live." The major developmental theories were based on observations of children in each theorist's particular culture. Therefore modifications must be considered relative to the multitude of cultures to which DAP might be applied in our ever more diverse society.

Theories of child development can serve as guides for assessing the developmental levels of any children (See Charlesworth, in press). They can help us know what children's competencies are and where we should begin instruction. Theories of development can serve as guides for planning instruction for individuals and for groups. The constructivist theories of Piaget and Vygotsky are especially helpful in guiding us to developmentally appropriate instructional practice. Concepts such as that of children constructing knowledge through their exploration of the world while adults determine their zone of proximal development and scaffold their learning experiences within the zone are invaluable guides. Piaget's periods of cognitive development provide clues to interpreting children's thinking as they move from sensorimotor to preoperational to concrete operational thought during early childhood. The period from ages five to seven, known as the *five to seven shift*, is very critical in assessing and planning for kindergartners and first graders (Golbeck, 2006). Erikson's stages help us understand the social/emotional development and behavior of young children beginning with basic trust, then the need for autonomy and independence and the need to be productive. These theorists all support the importance of play as the major vehicle for learning during early childhood. Other theorists also influence DAP. Maslow's hierarchy of human needs, Rogers' views on development of the self-concept, and Bandura's theories of social learning have all been applied to teaching practice. Interpretations of these theoretical guidelines may differ across cultures but provide a foundation for early childhood planning and practice.

Theory provides direction for program structure. Structure is necessary for any program in several areas: classroom space, guidance techniques, instructional methods, materials, curriculum, and assessment. Structure based on the development of young children includes some of the following factors that can be related to developmental theory:

- Classroom space is clearly divided into a variety of learning areas. The space includes table areas, a soft carpeted area, floor areas used as instructional space, and centers with open shelves where children can select materials. (Piaget and Erikson)

- Guidance techniques should be clear, consistent, positive and inductive; time blocks are broad and flexible but follow a consistent routine; children have choices of activities that fit their competencies, interests, and learning styles; children are involved in rule making. (Rogers, Bandura, Erikson, Piaget, and Vygotsky)

- Instructional methods include whole class, small group, and individual activities as appropriate; children are encouraged to construct their own knowledge; focus is on creative thinking and problem solving, peer interaction is encouraged, and play is the major vehicle for learning. (Piaget and Vygotsky)

- Materials are organized in space, are concrete and open-ended and promote creativity, and first-hand experiences are provided. (Piaget)

- Curriculum is guided by standards and scope and sequence but adapted for individual children's development, content is integrated, and there is equal emphasis on cognitive, affective, and psychomotor areas of development. (Piaget, Vygotsky, and Erikson)

- Assessment is done in an organized manner, mainly through observations and individual interviews as children work with appropriate materials. Observations are done on a daily basis to obtain information used for planning. Information for planning is obtained regarding children's current competencies and interests. Planning can then focus on age, individually, and culturally appropriate teaching strategies. (Piaget and Vygotsky)

Culture, the third dimension of DAP, has been at the center of many arguments against developmental theory as the foundation of DAP. Historically in the United States and other Western cultures an individualistic approach to education and development has been valued.

Individualism stresses independence and individual achievement, focusing on the needs of the individual, self-expression, and personal choice. (Zepeda, Rothstein-Fisch, Gonzales-Mena, & Trumbull, 2006, p. 4)

Most other cultures (about 70 percent) value a more collectivist approach (Zepeda et al., 2006). Zepeda et al. (2006, pp. 4–5) define collectivism as follows:

. . . most of the world tends to focus on the interdependence of groups and individuals. . . . Collectivism emphasizes social responsibility and the priority of group needs over individual needs. It stresses respect for authority and obligation to group norms.

They provide several examples of how these two views might result in different beliefs. For example, in the area of play and learning the individualistic view would see "Learning is child centered and involves play, exploration, and individual choice," while the collectivist view would be that "Learning is adult directed and depends more on observation than play, exploration, and child choice." The individualistic view appears to fit with Piaget and Erikson, the collectivist view with some of Vygotsky's and Bandura's ideas. Perhaps differences between collectivism and individualism can be bridged in order to provide a developmentally appropriate program for young children, one that considers culture and fully involves families in a partnership that respects cultural beliefs and child-rearing methods.

Just as DAP is a guide to practice, developmental and learning theories are *guides* to DAP, not rules. Planning for children is very complicated because children and families are complex and diverse. Many variables must be considered; one size doesn't fit all.

References

Bredekamp, S. (Ed.). (1987). *Developmentally appropriate practice in early childhood programs serving children from birth through age eight* (expanded edition). Washington, DC: National Association for the Education of Young Children.

Bredekamp, S., & Copple, C. (Eds.). (1997). *Developmentally appropriate practice in early childhood programs* (revised edition). Washington, DC: National Association for the Education of Young Children.

Charlesworth, R. (in press). *Understanding child development* (7th ed). Clifton Park, NY: Delmar Learning.

Golbeck, S. L. (2006). Developing key cognitive skills. In D. F. Gullo, Ed., *Kindergarten today*, pp. 37–46. Washington, DC: National Association for the Education of Young Children.

Zepeda, M., Rothstein-Fisch, C., Gonzales-Mena, J., & Trumbull, E. (2006). *Bridging cultures in early care and education: A training module.* Mahwah, NJ: Erlbaum.

Rosalind Charlesworth is professor and department chair in the Department of Child and Family Studies at Weber State University in Ogden, Utah.

For more activities and information, visit our Web site at http://www.EarlyChildEd.delmar.com

KEY TERMS

theory
hypothesis
nature/nurture controversy
psychodynamic theory
unconscious
psychosocial
autonomy
stimulus–response
reinforcement
socialization
modeling
classical conditioning
operant conditioning

reinforcers
assimilation
accommodation
equilibration
schema
myelination
transmission model
constructivism
transactional model
egocentric
sociocultural
zone of proximal
  development (ZPD)

scaffolding
private (inner) speech
bicognitive development
multiple intelligences
maturation
self-actualization
attachment
sociodramatic play
sex differences
dendrites
cortisol
stress

REVIEW QUESTIONS

1. Match the theorist with the appropriate description:

    B. F. Skinner   Ecological theory

    Abraham Maslow   Multiple intelligences

    Jean Piaget   Sex differences

    Albert Bandura   Attachment

    Mary Ainsworth   Social learning

    Eleanor Maccoby   Zone of proximal development

    Erik Erikson   Psychosocial development

    Arnold Gesell   Behaviorism

    Lev Vygotsky   Developmental norms

    Howard Gardner   Cognitive theory

    Uric Bronfenbrenner   Self-actualization

2. Describe Piaget's stages of cognitive development and their implications for early childhood education.

3. Name at least three psychologists who have contributed to the knowledge of development. Describe your reaction to each.

4. How is play beneficial to the child's development?

5. Define the common stages of play, and state at what chronological age each is likely to appear.

6. Given the eight theories of learning and development, which one would most likely advocate large blocks of free play? An early academic program? Open-ended questioning by teachers? Regular early mealtime?

7. Who said it? Match the theorist to the relevant quotation.

    Lev Vygotsky   "The first organ to make its appearance as an erotogenic zone and to make libidinal demands upon the mind is, from the time of birth onwards, the mouth."

    Erik Erikson   "There are problems when caregivers have low expectations for children based largely upon the children's membership in a low-status cultural group, rather than on the actual abilities of the children."

Jean Piaget	"From a sense of self-control without loss of self esteem comes a lasting sense of good will and pride; from a sense of loss of self-control and of foreign overcontrol comes a lasting propensity for doubt and shame."
Sigmund Freud	"Children acquire most of their concepts—the rules by which they live—from models who they observe in the course of daily life."
Sara Lawrence Lightfoot	"The young child's thinking manifests considerable activity that is frequently original and unpredictable. It is remarkable not only by virtue of the way it differs from adult thinking but also by virtue of what it teaches us."
Albert Bandura	"No matter how we approach the controversial problem of the relationship between thought and speech, we shall have to deal extensively with inner speech."

LEARNING ACTIVITIES

1. You are a teacher in a large urban child care center. Your children arrive by 7:00 and usually stay until after 5:00 each day. What would you do first thing in the morning? Use Maslow's hierarchy of needs to justify your answer.

2. What do you think of the influence of television on children's behavior? Consider the typical cartoons that the children you know are watching. From a social learning perspective, what are they learning? What else would you have them watch?

3. You are a teacher in a middle-class suburban preschool. What do you know about your group's needs and developmental stages? What assumptions, if any, can you make about development and social class? What does their cultural background tell you about what to teach? How will you find out about what each child is ready to learn?

4. Observe children in a child care center as they say goodbye to their parents. What can your observations tell you about their attachment levels? What can teachers do to support attachment and also help children separate?

5. Observe teachers as children play. What is the difference in play when (1) a teacher interacts with children in their play and (2) a teacher intervenes? What happens to the play immediately after teacher contact is made? How long does the play last? What is your conclusion?

6. Write a defense of play as a hallmark of early childhood philosophy and curriculum. How would you adapt the paper for parents? For a student of early childhood education? For teachers?

REFERENCES

General Texts

Berger, K. S. (2005). *The developing person* (6th ed.). New York: Worth.

Berk, L. (1996). *Infants, children, and adolescents.* Boston: Allyn & Bacon.

Fong, B., & Resnick, M. (1986). *The child: Development through adolescence.* Palo Alto, CA: Mayfield.

Santrock, J. W. (2001). *Child development* (9th ed.), Boston, MA: McGraw Hill.

Psychodynamic Theory

Erikson, E. H. (1963). *Childhood and society* (2nd ed.). New York: Norton.

Erikson, E. H. (1964). Toys and reasons. In M. R. Haworth (Ed.), *Child psychotherapy: Practice and theory.* New York: Basic Books.

Erikson, E. H. (1969). A healthy personality for every child. In P. H. Mussen, J. J. Conger, & J. Kagan (Eds.), *Child development and personality* (3rd ed.). New York: Harper & Row.

Freud, S. (1968). *A general introduction to psychoanalysis.* New York: Washington Square Press.

Mooney, C. G. (2000). *Theories of childhood.* Beltsville, MD: Redleaf Press.

Myers, J. K., et al. (1984). *Archives of General Psychiatry, 41,* 259–267.

Spitz, R. A., & Wolf, K. M. (1946). Analytic depression: An inquiry into the genesis of psychiatric conditions in early childhood, II. In A. Freud, et al. (Eds.), *The psychoanalytic study of the child* (Vol. II). New York: International Universities Press.

Behaviorist Theory

Bandura, A. (1963). Imitation of film-mediated aggressive models. *Journal of Abnormal and Social Psychology.*

Bandura, A. (1986). *Social foundations of thought and action: A social cognitive theory.* New York: Prentice Hall.

Skinner, B. F. (1953). *Science and human behavior.* New York, NY: MacMillan Co.

Suransky, V. P. (1982, Autumn). A Tyranny of Experts. *Wilson Quarterly,* 53–60.

Cognitive/Intellectual Theory

Dasen, P. R., & Heron, A. (1981). Cross-cultural tests of Piaget's theory. In H. C. Triandis & A. Heron (Eds.), *Handbook of cross-cultural psychology, Volume 4. Developmental Psychology.* Boston: Allyn & Bacon.

DeVries, R., & Kohlberg, L. (1990). *Constructivist early education: An overview and comparison with other programs.* Washington, DC: National Association for Education of Young Children.

Elkind, D. (1977). Giant in the nursery school—Jean Piaget. In E. M. Hetherington & R. D. Parke (Eds.), *Contemporary readings in psychology.* New York: McGraw-Hill.

Elkind, D., & Flavell, J. (Eds.). 1996. *Essays in honor of Jean Piaget.* New York: Oxford University Press.

Flavell, J. H., Green, F. L., & Flavell, E. R. (1989). Young children's ability to differentiate appearance-reality. *Child Development,* 60, 201–213.

Heuwinkel, M. K. (1996, Fall). New ways of learning = new ways of teaching. *Childhood Education,* 313–342.

Kohn, A. (1993). *Punished by rewards.* New York: Houghton Mifflin.

Kohn, A. (2005). *Unconditional parenting.* New York: Atria Books.

Mali, G., & Howe, A. (1980). Cognitive development of Nepalese children. *Science Education,* 64, 213–221.

Meade-Roberts, J., & Spitz, G. (1998). *Under construction.* Unpublished documents.

Voyat, G. E. (1982). *Piaget systematized.* Hillsdale, NJ: Lawrence Erlbaum Associates.

Sociocultural Theory

Berk, L. Vygotsky's sociocultural theory. In A. Gordon & K. W. Browne (2000), *Beginnings and Beyond* (5th Ed.). Clifton Park, NY: Thomson Delmar Learning.

Hale, J. (1986). *Black children: Their roots, culture and learning styles.* Baltimore, MD: The Johns Hopkins University Press.

Ramirez, M., & Castaneda, A. (1974). *Cultural democracy, biocognitive development and education.* New York: Academic Press.

Rogoff, B. (1990). *Appreciation in thinking: Cognitive development in a social context.* New York: Oxford University Press.

Vygotsky, L. S. (1978). *Mind in society: The development of higher psychological processes.* Cambridge, MA: Harvard University Press.

Ecological Theory

Bronfenbrenner, U. (2000). Ecological system theory. In A. Kazdin (Ed.), *Encyclopedia of Psychology.* Washington, DC: American Psychological Association & Oxford Press.

Multiple Intelligences Theory

Gardner, H. (1983). *Frames of mind.* New York: Basic Books.

Gardner, H. (1991). *The unschooled mind.* New York: Basic Books.

Gardner, H. (1993). *Multiple intelligences.* New York: Basic Books.

Gardner, H. (2000). *Intelligence reframed: Multiple intelligences for the 21st century.* New York: Basic Books.

Maturation Theory

Ames, L. B., & Ilg, F. (1979). *The Gesell Institute's child from one to six; The Gesell Institute's child from five to ten; The infant in today's culture.* New York: Harper & Row.

Gesell, A. (1940). *The first five years of life.* New York: Harper & Row.

Humanist Theory

Goble, F. G. (1970). *The third force: The psychology of Abraham Maslow.* New York: Grossman.

Maslow, A. H. (1954). *Motivation and personality.* New York: Harper & Row.

Developmental Topics

Ethnicity and Cultural Diversity

Caldwell, B. (1983). *Child development and cultural diversity.* Geneva, Switzerland: OMEP World Assembly.

Garcia Coll, C. (2003). "Cultural Perspectives on Parenting" *www.extension.iastate.edu* [12/04/03].

Garcia Coll, C., et al. (2005). In Cooper, et al. (Eds.). *Developmental attitudes and pathways through middle childhood: Rethinking diversity and contexts as resources.* NY: Lawrence Erlbaum Associates.

Gura, P. (1994). Childhood: A multiple reality. *Early Childhood Development and Care,* 98.

Hilliard, A., & Vaughn-Scott, M. (1982). The quest for the 'minority' child. In S. Moore & C. Cooper (Eds.), *The young child: Review of research* (Vol. 3). Washington, DC: National Association for Education of Young Children.

Hironaka Cowee, M. (2001). *Identity tied to culture.* CAEYC: Connections.

Lightfoot, S. L. (1978). *Worlds apart.* New York: Basic Books.

Markus, H., in Vaughan, L. J. "Culture as Sculptor: Markus Explores 'Models of Self'." Stanford University, *The Bing Times,* November, 2005.

Rodd, J. (1996). Children, culture and education. *Childhood Education, International Focus Issue.*

Rogoff, B. (2003). *The cultural nature of human development.* New York: Oxford University Press.

Sparks, L. D., & Phillips, C. (1997). *Teaching/Learning anti-racism: A developmental approach.* NY: Teachers College Press.

Tatum, B. D. (1995, February). *Stages of racial/ethnic identity development in the United States.* Paper presented at the National Association for Multicultural Education, Washington, DC.

York, S. (2005). *Roots and wings: Affirming culture in early childhood programs.* St. Paul, MN: Redleaf Press.

Attachment

Ainsworth, M. (1979, October). Infant-mother attachment. *American Psychologist,* 131–142.

Bowlby, J. (1969, 1973). *Attachment and loss* (Vols. I & II). New York: Basic Books.

Kagan, J. (1987). Perspectives on infancy. In J. D. Godowsky (Ed.), *Handbook on infant development* (2nd Ed.). New York: John Wiley & Sons, Inc.

Saxton, R. (2001). *Personal communication.*

Play

Bodrova, E., & Leong, D. J. (2003). Chopsticks and counting sticks. *Young Children, (58)*3.

Bowman, B. (1990). Play in teacher education: The United States perspective. In E. Klugman & S. Smilansky (Eds.), *Children's play and learning.* New York: Teachers College Press.

Frost, J. L. (1996). *Play and playscapes.* Clifton Park, NY: Delmar Learning.

Frost, J. L., & Sunderlin, S. (Eds.). (1985). *When children play.* Wheaton, MD: Association for Childhood Education International.

Hoffman, E. (2004). *Magic capes, amazing powers: Transforming play in the classroom.* St. Paul, MN: Redleaf Press.

Jones, E. (2000). What is the point of play? In A. Gordon & K. Browne, *Beginning & beyond: Foundations in early childhood education.* Clifton Park, NY: Thomson Delmar Learning.

Klein, T. P., Wirth, D., & Linas, K. (2003). Play: Children's context for development. *Young Children, (58)*3.

Rubin, K. H., Fein, G. G., & Vandenberg, B. (1983). Play. In E. M. Heatherington (Ed.), *Handbook of child psychology (Vol. 4, Socialization, personality and social development).* New York: Wiley.

Smilansky, S. (1990). Sociodramatic play: Its relevance to behavior and achievement in school. In E. Klugman & S. Smilansky (Eds.), *Children's play and learning.* New York: Teachers College Press.

Gender Differences

Bauer, P. J., Liebl, M., & Stennes, L. (1998). Pretty is to dress and brave is to suitcoat: Gender-based property-to-property inferences in 4–10 year-olds. *Merrill-Palmer Quarterly, 44,* 355–377.

Eisenberg, N., Martin, C. L., & Fabes, R. A. (1996). Gender development and gender effects. In D. C. Berliner & R. C. Calfee (Eds.), *Handbook of educational psychology.* New York: Macmillan.

Maccoby, E. E. (1998). *The two sexes.* Cambridge, MA: Harvard University Press.

Martin, C. L., & Fabes, R. (2001). The stability and consequences of young children's same-sex peer interactions. *Developmental Psychology, 37,* 431–446.

Wardle, F. (2004). The challenge of boys in our early childhood programs. *Early Childhood News* (January–February, 2004).

Moral Development

Buzzelli, C. A. (1992, September). Young children's moral understanding: Learning about right and wrong. *Young Children,* 47–53.

Eisenberg, N., Lenon, R., & Roth, K. (1983). Prosocial development in middle childhood: A longitudinal study. *Developmental Psychology, 23,* 712–718.

Gilligan, C. (1982). *In a different voice.* Cambridge, MA: Harvard University Press.

Kohlberg, L. (1981). *The philosophy of moral development.* New York: Harper & Row.

Brain-Based Research

Bruer, J. T. (1998). Brain science, brain fiction. *Educational Leadership, (56)*3.

Galinsky, E. (1997, Winter). *New research on the brain development of young children.* CAEYC Connections.

Gunnar, M. R., & Vasquez, D. M. (2001). Low cortisol and a flattening of expected daytime rhythm: Potential indices of risk in human development. *Development and Psychopathology, 13,* 515–538.

Jensen, E. (1995). *Brain-based learning and teaching.* New York: Brain Store.

Sanchez, M., Ladd, C. O., & Plotsky, P. M. (2001). Early adverse experience as a developmental risk factor for later psychopathology. *Development and Psychopathology, 13,* 413–450.

Shore, R. (1997). *Rethinking the brain: New insights into early development.* New York: Families and Work Institute.

HELPFUL WEB SITES

American Educational Research Association	http://tikkun.ed.asu.edu/aera/home.html
AskEric	http://ericir.syr.edu
ERIC (Educational Resources Information Center)	http://www.eric.ed.gov
Early Childhood Research Quarterly	http://www.udel.edu/ecrq
Early Childhood Education On-line	http://www.ume.maine.edu/ECEOL-L
National Association for the Education of Young Children	http://www.naeyc.org
Society for Research in Child Development	http://www.blackwellpublishers.co.uk/srcd

For more activities and information, visit our Web site at http://www.EarlyChildEd.delmar.com

Section 3

Who Are the Teachers?

TEACHERS AS ASSESSORS AND IMPLEMENTERS OF QUALITY: CREATING A CLASSROOM ENVIRONMENT THAT MEETS CHILDREN'S NEEDS

Thelma Harms, Ph.D.

It is now clear from educational, medical, and psychological research that the group care and learning environments our infants, toddlers, and preschoolers experience every day exert a long-term influence on their adjustment and achievement, not only on subsequent formal schooling, but ultimately on their adult lives. Based on this interdisciplinary input, the concept of what constitutes a high-quality early childhood classroom environment has been broadened to include meeting all three basic needs of young children:

- Protection of their health and safety
- Supportive interaction for emotional and social growth, and
- Stimulation of their cognitive and language abilities

None of these components can take the place of any other of these components. Having good social skills or competence in language development will not protect a child from coming down with a contagious illness due to inadequate handwashing in a preschool classroom. Since each component is important, a comprehensive observational instrument has to include specific items that can assess all three basic components of quality.

Health and safety assessment includes observing whether the meal or snack is served on a properly sanitized table, whether children and adults wash their hands, and whether the meal contains the approved nutritional components; nap issues include whether cots or cribs are placed far enough apart to prevent respiratory illness, and whether clean bedding is used.

Interaction items cover observing whether careful supervision is practiced outdoors and indoors, whether positive methods for discipline and guidance are used effectively, as well as the quality of staff-child and child-child interactions throughout the observation.

Appropriate stimulation is assessed by observing whether many materials for a wide variety of activities are accessible for children's use much of the day, and whether staff, through comments, questions, and additional information, bring language and learning out of children's play.

A comprehensive observational instrument will include items on the space and furnishings in the classroom, the way the personal care routines are carried out, the opportunities for children to practice language and reasoning, the activities and materials offered, the interpersonal interactions observed, the way the program schedule is organized, and the support given to parents and staff.

Since the majority of young children spend much of their day in out-of-home care, parental and public concern for assuring the daily quality of such settings has increased. Many states have added higher voluntary standards including a state-sponsored quality assessment to their relatively low mandatory licensing standards. This additional quality assessment usually requires an observation of ongoing practice in the classroom, conducted by a well-trained, reliable observer using a valid observational instrument. A thorough observation provides evidence of the actual functioning of a classroom, its "process quality."

Since the 1980s, research evidence has linked higher classroom process quality scores to better social skills and higher intellectual achievement by children, while they attended preschool as well as when they entered kindergarten, and during the elementary school years. Moreover, longitudinal studies that have followed children who were at risk for school failure into adulthood (such as the Abecedarian study of infants and the High Scope study of preschoolers) have proven the long-term positive effects of high-quality early care in group settings. Both projects have demonstrated that good early childhood practice not only improves children's academic achievement, but also their adult life adjustment skills such as successful employment and self-sufficiency. These encouraging results, based on programs conducted in university settings and assessed by researchers, have given the early childhood field verification of the value of high quality programs. The remaining challenge is how to prepare professional early childhood educators in real world settings to accurately assess their own daily practices and then follow through with the necessary changes.

A major portion of my long career has been devoted to developing process quality assessment instruments that can be used effectively by classroom teaching staff, directors, regulatory staff, providers of technical assistance and training, as well as researchers. These instruments, called the Environment Rating Scales, were initially used in research and evaluation to prove that positive social, cognitive, and language outcomes in children were linked to the quality of the group care they received. Now these scales are also widely used for program improvement efforts all over the United States and Canada, as well as in translation in Europe and Asia. Despite cultural differences, there seems to be a common consensus around the world about the core components of high-quality early childhood education that help prepare children to contribute positively to the global society by becoming healthy, productive, and competent adults. These scales include the infant-toddler environmental rating scale (ITERS-R) for children birth to two-and-a-half years of age, the early childhood environmental rating scale (ECERS-R) for preschool / kindergarten, the family child care environmental rating scale (FCCERS-R), and the school-age environmental rating scale (SACERS) for K–6 in out-of-school programs. The environmental rating scales have been used for research and evaluation, have been translated into several languages, and are used worldwide.

As early childhood education has taken significant steps toward becoming a recognized profession, credentialing of teaching staff, national accreditation of early childhood programs, and differential state reimbursement rates based on assessment of process quality are becoming accepted practice. Self-assessment of classroom practices by the teaching staff is a required part of most quality improvement efforts. Self-assessment is maximally helpful if the classroom staff has had training on the particular instrument or instruments used, and can compare their scores with those of an independent observer. Advice for improving lower scoring areas is provided by many states through on-site technical assistance or in targeted workshops and courses based on these observations.

The exemplary practices students learn in courses must become their daily practices as they become professionals and assume leadership roles in the field. Classroom teachers will always need the support of knowledgeable directors, principles, advisory boards, parents, legislators, and the general public, but delivering best practices on a daily basis can only be done by competent teachers who can create environments to meet the complex needs of children.

For more information:

The Environment Rating Scales
www.fpg.unc.edu/~ecers
The Abecedarian Project
www.fpg.unc.edu and click on Abecedarian
High Scope
www.highscope.org

THELMA HARMS, Ph.D., is the lead author of four widely used Environment Rating Scales (ECERS-R, ITERS-R, FCCERS-R and SACERS) and numerous other curriculum related publications. She has an M.A. in Child Development and a Ph.D. in Early Childhood Education from the University of California at Berkeley, where she served as head teacher of the H. E. Jones Child Study Center for 15 years. Dr. Harms subsequently served as director of curriculum development at the FPG Child Development Institute and Research Professor at the University of North Carolina at Chapel Hill for 30 years. Now Emeritus, she continues to lecture in the United States, Canada, Europe, and Asia and work on scales-related publications.

Teaching: A Professional Commitment

QUESTIONS FOR THOUGHT

What qualifications does a good teacher possess?

What are the essentials for successful teaching?

How is my own personal development related to my growth as a teacher?

What is a professional code of ethics, and why should we have one?

What does it mean to be a member of the teaching profession?

How can teachers be culturally competent?

What makes up a good teacher evaluation process?

WHO ARE THE TEACHERS OF THE YOUNG CHILD?

Margarita had always wanted to be an early childhood teacher. Right after high school she went to a community college and earned her A.A. degree. Shortly after her first child was born, she became a licensed family child care provider, and cares for infants and toddlers in her own home. It is important to Margarita that she feels she is making a contribution to the family's well-being as well as enjoying a satisfying career. She plans to pursue her B.A. degree in the evenings when her children are older.

Paul recently spent several years teaching in a school for emotionally disturbed children. He has been a lead teacher for four-year-olds at the child care center for two years, gaining experience with children whose developmental patterns are typical. Paul wants to remain a teacher but is concerned about the salary levels. He has given himself one more year before he will make a decision.

Kendra's four children were in parent cooperative nursery schools, where she enjoyed the companionship of so many other parents of young children. After a few years of teaching elementary school, she is now director of a parent co-op and teaches children from ages two to five. She particularly enjoys leading weekly parent discussion groups.

Elva was the most sought-after parent aide in the school after she began helping out when her two boys were ages four and five. This success stimulated her to get an A.A. degree in early childhood education, then a bachelor's degree in child development. She is now a kindergarten teacher in a bilingual program.

All of these people had different motivations, yet they all were drawn to the early childhood classroom. They may teach in different settings, have different educational backgrounds and skills, yet they do share common everyday experiences of the teacher of young children. They plan, observe, listen, help, learn, play, console, discipline, confer, comfort, and teach the children and adults who make up their particular world of early childhood.

Teacher Diversity

A longitudinal study (Whitebrook, Sakai, Gerber, & Howes, 2001) based on observations in the same child care centers in three California communities from 1994 to 2000 gives a glimpse of the diversity of teachers and caregivers in early childhood settings. The study is unusual as it is based on observations and data collected from the same centers in 1994, 1996, and 2000. The following picture emerged:

- 97 percent of the teachers were women.
- 33 percent were members of minority groups.
- 33 percent spoke a language other than English fluently.
- 68 percent had associate's degrees.
- 37 percent had bachelor's degrees or higher.
- 25 percent were under 30 years of age.
- 53 percent were between 30 and 40 years of age.

The study also noted that 44 percent of the classrooms had Spanish-speaking children, but only half were staffed by at least one Spanish-speaking teacher. Nearly 50 percent of the classrooms had Chinese-speaking children, yet only 7 percent had a staff member who spoke Cantonese or Mandarin. Not surprisingly, nearly 30 percent of the teaching staff in the sample reported that parents had difficulty communicating with the staff because of language barriers.[1]

According to the U.S. Bureau of Labor Statistics (2001), center-based care throughout the United States reflects a similar demographic picture in the gender, ethnic, age, and amount of education categories.

Comparison with Teaching in Other Educational Settings

The nature of teaching in the early years is unlike that of other age groups. At first glance, the differences in teaching preschool and older children may outweigh any similarities. There are some common elements, however, that link the two:

- Early childhood teachers teach what other teachers teach. The curriculum in the early years is rich in math, science, social studies, history, language, art, and geography, as it is in any other grade.
- Early childhood teachers and their elementary and high school counterparts share many of the frustrations of the teaching profession—long hours, low pay, and a people-intensive workplace.
- They also share the joy of teaching—the opportunity to influence children's lives and the satisfaction of meeting the daily challenges that teaching children provides.

1   We must continue to collect and use ethnic data on children and teachers in early childhood programs to ensure that we continually address equity and justice in the early childhood field.

Elements of Teaching and Learning	Early Childhood Settings	Elementary and High School Settings
How teaching and learning occur	Through teacher-child interactions and concrete use of materials	Through lectures and demonstrations that are often teacher dominated
	Guides children toward discovery	Teaches subject matter
Play opportunities	Primary learning medium is play	Usually just at recess
Opportunity for child to make choices	Many choices throughout the day both inside and outside	Few options—all students do same activity most of the day
Classroom environment	Abundant floor space, many activity centers, variety of materials for play	Rows of desks and tables
Daily schedule	Large blocks of time for unlimited exploration of materials and for play	45-minute to 1-hour periods on subject matter
Small group interactions	Majority of teaching	Much less frequent
Large group interactions	Few times a day	Majority of teaching
Outdoor activity	Teachers involved as intensively as they are in the classroom	Others usually supervise play yard—little direct teacher interaction
Parent relationships	Frequent, if not daily, contact	May see them once a year as child grows older
Working with other adults	Often works with aide, assistant teachers, and parents	Usually teaches alone or with part-time aide
Educational materials	Toys, games, natural materials, blocks	Textbooks and worksheets
Evaluating students	Observational and anecdotal assessments, portfolios	Grades, tests, and report cards
	Emphasis on growth of whole child	Standardized academic assessment
Age range of students	May have two- to two-and-a-half-year age span or greater	Usually same age
Art, music, and physical education	Available throughout the day as an ongoing part of curriculum	Restricted to a special class, time, or teacher
Teacher training	Strong child development foundation	Emphasis on subject matter

FIGURE 5-1 The nature of teaching in the early years is unlike that of other age groups.

Figure 5-1 highlights the similarities and differences between early childhood teachers and others.

THE TEACHER'S ROLE: PROFESSIONALISM IN ACTION

Definitions

The variety of roles early childhood teachers perform has been described in many ways:

storyteller
custodian
carpenter
adult educator
purchasing agent
staff supervisor
personnel director
psychologist

traffic director
file clerk
poet
parent resource
nurse
business manager
employee
sociologist

conflict mediator
plumber
musician
faculty member
program planner
treasurer
employer
scientist

This diversity is exactly what makes teaching in the early years so appealing. The multiple roles a teacher plays add challenge to the job. (The role of the teacher in relationship to parents and programs further discussed in Chapter 8.)

Two prominent early childhood teacher educators state the value of having teachers who have a theoretical and historical grounding. Jones (1994) tells us that teachers, like young children, are constructivists. The complexity and unpredictability of teaching, she says, call for on-the-spot decisions, and those decisions are based on developmental and learning theory and constructed from the teacher's own experience and practice. Spodek (1994) calls for teachers to know the history and traditions of the field along with theory but also stresses the need to know "the cultural, social and political contexts in which early childhood education functions."

Phillips defines teaching as those "daily acts of creation" (Phillips, 1994) that are constructed from the teacher's own repertoire of skills, knowledge, and training, added to what he or she observes about children and his or her interactions with their families. The teacher as a collaborator is a significant part of the teacher's role definition in the schools of Reggio Emilia, Italy (see Chapter 10). Collaboration reinforces the notion underlying many definitions that teachers are, first and foremost, lifelong teachers.

In her "Insights" article at the end of this chapter, Barbara Biglan tells a story of how students in an early childhood course learn a unqiue way to identify the many roles of an early childhood professional.

What teachers do with children is not all there is to teaching. Some of the work occurs outside the classroom. It is helpful to look at the teacher's role in another way. What are the things a teacher does with children? What are the things a teacher does after the children go home? How does the teacher interact with other adults in the early childhood setting?

In the Classroom

Interacting with Children

Teachers find their greatest satisfaction and challenges in their first role—who and what they are with children. The teacher-child interactions, the spur-of-the-moment crises, the intense activity, the on-the-spot decisions, the loving and nurturing, go far in making one "feel" like a real teacher. Helping Rhonda get a good grip on the hammer, soothing Josh and Benno after they bump heads,

and talking with Alexa about her drawing are at the heart of teaching young children. These encounters are enjoyable and provide moments for interactive teaching opportunities.[1] These times help establish good relationships with the children. It is during these spontaneous, anything-can-happen-and-probably-will times that teachers display their craftsmanship and professionalism.

The art of teaching comes on the floor of the classroom. All teaching skills are called on. Responses are automatic and ingrained. Teachers intuitively use their knowledge base, their experience, and their proven techniques. Almost unconsciously, they reach back in their minds for all those things they know about children. Throughout the school day they apply that combination of knowledge and know-how.

Managing the Classroom

Being a successful manager is a little like being a successful juggler. Both require the ability to think about and react to more than three things at once. With a simple gesture, a significant look, or merely moving nearby, the teacher maintains the ongoing activity.

Anticipating a clash between Nathan and Julie, the teacher, Miriam, intervenes, redirects them, and moves away. At the same time, she has kept a watchful eye on Bobby at the bathroom sink. Passing close to Francie, she touches the child's shoulder in brief acknowledgment, smiling down as Francie struggles with the doll's dress. Miguel and Lea run up to her, grab her by the skirt and hand, and pull her toward the science display. They need to ask her something about the snake . . . *now!* Jake, the handyman, has come into the classroom wanting to know exactly which of the climbers needs repair. Sarah, the parent volunteer, waves to her; it's time to check on the corn bread baking in the kitchen. Quickly, the teacher files a mental note of the names of the children who accompany Sarah to the kitchen. As she reaches for a copy of *Ranger Rick* (the one with the great snake pictures in it), she observes Angie and her father entering the room. They both look upset. Telling Miguel and Lea she will return, the teacher walks over to greet the latecomers. As she moves past Doug, the student teacher, she comments on how well his language game is going and suggests he continue for another five minutes. Glancing at the clock, she realizes it is almost cleanup time. Her assistant, Chuck,

---

 1 Teaching about the rich diversity that makes up our world can be an integral and spontaneous response when interacting with children.

Teachers model learning, listening, and loving.

watches her. She looks his way, and a nonverbal signal passes between them. Without a word, they both understand that snacks will be a little late today. Angie's father begins to explain their delay as the teacher bends down to invite the child to come and look at the new snake cage with her.

In this setting, the teacher has a major role in supervising a number of people. Aides and volunteers, student teachers, and visitors add to the richness of a program. But it is the teacher who coordinates and supervises their various functions. From the description, it is clear that the teacher's role as a supervisor and manager includes being:

- caretaker for a safe environment;
- observer of and listener to children;
- on-the-spot teacher trainer for students, aides, and volunteers;
- on-site supervisor for student teachers;
- a liaison and communicator with parents.

Setting the Tone

Teachers are responsible for what occurs in the classroom so they must have a finger on its pulse at all times and takes the pulse while moving around the class or yard. From the moment of arrival, the teacher puts into effect another vital element by setting the tone, creating an atmosphere in which teachers and children will work and play. The skill with which it is done can make the critical difference between a classroom that is alive and supportive and one that is chaotic or tense.

The teacher establishes what will be the **emotional framework**. This is done with body movements, by the tone of voice, facial expressions or lack of them, and gestures. The way this tone.

This interact the teacher creat the tone. Young adult moods and calm and confid inspire a mo sphere in which the teacher is punitive and harsh, classroom will reflect that. On the other hand, teachers act on their beliefs that children deserve respect and are intelligent, capable human beings, they will create an entirely different climate—and the children will respond in kind.

Normal behavior for the young child includes tantrums, crying, resistance, curiosity, impatience, emotional swings, noise, and self-centeredness. This is the time to achieve a sense of their own separate self. They need a place to work through the developmental stages that their needs and nature indicate. The atmosphere that a teacher creates is a key element in that process.

The way teachers handle conflict, react to tears, the words they use, and the voices raised communicate a direct message to the child. The understanding, the soothing, the warmth, and the acceptance, create a climate where children feel safe, secure, and guided. This requires teachers who respect childhood, the individuality of children, their growing patterns, their emerging feelings, and their special capacity to learn. Today we would also stress the need for teachers to become culturally competent: to accept and understand cultural differences, have a working knowledge of the cultural backgrounds of the children in the class, and appreciate that this may be the children's first experience outside their own culture.[1] The end result is that preschoolers will thrive in an atmosphere influenced by teachers who understand this time of tension and growth in their lives.

Planning and Evaluating the Curriculum

As teachers move through the school day interacting with children, managing the classroom, sensing the tone, they consciously or unconsciously evaluate what is happening:

- The relay race outdoors produced more tears than cheers; most of the children were

1 Emotional support is evident when children see that their family culture is valued.

in participating when the game
ut drifted away. Why?

Cuisenaire™ rods were never touched
y. How can we make this a more inviting
ctivity?

The toddlers are beginning to participate fully
in the "Eensy Weensy Spider" fingerplay.
What might they like to learn next?

- Several children have asked why Sasha "talks
funny." When would be a good time to talk
about his language and teach the class a few
words in Russian?[1]

The teacher notes where and how children played, the quality of their interactions, and possible "next steps" in curriculum. These notes are then discussed with other staff members at the end of the day or in weekly planning sessions. Effective ways to develop curriculum planning are discussed in Chapter 10.

It is important to note that the process has its roots in what the teacher sees happening in the classroom as children play and learn. It is constructivist theory in action: teachers watching and observing children to give meaning and support to their learning. Early childhood teachers use their observation skills, collect data as they work with children, and build curriculum around their knowledge of actual classroom practice and behavior.

Out-of-Class Responsibilities

Good classroom management is often dependent on how teachers spend their time away from the children. Many of the tasks that give added strength and depth to a teacher's curriculum are those that, out of necessity, must be accomplished after hours. The two most obvious jobs that fall into this category are record keeping and meetings.

Record Keeping

Early childhood teachers and caregivers keep a variety of records; the type and kind will vary from school to school. Although report writing and record keeping may be considered time-consuming, they are essential to any good early childhood program. Record keeping is based on a number of factors:

- *The purpose for which the records will be used.* In schools that rely on government funding, record keeping is not optional. The children's progress, the teacher's performance, and the program itself must be evaluated on a regular basis to ensure continued funding.

- *The philosophy of the school.* In laboratory schools and teacher training centers, teachers write periodical progress reports on the children to guide them in planning.

- *As part of a teacher-training process.* Documentation is critical for accreditation of early childhood programs. For years, CDA (Child Development Associates) candidates submitted a written portfolio of their experiences in the classroom as supportive evidence of their competency as teachers of young children.

- *As part of an accreditation process.* NAEYC's accreditation procedures require extensive documentation of the school's operation, ranging from governance and management issues to teacher effectiveness, space usage, parent involvement, school philosophy, and curriculum.

- *As a commitment to quality and appropriate child development practices.* Recording children's social and emotional growth provides information from which insights and interpretation can develop. It may be just a brief note taken on the run, a thoughtful anecdote written at length after class, or a checklist of the child's playmates for one day. All of these give teachers a greater understanding of the role they play in children's development.

- *As a means of family information and education.* Recorded observations, notes, and similar data collected over a six-month period may show that Abraham is not participating in any strenuous physical activity and studiously avoids activities that involve balancing and climbing. This information, when shared with parents, could lead to a medical evaluation and diagnosis of possible perceptual problems.[2]

- *As a means of developing curriculum.* Curriculum plans and learning activities sprout from such reports and records. It wasn't until such data were collected for entry into first grade that the kindergarten teacher realized most of the children in the class were not sufficiently proficient with scissors. Curriculum was planned around this need, and the class learned a necessary skill.

1 A goal of every early childhood program should be to foster positive attitudes and awareness of cultural differences.

2 Early childhood teachers are in a unique position to support early identification, prevention, and treatment of developmental problems.

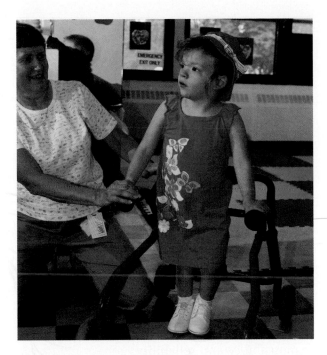

The teacher determines the quality of the child's school experience by providing a supportive atmosphere in which children can learn.

Attending Meetings

Meetings are probably the most time-consuming of all out-of-class jobs. The teacher may need to communicate with the other people who are involved in the lives of the children, directly or indirectly. Families, other teachers, baby-sitters, doctors, and social workers are some of the people with whom a teacher may want to confer. Teachers also attend professional meetings. Figure 5-2 lists the most common types of meetings.

Organizing and Collecting Materials

Some of a teacher's after-hours activities are intended to fortify and vitalize the classroom. Therefore, teachers:

- Organize and collect materials for use in class. They might collect space shuttle books from the library, find out if the bagel factory will allow field trips, or cut 18 pumpkin shapes. They might add pictures to the bulletin board, obtain new books and records, or replenish curriculum materials.

- Purchase materials and equipment that cannot be ordered. The kitchen needs new mixing bowls, the supply room is low on red construction paper, and someone has to pick up fabric for pillow covers.

Making Contacts

Teachers may call or e-mail families to check on children who are sick or absent, or return calls from parents and colleagues, or update a parent about a child's progress. For children with special needs, teachers may need to contact doctors, therapists, and other specialists. The popularity of e-mail has made some communications with families much faster and easier.

Staff Meetings

Held usually once a week for individual teaching teams. Purpose is to plan curriculum, set goals, and discuss children's progress. Faculty meetings for all school personnel may be held less frequently.

Parent-Teacher Conferences

May be offered on a scheduled basis or they may be called by either parents or teachers as needed. Each school defines its own policy as to the number and frequency of parent contacts.

Parent Education Meetings

Many schools offer evening programs for parents. Teacher attendance may or may not be required.

Professional Meetings

Attendance at workshops, seminars, in-service training. Local, state, and national conferences are sponsored by the National Association for the Education of Young Children, Association for Childhood Education International, and Child Care Coordinating Council.

Student-Teacher Conferences

In schools used as training sites, teachers arrange time with individual students assigned to their classes.

Home Visits[1]

May or may not be optional. Some schools schedule them before opening day. Otherwise teachers must arrange them on their own time.

FIGURE 5-2 Teachers attend many different types of meetings, which help them create better programs, learn more about children, and learn how to become better teachers.

1 Many parents welcome teacher's visits. Others may fear criticism or judgment about their home environment or family practices.

In addition to working with children, teachers support parents when they keep in touch. A brief, friendly phone call can make a family feel included in their child's education process.

Working with Families

Working with families may include working on multicultural issues, and organizing class fairs or school fund-raising events.[1] Further examples can be found in Chapter 8.

- Attend professional conferences and workshops and visit and observe other school settings. This type of ongoing professional education helps teachers keep abreast of the field.

- Attend in-service training events or study for an advanced degree in an area related to early childhood education.

These duties are a part of the job of teaching young children but many will be shared with other teachers on the team or at the school. Though time-consuming, these responsibilities add to the creativity and care that teachers express for their classes. Chapter 8 discusses the teacher-family relationship in depth.

PERSONAL AND PROFESSIONAL QUALITIES

Personal Qualities

Good teachers should have dedication, compassion, insight, flexibility, patience, energy, and self-confidence. Teachers should also be happy people who can laugh and use their sense of humor wisely. Liking children is part of wanting to work with them; teachers then feel that the job they are doing is important. Teachers should be fair-minded, showing concern for all the people they meet in an early childhood setting. Their personal qualities should foster the same learning in children: being kind, warm and loving, yet firm and consistent. Physical and mental well-being are important, as is a demonstrated sense of ethical responsibility and reliability.

The well-rounded teacher, while maintaining a professional commitment, has other interests as well. Good teachers have an involvement with the world outside the walls of the early childhood setting. They want to help children understand some of the real-life issues and concerns. They know that their interest in the world at large transmits itself to children.

Children deserve teachers who understand their nature and respect the limits of behavior. The best teachers are the ones who are struggling to become more than they are, on any given day, and who demonstrate to their students that this quest to learn and to grow, to accept failure and go on to new challenges, is what life is all about (LeShan, 1992).

Self-Awareness

To be the best teacher possible, understanding and accepting oneself is vital. **Self-awareness** will make a difference in the way teachers relate to children. Each teacher must ask: Who and what and why am I? And how does knowing this bring some meaning into my life? How does it affect my life as a teacher? What guides my moral and ethical decisions?

Teachers communicate an authentic appreciation of learning when they have a sense of it in their own lives. Teachers might well ask

1 Teachers are in a unique position to strengthen the bond between a child's school experience and family culture.

themselves: Do I see myself as a learner? Where does my learning take place? How? What happens to me when something is difficult or when I make a mistake? Do I learn from other teachers? Do I learn from children? Teachers' recognition of themselves as learning, growing persons gives an added degree of sincerity to teaching.

Asking—and then answering—these questions helps teachers gain insights into their own behavior as adults and as professionals who work with children. Pausing to look at their own behavior when faced with a difficult task or in handling a mistake helps teachers remember what children experience each day.

Opening themselves up to the possibility of learning from students stretches teachers' capacity to grow into relationships with children based on mutual respect and trust. This is especially important when teachers do not share the same cultural background or have no experience with a particular disability.[1]

Opening themselves to learning from other teachers creates a foundation for mutual support, collegiality, professional mind-stretching, and deepening of friendships.

The first step is self-awareness; the second step is self-acceptance. Adults who work with young children adopt these insights into their relationships with children, families, and other staff members. When teachers take the time to look at their own style of behavior and how it affects others, they place themselves on a par with children as learning, growing people.

Self-knowledge—examining values and personal qualities—takes courage and a willingness to risk oneself. Accepting oneself is where to begin in accepting children.

Attitudes and Biases

A teacher's values and attitudes weave their way into every relationship and is an indication of the ethical framework that guides the way they live and teach. This can be both positive and negative. Personal beliefs concerning race, culture, gender, handicaps, and economic status may negatively affect our teaching in ways of which we are not aware.[2] Facing prejudices about children and families based on long-held beliefs may be one of the most difficult things for a teacher to do. Most teachers will not have lived through the significant and powerful experience of adapting to a new culture, or learning a new language, or surviving on food stamps and aid to dependent children, or living in a wheelchair; therefore, they may be uncomfortable with people who are labeled "different" because they have faced these issues.

Adults have opinions, born of their own experiences, of what is "good" or "naughty" behavior. Personal histories are filled with biases. Children who are messy, who have odors, whose clothes are too big or too small, who eat strange food, who don't do what girls or boys are supposed to do, may bother some teachers. Some of these biases can be resolved, but only if a teacher takes the time to examine personal beliefs and biases.

A positive self-concept and a willingness to be open to new experiences are hallmarks of a good teacher of young children.

---

1 A teacher's lifelong learning includes self-awareness and the ability to learn from others.

2 Patricia Ramsey in her book *Teaching and Learning in a Diverse World* (2004) provides a format for the start of a thorough self-investigation of individual attitudes and biases.

There is a great deal of emphasis today on what is termed the "**anti-bias** approach"[1] to teaching young children (Derman-Sparks, 1989). (See sections in Chapters 9, 11, and 15 for further discussion.) This concern stems from several issues:

- significant changes in the ethnic makeup in the United States, especially in the last decade;
- widespread racial and ethnic prejudice still prevalent in this country; and
- concern on the part of early childhood educators of the harm being done to children's self-identity and self-esteem.

This important movement promotes the concept that all children are born equal and are worthy of our respect and it challenges teachers to examine beliefs, attitudes, and actions that might deny any child that unconditional respect.

The anti-bias approach affords teachers a tremendous opportunity to confront their own anxieties and biases. As they work with families of various religious and ethnic minorities they learn some of their cultural norms and practices, and promote greater global understanding with the children they teach.

As a way to begin, teachers might ask themselves a few questions:

- Am I aware of my own identity and its influences on my beliefs and behaviors?
- Do I have a set of ethical beliefs I follow? Is there a system of ethical behaviors related to working with children and families?

Teachers' values and dttitudes are reflected in the way they work with children.

- Do I truly foster a respect for the value of those who are somehow different from me? How?
- Do I examine my biases and look at ways I can change my own attitudes? When? How?
- Do I show a preference for children who most closely fit my own ethnic, cultural, and religious background? When? How?
- Do I somehow pass along my biases to the children I teach? When? How? With whom?
- Do I truly enjoy differences in human beings? When? With whom?

Figure 5-3 notes some critical issues teachers face when they work with families whose primary language is other than English. These suggestions reinforce the need for teachers to become more sensitive to their own attitudes about cultures other than their own.

Issues for Teachers When Families Speak Other Languages

1. Fluency in the child's language is critical to effective communication and to maximizing the child's learning experience.

2. Focus on the family's competency and learn to value the family's child-rearing practices.

3. Teachers' ability to preserve and enhance another families' culture by learning and valuing their own first.

4. Promote the use of multi-age groupings of children to foster social responsibility.[2]

5. Confront one's own personal attitudes and biases.[3]

FIGURE 5-3 Kuster (1994) suggests five critical issues for teachers who work with children and families who speak languages other than English.

1 All early childhood programs should be examined for discrimination, bias, and ethnocentrism so that children can develop a positive self-identity.

2 This activity may be developmentally appropriate practice that complements many diverse cultural traditions.

3 Teachers may need to learn new skills to effectively enhance a child's sense of self.

Teacher Burnout

Teacher burnout is an occupational hazard of substantial proportion and often results when a teacher is faced with a demanding workload, uncertain or inadequate rewards, and other pressures that damage work effectiveness. At its most extreme, teacher burnout can drive a good professional out of the field altogether, a common situation in early childhood settings and one that creates *one of the highest occupational turnover rates in the nation.*

When teachers feel that their efforts are not appreciated or they are not making the kind of impact with children and families, the results are low morale, stress, and disillusionment in a profession where staff quality is the most important single factor in program quality. Some consider that the No Child Left Behind plan (see Chapter 15) is causing increased stress with its emphasis on what they see as inappropriate state-induced standards which do not focus on the development of the whole child. This creates a conflict in values and in their ability to meet the requirements of their job.

In a climate where teachers can meet children's needs and program goals can be effectively addressed, feelings of job satisfaction and productivity will prevail. Bloom (2005) cites ten characteristics that produce a healthy and positive school climates:

- friendly, supportive, and trusting staff relationships
- emphasis on personal and professional growth
- leadership with clear expectations that encourages and supports staff
- clearly defined roles and policies
- fairness and equity regarding promotions, raises, and other rewards
- staff involved in decision making
- agreement among staff on philosophy, goals, and objectives
- emphasis on efficiency and good planning
- a physical environment that promotes responsible teaching and learning
- the ability to adapt to change and solve problems

It is the responsibility of all teachers on the staff to work together to create the kind of climate that enhances success and satisfaction in the workplace. Related discussions are in Chapters 10 and 15.

Professionalism

Professional attitudes and behavior contribute to successful teaching. Teachers should relate to one another as peers and professional colleagues, and keep personal grievances out of the early childhood setting. There is no place in the setting for petty gossip, ill will, or exclusive cliques.[1] Through written personnel policies, most schools have established appropriate procedures through which teachers may address conflicts and issues. The professional approach, however, is to first attempt to work out personal differences on a one-to-one basis.

Teachers should ask themselves: Do I behave in a professional manner? Can I keep confidences without being told to do so? Do I try to meet with those with whom I have differences in an attempt to work them out? Do I complain publicly about another member of the staff?

Barbara Biglan's "Insights" article at the end of this chapter looks at professionalism in a creative and exciting way.

A COLLABORATIVE EFFORT: TEAM TEACHING

The Team Approach

The heart of teaching is what happens when you begin to work in a classroom every day. The teaching role is not restricted to working with children, though. Numerous adults must be met, worked with, and included in the total teaching picture. Some of these people may be:

- other professional teachers, aides, and student teachers
- volunteers
- program directors and administrators
- school support personnel: clerical and janitorial staffs, food-service workers, bus drivers
- families
- consultants and specialists

The majority of these interactions will be with other teachers, and these relationships are among the most important a teacher can have. The beginning teacher may join a team of

---

 1 The teacher has an important role as a behavior model with other teachers as well as with children.

teachers or may teach in a small class alone. This will depend on

- the age level of the children,
- licensing or accrediting requirements,
- the size of the classroom, and
- the school's philosophy and practices.

The team approach is common in many nursery schools and child care centers where larger groups of children attend. Kindergarten, first-, and second-grade teachers generally teach alone in self-contained classrooms, sometimes with an aide. In extended-day, after-school programs, high school and college students may make up the rest of the team.

Team Composition

Most teams are composed of people with varying skills, experience, and training. A typical group will have a lead or head teacher—someone who is trained in child development or early childhood education. Assistants with less experience and training add support. Student teachers, interns, and volunteers may round out the group. A resource teacher—someone who specializes in art, music, or physical development, for instance—may also be available on a part-time basis.

Many state regulations mandate a minimum number of adults in the early childhood setting, and this minimum varies with the ages of the children. In infant programs, for instance, there is a higher ratio of adults per child (NAEYC suggests as optimal a ratio of 1:4), so it is more likely there will be several teachers in one classroom. Together the teachers will shape, direct, and participate in that program as a team of teachers.

The prescribed ratio of adult to children changes as the children mature and become able to function in more independent ways.

Role Definition and Satisfaction

To teach successfully, each person on the team must have a satisfying role to play. That means each person must be appreciated for the special something he or she brings to the classroom and the school. Beginning teachers might want to ask themselves: Is there a place in my school (or on my team) that is uniquely mine? How do my special talents and experiences contribute to the success of this program? These questions would make for a good staff meeting discussion so that all teachers could reflect on their special capabilities.

Professional attitudes and behaviors are crucial. Teachers and administrators work together in solving problems as colleagues and coworkers.

A written job description helps teachers understand the scope of their own position as well as those of other staff members. Clearly defined teacher roles also serve as a guard against legal and ethical problems, especially if children are injured at school. Teachers should ask themselves: Is my job description clearly written so I know the extent of my responsibilities? Do I fulfill my obligations, or are there areas where I am lax that might prove harmful to a child?

A clear understanding of the roles and responsibilities a teacher has is essential for the teacher's own sense of well-being and for the smooth functioning of the program.

Flexibility

Just as it is important to change with and adapt to the varying needs of children, so is it crucial to respond to the needs of other staff members with a give-and-take approach. Flexibility involves a willingness to offer and accept negotiation and compromise to preserve the effectiveness of the whole staff's effort. Teachers should ask themselves: Do I demonstrate a willingness to change with the changing needs of my co-workers, or do I adhere rigidly to preset plans or attitudes? Am I open to new ideas proposed by others? Do I help children become comfortable with flexibility and change?

Open and Frequent Communication

The ability to communicate thoughts, concerns, and feelings to others honestly and openly is perhaps the most important factor in promoting good personal relationships. Communication

Members of a teaching team need frequent communication with one another.

takes many forms: verbal and nonverbal, written and spoken, and body language.

Teachers must seek out opportunities for formal and informal communication with others on the staff. This may mean taking advantage of the staff/faculty lounge during lunch hour or arriving five minutes early to catch someone before children arrive. For those who work on teaching teams, set-up and cleanup times can be used to discuss issues, modify strategies, and resolve misunderstandings.

The three basic reasons for developing successful communication links with others on the teaching staff are:

1. *To share information*—about children and their families ("Sheila's grandmother died yesterday"), about changes in the schedule ("The dentist is unable to visit today; who wants to conduct group time?"), and about child development strategies ("Remember, we are all going to observe Leah's gross motor skills this week").

2. *To contribute new ideas*—teachers encourage one another to keep teaching fresh and alive when they share a recent article of interest, reports from a conference they attended, or a successful art activity.

3. *To solve problems*—accepting differences in opinions, approaches, personality, and style among people is part of the challenge of working closely with others. Open communication is an ongoing process in which people have honest and frequent discussion of their differences, respecting each other's feelings and integrity and working together for mutually agreeable solutions.

Who Am I?

Beginning teachers may feel uncomfortable or inadequate in their relationships with others on the staff; once they know more about

Sharing insights with colleagues helps the early childhood professional become more self-aware.

themselves and accept who they are, teachers can apply this self-awareness to their relationships with fellow workers.

To promote self-knowledge that contributes to success as a member of a faculty or teaching team, teachers might ask themselves: What are my strengths and weaknesses as a teacher, and how do they complement or conflict with others in this school? Do I prefer to follow or lead, to plan programs or carry out the plans developed by others? In what teaching situations do I feel uncomfortable, and why? What have I done lately that caused me to learn more about myself?

Mutual Respect

Appreciating and accepting the individuality of other team members are as important to the success of the program as are appreciating and accepting the individuality of each child. The climate of trust and the nonthreatening atmosphere gained through mutual respect allow each staff member to contribute openly and innovatively to the program. To develop that appreciation for one another, teachers should ask themselves: What do I have in common with my co-workers? Are their teaching philosophies different from mine and, if so, in what way? What are their social and cultural values?[1] What are their previous experiences with young children? What do I want them to respect and accept about me?

Team Support

A sense of being a team does not happen by accident, but by conscious effort. Every member of the staff must be committed to working together on a daily basis as well as to the long-term goals of the specific program and to being empathic to the feelings and needs of co-workers.

To develop staff relationships that enhance support for one another, teachers should ask themselves: How can I show support to my co-workers? What can I do to promote and sustain high morale among my fellow teachers? Where and how can I offer help to another staff member?

Sharing the Spotlight

Tension among staff members can arise from a sense of competition. Teachers must be willing to admit that others are just as dedicated to children and deserving of their affections as they are. There must be a feeling of shared success when things work well, just as there is a shared responsibility when problems arise. Teachers should ask themselves: How do I feel when a parent in front of me praises another teacher? How do I feel when a child prefers another teacher to me? Am I able to acknowledge my co-workers' achievements?

Evaluation

Evaluations are part of the privilege of claiming membership in the teaching profession. No teacher can become truly successful unless provisions are made for ongoing evaluations that provide a clear picture that confirms strengths and pinpoints areas for growth. Teachers should ask themselves: Do I accept evaluations as an essential part of teaching? Am I responsive to the suggestions made in my evaluations? When I evaluate others, am I fair, and do I share my observations in a supportive way?

The evaluation process is discussed in depth later in this chapter.

Advantages

There are many reasons why teaching in teams is such an integral part of so many early childhood programs. The advantages are numerous:

● *Variety of adult role models.* Teachers who are male, female, disabled, young, middle-aged, older, and varying in ethnic backgrounds bring equally diverse attitudes, approaches to children, interests, skills, and knowledge to share. This teaches children to accept differences in people as they watch adults interact with others on the teaching team.

● *Support for children.* The absence of one teacher is not as disruptive when the children can count on other familiar faces. This enables children to learn to trust the teaching environment because someone they know is always there.

● *Collegiality.* Teachers can find support from one another as they share planning problems and achievements and grow in admiration and respect for one another.

● *Lightened workload.* There is a sharing of all the teaching tasks, from curriculum planning

1 When we learn about the cultural norms and habits of our colleagues, we model a respect and concern for all.

and cleanup to parent conferencing and record keeping.

- *Enriched program.* Talents and resources of the team are used to best advantage so that team members will teach to their strengths, adding richness to the program.

Disadvantages

Good teachers are "complicated human beings with strengths and weaknesses, talents and limitations, good days and bad days" (LeShan, 1992). They work at becoming good teachers by developing skills in interpersonal relationships with other adults, just as they promote good social relationships between the young children they teach. Most of the disadvantages of **team teaching** stem from communication problems among team members.

Communication problems and conflicts arise in every teaching situation. The following section, "The Beginnings of Professionalism" is particularly useful for team situations. Teachers new to the team teaching process will want to discuss them with other team members.

THE BEGINNINGS OF PROFESSIONALISM

Eight essential attributes of successful teaching are:

1. knowledge and skills
2. abides by a code of ethics
3. continuing education and professional development
4. professional affiliations
5. knowledge of career options
6. cultural competency
7. advocacy
8. becoming a whole teacher

Knowledge and Skills

There is a body of knowledge, and educational foundation, that is assumed of anyone entering the early childhood professional. Some basic teaching skills are also necessary. These include methods and techniques appropriate for teaching the very young child.

Professional expectations start with having a common background with others in the field. This includes studying child development and human behavior, family relations, parent education and development, and curriculum planning.

Some practical teaching experience under the guidance of a master teacher is expected, as is familiarity with observation and recording techniques. This foundation of knowledge and experience provides the framework for professional development as teachers acquire further skills on the job.

The process of becoming a professional teacher is a progression along a continuum of development. The state you live in may or may not have regulations for early childhood teachers; some states offer a specialized certification for those in the early childhood field. Professional expectations mandated by the states provide some degree of professionalization of early childhood teachers.

Figure 5-4 is an example of the California statewide certification program. This *career lattice* has a number of levels, each with alternative qualifications for meeting the requirements. Within each level, there are a variety of teaching roles. Each state defines its own certification standards. Information is available through the state's Department of Education.

Figure 5-5 has some useful descriptions of the various roles teachers have in early childhood programs. While not a "career ladder," this chart shows how the progression from teacher aide to master teacher is matched to increasing responsibilities and education.

Abides by a Code of Ethical Conduct

As teachers mature, they turn their attention to issues and concerns outside themselves. Many of these issues are related to ethical conflicts and moral principles. Teachers are, after all, human beings, and that entails genuine conflict about behavior. Doing what is right becomes difficult at times; knowing what is right may be elusive. Even identifying what is right—an ethical conflict—may not be obvious. NAEYC's Code of Ethical Conduct (see Appendix A) is an important resource for all teachers and caregivers and can help their own personal code of ethics.

Every day, situations arise with parents, other teachers, and administrators that require teachers to make some hard choices. Some cases are clearly ethical dilemmas: suspected child abuse by a parent or teacher, talking about children and their families outside of school, or the firing of a staff member without due cause. Others, some of which are common

A Career Lattice: Child Development Permit Matrix

Level	Education Requirement	Experience Requirement
Assistant	6 units of ECE or CD	None
Associate teacher	12 units ECE/CD, including core courses	50 days of 3+ hours/day within 4 years
Teacher	24 units ECE/CD, including core clourses + 16 general education (GE) units	175 days of 3+ hours/day within 4 years
Master teacher	24 units ECE/CD, including 16 GE units + 6 specialization units + 2 units adult supervision	350 days of 3+ hours/day within 4 years
Site supervisor	A.A. (or 60 units) with 24 ECE/CD units, including core + 6 units administration + 2 units adult supervision	350 days of 4+ hours/day including at least 100 days of supervising adults
Program director	B.A. with 24 ECE/CD units, including core + 6 units administration + 2 units adult supervision	Site supervisor status and one program year of site supervisor experience

FIGURE 5-4 A combination of education and experience work together to form a career ladder for early childhood professionals in California who want a child development permit.

General Role Definitions for the Early Childhood Teacher

Title	Description	Minimum Qualifications
Apprentice/ Teacher Aide	Is responsible to teacher for implementing program	Entry level, no previous formal training but enrolled in early childhood education classes
Assistant or Associate Teacher	Is part of the teaching team under the direction of teacher; may implement curriculum, supervise children, and communicate with parents.	Child Development Associate (CDA) credential
Teacher	Is coleader who plans and implements curriculum, works with parents, and evaluates children's progress	Associate's degree in early childhood education or related field
Lead Teacher	Creates a model classroom, applies good early childhood education practices, supervises other team members, develops new curriculum, provides leadership to team	Bachelor's degree in early childhood education or related field; supervised teaching experience; additional coursework work in family life, assessment, supervision, etc.

FIGURE 5-5 There are many ways to reach the top of a career ladder. Each role has its own job description that will vary with the type of early childhood education setting. The qualifications will also be based on individual programs and their needs. (Adapted from *Blueprint for Action: Achieving Center-Based Change through Staff Development*, by P. J. Bloom, © 2005 New Horizons. Reprinted with permission.)

occurrences, may not seem as obvious. Some everyday examples are:

When parents:

- ask you to advance their child into the next class against your advice.
- want you to use discipline practices common to their family and culture but at odds with your own sense of what children need.[1]

- attempt to gossip with you about another staff member.

When another teacher:

- suggests a private staff meeting outside of school with a select group of teachers.
- refuses to take a turn cleaning out the animal cages.
- regularly is absent from staff meetings.

1 Teachers will need to become aware of child-rearing practices from many cultures.

- disagrees with the school's educational philosophy and continues to teach in ways that differ from the approved methods in that setting.

- goes to the school administrator with an inappropriate complaint about a staff team member.

When the administrator:

- insists on adding one more child to an already overenrolled class.

- makes personnel decisions based on friendship, not performance.

- backs a parent who complains about a teacher without hearing the teacher's side of the story.

Teachers may find it helpful to discuss their ethical concerns with colleagues. Some centers provide in-service programs for the staff where these issues are raised. Other schools have a code of ethics for their employees to follow.

Just what are **ethics**? Essentially, they are the moral guidelines by which we govern our own behavior and that of society. "Ethics—in the form of knowledge and skill in making responsible professional decisions—is one of the most fundamental qualities of a competent early childhood educator" (Smith, in Feeney & Freeman, 1999).

We can strictly define ethics as "the system or code of morals of a particular philosopher, religion, group, or profession." This definition suggests that a personal code of ethics can be supported by a professional code of ethics. A code of ethics is a set of statements that helps us deal with the temptations inherent in our occupations. It helps us act in terms of what is right rather than what is expedient (Katz & Ward, 1991).

Why might the early childhood profession need such a code? A primary reason is that the choices teachers make should be based not simply on personal values and preferences but "on values, judgments, and ethical commitments shared by the professional society or association of which they are a member" (Katz & Ward, 1991).[1]

A code of ethics provides collective wisdom and advice from a broad base in the profession. It states the principles by which each individual can measure and govern professional behavior. It says that a group or association has recognized the moral dimensions of its work. It provides teachers with a known, defined core of professional values—those basic commitments that any early childhood educator should consider inviolate. This protects teachers and administrators from having to make hard ethical decisions on the spur of the moment, possibly on the basis of personal bias. An established professional code supports the teacher's choice by saying, "It isn't that I won't act this way: No early childhood educator should act this way" (Kipnis, 1987).

NAEYC adopted a Code of Ethical Conduct and Statement of Commitment in 1989. It has since been revised, most recently in 1997. The four sections of the Code are: (1) Ethical responsibilities to children; (2) Ethical responsibilities to families; (3) Ethical responsibilities to colleagues; and (4) Ethical responsibilities to community and society. The Code of Ethical Conduct and Statement of Commitment may be found in Appendix A at the back of this text. Figure 5-6 shows a basic list of core values that has emerged from this work, values "that are deeply rooted in the history of our field" (NAEYC, 1997).

Continuing Education and Professional Development

Creative and stimulating classrooms are the product of teachers who continue to learn more about how to teach. After the initial stage of

Core Values of NAEYC's Code of Ethical Conduct

- Appreciating childhood as a unique and valuable stage of the human life cycle.

- Basing our work with children on knowledge of child development.

- Appreciating and supporting the close ties between the child and family.

- Recognizing that children are best understood in the context of family, culture, and society.

- Respecting the dignity, worth, and uniqueness of each individual (child, family member, and colleague).

- Helping children and adults achieve their full potential in the context of relationships that are based on trust, respect, and positive regard.

FIGURE 5-6 These core values form the basis of agreement in the profession about standards of ethical behavior. See Appendix A for the full version.

1 One of the values in NAEYC's Code of Ethical Conduct is the recognition that children are best understood in the context of family, culture, and society.

What do You Think?

What do you think the NAEYC Code of Ethics has to say about cultural diversity in early childhood programs? Which ideals and principles in the code would you use as references in making a decision related to cultural sensitivity and understanding? Look at the situations described on pages 204 and 205. How do you see the code of ethics supporting resolutions to those dilemmas? How does the code of ethics relate to your own sense of moral and ethical behavior?

Katz (1999) describes four distinct stages of teacher development, ranging from Survival to Maturity. The beginning teacher often feels inadequate and ill-prepared during the first year of teaching (Survival) but soon begins to focus on individual children and specific behavior problems (Consolidation). By the third or fourth year (Renewal) the teacher is ready to explore new ideas and resources and, within another year or two, has come to terms with teaching and searches for insights and perspectives (Maturity). At each stage, teachers need differing degrees of on-site support (mentoring), with increased exposure to professional conferences and organizations.

If time to pursue continuing education is not built into a teacher's schedule, there may be other options:

● In-service training programs may be brought into the school setting. Resource people can be invited to lead the staff in discussions about children's behavior, family relationships, assessment charts, science curricula, and creating multicultural classrooms.

teaching, many teachers begin to seek new challenges and new ways to improve the quality of their teaching. Usually this search leads to some form of **continuing education**, such as participation in workshops, courses, or seminars.

Ethical questions arise daily. This child has been taught to hit back if anyone hits him. What does the teacher say to him? How should this situation be handled?

- Members of the teaching staff can develop a program of their own, offering their expertise to fellow faculty at an in-service meeting.

- A computer specialist, art resource teacher, or multicultural expert can be invited to visit the classrooms, instructing children and providing staff with some useful ideas and plans.

- A family therapist can be invited to speak at a staff meeting about strategies for supporting families in crisis.

- A library for teachers, stocked with professional books, journals (such as *Young Children*), and newspapers (such as *Education Week*), can provide a teacher with the means to keep up with current trends and practices and to improve teaching skills in the classroom.

- Parents who are professionals in a variety of fields can be utilized whenever possible to enrich the knowledge and skills of the staff.

Look back at the career lattice (Figure 5-4) and see how many opportunities there are for advancement with the right education and experience. As you achieve each level, there are challenges to be met. A course in group dynamics, cultural sensitivity, or adult assessment portfolios will enhance your chances to move into more satisfying work and enlarge

Video VIEW Point 5-1

"Professionals in any field are inspired by conferences, seminars, workshops, courses, and meetings with their professional organization."

COMPETENCY: Professionalism

AGE GROUP: Infants and Toddlers

CRITICAL THINKING QUESTIONS:

1. Why do you think it is important for an early childhood educator to belong to a professional organization?

2. What associations and professional organizations might you consider joining?

your contributions to those you work with and to the profession as a whole.

Professional Affiliations

Early childhood professionals may choose to join one of the professional organizations related to the early childhood field. One of the largest, the National Association for the Education of Young Children (NAEYC), has local and state affiliate groups through which one can become a member. NAEYC offers a range of services to its members, including conferences and publications such as the journal *Young Children.* The Association for Childhood Education International (ACEI) has a similar function, whereas the Society for Research in Child Development (SRCD) focuses on child psychology, research, and development.

There are a number of organizations concerned with young children, teachers, and issues related to the early childhood profession. Abundant resources are available from these groups, and their Web sites at the end of this chapter and in Appendix C.

Knowledge of Career Options

The need for quality programs for young children has never been greater and the demand for early childhood specialists will continue, fostered by national attention to the issues of children and families. If you are considering a career in early childhood education (ECE), the options

Through frequent contacts with teachers and administrators, parents can become aware of the importance of professional training and development for early childhood educators.

Direct Services to Children and Families

Teacher in early childhood program
Director of child care facility nursery school,
    Montessori program
Family day-care provider
Nanny or au pair
Foster parent
Social worker/adoption agent
Pediatric nurse/school nurse
Family therapist/parent educator
Pediatrician
Parent educator
Early intervention specialist
Recreation leader
Play group leader
Home visitor

Community Involvement

State/local licensing worker
Legislative advocate
Child care law specialist
ECE environmental consultant
Interior designer for children's spaces
Government planning agent on children's issues
Consultant in bilingual education, multiculturalism
Nutrition specialist for children
Child care referral counselor

Indirect Services to Children and Families

Curriculum specialist
Instructional specialist—computers
Child development researcher
ECE specialist
Program consultant
Consumer advocate
Teacher trainer, two- and four-year colleges
Consultant
Resource and referral programs
State and national departments of education and/or human
    services

Other Options

Communications consultant
Script writer/editor
Freelance writer
Children's book author
Children's photographer
Microcomputer specialist/program consultant

FIGURE 5-7 There are many challenges in a variety of careers awaiting the early childhood professional. (Adapted from "Career Options in Early Childhood Education" by Dianne Widmeyer Eyer. In *Beginnings & Beyond: Foundations in Early Childhood Education* (3rd ed.), p. 170. Clifton Park, NY: Thomson Delmar Learning.)

are many and varied. Figure 5-7 lists some of the possibilities that exist in this profession.

Cultural Competency

Throughout this text, you will be exposed to cultural awareness and sensitivity in many contexts. In Chapter 1 (diversity, immigrant children, class differences); in Chapter 3 (cultural sensitivity and family cultural influences); in Chapter 7 (culturally appropriate guidance); Chapter 8 (the changing American family; Chapter 10 (culturally appropriate curriculum, inclusive curriculum, multicultural curriculum, and culturally responsive teachers); and Chapter 15 (multicultural education, bilingual education, the plight of the immigrant, class differences, equal play and gender issues, and sexuality).

The culturally competent early childhood professional must be aware of the issues addressed in those chapters. The population trends within the United States have changed

dramatically over the last few decades and the ability to adapt to a diversified group of families will be the challenge for the teachers of the 21st century.

This requires a pluralistic mindset and an ability to communicate across cultures and individual circumstances. We will make our own personal and professional journey through these remarkable times to prepare children to live in a world of diversity.

Advocacy

Children of America need advocates to speak for them and their families on issues ranging from health care to education to poverty to professional quality, staff, and wages. It is up to the early childhood professional to give voice to the issues concerning our young children and to educate the public about those issues. Public policy makers on the local, state, and national level need to hear from those who can speak out for those who cannot.

Video VIEW PoinT 5-2

"In their role as advocates, teachers demonstrate the vital importance of care and education for young children to their community."

COMPETENCY: Professionalism

AGE GROUP: Preschool

CRITICAL THINKING QUESTIONS:

1. What can you do to become an advocate for young children?

2. What early childhood education issues in your local community appeal to you as an advocate?

Advocates for children call attention to the moral and social responsibility our nation has to its young. Chapter 15 describes ways in which early childhood professionals can become greater advocates for today's families and children.

BECOMING A WHOLE TEACHER

At some point teachers emerge with their own point of view about teaching, based on self-knowledge of what calls them to teaching, why they teach the way they do, and what they know of the children they teach. This integration of knowledge and training, experience and life, is referred to by several names. Some say "real" teachers. Others refer to the "total" teacher. A common phrase is the "whole" teacher. Any one of these terms is an apt reflection of the relationship between how teachers view children and how they see themselves. There is a meshing of the emotional, physical, intellectual, and social aspects of each human being, adult or child.

Something happens when this blending occurs. During the first few years in the classroom, teachers consolidate their various official functions—merging their teacher training and experience with their personal style and nature. To discover and define the role of a teacher means to develop a personal teaching style. This is the sum of one's response to teaching, and it is unique to each teacher. When it happens, a beginning teacher becomes aware of "feeling" like a teacher. The strengths and convictions one has as a person blend with those one ... a teacher; they become inseparable. What ... ers do and what teachers are become wo ... together. And in adding the personal teach... to the professional teacher, the sum becomes greater than two, allowing the whole teacher the freedom to grow in insight and understanding.

EVALUATING TEACHERS: A KEY TO QUALITY

Teachers are the single most important factor in determining program quality. What makes "the effective teacher" has no one simple answer. Earlier sections in this chapter describe important attributes of the teacher. How these can be assessed is complicated, but assessing them is necessary to ensure the highest quality of teaching. There are ways to evaluate teachers that guide them toward more effective teaching in their work with children, co-workers, parents, and administrators.

Think of teachers as conductors of a symphony orchestra. They do not compose the music. They do not design or build the instruments, nor do they decide which ones will be played in the orchestra pit. They may even have limited choice of the music that will be played. Yet it is their job to lead a group of musicians through a medley of songs, bringing out the best in each musician, all under the intense scrutiny of a critical audience. Teachers must do this with care and expertise under the watchful eyes of parents and families, boards, supervisors and funding agencies.

As teachers' effectiveness is measured, they can learn better techniques for working with children and for planning quality environments and programs. The process for establishing and meeting these goals is evaluation. Teacher evaluation forms in this chapter can be adapted for use with student teachers and aides. Reread the introduction to evaluation in Chapter 2, on pages 79–84, for other insights.

A good evaluation process helps to:

- challenge methods, assumptions, and purposes;
- provide information by which to rate performance and quality;
- monitor progress, growth, and planning;
- set goals to meet for improving performance and quality;
- identify ways to support and provide follow-up for change.

COMPONENTS OF A GOOD EVALUATION

Certain elements are common to all evaluations. The following criteria serve as a guideline to an effective evaluation process:

1. *Select who and what will be evaluated.* Decide how often and under what circumstances the evaluation will take place.

2. *Have a clear purpose or motive.* Know the reasons for making an evaluation and consider who and what will benefit from the process. State what you expect to gain from it.

3. *Decide how the data will be collected.* Have a good understanding of the process or format that will be used. Be clear about who will collect the data and make the report. Some sample evaluations are found in this chapter.

4. *Know what use will be made of the evaluation.* Be aware of what decisions will be made from the results. Know who receives this information and how they will interpret it.

5. *State goals clearly.* Evaluators should make sure goals and objectives are outlined in ways that can be measured and observed easily and state behavioral goals in terms of what the person will do. The person being evaluated should be equally clear in his or her responses to the evaluation instrument(s).

6. *Make a plan.* Be prepared to act. Use the results to motivate people to put into action what they have learned from the evaluation. Set new goals based on the evaluation. Set up a timetable to check progress on a regular basis.

The important point to remember is that evaluation should be a continuous process, for without follow-through, long-lasting improvement is unlikely to occur. Take a look at Figure 5-8 to see how a **feedback loop** works for an evaluation process.

Why Evaluate?

It is a professional expectation in many programs that an annual assessment will be made of the teaching staff. Teacher evaluations are often part of an accrediting procedure. Continuing education and professional development can be the result of a good evaluation process to help the growing teacher gain greater experience and effectiveness. The

FIGURE 5-8 A feedback loop is a continuous cycle in which teacher behavior is observed for a performance evaluation. The evaluation is offered through growth goals, which are set in order to affect teacher behavior. Thus, the circle is continuous, with each part helping the next.

following sections describe the major reasons for teacher evaluations.

To Describe Job Responsibilities

It is essential for teachers to understand their job to do it well. A good job description outlines what is expected. One purpose of an evaluation is to see how those expectations are being met.

In an infant and toddler center, for example, teachers try to help children learn to separate comfortably from their parents. Evaluation in this setting could focus on the exact skills needed to implement this goal. How does a teacher help a parent separate from a young child? What environmental cues does the teacher prepare? How is the child in distress comforted? What teaching strategies are important?

Evaluation for specifying job responsibilities is a part of one's professional self-definition as well as a clarification of actual duties. Studying ourselves helps us know who we are and what we do. Assessing job responsibilities aids in this process.

To Monitor Job Effectiveness

Once clear guidelines are set for teaching expectations, a method is needed to monitor actual teaching. Most evaluation systems attempt to check teacher effectiveness. This process may vary from school to school. In some schools, teaching effectiveness is measured, in part, by child achievement, such as how children score on tests. Other centers may solicit parent opinion.

Evaluating teachers can help set professional growth goals and clarify a teacher's strengths and areas of improvement.

A teacher's co-workers may be part of an assessment team. For the most part, an evaluation for job effectiveness will include an observation of teaching time with children.

To Clarify Strengths and Weaknesses

An evaluation procedure preferred by many teachers is one that identifies specific areas of strength and weakness. Feedback about actual teaching and other job responsibilities is helpful to all teachers, whether beginners or experienced personnel. An assessment that offers teachers information about how to perform their job better contributes to job competence and satisfaction. By recognizing strengths, teachers receive positive feedback for high-quality work.[1] By identifying weaknesses, they can begin to set realistic goals for improvement.

To Create a Plan for Professional Development

One function of teacher evaluation is to foster professional development. Teachers do not become "good" and then stay that way for life. Regardless of their stage of development, teachers need goals in order to continually improve.

To be effective, goal setting must be embedded in an on-going system of professional development. Caruso and Fawcett (1999) note that staff development must also be integrated with the overall goals of the center or program for which a teacher is being evaluated.

Professional development takes into consideration the various stages of expertise and development of the individuals on the staff. A career-ladder plan, adopted by NAEYC in 1993, takes into account the diversity of education, training, and experience of early childhood professionals. The ladder sets out steps individuals can take to assume more responsibility as they become more qualified and prepared. This lattice framework promotes a system of professional development, which can motivate early childhood professionals at all levels toward professional growth (Willer, 1994).

To Determine Employment

An evaluation can also be used to decide whether teachers should be retained, promoted, or released. Assessment procedures are an administrator's most valuable tools in making that decision. A clear and effective evaluation tool enables the administrator to monitor performance and target specific areas for improvement. The administrator then has a fair and equitable way to determine the promotional status of each employee.

To Meet Accreditation Requirements

Many programs seek accreditation by organizations whose standards they embrace. NAEYC is the leading accrediting body for early childhood programs through its National Academy of Early Childhood Programs. The self-study aspect of the accreditation process includes a teacher's self-assessment, the director's assessment of the teaching staff, and the teacher's assessment of the director. The criteria in the self-study provides the standards against which these evaluations are made, providing concrete ways to measure quality.

Issues in Teacher Evaluations

How to evaluate is an important issue in teacher assessment. A system for evaluating employees can be one of trust and mutual respect or of anxiety and tension. The method often determines how successful the entire evaluation will be.

Preliminary Steps

To begin with, a school follows the same guidelines for developing a teacher evaluation as for child assessment (see Chapter 6). That

 1 Teacher expectations can have a substantial effect on children's behavior and self-esteem. Check yourself for biases: how you interact with children is key to your effectiveness, and discriminatory interactions must be noted and remedied.

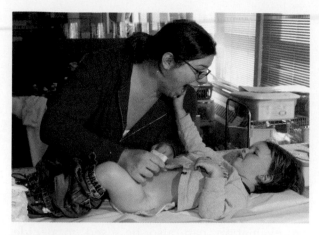

A teacher's self-evaluation provides an opportunity to improve her effectiveness with children.

is, the process includes determining a purpose, establishing who will collect the data and how, and clarifying how the evaluation will be used. In the assessment of teachers, the important components are: purpose (as described in Chapter 2), evaluators, process, and follow-through.

Evaluators

Several models have been developed around the issue of who will assess teacher performance.

Self-Evaluation. Self-assessment is used in the Child Development Associate's evaluation system for these reasons (Ward & CDA staff, 1976):

● The candidate is a valid source of information for use in assessment. Certain information is available only from the candidate's perspective.

● The candidate is able to clarify information on his or her performance, thereby adding to the assessment team's evidence for a valid decision.

● The candidate is better able to identify strengths and weaknesses and to receive recommendations for continued professional growth.

Figure 5-9 is an example of a staff evaluation form, which can also be used as a self-assessment tool. A less formal technique is to ask questions about yourself and your job, such as:

● How do I approach parent/family relationships?

● Have my guidance techniques been working well?

● Am I in a comfortable working relationship with my colleagues?

● What should be my next professional goals?

● How do I help children learn?

● Do I have a supportive relationship with my supervisor?

The answers to these few questions can provide a solid base for discussion between teacher and supervisor or assessment team.

One drawback of self-assessment is its subjectivity. We see ourselves too closely and too personally to be able to be entirely objective about our teaching. Therefore, self-assessment must be accompanied by other evaluating feedback.

Supervisory Evaluation. Job performance is an administrator's responsibility; therefore, teachers can expect their supervisor, director, or head teacher to be involved in their evaluation. Supervisors often use a single form combining a teacher's self-assessment and the supervisor's evaluation, such as Figure 5-9. This kind of form simplifies the paperwork and assures both teacher and supervisor that both are using the same criteria for evaluation. Caruso and Fawcett (1999) suggest a variety of formats used for evaluations; observations, conferences, videotapes, reports, portfolios, and storytelling are some of the ways to accomplish an assessment.

When selecting an appropriate format or tool, look for a balance in the categories on which a teacher is being evaluated. These usually include some of the following:

● knowledge and application of child development principles

● planning

● behavior management

● interactions with children

● interactions with adults (other teachers, administrators, and parents)

● interpersonal communication

● professionalism

● dependency

● cultural sensitivity

● respect for individual differences in adults and children

● preparing and maintaining appropriate learning environments

● health and safety

● personal qualities

Peer evaluation. Evaluation by others associated with the teachers is a welcome addition to the evaluation process. Often a system includes

Staff Evaluation

Employee _____

Evaluation Period _____

Key

How often observed:
C – Consistently
F – Frequently
O – Occasionally
N – Never

	C (90–100%)	F (60–89%)	O (30–59%)	N (0–29%)
General Work Habits				
1. Arrives on time				
2. Reliable in attendance; gives ample notice for absences				
3. Responsible in job duties				
4. Alert in health and safety matters				
5. Follows the center's philosophy				
6. Open to new ideas				
7. Flexible with assignments and schedule				
8. Comes to work with a positive attitude				
9. Looks for ways to improve the program				
10. Remains calm in a tense situation				
11. Completes required written communication on time				
Professional Development, Attitude, and Efforts				
1. Takes job seriously and seeks to improve skills				
2. Participates in workshops, classes, groups				
3. Reads and discusses distributed handouts				
4. Is self-reflective with goals for ongoing development				
Attitude and Skills with Children				
1. Friendly, warm, and affectionate				
2. Bonds low for child level interactions				
3. Uses a modulated, appropriate voice				
4. Knows and shows respect for individuals				
5. Is aware of development levels/changes				
6. Encourages independence/self-help				
7. Promotes self esteem in communication				
8. Limits interventions in problem solving				
9. Avoids stereotyping and labeling				
10. Reinforces positive behavior				
11. Minimal use of time out				
12. Regularly records observations of children				
Attitude and Skills with Parents				
1. Available to parents and approachable				
2. Listens and responds well to parents				
3. Is tactful with negative information				
4. Maintains confidentiality				
5. Seeks a partnership with parents				
6. Regularly communicates with parents				
7. Conducts parent conferences on schedule				
Attitude and Skills with Class				
1. Creates an inviting learning environment				
2. Provides developmentally appropriate activities				
3. Develops plans from observation and portfolio entries				
4. Provides materials for all curriculum components				
5. Provides an appropriate role model				
6. Anticipates problems and redirects				
7. Is flexible and responsive to child's interests				
8. Is prepared for day's activities				
9. Handles transitions well				
Attitude and Skills with Co-Workers				
1. Is friendly and respectful with others				
2. Strives to assume a fair share of work				
3. Offers and shares ideas and materials				
4. Communicates directly and avoids gossip				
5. Approaches criticism with learning attitude				
6. Looks for ways to be helpful				

Comments:

FIGURE 5-9 The quality and effectiveness of teaching is affected by the quality and effectiveness of the evaluation process. This form is useful for a self-evaluation and a supervisory evaluation. (From *The Visionary Director: A Handbook for Dreaming, Organizing, and Improvising in Your Center*, by Margie Carter and Deb Curtis (Redleaf Press, 1998). Copyright © 1998 by Margie Carter and Deb Curtis. Reprinted with permission from Redleaf Press, St. Paul, Minnesota, www.redleafpress.org. To order call 800-423-8309.)

more than a teacher's supervisor. Possible combinations are:

- Teacher (self-evaluation) and supervisor
- Teacher, supervisor, and parent
- Teacher, supervisor, and another team member (teacher, aide, student teacher)

A team evaluation is a more collaborative approach. More information is collected on the teacher's performance. A team approach may be more valid and balanced because a decision about teaching will be made by consensus and discussion rather than individual, perhaps arbitrary, methods. Figure 5-10 is an example of a peer observation form that might be used.

Peer or team evaluation does have its disadvantages, however. It is a time-consuming process because more than one person is asked to evaluate a teacher. Feedback may be contradictory; what one evaluator sees as a strength, another may view as a shortcoming. The system can be complicated to implement. For instance, how do teachers work in a classroom and evaluate another team member at the same time? Can funds be found to bring in substitutes? Do fellow teachers have the time to devote to evaluating each other? How and when does a parent evaluate a teacher? Clearly, a school must weigh these issues carefully as evaluation systems are devised.

Peer Observation

Name of colleague observed _____   Date _____

As you observe, please note comments about the following aspects of the classroom environment: interactions between teacher and children; interactions between the teacher and other co-workers or volunteers; interactions between the teacher and parents; the physical arrangement of space; the curriculum; and health, nutrition, and safety aspects of the classroom.

Aspects of this classroom I was impressed with include...

1. _____

_____

2. _____

_____

3. _____

_____

Aspects of this classroom that might be improved include...

1. _____

_____

2. _____

_____

3. _____

_____

Signed _____

FIGURE 5-10 An evaluation will have a wider perspective when it comes from more than one viewpoint. (Adapted from *Blueprint for Action: Achieving Center-Based Change through Staff Development,* by P. J. Bloom, © 2005 New Horizons. Reprinted with permission.)

Teacher Goal	Example
To help each child develop a positive self-concept	I greet each child with a smile and a personal comment.
To help each child develop socially, emotionally, cognitively, and physically	I have goals for each child in each developmental area, fall and spring.
To help provide many opportunities for each child to be successful	My parent conference sheets have examples; for instance, Charlie didn't want to come to group time, so I had him pick the story and help me read it—he comes every day now!
To encourage creativity, questioning, and problem solving	This is my weak point. I tend to talk too much and tell them what to do.
To foster enjoyment for learning in each child	I do great group times and give everyone turns.
To facilitate children's development of a healthy identity and inclusive social skills	I participated in our center's self-study and am taking an anti-bias curriculum class.

FIGURE 5-11 Performance-based assessment ties the goals of the program to the teacher's work. This example asks the teacher to do a self-assessment; a director, parent, or peer could observe and make a second assessment.

A Systematic Process

Many evaluations are based on observable, specific information about a teacher's activities and responsibilities. This is known as a **performance-based assessment**. Figure 5-11 is an example of performance-based assessment in regard to a teacher's work with children. When paired with specific goals and expectations, this system is known as **competency-based assessment**.

Competency-based assessments outline exactly what teachers must do to demonstrate their competency, or skill, in their job responsibilities. Criteria are set as a teacher begins working. Areas are targeted that pinpoint what knowledge, skills, and behaviors the teacher must acquire.

The evaluation tools or format determine how valid the information gathered will be. Informal techniques may result in unreliable conclusions. A process that is formalized and systematic, related to goal setting and professional development, has a greater chance of success. While it is important to select an appropriate method and assessment tool, keep in mind that it is the process through which the evaluation is conducted that matters most.

Portfolio-based assessments are becoming a popular tool for helping teachers make sense of the experiences that help them become better teachers. A **portfolio** is not an assessment tool in and of itself. It is the display or collection system used to demonstrate evidence of professional growth. Folders, boxes, files, and binders, are all used to house the collection of data. It is an intentional compilation of materials and resources, collected over a period of time that provides evidence for others to review. Campbell, Cignetti, Melenyzer, Nettles, and Wyman (1997) define a portfolio as "an organized, goal-driven documentation of your professional growth and achieved competence in the complex act called teaching."

Documentation is systematic and an important part of creating the portfolio. Concrete evidence of how a teacher understands and implements the best teaching practices, translates theory into action, and has a knowledge of the nature of teaching is the ultimate goal.

A portfolio is ever-changing and reflects the individuality of the teacher by virtue of what it contains. As an assessment tool, the portfolio is useful in many ways. It helps teachers clarify their values, keeps them focused on the goals they have set, provides an avenue for self-reflection, and demonstrates growth. By what is included and what is omitted, a portfolio shows an evaluator tangible evidence of a teacher's abilities, provides a framework for setting new goals, and gives a more personal sense of the teacher's commitment and professionalism. Figure 5-12 lists some of the items often included in a teacher's portfolio.

Cultural Awareness and Sensitivity

Cultural awareness has an effect on how a teacher relates to children, and this needs to be taken into consideration when assessing a teacher's performance. Insight about a teacher's

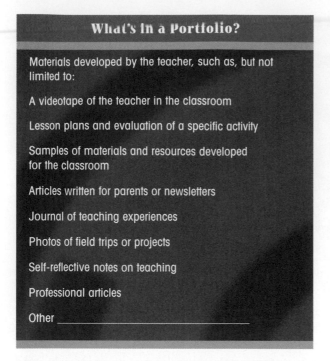

What's In a Portfolio?

Materials developed by the teacher, such as, but not limited to:

A videotape of the teacher in the classroom

Lesson plans and evaluation of a specific activity

Samples of materials and resources developed for the classroom

Articles written for parents or newsletters

Journal of teaching experiences

Photos of field trips or projects

Self-reflective notes on teaching

Professional articles

Other _____

FIGURE 5-12 A portfolio is a personalized assessment tool and contains a variety of materials and resources that reflect a teacher's professional growth. Some centers have their own criteria for a portfolio.

social and cultural background is particularly useful if the evaluator is a member of the majority population and the teacher is not.

Caruso and Fawcett (1999) define five specific cultural factors that can affect communication, particularly where supervisors and staff members are concerned. They are:

1. *Time sense.* Being on time and doing tasks in a timely fashion are high priorities for many people raised in mainstream American culture. Each culture has its own concept of time, and the teacher who is always late for meetings may be reflecting the cultural context in which he or she was raised.

2. *Space.* How close you get to someone while talking is also a function of cultural context. In some cultures, invading another's personal space (their "comfort zone") is considered rude. If a teacher backs away, she may be considered cold and unfriendly. If the teacher is the one getting too close, he may be seen as forward and aggressive. These perceptions may be innocent reactions based on their cultural sensibilities and should be viewed in that light.

3. *Verbal and nonverbal communication.* Eye contact is seen in some cultures to be disrespectful if prolonged; to others it may be

a sign of interest and attentiveness. Other facial expressions, such as smiling (or not), gestures, and body language, communicate different things from culture to culture. Silence, too, is used in different cultures in a variety of ways with an assortment of meanings. Speaking loudly may be a cultural norm or it may communicate anger and accusations. Teachers and their supervisors need to learn each other's communication styles and be particularly aware of those that are culture-bound.

4. *Values.* Our values drive our behavior and responses. If a teacher comes from a background that emphasizes dependency in the early years and the school philosophy is one that encourages early independence, a cultural conflict can erupt and affect a teacher's evaluation adversely. Supervisors and teachers must understand each other's value system and what causes each of them to make certain decisions.

5. *Concepts of authority.* The way people deal with authority is also culture-specific. Early childhood professionals who supervise and evaluate staff members from cultures different than their own need to be aware of what cultural expectations surround the issue of authority. In some instances, authority figures are often male, and females are raised not to question authority. A correct answer may be more culturally appropriate than expressing one's true feelings or ideas. The supervisor can avoid misunderstandings if he or she is aware that the teacher is used to an authoritarian style of leadership from supervisors and thus gear the conversation accordingly.

The evaluator has a rare opportunity to create bridges of understanding between and among many cultures. Jones (1993) notes that by seeing the connection "between their own cultural knowledge and their behavior as professionals in an early childhood setting," they can become "cultural brokers." Within their school community, they can create a two-way interchange about culturally relevant issues with children, parents, and other teachers.

Follow-Through

What follows an evaluation is critical to the overall success of an evaluation system. For instance, after gathering information for an evaluation session, a supervisor and teacher might discuss and evaluate concrete examples and live performance. Together they can establish goals for changing what may be ineffective or problematic.

Follow-through is the final part of the continuous feedback loop in a good evaluation system. Data are collected on teacher behavior and given to the teacher in person. Goals are set to improve teaching. A follow-up check is done periodically, to see how—and if—goals are being met. Teaching improves as recommendations are put into practice.

Follow-through makes the feedback loop complete as information about improvement is communicated. Refer back to Figure 5-8, which illustrates this cycle.

Techniques for Productive Evaluation Sessions

Evaluations take hard work, time, and dedication to a higher quality of teaching. It is also a shared responsibility. The supervisor must be explicit about a teacher's performance and be able to identify for the teacher what is effective and what is problematic.

Teachers themselves must value the process and understand its implications for their professional growth. The benefits of productive evaluation sessions are clear. They range from improved self-esteem, higher levels of job effectiveness, and less absenteeism and turnover to assessment-related salary raises and other job benefits. Certain techniques help make evaluation sessions productive for teachers:

1. Become involved from the beginning as the evaluation procedure is established. Know what is expected and how you will be evaluated.

2. Set a specific meeting time for your evaluation. Ask your supervisor for a time that works for you both.

3. Set some goals for yourself before meeting with your supervisor. If you know what you want to work on, you are more likely to get help achieving your goals.

4. Develop a plan for action. Be prepared to set a timeline for when and how you will work on your goals.

5. Establish a feedback loop (see Figure 5-8). Make a follow-up date, and make copies of your goal sheet for both you and your supervisor.

6. Approach the meeting with a sense of trust, respect, and openness. Planning ahead promotes these attitudes.

Better teaching and continued professional growth are the results of a good evaluation process. No two teachers are identical so each evaluation must be interpreted in terms of the behavior and stage of development of the individual person.[1] As teachers become more effective in their work with children; the quality of the entire program is improved.

THE BEGINNING TEACHER

Beginning teachers of young children cannot expect to successfully blend all of the many facets of teaching at once. However, beginning teachers must be committed to the time and energy needed to become proficient at their craft.

Beginning teaching can be a great deal of fun as well as a unique learning experience. Textbook theories come alive as children live out child development concepts. New teachers expect to learn about individual child growth and development; many are surprised to discover that they also learn how children function in groups and with adults. Working with an experienced teacher who models highly polished skills is an important part of the new teacher's experience.

Yet we know that first-time teaching is not always fun. It is a time for intensive self-searching and self-revelations.[2] Many teachers' own school experiences loom before them and undermine their confidence. There may still be doubts about being a teacher at all. It is uncomfortable to feel judged and criticized by others. This is a time of anxiety for most beginning teachers. But remember, even the poised, confident, and always-does-the-right-thing master teacher was once a beginner.

The Student Teacher

Many teacher training programs require a formal period of supervised work with young children either in the college's child development center

---

1 What teachers know about understanding and respecting diversity in children and families needs to be translated into working with colleagues.

2 This may be the first time some students confront their attitudes toward classroom diversity and inclusion.

The beginning teacher invests herself emotionally as well as physically.

Good teachers know when to help children learn new skills.

or in early childhood programs throughout the community. For students in such a program, practice teaching may be the first hands-on opportunity to work with children.

Beginnings for student teachers are just as important as they are for young children. A child's first days of school are planned very carefully; likewise, there are some strategies for easing the transition from student to student teacher. The following guidelines will help to make the first days of student teaching a satisfying and positive experience.

Before School Starts

● Contact the teacher and meet before school begins. Find out what time school begins, where the classroom is located, what the age group is, the size and makeup of the class, the daily schedule, and what hours you are expected to be on site. Ask if there are children with special needs and if there are cultural considerations of which you should be aware.[1] Find out what is expected of you the first few days. Be sure to meet the other administrative staff of the school.

● Visit the classroom to which you are assigned to become acquainted with its layout. Tour the yard as well. Find out where the janitor's room, kitchen, nurse's office, and storeroom are located.

 1 This may mark the beginning of a new teacher's pluralistic mindset.

Through experience, teachers learn how to handle large groups of children. Learning to develop story time and reading skills is an ongoing process.

● Share with the master teacher any special skills or talents you may have; let the teacher help you use these skills in new ways with young children. Let the teacher know about any other experiences with children: baby-sitting or camp counseling. Be sure to let the teacher know of any course requirements you must meet by this experience.

● Together, you, the master teacher, and your college instructor in student teaching will set goals and expectations for your student teaching experience. This will define more concretely what you would like to get out of the time you spend in the classroom, whether it is gaining experience with a group of children or learning to lead a group time by the end of the semester. By establishing common goals, the master teacher will be able to help guide a course so that these goals will be realized. An evaluation process related to those goals should be agreed on so that you will learn whether you have met the expectations of the teacher, the school, and the program.

SUMMARY

Teachers of young children share with other teachers a variety of subject matter. The curriculum in the early childhood school is rich in math, science, language, social studies, geography, and the like. The format for these learning experiences is a "hands-on" approach. Teachers set out materials, equipment, and activities that invite children's interest and interaction.

In some area the early childhood teacher differs from others in the field of education. Team teaching, teacher-child interactions, small-group emphasis, and adult relationships are more common in the early years than in other types of schools. The teaching role is not restricted to working just with children. Teachers must learn to interact with numerous adults—primarily parents, other teachers, and administrators. Teaching roles will vary, depending on whether you teach alone or on a team. Team teaching is common in many early childhood programs and has many advantages. By keeping in mind 10 essentials for successful teaching, all early childhood teachers can ensure themselves of optimal working conditions in their setting.

Early childhood teachers have multiple roles. They supervise and manage the classroom, interact with children and a number of adults, and set the emotional tone. Much of what they do occurs away from children. There are meetings to attend, reports to write, parent conferences to hold, and materials to purchase. These after-hours duties add to the depth of classroom experiences the teacher provides for the children.

Ethical situations arise frequently, calling on the teacher or administrator to make difficult choices about children and their lives. A professional code of ethics sets out standards of behavior based on core values and commitments all early childhood professionals share. It can support decisions individuals have to make in the best interests of children.

A systematic teacher evaluation process that is linked to professional growth opportunities is important. The process should include a self-evaluation by the teacher who, with a supervisor, sets appropriate professional goals. An evaluation by a supervisor and goal setting that relates to the program's philosophy and mission are also part of the process. Continuing growth within the professional field includes understanding the cultural context out of which teachers relate to the children, families, other staff members, and supervisors.

The student teacher gains valuable experience working directly with children under the supervision of a mature teacher. As they grow and gain confidence, teachers pass through several stages of professional development and search for ways to be more effectively challenged. As they integrate teaching style and personality, they become whole teachers.

TEACHING: A PROFESSIONAL COMMITMENT

by
Barbara Biglan, M.A., Ph.D.

As early childhood educators, we play many roles. We are surrogate parents, new friends, sources of comfort and support, providers of new and exciting learning experiences, and active learners committed to professional growth. All of these roles are played by the dedicated individuals who work with young children in a variety of educational settings.

In our class, Early Childhood Curriculum, we developed metaphors to explore these diverse roles of a teacher, to gain insight into the development of professional behaviors and to understand the meaning of commitment to the education of young children. There were common threads running through these descriptions: reflective learning, strategies for practice, and appreciating culture and diversity.

One metaphor that engaged all of us was that of the early childhood teacher as an artist. We worked as a class to add and expand the description. It became for us a way to think about our personal and collective commitment to the education of young children.

In our metaphor of teacher as artist, the canvas is the foundation knowledge required as a theoretical base for developmentally appropriate practice. The brushes are the variety of methods and strategies used to plan and implement educational activities. The composition of the work of art involves the balance of respect for each child, family, and culture, and provision of opportunities for each child to achieve the full potential of his or her unique talents in the context of a community of learners. Each artist uses color to express his or her own unique blend of talents. Bright yellows and reds express the excitement involved in new learning experiences, the blues and purples show the loving and supportive daily interactions,

the earth tones provide the background of a team of colleagues with a well-grounded sense of mission, and the greens remind all of us to keep growing in knowledge and ability. The final "professional" product is a result of talent, training, experience, and evaluation.

As we grow in our professional commitment, we will each "create" many works of art. Each work of art will express our belief that all children can learn and should be treated with dignity and respect. Each work of art will represent our journey of growth and development as teachers of young children.

We hope that all who prepare to become early childhood educators will find a meaningful metaphor to guide their growth and professional commitment to teaching.

Barbara Biglan, M.A., Ph.D., has been a classroom teacher, computer coordinator, the headmistress of an independent school (pre-K–6), and a college professor. She is currently a faculty member in the Education Department at Chatham College in Pittsburgh, Pennsylvania, and the higher education project director for the Math Science Partnership of Southwest Pennsylvania, an NSF funded initiative to improve the teaching and learning of science and math K–16. She started life as an educator 40 years ago with a BS in science as a junior high school science teacher, earned a master's in Education and then a Ph.D. in Science Education K–12.

For more activities and information,
visit our Web site at
http://www.EarlyChildEd.delmar.com

KEY TERMS

emotional framework	ethics	competency-based assessment
self-awareness	continuing education	portfolio-based assessment
anti-bias	feedback loop	portfolio
team teaching	performance-based assessment	

REVIEW QUESTIONS

1. What do you think are the five most important qualifications a teacher of young children should have? Why? Which do you possess? Which are most difficult for you?

2. How does a teacher "set the tone" for a classroom? How does being culturally competent fit in?

3. Give several reasons why team teaching is important in the early years.

4. Why is self-awareness important?

5. What does having a code of ethics mean to a teacher?

6. Who can be involved in evaluating teachers? Who would you prefer? Why?

7. How can teachers help to make their evaluation sessions productive?

LEARNING ACTIVITIES

1. Draw a picture of the first classroom you remember. Place furniture in it, and note where your friends sat, where you sat, and where the teacher sat. Down one side of the paper write one-word descriptions of what you felt when you were in that classroom.

2. Survey a classroom where you teach or observe. How many different cultures are represented? How does the teacher respond to the cultural diversity?

3. Have you ever had a teacher who was "different"? Describe the person. What did you like most about that teacher? What did you like least? Would you hire that teacher? Why?

4. Write your own code of ethics.

5. Read the ethical situations posed in the section on professional development. Think about how you would solve them. Discuss your answers with a member of your class, a teacher, and a parent.

6. Observe a teacher working in a team situation and one who works alone in a classroom. What seem to be the advantages of each? Disadvantages? Which would you prefer for your first year of teaching? Why? Your third year? Your seventh year?

7. Do you disagree with any core values listed in the section on code of ethical conduct? What are they? How would you change them? Discuss your response with another teacher, another student, or your class instructor.

8. In small groups, discuss the popular images of teachers as reflected in current movies and literature. Is there consensus of the portrait of teachers today? Where do early childhood professionals fit into the picture? Are issues raised about teachers being addressed anywhere? Where? How? By whom? What would you conclude about your role as a member of the teaching profession?

9. What elements would you add to Figure 5-1 on the basis of your observation of early childhood programs and teachers?

10. Try to establish goals for your own growth as a professional in the following areas:

Area	Goal	Objectives/Implementation	Timeline
Programmatic			
Administrative			
Staff Relations			
Professional Growth			

Ask your supervisor or a colleague to help you make a realistic timeline for each goal.

REFERENCES

Bloom, P. J. (2005). *Blueprint for action: Achieving center-based change through staff development.* Lake Forest, IL: New Horizons.

Campbell, D. M., Cignetti, P. B., Melenyzer, B. J., Nettles, D. H., & Wyman, R. M. (1997). *How to develop a professional portfolio: A manual for teachers.* Boston: Allyn & Bacon.

Caruso, J. J., & Fawcett, M. T. (1999). *Supervision in early childhood education: A developmental perspective.* New York: Teachers College Press.

Derman-Sparks, L. (1989). *Anti-bias curriculum: Tools for empowering young children.* Washington, DC: National Association for Education of Young Children.

Eyer, D. (1989). Career options in early childhood education. In A. Gordon & K. W. Browne (Eds.), *Beginnings and beyond: Foundations in early childhood education.* Clifton Park, NY: Thomson Delmar Learning.

Jones, E. (Ed.) (1993). *Growing teachers: Partnerships in staff development.* Washington, DC: National Association for the Education of Young Children.

Jones, E. (1994). Breaking the ice: Confronting status differences among professions. In J. Johnson & J. B. McCracken (Eds.), *The early childhood career lattice: Perspectives on professional development.* Washington, DC: National Association for the Education of Young Children.

Jorde Bloom, P. (1988b, September). Teachers need TLC too. *Young Children.*

Katz, L. G. (1999). *Talks with teachers of young children.* Norwood, NJ: Ablex.

Katz, L. G., & Ward, E. H. (1991). *Ethical behavior in early childhood education.* (Expanded ed.). Washington, DC: National Association for Education of Young Children.

Kipnis, K. (1987, May). How to discuss professional ethics. *Young Children,* pp. 26–30.

Kuster, C. A. (1994). Language and cultural competence. In J. Johnson & J. B. McCracken (Eds.), *The early childhood career lattice: Perspectives on professional development.* Washington, DC: National Association for the Education of Young Children.

LeShan, E. (1992). *When your child drives you crazy.* New York: St. Martin's Press.

National Association for the Education of Young Children. (1997). *Code of ethical conduct.* Washington, DC: National Association for the Education of Young Children.

Phillips, C. B. (1994). What every early childhood professional should know. In J. Johnson & J. B. McCracken (Eds.), *The early childhood career lattice: Perspectives on professional development.* Washington, DC: National Association for the Education of Young Children.

Ramsey, P. G. (2004). *Teaching and learning in a diverse world* (3rd ed.). New York: Teachers College Press.

Smith, M. M. (1999). "Foreword" in S. Feeney, & N. K. Freeman *Ethics and the early childhood educator using the NAEYC code.* Washington, DC: National Association for the Education of Young Children.

Spodek, B. (1994). The knowledge base for baccalaureate early childhood teacher education programs. In J. Johnson & J. B. McCracken (Eds.), *The early childhood career lattice: Perspectives on professional development.* Washington, DC: National Association for the Education of Young Children.

U.S. Bureau of Labor Statistics. (2001). *Child care workers/selected characteristics.* Washington, DC: U.S. Government Printing Office.

Ward, E. H., & CDA Staff. (1976, May). The Child Development Association Consortium's Assessment System. *Young Children,* 244–255.

Whitebrook, M., Sakai, L., Gerber, E., & Howes, C. (2001). *Then and now: Changes in child care staffing, 1994–2000.* Washington, DC: Center for the Child Care Workforce.

Willer, B. (Ed.). (1994). A conceptual framework for early childhood professional development: NAEYC Position Statement, adopted November 1993. In J. Johnson & J. B. McCracken (Eds.), *The early childhood career lattice: Perspectives on professional development* (pp. 4–21). Washington, DC: National Association for the Education of Young Children.

HELPFUL WEB SITES

Center for Child Care Workforce	http://ccw.cleverspin.com
Council for Professional Recognition (CDA)	http://www.cdacouncil.org
National Association for the Education of Young Children	http://www.naeyc.org
Association for Childhood Education International	http://www.acei.org
Child Care Information Exchange	http://www.ccie.com
ERIC Clearinghouse on Elementary and Early Childhood Education	http://www.eric.ed.gov
National Black Child Development Institute	http://www.nbcdi.org
Wheelock College Institute for Leadership and Career Initiatives	http://www.institute.wheelock.edu

For more activities and information, visit our Web site at http://www.EarlyChildEd.delmar.com

Observation and Assessment: Learning to Read the Child

QUESTIONS FOR THOUGHT

Why is observing children an important teaching tool?

How do observations help us understand people and their behavior?

What is the difference between fact and inference?

How can we record what we see to compare individual behavior and general developmental growth?

How can children be assessed?

What are early learning standards?

What are concerns about assessment and standardized testing and developmental or readiness screening?

How do we observe and record effectively?

What are the guidelines to follow when observing and assessing behavior?

Description	Interpretation/Inference
Jenny comes through the gate. She clutches her mother's hand. On the wall is a collection of road-building equipment; Jenny glances but does not stop or touch them. She is standing beside her mother and sucking her thumb.	Jenny is afraid of school. It's hard to let go of mom. She isn't interested because she is a girl. She doesn't like outdoor play.
Three children sitting at a table doing art project, S and C sitting on one side, D on the other. D asks S if she can have the red paint; S doesn't respond. D asks again; again, no reply. D then yells, "Did you not hear me?" and frowns. S looks startled, then pushes paint to D. C says "Doncha know? She got a ear, fection. You gonna break her heart." D clutches his chest—"No you breaking my heart." Everyone laughs as they all clutch chest and fall out of chairs.	Will D feel left out?
	D takes criticism well.
(Teacher asks: "How would you describe yourself?") I'm tall. My hair is very puffy. My two front teeth are very big. I have big feet. I have big muscles. I have a button nose. I have big black eyes. I like my very big cheeks.	Child has a positive self-image.
(Teacher asks: "What do you like about yourself?") I like that I'm good at karate. I like that I'm a nice girl. I'm good at school. I don't call people names. I like the way I approach people—I ask them how they're doing and their name. Hey, can you put this in? I like rice and lumpia.	Social success is important.
	Child has a well-developed interpersonal awareness.

FIGURE 6-3 Interpretation has its place in observation, but only after the behavior and description have been documented.

- What kind of social play is typical for the four-year-old?
- How does an infant move from crawling to walking upright?

Observation gives a feeling for group behavior as well as a developmental yardstick to compare individuals within the group. Teachers determine age-appropriate expectations from this. It is important, for example, to know that most children cannot tie their own shoes at age four but can be expected to pull them on by themselves. A general understanding aids in planning a thoughtful and challenging curriculum. Teachers in a class of three-year-olds, for instance, know that many children are ready for 8- to 10-piece puzzles but that the 20-piece jigsaw will most likely be dumped on the table and quickly abandoned.

Finally, knowledge of children in general gives teachers a solid foundation on which to base decisions about individuals. From observing many children comes an awareness of each child's progression along the developmental scale. Experienced teachers of toddlers will not put out watercolor sets, while the second-grade teacher will do so routinely. Teachers learn that it is typical of four- and five-year-olds to exclude others from their play because they will have seen it happen countless times. The three-and-a-half-year-old who is sure she is "too little" to use the toilet won't concern the knowledgeable teacher, who knows that this is developmentally appropriate behavior! Decisions about single children come from watching and knowing many children. This understanding is a valuable asset when talking to parents. [1]

Developmental Relationships

Observing brings about an understanding of the various developmental areas and how they are related. Development is at once specific and integrated. Children's behavior is a mix of several distinct developmental areas and, at the same time, an integrated whole whose parts influence each other. When we say the whole child we mean a consideration of how development works in unison.

When observing children, one must focus on these different developmental areas. What are the language abilities of three-year-olds? What social skills do preschool children acquire? Which self-help skills can children learn before

1 Keen observers of young children come to realize that there is a wide spectrum of ways in which children develop, with numerous ways in which parents support this growth—not good ways and bad ways, but many different ways.

What do YOU Think?

How can teachers shift their thinking and practice to become authentically child-centered? One way is to use what you see in children's behavior to reflect on what is going on for them and how you can capitalize on their interests to drive their learning.

Listen:

Nicolas slides down the climbing structure tube into the tanbark, stuffs handfuls into his jacket pockets, then hustles back up to Jack and Luis at the top. Together, they lay down the tanbark and watch it slide down, push the next handful, then throw the final pieces. They laugh, slide down themselves, and run to the side, where they pull off a three-foot-length of a tree branch and collect several sticks. With large grins, they race back to the foot of the tube and thrust it in, sweeping out the remaining tanbark. They repeat this regularly until a teacher stops them, admonishing them about safety around the slide.

What do you think is going on? Instead of continuing to redirect and correct, put on your "Teacher-as-Researcher" thinking cap. How can this interest be developed into curriculum?

Plan a staff meeting and put this behavior in the center. Recall together your own childhood experiences outdoors or with "loose parts." These teachers decided to focus on the interest of experimenting with gravity to build an outdoor activity area with plastic gutters, and indoors with small wooden ramps. This led to the children's suggestions of making a climbing structure for the pet hamster, a field trip to a local park, and a parent's visit as a hardware store clerk. The reflective approach helps teachers get away from planning in a vacuum, and puts the children in the center.

age six? How does fine-motor development interact with intellectual growth? Does gross-motor skill affect successful cognitive learning? How does self-concept relate to all of the other areas?

Observing helps teachers see how the pieces fit together. For instance, when given a set of blocks in various sizes, colors, and shapes, a four-year-old will have no difficulty finding the red ones or square ones, but may be puzzled when asked to find those that are both red and square. No wonder that same child has difficulty understanding that someone can be their best friend and someone else's at the same time.

Practiced observation will show that a child's skills are multiple and varied and have only limited connection to age. Derek has the physical coordination of a four-and-a-half-year-old, language skills of a six-year-old, and the social skills of a two-year-old—all bound up in a body that just turned three. A brief picture such as this "whole child" can be helpful to both parents and teachers.

Influences on Behavior

Careful observation gives us insight into the influences and dynamics of behavior.

Boaz has a hard time when he enters his child care each morning, yet he is competent and says he likes school. Close observation reveals that his favorite areas are climbing outdoor games and the sandbox. Boaz feels least successful in the construction and creative arts areas, the primary choices indoors, where his school day begins.

Mari, on the other hand, starts the day happily but cries frequently throughout the day. Is there a pattern to her outbursts? Watch what happens to Mari when free play is over and group time begins. She falls apart readily when it is time to move outdoors to play, time to have snacks, time to nap, and so on.

The environment influences both these children. The classroom arrangement and daily schedule impact children's behavior, because children are directly affected by the restraints imposed by their activities and their time. Boaz feels unsure of himself in those activities that are offered as he starts his day. Seeing only these choices as he enters the room causes him discomfort, which he shows by crying and clinging to his dad. By adding something he enjoys, such as a sand table indoors, the teacher changes the physical environment to be more appealing and positive. Boaz's difficulties in saying goodbye disappear as he finds he can be successful and comfortable at the beginning of his day.

The cause of Mari's problem is more difficult to detect. The physical environment seems to interest and appeal to her. On closer observation, her crying and disruptive behavior appear to happen just at the point of change, regardless of the activities before or afterward. It is the time aspect of the environment that causes difficulty for her. The teacher makes a special effort to signal upcoming transitions and to involve her in bringing them about. Telling Mari, "Five more minutes until naptime" or "After you wash your hands, go to the snack table" gives her the clues she needs to anticipate the process of change. Asking her to announce cleanup time to the class lets her be in control of that transition.

Adult behavior affects and influences children. Annika has days of intense activity and involvement with materials; on other days she appears sluggish and uninterested. After a week of observation, teachers find a direct correlation with the presence of a student teacher. On the days the student is in the classroom, Annika calls out to him to see her artwork and watch her various accomplishments. It is on the days that the student is absent that Annika's activity level falls. Once a pattern is noticed, the teacher acts on these observations. The student teacher offers Annika ideas for activities she could work on to show him when he returns to class. When he is absent, the teacher lets her write him a note or draw him a picture, and then reminds Annika of the plan and gets her started.

Children also influence one another in powerful ways. Anyone who has worked with toddlers knows how attractive a toy becomes to a child once another has it. The second grader who suddenly dislikes school may be feeling left out of a friendship group. Teachers need to carefully observe the social dynamics of the class as they seek to understand individual children.

Understanding of Self

Observing children can be a key to understanding ourselves. People who develop observational skills notice human behavior more accurately. They become skilled at seeing small but important facets of human personality. They learn to differentiate between what is fact and what is inference. This increases an awareness of self as

teacher and how one's biases affect perceptions about children.[1] Teachers who become keen observers of children apply these skills to themselves. As Feeney and colleagues (2001) note:

> In a less structured but no less important way, you also observe yourself, your values, your relationships, and your own feelings and reactions. When you apply what you know about observation to yourself, you gain greater self-awareness. It is difficult to be objective about yourself, but as you watch your own behavior and interactions you can learn more about how you feel and respond in various situations and realize the impact of your behavior on others.

The values and benefits of observation are long-lasting. Only by practicing observations—what it takes to look, to see, to become more sensitive—will teachers be able to record children's behavior fully and vividly, capturing the unique qualities, culture and personality of each child. The challenge of observation is high, but the benefits are well worth the effort.

RECORDING WHAT WE SEE

Once teachers and students understand why observing is important, they must then learn how to record what they see. Although children are constantly under the teacher's eyes, so much happens so fast that critical events are lost in the daily routine of classrooms. Systematic observations aid in recording events and help teachers make sense of them.

Understanding the child is the goal of observation. Noticing how children interact with each other and the materials enriches the teacher's own knowledge of growth and behavior.

 1 In the field of early childhood education, one is reminded repeatedly of the image of learning as a two-way, not a one-way, street. One teaches children and learns from children and families.

Teachers balance observing with interacting. When a child asks a question, the teacher is available but not intrusive so that the child's play is uninterrupted and the teacher can resume observation.

In recording what you observe, you need to learn how to look and to learn the language of recording. These are the "nuts and bolts" of observing and assessment. Learning to look, however, requires a certain willingness to become aware and to do more than simply watch. Although it is true that teachers rarely have the luxury of observing uninterrupted for long periods of time, they can often plan shorter segments. Practice by paying attention to the content of children's play during free periods—theirs and yours.

Next, try your hand at jotting some notes about that play. It is easy to get discouraged, especially if you are unaccustomed to writing. The language of recording gets easier as you practice finding synonyms for common words. For instance, children are active creatures—how many ways do they run? They may gallop, dart, whirl, saunter, skip, hop. Or think of the various ways children talk to you: they shriek, whisper, whine, shout, demand, whimper, lisp, roar. Once you have a certain mastery of the language (and be sure to record what you see in the language that comes easiest to you), describing the important nuances of children's behavior will become easier. For an example of such descriptions, look at Figure 6-5.

Common Elements of Observations

The key ingredients in all types of observations used in recording children's behavior are (1) defining and describing the behaviors and (2) repeating the observation in terms of several factors such as time, number of children, or activities. All observational systems have certain elements in common:

Focus

- What do you want to know?
- Whom/what do you want to observe?
  Child? Teacher? Environment? Group?
- What aspects of behavior do you want to know about? Motor skills? Social development? Problem solving?
- What is your purpose?
  Study the environment?
  Observe the daily schedule?
  Evaluate a child's skills?
  Deal with negative behavior?
  Analyze transitions?
  Do research?
  Confer with parents?
  Train teachers?

System

- What will you do?
- How will you define the terms?
- How will you record the information you need?
- How detailed will your record be?
- Will you need units of measure? What kind?
- For how long will you record?

Tools

- What will you need for your observations?
- How will you record what you want to know?
  Video or tape recorder? Camera? Pencil? Chart?

Environment

- Where will you watch?
- Classroom? Yard? Home?
- What restraints are inherent in the setting?

Using these building blocks of observational systems, teachers seek a method that yields a collection of observable data that helps them focus more clearly on a child or situation.

Four major methods of observing and two additional information-gathering techniques will be discussed. They are:

1. Narratives (baby biographies, diary descriptions, running records, specimen descriptions, anecdotal notes, logs/journals)
2. Time sampling
3. Event sampling
4. Modified child study techniques (checklists, rating scales, shadow study, experimental procedures, the clinical method)

Types of Observations

Narratives

At once the most valuable and most difficult of records, **narratives** are attempts to record nearly everything that happens. In the case of a young child, this means all that the child does, says, gestures, seems to feel, and appears to think about. Narratives maintain a **running record** of the excitement and tension of the interaction while remaining an accurate, objective account of the events and behavior. Narratives are an attempt to actually recreate the scene by recording it in thorough and vivid language. Observers put into words what they see, hear, and know about an event or a person. The result is a full and dynamic report.

Narratives are the oldest and often most informative kind of report. Historically, as Arnold Gesell reported, they were used to set basic developmental norms. They are a standard technique in anthropology and the biologic sciences. Irwin and Bushnell (1980) provide a detailed historical background that traces the narrative back to Pestalozzi (1700s) and Darwin (1800s). Jean Piaget watched and recorded in minute detail his own children's growth. His observations resulted in a full report on children's thought processes and development of intelligence. **Baby biographies**, narratives written by parents, were some of the first methods used in child study and reached their peak of popularity in the early 1900s.

Diary descriptions are one form of narrative. Just as the term implies, they are, in diary form, consecutive records of everything children do and say and how they do it. The process is a natural one. In the classroom this means describing every action observed within a given time period.

It might be a five-minute period during free play to watch and record what one child does. The child who is a loner, the child who wanders, and the child who is aggressive are prime candidates for a diary description. Another way to use this type of running record is to watch an area of the yard or room, then record who is there and how they are using the materials.

A more common form of the narrative is a modified version of a running record, or a specimen description as it is often called in research terms. The procedure is to take on-the-spot notes of a specific child each day. This task lends itself easily to most early childhood settings. The teachers carry with them a small notebook and pencil, tucked in a pocket. They jot down whatever seems important or noteworthy during the day. These anecdotal notes are the most familiar form of recording observations (see Figure 6-4). They often focus on one item at a time:

- A part of the environment—how is the science area being used?
- A particular time of day—what happens right after naps?
- A specific child—how often is Lucy hitting out at other children?

This system may be even less structured, with all the teachers taking "on-the-hoof" notes as daily incidents occur. These notes then become a rich source of information for report writing and parent conferences.

Another form of narrative is a log or journal (see Figure 6-4). Teachers write in details about each child or a critical incident. Because this is time-consuming and needs to be done without interruption, it helps to write immediately after the program is over. Sometimes teaching teams organize themselves to enable one member of the staff to observe and record in the journal

---

Journal Entry 4-2-99

Today three children spent the entire morning wrapping and unwrapping presents for me. All they needed were small objects, tape, scissors, and paper. They took great delight in my surprise as I opened each present and found lovely objects. So what are these three-year-olds thinking as they work so diligently? I listened to them from a distance as they chatted: "This is the best surprise . . . Susan won't know where we got this pretty necklace for her."

"You're not putting enough tape on that; let me tape it more."

"When we buy presents for my grandma, we find things she likes and doesn't have . . . then we give the store person a plastic card and then we go home and wrap it up for her . . . she cries when she opens presents."

"Maybe Susan doesn't like to cry at school."

They seem excited about what presents mean and maybe what it means to give someone something they really want. How can I extend their play, go beyond the repetitive activity and explore something that makes them think more deeply?

FIGURE 6-4 Susan's journal entry is a way of processing what she sees happening in her classroom, a way of examining what she sees as the children's interests, and a way of reflecting on where she wants to go with the interests demonstrated. (Excerpted from Barbour, 2000.)

during class time. The important point is that children's behavior is recorded either while it is happening or soon afterward.

The challenging part of this recording technique, the narrative, is to have enough detail so the reader will be able to picture whole situations later. Using language as a descriptive tool requires a large vocabulary and skillful recorder. Whatever notes the teachers use, however brief, need to be both clear and accurate.

At the same time teachers are recording in a graphic way, they need to be aware of the personal biases that can influence observations. When we look at children, what we see is in part a result of our personal experiences, the theories we hold, and the assumptions we make.[1] Teaching is an intensely personal activity, and what the children look like, do, and say may arouse strong feelings and reactions. Figure 6-1 compares two observations to illustrate this point. By becoming aware of our biases and assumptions, we can become more accurate and objective in our work as teachers. Figure 6-5 is an example of the narrative type of observation.

There are many advantages to this type of observation. Narratives are rich in information, provide detailed behavioral accounts, and are relatively easy to record. With a minimum of equipment and training, teachers can learn to take notes on what children do and say. To write down everything is impossible, so some selection is necessary. These "judgment calls" can warp the narrative. The main disadvantages of narratives are the time they can take, the language and the vocabulary that must be used, and the biases the recorder may have. Even though the narrative remains one of the most widely used and effective methods of observing young children today, many teachers prefer more structured procedures. These more definite, more precise techniques still involve some personal interpretation, but the area of individual judgment is diminished. The observational techniques discussed in the following sections also tend to be less time-consuming than the narrative.

Time Sampling

A **time sampling** is an observation of what happens within a given period of time. Developed as an observational strategy in laboratory schools in the 1920s, time sampling was used to collect data on large numbers of children and to get a sense of normative behaviors for particular age groups or sexes.

Time sampling appears to have originated with research in child development. It has been used to record autonomy, dependency, task persistence, aggression, and social involvement.

The Child Alone

Unoccupied Behavior. SH slowly walks from the classroom to the outside play area, looking up each time one of the children swishes by. SH stops when reaching the table and benches and begins pulling the string on the sweatshirt. Still standing SH looks around the yard for a minute, then wanders slowly over to the seesaw. Leaning against it, SH touches the seesaw gingerly, then trails both hands over it while looking out into the yard. (Interpretive comments: This unoccupied behavior is probably due to two reasons: SH is overweight and has limited language skills compared with the other children. Pulling at the sweatshirt string is something to do to pass the time, since the overweight body is awkward and not especially skillful.)

Onlooker Behavior. J is standing next to the slide watching her classmates using this piece of equipment. She looks up and says, "Hi." Her eyes open wider as she watches the children go down the slide. P calls to J to join them but J shakes her head "no." (Interpretive comments: J is interested in the slide but is reluctant to use it. She has a concerned look on her face when the others slide down; it seems too much of a challenge for J.)

Solitary Play. L comes running into the yard holding two paintbrushes and a bucket filled with water. He stops about three feet away from a group of children playing with cars, trucks, and buses in the sandbox and sits down. He drops the brushes into the bucket and laughs when the water splashes his face. He begins swishing the water around with the brushes and then starts wiggling his fingers in it. (Interpretive comments: L is very energetic and seems to thoroughly enjoy his outside playtime with water. He adds creative touches to his pleasurable experience.)

FIGURE 6-5 The narrative form of observation gives a rich sample of children's behavior; even though it risks teacher bias, it still records valuable information.

---

1   It is a given we all have biases. It is not realistic to think one can be bias-free. The goal is to be conscious of the bias we bring to our work and be open to multiple interpretations of observed behavior. In this way we do not let our individual bias dictate our observations and interactions with children from diverse backgrounds.

Time sampling has also been used to study play patterns and to record nervous habits of schoolchildren, such as nail biting and hair twisting (Irwin & Bushnell, 1980). The definitive study using time sampling is Mildred Parten's observation in the 1930s of children's play. The codes developed in this study have become classic play patterns: solitary parallel, associative, and cooperative play. These codes are used throughout this text (see Chapters 3, 10, and 14), as well as in the professional field to describe the interactions of children.

In a time sample, behavior is recorded at regular time intervals. To use this method, one needs to sample what occurs fairly frequently. It makes sense to choose those behaviors that might occur, say, at least once every 10 minutes. Figure 6-6 demonstrates a time-sampling procedure.

Time sampling has its own advantages and disadvantages. The process itself helps teachers define exactly what it is they want to observe. Certainly it helps focus on specific behaviors and how often they occur. Time sampling is ideal for collecting information about the group as a whole. Finally, defining behaviors clearly

Sharing children's portfolios with both children and families can be encouraging for all.

and developing a category and coding system, reduce the problem of observer bias.

Yet, by diminishing this bias one also eliminates some of the richness and quality of information. It is difficult to get the whole picture

PLAY WITH OTHERS

P = Parallel
A = Associative
C = Cooperative

Child	Time Unit																					Total		
	9:00			9:05			9:10			9:20			9:25			9:30								
	P	A	C	P	A	C	P	A	C	P	A	C	P	A	C	P	A	C				P	A	C
Jamal																								
Marty																								
Dahlia																								
Keith																								
Rosa																								
Cameron																								
Hannah																								

FIGURE 6-6 Time sampling of play with others involves defining the behavior and making a coding sheet to tally observations.

Observation techniques such as time and event sampling can help teachers capture important information about children, such as who they play with or how often they engage in particular behaviors.

those needs. When narratives or time samplings won't suffice, perhaps an event sampling will.

Event Sampling

Event sampling is one of the more intriguing techniques. With this method, the observer defines an event, devises a system for describing and coding it, then waits for it to happen. As soon as it does, the recorder moves into action. Thus, the behavior is recorded as it occurs naturally.

The events that are chosen can be quite interesting and diverse. Consider Helen C. Dawes's classic analysis of preschool children's quarrels. Whenever a quarrel began, the observer recorded it. She recorded how long the quarrel lasted, what was happening when it started, what behaviors happened during the quarrel (including what was done and said), what the outcome was, and what happened afterward. Her format for recording included duration (x number of seconds), a narrative for the situation, verbal or motor activity, and checklists for the quarrel behavior, outcome, and aftereffects (Irwin & Bushnell, 1980).

Other researchers have studied dominance and emotions. Teachers can use event sampling to look at these and other behaviors such as bossiness, avoidance of teacher requests, or withdrawal.

Like time sampling, event sampling looks at a particular behavior or occurrence (Figure 6-7). But the unit is the event rather than a prescribed time interval. Here again the behavior must be clearly defined and the recording sheet easy to

when one divides it into artificial time units and with only a few categories. The key is to decide what it is teachers want to know, then choose the observational method that best suits

Event Sampling Guidelines

1. Define the behavior to be observed.
2. Decide what information you want to know.
3. Make a simple recording sheet.

Children's accidents: spills, knock-overs, falls.
Child(ren) involved, time, place, cause, results.
To watch in early morning:

Time	Children	Place	Cause	Outcome
8:50	Shelley, Mike	play dough	M steps on S toes	S cries, runs to Tchr
9:33	Tasauna, Yuki	blocks	T runs through, knocks over Y's tower	Y hits T, both cry
9:56	Spencer	yard	S turns trike too sharply, falls off	S cries, wants mom
10:28	Lorena, Shelley	doll corner	L bumps table, spills pitcher S has just set there	S cries, runs to Tchr

Total 8:45–10:30 a.m. = 4

FIGURE 6-7 Event sampling can be helpful in determining how frequently a specific event takes place. For instance, sampling the number and types of accidents for a given child or time frame helps teachers see what is happening in class.

use. Unlike with time sampling, the event to be recorded may occur a number of times during the observation.

For these reasons, event sampling is a favorite of classroom teachers. They can go about the business of teaching children until the event occurs. Then they can record the event quickly and efficiently. Prescribing the context within which the event occurs restores some of the quality often lost in time sampling. The only disadvantage is that the richness of detail of the narrative description is missing.

Modified Child Study Techniques

Because observation is the key method of studying young children in their natural settings, it makes good sense to develop many kinds of observational skills. Each can be tailored to fit the individual child, the particular group, the kind of staff, and the specific problem. Teachers who live in complex, creative classrooms have questions arise that need fast answers. Modified child study techniques can define the scope of the problem fairly quickly. Some of the techniques are: checklist systems, rating scales, shadow studies, and modified processes that reach both the group and the individuals in it.

Checklists contain a great deal of information that can be recorded rapidly. A carefully planned checklist can tell a lot about one child or the entire class. The data are collected in a short period of time, usually about a week. Figure 6-8 is an example of an activity checklist. With data collected for a week, teachers have a broad picture of how these children spend their time and what activities interest them.

Observer _____ Date _____ Time _____

Learning Center	Anna	Charlie	Leticia	Hiroko	Max	Josie	Totals
Indoors Science Area					1		1
Dramatic Play	1	1	1			1	4
Art	1		1	1			3
Blocks		1					1
Manipulatives			1	1	1		3
Easels				1			1
Music			1		1		2
Outdoors Water/Sand/Mud		1	1			1	3
Blocks				1	1		2
Wheel Toys		1			1		2
Climbers	1		1			1	3
Woodworking				1			1
Ball Games	1						1
Animal Care	1	1				1	3
Totals	5	5	6	5	5	4	

FIGURE 6-8 An activity checklist. With date collected for a week, teachers have a broad picture of how children spend their time at school and what activities interest them.

If, however, teachers want to assess children's motor skills, a yes/no list is preferable. Figure 6-9 illustrates the use of such a chart.

Checklists can vary in length and complexity depending on their functions. To develop one, teachers first determine the purpose of the observation. Next they define what the children will do to demonstrate the behavior being observed. Finally comes designing the actual checklist, one that is easy to use and simple to set aside when other duties must take precedence.

Although they are easy to record, checklists lack the richness of the more descriptive

Motor Skills Observation (ages 2–4) Child_____ Date_____ Observer_____ Age_____	Yes	No
Eating:		
1. Holds glass with one hand		
2. Pours from pitcher		
3. Spills little from spoon		
4. Selects food with pincer grasp		
Dressing:		
1. Unbuttons		
2. Puts shoes on		
3. Uses both hands together (such as holding jacket with one hand while zipping with the other)		
Fine Motor:		
1. Uses pincer grasp with pencil, brushes		
2. Draws straight line		
3. Copies circles		
4. Cuts at least 2″ in line		
5. Makes designs and crude letters		
6. Builds tower of 6–9 blocks		
7. Turns pages singly		
Gross Motor:		
1. Descends/ascends steps with alternate feet		
2. Stands on one foot, unsupported		
3. Hops on two feet		
4. Catches ball, arms straight, elbows in front of body		
5. Operates tricycle		

FIGURE 6-9 A yes/no checklist gives specific information about an individual child's skills.

narrative. For instance, by looking at the checklist in Figure 6-8, teachers will know which activities children have chosen, but they will not gain a sense of how they played in each area, the time spent there, or whether and with whom they interacted. The advantages of checklists are that they can tally broad areas of information and teachers can create one with relative ease. Checklists are often used in evaluation, as in Figure 6-9.

Rating scales are like checklists, planned in advance to record something specific. They extend checklists by adding some quality to what is observed. The advantage is that more information is gathered. A potential problem is added because the observers' opinions are now required and could hamper objectivity.

Rating scales differ from checklists in several ways. Instead of simply recording where children are playing, the rating scales require the teacher to decide how they are playing. What is the extent of their involvement and the frequency or degree of their play? A rating scale may use word phrases ("always," "sometimes," "never") or a numerical key (1 through 5).

Developing a rating scale is simple, though a good scale can be difficult to make. The full range of behavior teachers will observe cannot always be easily reduced to discrete measurements. However, after deciding what to observe, teachers then determine what the children will do to demonstrate the action. A scale to measure attention at group times might include the categories in Figure 6-10. Each teacher's rating scale could include a series of checkmarks that record each group time for a period of two weeks. The

staff pools information by comparing notes. The result is a detailed description of (1) each child's behavior as each teacher sees it; (2) the group's overall attention level; and (3) an interesting cross-teacher comparison.

The **shadow study** is a third type of modified technique. It is similar to the diary description and focuses on one child at a time. An in-depth approach, the shadow study gives a detailed picture.

Each teacher attempts to observe and record regularly the behavior of one particular child. Then after a week or so the notes are compared. Although the notes may be random, it is preferable to give some form and organization. Divide a sheet of paper in half lengthwise, with one column for the environment and the other column for details about the child's behavior or response. This will make it easy to glance at 15-minute intervals to collect the data. Figure 6-11 illustrates this process.

The data in a shadow study are descriptive. In this, it shares the advantages of narratives. One of its disadvantages is that teachers may let other matters go while focusing on one child. Also, the shadow study can be quite time-consuming. Still, one interesting side effect often noted is how the behavior of the child being studied improves while the child is being observed. Disruptive behavior seems to diminish or appear less intense. It would appear that in the act of focusing on the child, teacher attention has somehow helped to alter the behavior. Somehow the child feels the impact of all this positive, caring attention and responds to it.

Two additional strategies are used to obtain information about a child. Because they involve some adult intervention, they do not consist strictly of observing and recording naturally occurring behavior. Still, they are very helpful techniques for teachers to understand and use.

Experimental procedures are those in which adult researchers closely control a situation and its variables. Researchers create a situation in which they can

1. observe a particular behavior,
2. make a hypothesis, or guess, about that behavior,
3. test the hypothesis by conducting the experiment.

For instance, an experimenter might wish to observe fine-motor behavior in seven-year-olds to test the hypothesis that these children can significantly improve their fine-motor skills in sewing if given specific instructions. Two groups

NEVER ATTENDS (wiggles, distracts others, wanders away)

SELDOM ATTENDS (eyes wander, never follows fingerplays or songs, occasionally watches leader)

SOMETIMES ATTENDS (can be seen imitating hand gestures, appears to be watching leader about half the time, watches others imitating leader)

USUALLY ATTENDS (often follows leader, rarely leaves group, rarely needs redirection, occasionally volunteers, usually follows leader's gestures and imitations)

ALWAYS ATTENDS (regularly volunteers, enthusiastically enters into each activity, eagerly imitates leader, almost always tries new songs)

FIGURE 6-10 A rating scale measuring attention at group times requires data in terms of frequency, adding depth to the observation.

Child's Name _____ Jeff _____		
Time	**Setting (where)**	**Behavior/Response (what and how)**
9:00	Arrives—cubby, removes wraps, etc.	"I can put on my own nametag" (enthusiastically). Uses thumb to push sharp end of pin, grins widely. Goes to teacher, "Did you see what I did?"
9:15	Blocks	Precise, elaborate work with small cubes on top of block structure, which he built with James. "Those are the dead ones," pointing to the purple cubes outside the structure. Cries and hits Kate when her elbow accidentally knocks tower off.
9:30	Wandering around room	Semidistant, slow pace. Stops at table where children are preparing snack. Does not make eye contact with teacher when invited to sit; Ali grabs J's shirt and tugs at it. "The teacher is talking to you!" J blinks, then sits and asks to help make snack. Stays 10 minutes.

FIGURE 6-11 A shadow study will profile an individual child in the class. This method is especially useful for children who seem to be having trouble in school.

of children are tested. One group is given an embroidery hoop, thread, and needle and asked to make 10 stitches. The other receives a demonstration of how to stitch and is then given the identical task. The embroidery hoops created by both groups are then compared. Some previously agreed-on criteria are used to quantify the fine-motor skill demonstrated by the two groups' work. The major criteria for a scientific experiment may be applied to this procedure as follows:

1. The experimenters can control all relevant aspects of the behavior. (In this case, the materials can be controlled, although previous experience with embroidering cannot.)

2. Usually, only one variable at a time should be measured. (Only fine-motor skill as it relates to embroidery is observed, not other skills such as language or information processing, or even fine-motor proficiency in printing or drawing.)

3. Children are assigned to the two groups in a random manner. (In other words, the groups are not divided by sex, age, or any other predetermined characteristics.)

Few teachers working directly with children will use the stringent criteria needed to undertake a true scientific experiment. However, it is useful to understand this process because much basic research conducted to investigate how children think, perceive, and behave utilizes these techniques.

The clinical method is the final information-gathering technique that involves the adult directly with the child. This method is used in psychotherapy and in counseling settings, as the therapist asks probing questions. The master of the **methode clinique** with children was Piaget, who would observe and question a child about a situation as described in Chapter 4. Two examples of this method are:

Three-month-old Jenna is lying in a crib looking at a mobile. Her hands are waving in the air. The adult wonders whether Jenna will reach out and grasp the mobile if it is moved close to her hands. Or will she bat at the toy? Move her hands away? The adult then tries it to see what will happen.

A group of preschoolers are gathered around a water table. The teacher notices two cups, one deep and narrow, the other broad and shallow, and asks, "I wonder which one holds more, or if they are the same?" The children say what they think and why. Then, one of the children takes the two cups and pours the liquid from one into the other.

In both examples, the adult does more than simply observe and record what happens. With the infant, the adult questions what Jenna's responses might be and then watches for the answer. The preschool teacher intervenes in the children's natural play to explore a question systematically with them, then listens for and observes the answers. The clinical method is not strictly an observational method, but it is an informative technique that, when used carefully, can reveal much about children's abilities and knowledge.

Observation and its various methods are used extensively in early childhood programs and, increasingly, in elementary education to assess children. Figure 6-12 summarizes these

"The NSACA has published Standards for Quality School-Age Care."

COMPETENCY: Professionalism

AGE GROUP: School-Age

CRITICAL THINKING QUESTIONS:

1. What kinds of observations would you conduct to document "Human Relationships" standards?

2. What might you look for to identify "trouble spots" in space or schedule at a school-age center?

systems. It is safe to say that whenever a teacher encounters a problem—be it a child's behavior, a period of the day, a set of materials, or a puzzling series of events—the first step toward a solution is systematic observation.

ASSESSMENT: EVALUATING CHILDREN

How do we evaluate children? What do we look for? How do we document growth and difficulties? How do we communicate our findings to parents? These questions focus our attention on children's issues, assessment tools, and the evaluation process.

Why Evaluate?

Children are evaluated because teachers and parents want to know what the children are learning. Evaluations set the tone for a child's overall educational experience. Highlighting children's strengths builds a foundation from which to address their limitations or needs. The process of evaluating children attempts to answer several questions: Are children gaining appropriate skills and behaviors? In what activities does learning take place? What part of the program supports specific learning? Is the school philosophy being met? Are educational goals being met?

Hills (1993) and others identify clear purposes for assessing children:

1. Educational planning and communicating with parents.
2. Identifying children with special needs.
3. Program evaluation and accountability.

In other words, evaluation processes can help teachers discover who children are, what they can (and cannot) do, and how we can help children grow and learn.[1]

In evaluating children, teachers first decide *what it is they want to know about each child, and why*. With an understanding of children in general, teachers then concentrate on individual children and their unique development. Goals for children stem from program objectives. For instance, if the school philosophy is, "Our program is designed to help children grow toward increasing physical, social, and intellectual competencies," an evaluation will measure children's progress in those three areas. One that claims to teach specific language skills will want to assess how speaking and listening are being accomplished.

Evaluations provide teachers with an opportunity to distance themselves from the daily contact with children and look at them in a more detached, professional way. Teachers can use the results to share their opinions and concerns about children with each other and with parents. For instance, an infant and toddler center might schedule parent conferences around a sequence of child evaluations: the first, a few weeks after the registration of the child; the second, six months after the child's admission into the program; and the third, just before the move up to an older age group (such as moving from the infant to the toddler class), which would include the parents and two teachers, the current and the receiving one. This concentrated effort expands everyone's vision of who and what the child can be, highlights patterns of the child's behavior, and helps in understanding the meaning of that behavior. It gives teachers the chance to chart growth and acknowledge progress and, in doing so, sets the child apart as an individual and unique human being. Evaluations are a reminder to all that they work with individuals and not just a group.

Of course, evaluations contain varying degrees of subjectivity and opinion. For an

---

1 The theoretical basis of "testing" is steeped in Western methods of thought. As a result, non-Western thought can easily be misinterpreted as deficient. Hilliard and others caution all teachers to pay close attention to tests in light of cultural diversity.

Method	Observational Interval	Recording Techniques	Advantages	Disadvantages
1. Narratives				
Diary description	Day to day	Using notebook and pencil; can itemize activity or other ongoing behavior; can see growth patterns.	Rich in detail; maintains sequence of events; describes behavior as it occurs.	Open to observer bias; time-consuming.
Specimen descriptions/ running record	Continuous sequences	Same.	Less structured.	Sometimes need follow-up.
Journal	Regular, preferred daily/ weekly	Log, usually with space for each child; often a summary of child's behavior.	Same as narratives.	Difficult to find time to do.
"On-the-hoof" anecdotes	Sporadic	Ongoing during class time; using notepad and paper in hand.	Quick and easy to take; short-capture pertinent events/details.	Lack detail; need to be filled in at later time; can detract from teaching responsibilities.
2. Time sampling	Short and uniform time intervals	On-the-spot as time passes, prearranged recording sheets.	Easy to record; easy to analyze; relatively bias free.	Limited behaviors; loss of detail; loss of sequence and ecology of event.
3. Event sampling	For the duration of the event	Same as for time sampling.	Easy to record; easy to analyze; can maintain flow of class activity easily.	Limited behaviors; loss of detail; must wait for behavior to occur.
4. Modifications				
Checklists	Regular or intermittent	Using prepared recording sheets; can be during or after class.	Easy to develop and use.	Lack of detail; tell little of the cause of behaviors.
Rating scales	Continuous behavior	Same as for checklists.	Easy to develop and use; can use for wide range of behaviors.	Ambiguity of terms; high observer bias.
Shadow study	Continuous behavior	Narrative-type recording; uses prepared recording sheets.	Rich in detail; focuses in-depth on individual.	Bias problem; can take away too much of a teacher's time and attention.
Experimental procedures	Short and uniform	May be checklists, prearranged recording sheets, audio or video tape.	Simple, clear, pure study, relatively bias-free.	Difficult, hard to isolate in the classroom.
Clinical method	Any time	Usually notebook or tape recorder.	Relevant data; can be spontaneous; easy to use.	Adult has changed naturally occurring behavior.

FIGURE 6-12 A summary chart of the major observational techniques that the early childhood professional can use to record children's behavior. (Adapted from Irwin, D. M., and Bushnell, M. M., *Observational Strategies for Child Study*. New York: Holt, Rinehart and Winston, 1980. Reprinted with permission of the author.)

evaluation to be reliable and valid, multiple sources of information should be used. Observing young children in action is the key to early childhood assessment, and readers will notice that most of the child evaluation instruments described in this chapter are based on what children do spontaneously or in their familiar, natural settings. As Schweinhart (1993) puts it, "the challenge of early childhood assessment is to apply the methods of the assessment field to the goals of the early childhood field." A proper evaluation of a child documents a child's growth over time (e.g., keeping a portfolio of the child's creations, dictations, and teacher observations—anecdotes of behavior or snips of conversations overheard). This chapter's section on authentic assessment and our "Insights" feature detail this process.

In general, evaluations are made to:

- Establish a baseline of information about each child by which to judge future progress.
- Monitor the growth of individual children.
- Have a systematic plan for intervention and guidance.
- Plan the curriculum.
- Provide parents with updated information on their child.
- Provide information for making administrative decisions.

To Establish a Baseline

One purpose of evaluating children is to establish a starting point of their skills and behavior. This is the beginning of a collection over a period of time of important information on each child. Through this cumulative record, teachers learn a great deal about the children: whom they play with, how they spend their time, how they handle problems, what fears and stress they show. In other words, they learn a lot about how children live their lives.

A baseline is a picture of the status of each child; an overview of individual development. It shows where the child is in relation to the school's objectives because the child is being measured according to program expectations. Baseline data give a realistic picture of a child at that moment in time, but there is a presumption that the picture will change.

A Baseline Tool. The beginning of the school term is an obvious time to start collecting information. Records of a child are established in the context of the child's history and family background. Parents frequently submit this information with an application to the school. Teachers can gather the data by visiting the child at home or holding a parent conference and speaking directly with the parents about the child's development.

An entry-level assessment made during the first few weeks of school can be informative, particularly when added to the child's family history. The evaluation itself should be done informally, with teachers collecting information as children engage naturally with materials and each other. A few notes jotted during the first month of school can serve as a beginning collection of pertinent data about the child. Or the format can be more structured, such as that used in Figure 6-13 for two- to five-year olds.

Application. Teachers then use this information to understand children and their various levels of development. They can see children's strengths and weaknesses and where future growth is likely to occur. When the information is shared with parents, they feel more relaxed about their child and even laugh when they recall those first few days of school. One must remember, however, that the entry assessment is only a first impression. Care must be taken to avoid creating a self-fulfilling prophesy by labeling children so that they become shaped into those beginning patterns. Again, teachers must be mindful of the cautions associated with all assessments as they document children's early behaviors. Still, so much happens in that short period of time; the rich information we gain from documenting this growth is invaluable.

Goals and Plans. Teachers use baseline data to set realistic goals for individual children. They tailor the curriculum to the needs and interests they have observed. An entry-level assessment is a vehicle for watching children's growth throughout the year. For instance, after setting a baseline of Mariko's language ability in English, teachers plan activities to increase her understanding and use of language. Then, they make periodic checks on her increased vocabulary as the school year progresses.

To Monitor Children's Progress

Teachers use evaluations to document children's growth. Data collected provide evidence of children's growth or lack of progress. A careful evaluation of each child furnishes the teaching staff

Entry-Level Assessment

1. Child's name_____ Teacher_____
   Age _____ Sex_____
   Primary language_____ Fluency in English?_____
   Any previous school experiences?_____
   Siblings/others in household_____
   Family situation (one/two parents, other adults, etc.)_____

2. Separation from parent:
   Smooth_____ Some anxiety_____ Mild difficulty_____ Unable to separate_____
   Did parent have trouble separating?_____
   Comments: _____

3. How does child come to and leave from school?
   Parent_____ Car pool_____ Babysitter_____ Bus_____

4. Physical appearance:
   General health _____
   Expression _____
   Nonrestrictive clothing _____
   Body posture _____

5. Self-care:
   Dressing: Alone_____ Needs assistance _____
   Toileting: By self_____ Needs help _____
   Eating: _____
   Toothbrushing: _____
   Sleeping/resting: _____
   Allergies/other health-related problems: _____

6. Child's Interests:
   Indoors:
   Clay_____ Books_____ Puzzles_____ Water play_____ Easels_____ Language_____
   Table/rug toys_____ Sensory choices_____ Art_____ Science_____ Blocks_____
   Outdoors:
   Swings_____ Climbers_____ Sandbox_____ Water play_____
   Wheel toys_____ Animals_____ Group games_____ Woodworking_____
   Group times (level of participation):

7. Social-emotional development:
   a. Initiates activities_____ Plays alone_____ Seems happy_____ Has to be invited_____
      Brings security object_____ Seems tense_____
   b. Plays mostly with children of: Same age_____ Younger_____ Older_____
   c. Moves into environment: Easily_____ Hesitantly_____ Not at all_____ Wanders_____
   d. Special friends: _____
   e. Does the child follow teachers?_____ Anyone in particular?_____

8. Cognitive development:
   Use of language: Follows directions_____ Clear pronunciation_____ Memory_____
   Curiosity_____ Holds conversations_____ Words/Phrases_____

9. Physical development
   Climbs safely_____ Uses scissors_____ Hand preference_____ Runs smoothly_____
   Uses pens, brushes_____ Foot preference_____ Handles body well_____

10. Goals/Points to remember: _____
    _____
    _____

FIGURE 6-13 Entry-level assessments collect baseline information. Once teachers and children have had some time together, these first impressions can be documented.

A baseline is a picture of a child framed at a particular moment. Children's use of materials, fine-muscle control, and task persistence can all be seen in these assessments.

with the necessary foundation from which they can plan the next steps.

> Hita has mastered the brushes at the easel. Now we can encourage her to try the smaller brushes in table painting.

> Enrico has been asking how to spell simple words. Let's see that he gets some time away from the blocks to work at the writing center.

All the children seem able to separate from their parents and say good-bye comfortably. How can we celebrate this progress with the group?

A Progress Tool. Figure 6-14 is a sample *mid-year evaluation*. Criteria for each area of development are included to build a profile of the whole child. Teachers note the intervention and guidance steps they plan, where appropriate.

Many states, national programs such as Head Start, school districts, and individual programs are developing and using assessment tools to establish and monitor progress. There has been a reluctance in the early childhood field to use the word "standards," so these tools are often called "essential learning," "developmental guidelines," or "learning goals." One such tool, the California Desired Results Developmental Profile (DRDP), has a profile form for several age groups:

- Infant/Toddler (birth through 36 months)
- Preschool (age 3 to kindergarten)
- Kindergarten through 7 years
- 8 years through 10 years

The DRDP describes four desired results for children; they are

- Children are personally and socially competent.
- Children are effective learners.
- Children show physical and motor competence.
- Children are safe and healthy.

For each age group, the tool outlines several indicators for those results, and contains space for observations and ratings. Many states have similar standards, and several national organizations have posted information about early learning

On his own! An evaluation can capture children's development in all skill areas, including self-concept.

A Tool for Monitoring Children's Progress

Check one of the evaluations below for each skill area; for those that need work, document with specific examples.

Developmental Area	Age Appropriate	Highly Skilled	Needs Work
Self-Management			
Personal care	Can feed, dress, toilet self well		
Making choices	Prefers indoors to outside		
Following routines	Does fine in routines		
Physical/Motor			
1. Fine Motor	Uses easels—brushes good grasp, pens also		
Art materials	Likes blocks, table toys		
Woodworking tools	Hasn't chosen woodworking, but watches often		
Manipulatives			
2. Gross Motor		Very cautious, seems fearful	
Ball handling		Won't swing, slide, use climber	
Balancing		Wanders outdoors, sometimes does music	
Jump/hop/skip		Runs away when wheel toys are rolled down hill	
Communication and Language			
Vocabulary		Exceptionally strong	
Articulation		Converses with adults daily	
Comprehension		Responds to children but rarely initiates talk	
English as a second language		Outstanding at group time—lots of ideas	
Converses with children		Talks around fears, but fears seem to keep him from trying	
Converses with adults			
Listens			
Expresses self (needs, ideas, feelings)			
Cognitive Development			
Sees cause and effect			
Processes and uses information			
Solves problems with:	Dylan has so much information to share, and lots of interest in problem-solving with indoor materials and interactions with teachers. We wish he could extend these skills into work with children and open up a bit more.		
objects			
peers			
adults			
Premath (sequencing, measuring, numbers)			
Prereading concepts (size, colors, shapes, letters, position)			
Social-Emotional			
Independence/initiative			
Positive self-concept	Does well on own, gets around		
Recognizes/accepts own feelings	Is comfortable and confident		
Deals with frustration	around adults		Seems hesitant/fearful outdoors
Flexibility			Is more solitary or onlooker; is this self-esteem or just fear?
Leadership			Don't know about leadership yet;
Initiates social contacts			have seen little because of lack
Prosocial behaviors (friendly, sharing, inclusive, cooperative, empathic)			of interaction with children
Child–child interactions			
Child–adult interactions			

OVERALL STRENGTHS: GOALS

FIGURE 6-14 A midyear evaluation is a more detailed description of the child. It highlights areas of concern and progress.

standards from across the United States. See "Helpful Web Sites" at the end of the chapter.

Application. Information about a child will be used to assess growth and change. How often this happens can vary. Although many changes occur in rapid succession in these early years, it takes time for a child to integrate life experiences and for teachers to see them expressed as a permanent part of behavior. Evaluating too frequently does not reveal sufficient change to make it worthwhile and places an added burden on the teaching staff as well. Once the initial baseline data have been gathered, a progress evaluation approximately every three to six months seems reasonable. In a normal school year, this would mean establishing a baseline in the fall and checking progress in the winter and/or spring. For centers operating on a year-round basis, an assessment could be done every six months. Figure 6-15 describes a sample measure in a format that could be used for a preschool child.

Goals and Plans. Goals are established for children as a result of an assessment. These goals are changed as growth takes place. A good assessment tool monitors progress in each developmental area so that plans can be made to challenge the child physically, socially, emotionally, creatively, and intellectually.

At the same time, theory reminds us that the child develops as a whole, with each area of growth influencing and being influenced by what changes take place in other areas. Evaluations that document growth include information so that all teachers see the interrelationships among areas of development. By assessing growth in individual areas, teachers relate that

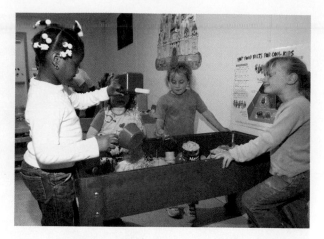

What do children need from a program? Evaluation can assess what each child needs, such as a wider range of materials to explore or guidance to connect with others.

development to the child's collective abilities, as in this example:

> Dylan's midyear report shows that he lacks dexterity in running and climbing and that he is exceptionally strong in verbal and listening skills. This influences his development in the following areas:
>
> *Emotionally.* He appears to lack self-confidence, and his self-esteem deteriorates the longer he feels inept at physical skills. He may even be afraid to master the art of climbing and running for fear he will fail.
>
> *Socially.* Children tease Dylan because he often cannot keep up with them while playing outside. He often ends up playing alone or watching the other children in more active pursuits.
>
> *Intellectually.* There is a lack of risk-taking in Dylan's whole approach to play. Because of his slow physical development, he seems unlikely to challenge himself in other ways.

Sample Preschool Assessment Form					
Developmental Area	**Child Outcome Standard**	**Not Yet**	**Emerging**	**Fully Mastered**	**Observation**
	Social and Emotional Competence				
Self-concept	1. Identity of self and connection with others				
	2. Self-awareness				
	3. Self-expression				
	4. Diversity awareness				

FIGURE 6-15 Child outcome standards describe the kinds of development and learning that should be taking place while children are being educated.

Dylan's progress report thus sets a primary goal in physical/motor skills, with the knowledge that such growth can positively affect learning in other areas. Teachers also plan the strategy of helping him talk about what he likes and dislikes about the outdoors and collecting some stories that depict characters persisting to master difficulties (such as *The Little Engine That Could*), using his strength as a springboard for growth.

Read "What Do You Think?" for another example of how observation can aid in assessment and appropriate action.

To Plan for Guidance and Intervention

A third purpose for evaluation is to help teachers determine guidance procedures. These are based on insights and perceptions brought into focus through the evaluation. This process serves as a primary tool on which guidance and planning are based. When teachers see a problem behavior or are concerned about a child, they plan for further assessment (see Chapter 7). If a developmental screening is done to assess if a child has a learning problem or needs special services,

What do You Think?

Meet Jody, age five.

Observations:

- He uses scissors in a "hedge-clippers" fashion.
- He has an awkward grip when using a pencil.
- He finds it difficult to fit puzzle pieces together.
- He does not choose the woodworking table, manipulative table, or cooking project during free choice.

Assessment: What would you do? Does he need intervention? How would you address this situation?

Results: The caregivers in his kindergarten after-school class were concerned about his fine-motor skill development.

A check with his parents revealed two important facts: Jody had trouble handling table utensils and couldn't button his sweater. They said there was no provision at home for him to pursue any fine-motor activities. Knowing of Jody's interest in airplanes, the teachers used that to draw Jody into areas of the curriculum he didn't ordinarily pursue. Small airplanes were added to the block corner, and airplane stencils were placed near the art table. A large mural of an airport was hung on the fence, and children were invited to paint on it. One day children cut airplane pictures out of magazines and used them on a collage. Simple airplane puzzles were placed on the puzzle table. Felt shapes and small plastic airplanes in the water table helped draw Jody toward activities requiring fine-motor skills. Jody's parents supplied him with a special art box at home, full of crayons, scissors, pens, water colors, and stencils. As his fine-motor skills increased and refined, Jody became a more confident and happier child. By the end of three months he was a regular participant in all areas of the school and seemed to be enjoying his newfound interest in art materials.

teachers will either refer the family to a proper specialist or agency or administer the screening themselves. Developmental screening tests will be discussed further in this chapter.

A Guidance Tool. Evaluations help in behavior management. Once a need has been pinpointed, the teaching staff decides how to proceed. Individual problems are highlighted when teachers make a point of concentrating on the child's behavior. Figure 6-16 illustrates a form used to determine intervention. Used at a team meeting, this form demonstrates what steps are to be taken in addressing the concern directly. It also helps teachers clarify how to talk to parents in a concerned and supportive manner.

Application. The following case studies demonstrate how information from evaluations is used for guidance and intervention:

> Elizabeth's recent evaluation revealed an increase in the number of toilet accidents she has had. The staff noted a higher incidence during midmorning

---

Child Guidance Form

Presentation of Problems (in behavioral terms)

What behaviors are causing the staff concern? Be specific. Limit to three problems or concerns.

1.

2.

3.

Family History (information from family, medical info if needed)

School History (child's relations to adults, children, materials, activities)

Intervention (What procedures have and have not worked? What strengths does the child bring to this issue?)

Future Plans (What is going to happen as a result?)

1. In classroom

2. With parents

3. Date for reviewing results

FIGURE 6-16 One purpose of evaluating children is to plan for behavior management. A good evaluation form will include how to follow through on plans made for intervention. (Adapted from McLaughlin & Sugarman, 1982.)

---

snacks but came to no conclusion as to the cause. They agreed to continue to treat her behavior in a relaxed manner and have one teacher remind Elizabeth to use the toilet before she washes her hands for snack. At the same time, they made plans to contact the parents for further information and insights. They will confer again afterward and agree on an approach.

> Trevor's parents report that he says he has no friends at school. At their staff meeting, the teachers make plans to suggest that Trevor's parents invite Ryan and Brooke to play with Trevor at home. Teachers have seen both children approach him, but he didn't seem to know how to respond. At school, the teachers will give Trevor verbal cues when children make attempts to play with him.

Goals and Plans. An evaluation tool, such as the Child Guidance Form in Figure 6-16, helps teachers set goals for children. Narrowing the focus to include only those behaviors that concern the staff enables the staff to quickly review the needs of many children.

TO PLAN CURRICULUM

Teachers plan the curriculum on the basis of children's evaluations. Translating the assessment to actual classroom practice is an important part of the teacher's role. A thorough evaluation helps teachers plan appropriate activities to meet children's needs. More importantly, observation itself drives curriculum development, particularly in the program models of Reggio Emilia, the Project Approach, and Emergent Curriculum (see Chapter 2). Figure 6-17 illustrates the connections between observation (listening to children's enthusiastic reports of a nearby construction project and their subsequent work in the block corner), curriculum development, and **documentation**.

Planning Tools. All three of the previous evaluation tools can be used to plan curriculum. The entry-level **assessment** and midyear report are often summarized in a group chart, as in Figure 6-18. One such chart, made at the end of the first semester of a prekindergarten class, revealed this pattern:

> At least one-third of the class was having trouble listening at group time, as evidenced by the group chart that identified "Group Time" and "Language Listening Skills" as areas for growth for nearly half

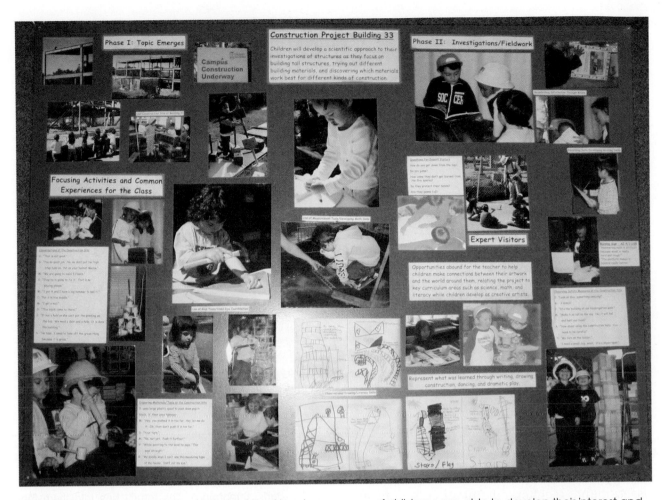

FIGURE 6-17 Thanks to the observational skills of teachers, a group of children were able to develop their interest and knowledge about building construction through curriculum development. Documentation panel by Maggie Lam and Kären Wiggins-Dowler (2006). Reprinted with permission from Mary Meta Lazarus Child Development Center, College of San Mateo.

the children. The staff centered their attention on the group time content. It was concluded that a story made the group times too long; the children were restless throughout most of the reading. It was agreed to move storytime to just before nap and shorten the group time temporarily.

Evaluation also applies to daily events, such as individual projects and the day as a whole. One tool for curriculum evaluation reviews the results of a specific activity. Figure 6-19 is a sample of that kind of curriculum assessment. Chapter 10 discusses curriculum planning in further detail.

Application. Evaluation results assist teachers in seeing more clearly the strengths and abilities of each child in the class. Curriculum activities are then planned that will continue to enhance the growth of that child. Also, areas of difficulty will be identified.

Jolene has trouble mastering even the simplest puzzle. Provide her with common shapes found in attribute blocks (small plastic shapes of varying color, thickness, size) and do some matching exercises with her.

The younger children in the class are reluctant to try the climbing structures designed by the older ones. Build an obstacle course with the youngest children, beginning with very simple challenges and involving the children in the actual planning and building as well as rehearsing climbing techniques with them. There are practical connections to be made in learning to "read" the children and actual curriculum planning. Reflective work is critical for making curricular connections. (See "What Do You Think?")

Goals and Plans. Each of the previous case studies demonstrates how evaluation tools can be used to plan curriculum. By analyzing both

Summary of Development/Fall Progress Reports (see forms for details)
Developmental Area: + = fine; − = needs work; ? = don't know

Child	Physical	Language	Cognitive	Social	Emotional	Creative
Greg	−	+	+	+	−	?
Anwar	?	−	+	−	−	+
San-Joo	+	?	?	−	+	+
Reva	+	+	+	+	+	+
Katy	−	+	?	?	?	−

Group Goals for Winter:

- Emphasize social and emotional areas of curriculum
- Plan physical games (indoor games because of weather)

Individual Goals for Winter:

Greg: Encourage some creative arts, games. Observe creatively in intellectual activities.

Anwar: Needs to be helped to feel confident and express himself; don't push too hard on physical risks yet.

San-Joo: Need assessment of language and cognitive skills; observe use of table toys, receptive language at group time.

Reva: What is the next step? Is she ready for helping the others? Involve her with 100-piece puzzles and the computer.

Katy: Need to focus on her overall development; too many unknowns—is she getting enough individual attention?

FIGURE 6-18 A group chart. Teachers can use individual assessment tools to plan for the entire group and for each child in the class.

group and individual skills through periodic assessment, teachers maintain a secure and challenging environment.

To Communicate with Parents

Plans for evaluating children should include the means by which parents are to be informed of the results. Once the teachers have identified a child's needs and capabilities, parents are entitled to hear the conclusions. The teaching staff has an obligation to provide a realistic overview of the child's progress and alert the parents to any possible concerns. See Chapter 8 for details about parents and teachers working together. Using the child guidance form (see Figure 6-15), teachers define problem behavior for a child and work closely with the parents to reach a solution:

Yum-Tong refuses to let his mother leave. The teachers agree that there are two issues: (1) Y.-T.'s screaming and crying as his mother leaves and (2) his inability to focus on an activity while she

attempts to go (though she stays as soon as he starts screaming). The family has told them that their other two children had separation problems as preschoolers. The previous school asked the parents to stay until the children stopped protesting, although the parents report that this took nearly six months and so was a hardship for them in their workplaces.[1]

The teachers choose to intervene by asking Yum-Tong's mother to plan ahead with Y.-T., deciding before school how they will spend five minutes together each morning. After playing and helping him to settle in, she will then say good-bye and leave Y.-T. with Pete, his favorite teacher. Pete will be prepared to be with him at the departure and stay with him until he calms down. They also plan to have a conference date after two weeks of this intervention plan to follow through and review how it is working for everyone.

A Tool with Parents. Teachers and parents need to talk together, especially when problems

---

1 Teachers need to examine theories of child development and practice for ethnocentricity (e.g., in Western-European and American culture it may be seen as a sign of secure attachment if a parent and child separate comfortably and quietly, whereas in another culture a secure attachment may be demonstrated by a passionate and emotion-laden farewell).

Evaluating Classroom Activity

Activity _____

How many children participated?_____ Did any avoid the activity?_____

How involved did children become? Very_____ Briefly_____ Watched only_____

What were children's reactions? Describe what they said and did._____
_____
_____
_____

What did you do to attract children? To maintain their interest?_____
_____
_____

How would you rate the success of this activity? Poor_____ Adequate_____ Good_____ Great_____

Why?_____

What skills/abilities were needed? Did the children exhibit the skills?_____
_____
_____

What parts of the activity were most successful? Why?_____
_____
_____

Describe any difficulty you encountered. Give reasons and tell how you would handle it if it happened again.____
_____
_____
_____

If you did this activity again, what would you change?_____
_____
_____

In light of your evaluation, what would you plan for a follow-up activity?_____
_____
_____

How did this activity compare with your goals and expectations?_____
_____
_____

FIGURE 6-19 Evaluating daily activities lets teachers use assessment as a curriculum planning tool. Although not every activity will need this scrutiny on a daily basis, careful planning and evaluation create effective classrooms. (Reprinted with permission from Julie Riess, Wimpfheimer Nursery School at Vassar College.)

are revealed by the evaluation. As parents and teachers share knowledge and insights, a fuller picture of the child emerges for both. Each can then assume a role in the resolution of the problem. The role of the teacher will be defined in the context of the parents' role, and the parents will be guided by the teacher's attitudes and actions.

Evaluation tools can help parents target areas in which their child may need special help. Chapter 8 discusses the parent-teacher relationship and offers guidelines for effective parent-teacher conferences. The tool that works best is one that summarizes the school's concerns and solicits high parent involvement.

Application. Aside from identifying normal behavior problems, evaluations may raise questions concerning a child's physical development, hearing and visual acuity, or language problems. Potentially serious problems may emerge from the evaluation, and parents can be encouraged to seek further professional guidance.

Goals and Plans. Because evaluation is an ongoing process, reevaluation and goal setting are done regularly. Communicating to parents both progress and new goals is critical for the feedback loop of an evaluation form to be effective, as shown in Chapter 5 on teacher evaluation.

To Make Administrative Decisions

Evaluation results can help a school make administrative decisions. They can lead to changes in the overall program or in the school's philosophy. For example, a child care component might be added to the half-day program after learning that most children are enrolled in another child care situation after nursery school. Or an evaluation might conclude that there is too little emphasis on developing gross-motor skills and coordination. To invite more active play, the administration might decide to remodel the play yard and purchase new equipment.

In the early childhood setting, both informal and formal methods are used for evaluating children. *Informal and homemade methods* include observation, note taking, self-assessments, parent interviews and surveys, samples of children's work, and teacher-designed forms. More *formal* kinds of *evaluations* may be used, although somewhat less frequently in the early years. These include standardized tests and various "screening" instruments. The yearly tests taken in elementary and secondary school, using a number-2 pencil, are an example of such procedures. Those and other standardized forms are

examples of formal methods of evaluation. Commercially developed, these tests usually compare the individual child's performance with a predetermined norm. There are problems associated with testing and screening of young children (see the section "Standards, Testing and Screening" later in this chapter).

It is important to choose assessment tools and techniques that are appropriate for the group or the child under consideration. Informal observations can be made more systematic or comprehensive to gain more information about a specific problem. Formal, commercially developed instruments need to be used more carefully if at all.

An Administrative Tool. Many kindergartens and some nursery schools use various kinds of **screening** tests before children begin school in the fall.[1] The usual purpose of these evaluations is to determine readiness: that is, to verify that the child will be able to cope with and succeed in school. These tools are best devised with the individual child in mind. Their purposes are positive: to highlight the skills the child has and to identify the areas in which the child may need help in the next class. Figure 6-20 shows a homemade screening evaluation that was developed for individual four- to five-year-old preschoolers who were leaving for kindergarten. The activity uses a one-to-one, gamelike approach in which a child and a favorite teacher can explore both strengths and difficulties in a safe, supportive setting.

Early Learning Standards. The first decade of the 21st century has seen a shift toward standards-based programming in American public schools. More than half the states now have standards that describe results (see DRDP), outcomes, or learning expectations for children under kindergarten age, and Head Start has a framework for Child Outcomes. It is essential that effective **early learning standards** (NAEYC & NAESC/SDE, 2003):

- emphasize significant developmentally appropriate content and outcomes.
- are developed and reviewed through informed, inclusive processes.
- gain their effectiveness through implementation and assessment practices that support all

1 It must be noted that "screening" tests can be biased, and their validity comes into question especially if they are developed locally. Additionally, teachers must know whether the purpose of the test is to check for handicapping conditions or to know children's skills; in addition, it might run the risk of simply excluding children.

Skills Inventory

Teacher _____

Child _____ Age _____ Date _____

TASK	**TEACHER COMMENTS**

Cognitive Skills

1. Can you say the alphabet?

2. Can you tell me what these letters are?

3. Can you count for me?

4. Please point to the number.

5. Can you put these in order from smallest to biggest? Which is the largest? Smallest? First? Last?

6. What color is this? If child cannot name the color, then ask to "Point to the red one," etc.

7. What shapes are these? If child cannot name the shape, then ask to "Point to the circle," etc.

8. Can you find your shoulders? Elbow? Thumb? Neck? Lips?

9. Name all the animals you can think of.

10. Please put these animals into two groups. One has the animals that live in water, and the other the ones that live on the land.

11. Here are a bear and a cube. Put the cube on top of the bear. Under the bear. Behind the bear. Beside the bear.

12. Here are three pictures. Can you put them in order so that they tell a story?

1. Sequence correct? Yes ____ No ____
   Length:

2. Number of letters correct ____
   Comment:

3. Note how far:
   Sequence correct how far? ____

4. 3-1-6-4-8-2-9-7-5
   How many correct? ____

5. Three sizes of triangles.
   Comments:

6. Point to red, blue, yellow, black, green, orange, brown, purple. Comments:

7. Point to circle, square, triangle, rectangle. Comments:

8. Comments:

9. Comments:

10. Giraffe, deer, cat, frog, alligator, shark, goldfish

11. Check correct responses:

12. Tree with green leaves. Tree with orange or red leaves, falling. Bare tree. Comments:

Auditory-Perceptual Listening Skills

1. Please repeat these numbers after I say them (Practice with 6-3-1-4):
   5-3-8-2
   2-7-9-3

2. Tell me the sentence in the same order as I say. (Practice with "The dog ran to the park.")
   The mother pointed to the airplane in the sky.

3. Listen to what I say, and then do what my words tell you. (Practice with "Put your hands on your head.")
   Stand up, go to the door, and walk back to me.

1. Sequence correct? Numbers correct?

2. Sequence correct? Words correct?

3. Comments:

Fine-Motor Skills

1. Print your name.
2. Draw a circle, square, triangle, rectangle.
3. Write the letters:
   O E P A J

1. Note grasp, hand preference.
2. Comments:
3. Comments:

(continues)

FIGURE 6-20 By creating effective tools for assessment, we are able to evaluate children's developing skills and their readiness for the next educational step.

TASK	TEACHER COMMENTS
4. Write the numbers: 1 3 7 2 5	4. Comments:
5. Cut out a circle.	5. Note scissors grasp, hand preference.
6. Draw the best person that you can. Have you left anything out?	6. Comments:

Gross-Motor Skills

1. Jump on two feet from A to B.	1. Note balance.
2. Hop on one foot from B to A.	2. Note balance.
3. Skip from A to B.	3. Comments:
4. Walk backward from B to A.	4. Comments:
5. Stand on one foot while I count to three.	5. Note balance.
6. Walk across this balance board.	6. Note balance.
7. Can you jump over these poles with your feet together?	7. Comments:
8. How high can you climb our climber? Go up our slide?	8. Comments:
9. Now run from the climber to the fence and back to me as fast as you can!	9. Note gait and balance.
10. Please throw the ball to me. Catch it. Kick it.	10. Comments:

FIGURE 6-20 *(continued)*

Assessing the group is one reason to evaluate children. How can you tell if these children are ready for more engaging and challenging group-time activities?

children's development in ethical, appropriate way.

● require a foundation of support for early childhood programs, professionals, and families.

The ethical use of assessment instruments and strategies cannot be overemphasized; see Appendix A for the Code of Ethics (Section I: Ethical Responsibilities to Children, I-1.6 and 1.7; Section II: Ethical Responsibilities to Families, I-2.7).

Some teachers conclude the year with a summary report. This evaluation serves as an overview of what a child has accomplished, what areas of strength are present, and what future growth might occur. These records are useful to parents as a summary of their child's learning experiences. Teachers may use them as references should they ever be consulted by another school about the child. Again, it is critical to administer these assessments in a sensitive and accepting manner, to keep the time period as brief as possible, and to communicate the results in the same tone. If this is not done, the child's self-esteem may be damaged and the

family trust may be lost. The disadvantages of these tools parallel those of standardized tests.

Application. Making administrative decisions based on evaluation results is a sound idea. Assessments give administrators specific and verifiable information on which to base decisions.

The issue of readiness or placement of children is difficult and complex. The next section describes the potential problems and misapplications of tests in this regard. Whether or not a child is ready to succeed in a program affects parents and children personally. Having a good evaluation tool helps in making such decisions equitably and in communicating results in a clear and kind manner.

Goals and Plans. The evaluation tool that gives a specific profile of a child's skills will allow an administrator to share information with a family clearly and honestly. By carefully choosing a tool, administrators give the parents information they can use to plan for the child's development.

Know the reasons for making an evaluation. Evaluations should avoid unfair comparisons, acknowledge individual differences and uniqueness, and not look at children in a competitive manner.

Concerns

Assessment is challenging! Of all the functions performed by teachers, probably none calls for more energy, time, and skill than evaluation. Anyone involved in evaluation should avoid:

- *Unfair comparisons.* Evaluations should be used to identify and understand the child involved, not to compare one with another in a competitive manner.

- *Bias.* Evaluations can label unfairly or prematurely the very people they are intended to help. Typecasting will not produce a useful assessment. Insufficient data and overemphasis on the results are two areas that need close monitoring. Evaluation tools should be free of language bias or other cultural bias.[1] For instance, an evaluation of children should not include experiences not familiar to the cultural group being assessed.

- *Overemphasis on norms.* Most evaluation tools imply some level of normal behavior or performance, acceptable levels of interaction, or quantities of materials and space. People involved in an evaluation must remember to individualize the process rather than try to fit a child into the mold created by the assessment tool.

- *Interpretation.* There is sometimes a tendency to overinterpret or misinterpret results. It must be clear what is being evaluated and how the information will be used (see Figure 6-21). It is particularly important to be sensitive to the feelings of those being evaluated when communicating the results of the assessment. Parents and teachers need to interpret evaluations clearly and carefully if they are to understand the findings and feel comfortable with them.

- *Too narrow a perspective.* An evaluation tool may focus too much on one area and not enough on others. Moreover, no single occasion or instrument will tell teachers all they need to know about a child's abilities, a teacher's performance, or a program's effectiveness. It is essential that information be gathered in many ways and on several occasions. Sampling only children's skills as the single measure would lead to conclusions that were neither reliable nor valid. An imbalanced assessment gives an incomplete picture.

- *Too wide a range.* An evaluation should be designed for a single level or age group and not cover too wide a range. It is appropriate to measure a child's ability to print at age six but not at age two. What is expected of the person or task should be taken into account and the evaluation method modified accordingly.

- *Too little or too much time.* The amount of time necessary to complete an evaluation must be weighed. The evaluation that is too lengthy loses its effectiveness in the time it takes. Time for interpretation and reflection must be included in the overall process.

Goals for children encompass all areas of development, and one measurement will not describe every area. Doing so also changes what happens in the program: "Teachers are very likely to shape their instruction to match a test's specific focus. This phenomenon, known as 'measurement-driven instruction,' [creates] a narrowing of the curriculum" (Meisels & Atkins-Burnett, 2005). Using a single yardstick to measure a child ignores the fact that young children do not always demonstrate what they know in a "testing" or single situation.

Educational Aims	Behavioral Goals
To achieve independence and autonomy.	Children separate from their parents successfully; can manage their own clothing needs; initiate own activities.
To become a functional part of a larger society.	Children participate actively in small and large groups.
To learn to live effectively with others.	Children develop social skills with peers and adults, show tolerance of differences.
To learn basic tools for acquiring knowledge.	Children show signs of curiosity, memory, and symbol recognition.

FIGURE 6-21 Teachers relate what happens in the classroom (behavioral goals) to traditional educational goals.

1 As we become aware of those we teach, we must adjust our evaluation systems to avoid bias and to reflect reality accurately.

Evaluations in programs with a wide age range may need to be individualized to adequately record children's skills.

AUTHENTIC ASSESSMENT: THE PORTFOLIO

The dictionary defines "authentic" as "of undisputed origin, genuine . . . made or done in a way that faithfully resembles an original" (*New Oxford American Dictionary*, 2005). For a child assessment to be authentic, it must try to capture who the child is, and what that child knows (or doesn't) and can (or cannot) do. Teachers must assess to know the child better in order to improve learning. How do we get there? Assessment must:

● Occur in a variety of settings over time, drawing on many sources of information.

● Focus on essential skills and dispositions valued by the program and families and community.

● Have teacher-designed assessment tools and methods that demonstrate the child in action and in the familiar setting.

Many early childhood educators have embraced the idea that children's work samples in a portfolio form are an excellent way to document children's learning and faithfully capture the child's development. In light of the concerns you have read in this chapter about the misassessment of young children and the "test mania"

that standardized tests in the primary grades have fomented, many professionals have looked for alternative assessment measures.

Danielson and Abrutyn (1997) identify three types of portfolios:

1. Display portfolios—scrapbooks that collect items without teacher comments.

2. Showcase portfolios—the best pieces of the child's work.

3. Working portfolios—include selections of typical work along with teacher documentation to show the child's progress. Gronlund (1998) recommends a working portfolio that combines work samples with teacher commentary. In our "Insights" article, Kären Wiggins-Dowler, an outstanding practitioner, describes this type of portfolio.

Collection Plan

Think carefully about a portfolio plan, a brief set of guidelines for collecting items for saving (see Figure 6-22). Since simple collection of work is not enough, here are some tips to expand upon collection (Pendowski, 2006):

● Do not try to collect everything. Look for work samples that demonstrate your educational objectives and a child's progress over time on a goal.

A Portfolio Policy

- Identify the purpose of the portfolio (improving communication with families, connecting with other teachers or programs).
- Identify the types of items to be collected (artwork, photos of block or dramatic play, etc.).
- Specify who will collaborate to create the portfolio (teacher, other caregivers, the child, family).
- Set a timetable (for instance, the first set by November 15, second set by April 30).
- Establish any standards or tool you will use (for example, Desired Results or Child Outcomes).
- Have in writing when any portfolio conferences will take place and who will be there (teacher, family, child?)
- Identify procedure for maintaining confidentiality, and for release of items.

FIGURE 6-22 Having a set of guidelines for developing and using portfolios keeps the process clear for all involved.

- Be organized when storing work samples. Ideas include pocket folders or even pizza boxes.

Implementation Plan

Plan your implementation so that you can collect children's work with purpose. In the Work Sampling System teachers look for work in several domains (see Figure 6-23). Many suggest you collect a piece of each child's work two or three times a year that demonstrates each area. This way each child's individual portfolio may have completely different work samples from others in the program, but every portfolio will still show growth over time in every developmental area.

Teacher's Evaluation

Finally, teachers add their written comments to the work samples. As Gronlund (1998) puts it:

The commentary enhances the documentation by giving the information necessary to assess the process of learning that is going on. Teachers have told me that a picture may be worth a thousand

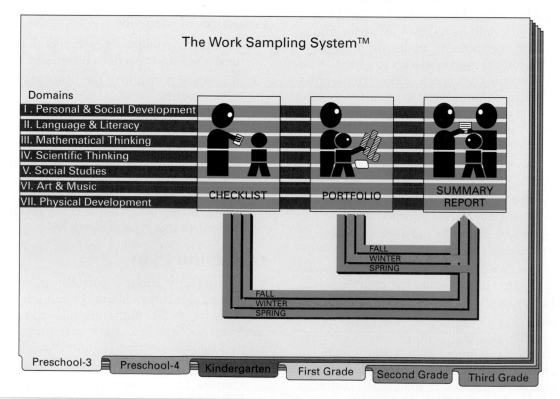

FIGURE 6-23 The Work Sampling System developed by S. J. Meisels and others (Meisels & Atkins-Burnett, 2005).

words; but for assessment purposes, the words are essential, not the photo!

At least, not the photo or drawing alone. Teacher commentary becomes a critical source of information to tell how the child did it, what it means, and how it shows growth or lack of it. Teacher observation and comments will document information for the teacher, the parents, and other program personnel to use in a confidential and ethical manner (Feeney et al., 1997).

Portfolios can provide a "history of learning, a structured record of learner accomplishment . . . as well as a method for assessing progress" (Fenwich & Parsons, 2000). While they must take considerable planning—setting up the organization and storage, and planning for what to collect to show your educational goals—they help you collect children's work intentionally. You can evaluate children on their work and play, as they are spontaneously, rather than with standardized tests or unnecessary screening.

STANDARDS, TESTING, AND SCREENING

"Standards, standards everywhere! . . . There are child outcome standards that define what young children should be learning, . . . What are the reasonable expectations that guide early educators in planning curriculum for preschool children and in assessing their progress in achieving these expectations? (Gronlund, 2006)

The practice of testing and screening for readiness and retention has increased dramatically in the last decade. With the passage of Public Law 94-142 (Education for All Handicapped Children Act) and the early childhood amendment to the law (P.L. 99-457), states now have the responsibility to establish specific procedures and policies to identify, evaluate, and provide services to all children with learning problems. Moreover, testing for admittance to kindergarten or promotion to first grade has become more common. The standards movement in K–12 that began in the 1980s has arrived at the early childhood doorstep. "The idea is to use standards to improve the odds that preschool programs will boost school readiness and lay a solid foundation for later achievement (Bodrova, Leong, & Shore, 2004). Yet the results are that more children are being denied entrance to a school system, being put in extra-year or pull-out programs, or being placed in kindergarten twice.

Standards

It is important to sort out these three issues. The idea of using standards for what children ought to learn and holding programs (and teachers) accountable is here to stay. Early learning standards are

statements that describe expectations for the learning and development of young children across the domains of: health and physical well-being; social and emotional well-being; approaches to learning; language development and symbol systems; and general knowledge about the world around them. (CCSSO, 2005)

What is a challenge is determining standards for children in the early years, since the ways children learn and what they are learning is different than those in elementary school. "In early childhood, the development of foundational skills (skills that lay the foundation for later learning) in just as important as mastery of content matter" (Bodrova et al., 2004). Figure 6-24 details the pros and cons to Early Learning Standards.

Testing

Ironically, the last decade has also taught us that standardized tests fail to reflect adequately what children learn (National Commission on Testing and Public Policy, 1998). Indeed, "children know so much more than they are "taught," and what is tested may not be the important learning that the children have done" (Bergan & Feld, 1993). Howard Gardner, whose work on multiple intelligences is described in Chapters 4, 12, and 13, puts it this way:

Over the past several decades the assumptions underlying the current testing edifice have been challenged by developmental, cognitive, and educational studies. There's a considerable body of scientific findings telling us that if we want to understand people's competence or knowledge about something, we should not examine them in an artificial way in an artificial setting. (Gardner, 1988)

Moreover, most formal testing engages only two (linguistic and logical mathematical) of the eight intelligences Gardner has identified. Such practices raise some practical and serious philosophical issues.

- Young children do not function well in common test situations, nor do the test results necessarily reflect children's true knowledge or skills.

Early Learning Standards

Pros

- They can provide richness to our conversation about children's growth and learning.

- We can match standards to what we are already doing.

- They can be linked to primary standards so that we are indeed contributing to children's school readiness.

- They help us identify next steps and transitions.

- They are a strategy for professionalizing our field.

- They help us communicate across the grades, among ourselves, and with our public.

- They help us to have higher expectations for children.

Cons

- They lead to teaching to the standards only in a cookie-cutter curriculum.

- They bring a pressure of accountability with the risk of a push-down in curriculum and inappropriate expectations for younger children.

- Direct instruction is assumed as the only way that standards are addressed.

- Learning in self-directed, exploratory ways is not trusted.

- They contribute to a "we/they" mentality between preschool and elementary teachers.

- They take time for early educators to learn and work through, to figure out how to integrate into good practices.

- They result in testing and other inappropriate assessment methods being used.

- There is little money to support education and training of early educators in the standards and how best to use them.

FIGURE 6-24 There are both benefits and problems with early learning standards. (Adapted from *Make Early Learning Standards Come Alive: Connecting Your Practice and Curriculum to State Guidelines,* by Gaye Gronlund (Redleaf Press, 2006). Copyright © 2006 by Gaye Gronlund. Reprinted with permisson from Redleaf Press, St. Paul, Minnesota, www.redleafpress.org. To order, call 800-423-8309.)

- These practices (often based on inappropriate uses of readiness or screening tests) disregard the potential, documented long-term negative effects of retention on children's self-esteem and the fact that such practices disproportionately affect low-income and minority children (National Center for Fair and Open Testing, 2006).

- Although the most needed and appropriate tests (teacher-made) are the hardest to create, the standardized ones are frequently misused and misunderstood by teachers and parents (Meisels & Atkins-Burnett, 2005).

- Teachers are pressured into running programs that overemphasize the testing situation and test items.

- Most tests focus on cognitive and language skills; such a narrow focus ignores other areas of development.

- Special training to administer tests is imperative, yet often overlooked. And standardized tests require specific protocols (Klein & Estes, 2004).

The practice of standardized testing has caused early childhood curricula to become increasingly academic. Early childhood educators and parents are alarmed that:

> Many kindergartens are now structured, "watered-down" first grades, emphasizing workbooks and other paper-and-pencil activities that are inappropriate for five-year-olds. The trend further trickles down to preschool and child care programs that feel that their mission is to get children "ready" for kindergarten. Too many school systems, expecting children to conform to an inappropriate curriculum and finding large numbers of "unready" children, react to the problem by raising the entrance age for kindergarten and/or labeling the children as failures (NAEYC, 1991).

The implications of such testing further erode the curriculum when teachers, wanting their classes to do well on the test, alter activities to conform to what will be tested. They then begin teaching children to learn "right" answers rather than to engage in active, critical thinking. Rather than making teachers more accountable, "the overuse (and misuse) of standardized testing has led to the adoption of inappropriate teaching practices as well as admission and

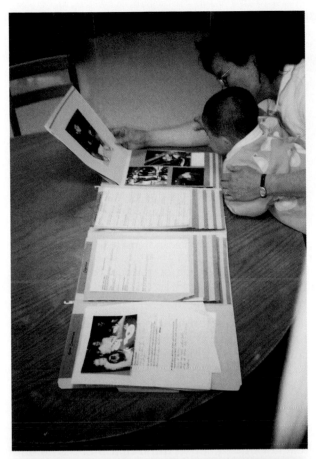

Fine-motor skills are one indicator of an ability to succeed in school and should be assessed as regularly as cognitive or socioemotional abilities.

Screening

Testing does have appropriate uses, such as using valid screening tests to "identify children who, because of the risk of possible learning problems or a handicapping condition, should proceed to a more intensive level of diagnostic assessment" (Meisels & Atkins-Burnett, 2005). Note that screening tests are *not* diagnostic tools; a properly developed screening only indicates if more investigative work is needed. The nonstandardized instruments in this chapter can be used to plan programs that respond to the individual children in them. At the same time, NAEYC has adopted specific guidelines for the use of standardized testing that include using only reliable and valid instruments and interpreting the test results accurately and cautiously to parents and others (NAEYC & NAECS/SDE, 2003; Bredekamp & Rosegrant, 1995).

Developmental screening instruments are not achievement tests, and are not meant to describe child learning outcomes.

Portfolio assessment is often the form of choice when doing authentic assessment.

retention policies that are not in the best interests of individual children or the nation as a whole" (NAEYC & NAECS/SDE, 2003).

Teachers and schools can respond to the overuse and inappropriate use of tests. The National Association of Elementary School Principals now urges limited use of formal tests and retention. The Texas Board of Education has barred retention before first grade, and in New York State a coalition of groups is urging a ban on mass standardized testing of children before grade three.

> Developmental screening tests identify at an early point which children may have learning problems or disabilities that could keep them from realizing their potential. . . . By triggering in-depth assessment, screening instruments help teachers and other professionals decide who needs additional

How to Use (Not Misuse) Results

- Do assess using multiple measures if the assessment information will be the basis for important educational decisions.

- Do use standardized screening tests only for initial screening and referral for further evaluation. Do link screenings to a follow-up that could provide needed services.

- Do use assessment results to *individualize* instruction.

- Don't make such important decisions based on just an assessment or two; *never* make them from a single test result.

- Don't use locally developed screening instruments and processes without examining their validity and reliability.

- Don't use assessment results to form unchanging groups or track children.

FIGURE 6-25 The basics of assessment include a plan for using the results to help children, not limit their opportunities to learn. (Adapted from *Basics of Assessment: A Primer for Early Childhood Educators* by O. McAfee, D. J. Leong, & E. Bodrova, Washington, DC: NAEYC, 2004, p. 69. Reprinted with permission form National Association for the Education of Young Children.)

support for learning, rather than potentially being used to judge whether classrooms are meeting standards set from the outside. (Meisels & Atkins-Burnett, 2005)

Head Start programs use an "Ages & Stages Questionnaire," for instance, so parents/adult family members can inform teachers about children's behaviors that allows for more accurate child monitoring. Meisels and Atkins-Burnett (2005) provide a detailed description about several well-known instruments.

Perhaps most important is the reminder to all teachers that tests have no special magic. Assessment is more than testing. A standardized test, a homemade tool, or a screening instrument should be only one of several measures used to determine a child's skills, abilities, or readiness. Any test result should be part of a multitude of information, such as direct observation, parental report, and children's actual work. (See Figure 6-25). Chapter 15 includes a discussion about the standards movement and the No Child Left Behind legislation. Above all, keep the testing to a minimum, thus guarding against "pulling up the plants to look at them before the roots take hold" (Cryan, 1986).

HOW TO OBSERVE AND RECORD

"The process of assessment is second nature for those teachers who view children in a holistic manner" (Barbour, 2000), and it includes observation at many levels. Learning how to observe is a serious activity and requires a great deal of concentration. Some preparations can be made beforehand so that full attention is focused on the observation. Thinking through some of the possible problems helps the teacher get the most out of the experience.

Observing While Teaching

To make observing workable at school, the teacher must keep in mind that there is no one right way to observe and record. Some teachers find certain times of the day easier than others. Many prefer to watch during free play, whereas others find it easier to watch individual children during directed teaching times. Although some teachers keep a pencil and paper handy to write their observations throughout the day, others choose to record what they see after school is over for the day. The professional team that is committed to observation will find ways to support its implementation.

Finding an opportunity for regular observations is difficult. Centers are rarely staffed so well that one teacher can be free from classroom responsibilities for long periods of time. Some ask for parent volunteers to take over an activity while a teacher conducts an assessment. In one center the snack was set up ahead of time to free up one teacher to observe during group time. The environment can be arranged with activities that require little supervision when a teacher is interested in making some observations.

When children know they are being observed, they may feel self-conscious initially, asking pointed questions of the observer and changing their behavior as if they were on stage. Observation helps keep most of the attention child-centered rather than teacher-directed and increases children's and adult's communication. When a teacher begins to write, some of the children will pay immediate attention.

"'What are you writing about?' asks four-year-old Nina as I sit down at the edge of the block area. 'I'm writing about children playing,' I explain. 'You're writing about what I'm doing?' Nina asks. 'Yes, I am.' She's pleased. She goes back to building a careful enclosure with the long blocks" (Jones & Carter, 1991). When effective observation strategies are used and regular observations are done by familiar adults, children will soon ignore the observer and resume normal activity.

Teachers can improve their observation and recording skills outside the classroom as well. Taking an "Observation of Children" class is helpful; so is visiting other classes in pairs and comparing notes afterward. Staff meetings take on added dimension when teachers role play what they think they've seen and others ask for details.

The teacher who makes notes during class time has other considerations. Be ready to set aside your recording when necessary. Wear clothing with at least one good pocket. This ensures the paper and pencil are available when needed and the children's privacy is protected. Take care not to leave notes out on tables, shelves, or in cupboards for others to see. They should be kept confidential until added to the children's records. Some teachers find the "low-tech" materials of pen and notebook or 3 × 5 cards easiest to find, carry, use, and set aside. Others find a camera, tape recorder, and even a video camcorder helpful, although the expense, storage, and distracting nature of such equipment need to be considered. Regardless of what teachers use, they must organize themselves for success:

- Gather and prepare the materials ahead of time: This may mean getting everyone aprons with large pockets or a set of cards or labeled spiral notebook.

- Consider where you will observe: Set up observation places (chairs, stations); in a well-equipped yard and room, you can plan strategically.

- Plan when you will observe: In a well-planned day, teachers can have the freedom to practice observing regularly during play time.

- Prepare every adult to be an observer: Give every teacher some regular opportunities to observe and reflect on children's play.

Respect the privacy of the children and their families at all times. Any information gathered as part of an observation is treated with strict confidentiality. Teachers and students are careful not to use children's names in casual conversation. They do not talk about children in front of other children or among themselves. It is the role of the adults to see that children's privacy is maintained. Carrying tales out of school is tempting, but unprofessional.

Beginning to Observe

In some schools, observers are a normal part of the school routine. In colleges where there are laboratory facilities on campus, visitors and student observers are familiar figures. They have only to follow established guidelines for making an observation (see Figure 6-26).

Many times students are responsible for finding their own places to observe children. If so, the student calls ahead and schedules a time to observe that is convenient. Be specific about observation needs, the assignment, the ages of children desired, the amount of time needed, and the purpose of the observation.

If you are planning to observe in your own class, several steps are necessary for a professional observation and a believable recording. First, plan the observation. Have a specific *goal* in mind, and even put that at the top of your recording sheet. Goals can be general ("Let's see what activities Ajit chooses today.") or specific ("Watch for instances of quarreling in the sand area."). Second, *observe and record*. To be objective, be as specific and detailed as possible. Write only the behavior—the "raw data"—and save the analysis and your interpretation for later. After class, reread your notes (transcribing them into something legible if anyone

Observation skills are honed when teachers have opportunities to work with a few children at a time.

Guidelines for All Observers and Visitors

1. Please sign in with the front office and obtain a Visitor's badge. **Your badge must be worn and visible at all times while at the center.**

2. Inform the front office when you have completed your visit.

3. **Be unobtrusive.** Please find a spot that doesn't infringe on the children's space.

4. If you are with a small group or another person, **do not observe together;** consciously separate and space yourselves. Do not talk to other visitors during observation, please.

5. Respond to the children, but **please, do not initiate conversations with them.**

6. **If a child seems upset that you are near him/her, please remove yourself from the area.** If you receive direct requests from a child to leave, please respond that you realize that he said you are in **his** space and will move.

7. **Please do not interfere with the teaching/learning process** during your observation. Either ask when you check out in the front office or leave a note in the teacher's mailbox requesting a time to meet. Please understand that we welcome questions but cannot interrupt the program to answer them immediately.

8. **Walk around the periphery of the outdoor area or classrooms rather than through them.**

9. **When possible, do not stand. Please do not hover over children.** Sit, squat, or bend down at the knees so you are at the children's level.

10. **Taking photographs is not permitted.** In special classes, permission for photographs may be given by the Dean of Child Development and Education.

Thank you for your help and consideration in making your visit to the center a pleasant one for everyone involved.

FIGURE 6-26 Establishing guidelines for observers and visitors helps remind us of the importance of teaching as watching, not just telling. (Courtesy of De Anza College Child Development & Education Department.)

else might need to read them) and make some conclusions. Your observation was what happened; the *interpretation* is the place for your opinions and ideas of *why* it happened. For instance, you may have found that three of the four quarrels were over holding the hose; this gives you a clear reason for the quarrels. The final step is implementing your solutions; plan what you will do next, and then *follow through* with your ideas. In our example, a five-pronged hose outlet could be purchased, a waiting list could be started for the "hose-holder job," or the teacher could be in charge of the hose.

Wherever an observation is planned, it is critical to maintain **professional confidentiality.** If observing at another site, call ahead for an appointment. Talk about the purpose and format of your observation with both director and teacher. Finally, in *any* discussion of the observation, change the names of the children and school to protect those involved.

How to Observe Effectively

The success of the observation depends on how inconspicuous the observer can be. Children

Learning to observe and record effectively takes time and practice. Remaining unobtrusive and recording quietly allow children to continue their natural behavior without distraction.

are more natural if the observer blends into the scenery. By sitting back, one can observe the whole scene and record what is seen and heard, undisturbed and uninfluenced. This distancing sets up a climate for recording that aids the observer in concentrating on the children.

There are two main reasons for an observer to be unobtrusive. First, it allows for a more accurate recording of the children's activities. Second, it does not interfere with the smooth functioning of the classroom, the children, or the teachers. In the case of teachers observing their own programs, you must plan ahead with co-teachers and have materials at hand that can be set aside quickly if necessary.

SUMMARY

Systematic observation and recording of children's behavior are fundamental tools in understanding children. What children do and say and how they think and feel are revealed as they play and work. By learning to observe children's behavior, teachers become more aware of the children's skills, needs, and concerns.

The ability to observe is a skill in itself; teachers examine their own beliefs, influences and attitudes to achieve a measure of objectivity. Recording the observations is another skill, one that requires facility with the written word and an understanding of the purpose for observing. To make a successful observation, teachers first decide what it is they want to find out about the child.

Key ingredients to successful observations include clear definitions of the behaviors to be observed and techniques for observing and recording them. These provide the tools for gaining a deeper understanding of individual children and the group. They also enhance knowledge about the interrelationships of developmental areas. Too, one gains insight into the dynamics of child behavior and what influences are brought to bear on it. Finally, observing children can give insight and greater understanding of self.

The general types of observational techniques explored in this chapter include narratives, time sampling, and event sampling. Modified child study techniques include checklists, rating scales, shadow studies, experimental procedures and the clinical method. Evaluating children involves assessing their growth in all of the developmental domains and over time. We evaluate children to establish a baseline, a starting point of their skills and behavior, and to monitor their progress. Evaluation helps us plan for guidance and intervention, to plan curriculum, to communicate with parents, and to make administrative decisions wisely.

Of all the functions performed by teachers, assessment is one of the most challenging, and many concerns arise as programs attempt to evaluate children. Early learning standards are a new and complicated addition to the teacher's job of observation and assessment. One method of authentic assessment is the portfolio, a promising way to document children's learning. Testing and screening, also used in many settings, can be inappropriate, costly, and can unduly affect teacher's curriculum and children's daily care and education.

As teachers observe and record the behavior of young children, they are aware of professional guidelines that protect children. The guidelines help ensure accurate observation and help the observer respect the privacy of the individual or group.

THE PORTFOLIO: AN "UNFOLDING" OF THE CHILD

by
Kären Wiggins-Dowler, B.A.

Early childhood portfolios are an excellent visual aid for showing the dispositions, strengths, and interests of a child as well as what universal skills and knowledge they have acquired under your care. They also serve as a history for each member of a shared community of learners. A portfolio organizes these samples into an integrated whole that offers parents and teachers a window into who the child is now and is becoming.

When you first think of portfolios, your initial reaction may be that it is too much work and that it adds one more responsibility to your already busy schedule. Instead, it can be a natural extension of your day and what you do with children. To have documentation become part of your regular day, keep clipboards, Post-it notes, cameras, and tape recorders handy and ready to use. Every time a staff member points out an "a-ha" moment of a child's life, you can write it down immediately. Items to look for include:

1. art samples
2. cutting samples
3. dictated stories
4. invented writing
5. photographs of constructions
6. written samples
7. emergent play activities
8. written conversations during science and math activities
9. social interactions with peers and adults
10. photographs of children using motor and self-help skills

When children see adults engaged in data collection, they begin to take part. They take clipboards from the writing table to "write down important things." I had a four-year-old child once who insisted I "support him." When I asked him to explain what he meant, he said, "Write down what I am doing: it's important."

Getting Started: What Works for Me

Recording what children say and how they interact can seem overwhelming. I use Post-it notes as a convenient, quick way to capture revealing moments. I attach these to my lesson plans as they are easily transferred to individual portfolios. Photographs can also supplement written documentation.

During the beginning stages of developing portfolios, the gathered information tends to be just snapshots of moments out of time and context. Pictures look like scrapbook portraits and not examples of professional documentation. Do not despair; teachers who have limited experience in observation and assessment practices can begin with simplicity and convenience. These samples add to the total picture of a child's growth and should not be discredited.

Remember to keep your writing legible—rewriting your notes takes additional energy and time, which most teachers don't have. If English is not your first language, it is often easier to write in your primary language and translate later. If writing is difficult, use a tape recorder to document. A few lucky centers have video, although one must use it regularly enough so a taping is easy for you and so it doesn't become a dramatic play scene when the camera arrives. All samples and records need names of those involved, time, and date. As you become more proficient, your observation skills become more specific and the samples you choose are not just their best work but now are indicative of that child's developmental process.

Finally, I use a folding document with five separate sections for each developmental domain. Each labeled section has a cascading file of four to eight pages (depending of the length of stay in the program) and on each of these cascading pages are examples of developmental landmarks or unique attributes of the child. The most historical work samples and observations are located on the bottom page, with each overlap showing the child's progressive development. Then, on the top of each file is a developmental checklist or a summary of growth. Thus, the portfolio can be an excellent visual "unfolding" of the child. What results is the amazing image of each child as a competent learner who actively constructs knowledge within a social and cultural context. Parents are so excited when presented with this in-depth reflection of their child's history and learning!

Kären Wiggins-Dowler, B.A., is a head teacher at the Mary Meta Lazarus Children's Center of the College of San Mateo, California, and a State Mentor Teacher. She has a degree in Anthropology and Elementary Education from California State University, Hayward, and has done post-baccalaureate studies at San Francisco State University. Karen has also modified the portfolios to highlight the development of English proficiencies with a group of Korean ESL elementary school students.

For more activities and information, visit our Web site at
http://www.EarlyChildEd.delmar.com

KEY TERMS

objectivity	running record	shadow study
bias	baby biographies	methode clinique
individualized curriculum	diary descriptions	documentation
connected knowledge	time sampling	assessment
intervention	event sampling	screening
norms	checklists	early learning standards
narratives	rating scales	professional confidentiality

REVIEW QUESTIONS

1. List four observational methods. Describe the advantages and disadvantages of each. Which would you prefer? Why? Which one(s) might best suit a beginning teacher? A parent? An experienced teacher? The director of the school?

2. Poor observations usually contain inferences, overgeneralizations, and/or opinions that cloud a complete, objective sampling of a child's behavior. Read the following segment and underline the language segments that contain such passages:

   C is sitting on the rug with four friends and he is playing with cars and he starts whining about his car. He is just having a bad attitude about its not moving correctly. C is crying because he just got hit with the car. Let me tell you something about him. He is a big whiner about anything and he always wants it his way. Then he goes over to the book corner and is very quietly reading a book and he is happy by himself.

3. Put this chapter to the test! Match the behavior with the category it describes:

Category	Behavior
Children in general	Matthew cries when his grandma says goodbye.
Influences on behavior	Most four-year-olds can pull up their pants on their own.
Understanding of self	To really know Celia, I'll have to observe her with scissors, at the climber, figuring out a problem, with her friends, in our small group time, when her mom leaves, and doing a painting.
Developmental relationships	I wonder why Mondays are so hard on Serena? Which weekends does she stay with her Dad?
Children as individuals	You know, I just overreact when I see children playing with their food.

4. What are the reasons for assessing children's progress? How can you communicate both strengths and weakness to parents?

5. What is a working portfolio?

6. Describe some of the problems with testing or screening of young children. How can you address these problems if you are required to administer a standardized test to your class?

7. What do you consider to be the three most important guidelines to follow when observing young children? Why?

LEARNING ACTIVITIES

1. Observe a group of children for 10 minutes engaged in block play. Record your observations in running record form. Now, go back over that running record and make a list of things you want to know about the children's thinking and behavior. How could you construct this list, using the clinical method, to obtain the information you need? Would you intervene nonverbally? What questions could you ask the children directly?

2. Observe a child for 10 minutes. Using language as your paintbrush, make a written picture of that child's physical appearance and movements. Compare the child's size, body build, facial features, and energy level with those of other children in the class. Record as many of the body movements as you can, noting seemingly useless movements, failures, partial successes, as well as final achievements.

3. Observe one child in your class and jot down a brief description of her language skills. Are they typical of her age level? How could you tell? Compare your notes with the perceptions of your supervising teacher.

4. Observe a children's quarrel. How did you feel when you watched? What does this tell you about your own influences in childhood? How did the teaching staff intervene? How would you? Why?

5. Try a time sample of children's play in your classroom. Observe 10 children for one minute each during free-play times, and record the type(s) of social behavior they show. Using Parten's categories, your chart would look like this one. Compare your results with the impressions of the other teachers with whom you work. Did you come to any conclusions on how children develop socially?

Child/Age	Unoccupied	Solitary	Onlooker	Parallel	Associative	Cooperative
1.						
2.						
3.						
4.						
5.						
6.						
7.						
8.						
9.						
10.						
Totals						

6. Choose two children, one you think is doing well and one who is having trouble. Observe the adult-child interactions of each. What are the differences from the children's point of view in the quantity and quality of those relationships? What generalizations about the importance of such relationships in the early years can you make?

7. If you can, try a shadow study on a child in your class. Choose a child you don't know much about, you have trouble working with, or who is exhibiting inappropriate behaviors. How did this study help you to see the class and school from that child's point of view?

8. Perceptions of a person's character are in the eyes of the beholder. These perceptions affect how teachers behave with children. What color are your glasses tinted? Divide a piece of paper in half, lengthwise. On one side, list some words to describe your feelings about childhood, school, teachers, children, authority, making friends, losing friends, hitting, and playing. One the other side, describe how these feelings may have influenced your teaching and helped create your own biases.

9. Does your own setting have an evaluation plan for child assessment? Analyze the goals of your plan and how the tools or implementation meet (or do not meet) those goals.

10. Develop an informal assessment tool to evaluate children's skills in a toddler class. Discuss how this would differ from one for a preschool and one for a school-age child care program.

11. Teachers have noticed that several children consistently interrupt at storytime with seemingly irrelevant questions and constantly grab onto children seated nearby. What's happening—and why? What observational tools would you use to find out? What clues from individual behavior would you look for? How would you look at the group as a whole? What other information would you need?

REFERENCES

Barbour, N. (2000). Focus box: Assessment. In A. Gordon & K. W. Browne, *Beginnings and beyond: Foundations in early childhood education* (5th ed.). Clifton Park, NY: Thomson Delmar Learning.

Benjamin, A. C. (1994, September). Observations in early childhood classrooms. *Young Children, 46*(6), 14–20.

Bergan, J. R., & Feld, J. K. (1993). Developmental assessment: New directions. *Young Children 48*(5), 41–47.

Bodrova, E., Leong, D., & Shore, R. (March, 2004). Child outcome standards in pre-K programs: What are standards: What is needed to make them work? In *Preschool Policy Matters.* National Institute on Early Educational Research (NIEER), www.nieer.org. Issue 5.

Bredekamp, S., & Rosegrant, T. (Eds.). (1995). *Reaching potentials* (Vols. 1 & 2). Washington, DC: National Association for the Education of Young Children.

California Department of Education, *Desired results developmental profile* (2006). www.cde.ca.gov.

Cartwright, S. (1994, September). When we really see the child. *Exchange,* pp. 5–9.

Cohen, D. H., Stern, V., & Balaban, N. (1997). *Observing and recording the behavior of young children* (4th ed.). New York: Teachers College Press.

Council of Chief State School Officers (CCSSO). Washington, DC, 2005.

Cryan, J. R. (1986, May/June). Evaluation: Plague or promise? *Childhood Education, 62*(5).

Danielson, C., & Abrutyn, L. (1997). *An introduction to using portfolios in the classroom.* Alexandria, VA: Association for Supervision and Curriculum Development.

Dawes, H. C. (1934). An analysis of two hundred quarrels of preschool children. *Child Development, 5,* 139–157.

Dowley, E. M. (n.d.). *Cues for observing children's behavior.* Unpublished paper.

Feeney, S., Christensen, D., & Moravcik, E. (2001). *Who am I in the lives of children?* (6th ed.). Englewood Cliffs, NJ:Prentice Hall.

Fenwich, T., & Parsons, J. (2000). *The art of evaluation: A handbook for educators and trainers.* Clifton Park, NY: Thomson Delmar Learning.

Gardner, H. (1988, September/October) Alternatives to standardized testing. *Harvard Education Letter.*

Gonzalez-Mena, J. (2000). Focus Box: Understanding what we observe: A multicultural perspective. In A. Gordon & K. W. Browne (Eds.). *Beginnings and beyond: Foundations in early childhood education* (5th ed.). Clifton Park, NY: Thomson Delmar Learning.

Gronlund, G. (1998). Portfolios as an assessment tool: Is collection of work enough? *Young Children, 53*(2), 4–10.

Gronlund, G. (2006). *Making early learning standards come alive.* St Paul, MN: Redleaf Press.

Hills, T. W. (1993, July). Assessment in context—Teachers and children at work. *Young Children, 48*(5), 20–28.

Irwin, D. M., & Bushnell, M. M. (1980). *Observational strategies for child study.* New York: Holt, Rinehart & Winston.

Jones, E., & Reynolds, G. (1992). *The play's the thing: Teachers' roles in children's play.* New York: Teachers College Press.

Jones, E. J., & Carter, M. (1991, January/February). The teacher as observer—Part 1, and Teacher as scribe and broadcaster: Using observation to communicate—Part 2. *Child Care Information Exchange, 35*–38.

Klein, A. S., & Estes, J. S. (2004, January/February). Using observation for performance assessment. *Early Childhood News.*

Lam, M., & Wiggins-Dowler, K. (2006). "Documentation Panel: Our Construction Curriculum Project." San Mateo, CA: MML Children's Center, College of San Mateo, 2005–2006.

McAfee, O., Leong, D. J., & Bodrova, E. (2004). *Basics of assessment: A primer for early childhood educators.* Washington, DC: National Association for the Education of Young Children.

McLaughlin, K., & Sugarman, S. Personal communications, 1982.

Meisels, S. J., & Atkins-Burnett, S. (2005). *Developmental screening in early childhood: A guide* (5th ed.). Washington, DC: National Association for the Education of Young Children.

National Association for the Education of Young Children (NAEYC) and the National Association of Early Childhood Specialists in State Departments of Education (NAECS/SDE). (2002). *Position statement on standardized testing of young children 3 through 8 years of age.* www.naeyc.org/resrouces/position_statements/pschape.pdf.

National Center for Fair and Open Testing (NCFOT). Cambridge, MA: Fair Test, 2006.

National Commission on Testing and Public Policy (CTTP). Boston, MA: Boston College, 1998.

New Oxford American Dictionary (2nd ed.). England: Oxford University Press, 2005.

Parten, M. B. (1932). Social participation among preschool children. *Journal of Abnormal and Social Psychology, 27,* 243–269.

Pendowski, J. L. (2006). Portfolios and their use in the early learning environment. *CAEYC Connections,* Spring, 2006.

Ramsey, P. G. (2004). Teaching and Learning in a Diverse World (3rd ed.). New York: Teachers College Press.

Saxton, R. R. (1998, April). Personal communication.

Schweinhart, L. J. (1993, July). Observing young children in action: The key to early childhood assessment. *Young Children, 45*(5), 29–33.

Seefeldt, C., & Barbour, N. (1997). *Early childhood education: An introduction* (4th ed.). New York: MacMillan College Publishing.

Special thanks to the following Early Childhood Education students for their observation samples: J. Gallero, C. Grupe, L. Hutton, C. Liner, C. Robinson, & M. Saldivar.

HELPFUL WEB SITES

National Association for the Education
of Young Children — http://www.naeyc.org

Early Childhood Education Assessment Consortium,
Council of Chief State School Officers — http://www.ccsso.org/ECEAstandards

Early Childhood Research Quarterly — http://www.elsevier.com/wps/find/journal
description.cws-home/620184/description

Early Childhood Research Online — http://www.ume.maine.edu/eceol/

ERIC Clearinghouse on Assessment and Evaluation — http://ericae.net

National Child Care Information Center — http://www.nccic.org/pubs/goodstart/
elgwebsites.html

National Institute for Early Education Research (NIEER) — http://www.nieer.org/standards/statelist.php

Work Sampling System — http://www.worksamplingonline.com

For more activities and information, visit our Web site at http://www.EarlyChildEd.delmar.com

CHAPTER 7

Understanding and Guiding Behavior

QUESTIONS FOR THOUGHT

Why do children behave the way they do?

What are some ways in which the classroom environment affects children's behavior?

What do teachers need to know about themselves so they can guide children effectively?

What is the difference between discipline and punishment?

Are behavior goals the same for all children? Why?

What are some common problem behaviors found in young children?

What are some effective ways to deal with behavior problems?

Why do some experts say spanking is harmful to children?

What should the teacher do if school and home guidance techniques differ?

THE GUIDANCE TRIANGLE

Guidance is the ongoing process of helping children learn to control their basic impulses, express their feelings, channel their frustrations, and solve their problems. There are no quick fixes or strategies that apply to all circumstances. Positive guidance methods are devised to fit a child, an adult (parent, teacher), and a situation. These three elements, when considered together, suggest the most appropriate guidance strategies. Figure 7-1 shows these three factors in relation to one another. Throughout this chapter, the relationship between the child, the adult, and the situation will be reflected in guidance theory and practices.

UNDERSTANDING BEHAVIOR

In the toddler class, two-year-olds Shawnsey and Kim are playing in the dress-up area. Kim grabs at one of the many necklaces Shawnsey has draped around her neck. Startled, Shawnsey lets out a cry, grabs Kim's arm, and bites her.

Malcolm, a five-year-old, rushes through the room, heading for the block area. For just a moment, he stands and watches Lorraine balancing blocks on

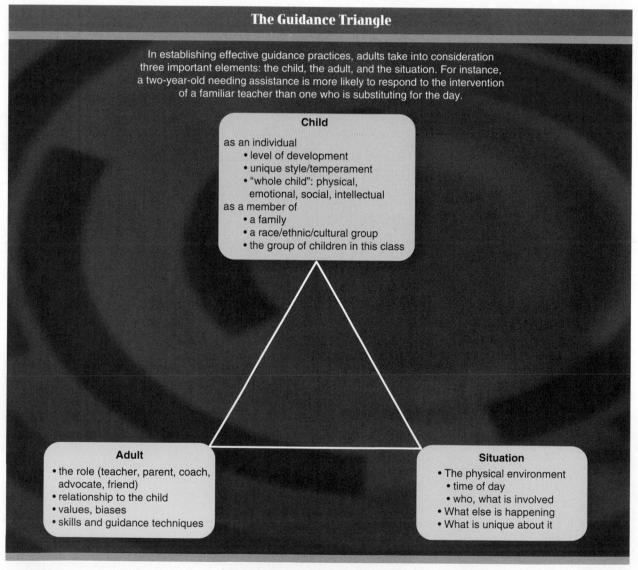

The Guidance Triangle

In establishing effective guidance practices, adults take into consideration three important elements: the child, the adult, and the situation. For instance, a two-year-old needing assistance is more likely to respond to the intervention of a familiar teacher than one who is substituting for the day.

Child

as an individual
- level of development
- unique style/temperament
- "whole child": physical, emotional, social, intellectual

as a member of
- a family
- a race/ethnic/cultural group
- the group of children in this class

Adult
- the role (teacher, parent, coach, advocate, friend)
- relationship to the child
- values, biases
- skills and guidance techniques

Situation
- The physical environment
- time of day
- who, what is involved
- What else is happening
- What is unique about it

FIGURE 7-1 The Guidance Triangle (From Ann Gordon & Kathryn Williams Browne, *Guiding Young Children in a Diverse Society*. Published by Allyn and Bacon, Boston, MA. Copyright © 1996 by Pearson Education. Reprinted with permission of the publisher.)

For guidance to be successful, a teacher must first understand children's behavior.

top of one another in a tall column. With a swift wave of his arm, Malcolm topples the structure.

Mac, a three-and-a-half-year-old, is busy with a puzzle. When a teacher stops at the table to tell the children it is nearly time to clean up for snacks, Mac replies, "My daddy says that cleaning up is a girl's job and I don't have to do it." He throws the puzzle on the floor and dashes away from the teacher.

These are typical scenes in any early childhood center. No matter how plentiful the materials, how many or well-trained the adults, or how preplanned the program, conflicts are sure to occur. Helping children learn how to cope with their anger, their fears, their frustrations, and their desires is one of the most challenging jobs for a teacher.[1]

To teach children to respect themselves and each other is a complex and difficult task. It takes experience, skill, and love and is a critical part of caring for children. Look at the examples again. What do they say about children in general? What do they say about Shawnsey, Malcolm, and Mac? How should teachers respond to these children, and how does that response influence future behavior? (See "What Do You Think?" on spanking on page 282 and Figure 7-10 for discussing solutions to these types of situations).

Theories

To guide children's behavior, a teacher must first understand it. This requires a solid background in child development, skills in observing, and understanding about why children behave and misbehave.

There are several ways of explaining what people do and why. One idea is that people's behavior is mainly a result of heredity (nature). Another is that experience and environment shape behavior (nurture). A third theory suggests that children go through "stages" at certain times of their lives regardless of their genes or home background.

All sides have valid arguments in the nature/nurture debate. It is useful to remember that both heredity and experience affect behavior. Age and stage theory is also familiar. People speak of the "terrible twos" or say that all four-year-old girls are silly. There may be some truth to those generalities, but that does not excuse the inappropriate behavior of the various developmental stages. Teachers and parents cannot ignore misbehavior (unless it is a specific guidance strategy) just because children are the "right" age or because of their home situations. That attitude implies adults are powerless to help children form new behavior patterns. Not true!

Adults can do something about children's behavior if they understand what is happening to the child. Where does appropriate behavior come from? Why do children misbehave?

Factors That Affect Behavior

Knowing what affects children's behavior and feelings helps adults understand and manage the misbehaving child. Teachers can anticipate problems instead of waiting for them to occur; preventive measures are part of guiding children's behavior. These factors combine aspects of both nature and nurture theories, as well as the theories of ages and stages of development. The three vignettes at the beginning of the chapter provide examples of all five factors, which are: (1) developmental; (2) environmental; (3) individual; (4) emotional and social; and (4) cultural.

1. **Developmental Factors.** Adults who work with children should be aware of developmental theory to know what type of behavior to expect of children at various ages. Developmental theory helps teachers anticipate what children will do and helps them maintain reasonable expectations. To see behavior as predictable and developmentally appropriate is to understand it more completely and guide it more effectively.

The facts are that Shawnsey, Kim, Malcolm and Mac have been in a group setting for more than

1   Different cultures have different ways of dealing with emotions. The educator needs an awareness of how he or she deals with particular emotions, as well as how the child's particular family culture deals with emotions.

Video VIEW PoinT 7-1

"Children's temperaments shape how they respond to others. Whereas some children are quite responsive and easygoing, other children are more withdrawn, slow to warm up to others, or difficult to please."

COMPETENCY: Social Development

AGE GROUP: Infants and Toddlers

CRITICAL THINKING QUESTIONS:

1. How would you describe your own temperament as a child?

2. What would you do to create a relationship with a toddler who was withdrawn?

"I'm the boss here!"

three hours and it is nearly snack time. Teachers know that preschoolers cannot be expected to be in control of themselves over extended periods of time. Conflicts and disagreements happen in any group of children. Hungry children are often ineffective problem solvers; Mac might be more manageable after snack. It is also clear to the teacher that the toddlers do not have the language or social development skills to talk problems out with other children as do Malcolm and Mac.

2. **Environmental Factors.** Through the intentional use of the environment, the teacher indirectly influences behavior in the classroom and the goals for positive behavior should be reflected in the classroom setting. The physical environment should tell children clearly how to act in that space. Child-size furniture that fits the preschool body encourages sitting and working behavior. Room arrangements that avoid spaces that could be used encourage children to walk from place to place. Low, open shelves create an expectation that children will take materials out and put them away after use.

Materials and equipment should be adequate and interesting to the age group. When children are occupied with stimulating and interesting age-appropriate materials, there are fewer opportunities for misbehavior. The materials can challenge children, overwhelm them, or bore

them. If materials and equipment are suitable, children will feel more at ease with themselves and be more willing to accept adults' limits and controls.[1] Adding materials and equipment can help prevent arguments over a favorite toy, create new and interesting challenges, and extend children's play ideas. Changing the environment when needed can help avert behavior problems. Removing attractive but breakable items reduces tears and conflicts. Some materials may prove to be too stimulating and may need to be removed for a while. Some activities may need to be limited to specific locations to control the level of activity and behavior. Look at Figure 7-2 to evaluate how the environment is related to your guidance philosophy and children's behavior. Chapter 9 contains a detailed discussion of many factors that should be considered when designing spaces for young children. Many of these environmental considerations directly influence children's behavior.

Shawnsey and Kim's teacher will want to add more necklaces to the dress-up area if there aren't enough to outfit several children.

The daily schedule and timing of events indirectly influence classroom behavior. When

---

1 Materials in the classroom reflect the attitudes of the teachers who select them. Those committed to multiculturalism will choose materials and equipment that reflect the diverse world.

Time

_____ Does the daily schedule provide enough time for unhurried play?

_____ Are those periods that create tension—transitions from one activity to another—given enough time?

_____ Is cleanup a leisurely process built in at the end of each activity, with children participating?

Program Planning and Curriculum

_____ Is there enough to do so that children have choices and alternatives for play?

_____ Is the curriculum challenging enough to prevent boredom and restlessness?

_____ Are there activities to help children release tension? Do the activities allow for body movement, exploration, and manipulation of materials?

_____ Are children included in developing the rules and setting guidelines? How is their inclusion demonstrated?

Organization and Order

_____ If children are expected to put things away after use, are the cabinets low, open, and marked in some way?

_____ Are the materials within easy reach of the children, promoting self-selection and independence?

_____ Are there enough materials so that sharing does not become a problem?

_____ Are the areas in which activities take place clearly defined so that children know what happens there?

_____ Does the room arrangement avoid runways and areas with no exits?

_____ Do children have their own private space?

_____ Are children able to use all visible and accessible materials? Are there materials about which children are told "Don't touch"?

Personnel

_____ Are there enough teachers to give adequate attention to the number of children in the class?

_____ Are the group size and makeup balanced so that children have a variety of playmates?

_____ Are the teachers experienced, and do they seem comfortable in setting limits and guiding children's behavior?

_____ Do teachers use their attention to encourage behavior they want, and do they ignore what they want to discourage?

_____ Do all adults consistently enforce the same rules?

FIGURE 7-2 Classroom checklist. By anticipating children's needs and growth patterns, teachers set up classrooms that foster constructive and purposeful behavior.

there are blocks of time to choose activities, children can proceed at their own pace without feeling hurried. They feel free to work, move, and play and are able to accept the teacher's control when it is necessary. The physical needs of eating, sleeping, and toileting are met by careful scheduling so that children are able to play without concern for the necessities of life. Schedules that do not allow enough time for cleanup and transitions produce a frantic climate.

> Mac, for instance, had just settled in at the puzzle table when the teacher told him that it was time to clean up. Uncooperative behavior is sometimes related to time pressures.

3. **Individual Factors.** Teachers of young children soon learn the temperamental characteristics of each child in the class.[1] Hondi works and plays with great intensity; Norman is easily distracted. Tawana fears any change, whereas Enrique thrives on challenges. The consistent patterns of temperament that emerge help define each child's individual style.

The teacher will want to support and comfort Kim at the same time she lets Shawnsey know that biting will not be tolerated. It is important to maintain a level of trust with Shawnsey so that she can help learn better ways to communicate her needs.

 1 Children's individual temperaments are an important consideration in developing an understanding of our diverse world. Differences in temperament may be less immediately obvious than differences in gender or race, but no less significant.

Research by Thomas and Chess (1977) has identified three types of temperament in babies: the easy child, the difficult child, and the slow-to-warm-up child. The traits used to classify these children were: activity level, regularity and rhythm of bodily routines, adaptability, physical sensitivity, intensity of reaction, ease of distraction, mood, and attention span. These differences were observed in very young infants and seem to remain consistent as the child grows.

The research supports the concept of individual differences that are present from birth and the importance of acknowledging those differences. If parents and teachers come to know the nature of a child's temperament, they can accept that as part of the wholeness of that particular child. Guidance measures can be tailored to meet the unique needs of a slow-to-warm-up child, for instance, or a difficult child. Those strategies will need to be different from techniques used to discipline the easy child. Children's temperament also affects the way people deal with them. An easy child is easy to respond to; a slow-to-warm-up child may be harder to reach. Difficult children may tend to be blamed for things they did not do. Identifying traits can be useful so long as adults are careful not to label children unfairly or prematurely.

> Malcolm is enthusiastic and plunges into activities spontaneously, sometimes without looking ahead or surveying the wreckage he leaves behind. His teacher is aware that he can be personable and cooperative if he is given options and a chance to make decisions. As they talk together about Lorraine's blocks, the teacher offers Malcolm a choice: to talk with Lorraine to see if she would like to have him help rebuild the same structure or start a new one. Both Malcolm and the teacher find satisfaction in working together in ways that acknowledge and respect Malcolm's personal style.

4. **Emotional and Social Factors.** Some behavior problems stem from the child's attempt to express social and emotional needs. These include the need to feel loved and cared for, the need to be included, the desire to be considered important and valued, the desire to have friends, and the need to feel safe from harm. Young children are still working out ways to express these needs and feelings. Typically, because they are only just learning language and communication skills, it is often through nonverbal or indirect actions that children let us know what is bothering them. It is also

What do YOU Think?

"Spanking may allow a parent to let off steam, but it doesn't teach a child the right way to behave. What's more, it is humiliating and emotionally harmful, and it can lead to physical injury. Worst of all, spanking teaches youngsters that violence is an acceptable way to communicate. The American Academy of Pediatrics strongly opposes hitting children" (American Academy of Pediatrics, 1997).

Spanking children is a controversial issue. Do you agree or disagree with the AAP? Why? Where in the Code of Ethical Conduct in Appendix A does it address this issue?

important to provide children with models of language for resolving these conflicts. It is important to let children know that we recognize they can be angry, jealous, or hurt. The supportive adult will help children find satisfying ways to cope with their social and emotional feelings.

> Shawnsey is an only child of older parents and has little opportunity outside of school to interact with others her age. Malcolm comes from a big, boisterous family where taking care of one's own desires and needs is instilled early on. Mac's parents are divorced and he is now living with his grandmother while his mother looks for work in another town. Their teachers understand their bids for attention and weigh each child's social and emotional history as they guide them toward positive behavior.

Other influences affect behavior. Weather seems to affect children. Wild, windy, gray, rainy days seem to stimulate children into high and excitable behavior. Bright, sunny days also seem to influence a child's mood and temperament. Problems that upset adults can make an impression on a child. A family crisis, a new baby, or a recent divorce have impact. Sharing a room, visits from relatives, illness, television and movie shows, brothers and sisters, and nutrition and health cause children to behave in many different ways. The longer teachers work with children, the more adept they become at

Teachers are called upon to deal with a variety of emotional needs.

Children are often able to work out their own solutions to conflict.

seeing how these various factors shape the behavior of the individual children in their class. In Chapter 14, the young child's social and emotional growth is further explored.

5. **Cultural Factors.** Today's children are growing up in a country of unparalleled diversity.[1] Many different cultures are converging and creating a nation of peoples, cultures, languages, and attitudes. Children and their teachers are living in a world of continual cross-cultural interactions. The ability to communicate across cultures is a critical skill to have when guiding children's behavior. (See also discussions in Chapters 2, 5, 8, and 15.) A review of Erikson's and Vygotsky's theories in Chapter 4 and Bronfenbrenner's in Chapter 15 underscores the connection between culture and behavior.

Discipline is deeply embedded within the values and beliefs of the family. The family's culture shapes how they raise their children, and each family is unique in the way it interprets its cultural values. Child-rearing practices ranging from the timing of toilet training to physical punishment are culturally influenced. The messages children receive about their behavior should be consistent between school and home. Yet conflict may be inevitable because the culturally influenced child-rearing practices of the family may be at odds with a teacher's ideas and expectations[2] (Gordon & Browne, 1996).

In some cultures, for instance, children are encouraged to challenge adult opinions, where this would be considered disrespectful in other cultures. Each child must be valued as part of a family system, no matter the origin of structure, and the teacher's role is to support the child's sense of security and identity within the family.

Children bring their unique individuality to the classroom, but they are also bearers of the context in which they are being raised: their family, culture, ethnicity, religion, socioeconomic status, and neighborhood. When we are aware of these influences we are better able to match who the child is with the most effective guidance approach (Gordon & Browne, 1996).

In some families, a sense of community is valued over individualism, a concept that can create difficulty in the early childhood classroom unless it is understood and appreciated. Early childhood educators, for the most part, do not force children to share personal possessions before they seem ready to, and they encourage children to become autonomous at an early age. This is at odds with families in which cooperation and sharing are valued concepts, as is dependency on other family members. Teachers

1 The ability to adapt to the needs of a diversified group of students will be the challenge for teachers of the 21st century.

2 Culturally sensitive teaching strategies will recognize the parent's perspective and the child's family experience.

will need to become culturally sensitive to some of the long-held assumptions of teaching young children. The sections on "Self-Awareness" and "Attitudes and Biases" in Chapter 5 suggest ways in which teachers can address stereotypes and prejudices that may interfere with their effectiveness in guiding children's behavior.

Schools must be inviting and safe places in which families from all cultures can express their perceptions, concerns, and expectations about their children. Teachers will need to be flexible and nonjudgmental as they work with the cultural implications of children's behavior. Figure 7-3 shows how different family cultural patterns relate to a child's behavior and an appropriate guidance strategy.

Kim (who was playing with Shawnsey) has a family culture that views the teacher as a respected authority figure and one who must be obeyed. This places Kim in an uncomfortable position if her teacher does not understand why Kim does not make activity choices easily and prefers to have the teacher tell her where to play and work each day. As teachers

Family Culture	Child's Experience and Behavior	Guidance Strategy
Power Structure		
Democratic family—members share in decision making	Child is encouraged to negotiate and compromise.	Offer real choices; use problem-solving techniques.
One family member makes all of the decisions	Child is expected to obey, follow commands, and respect adult authority. Child may be unable to choose activities, look adults in the eye, or call them by name.	Don't insist on eye contact. Child may need help in selecting an activity. Work with the family members who make the decisions.
Values		
Strong, close-knit family	Child learns that the family comes first; the individual sacrifices for the family.	Recognize that family matters may take precedence over school.
Honor, dignity, and pride	Child's behavior reflects family honor; child is disciplined for rudeness or poor manners.	Share achievements with parents; help child learn manners; be sensitive when discussing child's behavior problems.
Expressing feelings is accepted	Child is allowed to cry, scream, throw temper tantrums.	Accept child's crying as you give comfort; stay with child until he is calm.
Issue of Discipline		
Clear, direct discipline	Child learns to respect authority and does what he is told to do; child may not take positive guidance strategies seriously or ignore them.	Use a sense of humor; make firm statements.
Discipline motivated toward inherent goodness	Child has freedom to explore consequences and is warned of possible embarrassment due to behavior.	Child may be passive if disciplined harshly. Use natural consequences; ask rather than demand.
Discipline motivated from inherent self-interest	Child is scolded, threatened, and controlled by promises.	Model desired behavior; use "if/then" statements: "If you finish eating, then you can play." Praise good manners and good behavior.

FIGURE 7-3 Sample of culturally diverse family patterns that affect guidance and discipline. Knowledge of culturally diverse family patterns and guidance strategies to parallel these child-rearing styles can allow you to begin a dialogue with the children you teach. (From *Roots and Wings* (Revised Edition), by Stacey York (Redleaf Press, 2003). Copyright © 2003 by Stacey York. Adapted with permission from Redleaf Press, St. Paul, Minnesota, www.redleafpress.org. To order, call 800-423-8309.)

What do YOU Think?

Ask yourself: Do my classroom and teaching style reflect the patterns and relationships of one particular culture or many cultures?

become familiar with the customs and beliefs of the families in the program, they will gain insights into children's behavior and understand the reasons for the way a child responds.

GUIDING YOUNG CHILDREN

The overall process of guidance is a common concern of parents and teachers and can be the basis for a strong partnership as they learn together why Dominick whines or Carrie dawdles or Cleo disrupts group time.

What Is Guidance?

The children we meet in early childhood programs are just learning how strong their emotions can be and what impact they have on their own behavior and on others. Behavior is the unspoken language through which children act out feelings and thoughts. Until they learn to express themselves vocally, they use a variety of behaviors to communicate. They are just learning what kinds of behaviors are and are not acceptable and what adults expect of them. Using words (for instance, a resounding "No!" when someone takes a toy away) is slowly replacing biting, hitting, crying, and tantrums as a way to respond to frustration. Caring adults must help young children learn to behave responsibly and be respectful of others as they explore alternative behaviors, develop social skills, and learn to solve problems.

It is daily experiences that children use to construct their moral and social world, and need adult guidance. The concept of guide is an important one (Gordon & Browne, 1996). A guide is one who leads, explains, and supports. A guide points out directions, answers questions, and helps you get where you want to go. This is what teachers do as they guide children.

Implicit, too, is a sense of joint commitment of teaching and learning together. A positive guidance approach requires the active participation of both child and adult in order to be successful.

What Is Discipline?

The word **discipline** stems from disciple: a pupil, a follower, a learner. This suggests two important concepts, that of following an example versus following rules, and that of positive discipline. Children try to be like the adults they see; adults serve as models for children. How children see adults behave tends to become part of their own behavior. Adults help children learn appropriate behavior by setting good examples.[1]

Many people associate discipline with the word punishment. **Punishment** is generally thought of in negative terms. It is usually a penalty for an offense or misbehavior and can be harsh and punitive, but it doesn't have to be if blended with positive discipline practices. To some, the words discipline and punishment are synonymous. They are not, as Figure 7-4 shows how these terms mean very different things.

Toward Self-Discipline

One of the goals of a good guidance process is to help children achieve self-discipline. This happens only if adults lead in ways that support children's developing ability to control themselves. By gradually handing over to children the opportunity to govern their own actions, adults communicate trust. For young children, with their urge to prove themselves and their drive toward initiative, this is an important step to take. With added responsibility and trust comes an added dimension of self-respect and self-confidence. Such children feel capable and worthwhile.

Along with self-respect, the child must taste the freedom that comes with a lessening of adult controls. Children do not learn to handle freedom by being told what to do all the time. Only when they have an opportunity to test themselves and make some decisions on their own, will they know their capabilities. Young children must learn this in safe places, with adults who allow them as much freedom as they can responsibly handle.

An effective guidance approach is interactive. Adults and children both learn to change as they interact with one another toward a

---

 1 Good role models deliberately vary their teaching styles and strategies to accommodate different learning styles and cultural patterns.

Positive Guidance	Punishment
Emphasizes what the child should *do*	Emphasizes what the child should *not* do
Is an ongoing process	Is a one-time occurrence
Sets an example to follow	Insists on obedience
Leads to self-control	Undermines independence
Helps children change	Is an adult release
Is positive	Is negative
Accepts child's need to assert self	*Makes* children behave
Fosters child's ability to think	Thinks *for* the child
Bolsters self-esteem	Defeats self-esteem
Shapes behavior	Condemns misbehavior

FIGURE 7-4 Positive guidance encourages children's interaction and involvement; punishment is usually something that is done to a child.

common goal. Figure 7-5 summarizes some of the ways children and adults can learn from a guidance and positive discipline philosophy.

Developmentally Appropriate Guidance

Each developmental stage has shared characteristics, modified, of course, by a child's individual rate of growth. It is as typical for four-year-olds to test limits as it is for toddlers to have a strong sense of ownership about their possessions. To

have a developmentally appropriate guidance approach, teachers take this knowledge and understanding of child development principles into consideration as they contemplate how best to respond to a child's behavior.

Identifying the behaviors that are typical to a specific age group provides a context in which to understand the child and behavior that can be seen as normal and predictable. Guidance based on a developmental approach would help a teacher to know that first and second graders have an ability to consider others' points of view,

Guidance: An Interactive Approach

Guidance is an interactive process in which both children and adults may learn. Everyone benefits from disciplinary practices that foster changes in attitudes and behaviors.

We Teach	Adults Learn To	Children Learn To
Values	Express	Internalize
Self-control	Maintain own	Practice
Respect	Give to child	Accord to others
Appropriate behavior	Model	Observe and imitate
Limits	Be clear and consistent	Accept consequences
Feelings	Accept own and child's	Identify and label
Problem solving	Offer meaningful choices	Make decisions
Self-esteem	Protect and enhance	Respect and appreciate self
Rule setting	Share power	Participate in creating behavior controls
Taking another's viewpoint	Be sympathetic and understanding	To be empathetic
Collaboration	Involve child in solutions	Problem-solve cooperatively

FIGURE 7-5 Guidance is an interactive process in which both children and adults may learn. Everyone benefits from disciplinary practices that foster changes in attitudes and behaviors. (From Ann Gordon & Kathryn Williams Browne, *Guiding Young Children in a Diverse Society.* Published by Allyn and Bacon, Boston, MA. Copyright © 1996 by Pearson Education. Reprinted with permission of the publisher.)

so they would choose problem-solving methods that would ask children to think of how their behavior affected others.

A developmentally appropriate approach also requires that the teacher consider what is known about the individual child as well as what is typical for the age group. This ensures that the guidance techniques will match the capabilities of the child and that adult expectations will remain reasonable.

Culturally Appropriate Guidance

An emerging issue, as our population becomes more and more diverse, has to do with cultural values and guidance. Teachers may be confronted by parents whose guidance practices are contrary to the school's philosophy.[1] Pressure may be exerted on teachers to apply some of those same techniques at school that parents use at home. Teachers want to maintain the school's as well as their own standards without communicating to the family that their values are wrong or have children feel that something about their home and family is diminished in the teacher's eyes. Gonzalez-Mena (2001) emphasizes the teacher's responsibility to learn cross-cultural communication when child-rearing practices are in conflict between home and school and suggests the following strategies:

- Accept that both viewpoints are equally valid.
- Work together to figure out a solution to the situation.
- Resist assigning meaning and values to the behavior of others on the basis of your own culture.
- Remember that your behavior does not necessarily convey your own meaning and values.
- Educate yourself about the different cultures represented in your classroom. Learn how and what is communicated through facial gestures, touch, eye contact, physical closeness, and time concepts.
- Observe, ask, and talk about what the differences are; learn from the parents of the children in the classroom what you need to know about their culture.
- Maintain an open attitude that promotes respect and appreciation for each other's views.

Ethical issues involving culture-based differences are discussed in Chapter 5. The antibias curriculum, as described in Chapters 5 and 9, suggests some strategies as well. Also see "Child Development and Cultural Diversity" in Chapter 4. The NAEYC Code of Ethical Conduct is a useful resource for ethical concerns when working with families from many cultures. It is available in Appendix A.

The Language of Guidance and Discipline

Guidance has a language all its own.[2] As beginning teachers gain experience in handling problem behaviors, they learn to use that language. The result, in most cases, is a startling **interdependence**: the more practiced teachers become in the language of guidance, the more comfortable they become in developing their own approach to guidance problems. And the more comfortable they are in that approach, the more effectively they use language to solve behavior problems.

The language and communication techniques in guidance are both spoken and unspoken. Teachers discover how potent the voice can be; what words will work best and when. They become aware of facial expressions and what a touch or a look will convey to children. How they use their body reflects a distinct attitude and approach to discipline. Through experience, new teachers will learn how to use these tools in ways that will work best for them and the children.

Voice. Some adults feel that when they are speaking to children they must assume a different voice from the one they normally use. Talk to children in the same way you talk to other people. Learn to control the volume and use good speech patterns for children to imitate. To be heard, get close enough to speak in a normal tone; get down to the child's level. Often, lowering volume and pitch is effective.

Words. The fewer the words, the better. Simple, clear statements, spoken once, will have more impact. The child will be able to focus on the real issues involved. A brief description of what

---

1   There are *professional codes of guidance* versus *family socialization practices.* Parents and teachers have the same goals for the child, but the teacher is bound by professional standards and codes for behavior, whereas parental guidance has more latitude because of the strong bond of love, security, authority and loyalty.

2   The language of discipline may differ from culture to culture. Gender differences, which may be cultural, may emerge (e.g., boys are encouraged to "hit back," whereas girls are taught a more passive approach to conflicts).

happened, a word or two about what behavior is acceptable and what isn't, and a suggestion for possible solutions are all that is necessary.

Choose words carefully. They should convey to the child exactly what is expected. "Richy, move the block closer to the truck. Then Sarah won't bump into it again" tells Richy in a positive, concrete way what he can do to protect his block building. If he had been told, "Richy, watch where you are building," he would not know what action to take to solve the problem.

Body Language. When working with small children, the teacher must be aware of body height and position. Sit, squat, or kneel—but get down to their level. It is difficult to communicate warmth, caring, and concern from two or three feet above a child's head, or by shouting from across the room.

Guidance is founded on a loving, caring relationship between child and adult. To help children gain control over their impulses and monitor their own behavior, teachers must establish a sense of trust and well-being with children.

Body height and position are important. Getting down to the child's eye level provides for greater impact and involvement.

What do YOU Think?

- Do you think that all children will have problems, misbehave, and make mistakes?

- Do you think that children are capable of solving their own problems, and do you involve them in the process?

- Do you accept the child's right to independence and actively encourage self-reliance? Do you think this is always culturally appropriate?

- Do you think children misbehave deliberately to bother the teacher?

- Do you think you can help children accept the responsibility for their own actions without blaming them?

- Do you think problems can be solved and that you and the child can work them out together?

The way teachers use their body invites or rejects close relationship and familiarity. A child will find teachers more approachable if they are seated low, with arms available, rather than standing, with arms folded.

Making full use of the senses can soften the impact of words. A firm grip on the hand of a child who is hitting out, a gentle touch on the shoulder, tells children the adult is there to protect them from themselves and others. Eye contact is essential. Teachers learn to communicate the seriousness of a situation through eye and facial expressions. They also show reassurance, concern, sadness, and affection this way. Physical presence should convey to the child a message that the teacher is there, available, and interested.

Attitude. This is part of the unspoken language of guiding children. Attitudes are derived from experience.[1] Teachers find it useful to look at the way they were disciplined as youngsters and acknowledge their feelings about it.

 1 Attitudes affect expectations. Check to determine whether you may have any assumptions on how children behave depending on their race, gender, or culture.

As they begin to inhibit the behavior of the children in their classes, teachers should be aware of their own attitudes.

IMPLICATIONS FOR TEACHING

A teacher has *direct* and *indirect* influence on children's behavior. Some of the ways teachers deal directly with discipline are by what they say and what they do. Indirectly, a teacher's influence is felt just as strongly. Room arrangements and time schedules, attitudes, and behavior can work for or against good guidance practices. Teachers who are well grounded in the developmental process know that problem behaviors are normal and occur in every early childhood setting. They realize that growing children must have a safe, secure place in which to test themselves against the world.

The teacher as a **behavior model** is an important element in guidance. Children pattern their responses after adult behaviors. They are aware of how teachers respond to anger, frustration, and aggression; and how they solve problems and conflicts. Adults must be sure to model the desired behavior around the children they teach. To be successful models, teachers should be aware of their emotions and feelings; they do not want to compound a problem by their own reaction. Adults who express negative feelings to children must proceed carefully, stating their position clearly, honestly, and objectively, and in a low, calm voice.

● It bothers me when you call Roberto a dummy.

● You don't need to yell at me. I can hear you from right here. Tell me again in a quieter voice.

● I'm serious about this—no biting.

● Sometimes I get mad when children try to hurt each other.

● It makes me sad to see all that food going to waste. Please put just enough on your plate so that you will eat it all.

Remember that children are frightened by strong feelings; do not overwhelm them by your own behavior.

Being *consistent* is one of the key elements in good guidance practices. If adults want to develop mutual trust, the rules must be clear, fair, and enforced consistently and regularly. At the same time, children need to know what will happen if rules are not followed. Consequences too should be consistent.

Teachers should have *realistic expectations* for children, neither too high nor too low.

Sometimes they presume children have abilities and skills they do not yet possess and this may cause children to respond in inappropriate ways. It can be helpful to rehearse with children how they are expected to act. Practice sessions are especially useful when introducing a new topic or plan.

One teacher rehearsed the children for their first bus ride. They practiced singing, looking out the windows, having snacks, and talking with friends. A large outline of a bus was drawn with chalk on the patio floor. The children pretended to board the bus, walk down the narrow aisle, find a seat, and remember to take big steps getting up and down the steps. When the field trip day arrived, children knew several appropriate ways of behaving while on the long bus trip.

Many times children are asked to do jobs that are too complicated for them. The young child who is just learning to put on jackets and pants or to make a bed is a good example. Children may not be able to accomplish the entire job at first; it is helpful to them if the task is broken down into smaller steps. Straighten the sheet and blanket for Gordon, then let him pull the spread up over the pillow. Little by little have Gordon assume more of the bed-making job as he becomes capable.

As *active observers* in their classroom, teachers can learn a great deal about the effects of their guidance efforts. When teachers observe, they can time interventions, or move into a situation before it becomes problematic. Observations can also be used to help children see how their actions impact others. Chapter 6

"I get to be the first because I'm the biggest."

"I want my mommy."

"Gimme that, it's mine."

"Look, I won again, you dummy."

Good guidance practices involve children as active participants. How would you set limits in these situations?

has many good observation forms for teachers to use.

Preventing misbehavior is another part of the teacher's role. Effective guidance practices call for teachers to be alert to potential problems and situations before they result in children's inappropriate behavior. Even then, unpredict-

able situations occur: a child becomes tired in the middle of snack time; one of the teachers is called out of the room with a sick child; rain forces an activity to move indoors; or a scheduled event gets postponed. At these trying and typical times, a teacher's full range of abilities is called into play. Ways to help children maintain positive behavior patterns in these situations include:

1. *Recognize and label the problem or situation.* Acknowledge the difficulties it presents to the children. Example: "You seem tired, Gus, and I know you had to wait a long time for your snack. When you have finished your juice and cracker, put your head down on the table and rest for a minute."

2. *Ask children for their help.* Get them involved in working out the solutions. Example: "Mr. Gallo had to leave for a while. How can we continue with this cooking project when I need to watch the block area too? Who has an idea? What do you think would work, Henry?"

3. *Assign a job or a task to the children who are most likely to react to the crisis.* Example: "Lorraine and Paul, will you carry the special drums inside, please, while I help the toddlers put the wagons away?"

4. *Always being prepared with a story to tell, songs to sing, guessing games to play, or exercises to do.* Help children pass the time in an appropriate way modeled by the teacher. Give a new focus. Example: "Oh, dear. The fire truck hasn't arrived at school yet; we'll have to wait another five minutes. While we are waiting to go and see it, show me how firefighters climb ladders and slide down poles."

5. *Say what you would like to have happen.* Admit what you wish you could do to correct the situation. Example: "Oh, little Riko, I wish I could bring your mommy back right now but I can't. She has to go to work, but I will hold you until your crying stops."

These guidance practices apply equally to infants and toddlers, but there are some *special considerations* that teachers should remember. Infants cry—sometimes a great deal. It is their only means of communication. When they cry they should not be ignored or chastised, but comforted. It is helpful to talk to the baby, no matter how young, and begin to identify the steps you will take to ease the distress. "Oh, Fernando, you are crying and I don't know what's wrong. Let's take a look at your diaper; maybe a change will make you more comfortable. Perhaps you are teething; I know that can hurt. Maybe you are hungry; is it time for your bottle yet?" Those soothing words as a teacher changes diapers, rubs the baby's back, or cuddles and rocks ease this time of stress.

Toddlers, too, need adults to use words to express problem situations, and the preceding examples readily apply to working with this active and lively age group. One word of caution,

---

Being Positive

- Tell children what it is you want them to do. Make directions and suggestions in positive statements, not in negative forms. "Walk around the edge of the grass, Hilla, so you won't get hit by the swing" instead of "Don't get hit!"

- Reinforce what children do right, what you like, and what you want to see repeated. This helps build the relationship on positive grounds. "Good job, Sammy. You worked hard on that puzzle."

- Give indirect suggestions or reminders, emphasizing what you want children to do. Help them refocus on the task without nagging or confrontation. "I know you are excited about the field trip, Mickey. Looks like you are almost finished putting on your jacket so we can go" instead of "Hurry and button that jacket so we can go."

- Use positive redirection whenever possible. "Let's get a basket for you to toss those balls in. That way you won't bother other children who are playing nearby."

- Use encouragement appropriately, focusing on helping children achieve success and understanding what it is you want them to learn: "Harry, I notice you are being careful about where you put your feet as you climb that tree. It looks to me like you are finding good places to stand" communicates a supportive attitude and tells the child what he is doing well. Global praise, such as "great climbing, Harry. Good for you!" may leave children wondering what exactly it is they have been praised for and omits the learning they can derive from the experience.

- Give reasons for your request. Let children know in simple, straightforward statements the reasons behind your request. Children are more likely to cooperate when they can understand the reason why. "Tom, if you move those chairs, then you and Dee will have more room to dance" instead of "Move the chairs, Tom."

however. Removing infants and toddlers from the group or confining them to a playpen or crib is not appropriate. Very young children do not understand that kind of isolation. Guidance, to be effective, should be helpful, not punitive.

ESSENTIAL GUIDANCE PRACTICES

Inductive Guidance

There are a number of guidance approaches woven throughout the chapter. They have many similar components and fall under the definition of **inductive guidance**. The key elements in the use of inductive guidance are:

1. Guidance is an interactive process and involves children as much as it does adults;
2. Children are increasingly held responsible for their actions as they come to understand the impact of their behavior on others;
3. Teaching thinking and reasoning skills helps children achieve self-control and the development of a conscience;
4. Teaching children to think and reflect on their feelings and their actions;
5. Actively involving children in the process of solving the problem.

These goals are accomplished by providing choices (see "Giving Choices," p. 295), asking open-ended questions ("What would happen if you took her book?" "How do you think he would feel if you did that?"), and communicating trust and confidence in children to solve problems and control their own behavior.

The inductive guidance principles are based on the theories of Erikson and Piaget but owe particular credit to Vygotsky, who placed the child as a learner in the context of social interactions. The concept of the zone of proximal distance (see Chapter 4), for instance, reinforces the reciprocal relationship between adult and child implied in most inductive guidance techniques. Also, Thomas and Chess's (1977) "goodness of fit," where the adult works with the child's unique temperament to determine the best guidance approach to take, is reflected in the following material. Family context as well continues to be a priority when selecting appropriate guidance methods.[1]

"They won't let me play with them." A sensitive teacher will move in and help redirect a child's behavior before it becomes a problem. What would you do in this situation?

 1 The families in early childhood programs reflect a wide range of discipline and guidance beliefs and practices.

By integrating these methods into a positive guidance approach, teachers enlarge the child's capacity to become increasingly self-directed and self-reliant.

Power Assertive Techniques

At the other end of the positive guidance spectrum are **power assertive discipline** methods, which are harsh and rely on children's fear of punishment rather than the use of reason and understanding. Spanking, hitting, calling children names, and otherwise demeaning punishments exclude the opportunity for teaching and learning to take place or to promote problem-solving. See the following "Always Avoid" information.

Always Avoid

- Methods that will shame, frighten, or humiliate children.
- Physical abuse; physical punishment
- Comparisons among children. Comparisons foster competitiveness and affect self-esteem.
- Carryovers from the incident. Once it is over, leave it behind; do not keep reminding children about it.
- Consequences that are too long, too punitive, or postponed. Children benefit most from immediate, short consequences.
- Lots of rules. Set only enough to ensure a safe environment for all children.
- Making promises you cannot keep.
- Being overly helpful. Let children do as much as they can by themselves, including solving their own conflicts.
- Threatening children with the loss of your affection.

TEN ESSENTIAL GUIDANCE STRATEGIES

How do you decide which guidance strategy is the most appropriate for the situation? The following guidance methods are along a continuum that starts with the least intrusive, hands-off approach and moves to those that require greater intervention. They are valuable tools for enlarging the child's capacity to become increasingly self-directed and self-reliant.

Figure 7-6 illustrates how some of these guidance techniques may be used to the best advantage.

What do YOU Think?

- Do you think that all children will have problems, misbehave, and make mistakes?
- Do you think that children are capable of solving their own problems, and do you involve them in the process?
- Do you accept the child's right to independence and actively encourage self-reliance? Do you think this is always culturally appropriate?
- Do you think children misbehave deliberately to bother the teacher?
- Do you think you can help children accept the responsibility for their own actions without blaming them?
- Do you think that problems can be solved and that you and the child work them out together?

Ignoring Behavior

When misbehavior is of a less serious nature—for instance, when a child whines constantly—it may be best to ignore it. This kind of behavior, although mildly annoying, is not harmful. To use the technique successfully, the adult chooses not to respond to the child in any way and may even become occupied elsewhere while the behavior persists. This method is based on the learning theory that negative reinforcement (the adult ignoring the child) will eventually cause the child to stop the undesirable behavior. At first there might be an increase in the misbehavior as the child tests to see whether the adult will truly ignore the action. Once the child sees there is nothing to gain, the behavior disappears.

Active Listening and "I" Messages

Parents and teachers can learn the art of **active listening** to respond to a child's feelings as well as words. The adults listen carefully, trying to understand what the child is saying beyond the words being used. Then they reflect back in their own words what it is they think the child has said. The child has an opportunity to correct any misinterpretations. Further dialogue

If This Is the Behavior	Try This	For Example
Whining	Ignore	Do and say nothing while whining persists. Pay attention to child when whining stops.
Playing cooperatively	Positive reinforcement	"You two are sure working hard on this garden! What a good team you make."
Refusing to cooperate	Provide a choice	"Reva, do you want to pick up the Legos off the floor or help Charlie empty the water table?"
Restlessness, inattentiveness	Change the activity	"This story seems long today; we'll finish it later. Let's play some music and dance now."
Daydreaming	Indirect suggestion	"As soon as you get your coat, Winona, we'll all be ready to go inside."
Arguing over the use of a toy	Active listening	"You really wanted to be the first one to play with the blue truck today, didn't you, Lief?"
Dawdling, late for snack	Natural consequences	"Sorry, Nate, the snacks have been put away. Maybe tomorrow you'll remember to come inside when the other children leave the yard."
Pushing, crowding, running inside	Change room arrangement	Create larger, more open spaces so children have greater freedom of movement and do not feel crowded together.
Unable to take turns, to wait	Review daily schedule, equipment	Buy duplicates of popular equipment. Allow enough time for free play so children won't feel anxious about getting a turn.
Boisterous play	Positive redirection	"You and Sergio seem to want to wrestle. Let's go set the mats out in the other room. If you wrestle here you disturb the children who are playing quietly."

FIGURE 7-6 Varieties of guidance techniques. The astute teacher selects from the options available and individualizes the responses.

helps to clarify what the child meant. For example:

Rita: I hate school!

Teacher: Sounds as if you are really disappointed you didn't get a turn cooking today.

Rita: I really wanted to help make pancakes.

"I" messages are an adult's way of reflecting back to children how their actions have affected others.

Parent: When you scream indoors, it really hurts my ears.

Parent: I feel sad when you tell me you don't like me.

"I" messages are honest, nonjudgmental statements that place no blame on the child but that state an observation of the behavior and its results. They avoid accusing statements, such as "You made me . . ." and call for a framework that allows adults to state their feelings to that child (Gordon, 1970).

Reinforcement

Behavior modification is an organized approach based on the premise that behavior is learned through **positive and negative reinforcement** or rewards. The belief is that children will tend to repeat behavior for which they get the desired results (positive reinforcement) and are likely to avoid doing things that have undesirable consequences (negative reinforcement).

Positive reinforcement is used to teach new and different behaviors to a child and to help the child maintain the change. Negative reinforcement may simply involve ignoring or withdrawing attention when the child acts inappropriately. Initially, the reinforcement (or reward) must be swift and consistently applied, as often as the behavior occurs. If the desired behavior is for Janie to always hang her coat on the hook, praise and appreciate the effort each time Janie hangs up her wraps. Once this is a well-established routine, the reinforcement (praise) becomes less intense.

Reinforcers, or rewards, must be individualized to meet the needs of the child and the situation. Social reinforcers, such as smiling, interest and attention, hugging, touching, and talking, are powerful tools with young children. Food, tokens, and money are sometimes used as reinforcers in home and school settings. The goal, however, is that inner satisfaction will become its own reward regardless of the type of reinforcer one might use initially. If that does not occur, then other positive guidance measures should be explored.

Parents and teachers often take for granted the positive, desirable behavior in children and may forget to acknowledge these behaviors frequently. Behavior modification helps to correct that oversight. Whenever adults focus on a negative aspect of a child's behavior and make an attempt to change it, they also look at the positive qualities the child possesses and reinforce them. This keeps a balanced perspective while working on a problem.

Behavior modification enables adults to invite children to be part of the process, giving them an active part in monitoring their own behavior. Children are capable of keeping a chart of how many times they finished their plate, made the bed, or fed the dog. This chart serves as a natural reinforcer.

Redirecting the Activity

Sometimes the adult will want to change the activity in which the child is engaged to one that is more acceptable. If Pia and Elena are throwing books off the reading loft, the teacher will want to redirect them and may suggest throwing soft foam balls into a makeshift basket. This technique calls for the adult to make an accurate assessment of what the children really want to do. In this case, it appears they enjoy throwing from a height. Now the teacher can consider alternatives that permit the desired activity while changing the expression or form it takes: "It looks as if you two are enjoying dropping things from up there. Let's figure out a way you can do that so that books won't be damaged."

The substitute activity must be a valid one, acceptable to the adults and fulfilling to the children. In most cases children are not being deliberately malicious or destructive. More than likely they are expressing curiosity, imagination, and the need to explore. Positive redirection satisfies these needs in a way that enhances children's self-concept and self-control.

Giving Choices

Giving children choices whenever possible allows them some control so they do not always feel dominated by adults. Choices help children practice self-reliance, self-direction, and self-discipline. "Yes, Seth, the cooking area is too crowded. Looks like there is plenty of room at the clay table or writing table. Where would you like to play?"

You must give a choice only when you mean for children to make the choice and be prepared to accept the answer. "Some of the children are going in for music now. Would you like to join them?" This is a reasonable choice if there is another adult to supervise the outside.

Suggest two choices when there is the possibility of resistance. This lets a child know you expect him or her to comply with the request, but allows some decision making on their part. "It's time to go home now. Would you like to get your artwork before or after you put on your jacket?"

The choice must be valid. Acknowledge children's growing ability to deal with responsibility and help them practice making reasonable choices. "It's rest time for everyone now. Do you want to pick out some books before or after you brush your teeth?"

Children should be aware of the consequences of the choices they are making. "If you choose the computer now, you won't have time to finish your rain-forest project." Helping children make reasonable choices gives them a foundation for decision making throughout their life.

Setting Limits

To provide a safe and caring environment in which children can play and learn, teachers set limits on certain behavior. Limits are the boundaries set up to help children know what will or will not be tolerated. They are a necessary part of any group or society. Frequent exclamations of "Don't do this" or "Don't do that" need not be a part of the early childhood classroom when one understands the nature of setting limits. Teachers generally have two reasons for setting limits:

1. To prevent children from injuring themselves or others.
2. To prevent the destruction of property, materials, or equipment.

Limits are like fences; they are protective structures that help children feel secure. Fences and limits are erected and maintained to help people know how far they can go. When children know where fences are, and what limits and rules apply, they do not have to continually try to find out if fences are there and where they are. Inside the fences, children are free—and safe—to try out many behaviors.[1]

Children may not like fences; they may resist attempts to limit their behavior. Teachers must learn to set and maintain limits with confidence and authority. Children respond to how limits are set as much as to the limits themselves. Be sure children help determine limits. A positive guidance process involves children as active participants; this fosters self-discipline. Children also seem less resistant to following rules when they are a part of the limit-setting procedure. Figure 7-7 illustrates positive ways to set limits when working with young children.

When Setting Limits	For Example
1. Make sure that the limit is appropriate to the situation.	"Andrew, I want you to get down from the table. You may finish your snack by sitting in your chair or standing next to me. You may not stand on the table."
2. Fit the limits to the individual child's age, history, and emotional framework.	"Sheila, you've interrupted the story too many times today. Find a place at the puzzle table until we are finished. Remember, I told you earlier that you wouldn't be able to hear the end of the story if you yelled again." "Jamal, I know it's your first day back since you broke your arm, but it is time to listen to the story now. You and Sascha can talk together in a few minutes."
3. See that the limits are consistenty applied to all adults.	"I know you want to ride the red bike now but both teachers have said you already had a long turn today."
4. Reinforce the same rules consistently.	"Judy, remember, everyone *walks* inside. You can run outside."
5. Follow through; support your words with actions.	"I can't let you tear the books. Since this is the second page this morning, you'll need to make another choice instead of the book corner." If the child does not leave, begin to pick up books. Lead child firmly to another activity.
6. Use simple statements; be clear and state limits positively.	"Roger, use your gentle voice indoors. When your voice is too loud, people can't hear one another. You may use your big loud voice outside."
7. Respect the child's feelings and acknowledge them when you can.	"I know you want your mom to stay. She has to go to her job now. I'll stay with you while you feel sad and I'll take care of you until she comes back."
8. Act with authority; be sure of your purpose and be confident.	"I can't let you hurt other people. Put the block down." Instead of "I wish you wouldn't do that."
9. Be ready to accept consequences; have a plan for the next step, if needed. Maintain the limit. Don't avoid the situation or give in if the child threatens to fall apart or create a scene.	"I'm sorry, Sarah. You won't be able to play here any longer. Remember, we agreed earlier that you wouldn't call Gerry "Fatty" any more because it hurt her feelings. I'm sorry that makes you cry but I can't let you keep making fun of one of our classmates. When you are finished crying you can work in the writing center or go to the art room. Which do you want to do?"
10. Have children help in defining limits.	"We'll be taking a bus to the museum next week. What are some of the rules we should follow so that we can enjoy the trip? Wally, do you have an idea?"

FIGURE 7-7 Tips for setting limits. Children feel safe when appropriate limits are set on their behavior.

1 A good way to prepare children to live successfully and productively is to help them become increasingly responsible for their actions and their behavior.

A natural part of growing up is to stretch those limits and push those fences aside. For the child, limits are self-protective. Young children have not yet learned the skills to control themselves in all situations. Their behavior easily goes out of bounds. Children are just beginning to exert that inner pressure (self-control) that will help them monitor their own actions. Until then, they need adults to help them learn when and how to apply self-restraint. Limits keep them from going too far.

Children can frighten themselves and others with anger, frustration, and fear. They need adults to stop them from doing physical or emotional harm to themselves or others. Well-considered limits give the child freedom to try out, test, and explore avenues of self-expression in ways that will promote growth and protect budding autonomy.

Active Problem Solving

The principle in active problem solving is to actively engage children in confronting their differences and working together to solve their problems. The adult guides children toward solutions but does not solve problems for them. Posing open-ended questions, the adult helps keep the child focused so that they can suggest alternate solutions, for example:

"What could you do _____?"
"How might she feel when _____?"
"What might happen if _____?"
"How can you _____?"

All of the children's suggestions must be acknowledged seriously, even if they seem unreasonable. Young children are likely to start the discussion by suggesting extreme solutions. In the case of Malcolm, for instance (see the second example at the beginning of this chapter), they might initially suggest a radical alternative: "Don't let Malcolm come to this school anymore." These suggestions will become tempered as other children respond; fair and reasonable solutions will eventually emerge: "Anyone who knocks over somebody else's blocks has to help them build it back up again."

Rather than assessing blame, teachers help children think through a number of alternatives, including the consequences of their suggestions: "If we close the block area, what will happen when you want to play with your favorite trucks this afternoon?" By assisting them in anticipating the results of what they suggest, teachers can help children understand how their behavior influences and affects others. This is an early lesson in a lifelong quest to become responsible for one's own behavior.

Conflict resolution should become part of the child's daily life. Teachers can help children solve disagreements nonviolently and explore alternative ways to reach their goals. Figure 7-8 outlines a process for active problem solving and conflict resolution (see also Figure 7-6). It is useful for resolving differences through group discussion, as noted earlier, or when one or more children become embroiled in conflict. By following such a process, children learn to respect others' opinions, to express their own feelings in appropriate ways, and to learn tolerance for doing things in a different way.[1]

The process also suggests an important guidance principle: the adult role is to intervene as little as possible, allowing children the opportunity to come up with an acceptable solution.

When children help create a solution, they come away with a sense of commitment to it. This process also gives children a sense of power and control, a sense of independence, and a feeling of self-worth. Read Sue Warford's "Insights" article in Chapter 14 for a good example of active problem solving.

Distraction

Some problems may be avoided when the adult helps focus the child's attention elsewhere. Very young children, especially infants and toddlers, can easily be distracted from undesirable actions. Consider the example at the beginning of the chapter in which Kim grabs at one of the necklaces Shawnsey has. A fast-thinking teacher could present Kim with another attractive one. This method calls for well-timed intervention.

Natural and Logical Consequences

Natural consequences enhance children's ability to take responsibility for themselves. As implied, this approach lets children experience the natural consequences of their actions. Designed by Rudolf Dreikurs, it emphasizes the opportunity

1 Children should regard schools as places large enough and diverse enough to hold a regard for a variety of people whose background and experience are respected and understood.

The Six-Step Approach to Problem Solving

Scenario: Two children run outdoors to get the available wagon. They reach it simultaneously and start pulling on the handle, yelling, "Mine!" One child starts shoving the other child out of the way.

Step 1: Approach (Initiate Mediation)
- Approach the conflict, signaling your awareness and availability.
- Get close enough to intervene if nessesary; stop aggressive behavior or neutralize the object of conflict by holding it yourself.

Step 2: Make a Statement
- *Describe the scene.*
- Reflect what the children have said.
- *Offer no judgments, values, solutions.*

    "It looks as if you both want the wagon."
    "I see you are yelling at each other."

Step 3: Ask Questions (gather data, define the problem)
- Don't direct questions toward pinpointing the blame.
- Draw out details; define problems.
- Help kids communicate versus slugging it out. "How did this happen?" "What do you want to tell her?" "How could you solve this problem?" "How could you use it without fighting?"

Step 4: Generate Alternative Solutions
- Give children the job of thinking and figuring it out.
- Suggestions may be offered by disputants or observers.
- Ask questions: "Who has an idea of how we could solve . . . ?"

    "You could take turns"
    "You could both use it together"
    "You could both do something else."
    "No one could use it."

- Common mistake: rushing to this stage; give it the time it deserves.

Step 5: Agree on Solution
- When both children accept a solution, rephrase it ("So you both say that she will be the driver?")
- If any solution seems unsafe or grossly unfair, you must tell the children. ("It is too dangerous for you both to stand up and ride downhill together. What is another way you can agree?")

Step 6: Follow Through
- Monitor to make sure agreement is going according to plan. If the decision involves turn taking, you may need to be a clock-watcher.
- Tell the players and the group: "Looks as if you have solved your problem!"
- Use the power of language to:
    - Reinforce the solvability of the problem.
    - Note the ability of the players to do so.
    - Point out the positive environment to be successful.

FIGURE 7-8 Using these guidelines to help children solve problems, teachers listen more than talk, allow children the time to make mistakes and figure out solutions, and point out that diversity of viewpoints is natural, normal, and workable.

children have to learn from the way their environment functions:

> If Libby does not eat her dinner, she can expect to be hungry later.
>
> If Kara puts her hand on a hot stove, she is likely to get burned.
>
> If Tony grabs the book away from Ben, Ben may hit him.

This method allows adults to define the situation for children without making judgments and lets children know what to expect. The consequences are a natural result of the child's own actions.

Logical consequences, on the other hand, are a function of what adults impose. A logical consequence of disrupting group time is removal from the group. For the adult, this means a commitment to follow through; consequences, once stated, must be enforced. It is important to give children an opportunity to choose a course of action for themselves once

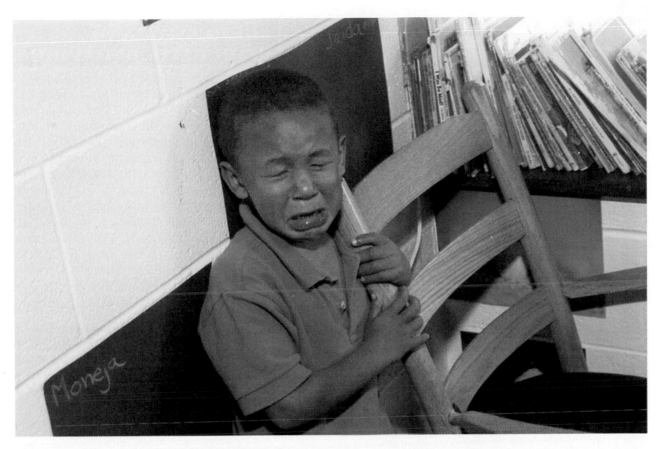

Young children should not be isolated for misbehavior in ways that damage their self-esteem.

they have some understanding of what is likely to happen.

Time Out

Removing a child from the play area is particularly appropriate when, owing to anger, hurt, or frustration, the child is out of control. Taking children away from the scene of intensity and emotion to allowing them time to cool off and settle down is sometimes the only way to help them. The teacher is firm and consistent as the child is quietly removed from play. It is important that this technique be used with a positive attitude and approach, not as punishment for misbehavior.

Used appropriately, the time-out period is very much like that used in athletic events: a brief respite and a chance to stop all activity and regroup. The teacher's role is to help the child talk about the incident—the feelings involved as well as the need for self-control—and to give the child an opportunity to gain self-control before resuming play. Children can monitor themselves and choose when they are ready to return to classroom activity. Noah, who persists in knocking down other children's block structures, might be told, "You may come back to the block area when you think you are ready to play without knocking over other children's work." Noah can then assume some responsibility for how he will behave and when he is ready to return to play.

Too often, time out is punitive. Children are pulled from an activity, pushed into a chair and told to "watch how the other children are playing nicely," or "sit there until you can behave."

Use this technique lightly. Adults can misuse it and leave the child with a sense of rejection. As with other strategies, it should be appropriate to the situation.

What do YOU Think?

Is time-out a useful strategy? Is it punishment, or can it be defined as guidance? Do you think children in "time-out" are thinking about their behavior? What might they be thinking? How do you think children learn to gain self-control?

Video VIEW PoinT 7-3

"Children need to feel powerful; it is part of the developmental design of growing up."

COMPETENCY: Guidance

AGE GROUP: School Age

CRITICAL THINKING QUESTIONS:

1. Why do you think it is important for a child to feel powerful?

2. What are some ways you could help a six-year-old feel powerful, within DAP and appropriate positive guidance guidelines?

AGGRESSIVE AND DISRUPTIVE BEHAVIOR

Every teacher has experienced the child who disrupts the class, throws tantrums, hurts other children, knocks over block structures, and provides wear and tear on equipment, materials, and the adult's patience. (See Elizabeth Crary's "Insight" article on tantrums at the end of this chapter). Children with a high degree of energy, short attention spans, who are easily distracted, demanding, and may be under stress, are some of the children who challenge our skills in guiding behavior. They need extra support as they learn to live in a group and become responsible for their actions. Figure 7-9 describes four areas on which to focus as you work with aggressive and disruptive children.

Area of Focus	What You Can Do
Observations	*Collect information about the behavior:* Identify the components that cause children to lose control. When does Nam throw a temper tantrum? Only before snack time? Just after her mother leaves? What prompts Rudy's resistance? What precedes it? How long does it last? How much attention does Arturo get when he interrupts story time? How many teachers intervene? For how long? How has his attention been sought prior to his disruption? Observe and learn also when these children are behaving appropriately, and record what and how much attention they receive from teachers at that time.
Modify the classroom	*Evaluate the classroom* on the basis of the observations you made. Is it orderly and free of clutter? Are there legitimate opportunities to move about and use large muscles? Can children select their own activities and make choices about where they will work and play? Is the curriculum challenging and appropriate to the age level? Is there advanced warning when activities will change? Is there an established routine that children can count on? Is there a cleanup time when the children help restore the play areas?
Teacher attention and language	*Give minimum attention* to a child during an aggressive episode, taking care of any injured party first. Use short, direct sentences, without judgment and without lecturing. Look at and speak to the child at eye level. Do not shame, ridicule, or use physical punishment.
	Good example: "No. I can't let you hurt children."
	Poor example: "It's not nice to hit other children. They don't like when you are mean. Why can't you play nice like they do? I'm gonna have to tell your momma you were bad when she comes. Can you promise me you won't hit anybody else today? Now tell Tomi you are sorry."
	Pay attention to disruptive, nonattentive, aggressive children when they are behaving appropriately. Talk over with them alternatives to their nonappropriate behavior.
	Examples: "Next time, tell someone you are angry instead of hitting." "When you are finished playing with the blocks, call me and I will help you find another place to play." "If you don't want to hear the story, what else could you do that wouldn't bother other people who want to listen?"
	Follow through. Help the child return to play, giving choices when possible, with activities that require energy (clay, woodworking, climbing) or those that are more calming (water play, painting), depending on what the child seems to need at the time. Support the child's involvement with relevant comments, interest, and suitable challenges.

(continues)

FIGURE 7-9 Managing aggressive, disruptive, high-energy behavior. (Adapted from Allen, K. E. (1992). *The exceptional child: Mainstreaming in early childhood education.* Clifton Park, NY: Thomson Delmar Learning. Used with permission. Taken from Gordon, A., & Browne, K. W. (1996). *Guiding young children in a diverse society.* Boston: Allyn & Bacon.)

Interacting with children

Examples: "Let's decide where you want to play now, Faisal. There's room for you at the water table or pounding the clay. I'll help you get started." (Later) "You look as if you are having a good time with that clay, Faisal. I bet you can squeeze it so hard it oozes out your fingers! I'll watch while you try."

Start with a child's known interests. Through observations, determine which activities consistently hold the child's attention so that you can reinforce positive behavior while the child is engaged. This technique also helps to increase attention span.

Example: "You sure have been having fun at the water table, Jessica. Here are some funnels and tubes. What could you do with them?"

Help the child plan where to go next and assist in getting started, if necessary. This is effective if the child's activity is changed before he loses interest or before he loses control.

Example: "Jay, it is nearly cleanup time and I know that sometimes it is a hard time for you when we stop playing. How about your helping me organize the children who want to move the tables. Could you be my assistant today and show everyone where to put the tables?"

Give time for response; take time to teach. Children need adequate time to respond to requests without being nagged and may need assistance in learning a skill or getting started with what was requested. Make the task manageable. If, after a reasonable time has passed and Shaquille still hasn't put his jacket on, the teacher restates the request and offers assistance.

Example: "You may go outside as soon as your jacket is on, Shaquille. If you put the jacket down on the floor like this, and slip your arms in here, you can pull it over your head."

Help children focus their attention. Get down to their eye level, call them by name, look at them, and speak directly to them. Give advance warning, clear and simple directions, and choices when possible. Do not overwhelm a child with rules and instructions.

Example: "Corretta, it will soon be time to go home. When you finish writing your story, you may choose to come over to the rug to sing songs or you may find a favorite book and look at it in the book corner."

Point out the consequences of their actions to help them understand other's feelings and become responsible for what they do.

Examples: "Linda is sad because you won't let her play with you." "Other children won't be able to use the paint when you mix the colors in the paint jar."

Remind children of the rules and expectations. Rehearse them in remembering appropriate behavior. Use positive phrases.

Example: "Before you go to the block area, remember how much space you need for the roads you like to build. Look around and see who else is playing and find a safe place for your road."

FIGURE 7-9 *(continued)*

SUMMARY

The early childhood educator provides opportunities for children to express their feelings in appropriate ways and to solve their social problems constructively. Young children are incapable of controlling their own impulses all the time, so caring adults are needed to guide them toward self-control. Teachers base their methods and guidance principles on an understanding of why children misbehave and what factors influence behavior.

Most guidance techniques begin by accepting the feelings the child expresses and verbalizing them. Then the adult sets limits on what form the behavior may take, guiding the action as needed and following through to conclusion.

The most effective methods of guidance are clear, consistent, and fair rules that are enforced in consistent, humane ways. Children should be aware of the consequences if the rules are broken.

Good guidance practices emphasize the positive aspects of a child's behavior, not just the problem behaviors. Guidance measures have greater meaning to children if they are encouraged to take responsibility for their own actions and are part of the problem-solving process.

TANTRUMS AS A TEACHING TOOL: WAYS TO HELP CHILDREN LEARN

by Elizabeth Crary

Marie doesn't want Stephanie to go home.

Josh wants the truck that Eli is playing with—right now!

David doesn't want his diaper changed, even though it stinks.

One of your jobs as a parent or teacher is to help children understand and deal with their feelings. There are several things you can do. During the tantrum you can acknowledge children's feelings and help them distinguish between feelings and behavior. Before the next tantrum you can begin to teach children ways to deal with their feelings and the situation.

1. **Acknowledge children's feelings.** You can do that by helping children develop a "feeling" vocabulary and by validating their feelings.

   - Label children's feelings: "You're disappointed that we can't go to the park today."

   - Share your feelings: "I feel frustrated when I spill coffee on the floor."

   - Read books that discuss feelings, such as the Let's Talk about Feelings series.

   - Observe another's feelings: "I'll bet he's proud of the tower he built."

   Validate children's feelings. Many people have been trained to ignore or suppress their feelings. Girls are often taught that showing anger is unfeminine or not nice. Boys are taught not to cry. You can validate feelings by listening to the child and reflecting the feelings you hear. Listen without judging. Remain separate. Remember, a child's feelings belong to her or him. When you reflect the feeling ("You are mad that Stephanie has to go home now"), you are not attempting to solve the problem. Accepting the feeling is the first step toward dealing with it.

2. **Help children distinguish between feelings and actions.** All feelings are okay. Actions may or may not be okay depending on the situation. For example, hitting a baseball is fine. Hitting a person is not acceptable. You can clarify the difference by saying, "It's okay to be mad, but I cannot let you hit Eli."

You can also model the difference between feelings and action. You might say, "This morning someone cut me off on the road. I was so mad I wanted to crash into them. Instead I . . ."

3. **Teach children several ways to calm themselves down.** If telling children to "Use your words" worked for most kids, grown-ups would have little trouble with children's feelings. Children need a variety of ways to respond—auditory, physical, visual, creative, and self-nurturing. First children need to practice different responses when they are calm. Then when children are familiar with different ways to respond, you may ask them which they would like to try when they are upset.

   For example: "You're real angry. Do you want to feel mad right now or do you want to calm down?" If your child wants to change her feelings, you could say, "What could you do? Let's see, you could dance a mad dance, make a card to give to Stephanie, talk about this feeling, or look at your favorite book." After you've generated ideas, let the child choose what works for her.

4. **Offer tools to resolve situations that are hard for them.** If Josh wants the truck Eli has, teach him to ask, wait, or trade for it. If Sonja gets frustrated putting puzzles together, teach her how to take breaks or to breathe deeply so she does not get upset. You can use books such as *I Want It, I Can't Wait* or *I Want to Play* to introduce options. Research has found that the more alternatives children have the better their social behavior.

Elizabeth Crary, MS, teaches parent education independently and at North Seattle Community College, and has written many books and articles on guidance, including Dealing with Disappointment *and* Love and Limits.

For more activities and information, visit our Web site at http://www.EarlyChildEd.delmar.com

KEY TERMS

discipline

punishment

interdependence

behavior model

inductive guidance

power assertive discipline

active listening

positive reinforcement

negative reinforcement

REVIEW QUESTIONS

1. What are some of the goals of children's misbehavior? What techniques can adults use to deal with children who exhibit these goals?

2. What developmental factors affect children's behavior? What environmental factors? How does a child's individual style affect behavior? What do developmental and learning theories (see Chapter 4) add to the discussion?

3. Why is it important to understand the child's family culture as you guide and direct behavior?

4. What is your own definition of discipline?

5. Why do teachers have to set limits on children's behavior? How does setting limits help the child?

6. Describe ways children differ in temperament.

7. Discuss in small groups the appropriate uses of time-out. Describe those ways in which this technique can be harmful to young children.

LEARNING ACTIVITIES

1. Your three-year-old daughter always interrupts when you talk on the telephone. She cries for you to play with her, hits her brothers, and crawls into cupboards. What is she doing and why? What is your reaction? How will you solve the problem?

2. List activities that channel aggressive feelings into acceptable ways to play. After each, note the emotion or feeling the specific activity might release.
   Example: Clay—anger, frustration

3. Finish this sentence: "When I was four years old, the worst thing I ever did was . . ." How did the adults around you react? What would you do if you were the adult in charge? Discuss and compare responses with a classmate.

4. Children's literature helps us focus on guidance and behavior problems. Select a book from the following list. Define the problem behavior and the person creating the problem. Do you agree with the author's way of handling the situation? Suggest alternatives. When and with whom might you use this story?

   Suggested books:

   Peter's Chair/Ezra Jack Keats
   Annie and the Old One/Miska Miles
   Jamaica's Find/Juanita Havill
   Momma, Do You Love Me?/Barbara M. Joosse
   Tree of Cranes/Allen Say
   Shy Charles/Rosemary Wells
   Bread and Jam for Frances/Russell and Lillian Hoban
   Where the Wild Things Are/Maurice Sendak

5. Observe a group of young children during play. See whether you can identify an example of a child who might be described as an easy child, a difficult child, and a slow-to-warm-up child. What guidance techniques do the teachers use with each child? Are they the same? If they are different, describe the differences. How successful are these techniques that are being used? What might you do differently?

6. How do you feel about spanking children? Were you spanked when you were a child? If so, what precipitated the spankings? Can you think of any other forms of behavior control that might have worked instead of spanking? Compare your thoughts and insights with those of another member of this class.

7. What can you find out about a technique known as "assertive discipline," and why do some early childhood educators consider it inappropriate for young children? Report your findings to this class.

REFERENCES

American Academy of Pediatrics. (1997). *A guide to your child's symptoms* (p. 35). Elk Grove Village, IL: Author.

Gonzalez-Mena, J. (2001). *Multicultural issues in child care.* Menlo Park, CA: Mayfield.

Gordon, A., & Browne, K. W. (1996). *Guiding young children in a diverse society.* Boston: Allyn & Bacon.

Gordon, T. (1970). *Parent effectiveness training.* New York: Peter H. Wyden.

Thomas, A., & Chess, S. (1977). *Temperament and development.* New York: Brunner/Mazel.

HELPFUL WEB SITES

Responsive Discipline	http://www.ksu.edu/wwparent/courses/rd
National Network for Child Care	http://www.nncc.org/Guidance
Urban Programs Resource Network	http://www.urbanext.uiuc.edu/behavior
Empowering People, Inc.	http://www.empowering.com/positivedisicpline

For more activities and information, visit our Web site at http://www.EarlyChildEd.delmar.com

CHAPTER

8

Families and Teachers: Partners in Education

QUESTIONS FOR THOUGHT

What are the benefits of an effective family-teacher partnership?

How can families get interested and involved in the classroom?

What are the ingredients for a good parent/family program?

What are the components for a successful parent/family-teacher conference?

What is the teacher's role in providing a supportive atmosphere for families?

How has the American family changed in recent years?

A HISTORICAL OVERVIEW

Working with families can be one of the teacher's most satisfying responsibilities, or it can be one of the most frustrating. It is usually both.[1] The potential is present for a dynamic partnership between the most important adults in a child's life. The common goal is obvious: the welfare of the child. Each has knowledge, skills, and a sense of caring to bring to that relationship. Each has a need for the other. Partnerships usually begin with such a need. So families and teachers become co-workers and colleagues in a joint effort to help the child develop fully.

Historical Precedent

There is a historical **precedent** for the partnership between families and teachers. Pestalozzi and Froebel, early 18th-century educators, detailed many of their procedures for home use (as noted in Chapter 1). The involvement of the mother in the education of the child was considered important even then. When kindergartens were organized in the United States, classes for parents and mothers' clubs were also started. The National Congress of Mothers evolved from that movement. Today it is the National Parents and Teachers Association. This well-known organization is an integral part of most school systems and continues to promote a union between school and home, teachers and parents.

Decades of Change

During the 1930s parent involvement in education was actively discouraged. Teachers were seen as experts who wanted to be left alone to do their job. In many cases, teachers felt they did little but remedy parental mistakes. That trend ended in the 1940s when the need for parent support and encouragement was recognized. Closer relationships between teachers and parents were established. This view of a need for closer ties between teacher and families, now over 50 years old, stands today as a commonly accepted principle.

In training, teachers were exposed to curricula that would help them appreciate and use parents as co-workers in the child's development. By the 1960s, Head Start programs required parental involvement and set about developing parent education and parent training programs.

Their commitment to children included a commitment to the families of those children.

Parent involvement and education were largely ignored in the education reform movement of the 1990s, and the typical parent education prevalent in early childhood programs is also being reassessed. That omission began to be addressed as parents became empowered in the creation of charter schools, a mid-'90s phenomenon that created greater parent involvement in public schools.

Mutual Collaboration

Two particular changes, collaborating with parents and working within the family context, are significant in today's school programs. For much of the century just past, the early childhood "professionally driven parent education tradition" dominated the method of parent-teacher relationships, preceded by the "child-saver" approach that early childhood programs made up for deficient home environments (Powell & Diamond, 1995).

Demographic data reinforces the need for families and teachers of preschool children to become full and equal partners and set the stage for future school/family partnerships. Increasingly, ethnic, racial, and cultural diversity will affect relationships between families and schools. Today's early childhood professional will need to be skilled in ways that will strengthen the family/school bond. Further discussion of the parent support movement follows.

At no other level of education is the responsiveness to the needs of parents so high, and there is a renewed effort to extend the role of families in their children's educational process. There is a broader emphasis from serving only children to serving children and their families. There is also a move to change the parents' role as one of just a volunteer to one of family support and a deepening of parent involvement. There is general agreement among early childhood teachers that at no other age is such a relationship more important than in the early years of a child's schooling, for children's needs are so interwoven with those of their parents. Strong parent-school relationships have always been a part of the early childhood educators' portfolio in ways that have not been understood or developed by teachers of other age groups.

Note: Throughout this chapter, the terms *parents* and *parenthood* are meant to include

1 Ellen Galinsky (1987) coined the word *parentist*. Just as educators must heighten their awareness of their sexist and racist bias, they must also be aware of individual bias toward particular "types" of parents.

Video VIEW PoinT 8-1

"Parents are their children's first and most important teachers."

COMPETENCY: Family Interaction, School and Community

AGE GROUP: Preschool

CRITICAL THINKING QUESTIONS:

1. What does this statement mean to you?

2. How would you describe the parent's role as "teacher" and how does that differ from your role as teacher?

mothers and fathers as well as other extended family members who have the responsibility for raising a child.[1]

STRENGTHENING THE PARTNERSHIP

What Families Contribute

Families have a unique contribution to make in the child's schooling. They have different knowledge about the child from what the teacher has. They know the child's history: physical, medical, social, and intellectual. They know the child as a member of a family and the role that child plays in the total family group, the extended family, and the community.

Families bring with them a sense of continuity about the child: they provide the context with which the teacher can view the whole child. As the teacher will soon learn, the family already knows what makes their children happy or sad or how they react to changes in routines. Thus, families have a wealth of intimate knowledge about their children that the teacher is only just beginning to discover.

How Families Benefit

One of the greatest values of a strong parent program is the opportunity for families to meet each other. They find that they share similar problems and frustrations and that they can support one another in finding solutions. Friendships based on mutual interests and concerns about their children can help them forge new relationships.

Through close home-school relationships, parents and families can find ways to become more effective as their children's teachers:

- They can observe modeling techniques that teachers find successful in dealing with children and can learn what behaviors are appropriate at certain ages.
- By observing how their children relate to other adults and children, families can come to know them better as social beings.
- They may become more aware of school and community resources that are available to them and, in the person of the teacher, they now have access to a consultant who knows and understands their child and can help them when they need it.

Parents and families are the child's teachers too. They teach by word, by example, by all they do and say. Through closer home-school relationships, families can be helped to see that their everyday experiences with their children provide teachable moments, opportunities for educating their children. Teachers can support families in their roles as teachers of their children by:

- keeping them informed about each stage of the child's development;
- showing them how to encourage language and thinking skills;
- educating them to children's social needs at any given age;
- providing lists of books and toys that encourage children's thinking and creative abilities;
- making sure parents have copies of children's favorite songs, recipes that are popular at school, and information, in a bilingual format as needed, on how to teach health and safety habits at home.[2]

Families need not teach a curriculum; they do need to use common household routines and experiences to encourage children's total growth. The teaching staff has a strong role to

---

1 As one works with our diverse world it is important to be mindful that many children are being parented by people other than their biologic or adoptive parents (e.g., grandparents, foster parents, aunts and uncles, legal guardians, or an adult living with the parent).

2 It is important to remember that fewer than half of the children under the age of five are being brought up in two-parent, middle-class, English-speaking, stay-at-home-mom households. Do parent-teacher policies reflect changing demographics?

A true partnership happens when parents and teachers share their strengths with one another for the benefit of the children they care for and love.

play in helping them learn how to do this. In Figure 8-1 a noted author and family counselor lists 10 of the most important things families can teach their children.

The Ten Most Important Things Families Can Teach Their Children

1. To love themselves.
2. To read behavior.
3. To communicate with words.
4. To understand the difference between thoughts and actions.
5. To wonder and ask why.
6. To understand that complicated questions do not have simple answers.
7. To risk failure as a necessary part of growing up.
8. To trust grownups.
9. To have a mind of their own.
10. To know when to lean on adults.

FIGURE 8-1 A list of important basics that children can learn at home. (Adapted from LeShan, E. (1992). *When your child drives you crazy.* New York: St. Martin's Press.)

A family-centered approach to school relationships supports the growth of the family as well as the child. When families have a meaningful partnership with their children's teachers, it raises their sense of importance and diminishes some of the isolation and anxiety of child rearing. By empowering families in a critical area of their children's lives, allowing them to participate in decisions affecting their children's education, teachers can help families see themselves as part of the solution.

Family Cultural Influences

Families today represent a wide range of cultural backgrounds, so it is more important than ever that their contributions be sought out, acknowledged, and used. This is one of the most pressing issues in teaching today. All of the subtle communication styles that exist within various cultures can be blocks to good family-school relationships, or they can be the basis on which teachers and families connect with each other.

All families have knowledge that the teachers need to know. Those whose linguistic and cultural backgrounds are different from the teacher need to share their perspectives so that issues relating to basic routines such as eating and sleeping may be understood in their cultural context.[1] The same is true for a family's expectations

---

1   Cross-cultural communications require sensitivity on the part of the teacher and a mind-set that is willing to be open, flexible, and eager to learn.

about their child's experiences in the classroom. Only through forging such a partnership can families of diverse cultural backgrounds become true contributors to their children's education and care. Chapter 10 discusses Culturally Responsive Teaching on pages 408 and 409.

What Teachers Contribute

Teachers bring another point of view to the partnership. As child development professionals, they see the child in relation to normal milestones and appropriate behaviors. They notice how each child plays with other children in the group—what seems to challenge Mickey and when Ramon is likely to fall apart. Unlike families, teachers see individual children from a perspective that is balanced by the numerous other children they have taught. They observe how the child behaves with a variety of adults, sensing children's ability to trust other adults through interactions with them at school. When families need help for themselves or for their child, teachers become resources. They work with the families to find psychologists, hearing and speech specialists, or other educational programs, if warranted.

Take a look at NAEYC's Code of Ethical Conduct (located in Appendix A at the back of this book), particularly at Section II on ethical responsibilities to families, for further clarification on standards for working with families of young children. Note which of the ideals and principles suggest how teachers might communicate with families regarding their child's participation and learning in the classroom. Supporting and encouraging families is part of the teacher's role. Good teachers are sensitive to parent concerns and understand their needs, similar to those expressed by Libby Miles's "Insight" article at the end of this chapter.

The majority of families today want to learn the best way to raise their children and want to improve their child-rearing skills. There are numerous opportunities for the early childhood teacher to work with families. Figure 8-2 cites a multitude of ways to begin to fulfill these needs.

How Teachers and Schools Benefit

Active family involvement benefits the teacher and school. Families are an untapped resource in most schools. The skills and talents in a group of families multiply the people resources available for children.[1] Some parents will want to work directly in the classroom with children, others may volunteer to help in the office, the schoolyard, or the kitchen. Family members can sometimes arrange to take some time off their job to accompany a class on a field trip. Some parents are willing to work at home, either sewing, typing, mending, building, or painting; others are available for a variety of fund-raising activities.

In an equal partnership, however, the parent level of involvement must go beyond volunteer participation in school activities to parent participation in decision-making roles, such as serving on school boards, parent advisory committees, and other groups that advocate for children's educational needs. Which of the ideals and principles of the Code of Ethical Conduct (see Appendix A) support the family's decision-making role?

Some parents may be unable to participate because of work schedules, small children to care for at home, lack of transportation, or inability to speak English.[2] If a school is serious about strengthening the family, these issues must be addressed and solutions must be found to involve all parents.

What Children Gain

The children whose families choose to take an active part in the school reap the rewards of such involvement. Decades of research show the positive effects on achievement when children's families are involved in their education. The family is the primary source from which the child develops and grows. It is needed to reinforce the learning, the attitudes, and the motivation if children are to succeed. Family visibility is especially important for low-income and minority children; their family's presence can heighten a sense of belonging. Children gain and family impact is increased when families are able to monitor their children's progress and reinforce the mission of the school at home.

The early childhood educator is often one of the first persons families turn to for help. Families come to the center or school looking for teachers who know about children and who will help them in raising their children. The ways in which teachers can help and their

---

1 Families are an excellent resource for bringing experiences of diversity into a classroom (e.g., a dad cooking an ethnic favorite with children).

2 It is important to help all families feel welcome, wanted, and involved.

A Checklist for Making Your School "Parent Friendly"

_____ Hold an orientation for familes at a convenient time.

_____ Provide a place for families to gather.

_____ Create a parent/family bulletin board.

_____ Give annual family awards for involvement.

_____ Create a family advisory committee.

_____ Allow families to help develop school policies and procedures.

_____ Schedule events on evenings and weekends.

_____ Provide child care for meetings.

_____ Establish a book or toy lending library.

_____ Make informal calls to families, especially to share a child's successes.

_____ Provide transportation for families who need it.

_____ Provide translators for families who need them.

_____ Send appropriate duplicate mailings to noncustodial parents.

_____ Survey families for issues of interest and need.

_____ Develop links to health and social support services.

_____ Provide resource and referral lists.

_____ Publish a school newsletter on a regular basis.

_____ Provide multilingual written communications as needed.

_____ Hire teachers with a strong commitment to supporting families and parents.

_____ Provide in-service training for teachers in working with families and parents.

_____ Hire teachers who are respectful of social, ethnic, and religious backgrounds of families.

_____ Hire staff that is reflective of the cultural background of students and families.

_____ Encourage regularly scheduled conferences between parents/family and teachers.

_____ Offer a variety of family support programs.

_____ Provide many opportunities for family members to volunteer.

_____ Provide frequent opportunities for parents/families to air their concerns.

_____ Encourage parents/families to ask questions, to visit, and to call.

_____ Encourage families to know what goes on in the classroom.

_____ Encourage families to report back on what works well.

_____ Encourage families to attend social events.

_____ Encourage teachers to make home visits.

FIGURE 8-2 A checklist for a family-oriented approach to meeting children's needs.[1]

response to family concerns should be carefully thought out. The following guidelines will help establish a supportive atmosphere for families. Again, Section 2, "Ethical Responsibilities to Families" in NAEYC's Code of Ethical Conduct can be found in Appendix A and suggests further ways to enhance collaboration between schools and families.

1   Many of the items on this list demonstrate an awareness of life in our diverse world. Can you think of others to add to make your school "parent friendly" in a diverse world?

1. *Prepare families* for what they can expect from their child's school experience and what is expected of them. School policies and a yearly calendar should be clearly written and reviewed with the family when the child first enters school so that they will know what their responsibilities are and where the school can be of assistance to them.

2. *Support all families,* including those with differing opinions. Acknowledge their concerns and questions calmly. There is a greater chance to discuss differences and effect change if there are areas where teachers and families find agreement, so try to find some common ground. Differences of opinion should be discussed out of the child's hearing, and teachers should do nothing that would undermine the family in the eyes of the child.

3. *Respect the values of all families.* Social, cultural, and religious differences, various lifestyles, family make-up, child-rearing methods, and educational philosophies are reflected in every classroom. It is important that families feel accepted. Focus on the similarities among families and develop an anti-bias approach to teaching (see Chapters 2 and 9).

4. *Keep a professional distance.* The temptation to move into a social relationship with some families in your class is one that many teachers face. You are better able to maintain a more realistic, objective picture of the child if there is some detachment. The child and the family will probably benefit the most if a close relationship is postponed until the child moves on to another class.

5. *Ask, don't tell.* Collaboration begins with the concerns of the family. A teacher's role is one of helping families clarify their own goals for their children and identifying the trouble spots, then encourage and support the family as they work together to solve the problem. Families may feel overwhelmed or inadequate if they think they must abandon their child-rearing practices. The sensitive teacher will observe the situation and help the family move toward a reasonable solution.

6. *Contact families frequently.* Keep the lines of communication open and flowing between the school and the home. Know the family members by name. Take advantage of the daily contact as they bring their child to and from school. It may be brief and breezy, but it is a good way to stay in touch. Find ways to touch base with those families who do not come to school every day, by telephone, e-mail, note, or home visit.

7. *Help families support each other.* Any group of families represents a multitude of resources and common concerns. Each family member has accumulated experiences that might prove helpful to someone else. Introducing two families to each other with the suggestion that their children play together outside of school is a good way to start. Family meetings, work parties, and potluck dinners are methods for getting families involved with one another. The teacher's role can be that of providing the setting, encouraging attendance, and then letting it happen.

8. *Enhance the family's perception of their children.* Families want teachers who know and enjoy their child, and who are an advocate for their child. That means acknowledging the child's strengths and those personality traits that are particularly pleasing. Help the family recognize the joys of parenthood rather than focusing on the burdens.

9. *Focus on the family-child relationship.* Help families learn the "how-tos" of their relationship with their child rather than the "how-tos" of academic skills. Concentrate on the nature of family-child interactions—how they get along with each other and how they interact as a family. These issues are the heart and soul of family interactions, and teachers have a role to play in enhancing the quality of those relationships.

10. *Listen to families.* Hear them out. Learn to listen to them with a degree of understanding; try to hear it from their point of view. Listen to families without judging them or jumping to conclusions; this is the basis for open communication.

FIGURE 8-3 Ten tips to effective interactions with families.

What do YOU Think?

Refer to the Code of Ethical Conduct (Appendix A) and reflect upon the Ten Tips in Figure 8-3. How is the code integrated into these guidelines? What additional guidelines would you include in this listing?

Becoming Full and Equal Partners

Families and schools are natural allies; together they claim the primary responsibility in educating and socializing children. They can and should be equal partners in that effort.

Family Support Movement

Early childhood educators have long recognized the importance of providing families with child-rearing information and support. Today, the task

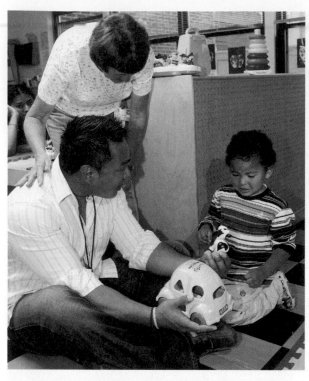

A parent's participation in his child's school life can heighten his child's sense of belonging.

Visits and participation in classroom activities are opportunities for parents and teachers to support a family-centered view of the child.

of raising children has become increasingly difficult, and the type of family education and participation is changing to meet current family's needs. What is termed a family support or "parent support" movement is evolving where the primary goal is to strengthen families to meet the challenges of parenting in the years ahead.

Parent/family education has often been achieved through lectures on discipline and guidance or age-appropriate characteristics. Family participation in school activities has been through fund raising, volunteering to help out in the classroom, and driving on field trips. Resource and referrals for children's special needs have defined family support. These are certainly important aspects of building good relationships between home and schools, but they are no longer enough for today's families. Gestwicki (2007) outlines five attitudes a teacher must have to form a successful partnership with families:

1. A concept of professionalism that believes in sharing responsibility and power with parents;

2. A strong sense of self based on clarifying their own values;

3. A sense of humility that allows them to be approachable and have an open mind;

4. A sense of compassion that recognizes the feelings families may have and the ability to empathize with them;

5. A genuine respect for others so that they treat each family with dignity as they acknowledge the family's experience and knowledge.

Factors that support the need of a more family-centered approach are: increase in the divorce rate, the growing number of single-parent families and families where both parents work, and increasing numbers of immigrant families. (See the following section, "Today's Families," and Chapter 15 for examples and discussion.) Long-held school perceptions of what constitutes a family may no longer correspond to the reality of today's definition of a family. Family support takes on new meaning when the differences in family styles are acknowledged and supported.[1] Figure 8-4 lists some important considerations for creating strong family programs.

Public Recognition

A growing awareness of the need for a family-centered approach to parent education has been recognized by several government agencies. From its beginning in 1965, Head Start mandated parent involvement as necessary for the health and welfare of many young children. More recently, the Education of the Handicapped Amendments (P.L. 99-457) in 1986

1 The more information the school has about the families of the children enrolled (preferred language, work schedules, particular challenges, areas of expertise, and so forth) the higher the likelihood of successful home-school relationships.

Four Components of a High-Quality Parent/Family Program

1. *Families and teacher collaborate* to ensure that parent/family program goals, methods, and content are responsive to family needs. The needs, concerns, and interests of families will vary according to the population the school serves. Families have many needs in common, but they do not all have the same needs at the same time. A good program for family involvement reflects those needs in the number, type, and kinds of opportunities it provides. An assessment of family needs is critical, as is family involvement in planning the program.

2. At the same time that the *familys' social services and community support networks are strengthened,* care must be taken not to overshadow the needs of the child. The interconnectedness of the child, the family, and the community must be recognized without disturbing the balance between meeting children's needs and the families needs. Teachers have a dual role of caring for and educating children while being sensitive and responsive to their families. As families and teachers develop a partnership, they should keep in mind that the children's best interests are the common goal of a good parent/family program.

3. *Programs must be tailored to the needs and characteristics of the specific family population, responding to cultural characteristics and values of ethnic populations.* To build on the family's strength and promote the family's contribution to their children's education, some programs will serve a targeted audience. Support groups for teenage parents, non-English-speaking families, and families who are working on their high school equivalency tests may be developed alongside

insights with one another are critical to only if teachers will respect their knowledge mutual respect; families have the freedom to opt for themselves.

rent/family program that promote the e equal and meaningful partnership. (From National Association for the Education

1 and 10). There is strong and active olvement at every level of school This is not surprising, since the re originally founded as parent coop-art of the guiding philosophy contin-old a model of equal and extended p. Malaguzzi (Edwards, Gandini, & 993) refers to this balanced responsi-eachers, parents, and children as a e center of education," who, in turn, he rest of the community to provide context for children's learning.

l-based management in the schools Emilia fosters meaningful participa-l families since the discussions and are made by the teachers and parents ch school setting. No area seems the property of either parents or teachers. m planning, for instance, depends on the family's involvement, interest, and contributions.

One of the best examples of school-family partnerships that bears witness to Powell's criteria for high quality programs and Gestwicki's attitudes for a successful partnership are the schools of Reggio Emilia, Italy (see discussions

Parents are the core of the individual school boards, and on the citywide school board as part

1 As American families continue to change, programs for young children will need to create linkages between family and school environments.

of an integral part of the decision making. Frequent meetings inform family's of the school's program and to bring them up to date on what their children are doing. Smaller groups of parents meet throughout the year with the teachers to talk about their children and the program; individual parent-teacher conferences, which either can request, are held to deal with specific concerns.

There are opportunities to be actively involved in the daily life of the school. Family members, teachers, and town residents build furnishings and maintain materials for the classrooms and the schoolyard and rearrange the space to accommodate program needs. In sessions with teachers and **pedagogistas**, parents learn various educational techniques necessary to the program, such as photography and puppet making, and they use these new skills in the classroom with their children. Using the whole town as a backdrop, families participate in many of the field trips to city landmarks, or as small groups visiting a child's home. Recording and transcribing children's activities and projects are often a parent's responsibility (see Chapter 10).

The meaning of family is communicated to the children of Reggio Emilia throughout their school environment. In classroom dramatic play areas and in the school's own kitchen there are displays of foods, materials, and utensils common to the region and found in the children's homes. Children are encouraged to bring special objects from home, and

Because half of the women with children younger than age six work outside the home, fathers often bring children to child care.

these are accorded special and beautifully arranged display space.[1] Photographs of children and families abound. These elements are the vehicles used to ensure a rich flow of communication between the school and the homes of the children of Reggio Emilia.

The schools of Reggio Emilia seem to have a unique reciprocal relationship with the families they serve. Family's have influence and help effect change; in turn, the schools influence and change families. Each becomes a stronger voice for what is in the best interest of the child.

TODAY'S FAMILIES

There is little preparation for the job of being a parent, and many parents feel inadequate in their role. Due to our mobile society, many couples do not live around the corner from grandparents or other family members so there is often no extended family to teach some of the traditional, time-honored child-rearing skills. There are few with whom parents can share their worries, frustrations, and concerns. So the pediatrician's phone number is etched in their minds, and they proceed to become the best parents they can.

An important change has taken place within today's young families. Raising children as a shared experience is becoming a commonly accepted way of life. Men, influenced by changing values and attitudes toward traditional sex roles, are taking an active part in raising their families. Fathers seem aware of the critical role they play in the child's life and are making appropriate changes to see that they have the time to be with their children.

Patterns of Child Rearing

Baumrind (1972) defined three types of parental styles: authoritative, authoritarian, and permissive. Authoritative parents were associated with the highest levels of self-esteem, self-reliance, independence, and curiosity in children. They provided a warm, loving atmosphere with clear limits and high expectations. In a follow-up study done when the children were eight or nine, Baumrind's findings persisted.

In contrast, authoritarian child-rearing patterns reflect high control and maturity demands combined with relatively low communication and nurturance. Authoritarian parents

  1 Diversity will be found and reflected through each child and family.

Characteristics of Successful Families

1. There is a healthy attachment and involvement with each other. Family members have a deep sense of commitment to one another and give time and attention to the family.

2. There is mutual nurturing that supports appropriate independence and healthy interdependence on one another. All family members get their needs met.

3. Self-esteem is important for all family members. It is cultivated in all interactions.

4. Effective communication allows family members to express and respond to feelings, resolve conflicts, and problem-solve together. They have the coping skills to deal with daily stress.

5. A secure, safe environment protects all family members, allowing them to connect with the rest of society in healthy ways.

6. The importance of passing on the culture, values, and goals of the family is accomplished through modeling, discussion, teaching, problem solving, and communication.

FIGURE 8-5 Enhancing healthy and successful families create a supportive atmosphere for children. (© 1993. Reprinted by permission of Pearson Education, Inc., Upper Saddle River, NJ.)

are dictatorial; they expect and demand obedience yet lack warmth and affection.

Permissive parents are essentially the reverse of authoritarian. There is a high level of warmth and affection but little control. Clear standards and rules are not set, nor are they reinforced consistently.

The positive effects of the authoritative parent model demonstrates that using reason over power, maintaining appropriate limits yet supporting appropriate autonomy, and encouraging give-and-take, create more successful children.

What makes a successful family? Gonzalez-Mena (2002) has identified characteristics that help each member function effectively both within the family and within society (see Figure 8-5). Note that these characteristics are similar to those of the authoritative child-rearing pattern.

The Changing American Family

Statistics gathered over a 35-year period show a dramatic picture of the changing American family. According to the U.S. Census Bureau, since 1970 the number of:

- divorced persons has more than tripled.
- children living with only one parent has more than doubled.
- children living with grandparents has increased 42%.
- single mothers has more than tripled.
- single fathers has increased nearly five times.
- births to unmarried teenagers nearly doubled.

The U.S. Department of Labor statistics for 2005 are equally informative regarding working mothers:

- 79% of mothers with children ages 6 to 17 are in the labor force.
- 71.5% of mothers with children ages 3 to 5 are in the labor force.
- 61% of mothers with infants (under age 1) are in the labor force.

Since the 1970s the United States has experienced a significant demographic transformation. Married couple families dropped from 69% in 1970 to 53% in 2000 (Spraggins, 2005). The challenge for the teacher is to be prepared to understand families in their various forms and to be part of a family support system.[1]

Families with Unique Needs

Parents are parents the world over and have mutual problems and pleasures as they go about bringing up their young. Their shared experiences create an automatic bond whenever they meet. There are some families who face additional challenges in child rearing and who may need added teacher support. These are:

- familes of children with developmental delays and disabilities
- single-parent families
- adoptive and foster families
- parents who both work outside the home
- divorced families
- gay/lesbian families

1   Teachers and caregivers should be familiar with the characteristics and issues that affect the families they serve and should be able to suspend any judgments based on their own ethnocentric views.

- homeless families
- teenage parent families
- grandparents raising grandchildren
- families who are raising children in a culture not their own
- families who do not speak English and whose child is in a setting where English is the predominant language
- multiracial families
- first-time-parent families
- blended and step-families

Many of these family characteristics place parents in situations where they do not have access to an extended family support system. Any one or combination of these situations can create complex challenges. Teachers should become aware of the forces at work within these families and be sensitive to their need and treat these families with the same respect as they do any other. It is not necessary to single them out, and, indeed, such an effort may be resented. For the most part, teachers can help these families by focusing on the many interests and concerns they share with other families.[1] In some cases, additional support for the family is needed, such as:

- Help them locate community resources to address their needs.
- Connect them with other families who have similar circumstances.
- Assist them in exploring school settings for the future.
- See that they are included in all school functions.
- Learn about their special needs.
- Seek their help and advice.

What do YOU Think?

Do you think parents are comfortable and welcome in the school where you work or observe? What are some stumbling blocks families might experience there? What would you change?

- Help them establish contact with other families who may be willing to assist in translating, transporting, babysitting, and sharing friendship.

Needs of Single Parent Families

2000:   26% of all children lived in families with only one parent
85% of single parents were women; 15% were men.

(U.S. Census Bureau, 2001)

Faced with the economic necessity to work, single parents must cope not only with raising children alone, but also with child care arrangements and costs. Particularly hard hit are women who head single-parent households. They are more likely than men to live below the poverty level, to never have married, not to have finished high school, and to be members of a minority population.

Single-parent families need the early childhood professional to be part of a support system for them and their children. To best serve the interests of children, educators must be sensitive to the unique aspects of raising children alone. This means reexamining school policies and attitudes that ignore the needs of single parents.[2] Overburdened child care professionals, some of whom are single parents themselves, need to be flexible in exploring new avenues of home-school collaboration. They need to ask:

- What kind of involvement in a child's classroom is possible for a working single parent?
- How can I help families feel connected even if they are unable to be at the center?
- What is appropriate support for single parents?
- How do I maintain the role of the professional, offering support, without getting involved with inappropriate friendships?
- How judgmental am I about single parents? About single mothers?
- How do I help parents and children deal with the absent parent?
- What are some of the best strategies for helping children cope with the transitions when visiting one parent or the other?

These and other similar questions must become an agenda of staff meetings, in-services for teachers, and parent/family-group meetings.

1 Many of the challenges and joys of parenting young children are universal, crossing the lines of the child's family structure, culture, ability, social class, and so on.

2 School policies can seem hostile or insensitive to the challenges faced by single-parent families (e.g., policies that require parent conferences during workday hours).

Needs of Immigrant Families

1970: 4.8% of the U.S. population was born outside of the United States.

2003: 11.7% of the U.S. population was born outside of the United States.

These immigrants come from:

Latin America	Over 50%
Asia	25%
Europe	13%
Other Regions	8%

These data from the U.S. Census Bureau (2003) highlight the extensive changes in immigration over a 35-year period. This has affected school populations across the country. A comparison from the National Center for Education Statistics (2005) tells the story in the following chart:

> 1972   22% of public school students were part of racial or ethnic minority groups
>
> 6% were Hispanic
>
> 15% were black
>
> 1% were other minority groups
>
> 2003   42% of public school students were part of racial or ethnic minority groups
>
> 19% were Hispanic
>
> 16% were black
>
> 7% other minority groups
>
> (U.S. Census Bureau: Foreign-Born Population in the United States, 2003)

The future of school population in this century will be defined by the lack of minority or majority groups. Today, about 65% of school-age children are non-Hispanic whites. That is likely to drop to less than 50% by 2040. The largest growth will occur among Hispanics, who are expected to reach 25% of the school-age population within 20 years (Olson, 2000). These data, added to existing ethnic populations already present in the United States, challenge the early childhood teacher to a multicultural sensitivity not yet realized.

These data also challenge the profession to aggressively recruit and train early childhood professionals within these cultures. A willingness to learn various cultural norms and a knowledge of languages will be helpful for teachers to communicate with children and parents whose primary language is not English.

Video VIEW PoinT 8-2

"Ethnic pride and cultural pride are important in the identity of school-age children."

COMPETENCY: Family Interactions, School, and Community

AGE GROUP: School-Age

CRITICAL THINKING QUESTIONS:

1. How does your family express its culture?

2. What are the types of family cultures represented in the school where you work or observe? How would you assist children in expressing their culture to others?

Because some studies suggest that teachers' stereotypes of social and racial subgroups influence their attitudes about a parent's ability and competence, teachers will want to examine their own biases (Powell, 1989). See the appropriate sections in Chapters 5, 9, and 10 for discussion of teacher bias, anti-bias curricula, and anti-bias environments.

Miscommunication may be a problem when teaching a classroom of diverse children. When cultural perspectives of the family and the school differ markedly, teachers can easily misread a child's attitude and abilities because of different styles of languages and behaviors. Also, teachers use classroom practices that may be at odds with a child's cultural norms. For example, in some preschool settings, children are encouraged to call their teachers by the teacher's first name. This informal style of addressing authority figures may make some parents uncomfortable. How adults and children interact with children, their teaching language, and the strategies they use to guide children's behavior are areas in which immigrant parents can help teachers learn the cultural differences that cause difficulties for children.

THE SEPARATION PROCESS

When parents leave a child at school, it may be a time of stress for all concerned. Each time this process occurs, the child, the family, and the teachers are entering into a new and unpredictable relationship.

The Child's Perspective

Each year, as school begins, a child enters a classroom and says good-bye to a parent. This is a new experience for that child, no matter how long he or she might have been enrolled in school. Even children returning to the same classroom will find some changes with which they must cope. There may be new teachers and new children along with some familiar faces or the school, teacher, and children may all be strangers. The room arrangement might be different enough to cause some anxiety. For most, school is a new and alien place. Each child will react differently to the situation, and it is difficult to predict how a child will respond. Some children will have had previous group experience to draw on; others will never have been a part of a group before.

Here are some scenes of children entering school for the first time:

Paul, clinging to his dad's trouser legs, hides his face from view. All efforts to talk with him are met with further withdrawal behind his father.

Sherry bounces in, runs from her mother over to the blocks area and begins to play there. Her mother is left standing alone, just inside the classroom.

Taryn clutches a stuffed animal as she enters school with her grandmother. She smiles when the teacher addresses her by name and looks surprised when the teacher asks to meet the rabbit she is holding. Taryn lets go of her grandmother's hand and moves forward to show the teacher her favorite toy. After a few moments, the grandmother tells Taryn good-bye, leaving her in conversation with the teacher.

The wide range of behavior these children exhibit is normal, predictable, and age appropriate. Each child has a natural way of dealing with the anxieties of coming to school. Their behavior will be as varied as they are themselves.[1]

The Teacher's Perspective

The **separation process** is one instance in which the teacher's role is to help the parents as much as the child. Parents and teachers must be especially clear with one another during this time. It is helpful to have written school policies and procedures so the teacher can go over the process step by step, on an individual basis, as each child enrolls, or at a general parent meeting held before the opening of school.

In some schools, teachers arrange to make a home visit to each child enrolled in the class before school begins. This helps the teacher know more about students before they enter school and gives children a chance to become acquainted with a teacher on their home ground.

The Family's Perspective

Most parents want their children to make a smooth transition from home to school. Adjustment is a gradual process; families need encouragement and guidance as their child moves toward independence. When families are reassured their child is acting normally, and their own anxieties are common, they relax and begin to help the child feel more comfortable.

Families encourage their child's participation in the program by asking questions and

Good communication is enhanced when parents and teachers leave notes for one another about important changes in the child's daily routine.

1 Early childhood educators are reminded regularly that there is not one right way; rather, there are many right ways.

talking together about school activities. They communicate their interest in ways to help their child meet the challenge with a minimum of stress and a maximum of enjoyment.

Working Together

In giving support and encouragement to both the family member and the child, the teacher helps them achieve independence from one another. Together, families and teachers make a plan, going over the guidelines and ground rules. The teacher takes the lead, encouraging the child to move out from the family member. The teacher is there to make the decisions regarding the time of actual separation. The parent and teacher prepare children and tell them when it is time. The teacher supports the family member's exit and stands by the child, ready to give comfort, if needed. This is a time when a teacher needs to act with conviction. Families appreciate firmness and confidence at a time when their own feelings may be *ambiguous*. Children are reassured by teachers whose attitudes express a belief in what they are doing.

Some parent-child attachment relationships are difficult to assess, and it is not always easy or obvious for the teacher to know what to do. Figure 4-5 may be helpful as a reminder of how patterns of attachment affect the separation process. For most children, the separation process is a struggle between their natural desire to explore the world and their equally natural resistance to leaving what is "safe." It is during these years that children are learning to move about under their own power and to trust themselves. Coming to school can provide each child with the opportunity to grow, starting with the separation from their family. Through careful planning, close communication, and sensitivity to one another, families and teachers will assure the child mastery of this task.

COMMUNICATING WITH FAMILIES

Parent/Family Education and Involvement

Almost any contact between the teacher and the parent can be perceived as parent/family education. Teachers interpret children's behavior to

Young children become intensely involved when parents participate in classroom activities.

their family, suggest alternative ways for dealing with problems, show them toys and games that are appropriate, hold workshops on parenting skills, mention books and articles of interest, and reinforce family interest and attention to their children's education. All of these activities are considered parent/family education. Some are planned, some are spontaneous.

Parent/family education happens frequently, whether in a class on positive discipline or in an informal chat about car seat safety, and is broadening to include any number of family support programs based on the needs of families and their children. Again, the Code of Ethical Conduct in Appendix A can be useful, especially the sections that outline the teacher's professional role to families. What does the code say about discriminating against families with unique needs or different family structures?

Keeping in Touch

There are many ways for families and teachers to increase their communication with one another.[1] In doing so, teachers demonstrate that they value the role families play in their children's lives, and families are made aware of what their children are doing in school. Five of the most common ways teachers can involve and inform families are:

1. *Classroom Newsletters.* They give a general idea of what the children are doing and

The Why and What of Classroom Newsletters

Why	What
To Keep Families Informed	Next Thursday is our first nature walk around the school and the neighborhood. Make sure your child wears boots or waterproof shoes to keep feet dry while we explore. Join us on our walk, if you can.
For Insights into Learning	The nature walk is part of our science curriculum. We want the children to explore the out-of-doors to stimulate their natural curiosity and delight in their discoveries. Firsthand experiences with the texture of tree bark or birds' nests help a child create a base of knowledge on which to build their understanding of the natural world around them.
To Bring Learning Home	You might want to try this at home with the whole family. Walk around your neighborhood and look at what is growing. Take a bag or basket to collect leaves and other natural materials. The children can make a collage out of them when you return home. Comment as the children make discoveries: "I wonder what makes the leaves so green." "What do you think happens to that flower when it snows?" Open-ended questions such as these help children clarify their own thinking and learning.
To Keep Communication Flowing	Several questions about our guidance philosophy came up at the last family meeting. We are putting together an insert for next month's newsletter and we would like your help on one of the topics. How do you deal with bedtime issues (delaying tactics, such as one more story, another glass of water, etc.) in your home? What works for you? Talk with Mrs. Olga or Miss Leona if you want to participate.

FIGURE 8-6 Classroom newsletters enlarge a family's understanding of what their child is experiencing and extends the learning between home and school.

any special events taking place in class, personal information about new babies, vacations, or other important events in the lives of the children. Be sure the newsletter is written in the language of the families in the class. See Figure 8-6.

2. *Bulletin Boards.* Posted where families can see them, these boards contain notices about parent/family meetings, guest speakers, community resources, child care, babysitting, clothing and furniture exchanges, and library story hours. Information regarding health programs, automobile and toy safety, and immunization clinics are also publicized. Post information on cultural events appropriate to the ethnic makeup of the school community.

3. *A Parent/Family Place.* Providing an area or room at the school set aside for family use can be an important step in letting families know they are wanted and needed. Some schools provide space for a parent/family lounge, complete with a library of resource books on child rearing. If there is no available space, set up a coffee bar in

the office or hall. The smallest amount of space—even a countertop with magazines—is a start.

4. *Informal Contacts.* These are the easiest and most useful lines of communication with families. All it takes is a phone call, a brief note, an e-mail, or a brief talk on a daily basis. For families who have difficulty attending meetings or who do not accompany their child to and from school, teachers can send home a note along with a sample of artwork, or a story the child has dictated, or a photograph of the child with friends.

5. *Home Visits.* Depending on its purpose, a home visit can be used to enhance communications. The visit might be set up to focus only on the relationship between the teacher and the child. Or the visit might have a purely social function—a way for teachers to meet the whole family and for them to get acquainted with the teachers. In any event, the teacher can use this as a bridge to build a pleasant, casual beginning with this family.

There are many avenues for parent–teacher communication. This bilingual bulletin board, located just outside the classroom door, holds newsletters, notices, and even children's art.

A good parent information program can inform parents of the need for greater child advocacy.

Parent/Family-Teacher Conferences

Parent/family-teacher conferences are the backbone of any good family-school relationship. They provide a way of coming together to focus on the needs of the individual child. Conferencing can be a mutually supportive link established between the adults who are most concerned about an individual child, with the purpose of helping the child reach the fullest potential possible.

Conferences between families and teachers are held for many reasons. The initial conference, when the child first enrolls in school, may focus on the family. Important information to share includes a brief overview of the child's development, daily habits, and interests, as well as the family's view of the child and their expectations. The teacher will want to assure the family that they are free to call at any time if they have questions about the school or their child. Further into the school year, both the family and teacher will want an up-to-date assessment of the child's progress, noting especially the strengths of the child and areas where improvement is needed. Several formats to help focus the discussion are cited in Chapter 6.

A conference may be called at any time by a family member or a teacher if there are concerns to discuss. A written outline listing the goals of the conference will help guide the discussion and direct it to problem areas. Every occasion when families and teachers get together to talk about a child is a step toward building trusting relationships between home and school.

For suggestions on a conference that is satisfying and productive to both parties, see Figure 8-7.[1]

Maintaining Privacy and Confidentiality

The more involved families are in the workings of the school, the more important it is to establish guidelines for protecting the privacy of all the families enrolled. Family members who volunteer in the office, the classroom, or on a field trip must understand they cannot carry tales out of school about any of the children, the teachers, the administration, or other parents. The school must be clear about its expectations for ensuring such privacy and communicate policies to families. Family members who work on advisory boards, planning committees, or other activities that allow them access to the school office should be sensitive to the confidentiality issue and respect the privacy of every family enrolled in the school.

1 All families want their children to do well yet may feel uncertain when dealing with a language and culture that is not their own.

Building Home and School Relationships through Effective Parent-Teacher Conferences

1. *Schedule conferences on a regular basis.* Parents and teachers should share some of the positive aspects of child growth and development and not meet only in crisis. This promotes better feelings about one another, not to mention the child, if meetings are at times other than when a problem occurs.

2. *Be prepared.* Discuss with the staff ahead of time any points they want to include. Gather any materials, notes, and samples of the child's work that might illustrate a point.

3. *Select a quiet place, free from interruption.* If necessary, sign up for use of a conference room. Make sure that someone is available to intercept phone calls and other appointments.

4. *Have a clear purpose.* Use a written format as a guide to keep focused on the intent of the conference. This gives a brief reminder of points to be covered and serves to keep parents on track.

5. *Put parents at ease right away.* Offer them a cup of coffee or share an amusing anecdote that just took place in the classroom. Acknowledge the important part they played in the school fair. These light, positive comments help relax both teacher and parent.

6. *Use up-to-date information and data.* Cite examples, from teacher's observations, that occurred when they were present: "Timmy is very empathic for a three-year-old; isn't he? That was so clear from the way you two were talking as you came through the door today."

7. *Give them a place to shine.* Tell them what they do well—their success with car-pool crowds or in mediating fights in the yard. If they have a special talent they have shared with the class, comment on its impact on the children.

8. *Ask—don't tell.* Get them talking by asking open-ended questions. "How is that new bedtime arrangement working?" "Tell me more about Katie's eating habits." Teachers will relate these to their own knowledge and experiences with the child and then share what has worked in school, but acknowledge the difference between school and home, teacher and parent. Learn how to listen. Concentrate on what the parents are saying. Don't listen with half an ear while planning an appropriate response or comment.

9. *Avoid blaming parents.* Keep the conversation based on mutual concerns and how to help each other. Look at some alternatives together and make a plan of action. Discuss ways to check in with each other or provide for follow-through at school or home. This way the parent will have a feeling of working together rather than of being blamed.

10. *Know where and how to secure community resources and referrals.* Many parents do not know where to get a child's speech tested, what an IQ test is, or where to secure family therapy. They may be unaware of play groups, gymnastic schools, library story hours, or children's museums. Be sure the school can provide this information for parents who need it.

11. *Take time to write a brief report after the conference.* Make special note of who attended and who requested the conference, what important issues were raised by either the parents or the teacher, what solutions and strategies were discussed, and what time was agreed upon for checking with each other regarding progress.

12. *Find a good role model.* Ask experienced teachers to share their ingredients for success. When possible, attend a parent conference with one of them. Observe what works for them and learn from their experience. Ask them to critique your own performance after a conference.

FIGURE 8-7 One of the most important responsibilities of the teacher is the parent conference. A good parent-teacher conference is focused and strengthens the relationship between home and school. (See Chapter 10.)

SUMMARY

The partnership in education between families and teacher has a long and varied history, with each partner recognizing the unique part he or she plays in the child's life. The value of sharing the information they have about the child highlights their separate but important functions.

In current practice, there is a movement to integrate parent/family education and family participation toward a more highly developed family-centered approach. An equal partnership, based on mutual respect for the strengths that both families and teachers bring to the relationship, requires a deepening of family involvement, particularly in the decision-making process.

One of the first and most intensive ways families and teachers work together is through the separation process that takes place when the child enters school. There are other basic skills teachers must have to work successfully with an increasingly diverse family population. Frequent and open communication, comfort with diversity, and planning for varied family education activities are but a few. Conferencing is a critical part of the parent/family-teacher partnership.

IT ALL STARTS WITH THE STORIES

by
Libby Miles, M.A., Ph.D.

Early childhood practitioners shine in their relationships with the children, and this is as it should be—your work with the children is the heart of what you do. Likewise, most students in a course like this one know how to build good working relationships with their own teachers. Chances are, you are as comfortable in your relationships with children as you are with your professors. But where do parents fit in? Relations among students and parents are rarely well defined and can be tricky territory to navigate. Nonetheless, it is worth it to try. All it takes to get started are a few stories.

I have been fortunate as a parent to have experienced wonderful caregivers in three different types of settings:

1. As an infant, my daughter spent several days a week with a family childcare provider.

2. As a toddler, my daughter was enrolled in a child care center owned and run by a national chain.

3. Now, as a full-fledged preschooler, Abra attends the lab school at the university where I teach.

In all three settings, I have been confident she was in good hands, that she was treated with respect and an affection for who she was at that stage of her life. In all three settings, I have learned—and admired—how sensitive caregivers connected with me as a parent. For you, as students of the field, I offer examples of some best practices culled from my three different child care experiences. Wonderful caregivers:

- Tell parents descriptive—not judgmental—stories about their children. I hunger for stories about my daughter; I want to know what she does and who she becomes during those hours we are apart. I can't get enough stories and appreciate those teachers (or the students learning to be teachers) who begin by telling me something Abra did that day. For example, she ate her own banana one day as an infant. She made up new lyrics to "Twinkle, Twinkle" as a toddler. The next day, she enjoyed painting a "bear cave." (It looked like a large brown blob to me.) At preschool, she laboriously lined up every peg during a manipulative activity, even though it took her 25 minutes to do so. Last week, she worked with friends to construct an enormous rainbow from colored paper. Each story helps me fill in the ever-changing picture of who my child is and helps me understand who my child might become.

- Exude an energetic affection for the children. The best caregivers really like the children with whom they work. They appreciate each for his or her strengths and challenges, and cheer through his or her struggles and successes. Their affection for the kids carries over into conversations with parents, often in the stories they choose to tell or the way they choose to tell them. I watch my daughter connect with the teachers who are open for hugs, with those who make their laps available for reading and cuddling, and with those who sparkle while she tells her elaborately thought-out plans.

- Ask me my name. As much as I love being "Abra's mom," I am always impressed with the college students who make a point to ask me my name. For some reason, I feel less like someone who impedes or undermines their work and more like I'm working with them. As a result, I tend to feel more comfortable with those students and often follow up with stories of my own.

- Make connections with other parts of our lives. They may say they saw us playing at the park or at a community concert. They may honk as they drive by us on campus or on the way to the grocery store. And, most importantly, they ask my daughter about everyday activities and listen attentively to her version of an event. They elicit her stories as well.

- Problem-solve with parents. Bolstered by a rich bank of stories, a strong sense of affection for the child, and an understanding that there are real constraints outside the child care setting, the best teachers engage me in helping my daughter through her current struggles, whether it is where and when to use the toilet or how to encourage her to rest quietly, or supporting her to stand up for herself when another child convinces her she is frequently wrong. With a solid foundation, we can work on these challenges together.

As I look back now, I see it all starts with the stories. Everything builds from there. Teachers (and students learning to be teachers) who take the time to tell me stories about my daughter stand out from the crowd. Teachers who illustrate for me where my daughter is in her social, emotional, cognitive, and physical development enable me to make better choices about what we can do at home. These teachers watch her, like her, interact with her, and translate their insights into stories for me since I can't be there to do it myself. Then, when she and I are together, their stories infuse what we do, how we do it, and who we are together. Those teachers and their stories have given us quite a gift.

Libby Miles, M.A., Ph.D., is a professor of writing and rhetoric at the University of Rhode Island, where she also directs the Writing Center. A working mom, she has been enriched by her daughter's committed and thoughtful caregivers. Abra, her kindergarten-aged daughter, now attends a public charter school focusing on social responsibility and environmental sustainability.

 For more activities and information, visit our Web site at http://www.EarlyChildEd.delmar.com

KEY TERMS

precedent   pedagogista   separation process

REVIEW QUESTIONS

1. What do you consider to be the most important reasons for teachers and families to have good relationships? Why should families be involved in their child's schooling? If you were a parent, how would you balance this involvement with your career and family responsibilities?

2. Describe three ways you would encourage families to participate in your classroom. Cite the advantages for the (a) children, (b) family, and (c) teacher. Are there any disadvantages?

3. What are some of your own "Myths about Parenthood"? Make two lists, one headed "Myths Teachers Have about Parents/Families" and another headed "Myths Parents/Families Have about Teachers." Compare the two and then discuss them with both a parent and a teacher.

4. What are some of the key elements in a successful family-member–child separation? What is the role of the teacher?

5. What would you do to help immigrant families feel welcome in your classroom? What are the difficulties you might have to overcome? What are the benefits to the class? To the family?

6. Describe the critical components of a high-quality parent/family education program. Give examples.

7. What is the value of a family-centered parent education program?

8. Outline what you would do in a parent/family conference that was (1) a routine get-together to discuss the child's progress, (2) to inform the family of recently observed behavioral problems, and (3) to recommend further assessment of a child's developmental delays in motor development.

LEARNING ACTIVITIES

1. Discuss the following in small groups, then share your responses with the rest of your classmates. Finish the sentences:

   a. "For me, the most difficult part of being a parent today is or would be . . . ."

   b. "When I have children, I plan to (work/stay at home/do both) because . . . ."

   c. "As a single parent, I will . . . ."

   d. "When I have children, I will raise them (just as my parents raised me/the opposite of the way I was raised) because . . . ."

2. Look at Figure 8-3, "Ten Tips to Effective Interactions with Families." Give an example of how you would apply each of the principles in your classroom. Do you see any examples of ways these guidelines are not being met in the school setting where you observe? What would you do to change that?

3. Are there ethnic minorities in your school setting? How are these families supported or not supported by school practices and policies? What changes would you make?

4. The last step in Figure 8-7 suggests that you find a good role model. Look around at the teachers you know and select one. Go through the steps suggested in number 12 and write your impressions.

5. As a teacher, how does the Code of Ethical Conduct in Appendix A influence your decision to report another teacher who uses harsh methods of behavior control and who yells at children when she is angry with them?

REFERENCES

Baumrind, D. (1972). Socialization and instrumental competence in young children. In W. W. Hartrup (Ed.), *The young child: Review of research* (Vol. 2). Washington, DC: National Association for the Education of Young Children.

Edwards, C., Gandini, L., & Forman, G., Eds. (1993). *The hundred languages of children.* Norwood, NJ: Ablex Publishing.

Galinsky, E. (1987). *Between generations.* Reading, MA: Addison-Wesley.

Gestwicki, C. (2007). *Home, school, and community relations.* Clifton Park, NY: Thomson Delmar Learning.

Gonzalez-Mena, J. (2002). *The child in the family and the community.* Upper Saddle River, NJ: Pearson Education.

LeShan, E. (1992). *When your child drives you crazy.* New York: St. Martin's Press.

Olson, L. (2000). Minority groups to emerge as a majority in U.S. schools. *Education Week,* September 27.

Powell, D. R. (1989). *Families and early childhood programs.* Washington, DC: National Association for the Education of Young Children.

Powell, D. R., & Diamond, K. E. (1995). Approaches to parent-teacher relationships in U.S. early childhood programs during the twentieth century. *Journal of Education 177,* 71–94.

Spraggins, R. E. (2005). *We the people: Women and men in the U.S. Census, special reports.* Washington, DC: U.S. Bureau of the Census.

U.S. Bureau of the Census. (March 2000). *Current population survey.* Washington, DC: U.S. Government Printing Office.

U.S. Bureau of the Census. (August 2004). *The foreign-born population in the United States: 2003. Population characteristics.* Washington, DC: U.S. Government Printing Office.

U.S. Department of Education. *The condition of education 2005. Racial/Ethnic distribution of public school students.* Washington, DC: National Center for Education Statistics.

U.S. Department of Labor. (2005). *Working in the 21st century.* Washington, DC: Bureau of Labor Statistics.

HELPFUL WEB SITES

U.S. Bureau of the Census	http://www.census.gov/population
Children's Defense Fund	http://www.childrensdefense.org
National Association for the Education of Young Children	http://www.naeyc.org
Center for Immigration Studies	http://www.cis.org
Center on School, Family, and Community Partnership	http://www.csos.jhu.edu
Especially for Parents	http://www.ed.gov/parents
National Coalition for Parent Involvement in Education	http://www.ncpie.org
Culturally and Linguistically Appropriate Services	http://www.clas.uiuc.edu
Zero to Three	http://www.zerotothree.org
Parent Soup	http://www.parentsoup.com
Child & Family Canada	http://www.cfc.efc.ca
Family Communications, Inc.	http://www.misterrogers.org

For more activities and information, visit our Web site at http://www.EarlyChildEd.delmar.com

CHAPTER

9

Creating Environments

QUESTIONS FOR THOUGHT

What does the term *environment* mean?

What criteria are used in planning the optimum environment?

What is a developmentally appropriate learning environment?

How do teachers create an anti-bias environment?

What is a self-help environment?

What is involved in an inclusive environment?

What health and safety measures must be considered when planning the total environment?

What are essential components of the physical environment?

What are basic materials for a classroom, and how are they selected?

What are adults' needs in a children's environment?

What are basic materials and equipment for a classroom and yard?

What room arrangements are appropriate and appealing?

In planning a temporal environment, what kinds of daily schedules should teachers consider?

In creating an interpersonal environment, how does the teacher create an atmosphere for learning?

WHAT IS THE ENVIRONMENT?

What does it mean to create an environment appropriate for young children? What makes up the environment? The environment is the stage on which children play out the themes of childhood: their interests, triumphs, problems, and concerns. An environment for children, therefore, includes all of the conditions that affect their surroundings and the people in it.

Each environment is unique. There is no such thing as a single model or ideal setting for all children. Each school has goals that reflect the values of its own program. When the goals and the setting mesh, the individual atmosphere of the school is created. But just what does environment mean? What do teachers mean when they say they want to create:

- environments for learning?
- optimal-growth environments?
- positive-learning environments?
- child-centered environments?
- favorable classroom environments?

Definition

The **environment** is the sum total of the physical and human qualities that combine to create a space in which children and adults work and play together. Environment is the content teachers arrange; it is an atmosphere they create; it is a feeling they communicate. Environment is the total picture—from the traffic flow to the daily

Each environment is unique, and children respond to whatever is offered. Does this equipment challenge the physical skills of young children? Is it safe for youngsters? Can it be properly supervised? For what age range would the playground be most appropriate?

Video VIEW PoinT 9-1

"The learning environment has a significant impact on how children play."

COMPETENCY: Learning Environment

AGE GROUP: Preschool

CRITICAL THINKING QUESTIONS:

1. How can you tell when children are overstimulated, and what changes would you make to the environment to address this?

2. How would you change the environment in the videoclip to provide for more self-help?

schedule, from the numbers of chairs at a table to the placement of the guinea pig cage. It is a means to an end. The choices teachers make concerning the **physical** setting (the equipment and materials, the room arrangement, the playground and the facilities available), the **temporal** setting (timing for transitions, routines, activities), and the **interpersonal** setting (number and nature of teachers, ages and numbers of children, types and style of interactions among them) combine to support the program goals.

The environments adults create for children have a powerful effect on their behavior. The environment speaks volumes to children, and their play is strongly influenced by settings and materials. Individual cubbies and children's art on the walls say "You belong here"; materials on low shelves tell children "You can do things on your own." Social interaction, independence, or imaginary play may all be fostered—or discouraged—by the ways the indoor and outdoor spaces are designed and used. The environments teachers create should be safe, effective, challenging, and in concert with the theoretical framework of the early childhood program.

"The environment," say Dodge, Colker, and Heroman (2002), "is the curriculum's textbook." It is the canvas on which children and teachers create their work. Teachers arrange the environment to promote what they feel is best in children. Early childhood educators assign significant credit to the role of the environment in their work with young children. For instance, When Reggio Emilia teachers describe the environment as a "third teacher," they are acknowledging a professional role that goes far beyond that of providing a safe and stimulating setting for children's learning. In Reggio Emilia, the environment serves an advocacy role on behalf of young children, inspiring adults—parents and community members as well as teachers—to work together to realize the potentials of children. (New, 2000)

Whether the environment is an adapted church basement, an elementary school classroom, or a space made especially for young children, it will be a powerful force in their lives.

CRITERIA FOR CREATING ENVIRONMENTS

All settings for the care and education of young children have the same basic environmental components and the same basic goals—meeting the needs of children—despite the fact that programs vary widely in the size of the group, age of children, length of day, program focus, and number of staff.

Such variation on this common educational theme is one of the reasons why our field is so diverse and interesting. Caution must be exercised, however, to ensure a quality experience for all children (Bredekamp & Willer, 1996). For instance, size does matter. Research conducted over 30 years ago (Prescott, Jones, & Kritschevsky, 1972) and corroborated more recently (Fowler, 1992) found that when a center gets too large, rules and routine guidance are emphasized, outdoor areas often have little variety, and children are often less enthusiastically involved and more often wandering. On the other extreme, too many of us know the problems associated with crowding and cramped conditions, little rooms that become "child care

The environment includes not only physical space and materials but also aspects of time and interpersonal relationships, such as who plays together and how much time they need to engage deeply in the play.

in a closet for ten hours a day" (Greenman & Prescott 1994).

Group size is recognized as one of the most important indicators of quality child care (Howes, Phillips, & Whitebrook, 1992; Bredekamp & Copple, 1997). As the National Association for the Education of Young Children (NAEYC) continues its work with accreditation of programs (see Chapter 2) and developmentally appropriate practices (DAP, see Chapters 2, 6, and 9–14), we continue the efforts to articulate what is quality for children in early childhood settings. Figure 9-1 gives recommended standards for group size and adult-child ratios. Although there are endless variations in planning for children, certain common elements must be considered:

1. the physical plant
2. available resources
3. program goals

Physical Plant

Before creating an environment for children, the early childhood teacher must analyze the physical plant. The building that is inviting and beautiful beckons children to enter; a space with color and light encourages children to play with both. Many settings use space designed for other purposes, such as a family home, a church basement, or an empty elementary school classroom. The size and shape of the designated space determine how to plan for safe and appropriate use.

To rescale the space, teachers shift from an adult perspective to a child's scale. Getting on one's knees provides a glimpse of the environment from the child's point of view; child space is measured from the floor and playground up. A child's stature determines what is available to and noticed by that child. For crawling infants, space consists primarily of the floor, whereas school-aged children can use and learn from the space up to about five feet, roughly their own height. It is this perspective that teachers must remember as they plan the physical space for children. (See the "Planning for the Environment" section in this chapter for details.)

Resources

In planning the environment, the teacher must know what kinds of resources are available. Rarely do teachers have unlimited dollars: "This year we can only afford . . ." determines many of

Teacher[a]-Child Ratios within Group Size

Age Group	Group Size									
	6	8	10	12	14	16	18	20	22	24
Infants										
Birth to 15 months[b]	1:3	1:4								
Toddlers/Twos (12–36 months)[b]										
12 to 28 months	1:3	1:4	1:4[c]	1:4						
21 to 36 months		1:4	1:5	1:6						
Preschool[b]										
2.5-year-olds to 3-year-olds										
(30–48 months)				1:6	1:7	1:8	1:9			
4-year-olds						1:8	1:9	1:10		
5-year-olds						1:8	1:9	1:10		
Kindergarten								1:10	1:11	1:12

NOTES: In a mixed-age preschool class of 2.5-year-olds to 5-year-olds, no more than two children between the ages of 30 months and 36 months may be enrolled. The ratios within group size for the predominant age group apply. If infants and toddlers are In a mixed-age group, the ratio for the youngest child applies.

Ratios are to be lowered when one or more children in the group need additional adult assistance to fully participate in the program (a) because of ability, language fluency, developmental age or stage, or other factors or (b) to meet other requirements of NAEYC Accreditation.

A group or classroom refers to the number of children who are assigned for most of the day to a teacher or a team of teaching staff and who occupy an individual classroom or well-defined space that prevents intermingling of children from different groups within a larger room or area.

Group sizes as stated are ceilings, regardless of the number of staff.

Ratios and group sizes are always assessed during on-site visits for NAEYC Accreditation. They are not a required criterion. However, experience suggests that programs that exceed the recommended number of children for each teaching staff member and total group sizes will find it much more difficult to meet each standard and achieve NAEYC Accreditation. The more these numbers are exceeded, the more difficult it will be to meet each standard.

[a] Includes teachers, assistant teachers-teacher aides

[b] These age ranges purposely overlap. Programs may identify the age group being used for on-site assessment purposes for groups of children whose ages are included in multiple age groups.

[c] Group sizes for this age group would require an additional adult.

FIGURE 9-1 Group size and staff-child ratio are two aspects of the environment that affect the quality of children's experience. (Reprinted with permission from the National Association for the Education of Young Children, *NAEYC Early Childhood Program Standards and Accreditation Criteria: The Mark of Quality in Early Childhood Education,* (Washington, DC: NAEYC, 2005), p. 83.)

the decisions made about the environment. Priority is usually given to teacher salaries and benefits, equipment and materials for the school, and other related services (maintenance, office help, bus service). Despite budget constraints, teachers must beware of operating on too low a materials budget. Lack of necessary materials can create increasingly passive, angry, and unhappy children out of sheer boredom. Only by knowing the extent of the fiscal boundaries and budget limits can a teacher plan a complete environment.

There are ways to stretch that budget, however. Good environmental principles do not depend on numerous or expensive equipment, materials, or buildings. A creative child-centered environment can happen in any setting, regardless of the lack of financial resources. Some equipment can be made, borrowed, or purchased secondhand. In church-based schools, annual rummage sales at the church provide a wealth of dress-up clothes, books, toys, and some appliances. Resource books are filled with ideas for recycling materials into usable equipment for young children. Parents and others can provide computer paper, wood scraps, or office supplies for dramatic play kits. Community sources, such as the public library storyteller or a senior citizens group, may be available for extended experiences for the children. Effective fund raising provides an added source of revenue in many schools and centers.

The human resources must also be identified. Adults do their best with children when their abilities, experience, and availability are matched with what is expected of them. Volunteers, for instance, will feel satisfied if their time is organized and spent in ways meaningful to them. A first-year teacher's resources are best expended in the classroom rather than on administrative projects. A master teacher is ready to be challenged in other ways, such as orienting parents or evaluating curriculum materials. When the entire community values its children, as in the case of Reggio Emilia, the school is a showcase, sending a strong message of how important children are in the life of its citizens. Just as we try to match children's developing skills to the tasks at hand, so, too, should we consider individual people as part of an environment's resources.

Program Goals

The program must be defined in relationship to the physical space because the goals and objectives of the program are expressed directly in the arrangement of the environment. Teachers of young children ask themselves: What sorts of goals should there be for children and families in our care? Harms (Harms, Clifford, & Cryer, 2005) names three general goals in designing environments: to plan soft and responsive settings that avoid behavior problems, to set up predictable environments that encourage independence, and to create a stimulating space for active learning. The physical space and materials should tell the children exactly what is going to happen and how they are to go about their work. In every program, consideration of what children are to accomplish puts goals and environments together.

The goals of an early childhood program will vary widely because early childhood settings contain such a wide range of age and experience. Some programs are housed in large centers, others in homes; children may attend all day or for part of the day and for educational, recreational, or even custodial reasons. The important point is that good environments for children must reflect clear and reasonable program goals. Once we know what we wish to do and why we want to do

it, we can create space, timing, and an atmosphere in which to meet those goals.

Reflecting Goals in the Environment

In creating an environment, teachers plan a program directed toward their goals:

1. The room and yard are arranged to give maximum exposure to the materials and equipment they want children to use.

2. They take care to arrange the daily schedule in ways that provide the time blocks needed to teach content when and how they want to teach it.

3. They see that a warm relationship exists among the teachers and in their interactions with children.

It is essential that teachers have a clear idea of their program goals before they begin to arrange the environment for children. When they invite children in to work, play, and learn, teachers must be sure that the way they have expressed goals through room arrangements, daily schedules, and personal styles matches what they believe. Blending all the factors that create an environment for children uses the environment to its fullest and demonstrates a belief in how and what children need for learning to occur.

If a goal of the program is to have children practice cognitive and fine-motor skills, games using prereading and writing materials should be prominent. Puzzles and table toys should have a central place in the classroom. Enough tables and chairs should be provided to accommodate all the children. Larger amounts of time should be made available for children to work on these activities every day, and teachers should be available to reinforce and encourage children as they play. Research on children's behavior in preschool settings (Moore, 1983) indicates that social participation and child involvement in activities can be influenced by equipment and materials placement, as well as by the teacher's interactive style.

When children walk into a classroom, the environment should communicate how they are to live and work in that setting. Children should receive clear messages about what they can and cannot do there as well as cues that tell them:

- where they are free to move to and where they cannot go.
- how they will be treated.

- who will be there with them.
- what materials and equipment they can use.
- how long they have to play.
- that they are safe there.
- what is expected of them.

Teachers communicate these messages in many ways. Figure 9-2 describes how teachers use the environment to tell children what is important there. For instance, when it is time to go outside, the doors are opened. If children need to stay off a piece of equipment, it is

Children Need to . . .	So the Environment Should . . .
Be treated as individuals, with unique strengths and developmental goals.	Ensure that the teacher-child ratio supports one-to-one interactions. Provide private as well as public spaces so children can experience group and solitary play. Ensure that children have ready access to teachers and materials. Be staffed by teachers who will set goals for each child on the basis of observation and assessment. Be equipped with materials that will match the developmental level of the group. Provide a balance of quiet and active times.
See themselves and their family culture represented positively in the environment; be exposed to cultural diversity in meaningful ways.	Include pictures, books, dolls, dramatic play materials, activities, and people that reflect many cultures and life experiences. Staff teachers who understand and value the children's home cultures and family practices. Provide opportunities for various cultural habits, activities, and celebrations to occur.
Have an opportunity to make choices and participate in independent learning.	Be arranged to encourage free exploration and a clear view of what is available. Offer a variety of activity centers so children can explore, manipulate, probe. Allow large blocks of time for child-initiated free play so children can make more than one choice. Provide an adequate number of trained teachers to support self-discovery.
Learn to be part of a group.	Be set up for group play with three to five chairs around the tables, easels, adjacent to one another, more than one telephone, carriage, wagon. Facilitate regular scheduling of small and large group times, which children are encouraged to attend and participate in. Include trained staff who select developmentally appropriate group activities for the group. Allow children to use each other as resources. Provide activities that will stress cooperation and social interaction.
Become responsible for the setting and take care of the equipment and materials.	Schedule cleanup times as part of the daily routine. Include teachers and children working together to restore order. Allow time for children to be instructed in the proper use of materials and be made aware of their general care.
Be aware of the behavioral limits of the school setting.	Ensure that the teachers and the daily schedule reflect the important rules of behavior. Include teachers who deal with behavior problems in a fair and consistent way. Allow plenty of time during transitions so that children can move from one activity to another without stress. Be arranged to avoid runways and dead ends created by furniture.
Be with adults who will supervise and facilitate play and encourage learning throughout the day.	Be set up before children arrive so teachers are free to greet them. Encourage teacher-child interactions through the use of small groups and a time schedule that allows for in-depth interactions.

FIGURE 9-2 The environment mirrors the goals of the program.

marked by dividers or a flag, and a teacher stationed nearby explains the instruction. Children know that they matter when they are welcomed each day, and they know their time is valued when teachers tell them how long they have to complete a project or play sequence and when that time is nearly up.

The teacher is the key element in making a creative environment. It is not the facility alone that counts, as much as the teacher's understanding of the use of all the environmental factors and how they are related to one another. The indicators of quality in a program, such as the adult-child ratio, the stability, education, and experience of the caregiver, and group size all contribute to an environment that meets its goals for children. Chapter 2 details these indicators, and Chapter 5 describes their place in teacher evaluation.

A room is just a room and a yard is just a yard until a teacher makes them environments for learning. The teachers themselves are the most responsive part of the environment; it is they who converse, hug, appreciate, give information, and see the individuality of each child. They are the ones who create the space, the time, and the atmosphere that will engage children's curiosity and involvement. Figure 9-2 summarizes these environmental goals.

Principles of Successful Environments

We are all affected by our environment, and for young children this is especially so. Since children live in the world of the senses, action, and feelings, they are greatly influenced by their immediate surroundings. While some children are particularly sensitive to stimulation (noise, light, clutter), all children's behavior is impacted by what is in front of them. Therefore, we must pay attention to what is in their environment and what happens during their stay there.

Developmentally Appropriate Learning Environments

The following are sixteen elements of such an environment:

1. *Create high-activity, low-stress, and brain-compatible environments.* In his book *Teaching with the Brain in Mind,* Jensen (1998) describes the positive changes that occur when a child is engaged in a learning experience and what happens in the brain when a threat is perceived. Rushton (2001) builds on this knowledge by suggesting that

the environment calls into use many of children's senses, choices and some autonomy, and cooperative learning. "The classroom environment determines, to some degree, the functioning ability of children's brains." Centers that allow small groups to form and focus on motor, intellectual, or social activity will stimulate learning without pressure or stress to perform or wait. "A developmentally appropriate learning environment is designed for *Individual* children to be messy, noisy and quiet, alone and social, and active and still," says Greenman (2000). "It is designed to accommodate much *Stuff*—loose parts—the raw materials of discovery for active hands and minds."

2. *Build culturally responsive environments.* First and foremost, it is important that the environment reflects the cultures of the children in the classroom. The Euro-American cultural value of independence will be expressed in aspects of a self-help environment (later in this section).

Programs and teachers that value interdependence may set up the learning environment to encourage children's reliance on adults. If the teachers don't look like the children, and their spaces don't look like home, it is critical that the interpersonal and temporal aspects of their environment complement their home culture. See Figure 9-3.

3. *Be sure children have access to enough toys and materials.* Help children imagine and live in alternative worlds, communities,

Appropriate learning environments include having enough toys in a culturally responsive atmosphere.

Overall Environment

1. In general, is the classroom hospitable?

2. What is hanging on the walls?
   If there is work done by children, does it all look alike? For example, are there bunnies or other animals that you have cut out and the children colored, or is the art *genuinely* done by the children?
   Yes _____ No _____
   Are the pictures of people hanging on walls or bulletin boards representative of a multicultural community?
   Yes _____ No _____
   Even if pictures *do* represent a diverse population, are they stereotypic in any way? For example, is there an alphabet chart that uses "Indian" to symbolize the letter "I" or a calendar that features little girls wearing dresses watching little boys involved in activities? Are there Hawaiians in grass skirts or people from South America sparsely clothed and with spears and painted faces?
   Yes _____ No _____

3. Are all of the pictures for children and the art hung *at children's eye level?*
   Yes _____ No _____

4. Are parents and/or family members involved in creating a hospitable classroom environment?
   Yes _____ No _____
   If yes, how do you include them? How might you make them feel even more a part of their children's school lives?

Blocks

1. Are the accessories in the block area representative of various cultural groups and family configurations?
   Yes _____ No _____
   List them below to be sure that no major cultural group or family configuration is missing.

2. Are the people block accessories stereotypic in terms of sex roles?
   Yes _____ No _____
   If yes, how will you change them?

Social Studies

1. Does the curriculum as a whole help the children increase their understanding and acceptance of attiudes, values, and lifestyles that are unfamiliar to them?
   Yes _____ No _____
   If yes, how?
   If no, what will you do to change your current curriculum so that it reflects a diversity of values?

2. Are materials and games racially or sex-role stereotypic—for example, black people shooting dice or

boys playing war games? Are women depicted only as caregivers while men do lots of exciting jobs?
   Yes _____ No _____
   If yes, what will you weed from your current collection? What materials and games can you add that decrease stereotypes?

Dramatic Play

1. Is there a wide variety of clothes, including garments from various cultural groups, in the dramatic-play area?
   Yes _____ No _____
   If yes, what are they?
   If no, what do you need to add?

2. Are the pictures on the walls and the props in the dramatic-play area representative of a diversity of cultures?
   Yes _____ No _____
   If yes, what is included?
   If no, what do you need to add?

3. Are the dolls in the dramatic-play area representative of a broad variety of racial groups?
   Yes _____ No _____
   If no, what do you need to add?

4. Are the dolls of color just white dolls whose skin color has been changed?
   Yes _____ No _____
   If so, which ones need replacing?

Language Arts

1. Does the classroom have a wide variety of age-appropriate and culturally diverse books and language-arts materials?
   Yes _____ No _____
   What are the strengths of the collection in general? Where are there gaps?

2. Are there stories about a variety of people from each of the following groups in the book corner?
   _____ Native-American cultures
   _____ Asian-American cultures
   _____ Black cultures
   _____ White ethnic cultures
   _____ Spanish-speaking cultures
   _____ Biracial or multiracial people
   _____ Family configurations, including biracial and multiracial families and gay and lesbian families

3. Are there any books that speak of people of diverse cultures in stereotypical or derogatory terms (e.g., describing Latinos as "lazy" or Japanese as always taking photographs)?
   Yes _____ No _____
   If yes, what are they? What new titles can you replace them with?

(continues)

FIGURE 9-3 A multicultural environment checklist provides questions for teachers to evaluate and monitor progress toward an anti-bias environment for children. (Adapted from *Diversity in the Classroom*, by F. Kendall, 2nd ed., 1996 with permission from Teachers College Press.)

Music and Games

1. Do the music experiences in the curriculum reinforce the children's affirmation of cultural diversity?
   Yes _____   No _____
   If so, how?

2. Are fingerplays, games, and songs from various cultural groups used in the classroom?
   Yes _____   No _____

3. Are there many varieties of musical instruments, including ones made by children, in the classroom?
   Yes _____   No _____

Cooking

1. Do the cooking experiences in the classroom encourage the children to experiment with foods other than those with which they are familiar?
   Yes _____   No _____

2. Are the cooking experiences designed to give young children a general notion of the connections between cultural heritage and the process of preparing, cooking, and eating food?
   Yes _____   No _____
   If so, how?
   If not, what can you do differently to help children make those connections?

FIGURE 9-3 (continued)

and homes where things are different. Show children respect by giving them the option to take care of themselves. Make sure that supplies are stored in such a way that adults do not have to hand them to children each time they will be used. Equipment placed at a child's height on open, low shelving permits children to proceed at their own pace and to select materials without depending on adults to serve them.

4. *Give children an opportunity to make choices.* Both indoors and out, children should be given an abundance of materials and a range of activities from which to choose so that they will decide how they spend their time. Choosing to play with the hamster rather than in the block corner helps children practice self-direction. Children should also be able to decide with whom they would like to play and with which teachers they would like to establish close relationships.

5. *Consider the developmental level of the children.* Recognize that there are many things young children will not be able to do for themselves, but allow them the chance to do all they can. Be developmentally aware—know what children in the class are capable of, where they are now in their development, and what the next step should be. Perhaps three-year-old Sophie can only zip her jacket now. Soon she will be able to put the zipper in the housing by herself. Recognize her readiness for taking the next step.

6. *Give families ways to identify their children's space.* Label cubbies with their names, a

photo, or a familiar picture so that they can see where to put up their wraps, artwork, and other personal belongings.

7. *See that children are responsible for caring for the equipment and materials.* Establish a cleanup time in the daily schedule and allow children time to help restore the room and yard. Label shelves and cupboards with pictures or symbols of what is stored there so that children can readily find where things belong. Outlining block cabinets with the specific shape of the blocks that are stored on each shelf will help develop children's self-help skills. Outdoor areas, clearly marked for wheel toys, help children function independently. A drying rack with large clothespins that is accessible to children tells children that they are expected to care for their own artwork.

8. *Involve children in the process of planning and setting up the environment.* Let the children help decide what they want to learn by developing areas and units around what they bring into class. For instance, if a child's pet has babies, encourage a visit and then send a newsletter asking for other pets, arranging a field trip to a pet store, and organizing a dramatic-play corner as a pet hospital or pet shop. When furniture or outdoor equipment needs moving, include the children in planning what the changes will be and then assist them in moving the pieces themselves. Make the yard more interesting by encouraging the children to rearrange climbing boards. Let them choose what game from the shed will be used that day. And the class feast is made more exciting

when the children themselves move all the tables together or plan the menu!

9. *Provide children with enough time.* One of the ways children learn is to repeat an activity over and over again. They explore, manipulate, experiment, and come to master an 18-piece puzzle, a lump of clay, or how to brush their teeth. Large blocks of time in the daily schedule—especially for routines—let children proceed to learn at an unhurried pace.

10. *Allow children to solve their own problems without adult intervention whenever possible.* See how far a child can go in discovering how to manipulate a pin so that it will close or to work out with another child who will use the red paint first. In solving social or mechanical problems, young children can begin to find out for themselves what is or is not successful. One mark of a good teacher is a person who can let a child struggle sufficiently with a problem before stepping in to help.

11. *Accept children's efforts.* To support children in their quest for independence, the adult must be satisfied with children's efforts and be ready to accept the way that Tom made his sandwich or that Shelley put her boots on the wrong feet.

12. *Communicate expectations. Let children know what they are expected to do.* Tell them in both verbal and nonverbal ways. "You don't have to hurry; we have plenty of time for cleanup" lets children know they can do a job without pressure. Prompt children by giving them clues that indicate how to proceed: "If you pull up your underpants first, it will be easier to get your trousers up," can be said to Raymond who is waiting for an adult to dress him. Give him feedback on what is working. "Good. You've got the back up. Now reach around the front." Focus on how Raymond is succeeding and communicate your confidence in his ability to finish the task.

13. *Be sure staff expectations are consistent.* The teaching team should set common goals for each child and reinforce them consistently. Janice will become confused if one teacher tells her to get her cot ready for nap and another teacher does it for her.

14. *Make it safe to make a mistake.* Children learn from their own actions and their own experiences. Let them know it is perfectly acceptable, indeed inevitable, that they will

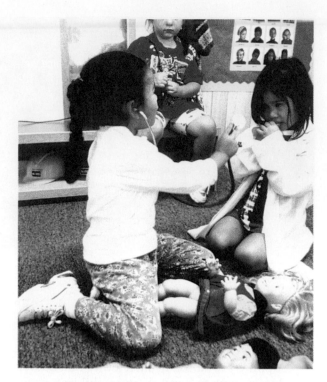

Allowing children to solve their own problems without interference is one principle of successful educational environments.

at times make mistakes. Children need to be accepted for who and what they are, and this includes when they are in error. Help them deal with the consequences of their mistakes. Adults in the preschool can provide models for children in coping with unexpected results and how to bring forth a positive resolution. When Chelo spills her juice, she is encouraged to find a sponge and clean up the table. The teacher reinforces Chelo's efforts and comments on her scrubbing ability or her swift action in preventing the juice from going on the floor.

15. *Give credit where it is due.* Provide feedback so that children will know when they have been successful. Compliment Chaz on the length of time he took sorting through the nails to find the one he wanted. Tell Ellen she worked hard at opening her own Thermos bottle. Let children take some credit for their own accomplishments.

16. *Let children teach one another.* Encourage children to share the skills they have mastered with their peers. Actively seek out each child's way of doing things; support a diversity of approaches. Those who can tie shoes enjoy helping their friends with stubborn laces or slippery knots. Whether reading or telling stories to one another, or showing a

friend a fast way to put on a jacket, children benefit from helping each other.

Adults who work with children should remember to interact with children in ways that will help them grow toward independence. To perceive children as helpless is to rob them of the satisfaction of achievement. A well-planned environment opens up infinite possibilities for children to achieve a feeling of self-satisfaction while they explore the boundaries of their own beings. Chapters 1 and 5 expand on educational ethics that serve as guidelines in working with children; Chapter 6 gives suggestions for how to evaluate children, teachers, and programs to check that these goals are met.

A final note: The environment in which children grow and learn should also be visually appealing and relaxing. There are so many assaults on our visual senses in schools: concrete, barred windows, heavy doors, tiny windows, clutter and chalkboards, to name a few. Children become numbed to balance, shape, form, line and color. While resources are limited, beauty does not need to be ignored. The environment is one of the few things that teachers can control and use to the children's (and adults') advantage.

The Anti-Bias Environment

Among the core values (see Appendix A) in any good early childhood program is the recognition of each child as unique, as deserving of respect, and as a part of a family.[1] Each child has the right to achieve full potential and to develop a positive self-esteem. Each family deserves support for the unique role it plays. Part of the commitment of the early childhood teacher is to help children learn to value one another's uniqueness, the differences as well as the similarities. Teachers do this, in part, by expressing such inclusive attitudes. Early learning standards (Gronlund, 2006, NAEYC, 2002) should be flexible enough to encourage teachers to embed culturally relevant experiences in the curriculum. Adaptations to standards will then promote success for all.

The anti-bias curriculum, developed at Pacific Oaks College, encourages children and adults to:

- Explore the differences and similarities that make up our individual and group identities, and

- Develop skills for identifying and countering the hurtful impact of bias on themselves and their peers (Derman-Sparks & the ABC Task Force, 1989).

The physical and interpersonal environment can be used to help children see that culture consists of the various ways people do similar activities. This approach is different from the "tourist curriculum," which provides only superficial information that is often detached from the child's own life. It is also different from an approach that is based only on the interests of the class and gender, racial, and cultural groups represented therein. The anti-bias environment incorporates the positive aspects of a multicultural curriculum and uses some of the activities that highlight other cultures, but it provides a more inclusive, ongoing approach. This approach avoids patronizing or emphasizing trivial, isolated, exotic differences. There is an inherent feeling of fairness to self and others in the anti-bias approach, as children explore the many ways people do the basic human tasks of everyday life. Think of the diverse cultures expressed in how babies and things are carried from place to place in different parts of the world. How many ways do people eat? Cook? Shop for food?

A value common to all early childhood programs is expressed in this anti-bias curriculum: that every person matters, so diversity is valuable and peaceful, and just cooperation among all is possible. The key here is the belief that "unity is the completed puzzle, diversity the pieces of the puzzle" (Hernandez, 1991). In this curriculum, the environment and the activities are derived from three sources: the children and their activities, the teachers' awareness of the developmental needs and learning styles of the group, and societal events. Teachers, of course, make general selections of what children are to learn and arrange the environment for learning to begin. Then, the environment, which includes the children themselves, begins to change. If children are especially interested in making things, perhaps the theme "All people live in homes" emerges, with activities that focus on how people build things, what they use the buildings for, and how they work to get something built.

Lessons about children's identity and budding attitudes concerning race, gender, disability, and age are learned early in life. With the

---

 1 The anti-bias and inclusive environments encourage children to learn tolerance and acceptance of the diversity in our world.

prevalence of stereotyping in society, and the impact of bias on children's development (Cross, 1985; Gutierrez, 1982; Kutner, 1984), early childhood educators have a responsibility to find ways to prevent, even counter, the damage done by such stereotyping. Teachers do this by arranging an anti-bias physical environment, as well as creating an atmosphere of problem-solving and learning in the day-to-day conflicts and interactions that arise naturally. Think about how teachers provide the materials and encourage an atmosphere of trust and time for conflict resolution in these examples:

> A kindergarten teacher shows the children a magazine picture entitled "Brides of America." All of the women pictured are Caucasian. She asks, "What do you think of this picture?" Sophia responds, "That's a silly picture. My mom was a bride, and she's Mexican." (Derman-Sparks et al., 1989)

> A toddler teacher sets up the water play table for washing babies. Choosing dolls that represent several racial and ethnic groups, she invites the children to soap and rinse them. One two-year-old begins to wash the teacher's arm, then scrubs it hard. "Do you wonder if my color will wash off?" the teacher asks. The child nods, and several others look up. "Does it? Go ahead and try. . . . See, a person's color is her own and stays with her. Try yours, too. That's one way people look different: we all have skin, and yet we each have our own color." (Gutierrez, personal communication, 1987)

The anti-bias approach to creating environments has its roots in the theories of Maslow, Piaget, and Erikson (see Chapter 4). Research data reveal that children begin to notice and construct classifications and evaluative categories very early; indeed, two-year-olds begin to notice gender and racial differences and may even notice physical disabilities (Froschl, Rubin, & Sprung, 1984; Honig, 1983). Early childhood programs must develop a child's basic sense of trust and mastery so that children can learn to understand themselves and become tolerant and compassionate toward others. Figure 9-3 is a multicultural classroom environment checklist that can help teachers evaluate their environment.

A Place at the Table

The anti-bias approach takes a broad view of a classroom, as a kind of "mini-society" in which children and adults work together to form a just world. There is a place for everyone at the table, no one is left out, but conflicts and problems are solved.

Further, injustices from the outside world are sometimes addressed. For instance, in one "anti-bias" video, a teacher helps children ticket parents' cars who improperly park in the class-made handicapped parking space (Derman-Sparks, 1989). See Figure 9-3.

An anti-bias classroom fosters:

● *Positive self-concept.* Curiosity and creativity stem from being able to affect the environment and what is in it. When Jamal says his baby's hair is fuzzy like his, his smile tells how good he feels about it.

The anti-bias environment encourages girls and boys to play together, respecting differences and including others in new ways.

- *Awareness.* All people have interests and feelings, both about themselves and about others. Yoko notices that her classmate Julie runs and throws her arms around her dad, but she prefers a less demonstrative greeting.
- *Respect for diversity.* This stems from the ability to classify similarities and differences and then to appreciate both. For example, when the children create self-portraits for their class books, some choose different colors of paper for drawing faces, but all of them use the same markers to draw in their features.
- *Skills in communication and problem-solving.* Learning how to express thoughts and feelings includes being able to hear others and finding peaceful ways to resolve conflicts. Jim and LaNell are quick to tell Eben he can't play, but they find out that telling him he is "too little" does not work. He does not accept that simply being three years old is enough reason to leave him out, and they must either try to include him or make a claim for privacy.

As Elizabeth Jones (personal notes, 1984) states:

> The pluralistic view assumes that (1) people are different from each other and (2) differences are valuable; they add to the richness of everyone's experiences. The task of the worker with children, then, is to acknowledge and appreciate differences. The developmental view assumes that growth and learning are spontaneously motivated. The task of the teacher is to provide a supportive environment that frees each individual to grow and learn—to empower children so that they will assert their needs and develop thoughtful strategies for meeting them.

The Self-Help Environment

One common goal in most early education programs can be demonstrated through the careful use of environmental factors. Promoting self-help and independent behavior in children is a widespread practice. In planning the environments, teachers attempt to create situations and settings where this is likely to happen.

A **self-help** environment has as one of its fundamental goals the development of children's own skills—fostering their mastery of basic abilities that will allow them to become responsible for their own personal care, their own learning, their own emotional controls, their own problem solving, and their own choices and decisions. A self-help environment gives children the feeling that they are capable, competent, and successful. It allows children

to do for themselves, to meet the challenge of growing up. A self-help environment reflects the belief that autonomy and independence are the birthright of every child.

I Can Do It Myself

Nothing renders people more helpless than not being able to maintain their own needs or to take care of themselves in basic ways. Children are still in the process of learning about what they can and cannot do. They need many different kinds of experiences to help them learn the extent of their capabilities. Most of all, they need adults who understand their tremendous drive to become self-reliant, adults who will not only encourage their abilities and provide the time for them to practice skills, but adults who understand that it is the nature of the child to develop this way.

Self-concept is based on what we know about ourselves, which includes the ability to take care of our own needs. To care for oneself, to feel capable of learning, to solve problems, are all related to feelings of **self-esteem**. Self-esteem is the value we place on ourselves; how much we like or dislike who we are. Helping children achieve a positive self-concept and self-esteem is the most important part of teaching. The development of a strong sense of self-esteem is a lifelong process; its origins are in the early years.

For all of these reasons, teachers establish settings that promote self-help. They want children to feel good about themselves and they want to foster that growing sense of self-esteem. This happens in classrooms that allow children to do what they are capable of doing. For the teacher, the reward comes from each child who says, "I can do it all by myself."

Planning an environment designed to promote self-help skills is the teachers' responsibility. Every aspect of the environment, from the room arrangement to the attitudes of the teachers, supports children in doing all they can for themselves. Each activity is designed to foster self-reliance, thereby building self-esteem. The supermarket is a good example of an environment created for maximum self-reliance. Shelves are accessible and the products are clearly marked and attractively displayed. It takes that kind of thoughtful preparation to create space that says to children, "Do me. Master me. You are capable." Teachers want to communicate to children that they value self-help skills as much as they appreciate an art project or science experiment. The ultimate goal is for children to see self-reliance as valuable. If Claudia feels that learning to tie her shoes is worth doing just because of the pleasure it gives her to manipulate the strings, weave them through the holes, and bring them together in a knot, then that becomes her reward. She becomes capable of reinforcing herself and leaves the way open for adults to praise her for other important learnings.

The Inclusive Environment

In 1975, the Education for All Handicapped Children Act (P.L. 94-142) called for an end to segregation for disabled students from kindergarten through high school. This policy filtered down to preschools and child care centers, and in 1986 an amendment made to this bill (P.L. 99-457) mandated that preschoolers with special needs be placed in the **least restrictive environment**. The practice of placing children with disabilities in the same classroom as children without disabilities is called *mainstreaming*. A more comprehensive method is known as *full inclusion,* in which both typically developing children and children with diverse abilities are taught together by a teaching staff with expertise in both normal child development and special education (see Chapters 3 and 8). The Americans with Disabilities Act of 1990 prohibits child care centers from denying admission to a child simply because the child has a disability. Together, these federal laws form part of the rationale for early childhood centers to become more inclusive environments.

Children with diverse abilities need the same things in their environment as their more typically-developing peers. They need an environment that is safe, secure, and predictable and one that provides a balance of the familiar and novel, so that there are materials and activities that provide for their development. "When a child with disabilities has different developmental needs than other children of the same age, adaptations must be made" (Youcha & Wood, 1997). These may require either adding something to the environment that is not already there or using something in the environment in a different way. Our Code of Ethical Conduct supports "the right of each child to play and learn in an inclusive environment that meets the needs of children with and without disabilities" (NAEYC, 2005).

Adaptations are changes that make the environment fit the child better, so they will vary with the children. Children with motor disabilities need different adaptations than those with hearing or language disabilities or with visual impairments. Physical changes may be necessary, modifications in the schedule may be recommended, or individualizing activities may be best. Parents will be the best source of information about the child, and other reading or specialists can be further guides. Three key concepts are helpful to remember: access, usability, and maximizing learning.

- Can the child get where she needs to be in the classroom to learn something?
- Once the child is in that location, can she use the materials and equipment and participate in the activity as independently as possible to learn something?
- Are the learning activities arranged and scheduled to meet the individual learning needs of the children, including the child with disabilities? (Youcha & Wood, 1997)

Figure 9-4 is an abbreviated checklist for adaptations to create an inclusive environment.

Come Together for a Child

Consider Andrew (Rogers, 1994), who, at five years of age had a motor/muscle disability with some speech difficulties. His cognitive skills were very strong and his social skills very weak. Andrew's mother talked to everyone during class about Andrew's needs and fears. If he fell down, he had a hard time righting himself. He needed help sitting and standing. He was afraid of getting bumped because he couldn't catch himself before falling very hard and then could not get up. The children all agreed to be careful about **roughhousing** around him. *The setting for success was being created.*

Because Andrew did not have much control of his fine-motor skills, we provided him with painting and play-dough. We kept up the crafts table; soon he was gluing pictures on paper, with or without order, and was very proud of his accomplishments. He even started using scissors on simple patterns. *The physical environment was responding to his needs.*

He was a wonderful puzzle builder, and the other children asked for his help often when they were stuck. It was wonderful to watch how they included him in many things. They accepted his differences right from the beginning and treated him just like all the rest—except they were careful when running and playing around him. His fear was apparent, and they respected it. *Thus the interpersonal environment was emerging.*

Checklist for an Inclusive Environment

Physical Environment

Questions to think about:
- How do different children use their bodies or the space around them for learning?
- How can we enhance or adapt the physical environment for children who have difficulty moving (or who move too much)?
- How can we capitalize on the physical environment for children who learn by moving?

Accessing the environment safely:

- ☐ Are doorway widths in compliance with local building codes?
- ☐ Ramps in addition to or instead of stairs?
- ☐ Low, wide stairs where possible (including playground equipment)?
- ☐ Hand rails on *both* sides of stairs?
- ☐ Easy handles on doors, drawers, etc.?
- ☐ At least some kids' chairs with armrests?
  - "Cube" chairs are great!
  - Often a footrest and/or seat strap will provide enough stability for a child to do fine-motor activities.
- ☐ When adapting seating, mobility, and/or gross-motor activities for a specific child with physical disabilities, consult a physical therapist.

Learning through the environment:

- ☐ Do the environment and equipment reflect variety?
  - Surfaces, heights (textured, smooth, low, high, etc.).
  - Space for gross-motor activity (open spaces, climbing structures, floor mats).
  - Quiet/comfort spaces (small spaces, carpet, pillows).
  - Social spaces (dramatic play area, groups of chairs or pillows, etc.).
- ☐ Are toys and equipment physically accessible?
  - Glue magnets to backs of puzzle pieces and attribute blocks and use on a steel cookie tray.
  - Attach large knobs or levers to toys with lids, movable parts.
  - Attach tabs to book pages for easier turning.
- ☐ An occupational therapist can provide specific suggestions for adapting materials and activities so a child with physical disabilities can participate.

Visual Environment

Questions to think about:
- How do different children use their vision for learning?
- How can we enhance the visual environment for a child with low or no vision?
- How can we capitalize on the visual environment for children who learn by seeing?

Accessing the environment safely:

- ☐ Are contrasting colors used on edges and when surfaces change (e.g., tile to carpet, beginning of stairs, etc.)?
- ☐ Can windows be shaded to avoid high glare?
  - Also consider darker nonglossy floors and tabletops.
  - Some children's behavior and learning may improve dramatically once a strong glare is eliminated.
- ☐ Is visual clutter avoided on walls, shelves, etc.?
  - Visual clutter can interfere with learning, predictability, and safety.
- ☐ Is "spot lighting" (e.g., swing arm lamp) in a dimmer room available?
  - Spot lamps help some children pay attention and work better on table tasks.
- ☐ Orientation and mobility specialists help children with visual impairments learn to navigate the environment.

Learning through the environment:

- ☐ Are objects and places in the environment labeled ("door," "chair," etc.)?
- ☐ Are the size and contrast of pictures and letters adequate for the children with visual impairments in your program?
- ☐ Are visual displays at the children's eye level?
- ☐ Are large-print materials, textured materials, and auditory materials available (e.g., big books, sandpaper letters, books on tape)?
- ☐ Is the daily schedule represented in words and pictures?

(continues)

FIGURE 9-4 When designing an inclusive environment, keep in mind that the environment needs to be safe and to help everyone participate, learn, and communicate. (Adapted from Haugen, K. (1997, March).)

- A Velcro schedule that allows children to post the schedule and then remove items as activities are completed can help children to stay focused and make the transition more easily from one activity to the next.
- ❑ Are children with low vision seated close to the center of activity and away from high glare?
- ❑ Teachers for the visually impaired assist in selecting and adapting materials for children with low vision.
- ❑ Children who are blind may need a "running commentary" of events, places, etc. Pictures in books and food on plates, for example, should be described.

Auditory Environment

Questions to think about:
- How do different children use their hearing for learning?
- How can we enhance the auditory environment for a child who is deaf, hearing impaired, or has poor auditory discrimination skills?
- How can we capitalize on the auditory environment for auditory learners?

Accessing the environment safely:

- ❑ Does background noise (from indoor or outdoor sources) filter into the area?
- ❑ Is there a way to eliminate or dampen background noise (using carpeting, closing windows and doors, etc.)?
  - Some kids are unable to do the automatic filtering out of background noises.
- ❑ Is "auditory competition" avoided?
  - Raising one's voice to compete with a roomful of noisy children is rarely as effective as using a "silent signal," for example, holding up a peace sign and encouraging children who notice to do the same until the room is full of quiet children holding up peace signs!
- ❑ Are nonauditory signals needed to alert a child with a hearing impairment?
  - Turning the lights on and off is a common strategy.
  - Ask the child's parents what strategies are used at home.

Learning through the environment:

- ❑ Are auditory messages paired with visual ones (e.g., simple sign language, flannel boards, picture schedules)?
- ❑ Are children with hearing impairments seated so they can see others' faces and actions?
- ❑ Teachers for the hearing impaired can provide strategies for modifying activities for children with hearing impairments.
- ❑ A child who is deaf and communicates through sign language will need a teacher or aide who uses sign language.

Social Environment

Questions to think about:
- How do different children use social cues for learning?
- How can we adapt the social environment for children with impulsive behavior, attention deficits, or other behavior problems?
- How can we capitalize on the social environment for children who learn by relating to others?

Accessing the environment safely:

- ❑ Is the schedule predictable? Are children informed of schedule changes?
- ❑ Does the schedule provide a range of activity levels (e.g., adequate opportunities for physical activity)?
- ❑ School psychologists and behavior specialists can help analyze misbehavior and modify the environment or schedule to minimize problems for children with attention deficits or behavior problems.

Learning through the environment:

- ❑ Does the environment have a positive impact on self-esteem?
  - Allows all children to feel safe?
  - Invites all children to participate?
  - Maximizes all children's opportunities for independence?
- ❑ Do learning materials and toys include representations of all kinds of people, including children and adults with disabilities?
  - People with disabilities should be represented in active and leadership roles, not just as passive observers.
- ❑ Does the schedule include opportunities for a variety of groupings (pairs, small groups, whole class) as well as quiet time or time alone?
  - Pairing or grouping children with complementary abilities eases the demands on the teacher and enables children to help one another.
  - When given a chance, peers often come up with the most creative ways for children with disabilities to participate.
  - Creative use of staffing may be needed to provide additional support for some children during some activities.
- ❑ Does the schedule provide both structured and open activity times?
  - Children who have difficulty with a particular type of activity may need extra support at those times.

FIGURE 9-4 (*continued*)

We had a regular P.E. time each day in the big room. We jumped rope, played "Simon Says," played "Red Light, Green Light," and ran obstacle courses. At first Andrew sat on the sidelines and watched. He cheered and looked interested, so I started asking him if he'd be my partner because I was a little afraid. At first he refused and told me to use someone else. I kept asking but would drop it as soon as he gave me his answer; then one day he said, "OK." We ran and jumped over the snake (rope), and all the kids laughed. We hugged, and that was the beginning. *When given the time that is needed (the temporal environment), the child triumphs.*

PLANNING FOR THE ENVIRONMENT

Who Is in the Environment?

Many people live and work in the early childhood environment. Cooks, bus drivers, office personnel, yard and building maintenance people are but a few. Each of these persons has special demands on the environment to do the job they are hired to do.

Teachers, parents, and children have the greatest influence on the early childhood environment; their needs are outlined in this section.

Children

Children's needs are met through the environment. The physical, social, emotional, and intellectual requirements of children suggest the type of building, the size of the furniture, the choice of equipment, the size and age range of

Children develop a sense of self when they have their own space, labeled with a photo or other visual clue so that they can easily identify it as their own.

the group, the number of teachers who lead and supervise, and the budget allocations. Guided by child development principles, teachers match the setting to the children who will learn and play there. The individuality of a particular group of children, of a school, and of its philosophy is expressed by the arrangement of the environmental factors. First and foremost, though, are the questions: Who are the children who will use this space? What are their needs? How can those needs be met in this particular setting?

Teachers

What has been done to meet the needs of the teachers? Do they have an office? A teachers' room? A place to hold conferences? Where do they keep their personal belongings or the materials they bring to use at school? Do they have a place to park? All teachers need room to create curriculum materials, to evaluate their programs, to review other educational materials, to meet with their peers. Research (Whitebrook, 1996) indicates that the working environment of caregivers (including the general context of the setting, opportunities for professional development, status, and wages) are important predictors of the quality of care children receive. How well teachers are provided for helps to determine the atmosphere they will establish in their classrooms. Adult space indoors is described in more detail later in the chapter.

Parents/Families

The needs of parents and other adults in children's families will differ, depending on whom the program serves. Adults who bring their children to child care or school need adequate and safe parking facilities. In settings where adults are free to stay, a reading room, resource library, or a comfortable place to talk with others is desirable. Those who participate in the class are welcomed by a teacher, shown a place to put their belongings, and given a name tag and appropriate directions.

There are many reasons parents may need to contact the school or center. Are there ways to reach teachers and children in emergencies? How welcoming is the environment as they enter the building? The office? The classroom? What does the environment say about family involvement and interest?

The teacher can make the school environment accessible and welcoming in several ways. Posting telephone numbers at which school authorities and teachers can be reached when

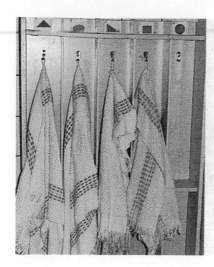

On the left, towels are color coded in easily recognizable shapes in a Russian child care center. On the right, toothbrushes and towels are accessible so that children in the Reggio Emilia centers in Italy can help themselves. (Courtesy of the city of Reggio Emilia, Italy.)

the school is closed assures parents that teachers are available whenever needed. A bulletin board for community notices and for family use can be put up along with mail pockets. Written communication can go between parents and teachers and among families. Working with families is vital to creating both an anti-bias and a self-help focus in children's education and care. Teaching from these perspectives is more likely to create positive changes in children's lives when families are included in the process. The classroom that offers parents both an authoritative teacher and other useful resources helps them feel that their children are important.

Health and Safety in the Environment

Regardless of how many children are in the setting and for how long, the first priority is to provide for their health and safety. Health, safety, and nutrition are closely related because the quality of one affects the quality of the others (Marotz, Rush, & Cross, 2001). Therefore, programs for children must establish policies that provide for the protection, service, and education of child health and safety at all times. Government regulations and professional recommendations vary, but all establish some kind of standards to ensure good health and safety practices. Key documents are noted in the reference section of this chapter.

Keeping Children Healthy

Sanitation. When groups of people live in close quarters, proper sanitary conditions are imperative to prevent the spread of disease. For an early childhood center, the physical plant must have adequate washing and toileting facilities for both children and adults. The number and size of toilets and wash basins are usually prescribed by local health or other regulatory agencies. Children don't realize their role in spreading germs, especially as their moist and warm hands touch and handle everything. Through gentle reminders and role modeling, teachers help children learn the habit of washing their hands at important times such as before snack and mealtimes.

The classrooms require daily cleaning, and equipment that is used regularly should be sanitized on a periodic basis. Nontoxic paint must be used in all circumstances, including on outdoor equipment, cribs, and for art activities with children. Classroom dress-up clothing, pillows, nap blankets, and cuddle toys all need regular laundering, either at school or at home.

The nature of preventive health care in educational settings has expanded in the last decade. Knowledge of how disease is spread and concern over infectious diseases such as hepatitis B and infection by the human immunodeficiency virus (HIV) have increased awareness of the kinds of practices teachers must engage in on a daily basis. These include hand washing (the number-one way to prevent unnecessary spread of germs) and an approach known as *Universal*, or *Standard Precautions*.

Because we cannot be guaranteed of the infectious state of an individual, it is very important to always follow universal safety procedures with all children. The steps that keep a barrier between persons and blood can apply to more than blood-borne infections. All programs should be equipped with sets of latex gloves and plastic bags to properly handle and dispose of anything with blood or fecal material. Because intact skin is a natural barrier against disease, it may not always be necessary or possible to use gloves, but it is essential that hands be washed immediately after any toileting activity. All areas for eating, diapering, and toileting must be cleaned and sanitized, using a bleach solution after cleaning away visible soiling.

Temperature, Ventilation, and Lighting. Heating and ventilation should be comfortable for the activity level of the children and should change when weather conditions do. Adequate, nonglare lighting is a necessity. Studies indicate that uniform, fluorescent lighting may not be the best environment for children; therefore, a mixture of lighting such as is in homes is preferable (Alexander, 1995). Rooms should have some means of controlling light (shades, blinds). Cross-ventilation is necessary in all rooms where children eat, sleep, or play. Proper heating and insulation are important.

Communicable Disease. This is an important issue when dealing with young children in group care. Some people question the advisability of early group care on the grounds that it exposes children to too much illness. Others claim that such exposure at an early age helps children build up resistance and that they are actually stronger and healthier by the time they enter primary grades. In the largest U.S. study to date on children's health, the Centers for Disease Control and Prevention concluded that, although infants and toddlers face a higher risk of colds and viruses, day care was not seen as increasing children's illnesses at older ages and not a risk overall (CDC, 1997).

Parents should be notified when normal childhood diseases (such as chicken pox) or common problems (such as head lice) occur in the classroom. Infections of special concern to adults include chicken pox, hepatitis A, and cytomegalovirus (CMV). A description of the symptoms and the dates of exposure and incubation period may be helpful to parents. They can then assist the school in controlling the spread of the disease in question.

In group care, children can contract a fair number of colds and viruses, especially when they are eating and sleeping close to each other. Figure 9-5 summarizes the 10 most common

Condition	Tips
1. Allergies and asthma	Post a list of all children with chronic conditions; check ingredient lists on foods; watch what triggers reactions.
2. Scrapes and cuts	Reassure and sympathize with child; supervise child's washing with soaped pad and caring comments; use packs of ice or frozen peas in towel for swelling.
3. Bumps on the head	Notify parents of any loss of conciousness and watch for signs for two to three days.
4. Sand in eyes	Remind child "Do not rub!," have child wash hands and cover eyes with tissue; normal eye tearing will bring sand to inside corner of eye; remove with clean tissue.
5. Splinters	Clean area with alcohol and remove with tweezers or cover with adhesive strip and let parent remove.
6. Conjunctivitis	"Pinkeye" is highly contagious; watch for excess eye rubbing and red eyes; have child wash hands; isolate with washable toys until parent takes child home and gets treatment.
7. Head lice	Distressing but not dangerous; wash shared clothing, stuffed animals, bedding; vacuum rugs and furniture; remove hats, combs, and brushes from dramatic-play area; send notices home and inspect children's hair for two to three weeks.
8. Chicken pox	Isolate child until parents pick up; alert all parents about contagious period; watch for signs on all children for three weeks after exposure.
9. Strep throat	Send home notices; wash all equipment that might carry germs.
10. Lingering coughs	At onset, send child home until evaluated; frequent drinks will soothe; coughs may last up to two weeks; if longer, may suggest infection or allergy.

FIGURE 9-5 Teachers need to be trained in first aid and cardiopulmonary resuscitation (CPR); in addition, a working knowledge of common health problems in school helps the teacher care for children. (Adapted from Needlman, R., & Needlman, G. (1995).)

health problems in school, with tips for dealing with them. The school and its staff have responsibility to ensure that good health standards are instituted and maintained to keep illness to a minimum.

Health Assessment and School Policies.

Every early childhood center should establish clear health policies and make them known to parents. A daily inspection of each child will help adults spot nasal discharge, inflamed eyes, and throat and skin conditions of a questionable nature. This daily check will screen out more serious cases of children too ill to remain at school and may be done by a teacher, nurse, or administrator. Educating parents about the warning signs of illness will encourage sick children to be cared for at home.

It is very important for the school to inform parents about what happens when children are refused admittance or become ill during the school day. Every school should provide a place for sick children where they can be isolated from others, kept under supervision, and be made comfortable until they are picked up. For their part, parents must arrange to have sick children cared for elsewhere if they are unable to take them home. School policies on these issues must be explicit and upheld consistently and compassionately, for the sake of all the children.

Teachers must be sensitive to parents' feelings and situations when sending a sick child home. This situation often produces guilt feelings in parents and work-related stress. Working parents may need school assistance in locating alternatives for care of a sick child.

Most schools require, under state or local laws, a doctor's examination and permission to participate in an early childhood education program before a child can enter the program. This includes a record of immunizations and the child's general health. Parents, too, should submit a history of the child, highlighting eating, sleeping, and elimination habits. It is critical to note any dietary restrictions or allergies and then post them in the classrooms for a reminder.

Nutrition.

What children eat is also important for proper health. Places where food is prepared and stored must be kept especially clean. The child who has regular, nutritious meals and snacks will likely be healthier and less susceptible to disease. Many children do not have the benefits of healthy meals and snacks. Some do not receive adequate food at home; others are used to sugar-laden treats and "fast foods." Education about nutrition becomes the responsibility of a school that is concerned with children's health and physical development. The need for educating parents regarding child nutrition exists in virtually all early childhood programs, regardless of social or economic status. Some centers establish food regulations in an attempt to ensure that nutritionally sound meals are served to children. Most schools attempt to provide a relaxed atmosphere at meal and snack time. Children are asked to sit and eat, sharing conversation as well as food. Because lifelong eating patterns are established early in life, teachers of young children have a responsibility to understand the critical role nutrition plays in the child's total development.

Clothing.

The health and safety of children are affected by the clothing they wear. A simple way to be sure children stay healthy is to encourage them to dress properly for play and for varying weather conditions. Children need clothing in which they can be active—clothing that is not binding and is easy to remove and easy to clean. To promote a self-help environment, parents and teachers should provide clothes the children can manage themselves (elastic waistbands, Velcro™ ties, large zippers). Pants are a good choice for both boys and girls; long dresses can become a hazard when climbing, running, or going up and down stairs. The safest shoes for active play should have composition or rubber soles. Whenever possible, it helps to keep changes of clothes at school.

Children need clothing in which they can be active, playful, and messy!

Health of the Staff.

A responsible early childhood center is one that supports and maintains a healthy staff. Teachers should be in good physical and mental health to be at their best with children. It is wise to check the health regulations and benefits of the individual school when employed there. Many states require annual chest X-rays as a condition of employment. Sick leave policies should be clearly stated in print. Early childhood education is an intense job involving close interpersonal contact. Most teachers work long hours, often with low wages and few health benefits, and with clients in various stages of health. Such working conditions produce fatigue and stress, which can lead to illness or other stress-related problems.

Guarding Children's Safety

Beyond the continual supervision of indoor and outdoor space, everything is planned with the children's safety in mind. Creating a hazard-free environment that still allows for risk and challenge for children takes careful observation and attention to detail. A quick walk around the room and yard will reveal potential problems:

● Are there any sharp corners at children's height?
● Are rug edges snagged or loose?
● Are absorbent surfaces used wherever there is water? Are mops and towels available for spillage?
● Is hot water out of the reach of children?
● Are children allowed to run inside?
● Are there rules governing the children's use of scissors, hammers, and knives?
● Are safety rules explained to children and upheld by adults?
● Are electrical outlets covered when not in use?
● Do open stairwells have gates?
● Do adults monitor the use of extension cords and appliances?
● Is broken equipment removed promptly?
● Are fences high enough to protect and safe to touch?
● Are there areas where wheel toys can move freely without fear of collision?
● Are swings placed away from traffic areas and set apart by bushes or fences?
● Can a child's foot or ankle be caught on equipment? Under a chain-link fence?

● Does playground traffic flow easily?
● Are the toys safe for children's use?

Approximately 20,000 children under the age of 12 are sent to an emergency room every year as a result of a playground accident (Consumer Product Safety Commission, 1997).

In addition, with an estimated 12 to 15 million children participating in organized sports each year (Nelson & Raymond, 1989), safety issues are paramount for school-aged children. The adults serve as the link between children and sports and are the chief means of prevention of injuries and accidents.

Be sure that swings are placed away from the traffic area and set apart so that other children can keep at a safe distance.

When planning for infants and toddlers, the teacher must check toys carefully, because children explore them with all their senses.

Safety List for Indoor Environments

_____ Person monitoring children (at entrances, indoors, outdoors)

_____ First aid and emergency
  _____ Materials readily available to adults, out of children's reach, and regularly stocked and updated
  _____ Adults trained in first aid and CPR regularly and familiar with emergency routines.

_____ Safety plugs on all outlets

_____ Cords
  _____ Electrical cords out of children's reach; avoid using extension cords
  _____ Curtain and window cords, window pulls and poles out of children's reach

_____ Floormat and carpet tacked down to avoid slippage

_____ Doors
  _____ Made to open and close slowly
  _____ All clear access, marked exits, and not blocked

_____ Cubbies and storage cabinets
  _____ Bolted to walls (or back-to-back together)
  _____ Any dangerous materials in locked area

_____ Toys
  _____ In good repair; no splinters or sharp, broken edges
  _____ Check for size with younger children (purchase safety-sizing gadget or estimate to keep at the size of a child's fist)
  _____ Check for peeling paint

_____ Plants and animals
  _____ Nonpoisonous plants _only_
  _____ Check animal cages regularly
  _____ Supervise animal handling carefully
  _____ Store animal food away from children's reach

_____ Adult materials
  _____ Keep adult purses, bags, and so on, away from children
  _____ Avoid having hot beverages around children
  _____ No smoking in children's areas

_____ Kitchen and storage
  _____ Children allowed in _only_ with adult supervision
  _____ Poisonous or hazardous materials stored in a locked area

FIGURE 9-6 Children's safety is of primary importance to teachers and caregivers. Careful evaluation and regular safety checks eliminate dangerous materials and conditions in children's spaces.

Figure 9-6 is a safety checklist for the indoor areas; Figure 11-7 shows how to make playgrounds safe.

First Aid. Every school should establish procedures for dealing with children who are injured on the property. First-aid instructions should be required of all teachers and made available as part of their in-service training. Teachers should know how to treat bumps and bruises, minor cuts and abrasions, bleeding, splinters, bites and stings, seizures, sprains, broken bones, and minor burns.[1] Each classroom should be equipped with two first-aid kits. One

 1 All teachers should receive training in using universal health precautions with all children. Teachers should not make assumptions about who is at risk and who is not for HIV infection and hepatitis.

is for use in the classroom and yard; the other should be suitable for taking on field trips. Each kit should be readily available to adults, but out of children's reach, and supplies should be replenished regularly.

Emergency numbers to be posted near the telephone in each room include those of the ambulance squad, fire department, police, health department, nearest hospital, and a consulting physician (if any). All families enrolled at the school should be aware of school policy regarding injuries at school and should provide the school with emergency information for each child: the name of their physician, how to locate the parents, and who else might be responsible for the injured child if the parents cannot be reached. The school in turn must make sure they notify parents of any injuries the child has incurred during the school day.

Natural Disaster. Most adults are familiar with the most common disaster preparation, the fire drill. Most local fire regulations require that fire extinguishers be in working order and placed in all classrooms and the kitchen area. Fire exits, fire alarms, and fire escapes should be well-marked and functioning properly. Children and teachers should participate in fire drills regularly. Other natural disasters vary by geographical location; helping children prepare for earthquakes, tornadoes, hurricanes, floods, and snowstorms will include participating in drills for those disasters. Proper preparedness will include eliminating potential hazards (e.g., bolting down bookcases), establishing a coordinated response plan (a "Code Blue!" emergency plan should involve children, parents, all staff, and local emergency agencies), and, in some areas of the country, conducting regular earthquake and tornado drills. These experiences can reinforce in parents the need for establishing similar procedures at home.

Automobile Safety. Automobile safety is a related concern when considering potential hazards for preschool children. The use of approved car seats and restraints for children riding in automobiles has received national attention in recent years. Some states have passed legislation requiring the use of specific devices to ensure safer travel for young children. Whether or not they walk to school, children should also be aware of basic rules for crossing streets. The school parking lot can be a source of danger unless the school articulates policies to parents

Video VIEW PoinT 9-2

"The National Fire Prevention Association and AAP recommend discussing safety issues relevant to school-age children."

COMPETENCY: Safety

AGE GROUP: School-Age

CRITICAL THINKING QUESTIONS:

1. What kinds of emergencies might occur at your school-age site, and how are they addressed? How often are drills performed and how do they take place? Make recommendations.

2. How can teachers discuss with school-age children issues and safety guidelines about being home alone? How might you involve the families in this issue?

regarding the safety needs of children. There are potential risks when cars and children occupy the same space. Children should not be left unattended in parking lots.

Maintaining Children's Well-Being

The overall environment for children takes into consideration many factors. To provide for children's health and safety, teachers look at the physical environment carefully—its materials, the equipment, and their arrangement and presentation (see Figure 9-6). Another factor in children's care and education is their well-being. Young children are growing up in a world threatened by violence abroad and at home, drug abuse, unresolved conflicts among adults, and constant bombardment of television and other media.

Since young children do not easily separate the home and school parts of their lives, early childhood educators learn about children's lives and family details readily. They are often at a loss as to what to do, either with information that a child shares or with the child's behavior in the program. Yet a situation does not need to be a crisis to affect a child's well-being. As a rule of thumb, when you feel the child's physical or emotional development is in jeopardy, you have a responsibility to take further action.

Children's well-being can be threatened by a difficult situation at school, such as being bitten, left out, or ridiculed. They are also at risk for the myriad of crises from home—problems with family members, separation or divorce, violence, or substance abuse. While much of our response will be with adults—parents, community resources, professional supports—we are also responsible for trying to provide a psychologically safe and positive environment. By design and by responsiveness, teachers provide an interpersonal environment that soothes and cares for young children.

CREATING THE ENVIRONMENT

The Physical Environment

Every educational setting is organized fundamentally around physical space. This means teachers work with the size and limitations of the facility, both inside and out-of-doors. The building itself may be new and designed specifically for young children. In Reggio Emilia, for example, it is the environment that creates an atmosphere of discovery. As founder Louis Malaguzzi explains (Edwards et al., 1993):

> There is an entrance hall, which informs and documents, and which anticipates the form and organization of the school. This leads into the dinning hall, with the kitchen well in view. The entrance hall leads into the central space, or piazza, the place of encounters, friendships, games, and other activities that complete those of the classrooms. The classrooms and utility rooms are placed at a distance from but connected with the center area. Each classroom is divided into two contiguous rooms . . . to allow children either to be with teachers or stay alone. . . . In addition to the classrooms, we have established the atelier, the school studio and laboratory, as a place for manipulating or experimenting.

More than likely, however, the space is a converted house or store, a parish hall, or an elementary classroom. Sometimes a program will share space with another group so that mobile furniture is moved daily or weekly. Family child care programs are housed in a private home; therefore, adaptations are made in the space both for the children and the family that lives there. There may be a large yard or none at all. Some playgrounds are on the roof of the building, or a park across the street may serve as the only available playground. (See the section on playgrounds in Chapter 11.)

Restraints also come in the form of weather conditions. Outside play—and therefore large-muscle equipment—may be unavailable during the winter, so room for active, vigorous play is needed inside during that time. Hot summer months can make some types of play difficult if there is little or no shade outdoors. Weather conditions must be considered when planning programs for children.

Early childhood programs have specific needs that must be met by the buildings they occupy. Although the choice of building is generally determined by what is available, at a minimum the setting should provide facilities for:

playing/working	food preparation
eating	storage
washing/toileting	office/teacher work space
sleeping/resting	clothing and wraps

Ideally, the setting should have enough space to house these various activities separately. In practice, however, rooms are multipurpose, and more than one event takes place in the same space. A playroom doubles as an eating area because both require the use of tables and chairs. When a school room serves many functions (playing, eating, sleeping), convenient and adequate storage space is a necessity.

General Requirements

Ground-floor classrooms are preferable for young children to ensure that they can enter and leave with relative ease and safety. For noise reduction, the walls and ceilings should be soundproofed. Carpeting, draperies, and other fireproof fabrics in the room will help absorb sound. Floors must be durable, sanitary, and easily cleaned. They should be free from drafts. Rugs should be vacuumed each day. Room size should be sufficient to allow for freedom of movement and the opportunity to play without interference. Some licensing agencies may suggest minimum room and yard size standards.

Many local and state agencies have regulations regarding the use of space for children in group care settings. The fire marshal, health department, and similar agencies must be consulted and their regulations observed. It is wise to consider their requirements when arranging space.

There are several key dimensions to any environment that are helpful to consider. If we are to offer children both balance and variety, these criteria need to be included in developing space both indoors and out. Figure 9-7 outlines these dimensions in detail.

The National Academy of Early Childhood Programs (NAEYC, 2005) has developed guidelines for indoor and outdoor facilities that promote optimal growth. Besides floor and play space (minimum 35 [and recommended 50] square feet indoors and 75 square feet outdoors), the guidelines suggest how to arrange activity areas to accommodate children and what kinds of activities and materials are safe, clean, and attractive. This document, along with *Designs for Living and Learning* (Carter & Curtis, 2003), *The Creative Curriculum* (Dodge, Colker, & Heroman, 2002) and the Environmental Rating Scales (Harms et al., 2005) are used extensively to develop this material.

Indoors

Interest Areas/Learning Centers

"A physical space divided into interest areas is an ideal setting for preschool children who want to explore, make things, experiment, and pursue their own interests" (Dodge, Colker, & Heroman, 2002). Ideally, the spatial layout reflects the program philosophy and the children's priorities. Realistically, most early childhood staff have restrictions as well. Deciding what interest centers you want and what kind of space you will need is good preparation to making a basic floor plan and sketching in the interest centers.

As you consider transforming your early childhood environment, start with an assessment of the way your space is designed now. First draw a

1. **Softness/Hardness**

   Soft: rugs, pillows, play-dough, finger paints, grass, sand, swings

   Hard: tile floor, wooden furniture, asphalt, cement

2. **Open/Closed**

   Open (no one right way to use it): sand and water, dress-up, collage materials, painting

   Closed (manipulated only one way to come out right): puzzles, many board games, most Montessori equipment

   In between: many manipulatives such as Legos®, Tinkertoys®, blocks, balls

3. **Simple/Complex**

   "Play equipment can differ in its holding power; i.e., the capacity to sustain attention . . . A simple unit has one manipulable aspect; a complex unit has two different kinds of materials combined; and a super unit has three different kinds of materials that go together."

   Simple: swings, climbers, sand pile with no toys

   Complex: dramatic play with only a kitchen

   Super: climbers with slides and ropes, playhouse with kitchen, dress-up clothes, dolls, and/or play-dough; sand area with equipment and/or water

   As you add more features to a unit, you increase its complexity and the children's interest in it. To simple play-dough, add cookie cutters; then add toothpicks or a garlic press and it becomes a super unit.

4. **Intrusion/Seclusion**

   Intrusion: places where children can enter or go through easily; blocks, housekeeping, even the entire environment are often highly intrusive areas

   Seclusion: places where children can be alone or with only one child or adult; cubbies, a fort, or under a table become secret places

5. **High Mobility/Low Mobility**

   High: whole-body places and activities, outdoors, climbers, trike lanes, gym mats

   Low: sitting-still places and activities; puzzles and games, story and group times, nap time

   In-between: dramatic play. Block corner, woodworking

FIGURE 9-7 Key dimensions when considering an early childhood environment. (Adapted from *Exchange Magazine*, E. Prescott, 1994.)

Early childhood programs provide for children to play and work alone and together, with friends and teachers, indoors and out.

simple floor plan of the room you are currently working in, one you are familiar with, or one you imagine using in a new job. As you sketch out the arrangements of the room, don't include a lot of detail. . . . Put yourself in the shoes of the . . . children who spend their days in your space. (Carter & Curtis, 2003)

You will consider their ages and needs of the group, and make a list of "I can" and "There are" statements as if you are those children. Now check your floor plan; if you had trouble finding any of the components in your room, it's time to make some changes.

Most programs will include basic areas for small group play, for flexibility, and for engagement. Learning centers are areas of the environment focused on different activities for different developmental experiences. For infants and toddlers, areas for movement and for sensory experiences will dominate; preschoolers will want more creative and manipulative choices; school-age children might include areas for academic stimulation or practice.

The teacher plays an important role in using and implementing the use of learning centers. They must be interesting, accurately reflect the goals for children, and take into consideration space, traffic flow, the number of people, and availability of equipment and materials. The teacher uses environmental cues to tell the children what may happen there, and make good use of the learning centers as places for observation and assessment (see Figure 9-8). Creating learning centers is a standard early childhood practice that has tremendous potential in school-age and primary settings.

Bathrooms

Bathrooms should be adjacent to the play and sleeping areas and easily reached from outdoors. Child-sized toilets and wash basins are preferable, but if unavailable, a step or platform may be built. In most early childhood settings, the bathrooms are without doors, for ease of supervision. Toileting facilities for children should be light, airy, attractive, and large enough to serve

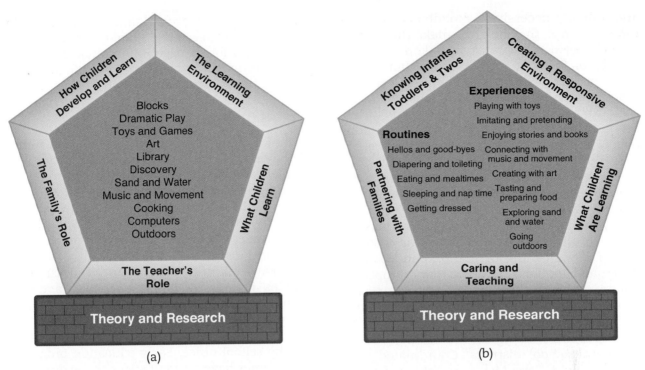

FIGURE 9-8 Teachers need to think about the features to be included in the environment but also the critical framework that helps build appropriate experiences for children in the early years. (a) Components for Preschool (From *The Creative Curriculum® for Preschool* (p. xiv), by D. T. Dodge, L. J. Colker, & C. Heroman, 2002, Washington, DC: Teaching Strategies, Inc. Copyright 2002 by Teaching Strategies, Inc. Reprinted with permission.) and (b) Components for Infants, Toddlers, & Twos. (From *The Creative Curriculum® for Infants, Toddlers & Twos*, 2nd ed. (p. 19), by D. T. Dodge, S. Rudick, and K. Berke, 2006, Washington, DC: Teaching Strategies, Inc. Copyright 2006 by Teaching Strategies, Inc. Reprinted with permission.)

several children at a time. An exhaust fan is desirable. Paper towel holders should be at child height and wastebaskets placed nearby.

If diapering is part of the program, areas for this purpose should be clearly defined and close to handwashing facilities. Handwashing regulations for the staff should be posted, and an area should be provided for recording children's toileting and elimination patterns. Closed cans and germicidal spray must be used, and diapering materials should be plentiful and handy.

Room to Rest

Schools that provide nap and sleeping facilities require adequate storage space for cots and bedding. Movable screens, low enough for teacher supervision, allow for privacy and help reduce the noise level.

Cots or cribs should be labeled with children's names and washed regularly. They should be placed consistently and in such a way that children feel familiar, cozy, and private—not in the center of the room or in rows. Teachers can develop a "nap map" that places children so they can get the rest or sleep they need while still feeling part of the group.

Food Service

"Good nutrition affects the health and well-being of individuals of all ages," states Marotz (2001). "Small children need nutrients for growth and energy . . . regardless of the guideline selected, the common factor necessary for good nutrition is the inclusion of a wide variety of foods." As early childhood classrooms have become more diverse and multicultural, routines and choices around food must take into consideration families' cultural practices and preferences.[1]

Feeding young children and teaching toddlers and older children about good food choices can be a challenge throughout the early childhood span. In an infant program, storing formula

1 Food preferences and customs, as well as toys and materials, need to reflect the cultures served.

and milk is a necessity. As toddlers assert their independence, they begin to make their preferences known. Care must be taken to offer a variety of foods at regular times, but avoid a battle of wills over what the child will eat. Preschoolers are influenced by a teacher who sets a good example of eating with balance and variety. School-aged children can understand nutritional concepts better but are more influenced by what their peers are eating.

Whether involved in a light snack or full meal program, the center must adhere to the most rigid standards of health protection and safety provisions. Every precaution must be taken to ensure maximum hygienic food service. Daily cleaning of equipment, counters, floors, and appliances is a necessity. Proper disinfecting of high chairs and tables requires half a cup of bleach to one gallon of water; bottles of this solution can be stored away from children's reach yet handy for teachers.

Local school districts, Coordinated Community Child Care (4Cs), or affiliates of the NAEYC may be consulted for guidelines on serving nutritional foods and may even offer financial subsidies. For infant and toddler programs, space for recording feeding information must be designated, and enough high chairs or low tables must be provided to prevent an unreasonable wait for eating.

Each age has its unique food-service needs. Infants will need to be held or seated near an adult. Toddlers should not be fed popcorn, nuts, or raw carrots because of the hazard of choking. All children must be served food on disposable dishes or on dishes cleaned in a dishwasher

Even the hallways serve a function in the Reggio Emilia Schools in Italy. (Courtesy of the city of Reggio Emilia, Italy.)

with a sanitation cycle. Lunches brought from home by school-age and full-day children must be checked for spoilage. Information about eating patterns, proportions, and nutritional needs should be regularly shared with parents.

Adult Space

"Oh, for a real 'teacher's desk,'" the early childhood caregiver moans. "I'm lucky if I can find a place to stash my bag in the morning!" A common issue for ECE programs is to donate nearly all the available space to child use and materials storage. Yet the personal and professional needs of adults deserve environmental support.

Few planning books or administrative guides include guidelines for how to create adult space in a classroom. Elementary classrooms include a desk and a bookshelf for the teachers, and a workroom or lounge for staff in the school office. Early education programs sometimes have an adult space in the director's area. An adult bathroom is also common. However, in programs for children under age five, even a desk can seem a hazard, taking up precious space for children.

Still, early childhood professionals deserve environmental support for their work. A safe place for their belongings, space for firstaid/emergency materials and information for families, and an area for a special adult project goes a long way in respecting the teachers' lives in the classroom. We show our priorities by the space and time we give them.

Out-of-Doors

"Children's access to outdoor play has evaporated like water in sunshine. It has happened so fast, along with everything else in this speed-ridden century, that we have not coped with it. . . . Some of our deepest childhood joys—those of field and stream, rocks and vacant lots; of privacy, secrecy, and tiny things that creep across or poke out of the earth's surface" (Rivkin, 1995)—can be experienced out of doors, and nowhere else. Free and fresh air, open space to move about at will, are often children's favorite spots in a program. Indeed, many a preschooler has been able to say goodbye easier when the great outdoors beckons.

The traditional playgrounds—typically on a flat, barren area with steel structures such as swings, climbers, a slide, perhaps a merry-go-round or seesaws, fixed in concrete and arranged

No matter what age the child is, snacks are a favorite part of the day.

in one row—are poor places for children's play from both safety and developmental perspectives (Frost, 1986). Children as young as toddlers and through the primary years much prefer the adventure or creative playground, spaces that have a variety of fixed and movable equipment. Raw materials, such as sand, water, tires, spools, sawhorses, bowls, or pans, in combination with larger superstructures or open-air "houses" with some flexible parts, stimulate a wide variety of both social and cognitive play (including constructive, dramatic, and games play).

A wide porch or covered patio is ideal for rainy days or days when the sun is too severe. Many activities can be extended to the outside area with this type of protection. The physical plant should include adequate playground space adjacent to the building. A variety of playground surfaces makes for more interesting play and provides suitable covering for outdoor activities. Tanbark can be used in the swing area, cement for wheel toys, and grass for under climbers. Sand is used for play in a large area and also in a sensory table. No matter what the surface, the yard should be constructed with a good drainage system. Trees, bushes, and other plantings will allow for both sunshine and shade. Fences are *mandatory*. They must be durable, an appropriate height, with no opportunity for a child to gain a foothold. Because there are no mandatory standards for the manufacture of play equipment, adults

What do YOU Think?

Close your eyes. Think back to the memories of places you liked to play when you were young. Was it outdoors? Was it a cozy spot near a loving adult? Did it involve other children? You may want to sketch these places, adding some notes about the feel or the sounds and smells. Can you help the children in your care find such places of delight?

who work with children must assume responsibility for playground design. Teachers can familiarize themselves with the literature, visit high-quality playgrounds, and consult with child development specialists when selecting equipment. Given the importance that young children attach to the outdoors, teachers are well advised to concentrate their efforts in a similar fashion. Chapter 11 discusses playgrounds and safety in detail.

Materials and Equipment

Selection of materials and equipment is based on a number of criteria. Out of necessity, most school budgets limit the amount of money available for such purchases. To make every dollar count, teachers select materials that:

- are age and developmentally appropriate.
- are related to the school's philosophy and curriculum.
- reflect quality design and workmanship.
- are durable.
- offer flexibility and versatility in their uses.
- have safety features (e.g., nontoxic paints, rounded corners).
- are aesthetically attractive and appealing to children (and adults).
- are easy to maintain and repair.
- reflect the cultural makeup of the group and the diversity of the culture overall.
- are nonsexist, nonstereotypical, and anti-bias.

Materials should be appropriate for a wide range of skills because children within the same age group develop at individual rates. "What makes good playthings? Simplicity of detail, versatile in use" (Community Products, 2004). Selecting equipment and toys to support development is important; because young children typically will try to play with everything in their environment, the selection of play materials involves many decisions. Many of the materials can be **open-ended**; that is, they can be used in their most basic form or they can be developed in a variety of ways. Unit blocks, clay, and Legos® are examples of materials that children can use in a simple fashion; as skills develop these materials can be

Basic Materials for Outdoor Playground/Yard
Grounds: Various surfaces (grass, asphalt, gravel/sand, tanbark), as much natural habitat as possible.
Equipment: Climbing apparatus with ramps, slide, pole, ladder; swings (various types); house/quiet area; ramps and supports to build; tires, "loose parts"
Sand/water area and toys
Riding area and various wheel toys
Large building blocks
Dramatic-play props
Balls and game materials
Workbench and woodworking/clay materials
Pet and garden areas
Infant-toddler: Have plenty of simple riding toys, eliminate woodworking, have apparatus correct size and simplicity and/or foam wedges
School-age: Increase game area, may eliminate number or kinds of wheel toys; substitute a stage, mural, boat, creek; increase "loose parts" for child-created forts.

FIGURE 9-9 The possibilities of creating outdoor space are endless; remember that children need space to run and group together, to experience first-hand nature, and to be reflective and alone to watch (see Chapter 11).

manipulated in a more complex manner. See Figure 9-9.

Toys and materials need to reflect the diversity of the class, the families, and the community.[1]

- From a DAP perspective, materials need to appeal to individual interests and also respond to children's cultural and linguistic strengths. "The nature of the classroom atmosphere contributes greatly to children's success in learning English as a second language" (Elgas et al., 2002). Materials and cultural artifacts help a child feel that the environment is familiar.

 1 Numerous resources are available to help the teacher select books, dolls, puzzles, and posters that will expose children in a positive way to people who are ethnically different, people with disabilities, and people who have different work and play habits from their own.

- From a self-help viewpoint, dressing frames and plenty of workable doll clothes will help children learn those self-care tasks. Children's books that demonstrate social values and attitudes that expand gender roles and family lifestyles show a value for an anti-bias environment.
- Modifications in the environment that promote inclusiveness might include ramp access for wheelchairs and materials to highlight tactile, auditory, and olfactory experiences for children with visual impairments.

Recall the Waldorf Schools in Chapter 1. Because Steiner believed the classroom is an extension of the family experience and was to be as free as possible from the intrusions of the "modern world," a Waldorf kindergarten might look like this (Waldorf, 1995):

> The feeling of warmth and security is largely created by using only natural materials: woods, cotton, wool in the construction of the decor and toys. The curtains transmit a warm glow in the room. Ideally, the walls and floor of the room are of natural wood. In this warm environment are placed toys which the children can use to imitate and transform the activities that belong to everyday adult life. In one corner stands a wooden scale and baskets for children to pretend they are grocery shopping; a pile of timber stands ready to be constructed into a playhouse, a boat, or a train; a rocking horse invites a child to become a rider; homemade dolls lie in wooden cradles surrounded by wooden frames and cloths the children can use to create a pretend family and play house. Pinecones and flowers are artistically dispersed. Lovely watercolors adorn the walls. The effect of this beautiful arrangement of decorations and toys is the feeling of stepping out of the business and clutter of modern life into a sanctuary where one can breathe easily, relax, and play according to the impulses of one's heart.

Try to avoid toys that have limited play value. TRUCE (2001–2002), which stands for Teachers Resisting Unhealthy Children's Entertainment, suggests that we steer away from toys that:

- make electronic technology the focus of play.
- lure girls into focusing on appearance.
- model violent and sexualized language or behavior.
- are linked to commercial products and advertisements.

Children are active learners, and their materials should provide them with ways to explore, manipulate, and become involved. Teachers encourage the use of fine- and gross-motor skills by providing equipment that involves their use. Children learn through all their senses, so the materials should be appealing to many of the senses. Children need opportunities for quiet, private time and space as well. For children in care for long hours or in large group sizes, a cozy corner is essential.

Organizing Space and Room Arrangements

There are many different ways to arrange and organize space in an early childhood setting; the final result expresses the diversity of the program. Most early childhood centers are arranged by **interest areas/learning centers** or activity areas. The room arrangement and the choice of activity centers show what is being emphasized in the program. The amount of space devoted to any one activity says a great deal about its value to the staff. For example, teachers at a child care center noticed the high interest in sociodramatic play with several new babies in children's families. They built up the housekeeping area, making sure there were at least six baby dolls, four telephones, and three doll buggies, and countless bottles, tippy cups and pretend baby food! As interests change, so do the room and yard—someone brings in a hamster and the discovery area blossoms, or family camping brings out tents around the grassy outdoor areas.

Room arrangement and choice of materials play such an important role in children's educational experience. A developmentally appropriate room will invite children in and welcome them at their level. Simplicity is a watchword in a toddler room. Notice how room arrangement changes with children's age ranges (Lowman & Ruhmann, 1998):

- A large-motor zone is essential in a toddler room.
- The dramatic-play zone is particularly conducive to pretend play.
- The messy zone is that area of the room where children are encouraged to "mess around" with a variety of fluid materials.
- Every toddler room needs a haven where children can unwind, kick back, chill out, sink in, and just relax. The quiet zone provides such a spot.

Video VIEW PoinT 9-3

"In this toddler room we see some examples of furniture arrangements, activities, and teacher expectations that are developmentally inappropriate."

COMPETENCY: Learning Environment

AGE GROUP: Infants and Toddlers

CRITICAL THINKING QUESTIONS:

1. Make a list of what you see as inappropriate in the environment, and recommendations for how you would change it.

2. Toddlers do not know how to play cooperatively. How would you arrange a room and a yard to take this into consideration?

Family child care homes present special challenges, both in the space and the mixed age ranges of children. Weinberger (2000) suggests that creating retreats, such as allowing children into a cabinet or behind the couch, allows moderate privacy while still insuring supervision.

Harms et al. (2005) list as important environmental supports for each of these areas for preschool and kindergarten:

1. space and furnishings
2. personal care routines
3. language-reasoning
4. activities (motor, cognitive, creative)
5. interaction (social, emotional)
6. program structure (schedules)
7. parents and staff (personal and professional needs)

School-age programs have special requirements, as those environments include children from kindergarten through third- and sometimes fifth- or sixth-grade. Their size, interests, and developmental needs require a different kind of classroom (Bickart, Jablon, & Dodge, 1999). The National School-Age Standards for Quality School-Age Care (NAA, 1998) recommends tables for projects and experiments, homework tables in a quiet corner, a place for snack and club meetings, art, blocks, house corner, and large group activity area.

A room that is arranged well with enough interesting materials will give children choices and open their eyes to possibilities.

- Self-help rooms will have materials on shelves for children to reach and perhaps a job chart that outlines children's responsibilities.
- Inclusive environments might prop boxes with materials for their children with visual or auditory special needs.

The placement of the interest centers is important. Balance the number of noisy and quiet activities, both indoors and out. Some activities are noisier than others, so place the noisier centers together and cluster the quieter ones together. Quieter activities, such as puzzles, language games, and storytelling, take place in areas away from blocks, water play, or dramatic play, because the last three tend to kindle animated, active, and sometimes noisy behavior. Some programs create a kind of layered room—entry, quiet, messy, noisy. See Figures 9-10 through 9-12.

Playground Designs

Environments must be arranged so that there are enough play spaces for the number of children in the group. When the number of play opportunities in school settings, both indoors and out, is analyzed, areas and activities can be assigned a value (Prescott, Jones, & Kritschevsky, 1972). A simple area (swings, climbers) counts as one play space, a complex area (housekeeping/dramatic play) counts as four play spaces, and a super area (sand and water play combined) counts as eight play spaces. The value assigned an area generally coincides with the number of children who might be accommodated in that space. When the total for the space is figured, it is matched against the actual number of children in the group to see if there is a place for everyone to play. See Figure 9-10.

Adult needs also should be met through proper organization. How can the teachers supervise all areas while ensuring cozy spots for children's privacy? Are the teachers deployed evenly throughout all the space? Is storage integrated so that equipment is located near the place where it will be used? Is the space arranged for cooperation and communication among the adults as well as the children? In other words, is this a workplace that is accepting, inviting, and challenging to all?

Clearly defined boundaries and obvious pathways make it easy for children to live and

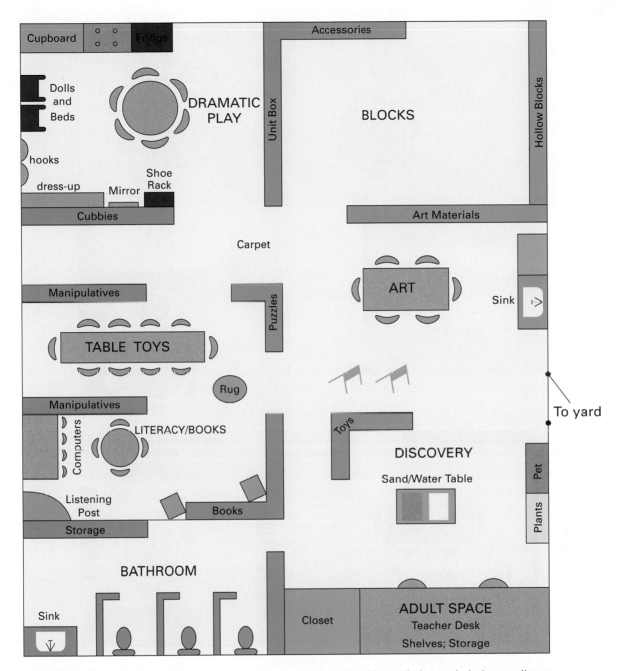

FIGURE 9-10 A preschool child care center needs clearly defined boundaries and obvious pathways to make it easy for children to use this space independently.

work in the space. There should be enough space for larger groups to gather together as well as small groups. Figure 9-10 shows a playground sketch for a preschool room and yard, Figures 9-11 and 9-12 are a school-age and toddler room, and Figure 9-13 shows a playground suitable for four- to eight-year-olds.

A good environment for children reflects the teachers' knowledge of how children play, what skills they possess, what they know, and what they need to learn. The settings are arranged to promote those aspects of child growth and development. They also reflect the teachers' values. A self-help perspective will have spaces and materials arranged for the children's access and use without undue teacher permission or help. With an anti-bias viewpoint, the environment would reflect images in abundance of all the children, families, and staff of that program as well as of the major racial and ethnic groups of the community and nation, with a balance of men and

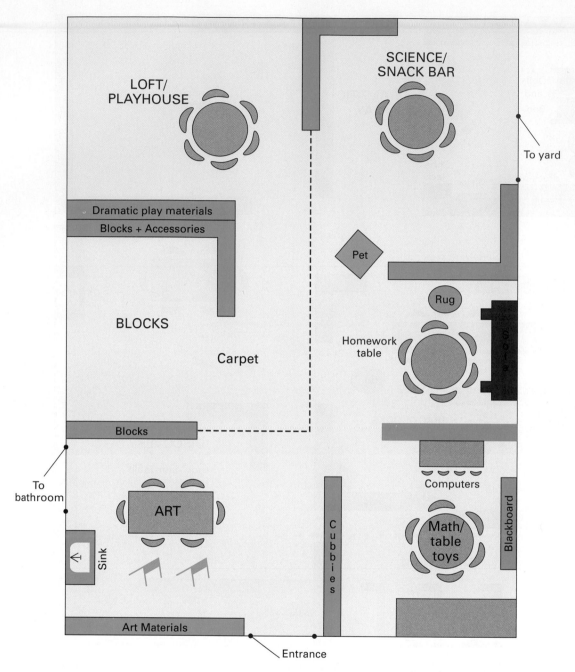

FIGURE 9-11 A school-age center has learning centers to allow children to make clear choices and engage in active learning through play.

 women as well as the elderly and disabled doing many jobs typical of daily life.[1] An inclusive environment could be reflected in the addition of cube chairs, easy handles on the doors, and puzzles whose pieces have magnets on the backs and are put together on a steel cookie tray. With peace education in mind, teachers provide materials to expand children's concepts, including those of similarity and difference, and help them develop a strong sense of self and the ability to cooperate and resolve conflicts peaceably.

One place in particular reflects the community's value of creativity and self-expression. On entering one of the community preschools in Reggio Emilia, one sees (New, 1990)

---

1 See the anti-bias curriculum resources listed in the bibliography.

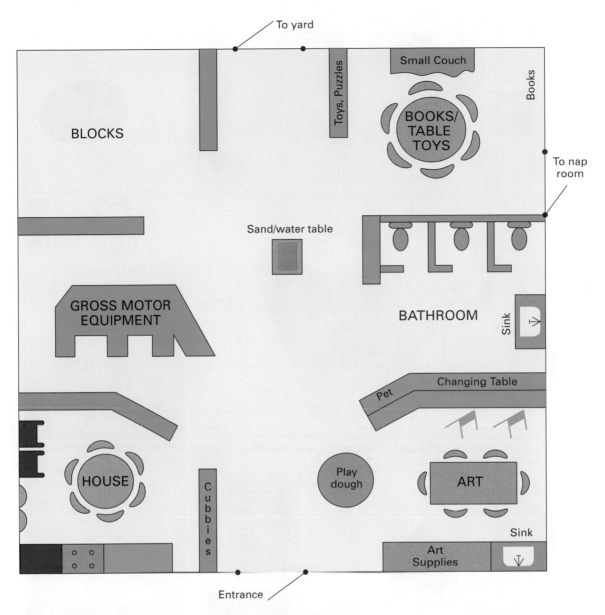

FIGURE 9-12 A toddler environment has safety and accessibility in mind, while helping children to work in small groups so they can be maximally involved with a minimum of distraction from others.

the work of children (drawings, paintings, sculptures) and their teachers (photographs and displays of projects in progress), often with the dramatic use of graphics. . . . Everywhere you turn, there is something else to ponder. Art supplies, including paints and clay as well as recycled or naturally found materials (leaves, bottle caps, fabric scraps) are pleasingly arranged, often by color, on shelves within children's reach. Groupings of found objects, including flower petals and plastic bags filled with "memories" from field trips, are carefully displayed so as to acknowledge the importance children attribute to the objects as well as the aesthetic qualities (shape, color, texture) of the objects themselves.

In summary, the physical environment should be organized for children according to these criteria:

- *Availability.* Open, low shelving with visual cues for placement of toys, equipment—aids in cleanup and room setup.

- *Consistency in organization.* Neat, systematic, in logical order.

- *Compatibility.* Noisy activities are grouped away from quiet ones; art needs natural light when possible; water play near a bathroom or kitchen; messy projects done on washable floors.

- *Definition.* Clearly defined boundaries indicating available space and what is to take place; obvious pathways outlined in class and yard;

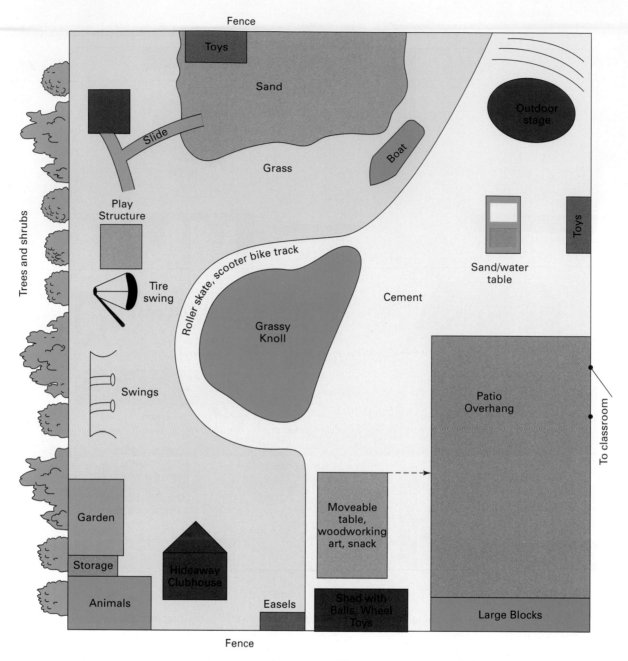

FIGURE 9-13 A playground/yard, suitable for ages four and older, will give children a sense of security and adventure, giving them "contact with nature, opportunities for social play, and freedom of movement and active physical play" (Adapted from Themes, 1999).

ways to get in and out of an area without disrupting activity in progress; no dead ends or runways.

- *Spacing.* Interest areas with enough space to hold the children who will play there; one-third to one-half of the surface should remain uncovered; materials stored near space where they are used; storage and activity spaces have visual cues.

- *Communicability.* Tells children what to do instead of relying on adult to monitor activities; communicates to children what behavior

is expected; arrangement suggests numbers of children, levels of activity.

THE TEMPORAL ENVIRONMENT

Daily Schedule: Time to Learn

The **daily schedule** defines the structure of each program. It creates the format for how children will experience the events of the day—in what order and for what length of time.

No two schedules are alike because each reflects the program it represents. The amount of time devoted to specific activities communicates clearly what value the school places on them. The amount of time given to certain aspects of the curriculum, the variety of events, and the flexibility tell children and adults what is important in this particular setting. Figure 9-14 and Chapter 10 expand on this issue of time.

In developing a schedule by which to function on a daily basis, teachers first decide what is important for children to learn, how that learning should take place, and how much time

Half-Day Toddler Program

9:00–9:30	Greet children Inside activities • playdough and art/easel • home living • blocks and manipulatives • books
9:30	Door to outdoors opens
9:45–10:20	Outdoor play • large motor • social play
10:20	Music/movement outdoors
10:30	Snack/"Here We Are Together" song • washing hands • eating/pouring/cleanup
10:45–11:45	Outside
11:15	"Time to Put Our Toys Away" song • all encouraged to participate in cleanup
11:20	Closure (indoors) • parent–child together • story or flannel board

Full-Day Program for Preschoolers

7:00	Arrival, breakfast
7:30	Inside free play • arts/easels • table toys/games/blocks • dramatic-play center; house, grocery store, etc.
9:00	Cleanup
9:15	Group time: songs/fingerplays and small group choices
9:30	Choice time/small groups • discovery/math lab/science activity • cooking for morning or afternoon snack • language art/prereading choice
10:00	Snack (at outside tables/cloths on warm days) or snack center during free play
10:15	Outside free play • climbing, swinging; sand and water, wheel toys, group games
12:00	Handwash and lunch

12:45	Get ready: toileting, handwashing, toothbrushing, prepare beds
1:15	Bedtime story
1:30	Rest time
2:30	Outdoors for those awake
3:30	Cleanup outdoors and singing time
4:00	Snacktime
4:15	Learning centers; some outdoor/indoor choices, field trips, story teller
5:30	Cleanup and read books until going home

Half-Day Kindergarten Plan

8:15–8:30	Arrival Getting ready to start • checking in library books, lunch money, etc.
8:30	Newstelling • "anything you want to tell for news" • newsletter written weekly
9:00	Work assignment • write a story about your news or • make a page in your book (topic assigned) or • work in math lab
9:30–10:15	Choice of indoors (paints, blocks, computer, table toys) or second-grade tutors read books to children • when finished, play in loft or read books until recess
10:15	Snack
10:30	Recess
10:45	Language: chapter in novel read or other language activity
11:15	Dance or game or visitor
11:45	Ending: getting ready to leave • check out library books • gather art and other projects
12:00–1:30	for part of group each day Lunch, then: • field trips • writing lesson • math or science lab

FIGURE 9-14 Daily schedules reflect the children's needs and ages while meeting the program's goals. The time and timing of the school day show what is valued in the program.

to allow in the daily program. If small-group work and individual attention are program goals, enough time will have to be set aside to ensure their success. More time is needed to allow children a number of curriculum choices than if they had only one or two activities from which to select. Three-year-olds need more time for toileting activities than do five-year-olds, who are considerably more self-sufficient.

The golden rule for child care is to treat children as we want them to treat us. Australian educator Anne Stonehouse (1990) notes that the children in child care today are the adults of tomorrow who will be taking care of us in our old age. Remembering that, it helps to think of how often children are asked to do and finish their tasks on others' schedules, to ask permission to do what they wish, to be required to participate in activities of someone else's choice. A children's program must be for children, on their timetable as much as possible. Stonehouse's five recommendations for a program's schedule reflect this respect:

1. Suitable choices are built in as much of the time as possible, avoiding the expectation that everyone should do the same thing at the same time. Flexibility . . . makes for a more humane environment.

2. The need for a sensitive and flexible settling-in period is taken into account. This starts with respect for the client and the client's family and the recognition that different people cope with change and new experiences in different ways.

3. Meaningless and sometimes mindless activities that simply "fill up the day," "help pass the time," or that have no intrinsic value are avoided.

4. A healthy balance between an individual's need for autonomy, freedom, and independence, on the one hand, and the need for rules that help us get along together, on the other, is strived for.

5. Staff balance the need for a routine, for the comfort and reassurance of the familiar, with the need for variety and novelty for change.

The physical plant itself may dictate a portion of the daily schedule. If toilet facilities are not located adjacent to the classroom, then more time must be scheduled to travel to and from the bathrooms. If the building or space is shared with other groups, some portion of the program may be modified. Many schools housed in church buildings schedule field trips during the annual church rummage sale to free up the space for the church's use.

The daily schedule is important for everyone in the setting. Two important aspects of a schedule are routines and transitions.

Routines. What is meant by a routine? **Routines** are the framework of programs for young children. A routine is a constant; each day, certain events are repeated, providing continuity and a sense of order to the schedule. Routines are the pegs on which to hang the daily calendar. When should children eat? Sleep? Play? Be alone? Be together? These questions are answered by the placement of routines. The rest of the curriculum—art activities, field trips, woodworking—works around them. Routines in an early childhood environment setting include:

- self-care (eating, rest/sleeping, dressing, toileting)
- transitions between activities
- group times
- beginning and ending the day or session
- making choices
- task completion
- room cleanup and yard restoration

Most routines are very personal and individual rituals in children's daily lives. Children bring to school a history firmly established around routines, one that is deeply embedded in their family and culture. Routines are reassuring to children, and they take pride in mastering them; they are also a highly emotional issue for some.

The self-care tasks—eating, sleeping, dressing, and toileting—can be difficult issues between adult and child, virtually from the moment of birth. Everyone can recall vivid memories associated with at least one routine. They seem to become battlegrounds on which children and adults often struggle. Many times this is where children choose to take their first stand on the road to independence.

The early childhood teacher must be able to deal with the issue of self-care routines in sensitive and understanding ways. Children adjust to routines when they are regularly scheduled in the daily program and when there are clear expectations.

Routines are an integral part of creating a good environment for children. All three environmental factors are influenced by routines:

1. *Physical.* Child-sized bathroom and eating facilities; storage of cots, blankets, and

sleeping accessories; equipment for food storage and preparation.

2. *Temporal.* Amount of time in daily schedule for eating, resting, toileting, cleanup.

3. *Interpersonal.* Attitudes toward body functions; willingness to plan for self-care tasks; interactions during activities and transitions; expectations of staff, parents, and children.

As teachers plan for children's basic needs, they are aware of the learning potential of ordinary, everyday routines. Figure 9-15 illustrates how self-care routines teach the young child important skills and habits. In the four curriculum chapters of the next section ("What Is Being Taught?," Chapters 10–14), there is specific planning for routines, transitions, and group times. It is these times that provide a sense of security for children. Beyond the planning for indoor and outdoor activities, careful teachers realize that helping children with the routines of daily living provides a solid underpinning so other learning can take place.

When the time sequence is clear to all, then everyone can go about the business of learning and teaching. Children are more secure in a place that has a consistent schedule; they can begin to anticipate the regularity of what comes next and count on it. In that way they are then free to move, explore, and learn without hesitation. Children can freely involve themselves without fear of being interrupted. Adults, too, enjoy the predictability of a daily schedule. By knowing the sequence of events, they are then free to flex the timing when unforeseen circumstances arise.

Routines: Learning Opportunities

- Eating Teaches Health:

  Introduction to new and different foods, good nutritional habits

- Eating Teaches Social Skills:

  How to manage oneself in a group eating situation, focusing on eating and conversing; acceptable mealtime behavior and manners

- Eating Teaches Fine-Motor Skills:

  Pouring; handling spoons, forks; serving self, drinking, eating without spilling

- Eating Teaches Independence Skills:

  Finding and setting one's place, serving self, making choices, cleaning up at snack and lunch times

- Eating Teaches Individual Differences:

  Likes and dislikes; choices of food; pace of eating

- Resting and Sleeping Teach Health:

  Personal care skills; relaxation habits; internal balance and change of pace; alternating activity to allow body to rest

- Dressing Teaches Independence Skills:

  Self-awareness: size of clothes, comparisons between clothes for girls and boys, younger and older, larger and smaller children, and children in and out of diapers or training pants
  Self-esteem: caring for one's own body; choosing one's own clothes

- Dressing Teaches Fine-Motor Skills:

  How to manage snaps, buttons, zippers; handling all garments; maneuvering in and out of a snowsuit or jacket; matching hands and feet with mittens and boots or shoes

- Toileting Teaches Emotional Skills:

  Self-awareness: body functions, learning the names and physical sensations that go with body functions
  Self-identity: comparisons between girls and boys (sit versus stand)
  Self-esteem: caring for one's own body without guilt, fear, shame
  Human sexuality: in a natural setting, promotes healthy attitudes toward the body and its functions, and that adults can be accepting, open, and reassuring about the body and its care

FIGURE 9-15 Every routine can be used as a vehicle for learning within the environment.

And it is the unforeseen that often does happen. Amidst the noise of children at work, the play is likely to be interrupted by a number of things that can affect the "best laid plans" of all teachers. For instance, a child unexpectedly decides that he doesn't want Dad to go—just as the teacher was helping someone onto the toilet for the first time. Or chaos breaks out in the block corner—at the moment a teacher was leaving with a group of children for the kitchen with several cookie sheets full of carefully constructed gingerbread people. A visitor is coming in the door—just as two children collide and bump heads. A parent is walking in the door with a special group-time activity—and this time a child refuses to clean up her play-dough creation.

Transitions

Humans are known as a species for their adaptability. And yet we are resistant to change. For young children, too, change is difficult. Teachers and caregivers can make the necessary changes easier for children if they focus their attention on those times. Rather than trying to rush through quickly to get to the next event, staff enough **transition** time. Helping children anticipate, figure out, work through, and successfully manage the changes in their day guides them to maturity. Figure 9-16 offers some strategies; Figure 9-15 shows how daily schedules honor the routines and transitions in a child's school day.

The plans and routines of a program do provide the security of the known; at the same time, spontaneous happenings of the day always occur and are often moments of intense learning. Good teachers prepare children for upcoming transitions, using a song or strumming of an instrument and the words, "Get ready to clean up soon." And they are also prepared for children's perceptions of time, immediacy, and closure to collide with the schedule. So if Chad doesn't want his dad to go, perhaps Shana's getting on the toilet will have to wait, or Dad can read him another story until Shana's "All done now!" has happened. The gingerbread sheets can be held momentarily so the quarrel can be resolved, or some of the "fighters" could be invited to be door-openers and help march the group to the kitchen. Perhaps Marisa could keep working on her masterpiece while the rest of the class joins the parent on the rug (at least, just this once?).

These examples all illustrate the common clash of "adult timetables and children's quest for engagement" (Ambery, 1997). Programs need to be designed to allow for both consistency and **flexibility**. Consistency brings security and closure, allowing for teacher authority and expertise to assert themselves; flexibility invites sensitivity to individuals and respectful agreements to be reached. As teachers work with schedules, they continually balance the needs of individuals with those of the group.

Developmentally Appropriate Schedules

Just as the arrangement of space should reflect the group of children within, so does the daily schedule allow for appropriate growth at the developmental level of the group. There are common factors to consider for all children in the early years, as well as some developmental distinctions at the various ages.

There are common elements in all schedules, whether they are designed for toddler groups or five-year-olds, all-day programs or half-day nurseries. Sound child development principles provide the framework on which the daily schedule is structured. The individual schools then adapt these requirements to their own philosophy as they work out their individual daily schedule. All schedules must:

- include time for routines (to eat, rest, wash, toilet) as well as time for transitions (what happens when there is a change from one activity to another) and **group times** (circle time to begin the day, song time for announcements, or story-time as closure).
- alternate quiet and active play and work to help children pace themselves.
- provide opportunities for both inside and outside play.
- allow children to participate in structured activities as well as those of their own choosing.
- make it possible for children to work individually, in small groups, or in larger ones.
- gear the time to the age and developmental levels of the group.
- provide for flexibility so that children's interests can be maintained and emergencies met.
- have a beginning and an end. Some provisions must be made for children to be met and greeted when they enter. The day is brought to closure with a review of the day's activities and a daily class anticipation of what will come tomorrow. Allow time for dismissal or transition to extended care.

Transition Times Made Easier

Questions for Planning

- Who is involved in the transition time (child, parents, teachers, other children, visitors, etc.)?
- What kind of activity has preceded the transition time and what will follow?
- What will the children be asked to do during transition?
- What will the teachers be doing *during* transition?
- How will the children be told or find out what to do during the transition?
- What do you know about child development and this particular child(ren) that can help with these questions?

Teaching Strategies

Arrival

- Greet each child with a smile, and welcome child and parent with what activities are available.
- Make name cards and/or an attendance sheet that child and parent can participate in as a starting point.
- Plan with parents, and alert the child, a simple and clear way for them to say goodbye and for the parents to leave (see Chapter 8 for details).

Cleanup Materials

- Give the children a five-minute "warning" to alert them to upcoming changes.
- Have a consistent and calm signal to start putting away toys.
- Use music as background and/or sing during cleanup.
- Consider having necklaces or cards of specific areas for children, or make teams.
- Construct the environment so that it is clear where things go and children can do the majority of it themselves.
- Occasionally thank the children publicly for cleaning up, noting individual efforts and specific chores done well.

Preparing Children to Attend

- Make a chart that shows the choices available.
- Sing a song or familiar fingerplay to get everyone's attention and participation.
- Ask the children to put on "elephant ears" (rabbit, etc.) or lock their lips and put the key in their pockets.

Ready to Rest/Nap Time

- Prepare the environment ahead of time to be restful—darkened room, soft blanket/cuddlies nearby, quiet music, teachers whispering and available to walk children to their places and stay with them.
- Read a story to the group in one place before they are to lie quietly, or split larger groups into small subgroups with a teacher reading to each.

Moving to Another Place/Building

- Gather the group and tell them exactly what will be happening.
- Ask for ideas of how to behave ("What will we need to remember? How can we stay safe and have fun together?") and reinforce with a few concrete rules.
- Have the children be a train, with adults as the engine and caboose, or a dragon with head and tail.
- Have the children choose a partner to stay with and hold hands.
- Ask preschoolers and early primary children to remember the "B" words ("beside or behind") in staying near adults.

Waiting for Others to Finish

- Prepare a part of the room for children to move to, such as a book corner or listening post, having an adult in that space with more than two children.
- Make an apron or hanging with several pockets filled with activity cards or small manipulatives for children to use alone.
- Plan a special table with folders or large envelopes with activities.
- Have a "waiting box" with special small items for these times only.

FIGURE 9-16 Transitions are a regular part of children's routines and should be learning times that are as well-planned as other parts of the day.

- involve the adults in daily planning and review; include a regular meeting time for more substantial discussion of children, long-range planning, and evaluation.
- include time for cleanup and room restoration.

- incorporate the teachers' roles and assignments so that they will know their area of responsibility.
- be posted in an obvious place in the classroom for all to see.

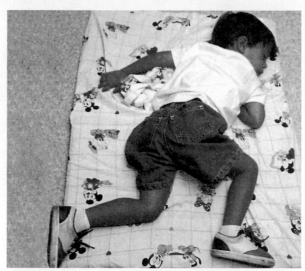

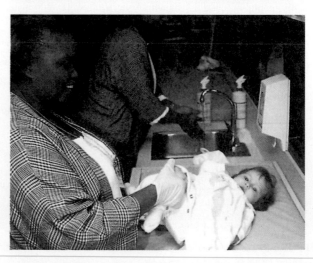

Every routine—handwashing, toileting, toothbrushing, eating, resting, diapering—has a place in the early childhood classroom.

All schedules have a great deal in common, but certain age-related differences can be seen. Figure 9-14 outlines three typical daily schedules for a half-day toddler class, a full day for preschoolers, and a kindergarten. (See also Chapter 2.) There are several important differences in schedules for the various age groups:

- *More choices* are available to children as they grow.
  Example: Two-year-olds could be overstimulated by the selection of materials that is appropriate for school-aged children.

- *Transitions* can be handled differently in the various age groups.
  Example: Older children can move through some transitions as a group, such as changing from one activity area to another or going out with a specialist in pairs or even in a single file. This is difficult for younger children, who would push or wander away. For them, the door to the yard opens quietly, allowing children to go out slowly.
  Example: A child care class of three- and four-year-olds is dismissed from song time to snack by the color of people's shirts, or the first letter of their names, rather than as one whole group. Figure 9-16 gives examples of handling transitions for all ages.

- *The structure* of the day changes with age.
  Example: The balance of free-play and teacher-directed activities shifts from relatively few directed activities for younger children to some more for the nursery school and child care ages. The kindergarten schedule provides more structure both in individual work projects and teacher-focused time. A first-grade schedule with some whole-group teacher instruction times is developmentally appropriate for those older children.

- *The content of group activities* changes with age.
  Example: In the toddler class, group times are simple: a short fingerplay, story with a flannel board or puppets, or a song to dismiss is adequate. Preschool group times include several songs, a dramatization of a favorite fingerplay, and a short story. By kindergarten, groups can last 15 to 20 minutes, with announcement and weather board, children's "newstelling," longer dramas, and even chapter stories.

Centers are very busy environments for children. So many things, so much learning, so much to do! Kielar (1999), a visiting storyteller, offers these suggestions as an "antidote" to such noisy times:

- Reserve an area of your school or center for those who want to sit quietly.
- Make lunch time a time for peace and quiet.
- Wake up children from naps a little sooner than is needed to give them time to transition.
- Don't decorate every window with paintings.
- Change room displays often.

The temporal environment thus mirrors the children's age and individual interests. In this regard it is useful to note that many programs divide the day into relatively small segments of time. This is done because adults believe that young children, particularly preschoolers, have such short attention spans that they cannot remain at an activity for long. However, we know that children can stay focused for long periods of time on activities of their choice or interest. Although they may last only a short time in teacher-planned, structured activities, children need and thrive with more time to get their own creative juices flowing. Children can spend hours with blocks, Legos®, sand, water, and dramatic play. Consult Figure 9-14 to see how the temporal environment allots time for such endeavors.

The Interpersonal Environment

A child responds to everything in school: the color of the room, the way the furniture is arranged, how much time there is to play, and how people treat one another. To the child, everything is a stimulus. The feeling in a room is as real as the blocks or the books. Thus, the interpersonal or social aspects of an early childhood setting are powerful components of the environment.

Defining the Tone

Children are the most important people in the setting; they should feel safe and comfortable. A warm, interpersonal environment invites children to participate and to learn. When children feel secure with one another and with the setting, they will be able to engage more fully in the total program.

Because it is understood that the single most important factor in determining the quality of a program is the teacher (see Chapter 5), it follows that teachers will be the key ingredient in determining the interpersonal "flavor" of a class. The first component of the National Academy's criteria for high-quality early childhood programs is the interactions among the staff and children (see Chapter 10). The human component, the connections among the people in a center or home, makes all the difference to young children, for they are the barometers of interpersonal tension or openness and freedom.

Parents matter in the life of school, especially in the early years. The way people feel about each other and how they express their feelings have an impact on children. Teachers have to see children within their family and social context, and to do so, they must invite families into the schooling process, as in these situations:

> You can't believe it; no matter how many times you tell Kai's Chinese grandfather that school starts at 9 a.m., he continues to bring him between 9:30 and 10 . . . until you find out that in China, old people are often late and the people respect their habits. Now you may need to flex your schedule to allow for this late arrival and support this family custom.
>
> Elena's father is large and speaks with such an accent you can hardly understand him. You'd like to just avoid talking with him, but then you'd connect only when there's a problem . . . and you discover that, in his Central American culture, teachers' ideas are to be solicited for parents to be seen as "good parents." Now you may need to overcome your discomfort and ask him respectfully to repeat what he is saying a bit more slowly.
>
> Every day Maryam brings her lunch, and it is so difficult to manage. These Iranian foods are not the same as the other children's, and there is often teasing that you have to keep redirecting. You wonder if you should simply tell her auntie to send her with a sandwich . . . only you realize that everyone wants to eat familiar foods, and letting Maryam eat what her parents want her to should also be coupled with having the other children learn some tolerance, too. Now you might use the lunch time situation to help everyone become curious and interested in new foods.

The interpersonal connection between parent and teacher can bolster what happens to the child within the classroom and can offer the child a smooth transition between school and home. Learning is enhanced when parents and teachers come to communicate in supportive, nonthreatening ways.

Just how important is the interpersonal environment? Although most experts agree that the relationship between teacher and child is important, extensive research has only recently begun to document exactly how teacher-child interactions occur and how variations in such interactions might be related to behaviors or other results in children. "Researchers demonstrate a pattern of positive relationships between children's sensitive, involved interactions with teachers and children's enhanced development. The impacts of these types of interactions are likely to be seen in children's cognitive, socioemotional, and language development" (Kontos & Wilcox-Herzog, 1997). Such research confirms the findings of recent brain-based research and theories of Erikson, Bandura, and Vygotsky (see Chapter 4) and confirms our belief that how teachers interact with children is at the heart of early childhood education.

Young children develop best through close, affectionate relationships with people, particularly adults. Although this is true for all young children, it is particularly important for children under three and those without facility in the dominant language spoken in the class. "The interpersonal aspect of environment is the central element affecting the quality of toddler play, more important than elaborateness of physical setting," declares Zeavin (1997). "Toddlers cannot talk about what is going on inside them. It is through their play that they externalize troubling feelings, work out emotional conflicts, and gain control of their world. . . . Every issue is a relationship issue." In a human and humane environment, people are respected, and the focus of the staff is on children's strengths and capabilities; limitations are seen as needs rather than liabilities. Teachers observe and engage children in interactions that include smiling, touching, listening, asking questions, and speaking on eye level. The language and tone of voice used are respectful and friendly, with children treated equally across lines of race, culture, language, ability, and sex.[1] Staff use positive guidance rather than punitive discipline techniques (see Chapter 7) and develop warm relationships with parents (see Chapter 8). What teachers do—and how they do it—determines what learning takes place in the class and how each child and family will respond.

---

 1 The first challenge is to recognize biases; the next is to restructure and expand perceptions; and the greatest challenge is the part that children are most likely to notice—how one speaks, truly feels, and behaves.

The teacher's posture and facial expressions show her respect for children and their learning pace and style.

A Quick Check

The attitudes and behaviors of teachers affect children's behaviors. Questions teachers can ask themselves as they evaluate the quality of the environment are:

- Is there a feeling of mutual respect between children and adults?
- Do teachers pick up on nonverbal and verbal expressions of both girls and boys? Of children with varying abilities? Of children of color?
- How do children treat one another?
- Do teachers model cooperative behavior with other adults and children? Do they show by example how to work through a disagreement or problem?
- Does the physical setup allow the teacher to focus on the children?
- Do housekeeping details keep teachers disconnected from children?
- Do teachers encourage children to use one another as resources?
- Do teachers take time to show children how to accomplish a task by themselves?

- Are girls complimented only on appearance and boys just for achievement? Are all children helped to appreciate similarities and differences?
- Do teachers use reasoning and follow-through?
- How and when do teachers interact with children?
- What are the teacher's posture and facial expression when involved in a problem situation?
- If I were a child, would I like to come to school here?

The answers to these questions provide teachers with a barometer of how well they are maintaining an atmosphere of positive social interaction. The most important thing to remember is that the way people feel about each other and how they express their feelings have an impact on children. Teachers must focus as much attention on the interpersonal part of the environment as they do on buying equipment or arranging the room. Chapter 10, on curriculum and play, and Chapter 14, on social and emotional skills, will emphasize the interpersonal aspects of the environment further.

SUMMARY

A good environment for young children is a combination of many factors. Teachers must consider the needs of the children, teachers, and parents as well as the program goals and objectives.

The physical environment includes the buildings and yard, the equipment and materials, and the way the space is organized and used. The setting is organized to support the program's goals and must meet necessary health and safety standards.

The daily schedule outlines the timetable of events. Time blocks are arranged around the daily routines of food, rest, and toileting. The temporal environment is balanced so that children alternate indoor and outdoor play, quiet and active play, and self-selected activities with teacher-directed learning. Good interactions between children and staff are characterized by warmth, personal respect, and responsiveness. It is the interpersonal relationships that set the tone in each environment. The size of the group, the number of teachers per child, and the quality of relationships affect the interpersonal environment.

It is essential to have a clear idea of program goals before arranging the environment. The environment mirrors those goals in the way the room is arranged, teachers are deployed, and the time schedule is framed. In early childhood settings where children's independence and self-reliance are valued, the environment is created to enhance the child's budding sense of autonomy. Anti-bias environments value individual differences in race, ethnicity, ability, and gender to help children develop positive identities. Inclusive environments help children and teachers alike see every child, regardless of ability, as competent and every place as adaptable for all. Such environments build attitudes and institutions that support social justice. A peace education framework encourages children to learn to cooperate and resolve conflicts peaceably, as well as increase an understanding of war and peace. All environments reflect the goals through careful application of many factors.

Creating good environments for young children does not require great sums of money or newly designed buildings. In most settings, teachers can adapt general principles of environments to create challenging, safe, and effective group settings for children.

THINKING ABOUT THE ENVIRONMENT: INSPIRATIONS FROM THE REGGIO APPROACH

by Louise Cadwell, M.E., Ph.D.

I have heard Carlina Rinaldi say, "The best environment for children is one in which you can find the highest possible quantity and quality of relationships." Reflecting on this idea while writing *Bringing Reggio Emilia Home* (Cadwell, 1997), I wrote,

> We interpret this to mean relationships between people—children, teachers, and parents; between people and materials and languages—words, numbers, pens, paper, clay, paint, wood; between people and ideas; between people and experience with the world in which they live. (p. 93)

When I look back over the last 10 years of our work in St. Louis at The College School and the other two schools in the St. Louis-Reggio Collaborative, The St. Michael School and Clayton Schools' Family Center, I see continual evolution in our interpretation of Carlina's words in our work. For example, every year, every month, and in fact almost every day, we have changed our spaces in school, and they have consequently changed us. We have developed environments based on who we are as individuals, and "who we are" is inseparably connected to where we find ourselves in space and time and what is important to us. Otherwise, we could live anywhere and we could be anybody.

The school environments we have created are actually made up of parts of all of us and fragments of the world in which we live. For example:

- Children's words and ideas.
- Teachers' and parents' words and ideas.
- Fabric patches from three-year-old Sam's baby blanket.
- My mother's button collection.
- Papers of every kind from every family, all sorted and displayed for use on an accessible shelf.
- A miniature tea set from my colleague, Jennifer's childhood.

I love Loris Malaguzzi's image of thinking with children as being a little like a game of tossing a ball back and forth. A child or a group of children have an idea or are drawn to something. If we are listening, we notice. Then perhaps we want to play a game, so we "toss" them a twist, a provocation, a wide-open question about their idea. They respond with something marvelous that we

did not anticipate, and the game continues. We don't know where the next idea will come from, but the game is fun and challenging for both child and adult, and we get better at playing it in many situations and scenarios.

The space can be like this as well. It is actually alive or dead depending on whether we are in a living, nourishing relationship with it or not. We make a change, the change alters the way we do things, and then new possibilities emerge. We are inspired to make another change, and so it goes. This is the way of an alive environment.

A basic, underlying principle that the educators in Reggio Emilia have incorporated into their schools, classrooms, piazzas, and dining rooms is: School needs to be comfortable, pleasant, orderly, inviting, and homelike. As children, teachers, and parents we have the right to spend our days in school surrounded by spaces that will enhance our lives, support our growth, and hold us in respectful ways. Little by little, we can examine the spaces that we have and shape them into more livable and amiable rooms.

As teachers in the St. Louis-Reggio Collaborative, we strive to look at our classrooms with critical and observant eyes as often as we can. We ask ourselves, "What needs care, repair, a new coat of paint, a sparkle of light, a splash of color? What areas of the room need to be enriched? What needs to be given away in order to make room for new life, energy, and new ideas? What aspects of ongoing experiences are unclear, left unexplained, or empty of meaning?"

One rule of thumb that guides us suggests that everything be out in the open so that we can see it and use it. On the high shelves there are Lucite boxes of fabric, ribbons, twines, and raffias of all colors. On nearby shelves you will find collections of clear folders of sparkly paper, patterned papers, handmade papers, white and cream colored paper curls. On the low shelves, transparent jars of shells, buttons, beads, wires, tiny pine cones, dried rose petals and sequins beckon. Children know where things are and can find them; so do the teachers and the parents. The abundance, diversity, order, and availability of materials seem to attract energy, ideas, connection, and possibility, all of which propel us in a positive direction.

Along with the evolution of our spaces a deep respect for the complexity and order of our environments has developed. The children here used to dump blocks in piles. They used to empty little plastic boxes of sequins or mix things up to be a bit mischievous or to see what would happen. Some even used to draw on the walls or color on the tables on purpose. Now, this rarely happens. Why? The children know that the materials wait like treasures to be touched, explored, transformed, and composed. The children recognize the materials for their power to hold stories, inventions, and layered ideas. Now, the children teach each other to care and respect the many aspects of our complex environment.

We have established, slowly but surely, with children and parents, a culture of respect, appreciation, interaction, care, and love of the spaces in which we live. The way the materials are displayed and used parallels the way ideas flow and circulate, gathering energy, excitement, form, and shape whether among children or adults. This phenomenon generates an atmosphere that feels electric and alive. Many elements of our life in school overlap and intersect, setting in motion a complex network of relationships of all kinds.

Louise Cadwell, M.E., Ph.D., is coordinator of curriculum and professional development at The College School in St. Louis, Missouri, studio teacher/researcher with all three schools in the St. Louis-Reggio Collaborative: The College School, The St. Michael School, and Clayton Schools' Family Center. She returned to St. Louis after a one-year internship in the preschools of Reggio Emilia, Italy. She is the author of Bringing Reggio Emilia Home: An Innovative Approach to Early Childhood Education *and* Bringing Learning to Life: The Reggio Approach to Early Childhood Education *and co-editor of* In the Spirit of the Studio: Learning from the Atelier of Reggio Emilia.

For more activities and information, visit our Web site at http://www.EarlyChildEd.delmar.com

KEY TERMS

environment	self-esteem	daily schedules
physical	least restrictive environment	routines
temporal	roughhousing	transition
interpersonal	open-ended	flexibility
self-help	interest areas	group times
self-concept	learning centers	

REVIEW QUESTIONS

1. Why is there no standard or ideal environment for early childhood schools? How would you describe a good environment for one-year-olds? For three-year-olds? For six-year-olds? Why?

2. What are the three aspects of environments to consider when planning programs for children? What do you think of first and why?

3. Why might educators want to create an anti-bias environment? How might that look in a multiethnic community? In a homogeneous setting?

4. Why is self-help a common goal in most early childhood settings? How can teachers support self-help in infants? In toddlers? In nursery schoolers? In school-aged children?

5. What kinds of adaptations might be needed to provide an inclusive environment for children with motor disabilities? With visual impairments?

6. Discuss three school health and safety policies that help keep illness and injury to a minimum. Include how you would explain these guidelines to parents and how you would handle a problem.

7. Outline at least six key interest areas in an early childhood environment.

8. Look at the daily schedule of an early childhood program. What transitions occur in the daily schedule, and how are they handled?

LEARNING ACTIVITIES

1. Hunch down on your knees and look at a classroom from the child's perspective. Describe what you see in terms of the principles of successful environments.

2. Examine a daily schedule from an early childhood center. What do you think are the program goals of the school? How can you tell? Compare this with a daily schedule of a family day-care home. How are they alike? How are they different?

3. The following list names some common problems that can be remedied by changing the environment. List at least one solution for each problem.

   a. too many children crowding into one area
   b. overcrowded shelves
   c. grabbing or arguments over the same toy
   d. hoarding of materials
   e. lack of cooperation during cleanup
   f. wheel toy collisions
   g. children crying when others' parents leave

4. Visit a toddler program, a four-year-old program, and a kindergarten. How are the learning centers defined? Name the centers of interest, and indicate which of them are for quiet play and which are for active play and work.

5. Check a classroom for diversity. Using the following checklist (de Melendez & Ostertag, 1997), enter a checkmark whenever you find something in the classroom that complies with the element of diversity.

Checking the classroom environment for diversity

ELEMENT OF DIVERSITY

	Culture	Gender	Social class	[Dis]ability	Age
Pictures/posters					
Books					
Housekeeping items					
Manipulatives					
Art materials					
Dramatic area					
Music					

Comments:

• Things I need to change:

• Things I need to add:

REFERENCES

Alexander, N. P. (1995, September). Turning on the light: Thinking about lighting issues in child care. *Exchange.*

Ambery, M. E. (1997, May). Time for Franklin. *Young Children, 52.*

Bickart, T., Jablon, J. R., & Dodge, D. T. (1999). *Building the primary classroom.* Washington, DC: Teaching Strategies.

Bredekamp, S., & Copple, C. (Ed.). (1997). *Developmentally appropriate practice in early childhood programs serving children from birth through age 8* (Rev.). Washington, DC: National Association for the Education of Young Children.

Bredekamp, S., & Willer, B. (Eds.). (1996). *NAEYC accreditation: A decade of learning and the years ahead.* Washington, DC: National Association for the Education of Young Children.

Carter, M., & Curtis, D. (2003). *Designs for living and learning: Transforming early childhood environments.* St. Paul, MN: Redleaf Press.

Centers for Disease Control and Prevention (1997). *The ABCs of safe and healthy child care.* Atlanta, GA: Author.

Community Products, LLc, "Children come first: Selecting equipment for early childhood education," Rifton, NY: 2004.

Consumer Product Safety Commission (CPSC). (1997). *National electronic injury surveillance system, 1990–94.* Washington, DC: Author.

Cross, W. E. (1985). Black identity: Rediscovering the distinctions between personal identity and reference group orientations. In Spencer, Brookins, & Allen (Eds.), *Beginnings: The social and affective development of black children.* Hillsdale, NJ: Erlbaum.

de Melendez, R. W., & Ostertag, V. (1997). *Teaching young children in multicultural classrooms.* Clifton Park, NY: Thomson Delmar Learning.

Derman-Sparks, L., & the ABC Task Force. (1989). *Antibias curriculum: Tools for empowering young children.* Washington, DC: National Association for the Education of Young Children.

Dodge, D. T., Colker, L. J., & Heroman, C. (2002). *The Creative Curriculum® for preschool* (4th ed.). Washington, DC: Teaching Strategies.

Edwards, C., Gandini, L., & Forman, G. (1993). *The hundred languages of children.* Norwood, NJ: Ablex Press.

Elgas, P. M., Prendeville, J., Moomaw, S., & Kretschmer, R. R. (2002). Early childhood classroom setup. *Child Care Information Exchange, 143,* 17–20.

Fowler, W. J. (1992). *What do we know about school size? What should we know?* Washington, DC: Office of Educational Research and Improvement.

Froschl, M., Rubin, E., & Sprung, B. (1984). *Including all of us: An early childhood curriculum about disabilities.* New York: Educational Equity Concepts.

Frost, J. L. (1986). Children's playgrounds: Research and practice. In G. Fein & M. Rivkin (Eds.), *The young child at play: Review of research* (Vol. 4). Washington, DC: National Association for the Education of Young Children.

Greenman, J. (2000). What is the setting? Places for childhood. In A. Gordon & K. W. Browne, *Beginnings and Beyond* (5th ed.). Clifton Park, NY: Thomson Delmar Learning.

Greenman, J., & Prescott, H. E. (1994). *Caring spaces, learning places.* Redmond, WA: Exchange Press.

Gronlund, G. (2006). *Make early learning standards come alive.* Washington, DC: NAEYC.

Gutierrez, M. E. (1982). *Chicano parents' perceptions of their children's racial/cultural awareness.* Unpublished master's thesis, Pacific Oaks College, Pasadena, CA.

Harms, T., Clifford, R. M., & Cryer, D. (2005). *The early childhood (revised), family day care, infant/toddler, and school age environmental rating scales.* New York: Teachers College Press.

Haugen, K. (1997, March). Using your senses to adapt environments: Checklist for an accessible environment: Beginnings workshop. *Child Care Information Exchange.*

Hernandez, A. (1991, July 8). What do we have in common? *Time.*

Honig, A. S. (1983). Sex role socialization in early childhood. *Young Children, 38*(6), 57–90.

Howes, C., Phillips, D., & Whitebrook, M. (1992). Thresholds of quality: Implications for the social development of children in center-based care. *Child Development, 63*(4), 449–460.

Jensen, E. (1998). *Teaching with the brain in mind.* Alexandria, VA: Association for Supervision and Curriculum Development.

Jones, E. (1984). *Personal notes about pluralistic and developmental viewpoints.* Unpublished.

Kendall, F. (1996). *Diversity in the classroom* (2nd ed.). New York: Teachers College Press.

Kielar, J. (1999, September). An antidote to the noisy nineties. *Young Children, 54*(5). Washington, DC: NAEYC, 28–29.

Kontos, S., & Wilcox-Herzog, A. (1997, January). Research in review: Teachers' interactions with children: Why are they so important? *Young Children, 52,* 4.

Kutner, B. (1984). Patterns of mental functioning associated with prejudice in children. Psychological Monographs, 72, 406.

Lowman, L. H., & Ruhmann, L. H. (1998, May). Simply sensational spaces: A multi-"S" approach to toddler environments. *Young Children 53*(3), 11–17.

Marotz, L., Rush, J. M., & Cross, M. Z. (2001). *Health, safety, and nutrition for the young child* (5th ed.). Clifton Park, NY: Thomson Delmar Learning.

Moore, G. T. (1983). *The role of the socio-physical environment in cognitive development.* Milwaukee, WI: University of Wisconsin.

National After-School Association (NAA). (1998). "National School-Age Care Alliance Standards for Quality School-Age Care," www.naaweb.org.

National Association for the Education of Young Children. (1995). Keeping healthy: Parents, teachers, and children. Washington, DC: Author.

National Association for the Education of Young Children. (2002). *Position statement: Early learning standards: Creating the conditions for success.* Washington, DC: Author.

National Association for the Education of Young Children. (2005). *Accreditation performance criteria* Washington, DC: Author.

National Association for the Education of Young Children. (2005). *Position statement: Code of ethical conduct* (Appendix A is the entire text of the Code). Washington, DC: Author.

Needlman, R., & Needlman, G. (1995, November/December). 10 most common health problems in school. *Scholastic Early Childhood Today.*

Nelson, M. A., & Raymond, B. (1989, September). Sports, kids, fun, & safety. *Good Housekeeping, 4,* 52.

New, R. (1990, September). Excellent early education: A city in Italy has it. *Young Children,* 4–10.

New, R. (2000). The role of the environment in Reggio Emilia. In A. Gordon & K. W. Browne, *Beginnings and Beyond.* Clifton Park; NY: Thomson Delmar Learning.

Prescott, E., Jones, E., & Kritschevsky, S. (1972). *Group care as a child-rearing environment.* Washington, DC: National Association for the Education of Young Children.

Rivkin, M. S. (1995). *The great outdoors: Restoring children's right to play outdoors.* Washington, DC: NAEYC.

Rogers, C. (1994, Spring). *Mainstreaming: Special needs—Special experiences.* Unpublished paper.

Rushton, S. P. (2001, September). Applying brain research to create developmentally appropriate environments. *Young Children 56*(5), 76–82.

"Standards for Quality School-Age Care." Charlestown, MA: National After School Association (NAA), 1998.

Stonehouse, A. (1990, November/December). The Golden Rule for child care. Exchange.

Teachers Resisting Unhealthy Children's Entertainment (TRUCE). (2001–2002). *Toys and toy trends to avoid.* West Somerville, MA: Author.

Themes, T. (1999). *Let's go outside: Designing the early childhood playground.* Ypsilanti, MI: High/Scope press.

Waldorf School (author unknown). (1995, January). *What is a Waldorf kindergarten?* Los Altos, CA: Author.

Weinberger, N. (2000). Overcoming obstacles to create retreats in family child care, *Young Children 55*(5).

Whitebrook, M. (1996). NAEYC accreditation as an indicator of quality: What research tells us. In S. Bredekamp & B. Willer (Eds.), *NAEYC accreditation: A decade of learning and the years ahead.* Washington, DC: National Association for the Education of Young Children.

Youcha, V., & Wood, K. (1997, March). Enhancing the environment for all children: Beginnings workshop. *Exchange.*

Zeavin, C. (1997, March). Toddlers at play: Environments at work. *Young Children, 52*(4), 72–77.

HELPFUL WEB SITES

Canada Institute of Child Health	http://www.cich.ca
Centers for Disease Control and Prevention	http://www.cdc.gov/nccdphp/ddt/tcoyd
Children's Health	http://www.kidshealth.org
	http://www.aboutkidshealth.ca
Child Development	http://www.nacd.org
Journal of Pediatrics	http://www.mosby.com
MyPyramid for Kids	http://www.fns.usda.gov/tn/kids-pyramid.html
National Program for Playground Safety	http://www.uni.edu/playground
National Safety Council	http://www.nsc.org/index/
U.S. Consumer Product Safety Commission	http://www.cdc.gov/ncipc/ncipchm
Zero to Three	http://www.zerotothree.org
Teachers Resisting Unhealthy Children's Entertainment	http://www.truceteachers.org

For more activities and information, visit our Web site at http://www.EarlyChildEd.delmar.com

Section  4

What Is Being Taught?

WHAT IS THE CURRICULUM?

Diane Trister Dodge

Over the past decade, the value of a written, research-based, comprehensive curriculum for providing care and education for infants, toddlers, two-year-olds, and preschool children has not only been recognized, but such a curriculum has become a requirement for programs that receive public funds, such as Head Start. It is also required for program accreditation from professional organizations such as the National Association for the Education of Young Children.

A number of factors have led to this recognition.

1. Extensive research findings—including new information about brain development—confirm the importance of the first five years of life as a time of enormous development and learning that is fundamental to future success. Children's development during this period is simply too important to be left to chance.

2. What children should know and be able to do before they enter kindergarten is now better understood. Every state has developed or is in the process of developing early learning standards. Teachers now have a way of evaluating their curriculum to determine whether it meets such standards.

3. Program quality is greatly affected by the degree to which teachers understand a research-based, comprehensive curriculum and implement it as intended. Opportunities for early childhood teachers to make real differences in the lives of young children—especially children who begin life in challenging circumstances—can only be realized if the programs are of high quality.

4. A comprehensive curriculum provides a crucial knowledge base for teachers, especially when it is used for ongoing professional development and support.

An early childhood curriculum is very different from a curriculum for older children. A traditional curriculum presents a scope and sequence for teaching each subject, outlining exactly what to teach each day and how. An appropriate curriculum for children under age five is more interrelated and comprehensive. This is because early childhood is a unique developmental period that requires adults to care for and teach children in ways that integrate learning in all developmental areas: social/emotional, physical, cognitive, and language. The curriculum must recognize the vast amount of development that occurs in the early years and young children's need to explore the objects, materials, and people in their immediate worlds. It must also enable teachers to take into account the huge variability in the rate at which children develop different skills and the many personal characteristics, personal experiences, and cultural influences that affect how a child relates to others and learns. A one-size-fits-all approach fails to meet the learning needs of all children.

An early childhood curriculum must include

- a discussion of the research and theories that form the foundation of the curriculum, so that teachers know not only what they are doing but why.

- an overview of children's social/emotional, physical, cognitive, and language development, and the characteristics and experiences that make each child unique.

- clear goals and objectives that align with state early learning standards and that are tied to a system of ongoing assessment that enables teachers to learn about and plan for each child.

- an explanation of how to create a responsive learning environment, including the materials and physical set-up of the room, the daily schedule and routines, experiences, and the social environment in which children learn to get along and build relationships with others.

- a discussion of what children learn, including an explanation of how the curriculum addresses content and skills in language and literacy, math, science, social studies, the arts, and technology through meaningful play and long-term studies.

- teaching approaches that range from child-initiated to teacher-directed learning.

- an explanation of how teachers use what they learn from observing children in order to respond to each child and to plan for each child and the group.

- strategies for building respectful partnerships with families and supporting them in promoting their children's development and learning.

The current move to offer prekindergarten programs for all four-year-olds has led to the publication of many new curriculum models. Some are comprehensive and developmentally appropriate. Others are narrow in scope and give teachers a script to follow as well as lessons plans for each day. The second approach seems to be an attempt to make the curriculum "teacher proof" and does not enable teachers to respond appropriately to the needs and interests of young children.

Scripts and prescribed lesson plans are unwise for a number of reasons. Teaching is both an art and a science. A curriculum should provide the structure that teachers need—especially new teachers—as well as the content to teach and how to provide meaningful, integrated learning experiences. The curriculum must also give teachers the tools to get to know and build a positive relationship with each child. Building the relationships that are critical to children's motivation, self-direction, and excitement about learning cannot be scripted. Teachers need a way to learn about each child, build on children's strengths and abilities, and respond to their individual interests and needs.

Young children are eager to learn and to form positive relationships. Our responsibility as teachers is to encourage and nurture children by allowing them to experience the joy of discovery; the power of making choices, decisions, and plans; the feelings of competence that come from persevering and completing a task; and the motivational force of meaningful learning experiences. Teachers should have a voice in selecting the curriculum that best addresses their goals and families' goals for children and their vision of effective teaching. This section of the book discusses the issues to consider in selecting a curriculum and implementing it well.

DIANE TRISTER DODGE

DIANE TRISTER DODGE is the founder and president of Teaching Strategies, Inc., a company that seeks to improve the quality of early childhood programs by designing practical, easy-to-use curriculum and training materials and providing staff development. She has been a preschool and kindergarten teacher, served as the education coordinator for Head Start and child care programs in Mississippi and Washington, DC, and directed national projects in education and human services. Diane is a well-known speaker and author of more than 25 books, including *The Creative Curriculum, Building the Primary Classroom,* and books for parents. Her work with teachers and administrators has taught her the value of curriculum and staff development materials that articulate a clear philosophy and practical approach to meaningful learning. Diane has served on numerous boards, including NAEYC and the Center for the Child Care Workforce.

CHAPTER

10

Curriculum Basics

QUESTIONS FOR THOUGHT

What factors define curriculum in the early childhood setting?

What is developmentally appropriate curriculum? Culturally appropriate curriculum?

What is the process of developing emergent curriculum?

What is the project approach to curriculum planning?

What role do learning styles play in curriculum development?

What is the role of the teacher in curriculum planning?

How does play support curriculum development?

What are four effective curriculum models?

CURRICULUM BASICS

What Is Curriculum?

> Ira, a two-year-old, is more interested in the process of pouring milk (especially what happens after the cup is filled) than in eating and conversing at snack time.

> Kindergartners Bert and Leo become absorbed in watching a snail make its way across the sidewalk, ignoring for the moment the lesson on running relays.

In an early childhood setting, the curriculum consists of the art activity and language game; it is also the spontaneous investigation of liquids at snack time, the song that accompanies digging in the sand, and the teacher's explanation of why the hamster died. The curriculum is the planned and the unplanned and includes all of the activities as well as the subject matter, the interactions with people, and all of the experiences of the child's day.

Young children absorb everything going on about them. They do not discriminate between what is prepared and structured for them to learn and whatever else happens to them at school. It is *all* learning.

Creating a good curriculum for young children is not simply a matter of writing lessons plans. It is understanding the process of how children interact with people and materials to learn. It is the sum of a teacher's knowledge about children's needs, materials, and equipment and what happens when they meet.

Bredekamp and Rosegrant (1995) provide an all-inclusive definition:

> Curriculum is an organized framework that delineates the *content* that children are to learn, the *process* through which children achieve the identified curricular goals, what *teachers* do to help children achieve these goals, and the *context* in which teaching and learning occur.

- The *content* is what is being taught—the subject matter reflects the interests, needs, and experiences of the children, as well as what children should learn.

- The *process* is how and when learning takes place, the choice of activities and how they integrate with one another, and the time frame within the daily schedule or yearly calendar. The process enhances children's learning through a hands-on, exploratory approach with a variety of open-ended materials. Play is the medium for the process.

Curriculum planning begins with children's interests and needs.

- The *teacher* is the person who creates the curriculum, planning and providing for activities and materials in relation to the age range of the group and observing and evaluating children's growth. Teachers are grounded in child development theory, have an understanding of how children learn, and are aware of the need to individualize to meet children's special needs.

Curriculum happens when child meets materials.

- The *context* is why certain projects and activities are chosen, based on the program's philosophy and goals, the cultural backgrounds of the children, and their family and community values and influences.

Curriculum must also be relevant to the child. Head Start classes on Native American reservations will develop curricula that represents the history and traditions of the tribes the students represent. Relevant curriculum for a preschool in Seattle may include field trips to the Pike Street Market to see the recent salmon catch, while a transportation unit for inner city Boston children may include subway rides.

Developmentally Appropriate Curriculum

Appropriate early childhood curriculum is based on the theory, research, and experience of knowing how young children develop and learn. An infant curriculum meets the basic needs of young babies; a toddler curriculum considers the emerging independence and mobility of toddlers. Four-year-olds require different materials and teaching techniques, as do five- or eight-year-olds. Each age level deserves special consideration when curriculum is being planned.

Developmentally appropriate programs, curricula, or practices have been defined by NAEYC (Bredekamp & Copple, 1997) as follows:

- *Appropriateness.* Programs and practices are based on knowledge of normal child development within a given age span.
- *Individual appropriateness.* Programs and practices are based on respect for the individual child, the individual rate of growth, and the unique learning style.
- *Social and cultural appropriateness.* Programs and practices provide meaningful and relevant learning experiences that are respectful of the backgrounds of the children and families in the group.[1]

A developmentally appropriate curriculum takes into account a knowledge of child development theory, research, and practice, including various related disciplines; cultural values; parental desires and concerns; community context; individual children; teachers' knowledge

Children enjoy and get involved with developmentally appropriate materials.

and experience; and it is related to overall program goals.[2]

The foundation for **developmentally appropriate practices** and curriculum content is historically rooted in John Dewey's vision that schools prepare students to think and reason in order to participate in a democratic society (see Chapter 1). Figure 10-1 lists 20 guidelines jointly endorsed by the National Association for the Education of Young Children and the National Association of Early Childhood Specialists in State Departments of Education to ensure developmentally appropriate curriculum. It can be used as a checklist as you move through the next three chapters, which focus on curriculum.

Culturally Appropriate Curriculum

If meaningful learning is derived from a social and cultural context (as Vygotsky asserts), then a multicultural atmosphere must be created where awareness and concern for true diversity (including ethnicity, gender, and abilities) permeate the

1 DAP is CAC. Developmentally appropriate curriculum is culturally appropriate curriculum.

2 There is no one "recipe" for developmentally appropriate practice; rather, sound practice is related to individual children, families, and the community in which one teaches.

Questions to Consider When Analyzing a Curriculum for Developmental Appropriateness

NAEYC and the National Association of Early Childhood Specialists in state Departments of Education jointly developed guidelines to ensure developmentally appropriate curriculum. Each of the guidelines suggests a question for analyzing developmentally appropriate curriculum. Teachers developing curriculum for young children should be able to answer "yes" to the following questions.

1. Does it promote interactive learning and encourage the child's construction of knowledge?

2. Does it help achieve social, emotional, physical, and cognitive goals and promote democratic values?

3. Does it encourage development of positive feelings and dispositions toward learning while leading to acquisition of knowledge and skills?

4. Is it meaningful for these children? Is it relevant to the children's lives? Can it be made more relevant by relating it to a personal experience children have had, or can they easily gain direct experience with it?

5. Are the expectations realistic and attainable at this time, or could the children more easily and efficiently acquire the knowledge or skills later on?

6. Is it of interest to children and to the teacher?

7. Is it sensitive to and respectful of the cultural and linguistic diversity? Does it expect, allow, and appreciate individual differences? Does it promote positive relationships with families?

8. Does it build on and elaborate children's current knowledge and abilities?

9. Does it lead to conceptual understanding by helping children construct their own understanding in meaningful contexts?

10. Does it facilitate integration of content across traditional subject matter areas?

11. Is the information presented accurate and credible according to the recognized standards of the relevant discipline?

12. Is this content worth knowing? Can it be learned by these children efficiently and effectively now?

13. Does it encourage active learning and allow children to make meaningful choices?

14. Does it foster children's exploration and inquiry, rather than focusing on "right" answers or "right" ways to complete a task?

15. Does it promote the development of higher order abilities such as thinking, reasoning, problem solving, and decision making?

16. Does it promote and encourage social interaction among children and adults?

17. Does it respect children's physiological needs for activity, sensory stimulation, fresh air, rest, hygiene and nourishment/elimination?

18. Does it promote feelings of physiological safety, security, and belonging?

19. Does it provide experiences that promote feelings of success, competence, and enjoyment of learning?

20. Does it permit flexibility for children and teachers?

FIGURE 10-1 (Reprinted with permission from the National Association for the Education of Young Children (NAEYC). "Suggestions for using the curriculum guidelines" from NAEYC & the National Association of Early Childhood Specialists in State Departments of Education (NAECS/SDE) 1990. Guidelines for Appropriate Curriculum Content and Assessment in Programs Serving Children Ages 3 through 8. Joint position statement. Copyright © 1990 NAEYC.)

program. This calls into question the familiar ways of doing things and requires new insights and ways of thinking about culture. Multicultural education is about "modifying the total school environment so that students from diverse ethnic and cultural groups will experience equal educational opportunities" (Banks, 1994). Figure 10-2 highlights the difference by comparing common characteristics of a dominant culture with an approach that would offer more perspectives from other cultures.

Culturally appropriate curriculum is also developmentally appropriate curriculum. The challenge is to develop a curriculum that reflects the plurality of contemporary American society in general and the individual classroom, in particular, and present them in sensitive, relevant ways. This does not necessarily mean creating a whole new curriculum.

Banks (1992) suggests the **infusion** of multicultural content within the current practices as a way to begin to develop a multicultural

Characteristics of a Multicultural Curriculum

Common Practices of Dominant Culture	For a Multicultural Approach
Focuses on isolated aspects of the histories and cultures of ethnic groups	Describes the history and cultures of ethnic groups holistically
Trivializes the histories and cultures of ethnic groups	Describes the cultures of ethnic groups as dynamic wholes
Presents events, issues, and concepts primarily from Anglocentric and mainstream perspectives	Presents events, issues, concepts from the perspectives of diverse racial and ethnic groups
Is Eurocentric—shows the development of the United States primarily as an extension of Europe into the Americas	Is multidimensional and geocultural—shows how many peoples and cultures came to the United States from many parts of the world, including Asia and Africa, and the important roles they played in the development of U.S. society
Content about ethnic groups is an appendage to regular curriculum	Content about ethnic groups is an integral part of regular curriculum
Ethnic minority cultures are described as deprived or dysfunctional	Ethnic minority cultures are described as different from mainstream Anglo culture but as rich and functional
Focuses on ethnic heroes, holidays, and factual information	Focuses on concepts, generalizations, and theories
Emphasizes the mastery of knowledge and cognitive outcomes	Emphasizes knowledge formation and decision making
Encourages acceptance of existing ethnic, class, and racial stratification	Focuses on social criticism and social change

FIGURE 10-2 A comparison of two different approaches to multicultural curriculum, one from a Eurocentric point of view, the other from a culturally sensitive perspective. (Reprinted with permission from James A. Banks, *Cultural Diversity and Education: Foundations, Curriculum, and Teaching* (5th Edition. Boston: Allyn & Bacon, 2006), page 238.)

curriculum. Infusion, according to Banks (1994), allows the teacher to continue using a developmentally appropriate curriculum while incorporating many perspectives, frames of reference, and content from various groups that will extend a child's understanding of today's society. This principle is demonstrated in Figure 10-3, in which the theme of "All About Me" is used for a dual purpose: to help children recognize their own unique self and to foster pride in their cultural diversity. This is a good example of using a common early childhood curriculum theme and infusing other cultural perspectives into it.

The infusion approach calls into question the common practice in many early childhood programs of cooking ethnic foods or celebrating ethnic or cultural holidays as isolated experiences, which often trivialize or stereotype groups of people. Folk tales, songs, food, and dress are symbols and expressions of a culture, not the culture itself. For children to gain any meaningful knowledge, the content must contribute to a fuller understanding of human diversity, not just a special-occasion topic. On the other hand, using music from various cultures for movement

and dance activities throughout the curriculum throughout the year incorporates the perspective of a pluralistic society into the established routines and rituals of the classroom.

de Melendez & Ostertag (1997) suggest ways to begin the process of infusion:

- List the topics/themes/units from your current curriculum guide or lesson plans.
- With your class list in hand, look for the traits that are descriptive of the cultural diversity of the students in your class (ethnicities, religion, languages, social class, exceptionality/abilities).
- Circle on the list of topics/themes/units those areas that lend themselves to infusion of diversity. Begin by incorporating those characteristics found in your own classroom, then consider those of others.
- Brainstorm how you could incorporate diversity into the selected topics. Ask yourself what other views could help children expand their understanding of this topic. Write down all responses.
- Refine the list of ideas and topics/themes/units including the additional perspectives. Put into action.

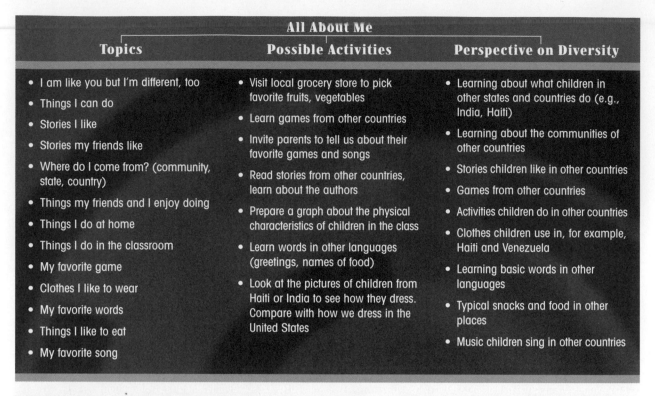

FIGURE 10-3 An example of curriculum infusion. (From de Melendez, R. W., & Ostertag, V. (1997). *Teaching young children in multicultural classrooms.* Clifton Park, NY: Thomson Delmar Learning. Used with permission.)

● Assess the results. Keep notes on children's responses and reactions. Revise your plan according to what you have learned.

To gain a greater sense of what multicultural curriculum can be in the early years, keep these questions in mind as you read through the rest of this chapter. Refer to the sections in Chapter 9 on anti-bias environments and inclusive environments and to the multicultural environment checklist (Figure 9-2) as well.

Classroom materials and activities need to be evaluated to ensure fair and sensitive portrayals of various cultures. Make sure they are consistent with the philosophy and goals of the program, and that they contribute to the understanding of life in our diverse society. de Melendez & Ostertag (1997) propose the following questions as a way of assessing the choice of a topic for infusion. Does the topic:

● present, elaborate, and/or expand concepts of diversity?

● fit logically into the child's learning and experience, giving a sense of real, not unimportant, learning?

● include the perspectives of how the people with diverse cultural views would behave or react to it?

● reflect issues that are common to the children in the classroom or the community?

● offer opportunities to present other positions that expose the children to divergent views?

● serve as a link to discuss emotions and feelings as perceived by the children?

● facilitate clarification of stereotypes and biases? How?

Inclusive Curriculum

Inclusive curriculum reflects an awareness of and sensitivity to diversity in all areas of a child's life: cultural, social, language, religion, gender, and capabilities. The inclusion of children with any and all varieties of disabilities and who reflect various cultural backgrounds has been built into the chapters of this text.

Cultural sensitivity is described in terms of developmentally appropriate practices in Chapter 3 and in defining the young child later on in that chapter. Chapter 7 includes cultural influences on children's behavior and various patterns of family behavior, and Vygotsky's theory that development and knowledge are culturally specific is discussed in Chapter 13.

Chapter 3 describes how a child with disabilities is included within the early childhood program. In Chapter 9 you will find suggestions for creating inclusive environments, with a checklist on pages 341; in Chapter 12, there are ideas for inclusion in physical activities.

Throughout the text there are references and examples of inclusion.

Arce (2000) describes "authentic inclusion" as an approach that builds upon and integrates multicultural and anti-bias strategies for a sensitive and culturally affirming program. Multiculturalism becomes a part of a whole area of inclusiveness, so that "no one is being left out" (Hall & Rhomberg, 1995).

The basic premise in this text is that children with disabilities, children from immigrant families, children from families whose first language is not English, girls and boys, and young children from all cultures need the same things in a learning environment. Quality early childhood education programs operate under the same sound principles, no matter what characteristics define the children who attend these programs. Adaptations are made to fit the capacities of each individual child as needed.

The curriculum philosophy becomes a crucial element in an inclusive environment. How are differences in children accommodated within the curriculum? The curriculum should be flexible and provide a variety of learning activities and opportunities for a wide range of skills and abilities all at one time. It needs to be a curriculum where children can participate at their developmental level, yet challenging enough to help them learn.

EFFECTIVE CURRICULUM: FOUR BASIC FACTORS

Effective curriculum consists of any number of factors. Four important features are curriculum that is (1) integrated; (2) emergent; (3) based on multiples intelligences; and (4) bears in mind differences in learning styles. With these in mind, the curriculum becomes more flexible and suited to all children in the class.

Integrated Curriculum

Do you remember back in Chapter 3 the discussion about the whole child? The developmental concept that growth is related is a significant point made on page 99, particularly in Figure 3-1. That drawing shows how one area of development affects and is affected by the others. As young children learn, the social, emotional, cognitive, creative, and physical areas of development work together to help children find meaning in and mastery of their world.

It is useful to think of integrated curriculum in the same way. Integrated curriculum coordinates many subject areas and utilizes a holistic approach to learning. It is curriculum that depends upon the individual differences in children, blending hands-on learning with the acquisition of skills. An integrated curriculum makes it possible for teachers to include skill development activities in context, not in isolation, weaving across many subject areas throughout the day. See Figure 10-4 for a good example of applying mathematical concepts in an integrated way.

Subject matter is not taught as separate and unique topics, such as math, science, art, and language. Instead, they are all planned components of the total curriculum. The subject areas cut across the learning activity and reinforce concepts in meaningful ways as children engage in their work and play. If this sounds familiar, go back to Chapter 1 and read about John Dewey's philosophy of education. The concept has been used in curriculum development for many years. The guidelines for developmentally appropriate curriculum found in Figure 10-1 contain many of the characteristics of an integrated curriculum.

It is easy to see how an integrated curriculum works. Experiencing the usefulness of numbers in a variety of contexts is a natural rather than a contrived way for children to learn. Other illustrations in this and the following four chapters demonstrate an integrated curriculum.

In music: Singing *Five Little Pumpkins*

In routines: Waiting for a turn because "too many" are brushing teeth already

In books: *Inch by Inch* by Lionni, *Millions of Cats* by Gag

In block play: Observing and using the fractions and wholes that make up a set of unit blocks

In physical development: Playing hopscotch

In cooking: Measuring and counting items in the recipe

In dramatic play: Noting there are only four hoses but five firefighters

In science: Counting the number of rainy/sunny/snowy days; recording temperatures (thermometers); time (clocks and calendars); and seasons (charts)

In art: Numbers: learning one-to-one correspondence by counting brushes, crayons, Magic Markers®, and colors

FIGURE 10-4 Young children learn best from an integrated approach to curriculum. Mathematical concepts are reflected throughout the classroom in a variety of activities.

An integrated curriculum provides numerous advantages (Gestwicki, 2007), Miller (1996), and Arce (2000) and

- reflects the natural way children develop at their own rate and not in all areas of growth at the same time.
- allows for a wide range of abilities within a classroom age range of one year as well as within a mixed-age group.
- accommodates individualization as children meet a variety of materials and experiences at their own unique development levels.
- maximizes the effect of rates of learning, different styles of learning, and multiple intelligences.
- provides for learning to take place within the context of meaningful activity.
- requires large blocks of time so learning can be more in-depth.
- promotes self-motivation and extension of learning.
- blends hands-on learning with skill acquisition.

Cooking projects promote a variety of curriculum subjects, such as math, literacy, science, physical coordination, and cognitive learning.

- lends itself to both a theme and project approach to curriculum planning.

Emergent Curriculum

Emergent curriculum is just what it says: curriculum that emerges—comes from or slowly evolves—out of the child's experiences and interests. The emphasis is on children's interests, their involvement in their learning, and their ability to make constructive choices. Teachers set up materials and equipment in the room and the yard, sometimes planning a few activities each day that will capture children's attention. For the most part, teachers then watch and evaluate what children do and then support and extend what use children make of their experiences.

Taking Cues from Children

A lively group time discussion one day in the three-year-old class involved a new bridge that was being built near the school. The teachers had noticed that the block area had sat unused during the week so they added books on bridges, paper, crayons, and scissors to the shelves near the blocks, and put up pictures of different kinds of bridges. These additions drew children to the block area where they drew bridges, made paper bridges, and counted the numbers of different kinds of bridges that were in the books nearby. The curriculum content in this example is apparent but an end product is not the major focus. It is an example of integrated curriculum as well as emergent curriculum because the process children go through in creating knowledge through the extension of bridge play fosters new insights and learning. The focus is always on the child, not on the activity.

This practice of taking cues from children—noting what they play with, what they avoid, what they change—is one of the components of emergent curriculum and stems from the belief that in order to be a meaningful learning experience, the curriculum should come out of the daily life in the classroom. Based on the principles of Erikson, Piaget, and Vygotsky, emergent curriculum assumes that children are active, curious, powerful learners, capable of taking the initiative and constructing their knowledge through experience. Children are encouraged to use whatever style of learning is most natural to them (Gardner, 1983), making use of the variety of materials in their own way. A materials-rich environment where play is valued forms the foundation for the curriculum.

Video VIEW Point 10-1

"Truly, the most fascinating, interactive, developmentally appropriate toys for infants are the adults and children in their lives."

COMPETENCY: Learning Environment

AGE GROUP: Infants and Toddlers

CRITICAL THINKING QUESTIONS:

1. What does this statement mean to you?

2. As an infant/toddler caregiver, how would you implement this statement?

Collaboration and Mutual Learning

The emergent curriculum calls for collaboration on the part of the teachers with children and with other adults who offer suggestions and ideas. The accent is on mutual learning for both children and adults. For example, when the first-grade class took a subway to the museum, this prompted a great many questions about subways and how they work. Because of the children's interest and the teacher's awareness of their developmental and educational needs, a project emerged and was developed over the next few weeks. It required the teachers to learn more about what the students wanted to know about subways, as well as to learn for themselves more about the topic so they could facilitate the children's learning and define the goals and objectives. The children helped plan the project. They asked questions, investigated, researched, explored, and, with the teacher's support and encouragement, formed small groups and completed assigned tasks. Books became an important resource, as did people. The teacher, knowing what the children needed and were ready to learn, guided the discussion to ensure that educational goals would be met.

For emergent curriculum to be successful, teachers have a responsibility to listen and observe carefully as children generate new ideas and then respond to what they hear and see that children have learned. Many observations methods were described in Chapter 6 and are appropriate ways to help teachers find ways and materials to advance and deepen what children learn. While emergent curriculum calls for collaboration and negotiation between children and teachers, it is the teacher who knows what is necessary for children's education and development and sets the goals for learning.

Sources for Curriculum Ideas

Children are only one of many sources of curriculum possibilities. A number of other sources feed into emergent curriculum, as noted by Jones (1994):

- Teachers' and parents' interests and skills.
- Developmental tasks of the age group.
- The physical and natural environment as well as people and things.
- Curriculum resource books.
- Family and cultural influences.
- Serendipity, or the unexpected.
- Daily issues of living together, problem solving, conflict resolution, routines.
- Values expressed by the school philosophy, the families, and the community.

Emergent curriculum seems to capture the spontaneous nature of children's play and blend it with the necessary planning and organization. In the discussion of curricular models that follows in this chapter you will see that emergent curriculum has many applications.

Multiple Intelligences

In Chapter 4, you read about Gardner's theory of multiple intelligences (MI). According to this theory, children are capable of at least eight distinct categories of intelligence. That is, they have many different ways of knowing or of being "smart." Refresh your memory by reviewing Chapter 4, page 153. The potential for developing the various intelligences is based on the child's experience, culture, and motivation. The following is a summary of this theory (adapted from Armstrong, [2000]) and The New City School [1994]. The eight MI categories with examples are:

1. *Linguistic Intelligence.* Sensitivity to the sounds, structure, meanings, and functions of words and language.

    Example: Children who enjoy word games, understand jokes, puns, and riddles, and enjoy the sounds and rhythms of language. They have a good vocabulary, spell easily, memorize readily, and are good storytellers. Examples: Adults such as Maya Angelou, Amy Tan, Martin Luther King, Jr.

FIGURE 10-5a Linguistic intelligence.

2. *Logical-Mathematical.* Sensitivity to, and capacity to discern, logical or numerical patterns; ability to handle long chains of reasoning.

   Example: Children who notice and use numbers, patterns, shapes and explore the relationships in them; they have a systematic approach to problem solving and organize their thoughts well. They think conceptually and are able to move easily from the concrete to the abstract. They like puzzles and computer games.

   Examples: Adults such as Stephen Hawking, Madame Marie Curie, Bill Gates

FIGURE 10-5b Logical-Mathematical intelligence.

3. *Spatial.* Capacity to perceive the visual-spatial world accurately and to perform transformations on one's initial perceptions.

FIGURE 10-5c Spatial intelligence.

   Example: Children who like to draw, build, design, and create things. They enjoy pattern and geometry in math as well as maps and charts. They think in three-dimensional terms and enjoy color as well as design. They love videos and photos.

   Examples: Adults such as I. M. Pei, Maria Martinez, Frank Lloyd Wright

4. *Bodily-Kinesthetic.* Ability to control one's body movements and to handle objects skillfully.

   Example: Children who are agile, coordinated, and have good body control and who take in information through bodily sensations. They are hands-on learners with good motor skills. They like to touch things, to run, and use body language.

   Examples: Adults such as Jackie Joyner Kersey, Marcel Marceau, Kristi Yamaguchi

FIGURE 10-5d Bodily-kinesthetic intelligence. (Photo courtesy of Kathleen Slaght.)

5. *Musical.* Ability to produce and appreciate rhythm, pitch, and timbre; appreciation of the forms of musical expressiveness.

Example: Children who like to sing, dance, hum, play instruments, and move their bodies when music is playing. They remember melodies, are able to keep and imitate a beat, make up their own songs, and notice background and environmental sounds. They enjoy listening and differentiating patterns in sounds and are sensitive to melody and tone.

Examples: Adults such as Stevie Wonder, Midori, and Cher

FIGURE 10-5f Interpersonal intelligence.

FIGURE 10-5e Musical intelligence.

FIGURE 10-5g Intrapersonal intelligence.

6. *Interpersonal.* Capacity to discern and respond to the moods, temperaments, motivations, and desires of other people.

Example: Children who have a lot of friends, who like to talk, who prefer group problem solving, and can mediate conflicts; who like to hear someone else's point of view; who volunteer to help when others need it.

Example: Adults such as Marion Wright Edelman, Mother Teresa

7. *Intrapersonal.* Access to one's own feelings and the ability to discriminate among one's emotions; knowledge of one's own strengths and weaknesses.

Example: Children who pursue personal interests and set goals; who identify and label feelings, are insightful, sensitive, reflective, intuitive; who may daydream and are comfortable being alone. They know their own strengths and weaknesses.

Examples: Adults such as Sigmund Freud, the Buddha, Maria Montessori

8. *Naturalist.* Expertise in distinguishing among members of a species; recognizing the existence of other neighboring species; and charting out the relations, formally or informally, among several species.

Example: Children who enjoy all the features of the outdoor world. They recognize and classify plants, animals, rocks, clouds, and other natural formations; they garden and like to have animals at home and school to care for. They enjoy zoos, aquariums and places where the natural world is on display and can be studied.

Examples: Adults such as John Muir, Jane Goodall, George Washington Carver

FIGURE 10-5h Naturalist intelligence.

In a group of preschoolers it is easy to notice the different strengths children have in the eight MI categories. Some children excel at puzzles and manipulative games while others are busy dictating stories, building a boatyard with blocks, or holding the guinea pig. There are children who cannot be still for very long and need to be actively and physically involved in play and work for much of the day. We all have the capacities for the eight categories of MI but we are not equally proficient in all of them.

MI theory is based on Gardner's belief that general intelligence is too narrowly defined and suggests that intelligence has more to do with the capacity to solve problems and engage in a wide variety of culturally valued activities (Berk, 2002).[1]

Through a wide variety of meaningful learning experiences, children's strengths (and primary intelligences) can be assessed, and curriculum can be developed that fosters new knowledge and thinking. Jmel is strong in spatial intelligence, and that can serve as a context for other learning in different intelligence categories. Her intrapersonal and linguistic intelligences can be encouraged through activities that include her telling or writing stories about something she drew and what it means to her. Bodily-kinesthetic and music abilities can emerge through dancing and moving the body through space in different ways. This allows Jmel to experience and reinforce her own strengths and increase her strengths in other areas as well.

The relationship of curriculum based on MI to integrated curriculum is fairly clear from the example of Jmel and from Figure 10-6. If children have different ways of knowing, they should experience a concept, lesson, or subject matter in a variety of ways. As teachers and caregivers expand their own thinking about children's abilities, they can vary what and how they teach and teach to many intelligences instead of just one, many developmental areas, not just one. An integrated MI curriculum makes it possible to involve many intelligences in a wide range of activities and enable more children to succeed by drawing on their own capacities to learn. The lesson plan in Figure 10-6 is a good example of planning curriculum with an MI emphasis.

Gardner (Woolfolk, 2001) has written about the good uses of MI theory when it is applied to teaching: "Schools should cultivate those skills and capabilities that are valued in the community and the broader society," he says, and, "At the heart of the MI perspective—in theory and in practice—(is) taking human difference seriously." In both comments, Gardner affirms criteria for DAP.[2]

Multiple Intelligences are also discussed in Chapter 4 and Chapter 12.

Differences in Learning Styles

Some people like going to lectures to learn about a new culture or country. Others prefer to watch a travelogue. Still others get the most out of traveling to that country and living among its people, eating the food, absorbing the atmosphere. Each of these is a legitimate method of learning

---

1 Cultural values and learning opportunities influence the degree to which a child's intellectual strengths are formed and how they are expressed (Berk, 2000).

2 This sensitivity to diversity should be an integral part of all early childhood curriculum.

and processing information, and each indicates the preferred style of that particular person. In Chapter 3, the discussion was about **learning styles** related to differences in children's behavior. In this chapter, we will focus on how basic learning styles affect curriculum planning.

Sensory Styles

Three basic sensory styles were mentioned in Chapter 3 and they follow here with examples (Schirrmacher, 2002). These are the preferred mode of each child but not the only method by which the child can integrate knowledge.

1. *The Visual Learner.* These are children who prefer pictures to words; photos, charts, and graphs provide the necessary clues; they like to represent their learning by reading, writing, drawing; the finished product is important.

2. *The Auditory Learner.* These are children who listen to others to learn and speak and discuss what they are learning. They are good at following directions in the appropriate sequence from one task to another.

3. *The Tactile-Kinesthetic Learner.* These children are active, full-body learners; they need hands-on activity and learn by doing, not listening or sitting still.

These modalities are the favored ways children learn through the use of their five senses. It seems clear that an integrated, emergent curriculum would be easily adaptable to all three learning modes. In fact, most early childhood experiences are heavily weighted toward the development of the five senses that provide many opportunities for children to learn through their preferred style.[1]

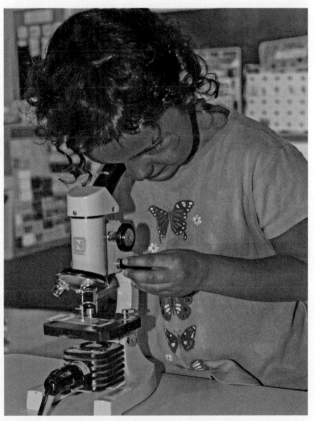

Play takes many forms: Three examples of play-based curriculum.

 1 Learning styles are also influenced by culture and gender. In some cultures where cooperation is more important than competition, students experience cultural conflict when the curriculum stresses competition.

Sounds of the City

MI Context: Students from diverse communities need to develop an awareness and appreciation for the unique nature of the urban environment.

Learner Outcomes: Student will recognize the sounds of the city.

Procedure

1. Elicit from students the sounds that are unique to an urban area and list these sounds on chart paper. Show pictures of different urban settings to enhance the activity. Some sounds that might be included in this list are airplanes, traffic, emergency sirens and street vendors.

2. Have students record city sounds on their empty playground if the school is located in an urban area. For homework, they could record city sounds from their neighborhoods or from the television.

3. Instruct the students to create a rhythm chant based on the sound word list created earlier and use the taped examples to enhance the mood of the chants. Percussion instruments may be used to accompany portions of the chants. Students perform their musical numbers for the class.

Materials

Pictures of city scenes, tape recorders, cassette tapes, percussion instruments, chart paper, markers

Assessment/Reflection

Are the students able to identify urban sounds? How are the sounds the students collected from the various locations the same and different? What generalizations are the students able to make from this information?

MI Extensions

Interpersonal: Help the students develop an awareness of how these city sounds affect their relationships with others.

Intrapersonal: How do city sounds affect moods?

Bodily-Kinesthetic: Use movement to complement the compositions.

Linguistic: Read *Apt. 3* by Ezra Jack Keats. List all the sounds that are heard within the story and who made those sounds. Use the sound hints to determine who lives on each floor.

Logical-Mathematical: Collect data on the number of times specific sounds can be heard within a community. Interview people and graph their reactions to these sounds. Propose a hypothesis as to how the frequency of sounds might affect the lives of the people they interviewed.

Spatial: Create cityscape murals that capture the city and its sounds.

A practical guide created by the faculty of The New City School © 1994

Everybody's Jumping

MI Context: This lesson is used as an extension for the book *Oliver Button Is a Sissy* by Tomie dePaola.

Learner Outcomes: Students will not only improve their skill at jumping rope but also recognize that it is valuable exercise for both boys and girls.

Procedure

1. Read *Oliver Button Is a Sissy* by Tomie dePaola.

2. Discuss the things Oliver did that were considered unusual for a boy, i.e., not liking ball games, walking alone, jumping rope. Brainstorm a list of activities that both girls and boys enjoy.

3. Provide different ropes for jumping and let the children practice different types of jumping including double dutch, singles, group and skip jumping.

4. Teach the children to count their breath rate. Compare rates before and after jumping.

5. Time the children and encourage them to improve on the length of time they can jump without missing.

Materials

Oliver Button Is a Sissy, ropes, stopwatch or a watch with a second hand

Assessment/Reflection

With practice, are the students able to jump for a longer time without missing? Can they name and perform different jump rope techniques?

MI Extensions

Interpersonal: Jump rope with a partner. Establish together when the positions will change and take turns being the turner and the jumper.

Intrapersonal: Discuss stereotypical girl games and boy games. Ask if they have ever been teased about their interests in a certain activity. How do they react to being teased?

Linguistic: Discuss jump rope jingles and have students write one of their own. Use the book *Anna Banana: 101 Jump-Rope Rhymes* by Joanna Cole to familiarize the students with other rhymes.

Logical-Mathematical: With a partner, students record how many times they can jump without missing. Do this three times. Find the average number of jumps. Graph the class's jump average. Check again a week later and note and discuss any changes.

Spatial: Students decorate their own plastic jump ropes.

A practical guide created by the faculty of The New City School © 1994

Teamwork

MI Context: Children develop interpersonal skills by working together to complete a task.

Learner Outcomes: Three- and four-year-old children will make decisions and compromises as they share materials.

Procedure

1. Divide the class into pairs. Keep in mind the personalities of the children: Put children together who might not choose one another. Place a child who can share easily with one who cannot. Put a verbal child with one less verbal.

2. Give each pair of children one puzzle to put together.

3. As children are working, talk to the pairs and to the whole class about how they are doing and if everyone is having a chance to work on the puzzle.

Materials

Ten- to twelve-piece puzzles, one for each pair of children.

Assessment/Reflection

Observe how well the pairs are able to complete the task and if they cooperated and compromised. Ask the pairs to talk about how well they think they did.

MI Extensions

Intrapersonal: Ask children to talk about what was easy and what was hard about working together to put together the puzzle.

Bodily-Kinesthetic: Give each pair one ball. They decide what they will play with it, i.e., throw, roll, bounce.

Linguistic: Read *Roxaboxen* by Alice McLerran. Discuss ways the children in the story might have cooperated as they played.

Logical-Mathematical: Give each pair one tray of several objects to sort.

Musical: Give each pair a container to use as a drum and two sticks. Ask them to make up a song on the "drum."

Spatial: Give each pair one piece of paper and two crayons to draw a picture of themselves.

A practical guide created by the faculty of The New City School © 1994

FIGURE 10-6 Planning curriculum around multiple intelligences. (Used with permission from New City School (August, 1995). *Celebrating multiple intelligences: Teaching for success.* St. Louis, MO: Author.)

A Teacher Provides Opportunities for:

Field Dependent Children to:

- Engage in global thinking
- Follow a given structure
- Be extremely directed
- Attend to social information
- Resolve conflict
- Be social
- Work with others
- Have friends
- Work with a provided hypothesis
- Work with facts
- Use others' decisions
- Be sensitive to others
- Use stress for learning

Field Independent Children to:

- Engage in analytical thinking
- Generate own structure
- Be internally directed
- Be inattentive to social information
- Think things through philosophically
- Be distant in social relations
- Work alone
- Have acquaintances
- Generate own hypothesis
- Work with concepts
- Use own decisions
- Be insensitive to others
- Ignore external stress for learning

FIGURE 10-7 A teacher must make use of learning styles for Field Dependence/Independence. (Adapted from Sharon L. McNeely, Ph.D. (1997), *Observing students and teachers through objective strategies.* Boston: Allyn & Bacon. Reprinted with permission of the author.)

Field Dependent/Independent Learning Style

One of the most useful aspects of this model of learning styles (Witkin, Moore, Goodenough, & Cox, 1977) is that it seems to be found in all cultures throughout the world. The two facets of this model, with examples (McNeely, 1997; Ramirez & Casteñada, 1974), are:

Field Dependent Learning Style (FD). FD children are able to grasp broad distinctions among concepts and they see relationships through a social context, working with others to achieve a common goal. They learn best through material that is related to their own experiences. FD learners are more person-oriented in their play and engage in social interactions sometimes for the sake of the interaction itself. They often use social conflict to make a social contact. They learn concepts through watching others, and their learning is reinforced by rewards such as verbal praise, helping the teacher, and showing the task to others. They depend on authority, seek guidance and demonstration from teachers, and need to have the performance objectives of the curriculum carefully explained.

Field Independent Learning Style (FI). These children look at things analytically, impos-ing their own structure to the task, and learn things for their own sake. They prefer self-defined goals and reinforcements and are motivated through competition, their own values, and are more assertive than FD learners. FI learners prefer to work inde-pendently, and rarely seek physical contact with teachers; they are more idea-oriented than people-oriented. They like to try out new tasks without help. These children like the details of concepts because they find meaning in the various parts. They focus on the materials and their uses; social interactions are not as important to them.

Figure 10-7 suggests some curriculum approaches that work well for these two learn-ing styles.

CURRICULUM: IT'S CHILD'S PLAY

Foundation for Learning

In Chapter 4 you learned about the value and process of children's play. You may want to review that section for a clear understanding of why play-based curriculum enhances chil-dren's potential for learning, and it is, in fact, the foundation for learning.

The vast knowledge of human development and behavior comes from researchers who spent countless hours observing and recording children playing. As noted by many, from Froebel to Vygotsky to Gardner, children need meaningful materials and activities in order to learn. They need to be physically as well as mentally and emotionally involved in what and how they learn, and they need to play. Through the use of activity centers, a variety of play opportunities are available throughout the school day. See Figure 10-8.

Cognitive/Language

Distinguishes between reality and fantasy
Encourages creative thought and curiosity
Allows for problem solving
Encourages thinking, planning
Develops memory, perceptual skills, and concept formation
Learns to try on other roles
Acquires knowledge and integrates learning
Learns communication skills
Develops listening and oral language skills

Creative

Fosters use of imagination and make-believe
Encourages flexible thinking and problem solving
Provides opportunity to act upon original ideas
Supports taking risks
Learns to use senses to explore
Re-creates images in buildings and art media
Sharpens observational skills
Provides variety of experiences
Learns to express self in art, music, and dance
Develops abilities to create images and use symbols
Acquires other perspectives

Social

Tries on other personalities, roles
Learns cooperation and taking turns
Learns to lead, follow
Builds a repertoire of social language
Learns to verbalize needs
Reflects own culture, heritage, values
Learns society's rules and group responsibility
Shows respect for others' property, rights
Teaches an awareness of others
Learns how to join a group
Builds awareness of self as member of a group
Gives sense of identification
Promotes self-image, self-esteem
Experiences joy, fun

Physical

Releases energy
Builds fine- and gross-motor skills
Gains control over body
Provides challenges
Requires active use of body
Allows for repetition and practice
Refines eye–hand coordination
Develops self-awareness
Encourages health and fitness

Emotional

Develops self-confidence and self-esteem
Learns to take a different viewpoint
Resolves inner fears, conflicts
Builds trust in self and others
Reveals child's personality
Encourages autonomy
Learns to take risks
Acts out anger, hostility, frustration, joy
Gains self-control
Becomes competent in several areas
Takes initiative

FIGURE 10-8 Play is the cornerstone of learning.

The Teacher's Role in Play

Interest and Understanding

Classroom teachers learn about children by listening to and observing spontaneous play activity and planning curriculum that encourages play. They discover each child's individual personality, learning style, and preferred mode of play.[1]

Genuine interest is one way teachers show their approval of the play process. Creating a safe environment where children feel physically and emotionally secure is another. To establish play as an important part of the curriculum, teachers must:

- *Understand,* appreciate, and value play experiences for young children.
- *Focus* on the process of learning rather than on the process of teaching.
- *Reflect* on their observations in order to know what activities, concepts, or learning should be encouraged or extended.

Frost (1996) reminds us of the excellent advice from one of the most able contributors to the field of human development:

> Erikson advises that play has a very personal meaning for each individual.[2] Perhaps the best thing that we as adults can do to discover this meaning is to go out and play; to reflect upon our own childhood play; to once again look at play through the eyes of the child.

Supporting Play

One of the most difficult tasks teachers face is knowing when to join children at play and when to remain outside the activity. They must ask themselves whether their presence will support what is happening or whether it will inhibit the play. Sometimes teachers are tempted to correct children's misconceptions during play:

> Abby and Salina, deeply involved in their grocery store drama, are making change incorrectly. A teacher must judge whether to explain the difference between nickels and quarters at that time or to create an opportunity at a later date. Teachers must be aware of what happens if they interrupt the flow of play and how they influence the

direction it takes. If Abby and Salina begin to talk about their coins, showing an interest in learning how to compute their change, the teacher can move into the discussion without seeming to interfere.

Many adults enjoy playing with the children in their class; others feel more comfortable as active observers. But every teaching situation will demand the teacher's involvement at some level. The hesitant child may need help entering a play situation; children may become too embroiled in an argument to settle it alone; play may become inappropriate, exploitative, or dominated by a particular child.

Vygotsky gives us other reasons to be involved with children as they play, particularly in relation to the interpersonal nature of teaching (see Chapter 4). The belief that learning is interpersonal and collaborative is exemplified by the teachers of Reggio Emilia (see Chapters 2 and 5), who guide and support children's learning by engaging in play and knowing what strategy will best help an individual child reach the next level of skill (*zone of proximal development*). The Reggio Emilia approach to curriculum (discussed at the end of this chapter under "Curriculum Models") finds an appropriate and appealing blend of Vygotsky's concern for individual exploration and assisted discovery. See Figure 10-9.

Setting the Stage for Play

Structuring the Environment

To structure the environment for play, teachers include uninterrupted time blocks in the daily schedule (at least 45 minutes to an hour) for free-play time. This allows children to explore many avenues of the curriculum free from time constraints. It is frustrating to young children to have their play cut off just as they are getting deeply involved.

Established routines in the schedule add to the framework of a day planned for play. The raw materials of play—toys, games, equipment—are changed periodically so that new ones may be introduced for further challenge.

- In choosing materials, teachers select dress-up clothes and accessories that appeal to all children's needs, interests, and emotions.

---

1 Observing children while at play helps a teacher understand how each child is unique *and* how all children are the same in our diverse world.

2 Curriculum should provide all children with continuous opportunities to develop a better sense of self.

Curriculum through Play for the One-and-a-Half-Year-Old

Sensory Stimulation

Objective: To help toddlers begin to explore and understand the five senses.

	Activity	Small-Group Focus	Optional Activities
Monday	Soap painting	Guessing game: textures. Distinguish soft from hard using familiar objects.	Play hide-and-seek with two or three.
Tuesday	Water table play	Guessing game: smells. Identify familiar scents in jars.	Blow bubbles.
Wednesday	Fingerpainting	Guessing game: weights. Distinguish heavy/not heavy using familiar objects such as book or doll.	Take walk to collect collage materials of different textures.
Thursday	Making collages of textures collected day before	Guessing game: shapes. Using puzzles of shapes and shape-sorting boxes.	Have a parade of sounds from many musical instruments.
Friday	Play dough	Food fest of finger foods: Try different textures, sizes, shapes, and flavors	Make foot or hand prints on large mural paper.

Water play is fun and promotes learning.

FIGURE 10-9 Example of teacher-directed activities to help toddlers explore their sensory skills.

 • Props are required for a variety of roles[1]: men, women, babies, doctors, nurses, grocers, mail carriers, teachers, and firefighters.

• Hats for many occupations help a child establish the role of an airline pilot, tractor driver, construction worker, police officer, or baseball player.

• Large purses are used for carrying mail and babies' diapers; they also double as a briefcase or luggage.

1 Choosing materials to place in a classroom should be done with an awareness of exposing children to images of diversity (e.g., male nurses, female construction workers, African American physicians, etc.) rather than fostering and reinforcing existing stereotypes. These materials are available to purchase or you can make your own photo albums and posters.

Guidelines for Facilitating Play

A Good Teacher

- Guides the play, but does not direct or dominate the situation or overwhelm children by participation.
- Capitalizes on the children's thoughts and ideas; does not enforce a point of view on them.
- Models play when necessary. Shows children how a specific character might act, how to ask for a turn, how to hold a hammer when hammering. Models ways to solve problems that involve children interacting on their own behalf.
- Asks questions; clarifies with children what is happening.
- Helps children start, end, and begin again. Gives them verbal cues to enable them to follow through on an idea.
- Focuses the children's attention on one another. Encourages them to interact with each other.
- Interprets children's behavior aloud, when necessary; helps them verbalize their feelings as they work through conflicts.
- Expands the play potential by making statements and asking questions that lead to discovery and exploration.

FIGURE 10-10 The teacher's role in play is to balance facilitating children's play and taking advantage of the teachable moments in which further learning is enhanced.

● Simple jackets or capes transform a child for many roles.

Props that represent aspects of the child's daily life are important; children need many opportunities to act out their life stories.

For younger children, teachers make sure there are duplicates of popular materials. Group play is more likely to occur with three telephones, four carriages, eight hats, and five wagons. Social interaction is enhanced when three space shuttle drivers can be at the controls.

Play is further enlarged by materials that are *open-ended*. These are materials that will expand the children's learning opportunities because they can be used in more than one way. Blocks, a staple of the early childhood curriculum, are a case in point. Children explore and manipulate blocks in many ways. The youngest children carry and stack blocks and also enjoy wheeling them around in wagons or trucks. They also enjoy the repetitious action of making small columns of blocks. Older preschoolers build multistoried structures as part of their dramatic play—offices, firehouses, and garages. Figure 10-10 summarizes ways to encourage play throughout the program.

Classroom Activity Centers

The **activity centers** in most early childhood programs consist of

Indoors	Outdoors
Creative arts	Climbing equipment
Blocks	Swings
Table toys/ manipulatives	Sand/mud/water
Science/discovery	Wheel toys
Dramatic play	Woodworking
Language arts/books	Hollow blocks
Math	Music
Music	Nature/Science

All of these centers offer activities and materials for children to choose from during free play time—the greatest portion of their school day. (See typical daily schedules in Chapter 2.) Paints are in the easel trays, puzzles on the tables, dress-up clothes and props in the housekeeping/dramatic play center, blocks and accessories in the block corner, and books and tapes in the language area. Teachers plan the resources and materials and place them so that children readily see the alternatives available

What do YOU Think?

What do you think are the most compelling arguments that play is a necessary part of any early childhood program? How would you respond to a first-grade teacher who thought too much time was devoted to play? What would you say to a parent who was interested in enrolling a child into your school but wanted to know why so much time was devoted to play.

A future businesswoman.

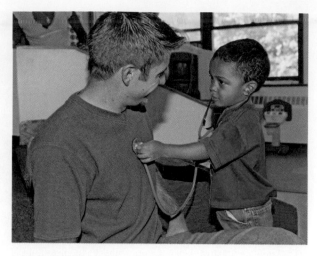

A future doctor.

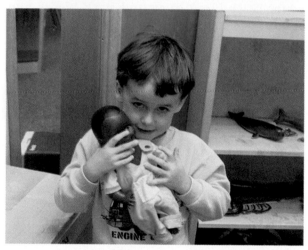

A future daddy.

A future computer expert.

A future civil engineer.

As they play, children learn. They may even be practicing for the future.

to them. Some of these activities might be teacher-directed: cooking snacks in the house-keeping area. For the most part, however, these activities will be self-initiating and child-directed. At all times, the emphasis will be on providing a child-centered curriculum.

Whatever the activity center, it needs attention and planning. Wherever children are present, learning and playing will take place. Because each play space will make a contribution to children's experiences, teachers should develop appropriate curriculum for that learning area.

Go back and review what Chapter 9 describes as the important principles in creating environments that reflect curriculum goals and see Chapter 2 for daily schedules.

Planning for Skills Acquisition

Just as curriculum can be developed by focusing on the activity or learning centers, so, too, can an early childhood program be planned around the skill levels of the children in the class. The next three chapters provide a more in-depth identification of the types of skills that children need to learn.

The first decision teachers must make concerns what particular skill they wish to help children develop. The skill can be in the area of physical, cognitive, language, creative, social, or emotional development. The nature of the individual class and the program philosophy will help teachers establish priorities for these skills. Teachers then select the activities and

materials that will enhance the development of any one or more of those particular skills.

Figure 10-11 shows how the cognitive skill of classification can be implemented in the classroom, making it the focus of the entire curriculum.

The next three chapters provide a more in-depth identification of the types of skills that children need to learn.

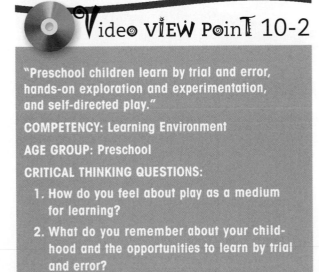

Video VIEW PoinT 10-2

"Preschool children learn by trial and error, hands-on exploration and experimentation, and self-directed play."

COMPETENCY: Learning Environment

AGE GROUP: Preschool

CRITICAL THINKING QUESTIONS:

1. How do you feel about play as a medium for learning?

2. What do you remember about your childhood and the opportunities to learn by trial and error?

CONSIDERATIONS FOR CURRICULUM PLANNING

Teacher Considerations

Factors in Preplanning

The aim of the curriculum is to help children acquire the skills and behaviors that will promote their optimal growth physically, socially, emotionally, and intellectually. Teachers consider a number of factors in developing a curriculum to provide maximum learning opportunities. Among these are the *educational philosophy and goals* of the program. A family day-care provider plans activities for a few children in an intimate setting while the kindergarten teacher arranges small working groups so that the large group will not seem overwhelming. The activities should support the goals of the program and result in those goals's being accomplished. Figure 10-12 lists ten curriculum goals and fifty curriculum objectives.

1. Probably the single most important determinant the teacher must consider is *the children themselves*. Their ages, developmental levels, individuality, and learning styles are barometers of what will be a successful and stimulating curriculum.

2. The *number* of children in the class will affect the teacher's planning,

3. The *ethnic and cultural backgrounds* of the children. Teachers like to plan curriculum experiences that draw on children's knowledge and experience but that also extend their thinking.

4. Effective curriculum planning stems from *a knowledge of young children*. Teachers ask themselves what concepts children should learn and how they will teach those concepts; what does the child already know, and how can the teacher build on that? What is the most effective way to teach a particular concept to this group of children?

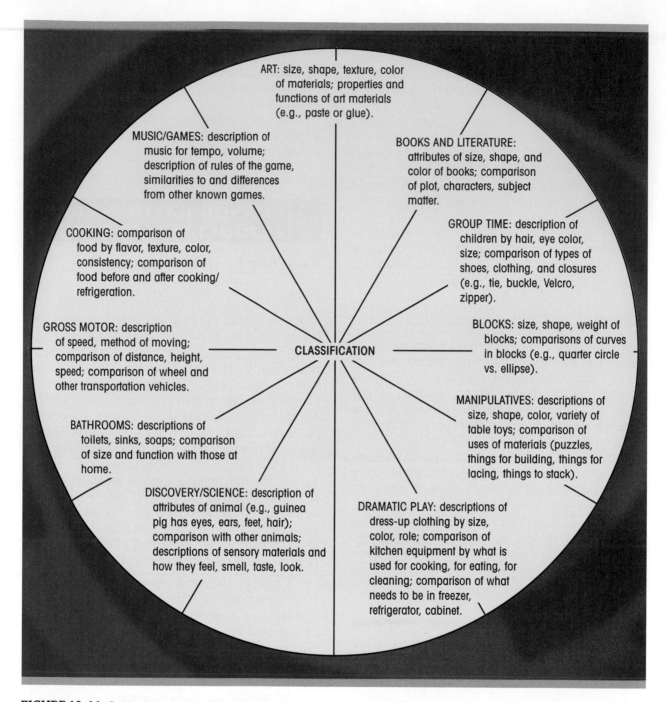

FIGURE 10-11 Curriculum can be developed with a focus on a particular skill. Classification skills can be enhanced throughout the curriculum and in activity centers. NOTE: This is a graphic way to demonstrate an integrated curriculum, not an example of a format for how to write curriculum plans.

In many ways, teachers start at the end: they look at what they want the child to accomplish or to learn as a result of this experience and then plan the curriculum to lead toward those results.

5. Planning for a *broad range of developmental skills and interests* is a key factor in creating a classroom curriculum. Because the abilities of children even of the same age vary,

activities must be open-ended and flexible enough to be used by a number of children with varieties of skills. Remember, too, that some children may not be interested in formal or organized art projects or science experiences. These children may learn more easily through self-selected play: by wearing a space helmet and fantasizing a trip to the moon, by building with

The Creative Curriculum® for Preschool Goals and Objectives at a Glance

Social/Emotional Development	Physical Development	Cognitive Development	Language Development
Sense of Self	**Gross Motor**	**Learning and Problem Solving**	**Listening and Speaking**
1. Shows ability to adjust to new situations	14. Demonstrates basic locomotor skills (running, jumping, hopping, galloping)	22. Observes objects and events with curiosity	38. Hears and discriminates the sounds of language
2. Demonstrates appropriate trust in adults	15. Shows balance while moving	23. Approaches problems flexibly	39. Expresses self using words and expanded sentences
3. Recognizes own feelings and manages them appropriately	16. Climbs up and down	24. Shows persistence in approaching tasks	40. Understands and follows oral directions
4. Stands up for rights	17. Pedals and steers a tricycle (or other wheeled vehicle)	25. Explores cause and effect	41. Answers questions
Responsibility for Self and Others	18. Demonstrates throwing, kicking, and catching skills	26. Applies knowledge or experience to a new context	42. Asks questions
5. Demonstrates self-direction and independence	**Fine Motor**	**Logical Thinking**	43. Actively participates in conversations
6. Takes responsibility for own well-being	19. Controls small muscles in hands	27. Classifies objects	**Reading and Writing**
7. Respects and cares for classroom environment and materials	20. Coordinates eye-hand movement	28. Compares/measures	44. Enjoys and values reading
8. Follows classroom routines	21. Uses tools for writing and drawing	29. Arranges objects in a series	45. Demonstrates understanding of print concepts
9. Follows classroom rules		30. Recognizes patterns and can repeat them	46. Demonstrates knowledge of the alphabet
Prosocial Behavior		31. Shows awareness of time concepts and sequence	47. Uses emerging reading skills to make meaning from print
10. Plays well with other children		32. Shows awareness of position in space	48. Comprehends and interprets meaning from books and other texts
11. Recognizes the feelings of others and responds appropriately		33. Uses one-to-one correspondence	49. Understands the purpose of writing
12. Shares and respects the rights of others		34. Uses numbers and counting	50. Writes letters and words
13. Uses thinking skills to resolve conflicts		**Representation and Symbolic Thinking**	
		35. Takes on pretend roles and situations	
		36. Makes believe with objects	
		37. Makes and interprets representations	

FIGURE 10-12 *The Creative Curriculum®* approach to planning ensures DAP. (From *The Creative Curriculum® for Preschool* (p. 530), by D. T. Dodge, L. J. Colker, and C. Heroman, 2002, Washington, DC: Teaching Strategies, Inc. Copyright 2002 by Teaching Strategies, Inc. Reprinted with permission.)

blocks for long periods, or by running and climbing out of doors.

6. The developmental word pictures of children from birth through age eight found in Chapter 3 can be useful in determining *what kinds of activities appeal* to young children.

7. All activities—especially those that are planned and formal—should be conducted in an *atmosphere of play* that offers the children options in choosing what they need to learn.

8. A **prerequisite** for planning is the *availability of people and material* resources and ways to use them. What are the strengths of the teaching staff? Are there enough supplies and equipment available? Are there enough adults to supervise the activities?

9. The *amount of time* available in the daily schedule and the *amount of space* in the room or yard affect a teacher's planning. Fingerpainting requires time for children to get involved, proximity to water for cleanup, and an area in which to store wet paintings. All of these elements must be considered in the planning process.

Teacher-Directed Learning

When is teacher-directed learning appropriate? Arce (2000) notes that it is a good teaching strategy when materials are complex or the concept is unknown to the children. Teaching certain skills, such as writing or cutting with scissors requires teacher guidance. The continuum that is shown in Figure 10-13 suggests a broad range of teaching behaviors, including teacher demonstration and directive teaching. Schirrmacher (2002) makes the point that all methods on the continuum are "valid at certain times for certain children and certain activities." Helm and Katz (2001) observe that teachers using the project approach often use teacher-directed instruction for teaching certain skills and concepts.

Group Times

There are certain times within the daily routine when teachers call children together. The size of the group is determined in part by how many teachers there are and how they want to present various learning experiences. The reverse is also true. Various types of learning experiences best lend themselves to small or large group discussions. In using the project

Video VIEW PoinT 10-3

"Children need to have good balance between challenge and mastery."

COMPETENCY: Learning Environment

AGE GROUP: School age

CRITICAL THINKING QUESTIONS:

1. What are some of the challenges a school-age child faces?

2. What help would you provide them in mastering one of those skills?

approach, for instance, small-group work seems to provide the best format for developing ideas and listening to one another's opinions. A presentation by a visiting parent or expert on the project theme would be more appropriate for the large group. Smaller groups could then form to discuss in greater detail the ideas presented.

Large-group times are used for a variety of reasons. Teachers may use them as opportunities to bring the entire class together to

- Provide transitions in the daily schedule.
- Bring in a special guest or presentation.
- Introduce new ideas and materials.
- Sing and do fingerplays.
- Read stories.
- Plan activities with children.
- Review the day's events.
- Initiate group problem solving.

Small groups, on the other hand, are opportunities for teachers and children to have a closer and more personal experience. This setting provides the teachers with ample opportunities to

- Help children practice a specific skill, such as cutting with scissors.
- Encourage children in their social interactions with one another.
- Enjoy conversations with children.
- Teach a new game to a few children at a time.
- Closely observe each child's growth and development.
- Hold discussions regarding their project work and move the project along.
- Explore topics in depth.

Nondirective			Mediating				Directive
Acknowledge	**Model**	**Facilitate**	**Support**	**Scaffold**	**Co-construct**	**Demonstrate**	**Direct**
Give attention and positive encouragement to keep a child engaged in an activity	Display for children a skill or desirable way of behaving in the classroom, through actions only or with cues, prompts, or other forms of coaching	Offer short-term assistance to help a child achieve the next level of functioning (as an adult does in holding the back of a bicycle while a child pedals)	Provide a fixed form of assistance, such as a bicycle's training wheels, to help a child achieve the next level of functioning	Set up challenges or assist children to work "on the edge" of their current competence	Learn or work collaboratively with children on a problem or task, such as building a model or block structure	Actively display a behavior or engage in an activity while children observe the outcome	Provide specific directions for children's behavior within narrowly defined dimensions of error

FIGURE 10-13 A continuum of teaching behavior. (Reprinted with permission from the National Association for the Education of Young Children. From S. Bredekamp & T. Rosegrant, eds., *Reaching Potentials: Appropriate Curriculum and Assessment for Young Children*, vol. 2, (Washington, DC: NAEYC, 1995), p. 21.)

- Eat a meal or have a snack with children and encourage the social process.
- Provide close supervision for some experiences, such as cooking.

What is common to all group times is the occasion for teachers to encourage listening and speaking skills; provide an arena in which children share thoughts and ideas with one another; and introduce any number of cognitive and social activities. Teachers must make the determination about which type of group best suits the experience.

Culturally Responsive Teaching

Positive attitudes toward self and others emerge when children know they are valued for their individuality and appreciated as members of a family and a culture. The school environment can reflect this in a number of ways. Figure 10-14 lists ways in which an early childhood program can use culturally diverse materials on a daily basis to foster the relationship between home culture and school.

Banks (2006) identifies five important characteristics of the effective teacher in a multicultural society. They are teachers who:

1. Will seek pedagogical knowledge of the characteristics of students from diverse ethnic, racial, cultural, and social-class groups; of prejudice and prejudice reduction theory and research; and of teaching strategies and techniques.
2. Have reflected upon and clarified an understanding of their own cultural heritage and experience and knowledge of how it relates to and interacts with the experiences of other ethnic and cultural groups.
3. Have reflected upon their own attitude toward different racial, ethnic, cultural, and social-class groups.
4. Have the skills to make effective instructional decisions and reduce prejudice and intergroup conflict.
5. Will devise a range of teaching strategies and activities that will facilitate the achievement of students from diverse racial, ethnic, cultural, and social-class groups.

Children with special needs are often able to use most of the curriculum materials typically found in early childhood classrooms. They, too, need their life mirrored in the school setting with dolls, books, and play accessories that signify acceptance and belonging.

Play Materials to Enhance Cultural Diversity and Inclusivity

Curriculum Area	Materials and Equipment
Music	Rainstick (Chile), marimba (Zulu), balaphon (West Africa), ankle bells (Native American), maracas (Latin America), Den-den (Japan), Shakeree (Nigeria), drums (many cultures), ocarina (Peru), songs of many cultures
Literature	Books on family life of many cultures, stories of children from far and near, legends and folktales from many countries, stories with common childhood themes from many lands, favorite books in several languages, wordless books, sign language, Braille books
Blocks and accessories	Variety of accessories depicting many ethnic people, aging people, community workers of both sexes in nonstereotyped roles and with various disabilities; Russian nesting dolls, Pueblo storytellers[1], animals from around the world
Art	Paints, crayons, markers, and construction paper in variety of skin-tone colors, child-size mirrors
Dramatic play	Anatomically correct dolls representing many ethnic groups; doll accessories, including glasses, wheelchairs, crutches, walkers, leg braces, and hearing aids; doll clothes, including cultural costumes and dress-up clothing from many cultures; cooking utensils, such as a wok, tortilla press, cutlery, chopsticks
Games	Language lotto, driedel game, lotto of faces of people from around the world, black-history playing cards, world globe
Outdoors	Elevated sand and water tables and ramps for wheelchair access, lowered basketball hoops, sensory-rich materials
Classrooms	Carp banners (Japan), paper cuttings from Mexico and China, photographs and magazine pictures of daily life from many cultures, artwork by artists from a variety of ethnic backgrounds, pictures of children from many ethnic backgrounds and cultures

FIGURE 10-14 A child's family and culture can be brought into the classroom through a variety of curriculum materials; so, too, can children with disabilities feel included.

Throughout this text, especially in Chapters 2, 5, and the upcoming chapters, cultural sensitivity on the part of teachers and curriculum goal is emphasized. Woolfolk (2001) suggests the following guidelines for culturally relevant teaching. They provide an accurate summary of many of the points found elsewhere in this book.

● Experiment with different group arrangements to encourage social harmony and cooperation.

● Provide a range of ways for children to learn material to accommodate a wide range of learning styles.

● Use direct-teaching methods for important information that everyone should know, such as telling children how to take care of materials, acceptable ways to disagree, and how to get the teacher's attention.

● Learn the meaning of different behaviors for your students; find out how they feel when

they are praised or corrected; talk with family members to discover the meaning of gestures, expressions, or other responses that are unfamiliar to you.

● Emphasize meaning in teaching; that is, make sure students understand the concept by using examples from everyday experiences.

● Get to know the customs, traditions, and values of your students; analyze different traditions for common themes; attend community fairs and festivals.

● Help students detect racist and sexist messages, analyze the curriculum for biases, and help children discuss ways that their communication with each other may be biased. Discuss expressions of prejudice.

A sound curriculum is the **linchpin** of a quality program for children. Curriculum planning and development is a creative act, one that is rewarding for teachers see Figure 10-15. In the

1   When using artifacts from other cultures, take care to avoid using materials or items that may have sacred or privileged status in that culture.

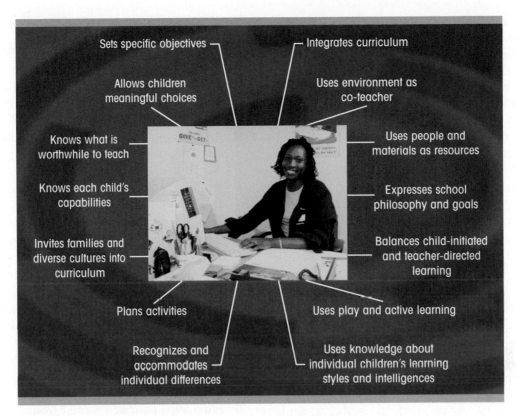

FIGURE 10-15 The effective teacher's role in creating curriculum.

next four chapters, curriculum implementations will be explored from another perspective, that of the major areas of development in the child's growth. In Chapter 11, the focus will be on how curriculum affects the growing body. Chapter 12 will emphasize the curricular role in developing the mind, and Chapter 13 and 14 will explore the curricular issues surrounding social and emotional growth.

State Standards

Curriculum planning, particularly in the primary grades, may be affected by a set of standards mandated by the state. Most states have developed some sort of explicit expectations for children to meet at various grade levels, often termed "outcomes" or "desired results." They describe the kinds of learning that should take place and often but not always, include most areas of developmental domains.

Gronlund (2006) notes some of the benefits of such standardization. To the public, they could reinforce the potential for learning in very young children and the importance of quality early childhood programs. They can provide a vehicle for demonstrating the breadth of learning that takes place in the early

years and, if used with thought and planning, they can work hand in hand with developmentally appropriate practices.

Many early childhood professionals have concerns over the potential misuse of these standards. They may foster "teaching to the test" rather than teaching to the child and cause pressure through inappropriate expectations. They may promote testing and other assessment methods inappropriate for young children.

Today's teachers will need to learn more about their own state's requirements and reflect with other early childhood professionals on the tension between meeting the standards and remaining true to developmentally appropriate practices.

Setting Goals

The process of developing curriculum begins with understanding what goals are set and then choosing the most pressing ones for attention. The following five steps are guidelines to setting and achieving curriculum goals:

1. *Set goals.* Decide what it is you want children to learn. What do you want them to know about themselves? About others? About the world? State goals clearly,

preferably in behavioral terms so results can be measured.

2. *Establish priorities.* Make a list of three to five goals or objectives you consider most important. State the reasons for your choices; your own values and educational priorities will emerge more clearly.

3. *Know the resources.* A rich, successful, and creative curriculum relies on a vast number of resources. To create a health clinic in the dramatic play area, for instance, you might need the following resources:

   - *Materials.* Props, such as stethoscopes, X-ray machines, tongue depressors, adhesive strips, medical gowns, and masks.

   - *People.* Parents and/or community people in the health care professions to visit the class.[1]

   - *Community.* Field trips to a nearby clinic, hospital, dentist's office.

4. *Plan ahead.* Set aside a regular time to meet for curriculum planning. This may be on a weekly, monthly, or seasonal basis. Discuss the curriculum activities as well as the daily routines in order to integrate the two.

5. *Evaluate.* Reflect on the outcome of your planning. Consider what worked and what did not, why it was successful or not. Look at the part of the experience that did not work as well as you would have liked. How can it be improved? What can you change about it? An evaluation should be immediate, precise, and supportive. Teachers need feedback about their planning and implementing skills. The needs of children are best served when the curriculum is refined and improved.

Written Plans

A written plan is an organized agenda, an outline to follow, a framework for the curriculum. It may include a list of activities, goals for children's learning experiences, the process or method of instruction, the teacher's responsibilities, the time of day, and other special notations. A plan may be developed for a day, a week, a month, or a specific unit or theme. Figure 10-16 illustrates a weekly curriculum. The four chapters that follow also contain many examples of written plans.

Advantages of Written Plans

Setting lesson plans to paper (see Figure 10-17) has many advantages. Doing so

- Helps teachers focus on the nature of the children they teach—their interests, their needs, their capabilities, their potential.
- Encourages thorough, in-depth planning of curriculum in a logical progression; provides a direction.
- Helps teachers clarify thoughts and articulate a rationale for what they do.
- Stimulates teamwork when teachers plan together, sharing their ideas and resources.
- Allows everyone to know what is happening; in case of absences, a substitute teacher can carry out the plans.
- Gives a foundation from which changes can be made; allows for flexibility, adaptation, and on-the-spot decisions.
- Allows for time to prepare materials, to see what is needed and what resources to gather or contact.
- Provides a concrete format from which evaluation and assessment can be made.
- Serves as a communication tool for the teaching staff, for parents, and for the governing agency.
- Allows teachers to see how much they have offered children, and the program's worth is communicated to others.

Planning by Objectives

Another approach to curriculum development requires more formal, organized planning. Comprehensive lesson plans are developed, sometimes for the whole year, and usually include objectives, the stated concepts that children will learn through this experience. These are commonly called behavioral objectives. The lesson plans include specific, stated, observable behaviors that children will be able to demonstrate to show that the teaching objective has been met. In other words, a behavioral objective states clearly what children will actually do (e.g., be able to hold scissors properly; grasp a pencil between thumb and first two fingers). If the behavioral objective is to improve fine-motor skills, the lesson plan includes activities and events that foster children's use

1 Involving parents in their work or professional role is a supportive and meaningful way to help them become involved in their child's learning.

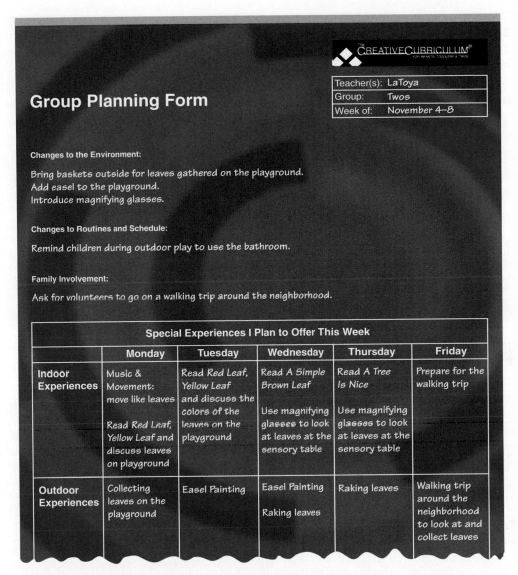

Group Planning Form

Teacher(s):	LaToya
Group:	Twos
Week of:	November 4–8

Changes to the Environment:

Bring baskets outside for leaves gathered on the playground.
Add easel to the playground.
Introduce magnifying glasses.

Changes to Routines and Schedule:

Remind children during outdoor play to use the bathroom.

Family Involvement:

Ask for volunteers to go on a walking trip around the neighborhood.

Special Experiences I Plan to Offer This Week					
	Monday	**Tuesday**	**Wednesday**	**Thursday**	**Friday**
Indoor Experiences	Music & Movement: move like leaves Read Red Leaf, Yellow Leaf and discuss leaves on playground	Read Red Leaf, Yellow Leaf and discuss the colors of the leaves on the playground	Read A Simple Brown Leaf Use magnifying glasses to look at leaves at the sensory table	Read A Tree Is Nice Use magnifying glasses to look at leaves at the sensory table	Prepare for the walking trip
Outdoor Experiences	Collecting leaves on the playground	Easel Painting	Easel Painting Raking leaves	Raking leaves	Walking trip around the neighborhood to look at and collect leaves

FIGURE 10-16 From *The Creative Curriculum® for Infants, Toddlers & Twos,* 2nd ed. (p. 103), by D. T. Dodge, S. Rudick, and K. Berke, 2006, Washington, DC: Teaching Strategies, Inc. Copyright 2006 by Teaching Strategies, Inc. Reprinted with permission.

of their fine-motor skills. Several objectives may apply to a given activity. It is then important to order the objectives so that the purposes of the lesson remain in focus. To plan successfully, the teacher needs to know developmental and behavioral theory (Chapter 4), to have good observational strategies (Chapter 6), and to possess tools to assess whether the objective has been accomplished (Chapter 6).

Figure 10-18 reflects the planning approach with the use of behavioral objectives. A more developed plan found in early childhood classrooms would include activities for the full range of curriculum areas, such as art, motor activities, and dramatic play, for each of the objectives.

Two important factors in developing curriculum objectives are (1) how much knowledge and understanding children have and (2) what children are interested in. The most effective curriculum grows out of the child's interests and experiences. As they play, children reveal their levels of experience and information as well as their misconceptions and confusions, providing the clues from which teachers can develop curriculum that is meaningful.[1]

---

1 Adults who are culturally sensitive can use this information to plan activities that deal with racism, sexism, and disabilities bias.

Ten Elements of Clearly Written Lesson Plans

1. Teacher-directed activities for large and small group times promote children's cognitive growth, attention spans, and socialization skills.

2. Activities where teachers work individually with children indicate individualized planning (see Figure 10-21 for an example).

3. Ample child-initiated free-choice time provides the opportunity for children to engage in activities offered by the teacher, balanced with opportunities for teacher-directed times.

4. An alternating flow of both active and quiet work and play experience meet children's developmental needs.

5. Activities for outdoor time focus children on outdoor benefits.

6. The teacher's goals and objectives connect with thematic units and/or projects to incorporate integrated planning.

7. Skill-focused learning activities should reflect the teacher's objectives.

8. Evidence of hands-on, concrete experiences provides discovery problem solving.

9. Regularly scheduled health, nutrition, and safety education activities provide essential knowledge.

10. Activities that promote the program's priorities should be evident.

FIGURE 10-17 Written lesson plans help teachers create an organized, cohesive curriculum which addresses children's needs, interests, and learning capabilities (Peterson, 1996).

Planning by Objectives

Activity	Teaching Objectives	Behavioral Objectives/Child Will
Painting with corn cobs	Tactile stimulation; awareness of textural design; fine-motor coordination; observational skills	Grasp, manipulate, and examine cob; use thumb and forefinger to hold cob while painting; compare with other textures; say how it looks and feels, using sensory words; compare its size, shape, and color to others
Outdoor obstacle	Spatial awareness; balance; gross-motor development; building confidence	Walk across 6' board at 2" and 4" heights; crawl through tunnel; jump from height of 2 1/2' without assistance; repeat the course on own; describe how it feels to balance, jump, crawl and make comparisons about the difficulty and ease of each challenge

FIGURE 10-18 Learning objectives define the goals and describe the desired behavior or outcome. (For guidelines in observation, see Chapter 6.)

Webbing

Webbing is the process through which teachers develop a diagram based on a particular topic or theme, highlighting key ideas and concepts (Katz and Chard, 1989). Ideas generated from brainstorming sessions flesh out the topic with many subheadings and lists of curriculum possibilities. Figure 10-11 illustrates a curriculum or topic web. Webbing is a planning tool that provides depth to a topic and creates a map of possible activities and projects. A web may be organized around a theme (water), into curriculum areas (language arts, music), or around program goals (problem solving, cooperation). By their very nature, webs foster an integrated curriculum approach and help teachers extend children's learning and experiences.

Creating a web can be fun, allowing teachers to use their imaginations and calling into play their knowledge, resources, and experience. Katz and Chard (1989) suggest the following process to develop a web, using examples from Figure 10-19:

1. *Brainstorming.* Using small slips of paper, teachers write down theme or topic ideas—each idea on a separate piece of paper. For the topic "Things that happen in fall and winter," for instance, the slips would contain ideas such as "cut jack-o-lanterns" or "rake leaves."

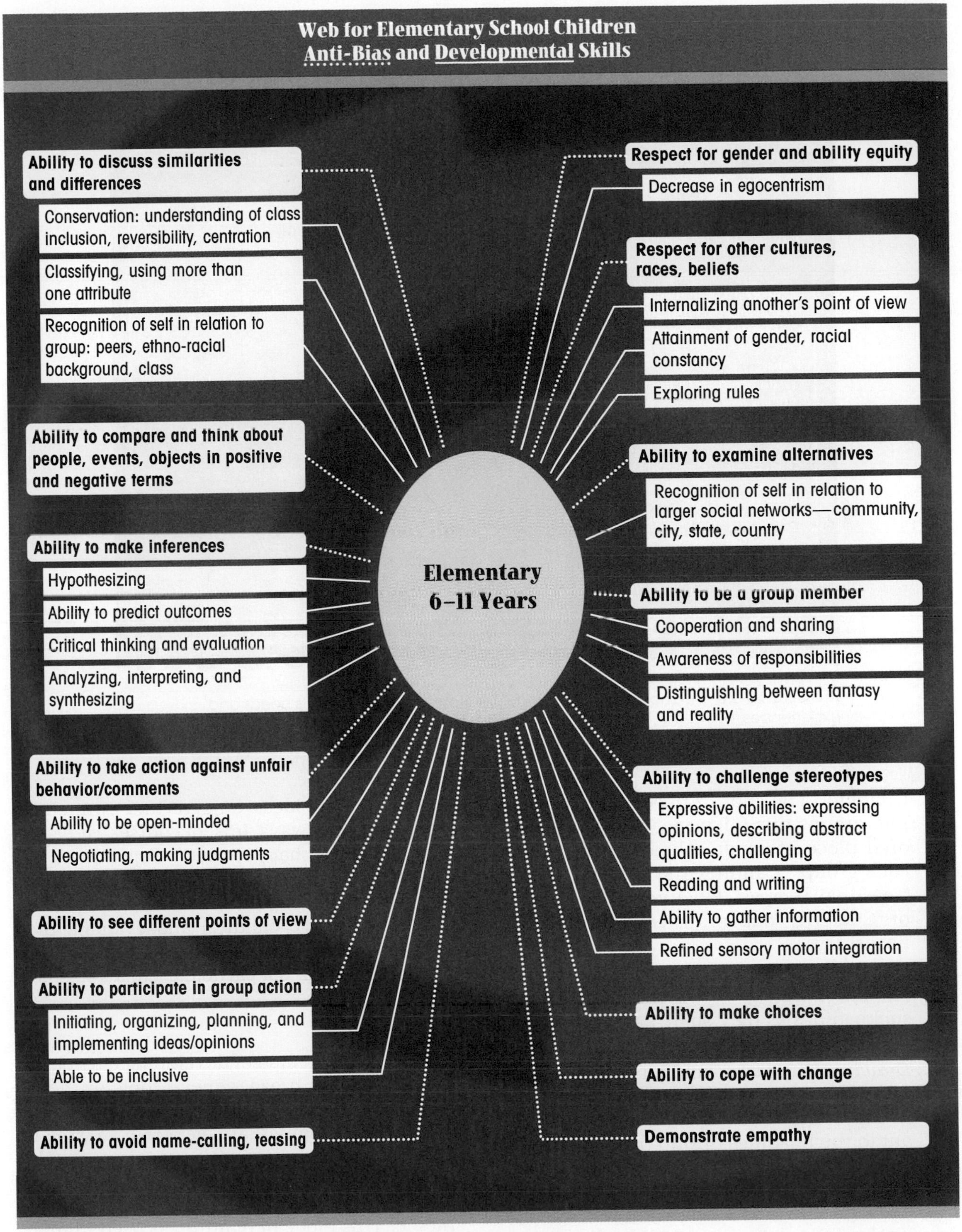

Web for Elementary School Children
Anti-Bias and Developmental Skills

Ability to discuss similarities and differences
- Conservation: understanding of class inclusion, reversibility, centration
- Classifying, using more than one attribute
- Recognition of self in relation to group: peers, ethno-racial background, class

Ability to compare and think about people, events, objects in positive and negative terms

Ability to make inferences
- Hypothesizing
- Ability to predict outcomes
- Critical thinking and evaluation
- Analyzing, interpreting, and synthesizing

Ability to take action against unfair behavior/comments
- Ability to be open-minded
- Negotiating, making judgments

Ability to see different points of view

Ability to participate in group action
- Initiating, organizing, planning, and implementing ideas/opinions
- Able to be inclusive

Ability to avoid name-calling, teasing

Elementary 6–11 Years

Respect for gender and ability equity
- Decrease in egocentrism

Respect for other cultures, races, beliefs
- Internalizing another's point of view
- Attainment of gender, racial constancy
- Exploring rules

Ability to examine alternatives
- Recognition of self in relation to larger social networks—community, city, state, country

Ability to be a group member
- Cooperation and sharing
- Awareness of responsibilities
- Distinguishing between fantasy and reality

Ability to challenge stereotypes
- Expressive abilities: expressing opinions, describing abstract qualities, challenging
- Reading and writing
- Ability to gather information
- Refined sensory motor integration

Ability to make choices

Ability to cope with change

Demonstrate empathy

FIGURE 10-19 Webbing is a useful way to create an anti-bias curriculum for the classroom. (From *Creative Resources for the Anti-Bias Classroom*, 1st edition, by SADERMAN-HALL. 1999. Reprinted with permission of Thomson Delmar Learning, a division of Thomson Learning: www.thomsonrights.com. Fax 800-730-2215.)

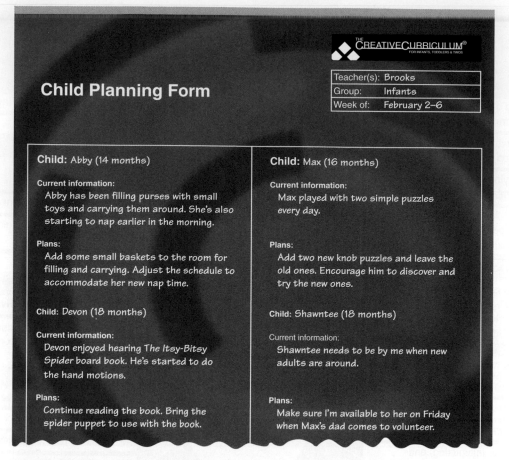

Child Planning Form

THE **CREATIVE CURRICULUM**®
FOR INFANTS, TODDLERS & TWOS

Teacher(s):	Brooks
Group:	Infants
Week of:	February 2–6

Child: Abby (14 months)

Current information:
Abby has been filling purses with small toys and carrying them around. She's also starting to nap earlier in the morning.

Plans:
Add some small baskets to the room for filling and carrying. Adjust the schedule to accommodate her new nap time.

Child: Devon (18 months)

Current information:
Devon enjoyed hearing *The Itsy-Bitsy Spider* board book. He's started to do the hand motions.

Plans:
Continue reading the book. Bring the spider puppet to use with the book.

Child: Max (16 months)

Current information:
Max played with two simple puzzles every day.

Plans:
Add two new knob puzzles and leave the old ones. Encourage him to discover and try the new ones.

Child: Shawntee (18 months)

Current information:
Shawntee needs to be by me when new adults are around.

Plans:
Make sure I'm available to her on Friday when Max's dad comes to volunteer.

FIGURE 10-20 The most effective curriculum grows out of the child's needs and experiences. (From *The Creative Curriculum® for Infants, Toddlers & Twos*, 2nd ed. (p. 97), by D. T. Dodge, S. Rudick, and K. Berke, 2006, Washington, DC: Teaching Strategies, Inc. Copyright 2006 by Teaching Strategies, Inc. Reprinted with permission.)

2. *Grouping.* The slips of paper are organized into groups of similar ideas, and, on a colored piece of paper, a heading is given to each group. "Canning and preserving" and "seasonal recipes" fall under the heading of "Cooking." Subgroups can be created, if necessary.

3. *Sharing.* Teachers can share their ideas with one another, rearranging the headings and subheadings as they share skills, resources, and information with one another.

4. *Drawing.* The ideas can be transferred to a piece of paper, placing the topic or theme in the center and drawing lines radiating out to the headings (group time, manipulatives, dramatic play). This creates a visual record of the relationships between and among the ideas and becomes what Workman and Anziano (1993) call "a living, growing resource."

Jones and Nimmo (1994) emphasize the organic nature of a web. First created as a response to children's ideas, it creates a picture in which ideas emerge and connect in any number of ways. It is, of course, a tentative plan, for what happens next depends on the children's responses. The web creates a flexible plan that can be altered and adapted as teachers observe children and evaluate their interests. See Figure 10-20 for a written plan that individualizes a particular child's needs.

Themes

A traditional method of developing curriculum is to focus on a broad, general topic or theme, also known as units. Though used interchangeably, themes are generally a smaller part of a unit, allowing for a more specific focus. For example, a unit on the body may have "What I can do with my hands" as one theme. This mode of planning is used in many early childhood and elementary settings; it is often a way to emphasize holidays. Focusing on themes, however, can and should be much more than an in-depth study of a topic. See Figure 10-21.

Theme: Familiar Things in Our World
Unit 2: Clothing Fasteners

Toy/Clothing Fastener Comparisons

Activity Purpose: Children develop a better understanding of how clothing fasteners work and see how the same mechanisms are used in other contexts.

Materials:
small shoe with Velcro fastening
several swatches of cloth with large
   snap set attached
several swatches of cloth with large
   hook and eye sets attached
several swatches of cloth with buttons
   and button holes
several Bristle Blocs
several Duplo and Lego blocks
several pieces of Links
several segments of Bits-O-Pieces
several pieces of Construx
   construction toys
several pieces of Brio construction toys
shallow trays and assorted containers
   to hold materials

Grouping of Children/Staffing: Children use the materials independently, during Activity Time, Arrival, and Dismissal periods. Adult interaction will facilitate children's exploration and comparison of the materials.

Materials Design and Activity Organization: Organize materials into sets for one child at a time to manipulate and explore. Each set has one each of the clothing fasteners and just enough of the other materials to allow children to experiment and compare them with the fasteners (but not enough to build something). Children manipulate the clothing fasteners and the toys and decide which work similarly.

Basic Procedure: Because these materials are not ordinarily used together, a child probably won't know what to do with them. A set of materials can be shown at meeting, and the teacher can tell the children that some of the clothing fasteners and some of the toys work in about the same way. Show how a snap works by fitting the two pieces together, then show that Lego blocks "snap" together in much the same way. After the introduction, place sets of materials in an appropriate area of the room. Interact with children as they explore the materials and ask which items they think work in similar ways, and why they think so.

Extensions: Teachers help children notice other things in their environment that work on the same principles as the clothing fasteners and toys. For example, hooks on doors or gates employ a hook and eye principle. Jewelry clasps often hook together. Bolts used to assemble an outdoor climbing toy employ a button and button hole principle although the bolts do not come out easily. Inspect the environment to find other examples.

Suggestions for Instruction: Teachers point out the shared principles between the clothing fasteners and some of the toys. It might be difficult for the youngest children to see the similarity in materials with such dissimilar appearances. Children probably haven't inspected closely the snap-like features of Duplo and Lego blocks, for example. They simply use them, moving the pieces until they fit together. Visual inspection of the construction toy features helps children see the similarities between the toys and the clothing fasteners. Teacher guidance prompts children to inspect the materials, especially if they have used them many times and are accustomed to fitting them together without thinking about how they actually work.
Four- and five-year old children rather than three-year-olds are more likely to be interested in learning about how their construction toys actually work.

Opportunities for Skill Development:

oral vocabulary
snap/unsnap, connect/disconnect hook and eye
Velcro, Bristle Blocs, Legos
teeth (Velcro and Bristle Blocs)
similar/different

oral expression
explaining in what ways the fasteners and toys are similar

problem solving
figuring out which clothing fasteners and toys work on the same principles

fine motor
manipulating the construction toys and the fasteners

FIGURE 10-21 Activity Plan: Familiar Things in Our World. (From Schickedanz et al. *Curriculum in Early Childhood: A Resource Guide for Preschool and Kindergarten Teachers.* Published by Allyn & Bacon, Boston, MA. Copyright © 1997 by Pearson Education. Reprinted by permission of the publisher.)

A thematic approach can utilize many of the attributes of an integrated curriculum:

- Children can help choose and plan themes, thereby constructing their own learning.
- Activities can be chosen to reflect the curriculum goals.
- The emphasis is on active learning.
- The most appropriate themes are those that have a meaningful connection to children's lives.
- Many subject areas can be integrated in the different activities.
- The program lends itself to flexibility, teacher permitting.
- It provides for an in-depth study of a topic.
- It can support the use of many learning styles through different media.
- It adds coherence and depth to the curriculum.
- It has the potential for good multicultural curriculum emphasis.

Holiday Themes or Not?

An inappropriate use of themes is to limit them to specific times of the year, such as Valentine's Day or Thanksgiving, or to celebrate holidays. Themes are not just for special occasions since they tend to isolate and narrowly define the topic.

Some holiday themes may not be appropriate to every family represented by the group. One teacher decided that making Easter baskets on Good Friday (a deeply religious day for many Christians) was offensive to those who practiced Christianity and was uncomfortable for the non-Christians in the class. The practice was dropped throughout the school in the name of cultural and religious sensitivity.

Some schools have adopted policies that do not permit celebrating holidays as part of the school curriculum. Holidays do provoke a particularly sensitive time for celebrating. There are many who believe that celebrating holidays from around the world brings a sense of multiculturalism to the curriculum.[1] York (2003) suggests that when done with thought and care, they can be an important addition to the curriculum. To ensure the most positive outcomes, according to York, all holidays are celebrated with equal importance; only those that have

Teachers of toddlers encourage touching and feeling, simple problem-solving, and choosing play materials. They remain patient as children explore the environment.

importance to the children and families in the class are observed; parents are enlisted to help; the celebration takes place within the context of the daily life of people and families; and sensitivity to the children and families who do not celebrate a particular holiday is observed.

Others might say this is a tourist approach to cultural diversity, or that it is a quick visit to another culture without follow-up and depth of exploration. Too often in early childhood programs, holiday curriculum units are the only expression of cultural diversity. According to Derman-Sparks (1989), there are no meaningful developmental reasons for the strong emphasis on celebrating holidays in most early childhood programs today. She further argues that this overuse of holiday themes actually interferes with a developmentally appropriate

What do YOU Think?

Should celebrating holidays be part of an early childhood curriculum? Justify your response with personal examples from your childhood, your teaching experiences, and your understanding of development. Debate your answer with a classmate who has a different opinion.

---

1 Some programs choose not to celebrate holidays at all, questioning whether it is DAP and how to adequately understand and explain the many holidays observed in the United States. Other programs invite members of the community to educate them about their particular observances. What is critical is to remember that, if holidays are celebrated, celebrations beyond the dominant culture should be included.

curriculum because too many foods or songs are used, bypassing the opportunity for children to learn about common areas of life. It seems that holiday themes paint a flat picture of a cultural or religious event without taking into account how people in those cultures live, work, sleep, or play in ways that are familiar or similar to other cultures.

Life-Oriented Themes

Themes that are of great interest to young children are those that directly concern themselves. The body as a theme suggests many avenues for development: body parts may be emphasized; exploration using the senses may be stressed; measuring and weighing children may be used to demonstrate growth of the body. Another subject to which children readily respond is that of home and family. Animals, especially pets, are appealing to young children and can lead into further curriculum areas of wild animals, prehistoric animals, and so on.

The more in touch with children the teachers are, the more their classroom themes should reflect the children's interests and abilities. Children who live in Silicon Valley in California, in Houston, Texas, or in Central Florida may have a local interest in space shuttles and computers.[1] The urban child of New York, Detroit, or Washington, DC, will relate more readily to themes about subways, taxis, and tall buildings. Children's interests often focus on, but are not necessarily limited to, what they have experienced. By choosing themes that coincide with children's daily lives, teachers promote connected and relevant learning. Take another look at Figures 10-6 and 10-11 from this perspective.

Some themes in an early childhood setting can address children's own issues. All young children share similar fears and curiosity about the world they do not know but imagine so vividly. The cues children give, particularly about their concerns, suggest to the observant teacher some important themes of childhood. During Halloween, for example, it can be helpful and reassuring to children if the theme of masks is developed. Select some masks that have a function, such as hospital masks, ski masks, safety glasses, sunglasses, snorkel masks, or wrestling and football helmets. Children can try them on and become comfortable with the

way their appearance changes. They can laugh with friends as they look in the mirror to see how a mask changes the appearance but does not change the person.

Gestwicki (2007) cites some disadvantages of using a traditional theme approach to curriculum. It can be restricted and narrow and too adult-directed, not allowing for children's curiosity and initiative. There is a danger of creating an artificial unit that has no relevancy to the children's experiences or interests. Teachers may find it hard to deviate from the curriculum plan and not be flexible enough to extend the topic further. When too rigidly applied, themes can isolate the experience into a particular subject or concept and miss the opportunities to broaden the learning potential. At its worst, a theme can be recycled every year without regard for the different group of children and their needs and interests.

Themes can be inclusive, integrated, and appropriate. It takes a teacher with a child-centered approach to respond to children's innate excitement and curiosity about learning.

The Project Approach

Much of what you have just learned about emergent and thematic curriculum as an integrated approach applies equally to projects. As you read ahead, keep in mind what you have learned about the advantages of an integrated curriculum (page 389), how to take cues from children as explained in the discussion on emergent curriculum (page 390), the concept of children and teachers collaborating (page 391), and the sources for curriculum ideas found on page 391. A **project approach** embodies these characteristics as well. On the continuum of teacher-directed versus child-directed learning, a project requires the greatest amount of child involvement.

Projects are the epitome of an integrated curriculum, embracing all of the key characteristics of integrated learning, and they allow for the incorporation of a wide range of subject areas. Katz (1994) defines the "project approach" as

> an in-depth investigation of a topic worth learning more about . . . usually undertaken by a small group of children within a class . . . the whole class . . . or even an individual child. The key

---

 1 A good multicultural curriculum should make maximize use of experiential learning, especially using local community resources.

A project emerged from the need for a new table. Children in Reggio Emilia, Italy, used their feet as a measuring device and drew up plans for the carpenter. Active exploration of the problem and art as a natural medium for children of all ages give the project approach meaning. (Courtesy of the city of Reggio Emilia, Italy.)

feature . . . is that it is a research effort deliberately focused on finding answers to questions about a topic posed either by the children . . . or the teacher.

A recent revival of this curriculum approach used in progressive schools (see Dewey, Chapter 1) is worth noting here. Based on the belief that "children's minds should be engaged in ways that deepen their understanding of their own experiences and environment" (Katz & Chard, 1989), the project approach consists of exploring a theme or topic (such as babies, dinosaurs, riding the school bus) over a period of days or weeks.

Preplanning by the children and teachers is the first step: they observe, question, estimate, experiment, and research items and events related to the topic. Together they make dramatic play and display materials they need. Children work in small groups throughout the process and have the opportunity to make numerous choices about their level of participation. The teacher often records the activity on tapes and with photographs. Project work has different levels of complexity so it meets the needs of children of different ages and abilities.

In the small town of Reggio Emilia in northern Italy, a similar approach to curriculum has received worldwide attention. The project approach is used in even greater depth as it permeates the entire curriculum and school environment. It will be discussed later in this chapter.

Projects emerge from children's own interests, teacher observations of children's needs and interests, and parents' suggestions. The topics reflect the local culture of the children.[1] In fact, Chard (1998) suggests that since life experiences and interests of the teacher and of the children are so strongly reflected in the project itself, it is a singular occurrence relevant only to that group. Another group may adopt the same topic, but it will not be a duplicate process due to the individual nature of the children and teacher planning the project.

This approach to teaching and learning easily lends itself to an inclusive classroom and curriculum, responding to diverse points of view as well as diverse cultures. Projects created by the children of Reggio Emilia, for instance, will differ from those of American children due to many cultural influences, in particular, the children's ability to argue their point and defend their ideas to others as the project emerges. In the Italian culture this is a natural part of discourse and is usual in the beginning of conversation between people; in American mainstream culture, it is usual when two people "agree to disagree" for the conversation to end.

The planning process is crucial to the success of the project approach as is the underlying philosophy that children can be co-constructors of their own education. This approach has much in common with the approaches of both Dewey and Summerhill (see Chapter 1). The teacher helps children explore what they already know about the topic, what they might need to know, and how they can represent that knowledge through various media, reinforcing Vygotsky's theory that interaction and direct teaching are important aspects of intellectual development. Teachers pose questions for children that lead them to suggest a hypothesis: What might happen if you do that? What do you think you could do to make that work? Children are encouraged to evaluate their own

1 The project approach provides the opportunity to avoid a "tourist" approach (emphasizing superficial facts or "foreign" customs) and provides children and teachers with an in-depth understanding of a particular culture and its traditions.

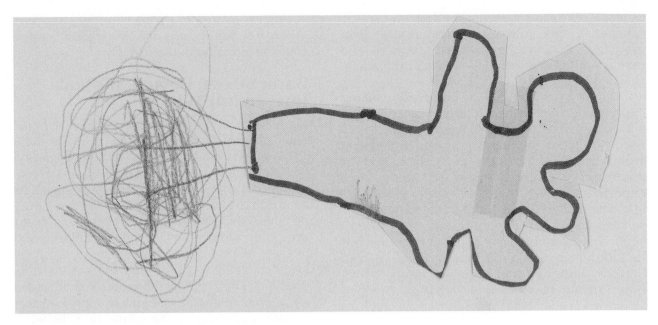

FIGURE 10-22 A child's representational drawing of a watering can.

Planning for physical skills is part of good curriculum development.

work and learn to defend and explain their creations to others.

The following is a summary of the process involved in a project approach as outlined by Chard (1998), Katz and Chard (1989), and Helm and Katz (2001). There are three phases to a project approach:

1. *Representation.* Children express and communicate their ideas. Through the use of drawing, writing, construction, dramatic play, maps, and diagrams children share their experience and knowledge. Representation documents what children are learning. See Figure 10-22.

2. *Fieldwork.* Investigations take place outside the classroom, through events, objects, places, and people, so that children build on their own knowledge through direct experiences.

3. *Investigation.* Using a variety of resources, children explore and research the topic. This includes fieldwork as well as closely analyzing, sketching, and discussing what they find.

4. *Display.* Exhibits of children's work on the project serve as a source of information and provide an opportunity to share their work and ideas with others. As the project progresses, the children are kept up to date on their progress by displays of their work.

CURRICULUM MODELS

High/Scope: Cognitively Oriented Model

The High/Scope curriculum stresses active learning through a variety of learning centers with plenty of materials and developmentally appropriate activities. Active problem solving is encouraged as children plan, with teacher's assistance, what they will do each day, carry out their plan, and review what they have done. Appropriately, this is known as the "plan–do–review" process. Teachers use small groups to encourage, question, support, and extend children's learning while emphasizing their communication skills.

There is a balance between child-initiated experiences and teacher-planned instructional activities. Teachers use observational techniques to focus on children and to understand children's play. Teachers are responsible for planning curriculum organized around key experiences that reinforce and extend the learning activities the children select for themselves. These key experiences are eight concepts that form the basis of the curriculum and include creative representation, language and literacy, initiative and social relations, movement, music, classification, seriation, number, space, and time (Hohmann & Weikart, 1995).

Children with special needs are integrated readily into High/Scope programs and with a curriculum developed especially for K–3 grades and early adolescents. High/Scope extends its active learning philosophy into further school years.

High/Scope's approach to children's learning is deeply rooted in Piagetian theory and supports Vygotsky's theory of social interaction and cognition: children learn when interacting with the people and materials in their environment. Core elements of the High/Scope philosophy are shared by the schools of Reggio Emilia. Both philosophies stress the importance of children's constructing their knowledge from activities that interest them; team teaching is an important concept, to allow the children access to adult support; and the process of planning, acting, recording, and reassessing is one that both approaches use to foster critical-thinking skills.

To document children's growth using a portfolio system (see Chapter 6), the High/Scope program uses the following categories (Schweinhart, 1993; Brewer, 1995):

- Initiative: Expressing choices, engaging in complex play.
- Creative representation: Making, building, pretending.
- Social relations: Relating to children and adults, making friends.
- Music and movement: Exhibiting body coordination, following a musical beat.
- Language and literacy: Showing interest in reading, beginning reading, beginning writing.
- Logic and mathematics: Sorting, counting objects, describing time sequences.

Teachers evaluate these abilities as they observe children's use of key experiences and plan the curriculum accordingly.

Bank Street: Developmental-Interaction Model

Bank Street was founded by Lucy Sprague Mitchell (see Chapter 1), and its roots reflect the thinking of Freud, Dewey, Erikson, Vygotsky, and Piaget, among others. There is a clear connection between education and psychology in its approach (Mitchell and David, 1992). It is developmental since knowledge of child development principles informs the curriculum planning, and interactive because of the connections made between children, adults, and the greater environment. The interaction between cognitive and social-emotional development is a key element as well, underscoring the connections between thinking and emotions (Mitchell & David, 1992).

Children are as seen as active learners who learn by interacting with and transforming the world about them. Play is the primary vehicle for encouraging involvement between and among children, adults, and materials. The teacher's primary role is to observe and respond to activities initiated by the children. Classrooms are organized into learning centers, where children can work individually or in groups.

The Bank Street model exemplifies an integrated curriculum. It is rooted in social studies (Mitchell & David, 1992) so that children learn about the world in which they live through concrete, first-hand experiences. Mitchell and David emphasize that the school is an active community connected to the social world of which it is a part and that "the school shares the responsibility with children's families and with other neighborhood institutions." Units and themes are used to focus the curriculum. There is freedom of movement and choice and easy access to materials (Epstein, Schweinhart, & McAdoo, 1996).

A teacher's knowledge and understanding of child development principles is crucial to this approach. Educational goals are set in terms of developmental processes and include the development of competence, a sense of autonomy and individuality, social relatedness and connectedness, creativity, and an integration of different ways of experiencing the world.

The Schools of Reggio Emilia

Respect for children's investigative powers and for their ability to think, plan, criticize, collaborate, and learn from all they do is the hallmark of the Reggio Emilia approach and is an excellent example of an integrated and emerging approach to learning. This collection of schools in Italy, with separate programs for infants to three-year-olds and three- to six-year-olds, has commanded worldwide attention for its philosophy and practices. "Nowhere else in the world," states Gardner (Edwards, Gandini, & Forman, 1993), "is there such a seamless and symbiotic relationship between a school's progressive philosophy and its practices." The curriculum takes the project approach to its highest levels.

Influenced by Dewey's progressive education movement, the philosophies and practices of Reggio Emilia owe a great deal as well to Piaget's constructivist theory, Vygotsky's belief in social discourse as a method of learning, and Gardner's theory of multiple intelligences (see Chapters 1, 4, and 13). Children are actively engaged in long-term projects that they initiate, design, and carry out with the support of the teacher. Art is the primary medium for learning.

Some of the key components of the Reggio Emilia approach are:

- a materials-rich environment that is aesthetically appealing;
- a community-based attitude involving the entire city;
- a family support system; and a commitment to process.

These elements are manifested in the program through astonishingly beautiful school settings, replete with the work of children and evidence of their projects elegantly displayed throughout; by support realized through a large portion of the city's budget; through small groups of children who stay together for a three-year period with the same teacher; and through intentionally bringing the children's culture into school life.[1]

Cadwell (1997) identifies eight fundamentals of the Reggio Emilia approach. Each has implications for creating a curriculum that is fully integrated and one that emerges from children's interests and ideas. These eight essential points are:

1. *The child as protagonist.* All children are strong and capable and have the potential and preparation to construct their learning. They are protagonists (i.e., central characters) with teachers and parents in the educational process.

The Reggio approach: order and beauty. (Courtesy of St. Louis-Reggio Collaborative. Copyright © 2001.)

Reggio Emilia: a materials-rich environment. (Courtesy of St. Louis-Reggio Collaborative. Copyright © 2001.)

2. *The child as collaborator.* There is an emphasis on working in small groups. This stems from the belief that we are social beings and form ourselves through interactions with people and things.

3. *The child as communicator.* Symbolic representation, through dance, art, painting, sculpting, building, dramatic play, music, and words help children discover and communicate what they know and what they question. Teachers support the use of these "many languages" to help children make their thinking visible.

4. *The environment as third teacher.* Every corner of the environment has an identity and purpose and encourages encounters,

---

 1 For example, common household objects and displays of pasta, fruits, and vegetables representing locally produced foods are often arranged in the lunch area.

communication, and relationships. There is order and beauty in the design of the equipment, the space, and the materials.

5. *The teacher as partner, nurturer, and guide.* Teachers listen and observe children closely in order to facilitate and guide their process of open-ended discovery. They ask questions to find out about children's ideas and theories and then provide the opportunities for their learning.

6. *The teacher as researcher.* Teachers work in pairs and collaborate with other members of the staff, engaging in continuous discussion and interpretation of their work and the work of the children. This provides ongoing staff development and deeper exploration of theoretical foundations. Teachers see themselves as researchers who prepare and document their work. They consider children researchers as well.

7. *The documentation as communication.* Thoughtful care is given to ways in which the thinking of children is presented. Teachers make transcripts of children's dialogue, take series of photographs of their projects, and arrange them in panels that hang throughout the school or in books. This documentation is a way to communicate to the rest of the school what the children's work is about, to help parents become aware of their children's work, to assist teachers in evaluating children's work, and to show children that their work is valued.

8. *The parents as partner.* Parent participation is considered essential, and parents discuss their ideas and skills with the teachers. This underscores the collegiality and collaboration between home and school and ensures a curriculum that represents the diversity of the children and their families.

The teacher's role is unique: two coequal teachers work with a class of 25 children. There is no head teacher or director of the school. The teachers are supported by a **pedigogista**, a person trained in early childhood education who meets with the teachers weekly. Also on the staff of every school is an **atelierista**, a person trained in the arts who teaches techniques and skills the children learn for their projects.

Process is highly respected as the way to plan and work together. Teachers and children, collaborators, listen to one another, and many points of view are encouraged. Debate and discussion are key elements in the process of deciding what project to do and how to go about it. The attitude that a child is a natural

researcher as well as an able learner and communicator has molded the organization and structure of the schools.

The schools of Reggio Emilia are worth knowing about just for the strong and powerful view they hold of the child and the concept of teacher and student learning from one another. There are a growing number of American models as well.

Cadwell (1997), who has assisted two schools in St. Louis to adopt the Reggio Emilia approach, pictured on these pages, offers a hopeful challenge: "We can learn from the Reggio educators to look at children differently, to expect more of them and of ourselves, and to offer them many more possibilities for full development."

Montessori Schools

In Chapter 1, Maria Montessori was discussed in relation to the history of early childhood education. What follows here is an explanation of the Montessori method as a program for young children.

Montessori's approach to learning has had a continuing influence in education since those early years. Of her work, three features stand out: (1) adapting school work to the individual rather than molding the child to fit the curriculum; (2) insisting on freedom for children in selection of materials and choice of activities; and (3) training of the senses and on practical life issues.

The Program

A common misunderstanding is that all schools with the Montessori name are the same. They are not. There are many variations and types of Montessori schools throughout the United States, reflecting an infinite variety of interpretations of the Montessori method. Within the Montessori movement itself, there are at least two factions claiming to be the voice of the true Montessori approach to education.

Although, the most common form of Montessori program is one in which three- to five-year-olds are grouped together, there are a growing number of schools for six- to nine-year-olds and even 9- to 12-year-olds. Teacher education programs now prepare Montessori teachers to work with infants and toddlers as well as high schoolers.

The most striking feature of the Montessori classroom is its materials. Many are made of wood and designed to stress the philosophy of learning through the senses. Color, texture, and quality of craftsmanship of the materials appeal to the hand as well as the eye; they demand to be touched. "Smooth" and "oval" take on new meaning as a child runs a finger around Montessori-designed puzzle shapes.

Montessori materials have other unique characteristics besides their tactile appeal. They are self-correcting; that is, they fit together or work in only one way so that children will know immediately whether they are successful. The Montessori curriculum presents the materials in a sequence, from simplest to most difficult. Many of the learning tasks have a series of steps and must be learned in a prescribed order. Whether sponging a table clean or using the number rods, the child is taught the precise order in which to use the materials. Montessori developed curriculum materials and tasks that are related to real life. "Practical life" activities range from cleaning tasks (hands, tables) to clothing tasks (lacing, buttoning, or tying garment closures).

In a Montessori classroom, children work by themselves at their own pace. They are free to choose the materials with which they want to "work"—the word used to described their activity. Children must accomplish one task before starting another one, including the replacing of the materials on the shelf for someone else to use.

The prepared environment in a Montessori program has child-sized furniture and equipment—one of Froebel's ideas that Montessori used. Materials are set out on low shelves, in an orderly fashion, to encourage children's independent use. Only one set of any materials—their shape, form, and the way they are presented for children to use—are the vehicles for learning.

The teacher in the Montessori setting has a prescribed role, one of observing the children. Teachers become familiar with skills and developmental levels, then match the children to the appropriate material or task. There is little teacher intervention beyond giving clear directions for how to use the materials. Group instruction is not common; learning is an individual experience.

Program Changes

Many changes have taken place in Montessori practices over the years, and today's best Montessori programs are those that are true to philosophical traditions of the Montessori method but constantly make small changes and adjustments. Many Montessori schools are adding curriculum areas of art, dramatic play, gross-motor development, and computers. There is also greater teacher flexibility to promote social interaction.

For years, Montessori was separated from the mainstream of American education. Today that has changed, with over 100 public school districts offering Montessori programs in their elementary schools and with the increased interaction between Montessorians and other early childhood professionals.

Maria Montessori has found her way into nearly every early education program in existence today. Whether labeled so or not, much of the material and equipment as well as many of the teaching techniques in use today originated with this dynamic woman nearly 100 years ago. She is firmly established in early childhood history and its future. The Montessori method should be weighed in light of contemporary knowledge and should be tailored to meet the needs of vigorous, eager, often needy children of the 21st century.

Waldorf Schools

The Waldorf curriculum, shaped by Rudolf Steiner in 1919 (see also Chapter 1), emphasizes the development of the whole child through "the head, heart, and hands." Based on the belief that young children learn primarily through observation, imitation, and experience, the curriculum provides a rich environment for children to explore and role models who provide appealing activities. A hallmark of the curriculum is learning through play, and large periods of time are devoted to creative play (Downs, 2003). Other defining features (WECAN, 2005) of a Waldorf curriculum include:

- Strong rhythmic elements based on the cycles of life and nature: A daily rhythm of play, work, circle time, outdoor play, ending with a nature or folk tale creates a consistent pattern for each session. The weekly rhythm evolves from activities, with one day for baking, another for crafts, and another for painting, and so on. Seasonal activities, such as planting bulbs, harvesting produce, or gathering leaves, stress nature's impact on our lives.[1]

 1 Seasonal celebrations mark the cyclical changes as well, and often include the families of the children in the class.

- Environments that nourish the senses: The walls of the classrooms are usually painted with soft watercolors, curtains may be made from plant-dyed fabrics, and tables and chairs are made of solid wood. The materials used are natural and real; the surroundings are simple and calming.

- Extensive use of natural materials: Wood, cotton, and wool are used throughout the classroom. Most of the toys are handcrafted from these natural materials, encouraging children to use their imagination. A piece of wood becomes ticket to ride the train, which is made from chairs and pieces of wood. It may also become a telephone, a piece of food, or animal in a barn made of similar materials. The Waldorf philosophy suggests that other, more "finished" toys limit the power of fantasy, imagination, and creativity that is natural in a young child.

- Play as an imitation of life: The curriculum fosters skills that imitate the work of adults. Children participate in activities focused on the home: cooking and baking, cleaning, washing and sewing, gardening and building. Engaging in meaningful life activities are seen as preparation for later academic challenges.[1]

- Enhancement of a sense of reverence and wonder: Children's natural sense of awe and wonder is fostered and deepened, primarily through activities, stories and festivals that celebrate the cycles of the seasons. In the fall, the classroom may be decorated with corn stalks and sheaves of grain; the seasonal table will be draped with beautiful fabrics in fall colors and hold gourds, pumpkins, acorns, and leaves. When parents join them for a harvest festival, songs of thankfulness and praise are sung before the feast begins. Each season this is repeated in order to expand the child's sense of reverence for life.

A Waldorf curriculum has much to offer, especially to those who put a premium on the use of imagination and an appreciation for the natural world. There are many elements common to the Montessori method and to the Reggio Emilia approach in particular, and to other curriculum models. Can you name them?

SUMMARY

Curriculum encompasses the planned and unplanned events children experience in group settings. Curriculum can include whatever happens to a child while in school or day care, or it can be a syllabus with detailed lesson plans. Today's teachers and caregivers ensure that children are exposed to developmentally appropriate, inclusive, and culturally appropriate curriculum.

Developing curriculum includes setting goals, establishing priorities, knowing what resources are available, planning ahead, and then evaluating the process. As teachers develop their curriculum plans, they may focus on the classroom activity or learning centers and the skills of the children. All three lend themselves to a basis for curriculum planning, and all are important vehicles for creative and effective curriculum for young children. Integrated curriculum provides opportunities for children of diverse skills and abilities to learn through the same experience. Emergent curriculum takes its cues from the children's interests, and the teacher helps them to explore their ideas in more depth. An extension of this is the project approach, which may last for weeks and months. There are many ways of learning, and the multiple intelligence theory helps teachers understand how to create curriculum that covers a broad range of abilities and interests. Various curriculum models demonstrate the application of curriculum development theory to practical use.

Play is the way curriculum is expressed in the early childhood setting. Teachers, aware of play as a foundation for learning, provide an atmosphere that supports the play process. They provide a setting in which play is recognized as the curriculum of the child, the primary process through which children learn. Curriculum comes alive as children discover and take pleasure in learning.

Teachers demonstrate their appreciation of diversity by carefully selecting materials and planning experiences that are culturally responsive and inclusive and provide opportunities for learning in large and small groups.

1 Waldorf teachers are good role models in the ways they participate in meaningful work with the children in the hopes that children will imitate good work habits and a sense of responsibility for others.

MAKING A DIFFERENCE IN YOUNG CHILDREN'S LIVES

by
Marjorie Kostelnik, Ph.D.

Nurturing children's development and learning throughout the early years is an exciting and awesome responsibility. As an early childhood educator, you will constantly be faced with situations in which you must make judgments about how to support and guide the children in your care. On any given day, you may wonder:

- Should I insist that all children play together and that everyone be "friends"?

- What should I do to help a child who has difficulty cutting with scissors?

- When is it reasonable to expect children to begin recognizing the letters in their names?

- What are sensible expectations when it comes to children following rules?

- How can I help children develop empathy and respect for all kinds of people?

How you answer questions like these and the actions you take can be more or less helpful to children. Your actions could enhance children's feelings of self-worth or detract from them. Your responses could increase children's interpersonal abilities or leave children at a loss about how to interact effectively. You could either promote or inhibit children's developing literacy, numeracy, or motor skills. Although there is not just *one* right answer for any of these situations, the things you say and do will make a real difference in children's lives.

What resources are available to help you frame the most effective responses? Your past experiences with children, advice or models provided by colleagues, and your intuitive feelings about what is best all contribute to your knowledge base. However, it is not sufficient to guide your actions professionally. Your personal qualities and experiences must be supplemented by theory and research regarding how children develop and learn. This knowledge extends beyond what you have absorbed from encountering the 5, 10 or even 100 children with whom you have interacted so far. It encompasses the accumulated wisdom of our profession that goes back further than any of us have been alive. Such knowledge includes terms, facts, principles and concepts that will help you understand how and why children think and behave as they do. It will also provide evidence-based insights into potentially useful intervention techniques. Ultimately, this combination of personal, conceptual, and research-based understandings will help you make the transition to bona fide early childhood professional.

As part of your professional education you will become familiar with common sequences of development and what characterizes typical development in various domains (cognitive, emotional, language, social, physical) at different ages. This knowledge helps determine reasonable expectations for children, so you can plan educational activities that are age appropriate. You will also learn how rates of development vary from child to child. This will sensitize you to the wide range of abilities represented among the youngsters in your group and help you create activities that are best suited to children's individual needs.

Likewise, there are theories and research describing how young children learn. For instance, as you become more familiar with children's learning styles and the role of play in children's learning you will be able to create educational environments that suit how children learn best. Finding out what researchers think about teaching by example, the use of rewards and consequences, and different ways to coach children in the learning process will give you much to think about regarding your interactions in the early childhood setting. In addition, becoming more aware of research that describes how children's families and cultural contexts impact the educational process will help you develop approaches that are socially and culturally relevant.

Some of the professional knowledge base seems logical, but some is counterintuitive. For example, common sense might tell you that praising children when they do something well is a good strategy for increasing positive behaviors in the future. Yet, researchers have found that certain kinds of praise actually interfere with children's learning and make it less likely that they will repeat desired actions.

Finally, you need to put these learnings into practice. You need to gather both time-honored curriculum and innovative ways to organize the environment and the daily schedule. You must work to plan activities that help all children learn in every domain. *While professionals* in the field have attempted to catalogue such practices in a variety of documents, you will have to do more than memorize or copy them. There is more than one way to think about things; there are contradictory ideas to consider; different contexts will demand different approaches. In the end, you have to make your own judgments about how to interpret and respond to children in a variety of circumstances. And that will help you define what is being taught to young children.

Marjorie Kostelnik, Ph.D., has been an early childhood educator for 30 years. Currently, she is Dean of the College of Education and Human Sciences at the University of Nebraska. Most recently, she and her coauthors have written Guiding Children's Social Development (5th ed.), Delmar Publishing, and Developmentally Appropriate Curriculum: Best Practices in Early Childhood Education, Merrill/ Prentice Hall.

For more activities and information, visit our Web site at http://www.EarlyChildEd.delmar.com

KEY TERMS

developmentally appropriate
   practice (DAP)
culturally appropriate
   curriculum
infusion

inclusive curriculum
emergent curriculum
learning styles
activity centers
prerequisite

linchpin
webbing
project approach
pedigogista
atelierista

REVIEW QUESTIONS

1. Define developmentally appropriate curriculum for early childhood programs. What three principles determine whether a curriculum is "appropriate"?

2. Name 10 guidelines for developing curriculum for young children.

3. Observe several early childhood programs (e.g., a family child care home, a child care center, and an after-school program for primary-age students) for examples of multicultural infusion in the curriculum. Describe the way the content does or does not expand the children's understanding of diversity.

4. What is emergent curriculum, and why is it appropriate for early childhood teachers?

5. What are some appropriate uses of themes when developing curriculum?

6. How does knowledge of multiple intelligences and learning styles inform curriculum planning?

7. Describe the project approach, including how it can be incorporated into the curriculum. Be sure to show how it can affect every major curriculum area.

8. Which curriculum model best represents your own thinking? Why?

LEARNING ACTIVITIES

1. Create a curriculum web with several classmates following the process described on pages 413–415.

2. Develop a project for (a) three-year-olds in a half-day nursery school; (b) six-year-olds in an after-school extended-day program; (c) a family day care home. Use a nonholiday theme.

3. Observe teachers as children play. What is the difference in the play when (1) a teacher interacts with children in their play and (2) a teacher intervenes? What happens to the play immediately after teacher contact is made? How long does the play last? What is your conclusion?

4. Use Figure 10-5 to determine your own style of learning. How has this style affected your abilities as a student?

5. Use Figure 10-17 to plan an activity for (1) toddlers; (2) four-year-olds; (3) first graders.

6. What materials do you find in early childhood classrooms that enhance cultural diversity? What would you add? Take away? Why?

REFERENCES

Arce, E. (2000). *Curriculum for young children: An introduction.* Clifton Park, NY: Thomson Delmar Learning.

Armstrong, T. (2000). *Multiple intelligences in the classroom.* Alexandria, VA: Association for Supervision and Curriculum Development.

Banks, J. (2006). *Cultural diversity and education: Foundations, curriculum and teaching.* Boston: Allyn & Bacon.

Banks, J. A. (1992, November/December). Reducing prejudice in children: Guidelines from research. *Social Education,* pp. 3–5.

Banks, J. A. (1994). *Multiethnic education: Theory and practice.* Boston: Allyn & Bacon.

Berk, L. E. (2002). *Child Development.* Boston: Allyn & Bacon.

Bredekamp, S., & Copple, C. (1997). *Developmentally appropriate practices in early childhood programs.* Washington, DC: National Association for the Education of Young Children.

Bredekamp, S., & Rosegrant, T. (Eds.) (1995). *Reaching potential: Transforming early childhood curriculum and assessment* (Vol. 2). Washington, DC: National Association for the Education of Young Children.

Brewer, J. (1995). *Introduction to early childhood education.* Boston: Allyn & Bacon.

Cadwell, L. (1997). *Bringing Reggio Emilia home.* New York: Teachers College Press.

Chard, S. (1998). *Practical guide to the project approach.* New York: Scholastic.

de Melendez, R. W., & Ostertag, V. (1997). *Teaching young children in multicultural classrooms.* Clifton Park, NY: Thomson Delmar Learning.

Derman-Sparks, L., & the ABC Task Force. (1989). *Anti-bias curriculum: Tools for empowering young children.* Washington, DC: National Association for the Education of Young Children.

Downs, M. (2003). The Waldorf preschool curriculum: An engaging path to academic success. *Southern Journal of Teaching and Education.*

Edwards, C., Gandini, L., & Forman, G. (1993). *The hundred languages of children: The Reggio Emilia approach to early childhood education.* Norwood, NJ: Ablex.

Epstein, A. S., Schweinhart, L. J., & McAdoo, L. (1996). *Models of early childhood education.* Ypsilanti, MI: High/Scope Press.

Frost, J. L. (1996). *Play and playscapes.* Clifton Park, NY: Thomson Delmar Learning.

Gardner, H. (1983). *Frames of mind: The theory of multiple intelligences.* New York: Basic Books.

Gardner, H. (1998). *Reflections on multiple intelligences: Myths and messages.* In Woolfolk, A. (Ed.) "Readings in Education Psychology," pp. 64–66. Boston: Allyn & Bacon.

Gestwicki, C. (2007). *Developmentally appropriate practice: Curriculum and development in early education.* Clifton Park, NY: Thomson Delmar Learning.

Gronlund. G. (2006). *Making early learning standards come alive: Connecting your practice and curriculum to state guidelines.* St. Paul, MN: Redleaf Press.

Hall, N. S., & Rhomberg, V. (1995). *The affective curriculum.* Clifton Park, NY: Thomson Delmar Learning.

Helm, J. H., & Katz, L. (2001). *Young investigators: The project approach in the early years.* New York: Teachers College Press.

Hohmann, N., & Weikart, D. P. (1995). *Educating young children: Active learning practices for preschool and childcare programs.* Ypsilanti, MI: High/Scope Press.

Jackman, H. L. (2007). *Early education curriculum: A child's connection to the world.* Clifton Park, NY: Thomson Delmar Learning.

Jones, E. (1994). An emergent curriculum expert offers this afterthought. *Young Children, 54,* 16.

Jones, E., & Nimmo, J. (1994). *Emergent curriculum.* Washington, DC: National Association for the Education of Young Children.

Katz, L. G. (1994). *The project approach.* Champaign, IL: ERIC Clearinghouse on Elementary and Early Childhood Education.

Katz, L., & Chard, S. (1989). *Engaging children's minds: The project approach.* Norwood, NJ: Ablex.

McNeely, S. L. (1997). *Observing students and teachers through objective strategies.* Boston: Allyn & Bacon.

Miller, R. (1996). *The developmentally appropriate inclusive classroom.* Clifton Park, NY: Thomson Delmar Learning.

Mitchell, A., & David, J. (Eds.) (1992). *Explorations with young children.* Mt. Ranier, MD: Gryphon House.

New City School. (1994). *Celebrating multiple intelligences: Teaching for success.* St. Louis, MO: The New City School.

Peterson, E. A. (1996). *A practical guide to early childhood planning, methods, and materials.* Boston: Allyn & Bacon.

Ramirez, M., & Casteñada, A. (1974). *Cultural democracy, bicognitive development, and education.* New York: Academic Press.

Schickedanz, J. A., Pergantis, M. L., Kanosky, J., Blaney, A., & Ottinger, J. (1997). *Curriculum in early childhood.* Boston: Allyn & Bacon.

Schirrmacher, R. (2002). *Art and creative development for young children.* Clifton Park, NY: Thomson Delmar Learning.

Schweinhart, L. J. (1993, July). Observing young children in action: The key to early childhood assessment. *Young children,* pp. 29–33.

WECAN (Waldorf Early Childhood Association of North America) (2005). *The Waldorf kindergarten: The world of the young child.*

Witkin, H., Moore, C., Goodenough, D., & Cox, P. (1977). Field dependent and field independent cognitive styles and their educational implications. *Review of Educational Research, 47,* 1–64.

Woolfolk, A. (2001). *Educational psychology.* Boston: Allyn & Bacon.

Workman, S., & Anziano, M. C. (1993, January). Curriculum webs: Weaving connections from children to teachers. *Young Children,* pp. 4–9.

York, S. (2003). *Roots and wings: Affirming culture in early childhood programs.* St. Paul, MN: Redleaf Press.

HELPFUL WEB SITES

High/Scope	http://www.highscope.org
NAEYC	http://www.naeyc.org
ERIC/EECE	http://www.ericeece.org
The Creative Curriculum®	http://www.TeachingStrategies.com
Project Approach	http://www.ualberta.ca/schard/projects
Multiple Intelligences	http://www.newcityschool.org
National Black Child Development Institute	http://www.nbcdi.org
National Latino Children's Institute	http://www.nici.org
The Anti-Defamation League	http://www.adl.org
Reggio Emilia	http://www.reggiochildren.org

For more activities and information, visit our Web site at http://www.EarlyChildEd.delmar.com

CHAPTER

11

Planning for the Body:
Physical/Motor Development

QUESTIONS FOR THOUGHT

How does physical growth differ from motor development?

What are the physical and motor skills children learn in an early childhood setting?

What should the teacher of young children consider when planning for physical/
motor development?

How is physical/motor development integrated into the curriculum?

Why is outdoor play important?

LEARNING THROUGH MOVEMENT

One of the first things you notice about young children is their energy and movement. Teachers often characterize children through their movements. "Trina never walks . . . she runs!" Pregnant mothers are aware of fetal motions and often assign personality traits to their children by these movements. "This baby is so active I think it must be in training for the Olympics." Infants show the extent of their full-bodied, random movements when they cry, roll over, and reach for a crib mobile.

In the Beginning

Basic motor skills develop in the early childhood years and form the foundation for movement and motor proficiency. If children do not develop them during the early years, these skills often remain unlearned.

A child's first few years of life are an astounding time of physical growth and acquisition of motor skills. The many milestones, such as rolling over, sitting up alone, crawling, walking, and running, are reinforced daily by parents and caregivers. This reinforcement strengthens the network of synapses, and they become a permanent part of the brain. By adolescence, the brain is beginning to rid itself of excess synapses. Those that have been activated and experienced most often are the ones that will survive (Shore, 1997). This research makes a strong case for activities and experiences, which foster physical growth and motor skills in young children. As

Children are the picture of movement, spending the greatest portion of their day in physical activity.

Greenman says, "Movement is as necessary to their learning as air and light" (2000).

Physical growth and motor development are partly determined by a child's genetic make-up. Equally important are environmental factors, such as nourishment, health, safety, stimulation, opportunity, practice, encouragement, and instruction. The crucial interplay of heredity and environment guides the child's progress through life.

Learning Is Integrated

Motor abilities affect other areas of development. Current research reinforces the notion that physical and motor development is integrated with a child's cognitive development and that this relationship between movement and learning continues throughout life (Jensen, 1998). Complex movements such as dancing or throwing a ball engage areas of the brain used for problem solving, planning, and sequencing new things to do. This mind-body integration can be seen in other areas of development as well:

> Tim is reluctant to climb outside. He frightened when he—or anyone else—is up in a tree or on any climber. Because he cannot risk using his body in space, he stops himself from playing with anyone who invites him to try these activities. Thus, Tim's lack of gross-motor development is affecting his social skills. Samantha loves to draw and cut. She chooses the art area every day she attends the two-year-old class. Not only are her fine-motor skills well developed for her age; she takes great pride in her creations. Her motor skills enhance her self-confidence in school. In turn, she receives praise and attention from others as she communicates with both adults and children through her work.

Program Needs

The greatest portion of the young child's day is spent in physical activity. Quality early childhood programs recognize this, providing for a full range of physical and motor experiences, planned and spontaneous. Indoors, children use puzzles, scissors, and dressing frames as they practice fine-motor skills. They dance with scarves and streamers to music. **Perceptual-motor development**, as with body awareness, occurs when children learn songs and games ("Head and Shoulders, Knees and Toes" or "Mother May I Take Two Giant Steps?") or while fingerpainting. Outdoors, gross-motor skills are refined by the use of climbers, swings, hopscotch, and ring-toss.

Movement Exploration Enhances Children's Ability to

- Problem solve.

- Exercise divergent thinking.

- Respond at their own age and developmental level.

- Learn to cooperate with others.

- Become more aware of others' viewpoints and ideas.

- Share, take turns.

- Be self-expressive.

- Be creative.

- Gain confidence.

- Develop strong muscles.

- Refine motor skills.

Children need time as well as equipment and activities to practice their skills. The value teachers place on physical and motor development is directly related to the time allotted in the daily schedule for children to pursue them.

For years, early childhood programs have made an outdoor environment available to children, assuming a great need for physical activity and that children will find ways to fill that need themselves. However, many school outdoor areas contain few challenges, perhaps only a blacktop for bouncing balls and a small metal climber for hanging and climbing. Moreover, American children are exposed to a value system in which physical/motor fitness is not always a high priority. Children are often encouraged toward sedentary activities at an early age, such as watching television.

Physical/motor development is the central focus of the needs and interests of young children; it should play a central role in planning the curriculum.

PHYSICAL GROWTH/ MOTOR DEVELOPMENT

Physical Growth

Understanding of physical development is important to teachers and parents for a number of reasons. For example:

- New behavior is made possible through physical change: A toddler can be toilet-trained once anal sphincter muscles develop.

- Growth determines the child's experiences: Observe the new vistas that open up to the brand new walker.

- Growth changes the way people respond to the child: The mobility of crawlers and toddlers leads to more restrictions from parents.

- Self-concepts are profoundly related to physical development: An obese kindergartner avoids the running and chasing games during recess.

Development follows a directional and sequential pattern. Large muscles develop before smaller ones—one reason why most preschoolers are more proficient at running than at cutting with scissors. Growth also starts at the center of the body and moves outward. Watch a toddler walk using whole-leg action and compare that with a five-year-old whose knees and ankles are involved in a more developed response. Children also tend to develop in a head-to-toe pattern. Infants move their eyes, head, and hands long before they learn to creep or crawl. It is important to remember, however,

Self-concept is related to physical development.

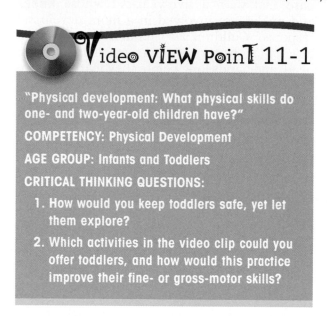

Age	Weight	Height	Proportion	Teeth
Newborn	7 lb.	20 in.	Head = 1/4 of length	None
Infancy (up to 18 months)	Gains 15 lb. (now 20–25 lb.)	Adds 8 in. (now 28–29 in.)	About the same	6
Toddler (18 mo. to two-and-a-half years)	Gains 5 lb. (now 28–30 lb.)	Adds another inch or two (now 29–33 in.)	Legs = 34% of body	20
Preschool (two-and-a-half–five years)	About 5 lb./yr. (now 30–40 lb.)	Add 14–15 in. from birth; at age 2 = half of adult height (now 35–40 in.)	Head growth slows; legs at age five = 44% of body	20
Early-middle childhood (five–eight years)	Doubles before adolescence (age six = 45–50 lb.)	Adds 9–10 in. (age six = 44–48 in.)	Continues to move slowly toward adult proportions	Begins to lose baby teeth; replaced by permanent teeth (age six = 20–24 teeth)

FIGURE 11-1 An overview of growth shows how rapid physical growth is in childhood.

Video VIEW Point 11-1

"Physical development: What physical skills do one- and two-year-old children have?"

COMPETENCY: Physical Development

AGE GROUP: Infants and Toddlers

CRITICAL THINKING QUESTIONS:

1. How would you keep toddlers safe, yet let them explore?

2. Which activities in the video clip could you offer toddlers, and how would this practice improve their fine- or gross-motor skills?

that growth does not occur in a smooth and unbroken pattern.

See also Chapter 3 for an overview of developmental norms. Figure 11-1 shows an overview of the dramatic changes in growth for children up to age eight.

Gender Differences

There are gender differences as well. Boys have a larger proportion of muscle tissue than girls, and from the beginning girls have more fat tissue than boys. Each of these differences becomes more obvious in adolescence. In regard to physical development, girls mature earlier than boys, and their growth is more regular and predictable. In motor skills, preschool girls have an edge in fine-motor skills, such as writing and drawing, and gross-motor skills, such as hopping and skipping. By age five, boys can jump slightly farther, run slightly faster, and throw a ball about five feet farther than girls. These gender differences remain small until adolescence (Berk, 2002).

Cultural Differences

There is some indication that physical development differs among ethnic groups.[1] African American infants and toddlers seem to walk earlier and as a group are taller than Euro-Americans. Asian children also seem to develop physically earlier than Euro-American babies but are smaller and shorter overall (Bee, 1997). Some researchers suggest that because African American children have longer limbs, they have better leverage, which accounts for their superior performance in running and jumping (Berk, 2002).

While looking at general growth patterns of children, parents and teachers must keep in mind the wide individual differences in the rates at which children grow and in the timing of each change. As a general rule, the pattern within individuals is consistent; that is, a child

---

1 Be aware of the possibilities in the way children grow, but be careful not to stereotype them.

who is early, average, or late in one aspect of physical development will be so in all aspects. There are sex differences as well in rate and patterns of physical growth. The most obvious of these is that girls generally begin puberty two years ahead of boys (Bee, 1997). Bee also found that as a group, poor children grow more slowly and are shorter than middle-class children, a finding attributed to diet. Even though the rate of physical development may differ, however, the sequence of development remains the same. This holds true even for children who are physically or mentally disabled.[1]

Including Children with Special Needs

Every classroom is likely to have children who have special needs that must be met. It has already been established (see Chapters 3 and 9) that inclusion of children with special needs in early childhood programs is not only appropriate but is mandated by law. Physical education is the only subject area cited in the definition of an "appropriate education" in Public Law 94-142 (Gallahue, 1996), providing an opportunity for children to grow and develop through movement and physical activities.

Children with physical, cognitive, emotional, or learning disabilities are faced with a variety of challenges, many of which may be met by adapting the environment and planning for activities that help children function within their range of abilities. "The Inclusive Environment" and Figure 9-4 in Chapter 9 offer a number of ways for teachers and caregivers to individualize the setting for a variety of needs. In Chapter 3 many types of disabilities are discussed.

There are a number of teaching strategies that can enhance the participation of children with special needs in regular classroom activities in Figure 11-2. These brief examples make it clear that including children with special needs takes some careful thought about what kinds of movement experiences and physical development activities are within their abilities. Many of the suggestions are appropriate for all children, reminding us that the needs and interests of all children are essentially the same. Figure 11-3 expands

Teaching Strategies for Children with Special Needs

1. *For Children with Learning Disabilities*

   Help children gain a better understanding of their body, the space it occupies, and how it can move.

   Structure personalized activities that work within the child's present level of abilities.

   Progress from simple to more complex activities in small increments.

   Make frequent use of rhythmic activities, stressing the rhythmical elements to movement.

2. *For Children Who Are Visually Impaired*

   Use many auditory cues to help children gain a sense of space and distance.

   Include strenuous, big-muscle activities.

   Modify activities that require quick directional changes.

3. *For Children with Cognitive Disabilities*

   Stress gross-motor activities.

   Focus on fundamental stability, locomotor, and manipulative skills.

   Allow children to repeat their successes to enjoy the accomplishment.

   Avoid activities in which participants are eliminated from the game.

FIGURE 11-2 Many physical activities are appropriate for all children and encourage those with special needs to take an active part in the daily program. (From Gallahue, D. L. (1996) *Developmental Physical Education for Today's Children.* Madison WI: Brown and Benchmark.)

these strategies with an example of one child's developmental needs.

Motor Development

Motor development "is the process of change in motor behavior brought about by interaction between heredity and environment" (Gallahue, 1996). It is a lifelong process of continuous change based on the interaction of (1) maturation (i.e., the genetically controlled rate of growth); (2) prior experiences; and (3) new motor activities. Like physical growth, motor development is a sequence of stages that is universal but still allows for individual differences.[2] Each stage is different from, yet grows out of, the preceding level. Figure 11-4 charts motor development through the early years.

---

1 Variations in growth patterns are influenced by environment and genetic make-up. This holds true for all children.

2 One is reminded of the definition of developmentally appropriate practice—some characteristics of development are universal and sequential, and other characteristics are highly individual.

Planning Inclusively for Children with Special Needs

Nathan is a short-statured four-year-old, approximately two-thirds as tall as his peers. His legs are short in proportion to his body size and he loses his balance easily. Ana's physical development is normal, but she is quite shy and prefers to watch others rather than participate in activities. A step-by-step process that builds on children's strengths and skills helps teachers plan meaningful activities for each child.

1. *Ascertain child's strengths.*

   Nathan—imaginative, agile, healthy, outgoing, demonstrates positive self-image

   Ana—perservering, patient, compliant, methodical, each small success is evident in her expression

2. *Ascertain child's needs.*

   Nathan—to prove that he is as competent as his peers, despite short stature; to improve poor balance due to disproportionately short legs

   Ana—to improve large-motor skills; to gain confidence in joining groups

3. *Set goals.*

   Nathan—to gain better balance and to be offered the chance to feel tall and big

   Ana—to become a bit more adventurous, more sociable, and more comfortable with her body in space

4. *Brainstorm: What group activities are suitable?*

   Nathan—physical activites that require stretching and balancing

   Ana—noncompetetive experiences that require different kinds of motor planning and that allow her to proceed at her own pace while participating with her peers

5. *Select an activity* (e.g., an outdoor obstacle course).

6. *Plan the activity* (see "Planning an Outdoor Obstacle Course").

7. *Implement the activity* (see "Building an Obstacle Course").

8. *Evaluate the activity.*

   Nathan—Was he able to stretch sufficiently to climb the rungs and reach across the empty spaces between obstacles? Did he work on his balancing skills?

   Ana—Was she willing and able to work through the course? Did she need a teacher's hand throughout? Did she interact with her peers?

   Both—Did they do the whole course, or did they skip some obstacles? Did they return to a favorite spot? Did they voluntarily repeat the whole course?

   All—Did everybody have fun?

9. *Refine the activity—and try again!*

FIGURE 11-3 Planning inclusively for children with special needs. (Adapted from C. S. Kranowitz, "Obstacle Courses Are for Every Body," in *Alike and Different: Exploring Our Humanity with Young Children*, ed. B. Neugebauer (Washington, DC: NAEYC, 1992), p. 23. Reprinted with permission from the National Association for the Education of Young Children (NAEYC).)

Any discussion of motor development should include reference to bodily-kinesthetic intelligence, part of Gardner's multiple intelligence theory (see Chapters 4, 10, and 12). Bodily-kinesthetic intelligence occurs when children use their bodies to help them process information and communicate their understanding of school. For instance, children who learn best through bodily-kinesthetic intelligence need active manipulation of materials. Drama, creative movement, dance, manipulatives, games, and exercises, both indoors and out-of-doors, benefit the bodily-kinesthetic learner (The New City School, 1994).

Gross-Motor Development

Gross-motor activity involves movements of the entire body or large parts of the body. Using various large muscle groups, children try to creep, crawl, roll, bounce, throw, or hop. Activities that include balance, agility, coordination, flexibility, strength, speed, and endurance foster gross-motor development.

Fine-Motor Development

Fine-motor activity uses the small muscles of the body and its extremities (the hands and feet). Such movement requires dexterity, precision,

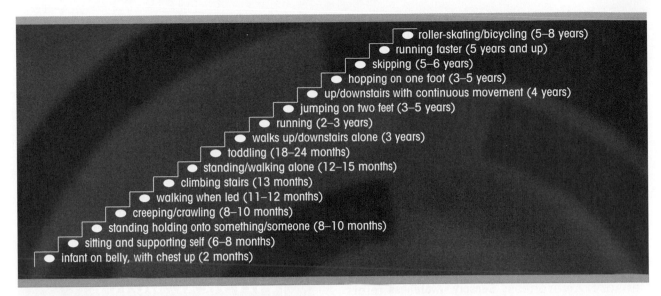

roller-skating/bicycling (5–8 years)
running faster (5 years and up)
skipping (5–6 years)
hopping on one foot (3–5 years)
up/downstairs with continuous movement (4 years)
jumping on two feet (3–5 years)
running (2–3 years)
walks up/downstairs alone (3 years)
toddling (18–24 months)
standing/walking alone (12–15 months)
climbing stairs (13 months)
walking when led (11–12 months)
creeping/crawling (8–10 months)
standing holding onto something/someone (8–10 months)
sitting and supporting self (6–8 months)
infant on belly, with chest up (2 months)

FIGURE 11-4 Motor development follows a developmental sequence. (Adapted from Allen, K. E., & Marotz, L. (2003). *Developmental profiles: Prebirth through eight*. Clifton Park, NY: Thomson Delmar Learning.)

and manipulative skill. Grasping, reaching, holding, banging, pushing, spinning, and turning are all activities that refine these skills.

Perceptual-Motor Development

Perceptual-motor development is a process in which the child develops the skill and ability to take in and interpret information from the environment and respond to it with movement. Children obtain data and impressions primarily through their senses. How often have you seen babies mimic a parent's or caregiver's mouth movements—taking in visually the various expressions, then physically responding in kind?

In a sense, every moment is perceptual-motor activity because the body and mind must work together to complete all motor tasks. The perceptual task is to process information; the motor response activates what is received in a physical way although perceptual and motor abilities do not necessarily develop at the same time or the same rate (Gallahue, 1996). The complex nature of perceptual-motor development can be seen when examining the three basic categories of spatial, temporal, and sensory awareness, which also include perceptual-motor concepts of body and directional, visual, and auditory awareness.

Spatial Awareness. For children, **spatial awareness** means a sense of body awareness and the body's relationship to space, as well as a knowledge of what the body parts can do.

- For the toddler, concepts of spatial relationships are developed through motor activity:

dropping objects from a highchair or forcing a large stuffed animal into a small box. Their definition of space is related to the action and movement involved in specific activities.

- A sense of relationship to less immediate things and places (knowing a specific route to school and home, making simple maps) develops in the preschool years. To illustrate, let us look at three-year-old Tamara. She demonstrates her awareness of spatial relationships as she moves herself up to a table (without bumping into it), reaches to her left to pick up a ball of clay, and turns around behind her to choose a rolling pin.

- Not until ages six to eight do children develop the more abstract spatial ability of distinguishing left from right on their own bodies and

Gross-motor activity uses the various large-muscle groups so that children can move their entire bodies.

others' Specifically, directional awareness refers to left and right, up and down, front and behind, over and under.

Temporal Awareness. Temporal awareness is the child's inner clock, a time structure that lets the child coordinate body parts. Dancing to a rhythmic beat, speeding up and slowing down, develops this kind of skill. It is also a force that helps children predict time. For instance, seven-year-olds Luis and Aref ask if it is time to clean up as they finish their game of soccer. The after-school center has sports time for about an hour before getting ready for snack; the children have an inner sense of time that parallels their knowledge of the daily schedule.

Sensory Awareness. **Sensory awareness** refers to use of the senses. It is another way the body gives the mind information. Vision is the dominant sense for young children. Visual awareness is the ability to mimic demonstrated movements and to discriminate faces, emotions, sizes, shapes, and colors. It is the ability in

Fine-motor activity requires using the small muscles of the body with dexterity and precision.

three-month-old babies to recognize their mothers. Auditory awareness includes the ability to understand and carry out verbal directions and to discriminate among a variety of sounds ("Is this loud? fast? soft?" "Is that Josie or Dominick who called you?"). Auditory skills help children process information about language. From infancy, children seem to be able to combine visual and auditory awareness. Further sensory awareness develops through touch. Babies seem to put everything in their mouth to learn. When four-year-old Stephanie picks up each object at the display table, she is using her sense of touch to discover size, shape, and volume.

PHYSICAL/MOTOR SKILLS IN EARLY CHILDHOOD

Types of Movement

Physical/motor skills involve three basic types of movement: locomotor, nonlocomotor, and manipulative abilities:

1. *Locomotor* abilities involve a change of location of the body (Gallahue, 1996) and include the skills of walking, running, leaping, jumping, climbing, hopping, skipping, galloping, sliding, and tricycling.

2. *Nonlocomotor* abilities (sometimes referred to as balancing or stabilizing) are any movements that require some degree of balancing (Gallahue, 1996). These skills are turning, twisting, pushing, bending, stretching, pulling, swinging, rolling, dodging, and balancing.

3. *Manipulative* abilities include the operation and control of limited and precise movements of the small muscles, especially those in the hands and feet. Manipulative skills include throwing, catching, reaching, bouncing, striking, kicking (gross-motor manipulation) and holding, grasping, cutting, and sewing (fine-motor manipulation).

These three basic movements are necessarily combined when children are active in physical play:

With doll buggy: Holding onto buggy—
                     Manipulative
                     Pushing buggy—
                     Nonlocomotor
                     Walking with buggy—
                     Locomotor

Playing ball: Bending down for the
                    ball—Nonlocomotor
                    Throwing the ball—
                    Manipulative
                    Running to base—
                    Locomotor

Jumping rope: Holding and turning the
                    rope—Manipulative
                    Jumping—Locomotor
                    Balancing self after
                    jump—Nonlocomotor

Breaking a piñata: Holding the bat—
                    Manipulative
                    Swinging the bat—
                    Nonlocomotor
                    Running to get the prize—
                    Locomotor

Figure 11-5 shows age-appropriate toys and games that foster the development of the three types of basic motor skills.

Learning Motor Skills

Children must use their bodies to learn motor skills. They acquire these skills by making comparisons between their past experience and new actions. Such comparisons use memory and experience.

Memory and Experience

Memory plays an important part in learning motor movements because children need to recall what they just did to make corrections or refinements. The ball that does not reach the basket is tossed farther on the next shot. To get the puzzle piece to fit, a child remembers other ways to manipulate the pieces. A long-term memory of movement is one that may go unrehearsed for long periods of time. The experience of swimming, for example, may be recalled only in the summer.

Type of Motor Skill	Infants Zero to One-and-a-Half Years	Toddlers One-and-a-Half Years to Three Years	Preschoolers Three to Five Years	Early School Six to Eight Years

Locomotor:
Walking
Running
Jumping
Hopping
Skipping
Leaping
Climbing
Galloping
Sliding
	Safe areas to explore
	  body movements
	Balls to roll
	Hanging jumpseats
	Walkers on wheels
	Simple obstacle course
		Walker wagons
		Pull/push toys
		Dancing
		Wide balance board
		Toddler gym—stairs
		  and slide
		"Ring around the Rosey"
			Hippity-hop balls
			Sled
			Beginning skis
			Trampoline
			Roller skates
			Jump rope
			Balance beam
			Climber
			Dancing
				Jump rope
				Roller skates
				Ice skates
				Climbing rope
				Tumbling mats
				Hopscotch

Nonlocomotor:
Pushing
Pulling
Bending
Balancing
Stretching
Rolling turning
Twisting
	Large, safe areas
	  for exploration
	Parent/caregiver
	  play: holding,
	  pushing arms,
	  legs, sturdy
	  push toys
	Soft obstacle
	  course of pillows
		Pounding board
		Simple, low rocking horse
		Ride-on toys
		Toddler-type swing
		Large Legos®
		Sturdy doll buggy
		Wagon
		Fabric tunnels
		Blocks
		Cars, trucks to push
			Shopping cart/doll
			  carriage
			Wheelbarrow
			Pedal toys, trike
			Rakes, shovels
			Slide
			Swing
			Punching bag
				Scooter
				Two-wheel bike
				Sled, toboggan
				Exercise mat
				Acrobatics
				Diving mask for
				  swimming
				Doorway gym bar

Manipulative:
Grasping
Throwing
Catching
Kicking
Receiving/moving
  objects
Bouncing
	Mobile attached to crib—
	  kicking feet moves it
	Rattles, teething rings
	Crib activity board
	Soft foam blocks
	Snap beads
	Floating bath toys
		Variety of balls
		Stacking, nesting toys
		Activity box—on floor
		Shape sorters
		Large, fat crayons
		Large pegs and board
		Water/sand table
			Crayons, markers
			Clay, dough
			Bowling games
			Puzzles
			Woodworking tools
			Balls
			Lacing board
			Water/sand table
				Baseball glove/bat
				Ring toss game
				Full-size balls
				Oversize bat
				Frisbee
				"Miss Mary Mack"

FIGURE 11-5 Toys and games help develop specific motor skills in young children.

To learn a motor skill, children must combine memory with experience, taking advantage of opportunities to try something new, and practice what has already been learned.

The experiences children have and the ability to recall those experiences are necessary to the process of gaining motor skill. Rehearsal is as important to the young child as it is to the actors in a play. "Overt practice, repeating a specific movement over and over again, provides a motor rehearsal young children display every day" (Clark in Ridenour, 1978).

Practicing Basic Skills

A child's typical day, at home or at school, provides numerous opportunities to practice motor skills. Through play, the child can practice fine-motor skills such as:

● Holding a paintbrush, scissors, or rattle.
● Tiptoeing to music.
● Grasping a bottle, a hand, a toy.
● Threading a bead or a wide needle.

and gross-motor skills such as:

● Pumping on a swing.
● Climbing a tree.
● Digging a garden.
● Balancing on a board, on one foot.

Through self-help activities the child can practice fine-motor skills such as:

● Buttoning a coat or doll's clothes.
● Brushing teeth, hair.
● Turning a faucet handle or doorknob.
● Feeding self with utensils.

Gross-motor practice includes:

● Moving a nap cot or table.
● Kicking covers off.

Teachers provide many opportunities to practice motor skills through fingerplay, games, and songs.

- Walking, holding onto furniture.
- Climbing into crib, bed.

Children learning motor skills need experience in basic skills; they must learn simple skills before combining them into complex activities. Children must have time to try, refine, and try again.

Feedback

Children modify and improve their motor skills as they receive information about their movements, both **intrinsic** (the paintbrush makes marks when it is pushed across the paper) and **extrinsic** ("I notice that your legs are very far apart as you try to somersault; how about holding them together as you roll next time?").

A Range of Developmental Levels

Any group of young children will have various levels of motor growth and physical development. An individual child may have different abilities and skills in gross-, fine-, and perceptual-motor areas; activities should be offered on several developmental levels. Play materials and equipment, such as balls, climbers, and ladders, should accommodate a variety of skill levels, particularly if children with physical disabilities are in the class. Climbing boards put on several levels and puzzles ranging from 6 to 60 pieces are two examples of how teachers can meet the need for success and challenge.

ROLE OF THE TEACHER

Considerations

As teachers plan programs for physical/motor development, they reflect on several important issues. One often overlooked area is that of gross-motor development as an everyday occurrence. Teachers sometimes take for granted children's progress as they walk up and down stairs, climb on and off platforms and benches, and dance with abandon. Favorite rainy-day activities such as moving around like Tyrannosaurus rex or spinning like a top are exercises in physical/motor development using gross-motor skills. Remember that the normal classroom setting can promote physical development every day through established routines and curriculum.

Childhood Obesity

According to the American Academy of Pediatrics (AAP) (2003), there is an epidemic of childhood obesity in the United States. The frequency of childhood overweight and obesity has increased alarmingly, having doubled in the past two decades. Part of the problem is that children are less active on a daily basis than in previous generations. Health risks include heart disease, high blood pressure, diabetes, depression, and low self-esteem.

While there are many factors influencing obesity, such as socio-economic status, family eating habits, heredity, and television viewing, a key factor seems to be whether or not one of the parents is obese (Berk, 2002). The AAP (2003) notes that if one parent is obese, the child is three times as likely to be obese in adulthood; if both parents are obese, the risk is ten times likely that the child will be an obese adult.

The dramatic increase in childhood obesity only serves to underscore the need for regular physical exercise in programs for young children. Sanders (2002) suggests structuring physical activity into the schedule to help children maximize their movement experiences. Children do not learn by play alone. Organized movement experiences provide certain skill development that unstructured play cannot.

The National Association for Sport and Physical Education (NASPE) and the Council on Physical Education for Children (COPEC, 2000) established developmentally appropriate guidelines for preschool-age children. See Figure 11-6.

Sex-Role Stereotyping

Is motor behavior different for boys and girls? If so, why? Research indicates that there are differences between girls and boys in these areas. For example, behavioral differences in motor development are apparent in early life: one-year-old girls already spend more time in fine-motor tasks, while baby boys are more engaged in gross-motor activity. Around the age of two, children begin to identify people by their gender. Preschoolers often characterize many toys, articles of clothing, occupations, and behaviors with one sex or the other (Huston, 1993; Picariello, Greenberg, & Pillemer, 1990). Girls of this age increasingly seek out other girls to play with in quieter pursuits, while boys seem to prefer more active, aggressive play (Bennenson, 1993; Maccoby & Jacklin, 1987).

Why does this happen? Probably some sex differences are the result of genetics. At the same time, **sex-role stereotyping** expectations profoundly affect the motor and physical development of young children. This is the crucial

Developmentally Appropriate Practices for Preschool Movement Programs

1. Toddlers should participate in at least 30 minutes a day of structured play and one to several hours a day of unstructured physical activity. Preschoolers should participate in at least one hour of daily structured physical activity.

2. Preschoolers should not be sedentary for more than one hour at a time and be engaged in unstructured physical activity whenever possible.

3. Basic movement skills should be the building blocks for more complex movement abilities.

4. Indoor and outdoor environments should exceed recommended safety standards for performing large-muscle, gross-motor activities.

5. Teachers and caregivers should understand the importance of physical activity and integrate movement programs as part of the daily educational program.

6. Teachers serve as facilitators, encouraging children to explore and discover a range of movement possibilities.

FIGURE 11-6 From *Appropriate Practices in Movement Programs for Young Children, Ages 3–5*. The Council on Physical Education for Children (Reston, VA: a position statement of the National Association for Sport and Physical Education/NASPE, 2000, pages 8–9, 11, 15, 17) and Sanders, S. W. (2002), *Active for Life: Developmentally Appropriate Movement Programs for Young Children* (Washington, D.C.: The National Association for the Education of Young Children).

issue for teachers, for their attitudes can either encourage or discourage children from developing to their fullest potential. Teachers must acknowledge the differences that exist, and then ask themselves:

- What messages do I give children about physical activity? Do I value it for myself? For children? Do I value physical expression for girls as well as boys?

- Do I emphasize sports as a way to have fun? A way to be healthy? Do I praise only the "winner"?

- Can I provide male and female role models for physical activities using parents, grandparents, older siblings, staff, visitors, and guests?

- Do I encourage children to wear clothing that allows them the freedom to run, climb, tumble? What do I do when girls arrive in long dresses and party shoes?[1] What should I wear?

- Are all physical/motor activities made equally available and attractive to boys and girls? What should I do if some children dominate these activities, while others never choose them?

- How do I actively engage all children in every form of physical activity? Do I let them know I think it is important?

Pica (2004) notes that children between the ages of 6 and 8 usually play with others of the same sex. She further suggests that this

What do YOU Think?

Are you physically active? Do you participate in a sport or exercise on a regular basis? What would you do to create opportunities for all children to be physically active for some part of each school day? List some examples that would be especially appropriate indoors.

growing gender awareness can be addressed by assigning play partners of the opposite sex for certain games or suggesting that all children take on the roles of people in various occupations (firefighters, police officers, hairdressers, dancers) regardless of gender. See Chapter 15 for further discussion on gender-related issues.

A Safe and Challenging Environment

First and foremost, teachers ensure the safety of the children. To maintain a safe physical environment, they see to it that materials and equipment are in usable condition and that overall traffic patterns are free of hazards. For example, to make a gymnastic activity safe, teachers would provide mats and make sure that only one child is tumbling at a time.

1 Be sensitive to family and cultural influences about gender typing.

Psychological safety requires an even finer sensitivity on the part of the teaching staff. Fear is a learned response, and teachers must be careful not to discourage children from using their full range of abilities, creating overly anxious and fearful children. The new teacher is often concerned about children's safety, particularly when they are climbing. It helps to remember that children generally climb to heights that are comfortable for them; in other words, they set their own limits.

The practice of picking children up and placing them on equipment, often at their own request, is questionable. If teachers comply with children's wishes to be lifted and set somewhere high, they are placing those children in situations outside of their natural limits. The children may see this as saying, "You are incapable of climbing up there yourself," or "It is too dangerous for you to try that alone." Also, this does not allow children to gain experience in basic skills first, but puts them in a situation that calls for skills more complex than they have at the time. This denies the child the opportunity to practice those skills. Children learn their capabilities by being held responsible for what they do. When they must seek solutions to getting up, out, in, or down, they learn to handle realistically their current level of physical and motor development. Teachers lend encouragement and confidence to children by saying, "I can't put you up there, but I will help you try." Making playgrounds safe is a good way to promote physical growth and sets the stage for learning through motor development (Figure 11-7).

Playground Enrichment

The playground is the natural arena for optimal physical development and the ideal environment to promote physical fitness. On the playground, all motor skills are called into play.

> Carmine grabs a scarf and begins to dance, *twirling* and *whirling*, *hopping* and *bending* in time to the music. Following the teacher's lead, Carmine *balances* on his toes and *waves* his scarf high over his head.

> Tina *walks* to the climber, *grasps* the highest rung she can reach, *pulls* herself up by *lifting* one leg and then the other until she *stretches* vertically full-length along the climber bars. Satisfied, she *pushes* off with her feet and *jumps* backward to the ground. She *bends* her knees as she lands, *balances* herself to an upright position, and *runs* off.

> Ramon *toddles* over to *pick up* the large red ball. Momentarily overwhelmed by its size, he *falls* backward to *sit* on the grass. As a teacher approaches him, he *rolls* the ball toward her. She *throws* it back to him and Ramon imitates her movements. Soon they are involved in *kicking* and *tossing* the ball to each other.

Using both small and large muscles, children gain control over their bodies as they run and play. The playground provides open space where full-bodied action takes place, providing many opportunities to develop balance and coordination.

Physical skills, however, are not the only benefit of outdoor play. Social and cognitive skills are enhanced as well. On the playground, children must negotiate turns with the wagons, ask for a push on the swing, and wait in line going up the slide. Some of the most intricate and involved dramatic play takes place outdoors. Problems get solved when two trikes collide. Science experiences are all around—finding a bird's nest or planting a garden. According to Frost (1992), "good playgrounds increase the intensity of play and the range of play behavior."

On the playground no one says "Be quiet!" or "Quit wriggling!" It is a place of motion and space, filled with the special sensations found only outdoors.

When creating and maintaining a challenging environment, teachers consider both variety

Playground equipment should be challenging, and it should provide a variety of movement experiences and a significant amount of physical activity.

Making Playgrounds Safe

Safety in the yard means:

- Enough room for the number and age of children who will use it.
- Adequate empty space.
- Availability of both hard and soft surfaces.
- Soft surfaces under any equipment from which a child might fall.
- Shady areas alternating with sunny spots.
- No standing water—good drainage.
- No poisonous or thorny plants, or litter or debris.
- Areas of play clearly defined and differentiated from one another.
- Sand area protected at night from animals.
- Fences high enough and in good repair.
- Gates secure with latches out of children's reach.

Equipment is:

- Well maintained—no exposed nails, screws, sharp edges, chipped paint.
- Chosen with children's ages in mind in regard to height and complexity.
- Stable and securely anchored.
- Repaired immediately or removed if damaged.
- Varied to allow for wide range of skills.
- Not crowded.
- Smooth where children's hands are likely to be placed.
- Checked frequently.
- Placed appropriately: sides facing north, swings away from other structures and busy areas.
- Scaled to age level: steps and other openings are 4 inches or less apart or 8 to 10 inches apart.
- Modified for age levels: swings have soft seats.

Teachers:

- Reinforce safe practices.
- Wear appropriate outdoor clothing.
- Check frequently where children are playing.
- Involve children in safety checks of yard, equipment, and grounds.
- Provide continual, adequate supervision.
- Avoid congregating to talk.
- Get involved with children.
- Provide enough activities and challenges.
- Watch for sun exposure, especially with toddlers.
- Assist children when they want to rearrange movable equipment.

FIGURE 11-7 Before children are allowed to use a playground, teachers should use a checklist such as this to ensure that safety standards are met. A safe playground stimulates physical development, social interaction, and full exploration of the materials and environment.

and level of challenge. A choice of surfaces encourages a variety of movements. Cement may be appropriate for transportation toys, but tanbark and rubber mats are better for climbing, hanging, and dropping.

Varying the equipment also stimulates motor activity. Equipment that is mobile allows for greater range of uses and allows children to manipulate their own environment. By creating their own physical challenges with wooden crates, children make platforms, caves, and houses to crawl in, over, and through. Another way to provide variety is to focus on the less-developed skills, such as catching and throwing, rolling, latching, snapping, or zipping.

When children are encouraged to discover their own physical potential, they learn to solve problems of movement defined by the limits of

Parents and teachers encourage physical play from early infancy.

their own abilities rather than by performance. This kind of learning encourages self-confidence as children find success through their own challenges.

A Child's Self-Concept

The image of physical self is an important part of self-concept. How people feel about themselves is rooted in the way they feel about their bodies and what they can or cannot do with them. Attitudes about the body and its abilities directly affect the types of activities children will try. Studies show that skill in games appears to be tied to peer-group acceptance (Gallahue, 1996). Psychologists and teachers often notice a link between learning problems and clumsiness. Children with problems seem to have motor difficulties more often than those who do well in the classroom (Cratty, 1986).[1]

Physical activity, then, contributes to a child's self-concept. With practice comes a sense of competence. Children can learn to relax as they gain experience in physical activities, and thus reduce the stress of anticipating failure. Competence breeds self-confidence and a willingness to try greater challenges. As children try new activities, they learn more about themselves. And physical activity increases awareness of what fun it is to move—to run through a field or pump a swing just for the sheer joy of it!

Teachers support positive self-concept through physical and motor development in several ways. They let children discover their own physical limits, rather than warning or stopping them from trying out an activity for themselves.

- *"I'm stuck!"* A child shouts across the yard. Rather than rushing to lift the child down, the teacher walks over to the child and replies, "Where can you put your foot next?" "How can you find a way to get across that branch?"

- *"I'm afraid!"* The teacher stands close to the child who is climbing and responds to the fear. "I'll stand close to the climbing ropes so you will feel safe."

- *"Look what I can do!"* Teachers reinforce children who try something new. "Greg, it's good to see you cutting out that pumpkin all by yourself."

- *"I tried."* Teachers congratulate efforts for the achievement they really are. "Your hands reached the top this time, Shannon. I'll bet you are feeling proud of yourself."

- *"I can't do it."* Children who stand on the sidelines observing others may need some encouragement from the teacher to take the first step in mastering the climbing frame or slide. "Here's a good place for you to put your foot, Arturo. I'll hold on to your hand until you get me to let go."

It is often not so much what teachers say to children that influences their feelings about themselves as it is the way in which children are treated. Children value themselves to the degree they are valued by others. The way teachers show how they feel about children actually builds their self-confidence and sense of self-worth. Children create a picture of themselves from the words, attitudes, body language, and judgment of those around them.

Games that promote competition may affect a child's self-concept. Rae Pica's "Insight" article at the end of the chapter raises questions about the use of competitive rather than cooperative games with young children.

Encouraging Physical Play

The vital role of physical activity is best fulfilled when teachers:

- Create time in the daily schedule for periods of physical activity, preferably, but not limited to, outdoors.

- Actively participate while supervising and encouraging all children to become involved in strenuous activity.

1 A skilled early childhood educator carefully observes children, documents observations, and makes a referral if an assessment is needed for an individual child.

Check Whether Child

☐ 1. Has trouble holding or maintaining balance

☐ 2. Appears to have difficulty balancing and moves awkwardly

☐ 3. Cannot carry self well in motion

☐ 4. Appears generally awkward in activities requiring coordination

☐ 5. Has difficulty making changes in movement

☐ 6. Has difficulty performing combinations of simple movements

☐ 7. Has difficulty in gauging space with respect to own body; bumps and collides with objects and other children

☐ 8. Tends to fall often

☐ 9. Has poor eye-hand coordination

☐ 10. Has difficulty handling the simple tools of physical activity (beanbags, balls, other objects that require visual-motor coordination

FIGURE 11-8 A checklist of possible problems in physical/motor development serves as a guideline when devising a developmentally specific profile for spotting problems.

- Set goals for children's motor development and physical fitness.
- Use a variety of activities on a daily basis, including science, art, and music, to stimulate physical development.
- Select age-appropriate equipment and materials, providing a variety of props to enhance their use.
- Give children opportunities to repeat, practice, and refine the skills they learn.

When children develop their physical and motor skills under this kind of encouragement, their confidence and sense of competence grow.[1]

Observing children while they play outdoors allows teachers an opportunity to assess potential problems in motor development. The checklist in Figure 11-8 indicates some areas to observe.

Curriculum Planning for Physical/Motor Development

Teachers plan activities that promote physical/motor skills in the areas of gross-motor, fine-motor, and perceptual-motor development.

Video VIEW Point 11-2

"The teachers in this preschool planned physical activities that can take place indoors or out."

COMPETENCY: Program Management

AGE GROUP: Preschool

CRITICAL THINKING QUESTIONS:

1. How was this demonstrated in the video?

2. Describe the range of activities and how they reflect the use of large and small motor skills.

3. What would you add to the indoors and the outdoors to provide for greater physical activity?

They look at the environment, both indoors and out, to see that all three areas of physical growth are encouraged.

In the Classroom Setting

When thinking of physical/motor development in the classroom, teachers tend to focus on the fine-motor (or small-muscle) tasks for the classroom and on gross-motor (or large-muscle) tasks for the outdoor play space. The indoor area lends itself more readily to activities with less movement, and the outdoor area encourages whole-body play. Yet children can have a wider variety of activities if teachers remember that both gross-motor and fine-motor projects can happen everywhere in the environment.

Indoor Areas. Indoors, the art area is stocked with pens, crayons, scissors, and hole punches that develop the fine-motor skills.

1. Add large brushes or rollers to the easel, or plan fingerpainting, and the art area now includes gross-motor development.

2. When children use templates to trace both inside and outside spaces, they practice perceptual-motor skill.

3. In the science area, getting "just a pinch" of fish food is a fine-motor activity; cleaning out the turtle house requires larger muscles to move rocks and sand.

 1 For all children, a sense of personal worth is at the core of their existence.

4. Perceptual-motor development occurs as children use pitchers to fill the fish tank or turtle tub and learn about water levels.

5. At the manipulative table, when a child puts a peg into a pegboard, fine-motor skills are used.

6. Removing puzzles from a shelf and carrying them to a table brings in gross-motor skills. Add nuts and bolts, and the child's perceptual-motor skills are called into play.

7. The block area has endless possibilities, from lifting and carrying (gross-motor), to balancing and stacking (fine-motor), to building a space so that an animal or car will fit through (perceptual-motor).

8. The language and library areas are places for turning pages or looking at words and pictures (fine-motor). They also involve taking books off shelves and replacing them and trying out the movements and activities read about in books. For instance, Tana Hoban's book, *Is It Hard? Is It Easy?*, encourages children to act out the scenes pictured in the story, all gross-motor tasks. With a listening post nearby, children listen for the "beep" and coordinate what they hear (perceptual) with turning the pages (motor).

Outdoor Areas. Outdoors, children develop motor skills of all kinds.

1. In the sand, children dig, a gross-motor activity. As they judge how big a hole is, or how much water will fill it, they are practicing and improving their perceptual-motor skills. Turning on a faucet, planting seeds, and making mudpies are for fine-motor development.

2. Wheel toys offer children opportunities in all motor areas.

3. Pushing someone in a wagon develops arm and leg strength—gross-motor development.

4. Guiding tricycles and carts on a path and around obstacles requires perceptual-motor skill.

5. Trying to "repair" or "paint" a wheel toy with tools or with large brushes, tying wagons together, or weaving streamers through the spokes of a bicycle all use fine-motor skills.

6. By looking at the classroom and yard with one eye to physical and motor development, teachers can plan activities that support growth in all skill areas.

Transitions and Group Times. Every part of the daily schedule can be planned to use all physical/motor skills. For instance,

1. Getting in and out of coats and snowsuits is a large-muscle activity. Children learn perceptual-motor skills as they try to get their arms in the correct sleeves.

The outdoor area has great potential for developing gross-motor skills (climbing, bending, sliding), fine motor skills (grasping, reaching, holding), and perceptual motor skills (eye–hand coordination, directionality, tempo).

2. Buttoning, zipping, and tying are fine-motor activities.

3. As children get ready for group time, often a difficult transition, they might practice drawing faces in the air or making their bodies into the shapes of letters, both perceptual-motor tasks.

4. Group times also include activities for motor development.

5. When there are balloons, scarves, or a parachute at music time, children practice gross-motor skills.

6. Fingerplays at group time are a fine-motor task. Activities for developing the senses of hearing and sight are two areas of sensory growth that can be utilized as content for group times.

Focus on Skills

The physical/motor skills include those that use large and small muscles and that coordinate perception and motor response. Teachers planning activities for children can focus on any one of these as a basis for curriculum planning. For example, the skills of eye–hand coordination (perceptual-motor) and of walking on a balance beam (gross-motor) are elaborated as follows. They show how teachers can focus on a single skill and develop a rich curriculum for children. Figure 11-3 outlines a process for developing activities to meet the needs of children with a wide variety of skills and considers each child's strengths and needs.

Eye–Hand Coordination. Developing stitchery skills uses the perceptual-motor skill of *eye–hand coordination*. A series of activities can be planned to help children learn these skills.

1. It begins in infancy, when the baby first begins to manipulate and examine an object, learns to grasp with thumb and forefinger (pincer grasp), and shows a hand preference.

2. Stringing large wooden beads is a first step and leads to using pieces of straw and punched paper, with somewhat smaller holes. Macaroni can be strung on shoelaces or on stiff string, then onto yarn, which is softer and more challenging.

3. Sewing cards made by punching holes in polystyrene trays can be introduced as the next activity. Large, plastic needles can be used with the lacing cards or with the trays; large embroidery needles with big eyes can be used for stitching yarn onto burlap.

4. Children may be ready to use embroidery hoops with which they can make a design on burlap first and then stitch over the outlines. Buttons can be sewn on burlap or other fabric. Popcorn or packing material can be strung using a needle.

5. A final project might be to make a group wall hanging, with squares of children's stitchery sewn together. Simple backpacks and coin purses might be made, with the children sewing most of it themselves.

Walking on a Balance Beam. Teachers might want to focus on the skill of walking on a balance beam, a gross-motor and perceptual-motor activity. Using any kind of beam requires more balance and slower movements than regular walking.

1. Teachers place tape on the floor and ask children to walk forward and backward on it. Use a rope on the floor and everyone can pretend to be a tightrope walker.

2. Place a wide board flat on the floor, then substitute a narrow one (still on the floor

At an early age, children take pride in their physical accomplishments. Feeling strong or capable enhances self-confidence.

itself) after children have mastered the first board.

3. Next, place the wide board at a minimal height (perhaps two inches off the ground). Once children have successfully walked on this board, they are ready to try a narrower board at the same height.

4. Set some boards at a slant, from the ground level up, providing a challenge that allows children to move their bodies off the ground as gradually as they wish.

By planning activities for walking on wide and narrow boards of various heights, teachers help children of all levels acquire the gross-motor skills necessary to master these tasks. Figure 11-5 lists age-appropriate equipment that fosters the development of motor skills.

Use of Themes

When beginning teachers plan activities, they often have a theme or unit as their focus. Themes can be used to encourage physical and

motor involvement. A unit of "Outerspace" involves ample opportunity to involve all the motor skills.

- Gross-motor skills are used in jumping around on the moon, taking a space walk, getting in and out of the rocketship, and building a space-ship with large blocks.

- Fine-motor skills are needed to manipulate knobs on the instrument panel, to draw maps of the stars, or to write out a countdown on a chalkboard.

- Perceptual-motor skills are needed to work out how to get ready for a trip to Mars, what happens on the trip, and when and how to get back to Earth.

- Use the sample forms in Chapter 10 to develop an outer-space unit as well as other appropriate themes to encourage motor skills.

Once teachers realize which physical/motor skills the children possess and what the group is ready to learn, they can plan activities around a classroom unit.[1] See Figure 11-9.

Appreciating Cultural Diversity through Motor Development

For Indoor and Outdoor Play

Activity	Motor Skill Practice	Culture
Lion or dragon dance	Gross-motor	Chinese (New Year)
Making and flying carp kites	Fine- and gross-motor	Japanese
Dodgeball	Gross-motor	Euro-American
Chinese jump rope	Gross-motor	Chinese
Breaking the piñata	Gross-motor	Latino
Spinning like a dreidel	Gross-motor	Jewish (Hannukah)
Origami art	Fine-Motor	Japanese
Activity	**Motor Skill Practice**	**Culture**
Weaving	Fine-Motor	Native American
Country/Western dance step	Gross-motor	Euro-American
Make mariachi instruments	Fine-motor	Latino
Dancing to mariachi band music	Gross-motor	Latino
Hokey pokey	Gross-motor	Euro-American
Make and twirl a grager	Fine-motor	Jewish (Purim)
Cooking; stir-fry rice	Fine-motor	Chinese
Making fry bread	Fine-motor	Native American
Kick the can	Gross-motor	Euro-American
Making and beating drums	Fine-motor	Native American

FIGURE 11-9 A variety of activities that reflect many cultures can be integrated into the curriculum for motor and physical development. Note: These activities are, at best, an approximation of traditional cultural expressions and not authentic presentations, yet they can enlarge the child's worldview through physical play.

 1 Parents are an excellent source of ideas for ensuring that activities will reflect a true multicultural experience.

Curriculum planning for motor and movement skills requires teachers to know principles of physical growth and motor development. They then can use this knowledge to plan activities that encourage children to master their own movements and to learn other skills through movement. In the early childhood setting, curriculum can be planned by concentrating on activity areas, focusing on a specific motor skill, or using a classroom theme.

SUMMARY

Children are in motion virtually from conception and develop their abilities to move their bodies as they grow. Young children spend most of the day in physical activity; therefore, the development of physical and motor skills must take a high priority in early childhood programs. Physical growth, that which pertains to the body, is for teachers an issue of fitness and health. They need to have an overview of growth to help children develop functional and flexible bodies. Motor development means learning to move with control and efficiency. Development involves maturation and experience. Teachers must know the sequence of development and what part they play in providing physical and motor experiences for the young child.

Muscular development can be categorized as gross-motor, fine-motor, and perceptual-motor. Gross-motor movements use the entire body or large parts of it, such as the legs for running or the arms and torso for throwing. Fine-motor movements, such as manipulating objects, are those that use smaller muscles and that require precision and dexterity. Perceptual-motor movements are those that combine what is perceived with a body movement. Spatial, temporal, and sensory awareness all play an important part in the development of perceptual-motor skills.

In the early childhood years, children need exposure to many motor activities. They need a chance to practice, to get feedback, and to have a broad range of experiences of variety and challenge. Because children acquire motor skills through short- and long-term memory, rehearsal plays an important role as well.

When planning curriculum, teachers must have an awareness of sex-role stereotyping and must consider safety as well as challenge. A child's self-concept is linked with the concept of physical self and skill, so teachers keep in mind which behaviors should be encouraged and which behaviors may indicate potential problems. As they plan activities for children, teachers use classroom and yard areas, focus on a specific skill, or use a theme to develop curriculum for physical/motor skills.

IS COMPETITION DEVELOPMENTALLY APPROPRIATE?

by
Rae Pica

The subject of competition is one that provokes some pretty strong feelings in the United States. The prevailing belief is that competition is good for us and that being competitive is human nature. But is it human nature, or is it learned behavior?

The research shows that, given a choice, most preschoolers prefer cooperative to competitive activities. This would seem to indicate that competitive behavior is not a natural inclination. Also, in a *New York Times* essay, Nicholas Kristof told a hilarious story about trying to teach the traditional game of musical chairs to a group of 5-year-old Japanese children who kept politely stepping out of the way so their peers could sit in the chairs! This would seem to indicate that competitive behavior is taught in some societies—and not taught in others.

It's no wonder the research has determined that competition fosters such antisocial behaviors as aggression and cheating. In case you don't recall from your own childhood (or you were always the one winner among many losers), being eliminated feels terrible, as does feeling like a loser. And those other kids you're playing with? For the duration of the game, they're not your friends; they're what's standing in your way. Children only have to play an elimination game once to know that, if they're not going to be labeled losers, they have to do whatever it takes to win. And we've all seen what that can mean: punching, poking, kicking, scratching, screaming, and shoving.

When the important adults in their lives consistently place children in situations where winning is the ultimate goal—where the winners are considered heroes and the losers "losers"—winning is what children come to value. They learn that only the end result (the product) counts—not enjoyment of the game (the process). This, in turn, places more emphasis on extrinsic, rather than intrinsic, reward. Yes, winning feels good when everyone around you is making a big deal out of it. But does that feeling last? What happens when the possibility of being "number one" becomes the only reason for doing something? And what about the children who aren't winning?

Consistently playing cooperative, rather than competitive, games with the children lets them know you value the process. It lets them know you value collaboration. Moreover, when children participate in games like Footsie Rolls (which requires partners to perform log rolls with the soles of their feet together) or Body Balance (which requires a group to work together to maintain a steady balance through a series of challenges), they come to realize how good it feels to work and be together. In place of the punching, poking, and kicking, there is problem solving, encouragement, and a whole lot of laughter. As a result, they want to experience more of it!

Musical chairs actually has a great deal to offer children—in all three developmental domains—but only when the children have the opportunity to continue playing! With a simple modification—challenging the players to find a way to *share* the remaining chairs—the children develop listening skills, learn to discriminate between sound and silence, and learn to solve problems (the cognitive domain). Because no one is eliminated, they experience feelings of belonging. They're also developing their cooperative skills (the social/emotional domain). And the activity gives them a chance to get their blood flowing, while also offering practice with stopping and starting (the physical domain).

Dare I say it? Winning isn't everything—particularly in early childhood. Because I consider it more important for children to grow up to be self-assured, character-driven adults—who also happen to have positive feelings about physical activity—I prefer that the children participate in games and activities without competition, elimination, or humiliation.

I believe that, because we've been entrusted with the education of the whole child, we should regard the activities we present in light of what they offer children cognitively, socially, emotionally, and physically. I believe we should select games and physical activities just as we select the other parts of the curriculum—based on whether they are developmentally appropriate.

Rae Pica is a children's movement consultant and the author of 15 books, including Experiences in Movement, Moving & Learning across the Curriculum, *and* Great Games for Young Children. *For more ideas and activities, visit www.movingandlearning.com.*

For more activities and information, visit our Web site at http://www.EarlyChildEd.delmar.com

KEY TERMS

perceptual-motor development   spatial awareness   extrinsic

gross motor   sensory awareness   sex-role stereotyping

fine motor   intrinsic

REVIEW QUESTIONS

1. How does physical growth differ from motor development in young children?

2. What factors influence motor development in young children?

3. What physical/motor skills are appropriate for young children to develop?

4. How can the teacher of young children support motor development in classroom areas?

5. How can the teacher support acquisition of specific motor skills in young children?

6. Follow (a) an infant or toddler, (b) a three-and-a-half-year-old, and (c) a six- to eight-year-old during a typical play period at school or at home. Try to observe for one hour. Does the child exhibit all three basic types of movement (locomotor, nonlocomotor, and manipulative)? Describe the action of each, including any toys or materials the child uses.

7. How would you present the activities in Figure 11-3 to visually impaired children?

8. Have you observed gender differences in the physical development of young children? If so, what implications are there for teachers planning motor activities?

LEARNING ACTIVITIES

1. Map the classroom in which you are currently working. List at least one activity in each area that develops physical motor skills. Add one more activity of your own that widens such development.

2. In what ways does a school program you know reinforce sex-role stereotyping in motor activities? What could be done to change this?

3. Try to develop the theme of "at the beach" or "camping" in your setting in such a way that physical/motor skills are used. Be sure to include gross-motor, fine-motor, and perceptual-motor activities. List at least six other themes around which you could build a similar curriculum.

REFERENCES

Allen, K. E., & Marotz, L. (2003). *Development profiles: Prebirth through eight.* Clifton Park, NY: Thomson Delmar Learning.

American Academy of Pediatrics Policy Statement: *Pediatrics* Vol. 112, No. 2, Aug. 2003, pp. 240–243.

Bee, H. (1997). *The developing child.* Menlo Park, CA: Addison-Wesley.

Bennenson, J. F. (1993). Greater preference among females than males for dyadic interaction in early childhood. *Child Development, 64,* 544–555.

Berk, L. E. (2002). *Infants and children.* Boston: Allyn & Bacon.

COPEC (Council on Physical Education for Children). (2000). *Appropriate practices in movement programs for young children ages 3–5: A position statement of the national association for sport and physical education.* Reston, VA: NASPE.

Cratty, B. J. (1986). *Perceptual and motor development in infants and children.* Englewood Cliffs, NJ: Prentice-Hall.

Frost, J. L. (1992). *Play and playscapes.* Clifton Park, NY: Thomson Delmar Learning.

Gallahue, D. L. (1996). *Developmental physical education for today's children.* Madison, WI: Brown and Benchmark.

Greenman, J. (2000). Guest Editorial: Places for Childhoods. In A. M. Gordon & K. W. Browne, *Beginnings and Beyond: Foundations in Early Childhood Education*. Clifton Park, NY: Thomson Delmar Learning.

Huston, A. C. (1993). Sex typing. In E. M. Heatherington (Ed.), *Handbook of child psychology* (Vol. 4, pp. 387–467, Socialization, personality, and social development). New York: Wiley.

Jensen, E. (1998). *Teaching with the brain in mind*. Alexandria, VA: Association for Supervision and Curriculum Development.

Kranowitz, C. S. (1992). Obstacle courses are for every body. In B. Neugebauer (Ed.), *Alike and different: Exploring our humanity with young children*. Washington, DC: National Association for the Education of Young Children.

Maccoby, E. E., & Jacklin, C. N. (1987). Gender segregation in childhood. In E. H. Reese (Ed.), *Advances in child development and behavior* (Vol. 20, pp. 239–287). New York: Academic Press.

[The] New City School, Inc. (1994). St. Louis, MO: Author.

Pica, R. (2004). *Experiences in movement: Birth to Age 8*. Clifton Park, NY: Thomson Delmar Learning.

Picariello, M. L., Greenberg, D. N., & Pillemer, D. B. (1990). Children's sex-related stereotyping of colors. *Child Development, 61,* 1453–1460.

Ridenour, M. V. (Ed.). (Contributing authors: Clark, Herkowitz, Roberton, Teeple). (1978). *Motor development: Issues and applications*. Princeton, NJ: Princeton Book Company.

Sanders, S. W. (2002). *Active for life: Developmentally appropriate movement programs for young children*. Washington, DC: National Association for the Education of Young Children.

Shore, R. (1997). *Rethinking the brain: New insights into early development*. New York: Families and Work Institute.

HELPFUL WEB SITES

American Academy of Pediatrics	http://www.aap.org/policy/re9741.htm
National Program for Playground Safety	http://www.uni.edu/playground
National Association for Sports & Physical Education	http://www.aahperd.org/naspe

For more activities and information, visit our Web site at http://www.EarlyChildEd.delmar.com

CHAPTER

12

Planning for the Mind: Cognitive Development

QUESTIONS FOR THOUGHT

What is cognition?

What do the theories of constructivism and multiple intelligences, sociocultural theory, and brain-based research offer to curriculum development?

What are the cognitive skills of early childhood?

How can the teacher support cognitive development?

How might computers be used with young children?

INTRODUCTION

Ah, to be a child again! The world is a place of wonder and promise. There are worlds and people to discover, explore, and understand. Childhood is a time

- *Of self* . . . a baby plays with his hands and feet for hours and rolls over just for the sake of doing it.
- *Of things everywhere* . . . a toddler invades the kitchen cabinets to see what treasures can be found.
- *Of people* . . . a preschooler learns the teachers' names and then makes a first "friend."
- *Of faraway places* . . . a kindergartner packs for the first "sleepover."

The amount of learning that takes place in early childhood is staggering. How do children manage to absorb the sheer quantity of information and experience they accumulate in their first few years of life?

Every child accompanies this mighty feat by thinking. Early theories about cognition have been based on the idea that intelligence is a general capacity or potential that can be measured by standardized tests (such as IQ tests) and, therefore, that cognition can be developed by a specific, rather narrow, set of teaching techniques. During the last half of the 20th century, however, new ideas began to emerge. All of the recent theories revolve around the same fascinating question: What accounts for the remarkable changes in thinking, language, and problem solving in young children? Jean Piaget's theories (see Chapter 4) are an important part of early childhood educational philosophy. Recent research on the brain and information-processing, and the theories of Piaget, Vygotsky and Gardner have broadened our notions of thinking and intelligence.

Cognition is the mental process or faculty that children use to acquire knowledge. To think is to be able to acquire and apply knowledge. By using conscious thought and memory, children think about themselves, the world, and others. Educating the thinking child is a critical function of parents and teachers. Curriculum in the early years must address the thinking, or cognitive, skills.

The relationship between cognition and language is important. Typically, we find out

As children investigate the world of people and places, they ask themselves and others what they want to know.

what children think by listening to them talk or asking them to tell us what they know. Cognition *can* occur without the language to express it. For example, an infant's laughter during a game of peek-a-boo indicates the child's knowledge that the hidden face will reappear. Conversely, the use of language can occur without cognition (i.e., without knowing the meaning). A child's counting from 1 to 20 (". . . 11, 13, 17, 19, 20!") is a case in point. At the same time, language and thought are intertwined. The growing child communicates through meaningful language. Children get their needs met better when they can name them. Their thoughts are expressed clearer to adults when they are put in words, and feelings can be mediated through language. Cognition and language generally become more interdependent as development progresses. Children expand their knowledge base through language. They listen, question, tell. The child with good language skills can thus apply them to widen the horizons of knowledge.

Cognition is related not only to the developing mind but also to all areas of the child's growth. Young thinkers are at work no matter what they are doing. For example, physical/motor development is also a cognitive process. Learning to roller skate involves skinned knees and learning to balance (motor tasks), along with analyzing, predicting, generalizing, evaluating, and practicing the art of locomotion on wheels (cognitive skills). When trying to enter into group play (a social task), children will think of strategies for how to get started (cognitive skill).

This chapter explores in depth the framework for planning curriculum for the mind. Chapters 3 and 4 describe cognitive development in early childhood; this chapter takes this into curriculum planning by elaborating on

- the development of cognition in the early years,
- the skills acquired by children from birth to age eight,
- specific curriculum content.

For the purposes of clarity, cognition and language will be separated into two categories. However, teachers must remember that these work together. Planned programs for early childhood will be more successful if that link is

recognized. Both cognitive and language development are nurtured through a rich environment of stories—both told and read—environmental print, and the writing process that begins with scribbles and meaningful print (see Chapter 13).

THE DEVELOPMENT OF COGNITION: A PERSPECTIVE

An Eclectic Point of View

In trying to enhance cognitive development, early childhood educators draw on developmental and learning theories and their direct experiences with children.[1,2] By combining theoretical and practical viewpoints, teachers take a blended, or eclectic, perspective on the development of the thinking process. They work with children to encourage their ability to formulate ideas and to think rationally and logically. Regardless of theoretical viewpoint, the early childhood professional works toward helping children acquire skills that will lead to the development of:

Concepts: Labeling or naming an idea, moving from the specific to the abstract.
"What is a grape?"

Relationships: What is the association between two or more things? How are they similar or different? What are their functions, characteristics, attributes?
"How many colors of grapes are there? Do all of them have seeds? Are they different sizes? Do they taste alike?"

Generalizations: Drawing conclusions from relationships and concepts/ideas. This means grouping things into classes and finding common elements.
"Are grapes a fruit or meat? How do grapes grow?"

The primary viewpoints that inform teachers in planning curriculum for cognitive development in early childhood are cognitive, multiple intelligences, and sociocultural theories, and brain-based research.

---

1 Teachers must blend what they know about theory and concepts with what they learn about individual children and culture; see Chapter 3 for descriptions of learning styles and how children develop attitudes regarding race, gender, and ability.

2 The role of culture in cognition is one of several major diversity areas in this chapter. For instance, Piaget's constructivism informs educators about how they should teach; because children construct knowledge from their own personal experiences, their culture will have a major impact on how they come to know.

A Piagetian Perspective

Developmental psychology, particularly through the works of Jean Piaget, has provided a deeper understanding of cognitive development. Piaget's view of cognition is twofold. First, learning is a process of discovery, of finding out what one needs to know to solve a particular problem. Second, knowledge results from active thought, from making mental connections among objects, from constructing a meaningful reality for understanding.

For Piaget, knowledge is "an interpretation of reality that the learner actively and internally constructs by interacting with it" (Labinowitz, 1980). Piaget divided knowledge into three types: physical, logical mathematical, and social. Physical knowledge is what children learn through external sensory experiences. Watching leaves blow in the wind, grabbing a ball, sniffing a fresh slice of bread are all instances of children learning about different physical objects and how they feel, taste, smell, move, and so on. The basic cognitive process involved in the development of **physical knowledge** is discrimination. For example, by touching magnets to paper clips, puzzles, and paper dolls, children learn first-hand about magnetism. They learn to discriminate between those objects that "stick" to the magnet and those that do not.

Logical mathematical knowledge derives from coordinating physical actions into some kind of order, or logic. This is not to be confused with formal mathematics; rather it is the kind of mathematical thinking children use in making connections about what they see, such as an infant's lifting the blanket to find a hidden toy. The logic of the young child is seen in the coordination of actions to make an **inference**. Think back to the magnets example. If a child deliberately takes a magnet to the metal drawer pulls and metal climbing bars, we can see the logical knowledge used: the child has made the inference that it is the metal things that "stick" on the magnet.

Social knowledge comes from our culture, the rules of the game, the right vocabulary, the moral codes. It includes learning vocabulary and being taught or told things, as well as knowledge about the social aspects of life. Value-laden and often arbitrary, it can rarely be constructed logically but is learned through life. With the aforementioned magnets, social knowledge would need to be used to decide who gets to play with the magnets, or when it is somebody else's turn.

In developing cognitive curriculum, teachers plan experiences that enhance those types of knowledge. They can teach using different forms of knowledge. **Rote knowledge** is information given with no particular meaning to the learner—that which could be learned meaningfully but is not. A teacher talking about magnets or telling children what attracts or repels gives children rote knowledge. **Meaningful knowledge** is what children learn gradually and within the context of what they already know and want to find out—like the example of letting the children handle the magnets themselves if they choose, and answering their questions as they arise. Both telling (rote) and asking or allowing (meaningful) can be useful; the question for the children is the balance between the two in everyday educational encounters.

As you may recall from Chapter 4, a special topic of Piaget's theory of cognitive development was constructivist theory. How does this theory apply to curriculum? The constructivist classrooms will vary greatly in their organization and activities, but the following characteristics are likely to be consistent (adapted from Roberts & Spitz, 1998):

- *Choice.* It is crucial to practice life in a democracy and to learn to evaluate choices and decisions from a variety of materials or activities so they can focus on formulating their own real questions and learn how to find genuine answers.

- *Play.* Through play experiences children will develop their own thinking because it will allow for self-selection and create situations where children must exchange views and solve problems.

- *Materials and Activities.* Concepts will be developed through interactions and experimentation with real objects, materials, and people and thus will need an environment that provides materials both appropriate and interesting as well as many activities that stimulate interaction with peers.

- *Time.* Each day will allow long blocks of uninterrupted time for child-initiated activities.

- *Teacher.* The teacher's role is to facilitate and to impart information and social knowledge, along with providing an emotionally safe and intellectually stimulating environment.

- *Curriculum Content.* The content arises from the issues of the students' real lives, their interests, family, and events so that learning is in the context of meaning for each child.

Gardner's Multiple Intelligences

Research in cognition documents that children possess different kinds of minds and therefore understand, learn, remember, and perform in different ways. Most experts agree that **intelligence** is complex and that traditional tests do not measure the entire host of skills or abilities involved. This alternative suggests that there are eight "frames of mind" (see Figure 12-1).

"Gardner's theory is a dream come true for teachers," says Nelson (1995), "because it means many intelligences can be nurtured. And with that in mind, I [can] reinvent my curriculum and the way I teach it so that it meets the needs of a wider range." Multiple intelligences theory acknowledges that people learn and use knowledge in different ways. In practice, it is a systematic approach to basic skills. "Project Spectrum" was founded to develop an innovative approach to curriculum and assessment in the preschool and early primary years. "The work was based on the conviction that each child exhibits a distinctive profile of different abilities, or spectrum of intelligences. The power of these intelligences is not fixed, but can be enhanced by educational opportunity and an environment rich in stimulating materials and activities (Chen et al., 1998).

Because MI is neither a curriculum nor a model of pedagogy, there are many ways that the intelligences can be brought into the classroom. The overall framework involves four steps:

1. Introduce children to a range of learning areas;
2. Identify each child's strengths;
3. Nurture those strengths;
4. Bridge their strengths to other subject areas.

A relatively easy start is to create the various learning centers that correspond to the different intelligences. The learning centers can be designed to give all children a roughly equal opportunity to explore all available materials in all eight domains.

> Students who need to learn counting, one-to-one correspondence, or math facts can do so, for example, through centers which tap into their spatial talents: students draw items—or group already-drawn images—to capture the math concepts. Students might go to a bodily-kinesthetic center to snap fingers or jump as they count by twos. Or perhaps student listen to music, clapping hands to catch the rhythm and beat of the numbers (Hoerr, 2004).

This does not mean that teachers must develop every activity to all eight intelligences! Rather, teachers learn about each individual child and then tailor their curriculum to build on their children's strengths. Figure 12-1 gives examples of how an MI approach can build a bridge between children's curiosity and the school curriculum.

Vygotsky, Thinking, and Culture

Focusing on how our values and beliefs affect what we transmit to the next generation, Vygotsky's sociocultural theory claims that much of children's development and knowledge is culturally specific (see Chapter 4). Because

The MI approach: Sample Early Learning Activities

Learning Center	Sample Activity	Intelligence Area
Mechanics/Construction	Making Wire Designs	Spatial
Science	Tools for Biologists	Naturalistic
Music	Sound Cylinders Match-up	Musical
Movement	Statue Game	Body-kinesthetic
Math	Weights and Measures	Logical
Social Understanding	Making Silhouettes	Interpersonal
Language	"Reporting the News"	Linguistic
Visual Arts	Making an Art Portfolio	Intrapersonal

FIGURE 12-1 Sample activities from Project Spectrum (Chen, Isberg, & Krechevsky, 1998), based on a year-long research project aimed at improving the academic performance of at-risk first graders in a Boston-area public school.

children learn from more knowledgeable members of the community, they come to know those skills that are socially valued. In today's America, the most salient sources of knowledge are family members, the media, and school. The psychological tools children need to learn higher mental functions, such as symbolic thought, memory, attention, and reasoning, need the mediation of someone who knows the tools of that particular society.

Vygotsky adds an important element to our understanding of thinking.[1] If knowledge is connected to what a culture values, then learning must be done in a collaborative style. Teachers and parents must have some agreement about what is important to teach children. The best way of teaching is a kind of assisted learning, that allows for scaffolding, a natural learning technique known as "apprenticeship." Such learning can occur via physical or verbal interaction and as long as both the learner and the teacher are motivated (one to learn and other to assist). An older child or adult serves as a guide who is responsive to what the child is ready to learn. There are three implications of this theory for curriculum.

1. Mixed-age groupings so that young children can learn from older ones, and the more advanced ones have opportunities to help others. Indeed, the most effective strategy for preventing early reading failure is one-to-one tutoring.

2. Play is a valuable way for children to work with the symbols and other higher forms of thinking. With other people alongside, the child practices what is to be expected and valued in society.

3. The teacher can be both observer and participant. For instance, if a child builds with blocks, the adult might sketch the building and then encourage a joint effort to make a map or use measurement tools.

Research from cognitive-developmental psychology and brain research supports these alternative findings. The biologic evidence strongly suggests that there are sequences in children's thinking, that there are at least multiple expressions of intelligence, and that the context of learning affects what children know. These theories all attempt to describe some of the incredible diversity of human cognitive ability.

Brain-Based Research

"The human brain is the most fascinatingly organized three pounds of matter on this planet" (Schiller, 1998). The only unfinished organ at birth, it continues to grow throughout the life cycle. The principal task of the brain in early childhood is the connection of brain cells, as a child's brain is two-and-a-half times as active as an adult's. "Cognitive science unites psychology, computer science, and neuroscience to produce research and insights about the science of children's minds" (Gopnik, Meltzoff, & Kuhl, 1999). During the first three years of life, an infant's brain creates an estimated 1,000 billion synapses. Providing quality experiences and relationships will create lasting effects on how the brain gets wired.

As noted in Chapter 4, a child is born with a billion cells (neurons) not yet connected in a meaningful way. Over the next few years, the brain forms trillions of networks (synapses), many more than a child will ever need. As they multiply and connect, a sophisticated network of neural pathways is created (Shore, 1997). New research on the brain development of young children (see Figure 4-19) has important implications for curriculum. Indications are strong that children's brains need to be stimulated for the network of connections to grow and be protected from being discarded. "Brain connections that have been reinforced by repeated experience tend to remain while those that are not are discarded" (Galinsky, 1997). We need to develop curriculum that brings children to interesting places and brings interesting things to children. Brain functions—information-processing skills of attention and memory—are getting serious attention from neuroscience. Teachers then translate new findings into curriculum planning (see Figure 4-20):

● *The brain is strongly run by patterns rather than facts.* Children learn best with curriculum developed around themes, integrated learning, whole experiences. The key to our intelligence is the recognition of patterns and relationships.

Conclusion: Develop meaningful themes for activity planning. Uninteresting or abstract pieces of information (e.g., drilling young children on alphabet letters) will not provide understanding. Plan some kinds of "immersion

1 Vygotsky's approach to development recognizes the social origins of an individual's thinking functioning: for instance, taking into account children's home language experiences can turn passive learners into lively participants (Berk & Winsler, 1995).

experiences" that encourage children to go deeply into their play and work.

- *Stress and threat affect the brain in many ways.* Emotions run the brain, and bad emotions reduce the capacity for memory and understanding as well as reducing higher-order thinking skills. Good emotions create excitement and love of learning.

  Conclusion: Make a positive, personal connection with each child, and avoid threats by loss of approval, hurried schedules, or implying children are helpless or bad. A secure environment counteracts the problems that may occur when the stress regulation mechanisms are triggered too often. Good emotions enhance memory.

- *The brain runs better when food intake is steady.* Insulin levels stay more even, cortisol levels are lower, and glucose tolerance is better. Diet activates memory; children need diets rich in proteins (meats, nuts, cheese), omega-3 fatty acids, and selenium and boron (leafy green vegetables), as well as enough restful sleep so the brain can reorganize itself (Schiller, 2001).

  Conclusion: Snacks are good! Regular snack times may lead to better cognitive functioning, fewer discipline problems, and an enhanced sense of well-being.

- *All learning is mind-body.* A child's physical state, posture, and breathing affect learning. Our brain is designed for cycles and rhythms. Practice makes permanent, and memory is kept more accurate when information is revisited.

  Conclusion: Keep track of and teach to children's bodily functions and body states and how long they are expected to sit or nap. Plan a daily schedule with both variety and balance, and work in regular routines and productive rituals.

Brain research findings parallel our Code of Ethics: "The basic elements of interpersonal relationships—collaboration, reflection, repair, coherent narratives and emotional communication—help to shape the growing mind of the child" (Siegel, 1999). A core value is to recognize and respect the unique qualities, abilities and potential of each child (Appendix A, I-1.3). Curriculum ideas based on brain research are shown throughout the chapter.

In general, teachers of children can keep these ideas in mind:

- *Birth to age four.* Provide for healthy sensory stimulation. This means all the senses need to be included in a child's exploration of the world. "There is a very important time in a child's life, beginning at birth, when he should be living in an enriched environment—visual, auditory, language, and so on—because that lays the foundation for development later in life" (Weisel in Caine & Caine, 1997). Further, "there are circuits that are responsible for emotional and social functioning (not just perception and motor action) that come 'on line' during the first years of life" (Siegel, 1999).

- *Age four to eight.* The brain is eagerly searching for stimulation; "schooling from kindergarten through fifth grade, therefore, must be richly stimulating with activities that reward the brain's insatiable appetite for meaning" (Kotoulek in Phipps, 1998). Give children plenty of opportunities to use stories, explore ideas, and master tasks rather than use worksheets or other repetitive tasks that kill enthusiasm for learning.

- *All ages.* Develop curriculum that emphasizes choices. "Exercise and positive social contacts, such as hugging, music, and the supportive comments of friends, can elevate endorphin levels and thus make us feel good about ourselves and our social environment" (Leventhal in Sylwester, 1995). Create opportunities for "collaboration" and cooperation, both among children and between children and teachers.

COGNITIVE SKILLS IN EARLY CHILDHOOD

The actual skills children acquire as they learn to think are considerable. A basic skill is defined by two fundamental qualities:

- A skill is basic if it is **transcurricular**: that is, if the child can use it in a variety of situations and activities throughout the school day. For example, children who can express feelings and opinions clearly—who can let adults know when they are having difficulties with a particular task or social situation—have acquired a skill that is useful anywhere.

- A skill is also basic if it has **dynamic** consequences: that is, if it leads to other worthwhile responses. For instance, children who are articulate tend to elicit more verbal responses from adults. Consequently, they are exposed to more verbal stimulation, which in turn strengthens their verbal abilities, and so on. Thus, having this skill leads to major dynamic consequences in a favorable direction, whereas not having the skill leads to dynamic consequences in an unfavorable direction.

Most skills fall into the nine categories that follow. The list, though long, is comprehensive; what children learn in the thinking realm of their development will fall into one of these categories. The teacher plans activities for all cognitive skills to ensure challenging children's thinking.

Skills of Inquiry

Young children are curious, watching the world carefully. Through exploration and examination, they increase their attention span. Inquisitive children begin to organize what they see, analyzing and identifying confusions or obstacles for themselves. All the senses function at birth, and both *sensation* and *perception* are used to make sense of the world.

> Cognition is one step beyond perception. It occurs when a person actually thinks about what he or she has perceived. Thus there is a sequence, from sensation to perception to cognition. A baby's sense organs must function if this chain of comprehension is to begin. No wonder the parts of the cortex dedicated to the senses develop rapidly: This is what allows all other developments to occur. (Berger, 2005)

Thus the skills of inquiry include the development of *attention span* and *memory*. The next step is communication; the child asks questions, listens, gets ideas, and makes suggestions. This includes interpreting what others communicate. Then children are ready to use resources, seeking assistance from other people and materials.

Piaget called these skills of inquiry; several of Gardner's intelligences would also be included, as would Vygotsky's notion of cultural ways of learning. Organizing and finding patterns, reasoning, and problem solving are also inquiry skills. As children examine alternatives, they choose a course of action, revising their plans as needed. The National Education Standards of Kindergarten–Grade 4 has been translated into early childhood and concentrates on an inquiry-based approach. This means we develop this skill by helping children build what they already know in order to construct new knowledge.

Young children thrill in making educated guesses, then checking their hypotheses by experimenting and taking risks. In doing so, they learn to evaluate, to use judgments and opinions, and to distinguish between fact and opinion, reality and fantasy. These basic skills of inquiry are the foundation for thinking; as such, they are far more important to develop than are simple prereading or number skills.

Knowledge of the Physical World

How do children learn about the physical world? First, they use objects, spending plenty of time exploring, manipulating, choosing, and using toys and natural materials. Babies search for something to suck; they begin to grasp objects and let them go. Toddlers will pick up and throw things or drop objects from a highchair to see what happens. Children observe reactions, discover relationships, and try to predict what will happen. Six-year-olds with balloons and water explore how to fill, roll, throw, and burst the balloons. This knowledge is part of Gardner's logical-mathematical intelligence, for knowledge of the physical world is essential to making order of it. We have learned that participation in an environment filled with interesting sights, sounds, and people enriches a child's schemes of thought and action (Lally, 1998).

As they learn the properties of objects, children gain a better understanding of the concept of cause and effect. Experience with the physical world gives children a base for comparing and contrasting, key skills for mathematical classification and scientific thinking.

Knowledge of the Social World

Relationships are primary to development. "Early experience significantly influences social and emotional brain functions" (Lally, 1998). Learning about others is hard work because the social world is not concrete and is often illogical. The child needs an awareness of self before developing an awareness of others and how to interact socially. To Gardner, this kind of knowledge requires two types of intelligence. The first is intrapersonal, having access to one's own feelings and a range of emotions, and the second is interpersonal, being able to notice others, making distinctions among individuals, particularly their moods and motivations. "Attachment relationships are important in the unfolding of the emotional and social development of the child. . . . it is not a matter of overwhelming enrichment or excessive sensory stimulation that is needed during this time, but one of attunement between adult and child" (Siegel, 1999).

Infants begin by distinguishing friends from strangers. Toddlers learn to use "mine" and then to use others' names as well. The next step is to expand their knowledge of roles to include those of family, school, and the community. Four- and five-year-olds are provided with daily opportunities to cooperate, to help, and to negotiate with

Being able to explore actual materials and objects encourages children to assimilate and use new knowledge.

others about their needs and wishes. According to Vygotsky, preschoolers learn appropriate actions by playing with older children. Also, make-believe is a major means through which children extend their cognitive skills.

In the best of circumstances, children are encouraged to notice both similarities and differences in people and then are led to develop tolerance for both. "Contextual intelligence" describes the ability to understand and manipulate the environment to suit oneself.[1] School-aged children seek small-group teamwork and moments of private time with a close friend. Children in the primary grades experience the development of conscience and learn rules for social living. In these ways children learn what is appropriate conduct in various situations—indoors or out, happy or sad, at the grocery store or at the dinner table.

CLASSIFICATION

Knowledge of the physical world teaches children to have different responses to different objects. **Classification** is the ability to group like objects in sets by a specific characteristic

(see Gardner in Chapter 4). Throughout their first year, infants use their senses to sort and classify their many experiences. As children develop, they initially classify by sorting groups of completely different objects, using a logic that only the child understands. During the preschool years, they begin to sort objects using consistent criteria. Once they develop language proficiency, they can name and classify objects. Gradually, and with help from adults who stimulate describing and manipulating, they learn that objects have more than one attribute and can be classified in more than one class. To clarify this process, consider how two-year-old Tisa learns to classify:

> What can Tisa do to the stuffed bear and the pet dog? What can she do with one and not the other? Which are her toys? Which are Rover's? Which ones have fur? What is different about them?

Tisa learns the attributes of the objects by exploring, learning the class names of "toy" and "pet." Tisa makes collections, sorting by similarity those that are Rover's toys and those that are her own. She uses class relationships to understand that both animals have fur, but she

  1 Social knowledge is a critical factor in children's development, enabling them to function in our diverse world.

can tug on only one animal's ears without encountering a problem.

Seriation

Seriation is "the ability to put an object or group of objects in a logical series based on a property of those objects" (Geist, 2001). Like classification, seriation can appear confusing at first glance. To illustrate its development, look at some of the materials designed by Montessori. These toys were developed to make clear to children exactly what seriation is and how it can be learned. Many of these toys distinguish grades of intensity by size, color, weight, number. Children build pyramid towers, fit nesting blocks together, and use the counting rods. By noting differences, often through trial and error, children learn seriation systematically. For instance, the pyramid tower is ordered from largest piece to smallest as it is built. Boxes are nested, one inside the other, by their graduated size or volume. The counting rods can be put into a staircase array, the units building on each other from one to ten. Children can arrange several things in order and fit one ordered set of objects to another. Gardner's category of musical intelligence requires seriation, as well as the skill of inquiry ("How do I make noise? Rhythm? Musical song?") and a knowledge of the social world ("How can we make music together? A real band?").

Numbers

Understanding the concept of number means learning about quantity: that is, understanding amount, degree, and position. Mathematical knowledge is now being seen as an emergent understanding of concepts, as we already think of literacy development (see Chapter 13). Once infants develop an understanding of object permanence (that an object exists whether or not it can be seen), they are ready to learn about quantity as they compare objects—for example, by stacking rings on a stick. Toddlers and twos can sort by groups (large versus small, hard versus soft) and start noticing what is "more."

Children under five have plenty of songs, chants, and fingerplays that include numbers ("One Potato, Two Potato" or "Five Speckled Frogs"). Once children comprehend numbers, they are ready to use mathematical terms and forms of expression. For instance, after singing about the frog that jumped into the pool in the song "Five Speckled Frogs," Chantel can begin to understand that four is one less than five.

Cognition in action! The concepts of the world come to life through Montessori materials.

But a knowledge of numbers is neither complete nor meaningful unless children have direct experience with materials and objects. "Quantification is the basis for formal mathematics, and is a synthesis of order, the basic understanding that objects are counted in a specific sequence and each object is counted only once" (Geist, 2001). Learning about quantity also means comparing amounts (as when children work with table toys, blocks, sensory materials, and the like) and arranging two sets of objects in one-to-one correspondence ("Each person needs one and only one napkin for snack, Tyler"). Children can also count objects and begin computation ("Parvin, you have three shovels. Here is one more; now how many do you have?"). With countless experiences such as these, children in kindergarten through third grade will be ready and excited to learn more mathematical skills.

Symbols

A symbol stands for something else; it is not what it appears to be! Young children have to think hard and long to symbolize. It is a task of some skill to imitate or use one object to represent something else. "The value of revisiting and re-representing children's symbolic representations for both teachers and children has been well-documented" (Moran & Jarvis, 2001).

Children begin by using their bodies. Infants and toddlers love to play peek-a-boo, reacting to "Boo!" with full-bodied excitement each time it is said. Preschoolers revel in playing favorite characters. Primary school children make up plays and puppet shows. Make-believe helps in the process of symbolizing, as does making sounds to represent objects ("Choo-choo" is a train, for example). Using and making two- and three-dimensional models are other ways children symbolize, when they transfer what they see to the easel or to the clay table. Children are also symbolizing when they dress up in costumes and uniforms. The Reggio Emilia approach (see Chapters 2, 9, and 10) encourages children to use a variety of media to express their thinking and deepen their understanding.

Teachers add to the symbolizing process when they use descriptive words. Description games encourage children to do the same. For example, "It is round and red and you eat it. What is it?" (An apple!) After all these skills have been mastered, children are ready for written symbols, when they can use the written word to label, take dictation, or write notes. Using Gardner's and Vygotsky's ways of thinking, educational environments for school-age children might take the form of discovery centers, a kind of museum, where apprentice-groups with children of different ages would help children with numerical and computer skills.

Spatial Relationships

Spatial relationships develop early. Infants visually track what they see, trying to reach and grasp. As they experience one object's position in relation to another, they begin to have a mental picture of spatial relationships. Toddlers find this out as they learn to steer themselves around tables and seat themselves on the potty. The concept of "close" (the chair) and "far away" (the quesadilla cooling on the counter) give clues to length and distance. ("How far do I have to reach to get one?"). As spatial skills develop, children learn to fit things together and take them apart. They rearrange and shape objects. They observe and describe things from different spatial viewpoints. This perspective is learned only through experience. The child under five needs to describe and then try out the notion that what one sees from the side of the hill is not what can be seen from the top.

Adults help children learn such skills by letting them locate things at home, in the classroom, in the department store. Both Piaget and Gardner would agree that body and kinesthetic knowledge are used in this type of activity. In Reggio Emilia, for instance, mirrors are placed around corners, found at the school entrance, and embedded in the floors, giving children a sense of self in space in a number of ways. Teachers encourage children to represent such spatial relationships in their drawings, with pictures, and in photographs.

Time

Understanding time is a complicated affair because time is composed of at least three dimensions: time as the present, time as a continuum, and time as a sequence of events. Children must learn each of these to fully understand the concept of time. In some settings, children learn to stop and start an activity on a signal (when the teacher strikes a chord on the piano for cleanup time). They try to move their bodies at different speeds, indoors and out. Older children begin to observe that clocks and calendars are used to mark the passage of time. Specifically, children come to know the sequencing of events in time: which comes first, next, last? Having an order of events through a consistent daily schedule helps children learn this aspect of time. They also benefit from anticipating future events and making the appropriate preparations. Planning a course of action and completing that plan give meaning to the idea of time.

What children learn intellectually in the early years is massive in quantity and quality. Yet young children are ready—eager, in fact—to engage themselves with the world around them to acquire these cognitive skills. Figure 12-2 gives

When considering intellectual development, teachers should keep in mind that, to children, education is exploration. Let children use their imagination to use materials in new and different ways.

Cognitive Skills into the Curriculum

Cognitive Skill	Sample Activity	Age
Inquiry: senses, perception, attention, memory	Playing with water: what can you find out?	Toddler, Preschool
Knowledge of the Physical World	Take an outdoor sound walk	Toddler, Preschool
Knowledge of the Social World	Make a Wheel of Feelings; read Aliki's *Feelings* book	Preschool, School-Age
Classification	Collections: put together, identify describe, and classify a nature collection	Preschool, School-Age
Seriation	Yeast grows: see which expands most, with flour, sugar, salt, juice	School-Age
Numbers	Play "fives" game with playing cards numbered 1–4	School-Age
Symbols	Making shapes: bodies and shape cards	Preschool, School-Age
Spatial Relationships	Geoboards	Preschool, School-Age
Time	Play "Stop & Go" with music	Preschool, School-Age

FIGURE 12-2 Every cognitive skill has a place in planning curriculum.

examples of activities that address the nine cognitive skills. By remaining aware of how much is to be learned, educators keep a realistic—and humble—appreciation for the "work" of children.

THE TEACHER'S ROLE

Considerations

When considering children's intellectual development, teachers should keep the following in mind:

● *Education is exploration*. The process of education is more than its products. Teachers enhance learning by allowing children to interact with the environment. The teacher is a source of information and support rather than one who gives answers or commands. A project approach, based on the belief that children's minds should be engaged in ways that deepen their understanding of their own experiences and environment, may be used. Consisting of exploring a theme or topic (such as shadows, houses, building a table) over a period of weeks, this approach reflects Dewey's progressive education and the British Open Schools (see Chapter 1) and is implemented regularly in the Reggio Emilia schools. The

goal is to have children ask their own questions and create their own challenges.

● *Children do not think like adults*. Children think and perceive in their own ways, as Piaget believed. They think in sensory and concrete terms and come to conclusions based on what they see and touch.

● *Children's thinking is legitimate and should be valued*. Their thought processes and perceptions are as valid as adults'. Teachers support those processes by asking questions to stimulate further thought and by providing materials for exploration.

● *The language of the teacher should support cognitive development*. Throughout their interactions with children, teachers help children use words, terms, and concepts correctly:

> Mariko (at water table): I need that suckup.
> Teacher: The baster really does suck up water, doesn't it?

Teachers' questions are open-ended; they are not to be answered with a simple yes or no. For example, when teachers in Reggio Emilia question children, it is usually in small groups of three or four so that they explore together what the children are doing in greater depth. The goal is to use language to help children *think*.

What do YOU Think?

"Back to basics" is a phrase commonly heard in conjunction with academic and cognitive curriculum. Its intention is to focus attention on what is fundamental to be learned, and often refers to intellectual skills. Fondly known as the 3Rs—reading, 'riting, and 'rithmetic—these skills are often taught by whole-group telling and by drill-and-skill repetition.

But what should early childhood professionals be doing? Surely, the 3Rs cannot be taught as such in programs for children under five, and a program of only direct instruction has been criticized by developmental advocates. How do we teach "before the basics"?

One ECE educator, Bev Bos, has been teaching and demonstrating just this notion for over 20 years. She suggests giving one's curriculum a "child-centeredness test." While these questions are good for all curriculum, they are especially important for those activities and times we designate for cognitive development. See how your cognitive curriculum holds up (Bos, 1983):

- Does this activity help the child's sense of identity?
- Is the activity open-ended—that is, can the child change this material?
- Does this activity allow the child to create?
- Does this activity provide a framework for the child to cooperate with others while retaining a sense of self?
- Is the activity fun? Will it inspire laughter and a love of learning?

Teachers can use language to define a problem, help children figure out what they are doing, and decide what they need to do next. They leave the child with something to ponder.

Teacher: I wonder why the turtle's head went back in its shell when you put your finger close by.

Teacher: If you want to play with José, how can you let him know?

Teacher: What do we need from the woodworking shelf to make a spaceship?

The teacher must match the child's cognitive capacity with the instruction. Child-centered, self-initiated learning (see Chapter 10) is a great motivator, so observing children's intensity with materials and asking questions to extend their thinking is recommended. Current research (Landry & Forman, 2000) suggests using conversation, documenting children's thinking, using drawing, and incorporating problem-solving.

Figure 12-3 shows further how teachers' use of language helps children think and develop cognitive skills as part of their early childhood experience.

The teacher must consider, include, and plan for children with learning disabilities and other varied learning "styles." Each type of learning disability (see Chapter 3) has its own description and treatment. Teachers must develop a wide range of techniques to address such disabilities. After the identification and assessment phases, teachers and families need to work with specialists and devise options (an individualized education plan, or IEP) that include the child and establish reasonable learning goals.

Curriculum Planning for Cognitive Development

In the Environment

Teachers can plan cognitive curriculum for their children by considering the class setting, both indoors and out, throughout the daily schedule. Each activity center can be used to encourage intellectual development with a variety of curriculum materials and methods (see High/Scope in Chapter 2). The environment and methods required to help children think

Skill	Teachers Can
Inquiry	• Ask questions so children make statements about their conversations. *Example:* "What do you notice about the guinea pig?" • Try to be more specific if such questions seem overwhelming or if they elicit little response. *Example:* "What sounds do you hear? What can you find out by touching her?" • Ask how children arrived at their answers. *Example:* "How did you know that the marble wouldn't roll up the ramp?"
Social Knowledge	• Try not to respond to unstated needs. *Example:* "Do you want something? Can I help you?" • Help children define what they want or need, so that they learn how to ask for it. *Example:* Marie: "I wonder who is going to tie my shoes?" Teacher: "So do I. When you want someone to tie your shoe, you can say, 'Would you tie my shoe?'" Marie: "Would you tie my shoe?" Teacher: "I'd be glad to."
Classification	• Ask questions that will help children focus on objects and see differences and details. *Example:* While cooking, ask "Which things on the table do we put in the bowl?" "What are made of plastic?" "Which go in the oven?" "What on the table is used for measuring? How do you know?" "Now look carefully—what do you see on the measuring cup?" "What do those little red lines mean?"
Spatial Relationships	• Ask for the precise location of an object the child asks for or is interested in: *Examples:* "Where did you say you saw the bird's nest?" "You can find another stapler in the cabinet underneath the fish tank."
Concept of Time	• Use accurate time sequences with children. *Example:* Teacher: "Just a minute." Milo: "Is this a real minute or a 'wait a minute'?" Teacher: "You're right. I'm with Phoebe now. I'll help you next."

FIGURE 12-3 Teachers' use of language affects how children develop cognitive skills. The more children are allowed and encouraged to think for themselves, the more their cognitive skills will develop.

include challenging situations, enriching materials, and supportive adults. Young children have special ways of thinking (see Chapter 4) that expand with age. The children's active participation in self-directed play with concrete materials is very important for early perceptual, fine-motor, and cognitive development (Moore, 1997). Some children under age three have a limited attention span and can be overstimulated unless the environment is kept simple. Three- to five-year-olds can absorb more and in finer detail as they have more developed motor and perceptual skills. Older preschoolers and kindergartners learn best trying to solve real problems, and the six- to eight-year-old still benefits in discovery-oriented, "learn by doing" situations. Figure 12-4 shows how one activity (which can be done with nearly all ages) contributes to the development of children's thought processes.

Video VIEW PoinT 12-1

"As adults move and observe children engaged in activity, they see opportunties to reinforce and enrich children's learning experiences."

COMPETENCY: Cognitive Development

AGE GROUP: Preschool

CRITICAL THINKING QUESTIONS:

1. What kinds of questions or comments stimulate cognitive thinking? How do teachers start to ask without interrupting the play?

2. How do teachers get ideas for curriculum? When during the preschool day would be good times for curriculum opportunities?

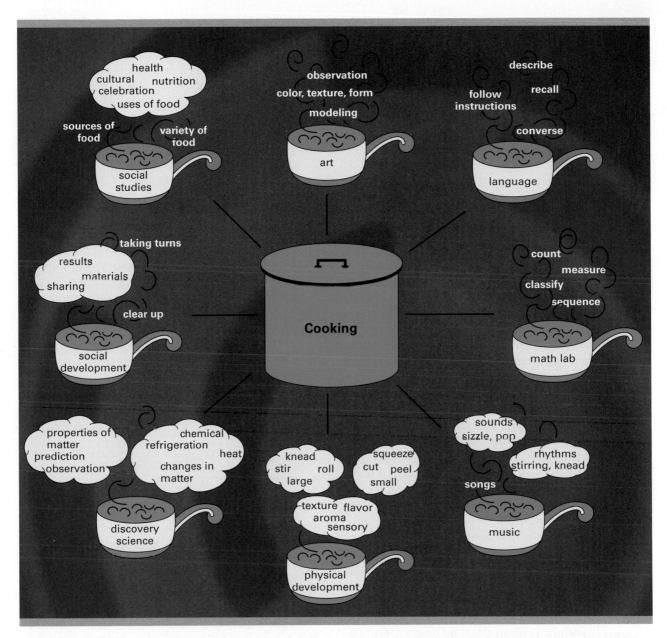

FIGURE 12-4 Each activity, such as cooking, can enhance cognitive development throughout the curriculum. A trip to the market can be an experience in classification and calculation. (For further reading, see Dahl, 1998.)

Classroom teachers can create what Jensen (1998) calls high-activity, low-stress, brain-compatible learning environments. An optimal environment will have several learning centers for the children to choose from so that the brain is stimulated to be attentive, absorb new information, and to store this information in long-term memory.

Teachers should aim to create a balance between meaningful experiences and optimal stimulation of the brain in their classrooms. . . . Such an environment offers children experiences with real-life, hands-on, theme-based activities oriented to solving problems, such as children counting out play money when shopping at the store in the dramatic play center (Rushton, 2001).

Indoor Areas. The indoor environments described in Chapter 9 include the basic ingredients of a stimulating cognitive environment. The indoor areas might have some of the following materials and activities:

- *Art.* Include a "help-yourself" shelf for child-chosen projects. A variety of paper, drawing implements, and tools encourages children to re-create their own reality, using representational art forms that show how children see the physical and social worlds.

- *Blocks.* Have paper models of each block shape on storage shelves to help children with classification by shape and size. Be sure you put a priority on having enough unit blocks (a 600+ piece set for a preschool class of 16) and provide enough space (40–80 square feet per group) with a firm carpet that supports balancing towers and controls noise. Accessories, such as animals and homemade trees and lakes, help children symbolize. As they experiment with blocks, they learn about physical laws and reality and have experiences in cooperative learning and living, all of which are cognitive tasks. Counting blocks, which builds on one-to-one correspondence rather than rote memorization, contributes to genuine understanding.

- *Discovery/science.* Rotate a display of "touch me" materials. This gives children firsthand experience with plants, seeds, animals, magnets, sea shells, foods, and so on. Have a "Fix-it Shop" or "Disassembly Line" with nonworking appliances and radios, equipped with plenty of screwdrivers, pliers, and containers for small parts (Ross, 2000). Help children formulate questions and then experiment or observe to seek the answers. School-age children can find out which plants grow in saltwater or freshwater by setting up plants in each environment and watching daily ("Today something has changed!" wrote a seven-year-old. "The duckweed is not relly grren anymore. A scnd root is hanging."). If you can, have a computer available with developmentally appropriate software.

- *Dramatic play.* Stock this area with materials for role playing, puppet making, and acting out adult activities. Have anatomically correct boy and girl dolls of a variety of races and some with disabilities. Include clothing for all types of work, equipment for carrying things and babies, that reflect the homes of all the children in the group but also extend the play to include new ways of dressing, eating, and playing.[1] When several pre-kindergarten children got haircuts, the class developed a "Hairy Heads" theme, transforming this area into a hair salon with brushes, barrettes, and wigs. The dolls got plenty of shampoos that month!

- *Language/library.* Choose books that focus on both the physical and social worlds. Children's interests in numbers, symbols, and time can also be extended by selecting literature that reflects their level of understanding. Look for the message in children's books and choose good stories that reflect diversity, such as *Helping Out* (Ancona) and *George the Babysitter* (Hughes). Be sure to listen to the group's interests, and make a point to place books that respond to those interests in the library.

- *Manipulatives (table toys).* The manipulatives area is an ideal place for materials that encourage cognitive development; highlight this area with both favorites (Legos® or Crystal Climbers®) and new items (Construx® or sewing cards). Counting cubes aid in classification and seriation, while puzzles or nesting blocks focus on spatial relationships. Information-processing theory emphasizes the importance of experiences that develop children's working memory and familiarity. Manipulative materials (including beads, tiddledywinks, and so on) and games give children hands-on experiences with counting, sorting, and organizing that are both meaningful and socially natural. Homemade lotto games or puzzles with the children's photos encourage self-esteem and group identity as well as cognitive and motor development.

Outdoor Areas. The outdoor area provides opportunities for children to plan and organize their own thoughts. Offer your yard as a place for discovery. "A kinder garden needn't be manicured or tamed. Shrubs and viney tangles are secret hideouts. Fallow beds are places where worms, roots, and rocks can be explored. Vegetables sometimes ignored at dinner are trailside snacks. Pests are pets" (Ross, 2000).

Toddlers can classify what they find as they look for balls, sand buckets, and toy trucks hidden around the yard. Kindergartners playing tag need inquiry skills. Preschoolers in the sand pit predict how water will affect the sand, using their growing knowledge of the physical world. Children learn to classify water table and wheel toys; they learn seriation when they select sand buckets by size. Counting shovels to see that there are enough to go around, building with large, hollow blocks, and watching the seasons change are all cognitive skills children gain as they play outside.

Physical- and logical-mathematical activities are thus easily incorporated into the curriculum outdoors. A Piagetian approach of asking "I

1   Children's learning environments should be rich with images of diversity. This diversity adds to the complexity of their thinking!

wonder why . . .?" or "What would happen if . . .?" inspires experimenting and reasoning in young children. The water table outdoors could have a large block of ice, a variety of materials such as wood, cotton balls, straws, and cardboard, or containers of colored water and eyedroppers. Balancing activities might mean hollow blocks, milk cartons, or beanbags (or all three). A hillside or long plank can become a site for predicting and trying out rolling, using different sizes of balls or even bodies.

Routines, Transitions, and Groups

Groups, transitions, and routines all play a part in developing children's knowledge of the social world. As children learn to conduct themselves in school, they learn:

- To enter a class and start to play (transition).
- To take care of their own belongings and those of their school (routines).
- To concentrate on an activity with others around (group times).
- To interact with others while at the same time paying attention to a leader or task (group times).
- To end an activity, an interaction, a school day (transition).

Teachers plan environments, activities, and grouping of children to give the class experience in all these cognitive challenges. Look back at Figure 9-16. It describes strategies for helping children learn concrete and comfortable ways to think and live with transitions. Teachers use signs, their own words, and helpful tips that illuminate for children what is happening, what is expected of them, and how they can express themselves in all three of these daily segments.

Moreover, many routine activities offer wonderful opportunities for cognitive learning. For example, consider the snack table. Incorporating math concepts into snack time will engender enthusiasm and skill development. Whether as a part of free-choice time or a time period on its own, snack time becomes "think time" as children:

- Fill out and use menu cards.
- Learn the concept of sets ("*Everyone* needs five of *everything*, huh?").
- Work with the concept of uniform units ("Are the ham and cheese pieces the same?").
- Understand the concepts of equal, less, and more.

- Learn how to count "wet stuff" and to count by the spoonful or handful.
- See geometry and fractions at work (circles for raisins, triangles for sandwiches, "Break the graham cracker in pieces for everyone . . . fair!").

Focus on Skills and Problem Solving

How can teachers help children develop specific cognitive skills? After observing the children carefully, teachers identify a particular skill and then list those processes, concepts, and vocabulary involved. For instance, the skill of inquiry can be encouraged in every part of the curriculum by asking questions. Teachers model curiosity by observing and asking questions about what they see and what children may be thinking. This stimulates children to look, wonder, and interact:

Teacher: I wonder which piece of wood you'll choose to glue on your board next.

Teacher: What part do you want to play in our grocery store?

Teacher: How can we find out how long your road of blocks is?

The processes of mathematical literacy involve using representation, performing manipulations, making sense in math reasoning, and problem solving (Diezmann & Yelland, 2000). For instance, help children as they use markers to "stand for" people or animals or dolls in place of real babies—this representational thinking is a hallmark of the preschool period, and fantasy play can help in mathematical thinking if the teacher makes children aware. Using manipulatives can help children add and subtract, and will make such operations understandable. Guessing games can be a fun way to elicit reasoning, because "they often involve children in reflecting on and modifying their ideas (see Figure 12-5). Remember that children have limited knowledge and need to be encouraged to keep guessing, while you stimulate them to offer, justify, and question their ideas.

Problem solving is mentioned often in early childhood education circles, in social and artistic contexts as well as for cognitive development. For this to be successful, two issues must be addressed: problem-posing and investigations (National Council of Teachers of Mathematics, 2000). Problem posing is difficult for many children and they will need guidance, so that the problem is clear before the group or individual launches into looking for a solution. Investigations are "authentic problem-solving

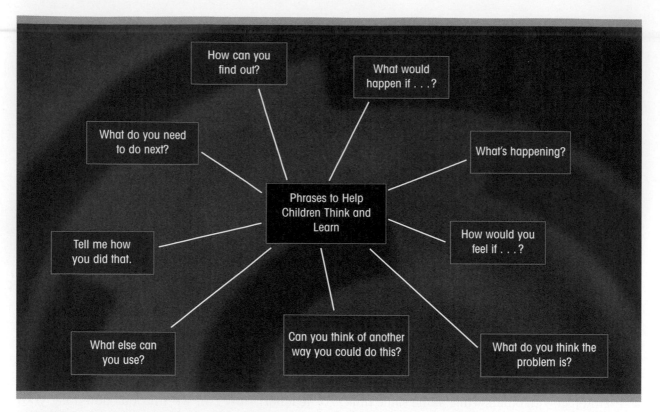

FIGURE 12-5 Teachers encourage children's thinking when they ask questions. Posted in the classroom or given to students and parents, this chart serves as a reminder that to TEACH is to ASK more often than to TELL.

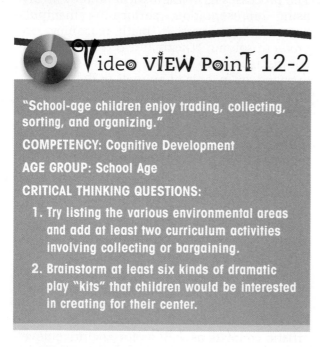

Video VIEW PoinT 12-2

"School-age children enjoy trading, collecting, sorting, and organizing."

COMPETENCY: Cognitive Development

AGE GROUP: School Age

CRITICAL THINKING QUESTIONS:

1. Try listing the various environmental areas and add at least two curriculum activities involving collecting or bargaining.

2. Brainstorm at least six kinds of dramatic play "kits" that children would be interested in creating for their center.

situations in which children work as mathematicians and have opportunities to develop mathematical power" (Diezmann & Yelland, 2000). Help children set a course for finding out so that they will end their investigation with a real discovery. And be sure to reward the efforts and process, regardless of the outcome!

When children see that it is all right to ask "Why?" they feel encouraged to ask questions themselves. Brainstorming is a technique that helps children get ideas and use resources to find out how many ways there are to make a kite or build a castle.

Outdoors, inquisitive children explore their environment. Children ask questions: "Can we turn on the water? What if we bury all of the toy bears in the gravel? Could we use the ladder to see over the fence? Let's all hide from the teacher!" The way teachers handle inquiries from children about what they want to do sends a message that supports—or discourages—this cognitive skill. When there is no harm in asking (though the answer may be "No"), children are encouraged to develop further the skill of inquiry. Figure 12-6 illustrates exactly how the cognitive skills of reasoning and problem solving could serve as the basis for curriculum development around the entire classroom.

Use of Themes

A specific theme can be chosen for cognitive development. Themes that bubble up from the children's interests will engage their thinking more than those imposed from the teachers.

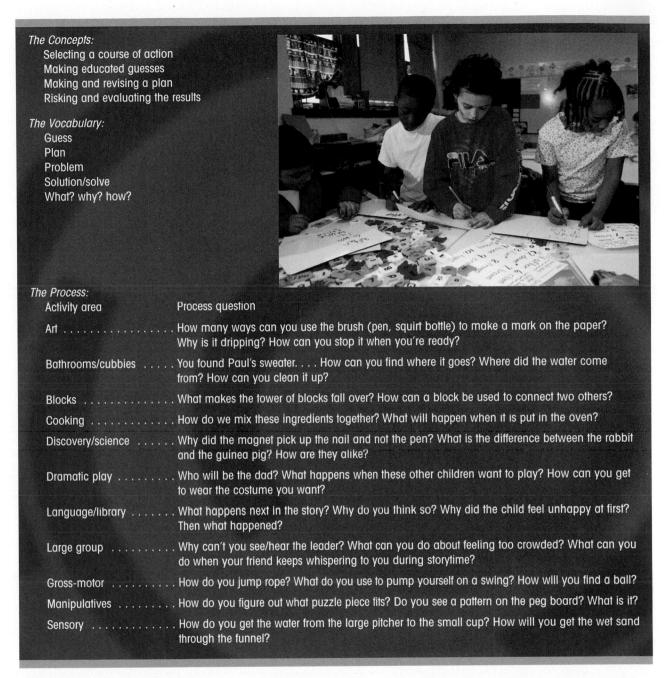

The Concepts:
- Selecting a course of action
- Making educated guesses
- Making and revising a plan
- Risking and evaluating the results

The Vocabulary:
- Guess
- Plan
- Problem
- Solution/solve
- What? why? how?

The Process:

Activity area	Process question
Art	How many ways can you use the brush (pen, squirt bottle) to make a mark on the paper? Why is it dripping? How can you stop it when you're ready?
Bathrooms/cubbies	You found Paul's sweater. . . . How can you find where it goes? Where did the water come from? How can you clean it up?
Blocks	What makes the tower of blocks fall over? How can a block be used to connect two others?
Cooking	How do we mix these ingredients together? What will happen when it is put in the oven?
Discovery/science	Why did the magnet pick up the nail and not the pen? What is the difference between the rabbit and the guinea pig? How are they alike?
Dramatic play	Who will be the dad? What happens when these other children want to play? How can you get to wear the costume you want?
Language/library	What happens next in the story? Why do you think so? Why did the child feel unhappy at first? Then what happened?
Large group	Why can't you see/hear the leader? What can you do about feeling too crowded? What can you do when your friend keeps whispering to you during storytime?
Gross-motor	How do you jump rope? What do you use to pump yourself on a swing? How will you find a ball?
Manipulatives	How do you figure out what puzzle piece fits? Do you see a pattern on the peg board? What is it?
Sensory	How do you get the water from the large pitcher to the small cup? How will you get the wet sand through the funnel?

FIGURE 12-6 Children want to know how to solve problems, such as, "Which letters and numbers do I need to match my list?"

Units based on things in the physical world (season changes, pets, the garden), on unexpected or current events (a new load of sand, a community fair, road work nearby), or the special interests of the children (sharing the African masks or spacesuits, using the puppet stage, studying reptiles) are all appealing. Figure 12-7 illustrates a dinosaur theme.

Current events must be chosen carefully because young children may have only passing knowledge or interest in most of them. Meaningful events might be a space shuttle mission or a solar eclipse. More likely, the event will be a local one, such as a windy day or someone's new baby. Units based on these happenings might be named "Space and Travel" or "Our Beginnings as Babies." Events such as the discovery of ants on the playground have a high level of interest and are worth pursuing. See Figure 12-8.

Themes can change with the seasons, and can capitalize on the five scientific thinking processes of observing, comparing, classifying, measuring, and communicating.

Theme: Dinosaurs

Area	Cognitive Skill(s)	Activity
		Indoors
Art	Organization	Papier mâché model of a dinosaur, make a "dinosaur world" mural.
Blocks	Seriation	Use blocks to compare relative sizes of dinosaurs.
Cooking	Relationships	Prepare vegetarian snack (herbivores), then meatballs for the carnivores.
Discovery	Observation	Get fossils, other skeletons. Collect books on how scientists learn about dinosaurs. Compare relationships (size, stature, etc.) of prehistoric to common animals. Hide bones in the sand table to dig up and role play paleontologist.
Dramatic play	Symbols	Dinosaur puppets. Masks of dinosaurs.
Library	Label/recall; use of resources	Provide books about dinosaurs. Make dinosaur books with stamps and children's words.
Manipulatives	Reasoning; problem solving	Individual and floor dinosaur puzzles. Templates to trace and cut.
		Outdoors
Sensory	Symbols	Rubber dinosaurs in pebbles; dinosaur cookie cutters in clay/play dough.
Gross-motor	Symbols	Measure children's bodies with a rope the length of various dinosaurs.
Sand	Symbols	Act out digging up dinosaur bones.
Games	Social world	"Tyrannosaurus, May I?" game, naming and taking steps of various dinosaurs.
		Groups
Large	Label/recall; educated guessing	"Who Am I?", verbally describing dinosaur. Mystery Pictures, showing parts of dinosaurs and having children guess.
Music	Symbols	Acting out dinosaurs to a record, or to music of various tones.

Small	Label/communicate	Draw your favorite dinosaur, dictate what you like about it and what you know.
		Dinosaur sheet, folded in quarters, with a sentence to fill in and space to draw:
		   The dinosaurs laid . . .
		   Some dinosaurs lived . . .
		   Dinosaurs ate . . .
		   Dinosaurs died because . . .

FIGURE 12-7 Using a theme of special interest, such as dinosaurs, teachers can develop children's cognitive skills in many classrooms areas.

Fall: "Harvest Time," "Changes, Changes"

Winter: "Water, Water Everywhere"

Spring: "Green and Growing Things"

Summer: "The Seashore," or at least the local lake or river.

The critical point is to have a meaningful theme for children; rehashing the same old themes year after year may be easy for adults, but can crowd out other interests of each unique group.

The theme of "Friendship" expands children's knowledge of the social world, as they increase their awareness of others through the giving and receiving of letters and cards. Cooperation and group conflict resolution expand the friendship theme. A unit can also focus on symbolizing through use of names, letters on a "post box," or the numbers and location of people's houses and apartments. When this happens is less important than the fact that it is meaningful and engaging to children.

Throughout the year, teachers observe the interests of the particular group and notice what is relevant to their lives. For a group interested in the passage of time, "Watches and Calendars" could be a theme, with timepieces from hourglasses to digital watches and clanging timers and calendars from around the

Discovery Learning About Ants: Curriculum Planning for Primary Cognitive Development

The Setting:

- The playground after a rain and in the sidewalk cracks.
- The classroom, especially around the wastebasket.

The Discovery:

Ants everywhere!

Children: "Let's smash them!"

Teacher: "Wait—let's get to know them."

The Process:

Asking what you want to know about ants (RESEARCH QUESTION)

1. What do ants eat?
2. Why do they go into an anthill?
3. Do ants sleep?
4. Where do ants go when it rains?
5. What does an ant's body look like?
6. What is inside an anthill?

Finding out about these things (METHODOLOGY, PROCEDURE)

1. Consult experts (a library visit, checking at home, asking parents, looking at class copies of *Ranger Rick,* and so on).
2. Observe them (watch ants, collect them, put them in containers.)
3. Collect information (write journals, do group stories and reports).
4. Do experiments on ants ("Do ants hear?" Try blowing a trumpet; "Can ants swim?" Put them in a bowl of water; "How strong are they?" Give them various sizes of bread and see what they can carry.)

Telling what you know (RESULTS, CONCLUSIONS, NEXT STEPS)

1. Write reports.
2. Make a drama or play and act it out.
3. Take photos or draw pictures.
4. Make a book.

FIGURE 12-8 A lesson that uses the discovery method engages the children in scientific thinking and is related directly to their own thinking. Children's innate curiosity, the foundation for scientific thinking, is thus extended into the primary years. (Adapted, by permission, from A. Klein, "All about Ants: Discovery Learning in the Primary Grades," *Young Children 46* (July 1991): 23–27.)

world. Having children build ramps from cardboard tubes in the block corner, for instance, stimulates a discussion about slides and ramps that expands into a unit (remember Nicholas in Chapter 6?). The "School Bus" theme can include field trips, a big cardboard prop to be made, outdoor building, new block accessories, with a memory book of photos, stories, and drawings as a class keepsake. The Project Approach (see Chapter 10) describes the use of themes in curriculum, making it accessible so that the children can interact and "own" it.

Young children, particularly those under age five, use themselves as a starting point. Working their way into the world from there, they are often interested in their bodies, and a loosely formed theme of "Our Bodies, Ourselves" allows for learning about physical and gender similarities and differences as well as differences in physical abilities.[1] Expanding this unit to "My

1 What better time to deal with the potential of children's misconceptions and pre-prejudice attitudes and create an understanding and celebration of diversity!

Curriculum Planning for Cognitive Development with Infants and Toddlers

The Environment

- Contains soft items (such as pillows) and hard elements (such as mirrors) to see, taste, and touch.
- Has contrasts of color and design.
- Changes periodically, from the floor to strollers to swing.
- Is decorated with pictures of people's faces, animals, families.

The Skills

- Include self-help activities of eating, toileting/changing, and dressing.
- Highlight language and thinking as the adults label objects, describe events, and reflect feelings in a simplified, conversational manner.
- Encourage listening to a person, a story, a flannelboard song, fingerplay.
- Use appropriate art media to explore and manipulate, not to produce a finished product.

The Themes

- Are loosely defined and flexible, as is the schedule.
- Are of family and belonging, of self and bodies, of babies.
- Are dictated more by children's needs than by adults'.

FIGURE 12-9 Planning for infants and toddlers involves understanding specific development and intimate knowledge of the individual child. Consistent caregiving and flexibility are as important to effective planning for children under two years of age as are the actual activities offered.

family" and "My Neighborhood Community" is a natural process that builds on a solid base. Another way to plan curriculum is to focus on the children's developmental level. Infants and toddlers have less need for a theme curriculum; curriculum ideas for them concentrate on cognitive stimulation at their particular level of development, as in Figure 12-9.

COMPUTERS IN THE CLASSROOM

A computer can be as nonthreatening as a watercolor brush. In the hands of a child it can be a tool for experiencing the world. Early childhood classrooms are arranged so that children learn about the world directly, by piling blocks, molding sand and clay, bouncing a ball. Through these experiences, children gradually form concepts about how the world works and how they can affect it. As children touch the keys of a computer, they are challenged to explore and discover in ways never before possible.

"There are two reasons why every classroom or child care center should have a computer—children love them and they can provide a positive learning experience for even the most hard-to-work-with child" (Buckleitner, 1995). Unfortunately, many professionals are skeptical of computers. They worry that children will become passive for long periods of time, unwilling and unable to disengage and become involved in physical and social play. Indeed, specialists such as Elkind (1998) and Haugland (1999) do not recommend computer use for children under three, maintaining that children at those ages need to be learning through their bodies and motor manipulation of objects. NAEYC has published a position statement on Technology and Young Children for ages three to eight (2005).

Computers will have the most positive impact when

- They provide concrete experiences.
- Children have free access.
- Children and teachers learn together.
- Peer tutoring is encouraged.
- Children control the learning experience. Computers are used to teach powerful ideas (Haugland, 1999).

Discovery-oriented experiences with computers enhance children's learning, especially in

Using the computers in a classroom can individualize a program and offer social experiences.

 stimulating their cognitive thought processes.[1] Children design and control places and things of their own choosing, such as a house, the seashore, or a face. Then they create events that challenge them to think through the conse- quences of their actions. Moreover, computer programs can be "process highlighters" for children; the program can speed up or detail hidden processes and cause-and-effect relation- ships that are more difficult to observe, such as a plant growing, a face changing expression on command, or a dance put together with a spe- cial sequence of steps.

Although relatively new to the early child- hood classroom, computers and other technol- ogy have created a great deal of interest. Parents support computers in the classroom, most believing that computers can have a pos- itive effect on their children's learning (Milken & Hart, 1999). To integrate computers and take advantage of what they can offer children, Haugland (2000) recommends four steps:

- Select developmental software.
- Select appropriate Web sites.
- Integrate resources into the classroom.
- Select computers to enhance learning.

Further, technology is especially meaning- ful in primary classrooms. "Appropriate use of technology [includes] documenting events in the classroom using digital still or video cameras, creating multimedia electronic portfolios that document children's learning, using informa- tional software or Websites to find the answers to questions that come up in the course of ongoing learning, or working with children to create multimedia slide shows to present to families during open house or parent events" (Murphy, DePasquale, & McNamara, 2003). School-age programs can create a Website or make newsletters that increases communication with families while creating interesting curriculum experiences. Using Kidspiration and KidPix software allows children to create curriculum webs and draw pictures of their experiences. Innovative teachers involve children in creating PowerPoint slides to illustrate their strengths, interests, and challenges for a teacher-family- student conference.

Developmentally Appropriate Software

Along with blocks and paints, the computer can become an expressive medium that encourages skills in a variety of ways. It is important that the computer be used in addition to other con- crete experiences, not instead of them. For instance, children need to have real materials on the art and manipulatives tables; only then is it meaningful to manipulate images of those same kinds of materials at the computer table. Children need to have many experiences with *concrete* items such as paint, crayons, and markers. They are then ready to try their cre- ative hand at computer graphics.

To use computers appropriately in the classroom, teachers must first be *comfortable* with the computer themselves.

1. Put the computer area in a quiet spot of the classroom (such as in or near the library/ listening spot), against a wall to minimize damage to the equipment or cords.
2. To introduce the computer, show small groups of children the basic care and han- dling of the computer.
3. The computer can be one of many choices offered during free play, or it can be a more limited choice with a waiting list.
4. Interaction between children can be encouraged by
   a. including space for two or more at the computer,
   b. assigning turns to a pair or small group of children, particularly if the computer seems to be dominated by a few, and

---

1 Unlike a teacher or a playmate, computers can wait patiently for a child in a nonjudgmental way; thus computers can provide another avenue for learning and teaching to a diversity of children, even adjusting automatically to a child's abilities.

c. watching to ensure that no one becomes "stuck" at the computer or any other area.

It is in the area of **software** that teachers of young children have many choices. These choices must be carefully made. Not every program intended for children is developmentally appropriate, and teachers must pay thoughtful attention to the program and to what they know about their own group of children. Teachers must know what to look for and how to choose programs that will be useful and appropriate for the specific age of the group. Haugland and Shade (1990) suggest 10 criteria for evaluating computer programs. Computer software should

1. Be age appropriate.
2. Allow children to control it (children setting the pace and being active participants).
3. Include clear instructions.
4. Have expanding complexity.
5. Support independent exploration.
6. Be "process oriented" (having the software program be so engaging that the product of using it is secondary).
7. Include real-world representation.
8. Have high-quality technical features (colorful, uncluttered, and realistic).
9. Provide trial-and-error opportunities.
10. Have visible transformations (being able to affect the software, for example, by transposing objects).

Selecting software can become easier by using a rating system. Haugland (1997) has since made a Developmental Software Scale and evaluated an abundance of software to that date. The Web site Children and Computers (http://childrenandcomputers.com) can also help with software recommendations.

Web Sites

Many centers will use a computer simply with software; others, particularly those with primary-age children, may be interested in using the Internet. The Internet has been less researched than software, and its potential is untapped. There are a variety of learning opportunities using the Internet; however, as Haugland (2000) reminds us, "the sheer volume of Internet sites is overwhelming. Also, they have not been screened by anyone. Some sites are developmentally appropriate while others are simply terrible."

There are four types of children's Web sites:

1. *Information.* Information sites are great reference resources; for instance, the National Zoo from the Smithsonian (http://www.si.edu/natzoo) would be a wonderful introduction or follow-up to a field trip.
2. *Communication.* These sites connect children to experts to answer questions on projects, such as "Ask an Astronaut" (http://www.nss.org/askastro/home.html) for an Outer Space theme.
3. *Interaction.* These work like software programs, only more slowly.
4. *Publication.* These sites can post children's work, such as Kid Pub (http://www.kidpub.org/kidpub).

In addition, there are many online resources on technology as a learning tool; while many websites change, a few that have stood the test of time include the Center for Media Literacy (www.medialit.org), Children and Computers (www.childrenandcomputers.com), and NAEYC's Beyond the Journal (www.journal.naeyc.org).

When Child Meets Computer

Specific methods have been devised for teaching young children to work successfully with computers. For instance, a child must be able to maneuver a joystick or mouse, find the keys on the keyboard, or even insert a disk into the computer correctly. Because very young children cannot read, they will need help getting started. Teachers must be able to help children learn by setting up their classrooms with a computer positioned in a safe yet accessible place, structuring activities and the daily schedule to give children plenty of time to manipulate the machinery and programs, and choosing specific hardware and software that work with the class.

Integrating the Computer into Learning

One of the most exciting aspects of computers in the classroom is their ability to support other learning. Teachers who use the computer effectively as an educational tool integrate their program goals to use the computer with individual children. Davidson (1989) suggests using computers to support a classroom unit on three levels:

1. Specific software can provide unit-related information. For instance, the program "Dinosaurs" can be in place while developing a theme such as the one in Figure 12-7.

2. Tool software—such as graphics or writing programs—can be used for creating unit-related products. For example, a program such as "Explore-a-Story" can help primary-age children write stories about their own interests and responses to whatever unit is being studied. With a younger group, the teacher could help the class make a group story to send home.

3. Computer-related activities can be designed to support the unit theme. One idea is using the program "Name-Jumping," which asks children to jump around a floor-sized keyboard.

To maximize the benefit computers can give children, teachers should attend to three components: access, availability, and home collaboration. In the classroom, be sure the computer is open regularly, enough so that the issue of crowding or frantic behavior around access is eliminated. Pay close attention to who is using the computer: by the time children are 10, boys spend more time at computers than do girls. Although this difference is not significant at preschool age (Haugland, 1992), teachers need to ensure that girls get access, and that selected software is not catering to males only. Finally, regardless of your family population, be sure to communicate to parents about computer use and learning, and be ready to offer ideas where appropriate about quality software, supervision, and using the Internet.

SUMMARY

Cognition is the ability to learn, remember, and think abstractly. Children's cognitive development is related to learning in all other skill areas. Early childhood educators see cognitive development from an eclectic point of view and draw heavily from the works of Jean Piaget.

Cognitive skills in the early years can be put into several categories. The teacher's role is to understand how cognition develops in children and to put that knowledge to work in the classroom. While creating curriculum, teachers keep certain attitudes and ideas in mind. Then, they set about planning for their programs.

The methods of developing children's cognition skills are as varied and creative as the teachers—and children—can be. By focusing on the class setting, a specific skill, or a theme, teachers help children acquire and use the skills of thinking to understand themselves and the world around them.

Ask yourself:

- What perspective do early childhood teachers have on the development of cognition?
- What are nine cognitive skills of the early years?
- What should teachers consider when defining their role in cognitive development?
- How can cognitive curriculum be developed in the class setting?
- What skills could be the focus for curriculum planning?
- What are three themes that encourage the development of cognitive skills?

TECHNOLOGY AND YOUNG CHILDREN'S LEARNING: HOW DOES TECHNOLOGY IN THE EARLY CHILDHOOD CLASSROOM RELATE TO CHILDREN'S LEARNING?

by
Arleen Prairie, M.Ed.

In most early childhood classrooms the computer center is where children freely choose to explore selected children's software. This is a worthwhile activity for children to realize their skills in using software. Yet the possibilities for learning go far beyond the limits of the classroom when teachers use technology to create opportunities to examine and explore ideas, find information, and communicate ideas. Along with the children, teachers can access software programs designed for classroom use, the digital camera and PhotoSuite, the Internet, and e-mail.

Just imagine . . .

With technology, teachers, along with the children, can find more information and view pictures on practically any topic through accessing the Internet: When a small group of children found a strange-looking tiny insect on the classroom wall, the teacher heard the children's attempt to label it. "It's a-a-a ant," "A frog 'cause it has back legs." "I know. It's an *ugly* spider." Mr. Ed had no idea what it was. They put the strange creature in a collection jar for the afternoon. With children excitely looking on, Mr. Ed downloaded photos and a large diagram of an ant, a frog, a spider, and an insect. They compared the pictures and the creature. They discussed the body parts and counted legs. "You found out it was an insect. Let's search the Internet some more."

With technology a group of children can generate ideas and develop plans: While developing the new topic about the study of earthworms, the group listed what they knew about earthworms as the teacher entered them on computer using a computer program. To add to the list, one child announced. "They have eyes." Several children agreed. Others did not. The group posed several questions they could explore to determine whether worms have eyes. This started a lengthy investigation over several days, looking at them through the magnifying glass, looking at diagrams, taking close-up photos and enlarging them using PhotoSuite, and asking the worms if they see their reflection in the mirror they held up to it.

With technology, teachers can communicate the ideas and learning of children with parents: When the children returned from their short trip to visit "their class tree" in December, Renee was particularly concerned about what she called "our dead tree." When Ms. Jonel, her teacher, sent a photo of the tree from this short trip via e-mail to parents she also suggested that parents and children together look at trees around their house. She added a note to Renee's mother about her daughter's comment. Later that evening, Renee's mother viewed the e-mail

and the photo with her daughter. Together they looked out the window at trees and bushes nearby. Renee noted the difference between the green of the "growing trees" (evergreens) and "dead trees." Outside they found dead leaves and small branches from "dead" and "alive" trees. Back inside, Renee looked at, smelled, and bent the deciduous branch. Later Renee thought aloud, "Maybe it's sleeping in the cold."

"Rather than being merely an enrichment or add-on to the curriculum, technology has taken a central place in early childhood programs" (NAEYC, 2003). Teachers develop the knowledge and skills to use technology as a teaching tool. In this way, they show children how to use both the computer and other learning tools to discover more about their world.

References

National Association for the Education of Young Children. (2003). NAEYC standards for early childhood professional preparation: Initial licensure programs. In M. Hyson (Ed.), *Preparing early childhood professionals: NAEYC's standards for programs* (17–64). Washington DC: Author.

Prairie, A. P. (2005). *Inquiry into math, science, and technology for teaching young children.* Clifton Park, NY: Thomson Delmar Learning.

Arleen Pratt Prairie, professor emeritus, taught Child Development in the City Colleges of Chicago for 25 years. In her teaching she focused on preschool education, infant and toddler care, and brain development in the early years. She developed a series of videos in Infant and Toddler Care, and also worked with the production of the video course, The Developing Child, of which she recently revised 12 of this series. She is co-author of Emotional Connections: How Relationships Guide Early Learning by Perry M. Butterfield, Carole A. Martin, and Arleen Pratt Prairie. And she is author of Inquiry into Math, Science, and Technology for Teaching Young Children. Arleen Prairie earned a B.S. in Child Development from Iowa State University and a M.Ed. in Early Childhood Education from Erikson Institute. She resides in Chicago where she enjoys her two grandchildren and her love of sailing.

For more activities and information, visit our Web site at
http://www.EarlyChildEd.delmar.com

KEY TERMS

cognition

physical knowledge

logical mathematical
  knowledge

inference

social knowledge

rote knowledge

meaningful knowledge

intelligence

transcurricular

dynamic

classification

seriation

software

REVIEW QUESTIONS

1. How are cognition and language related?

2. Match the cognitive skill with the appropriate activity.

    inquiry

    physical world

    social knowledge

    classification

    seriation

    numbers

    symbols

    spatial relationships

    time

    being aware of others

    learning to locate things

    pretending to be a puppet

    asking questions

    sequencing events

    using nesting blocks

    expressing amounts

    sorting objects

    manipulating materials

3. How does the teacher's use of language affect how children develop cognitive skills? Give several examples of what discourages such growth; counter that with how what a teacher says encourages skills.

4. Name three considerations when planning for computer use in a classroom.

5. What is an activity in each environmental area that stimulates cognitive development?

LEARNING ACTIVITIES

1. Look at the program in which you now teach, or recall your own first classrooms. Find at least one example of rote knowledge, social knowledge, and meaningful knowledge.

2. Take one cognitive skill and trace how it could be developed in each curriculum area of the program you used in Activity 1.

3. Observe block play at your school. Make a chart, as in Figure 12-2, that describes the learning processes involved.

4. Make a list of the classroom areas. Beside each, name one activity that would foster cognitive development and one that calls for language skills.

5. One theme often used in early childhood programs is that of the changing season in the fall. How can that theme develop language and thinking skills in preschoolers?

6. Consider the use of a computer in the following classrooms:

toddler child care program

preschool half-day program

kindergarten

after-school primary program

Is a computer appropriate in each of them? Why and how? What guidelines, if any, would be needed in each setting? What would be the adult's role in each?

REFERENCES

Berger, K. S. (2005). *The developing person through the life span* (6th edition). New York: Worth Publishers.

Berk, L. E., & Winsler, A. (1995). *Scaffolding children's learning: Vygotsky and early childhood education.* Washington, DC: NAEYC. (ERIC Document No. ED384443).

Bos, B. (1983). *Before the basics.* Roseville, CA: Turn the Page Press.

Buckleitner, W. (1995, January). Getting started with computers and children. *Exchange.*

Caine, R. N., & Caine, G. (1997). *Unleashing the power of perceptual change: The potential of brain-based teaching.* Alexandria. VA: Association for Supervision and Curriculum Development.

Chen, J.-Q., Isberg, E., & Krechevsky, M. (1998). *Project Spectrum: Early learning activities.* New York: Teachers College Press.

Dahl, K. (1998). "Why cooking in the classroom?" *Young Children* (53) 1.

Davidson, J. I. (1989). *Children and computers together in the early childhood classroom.* Clifton Park, NY: Thomson Delmar Learning.

Diezmann, C., & Yelland, N. J. (2000). *Developing Mathematical Literacy in the Early Childhood Years, in* Yelland, N. J. (Ed.) *Promoting Meaningful Learning.* Washington, DC: NAEYC.

Elkind, D. (1998). Computers for infants and young children. *Child Care Information Exchange* (123), 44–46.

Galinsky, E. (1997, Winter). New research on the brain development of young children. *CAEYC Connections.*

Geist, E. (2001, 4 July). Children are born mathematicians: promoting the construction of early mathematical concepts in children under five. *Young Children* (56).

Gopnik, A., Meltzoff, A. N., & Kuhl, P. K. (1999). *The scientist in the crib.* New York: HarperCollins.

Haugland, S. W. (1997). *The developmental scale for software.* Cape Girardeau, MO: K.I.D.S. & Computers.

Haugland, S. W. (1999, November 6) What role should technology play in young children's learning? *Young Children* (54).

Haugland, S. W. (2000, January 1). Early Childhood Classrooms in the 21st Century: Using Computers to Maximize Learning. *Young Children* (55).

Haugland, S. W., & Shade, D. D. (1990). *Developmental evaluations of software for young children.* Clifton Park, NY: Thomson Delmar Learning.

Hoerr, T. (2004). MI: A way for all students to succeed. In A. Gordon & K. Browne, *Beginnings and Beyond* (6th ed.). Clifton Park, NY: Thomson Delmar Learning.

Jensen, E. (1998). *Teaching with the brain in mind.* Alexandria, VA: Association for Supervision and Curriculum Development.

Klein, A. (1991, July). All about ants: Discovery learning in the primary grades. *Young Children, 46*(5).

Kotoulek, A., in Phipps, P. A. (1998). *Applying brain research to the early childhood classroom.* New York: McGraw-Hill Learning Materials.

Labinowitz, E. (1980). *The Piaget primer: Thinking, learning, teaching.* Menlo Park, CA: Addison-Wesley.

Lally, J. R. (1998, May). Brain research, infant learning, and child care curriculum. *Child Care Information Exchange* (121).

Landry, C. E., & Forman, G. E. (2000 Fall). Research on Early Science Education. *Early Childhood Research & Practice (2),* 2. ED436256 PS02092

Milken E., & Hart, P. D. (1999). Public opinion poll, 1998. Available online at: http://www.milkenexchange.org/publications.

Moore, G. T. (1997, May). A place for block play. *Child Care Information Exchange* (115).

Moran, M. J., & Jarvis, J. (2001, September 5). Helping young children develop higher order thinking. *Young Children* (56).

Murphy, K. K., DePasquale, R., & McNamara, E. (2003). Meaningful connections: Using technology in primary classrooms. *Beyond the Journal: Young Children on the Web.* November, 2003.

NAEYC. (2005). Position statement on technology and young children—ages three through eight. Washington, DC: Author.

National Council of Teachers of Mathematics. (2000). "Principles and Standards for School Mathematics." Reston, VA: NCTM, nctm@nctm.org.

Nelson, K. (1995, July/August). Nurturing Kids: Seven ways of being smart. *Instructor.*

Roberts, J. M., & Spitz, G. (1998). *What does a constructivist class look like?* Unpublished paper developed with the Advisory Board of "Under Construction." Monterey, CA.

Ross, M. E. (2000, March 2). Science their way. *Young Children* (55).

Rushton, S. P. (2001, September 5). Applying brain research to create developmentally appropriate learning environments. *Young Children* (56), 5, September, 2001.

Schiller, P. (1998, May). The thinking brain. *Child Care Information Exchange* (121).

Schiller, P. (2001, July). Brain research and its implications for early childhood programs. *Child Care Information Exchange* (140).

Shore, R. (1997). *Rethinking the brain: New insights in early development.* New York: HarperCollins.

Siegel, D. L. (1999, November). Relationships and the developing mind. *Child Care Information Exchange* (130).

Sylwester, R. (1995). *A celebration of neurons: An educator's guide to the human brain.* Alexandria, VA: Association for Supervision and Curriculum Development.

HELPFUL WEB SITES

Carnegie Corporation of New York: New Directions in Education	http://www.carnegie.org/starting_points/
Center for Media Literacy	http://www.medialit.org
Children and Computers	http://www.childrenandcomputers.com
I Am Your Child Foundation	http://www.iamyourchild.org
K.I.D.S. & Computers, Inc.	http://childrenandcomputers.com
National Association for the Education of Young Children	http://www.naeyc.org
Beyond the Journal (NAEYC)	http://www.journal.naeyc.org.
National Child Care Information Center of the U.S. Dept of Health and Human Services	http://www.nccic.org
SuperKids® Educational Software Review	http://www.superkids.com
Zero to Three	http://www.zerotothree.org

For more activities and information, visit our Web site at http://www.EarlyChildEd.delmar.com

CHAPTER
13

Planning for the Mind:
Language Development

QUESTIONS FOR THOUGHT

How are language and thought connected?

What does linguistic and brain research tell us about children's language?

What are the stages of language development?

What language skills are developed in an early childhood setting?

What is the teacher's role in supporting and extending language development in young children?

How does the teacher introduce and develop reading and writing in the early childhood setting?

What can children's literature offer young children?

485

INTRODUCTION

Alexis: Laleña, will you help me full this pitcher up?

Laleña: No, because my ponytail is keeping me in bothers.

Veronique: Hey, come here! I accidentally dropped a piece of bread and the birds yummed it right up!

Abhi: I know, that's what the tooth fairy did to my tooth.

Marty: I'm going to keep all my baby teeth in a jar and the next time a baby comes along, I'll give him my baby teeth.

Language is the aspect of human behavior that involves the use of sounds in meaningful patterns. This includes the corresponding symbols that are used to form, express, and communicate thoughts and feelings. Any system of signs used for communication is language. For the developing child, language is the ability to express oneself. Language is both **receptive**—listening, understanding, and responding—and **expressive**—articulation, vocabulary, grammar, and graphic language. In other words, as illustrated above, language is meaningful, enjoyable communication.

Language and thought are closely related. Thoughts are produced when people internalize what they experience, and language is how they express or describe it. Language shapes the way thoughts are produced and stored.

"Language is a logical and analytical tool in thinking" (Vygotsky, 1962). Farmers who work the land develop tools to till the soil and language to describe their work. The child who comes to the bazaar with her mother learns the language of bargaining better than one who is in a shopping cart in a grocery store. Tribes who are snowbound develop tools to deal with the ice, and language to describe the many kinds of water conditions. Language and thought are tools to make sense of and interact with the world.

A baby may not start life with language, yet always communicates. Crying, laughing, smiling, and wiggling are body language to express and transmit information. Some communication is nonsymbolic (gestures or pointing), and some is symbolic (words). A child progresses naturally from nonsymbolic communication (pointing at the window to mean *go outside*) to symbolic communication, when the child says "out go" or "me go out." "Spoken language is by far the most common form of symbolic language." (Willis, 1998). The growing child learns to use meaningful language to communicate thoughts; thus language and thought are intertwined.

Language is also related to other areas of development. Children learn to offer an idea as well as a prop to get social play started. They use language in developing emotionally, as they learn to label, describe, question, and demand when they tell each other how they feel and what they want. Anyone who has heard a child talk himself down from a tree knows how language can be a great help in using physical skills.

THE DEVELOPMENT OF LANGUAGE

Language seems to be an innate characteristic of humankind. Wherever people live together, language of some form develops. Languages worldwide vary remarkably in their sounds, words, and grammatical structure. Nonetheless, young children around the world acquire language.

What Research Tells Us

Research into language development and expression reveals several interesting characteristics. First, *the language of children is different from adult language.* Children's language deals with the present and is egocentric, taking into account only the child's own knowledge. There appears to be a lack of awareness on the child's part of language form. Preschool children do show awareness of language structure (for instance, "feets" to mark the plural form) but do not seem to know the parts of speech. In other words, children use language to communicate but seem to have no understanding of language as an entity itself.

Second, *language is not learned simply by imitating adult speech.* Child language is not garbled adult language, but rather is unique to the child's age and linguistic level. Gardner lists language ability as one form of cognition (linguistic intelligence), and most language development theorists agree that there seems to be an innate human tendency toward language (Chomsky, 1993). Children are not just trying to imitate others and making mistakes but are trying to come to terms with language themselves. A child will try out theories about language in attempts to understand its patterns. In language, as in so many areas of cognition, children are involved as active participants in their own learning. The use of speech is not merely imitative but productive and creative.

Third, *experiences help build language.* The more experiences a child has, the more she has to talk about; thus vocabulary is built on first-hand life.

> The size of a child's vocabulary is strongly correlated with how much a child is talked to, cuddled, and interacted with. Recent research show that at 20 months of age, children who have mothers who frequently talk to them average 131 more words than children of less talkative mothers (Willis, 1998).

Fourth, *the language experiences during the first five years are reflected in later literary success.* High quality programs can reduce the degree of delay for high-risk children in communicative skills, and personal interactions in a stimulating environment increase children's communication effectiveness (Isbell & Phillips, 2001). Three dimensions of children's experiences that relate to later literary success (Dickenson & Tabors, 2002) are:

- Exposure to *varied* vocabulary.
- Opportunities to be part of conversations that use **extended discourse**.
- *Home* and *classroom environments* that are cognitively and linguistically stimulating.

The level of language and literary skills that young children acquire provide a strong base for their later years; indeed "the scores that the kindergartners achieved on the measures were highly predictive of their scores on reading comprehension and receptive vocabulary in fourth and in seventh grade" (Dickenson & Tabors, 2002).

Finally, *language development is a process of experience and maturation.*[1] Just as in the development of cognitive skills, there are stages of language growth that follow a specific sequence. There are also variations in timing that are important to remember.

Stages of Language Development

Children follow a six-step sequence in language development. Except in cases of deafness or trauma, this sequence seems *invariable* regardless of what language is being learned.

1. *Infant's Response to Language.* Babies begin by attending to speech, changes in sound, rhythm, and intonation. These are the **precursors** of speech, and young infants are especially sensitive to some sound differences. Infants need to hear speech, and plenty of it, to develop the foundations of sound.

2. *Vocalization.* By three to four months of age, infants begin cooing and babbling. Babbling increases with age and seems to peak around 9 to 12 months. This is a matter of physical maturation, not just experience; children who are deaf or hearing impaired do it at the same time as those whose hearing is normal. Furthermore, similar vocalization patterns are seen among different languages.

3. *Word Development.* The child must first separate the noises heard into speech and nonspeech. The speech noises must be further separated into words and the sounds that form them. The growing infant starts to shift from practice to playing with sounds. The end result is planned, controlled speech.

   Children begin playing with sounds around 10 to 15 months of age. From this point, the development of speech is determined as much by control of motor movements as by the ability to match sounds with objects.

   Most children can understand and respond to a number of words before they can produce any. Their first words include names of objects and events in their world (people, food, toys, animals). Then the child

Video VIEW Point 13-1

"A toddler who is developing normally will have certain language skills."

COMPETENCY: Communication Development

AGE GROUP: Infants and Toddlers

CRITICAL THINKING QUESTIONS:

1. What might be effective tools for teaching children new words?

2. How can a teacher reinforce the meanings of words?

---

 1 Teachers must be aware of the children they teach and alert for a diversity of language issues and skills, particularly in the area of bilingualism, speech or language disorders, and dialects (see later in this chapter).

begins to overextend words, perhaps using "doggy" to refer to all animals. Finally, single words can be used as sentences: "Bye-bye" can refer to someone leaving, a meal the child thinks is finished, the child's going away, a door closing.

4. *Sentences.* Children's sentences usually begin with two words, describing an action ("Me go"), a possession ("My ball"), or a location ("Baby outside"). These sentences get expanded by adding adjectives ("My big ball"), changing the verb tense ("Me jumped down"), or using negatives ("No go outside"). Children learn grammar not by being taught the rules, but as they listen to others' speech and put together the regularities they hear.

Child language, though not identical to that of adults, does draw on language heard to build a language base. Children incorporate and imitate what they hear to refine their own language structures.

5. *Elaboration.* Vocabulary begins to increase at an amazing rate. Sentences get longer, and communication begins to work into social interaction. In the hospital corner of a nursery school, this conversation takes place:

Chip: I'm a nurse.

Brooke: I'm going to try to get some patients for you.

Megan: Do I need an operation?

Chip: Yeah, if you don't want to be sick anymore.

6. *Graphic Representation.* By late preschool and kindergarten, reading and writing emerge as children become aware of language as an entity itself and of the written word as a way of documenting what is spoken. Awareness of print and emerging literacy are the outgrowth of this last stage of development.

In fact, alphabet knowledge and **phonemic awareness** are predictors of early reading success (Wasik, 2001). Children who learn to read well and most easily in first grade are those with prior knowledge of the alphabet and the understanding of the sounds that letters represent. Within the guidelines of developmentally appropriate practice, the teaching focus must be on creating meaningful experiences, and will be addressed in the section on "Early Literacy," which begins on page 505.

As children create a linguistic representation of their cognitive understanding, they see

Research tells us that language experiences during preschool and kindergarten are reflected in later literacy success.

the potential of language reading and writing as a tool for communicating. Known as "literate thinking," this is the hallmark of the last early childhood developmental stage in language development (Salyer, 2000). See the sections on "Reading and Writing," and "Children's literature," which address the issue of language and literacy. Figure 13-1 is a sample of a child's developing language skills.

Bilingualism

In early childhood terms, **bilingualism** (or multilingualism) is the ability of a person to communicate in a language other than their native language with a degree of fluency.

> There is not just one dimension of language. We can examine people's proficiency in two languages in their *listening (understanding), speaking, reading and writing* skills. . . . Calling someone *bilingual* is therefore an *umbrella term*. Underneath the umbrella rest many different skill levels in two languages. Being bilingual is not just about proficiency in two languages. There is a *difference* between *ability and use* of language. . . . In practice, a person may be bilingual, although ability in one language is lacking (but improving steadily). (Baker, 2004)

A bilingual child must learn to comprehend and produce aspects of each language and to develop two systems of communication. This is a "lengthy and complicated process of getting used to a new culture and a new language" before feeling comfortable enough to use it in a classroom (Tabors, 1998).

Second-language learning occurs in two general ways. **Simultaneous acquisition** happens if a child is exposed to two languages from birth. These bilingual children tend to lag behind in vocabulary development in the early years, often mixing sounds or words. By four or five years, however, most children have separated the languages successfully.

The second pattern is known as **successive acquisition.** This occurs as a child with one language now enters the world of a second language, as when children with one home language enter a school that uses another language. A common pattern among immigrants and many children in the United States, this learning seems to favor younger children in their accent and grammar, but there is no evidence that younger children are any more successful with vocabulary and syntax.

With more bilingual/bicultural children in early childhood classrooms, it helps to understand how children learn a second language and

Stage	Age (Approx.)	Sample
1. Response	Zero–six months	Smiles, gazes when hearing voices
2. Vocalization	Six–10 months	Babbles all types of sounds, creating babble-sentences Uses vocal signals other than crying to get help
3. Word Development	10–18 months	Mama, Dada, Doggie Bye-bye, No-no
4. Sentences	18 months–three years	Me want chok-quit (I want chocolate) She goed in the gark (She went in the dark)
5. Elaboration	Three to five or six years	You're my best Mommy, you can hold my turtle at bet-bis (breakfast) (Cough) That was just a sneeze in my mouth
6. Graphic Representation	Five plus to eight years	

FIGURE 13-1 Children's language skills develop with both age and experience.

Myths	Truths
Children who are exposed to more than one language get confused.	Young children have the brain capacity and the neural flexibility for learning two or more languages without becoming confused.
Bilingual children are slower than monolingual children in developing speech.	There is no evidence regarding a later age in developing speech for bilingual children.
Mixing languages or "code switching" is a sign of the child being confused.	"Code switching" is a normal part of bilingual language development and a common communication strategy for bilingual children and adults.
Home language interferes with children's ability to learn English.	Home language does *not* interfere with the ability to learn English. In fact, a strong foundation in the home language positively impacts the learning of a second language.
Children can learn a second language very quickly.	It takes *two* years for children to incorporate a conversational level in a second language, and *five to seven* years to achieve an academic level (e.g., school-related skills, language of text).

FIGURE 13-2 Myths and truths related to bilingualism. (Developed by the Early Childhood Language Development Institute, a project of San Mateo County Office of Education, Redwood City, California. June 2005. Reprinted by permission of the author, Soodie Ansari.)

how to apply this research in practical ways. Since language is key to every child's success, teachers must understand the myths and truths relating to bilingualism (Figure 13-2). Research (Diaz-Soto, 1991; Garcia, 1986; Chang-Chu, 1983) shows that the process of learning a second language in childhood depends, in part, on the individual child. Cognitive, social, and linguistic skills are all at work in acquiring a second language. Moreover, the child's culture, unique temperament, and learning style play a part as well. For instance, Tjarko is of Swiss-German ancestry, so is it any wonder he pronounces an English "v" like an "f," as in "Can I *haff* one of those?" Sachiko, who has moved from Japan within the year, complains, "My *neck* hurts when I drink," and disagrees that it is a sore throat, since "neck" is the word she knows.

First- and second-language acquisition are similar in many ways. Language acquisition is a natural process. However, children need to be exposed to language in meaningful ways. A particular important point for all early educators to understand is the effect of a new language on a child in the classroom and at home. First, children of linguistically and culturally diverse backgrounds may face isolation at school. In an English-speaking school, for instance, the child who does not yet understand or speak English may find it difficult to interact appropriately with children and teachers. Lack of a mutual language can result in the child being treated as nearly invisible, or like a baby, by other children, or as less intelligent or able by teachers.

They are caught in what I call the double-bind of second-language learning: To learn a new language, you have to be socially accepted by those who speak the language; but to be socially accepted, you have to be able to speak the new language. (Tabors, 1998)

Moreover, children acquiring language in an English-dominant classroom often begin to isolate themselves from their families. They may refuse to use their home language anymore, as it is difficult to use both, and English may have greater status in the children's eyes. Families sometimes promote this, as they wish their children to learn English. However, if they themselves do not speak English, they become unable to communicate at length with their children. The lack of a mutual language then grows at home, creating problems of family cohesiveness and harmony.

Teachers need guidance in educating second-language learners. Support for second-language acquisition includes environmental organization, language techniques, classroom activities, and family contact (see Figure 13-3). The following recommendations serve as guidelines for teachers of children who are acquiring a second language:

1. *Understand how children learn a second language.* There is a developmental sequence of second-language acquisition. First, children may continue to speak their home language with both those who speak it and those that do not. Next, children begin to

Checklist for Language-Friendly Classroom Practices

1. Help children make sense of language.
   ___ What is their "Language Dictionary"?
   ___ What can their family experts tell you?

2. Provide comprehensible input.
   ___ What information talk can you provide in the moment?
   ___ What multisensory experiences can you plan?

3. Be prepared for the "silent period."
   ___ How do they communicate when they aren't speaking?
   ___ What sign of progress and learning do you see?
   ___ In what ways is the child able to communicate?

4. Be sensitive to the affective filter.
   ___ How can you tell when the child is in emotional discomfort?
   ___ When do you invite participation?

5. Create a connection.
   ___ What is your morning greeting?
   ___ What is the predictable schedule?
   ___ When does the child need your support?

6. Build a community of acceptance.
   ___ Does the environment reflect the child's life?
   ___ How is the child's home language validated?
   ___ Have you helped the child find buddies?
   ___ How have you worked with the family?

7. Examine teacher behaviors.
   ___ When/how are teachers helpful and encouraging?
   ___ When/how have teachers ignored or been unhelpful?

FIGURE 13-3 A checklist for teachers to examine their own daily practices with children who are acquiring a second language (with help from Soodie Ansari, 2005).

Providing books that are in tune with all children's cultures and language backgrounds expands everyone's world.

understand that others do not understand their language and give up using it, substituting nonverbal behavior that may appear less mature. Allowing them to watch and listen and also interpreting and inviting children into play will help. Third, children begin to break out of the nonverbal period with a combination of telegraphic and formulaic language. One-word phrases such as "no, yes, mine, hey" all telegraph meaning, as do catch-words such as "ok, lookit, I dunno" that are used as formulas for communicating. Finally, productive use of the new language appears.

She describes an activity ("I do an ice cream"), an idea ("I got a big"), or a need ("I want a play dough"). Because she is no longer using memorized phrases, it may seem that her language ability has actually decreased because there will be many more mistakes. (Tabors, 1998)

The perceptive teacher will see that it is a positive step in a cumulative process.

2. *Make a plan for the use of the two languages.* Try to have bilingual staff, or at least one teacher who specializes in each language. The children are then exposed to models in both the home language and English. Many programs in communities where the children and educators come from the same first-language background use the children's home language while learning English in a naturalistic setting. They may start a year with the language of the children and gradually use more English until the languages are equal. Our Code of Ethics reminds us to "provide all children with experiences in a language that they know, as well as support children in maintaining the use of their home language and in learning English" (see Appendix A, 1.11).

3. *Accept individual differences.* Take note of both the style and the time frame of language learning. Children bring a range of individual differences to learning a second language. Motivation to learn, exposure to the dominant language, the age of the child in relationship to the group, and temperament can all affect language acquisition.

Don't insist that a child speak, but do invite and try to include the child in classroom activities. Assume developmental equivalence: that is, that the children, although different, are normal. For example, Maria Elena just will not come and sit at group time. Allow her to watch from a distance and believe that she is learning, rather than be worried or irritated that she isn't with the group yet.

4. *Support children's attempts to communicate.* Encouraging children's communication bids rather than correcting them will help children try to learn. Recognize developmentally equivalent patterns. For instance, Kidah may not say the word "car" but can show it to you when you ask. Receptive language precedes expressive language.

5. *Maintain an additive philosophy.* Recognize that children are acquiring more and new language skills, not simply replacing their primary linguistic skills. Asking Giau and his family about their words, foods, and customs allows teachers to use a style and content that are familiar to the Vietnamese, thus smoothing the transition and adding onto an already rich base of knowledge.

6. *Provide a stimulating, active, and diverse environment.* Give many opportunities for language in meaningful social interactions and responsive experiences with all children.

> Two aspects of classroom organization can help second-language-learning children. The first is to have a set routine for activities so that children can catch on and get into the flow of events. . . . The second is to provide safe havens in the classroom [so that] children can spend some time away from the communicatively demanding activities and develop competency in other skill areas besides language. (Tabors, 1998)

> Make use of story time, increasing the amount of time when you tell or read aloud stories; the predictable plot and repetitive language help children follow along and understand. Choose chants, finger play, and songs for the same reasons. Allow children to "assume a new identity—second language learners are often willing to speak when they can use another identity (puppets, masks, costumes)". (Chesler, 2002)

7. *Use informal observations to guide the planning of activities.* Provide spontaneous interactions for speakers of other languages. Teachers will need to expand the types of observations used for assessment to see a child's physical, cognitive, or emotional abilities in language-free situations. Additionally, a home visit observation may help to learn how a child is doing in first-language development. Also, only by actively watching will a teacher find special moments in a classroom to help a child be accepted and join in. Seeing a group of girls building a zoo, a teacher gives a basket of wild animals to Midori. Walking with her to the block corner, she offers to stock the zoo and then helps all the girls make animal signs in Japanese and English. Thus does Midori enter the play in a positive and strong way.

8. *Find out about the family.* Establish ties between home and school. "School learning is most likely to occur when family values reinforce school expectations" (Bowman, 1989). Parents and teachers do not have to do the same things, but they must have a mutual understanding and respect for each other and goals for children. For example, Honwyma's parents and his teacher talk together about what of the Hopi language and culture can be brought into the classroom. Where there are differences between the Hopi patterns and those of the school, teachers will try to accommodate. "We shall make every effort to communicate with all families in a language they understand" (see Appendix A, Code of Ethics, p. 627).

9. *Provide an accepting classroom climate.* It must value culturally and linguistically diverse young children. Teachers must come to grips with their own cultural ethnocentricity and learn about the languages, dialects, and cultures beyond their own. It is critical to value all ways of achieving developmental milestones, not just those of the teacher's culture or educational experience.

The challenge to young children and their teachers is enormous. With informed, open-minded teaching, children can learn a second language without undue stress and alienation. As of this date we can conclude that:

- Children can and do learn two languages at an early age, though the process and time vary with the individual child.
- Two languages can be learned at the same time in a parallel manner. The depth of knowledge of one language may be different from that of the other, or the two may develop equally.

- The acquisition of languages may mean a "mixing" of the two, as heard in children's speech when they use words or a sentence structure of both languages.

- Learning two languages does not hurt the acquisition of either language in the long run.

Dialect Differences. Teachers may encounter differences in the way words are pronounced or grammar is used, even among English-speaking children. These differences reflect a **dialect**, or variation of speech patterns within a language. When we travel to New York, for example, our ear is attuned to the unique pronunciation of "goyl" (girl), and when we move north we hear "habah" (harbor). Southern speakers are easy to identify with elongated vowel sounds such as "Haiiiii, yaaw'll!" In addition to regional dialects, there are also social dialects that are shared by people of the same cultural group or social class. Inner-city children may express their enthusiasm for reading with a statement such as "I been done knowed how to read!"

Italian, Russian, and numerous other languages have regional and social dialects. Linguists, the scholars who study languages, argue that there is no such thing as a good or a bad language. Each language and dialect is a legitimate system of speech rules that governs communication in that language. Some dialects, however, are not viewed favorably within the larger society and often carry a social or economic stigma. In the United States the dialect that has received the most attention and controversy is **Ebonics**, or black English.

The unique linguistic characteristics of African American children have been studied for decades (Thomas, 1983). The name "Ebonics" is made up of the words ebony and phonics. "It has a West African base with English vocabulary superimposed on top," says Hoover (1997). "It's based on the grammar of West African languages." Elementary schools have traditionally grappled with the dual missions of doing everything within their power to help all students succeed and, at the same time, respect the cultural and linguistic backgrounds of everyone. One way to respond to this is to improve the instructional strategies for those whose linguistic background is not standard English.

The debate over the significance of Ebonics was thrust into the public spotlight in 1997 when the Oakland, California, school district voted to view Ebonics as a separate language and adopt it to help improve student learning. Critics cite educators who claim the dialect will interfere with reading achievement, whereas supporters insist that the real barrier to academic success is teachers' low expectations of dialect speakers. The National Head Start Association has spoken out against Ebonics, emphasizing that all children must be taught to use language in ways to increase their power, not to segregate.

Often cited in the argument is the concern for how nonstandard speakers will fare in our future high-tech society. Negative views of black English or any nonstandard dialect held by prospective employers have been documented (Atkins, 1993) and are of concern to parents who want better opportunities for their children. Certainly there is much in our early childhood education history and in our current work on developmentally appropriate practices that points in the direction of respecting and welcoming children's individual dialects while also addressing any linguistic differences that limit children. As the controversies over the role of dialect in education wax and wane, the early childhood educator would be prudent to develop the goal of "communicative competence" (Cazden, 1996) or "language power" (Saxton, 1998) for all students. This goal would strive to empower each child to be a comfortable and capable speaker in any situation demanding "standard" English or the language of his own "speech community."

LANGUAGE SKILLS IN EARLY CHILDHOOD

Teachers translate language development theory into practice as they work with children. Language skills in the early childhood setting include articulation, receptive language, expressive language, graphic language, and enjoyment. Children's conversations, their ways of talking, some children's lack of expressive language, and their ways of asking questions all offer glimpses into children's language skills.

Articulation

Articulation is how children actually say the sounds and words. Children's ability to produce sound is a critical link in their connecting the sounds to form speech. Mispronunciation is common and normal, especially in children under five years of age. The preschool teacher can expect to hear "Thally" for Sally, "wope" for rope, and "buh-sketty" for spaghetti. Children who repeat sounds, syllables, or words in preschool are not stutterers; 85% of two- to six-year-olds hesitate and repeat talking. As children talk, teachers listen for their ability to hear and reproduce sounds in daily conversation. Can they hear and produce sounds that differ widely, such as "sit" and "blocks"? Can they produce sounds that differ in small ways, such as in "man" and "mat"?

How adults respond to *dysfluencies* can help a child through this normal stage of language development. Chesler (2002) suggests:

- Pay attention to the child when she talks to you. Don't rush her.
- Don't demand speech when a child is upset or feels stressed.
- Don't put children on exhibition by asking them to recite or talk when they don't want to.
- Avoid interrupting a child when she is talking; avoid completing a sentence for her.
- Statements like "slow down" or "think before you talk" draw attention to his speech and usually cues the child that there is something wrong with the way he talks.
- Do make an example of your speech by talking slowly, smoothly, and distinctly.

Receptive Language

Receptive language is what children acquire when they learn to listen and understand. It is what they hear. With this skill children are able to understand directions, to answer a question, and to follow a sequence of events. They can understand relationships and begin to predict the outcome of their behavior and that of others. They develop some mental pictures as they listen.

Video VIEW PoinT 13-2

"Listening is not simply a generalized skill but is a group of skills that are closely related."

COMPETENCY: Communication Development

AGE GROUP: School Age

CRITICAL THINKING QUESTIONS:

1. What behaviors can you observe that tell you if children are listening, not hearing, listening but not understanding, or listening but choosing not to respond?

2. How can children's use of symbols help them develop listening skills?

Children begin early and can become experts in reacting to words, voice, emphasis, and inflection. How many times does the child understand by the way the words are spoken?

"You finally *finished* your lunch." (Hooray for you!)

"You *finally* finished your lunch?" (You slowpoke.)

Children learn to listen for enjoyment, for the way the wind sounds in the trees, the rhythm of storytelling, or the sound of the car as it brings Mom or Dad home.

Expressive Language

Expressive language in the early years means the process and steps involved in expressing ideas, feelings, and intentions in language. This includes words, grammar, and elaboration.

Words

Expressive language is the spoken word. Children's first words are of what is most important to them (Mama, Da-Da). Adults help children extend their knowledge and vocabulary by using the names of objects and words of action (walk, run, jump) and feelings (happy, sad, mad). By describing objects in greater and greater detail, teachers give children new words that increase their skills. Children are then ready to learn that some words have more than one meaning (the word "orange," for example, is both a color and a fruit) and that different words can have the same meaning (such as "ship" and "boat" as similar objects, or "muñeca" and "doll" as the same word in different languages).

Grammar

Basic grammatical structure is learned as children generalize what they hear. They listen to adult speech patterns and use these patterns to organize their own language. It helps to hear simple sentences at a young age, with the words in the correct order. Next, children can grasp past tense as well as present, plural nouns along with the singular. Finally, the use of more complex structures is understood (prepositions, comparatives, various conjugations of verbs).

Elaboration of Language

Elaboration of language takes many, many forms. It is the act of expanding the language. Through description, narration, explanation, and communication, adults elaborate their own speech to encourage children to do the same. For instance, communication for children includes talking to oneself and others. When a teacher verbalizes a process aloud, children see how language helps them work through a problem. ("I am trying to get the plant out of its pot, but when I turn it upside-down, it doesn't fall out by itself. Now I'll use this trowel to loosen the dirt from the sides of the pot, and hope that helps.") Communicating with others involves giving and following directions. ("It's time to make a choice for cleanup time. You find something to do and I'll watch you.") It means asking and answering questions. ("How do you feel when she says she won't play with you? What can you say? What can you do?") Sticking to the subject keeps communication flowing. ("I know you want to play kickball, but first let's solve this problem between you and Conor about the wagon.") Children are encouraged to communicate verbally with others as they see teachers using speech to get involved in play themselves. ("What a great house you have built. How do you get inside? Do you need any dishes?")

Graphic Language

"Talk written down" is the essence of graphic language. The child now learns that there is a way to record, copy, and send to another person one's thoughts. Learning to put language into a symbolic form is the gist of the reading and writing process. Children learn about print when they are read to regularly, when they see adults reading and writing, and when they are surrounded with a print-rich environment. Because words and letters are simply "lines and dots and scribbles" to young children, the teacher and parent must demonstrate how meaningful graphic language can be. Moreover, the translation of talk into print is a cognitive task (that of symbols, see previous section), so children's intellectual development as well as their language abilities are at play when learning about the printed word.

Enjoyment

To encourage language is to promote enjoyment in using it. Teachers converse with children, parents, and other adults, modeling for children how useful and fun language can be. Knowing the power and pleasures of language gives children the motivation for the harder work of learning to read and write. In fact, creating readers can be an enjoyable process for children if teachers:

- Surround themselves with books and other reading materials.
- Set up inviting library learning centers.
- Establish regular visits to the local library.
- Encourage children to share favorite books.
- Take time for conversations (Curry-Rodd, 1999).

Children learn to enjoy language by participating in group discussion and being encouraged to ask questions. Reading and listening to stories and poems every day is an essential part of any program. The program should also include children's literature and stories children dictate or write themselves.

Word play and rhyming arc fun as well as educational. Group language games are useful, such as asking the question "Did you ever see a bat with a hat? a bun having fun? a bee with . . . ?" and letting the children add the rest. Begin a song, for instance, "Do You Know the Muffin Man?," and add the children's names. Whatever contributes to the enjoyment of language supports its growth, from varying voice and tone to fit the situation (in storytelling, dramatic play, and ordinary activity periods) to spontaneous rhyming songs.

THE TEACHER'S ROLE

Considerations

When considering how to work with young children in language development, teachers should keep several things in mind:

- *Children need an "envelope of language."* "Babies already read; think about how they read you,"

Teachers and children can share intimate moments when they enjoy using language together.

says Miller (2001). "Before we talk about a print-rich environment we must first ensure a language-rich environment. Magda Gerber encourages people to be a play-by-play announcer, providing language labels for everything the child does and touches." When you expose children to quality literature everyday, be sure there is an emotional response to reading that conveys:

- It is a warm and pleasant thing to do.
- They are learning how books work.
- They are gaining vocabulary and learning to focus their attention (Miller, 2001).

- *Children must use language to learn it.* Adults often spend much of their time with children talking—to, at, for, or about them. Yet, to learn language, children must be doing the talking. Children need time, a place, and the support for practicing language.

  Children's conversations with each other are important in learning the basics of how to take turns and keep to one topic and of saying what they mean, getting their ideas and themselves heard and accepted. Time with peers and adults, in both structured (group times) and nonstructured (free play) situations, allows children to practice and refine language skills. Selman (2001) describes one two-year-old class that has "talk time" at each snack table.

  "Our talk time program has three governing rules:

  1. Only one person at a time may speak.

  2. Everyone gets a turn to choose a subject.

Children can use storytime as "talk time" as well as for engaged listening.

3. We don't leave the talk time table until everyone has had a turn and the activity is officially over."

"Talk time" cannot be used to correct children's language or ideas and yet is a useful way to help delayed talkers. A number of themes developed in a toddler class that the children can choose: "Mommy," "Doing things all by myself," "Nonsense talk." Imagine the themes a five-year-old class might have!

- *The most verbal children tend to monopolize language interactions.* Research shows that teachers interact verbally with the children who are most skilled verbally. Seek out and support language development in those with fewer skills, generally by drawing them out individually through (1) reading the unspoken (body) language that communicates their ideas, needs, and feelings and (2) helping them express verbally those ideas, needs, and feelings.

- *Adults should know the individual child.* Consistency in adult–child relationships may be as important for language as for effective development during the early years. If so, teachers must have a meaningful relationship with each child. This includes knowing the parents and how they communicate with their child.

- *Home languages are to be invited into the classroom.* "The explanations for home language are severalfold," writes Chang (1993). "First, when centers do not use the home language, they reinforce existing societal messages that a child's language is lower in status than the dominant language, English. . . . Language and culture are closely related since the language of an ethnic group is usually the vehicle through which the community transmits to its young its customs and beliefs. . . . The development of a child's primary language skills is integral to helping a child succeed academically and to eventually develop skills in English."

- *Dialect differences expand your speech community.* Dialects are as much a part of children's culture and identity as is their home language. Smitherman (1977) note:

  > Black Language is Euro-American speech with an Afro-American meaning, nuance, and gesture. . . . The ability to speak Black English often serves a crucial source of connection to the community and the inability to speak in the vernacular can be interpreted as a sign that an individual has rejected his or her African American identity.

Providers may mistakenly see children speaking their own dialect as less capable, or even delayed. Yet we need to not make the assumption that different means "less than."

- *Some children may have speech and language disorders.* Early detection of and intervention for speech and language disorders is possible without the teacher being a speech therapist. With a basic knowledge of typical speech development and signposts of speech and language problems, the perceptive teacher can alert families and recommend specialist assessment and input. Once a child with a disability comes into a program with specific learning objectives, the staff needs to plan how to address those needs in the curriculum and with the children. "For children with learning challenges, adult communicative input can often make or break the child's chances for optimizing learning potential" (Klein, Cook, & Richardson-Gibbs, 2001). They suggest the following strategies:

- Follow the child's lead.
- Use progressive matching (also known as expansion: modeling language just slightly more complex than the child's current capability).
- Use labels and specific descriptors.
- Repeat key words and phrases.
- Use appropriate pacing.

- Give children ample time to respond.
- Create the need to communicate.

    See Figure 13-4 for an example of how this can happen.

- *The language of the teacher influences the classroom.* What teachers say—and how they say it—is important. Moreover, it is often what they do not say that communicates the most to children in their struggle to gain mastery of the language. Teachers provide a rich environment and a high quality of interaction with the child that encourages all language skills.

To articulate means to speak distinctly and with moderate speed. Teachers reinforce clear speech by giving frequent opportunities for children to practice speech. They alter their way of speaking when addressing children under three. This "parentese" includes a higher pitch, short utterances, and repeating the child's language attempts. The effects of this are debated, but "a number of [its] features are likely to facilitate language learning" (Baron, 1989).

Receptive language can be developed by using the six strategies outlined in Figure 13-5.

Expressive language is encouraged when teachers focus on the spoken word. They use short, concise sentences to frame or highlight

Curriculum Planning for Language Development: The Teacher Talks

Description

- Use nouns for people, places, events, "We are going to visit Grandma now. That means we need to get dressed and walk to her apartment."

- Use modifiers: "That is your uncle's truck outside" or "Can you find your sister's teddy bear?"

- Use more relational terms: "You are taller than the chair; the wagon is wider than the bed."

- Try more differentiated words to express differences: Instead of just "big/little," try "fat/thin" and "tall/short."

Narration

- Describe simple relationships of time: "Yesterday you stayed home. Today is a school day. Tomorrow is Saturday, a stay-home day."

- Clarify a sequence of events: "When you come to school, first you put your things in your cubby, then you make an inside choice."

- Use words to describe repetition, continuation, and completion: "We are going to the store again, to buy food for dinner" or "I see that you and Juana are still playing together today" or "You finished building the box last time; now you are ready to paint it."

Explanation

- Point out similarities and differences: "Both Cathi and I have brown hair, but what is different about us? Yes, she has on shorts and I am wearing overalls."

- Try classifying what you see as well as asking children to do so: "I notice that all these shells have ridges on the outside; what do you see that is different about them?"

FIGURE 13-4 Several aspects of language development affect how teachers speak to children in the early years.

Helping Children with Receptive Language

1. *Give clear directions.* "Please go and sit on the rug next to the chairs," instead of "Go sit over there."

2. *Let children ask questions.* Give them acceptable answers. For example, repeat a phrase from the child's last sentence that asks the child to try again: "You want what?" or "You ate what?" Or cast the question back to a child by changing the phrase "Where did you put it?" into "You put it where?"

3. *Give instructions in a sequence.* "Put your lunch on your desk, then wash your hands. Then you are ready to go to lunch." It often helps to ask the children what they think they are to do: "How do you get ready for lunch? What comes first? Next?"

4. *Try to understand what the child means, regardless of the actual language.* Look for the purpose and intent beyond what the child may have said. This is particularly important with toddlers, non-English speakers, and newcomers.

5. *Ask children to state their thoughts out loud.* "Tell me what you think is going to happen to the eggs in the incubator. Why do you think some might hatch and some might not?"

6. *Use literature, poetry, and your own descriptions.* Give children an idea of how words can be used to paint verbal and mental pictures. Ask questions about children's own images and dreams. To older children read aloud from books without pictures.

FIGURE 13-5 Teachers do more than insist "Listen to me" to encourage receptive language.

a word. If a child says, "Look at that!", teachers reply, "That's a butterfly," or "I see; do you think it's a butterfly or a bee?"

One way children gain a greater awareness of themselves is by describing their own actions in words. To make sure that all children experience the art of conversation, be sure to provide plenty of opportunities for them to converse with adults as well as peers to help them learn the reciprocal nature of communication. Ask them to say what they are doing. Make a statement describing the child's behavior or actions. This is particularly helpful when dealing with feelings, such as the statement "It looks as if you are feeling angry" (when confronted with a frown and clenched fists).

Teachers help children by directing their attention to objects, events, and relationships.

Michelle: I have something to show you.

Teacher: Can you give us some clues?

Michelle: It's not a record and it's not a book, and you can't play with it.

Teacher: Can you hold it in your hand?

Michelle: No, silly, it's a kiss!

Give children opportunities to describe what they are going to do and what they have done. Through this, teachers discover what is meaningful to children and what they remember, and it gives them the chance to plan and review. When the class celebrates a birthday, children will want to discuss when their birthday is, what they will do, or how they feel. The answers may range from "July thirty-last"

to "We're going to the moon" to "On my birthday my heart is filling me with lightning." Figures 13-4 and 13-5 demonstrate the adept teacher at work on language development.

Developing communication skills with others is particularly important for children in the early years. Encouraging active listening and repeating one child's words to another ("Bahrain, did you hear what Joanna said about the sandtruck?") give children support. Expressing thoughts and feelings in words offers a model. By telling a child what works for you ("I like it when you listen to my words"), a teacher provides a good example of how to communicate. Helping children stick to the subject shows that there is a topic at hand: "Stevie, now we're talking about our field trip to the track. You can tell us about your new dog next."

Graphic language can be developed in hundreds of ways. What is now called "emergent, or early literacy" is a broad view of reading and writing as developing, or emerging, out of language development as a whole. Rather than a simple set of skills, early literacy involves a set of attitudes, behaviors, and understandings related to written language. Courses such as the National Head Start Association's "Heads Up! Reading" provide professional training in leading children through the early steps to reading. Programs such as "Raising a Reader" and other take-home book bag preliteracy programs help children and families access books in an enjoyable, consistent way. Look in "Helpful Web Sites" for several resources.

What do YOU Think?

What is your home language? What do you remember of your first schooling experiences and language? Was it easy to speak up? How did you interact with your teacher and with other children when using language? What can you remember about learning to read? Was it easy or difficult? Can you recall reading aloud to others? How do these memories inform your educational practices?

Teachers use their own language as a way to direct children in a variety of symbol-using activities, such as making grocery lists for a dramatic play corner or the zoo signs in the previous example of bilingual education. "Remember that reading is more than sounding out and identifying words, it is about communicating ideas, images, and feelings," asserts Escamilla-Vestal (2002).

All learning happens in the context of meaningful relationships. As early childhood educators we want to model for children how we use reading and writing to communicate our feelings and ideas to others. We want to model how reading and writing can build bridges between cultures; for example, having books in the classroom/family child care home which depict individuals from different cultures involved in everyday activities, or posting "Hello" and "Welcome" signs in different languages.

Curriculum Planning for Language Development

Teachers who plan curriculum for language skills, just as for cognitive development, focus on the class setting, specific skills, and themes. They organize the environment and activities to help children acquire linguistic skills of their own (NAEYC, 2005).

In the Environment

Indoors. Teachers arrange space so that children will practice speaking and listening and, in programs for older children, reading and writing.

Indoor areas can be arranged to enhance language development as follows:

Art
- Have signs and pictures that show where things are kept.
- Ask children to describe the materials they use.

Blocks
- Ask children to give each other directions for where blocks go and what they are used for.
- Label block shelves with shapes and words.
- Sketch children's structures and then write their verbal descriptions.

Cooking
- Label utensils.
- Describe actions (pour, measure, stir).
- Use recipe cards with both pictures and words.

Discovery/Science
- Label all materials.
- Ask questions about what is displayed.
- Encourage children's displays, with their dictated words nearby.
- Graph growth and changes of plants, animals, children, and experiments.

Dramatic Play
- Provide a variety of equipment for a diversity of gender play, including male and female clothes.
- Set up spaces in addition to a "house/kitchen," such as a "reader's theater" in which children choose a story to act out and eventually write their own scripts.
- Offer cooking and eating utensils, objects, and tools that reflect cultural and linguistic diversity,

Grouptimes are language-intensive activities that call for teachers to provide material and experiences in everyone's home language.

such as a tortilla press and molcajete in the kitchen and different kinds of combs and brushes for the dolls, beginning with the cultures of the children in your program and then adding other groups.

- Have plenty of child-sized mirrors.

Language/Library

- Label the bookshelf, cassette player, and computer in children's languages.
- Help children make their own books that involve description (My family is . . .), narration (It is winter when . . .), and recall (Yesterday I . . .).
- Have children "write" notes, lists, or letters to one another, the teachers, and their families.
- Develop a writing center with a typewriter, office supplies, etc. (see Figure 13-14)

Manipulatives

- Recognize this area as a place for self-communication, as children talk and sing to themselves while they work.
- Explain similarities and differences of materials and structures.

Outdoors. Outdoors, motor skills can be described and pointed out by teachers and children, as both use words of action and of feeling. For example, what actions does it take to get a wagon up the hill? How does a child's face feel when swinging up high? How do people sit? move? carry things?

Routines, Transitions, and Groups

Transitions and routines are more manageable if the children understand what is happening and exactly what they are to do. Teacher language helps talk children through the process so that they can internalize what they are asked to do. Arrival is an easy time to reinforce name recognition. Mark cubbies with names and photos:

> Each day, encourage children to find their own cubby. Point out their printed name. It is also helpful to point out other children's names and to notice the differences. "Oh look, here's Robert's name. His starts with an R just like yours. And here is Ann's. Her name starts with an A. Her name is very short." (Klein, Cook, & Richardson-Gibbs, 2001)

Children's belongings should also be labeled. These steps take a little time to make, but can increase children's awareness of print.

A chart that shows in pictures and written language the steps children are to take from lunch to nap is invaluable, and children will refer to it daily. "Pillow Talk" is another ritual one Head Start class began to ensure that children

---

Environmental Elements that Promote Acceptance

Classroom posters, signs, bulletin boards

a. Hello, Buenos Dias, Ciao, Jambo . . . in as many languages as you have or want to learn.

Children as ambassadors

a. Every new child gets a "buddy for the day" for as long as they want.

b. The small group builds a "Talkalot Kit" for a new child to take home, a collection of materials that they can talk/show/add to at home.

Reading, math, science materials

a. Plenty of books and signage in several languages.

b. For older children, a "Writer's Briefcase" filled with stationery items such as paper, blank books, pens or crayons, envelopes, paper clips and brads, scissors and stapler, stickers; children check it out overnight, and their creation is shared at school.

c. A preschool alternative is "My Sleepover," a favorite toy, such as Curious George, takes turns going home in a bag with a journal. Families write or listen to their children's adventures with George, to be read in school.

Music, dance, and activities

a. Families bring in music or teach songs and dances to the teachers and children.

b. Teachers bring in materials that honor diverse cultures, teach songs in more than one language, incorporate both in daily activities.

FIGURE 13-6 Teachers consider environmental elements to promote a sense of acceptance and belonging.

A language-rich environment includes a welcoming spot for books and reading.

have regular and predictable one-on-one conversations with a teacher:

> Once children are settled on their cots, Nancy sits on the floor next to a child. Her prompt, "Do you have anything you want to talk about today?" initiates the conversation. Most children are eager to share a personal statement about themselves or their families. . . . Nancy closes the conversation with a warm and affectionate gesture, such as a light pat on the shoulder. The final step in the routine is to tell the child that it is time to be very quiet and take her nap, accompanied with the message, "I'll see you when you wake up." (Soundy & Stout, 2002)

Finally, a teacher can write a note to "Please save" for the child who does not have time to finish a project, or they can write children's dictated notes to parents.

Group times, with fingerplays, songs, and stories, are language-intensive activities. Children's articulation skills are strengthened, as is receptive language through listening to others. Group times are also opportunities for children to express themselves. When children discuss daily news and important events, brainstorm ideas about a subject, or report on what they did earlier in the day, they gain experience in listening and speaking. Children can also dramatize familiar stories and fingerplays. Snack tables at one preschool began to exchange notes ("Dear Teacher Adrienne's Table: What are you doing? What are you eating?") and pass notes to each other's groups, including the sign language two children used ("How do you sign banana? What's the sign for graham crackers?" came the next note). As a result, the class created a book with pictures of children signing and written descriptions of the hand positions (Lomangino, 2005).

"Persona dolls" (Derman-Sparks, 1989) encourage language involvement. Each doll has his/her own story that can reflect the composition of the class and can offer experiences that extend the children's learning. All dolls are introduced with their own lives, and a teacher introduces each one and tells its story. Children ask questions, which expands the story, and the teacher can tell a story that arises from the everyday interactions in class, "hot topics" that parents are talking about or occur in the news, things the teacher decides are important to think and talk about, or stories based on history.

Using visual aids or name cards gives children experience in graphic language. These might include having felt letters for the song "B-I-N-G-O," numbers for the fingerplay "One, Two, Buckle My Shoe," or name cards for the activity "I'm Thinking of Someone...." And children enjoy the cadence and rhythm of language spoken or chanted.

A "Topic Web" (Chard, 1998) is a way to begin a project; teachers often make these webs as a teaching team to chart the ideas they want the children to learn and then translate them into activities. Including the children helps them brainstorm both what they know and what they'd like to learn. They get excited about what they are hearing and also are motivated to get their own ideas written down. Topic webs are then revised and used to plan and record the work. They can also be posted on a classroom wall for reinforcement. (See Figure 13-7.)

Focus on Skills

Recall that language skills are the ability to articulate, to learn vocabulary and put words together into complete sentences, and to understand when others speak. It also refers to the pragmatics, the appropriate and effective use of language in social communication. Speech skills refer to the ability to produce sounds (**phonemes**) that make words and articulate those sounds in meaningful, understandable ways (Klein, Cook, & Richardson-Gibbs, 2001).

Teachers can plan curriculum based on any one of the skills. For *receptive language* (listening) skills, have children bring a favorite item from home or choose something from the class or yard and hide it in a Guessing Bag. Children take turns looking into the bag and describing their item until others guess. They can then pull it out and talk about it with the group. To increase vocabulary and awareness of other languages, get a familiar book such as *The Very Hungry Caterpillar* (Carle) from the Children's Braille Book Club and also make name cards in Braille for every child.

> Discuss with the children the fact that a book can be written in two languages. Let them explore the raised braille patterns and then identify the configurations on their individual name cards. Talk about how people who are visually impaired use their fingers to read. Invite a visitor from the community to demonstrate how braille is read. (Hall, 1999).

To emphasize expressive language, teachers allow children to express themselves by practicing words and grammatical structure and by elaborating on their own expressions. A teacher asks three-year-old Ceva to describe what she is doing with the art materials. "I'm dripping my paint," she replies. Outdoors, two-year-old Hadar describes her actions: "Teacher, look at me! I'm taller than you!" The teacher responds, "You climbed up the ladder to the top of the tunnel. Now, when you stand up, your head is above mine."

For *graphic language*, the kindergarten class makes a group story about "The Mystery of Space." Then they separate into small groups with second-grade helpers to write their own books in story form, complete with illustrations. Two after-school programs developed programs to help children with English language acquisition. In one, staff from a local university was recruited who both spoke the language and understood the culture of the students. They developed a series of reading exercises and games and provided peer-to-peer help. In the other, they used their multilingual skills to speak with the parents in their primary language while introducing them and the children to the program Afterschool KidzLit, which integrates art, games, and reading with over 120 books, including such favorites as *Green Eggs and Ham*. "Overcoming language barriers in afterschool programs need not be overwhelming," says Parker (2006). "They take advantage of the children's natural tendency to socialize in afterschool, while giving parents the tools and resources to help their children at home and at school."

Projects/Themes

How could an emerging project or theme for curriculum planning be used to develop language skills? One unit with universal appeal is "Babies," charted in Figure 13-8. Other units that elicit an extensive use of language are:

● *Harvest.* Activity: Ask preschool and kindergarten children to bring food from home for a "feast corner." Make a display of food from a harvest feast in the past or change the housekeeping corner into a "feast for all" area.

Group time: Begin a group story using the sentence "I am thankful for . . ."

Special project: Plan a feast, with the children creating the menu and preparing both the food and the table for their families at the school.

● *Friends.* Activity: Choose a favorite book to introduce the topic; the Story Stretchers book series (Raines & Canady, 1989) has several suggestions, such as Heine's *Friends*.

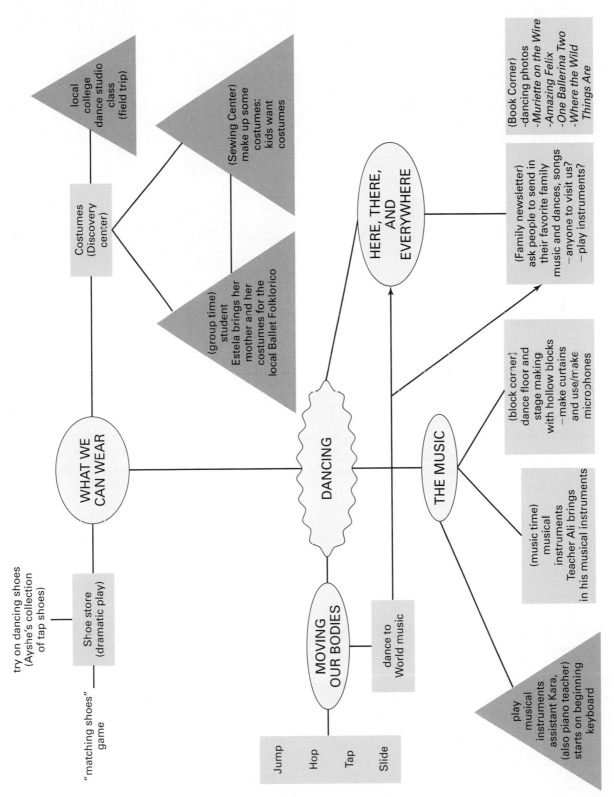

FIGURE 13-7 Children's topic of interest generates child and adult ideas for curriculum.

Theme: Babies

Art: Limit art materials to just what toddlers and infants can use.

Cooking: Make baby food.

Discovery/science: Display baby materials, then bring in baby animals.

Dramatic play area: "The Baby Corner" with dolls, cribs, diapers.

Manipulatives: Bring in several infant and toddler toys.

Gross-motor/games: Make a "crawling route," an obstacle course that requires crawling *only*.

Field trip/guest: A parent brings a baby to school to dress, bathe, feed.

Large group time: Sing lullabies (*Rock-a-Bye-Baby*)

Small/large group: Children discuss "What can babies do?"

Joshua: Babies sleep in cribs. They wear diapers. Babies can't talk.

Becky: They sometimes suck their thumbs. Babies cry when they are hungry.

Dennis: Babies go pee in their diapers.

Stevie: Babies sit in highchairs. Babies eat baby food that looks like squashed bananas.

Corey: Babies sleep in a bassinette. Then they crawl and bite your finger.

FIGURE 13-8 Teachers plan a unit to promote the skills they are focusing on in the class. A "babies" theme brings out the expert in all children and encourages language.

Group time: Talk with the children about the kinds of things friends like to do together. Make a list, then read the book. Later, select children to act out the animal parts. Don't worry about reading lines; keep it imaginative!

Special projects:

— Library Corner: Flannel board with characters and props from the book. Encourage the children to tell the story from the perspective of the various animals and then the farmer.

— Dramatic play corner: Re-create the area into a boat, and play "pirates."

— Science/Sensory table: Make the table into a "village pond" and see what floats and sinks; encourage plenty of conversation.

— Outdoors: Play hide-and-seek.

● *The Earth Is Our Home.* Activity: Kindergarten and primary children can make a large circle in a shade of blue, sketching the continents. Provide brown, green, and blue paint in pie tins and let children make a hand print on the ocean or land. Next, have the children bring from home the names of the countries of their family's ancestry.[1] Help them locate those areas and attach their names to those parts of the world.

Group time: Sing "The Earth Is Our Home" (Greg & Steve) and "One Light, One Sun" (Raffi). Read *Just a Dream* (Van Allsburg) and *Where the Forest Meets the Sea* (J. Baker).

Special project: Help make a class recycling area or compost heap. Take a field trip to recycle the materials, or visit a garden that uses compost. Young children can learn about endangered species through Burningham's *Hey! Get Off Our Train;* older children can do research on an animal and make its natural habitat in a shoebox.

● *Favorite Foods.* Activity: Make a salad from everyone's favorite vegetable, or follow the story line of *Stone Soup*.

Group time: Discussion topic can be "My favorite fruit is . . ." (Example: "An apple because it is crunchy and is big enough to share.")

Special project: Make recipe cards to send home. (Example: Chicken—"First you get seven pounds of skin. Then you get flat pieces of roast chicken. Then you put some bones in. Then you get one pound of pickle seeds and put them on the chicken. Then cook it in the oven for about five hours!") Any theme can be developed, so long as it brings out oral and graphic language experiences.

Although preschool and school-age children are challenged by specific themes, curriculum for infants and toddlers does not always need

---

1 Be sensitive to the fact that some families do not have a strong attachment to a national heritage or ancestry beyond the United States.

Curriculum for Language Development of Infants and Toddlers

The Environment

1. Is gentle and supportive, with adults who listen and respond to sounds made and who let the children initiate language.

2. Is explained simply, such as what caregiver is doing during clothing or diaper changing.

3. Is responsive, as adults respond quickly to crying and redirect what the children can do and express.

The Skills

1. Adults expand on the children's own words. Toddler: "The shoe." Adult: "Oh, that's your shoe you are holding."

2. Adults model for children the words to say. Adult: "Elenora, I want the puppet now."

3. Children listen in small groups of two or three, on laps, or next to adults, and are allowed wide variation in their participation.

The Themes

1. Revolve around the children's individual interests.

2. Include favorite stories presented in several ways: reading *The Three Bears,* doing a flannelboard story, singing a fingerplay, having bear puppets and stuffed animals

FIGURE 13-9 Language experiences for infants and toddlers consider the developmental milestones and the individual child's level of self-expression.

this kind of focus. Curriculum for younger children should emerge naturally from their developmental level and interests. For instance, a project on body awareness can develop from the children's interest in dolls. In one setting, "the teachers decided to offer each child a hand-made cloth doll without distinguishing features" (Wien, Stacey, Keating, Rowlings, & Cameron 2002). An art consultant made dolls of varying skin tones and body shapes, and features such as eyes, noses, ears, lips, and hair separately. Children's conversations were audiotaped, their drawings displayed, their visits to a hair salon and hotel (to investigate beds) all recorded. Over time, each doll received the features chosen by the children. The project lasted nearly six months because of the sustained interest of the children, all from 27 months to three-and-a-half years of age! Figure 13-9 describes curriculum ideas for language development in an infant/toddler class.

EARLY LITERACY

The ability to read and write does not just happen when children reach a certain age. Their readiness for graphic language must be nurtured. A child's language proficiency will determine readiness for reading. Teachers identify this readiness by knowing how well a child understands the structure and vocabulary of the language. Therefore, a program to encourage

beginning reading will offer experiences in oral language. Research shows that successful readers see a relationship between spoken language and the written word. They are aware that sounds are how language is put together. So teachers plan activities that make connections between what is said and what is written. With the emphasis on early reading, the growth of early learning standards, and the advent of legislation such as No Child Left Behind (see Chapter 15), teachers are feeling pressured to bring direct instruction into their early education programs. It is important to emphasize that early literacy is *not* equivalent to early direct instruction.

How exactly do infants (and adults) strive to make sense of everything they encounter in the world? They *read* it. Reading is the most natural activity in the world. . . . We read the weather, the state of the tides, people's feelings and intentions, stock market trends, animal tracks, maps, signals, signs, symbols, hands, tea leaves, the law, music, mathematics, minds, body language, between the lines, and above all we read faces. "Reading," when employed to refer to interpretation of a piece of writing, is just a special use of the term. We have been reading—interpreting experience—constantly since birth and we continue to do so. (Smith, 2004)

Teachers must ensure that children's needs are addressed, as well as their ways of learning

Essential Early Literacy Teaching Strategies

Rich teacher talk	Engage in conversation, use rare words, extend their comments.
Storybook reading	Read aloud once or twice a day.
Phonemic awareness activities	Play games or sing songs that involve rhyme, alliteration, match sounds.
Alphabet activities	Use magnetic letters, alphabet blocks and puzzles, alphabet charts and books.
Support for emergent reading	Provide a well-designed book center, repeat reading children's favorites, have functional and play-related print.
Support for emergent writing	Encourage scribble writing, invented spelling, provide a well-stocked writing center and play-related writing materials.
Shared book experience	Read Big Books, draw attention to basic concepts of print such as left-to-right and top-to-bottom, cover and title page.
Integrated, content-focused activities	Investigate topics of children's interest, helping children gather data and record it, engage in dramatic play, use emergent writing to record what they learn.

FIGURE 13-10 The pressure of early reading instruction can be relieved by encouraging early forms of reading and writing that also give play a prominent role (Roskos, Christie, & Richgels, 2003).

preserved. Language-rich interactions and relationships with peers; challenging, well-planned curriculum offering depth, focus, choice, engagement, investigation, and representation; teachers' active promotion of concept and skill development in meaningful contexts can be achieved only in connection to young children's interests and abilities. Figure 13-10 describes some of these strategies.

There is an important role for teachers of young children in the early stages of reading and writing. Teachers can influence positive attitudes toward reading and writing. They encourage children to talk and converse with others about what they see and do; this gives them increasing experience in using and attaching experiences to words. Taking the time to write down what children say and then reading it back gives a sense of importance to children's language and their ability to express themselves. Organizing the environment to support literary development and learning to teach toward reading in developmentally appropriate ways are all part of building an early literacy curriculum. In these ways, teachers can help children get involved with print in natural and unpressured ways.

Children and Reading

The role of the adult is one of engaging children with print in ways that make sense to them. By creating an environment that provides rich opportunities to use the printed word, teachers help motivate children toward reading. Research tells us that early literacy learning is closely associated with achievement in later schooling, social relations, and work (National Research Council, 1998; IRA/NAEYC, 1998).

Adults and even children often have a stereotypical concept of reading. They think the ability to read is only the literal translation of signs and symbols on a printed page (called **decoding**). Learning to read is also attaching experiences and knowledge to words and understanding the use of the written word in daily life. In fact, learning to read is a complex process that includes both language and literary competencies. Building upon these skills takes time and has tremendous individual variation; thus, it is known as **emergent literacy**.

Emergent Literacy

Emergent literacy involves the "skills, knowledge, and attitudes that are developmental precursors to conventional forms of reading and writing. These skills are the building blocks for learning to read and write. Interventions in preschool should focus on emergent literacy skills since very young children are not yet engaged in conventional literacy" (Shanahan, 2005). In the last several years, early childhood professionals have begun to articulate the processes involved in helping children with emerging literacy.

Adults encourage children's writing by taking their attempts seriously.

1. Young children begin the process of literacy development before they enter [elementary] school.
2. Reading and writing develop concurrently and in an interrelated manner.
3. Literacy develops in everyday activities.
4. Children learn about literacy through interaction with their world. Furthermore, literacy development is part of the total communication process that includes listening, speaking, reading, and writing.

We need to change our definition of reading from a *technical skill* (translating print to spoken language) to the conception of a different mode of language use. The International Reading Association (IRA, 2006) declares that most children pass through five stages of early literacy development:

1. Awareness and exploration
2. Experimenting with reading and writing
3. Early reading and writing
4. Transitional reading and writing
5. Conventional reading and writing

Teachers can help children succeed as they travel these stages (Early Childhood Resources, 1995). First, help them learn that print is a form of language. Read them books filled with magic, messages, and mystery (prereading). Next, be sure they hear stories, poems, chants, and songs many times. Help them rehearse by chanting, singing, resaying, and "reading along" as we read to them (prereading). Third, observe as they learn to recognize words (see Figure 13-11). They read and know the text, and begin to use some phonics to discover which words say what (beginning reading). Finally, children start to read more and more on their own, or with a friend. Now the task is to make them better readers (reading).

Starting Out Right (1999) outlines the findings of a major report of the National Research Council entitled "Preventing Reading Difficulties in Young Children" (1998). It divides the reading process into two stages in the early years.

1. *Growing up to read* (zero to four years old). Falling in love with words and using everyday narrative are followed by first attempts: pretending to read, learning about print, and nourishing the mind with high-quality books. Toward the end of this period children know that alphabet letters are a special category of visual graphics and may recognize some. They pay attention to separate and repeating sounds in language, show an interest in books and reading, and display reading (signs in the local environment) and writing attempts (name on a birthday card; taking orders in a pretend restaurant).

2. *Becoming real readers* (kindergarten through grade three). To become real readers, children need well-integrated instruction that focuses on three core elements: (1) identifying words using sound-spelling correspondence and sight word recognition, (2) using previous knowledge, vocabulary, and comprehension strategies to read for meaning, and (3) reading with fluency.

   ● During kindergarten, children should gain a solid familiarity with the structure and uses of print, be familiar with sound-by-sound and word-by-word analysis of language, and have an interest in the types of language and knowledge that books can bring them.

   ● First grade makes a transition from emergent to "real" reading. Children continue phonemic awareness, letter knowledge, and print awareness to help with writing attempts and fluent reading. Spelling becomes a focus during the year, starting with **invented spelling** and growing into a sensitivity to conventional spelling. Literacy activities are done voluntarily,

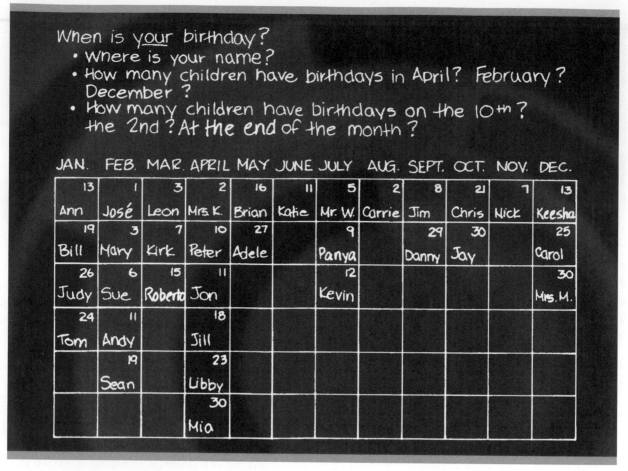

FIGURE 13-11 A language experience chart involves children through the subject matter and the way in which information is displayed.

such as choosing stories to read or writing a note to a friend.

- Second and third grades help children build automatic word recognition, spelling skills, and reading fluency. Comprehension improves, as does recall of facts and participation in creative responses to texts, and children move toward producing a variety of written work. "Learning to read" is now shifting toward "reading to learn."

In her book *Teacher*, Sylvia Ashton-Warner describes one technique for introducing printed language to young children. A kindergarten teacher who believed strongly in children's innate creativity and curiosity, Ashton-Warner developed a system of "organic reading" in which the students themselves build a key vocabulary of words they wish to learn to read and write. This method was effective for her classes of native Maori children in New Zealand, for whom the British basal readers held little meaning.

Ashton-Warner's personal, culturally relevant teaching works well, because it flows naturally from the child's own life and interests.[1]

Combination Strategies. Many teachers use a combination of key words, journals, and phonics (Tanaka in Jones, 1988) along with holistic strategies such as DEAR (Drop Everything and Read), huddle groups (you choose who to work with), book bragging time (either in large or small groups), and BEAR (sustained silent reading with a timer, usually done in grades 1 through 3) as they teach reading in developmentally appropriate ways (Bobys, 2000; Reisner, 2001).

A Print-Rich Environment. Labels, lists, signs, and charts can make print a meaningful part of the classroom environment. Often, children are involved in making the signs to indicate where things go and what things are. Using the languages of the group expands this "literate room," as do helper charts, daily schedules, and even

Adults encourage children's writing by taking their attempts seriously.

attendance charts. Road signs can be made for the block corner, recipe cards for cooking. "Do not touch" may be written for an unfinished project, as can "Inside voices here" for the library corner. For specific literary practice, Schickedanz (1999) suggests labeled picture cards for rhyming games, alphabet puzzles, magnetic letters, and scrabble games, as well as opportunities for children to give dictation, write grocery lists, and compose letters to friends and family (see Figures 13-12 and 13-13).

The child's readiness to read is related to the development of certain skills (see Figure 13-12). Readiness skills can be acquired through planned experiences in the school program that:

- Promote meaningful interaction with words.
  Example: Writing children's names on their drawings; labeling cubbies with children's names and pictures.

- Are age-level appropriate.
  Example: For two-and-a-half-year-olds, play lotto games using pictures of familiar objects; for four-year-olds, use animal pictures; for six-year-olds, use alphabet letters.

- Are fun and enjoyable for children.
  Example: Creating a class newspaper to take home.

- Take a gradual approach through the use of nonreading materials.
  Example: Label toy storage boxes with pictures. Later in the year, add the words alongside the pictures.

- Acknowledge the child's ability to read the environment, to read events, to read other people.
  Example: Clark, looking out the window at the darkening sky, says, "Looks like it's gonna rain." Margo "reads" her painting as she describes the vivid monster to the teacher.

- Involve the use of children's senses.
  Example: Display baskets of vegetables and foods along with the book *Stone Soup*.

The school will have many activities in the area of "reading readiness." An early childhood program promotes an awareness of the graphic aspects of language by:

1. Developing children's speaking and listening proficiencies through the use of conversation, descriptive language, oral feedback, and meaningful listening comprehension activities.

2. Helping children hear phonemes (language sounds) through oral language activities such as rhyming, initial consonant substitution, and the use of alliteration in jingles and language play.

3. Providing many opportunities for children to make the connection between spoken and written language.

4. Emphasizing children's own language in beginning reading activities.

5. Filling the environment with printed words and phrases, so children become familiar with meaningful print.

Reading Readiness Is	Teachers
1. Oral vocabulary	1. Encourage talking, learning new words and phrases, singing, fingerplays, remembering and reflecting verbally.
2. Curiosity about/for reading	2. Provide a separate area for books (and are available to read to children), language games (lotto), dictation from children ("If I could fly I would . . . "), notes about children that the children deliver themselves to other adults.
3. Auditory discrimination (the ability to detect sound differences)	3. Create sound discrimination boxes in the science area, a "listen-to-the-sound" walk, guessing games with musical instruments, activities that teach letter sounds by using the children's names.
4. Visual discrimination	4. Support directionality: left and right (in the "Hokey-Pokey" dance and labeled on shoes and mittens), up and down, top and bottom, likenesses and differences.
5. Awareness of print	5. Help the children name and label the classroom (door, tables, book corner), with bilingual signs as appropriate. Bring children's native language into print by asking parents for the names of common objects, numbers and so on for use around the classroom and in song and fingerplay charts. Encourage children to help print their own names on creative works. Write group newsletters to send home. Make flannelboard letters for free play and for use in songs, such as "Bingo."

FIGURE 13-12 Children gain reading readiness skills through activities for oral vocabulary, curiosity about reading, and auditory and visual discrimination.

Early Literacy Comes to the Classroom

1. Have a cozy library corner, giving children lots of time to explore and read all kinds of books.

2. Make a writing corner with different kinds of supplies, using this area to develop grouptime activities (children's stories), meaningful themes (post office), and connected learning (writing and sending letters).

3. Take field trips, pointing out print as they find it (street signs, store shelves, bumper stickers) and writing about it afterward.

4. Use large charts for poems, fingerplays, and songs as well as for listing choices available and for group dictation.

5. Plan activities that incorporate print: read recipes for cooking projects, make menus for lunch and snack, follow directions in using a new manipulative toy, write sales tickets for dramatic play units, bring books into science displays.

6. Use written notes regularly, sending a regular newspaper home that the children have written or dictated, writing notes to other team teachers that children deliver, encouraging children to send notes to each other.

FIGURE 13-13 Whole language in the primary classroom means integrating graphic language activities in a natural, meaningful way.

6. Highlighting the language used in beginning reading instructions; for example, use the terms "letter," "sound," "word," and "sentence."

Whole Language or Phonics?

The concept of **whole language** has many familiar and exciting elements from the early childhood tradition. An approach that was popular in the early 1980s but has suffered in the early 21st century as direct instruction has dominated, whole language (Cruikshank, 1993):

> is different in both theory and practice from the traditional basal [direct instruction] approach. Because it is child-centered rather than teacher-dominated, curriculum activities arise from children's current interests, needs, and developmental levels. Making connections is emphasized, and it is through meaningful integrative themes that students acquire knowledge and skills. Children are

also encouraged to share ideas and work with others, as socialization is valued. Evaluation focuses on the child's growth over time, and both pupil portfolios and anecdotal reporting are common assessment tools.

Goodman (1986) offers key principles of the whole language approach:

- Whole language is a way of viewing language, learning, and people (children, teachers, parents) in a *holistic, integrated* way. All the language arts are related to each other. For instance, a teacher might read a story to the children, then ask them to make up their own endings. The class would be *listening* (to the story), *speaking* (telling their ideas), *writing* (trying their hand at spelling and handwriting), and *reading* (their creations to a friend or the class at the end of the lesson).

- *Meaningful* content is when children use language in a purposeful way, developing naturally through a need to communicate. The young child who is read stories and engaged in conversations from infancy is then led smoothly to reading and writing as another extension of language use.

- Whole language encourages this extension of *function into form*; that is, children's own mastery of oral language and unique interests are drawn on in teaching the "rules" of sounds, letters, and words.

Critics of whole language argue that this approach leaves out teaching the decoding skills, which a traditional phonics approach emphasizes. Current knowledge concludes that to learn, primary children benefit from both specific phonics instruction and a rich background in literature (such as being read stories). This approach blends early phonics instruction in the teaching of reading while at the same time stressing the importance of balance (see Figure 13-13). In addition, it must be repeated that children under five years of age are not yet ready for an onslaught of conventional, direct instruction methods. There is a lack of agreement in the field over what count as "emergent literacy skills," and more research is needed along with more refined understanding of the skills involved. Learning graphic language is a creative process that involves both an "art" (literature, rhyming songs, invented spelling) and a "science" (the nuts and bolts of decoding). It is the teacher's job to be the master craftsperson in helping children put the two together.

Children and Writing

Children learn about words in print much the same as they learn about reading and other aspects of language: that is, by seeing it used and having plenty of opportunities to use it themselves. Writing can be as natural for children as walking and talking. "What is written language? For a child, print is just another facet of the world, not yet comprehended, perhaps, but not different from all the complex sights, sounds, smells, tastes, and textures in the environment—not especially mysterious or intimidating" (Smith, 2004). Children begin to write when they first take a pencil in hand and start to scribble. Later, they can write a story by drawing pictures or by dictating the words and having someone else write them down.

The early childhood classroom heightens an interest in writing through a writing center. It can be part of a language area or a self-help art center. Wherever it is located, this center will include a variety of things to write with, to write on, and "writing helpers." Children write with pencils (fat and thin, with and without erasers), colored pencils, narrow and wide marking pens, and crayons. They enjoy having many kinds of paper products, including computer paper, old calendars, data-punch cards, and colored paper. Children also enjoy simple books, a few blank pages stapled together. Carbon paper, dittos, and lined paper will add variety. "Writing helpers" might be a picture dictionary, a set of alphabet letters, a print set, an alphabet chart, a chalkboard, or a magnetic letter board. All of these serve to help children practice writing skills (see Figure 13-14).

Children's first attempts at writing will likely include drawing or scribbling. Because drawing helps children plan and organize their thoughts (and, thus, their text), teachers encourage children to tell them about their stories and can ask for a child's help in "reading" these writings. As children begin to work with words themselves, adults can help them sound out words or spell words for them. Spelling development is similar to learning to speak: adults support the efforts, not correct the mistakes, and allow children to invent their own spelling of words. Picture dictionaries and lists of popular words help children use resources for writing. Figure 13-15 is a sample of invented spelling in a kindergarten.

Writing materials can be available throughout the room and yard. Paper and pencils come in handy in the dramatic play area. Menus,

Suggested Writing Center Materials

- Alphabet board
- Alphabet stamps
- Binders—yarn, string, "twist ties," to bind homemade books
- Book-binding machine (used by adults to bind special books)
- Cardboard—cereal/cracker boxes provide cardboard for covers
- Clipboards
- Collage materials—magazines, wall paper, and wrapping papers
- Colored pencils
- Crayons
- Envelopes (local card store will sometimes donate leftovers)
- Fabric
- Laminate (factories will sometimes donate end rolls)
- Magnetic letters
- Markers
- Mini books ($\frac{1}{2}$ and $\frac{1}{4}$ size sheets of paper, about 4–5, stapled. Another recommendation, half sheets of lined paper, about 30 pages for longer works.
- Name cards (children's names)
- Notebooks, notepads, stationary, odd-shaped/colored papers (printshops will sometimes donate these)
- Office-style rubber stamps and ink pads
- Old cards, invitations, and business cards
- Old date books and calendars
- Paper crimping tool (roll a piece of paper through and it comes out corrugated—found at a rubber stamping or craft store)
- Paper punches (with large button that can be easily pushed by children)
- Recycled paper (different sizes)
- Rulers
- Scissors
- Stamps: wildlife and other nonpostage stamps. (Homemade stamps can be made by painting the backs of pictures with "lick'em, stick'em"—one part strawberry gelatin and one part water. Apply to shiny magazine pictures, dry and then they can be licked and used as stamps.)
- Stapler (kindergarten)
- Stencil shapes
- Stickers
- Word wall (words and their corresponding pictures—whenever the children need to know how to write a new word, it goes up there.)

FIGURE 13-14 A writing center needs plenty of materials to stimulate graphic language development (Chesler, 1998).

shopping lists, prescriptions, and money are but a few uses children will find for writing equipment. The block corner may need traffic signs; the computer, a waiting list. Outdoors, pictures can label the location of the vegetables in the garden; markers indicate where children have hidden "treasures" or where the dead bird is buried.

The "language experience" approach involves taking dictation, writing down and reading back to children their own spoken language. It is important to use the child's exact words so

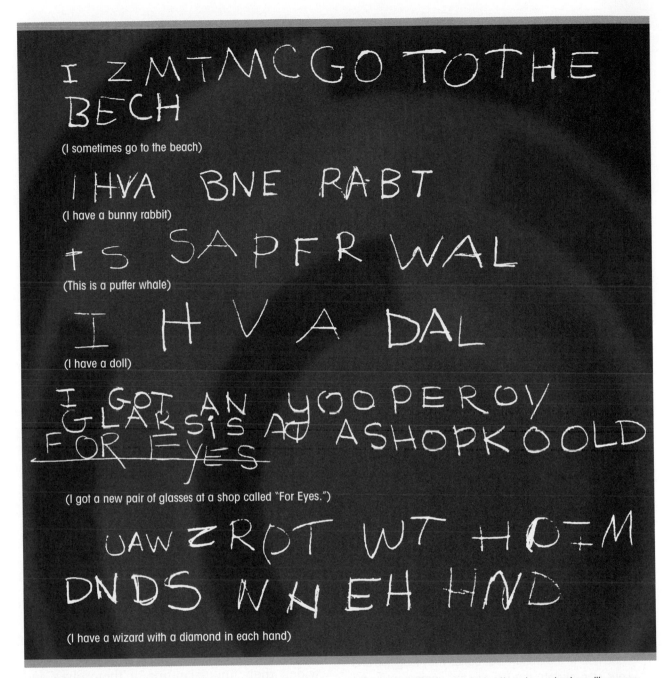

I ZMTMCGO TOTHE BECH

(I sometimes go to the beach)

I HVA BNE RABT

(I have a bunny rabbit)

TS SAPFR WAL

(This is a puffer whale)

I H V A DAL

(I have a doll)

I GOT AN YOOPEROV GLARSIS AT ASHOPKOOLD FOR EYES

(I got a new pair of glasses at a shop called "For Eyes.")

UAW ZROT WT HOFM DNDS NH EH HND

(I have a wizard with a diamond in each hand)

FIGURE 13-15 Early writing usually involves children's attempts at words of their own invention. Invented spelling can be treated with respect for the efforts and as a foundation for successful writing experiences. (Courtesy of Kim Saxe. Reprinted with permission.)

they can make the connection between their speech and the letters on the page. This is true for group stories, for children's self-made books, or for descriptions of their own paintings. A useful technique in taking dictation is to say the words while writing them, allowing the child to watch the letters and words being formed. When the content is read back, the child has a sense of completion. Figure 13-16 is an example of these kinds of language experiences in classrooms of three-, five-, and six-year-olds.

Story maps help children see the parts and sequencing of the writing process. Depicted as a body, the head serves as the beginning (with facial features called "topic," "characters," and "setting"), the body as the middle, and the legs as the end ("Finally . . .") A primary child can write in the various parts of the story and read it from the map or continue to elaborate with full sentences in a more traditional manner. In these ways, teachers help raise awareness of the use and enjoyment of the printed word.

The Language Experience Approach

1. Start with a leading sentence.

If I were an instrument . . .

Michelle: I would be a piano with strings and lots of sparklies on top. And you could play me even if you were blind.

Janette: I would be a drum. I would be hit and I wouldn't be happy because they would make me hurt.

Dennis: I would be a violin. Someone would play me with a bow and I would make a beautiful sound.

2. Take dictation on topics and pictures of their making.

"On Our Halloween Nights"

Ehsan: There was a witch and skeleton and ghost in my room on Halloween night.

Lionel: Costume night. A cow jumping over the moon. The little rabbit sleeping.

Martine: There was a big pumpkin and a big bat and a bear and a pirate. There was a jack-o-lantern and the light glowed.

Andrew: There was a smiley monster and Aka-Zam!

Luke: We went to my church for hot dogs and cider.

3. Ask for stories of their own.

Once upon a time there's a boy named Timothy and he punched all the bad guys dead. And he was very strong and he can punch anything down. And he can do anything he likes to. And he makes all the things at winter. And he was so strong he could break out anything else. And he had to do very hard work all day long and all day night. And he had to sleep but he couldn't. And he had a very small house and cup. And then he did everything he want to all day long. The End. Tim (signed)

4. Make a group book (including illustrations).

All By Myself (our version of the book by Mercer Mayer)

"I can put on my overalls all by myself" (Stephanie)

"I can brush my hair all by myself" (Lindsey)

"I can make pictures all by myself" (Jessica)

"I can buckle my jeans all by myself." (Megan)

"I can make a drill truck with the blocks all by myself." (Lionel)

"I can jump in the pool all by myself." (Andrew)

FIGURE 13-16 The language experience approach takes many creative forms in a classroom. (Special thanks to Gay Spitz for example 1 and to Ann Zondor and Lynne Conly Hoffman and the children of the Children's Center of the Stanford Community for several of the examples in 2 and 4.)

CHILDREN'S LITERATURE

Children's books bring us back to ourselves, young and new in the world. "Our bones may lengthen and our skin stretch, but we are the same soul in the making. . . . Children's books are such powerful transformers because they speak, in the words of the Quakers, to one's condition, often unrecognized at the time, and remain as maps for the future. . . . In children's books we preserve the wild rose, the song of the robin, the budding leaf. In secret gardens we know the same stab of joy, at whatever age of reading, in the thorny paradise around us. (Lundin, 1991)

Literature does indeed have an important place in the curriculum today. Through the use of good books, teachers can help children broaden their interests and concepts. Books that are primarily used for transmitting information expand the child's knowledge base. Thoughtful books that draw on children's everyday experiences widen their understanding of themselves and others. Through books, children can learn to see things in an endless variety of ways. Five different books will describe and illustrate the behavior of cats in five different ways. Exposure to *Millions of Cats* (Gag), *Angus and the Cats* (Flack), and *The Cat in the Hat* (Dr. Seuss), as well as to the cats portrayed in *Peter Rabbit* (Potter) or *Frog Went A-Courtin'* (Langstaff), will enlarge the child's concepts of cats. Different cultures are also represented in any number of children's books, teaching a greater awareness of all of humankind[1] (see Figure 13-17 and the Voice of Experience at chapter's end).

 1 Children's literature provides a window and a mirror to our diverse world.

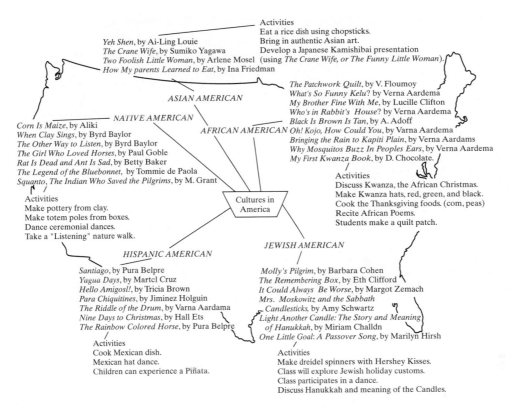

Activities
Eat a rice dish using chopsticks.
Bring in authentic Asian art.
Develop a Japanese Kamishibai presentation
(using *The Crane Wife,* or *The Funny Little Woman*).

Yeh Shen, by Ai-Ling Louie
The Crane Wife, by Sumiko Yagawa
Two Foolish Little Woman, by Arlene Mosel
How My parents Learned to Eat, by Ina Friedman

ASIAN AMERICAN

The Patchwork Quilt, by V. Floumoy
What's So Funny Kelu? by Verna Aardema
My Brother Fine With Me, by Lucille Clifton
Who's in Rabbit's House? by Verna Aardema
Black Is Brown Is Tan, by A. Adoff
Oh! Kojo, How Could You, by Varna Aardema
Bringing the Rain to Kapiti Plain, by Verna Aardams
Why Mosquitos Buzz In Peoples Ears, by Verna Aardema
My First Kwanza Book, by D. Chocolate.

NATIVE AMERICAN

Corn Is Maize, by Aliki
When Clay Sings, by Byrd Baylor
The Other Way to Listen, by Byrd Baylor
The Girl Who Loved Horses, by Paul Goble
Rat Is Dead and Ant Is Sad, by Betty Baker
The Legend of the Bluebonnet, by Tommie de Paola
Squanto, The Indian Who Saved the Pilgrims, by M. Grant

AFRICAN AMERICAN

Activities
Discuss Kwanza, the African Christmas.
Make Kwanza hats, red, green, and black.
Cook the Thanksgiving foods. (com, peas)
Recite African Poems.
Students make a quilt patch.

Activities
Make pottery from clay.
Make totem poles from boxes.
Dance ceremonial dances.
Take a "Listening" nature walk.

Cultures in America

HISPANIC AMERICAN

JEWISH AMERICAN

Santiago, by Pura Belpre
Yugua Days, by Martcl Cruz
Hello Amigosl!, by Tricia Brown
Para Chiquitines, by Jiminez Holguin
The Riddle of the Drum, by Varna Aardama
Nine Days to Christmas, by Hall Ets
The Rainbow Colored Horse, by Pura Belpre

Molly's Pilgrim, by Barbara Cohen
The Remembering Box, by Eth Clifford
It Could Always Be Worse, by Margot Zemach
*Mrs. Moskowitz and the Sabbath
Candlesticks,* by Amy Schwartz
*Light Another Candle: The Story and Meaning
of Hanukkah,* by Miriam Challdn
One Little Goal: A Passover Song, by Marilyn Hirsh

Activities
Cook Mexican dish.
Mexican hat dance.
Children can experience a Piñata.

Activities
Make dreidel spinners with Hershey Kisses.
Class will explore Jewish holiday customs.
Class participates in a dance.
Discuss Hanukkah and meaning of the Candles.

FIGURE 13-17 Using multicultural literature helps each child get connected with books and expands all children's outlooks (courtesy of de Melendez & Ostertag, 1997).

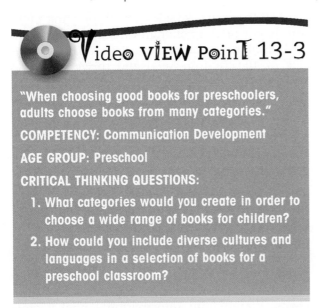

Video VIEW Point 13-3

"When choosing good books for preschoolers, adults choose books from many categories."

COMPETENCY: Communication Development

AGE GROUP: Preschool

CRITICAL THINKING QUESTIONS:

1. What categories would you create in order to choose a wide range of books for children?

2. How could you include diverse cultures and languages in a selection of books for a preschool classroom?

Teachers have an opportunity to encourage divergent thinking through the use of children's literature. Children gain more than facts from books; they learn all manner of things, providing they can interpret the story rather than just hear the individual words. Quizzing children about whether the dinosaur was a meat- or plant-eater will bring about responses that are predictable and pat, but comprehension does not have to be joyless. Zingy questions will

provide not only thought but also interest (see Figure 13-18).

"Would a brontosaurus fit in your living room?" will get children to think about *Danny and the Dinosaur* (Hoff) or Kent's *There's No Such Thing as a Dragon* or Most's *If the Dinosaurs Came Back* in a new way. "Is the troll bigger or smaller than your brother?" might be a point of discussion after reading *The Three Billy Goats Gruff.* The point is not to have children feed back straight factual information but to get them involved in the story.

Selection of books is important (see Figure 13-19). The wise teacher will choose books that invite participation. Everyone can "roar a terrible roar, gnash their terrible teeth, and show their terrible claws" during a rendition of *Where the Wild Things Are* (Sendak). Meaning for children lies more in action than in words. Children will be more apt to talk about stories that have in some way touched them and stimulated their involvement.

When Andrea was struggling to find the words to describe a large amount, Mitra began to recite: "Hundreds of cats, thousands of cats, millions and billions and trillions of cats!" (*Millions of Cats,* Gag)

Riding home in the car after school one day, Parker chanted: "Tik-ki tik-ki tem-bo no sa rembo, chari bari ru-chi, pip peri pembo." (*Tikki Tikki Tembo,* Mosel)

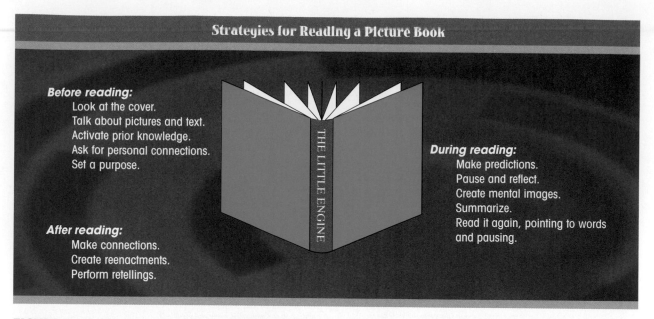

Strategies for Reading a Picture Book

Before reading:
Look at the cover.
Talk about pictures and text.
Activate prior knowledge.
Ask for personal connections.
Set a purpose.

During reading:
Make predictions.
Pause and reflect.
Create mental images.
Summarize.
Read it again, pointing to words and pausing.

After reading:
Make connections.
Create reenactments.
Perform retellings.

FIGURE 13-18 Getting and keeping children emotionally engaged with a picture book has several parts to the process (derived from Owocki, 2001).

Selecting Children's Books

1. ____ Could I read this book enthusiastically?

2. ____ Are the contents of the book appropriate for the children?

    ____ Is it age appropriate?

    ____ Is it suitable for the individual child(ren)?

    ____ What are the cultures and languages of the group?

3. ____ Is this book biased?

    ____ Are illustrations stereotyped or showing tokenism?

    ____ What is the story line: what is the standard for success, how are problems presented and resolved, what is the role of women, people of color, the heroes?

4. ____ Is the book written with an understanding of my group's age characteristics?

5. ____ Is the author's style enjoyable?

    ____ Can the children understand the sequence?

    ____ Is there repetition of words or actions?

    ____ Does it end in a satisfying way?

    ____ Are there humorous parts?

6. ____ Does it have educational value?

FIGURE 13-19 Selecting books for children involves careful study (excerpted from Machado, 1999, and Derman-Sparks, 1989).

Derek and Shigeo were playing grocery store. To attract customers they called out: "Caps for sale! Fifty cents a cap." (*Caps for Sale,* Slobodkina)

As Trelease (1982) puts it, "If our first problem is not reading enough to children, our second problem is stopping too soon." Whether age one or 10, children need and thrive on being read aloud to regularly. Teachers could ask for no better activity to promote good listening habits than a wealth of good children's books.

Creating a Rich Literary Environment

The comics of yesterday are far outdistanced by the television and video games of today. How can teachers give children experiences in literature in the face of such competition?

The field of children's literature is rich in its variety, including both great classic stories and those of present-day situations and concerns. Fiction and informational books, children's magazines, and poetry add balance to the literary curriculum. Every classroom should contain representative works from each of these areas and should:

● *Provide plenty of time for using books and other materials.* Children need time to browse, to flip through a book at their own pace, to let their thoughts wander as they reflect on the story line. They also enjoy retelling the tale to others.

Be sure to plan enough time for children to be read to every day.

- *Make a space that is quiet and comfortable.* In addition to soft pillows or seats, locate the reading area where there is privacy. Crashing blocks and messy fingerpainting will intrude on the book reader. A place to sprawl or cuddle up with a friend is preferable.

- *Have plenty of books and supporting materials.* The language arts center might contain a listening post, with headsets for a CD or tape player. Perhaps there is even a place where books can be created, a place supplied with paper and crayons. There may even be a typewriter, puppet stage, or flannelboard nearby so that stories can be created in new ways.

- *Display children's literary creations.* The efforts of children's stories and bookmaking should be honored by establishing a place in the room where they can be seen and read. Children then see how adults value the process of literary creation and the final product.

- *Model how to care for a book and keep classroom books in good repair.* Children can come to realize that a book is like a good friend and should be given the same kind of care and consideration.

- *Foster children's reading at home.* This is one of the important contributions a teacher can make to the reading process. Family literacy programs are developing for all families to gain skills in English; check your local community for availability. Attitudes about reading are communicated to children from the important people in their lives. Figure 13-20 gives parents ideas of helping children at home.

    Teachers encourage this enthusiasm in a number of ways. Encourage parents to read good-quality literature by making "book bags," large plastic bags that the children can use to hold a book borrowed from the classroom to read overnight and return the next day. Posting the local library hours, establishing a lending library, and providing parents with lists of favorites will reinforce the child's interest in literature.

- *Use books around the room.* Don't confine them to just the book corner or the book shelf. Demonstrate their adaptability to all curriculum areas by displaying a variety of books in the activity centers. Ask children to help you

12 Things Parents Can Do to Help Their Preschooler Become a Reader

1. Have daily conversations with your child.
2. Keep lots of printed materials and writing materials in your home.
3. Set up a reading and writing space for your child.
4. Let your child see you read and write.
5. Read with your child every day.
6. Call your child's attention to reading and writing in everyday activities.
7. Make a message board.
8. Encourage your child to read.
9. Display your child's writing.
10. Make a bank or file of words your child likes to write.
11. Go to the library with your child.
12. Use television and technology wisely.

FIGURE 13-20 Teachers foster reading at home by offering families practical ideas (Epstein, 2002).

retell or emphasize parts of a story (see the storytelling section), and ask them questions informally afterward: "How many bowls of porridge were on the kitchen table? Which one did Goldilocks like best? How did you know?" Figure 13-21 shows how books can enhance play and learning throughout the school room.

Extending Literary Experiences

Good literature comes in many forms and can be presented in a variety of ways. A creative teacher uses books and literature to develop other curriculum materials. Translating words from a book into an activity helps a child remember them. Books and stories can be adapted to the flannelboard, storytelling, dramatizations, puppets, book games, and audiovisual resources.

Storytelling

Storytelling is as old as humanity. The first time a human being returned to the cave with an adventure to tell, the story was born. Storytelling is the means by which cultural heritage is passed down from one generation to another.[1] Children's

  1 In many cultures, other than Western European-American culture, there is a high value placed on learning through oral storytelling and rhyming and chanting; a higher value than on learning based on playing with objects.

Living Together: Reflecting Diversity

Knots on a Counting Rope (Martin, Jr., & Archambault)
The Legend of Bluebonnet (de Paola)
The Quilt (Jones)
The River That Gave Gifts (Humphrey)
The Big Orange Splot (Pinkwater)
Mei Li (Handforth)
Gilberto and the Wind (Ets)
Stories for Free Children (Pogrebin)

Creating Art

Black Is Brown Is Tan (Adoff)
Start with a Dot (Roberts)
Little Blue and Little Yellow (Lionni)
My Very First Book of Colors (Carle)

Dramatic Play: On Our Heads!

Martin's Hats (Blos)
Caps for Sale (Slobodkina)
Hats Hats Hats (Morris)

Discovery/Science: Grow, Growing, Growest!

Growing Vegetable Soup (Ehlert)
The Carrot Seed (Krauss)
From Seed to Pear (Migutsch)
Here Are My Hands (Martin, Jr., & Archambault)
Window into an Egg (Flanagan)

Math Lab: 1,2,3, Count with Me!

How Much Is a Million? (Schwartz)
Roll Over! A Counting Song (Peek)
Ten, Nine, Eight (Bang)
Have You Seen My Duckling? (Tafuri)
The Doorbell Rang (Hutchins)

Making Music

Hush Little Baby (Aliki)
Ben's Trumpet (Isadora)
One Wide River to Cross (Emberley)
Over in the Meadow (Wadsworth)
I Know an Old Lady (Bonne)

Books for Zero to Threes

Goodnight Moon (Brown)
Brown Bear, Brown Bear (Martin, Jr.)
Duerme Bien, Pequeno Oso (Buchholz)
On the Day You Were Born (Frasier)
Ten, Nine, Eight (Bang)
Spot (Hill)

Building Blocks

Changes Changes (Hutchins)
The Big Builders (Dreany)
Who Built the Bridge? (Bate)
Boxes (Craig)

Families

When You Were a Baby (Jonas)
All Kinds of Families (Simon)
Whose Mouse Are You? (Kraus)
Five Minutes Peace (Murphy)

ABC, Just Like Me!

K Is for Kiss Goodnight: A Bedtime Alphabet (Sardegna)
A to Zen (Wells)
Grandmother's Alphabet: Grandma Can Be Anything from A to Z (Shaw)
Action Alphabet (Rotner)

Having Friends

Friends (Heime)
George and Martha (Marshall)
Best Friends (Cohen)
Frog and Toad Are Friends (Lobel)
I'll Build My Friend a Mountain (Katz)

Books for Early Primary

Charlotte's Web (White)
How Many Days to America? (Bunting)
Ramona (Cleary)
The Stories Julian Tells (Cameron)
Like Jake and Me (Jukes)

FIGURE 13-21 When literature is a natural part of the environment, children learn to appreciate and use it. (See also Ramirez & Ramirez, 1994.)

involvement with a story that is being told is almost instantaneous. The storyteller is the medium through which a story comes to life, adding a unique flavor through voice, choice of words, body language, and pacing.

"The experience of hearing a story told is more personal and connected to the reader," states Isbell (2002). "Storytelling promotes expressive language development—in oral and written forms—and presents new vocabulary and complex language in a powerful form that inspires children to emulate the model they have experienced." The oral tradition is strong in many cultures, and the telling of the tale is memorable.

Instead of focusing on a book page, the teacher involves the children directly, with expressions and gestures that draw in the children. Repetition and questions get the children so involved they feel that they have created the story. Young readers will want to find the book, and young writers will want to draw and retell the story or create their own.

Teachers can use any familiar story, be it *The Three Little Pigs* or *Madeline*. Props can be added to draw attention to the story. Flannel-board adaptations of stories are helpful; they give the storyteller a sense of security and a method for remembering the story. Children can be involved in the action by placing the characters on the felt board at the appropriate time. Puppets or an assortment of hats can be used as props. Good storytellers enjoy telling the story and communicate their enthusiasm to children.

Dramatizing Stories

Acting out characters from a favorite story has universal appeal. Young preschoolers are introduced to this activity as they act out the motions to fingerplays and songs. "The Eensy-Weensy Spider" and its accompanying motions is the precursor for dramatization. Story reenactment helps children learn to work together so that their *social development* is enhanced, as is the cognitive ability to engage in *collective representation*. As an extension of Steiner's theories, Waldorf kindergartens include fairy and morality tales. "Fairy tales are told to the children on successive days for up to two weeks, culminating in the tale as a puppet show offered to the children by the teacher or as a play with costumes acted out by the children with the teacher narrating" (Waldorf Staff, 1994). Whether the child is an observer, walk-on, mime, or actor, the learning is real in each step of the continuum.

Stories such as *Caps for Sale* (Slobodkina) and *Swimmy* (Lionni), as well as fairy tales, are popular choices for reenactment by four- and five-year-olds. They need plenty of time to rehearse, and simple props help them focus on their role. A red scarf helps Jeannada become *Little Red Riding Hood*; an old pair of sunglasses transforms Joaquin into a character from *Goggles* (Keats).

Older children may choose to write (or dictate) parts or scripts; it is appropriate for six- to eight-year-olds to have their playmates act out original stories. Once the "right" story has been chosen, the teacher helps the children to retell the story together, set the stage, and let the play begin.

Puppet Shows

Puppet shows can involve a large number of children as participants and audience. Children of all ages enjoy watching and putting on a puppet show. Because puppets are people to young children, they become confidants and special friends. Children will confide in and protect a puppet, engaging in a dialogue with one or more puppets that is often revealing of the child's inner struggles and concerns. Teachers can support their efforts by helping them to take turns, suggesting questions and dialogue to them, and involving the audience. The project of puppet making can be quite elaborate and very engaging for older children.

Book Games

Book games are a good way to extend the literary experience. Buy two copies of an inexpensive book with readable pictures, such as *The Carrot Seed* (Krauss). Tear out the pages, and cover each page with clear plastic. Children must then read the pictures to put the book into proper sequence. A book of rhymes, *Did You Ever See?* (Einsel), lends itself to rhyming games. Children can act out the rhymes from the story line or match rhyming phrasing from cards the teacher has made.

Audiovisual Resources

Cassettes and videos enlarge the child's experience with books. The auditory and the visual media reinforce one another. Putting in a "listening post" so that a few children can listen to a story with headphones adds interest to stories.

Music brings literature alive; besides tapping into the musical aspect of intelligence, it appeals to all children to move and express themselves and thus enjoy literature and books even more. The pictures can show children new aspects of the words; sometimes the music or the voices bring the book to life. Often both happen. Hundreds of children's stories—classics and modern–day—have been translated to these media.

SUMMARY

Planning for language development is a huge part of a teacher's curriculum work. Language and thought are interwined, and recent research on brain development and early literacy both indicate the importance of the early years in language acquisition and literacy skills. Children follow a sequence of language development. Language skills in early childhood include articulation, receptive and expressive language, graphic representative, and enjoyment.

The teacher's role requires an understanding of several considerations. Knowing language development and the role of home language is critical. Keeping individual children in mind and being watchful for dominance by the most verbal children helps. The teacher also needs an understanding of bilingualism and dialect differences, and a working knowledge of speech and language disorders. The language of the teacher—both spoken and nonverbal—will influence children's use of language in a program.

Children and books belong together. Good literature gives insight into human behavior. Books teach children less important though exciting things such as how to play peek-a-boo or escape a hungry lion. But they also teach matters of substance and character such as how to go to sleep, make a friend, be brave. The early years should lay a foundation in literature upon which children can build throughout their lives.

A listening past can provide additional interest in books and stories.

Books are no substitute for living, but they can add immeasurably to its richness. When life is absorbing, books can enhance our sense of its significance. When life is difficult, they can give a momentary relief from trouble, afford a new insight into our problems or those of others, or provide the rest and refreshment we need. Books have always been a source of information, comfort, and pleasure for people who know how to use them. This is as true for children as for adults. (Arbuthnot & Sutherland, 1972)

Reading and writing are part of the language and thought processes. Adults in early childhood education seek ways to involve children with the printed word in ways that have here-and-now meaning in the children's lives. Literature and computers further the development of reading and writing skills and provide enjoyable tools for the enhancement of cognition and language.

WELCOMING ENVIRONMENTS FOR YOUNG ELL CHILDREN

by
Wilma Robles de Meléndez, Ph.D.

With a continuous high rate of immigration, cultural and linguistic diversity is already a pattern that characterizes early childhood education where an increasing number of young English language learners (ELL) are commonly found in preschool and primary classrooms around the country. Working with ELL calls for teachers to be mindful and sensitive about the child's needs as they encounter a new context. Getting a sense that one belongs and that you are part of the group is an important factor that influences individual achievement. It is important to consider that some may come from settings with different cultural behaviors and that, in addition, they may have limited or no exposure to English. Coming into a classroom where social behaviors differ from those they know and where interactions are in a language different from theirs could be a challenging and, to an extent, a frightening experience. How to address these needs begins with the careful planning and organization of the environment. Environments are a powerful teaching and learning element that communicate ideas and expectations. They also help to validate the child's first language and heritage. Literally, environments "speak" to the child, a reason why at all times they should say, "This is your classroom." Successful environments for ELL children are characterized by having welcoming messages, meaningful content, and high child-appropriate expectations. Careful planning is the key to creating contexts that meet the needs of young children who are learning English.

A first step in planning a welcoming environment for young ELLs, as well as all children, is to think about the messages and impressions that the classroom communicates. Ask yourself if what hangs on the walls, what is displayed, and the materials offer a welcoming feeling for culturally and linguistically different children. Check the charts, bulletin board, and signs and see if they include postings in languages other than English and especially those reflective of the children's first languages. This would already communicate to the child "your language is valued!" For the ELL child, it also means finding something familiar, which is reassuring, helping her to feel a part of the setting. Visual impressions are compelling communicators of ideas, too, so take time to examine the images and illustrations posted. Check if these are representative of children and families from diverse backgrounds. Also, be sure to provide images that are inclusive of different social groups. You want to make everyone feel welcome!

Best practices remind us about the importance of making learning meaningful to the young ELL child. Effective environments for ELL should foster opportunities to connect experiences with what they know, which is another key step in creating a well-planned context. Take time to examine the themes that are explored in your classrooms. See if these relate to the children's experiences and backgrounds. Meaningful connections happen when the context includes opportunities such as listening and reading stories with themes and characters representative of the children's backgrounds. This supports their culture and language and provides experiences familiar to the child where opportunities abound to activate and link prior knowledge with what is learned in the classroom. Use of realia and manipulatives carefully linked to what is explored also contributes to connecting concepts and content in meaningful ways.

Environments are also characterized for communicating expectations, another essential step in planning a supporting context for ELL children. Interactions with children and peers, use of materials, and nonverbal exchanges all communicate expectations in different ways to the young English language learner. Classroom contexts for children who are learning English should communicate and encourage them to participate in experiences fostering the sense "Yes, I can!" While building their linguistic proficiency, they should also explore rich and challenging content. Take time to reflect on the expectations that you hold for the young ELL child. Remember, knowledge about the individual needs and progress level guides the planning and selection of content that should match the child's learning level. Maintaining equitable expectations requires early educators to balance activities while setting up engaging and challenging experiences.

While these three aspects—environment, content, expectations—are essential, the key to a welcoming context is a sensitive and caring early childhood educator who will find that working with young ELL children is another exciting experience that calls for attention to meeting the child's linguistic needs.

Wilma Robles de Meléndez, Ph.D., is program professor of early childhood education at the Fischler School of Education and Human Services of Nova Southeastern University (FL) where she teaches and coordinates the graduate program in early childhood education and early literacy. Her research interests include research in services for young children with cultural and linguistically diverse backgrounds, multicultural education, social studies for young children and early literacy development. She is the author of Teaching Young Children in Multicultural Classrooms *(2007) and of the* Lee y serás' Child Care Providers Conversations Series *(2005), a national Latino early literacy initiative.*

For more activities and information, visit our Web site at http://www.EarlyChildEd.delmar.com

KEY TERMS

receptive language	simultaneous acquisition	phonemes
expressive language	successive acquisition	decoding
extended discourse	dialect	emergent/early literacy
precursors	Ebonics	invented spelling
phonemic awareness	articulation	whole language
bilingualism	elaboration	

REVIEW QUESTIONS

1. How are language and cognition related?

2. How does the teacher help children develop speech and language skills in planning curriculum? How is curriculum planning affected in a class with children whose primary language is not English?

3. The way teachers use language is critical in encouraging children's own language. Name the four areas of language and what a teacher can say to encourage growth in those areas.

4. Describe some curriculum activities for cognition and language development. Simplify them for infants/toddlers/twos and elaborate for the primary-aged youngsters.

5. Name two major steps in the development of children's reading, and at least two aspects of learning in each step.

6. What is a "print-rich environment"? Give at least five examples.

7. How does one select good children's books?

LEARNING ACTIVITIES

1. Observe the children in your care. Identify the stages of language development of three children. Give concrete examples that validate your assessment.

2. Choose a child in your care whose primary language is not English. How is that child processing language? What are you doing to foster the child's emerging English skills? How is that child's first language being supported in your program? What can you do to involve the family?

3. Teaching reading readiness involves trying to develop oral language and listening skills. What could a teacher of toddlers plan for each? A kindergarten teacher?

4. Describe three ways children's books and literature help to develop intellectual skills and language proficiency. Through what techniques can literary experiences be extended in the curriculum?

5. Select four or five books from a bibliography of multicultural children's books. What themes are addressed? How does the vocabulary or speech style of the story characters teach children about diversity?

REFERENCES

Ansari, S. (2005). English Language Development Institute. Redwood City, CA: San Mateo County Office of Education.

Arbuthnot, M. H., & Sutherland, Z. (1972). *Children and books* (4th ed.). London: Scott, Foresman.

Atkins, C. P. (1993, September). Do employment recruiters discriminate on the basis of nonstandard dialect? *Journal of Employment Counseling, 30*(3), 4 (bibliography).

Baker, C. (2004). *A parents' and teachers' guide to bilingualism* (2nd ed.). Clevedon, ENG: Multilingual Matters Ltd.

Baron, N. S. (1989). *Uses of baby talk.* ERIC. ED 318230.

Bowman, B. T. (1989, October). Educating language-minority children: Challenges and opportunities. *Phi Delta Kappan.*

Cazden, C. B. (1996, March). *Communicative competence, 1966–1996.* Paper presented at the annual meeting of the American Association for Applied Linguistics (ERIC No. ED 399764), Chicago.

Chang, H. (1993). *Affirming children's roots: Cultural and linguistic diversity in early care and education.* Oakland, CA: California Tomorrow.

Chang-Chu, M. (Ed.). (1983). *Asian- and Pacific-American perspectives in bilingual education: Comparative research.* New York: Teachers College Press, Columbia University.

Chard, S. C. (1998). *The project approach: Making curriculum come alive.* New York: Scholastic.

Chesler, P. (1998). *Literacy development and activities for the young child.* Unpublished.

Chesler, P. (2002). *Bilingualism: Literacy development and activities for the young child.* Unpublished.

Chomsky, N. (1993). *Language and thought.* Wakefield, RI: Moyer Bell.

Curry-Rodd, L. (1999, September/October). Creating readers. *Child Care Information Exchange* (129).

Diaz-Soto, L. (1991, January). Research in review: Understanding bilingual/bicultural young children. *Young Children, 46*(2).

Dickenson, D. K., & Tabors, P. O. (2002, March). Fostering language and literacy in classrooms and homes. *Young Children, 57*(2).

Epstein, A. (2002). *Helping your preschool child become a reader: Ideas for parents.* Ypsilanti, MI: High/Scope Press.

Escamilla-Vestal, P. (2002, May). Early steps to reading success update, www.caeyc.org/connections. *Newsletter,* May, 2002.

Goodman, K. S., & Buck, C. (1997, March). Dialect barriers to reading comprehension revisited. *Reading Teacher, 50*(6).

Hall, P. (1999). *Because books matter.* Boston, MA: National Braille Press.

Hoover, M. (1997, March/April). Ebonics insider. *Stanford Magazine.*

International Reading Association. (2006). *Position statement: Literacy development in the preschool years,* www.reading.org.

Isbell, R. T. (2002, March). Telling and retelling stories: Learning language and literacy. *Young Children, 57*(2).

Isbell, R., & Phillips, L. (2001, Spring/Summer). Oral language development in learning centers. *Play, Policy, and Practice Connections, VI*(1).

Klein, M. D., Cook, R. E., & Richardson-Gibbs, A. M. (2001). *Strategies for including children with special needs in early childhood settings.* Clifton Park, NY: Thomson Delmar Learning.

Miller, K. (2001, September/October). Caring for the little ones: When do you teach them to read? *Child Care Information Exchange* (141).

NAEYC. (2005). *Position statement on responding to linguistic and cultural diversity: Recommendations for effective early childhood education.* Washington, DC: Author.

Owocki, G. (2001). *Make way for literacy.* Clifton Park, NY: Thomson Delmar Learning.

Parker, N. (2006). "Language Barriers in Afterschool." *CAEYC Connections,* Spring, 2006.

Roskos, K. A., Christie, J. F., & Richgels, D. J. (2003). The essentials of early literacy instruction. Washington, DC: *Young Children.*

Salyer, D. M. (2000, July). "I disagree!" said a second-grader: Butterflies, conflict, and literate thinking. *Young Children, 55*(4).

Saxton, R. R. (1998, July). Different dialects. Personal communication.

Selman, R. (2001, May). Talk time: Programming communicative interaction into the toddler day. *Young Children, 56*(3).

Smitherman, G. (1977). *Talkin' & testifyin': The language of black America.* Boston: Houghton Mifflin.

Soundy, C. S., & Stout, N. L. (2002, March). Pillow talk: Fostering the emotional and language needs of young learners. *Young Children, 57*(2).

Tabors, P. O. (1998, November). What early childhood educators need to know: Developing effective programs for linguistically and culturally diverse children and families. *Young Children, 53*(6).

Thomas, G. T. (1983). The deficit, difference, and bicultural theories of black dialect and nonstandard English. *Urban Review, 15*(2).

Vygotsky, L. S. (1962). *Thought and language.* New York: MIT Press and John Wiley & Sons.

Wasik, Barbara, A. (2001, January). Teaching the alphabet to young children. *Young Children, 56*(1).

Wien, C. A., Stacey, S., Hubley Keating, B., Deyarmond Rowlings, J., & Cameron, H. (2002, January). The doll project: Handmade dolls as a framework for emergent curriculum. *Young Children, 57*(1).

Willis, C. (1998, May/June). Language development: A key to lifelong learning. *Child Care Information Exchange* (121).

Early Literacy

Bobys, A. R. (2000, July). What does emerging literacy look like? *Young Children, 55*(4).

Cruikshank, S. (1993). Whole language: A developmentally appropriate alternative. In A. Gordon, & K. B. Browne (Eds.), *Beginnings and Beyond* (3rd ed.). Clifton Park, NY: Thomson Delmar Learning.

de Melendez, W. R., & Ostertag, V. (1997). *Teaching young children in multicultural classrooms.* Clifton Park, NY: Thomson Delmar Learning.

Derman-Sparks, L., & ABC Task Force. (1989). *The anti-bias curriculum.* Washington, DC: NAEYC.

Early Childhood Resources. (1995). *Implementing developmentally appropriate practice kindergarten through third grade.* Corte Madera, CA: Author.

Goodman, K. (1986). *What's whole in whole language.* Portsmouth, NH: Heinmann Educational Books.

International Reading Association and NAEYC. (1998, July). Learning to read and write: Developmentally appropriate practice for young children. *Young Children, 53*(4).

Lomangino, A. G. (2005). "Passing Notes and Signing Words at Snack Time," Stanford University: *Bing Times,* November, 2005.

Lundin, A. (1991, Summer). Secret gardens: The literature of childhood. *Childhood Education, 67*(4).

Machado, J. M. (1999). *Early childhood experiences in language arts.* Clifton Park, NY: Thomson Delmar Learning.

National Research Council. (1998). *Prevention of reading difficulties in young children.* Washington, DC: National Academy Press.

Raines, S. C., & Canady, R. J. (1989). *Story stretchers.* Mt. Rainier, WA: Gryphon House.

Ramirez, G., Jr., & Ramirez, J. L. (1994). *Multiethnic children's literature.* Clifton Park, NY: Thomson Delmar Learning.

Reisner, T. (2001, March). Learning to teach reading in a developmentally appropriate kindergarten. *Young Children, 56*(2).

Schickedanz, J. (1999). *Much more than the ABCs: The early stages of reading and writing.* Washington, DC: NAEYC.

Shanahan, T. (2005, February 14–16). *What the national early literacy panel tells us about early literacy.* At IRA-NICHD Conference on Early Childhood Literacy Research, Washington, DC.

Smith, F. (2004). *Understanding reading—The psycholinguistics of reading and writing* (6th ed.). NJ: Lawrence Erlbaum Associates.

Tanaka, M. D. (1988). Literacy learning in kindergarten: Key words, journals and phonics. In E. Jones, (Ed.). *Reading, writing and talking with four, five and six year olds* (1988). Pasadena, CA: Pacific Oaks.

Trelease, J. (1982). *The read-aloud handbook.* New York: Penguin Books.

Waldorf Staff of Los Altos, CA. (1994). *Understanding the Waldorf curriculum.* Pamphlet for parents.

HELPFUL WEB SITES

American Library Association	http://www.ala.org
Braille Institute	http://www.brailleinstitute.org
Children's Book Council	http://www.cbcbooks.org
Children's Book Press (multicultural literature)	http://www.cbookpress.org
Education Development Center/Center for Children and Families/ Latinos	http://www.edc.org/ccf/latinos
Head Start Information and Publication Center	http://www.headstartinfo.org
HeadsUp!	http://www.huronline.org
International Reading Association	http://www/rcading.org
National Association for Bilingual Education	http://www.nabe.org
National Association for Multicultural Education	http://www.nameorg.org
National Association for the Education of Young Children	http://www.naeyc.org
National Black Child Development Institute	http://www.nbcdi.org
National Center for Family Literacy	http://www.famlit.org
National Institute for Literacy	http://www.nifl.gov
Office of Education, Federal Level	http://www.ed.gov/index.jsp
Raising a Reader Early Literacy Program	http://www.raisingareader.org
Reading Is Fundamental	http://www.rif.org

For more activities and information, visit our Web site at http://www.EarlyChildEd.delmar.com

Planning for the Heart and Soul: Emotional, Social, Creative, and Spiritual Growth

QUESTIONS FOR THOUGHT

What is the connection between a child's well-being and affective development?

What are the components of self-esteem?

What is emotional growth in the early childhood years?

How do teachers handle the expression of feelings in the class setting?

What is social competence in the early childhood years?

How are social skills developed through the curriculum?

What is creativity?

How is creativity expressed in the early years?

How can teachers care for children's spiritual growth?

INTRODUCTION

The heart and soul of any good program for young children is a commitment to help children as they struggle with (1) the reality of emotions, (2) the awareness of the need for social skills, (3) the creative urge, and (4) acknowledgment of the spirit. Together, these four areas comprise the affective side of development. Closely related to the child's self-concept and self-esteem, affective growth takes place in the context of personal identity. "Identity is tied to culture. In the critical early years, children begin to develop a sense of self as families hand down beliefs, attitudes, and behaviors (Nakahata, 2001). It is primarily through affective experiences that children learn who they are; only then can they see themselves successfully in relation to others." "K–12 standards have often focused on academic subject matter rather than including other domains. . . . Because research has emphasized how powerfully early social and emotional competence predicts school readiness and later success, and because good early environments help build this competence, this domain should be given explicit attention in early learning standards" (NAEYC, 2002).

Each section of this chapter—emotional, social, creative, and spiritual growth—is explored individually to give a greater understanding of its importance to the developing child. An overview of development is followed by a discussion of the skills children learn in the preschool years. The crucial role of the teacher is emphasized next, followed by curriculum planning to reinforce each developmental area.[1]

The Affective Domain

The first thing one notices on entering an early childhood classroom is the children at play. A quick survey of the area shows who is playing together, whether there is crying or fighting, and how happy or sad the children look. This overview gives an immediate sense of the emotional, social, and creative climate in that early childhood setting.

- *Emotional.* Toddler Abier giggles as she runs her hands across the water table, then cries after she splashes soapsuds in her eyes and needs to be comforted.

- *Social.* Preschooler Danny wants his favorite red wagon so Pat, the student teacher, helps him negotiate a turn with Christa.

- *Creative.* Kindergartners Fabio, Erika, and Benjy work steadily to build a tall, intricate block structure. When it is finished, the three children stand back and marvel at their creation.

- *Spiritual.* The children see a nest being built in the backyard of Teresa's family childcare home. "How do the birds know how to make the nest?" wonder the children. They make daily checks and then hear the peeping sound of the newly hatched baby birds. "It's magic!" whispers Neefara, and the children sit quietly and reverently every time they see the mother return.

Together these factors—emotional mood, social dynamics, creative, and spiritual tone—define the overall atmosphere in which children play and work.

The components of well-being are woven together in the developing child. Children who are sensitive to their own feelings and moods are able to begin understanding other people and thus become more socially effective and successful. Children with experience in many creative endeavors have the self-confidence that comes from having an outlet for self-expression. Children who are spiritually curious are likely to ask questions such as "How did the little seed do that?" when gardening, or they want to write a letter to their dead pet to make sure all is at peace.

These four areas are also linked to other aspects of the child's growth. Below are four examples of how the developmental domains connect

- *Creative/Physical.* Physical skills can define and limit children's creative abilities. Two-year-old Andrea, whose physical skills do not yet include balancing objects, plays with blocks by piling them on top of one another, filling her wagon with blocks, and dumping them or lugging them from place to place.

- *Social/Cognitive.* It is hard for five-year-old Karena to share her best friend Luther with other children. Her intellectual abilities do not yet allow her to consider more than one idea at a time, so she cannot understand that Luther can be her friend and Dana's at the same time.

- *Emotional/Language.* Tyler is upset with his teacher's refusal to let him go outdoors during

---

1 "As children are forming their identity and self-worth, they often struggle with conflicting messages from home, media, school and peers about who they are and what they are worth" (Nakahata, 2001). Caregivers help children grow by first attending to their home cultures and languages as they develop curriculum.

storytime. "I hate you!" he screams, "and you aren't the boss of me!" Children learn to label and express their emotions through words.

● *Spiritual/Creative.* The children make their daily trek to the henhouse as soon as outside time begins. They first gasp as they discover a raccoon has pried open the wire and killed their pet. After all the queries about what happened, Ellie speaks up, "I want to make a picture for Henny-Penny to take with her." The group paints a multicolored mural, where each one dictates ideas. "I am sad you died," says Ellie. "But don't worry, you will rise again!" A child's spiritual notions are allowed to express themselves in creative ways.

It is difficult to measure the child's growth in these areas; it is easier to determine a child's progress in physical, cognitive, and language development. After all, a child counts or doesn't count, is either 40 inches tall or is not, and speaks in full sentences or in short phrases. Affective expressions are more subtle and subjective. Talbot may feel rejected and sad if no one greets him as he enters the playhouse. He may mistake the children's busy-ness as an act of exclusion. In reality, the children did not even notice he was there. Teachers can play a critical role in helping children express their inner selves and feelings.

Traditionally, early childhood educators have concerned themselves with children's well-being, knowing that in the early years the foundations must be laid for children to understand themselves and others. Social growth, creative expression, and experience with a wide range of emotional behaviors also help children develop a strong self-concept with positive self-esteem.

Building self-image is complex, multidimensional, and ever-changing. It affects everything we do and is affected by everything we do. Crucial to children's self-image is how children interpret the response of the environment to their actions. And much of a self-image is based on the way society views the child. Teachers take an important role as they provide an essential ingredient of self-image: the quality of human interactions.[1]

Curry and Johnson (1990) have identified several key experiences for children in the early years to have in order to develop and consolidate a sense of self (see Figure 14-1).

"Kindness and hostility go hand in hand as children exercise their growing abilities to understand and affect the feelings of others" (Curry & Johnson, 1990). At the same time, this age is looking at themselves in terms of moral worth, wrestling with good/nice and bad/mean.

Early childhood curriculum can be transforming if it fosters the development of the whole child. This will mean including the

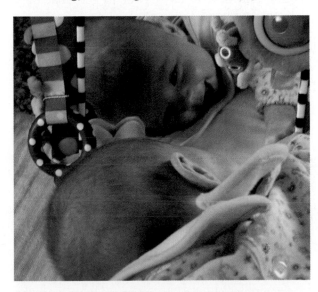

Building self-image is complex, multidimensional, and ever-changing. (Courtesy of Chris and Stephanie Kelly.)

Age	Growth Focus	Help Children with . . .
Infants	Relationship	Attachment
Toddlers	Awareness	Self-regulation
Twos	Curiosity	Interactions with others
Preschool	Self-concept	Testing and evaluating self
	Authority	Testing their limits in play, making friends
Kindergarten	Self-in-the-world	Feeling effective
Primary	Competence	Managing failure/ mistakes, finding their strengths

FIGURE 14-1 Children's emotional and social growth is an ongoing challenge as they enter new settings in their expanding world.

 1 While secure attachment has been identified as a requirement for positive emotional development, there are many pathways to self-esteem, all of which occur within the particular values and goals of a child's culture. Responsive, supportive adult contact comes in many forms.

children's and their families' lives and incorporating multicultural and anti-bias elements (see Chapters 9 and 10).

> Transformative education recognizes that all of us are socialized to take our place in society. Our sense of self is influenced by prevailing social values and our social skills are shaped by social practices. The social realities of sexism, racism, classism, ethnocentrism, and heterosexism shape children's self-identity and the formation of prejudice and discriminatory behavior. Transformative education fosters a positive and knowledgable self-identity by strengthening children's connections to their families, cultural communities, and geographic communities. (York, 1998)

An affective curriculum that prepares children to be active and involved and promotes social action and problem solving helps children develop into involved citizens with a positive self-identity. In curriculum for infants and toddlers, the emphasis is on relationships. In preschool, it is part of the traditional emphasis on social and emotional development. For school-age programs, it is often known as "Character Education." Our Code of Ethics reminds us to "recognize that children and adults achieve their full potential in the context of relationships that are based on trust and respect" (Core Values, see Appendix A).

Affirming Identity

As children experience messages from others and through their own perceptions, they construct an understanding of race, ethnicity, gender, and ability. This will shape their self-image and, by extension, their relationships to others. Starting Small (1997) suggests activities to assist in promoting children's identity, which are incorporated in the theme/project in Figures 14-1 and 14-7.

Self-Esteem

An individual's sense of personal worth and an acceptance of who one is helps them make judgments about themselves as they confront the world. To the extent that children feel worthy and capable, they are ready to succeed. If children disapprove of themselves, they may feel like failures and expect to do poorly.

Self-esteem develops as a reflection of experiences: The way people respond to you gives you some indication of your importance or value. Newborn infants have no concept of self

and no past experience to judge their own worth. A young child who has positive experiences with others will more likely have a high sense of self-esteem than one who has felt unloved or unnoticed.

There appear to be four components of self-esteem:

1. A sense of one's own identity.
2. A sense of one's uniqueness.
3. A sense of self (power).
4. A sense of belonging (connectedness).

Early in life, self-esteem is tied to family, friends, and other important people, such as teachers. Figure 14-2 shows how curriculum can develop each of these characteristics. Planning for children's success builds self-esteem. It includes the following four components, which we call the "Four I's":

- *I.* When children enter the classroom, the message they receive is "I am important and this is my place." The physical environment, the daily schedule, and the curriculum are designed to give all children permission to express themselves. This gives children a sense of identity and uniqueness.

- *Initiative.* Children are encouraged to initiate their own learning, to make contact with others, to take action, and to make choices. Power is important to young children; they want to know how to take (and when to let go) of control, and how to use power to get what they want and need.

- *Independence.* Self-management tasks of dressing, eating, toileting are given an important place in the curriculum. Children are assisted in taking care of their own belongings and in developing independent judgment about events and activities. Every culture and group has its own intricate rules about when and how to be independent, and an early childhood group can give them experience.

- *Interaction.* Social interaction has a high priority in the program. The room and yard are busy places, with children moving about and talking among themselves and with adults. Conflicts are accepted as a natural consequence of social life. In the spirit of John Dewey (see Figure 1-1, Chapter 1), democratic group living will encourage children to interact. In respect for cultures that value collaboration and group harmony, such interaction fosters a consciousness of interdependence. The need for relationships with other people is crucial, and interaction gives children a sense of connectedness.

Emotional Skill Development	Curriculum: Activity (Use of Sense)
Self Esteem 1. *Identity:* "Look at what I can do, the noise I can make, the weight I can pick up and move!" 2. *Connectedness:* "I can make the sames snakes as you; we can all make cakes." 3. *Uniqueness:* "I'm pouring mine; you're dripping yours; and she is squeezing her stuff out her fingers!" 4. *Power:* "I can make this water go anywhere I want; look out for the tidal waves!" **Deal with Feelings** 1. *Identification* (to notice and label): "Does it feel very smooth, slippery, slidy? Is it soft and soothing?" 2. *Mastery* (to accept): "She took your baker's dough and that made you angry. You can tell her you don't like it when she grabs what you are using." 3. *Expressing* (to express appropriately): Child: "Tami has all the big pitchers." Teacher: "How can you let her know you want one?" Child: "And she splashed me two times!" Teacher: "If you feel too crowded, you need to tell her so." 4. *Feelings* (to deal with others): "Whee! Yuk! Mmm! Ha!"	• Use rocks of various sizes with balances, so that children can touch and hear when they move things around. • A malleable material such as play dough can be used first alone, then with tools. • Make "oobleck," a mixture of cornstarch and water, in separate tubs for each child. Children can manipulate it in their own ways. • Water play offers the child choices: pour into any of several containers, fill or empty the jug, use a funnel or a baster to squirt the water, make waves or splash hands. • When fingerpainting, the teacher can describe what it appears the child is feeling. Children can identify their feelings as the teacher describes them while they use the materials. • Whether the sensory material is clay, soapy water, or fine sand, the issues of ownership and use of materials arise. Then, teachers reflect children's feelings and help them take responsibility for their own feelings. • As children begin to use the sensory materials, they need to communicate to others. Usually the issues are about wanting more material and personal space. • When children share in a sensory activity, such as a feeling walking through tubs of small pebbles, sand, and soapsuds, they have the delightful experience of enjoying their own feelings with another.

FIGURE 14-2 An affective curriculum offers sensorimotor opportunities to deal with materials in a nonstructured way. Because children relax with open-ended activities, they will often share their feelings as they use sensory materials in a comfortable atmosphere.

A positive sense of self is critical for young children. Research (Marshall, 1989) shows that low self-image is correlated with poor mental health, poor academic achievement, and delinquency. In contrast, a positive self-concept is correlated with good mental health, academic achievement, and good behavior. Children with a positive self-image are ready to meet life's challenges. They will have the self-confidence to deal with the reality of emotions, the changing nature of social interaction, the joys of creativity, and serenity of spirituality

THE DEVELOPMENT OF EMOTIONS AND EMOTIONAL GROWTH

Emotions are the feelings a person has—joy and sorrow, love and hate, confidence and fear, loneliness and belonging, anger and contentment, frustration and satisfaction. They are responses to events, people, and circumstances. Feelings are an outgrowth of what a person perceives is happening. Emotionally healthy people learn to give expression to their feelings in appropriate ways. They do not allow their feelings to overshadow the rest of their behavior. The optimal time to learn these skills is in the early years.

Research in brain development (Pool, 1997; Chapters 4 and 12) and the theoretical work in multiple intelligence (see Chapter 4) were expanded by Daniel Goleman as he wrote about emotional intelligence (1995). An area in the limbic section of our brains is the control center of our emotions. Two almond-shaped organs behind our eyes, called the amygdala, are in constant communication with the rest of the brain (for thinking and perceiving).

The emotional brain scans everything happening to us from moment to moment to see if something that happened in the past that made us sad or angry is like what is happening now. If so, the amygdala calls an alarm—to declare an emergency and to mobilize in a split second to act. And it can do so, in brain time, more rapidly than the thinking brain takes to figure out what is going on, which is why people can get into a rage and do something very inappropriate that they wished they hadn't. It's called an "emotional hijacking."

Children experience this constantly, and we need to help develop what Goleman identifies as five dimensions of emotional intelligence into everything we do in school and group settings: self-awareness, handling emotions generally, motivation, empathy, and social skills. Each of these is discussed in this chapter, with suggestions of how to put emotional health into our curriculum. The amygdala doesn't mature until the midteens, so teachers can help develop emotional intelligence in young children successfully.

For example, infants respond in agitated emotion whether wet, hungry, hurt, or bored. Gradually, the expression of the emotion becomes more refined and varies with the situation. A toddler's cry of distress is different from the cry of discomfort or hunger. As children get older, their emotional expressions change as they gain control over some of their feelings and learn new ways to express them.

Strong external forces are also at work. Parents, family members, teachers, and friends are social influences, helping the young child learn socially acceptable behavior. Much of what children learn is by example (see Chapter 4). Therefore, children learn more from adult models than from simply being told how to behave and feel.

EMOTIONAL SKILLS IN EARLY CHILDHOOD

The emotional skills children learn in their early years are substantial. Research shows that some emotions—interest, disgust, distress, to name a few—are observable in the newborn, and it is posited that all the **basic emotions** are present within the first few weeks of life. These include happiness, interest, surprise, fear, anger, sadness, and disgust. The more **complex emotions** of shame, guilt, envy, and pride emerge later, once children have had the social experiences of observing these emotions in others or have been in situations that might evoke such feelings. These expressions have been observed in a wide range of cultural and ethnic groups.[1]

In early childhood, children learn to respond to new situations and to react and connect with a teacher, both very emotional experiences. Good teachers stimulate an emotional response to themselves and the curriculum that is a balance between interest and overwhelming fear. Creating the "right" emotional conditions is a primary way to gain access to a child's capacity for learning. Young children are not yet limited by **social mores** and standards of conduct that prevent them from sincere and truthful self-expression. Teachers observe children and learn how youngsters feel about facing their own feelings, the feelings of others, and the range of skills categorized as emotional growth.

Ability to Deal with Feelings

Dealing with feelings involves four steps. Each builds on the other so that they follow a developmental sequence; the learning that takes place at one level affects the development of what follows. Figures 14-2 and 14-4 describe how the early childhood classroom and teacher help children deal effectively with their feelings.

Video VIEW PoinT 14-1

"Infants and toddlers express a wide range of emotions."

COMPETENCY: Emotional Development

AGE GROUP: Infants and Toddlers

CRITICAL THINKING QUESTIONS:

1. What would be appropriate curriculum for such young children that would help them learn to express feelings?

2. How can you take into consideration different family and cultural beliefs about the expression of emotion?

---

 1 Because a child's self-image begins with where she belongs—family, community, culture—it is critical that early childhood programs support a child's home environment—culture, race, language, lifestyle, and values (Wardle, 1993). One is reminded of the universal qualities to be found in each of us in our diverse world. The challenge is to notice and celebrate our similarities and our differences—both are gifts.

To Notice and Label Feelings

This ability is the first step and corresponds to Goleman's "self-awareness" dimension. The sobbing one- or two-year-old may have many reasons for feeling in distress. As parents recognize the cries of hunger, hurt, and fear, they name these feelings. The child will learn to notice what the feeling is and recognize it. Teachers know how to "read" children's faces and body language to give them the words for and ways to express those feelings. Chapter 6 has suggestions for becoming a skillful observer. For instance, we can help young children produce a label for their feeling of anger or sadness by teaching them that they are having a feeling and that they can use a word to describe their angry feelings. We can ask them to "Use your words" only after we have helped them learn and find those specific words (Marion, 2003).

Preschoolers are quite verbal and curious about language and ready to learn words that describe a wider range of feelings. They can learn "lonely," "scared," "silly," "sad," and "happy." Labeling what one feels inside is a critical skill to learn. It is a healthy first-grader who can say, "I have tried to cut this string three times and the scissors aren't working. I am frustrated. I need some help!"

To Accept Feelings

Teachers recognize that children are capable of strong feelings. Children can feel overwhelmed by the very strength and intensity of a feeling, be it one of anger or of love. As children come to

Young children feel their emotions strongly. Learning to read faces and body stance is essential to guiding emotional development and for children to be successful socially.

accept feelings, they learn how to handle the depth of the feeling and not let it overpower them. The changing nature of feelings is also part of accepting the feeling. It can be a source of comfort and relief for young children to discover that the strong emotion they experience now will pass. Adults who work with young children help them work through those feelings safely.

Carlos feels sad as his mother prepares to leave. His teacher walks them to the door, then bends down and puts an arm around him as his mother waves good-bye. Acknowledging that he is sad, the teacher stays with Carlos, reminding him that his mother will return and that the teacher will take care of him while he is at school. Because the child is allowed to feel the sadness that is natural in leave-taking, the tense feelings are over in a few minutes. The teacher smiles and encourages Carlos to find something fun to do. Once he has recovered his composure, the teacher can point out that he's "okay now," and Carlos can feel proud for having lived through and grown from saying good-bye. Goleman's dimension of motivation is at work, for Carlos now feels hope. He is motivated to learn, and now has zeal or persistence to work through future scared or sad moments. Acknowledgment of the feeling and his ability to accept it help give Carlos the confidence to move on.

To Express Feelings in an Appropriate Way

Expressing feelings appropriately is a two-part process. First, children must feel free to express their feelings; second, they must learn ways of expression that are suitable to their age and to the situation. Many beginning teachers are uncomfortable because children express themselves so strongly (and often aggressively). Yet the child who is passive and unable to express feelings freely should be of equal concern and should be encouraged in self-expression.

When teachers create a safe emotional climate, they can effectively help children learn to understand and express themselves. "Adults who most effectively socialize . . . convey a simple, firm, consistent message, [for example] acknowledging a child's right to feel anger while prohibiting expression of anger in destructive

or hurtful ways" (Marion, 1997). Goleman describes this as handling emotions generally. Knowing how to handle upsetting feelings, or impulses, is the root of emotional intelligence. "I can see you are upset about Joaquin taking the zoo animal," you might say, "But I can't let you hit him—and I won't let him hit you, either."

As children grow, they acquire the modes of expression that are developmentally appropriate for their age. Babies and toddlers without language cry to express their feelings; thus this type of crying calls for the same kind of immediate response given to other forms of communication in later years. Two-year-olds express their displeasure by pushes and shoves; four-year-olds use their verbal power and argue. By six or seven, children learn to tell others—clearly and with reasons—what they are feeling. The ability to express feelings is intact, but the methods of expression change as children grow. Expression of feelings also has a cultural dimension. Some cultures are open in their display of emotions, whereas others are reserved.[1]

To Deal with the Feelings of Others

Dealing with the feelings of others is the culminating step in the development of emotional skills. Feelings are the spark of life in people: the flash of anger, the "ah-hah" of discovery, the thrill of accomplishment, the hug of excitement. Because recognizing and expressing emotions are closely interwoven, children who can distinguish among different emotions and have some experience in taking the perspective of others by observing their feelings develop empathy. *Empathy* can happen at a young age. Very young children may cry or gather near the teacher when a playmate is hurt or sad; preschoolers smile at another's laughter; and kindergartners imagine themselves vividly in another's predicament during a story. Like the complex emotions discussed earlier, empathy requires cognitive abilities, such as seeing oneself as separate from other people (see Erikson in Chapter 4) and also as connected in some way to others (see Vygotsky in Chapters 4 and 12). Two- to five-year-olds can respond with empathy to the emotions of others.

Older children, who are better able to put themselves in another's place (see Piaget in

---

Chapters 4 and 12) and who understand a wider range of emotions, can respond to others in distress. Conducting class meetings to help children "Talk It Out" (see Figure 14-11) guides children through a process that builds problem-solving, compassion, and community. Empathy is affected by early experience (Berk, 1999) and needs nurturing to grow. Helping children to tolerate and appreciate how different people express their emotions leads to understanding and cooperation.

Ability to Handle Change

Isn't it remarkable that, as one of the most adaptable species on the planet, we humans resist change so much? Even as our brains are programmed to find pattern and sameness, it is change that is inevitable.

The very act of being born is a change, marking the beginning of a life in which stress is part of the act of developmental achievement. Witness the toddler's numerous falls toward walking, the separation of parent and child at the nursery school doorway, the concentration and frustrations of the six-year-old on roller skates. A measure of **positive stress** encourages a child to strive and achieve, to find out and discover.

Stress can arise from several factors, both internal (severe colic) or external (moving to a new home). Some stresses are acute in a child's life, such as a hospitalization, whereas others are chronic, such as living in an alcoholic household. Many variables are associated with different kinds of stress in children's lives. For instance, age, intellectual capacity, and gender can influence a child's response to a stressful situation; research seems to indicate that male children are more vulnerable than female children (Honig, 1986). Inadequate housing, poverty, and war are ecological stressors (see Chapter 15 for a discussion of violence). Family changes—the birth of a sibling, death or loss of a close family member, marriage problems and divorce—are sources of stress on a personal level.[1,2] Inept parenting practices that neglect or abuse children are especially troublesome as they hurt children and provide them with poor role models for learning how to cope with stress.

Children learn to appreciate and understand feelings as their feelings are accepted by teachers who can show them how to deal with feelings and changes.

Dealing with stress and coping with new information are part of the ability to handle change. Indeed, as early as the 1970s researchers were looking into the concept of resilience, the idea that some children, in spite of adversity, appeared psychologically invulnerable. The capacity to cope effectively with adversity and bounce back is a combination of nature and nurture. The protective mechanisms that promote resiliency fall predominantly into three categories (Weinreb, 1997):

1. The individual's personality and behavior
2. Family attributes
3. The social environment

Resilient children have hope, and good self-esteem. Both of these are under the influence of the teacher and curriculum. Helping children find a haven and creative interests also help develop a protective buffer against difficulties in school or home. "Caring schools value and

---

1 In working with children from potentially stress-producing situations, teachers recognize and acknowledge the level of coping and resiliency so many children and their families possess.

2 Simply living in American society is stressful for many children. For instance, the Native American child lives in "a conflict of cultures. She must 'make it' in the white world to survive, and she must recognize her Indian heritage to affirm her own identity. A teacher must accept the total child and help her function effectively in both worlds" (Sample, 1993).

Stage	Behavior	The Teacher Helps
Alarm	Feels arousal, fear, confusion. Has swift mood changes.	Notices when child is stressed (sees changes in behavior). Listens. Offers words for child's feelings. Offers age-appropriate explanations. Is accepting of unpredictable behavior. Reassures child of teacher's constant availability. Alerts parents and others of child's state. Takes preventive actions to lessen other stressful events.
Appraisal	Attempts to understand the problem.	Listens. Offers age-appropriate explanations. Helps child see situation more positively. May make a simple list of the problem. Reassures that the problem *will* be solved. Alerts other adults to the importance of child's work.
Search	Looks for coping strategy. Selects from what is at hand.	Listens. Asks for the child's ideas. Helps child list possible solutions. Tells parents and others of child's solutions. Demonstrates self-control and coping skills him/herself. Encourages and enhances child's self-esteem.
Implementation	Tries out a coping strategy. Applies a solution to the problem.	Listens. Observes child's implementing a solution. Gives supportive feedback about relative success or failure of the plan. Helps child refine or revise strategy as needed. Encourages child's efforts.

FIGURE 14-3 Stages of and strategies for coping with stress: the teacher is observant of the child throughout, makes regular time to talk individually, and encourages the child to use art, books, and class members as supports.

promote artistic endeavors, and the products are displayed proudly and masterfully. . . . Less physical crowding . . . outdoor space for running or a clutter-free classroom environment" (Weinreb, 1997) can help children live without turmoil at school or childcare. Perhaps the single most important intervention is you, the teacher, who is a confidant or a positive role model. Figure 14-3 lists the stages of stress and teacher strategies.

Teachers can help children accept change in several ways.

- Anticipate changes that are likely to occur and identify the process for children. "Junko, your mother will be leaving soon. We'll go looking for that favorite puzzle after you say good-bye to her."
- Notify children of changes in the daily routine. "We won't be having snacks inside today; let's use the patio table instead."
- Model acceptance of unanticipated changes. When children are informed that change is

anticipated, accepted, and not necessarily disrupting, they become more relaxed about handling the unpredictable.

- Be a resource for helping children cope in ways that are appropriate to the child and the situation at hand. "It's OK to cry when you're sad or scared, Akbar. It's hard to figure out what to do when they say they don't want to play."

Ability to Exercise Judgment

The ability to exercise judgment is an important skill, for it helps children to make decisions and figure out what to do in new situations. On entering school, a child faces many decisions: Where shall I play? Who shall I play with? What if my friend wants to do something I know is wrong? Who will I turn to for help when I need it? Judgment is selecting what to do, when to do it, with whom to do it, and when to stop.

Making choices is an essential part of decision-making. Children are bombarded with choices in America—too many choices, some people say. Some children must decide about issues that, in other times, only adults handled. But children "have difficulty discriminating between big choices and little choices. Every choice is a big one for most children" (Simon, 1994). So, as does any skill, learning to make good choices takes thought, guidance, and lots of practice.[1]

There is no easy way to teach children how to make decisions because each situation must be dealt with on an individual basis. The judgment a child exercises in choosing a friend to play with today may have other factors to consider tomorrow. Instead, teachers help children base their decisions on the best judgment they are capable of in each instance. One way to encourage decision making is to provide opportunities for choice (see "Focus on Skills" for specific suggestions).

Another aspect of judgment is a child's **self-regulation**. Research (Bronson, 2000) suggests that children can develop the capacity to plan and guide themselves. In contrast to self-control, in which we teach children to respond to an external rule, children's self-regulation is a combination of the cognitive and emotional realms.

> During the early childhood years, there is a great increase in self-regulation . . . [T]his increase is a "central and significant" developmental hallmark of

the early childhood period. During these years the child makes tremendous progress towards regulating emotional responses and is increasingly able to comply with external requests, control behavior in familiar settings, control attention, and engage in self-directed thinking and problem-solving self-regulation. (Bronson, 2000)

The teacher can encourage this process by serving as a Vygotsky-like mediator, making children participants in their own learning (thinking), and by supporting children's focus on self-competence (emotional). As they mature, children are able to sort out what judgments might be made here, what factors need to be considered there.

Enjoying One's Self and One's Power

Teachers want children to feel powerful—to know that they can master their lives and feel confident in their own abilities. This feeling of power is particularly important in the early years, when so much of what a child can see is out of reach, both literally and figuratively.

Responsibility and limits, however, go hand in hand with power. The child who is strong enough to hit someone has to learn not to use that strength unnecessarily. The child who shouts with glee also finds out that noise is unacceptable indoors. By holding children responsible for their own actions, teachers can help children enjoy their power and accept its limitations.

One kind of fantasy play most teachers encounter is that of **superheroes**. Common to children as young as two, superhero play is exciting and rowdy, usually active and loud, playacting of heroic roles that give children powers they lack in everyday life. Superhero play attracts children who are (Hoffman, 2004)

- Investigating power and autonomy
- Balancing the desire for power with the need for friendship
- Testing physical limits
- Exploring feelings
- Answering big questions about the world such as
  - What is right and what is wrong, good and bad?
  - What is fair and what is unfair?

Enjoying one's self includes being aware of one's power and learning to use it well, making important things happen without harming self or others.

 1 Teachers can help children with some emotionally difficult choices as they work with issues of bias and stereotyping. Social action (see next section) is one way to teach about choices that benefit others as well as helping children express their feelings and ideas.

- What is life and what is death?
- What is a boy and what is a girl?
- What is real and what is fantasy?

Children's natural struggles for mastery and the attraction of rough-and-tumble play collide with teachers' concerns about fighting, aggression, and letting the play get out of hand. This special type of dramatic play calls for special handling (Kostelnik, Whiren, & Stein, 1986):

- Help children recognize humane characteristics of superheroes.
- Discuss real heroes and heroines.
- Talk about the pretend world of acting.
- Limit the place and time for superhero play.
- Explore related concepts.
- Help children de-escalate rough-and-tumble play.
- Make it clear that aggression is unacceptable.
- Give children control over their lives.
- Praise children's attempts at mastery.

Imaginary companions often join superheroes, although they just as often accompany children on their own. This second type of fantasy play sometimes concerns adults. Piaget believed that they reflected immature thinking of the preoperational stage and should disappear by the time a child began elementary school (Chapter 4). More recent research (Taylor, 1999; Carlson & Taylor, 2005) suggests that imaginary friends offer companionship and entertainment, and can help children through difficult times.

> [T]he creation of an imaginary companion is healthy and relatively common. . . . [C]hildren with imaginary companions appear to be less shy, more able to focus their attention, and to have advanced social understanding when compared with other children. . . . The bottom line is that although imaginary companions and other fantasies have sometimes been interpreted as signs of emotional disturbance, a break with reality, or even the emergence of multiple personalities, they are really just a variation on the theme of all pretend play.

Fantasy play is an important component of children's cognitive and emotional development. Still, teachers and parents are rightfully concerned if children's fantasy behavior turns aggressive. They wonder if this kind of play increases an and exposure to war or violence, stimulated from both the media and home. However, *roughhousing* and aggression have distinctly different patterns of behavior and should be recognized as such. Chapter 15 discusses the concerns of war play and violence and disaster in children's lives. Children need guidance to learn how to express themselves appropriately and exercise their growing powers responsibly.

Teachers can help children learn to appreciate and enjoy themselves. Each time a child is acknowledged, a teacher fosters that sense of uniqueness: "Carrie, you have a great sense of humor!" "Eric, your power bracelets are helping collect all the trash here." "Freddie, I love the way you and your 'dog-friend Dan' sing so clearly." Saying it aloud reinforces in children the feeling that they are enjoyable to themselves and to others.

THE TEACHER'S ROLE

The first step in helping children develop healthy emotional patterns is for adults to acquire such good patterns themselves. For instance, are you a person who labels others? What happens when a child is difficult, or doesn't meet your expectations? Looking inside, stepping back to think about what we are feeling, is helpful. Coming up with a *positive* label for every child may also help teachers deal better with the emotions and behavior of the children in their care (Greenman, 1991). Another step is to develop and use a "feeling" vocabulary. Words of an emotional nature can be used to label and identify feelings as teachers talk with young children.

There are many ways to develop a list of words related to emotions. Figure 14-4 illustrates one way. Identify some of the feelings children express; then describe how the children look and act when experiencing those emotions. This practice helps to build a vocabulary and an understanding of children's emotional expressions.

Making the classroom a comfortable place for children is the third step to a healthy emotional climate.[1] Teachers can also become more attuned to the emotional climate in the

---

1 To feel they belong, children need to have their culture and some of their family rituals and traditions incorporated into their program. For instance, "the rituals of mealtimes, the greetings and goodbyes, are all distinctly Hispanic . . . Ask children how to acknowledge persons who come to the door, especially older persons. Children should always greet each other's parents and each other" (Barrera, 1993).

Feeling	Behavioral Definition
1. Fear	Pale face, alert eyes, tense mouth, rigid body.
2. Surprise	Wide eyes, eyebrows uplifted, involuntary cry or scream, quick inhale of breath.
3. Anger	Red face, eyes staring, face taut, fists and jaw clenched, voice harsh or yelling, large gestures.
4. Joy	Smiling face, shining eyes, free and easy body movements, laughing.
5. Pride	Head held high, smiling face, jaunty walk or strut, tendency to announce or point out.
6. Embarrassment	Red face, glazed and downcast eyes, tight mouth, tense body, small and jerky movements, soft voice.
7. Sadness	Unsmiling face, downturned mouth, glazed and teary eyes, crying or rubbing eyes, limp body, slow or small movements, soft and trembly voice.
8. Anxiety	Puckered brow, pale face, tight mouth, whiny voice, jerky movements, lack of or difficulty in concentration.
9. Curiosity	Raised brow, shining eyes, perhaps tense body in absorption of the object of curiosity; often hand movements to touch and pick up object; sometimes mouth agape.

FIGURE 14-4 As we observe children's behavior, we understand how their feelings are expressed. Expressions of fear, anger, sadness, disgust, and happiness are universal, and the face can be read and understood long before children understand language.

classroom by knowing when and how feelings are expressed. "Caring as total presence is a matter of attitude. Sometimes doing 'less' is doing 'more'" (Rofrano, 2002), particularly important in curriculum for young children. To gain insights, teachers might ask themselves:

- What causes children in the class to become excited? Frightened? Calm? Loud? How does this knowledge guide curriculum planning? How can it help a teacher handle an unplanned event or change in the schedule?

- How do I anticipate children's emotional behavior? How do I follow through?

- What can teachers do to handle children's emotional outbursts and crises?

- What happens to the rest of the class when one teacher is occupied in an emotional incident with one or more children?

- What do I do when a child shows emotion? How do I feel when a child displays emotion?

- What types of emotions are most common with the young child?

In the early childhood setting, teachers help children come to grips with their strong feelings by discussing those feelings openly. They take the time to help children find names for feelings, to speak of their own feelings, and to begin to be aware of the feelings of others (see Figure 14-5).

When teachers perceive that children are ready to talk about their feelings, small-group discussions or individual conversations can be helpful (see Figure 14-6). Good books that touch on sensitive issues (being excluded, being blamed, caring for others) offer possibilities for teachers and children to talk about feelings. Games, joking, and teasing can help children to

Observing children's feelings, such as the joy and pride in this child's face, helps teachers understand the children they teach.

The Teacher's Role in Children's Anger Management

1. Create a safe emotional climate . . . by having clear, firm, and flexible boundaries.

2. Model responsible anger management . . . by acknowledging when you are upset.

3. Help children develop self-regulatory skills . . . by giving children age- and skill-appropriate responsibilities and encouraging problem-solving with support.

4. Encourage children to label feelings of anger . . . start with "mad" and expand to include "upset, annoyed, irritated, furious, steamed," etc.

5. Encourage children to talk about anger-arousing interactions . . . by talking about situations when they aren't happening. "I felt mad when . . . " can start a lively conversation; cards with realistic scenarios can do the same, as can puppets.

6. Use appropriate books and stories about anger to help children understand and manage anger . . . see Figure 14-6.

7. Communicate with parents. . . . Introduce the books or puppets, let them borrow them overnight. Tell them what you do in your program, and ask what they do.

FIGURE 14-5 When children come to grips with their strong feelings, their emotional growth is encouraged (categories from Marion, 1997).

feel relaxed and to explore feelings in an accepting way. Classroom problems (not sharing materials, pushing on the climbers) offer topics for discussion. The ability to express emotions verbally gives children the power to deal with them without resorting to inappropriate behavior. Be a "resiliency mentor; help children by modeling, providing, and strengthening those protective buffers" (Weinreb, 1997). Remind children you believe that "all children are inherently loving, cooperative, and full of life-spirit and intelligence, [as well as] sensitive and vulnerable to hurts" (Bowling and Rogers, 2001).

Social referencing involves "relying on another person's emotional reaction to form one's own appraisal of an uncertain situation" (Berk, 1999). Making use of others' emotional cues can help infants to deal with stranger anxiety,

toddlers to calm themselves after saying goodbye, preschoolers to avoid overreacting to a fall, and school-aged children to begin to recognize that people can feel more than one emotion at a time. Social referencing is a vital strategy in learning how to respond emotionally. The teacher who runs to the rescue after a minor spill can engender "learned helplessness" and overreaction. Conversely, the teacher who fails to respond to children when they express emotions may give children the message that others' distress is to be ignored.

When adults show an understanding of feelings, children come to believe that adults are able to help them with their emotions, and the children become more at ease with their own feelings. When something painful happens to a child, adults can express what the

---

"Let's Eat: Learning at Snack Time"

1. Choose a small-group or whole-group snack routine. Try for small-group in full-day, set up in a corner without distractions. A whole-group snack is often better for part-day when time is at a premium.

2. Organize snack trays. A well-organized snack, attractively displayed with all items already gathered makes for a respite for children and adults alike.

3. Plan a transition ritual before snack. Cleaning tables can be soothing and allows children to be directed to hand washing without line-ups or shoving matches.

4. Define each child's personal space. Getting seated and getting ready can be challenging. Think: placemats? napkin in cup already?

5. Sit at eye level with the children. Too many teachers stay standing! When you sit, you are the anchor, the stage manager, the face-to-face model.

6. Teach genuine respect and care with social skills. You teach "good manners" better when you sit with them, modeling *and* praising, encouraging the delight in both giving and receiving expressions of gratitude.

7. Teach independence in small steps. Start tight and loosen: Begin a year or group by serving the food yourself, then teach them the skills in small steps as you loosen up. As Montessori put it "the directress must at the beginning intervene, teaching the child with few or not words at all, but with very precise actions" (Montessori, 1914).

8. Offer food choices to strengthen self-identity. After the routines are established, start to offer food choices; talk about "things I like" and "things I don't like"; use snack time to further the children's developing projects or books.

9. Observe and reflect. Ask yourself: "Do the children appear relaxed? Are they content in this time?"

10. Let spontaneous conversation flow. Don't sacrifice spontaneous child-generated language for teacher topics.

FIGURE 14-6 Snack time is a chance to care emotionally for children and adults alike.

child is feeling. "It really hurts to bend your knees now that you have scraped them." "You look so sad now that Gabi is playing with someone else." Children then become familiar with ways to express how they feel in a variety of emotional situations.

Adults can also help children become aware of the emotional states of others. "Look! Paul is crying. Let's go over and see if we can comfort him." Teachers can encourage children to help care for each other's hurts and needs. A child can ease the pain of a friend by sitting nearby as a wound is cleansed or by giving a hug when an achievement is made. Teachers must be sure to allow children to express their concern and to help them learn ways to respond to the emotional needs of others.

CURRICULUM PLANNING FOR EMOTIONAL GROWTH

In the Environment

Teachers set up their classrooms and yards to promote emotional growth. Materials and activities enhance self-esteem and self-expression. How activities are presented and carried out is also a factor. In the class setting, the "how" is as critical as the "what" in curriculum planning for emotional development. Refer to Figure 14-8 to see how curriculum can be developed to encourage emotional growth.

Indoors. Select materials that enhance self-expression. Indoors, children's inner thoughts and feelings are best expressed through:

- *The Arts.* Clay or dough lets children vent feelings, because it can be pounded, pinched, poked, slapped, and manipulated. Fingerpainting and painting on broad surfaces with large brushes encourage a freedom of movement that permits children to express themselves fully.

- *Blocks/Manipulatives.* Vary the materials regularly to help children adjust to change and to allow them to exercise judgment about playing with different materials. A variety of props—motor vehicles, animals, people, furniture—gives children the opportunity to reenact what they see of the world.

- *Discovery/Science.* Often, science projects are geared toward cognitive and language development. They need not always be; some activities can focus on feelings. Caring for pets, for instance, brings out feelings of nurturing and protectiveness. Making "feeling clocks" can emphasize emotions. Blank clock faces are used as a base upon which children draw or paste pictures of people showing various emotional states. Display these at children's eye level so they can be changed frequently.

- *Dramatic Play.* Home-life materials give children the props they need to express how they see their own world of family, parents, siblings. Through play, the child who is afraid of being left with a sitter may become the parent leaving the child–doll at home and then returning; the child who is afraid of the doctor can sometimes be seen gleefully giving shots to all the stuffed animals. Turnabout is indeed fair play" (Hyson, 1986). Mirrors, telephones, and dress-up clothes encourage children to try out their emotional interests on themselves as well as each other.

- *Language/Library.* Stories and books in which characters and situations reflect a wide range of emotions are readily available (see Figure 13-20 and Figure 14-7 for some suggested titles). Children enjoy looking at photographs of people and guessing what the person in the photo is feeling. This activity encourages children to find words that label feelings; their responses can be recorded and posted nearby. Once children seem at ease in using feelings words, the discussion can continue when the teacher poses the question "Why do you think this person is sad/happy/angry?"

- *Music/Movement.* Music of all kinds encourages self-expression and permits an endless variety of movement and feelings to be shown openly and freely. Children can be introduced to classical, ethnic, jazz, or rock music while dancing with scarves or streamers or marching with rhythm sticks, as well as singing and dancing to children's recordings.[1] Because musical knowledge is the earliest of human intellectual competencies (see Chapter 12), music can be part of the curriculum for children as young as toddlers. Pounding on drums and dancing both relieve tension in a socially acceptable manner. More structured activities, such as showing children how to use musical instruments, must be balanced by plenty of freedom for individual musical expression.

Outdoors. The environment itself encourages self-expression. Whether in the sand or on a swing, children seem to open up emotionally as they relax in the physical freedom the out-of-doors fosters. Outdoor games are usually highly emotionally charged. Running, chasing, and the dramatic play of superheroes provide emotional release for children.

The outdoor area is an ideal place for large, noisy, and messy activities. It is ideal for tracing body outlines, for instance. These life-size portraits of each child reinforce self-concepts and encourage a feeling of pride in one's self. Woodworking is an outdoor activity that allows children to vent anger and tension. Nails won't be hurt no matter how hard they are pounded; there is satisfaction in sawing a piece of wood into two pieces. Music offers numerous opportunities for self-expression. Children can dance with scarves or streamers, march through the yard with drums pounding, imitate Wild Things, make a maypole around the tree, and create a dragon for a parade. A rich musical repertoire of band instruments, phonograph records, tapes, and voices can stimulate children to pretend to be elephants, tigers, and dinosaurs, as well as circus performers and ballet artists. Even a simple project such as water painting becomes an avenue for self-expression as children use paint brushes and buckets of water on trees, cement, and buildings, giving them all a fresh coat of "paint."

Routines, Transitions, and Groups

Routines, transitions, and group times have one thing in common: change. Because they all involve shifts from one kind of activity to another, there is a sense of uncertainty and they are emotionally charged. Children's behavior in these times is most likely to be unfocused. Here you will find the wandering and chasing, even oppositional or withdrawn behavior.

Teachers help children best by creating an atmosphere of trust and clarity. Giving a child ideas of what to do ("Each of you can sponge a table now," or "You can sit on my lap while your dad leaves today") helps a child feel a sense of confidence in managing through a routine or transition. Specific suggestions for group behavior, including those generated from the class itself, inspire success. One specific routine, snack time, is familiar to most teachers and children in group care. Yet it is often a time of stress and chaos rather than a coming together of people to be nurtured by food and

---

 1 Music provides the perfect way to celebrate our diverse world—all cultures have music *and* it is all different. Carefully choose tapes for group times, for nap times, and for background music, with an awareness of and ear for diversity.

company. Murray (2000) reminds us that "the foundation of self-development begins in an environment that sensitively responds to the child's most basic needs. Physical needs are met by providing nutritious food to the hungry child. Emotional needs are considered as we create a comforting and inviting atmosphere." Figure 14-6 gives some suggestions for using snack time for emotional growth.

Finally, changes require teachers to be alert and flexible. As family caregiver McCormick (1993) puts it:

> Flexibility is the cornerstone of successful home child care, and an essential building block in provider/child relationships. Flexibility allows me to adapt to parents' changing schedules, children's changing sleep patterns, and even to alter the day's activities with the changing weather. By remaining flexible, especially to the children's needs, I have built a deep, personal relationship with each of the children I care for. I find ways to adapt to their schedules as much as possible instead of [always] forcing them into a [rigid] routine of the center.

Acknowledging a child's right to strong emotions and understanding a child's reactions to changes in these daily activities help children become comfortable and competent. Figure 14-8 outlines how specific materials and activities can be developed for emotional growth.

Focus on Skills

Emotional development is a lifelong process that requires experience with one's own feelings. To help children learn to express and control their emotions, teachers plan programs such as those illustrated in Figure 14-7. Each child has a unique emotional foundation, which the knowledgeable teacher assesses. Only after assessment can teachers plan curriculum with realistic goals in mind for the children in that class. The goals teachers set for children will determine which emotional skills will be the focus as they individualize the curriculum. Maggie has difficulty with changes in the routine; Caroline never cries, no matter how she hurts; and Clyde screams when he is frustrated.

Making choices is another worthwhile skill with an emotional focus. As does any skill, it takes thought and practice. To teach children to make choices, Simon (1994) suggests examining the process you use to make your own. "Think about your choice to become a teacher. What influenced your choice? What other options did you consider? What were the pros and cons of each of your options? Did your choice turn out as you expected? Would you make the same choice today? Why or why not?" To help children make choices and decisions, focus on a step-by-step process:

1. Help children define the situation by turning it into a question. (What can we do to fix up our playground?)
2. Make a list of options or alternatives. (Plant flowers, get more bikes, add more sand toys.)
3. Ask the children to think of what might happen for each option. (Flowers would look pretty, but we would have to water them.)
4. Make a choice. (This is the key point!)
5. Check later to see how the choice turned out. (Look how nice the yard is! or Darn, when we forgot to water, they died.)

Figure 7-9 offers a more detailed example of this process in social problem-solving.

Finally, encouraging children to create and tell a story can help them with difficulties. Research (Cook, 2001) shows that story-telling can be therapeutic, helping children with issues of compliance, anger management, and fears. Further, by following a five-step process, caregivers can give children the opportunity to identify their fears and problems and come to resolution in satisfying ways. Be sure to elaborate and even let children add details along the way:

1. Introduce the main character. "Once upon a time there was a girl named Ning . . ."
2. Tell about the problem. "One day Ning ran away from school because . . ."
3. Talk to a wise person. "Ning's auntie knew just about everything, so . . ."
4. Try out a new approach. "So Ning decided she would try . . ."
5. Summarize the lesson. "Now Ning felt better. She told her friend . . ."

Use of Themes

One particular theme, that of "Who Am I?", is useful when developing curriculum for emotional growth. Figure 14-8 outlines how this theme can be incorporated in many ways, both indoors and out. A number of other units can be developed to extend the theme of "Who Am I?" Some of these are: "My Body," "The Senses," "The Community Where I Live," and so on.

One school, serving children three through elementary school age, has developed a kind of

Curriculum for Emotional Skill Development

Indoor Activities

Art: Reflect children's expressions and see how they are feeling.
- "You look as if you are enjoying yourself."
- "Your face tells me that was funny (disappointing, etc.) to you."

Blocks: Be there/be aware/ask them how it feels when:
- You make a structure by yourself
- It falls down
- Someone knocks it over (accidentally or on purpose)
- Someone laughs

Discovery/Science:
- Use the words "curious" and "proud" to describe what children do as they experiement with materials.
- Use computer program "Choices, Choices."

Dramatic Play: Give children freedom, variety, and reflection.
a. Have books that reflect a variety of feelings and ways to deal with them, such as:
   Anger: *When Sophie Gets Angry—Really, Really Angry* (Bang); *The Grouchy Ladybug* (Carle); *My Name Is Not Dummy* (Crary).
   Fear: *There's a Nightmare in My Closet* (Mayer); *Storm in the Night* (Stolz)
   Self Esteem: *The Growing Story* (Krauss); *Ruby* (Glen); *Things I Like* (Browne); *Amazing Grace* (Hoffman)
   Loss: *The Maggie B* (Keats); *Amos and Boris* (Steig)
   Change: *Changes, Changes* (Hutchins); *Sam Is My Half-Brother* (Boyd)
   Friendship: *Two Is a Team* (Bemelman); *That's What Friends Are For* (Kidd); *Big Al* (Clements)
   Security: *One Step, Two* (Zolotow); *The Bundle Book* (Zolotow); *Rise and Shine, Mariko-chan* (Tomioka)
   Choice: *Best Enemies* (Leverich); *Did You Carry the Flag Today, Charly?* (Claudill)
b. Include books on themes, particularly when a child or group is dealing with an emotional issue:
   Death: *Death and Dying* (Stein); *The Dead Bird* (Brown); *Nana Upstairs, Nana Downstairs* (dePaoli)
   Divorce: *Two Places to Sleep* (Schuchman)
   Doctor/Dentist: *Curious George Goes to the Hospital* (Rey); *Your Turn, Doctor* (Robinson & Perez); *My Doctor* (Harlow)
   Moving: *Mitchell Is Moving* (Sharmat); *Jamie* (Zolotow); *The Leaving Morning* (Johnson)
   New Baby/Adoption: *Baby Sister for Frances* (Hoban); *I Want to Tell You about My Baby* (Banish); *Peter's Chair* (Keats); *The Chosen Baby* (Wasson)
   Nightmares: *Where the Wild Things Are* (Sendak); *In the Night Kitchen* (Sendak); *There's a Nightmare in My Closet* (Mayer)
   Spending the night: *Ira Sleeps Over* (Waber)
c. When reading stories, stop and ask how a particular character is feeling.
d. Tie in children's lives to books. For example, have children bring a special object or toy to share. A warm cuddly can be tied into the stories of *Goodnight Moon* (Brown) or *Teddy Bear's Picnic* (Kennedy).

Outdoor Activities

Movement:
a. "How would you walk if you were glad?" (sad, mad, worried, giggly?)
b. "A Tiger Hunt" (this game is known by many names). Go on a "hunt" with children, using their bodies to describe such movements as opening/shutting a gate, swishing through tall grass, climbing a tree, swimming in water, going through mud, looking in a cave, running home so that the "tiger" doesn't catch us.

Music:
a. Choose several cuts of music that differ in tone and type. Ask children how each makes them feel, then have them show you with their bodies.
b. Write songs or chants about feelings.

(continues)

FIGURE 14-7 Whether two years old or in grade two, children learn about their feelings when teachers plan programs that encourage self-expression.

Routines and Transitions

1. Respect children's feelings of anticipation.
   - Have a chart of daily activities.
   - Discuss upcoming field trips or visitors ahead of time when possible.

2. When unexpected changes occur, discuss them with individuals and the group.
   - "Andy isn't here today. He has a sore throat, so he is staying home. Esther will be the teacher in his group today."

3. When possible, let the children take responsibility for known sequences.
   - Set their own snack table.
   - Get flowers for the table.
   - Help clean a place for the next children.

4. Provide time for self-help *without unnecessary hurry*.
   - Put on their own name tag.
   - Wash and dry their own hands.
   - Dress themselves—jacket for outdoors, shoes after nap, and so on.
   - Take care of their rest items—blanket and stuffed toy in a labeled pillowcase, books back in a basket or bookshelf, and so on.

Group Times

1. Use children's faces as a focus.
   - Practice facial expressions with mirrors.
   - Call out feelings, having them show you on their faces.
   - Sing "If You're Happy and You Know It, . . ." with a variety of feelings. Ask children what situations have them feel each.
   - Show photographs of children's faces and expressions and ask the group to tell you how that person is feeling, why, and so on. OR do the same with the children's own drawings.

2. Try idea completions.
   - "I feel glad when . . ." (also mad, bad, sad, safe, excited, scared, silly)
   - "I like school when . . ." (also don't like, also my friend, mom, it)
   - "I wish . . .", "The best thing I can do . . ."

3. Use situations to elicit feelings.
   - "Here's a picture of a family. What are they doing? How does each person feel?"
   - "I'm going to cover part of the picture of the face to see if you can guess what expression it's going to be."
   - "These are cards of situations that the teachers have seen happen in our class. Let's read them and then ask ourselves, 'How do I feel? What can I say? What can I do?'"

FIGURE 14-7 (continued)

emerging theme of celebrating emotions that they labeled "Hurt & Healing."

> The most powerful way we have found to help children heal emotionally is to give them complete focused attention with no interruptions. . . . We call this special time and talk about when it will be and for how long. We follow the child's lead in this special-time play, doing whatever he or she chooses (Bowling & Rogers, 2001).

Children and teachers generate ideas for special feelings-releasing activities called "moosh plans." Since everyone uses this phrase, children and adults can brainstorm activities to do. One group's list included throwing water baggies at targets, kicking stacks of boxes, stomping on egg cartons, pounding anger out into clay, throwing colored water at a painting. Dramatic play included acting out scared reactions; stories were dictated, pictures drawn, games made-up. Children bring their troubles to school, and the school welcomes them as curriculum.

CONCLUSION

Emotional growth is a crucial part of children's development in the early years. Emotions develop as children respond to life experiences with a full range of feelings. An undifferentiated state of emotions during infancy evolves into a

Theme: Who Am I ?

1. *Art:* Body outlines
   Facial expressions pictures—variations (a) provide handheld mirrors, (b) give a blank face and let them draw in the features, (c) self-portraits: make them throughout the year, using "people colors," (d) cut out faces in magazine for collage
   Face painting
   Fingerprinting (hand and foot)

2. *Blocks:* People, furniture, structures people live in
   Pictures of same

3. *Cooking:* Share ethnic dishes (tortillas, pasta, things you like to cook at home)

4. *Discovery/Science:* Height-weight charts
   Drawing around hands and feet and comparing sizes
   Doing body outlines of a large group of children, each with a different color, and comparing sizes
   Mapping—charting where people live, charts of phone numbers, put out a globe
   Weather—make connections to types of homes

5. *Dramatic Play:* Lots of mirrors
   A variety of dress-up play for taking on a variety of roles and seeing how they feel

6. *Language/Library:* Have children write books about themselves—variations: (a) use *Is This You?* (Krauss) as model
   (b) loose-leaf binder of their own books they can add to themselves, (c) "Where I Live" as title,
   (d) families
   Books on children and families with diverse backgrounds (*Corduroy* [Freedman] lives in an apt.)
   Where animals live
   Feelings about where children live

7. *Manipulatives:* Puzzles with body parts, with people and clothing
   Self-help skills with dressing frames
   Encourage children to build a structure that things could live in (e.g., using Lincoln Logs).

8. *Sand and Water Play:* Bubble-blowing
   Using your bodies to build—digging with hands and feet, encouraging sensory exploration
   Use body parts to help you (e.g., using your foot on the shovel).

9. *Swinging/Climbing:* Both of these activities use body parts; teachers help the children become aware of how they do
   physical activity.

10. *Games:* Rolling the barrel, rolling yourself   Hide and Seek, Tag
    Mother May I?   Dramatic play games with family members
    Guessing games: Make "Who am I?" snapshots of the backs of children's heads or their hands. Use a shoe from each
    child, having them all tuck their feet under them.

11. *Large Block-Building:* Making house-like structures
    Using vehicles that need your body's force to move

12. *Woodworking:* Using body parts
    Make a map board of school, neighborhood, a city

13. *Routines:* Self-help: Awareness of what you can do by yourself by deinition of "Who Am I?" tasks; teachers use verbal
    and musical reinforcement

14. *Transitions:* Use physical characteristics of children for transitions—"Everyone who has brown eyes/freckles/blue jeans can
    go outside."

15. *Group times:* "Head and shoulders"
    Description games—describe someone and guess who it is as a game "I'm thinking of someone" or with
    song "Mary Has a Red Dress"
    "Little Tommy (Tina) Tiddlemouse," voice recognition
    "Good morning little Teddy Bear," with bear going around circle and saying names

16. *Snack time/bedtime:* Mark places with names and pictures, such as beds or placemats
    Try to coordinate the name tag, bed, or placemat with symbol on cubby

FIGURE 14-8 A child's school experience is strongly related to how emotional events are handled.

more refined array of feelings in childhood. Children gain control of their emotions through maturation and experience.

Emotional skills learned in the early years are: the ability to deal with feelings and with change, to be able to exercise judgment, to know and enjoy one's power. Teachers help children develop these skills by building a vocabulary of feeling words, by an awareness of the emotional climate in the classroom, by talking with children about their feelings, and by helping children sense the emotional framework of others. Self-esteem and self-concepts are enhanced by positive emotional growth.

Curriculum planning for emotional development involves an emphasis on many avenues for self-expression in the class setting, sometimes focusing on one particular emotional skill or theme that emphasizes emotional expression.

Ask yourself:

- What are the principles of emotional development? How will the four I's of *I, independence, initiative,* and *interaction* help in my teaching?
- What emotional skills are learned in early childhood?
- What is the role of the teacher in emotional development?
- What are three ways to plan curriculum that will enhance emotional growth?

SOCIAL GROWTH: THE DEVELOPMENT OF SOCIAL COMPETENCE

Social development is the process through which children learn what behavior is acceptable and expected. A set of standards is imposed on the child at birth that reflects the values of the family and the society in which the child lives.

Theorists from Freud and Piaget to Bandura and Gardner (see Chapters 4 and 12) acknowledge the relationship between social competence and learning. Indeed, enhancing social intelligence builds a set of skills that may be among the most essential for life success of many kinds. How is it done?

Social development begins at birth. Within the first few months of life, the infant smiles, coos, and plays in response to a human voice,

face, or physical contact (see Attachment, Chapter 4). Young children are influenced from birth by a deliberate attempt on the part of adults to guide them in ways that society expects. Parents attempt to transmit behavior patterns that are characteristic of their culture, religion, gender, educational, and ethnic backgrounds.[1] Children imitate what they see; they adapt social expectations to their own personality.[2] The family, caregivers, teachers, peers, and the community all contribute to children's social world and to the values and attitudes that are developed. "Cooperation, generosity, loyalty, and honesty are not inborn. They must be passed on to the child by older people, where they are parents, other adults, or older youngsters" (Bronfenbrenner in Kostelnik, 2002). There are such cultural variations in how people relate to each other, what and when to eat, how to dress, what feelings are to be expressed, how to think about time and personal space, how and who to touch, and how to respond to personal events. It is critical for programs to inquire about family culture, language, and priorities for each child.

This process—called *socialization*—includes learning appropriate behavior in a number of different settings. Children learn very early to discriminate between the expectations in different environments. At school, free exploration of play materials is encouraged, but in a church pew it is not. Grocery stores, circuses, libraries, and Grandma's home call for a repertoire of fitting behaviors. Children's understanding of others is critical for their social growth. Very young children show awareness of what other people feel, as infants pay special attention to emotional expressions of adults. Toddlers can ascertain if someone is happy, sad, or angry, and can try to comfort someone in distress. Three-year-olds know that if someone gets what he wants, he will be happy, and if not, he will be sad. Older preschoolers begin to understand that what they (or others) believe may turn out to be false. By then one can see that children are forming the notion of another's mind.

Research suggests that children who understand others' minds at an early age may be more able to get along well with others and that parents and teachers can support the development of this

---

1 The socialization of children ensures that the values and traditions of the culture are preserved.

2 As you gather cultural information, be careful not to stereotype. "Cultural information only provides clues, not concrete data, about particular people; and so, even though you have information about a specific culture or ethnic group, it won't necessarily apply to all the people in that group" (Kendall, 1996).

understanding by encouraging pretend play and discussing mental states with them from story-books or real-life encounters. (Lillard & Curenton, 1999)

In general, the socialization process in a school setting revolves around a child's relationships with other people. During this time of their lives, children work out a separate set of relationships with adults other than their parents. They establish different relationships with adults than they do with other children and, most important, they learn to interact with other children.

Through socialization, the customary roles that boys and girls play are also transmitted. Children come to understand how teachers, mommies, daddies, grandparents, males, and females are expected to act.[1]

Children also learn social attitudes at an early age. They learn to enjoy being with people and participating in social activities. At the same time, young children can also develop attitudes of bias, and it is in these early years that prejudicial behavior often begins now. Be honest about your feelings, for how the teachers respond to negative comments, unfair acts, exclusivity based on race, gender, or ability is crucial in combating this kind of socialization. Favorable attitudes toward people and a strong desire to be part of the social world and to be with others, are established in the early years.

Another important facet of socialization involves the development of a sense of community. A program's emotional climate and teacher's behavior contribute not only to children's sense of personal safety and belonging but also to the value of "a web of relationships that is sustained by a process of communication" (Gilligan, 1982). Moreover, teachers who strive for community awareness and bonding often do so by adhering to an anti-bias philosophy (see Chapter 9, among others) that promotes empathic interaction with people from diverse backgrounds and standing up for self and others in the face of bias.

Social Competence

Social competence involves the skills and personal knowledge children develop to deal with the challenges and opportunities they face in life with others. Adds Katz and McClennan (1007), "they generally focus on an individual's ability to initiate and maintain satisfying, reciprocal relationships with peers." Our definition includes relationships with all other people, including family, teachers, caregivers, peers, and the community at large. Through their social interactions, children learn a sense of personal identity, adopt family and cultural values, acquire interpersonal skills, and learn how to "live in the world."

There are several components to social competence. These are:

- *Emotional regulation.* The ability to regulate emotions (see earlier in this chapter).
- *Social knowledge and understanding.* Knowledge of enough language and norms to interact successfully; understanding others' reactions and their feelings (empathy).
- *Social skills.* Social approach patterns, attention to others, exchange of information, handling aggression.
- *Social dispositions.* Habits or characteristic ways of responding to experiences.

The elements of social competence are illustrated in Figure 14-9.

Why is social competence important? Such children are happier than their less competent peers. Children's social relations have been linked to academic achievement. Lack of social competence has been linked to rejection by peers, poor self-esteem, and poor academic performance (Kostelnik, Whiren, Soderman, Stein, & Gregory, 2002). "Indeed, the single best childhood predictor of adult adaptation is not IQ nor school grades, but rather the adequacy with which a child gets along with others" (Hartup, 1992).

Social Development

All areas of children's development play a part in learning social skills:

- Having the confidence to try joining a group calls upon emotional skills.
- Remembering children's names or how a game works is a cognitive task.
- "Using your words" to express an idea or feeling requires language.
- Being able to play chase or walk in high heels for a dress-up game requires certain physical dexterity.

---

1 Early childhood professionals need to be aware of the difference between a child's developing a gender identity and a child's sex role development. One needs to be able to communicate the difference to parents and to be aware of how different cultures may have differing notions about sex role development.

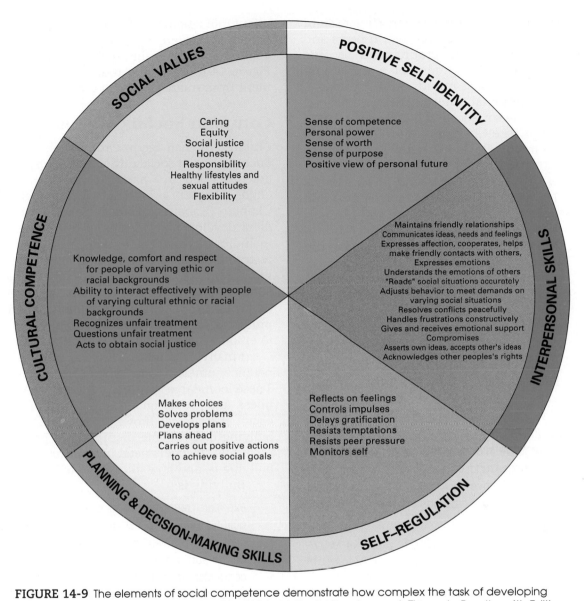

FIGURE 14-9 The elements of social competence demonstrate how complex the task of developing socially is for young children. (From *Guiding Children's Social Development: Theory to Practice,* 4th Edition by Kostelnik/Whiren/Soderman/Stein/Gregory. 2002. Reprinted with permission of Delmar Learning, a division of Thomson Learning: www.thomsonrights.com. Fax 800 730-2215.)

There are many variations that arise in social situations. For instance, children can sustain complex play without much language, and games can be adapted to include children with a variety of physical skills. Understanding the principle of interrelated development, however, helps teachers appreciate the process of social learning and recognize opportunities to guide their social development.

In the early years, children mature socially in discernible developmental stages. From birth to age three, children's interest in others begins with a mutual gazing and social smile in the early months (birth through 8 months), continues with an exploration of others as well as some anxious behavior around strangers in the crawler and

walker stages (8 to 18 months), and develops into an enjoyment of peers and adults along with an awareness of others' rights and feelings as a toddler and two-year-old (18 months to 3 years).

In the preschool years, children learn to control their aggressive impulses, think about others besides themselves, and resist doing what they shouldn't. This learning translates into four basic expectations. They will:

1. Show interest in others.
2. Learn right from wrong.
3. Learn to get along with others.
4. Learn a role for themselves that takes into consideration their own unique self—gender, race, ethnicity, and abilities.

Children of the primary years (five to eight years) show an increased interest in peers and social competence, and group rules become important. The development of a social conscience and of fairness rounds out the primary-grade developmental milestones.

Children learn social skills in several predictable ways (see Chapters 4 and 12). First, the brain is wired to look for patterns. When an infant smiles and is met with a reciprocal smile, a pattern of responsiveness and attachment is begun. The preschooler who grabs for toys and usually gets to keep them at home will be surprised (and unhappy) when the pattern is broken at the center and the toy is returned to the one who was using it. As a result of their experiences, children form ideas about how the social world works. They are active learners, asserted Piaget and others, who will observe and experiment, learning firsthand what happens when they try something. In-the-moment, on-the-spot lessons will greatly help children learn socially.

> Sarda wants to play in the block corner, but stands hesitantly as four boys shout and vroom the cars around. "Do you want to play here?" inquires the observant teacher. When she nods, the teacher helps her move in and the two begin building. Soon, the boys notice and come to see a garage being built, so they drive their cars over. The teacher slowly steps aside. Sarda has experienced one way to get started.

Next, children have *multiple ways of learning*. As Gardner (see Chapters 4 and 12) points out, there are at least eight ways to express intelligence. Since teachers often do not know each child's ways of learning, it is best to try a variety of approaches when teaching social skills. Talking helps some (linguistic), others learn better by seeing patterns (logical-mathematical), and many learn by your model (see example just given). Rehearsing how to do or say the words helps the kinesthetic learner.

It is through play (as discussed in Chapter 4) that children learn much of their social repertoires. Dramatizations, role playing, and dramatic play provide opportunities to act out many roles and help children deal with some of the demands placed on them. In play, the child experiments with options: finding out what it feels like to be the boss, to be the baby, to behave in ways that might otherwise be unacceptable. Carla was the oldest of three children and had many "big girl" expectations placed on her within the family setting. At school, Carla enjoyed being the baby, acting out a helpless

infant role whenever she could. Under the guise of play, children, like Carla, rehearse for life without suffering the real-life consequences. Figure 14-10 traces the route of social development from infancy through the primary years.

Common Social Challenges

Children of each age in early childhood experience a range of social difficulties. Many of these are described in Chapter 3 about the young child, Chapter 4 in child development, and Chapter 7 about guidance. For instance, toddlers develop many forms of testing behavior, including saying "No" to adult rules and other restraints. Grabbing, biting, and hitting are common forms of aggression and self-expression. Some of this occurs in preschoolers, as well as other forms of self-determination. There are problems children encounter when responding to emotions, both theirs and those of others.

Finally, two critical aspects of social competence emerge: peer status and friendship. These loom large in primary school, where loneliness and exclusion, teasing and bullying all occur. (Gordon & Browne, 1996). Teasing and bullying can become disruptive in groups and programs. Teachers need to be clear about what bullying is, and how to respond to it early.

Bullying is:

> exposure repeatedly and over time, to negative actions (words, physical contact, making faces, gesturing, or intentional exclusions from a group) on the part of one or more other[s]. . . . In a study conducted in grades K–3 by Educational Equity Concepts and the Wellesley College Center for Research on Women, boys initiated 78% of incidents observed, more than three times as many incidents as started by girls, although boys and girls were equally likely to be recipients of such incidents. (Froschl & Sprung, 1999)

This is not to be thought of as boys being bad. But we must take notice and do a better job of dealing with the behaviors. Consider this activity teachers use with school-age children who are bullying others. Children are paired and asked to make faces at each other that show different feelings (angry, sad, surprised, neutral, and hostile). Then they are asked to identify what feelings the faces communicated. They teach the group how to enter play, to ask other children about themselves, and how to take turns. After this intense small-group work (called "the buddies club"), the bullying diminishes (Pool, 1997).

Social Development Timeline

Infant–Toddler	Preschooler	Primary Child
Response to Other's Distress		
Reacts emotionally by experiencing what the other seems to feel.	Begins to make adjustments that reflect the realization that the other person is different and separate from self.	Takes other's personality into account and shows concern for other's general condition.
Peer Interaction		
• First encounters mutual inspection • First social contacts • (18 months) Growth in sensitivity to peer play • (Two years) Able to direct social acts to two children at once (beginning of social interaction)	• Adjustment in behavior to fit age and behavior of other • (More than three years) Friendship as momentary • (Three to five years) Beginning of friendship as constant	• Friend as someone who will do what you want • Beginning of friend as one who embodies admirable, constant characteristics
Social Roles		
• (10–20 days) Imitation of adults • (Three months) Gurgles in response to others • (Six months) Social games based on imitation • (18 months) Differentiation between reality and pretend play • (Two years) Makes doll do something as if it were alive	• (Three years) Makes a doll carry out several roles or activities • (Four to five years) Acts out a social role in dramatic play and integrates that role with others (mom and baby)	• (Six years) Integrates one role with two complementary roles: doctor, nurse, and sick person • (Eight years) Growing understanding that roles can influence behavior (doctor whose daughter is a patient)

FIGURE 14-10 A timetable of social development for the ages of infancy through the primary years. (Special thanks to Gay Spitz. Reprinted by permission.)

Preschool and school-age programs can also implement conflict resolution programs that teach children how to express themselves and listen to others in socially intense situations (Gordon & Browne, 1997; Porro, 1996). Systematic work with children to teach them these social competence skills helps them deal with what might be called the "garden variety" conflicts—issues of property, territory, and power such as teasing, put-downs, hitting, not sharing, who's the boss. Figure 14-11 is a sample chart used in such programs, preschool through elementary school.

Peer Relationships

For the young child, social development means the steady movement away from the *egocentric* position of self (and parents) as central points toward a more **sociocentric** viewpoint that involves others—both adults and, especially, children. During the early years, the child learns to socialize outside the family; social contacts outside the home reinforce the enjoyment of social activities and prepare the child for future group activity.

Peer interactions, that is, associations with friends of the same age group, become important to the child once infancy and early toddlerhood are past. Through peer interactions, children can identify with models who are like themselves and can learn from each other's behavior. Friends provide models for imitation, for comparison, and for confirmation of themselves, and they are a source of support.

Playing with other children begins with solitary parallel play at around two years of age, where two or more children are in the same area with each other but do not initiate social interaction. By the ages of three and four, more interaction takes place: There are conversation and conflict as well as cooperation in playing together.

There are stages in children's friendships. In the early years, friendship starts at an

FIGURE 14-11 A "Talk It Out" poster helps teachers mediate conflicts and teach children resolution skills (From *Talk It Out: Conflict Resolution in the Elementary Classroom,* Copyright © 1996 by Barbara Porro. Reprinted with permission from ASCD. The Association for Supervision and Curriculum Development is a worldwide community of educators advocating sound policies and sharing best practices to achieve the success of each learner. To learn more, visit ASCD at www.ascd.org.).

undifferentiated level, when children are egocentric and a friend is more of the moment. This gives way to a **unilateral** level; a good friend does what the child wants the friend to do. Toward the end of early childhood, friendship becomes more **reciprocal**, involving some give-and-take in a kind of two-way cooperation. Listen to these children trying out their friendship:

Chris: I'll be the teacher, you be the kid.

Suzanne: NO! I want to be the teacher, too.

Chris: No! No! You can't be the teacher, too, cause then there'd be no kids.

Suzanne: OK. Next time, I get to be the teacher.

Chris: Maybe! OK, everybody go wash your hands for snack time. Suzanne, you can pass out your very nutritious snack to everybody.

Suzanne: Superfasmic, I'm the boss of snack.

A peer group is important for a number of reasons. Social development is enhanced because a child learns to conform to established social standards outside of his home setting. The expectations of the larger society are reinforced. To become autonomous, the child must also learn to achieve independence from the family, especially parents. Young children must also come to understand themselves as part of society. Their self-concepts are enlarged by a group of peers as they see how others respond to them and treat them.

Making and keeping friends are essential to children's positive social development, so important that children without friends by the primary years are considered at risk for overall school success. Understanding friendship and social interaction is basic required knowledge of every early childhood teacher, for children's constructed knowledge about how to interact with people is more complicated than that of objects or materials. Adults can promote basic skills, take responsibility for guidance and instruction, model constructive and inclusive interactions, and keep track of each child's developing friendships.[1]

Smith (1982) states that three trends emerge in the way children relate to each other. First, children become more sensitive to their play partners. Second, they begin to use language more effectively in their interactions. Finally, cooperative play increases as parallel play decreases. Children pass through three stages of social understanding in the early years: (1) they shift from a preoccupation with self to an awareness of the thoughts and feelings of another; (2) they shift from the observable, physical qualities of the play partner to an awareness of their friend's less obvious characteristics; and (3) they begin to perceive the friendship as long lasting.

SOCIAL SKILLS IN EARLY CHILDHOOD

Social skills are strategies children learn that enable them to behave appropriately in many environments. They help children learn to initiate or manage social interaction in a variety of settings and with a number of people.

Social cognition is the application of thinking to personal and social behavior; it is giving meaning to social experience. Notice how these two children use social cognition: Nadia used the cognitive skill of memory when she wanted

1 Developing friendships is more than teaching general interpersonal skills and is especially important for children with special needs (Lowenthal, 1996). Facilitating friendship development in inclusive classrooms requires teacher awareness and interaction as well as careful environmental and schedule planning.

to play with Paul, a very popular four-year-old. She remembered Paul's interest in the rope swing and challenged him to swing higher than she did. Bruno, on the other hand, is well known throughout the group for his inability to share materials. When Sandy wanted to play with the small fire trucks (Bruno's favorite toys), she used cognitive skills to negotiate the use of one truck.

Social cognition requires children to interpret events and make decisions, to consider the impact of their behavior on others, and to consider the cause as well as the consequence of an action. Cognitive skills are necessary when we ask children to seek alternative solutions to social problems: "How else could you ask him for a turn, Pete?" These are all social cognition skills, and they serve as the basis for the acquisition of other skills.

Social Intelligence

Building on Gardner's multiple intelligences theory (see Chapters 4 and 12), Daniel Goleman outlined five dimensions of emotional intelligence (see previous section). The fifth element of emotional intelligence, noted Goleman, is social skills. Teachers who can help children handle their emotions (self-regulation) and learn to "read" other people's feelings by their body language or tone of voice (empathy) can then lead children to gain social skills. As mentioned earlier in this chapter, children who bully can be taught better social skills. And the early childhood setting is just the place to do so. Paley (1992) has written extensively about the social climate of classrooms:

> "Are you my friend?" the little ones ask in nursery school, not knowing. The responses are also questions. If yes, then what? And if I push you away, how does that feel?
>
> By kindergarten, however, a structure begins to be revealed . . . certain children will have the right to limit the social experiences of their classmates. . . . Long after hitting and name-calling have been outlawed by the teachers, a more damaging phenomenon is allowed to take root, spreading like a weed from grade to grade.

With more social intelligence than most, Paley as kindergarten teacher decided to post a sign outside her door one year. "You can't say you can't play" turns the class upside-down and requires both adults and children to learn new ways to interact.

Social skills can be viewed in different ways. The "Four Hows" is one set of categories for such a complex array of skills:

1. *How to approach.* Getting and being included.
2. *How to interact.* Sharing, cooperating.
3. *How to deal with difference.* Including others, helping, bullying, and teasing.
4. *How to manage conflict.* Handling aggression, problem solving.

Another is to realize that there is a skill set learned in every kind of interaction.

Skills Learned with Adults

In their relationship with adults, children learn:

- They can stay at school without parents.
- They can enjoy adults other than parents and respond to new adults.
- Adults will help in times of trouble or need.
- Adults will help them learn social protocol.
- Adults will keep children from being hurt and from hurting others.
- Adults will help children learn about ethnic differences and similarities, disabilities, gender identity, and language diversity.

Peer relationships are a source of pleasure and support. As social understanding develops, children shift from a preoccupation with themselves to an awareness of the thoughts and feelings of their friends.

Rejection is a common form of social behavior in young children. In the early years children need to deal with the feelings that arise when they are told, "You can't play with us."

- Adults will resist bias and stereotyping and teach children to actively do the same.
- Adults will not always take a side or solve the problem.
- Adults will work with them to solve problems.
- Adults believe that every child has a right to a satisfying social experience at school.

Skills Learned with Peers

In their relationship with other children, children learn:

- There are different approaches to others; some work, some don't.
- Interactive skills, and how to sustain the relationship.
- How to solve conflicts in ways other than retreat or force.
- How to share materials, equipment, other children, friends, teachers, and ideas.
- How to achieve mutually satisfying play.
- Self-defense, and how to assert their rights in socially acceptable ways.
- How to take turns and how to communicate desires.
- How to negotiate.

- How to be helpful to peers with tasks, information, and by modeling behavior.
- How to anticipate and avoid problems.
- Realistic expectations of how other children behave and respond toward them.
- Ways to deal with socially awkward situations and with socially difficult situations and children.
- How to make, be, share, and lose a friend.

Skills Learned in a Group

In groups, children learn:

- How to take part as a member and not as an individual.
- That there are activities that promote group association (stories, music).
- A group identity (center room class, Mrs. T's group, four-year-old group).
- To follow a daily schedule and pattern.
- To adapt to school routines.
- School rules and expectations.
- Interaction and participatory skills: how to enter and exit from play.
- To respect the rights, feelings, and property of others.
- To become socially active, especially in the face of unfair or biased behavior and situations.
- How to work together as a group, during cleanup time, in preparation for an event, etc.
- How to deal with delay of gratification: how to wait.

Skills Learned as an Individual

As individuals, children learn:

- To take responsibility for self-help, self-care.
- To initiate their own activities and to make choices.
- To work alone, close to other children.
- To notice unfairness and injustice and learn how to handle them.
- To negotiate.
- To cope with rejection, hurt feelings, disappointment.
- To communicate in verbal and nonverbal ways, and when to use communication skills.
- To test limits other people set.
- Their own personal style of peer interaction: degree, intensity, frequency, quality.
- To express strong feelings in socially acceptable ways.
- To manage social freedom.

Specific skills within these four areas include the social and moral aspects of nurturance, kindness, and sharing. As children get older, these skills become more specific: telling the truth, taking turns, keeping promises, respecting others' rights, having tolerance, and following rules.

Another social skill that has taken hold is that of **social action**. In an anti-bias curriculum (see Chapter 9), children can learn how to take social action to make unfair things fair. For instance, preschoolers discover that their adhesive strips are labeled "flesh-colored" but match the skin of only a few children; they take photos and send them to the company (Derman-Sparks, 1989). Promoting activism may not always bring successful results, but the activity and the model are powerful learning experiences.

Cooperation: "I'll help you, then you'll help me."

THE TEACHER'S ROLE

A major role for the early childhood teacher is to see that children have enjoyable social contacts and to help motivate children toward a desire to be with others. The early childhood setting affords children numerous learning opportunities for social development.

The teacher has an important role to play as children learn the give-and-take of social interaction. In the role of social organizer, the teacher creates a physical and interpersonal environment that promotes the development of children's social skills.

Plan and arrange a social environment. Child-initiated activities, self-care, and group responsibility are stimulated by the use of low, open shelves and furniture scaled to size. Group activities, toys, materials, and placement of furniture should be structured in ways that allow children to play alone or with someone. Establishing a **coacting** environment, declares Bos (1990) helps

Friendship: "The more we get together, the happier we'll be!"

Helping: "I'll help clean up."

children in "a way of interacting with others, more often one-on-one than in larger groups, with an emphasis on process rather than product. The placement of two telephones, three wagons, and eight firefighter hats fosters child–child interactions. Cooperation, which implies a mutually recognized goal, is an outgrowth of coacting (see Figure 14-15). Children will often act together in a spontaneous way; they get organized toward a planned end when they decide to build a single tower together. The teacher must also allow enough time in the daily schedule for children to get thoroughly involved in playing with one another.

Help children develop trust. Trusting, in themselves, their peers, and their teachers, is a part of learning about social relationships. Teachers enhance children's social knowledge as they gradually improve their sense of trust. General recommendations are:

1. *Help children recognize their own needs.* Notice children who need to clarify their wishes; ask uninvolved children with whom they'd like to play; help arguing children say how they feel and what they want.

2. *Increase children's awareness of their social goals and the goals of others.* Teachers can aid children by helping them recognize their choices; they can also mediate so that others can express themselves.

3. *Help children develop effective social skills.* Provide a model for listening, for choosing another place to play, or for going along with another's ideas; help children find ways to stand their ground and also accommodate and learn to use conflict resolution, cooperation, coping, and helping skills (see Chapter 7 and this chapter's "Insights" section).

4. *Teach children to recognize others' emotions and intentions.* Children become flooded with their own strong feelings and are not likely to notice someone else's emotions in the heat of the moment; teachers can help children see another's face or hear a tone of voice, thus beginning to "read" another person.

5. *Reflect with children on how their behavior affects others by pointing out what is predictable in their interactions.* Young children do not always "connect the dots" between their behavior and others' reactions. When a teacher makes a statement without disapproval, the child can then understand the effects of her or his behavior on others:

"Wow! When you use that loud voice, I see the kids looking scared, and then they tell you not to play here."

6. *Highlight children's success by helping them learn to monitor their own behavior.* It can help children to see their successful social encounters as well as the strategies that didn't work. "When you asked them if you could play, they said, 'No!' But then you went and got shovels for everyone and that worked!"

7. *Avoid telling children who their "friends" are.* Early childhood teachers encourage children to learn about friendship; however, "legislating friendship" often backfires. Telling children "We're all friends here," or "Friends share their things with everyone" denies the distinction between positive, friendly experiences and friendship. Classmate and friend are not the same word.

8. *Develop a set of strategies to help the socially awkward and troubled in your class.* Although each child is unique, there are certain situations that arise time and again in an early childhood classroom. Children who are socially inept often do not use nonverbal language effectively and are "out-of-synch" because they miss the signs.

9. *Do not stay uninvolved or ignore teasing and bullying.* A lack of response can signal all children that it is "OK" to engage in these behaviors and acceptable to fall victim to it. Talk about it; read books such as *Rosie's Story* (Gogoll) or *Oliver Button Is a Sissy* (de Paola); make an experience chart ("I Feel (Un)Welcome When . . .") and help the class with fair rules. In noncompetitive games, children learn to help each other rather than trying to win or gain power over others. Finally, foster friendships between girls and boys and actively counter gender bias.

10. *Work to provide a caring community in your class.* "In order for children to have the confidence to take the risks inherent in learning . . . they must experience a consistently accepting, inclusive and predictable atmosphere in the classroom" (Maniates & Heath, 1998). Brain research (see Chapter 4) confirms this point, and an anti-bias approach (see Chapters 3 and 9) supports the development of social action as an extension of "making right" the classroom and beyond.

11. *Invite parents and families into the process of children's socialization.* Both teachers and families share in the responsibility of

helping children develop social skills; neither one can do it alone. There are many ways to make your program family friendly; see Chapter 8 for suggestions.

Facilitate children's interactions and interpret their behavior. To help young children understand each other and to pave the way for continued cooperation, the teacher reports and reflects on what is happening. In the classroom setting, during an active, free-play period, the teacher might:

Reflect the Action:	*Say:*
Call attention to the effect one child's behavior is having on another.	"Randy, when you scream like that, other children become frightened and are afraid to play with you."
Show approval and reinforce positive social behavior	"I like the way you carefully stepped over their block building, Dannetta."
Support a child in asserting her rights.	"Chrystal is hanging on to the doll because she isn't finished playing yet, Wilbur."
Support a child's desire to be independent.	"I know you want to help, Keyctta, but Sammy is trying to put his coat on by himself."
Acknowledge and help children establish contact with others.	"Omar would like to play, too. That's why he brought you another bucket of water. Is there a place where he can help?"
Reflect back to a child the depth of his feelings and what form those feelings might take.	"I know George made you very angry when he took your sponge, but I can't let you throw water at him. What can you tell him? What words can you use to say you didn't like what he did?"

Adult responses to children's play are particularly critical in supporting positive social development. The teacher has a powerful, emotional role in children's lives at school. When children make judgments in error, coming to false conclusions about children on the basis of race, gender, native language, or ability, the teacher must intervene, for silence signals tacit approval. This is perhaps the most dynamic and challenging part of teachers' jobs, the heart of the profession. "Facilitation is fundamental to helping children achieve greater social competence. You engage in facilitation when you demonstrate empathy, warmth, respect, and authenticity in your interpersonal relations with children" (Kostelnik et al., 2002).

Illustrated in Chapter 7, the social problems in early childhood range from possession of toys, to hitting others, to keeping promises. How a teacher helps children identify and resolve their own conflicts is often more important than the specific problem or solution.

Teaching strategies that facilitate social competence will be developmentally appropriate when teachers recognize age-related variables as well as individual differences and the cultural context in which children live. Think about the age of the children when you prepare the environment. Understand the general characteristics and capacities of the age-range. Then, consider the individual child(ren) involved and what language, patterns of response, and social expectations each one brings. It's a big job, but the best way to encourage positive social interaction. See Figure 14-12 for a list of Dos and Don'ts.[1]

Curriculum Planning for Social Growth

Social curriculum happens everywhere in an early childhood program. One of the goals of curriculum is:

> to help the young child move from her or his sheltered family unit into a much more complex environment. . . . The curriculum should develop the knowledge and perspective which is commensurate with the kind of world in which we live, a world that . . . is composed of an unlimited variety of outlooks, backgrounds, and standard of living. [Early education programs] can be a step in socializing the child, in helping the child change from an egocentric, ethnocentric person to one who understands and is sympathetic to people of considerable diversity. (Kendall, 1996)

---

1 In helping children do well in groups, teachers look for several clues to patterns that might be affected by culture, such as the child's manner in participating (on the sidelines or in the thick of things), the manner in which thoughts are presented to others, the ways the child asks questions (carefully, fearfully, with abandon, etc.) and the kinds of questions asked (from intimate to careful). (Adapted from Longstreet in Kendall, 1966.)

Social Competence: The Teacher's Role	
Do	**Don't**
• Respect individual timetables and feelings.	• Make implied comparisons
• Establish authority and credibility.	• Issue empty threats.
• Express expectations simply and directly.	• Hover.
• Redefine children's characters in positive terms.	• Make teacher-child interaction be all about misbehavior.
• Encourage impulsive control.	• Motivate children by indirect disapproval.
• Appeal to children's good sense.	• Lose your sense of humor.
• Invoke ground rules.	• Allow a rigid curriculum to narrow possibilities for social interaction.
• Mix it up: Arrange things to get one child next to another.	
• Move it: people, toys, you	
Question everything you do: Could I open this up for more than one child?	

FIGURE 14-12 The Dos and Don'ts of facilitating social competence (adapted from Bos (1990) and Katz & McClelland (1997)).

In the Environment

Teaching social behavior in most classrooms usually occurs in response to spontaneous situations. The teacher's direct involvement in children's social interactions is the most frequent method used. Occasionally, teachers will approach the acquisition of social skills in a more formalized way through planned curriculum activities. The way the environment is arranged has a profound effect on social interaction among children.

Indoors. Most indoor activities are planned and set up to encourage participation by more than one child at a time. Adjusting interior space can promote social development. If the space is hard and unattractive or makes people feel closed in or is too noisy, children are not encouraged to interact in a relaxed and sustained manner. "Variation in texture usually influences the sound level and tends to humanize the environment" (Kostelnik et al., 2002); adults can modify the walls and floors, as well. Arrange the space into learning centers that provide for coactivity, with clear physical boundaries and ways to get around (see Chapter 9). Remember, the environment is one of the teachers.

- *The Arts.* At the art table, four or more children will share collage materials, paste, and sponges that have been placed in the center of the table. When easels are placed side by side, conversation occurs spontaneously among children. A small table, placed between the easels, on which a tray of paint cups is placed, also encourages children's interactions. If there is only one of each color, the children will have to negotiate with one another for the color they want to use.

- *Blocks/Manipulatives.* A large space for block cabinets gives children a visual cue that there is plenty of room for more than one child. Puzzle tables set with three or four puzzles also tell children that social interaction is expected. Many times children will talk, play, and plan with one another as they share a large bin full of Legos® or plastic building towers. A floor puzzle always requires a group: some to put the picture together, others to watch and make suggestions. As children build with blocks next to one another, they soon share comments about their work; many times this sharing leads to a mutual effort on a single building.

- *Discovery/Science.* Many science projects can be arranged to involve more than one child. A display of magnets with a tray of assorted objects can become the focus of several children as they decide which objects will be attracted to the magnets. Cooking together, weighing and measuring one another, and caring for classroom pets can be times when teachers reinforce social skills.

- *Dramatic Play.* This area more than any other seems to draw children into contact with one another. Provide an assortment of family life accessories—dress-up clothes, kitchen equipment and utensils—and children have little trouble getting involved. A shoe needs to be tied or a dress zipped up. Someone must come eat the delicious meal just cooked or put the baby to bed. A medical theme in this classroom area also enhances children's social skills. They learn to take each other's temperature, listen to heartbeats, and plan operations, all of which require more than one person. Sociodramatic play can provide curriculum integration in the primary grades as well. In one first grade, the teacher started a "card shop" that could "provide a non-threatening, child-centered environment where children teach, learn, and experience real-life roles. . . . The social interaction inherent in socio-dramatic play provided opportunities for the children to collaborate (Cooper and Dever, 2001).

- *Language/Library.* Children enjoy reading books and stories to one another, whether or not they know the words. Favorite books are often shared by two children who enjoy turning the pages and talking over the story together. Lotto games encourage children to become aware of one another, to look at each person's card in order to identify who has the picture to match. Name songs and games, especially early in the year, help children learn to call each other by name.

- *Music Movement.* Build in regular times for music and movement activities. The entire group can participate in familiar songs; a sense of community is built by everyone's participation. Activities during the free choice times usually involve smaller numbers, where group members can challenge one another to new ways to dance with scarves or use the tumbling mat. Finally, one-to-one experiences encourage new friendships as the intimacy of a shared musical experience brings two children or a teacher and child together.

Outdoors. "Children need a space to run, a place to yell, a place where adults are not hovering and directing each activity" (Bos, 1990). The pretend play of boys, in particular, is usually richer than inside and many of the rough-and-tumble activities prohibited indoors are safe here (Kostelnik et al., 2002). It may be more difficult to observe children, and directions are often harder to give with distance. The outdoor environment can be structured in ways to support group play.

- *Painting or Pasting.* Painting or pasting on murals or drawing chalk designs on the cement are art activities that promote social interaction.

- *Planning and Planting a garden.* Planning and planting a garden is a long-range project that involves many children. Decisions must be made by the group about what to plant, where to locate the garden, how to prepare the soil, and what the shared responsibilities of caring for the garden will be.

- *Gross-Motor Activities.* Most gross-motor activities stimulate group interactions. Seesaws, jump ropes, and hide-and-seek require at least two people to participate. A-frames, boards, and boxes, as well as other movable equipment, need the cooperative effort of several children in order to be rearranged. Sand play, when accompanied by water, shovels, and other accessories, draws a number of children together to create rivers, dams, and floods. Ball games and relay races also encourage social relationships.

Routines, Transitions, and Groups

Routines and transitions are often social experiences, as they provide children with an opportunity for support and peer interaction. Teachers use these times as an opportunity to build social skills. For instance, the routine of nap preparation can be structured with a "buddy" system so that older children are paired with the younger ones to set up the cots, choose a cuddly or books, and get tucked in. A cleanup time transition can be made fun and successful if children can wear a necklace to depict the job or area. Another way is to provide a basket of "pick-up" cards; bringing out the basket signals cleanup time and allows children to choose their chores. Children with similar cleanup cards get a sense of teamwork when putting an activity area back in order. Figure 14-13 shows another way to build community through noticing kind acts at class meetings.

As a directed learning experience, small-group times afford an opportunity to focus on social skills in a more structured way. Small groups provide a setting for children and teachers to participate in more relaxed, uninterrupted dialogue. The intimacy of the small group sets the stage for many social interactions.

Grouptime discussions, such as circle time in preschool and class meetings for school-age children, can focus on problems that children can solve. Too many children crowding the water table, a child's fear of fire drills, or the noise level on a rainy day are subjects children will talk about in small groups. The most relevant situations are ones that occur naturally in the course of a program. Another curriculum idea is to make "Situation Cards" of these and other common

Transition:
The first day of kindergarten

Routine:
The teacher makes notes of kind acts, talking aloud as she writes, and puts them in the jar.

Group:
At circle time, the teacher reads them aloud before lunch and at the end of the day.

Curriculum Variations:
• Children become "kindness reporters."
• They begin to make notes for the jar.
• Then they make their own kindness jars.
• Children elaborate on conflict resolution as it happens.
• They create their own routine called "team kindnesses."

FIGURE 14-13 Kindness in a jar. (Adapted, by permission, from P. Whitin, "Kindness in a Jar," *Young Children 56* (September 2001): 18-21. Figure from p. 19. Copyright © 2001 National Association for the Education of Young Children.)

incidents. For instance, teachers can create illustrated cards that pose situations such as:

● You tell your friends to "stop it" when they take part of the toy you are using, but they do it again.

● You open your lunch and your mom or dad has packed your favorite foods.

● You come down the slide and your teacher calls "Hooray for you!"

● You promise your friend you'll play with him at recess, but then someone else you like asks you to play with her.

The teacher then guides a discussion around the questions "How do you feel? What can you say?

What can you do?" This activity can be simplified or elaborated depending on the individuals and group involved.

Solutions may emerge when the teacher supports active and involved participation. Teachers pose the problem and ask children to respond in several ways: "How does it make you and others feel when that happens? What can you and others do about it? What are some alternatives?" The problems must be real, and they must be about something that is important to children. Figure 14-14 is an example of a sequentially planned curriculum that fosters the development of social skills in small group settings.

Curriculum for Social Skill Development

Time	Skill	Activities
Week 1	Developing a positive self-image	Do thumbprint art.
		Make foot and handprints.
		Compare children's baby pictures with current photos.
		Play with mirrors: Make faces, emotional expressions.
		Dress felt dolls in clothing.
		Sing name songs: "Mary Wore Her Red Dress."
		Make a list: "What I like to do best is . . . " Post in classroom.
		Do a self-portrait in any art medium.
		Make a silhouette picture of each child.
Week 2	Becoming a member of a group	Take attendance together: Who is missing?
		Play picture lotto with photographs of children.
		Play "Farmer in the Dell"
		Share a favorite toy from home with older children.
		Tape record children's voices, guess who they are.
		Have a "friendly feast": Each child brings a favorite food from home to share.
Week 3	Forming a friendship within the group	Provide one puzzle (toy, game, book) for every two children.
		Take a "Buddy Walk": Return and tell a story together of what you saw.
		Play "Telephone Talk": Pretend to invite your friend over to play.
		Play "copy cat": imitate your friend's laugh, walk, cry, words.
		Practice throwing and catching balls with one another.
		Form letter together with two children's bodies: A, T, C, K, etc.
		Play tug-of-war with your friend.
		Build a house out of blocks together.
		Make "mirror images" movements with your friend.
Week 4	Working together as a group	Play with a parachute; keep the ball bouncing.
		Make snacks for the rest of the class.
		Plan and plant a garden.
		Make a mural together to decorate the hallways.
		Play "Follow the Leader."
		Sing a round: "Row, Row, Row Your Boat."
Week 5	Learning a group identity	Make a map of the town and have children place their house on it.
		Take a field trip together.
		Print a newspaper with articles by and about each child.
		Select and perform a favorite story for the rest of the class.
		Take a group snapshot.
		Make a "family tree" of photos of children in group.
		Learn a group folk dance.
		Make a mural of handprints joined in a circle.

FIGURE 14-14 Building social skills through small-group experiences, beginning with an understanding of self and moving toward an appreciation of group membership. (See Chapter 10 for specific guidelines to curriculum planning.)

Focus on Skills

Social development for the preschool child includes gaining an awareness of the larger community in which the child lives. The early childhood curriculum contains elements of what is often in the later grades called social studies. Visits from police officers, mail carriers, firefighters, and other community helpers are common in many programs. Learning about children from other cultures, exploring the neighborhood around the center, and making maps are other ways children learn social studies skills.[1]

Sharing. Learning to share involves using or enjoying something in common with others. Although sharing may seem simple to adults, it is not a skill that is learned overnight, nor is it easy to orchestrate in young children. In America where the dominant culture is one of individualism, competition, material acquisition, and ownership, children get particular messages that can make teaching "sharing" difficult. "The culture in which a child grows up influences what that child learns about sharing" (Davis & Keyser, 1997). Young children understand sharing in different ways at different ages.

What does sharing mean to you? To a young child:

- giving up one's possessions   OR taking turns?
- holding onto a power position   OR bringing in more power?
- losing what you have   OR dividing everything equally?
- defining who I am   OR being the me who can give?
- losing the thread of the play   OR adding to the play?

Toddlers and the two-year-olds are rarely ready to share on their own. Grabbing what they want makes sense to them, and sharing a toy or space may feel like giving it up forever. Preschoolers share more readily because of the experiences they have had in "getting it back," and because of the fuss they have seen occur when they do not share. School-age children begin to be aware that some children feel the same as they do and that others may have needs and wishes different from their own.

What do YOU Think?

"Nobody likes to think about it, even though we know it is not okay to hurt a person with words, or things, or with the way we behave. So when some kids in my class started picking on Ray when the teachers were busy and just couldn't see, nobody knew what to do." Thus begins Becky R. McCain's picture book entitled *Nobody Knew What To Do* (Morton Grove, IL: A. Whitman & Co, 2001). What do you think? Do you advise children to "fight back"? Do you shrug off "tattling" about these incidents? How do you think bullying can be prevented? Dealt with when it happens?

Thus, sharing makes more sense over time. In the classroom, teachers can help by:

- *Understanding child development* and that it is normal not to want to share and to have trouble doing so.
- *Explaining in simple terms what they want the child to do.*
- *Making sure that children "get back"* what they have shared so that taking turns really works.
- *Being an example of sharing* because "Do as I do" is more powerful than "Do it because I told you to."
- *Giving children experience of there being enough.*
- *Letting the children experience ownership,* too, because children can't really know what it means to share until they know what it means to own something.

Cooperating. Learning how to cooperate with others is one primary social skill in which young children need plenty of practice. Toddlers and two-year-olds can begin to see the benefits of cooperation as they become more aware of others' feelings and wishes, and as teachers help all children get what they want through taking turns, dividing materials, looking for another item when it is in demand. Three- to five-year-olds become more cooperative as they learn

1 Notice that these job titles are not gender specific. Try to invite men and women in nontraditional jobs to visit and talk about or demonstrate their work.

Video VIEW PoinT 14-2

"Preschool children are able to cooperate with each other."

COMPETENCY: Social Development

AGE GROUP: Preschool

CRITICAL THINKING QUESTION:

1. How can teachers bring into the curriculum the social conflicts that are common in children's play?

2. How can children's interest in cooperative play be built into the environment and schedule?

more self-help skills (motor development) and can express themselves (language development) as well as remember guidelines and understand reasons for prosocial behavior (cognitive development). School-age children develop an emotional sense of competence (see discussion of Erik Erikson's work in Chapter 4). They do this by acquiring knowledge and skills recognized by our culture as important (e.g., reading and writing in elementary school) and then using them with peers.[1] Children can learn and rehearse their skills in many areas of the program (Figure 14-13).

In preschool and primary classrooms, teachers often involve children in "cooperative learning" as a strategy that enhances cognitive learning through social interaction. Involving children's participation in small group learning activities, cooperative learning promotes social and academic interaction, increases enthusiasm and motivation, and rewards group participation.

Structured activities that promote cooperation (see Figure 14-15) help children become aware of and learn to work with others and to see viewpoints other than their own. Although most children spontaneously interact in free play periods (thus learning social skills in the process), some children need the structure of a more teacher-directed group activity to promote social development. Moreover, children's friendships can be expanded by the guided affiliation determined by a teacher and a project.

Successful implementation of cooperative learning activities in both older preschoolers and early elementary children usually needs a clear focus of project or activity (such as eating a snack, writing a newsletter, building a model, or catching a hamster on the loose). The group size and, often, members are determined by the teacher, who also needs to make the expectations for group behavior known. The teacher then monitors the interaction, providing assistance, clarification, or problem solving as needed. Evaluation is based on observation, and the group is rewarded for its success.

Being Included. Young children get involved in a variety of interpersonal situations that are beyond their capacities to handle with grace. An overly aggressive child, one who withdraws or stays apart from social opportunities, someone who chronically interrupts or disrupts the play, children who deliberately leave another out—all may end up becoming rejected by their peers. These socially awkward or troubled children need special help to learn the strategies for being included that all children have to learn.

Developing a conflict resolution curriculum will help all children learn the communication and coping skills necessary for being included. Children who learn good observation and body language skills can then be helped to participate successfully in situations that require prosocial behaviors. In addition, children will need guidance and practice in deciding how to include others whose appearance, interests, age, or behavior differs from their own (Paley, 1992). Chapter 7 has additional suggestions.

Children's literature can be used to facilitate social understanding of those who seem to differ from themselves. Research findings on guided reading indicate that books and reading can change attitudes as well as shape as child's character (Sawyer & Comer, 1996). For instance, use books that help inform children about disabilities; *I'm the Big Sister Now* (Emmert) helps school-aged children learn about multiple handicaps. At the same time, there is a body of books known as "inclusionary literature, where the intent is not to inform, [but rather] a person with a disability is included in story much like a person might be a neighbor, a classmate, or a friend" (Blaska & Lynch, 1998). Examples include *Lester's Dog* (Hesse) and *Mama Zoom* (Cowen-Fletcher).

---

 1 Be sure to include skills that are important to each child's culture and family.

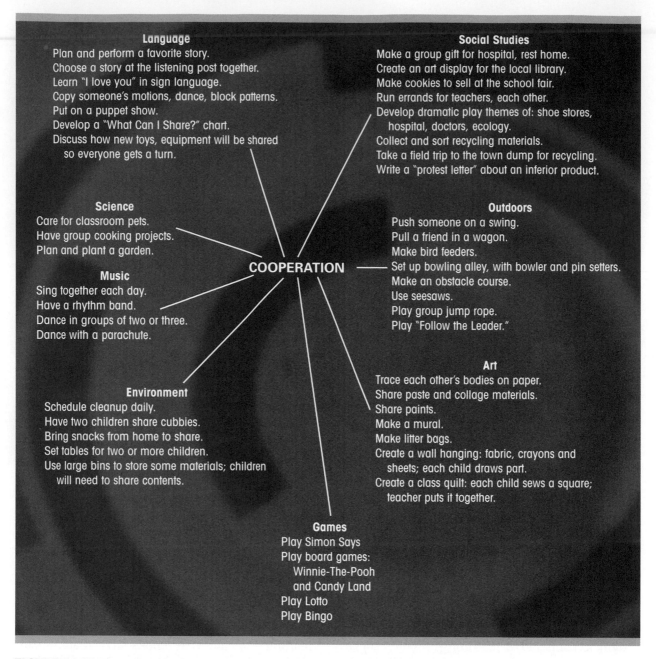

Language
Plan and perform a favorite story.
Choose a story at the listening post together.
Learn "I love you" in sign language.
Copy someone's motions, dance, block patterns.
Put on a puppet show.
Develop a "What Can I Share?" chart.
Discuss how new toys, equipment will be shared
    so everyone gets a turn.

Social Studies
Make a group gift for hospital, rest home.
Create an art display for the local library.
Make cookies to sell at the school fair.
Run errands for teachers, each other.
Develop dramatic play themes of: shoe stores,
    hospital, doctors, ecology.
Collect and sort recycling materials.
Take a field trip to the town dump for recycling.
Write a "protest letter" about an inferior product.

Science
Care for classroom pets.
Have group cooking projects.
Plan and plant a garden.

Outdoors
Push someone on a swing.
Pull a friend in a wagon.
Make bird feeders.
Set up bowling alley, with bowler and pin setters.
Make an obstacle course.
Use seesaws.
Play group jump rope.
Play "Follow the Leader."

COOPERATION

Music
Sing together each day.
Have a rhythm band.
Dance in groups of two or three.
Dance with a parachute.

Art
Trace each other's bodies on paper.
Share paste and collage materials.
Share paints.
Make a mural.
Make litter bags.
Create a wall hanging: fabric, crayons and
    sheets; each child draws part.
Create a class quilt: each child sews a square;
    teacher puts it together.

Environment
Schedule cleanup daily.
Have two children share cubbies.
Bring snacks from home to share.
Set tables for two or more children.
Use large bins to store some materials; children
    will need to share contents.

Games
Play Simon Says
Play board games:
    Winnie-The-Pooh
    and Candy Land
Play Lotto
Play Bingo

FIGURE 14-15 The social skill of cooperation can be fostered throughout the curriculum. (How to plan a lesson and build a unit are discussed in Chapter 11.)

Helping. One area of social development that is sometimes not emphasized in an individualistic society or classroom is that of helping others. In the past, it was thought that children's egocentric thinking prevented them from developing empathy or helping one another in a genuine way until later in childhood. Good early education programs, however, emphasize cooperation (see earlier section in this chapter) and find that children spontaneously offer help and sympathy to those in need. Snack-time is a natural setting for practicing helping others, both by having a conversation and helping one another, in both words (please pass the fruit; no, gracias) and deeds (handing someone the pitcher or a sponge). Remember to sit face-to-face, rather than hover behind. Teachers who stand behind often fall into the trap of withholding food while eliciting rote words, rather than genuine or spontaneous positive social interaction. Curriculum can be developed from the classroom ("What can we do when someone's sad to say good-bye to Mom?") and the larger world ("Some children have noticed a lot

Theme: Friendship

Concepts Children Will Learn	Activity
Everyone has a name and likes to have it used.	Friendship songs, using children's names.
Each person is something special and unique.	Make a "Friend Puppet" with paper plates, tongue depressor handles. Child decorates it with felt pieces and yarn to look like a friend.
Friends are different; they do not all look the same.	Children respond to "Tell me about your friend Alice. She . . . " (Child describes a friend as teacher writes the words.)
Having friends is fun.	Make a friendship ring: Each child traces own hands on mural making a circle.
Friends enjoy doing things together.	Go on a scavenger hunt with a friend.
Adults can be your friends.	Teacher helps child solve conflict or gives comfort when child is hurt.
Animals and pets can be your friends.	Children have an opportunity to bring small house pets to school to share with rest of class.
To have a friend is to be a friend.	Children respond to: "A Friend Is Someone Who ..." (They describe their impressions while teacher writes down their words.)
Friends enjoy doing things for one another.	Children respond to "Being a Friend with Someone Means ..." (Teacher writes down children's dictation.)
Everyone can have a friend.	Teacher reads stories about friendships. *Will I Have a Friend?* (Cohen), *Corduroy* (Freeman), *Play with Me* (Ets), *Little Bear's Friend* (Minarik), *A Letter to Amy* (Keats), *Hold My Hand* (Zolotow), *Jessica* (Henkes), *Harry & Willie & Carrothead* (Caseley).
You can show someone you want to be friends.	Write a letter to a friend; invite a friend over to play.
Friends will help you.	Form a relay team and have a race.

FIGURE 14-16 A friendship unit can encourage children to express positive emotions while they use their cognitive, language, and motor skills to enhance their social development.

 of trash in the park next door.") to enhance children's helping skills.[1]

Use of Projects/Themes

A popular theme that lends itself to social growth is that of friendship. One second-grade teacher started an intergenerational program she calls "Forever Friends." Early in the year, Ms. Power introduces her class to a group of residents of a retirement center.

> The elders visit the school throughout the year, participating first-hand in the students' studies and activities. They share oral histories, favorite memories and stories, and introduce the children to their talents and hobbies, such as photography, playing musical instruments and collecting coins and model trains.

There are discussions about what each group thinks about age issues ("What is old?") and take an attitude survey. They visit museums together, the children invite the elders to an art show of their paintings, and there is a musical review at the end of the year, including a song "Forever Friends" the teacher wrote (Holland, 2000). Figure 14-16 illustrates how a unit on friendship can be developed for a setting with children as young as three and as old as third grade. Other themes can be generated from the children:

"Make It Fair"	Not enough raisins in the cereal, complained a kindergartner, sparking a class letter-writing campaign.
"The Girl No One Wanted to Play With"	Preschoolers rejecting another, so they wrote, made costumes and performed a play.
"Saving the World"	Third-graders put on a sale to buy rainforest acreage.

Figure 14-17 shows a "Family" unit for the early primary (K–1) level.

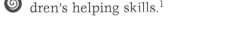 1   Be aware that some cultures in your classroom have a more cooperative orientation and can offer help to the teacher who is trying to expand from an individualistic focus to a more communal one.

Theme: About Families

Step 1:   **Establish Background Knowledge**

Large Group Brainstorm: What is a family?
    What are they called (Dad, Mama, Hermano, Nona, etc.)?
Individual List: Your own family and their names
    A picture of your family
Small Group Discussion: Feeling words for families
    Family jobs in the home
    Charades depicting family jobs
Think-Pair-Share: List, then draw how families have fun together
    List, then draw the tough times families have

Step 2:   **Decide the Theme Focus (e.g., "Family Fun")**

Step 3:   **Review Knowledge, Make a Plan**

Large Group: Review how families have fun
Pairs: Cut pictures from magazines showing family fun, make collage for classroom bulletin board.
Small Group Discussion: Brainstorm, then list and prioritize list of a family activity the class can do as a "family"
Large Group: Small groups present ideas, class vote (e.g., campground)

Step 4:   **Plan**

List what is needed, vote on placement of areas, make assignments for building and map-making.

Step 5:   **Building**

Create areas in classroom (e.g., campground, forest, lake, camp store, ranger station, cave, trails, etc.).

Step 6:   **Play!**

Step 7:   **Review and Conclusion**

Ongoing: Teacher observes and evaluates individual participation
At the end: Group discussion on what went well and didn't work; suggestions for future projects and taking
    down of building.

FIGURE 14-17 Cooperative learning activities involve children socially in their own academic learning. An *early primary* theme that is derived from the children and executed by them increases both learning and participation. (Thanks to Amy Buras for the kindergarten unit.)

CONCLUSION

Early in life children become aware of their social nature. The socialization process begins under the guidance of parents and family members. When children enter group settings, they are further exposed to behavior, social rules, and attitudes that foster social development. Much of a child's social repertoire is learned by playing with other children.

Children learn a great many social skills in these early years. They learn to enjoy and trust adults other than their parents. In their relationships with others, children learn ways to cooperate, disagree, share, communicate, and assert themselves effectively.

Children also learn how to be a member of a group—to take part in group activities, to adapt to school expectations, and to respect the rights and feelings of others. The young child also learns to express feelings in appropriate ways and to begin self-care tasks.

Teachers plan and arrange the early childhood environment in ways that will promote social growth and interaction. The adults help children understand each other's actions and motivations by interpreting the behavior to children as they play.

Curriculum to develop social skills in young children can be spontaneous as well as planned. Much of the focus in an early childhood setting is on social interactions throughout the day. At other times, social growth is enhanced by grouptime discussions, awareness of the community and society at large, and an emphasis on specific social skills.

Ask yourself:

1. What are social expectations of infants and toddlers? Preschoolers? School-aged children?

2. Why is peer group experience important?

3. What social skills do children develop with adults? With other children? In a group? As individuals?

4. How do teachers help children develop social skills?

5. How are social skills fostered in the curriculum?

CREATIVE GROWTH: THE DEVELOPMENT OF CREATIVITY

It's OK to try something you don't know.

It's OK to make mistakes.

It's OK to take your time.

It's OK to find your own pace.

It's OK to bungle—so next time you are free to succeed.

It's OK to risk looking foolish.

It's OK to be original and different.

It's OK to wait until you are ready.

It's OK to experiment (safely).

It's OK to question "shoulds."

It is special to be you. You are unique.

It is necessary to make a mess (which you need to be willing to clean up!).

"Permissions," by Christina Lopez-Morgan (2002) opens our discussion of creativity, to give the tone for what creativity is and how it develops.

In this section, we will discuss the development of creativity and creative skills, then look at the role of the teacher and creative curriculum.

Creativity is the ability to have new ideas, to be original and imaginative, and to make new adaptations on old ideas. Inventors, composers, and designers are creative people, as are those who paint and dance, write speeches, or create curriculum for children.[1] Thinking in a different way and changing a way of learning or seeing something are all creative acts.

Creative thinking is a cognitive process, expressed by children in all developmental areas. Picture the two major ways of thinking as vertical or lateral. Vertical thinking involves learning more about something, and tends to lead toward an answer. It is also known as convergent thinking, used when asked, "What shape is this block?" Lateral thinking is a process used to find the creative solution or unusual idea. Such **divergent thinking** tends to broaden the field of answers, as when responding to "how many different ways can you surprise your mother?"

Creativity engages certain parts of the brain. The left hemisphere controls the right side of the body and controls such operations as concrete thinking, systematic planning, language and mathematical skills, what we might call the more rational and cognitive parts of thinking. It is the right brain that engages in more spontaneous ideas, and thinks in nonverbal, intuitive ways. Of course, we need both sides to engage to develop, but clearly, the right side is the creative information processor.

The roots of creativity reach into infancy, for it is every individual's unique and creative process to explore and understand the world. Infants' creativity is seen in their efforts to touch and move. Toddlers begin to scribble, build, and move for the pure physical sensation of movement. Young preschoolers create as they try for more control, such as scribbling with purpose or bobbing and jumping to music. Older preschoolers enjoy their budding mastery. Their drawings take on some basic forms, and they repeat movements deliberately while making a dance. As they grow, five- to eight-year-olds communicate to the world through artistic and expressive creation. With advanced motor control and hand-eye coordination, their drawings are representational and pictorial, their dramatic play more cohesive.

Creativity is a process; as such, it is hard to define. As one becomes involved in creative activity, the process and the product merge.

> It is probably best to think of creativity as a continual process for which the best preparation is creativity itself. . . . there is real joy in discovery—which not only is its own reward, but provides the urge for continuing exploration and discovery. (Lowenfeld & Brittain, 1975)

---

 1 Introduce children to a diverse range of creative adults—men and women from a variety of cultural backgrounds. When we become too concerned with molding children to "fit," we miss the fact that accepting and developing the differences among children enhance creativity.

The young child is open to experience, exploring materials with curiosity and eagerness. For young children, developing the senses is part of acquiring creative skills. Children are also quick to question, wonder, and see things that do not quite match up. In the early years, it is delightful to watch confident children elaborate in their creative expression with increasing detail, and using more complex forms.

CREATIVE SKILLS IN EARLY CHILDHOOD

There are characteristics common to creative people. For the teacher interested in fostering creative growth in children, these are the skills they should help children learn.

Flexibility and Fluency

Flexibility and **fluency** are dual skills that allow for creative responses. Flexibility is the capacity to shift from one idea to another; fluency is the

Creativity is the ability to be original and imaginative, to soar above the commonplace. (Courtesy of the city of Reggio Emilia, Italy.)

ability to produce many ideas. "How many ways can you move from one side of the room to another?" is a question likely to produce many different ideas, one example of fluency. Children who must think of another way to share the wagons when taking turns doesn't work learn flexibility.[1]

Sensitivity

Being creative involves a high degree of sensitivity to one's self and one's mental images. Creative people, from an early age, seem to be aware of the world around them; how things smell, feel, and taste. They are sensitive to mood, texture, and how they feel about someone or something. Creative people notice details; how a pinecone is attached to the branch is a detail the creative person does not overlook.

A special aspect of this skill is a sensitivity to beauty. Also known as **aesthetics**, this sensitivity to what is beautiful is emphasized in some programs (such as Reggio Emilia) and some cultures (such as tokonoma, an alcove dedicated to display, in Japanese homes).[2] Growing evidence (Spodek et al., 1996) indicates that children have an awareness and value about their natural environment and what is aesthetically pleasing.

Creative children take delight and satisfaction in making images come to life. Their creative response is in the way they paint a picture, dance with streamers, or find a solution to a problem. Figure 14-18 shows how a five-and-a-half-year-old's sensitivity to perspective and detail comes out through a drawing.

Use of Imagination/Originality

Imagination is a natural part of the creative process. Children use their imagination to develop their creativity in several ways.

- *Role Playing.* In taking on another role, children combine their knowledge of the real world with their internal images. The child becomes a new character, and that role comes to life.

- *Image Making.* When children create a rainbow with a hose or with paints, they are adding something of their own to their understanding of that visual image. In dance, children use their imagination as they pretend to be objects or feelings, images brought to life.

- *Constructing.* In building and constructing activities, children seem to be re-creating an

1 Creative individuals defy being placed in categories because their special ability to solve problems in new ways is not measured by intelligence tests or by cultural, gender, or ability stereotyping.

2 Teachers can ask the families of children in their care about special places, objects, and rituals that celebrate beauty and help children acquire an aesthetic interest in their environment.

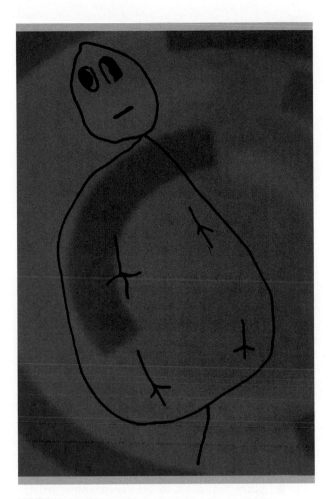

FIGURE 14-18 Sensitivity to one's own mental images, such as perceiving direction and movement, are part of creativity in the young child. A five-and-a-half-year-old sketched how a pet rat looked from below after picking it up often and watching it run on its exercise wheel.

image they have about tall buildings, garages, or farms. In the process of construction, however, children do not intend that the end product resemble the building itself. Their imagination allows them to experiment with size, shape, and relationships.

A Willingness to Take Risks/Elaboration

People who are willing to break the ordinary mental set and push the boundaries in defining and using ordinary objects, materials, and ideas are creative people. They take risks. Being open to thinking differently or seeing things differently is essential to creativity.

When children create, they are revealing themselves. Art, for instance, is a form of cultural communication, one of the basic language skills children need to participate in a multicultural democracy (Schirrmacher, 2006). Increasing opportunities for creative expression

allows for nonverbal response and success without directions. It encourages children (and families) to share themselves in enjoyable ways. It is, therefore, a good way to teach about cultures and learn about each other in a relaxed, accepting atmosphere.

Self-esteem is a factor in risk-taking because people who are tied to what others think of them are more likely to conform rather than follow their own intuitive and creative impulses. People usually do not like to make mistakes or be ridiculed; therefore, they avoid taking risks.

A teacher concerned about creative growth in children realizes that it will surface if allowed and encouraged. When a child is relaxed and not anxious about being judged by others, creativity will more likely be expressed. With support, children can be encouraged to risk themselves.

Using Self as a Resource

Creative people who are aware of themselves and confident in their abilities draw on their own perceptions, questions, and feelings. They know they are their own richest source of inspiration. Those who excel in creative productivity have a great deal of respect for themselves and they use the self as a resource.

Experience

Children need experience to gain skills in using materials creatively. They must learn how to hold a paint brush before they can paint a picture; once they know how to paint, they can be creative in what they paint. Teachers of young children sometimes overlook the fact that children need competence with the tools to be creative with them. A little sensitive, individual demonstration on proper use of a watercolor brush, sandpaper, or ink roller can expand a child's ability to create and eliminate needless frustration and disappointment. The teachers of Reggio Emilia, for instance, demonstrate how to use the tools so that the children can then make outstanding creations, (Figure 14-19). Anecdotes from highly accomplished people in creative endeavors (pianists, mathematicians, Olympic swimmers) highlight the value of long-term systematic instruction in a sort of apprenticeship with inspiring teachers as well as parents who are committed to assist. As teachers we can see how Vygotsky's theory applies in the arts and can provide the initial palette of creative activities so that children can dabble and become experienced. When the skill of the medium is mastered, the child is ready to create.

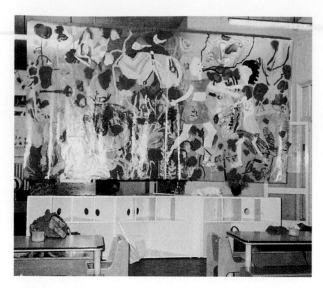

FIGURE 14-19 When children have a chance to create, with permission to use an abundance of materials, the results are creative. (Courtesy of the city of Reggio Emilia, Italy.)

THE TEACHER'S ROLE

Teachers affect the creative process for children in several distinct ways:

- By how they set up the environment.
- By the choices and kinds of activities they provide.
- By the types of interactions they have with the children during creative activities (Lopez-Morgan, 2002).

Early childhood professionals consider their roles carefully. Think about how you can encourage creativity.

Teachers can follow these eight tips to encourage creative development.

1. *Provide continuous availability, abundance, and variety of materials,* as is done in Reggio Emilia (see Chapter 2).

2. *Give children regular creative opportunities to experience and the skill necessary to be creative.* Children need frequent occasions to be creative to function in a highly creative manner. When children have a chance to create, their skills in perceiving the world are enhanced.

3. *Encourage divergent thinking.* Don't interfere. "Children need to please only themselves. . . . Once you've presented the materials, forget how you intended them to be used" (Bos, 1978). Where there are no "right" or "wrong" answers, children are free to create. Avoid models, making things

for children to copy. It insults children, and can make them feel inadequate in the face of something you can do so much better.

The "creativity questions" in the curriculum section are examples of divergent thinking. Also, notice the children's responses to a fight over the swings.

4. *Help foster conversation on issues and seeking solutions to problems:*

    Teacher: How do you think we could share the swings?

    David: The kids who give me a turn can come to my birthday party.

    Sabrina: No. We will have to make a waiting list.

    Xenia: Only girls can use the swings. The boys can have all the cars.

    Frederico: Buy a new swing set.

5. *Talk with young children about what they create.* Whether it is their artwork, table toy creations, or dramatic play sequences, talk helps creativity considerably. Schirrmacher (2006) offers some suggestions about talking with children about art; these hints could apply to all creative endeavors. Rather than approach children's work with compliments, judgments, or even questions:

    - Allow children to go about their artistic discoveries without your comparing, correcting, or projecting yourself into their art.
    - Shift from searching for representation in children's art to a focus on the abstract, design qualities.
    - Use reflective dialogue.
    - Smile, pause, and say nothing at first.

6. *Allow children to take the lead* in their own creative works from start to finish. Adults do not need to take over at any point, particularly at the end with questions ("What is it?") or praise ("I like it!"). If a child seems to want more response, comment on the color ("What a lot of blue you used"), texture ("I see wiggly lines all down one side"), or the child's efforts ("You really worked on this painting, huh?"). "Listen carefully to each child, and try to provide what the child asks for. I try never to say, 'We're not doing that today'." (Bos, 1978).

    Child: The monster's gonna get you and eat you up!

    Teacher: You made a monster with the wood scraps.

Child: Yes, and it's for my daddy.

Teacher: Let's put it on the counter so it will be dry when he picks you up.

7. *Integrate creativity and learning in the classroom.* Early childhood theorists from Dewey and Piaget to Montessori and Malaguzzi (see Chapter 1) have advocated multisensory learning through experimentation and discovery. See the Art section later in this chapter.

8. *Teacher timing and attitudes stimulate creativity.* Don't delay; children want to see immediate results and act on their ideas now. Teacher timing and attitudes are important in stimulating creative development. Give plenty of time for a dramatic theme to develop, to pursue the props needed, or to find the players and audience. The early childhood years are probably the most crucial time to encourage creative thinking; one study found that kindergartners gave a higher proportion of original responses to creativity tasks than did second-graders (Moran, Milgram, Sawyers, & Fu, 1983). "It is here that initial attitudes are established . . . and school can be a fun place where the individual's contribution is welcome and where changes can be sought and made" (Lowenfeld & Brittain, 1975).

Children need plenty of time and a relaxed atmosphere to be creative. They need encouragement and respect for the process and products of their creative nature. The teacher's attitude tells the children that what they do is important and that how they do it makes a difference. Rather than expecting a predetermined right answer, the teacher encourages creativity by valuing the answers the children give even when they appear unusual or illogical.

Note: The Reggio Emilia approach to curriculum (see Chapters 2 and 10) emphasizes children's creative and cognitive expressions. They have a special art teacher (atelierista) who operates an art studio within the school. The studio is stocked with art materials, and children work alongside this teacher. While most groups will not have this arrangement, the idea of children talking and learning with a more experienced adult can help them excel in creating.

Curriculum Planning for Creative Growth

The early childhood curriculum offers many rich avenues for self-expression and creativity.

Beyond art and music, there is the ability to think and question, to find more than one answer to a problem. Blocks, climbing equipment, and social relationships offer risk-taking opportunities. Children use themselves as resources as they play outdoor games, experiment with science projects, and participate in dramatic play. Taruna exhibits many creative traits as she attempts to enter into play with two other children. She first asks if she can play, and when met with rejection, she demands to be one of the mommies. Taruna finally offers her doll as a prop and is accepted into the group. Her persistence is exceeded only by her creative problem solving.

In the Environment

Teachers create the atmosphere and the environment for creative endeavors. "Studies show that teachers plan areas for discussions, walls for displays, centers for activities, and areas for supplies. In the organization of these classroom areas by teachers and their use by children, the spaces and artifacts take on meaning and influence learning" (Taunton & Colbert, 2000).

Open-ended materials provide a continuing challenge as children use them repeatedly in new and different ways. Clay, play dough, paints, crayons and pens, blocks, water, sand and other sensory materials, and movable outdoor equipment are good examples of open-ended materials that stimulate creativity. Particularly in the area of creative art, it is

Video VIEW Point 14-3

"A teacher needs to know how to create a space that invites children to explore."

COMPETENCY: Creative Development

AGE GROUP: School Age

CRITICAL THINKING QUESTIONS:

1. How can teachers foster creativity and divergent thinking in a school-age environment and still respond to family requests to get homework done after school?

2. What movement challenges can teachers give children that teach skills but also encourage individual expression?

important to avoid projects that masquerade as creative activities, such as duplicated, photocopied, or mimeographed sheets, cut-and-paste activities, tracing patterns, coloring-book pages, dot-to-dot books (Schirrmacher, 2006), and any art "project" that is based on a model for children to copy or imitate. Children are motivated to try new ways to use materials when a project is flexible and challenging.

Offer many materials to create an open-ended art center.

When a community values creativity, it puts creative skill development high as a school priority. (Courtesy of the city of Reggio Emilia, Italy.)

Indoors. Every classroom has a potential for creative activity.

- *The Arts.* A wide variety of materials and opportunities to choose how they will be used is the basis of the creative process. An open table with a shelf of simple, familiar materials that can be combined in many ways will lead to inventiveness. Two-year-olds like crayons, paste, and colored paper pieces; three- to five-year-olds will enjoy the addition of markers, string, hole punches and scissors, and tape. Older children can manage staplers, rulers, and protractors. Plenty of paper, such as recycled computer paper and cardboard, round out an open-ended, self-help art shelf. More organized art activities can also be offered, particularly for the preschool child, as long as the focus is on the child's process, rather than an end product or model. As they approach the primary years, children become interested in what their creations look like and then are ready for practical help and advice on getting started. *Creativity question: What other ways can you think of to use the paint?*

- *Blocks/Manipulatives.* Children use their imagination when blocks become castles, tunnels, corrals, and swamps. These areas encourage creativity when children have enough materials of one kind to "really" make something; one long block is just not enough for a road. Also, creations have a sense of permanence when they are noted and kept. Sketching or photographing a block structure, attaching signs (including taking dictation) for the day, even rethinking cleanup periodically shows how valuable these creations are. *Creativity questions: How can you use the blocks to make a forest? A stairway? Can you think of a design using the pegs?*

- *Discovery/Science.* Building geoboards or making tangrams and cube art all blend math and art. Art activities can lead children to discover scientific principles, such as color mixing, dissolving powder paint in water, and having water available with clay. Natural materials can be used for rubbings, mobiles, and prints. Collecting materials during a "litter walk" makes interesting and informative collages. *Creativity questions: What do you think will happen? Now, how can you find out why it happened that way?*

- *Dramatic Play.* The dramatic arts offer opportunities for children to express themselves. Every "unit" in the dramatic play corner brings out children's own interpretations of their world, be it a house, shoestore, market, or a campout, dinosaur cave, or space shuttle.

Favorite books and stories can be acted out in the dramatic play area. This will work better with children who have interacted together in socio-dramatic play. Start with a simple nursery rhyme, and move to short stories with a few characters, simple plots, and manageable speaking lines (Schirrmacher, 2006).

Help children create costumes, props, and a stage. Be sure to stay creative in the roles; there is no reason girls can't play the Wild Things or Max! *Creativity questions: What could you use to help you pretend you are the grandpapa? How could this scarf be used in your house?*

- *Language/Library.* Besides a variety of books and children's literary experiences (see Chapter 13), the booknook can be a place for teachers to ask open-ended questions for fun and pondering. "What if you were a twin? What would you wear or eat? Where would you live?" is a social creation; "If I were a hat, I would . . ." is physical creativity; "How many ways could we make triangles with these materials on the table?" challenges a child to cognitive creativity. Creative responses for language development can use a familiar storyline: For instance, the book *Did You Ever See?* (Einsel) or the song "Down by the Bay" can be used to ask children to make a rhyme to end the sentence "Did you ever see a whale . . . ("flipping its tail!") *Creativity question: What do you think will happen next in the story?*

Outdoors. Creativity happens out-of-doors also. Large, hollow blocks can become a stairway, and wagons and carts become fire engines, buses, doll carriages, moving vans, or trucks. Dancing with ribbons, making a banner for a parade, rearranging equipment to make a tumbling or obstacle course all combine children's motor skills with music for creative growth. The use of these activities is limited only by the creativity of the children. Sand, water, and mud provide a place for children to dig, haul, manipulate, and control in any number of ways. *Creativity questions: How many parts of your body can you use to get the ball to your friend? How many ways can you think of to cross over on the climber? I wonder how you could get the wet sand into the bucket? What is your tricycle going to be today?*

Routines, Transitions, and Groups

Teachers can apply their own creativity to many routine situations. Children looking for a lost mitten organize a "hunt." Pretending to be vacuum cleaners, dump trucks, or robots gets the blocks picked up faster. Saying good-bye can be an exercise in creativity; the child can say, "See you later, alligator," and the adults (parents and teacher) can make up a silly response. Another day, the child and parent can reverse roles.

Schirrmacher (2006) has devised several creative-thinking games that can be part of any transition time. Since teachers are looking for unusual responses, children will stay engaged and the game stays fresh over time. "What would happen if . . ." is the prompt; provide endings such as "refrigerators ate food? bathtubs could talk? you could be invisible?" Another game called "Just Suppose" asks children to come up with endings to such short stories as "You found a magic flying carpet. Where would you go? What would happen?" or "You could be any animal." A third game, "Make It Better" uses a prop. The teacher brings a stuffed animal, race car, or other familiar toy. Pass it around carefully, then ask, "How could we make it a better toy? What could we do to make it more fun to play with?"

Creativity does not respond well to the clock. These three issues—routines, transitions, and groups—must be handled so as not to interrupt children too often. "Children's own sense of time and their personal rhythms are considered in planning and carrying out activities and projects" (Gandini in Gillespie, 2000). *Creativity question for dismissal transition: How can you use one foot and one hand in some way to go to your snack groups?*

Music is a special outlet for children's creative expression in groups. Music is a universal language that develops every aspect of affective development. It allows the expression of emotions and provides the opportunity to take roles as well as a delightful time to create with movement. There is a kind of developmental sequence in the creative expression of music.[1] The very young child is receptive to music, responding by listening, singing, and making noise with instruments. "One of the most satisfying rewards of teaching 2-year-olds is witnessing their rapid growth," states one teacher. "Keeping pace with this growth is a challenge for

---

1 Sharing music and dance from home is an ideal way to incorporate children's individual cultures into the classroom. Translate a simple song into another language; teach the children the song, working in the language that is "home base" for most of the children, then reteach it. Words and phrases made familiar by melody are remembered and made valuable.

parents and teachers, especially since not all children advance at the same rate. Music offers a solution to this challenge . . . It can help children adjust to a large group activity. With one voice, the children can express themselves in joyful song and movement that truly realizes the feeling of community. Both the vociferous, active child and the quiet one 'singing' the words silently feel a sense of accomplishment" (Pecka, 2005).

Preschoolers move to rhythmic music, often singing spontaneously in play and responding to repeated songs or repetitious phrasing. Their interest in musical instruments precedes their skill, and they often need instruments to be introduced and their proper use demonstrated. Older preschoolers and school-age children are more accurate in matching their pitch and tempo to the group or played music.

Music can permeate the entire program. It can set the tone at nap time, signal that a cleanup task is at hand, summon children to a group, and offer cultural experiences that are meaningful and enjoyable.[1] For instance, New Year is often a noisy time; it can be celebrated by making ankle bells and doing a Sri Lankan dance or making a West Indian Conga line. In Waldorf schools, music is quite important. Children are engaged daily in eurythmy exercises (developed by Steiner, see Chapter 1). Taught by a specialist, it is a kind of creative form that translates music and speech into movement. (See Figure 14-20.)

Stage of Musical Development	Appropriate Music/Movement Activity
Two-year-olds	
Use their bodies in response to music	Bounce to music with different tempos
Can learn short, simple songs	Repetitive songs like "Itsy-Bitsy Spider" or "If You're Happy and You Know It"
Enjoy experimenting with sounds	Pound on milk cartons, oatmeal boxes
	Make shakers with gravel in shampoo bottles
Three-year-olds	
Can recognize and sing parts of tunes	Select songs that include their names, such as "Do You Know the Muffin Man?"
Walk run, jump to music	Use Ella Jenkin's recordings or try "Going on a Bear Hunt"
Make up their own songs	Start "Old MacDonald" and let them make their own additions; dance with scarves or use shakers to sing along with a child
Four-year-olds	
Can grasp basic musical concepts like tempo, volume, pitch	Be a flying car, trees swaying in the wind, sing "Big, Bigger, Biggest" with variations
Love silly songs	Change "Where Is Thumbkin" to "Where Is Fi-fo" and improvise with their ideas
Prefer "active" listening	Accompany music with instruments, "Green Grass Grew All Around" with action
Five- to six-year olds	
Enjoy singing and moving with a group	Use a parachute to music
Enjoy call-and-response songs	Try "Did You Feed My Cow?"
Have fairly established musical preferences	Be sure to ask the group and use them in selecting music activities
Seven- and eight-year olds	
Are learning to read lyrics	Use large word charts
Enjoy musical duets with friends	Do partner games
	Children pick instruments in pairs

FIGURE 14-20 Creative experiences in music and movement engage the whole child and offer children integrated experiences throughout the curriculum (adapted from Schirrmacher, 2006).

1 Improvised music and lyrics can sustain sociodramatic play between children with developmental delays and nondelayed peers (Gunsberg, 1991).

Focus on Skills

The wide range of skills necessary for creative development can be supported throughout the early childhood program. The creative thinker is one who finds many ways to solve a problem, approach a situation, use materials, and interact with others. The teacher's role is one of supporting imaginative use of equipment and using a multisensory approach to deepen learning. The Creativity Questions in the previous section demonstrate some of the ways teachers focus on children's creative skills through the use of questions.

Use of Projects/Themes

As teachers plan curriculum around a theme, they keep in mind what creative skills can be developed. Figure 14-21 charts the theme of "Green and Growing Things" and can bring out the child's creative nature. In addition, such a theme touches on aspects of social responsibility (see previous section) by promoting ecological responsibility through the arts and nurturing an environmental and social ethic.

One teacher (Bovard, 2000), whose personal interest took her to an acting workshop, brought an activity back to her class of older primary

---

Theme: Green and Growing Things

Outdoor Activities

1. Plant a garden in a corner of the yard, in an old barrel, or in a box flat on a table. Children learn through experimentation why some things grow and others don't. Make space for a compost heap.

2. Add wheelbarrows to the transportation toys.

3. Take a field trip to a farm, at planting time if possible, or a garden center.

4. Add gardening tools to the sand area. With proper supervision, children can see how trowels, hand claws, rakes, and shovels can be used to create new patterns in the sand and mud.

5. Plan group games that emphasize green and growing things. Older children could run wheelbarrow races, using one child as the wheelbarrow and another as a driver.

6. Play "musical vegetables" with large cards or chalk drawings. Dance with gourds, coconut instruments, sugar cane rhythm sticks.

7. Have children select a potted plant (have older children pick a partner), then have them draw, paint, or collage what they see. Let children look, talk and compare, then make another creation.

Indoor Activities

1. Leaf rubbings, printing with surplus apples, onions, carrots, potatoes, lemons, oranges, and celery, and painting with pine boughs are ways children can create art with green and growing things, make cornhusk dolls, avocado seed porcupines.

2. Book accessories might include blue felt forms for lakes, hay for corrals and barns.

3. In the manipulative area, match a photo of familiar plants with a sample of the plant. Add sorting trays with various kinds of seeds to count, feel, mix, and match. Match pictures of eggs, bacon, milk, and cheese, with other animals from which they come.

4. In the science area, grow alfalfa sprouts and mung beans. Let children mix them in salads and feed to classroom pets. As the sprouts grow, children can chart the growth. This activity can lead to charting their own development, comparing it with when they were infants.

5. The dramatic play center can be transformed into a grocery store to emphasize the food we buy to eat, how it helps us, and why good nutrition is important. Other dramatic play units are a florist shop or nursery, stocked with garden gloves, seed packets, peat pots, and sun hats.

6. The language area can be stocked with books about how plants, baby animals, and children grow. In small groups, children can respond to "When I plant a seed . . . " or "When I was a baby I . . . Now I . . ." to stimulate creative expression.

7. Songs and fingerplays help focus on green and growing things, children's growth, and animals. "The Green Grass Grows All Around" can be sketched by a teacher so that children will have visual cues to each successive verse. A favorite fingerplay, "Way Up in the Apple Tree," can be adapted to a number of fruits and vegetables.

FIGURE 14-21 Creativity around the classroom. Creativity and problem solving may stem from the same source. Real-life experiences, such as planning and building a garden, expand to provide creative thinking and logic in the classroom.

children known as the "Emotion Map." After leading a discussion about imaginative maps (*The Hobbit, Harry Potter*), she listed their suggestions ("Slump Swamp," "Guilt Garage," "Boring Boulevard," "Bridge of Joy"). Rolling out a piece of paper on the floor, they began to sketch and talk. Once the map was made and elaborately decorated, the students used it to plot how they felt daily, using a Post-it® they had drawn of themselves. Discussions were frequent. New ideas cropped up: Children wanted "emotion maps" made into books for journaling and to plan for performances about different emotions.

In a younger group, a preschool team noticed the children's interest in shoes. They helped the children brainstorm what they knew about shoes and what they wanted to learn and do about them. The group built a shoe store, created a song and game called "Whose shoe are you?" and made elaborate "houses" out of old, donated adult shoes modeled after "I Know an Old Woman Who Lived in a Shoe." The project lasted nearly a month!

ART

"Just as the spirit of the artist is in the things the artist makes, the spirit of the child is in the things the child makes. True education helps children discover and revel in that spirit" (Froebel in Feinberg, 2003). Art touches the whole child.

Whether the sweeping motion of a brush onto an easel, pounding the fist into clay, or rhythmic scissoring, art is a physical activity. Art may be an individual experience, but in the early childhood classroom, it is a social one as well. Children learn how to interact with others when sharing materials, taking turns, and exchanging ideas with others. Emotionally, children express their inner selves and work through feelings, both positive and negative, in their artwork. Indeed, art therapy has a long history in helping therapists understand children. Art reflects what the child knows; planning and organizing, revising and finishing are all cognitive tasks. Moreover, early childhood professionals can encourage children to talk about their processes and making art a language activity as well. Finally, children's artistic creations may be similar in their development (see next section), but are unique expressions of each child's creativity.

Rhoda Kellogg (1969) described the developmental stages of art, after having analyzed literally millions of piece of children's art from around the world over a 20-year period. Briefly, they are:

- *Placement stage:* Scribble, ages two–three
- *Shape stage:* Vague shapes, ages two–four; actual shapes, ages three–five
- *Design stage:* Combined shapes, ages three–five; mandalas and suns, ages three–five
- *Pictorial stage:* People, ages four–five; beginning recognizable art, ages four–six; later recognizable art, ages five–seven

Figure 14-22 illustrates these stages.

The process of creating art follows a predictable four-step pattern, although there are as many variations on the theme as there are children and art experiences.

1. *Preparation.* Gathering materials and ideas to begin.
2. *Incubation.* Letting ideas "cook" and develop.
3. *Illumination.* The "a-ha" moment when everything gels; the "lightbulb."
4. *Verification.* When exhilaration has passed and only time will confirm the effort.

When Howard Gardner began his studies of intelligence (see Chapters 4 and 12), he became intrigued with artistic capacity. Project Zero was the implementation of this interest. A program to study intelligence, the arts, and education for the last 30 years, the project (Gardner, 1993) has helped identify some key ideas about art education:

1. In the early childhood years, production of art ought to be central. Children need to work directly with the materials.
2. The visual arts ought to be introduced by someone who can think visually or spatially. An ECE team ought to be diverse enough to have someone with this intelligence on board.
3. Whenever possible, artistic learning should be organized around meaningful projects. Both the project approach and emergent curriculum address this (Chapter 10).
4. Artistic learning must entail emotional reflection and personal discovery along with a set of skills. Integration of development is encouraged.

Taken together, these observations help teachers create developmentally appropriate art activities. If you work with infants or toddlers, be sure to help children explore materials and places with all their senses, and expect scribbling by 15–20 months. Young preschoolers will work in manipulating tools and materials, discovering what can be done and needing lots of repetition. Do not expect

1. Scribbling:

2. Drawing a single shape:

3. Combining single shapes into designs:

4. Drawing mandalas, mandaloids, and sun figures:

5. Drawing a human figure with limbs and torso:

FIGURE 14-22 Children's art follows a sequence of stages (From *Art and Creative Development for Young Children* (4th Ed.) by Schirrmacher. © 2002. Reprinted with permission of Delmar Learning, a division of Thomson Learning: www.thomsonrights.com. Fax 800 730-2215.)

much concern about the final product. By four–six years, children's art becomes more symbolic and planned; more detailed work with forms and shapes may be seen. Children become interested in what they are doing and how it turns out.

Giving art its place in early childhood curriculum will require space, time, and attention. An art center (Schirrmacher, 2006) is:

1. An artist's studio.
2. Conveniently located and easily accessible.
3. Well-stocked with developmentally appropriate materials.
4. Orderly and organized.
5. A place with rules and limits.

See Chapter 9 for more details on space. Basic categories of art materials include:

- tools for mark making,
- papers in a variety of shapes/sizes/textures,
- modeling and molding materials such as play dough/clay,
- items for cutting, fastening and attaching such as scissors and string,
- items for painting,
- and collage items.

Adapting Art for Children with Special Needs

___ **Visual:**

Verbally describe materials and how they might be used.

Provide a tray that outlines the visual boundaries.

Offer bright paint to contrast with paper.

Go slowly and encourage children to manipulate the items as you talk.

___ **Auditory:**

Model the process, facing the child and using gestures for emphasis.

Use sign language as needed.

___ **Physical:**

Make sure there is a clear path to the art center.

Provide adaptive art tools such as chunky crayons, large markers.

Provide double ambidextrous scissors so you can help, or a cutting wheel.

Velcro can be attached to marking instruments or paintbrushes.

Use contact paper for collage, or glue sticks instead of bottles.

___ **Attention-deficit and/or behavioral:**

Provide children with their own materials and workspace, minimizing waiting and crowding.

Offer materials like play dough to express feelings and energy.

Limit children to few choices rather than overwhelming them with everything in the art center.

FIGURE 14-23 The value of art activities for children with special needs cannot be overemphasized.

Figure 14-23 gives some suggestions for adapting art for children with special needs. "Merely labeling an activity art is no guarantee that the activity will have artistic merit," warns Schirrmacher (2006). Uncreative activities are masquerading as creative, and should be avoided. Some adults defend these activities by claiming that children like them. The same holds true for candy and violent play, but alert adults do not allow unfettered use of either one. Moreover, highly structured, teacher-directed art activities may have a purpose for creating a finished product that teaches discouragement ("Mine doesn't look like the teacher's.") and inhibits creativity ("I'm not a good artist."). Again, Schirrmacher:

> Crafts are often given as holiday gifts. Most parents would be delighted to receive a paperweight or pencil holder constructed by their child. Although it is important to please parents, it is equally important to meet the creative needs of children. Providing for child input, planning, decision-making, and creative processing guarantees that each finished product will be as unique and individual as the child who produced it.

Taking the time to talk with families about children's art and creativity will help them appreciate the unique nature of children's creations.

CONCLUSION

Young children are open to the creative process and to creative experiences. The early years are a good time to acquire the skills of flexibility, sensitivity, imagination, risk taking, resourcefulness, and experience.

The greatest challenge for adults in nurturing children's creativity is to help children find and develop their "creativity intersection"—the area where their talents, skills, and interests overlap (Amabile, 1989). The role of the teacher is to plan curricula that will help develop children's creativity. An atmosphere conducive to creative work is one that supports children's divergent thinking, encourages them to take risks, and provides ways they can use themselves as resources.

Ask yourself:

● What are the creative skills learned in early childhood?

● What is the teacher's role in the development of creativity?

● What classroom area, skill, or project promotes creative thinking?

● What is in an art center, and how can art promote creativity?

SPIRITUAL DEVELOPMENT

Spiritual development is rarely discussed in early childhood or developmental texts. In the United States, where the separation of church and state is mandated, the public classroom has avoided involvement in things spiritual or religious. Private schools are not under such legal restraints, and many (see Chapter 2) actively support or are sponsored by religious organizations. Still, the spiritual side of formal schooling is usually left to religious institutions and families.

Often adults tend to see children as not particularly spiritual. Without higher reasoning and abstract thinking skills, young children are seen as not able to have a spiritual life. Moreover, many think of spirituality solely in terms of religion, and "this focus on the 'religious' end of spirituality may be developmentally 'off target'" (Nye in Dillon, 2000). By seeing children as faulty thinkers (since they cannot articulate or conceptualize like adults) or by focusing only on organized religion and its ways of explanation, we may overwhelm or overlook children's spiritual experiences.

Some of the earliest contributors to the field have mentioned spiritual development. Froebel saw the child as having an innate spiritual capacity. Education was meant to build on the living core of the child's intrinsic spiritual capacity. Steiner developed the three spiritual dimensions of selfhood, and felt that children of all levels of development were capable of spiritual experience. Montessori (in Wolf, 2000) wrote:

> If education recognizes the intrinsic value of the child's personality and provides an environment suited to spiritual growth, we have the revelation of an entirely new child whose astonishing characteristics can eventually contribute to the betterment of the world.

It would appear that "profound levels of spiritual reality are accessible even to the youngest human being. . . . These experiences typically involve unity, joy, mystery" (Dillon, 2000). Take, for instance, the children's awe as they see a banana slug inching its way up a redwood tree. Or the wonder in their eyes at the many colors of autumn maple leaves. Their gasp when they find a dead bird, or the sheer joy and outstretched arms (and tongues!) to catch snowflakes.

Saxton (2004) reminds us of the religious or spiritual influence on a child's cultural identity. Robert Coles (1990) conducted an inquiry of the spiritual life of children in the United States, Central and South America, Europe, the Middle East, and Africa. He concluded that children are "seekers, as young pilgrims well aware that life is a finite journey and as anxious to make sense of it as those of us who are farther along in the time allotted us."

Spiritual development in an early childhood program includes the child's deep experience with self and the world, with the mysterious and invisible and with the joy and pain that real life offers. It can also be expressed through the emotional and social curriculum. Early childhood programs address general spiritual development in these four ways:

1. *Teaching about right and wrong.* Caring adults contribute to children's moral education by encouraging integrity. In their book *Moral Classrooms, Moral Children* (1994) DeVries and Zan assert

> Interpersonal conflict can provide the context in which children become conscious of others as having feelings, ideas, and desires. . . . Piaget stated that conflict is the most influential factor in the acquisition of new knowledge structures. Conflict may thus be viewed as a source of progress in development.

Children then learn issues of "right and wrong" in a caring setting, balancing their own wishes with those of others.

> It is possible to train and habituate the young with respect, generosity of spirit, and intellectual curiosity. . . . When the habit of justice becomes second nature, it inspires the habit of compassion—the habit of real sensitivity to the pain or suffering of others. (Delattre, 1990)

2. *Matters of death.* "For children . . . death has a powerful and continuing meaning" (Coles, 1990). Whether it be a class pet, an accident or injury to a classmate or family member, even a teacher's absence due to illness, children's curiosity about death is inevitable. For instance, a kindergarten pet rabbit died; the janitor had found it dead the night before. The group talked, asked questions, drew and painted pictures, made books and signs, and asked for stories and reassurance. "Had the teachers taken over, much of this rich experience would have been lost . . . The children had different needs and different ways of expressing and processing those needs (Sandstrom, 1999).

3. *Peace education.* "Peace education curricula generally include instruction in conflict resolution; global awareness; and social and ecological responsibility" (Johnson,

1998). Teaching respect and tolerance (see Chapter 7) has become an educational focus of the peace movement, and is certainly appropriate for the early childhood classroom.

4. *Love of nature.* One way to connect with children spiritually is through a love of nature and appreciation of the environment. Give children the firsthand experiences of a seed sprouting a plant, a live animal to care for, a running stream to play in, and a sunset to watch, and they will get closer to their spiritual side.

The Teacher's Role

Teachers are often unsure of their role in spiritual development. Juggling what is appropriate and lawful with what is respectful of diverse family values and affiliations is difficult. A teacher's own identity and beliefs must be considered (Saxton, 2004). "One of the most helpful things we can do for ourselves and our children is to keep in mind the difference between nurturing spiritual growth and passing on a religion" (Fitzpatrick, 1991). As Elkind (1992) puts it

> Spirituality can be used in either a narrow sense or a broad one. In the narrow sense spirituality is often used to indicate a particular set of religious beliefs. . . . Spirituality, however, can also be used in a much broader sense. Individuals who, in their everyday lives, exemplify the highest of human qualities such as love, forgiveness, and generosity might also be said to be spiritual. It is spirituality in the broad, nondenominational sense that I believe can be fostered by educational practice.

Families provide a vital ingredient in the development of children's spirituality. Working with families around spiritual issues is a delicate matter. Making clear your distinction between religion and spirituality helps parents see your priorities. Emphasize that you are thinking about the adults they may become and that you are trying to give them a kind of framework to face the state of the world as it is becoming.

A child's spiritual growth can be measured in terms of his/her ability to trust, to give love willingly, and accept self and others. Families may disagree with the teaching of some of those concepts, but the dialogue will be useful. In the end, teachers usually find that there is more agreement about these kinds of ideas than they expected. Once made clear, parents often

have questions themselves about how to promote family spirituality.

Whether at home or in the classroom, spiritual nurturing does not happen according to schedule and does not entail a sense of teaching in the formal sense. "Spiritual nurturing can never be reduced to a set of techniques or a routine curriculum. It can only flow freely from the teacher's own inner essence and from his or her belief that each child is truly a spiritual being" (Wolf, 2000). Teachers and families have something to share, a way of setting the environment and the tone that opens up the process of self-knowledge, morality and relationship with others, and a reverence for life and spiritual experience.

Children as a Spiritual Resource

Children as a spiritual resource are active participants in their own experience and learning. As the teacher plans, he or she must also be prepared to listen and sit back. "Interactions with children present us adults with the opportunity to regain a sense of connectedness, spontaneity, emotional sensitivity, philosophical wonder and mystery, and attentiveness to value that we have long since left behind" (Dillon, 2000). Time to wonder, to be in awe, and to reflect need to happen and be in place in a program. A hurried or overscheduled program is unlikely to provide such times.

The basic curriculum of the early childhood program is to provide every child with repeated experiences of being loved, accepted, and understood, of finding people trustworthy and dependable, of discovering the world to be a place that loves him and cares for her deeply. Spirituality is concerned with directly experiencing life via intuition and feeling. Early childhood educators can set the stage for these experiences in many ways. Figure 14-24 provides several suggestions.

Spiritual expression in educational programs is new for many educators. Saxton and McMurrian (2002) suggest teachers ask themselves:

1. To what extent are you aware of the religious/spiritual diversity of students in your classroom?
2. Have students asked questions or made comments about religious or spiritual topics?
3. What is the source(s) of your information and support concerning the handling of religious/spiritual expression in the classroom?

Quiet Corner
Set aside a corner space or alcove, perhaps behind a shelf that holds the fish tank. Place a small table and chair where a child can sit alone, gaze at the water or out the window.

A Kindness Plant
Put a live plant next to a basket of artificial flowers. Each time a child receives a kindness, they put a flower in the plant.

The Peace Rose
Keep a lively silk rose in a vase within children's reach. Whenever two children have a quarrel, one of them, or a third child, collects the peace rose. Each child holds the rose while talking: Once they reach solution or simply get over it, together they put their hands on the stem of the rose and say, "We declare peace."

Guided Meditation
Have the children sit or lie down quietly and close their eyes. Lead them through a reflection, asking each child to think about his or her heart—the place where love lives.

The Garden
Plant seeds together, ask how things grow, and how could a seed do that. Check as they sprout. Plant a button, a seed, and a penny—and see the power of the seed.

I Spy
Play the game of "I Spy" with the children you have observed helping others. "I spy someone who helped Danny clean up the paint he spilled."

The Universe Star
Make a star in your classroom. Taking turns, each child carries the star home, waits for a clear night, and goes outside at dark with a parent to look at the night sky. When the child brings back the star, take time as a class to talk about the wonder and size of the universe.

A Silence Game
At a time when the children are engaged and behaving well, give them a new challenge. Ask them to stop all talking and sit perfectly still for several minutes. Each time you initiate this activity, lengthen the time. When the time is up, children will report what they heard.

FIGURE 14-24 Aline Wolf (2000) offers several curriculum ideas for nurturing the spirit.

What do YOU Think?

Can teachers remain spiritually neutral? Are there topics that are best left unmentioned or undeveloped in an early childhood program? How will you help children develop their spiritual sense? How do you involve familes?

4. Have you observed instances of religious bias in the classroom? Religious tolerance?

Questions such as these help teachers probe their own feelings and attitudes about spiritual development and its expression in a classroom.

SUMMARY

Affective development is at the center of the early childhood curriculum. Planning for emotional, social, creative, and spiritual growth involves an understanding of how each develops in the young child and how they are interrelated. Children learn many skills in these areas as they interact with each other, with adults, and in the environment.

Planning curriculum for affective growth calls upon teachers to play a supportive role, facilitating children's involvement with the materials and each other. Only then can children discover themselves, explore their relationships, develop the ability to use their imagination and resources, and explore deeper questions of self and spirit.

THE PEACE TABLE IN ACTION

by
Sue Warford, M.Ed.

How can early childhood educators support children's development of a peaceful approach to conflict resolution? How can we help children in choosing peaceful solutions to interpersonal problems? How can the social emotional environment be structured in such a way that children's first impulse is to reconcile their differences and generate a solution to problems where everyone is satisfied? How can we support children's development of nurturing, tolerant, accepting, mutually empowering approaches to conflict? Do we expect to eradicate conflict from children's lives? No, that would be completely unrealistic and would eliminate many wonderful opportunities for children's growth in their ability to be peacemakers. Watch what happens with four-year-olds Rose and Lydia...

Rose: Lydia, I was using that doll.

Lydia: But Rose, you weren't holding it. It was in the crib.

Sharon, the teacher: It sounds like there is a problem here. Let's take this doll over to the Peace Table and you two can try to work out this problem.

Lydia: Rose, you weren't holding that doll or near that doll so I thought you weren't using it.

Rose: Lydia, my baby was taking a nap and I was doing some cooking while she slept. You can't take my baby.

Sharon: We have some new information. Rose was still using that doll but Lydia thought she was done because Rose wasn't near the doll. What are we going to do about this problem?

Rose: I know. Lydia can have a turn when I'm done.

Sharon: What do you think about that, Lydia?

Lydia: No...I want a turn now. I know, Rose, you can be the mom and I can be the babysitter.

Rose: O.K., and you can have a turn when I'm done.

Sharon: So Rose is going to be the mom and Lydia is going to be the babysitter and Lydia will have the baby when Rose is done.

Lydia: We solved the problem!!

Rose: Yeah.

Why did this episode end so peacefully? Does simply adding a Peace Table to a classroom insure there will be peaceful solutions to every problem? Actually, these two children have had two years of experience using the Peace Table at the University of Rhode Island Child Development Center as a safe and peaceful place to go to solve problems nonviolently with their peers. At first, children require a great deal of adult support and input in negotiating their problems, and often, it is the adult who guides the discussion. The steps which can be followed to guide these conflict resolution discussions are:

- *Initiate the mediation. It looks like there is a problem here. Or, what's happening here?*
- *Clarify each child's perspective.* In this step each child is given the opportunity to explain his/her perspective on the situation.
- *Summarize.* In this step, the teacher clearly articulates a summary of each child's perspective.
- *Generate alternative solutions. What can we do about this problem?* In this step, the teacher supports *children's* generation of alternative solutions.
- *Agree on a solution.* Here, both children agree on a solution to the problem. It is critical to allow sufficient time for *children* to arrive at a mutually satisfying solution.
- *Follow through.* The teacher checks with the children later to be sure that the solution actually satisfied everyone. *You had a problem with that doll before. You two solved that problem. Did your solution work?*

These discussions provide opportunities for everyone involved in a conflict to feel empowered and to participate in generating solutions to the problem. This process is effective with many types of problems and conflicts that arise daily in an early childhood classroom. Some of these conflicts involve possessions (two children want the same truck at the same time), position (two children want to sit on the teacher's left side at the same time), exclusion (*you can't play at the texture table with us*), and misunderstandings or accidents (*I didn't mean to hurt you when I stepped on your finger*). As time goes on and children gain more experiences with the problem-solving process, they are able to become more and more independent in clarifying misunderstandings and nonviolently solving their problems at the Peace Table.

The Peace Table is one tool used at the University of Rhode island Child Development Center as part of the overarching approach to social interactions that encourages children to peacefully interact with each other. This method encourages children to accept diversity and to attempt to understand differing perspectives. This approach helps children to see all problems as solvable and scaffolds children in their attempts to "solve the problem." Within an environment where adults assist children to feel empowered to actively solve interpersonal problems, children like Lydia and Rose quickly become peacemakers.

Sue Warford is the coordinator of the University of Rhode Island's Child Development Center, a part of the Department of Human Development and Family Studies. She has worked at the CDC for 16 years, while also teaching courses in early childhood education. Sue has a master's in Education from the University of Massachusetts, Amherst.

For more activities and information, visit our Web site at http://www.EarlyChildEd.delmar.com

KEY TERMS

basic emotions

complex emotions

social mores

positive stress

self-regulation

superhero

social referencing

sociocentric

peer interactions

undifferentiated

unilateral

reciprocal

social skills

social cognition

social action

coaching

divergent thinking

fluency

aesthetics

REVIEW QUESTIONS

1. How are emotional, social, creative, and spiritual growth related to each other?

2. How can teachers help children articulate their feelings?

3. What are some curriculum ideas for emotional development at circle time?

4. List some of the social skills that are learned in the major indoor areas of the environment.

5. How can teachers support conflict resolution and problem solving?

6. What kinds of activities masquerade as creative art?

7. Write three examples of a child's divergent thinking. How do these show the "creativity intersection"?

8. How can teachers nurture the spirit in nonsectarian environments?

LEARNING ACTIVITIES

1. How does your center promote positive self-concept? What else could be done?

2. Make behavioral definitions of emotions you think you will see in the children you teach. Observe the children, then check the accuracy of your definitions.

3. Observe a group of four-year-olds at play. How do they decide what roles each one takes? Are they clear in their expectations of what sex roles are appropriate for boys and girls? Is there sex-role stereotyping?

4. Taking turns and sharing equipment and materials are difficult for young children. Cite three examples you have seen where children used their social skills to negotiate a turn. Was teacher intervention necessary?

5. Name five people you consider creative. Match their skills with those we have identified in early childhood. Where are they similar? Different?

6. Give three examples of children in your center trying to "break mental set." In what area of the classroom did it occur? What were the adults' responses?

7. How do teachers in your setting plan for creativity? What place does such expression take in the priority of the school philosophy?

8. If spirituality includes the embodiment of the highest human qualities, name three and offer an idea of how to put this into the curriculum.

REFERENCES

General

Berk, L. E. (1999). *Infants, children, and adolescents* (3rd ed.). Boston: Allyn & Bacon.

Curry, N. E., & Johnson, C. N. (1990). *Beyond self-esteem: Developing a genuine sense of human value.* Washington, DC: NAEYC.

Marshall, H. H. (1989, July). Research in review: The development of self-concept. *Young Children, 44(5).*

Nakahata, A. (2001, Fall). *Identity is tied to culture.* Interview by Marion Hironaka Cowee in Connections: California AEYC Newsletter.

Teaching Tolerance Project. (1997). *Starting small: Teaching tolerance in preschool and the early grades.* Montgomery, AL: Southern Poverty Law Center.

York, S. (1998). *Big as life: The everyday inclusive curriculum.* St. Paul, MN: Redleaf Press.

York, S. (2003). *Roots and wings: Affirming culture in early childhood programs* (2nd ed.). St. Paul, MN: Redleaf Press.

Emotional Growth

Barrera, R. (1993, March). Retrato de mi familia: A portrait of my Hispanic family. *Exchange.*

Bowling, J. H., & Rogers, S. (2001, March). The value of healing in education. *Young Children, 56(2).*

Bronson, M. R. (2000, March). Recognizing and supporting the development of self-regulation in young children. *Young Children, 55(2).*

Carlson S. M., & Taylor, M. (2005). Imaginary companions & impersonated characters: Sex differences in children's fantasy play. *Merrill-Palmer Quarterly, 51,* 93–118.

Cook, J. W. (2001, January). Create and tell a story: Help young children who have psychological difficulties. *Young Children, 56(1).*

Cooper, R. M. (1992, November). The impact of child care on the socialization on African American children. Paper presented at the NAEYC Annual Conference, New Orleans.

Goleman, D. (1995). *Emotional intelligence.* New York: Bantam Books.

Greenman, J. (1991, January/February). Seeing children: A question of perspective. *Exchange.*

Hoffman, E. (2004). *Magic capes, amazing powers: Tranforming superhero play in the classroom.* St. Paul, MN: Redleaf Press.

Honig, A. S. (1986, May and July). Stress and coping in children. *Young Children, 41(1 & 5).*

Hyson, M. C. (1986). Lobster on the sidewalk: Understanding and helping children with fears, in McCracken, J. B. (Ed.), *Reducing stress in young children's lives.* Washington, DC: NAEYC.

Kostelnik, M., Whiren, A. P., & Stein, L. G. (1986, May). Living with he-man: Managing superhero fantasy play. *Young Children, 41(4).*

Marion, M. (2003). *Guidance of Young Children* (6th ed.). Columbus, OH: Merrill Publishers.

McCormick, J. (1993). Family child care. In A. Gordon & K. B. Browne (Eds.), *Beginnings and beyond* (3rd ed.). Clifton Park, NY: Thomson Delmar Learning.

Murray, C. G. (2000, March). Learning about children's social and emotional needs at snack time—nourishing the body, mind, and spirit in each child. *Young Children, 55(2).*

Pool, C. R. (1997, May). Up with emotional health. *Educational Leadership, 54(8).*

Rofrano, F. (2002, January). "I care for you": A reflection on caring as infant curriculum. *Young Children, 57(1).*

Sample, W. (1993, March). The American Indian child. *Exchange.*

Simon, T. (1994, September). Helping children make choices. *The creative classroom.*

Taylor, M. (1999). *Imaginary companions and the children who create them.* NY: Oxford University Press.

Wardle, F. (1993, March). How young children build images of themselves. *Exchange.*

Weinreb, M. L. (1997, January). Be a resiliency mentor: You may be a lifesaver for a high-risk child. *Young Children, 52(2).*

Social Growth

Blaska, J. K., & Lynch, E. C. (1998, March). Is everyone included? Using children's literature to facilitate the understanding of disabilities. *Young Children, 53(2).*

Bos, B. (1990). *Together we're better: Establishing a coactive learning environment.* Roseville, CA: Turn the Page Press.

Buras, A. (1991, Spring). Social settings in the classroom. *ACEI Focus, 3(3).*

Cooper, J. L., & Dever, M. T. (2001, May). Sociodramatic play as a vehicle for curriculum integration in first grade. *Young Children, 56(3).*

Davis, L., & Keyser, J. (1997). *Becoming the parent you want to be.* New York: Broadway Books.

Derman-Sparks, L. (1989). *The anti-bias curriculum.* Washington, DC: National Association for the Education of Young Children.

Froschl, M., & Sprung, B. (1999, March). On purpose: Addressing teasing and bullying in early childhood. *Young Children, 54(2).*

Gilligan, C. (1982). *In a different voice.* Cambridge, MA: Harvard University Press.

Gordon, A. M., & Browne, K. W. (1996). *Guiding Young Children in a Diverse Society.* Boston, MA: Allyn & Bacon.

Hartup, W. W. (1992). *Having friends, making friends and keeping friends: Relationships as educational contexts.* ERIC Digest. Urbana, IL: ERIC Clearinghouse on Elementary and Early Childhood Education.

Holland, H. (2000, Spring). These guys are fun! *Teaching Tolerance, 17.*

Katz, L. G., & McClennan, D. E. (1997). *Fostering children's social competence.* Washington, DC: NAEYC.

Kendall, F. E. (1996). *Diversity in the classroom: New approaches to the education of young children* (2nd ed.). New York: Teachers College Press.

Kostelnik, M. J., Whiren, A. P., Soderman, A. K., Stein, L. C., & Gregory, K. (2002). *Guiding children's social development: Theory to practice* (4th Ed.). Clifton Park, NY: Thomson Delmar Learning.

Lillard, A., & Curenton, S. (1999, September). Research in review: Do young children understand what others feel, want, and know? *Young Children 54 (5).*

Maniates, H., & Heath, M. (1998, Spring). Creating a climate for learning. *Early Childhood Resources.*

Paley, V. G. (1992). *You can't say you can't play.* Cambridge, MA. Harvard University Press.

Porro, B. (1996). *Talk it out: Conflict resolution in the elementary classroom.* Alexandria, VA: Association for supervision and curriculum development.

Sawyer, W. E., & Comer, D. E. (1996). *Growing up with literature.* Clifton Park, NY: Thomson Delmar Learning.

Smith, C. A. (1982). *Promoting the social development of young children.* Palo Alto, CA: Mayfield Publishing.

Whitin, K. (2001, September). Kindness in a jar. *Young Children.*

Creative Growth

Amabile, T. M. (1989). *Growing up creative.* New York: Crown.

Bos, B. (1978). *Don't move the muffin tins.* Roseville, CA: Turn the Page Press.

Bovard, K. (2000, Spring). The emotion map. *Teaching Tolerance, 17.*

Feinberg, S. G. (2003, May). All about art inside and out! *Scholastic: Early Childhood Today.*

Gillespie, C. W. (2000, January). Six Head Start classrooms begin to explore the Reggio Emilia approach. *Young Children, 55(1).*

Gunsberg, A. (1991). Improvised musical play with delayed and nondelayed children. *Childhood Education (67),* 223–226.

Kellogg, R. (1969). *Analyzing children's art.* Palo Alto, CA: Mayfield Publishing.

Lopez-Morgan, C. (2002). *Creative arts for the young child.* Cupertino, CA: De Anza College.

Lowenfeld, V., & Brittain, W. L. (1975). *Creative and mental growth.* New York: Macmillan.

Moran, J. D., Milgram, R. M., Sawyers, J. K., & Fu, V. R. (1983). Original thinking in preschool children. *Child Development.* 921–926, p. 54.

Nabors, M. L., & Edwards, L. C. (1994, Fall). Creativity and the child's social development. *Dimensions in Early Childhood.*

Pecka, K. (2005, November). Two-year-olds grow with music, Stanford University: *Bing Times.*

Schirrmacher, R. (2006). *Art and creative development for young children* (5 ed.). Clifton Park, NY: Thomson Delmar Learning.

Spodek, B. S., et al. (1996, March). Beginnings workshop: Art experiences. *Exchange.*

Taunton, M., & Colbert, C. (2000). Art in the early childhood classroom: Authentic experiences and extended dialogues, in Yelland, Nicole (Ed.). *Promoting Meaningful Learning.* Washington, DC: NAEYC.

Spiritual Growth

Coles, R. (1990). *The spiritual life of children.* Boston, MA: Houghton-Mifflin.

Delattre, E. J. (1990, September 5). Teaching integrity: The boundaries of moral education. *Education Week.*

DeVries, R., & Zan, B. S. (1994). *Moral classrooms, moral children.* NY: Teachers College Press.

Dillon, J. J. (2000, Winter). The spiritual child: Appreciating children's transformative effects on adults. *Encounter: Education for Meaning and Social Justice, 13(4).*

Elkind, D. (1992). *Spirituality in Education. Holistic Education Review* (Spring).

Fitzpatrick, J. G. (1991). *Something more: Nurturing your child's spiritual growth.* New York: Viking Press.

Hart, T. (2000, Summer). Teaching for wisdom. *Encounter: Education for meaning and social justice, 14(2).*

Johnson, M. L. (1998). Trends in peace education: ERIC digest. Bloomington, IN: ERIC Clearinghouse, ED417123.

Sandstrom, S. (1999, November). Dear samba is dead forever. *Young Children 54(6),* 14–16.

Saxton, R. R. (2004). A Place for Faith in Gordon & Browne, *Beginnings & Beyond* (6 ed.). Clifton Park, NY: Delmar Publishers.

Saxton, R. R., & McMurrain, M. K. (2002). *Spiritual diversity in the classroom.* Atlanta, GA: Georgia State University Research Project.

Wolf, A. D. (2000, January). How to nurture the spirit in nonsectarian environments. *Young Children,* 55(1).

HELPFUL WEB SITES

Biocultural Diversity	http://www.terralingua.org
Collaborative to Advance Social and Emotional Learning	http://www.casel.org
Creative Curriculum	http://www.teachingstrategies.com
Cultural Survival	http://www.cs.org
Educators for Social Responsibility	http://www.esrnational.org
Intuitive Knowing	http://www.noetic.org
M.U.S.I.C.	http://www.learningfromlyrics.org
Peace Education/Atrium Society	http://www.atriumsoc.org
Society for Myth and Tradition	http://www.parabola.org
Southern Poverty Law Center	http://www.teachingtolerance.org

How Do We Teach for Tomorrow?

Chapter 15
Issues and Trends in Early Childhood Education ∗ 589

HOW DO WE TEACH FOR TOMORROW?

Sharon L. Kagan, M.A., Ed.D

Arguably, nothing—but nothing—in the field of early care and education deserves more attention than the way in which we teach young children. Not only are early childhood curriculum and early childhood pedagogy at the center of early childhood education, they are a key determinant of the enduring results young children will derive during and after their experiences in early care and education settings.

In speaking about how we teach for tomorrow, we must consider who the children of tomorrow will be. In a landmark volume, *Children of 2010*, Washington and Andrews (1998) clearly point out that tomorrow's children are not the children of today. Yes, of course at the core, children are children from one century to the next; their development proceeds in fairly predictable ways, they are more dependent than adults, and they always have and always will need love to thrive. Beyond these fundamentals, however, children of the future will be different in the aggregate and they will be different from children who grew up but a few short years ago.

In the aggregate, American children of the future will be more diverse, with many more being of color. They will come from families where, increasingly, the home language is not English. Many will come to early childhood programs having had no prior experience in the United States. Many will come from familial and community environments characterized by abuse, drugs, and violence.

Simultaneously, many young children will come from families where, for the first time in generations, mothers are working out of the home. Others will come from homes where technology is readily available, if not a pervasive element of the environment. Still others will come from families where substantial wealth has recently been amassed. All these children come to our doors, each with different, unique needs that require equally different and unique approaches in order to cohere their talents into a collective, well-functioning citizenry.

Given this diversity, what and how should early childhood teachers teach? Fortunately, we have some strong guidance on these matters. First, regarding *what* should be taught: The National Education Goals Panel has codified what children need to learn so that they will be ready to enter school. These necessary learnings are divided into five dimensions:

1. Physical and motor development.
2. Social and emotional development.
3. Approaches toward learning.
4. Language, literacy, and communication skills.
5. Cognition and general knowledge.

We know that learning in all five of these areas is equally important, and that no one area should take precedence over the others, although at certain times in the developmental trajectory, it is important to focus a bit more on one domain than another. A rounded and high-quality early childhood program must have exciting content that addresses each of these domains.

With regard to *how* young children should be taught, I suggest that if we simply understand how little children learn we will have the key to how they should be taught. For example, we know that little children cannot master abstract thinking until they have mastered concrete thinking. As a result, it is critical that all programs that serve young children (be they in museums, libraries, family child care homes, or early childhood centers) provide abundant opportunities for hands-on learning. It is true that little children learn by doing. It is also true that they are episodic learners; that is, they often learn something one day, only to "forget" it the next day. While they don't actually forget, little children do store knowledge, often retrieving it at odd time frames and in nonlinear ways. This is why it is inappropriate to rely on test results taken at a single point in time; children's learning is very variable. For the teachers, this means we must be keen and constant observers; we must be informants for parents who often worry unnecessarily about the natural fits and starts that characterize children's development.

We also know that young children learn according to their own timetables, with some learning some facts quickly and needing more time to master other facts. This means that as we teach, we must provide opportunities for different learning styles. We also know that children's learning is reinforced by repetition. This is why, innately, little children love to repeat stories, songs, and experiences; they derive pleasure (as do adults) from that which is familiar. Finally, we know that little children are constant learners; that is, they pick up ideas, facts, and gestures from all that is around them. This is why we must remember that as teachers, above all, we are role models. While it is axiomatic to early childhood educators that children learn by doing, it is also important to remember that children learn a great deal by watching.

All of this means that the early educators' task is enormous. Little children don't miss a trick; they want to learn, and they do learn. Our job as educators and caring adults is to be sure that *what* they are learning is important and that *how* they learn matches their developmental capacities and predilections to learning.

BIBLIOGRAPHY

Washington, V., & Andrews, J. D. (Eds.). (1998). *Children of 2010.* Washington, DC: National Association for the Education of Young Children.

SHARON LYNN KAGAN

SHARON LYNN KAGAN is the Virginia and Leonard Marx Professor of Early Childhood and Family Policy at Teachers College, Columbia University, and a Professor Adjunct at Yale University's Child Study Center. Author of over 100 articles and 12 books, Kagan's research focuses on the institutions and policies that impact child and family life. Kagan consults with numerous federal and state agencies, Congress, governors, and legislators; is a member of 40 national boards; and is past president of the National Association for the Education of Young Children and Family Support America.

CHAPTER
15

Issues and Trends in Early Childhood Education

QUESTIONS FOR THOUGHT

What are the major issues facing early childhood educators today?

How are the major themes of early childhood education reflected in the issues facing children, families, and teachers today?

INTRODUCTION

Early childhood education has undergone remarkable changes in the past 40 years. It has evolved from being an option for middle-class preschool children to a necessity for millions of families with children from infancy through the primary years.[1] Such transformations are a reflection of the economic, social, and political climate of the times, as well as research in child development and early education. Changes in education historically have been linked to societal reform and upheaval. Issues of today and trends for tomorrow grow out of the problems and solutions of the past.

In the 1960s, social action and the War on Poverty captured the American interest and spirit. Head Start programs opened around the country and were the symbols of social action of that era. The 1970s brought changes related to economic crisis. The family unit was affected by the job market, the end of the Vietnam War, an energy crisis, inflation, rising divorce rates, and the feminist movement. All of these factors led more women into the workplace rather than in the home. One of the expansions in public funding at this time was in the services to the handicapped and bilingual populations.

The 1980s meant further budget cuts, and reduced services for children and families. Many children were now in group care for most of their waking hours. They grew up with change, rather than stability, as a constant in their lives. Child abuse became a national cause for alarm. The need for early child care and educational services was well established. The education reforms that began in the early 1980s brought about some rethinking in early childhood education. Interest in young children flourished along with reforms at other grade levels. As the 1990s ended, there was an expanded acceptance of child care for children under five and an increasing awareness of the needs of the whole child in the early primary years. The quality and cost of programs for young children became an issue.

The turn of the century saw many of the issues unresolved. Home schooling is an increasingly popular option. Due to lack of funding, Head Start and Early Start can enroll only a small percentage of the children who need the programs. Education reforms have defined new standards; government-mandated standards and testing are pressuring programs to put more emphasis on academics. Professionalism is making its way into early childhood certification. All these issues are making inroads into early childhood programs at every level.

It seems appropriate to discuss current issues in light of the history of the early childhood profession. Look back at Chapter 1. For all its diverse and varied pasts, early childhood education has had a consistent commitment to four major themes: the ethic of social reform, the importance of childhood, transmitting values, and professionalism. These four themes are the same ones facing early childhood educators today (see Figure 15-1):

- **Ethic of Social Reform**: the quality of programs and services needed for children under eight and the education reforms that provide it

What is the role of family in a child's early life?

1 Early childhood education and care continue to be on the forefront in dealing with the outcomes of immense social change in American society.

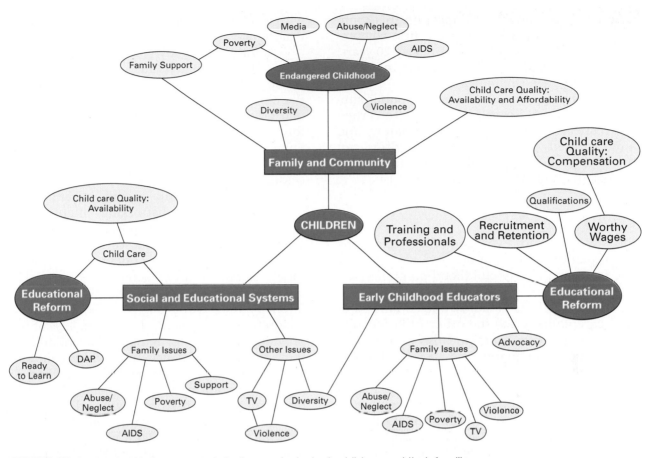

FIGURE 15-1 A web of influences and challenges for today's children and their families.

- **Importance of Childhood**: children's health and welfare and the changes in family life.
- **Transmission of values**: challenges presented by the media culture, violence, disaster, and diversity;
- **Professionalism**: standards for children's programs and teacher preparation.

ETHIC OF SOCIAL REFORM

The first theme suggests that schooling for young children will lead to social change and improvement. Maria Montessori, the McMillan sisters, Patty Smith Hill, and Abigail Eliot were pioneers in improving children's lives through a comprehensive approach to education. Today, Marion Wright Edelman, by creating the Children's Defense Fund 40 years ago, is continuing the efforts started nearly one hundred years ago. Louise Derman-Sparks and colleagues enlarged the issue when they published the *Anti-Bias Curriculum* in 1989 and challenged our thinking about bias as a social issue for young children.

Child Care

- 71% of mothers with children under the age of 18 were in the labor force in 2004 (Children's Defense Fund, 2005).
- Between 1964 and 1999 enrollment rate in nursery schools rose from about 5% of the preschool population to about 50%, reflecting a significant societal shift (U.S. Census Bureau, October, 1999).
- At least one-third of states place eligible families who apply for help on waiting lists or turn them away without even taking their names because there are not enough funds to provide services (Children's Defense Fund, 2005).
- The use of center-based child care has progressed from the least popular form of child care to the most popular choice for parents today, with over 60% of parents choosing this option (Neugebauer, 2002; USDE, 2001).

Without question the need for child care has been firmly established. Look back at "Quality and Cost" in Chapter 2. The significant increase in enrollment in child care centers over the last 40 years, underscored by the demographic facts, has had a profound impact on this country: In 1990 Congress passed the first comprehensive child care legislation in nearly 20 years; a year later Head Start funding was increased significantly (see Chapter 2).

It is obvious that child care has public support. Quality child care programs have earned the respect of parents and legislators and demonstrated to society that children can thrive in good early childhood programs. (See discussion on child care in Chapter 2.)

Quality and Cost

The key word, however, is quality—the terms "good quality" and "high quality" identify specific features in early childhood programs (see Chapter 2).

Two broad-based studies, one conducted in child care centers and the other in family day care settings, have examined the critical relationship between quality and cost and present a disturbing picture.

Inadequate child care was found to be rampant in the first study, which was conducted in hundreds of centers in California, Colorado, Connecticut, and North Carolina (Costs, Quality and Child Outcomes Study Team, 1995). In a dramatic conclusion, the study found that most child care centers provided mediocre services and that some were of such poor quality that they threatened children's emotional and intellectual development.[1] Infants and toddlers were most likely to be at risk for poor care in these centers; nearly half of their settings failed to meet basic health and safety needs. Yet 90% of the parents rated the care as "good."

The report was the first of its kind to examine the relationship between the costs of child care and the nature of children's experiences in child care settings (quality). In centers in which researchers found high-quality care, the center staffs were paid higher wages, there were more personnel, and more of them were trained in early childhood education. They were also programs that were subsidized in some way, by the government, a university, or employers of families using these services. The states that had more demanding licensing requirements had few poor-quality programs. According to this report, these factors, along with teachers' salaries and administrators' prior experience are strong determinants of quality.

A follow-up study, "The Children of the Cost, Quality, and Outcomes Study Go to School" (Peisner-Feinberg et al., 1999), followed the children in the original study through second grade. The findings from this study reinforced the notion that high-quality child care enhances cognitive and social skills that, in turn, help children be more prepared and successful in school.

The results of a major study of family day care are similarly distressing, highlighting uneven and poorly regulated conditions. Conducted by Galinsky and co-workers (1994), the study concluded that only 9% of the homes they observed were of good quality and that over one-third of the providers were so indifferent in their caregiving as to be harmful to children's development.[2] More than 40% of the providers planned no activities for children in their care, and only half the children showed signs of trust or attachment to the caregiver.

The more a provider was paid, the better the care; the licensed or regulated providers were more likely to be warm and attentive to children, communicate with parents, and provide a safe home. Look at NAEYC's criteria for high quality programs in Figure 2-2 (Chapter 2) to see the relationship with the findings of these two studies.[3] The good news is that between 1990 and 2002, licensing of family child care homes increased by 37% (The Children's Foundation, 2001).

These two forms of child care—child care centers and family day care—are equally popular; they are the programs of choice by America's working families, who, according to this research, either do not recognize what makes a quality program or who think they cannot demand it. Quality is a function of group size, low teacher-child ratios, trained and experienced staff, adequate compensation, and safe and stimulating environments. Yet these are not the first things parents look for.

The family child care study found that parents rate safety as the most important factor in choosing a provider, communications with parents second, and warm attention to children as third. Adult-child ratios, professional training, and licensing rank much lower. Geographical

1,2 Hundreds of thousands of children are spending their critical years in environments that compromise their optimal growth and development.

3 The National Academy of Early Childhood Programs—the accreditation department of NAEYC—base their criteria for quality on the knowledge and experience of thousands of early childhood professionals.

The quality of child-care program is directly related to the experience and training of the teachers.

distance and price have been cited by others as the primary criteria for choosing a child care setting (Hofferth, 1994).

To improve the quality of family child care, the reports call on government and business to increase their support in a number of ways: help parents pay for good care, establish training programs for providers, bring providers into regulation, and educate parents about high-quality care.

All of the studies share a common concern that parents must be able to distinguish good from poor quality centers and demand higher quality care before the centers will increase their fees to cover the costs of providing better care.

A National Crisis

Quality care and education of young children has a cost that must be addressed. The cost of quality is directly related to the needs of the families served by the specific program. In some programs, securing the basic needs of food, housing, and health care is an important obligation. The added costs of helping families connect with the right resources and providing the necessary comprehensive services will contribute to a higher cost for quality in that program. Fee reductions and financial aid for low-income families also add to the costs for a quality program.

Quality is significantly related to staff: how many adults there are compared with the number of children in a class; whether the salaries and benefits provide incentive for teachers to be retained for a number of years; the level of the staff's education and training and their years of experience. These factors have created a staffing crisis of major proportion in the country today. Refer to the section "A Trilemma" in Chapter 2 for more discussion on the quality, cost, and compensation factors.

The crisis refers to the difficulties of recruiting and retaining qualified staff for good early childhood programs. A program's budget centers around the costs of providing for quality teachers and staff. Salaries for early childhood employees are disgracefully low, and pension plans and health care benefits are nonexistent for many.

According to the Center for the Child Care Workforce, the national employee turnover rate stays at about 30% and that fewer than one-third of child care employees have health benefits. They also report that child care programs are having difficulty recruiting and hiring qualified replacement staff for those who leave. For further discussion, see Chapter 2 and the report Then and Now: Changes in Child Care Staffing, 1994–2000. (Whitebook, Sakai, Gerber, & Howes, 2001).

At the same time, there is an unprecedented demand for child care services. The increased recognition of the need for high-quality child care, however, does not solve the problem of how to keep fees low enough to provide the necessary services yet.

Quality 2000: Advancing Early Child Care and Education is an initiative whose goal is to provide high-quality early care and education to all children from birth to age five, by 2010 (Kagan & Neuman, 1997). Creating an early child care and education system requires a comprehensive vision that includes factors such as:

- Promoting cultural sensitivity and cultural pluralism
- Increasing the number of accredited programs
- Linking programs to support services and other community resources
- Creating three separate types of licenses for early childhood care and education workers and developing national licensing guidelines

- Focusing staff training and preparation on children and families, with respect to cultural and linguistic diversity
- Funding that is commensurate with per-child levels for elementary school children
- Establishing governance and accountability structures in every state and locality

Addressing these factors will help ensure that families have equal access to good programs where consistent standards at a national and local level guarantee equality and excellence for all children.

Education Reform

One of the primary functions of the public school system in the United States is to prepare students for productive roles in society—to produce skilled workers who will enter the job market and contribute to a healthy, competitive economy worldwide.

The trend since the 1990s has been toward a national agenda.[1] In 1989, a national summit on the future of American education resulted in the creation of eight national goals, the first of which was that by 2000, every child will start school ready to learn. It was the first time in history that we have had a national consensus on a vision of public education.

The first goal, "Ready to Learn," included the provision that all children would have equal access to high-quality and developmentally appropriate preschool programs that help prepare children for school. Strong parent involvement with training and support and comprehensive health care, primarily through enhanced prenatal health systems were also a part of the agenda.

No Child Left Behind

As the new century began, a new administration passed the reauthorization of the Elementary and Secondary Education Act of 1965 to close the achievement gap between disadvantaged and minority students and their peers (U.S. Department of Education, 2001). Since then a national education problem has been identified and a sense of urgency instilled in the public mind. At the federal level, it is known as the No Child Left Behind Act (NCLB).

The major provisions of the act pertaining to early childhood are:

- *Adequate annual progress*: Children will be assessed in reading and math (plus a third area by state choice) beginning in the third grade. The trickle-down of inappropriate testing or imbalanced curriculum for younger children is a valid concern of early educators.
- *Highly qualified teachers*: By the 2005–06 school year, all teachers in core academic subjects must have a B.A. degree, and be fully certified (by state definition) in their areas of teaching assignment. The early learning field, plagues by high turnover and low pay, cannot meet these standards without significantly more funding.
- *Reading/literacy*: There are significantly increased funds aimed at having all children achieve reading proficiency by grade three. An early childhood concern is that other critical domains of child development will be undervalued or overlooked altogether.

Critics of NCLB cite many reasons to be concerned about this plan. (1) They worry that the narrow focus on reading and literacy and math will create an imbalanced curriculum that loses focus on the whole child and that

How do we know that children will start school ready to learn? How can good-quality early childhood programs help No Child Left Behind reach its first goal?

other critical domains of child development will be undervalued or overlooked altogether. (2) Critics also question whether or not teachers will be forced to "teach to the test" in order for a school to avoid sanctions. (3) The sanctions for not meeting the NCLB standards seem punitive to some and seem to impact the most seriously disadvantages schools. And (4) overall, there is the threat of facing sanctions without adequate resources or support to meet the requirements that are imposed by this plan.

Standards and high-stakes testing are realities in the primary grades. Preschool educators are feeling these pressures as well. It remains to be seen how this complicated and ambitious plan will fare over the coming years and how it relates to early education from zero to age five.

Universal Preschool

Early learning opportunities are unavailable to many children who could benefit from a quality early childhood program.[1] Families throughout the country put together a patchwork of child care situations. Programs are unequal in quality and the low-income working families who would benefit the most from quality child care are unable to afford it. There is a "disconnect," according to the Children's Defense Fund (2005), between the need and demand for quality child care and the government's willingness to fund it.

Universal Preschool, called Preschool For All in some areas, is an effort in many states across the country to address this inequality. If successful, it would mean that there would be universal access to publicly funded, high-quality preschool education for one or two years prior to kindergarten. Three-quarters of the states, plus the District of Columbia currently have such initiatives, while Georgia, Oklahoma, and Florida already provide voluntary preschool for all four-year-olds. It would appear that this effort has every chance to succeed within the next few years.

We believe that it is time for the United States to acknowledge society's stake in and responsibility for early education, as it long has for older children, by making publicly-funded prekindergarten, offered by a variety of providers, available to all children age 3 and over whose parents want the to participate. (Committee for Economic Development, 2005)

Reform Strategies

To meet the needs of working parents and ensure that children are ready to learn, reform strategies should be enlarged to include the following:

- *Link education and child care.* The dichotomy between care and education must be eliminated, as learning in the early years includes both caregiving and educational aspects of teaching.
- *Establish continuity between early childhood programs and kindergartens.* The perception that preschools are "only about play" and that primary schools are "all about academics" negates the whole child philosophy of the early childhood years.
- *Address children's nonacademic needs.* Unless more is done to meet the early health and social needs of children, school reform is likely to fail.

Good early childhood programs do not distinguish between education and care but understand that both are vital to the growing child.

---

   1 Eliminating inequalities such as this requires a national agenda for children.

- *Promote developmental learning.* Get schools ready for young children as opposed to having children be pressured and pushed to get ready for school.
- *Initiate programs and policies that strengthen the family.* The family support for learning should be addressed by focusing on parental attitudes and involvement at home as well as at school and on the parents' responsibility for meeting the basic care and needs of their children.[1]
- *Develop partnerships with the community and with business.* Coordinating with providers of child care services and collaborating with other community agencies that service young children and their families, make better use of public funds and improve the quality of all programs (National Association of State Boards of Education, 1988).

THE IMPORTANCE OF CHILDHOOD

The second theme is the importance and uniqueness of childhood. In fact, the entire notion of the importance of childhood rests on the concept of the child as a special part of human existence and therefore a valuable part of the human life cycle. When a society values its children, it takes the responsibility for providing a quality of life for them.

The impact of social changes in the last 40 years has been hardest felt by the children. The increase in the divorce rate, poverty and homelessness, and the dangerous effects of the media culture, drugs, and worldwide violence have thrust children into adult situations with adult troubles. Dual-parent careers and single working parents, together with the lack of extended families, have meant that children's behavior is not as closely monitored as it once was.

Children and childhood have changed. Gone are the days when the majority of children arrived home from school to be greeted by Mom in the kitchen, serving milk and homemade cookies. Today's child spends the bulk of time in child care centers or elsewhere while the parent is at work. Too many children arrive at empty homes and spend the next few hours alone or caring for younger siblings. As often as not, the child of today lives with just one parent.[2]

Every child has the right to a full and wondrous childhood.

Childhood Stress

Common experiences that produce stress in young children are family related. Divorce, and remarriage, a move to a new home, prolonged visits from a relative, and a new sibling are classic stress situations for children. Yet there are less dramatic sources of stress, the simple everyday occurrences that children face: being told not to do something, not having a friend, being ignored by a parent, experiencing changes in the routine, not being able to read or zip a zipper or put a puzzle together.

Stress may also occur in families where both parents pursue high-powered careers and children feel the need to live up to exceptional standards in academic achievement or sports proficiency. Apathetic parents, parents who ignore their children or have no time for them, and parents who push children into frantic schedules of activity also cause stress in their children. Stress can result from happy occasions as well—holidays, vacation, or a new

---

1 Through these efforts, the values and needs of all parents can be represented.

2 Do we as a society have a mindset of our diverse world, or an image/mythology based on middle-class family life of the mid-1990s?

How do we help children cope with stress?

puppy may be overanticipated, overstructured, and overstimulating to a child.

Children respond to stress in many ways. Signs of stress include sleeping problems (such as nightmares or sleepwalking), depression, regression to the behavior of an earlier stage, aches and pains, acting out, eating problems, and overreactions, as well as medical problems (such as headaches, upset stomach, and bleeding ulcers).

Brazelton and Greenspan (2000), in response to the overwhelmed, stressed-out life of children and parents today, defined seven irreducible needs of children:

1. The need for ongoing nurturing relationships

2. The need for physical protection, safety, and regulation

3. The need for experiences tailored to individual differences

4. The need for developmentally appropriate experiences

5. The need for limit setting, structure, and expectations

6. The need for stable, supportive communities and cultural continuity

7. Protecting the future (on behalf of the world's children)

Stress is a natural part of life and is a factor in every child's development. It needs to be identified and addressed by the families, teachers, and other adults who care for them.

Child Abuse and Neglect

The Crisis

An estimated three million children were reported for **child abuse** and neglect in 2003, at the rate of one child every 35 seconds (Children's Defense Fund, 2005). More than 80% of victims are abused by one or both parents (U.S. Department of Health and Human Services, 2002). These horrendous statistics tell us that child abuse and neglect are significant problems in this country.

A neglected child may be one whose waking hours are mostly unsupervised by adults, in front of the television or simply unconnected with—and unnoticed by—parents or an important caregiver. **Child neglect** takes other, more hazardous, forms, however. When the basic needs of adequate food, clothing, shelter, and health are unmet, parents are being neglectful. Failure to exercise the care that children need shows an inattention to and lack of concern for children.

Child abuse is the most severe form of disrespect for children. Violence in the form of physical maltreatment and sexual abuse are improper treatments of children, regardless of their behavior. Abusive language and harsh physical aggression are other forms of child abuse that occur in families and, unfortunately, some settings for child care. Publicized investigations into sexual abuse of children in child care centers, preschools, and family situations have brought national attention to this hideous violence. Yet reports of abuse in day care, foster care, or other institutional care settings represents only about 3% of all confirmed cases in 1997 (Wang & Daro, 1998).[1] Whether or not its increased incidence is due to a change in reporting practices, it is clear that the abuse of children knows no social, racial, or economic barriers. It is happening to children at all levels of the social spectrum.

Standards of Care

A national call to action to increase public awareness and understanding of child abuse is under way. Standardized licensing procedures, upgrading of the certification of child care workers, and national **accreditation** of all preschools are some of the most frequently mentioned solutions to the problem. Helping parents identify what qualities to look for when placing their children in someone else's care is another way to prevent child abuse in centers.

Role of the Teacher

Reporting suspected child abuse is mandated by law in all states. Educators must assume the responsibility to inform the proper authorities if they suspect that a child in their care is being abused by adults. Figure 15-2 lists the warning signs a teacher should be aware of.[2] Figure 15-3 discusses the steps to take if child abuse is suspected.

The mandate to report suspected child abuse applies to teachers, principals, counselors, school nurses, and staff members of child care centers and summer camps. Certain knowledge that abuse took place is not required; reports are legally required if there is reasonable cause to suspect a child has been mistreated. For the protection of anyone reporting abuse or neglect, the person filing the report is held immune from civil or criminal liability if the report was made in good faith.

In 1996, NAEYC adopted a "Position Statement on the Prevention of Child Abuse in

Child Abuse Should Be Suspected If a Child:

- Is constantly late, stays away from school for long periods of time, or arrives early and stays late, avoiding going home
- Is withdrawn passive, and uncommunicative or aggressive, destructive, and nervous
- Has unexplained injuries, too many "explained" ones, or has an injury that is inadequately explained
- Complains of numerous beatings, of someone "doing things," whether or not the parents are home
- Goes to the bathroom with difficulty; has burns, lumps, or bruises, patches of hair missing, bad teeth
- Wears clothing that is too small, soiled, or inappropriate for the weather, or uses clothing to cover injuries
- Is dirty, smells, is too thin or constantly tired, exhibits dehydration or malnutrition
- Is usually fearful of other children or adults
- Has been fed inappropriate food, drink, or drugs
- Is often tired or listless or sleeps in class
- Is often hungry
- Has torn, stained, or bloody underclothing; has bruises or is bleeding in genital areas
- Has unattended physical problems or lacks routine medical care
- May seem unduly afraid of parents, may take on the protective role with parent(s), and/or lack parental supervision at home
- Has learning problems that cannot be diagnosed

FIGURE 15-2 A child who exhibits several of these signs should be investigated as a possible victim of child abuse. (Adapted from *Child Abuse: Betraying a Trust*, 1995.)

1 These cases often become sensationalized in the press. Low numbers of incidence, however, do not eliminate the need for clear policies and procedures in all early childhood programs.

2 A study of teachers' knowledge of the signs of child sexual abuse found that 15% could not recognize even the most obvious signs (Harvard Education Letter, 1995). Lung and Daro (1996) report that three children die each day because of parental abuse and credit the increase in poverty, substance abuse, and violence as causes.

What to Do If You Suspect Child Abuse

- Make notes of child's appearance—any bruises, marks, or behaviors that cause you concern.

- Inform the director of the program and/or your immediate supervisor; plan together who will inform the proper authorities and how to contact the parent(s).

- Discuss ways to support the staff members who make the report, the parent(s), and the child.

- Call the locally designated agency for child abuse. A written report may be required within 24 to 48 hours.

- Support the parent(s) throughout the investigation. Be available to the parent(s) and the child as they deal with the other agencies that are trained and equipped to handle this problem.

- Follow through with assistance or support if requested to do so by the child protective services agency. Help the family by working with others who are counseling them and performing parent support services.

What to Do If a Child Tells You He or She Has Been Abused

- Believe the child; children rarely lie about sexual abuse.

- Commend the child for telling you what happened.

- Convey your support for the child. Children's greatest fear is that they are at fault and responsible for the incident. It is important to help children avoid blaming themselves.

- Temper your own reactions, recognizing that your perspective and acceptance are critical signals to the child. Do not convey your own feelings about the abuse.

- Report the suspected abuse to the child's parent(s), the designated social service agency, and/or the police.

- Find specialized agencies that evaluate sexual abuse victims and a physician with the experience and training to detect and recognize sexual abuse.

FIGURE 15-3 Recommendations for teachers about child abuse. (Source: *Child Sexual Abuse Prevention.* Washington, DC: U.S. Department of Health and Human Services, 1998.)

When basic needs such as food and shelter are met, children are free to develop interests in other people and other things.

Early Childhood Programs and the Responsibilities of Early Childhood Professionals to Prevent Child Abuse" urging that early childhood programs in homes, centers, and schools adopt a set of policies based on guidelines such as employing adequate staff and adequate supervision of staff; environments that reduce possibility of hidden places; orientation and training on child abuse detection, prevention, and reporting; defined and articulated policies for a safe environment; avoidance of creating "no-touch" policies by the caregivers and staff.

In regard to staff recruitment, NAEYC recommends that early childhood programs in the home, center, or school initiate policies that require personal interviews, verification of references and education background and qualifications, criminal record checks, and disclosure of previous convictions. New employees should serve a probationary period, and programs should have policies that provide for the removal of anyone whose performance is unacceptable. Procedures must also be in place for responding to an accusation of child abuse and provide due process for the accused (NAEYC, 1997).

All those involved in early childhood care and education would be well advised to secure a copy of the statement and use it to reflect on the effectiveness of their own program's policies and procedures.

Children and AIDS

Acquired immunodeficiency syndrome (AIDS) is a communicable disease that breaks down the body's immune system, leaving it unable to fend off harmful bacteria, viruses, and the like. Illnesses that are not usually life-threatening to a healthy person can result in death for someone who has AIDS.

AIDS is caused by the human immunodeficiency virus (HIV), which is primarily sexually transmitted, although it can pass from one person to another by contact with blood, blood products, or through bodily secretions that mix with a person's blood. The AIDS virus may be present in the blood even though the full AIDS syndrome does not develop. The infection, however, can be transmitted to someone else even if the person carrying it has no symptoms.

In the United States the disease is prevalent among males (85% of the AIDS victims are men) and occurs primarily in homosexuals, in intravenous drug users, and in hemophiliacs and other persons who receive contaminated blood transfusions. Children, too, can be infected with AIDS. Those at greatest risk are:

- Infants born to mothers who have AIDS.
- Infants who are breast-fed by mothers with AIDS.
- Infants and children who receive blood transfusions (blood screening programs may have reduced this risk).
- Sexually abused children.

Prenatal care and preventative treatment in the mid-1990s drastically reduced the number of babies born with AIDS by 75% between 1992 and 1998. Mother-to-child transmission of the disease accounted for over 90% of all AIDS cases among U.S. children (Center for Disease Control, 1999).

The greatest fears—and misconceptions—about AIDS are how contagious the disease is and how it is transmitted. Sexual contacts and mingling of blood are the two known routes of infection, and not one case is known to have been transmitted any other way, even to close family members of AIDS patients. No children have contracted AIDS from ordinary contact with other children. None of the cases of pediatric AIDS in the United States has been transmitted in a school or child care setting or through hugging, sharing a glass or a plate, sharing bathrooms, or in kissing that is not mouth-to-mouth kissing (Centers for Disease Control and Prevention, 1999).

Role of the Teacher

Early childhood professionals have a role to play regarding this misunderstood disease:

- Be an informed resource to parents and other teachers. Keep abreast of current data and educate others about the facts of AIDS.
- Know how to answer the questions a preschooler will ask. Begin to educate children.
- Examine your own attitudes about sexually transmitted diseases, homosexuality, and drug usage.
- Keep up to date on research about AIDS; information changes rapidly and is released frequently.
- Take appropriate precautions—careful handwashing and use of plastic gloves when contact with blood may occur.
- Be prepared to counsel children and their families through long illness and death in the same way as with other fatal diseases.
- Develop school policies that reflect the current knowledge and recommendations of medical experts.

Poverty

There is a group of Americans who are destined for limited participation in the social, political, and economic mainstream of national life. The children who are at risk for academic failure are likely to be: those who live in poverty, members of minority groups in racial isolation, children with various physical and mental disabilities, children with limited English proficiency, children from single-parent families, or children attending schools with a high concentration of students who live in poverty (Casey Foundation, 2005).

One in five children is poor in the United States (see Figure 15-4).

- An American child is born into poverty every 43 seconds, one in five children is poor during the first three years of life—the time of greatest brain development.

Poor Children Come in All Colors and Live in Every Family Type and Geographic Area of America

74% live in families where somebody worked all or part of the time in 1998, up from 61% in 1993.

59% live in female-headed families, up from 45% in 1969.

35% live in two-parent families, down from 38% in 1988.

41% live in two-parent or father-only families, down from 55% in 1969.

30% live in young families headed by a person under 30.

62% are white, up from 60% in 1969.

32% are black, down from 39% in 1969.

29% are Hispanic, up from 14% in 1973.

4% are Asian or Pacific Islander.

55% live in suburban and rural areas, down from 67% in 1969.

FIGURE 15-4 Poverty affects all children in America (courtesy of C.D.F., 2002).

- Nearly 12 million children are poor, and millions are hungry, at risk of hunger, living in worst-case housing, or homeless.

- Almost 80% of poor children live in working households (CDF 2002).

   There is a striking correlation between poverty and school failure. Children who start out at a disadvantage fall farther behind in academic achievement throughout their school years.[1]

The changing school population suggests that these problems will only increase as the proportion of minority groups expands (because they are overrepresented among the poor), as a larger and larger percentage of children fall below the poverty line, and as traditional patterns of child rearing and marriage change so that fewer children will have the emotional and educational advantages of a two-parent family.

The National Institute of Child Health and Human Development Study of Early Child Care conducted a three-year study of 1,000 children in 10 cities, examining maternal sensitivity, home environment, hours in child care and quality of child care. Children were then given a school readiness test, and the data were compared with children in similar settings. In a report entitled "Growing Up in Poverty" (Center for Children and Families, 2000), researchers from Berkeley, Columbia, Stanford, and Yale Universities found that early maternal employment had negative effects on children's intellectual development. Children whose mothers worked by the time the babies were nine months old, had insensitive mothers, and poor-quality child care had scores significantly lower than those with sensitive mothers who were not employed by the ninth month and had good-quality child care. While the study did not take into consideration such factors as father involvement or how much the mother wants to be employed, it certainly has serious implications for families at risk.

A dramatic and intensive reform effort is needed for these children, and a number of solutions are being considered. As the National Commission on Children (1990) states:

> Too many of today's children and adolescents will reach adulthood unhealthy, illiterate, unemployable, lacking moral direction and a vision of a secure future. This is a personal tragedy for the young people involved and a staggering loss for the nation as a whole. We must begin today to place children and their families at the top of the national agenda.

Family Support

The family of today has many shapes, sizes, and styles. A family can be:

- A dual-career family, with two parents working outside the home and children in child care

- A single parent supporting children, with little or no help—either financial or personal—from the absent parent

- Older parents raising their grandchildren

- Teen parents living with, or without, family support

- A blended family—adults with children remarried to form a new structure, with children living full- or part-time in residence

- An extended family (or several families) living together in a small dwelling

- A gay or lesbian couple raising children

- An unmarried person living either alone or with others who do not have children

---

1 It is a paradox of the 21st century that nearly half of our school population is considered to be "at risk." As we learn more about what constitutes difficulty in achieving school success, and make assessments on more than simple grade level academic performance, our concept of "at risk" diversifies and requires a stronger commitment to school reform.

In fact, the American family has evolved so extensively over the last few decades that the Children's Defense Fund (2002) reports:

- One in two preschoolers has a mother in the labor force.
- Two thirds of mothers of young children [six and under] work outside the home; 55% of working women provide half or more of the family's income.
- One in two children will live in a single-parent family at some point in childhood.
- Families with children accounted for more than a third of the homeless Americans in urban areas who seek shelter.
- One in three children will be poor at some point in childhood.
- The United States ranks first among industrialized countries in gross domestic product, but 18th in the income gap between rich and poor children.

The changing family structure and circumstances affect early childhood professionals in several ways. Chapter 8 discusses issues around the changing family and makes recommendations for the role of the teacher.

Divorce and Family Structures

Perhaps no one single change has affected children as much as the divorce rate. DelCampo & DelCampo (2006) note that, in some studies, "children rate divorce second only to the death of a parent as the most stressful event in their lives, and most of them end up not having a close relationship with one of their parents." The trend toward more divorce is significant. Nearly 50% of marriages end in divorce, and five of ten children born in the 1990s will spend part of their growing years in a single-parent home (Children's Defense Fund, 2002).[1] One school child in three has parents who are divorced; 30% of these are children in stepfamilies and the other 70% live with their mothers or fathers alone (Clarke-Stewart, 1989). The effects of divorce are felt for years. Getting over divorce and onto a productive life is critical for both child and parent; teachers can help.

The effects of divorce are felt by children well before the event itself. Children exhibit "predivorce family stress" by increased impulsive or aggressive behavior, and parents show the stress with headaches, fatigue, mood swings, or depression. Children's initial reaction to their parents' separation is traumatic—shock and distress (the "stage 1" responses to stress as described in Chapter 14). Even if parents are not in violent conflict with each other, no child is happy about divorce. After divorce, many parents become overworked and overwhelmed. Children are often neglected or left with less than what both parents could provide, including emotional and financial support.

> Among employed adults, unmarried women who support families have the greatest risk of living in poverty. . . . Moreover, unmarried mothers often have time constraints that can affect their ability to supervise their children, offer emotional support, take an active part in their education, and arrange other activities for them. When children live with one parent, it is still most often the mother. (Casey Foundation, 2005)

Adjustment to divorce is difficult, and the psychological effects of divorce on children are often felt well into adulthood. "Divorce is a cumulative experience for the child. Its impact increases over time," writes Wallerstein (2002), reporting on a 25-year research project initiated in the early 1970s. For instance, of the people who were two-and-a-half- to six-years-old when their parents divorced, one-third did not pursue any education beyond high school, though 40% of them did graduate from college.

Growing up in a divorced home does not mean children cannot live happy lives. Fortunately, children are amazingly resilient. The age and gender of the children involved seem to have some bearing on their adjustment. Very young children recover more easily than older ones, and boys react more intensely than girls to the loss of their fathers from the home (Wallerstein, 2002). The parents' ability to be caring and available makes a difference, as does the parents' relationship with each other and the quality of the children's relationship with both parents.

What can teachers do?

1. Read and understand the effects of divorce (DelCampo & DelCampo [2006] have an extensive suggested reading list).
2. Be informed about what to expect from children in a divorce cycle (see Chapter 14 about stress).

1 Consider the stories read to young children. Is this reality reflected? Is this reality reflected in messages sent from program to home? When scheduling parent-program meetings?

3. Help parents get access to outside help (parent support groups, community welfare services, or a parental stress hotline).

4. Plan strategies for family involvement that takes into account the work demands, resources, and expertise of parents.

5. Provide a place and time to heal:

- *Know your children.* Confer with families as often as possible and be aware of family stresses and crises.

- *Talk about feelings.* Anger and sadness are predominant, along with guilt, loss, helplessness, and loneliness; an understanding teacher can go a long way to help a child feel less alone and can offer appropriate opportunities—through intimate moments, puppets and dolls, unstructured drawings, role playing and creative drawing—for expression.

- *Use bibliotherapy.* Books are powerful tools to connect with children, with understanding and kindness. They are also wonderful resources to families.

- *Keep aware of family diversity.* Be sure to include many family structures in the curriculum, during informal discussions, with any correspondence to home.

- *Include open communication with parents and family members.* Divorce tends to complicate communication between teachers and parents. Make adjustments in conferences, newsletters, and notes about the child so both the primary and noncustodial parents are included as much as possible.

The Working Parent

Two-thirds of all preschool children under six have mothers in the work force (Children's Defense Fund, 2002), and the percentage rises when considering school-aged children as well. Mothers at work affect the family and the teacher.

The implications for families are considerable. For women, the double roles of job or career and family nurturer can be overwhelming, creating great conflict and the stress of chronic fatigue. Men are looking at their role in a different light; many are learning about greater involvement in child rearing and how to adjust to a new financial provider role.[1] For

both parents, three issues loom large: the concern for good child care, the struggle to provide "quality time" with children and as a family unit, and the financial burden. Without parental leave, parents are forced to return to work during the critical early months of infancy or lose income and even their job. Further, while many mothers go to work from welfare, there are still few gains in the family's broader economic well-being. Women report still needing to use local food banks and taking second and third jobs. Self-sufficiency without income supports is rarely achieved.

For educators, working families have special new issues. As more parents are fully occupied with work during the school day, they are less available for direct participation in a classroom or on a constant basis. Teachers plan flexible opportunities for them to become involved in their children's education.

In the public sector, several proposals gained momentum in the 1990s. The most successful so far, the ABC Bill of 1990, allotted federal dollars to the states to provide support for centers, improving the quality of children's services available. Child tax credits and pre-tax dependent care credits are governments and employer supports. Leading pediatrician T. Berry Brazelton's Washington-based lobby group, Parent Action, is garnering support for family medical leave that would enable parents of newborns several months of unpaid leave from their jobs to be at home and establish an attachment bond and family setting so critical to infants' well-being and survival.

Public policy is a reflection of the attitude and values we as a nation hold toward children and families, and the inequities are glaring. Most European countries fund public programs for children and support services for parents at a much higher rate than in the United States. We look toward a future trend of clearer and more supportive public policies.

Community and School Support

The relationship between schools and the community at large and the families they serve dictates the role schools play in the lives of families. Yet, as the Children's Defense Fund (2000) points out, "our communities, our work places, and our nation offer little support for parents

---

1 The sweeping changes in social behavior have resulted in changing attitudes about adults. However, there are vast differences among the various cultural groups and individual adults about the value of and care for children. Do not assume that a change in what you consider a "traditional" family pattern equals an inferior commitment to children.

engaged in the extraordinarily difficult task of caring for young children."

At the same time, the history of education in the United States is the story of the "progressive assumption" (Elkind, 1991). This means that the trend over time is for educational institutions to assume functions once performed by the family. There are difficulties in this progression, however, as schools are reluctant to assume some of these responsibilities, parents are wary of giving them up, and it is unclear if children gain from such a "handoff" of responsibility.

In colonial times, schools were primarily private, church-based programs for boys. After the American Revolution the government began forming a national public school system, based on the belief that a democracy demands literate participants. This trend continued as the "public" came to include women and people of color. The 21st century has seen governments provide subsidies to schools to provide free or low-cost meals, medical and dental services, and physical education programs.

In the last 30 years, schools have continued to take on more child-rearing functions. Schools have a key role to play in nurturing parental involvement in education and family life. Coleman (1991) describes this role as rebuilding the "**social capital**" both within the family and in the community. Drawing on an economic model, social capital refers to the richness and resources that social relationships provide for a child. The strength of these social relations helps shape a child's habits, establish norms of acceptable behavior, and encourage the development of children's character, long-range goals, and even educational attainment.

One example of the school as a reflection of community life is the Reggio Emilia system (see Chapter 2). Founder Malaguzzi understood that the child cannot be thought of in the abstract, but as tightly connected to the world of relationships and experiences. Both Vygotsky (see Chapters 4 and 12) and Bronfenbrenner (see Chapter 2) emphasize these ties.

The issue today in the United States is to define a new role for schools. Some specific ways include taking a comprehensive approach to families, so that the early childhood program is fully integrated into the families it serves. School systems can help parents get needed medical, dental, mental, job-related, and social services by collaborating with other agencies and individuals. Head Start models this resource-rich type of program.

"It takes a village to raise a child." This old adage has new significance in today's society.

What responsibility does the community have to young children and their families? How do families with young children influence the community in which they reside? They join forces to advocate for important early childhood issues. (Courtesy of Stand For Children.)

The factors of positive experiences, relationships, opportunities, and personal qualities help children grow up to be healthy, caring, and responsible. These include:

- External assets (those positive experiences that young children receive from the people and institutions in their lives) of *support, empowerment, boundaries and expectations,* and *constructive use of time)*
- Internal (the internal dispositions that guide children's choices and create a sense of centeredness and purpose) of *commitment to learning, positive values, social competencies,* and *a positive identity.*

Children who have positive family communication, supervised time at home, as well as stimulating activities with useful roles for children outside of home in a community that is safe and that values children have experiences that enhance positive development. When put together, the assets offer a set of benchmarks for positive child development. The roles that families, schools, congregations, neighborhoods, youth organizations, and others in communities play in shaping young people's lives contribute to both external and internal supports. As part of this effort, early childhood professionals provide not only the knowledge and understanding of

When both parents work outside the home, new roles for fathers emerge.

child development, but also the ability to relate to all children, parents, and coworkers with compassion, empathy, and understanding.

Early childhood programs can help articulate the shared values of the community and the support for diversity of the whole community. The trend is for the role of the teacher to become greater with families. Teaching is a two-client job: a teacher of the child and a resource for the family.

TRANSMITTING VALUES

As with the other themes in early childhood education, the issue of transmitting values is not for the teacher or school alone. A deep and primary source of values is that of the family and culture. The school must work with the family to provide a sense of shared values; nonetheless, both parents and teachers must acknowledge other sources that shape children's values and behavior. Three other critical sources are the media culture, violence and disaster, and social diversity.

The Media Culture

In many homes, the television set has replaced adult supervision.

> Ninety-nine percent of American households contain at least one TV, with two-thirds containing two or more sets. Children and adolescents comprise between 10% and 20% of the prime-time viewing audience, and they spend more time watching TV (15,000 h) than they do in school

(11,000 h). During this time they witness 180,000 murders, rapes, armed robberies, and assaults. (Johnson, 1996)

The Nielsen Report on Television (1989) commented that children age 2 to 5 viewed approximately 27 hours/week, and children age 6 to 11 years viewed more than 23 hours/week. Television and, for school-age children, the Internet and other media, represents an influential force in the lives of children.

There are four basic concerns that parents and teachers express about children's viewing of media:

1. Media violence can lead to aggression and desensitization to violence.
2. Media viewing promotes passivity, slowing intellectual development and stifling imagination.
3. Media promote racist and sexist attitudes.
4. Television promotes materialistic consumerism.

Research highlights the powerful effects on children of the models they see, whether they be of children, adults, or fantasy characters (see section on Bandura in Chapter 4); it is generally accepted that media images can have similar influences. The Center for Media Literacy (1993) documents four effects of viewing media violence:

1. Increased aggressiveness and antisocial behavior. *"There is absolutely no doubt that higher levels of viewing violence on television are correlated with increased acceptance of aggressive attitudes and increased aggressive behavior."*
2. Increased fear of becoming a victim. *"Viewing violence increases the fear of becoming a victim of violence, with a resultant increase in self-protective behaviors and increased mistrust of others."*
3. Desensitization to violence and victims of violence. *"Viewing violence increases desensitization to violence, resulting in a calloused attitude towards violence directed at others and a decreased likelihood to take action on behalf of the victim when violence occurs."*
4. Interest in more violence in entertainment and real life. *"Viewing violence increases viewers' appetite for becoming involved with violence or exposing themselves to violence."*

As to the passivity argument, one need only see the enthralled look on children's faces to know that the screen images are engaging. Children do spend large amounts of time with

Antidotes to television.

television, but the research available seems to indicate that children actually do many other activities while the set is on and that their attention to TV is variable. Preschool children seem to attend to minute details of a show that interests them; most parents report very young children learning advertising jingles or details of slogans. Research about the cognitive effects of television viewing reveals that TV viewing seems to be a fairly complex cognitive activity. Still, there is little consistent evidence concerning television's influence on imagination and creativity.

In the area of bias and stereotyping, children's television is an arena "where boys are king" (Carter, 1991). Networks generally assert that boys will not watch female-lead shows, but girls will watch shows with a male lead. With children's television shows, the Euro-American and male attitudes and behaviors are reinforced.[1]

Does television promote consumerism? As Bob Keeshan, affectionately known as Captain Kangaroo, once put it, "In America, television is not a tool for nurturing. It is a tool for selling" (Minow, 1991). After the deregulation of the

  1 An important task of early childhood educators is to actively counteract gender and ethnic group stereotypes.

television industry in 1985, the amount of commercial time in children's shows increased, and the "program-length commercial" was introduced, whereby a show was developed based on a line of consumer toys and products aimed at the children's market. Proponents of deregulation had reasoned that a free market and competition would improve the quality of television. "Competition, it is said, brings out the best in products and the worst in people. In children's television, competition seems to bring out the worst in programs and the worst in children" (Minow, 1991). Therefore, in 1990 the Children's Television Act became law, requiring that stations submit an assessment of children's television offerings when they apply for license renewal with the Federal Communications Commission (FCC). Another is the 1996 ruling by the FCC requiring broadcasters to provide three hours of educational programs for children each week and limit the amount of advertising during children's shows.

Television and the lessons it teaches are and will be a part of children's lives. "Perhaps if parents [and teachers] could accept the inevitable, that television is not only here to stay but viewing choices are expanding almost daily, then society could move past this dichotomy of thinking of television as simply good or bad. Television viewing could be thought of as an active endeavor rather than a passive one" (DelCampo & DelCampo, 2006).

Families and teachers can use guidelines for television viewing and for dealing with the hazards of media culture (video games, computer games, assorted toys and games, etc.) (NAEYC, 1990).

1. *Set limits.* Know how many hours of TV children watch, and set limits. The American Academy of Pediatrics suggests a maximum of one to two hours daily. Keep the TV turned off unless someone is actively viewing; TV can easily become more of a habit than a choice. Involve your children in discussions about video-game systems or computer games; consider establishing rules (for instance, "Game-playing counts as 'screen time'" and "I can't play when a friend comes over.")

2. *Plan and participate.* Work together with children to decide what to watch. Help children choose shows with an age-appropriate viewing length, bias-free content, and peaceful action. Consider watching shows

Video VIEW PoinT 15-2

"Media: Much has been written on the effects of media on children."

COMPETENCY: Family Interactions, School and Community

AGE GROUP: School-Age

CRITICAL THINKING QUESTIONS:

1. How should programs deal with children's interests in using media games and toys in their after-school programs?

2. How would you respond when children talk about and act out television shows and movies that promote violence?

together, pointing out parts that are prosocial and asking about those parts you wonder about or disagree with. Use the "pause," "rewind," and "mute" buttons as part of the process. Watch carefully what children are doing with video and computer games.

3. *Resist commercials.* Children do not distinguish easily between the sales-pitch commercial and the ordinary show. Help them become "critical consumers" by pointing out the exaggerated claims. Even three-year-olds can answer the question "What are they trying to sell us?"

4. *Express your views.* Call a station that airs a show or commercial you find offensive, or write a letter to the Children's Advertising Review unit of the Better Business Bureau. Action for Children's Television in Cambridge, Massachusetts, has been a leading public interest group for more than 20 years and has valuable suggestions for how adults can influence children's television programming.

Violence and Disaster

Trends

The trend of children's increasing exposure to violence is alarming. Families speak of what is shown in the media and the kinds and choices of toys that give them a sense of being out of control in limiting or influencing children's behavior. Teachers notice changes in children's play, commenting that the weapon and war play in classrooms is so single purpose and intense that it is difficult to redirect; rule setting and controlling overzealous play take an inordinate amount of teachers' energy.

Tragically, there is an alarming rash of unexplainable attacks in school of children wounding and killing other children and teachers. Access to real guns has fueled this deadly phenomenon. It is no wonder that Dr. Jocelyn Elders, when Surgeon General, declared that the primary health concern of our society is violence (Hoot & Roberson, 1994).

When a catastrophe happens, whether personal or societal, children need help making sense of the calamity and then support in recovery. Shock, confusion, fear, anxiety, grief, anger, guilt, helplessness are all common emotional responses to trauma. As Greenman (2001) notes:

> The events of that day (September 11th) touched everyone. Certainly the millions in New York, Washington, DC, and Pennsylvania who experienced the blast and the aftermath know first-hand the trauma. Anyone who commutes to those cities, travels by air, works in a tall building or a federal building, visits New York or Washington, or knows someone who does, is also affected. And, as the fear of further acts of terrorism grows, anyone who can say, "That could have been me or someone I love" is joined by many others who will worry, "That could be me or someone I love next time."

Such reactions will generate changes in behavior, both in adults and in the children we care for.

How much children are traumatized varies; research has shown that five factors seem to determine the amount of suffering children experience during war. The child's own biological and psychological makeup, the level of disruption of the family unit, the breakdown of the community, cultural influences (especially positive), and the intensity, suddenness, and duration of the war affect how deep the scars will be on one's childhood. How children see their parents and teachers react, a child's age, and how much destruction and/or death is seen will also make an impact (AACAP, 1999). Chapter 14 discusses children's reactions to stress, and the role of the teacher in helping children process and cope with child trauma. Figure 15-5 gives suggestions for how to help children in case of a disaster.

The increasing violence of American society has so alarmed educators and parents alike

(Levin, 1998) that programs are being developed for children and for teachers. Organizations such as Adults and Children Together (ACT) Against Violence, the Educators for Social Responsibility, and the National Association for Mediation Educators serve as both clearinghouses for information and material and as training institutes for teachers. Additionally, in California a "Safe Start" program is in place for teachers-in-training and those already in the field to work more effectively with both children and families living in a violent world.

Thoughtful adults find themselves in a dilemma. Should they allow war play to continue (unchecked? with limits? with intervention?)? Or ought this kind of play be altered (redirected? contained? banned?)? This dilemma illustrates children's play from two different viewpoints, a developmental one and a sociopolitical one. The developmental viewpoint states that play, including war play, is the primary vehicle through which children work on developmental issues. Because children need to develop a sense of how the world works, of fantasy and reality, of good and bad, war play is an extension of "superhero" play (see Chapter 14), and is, therefore, a necessary part of children's play. The sociopolitical view assumes that children learn basic social and political behavior at an early age and, therefore, will learn militaristic concepts and values through war play. This viewpoint contends that children learn about conflict and resolution, the use of fighting, and the meaning of friends and enemies in their play, and that allowing war play endorses the use of force (Carlsson-Paige & Levin, 1987).

These two ideas give teachers the basic building blocks for how to deal with the issue of developing shared values and for engaging in a dialogue with fellow teachers and parents. Whatever your viewpoint, remember that early learning is powerful. Being exposed to violence is harmful, particularly when children are victims.

When disaster strikes, what children need most is reassurance, to know they will be safe and that caring grown-ups will still take care of them. Constancy and predictability, in the form of a consistent routine and continued habits of behavior and tradition, will help children feel anchored in their lives. Listening carefully, answering children's questions in simple ways, asking questions to elicit their thoughts all encourage communication and a dialogue about their feelings. Most educators

When a Child Experiences Disaster

For all children . . .

Stop, look, and listen.

Spend time with the child, be aware of actions and feelings.

Be aware of your feelings and reactions.

Ask open-ended questions.

Give reassurance and physical comfort.

Welcome children's talking about it.

Provide structure throughout the day.

Work with parents and significant adults.

Adapt the curriculum:

- Give them more time for relaxing, therapeutic experiences of playing with sand, water, clay, and play dough.
- Allow plenty of time to work out their concerns through dramatic play.
- Spend more time in physical activity for emotional release.

For children under age three . . .

Resume normal routines and favorite rituals.

Give limited exposure to the media and adult conversations about the crisis.

For children under age five . . .

Be reassuring verbally that you and they will be okay.

Make sure they know where you are at all times.

Model peaceful resolution to conflict.

Make opportunities for children to write, dictate stories, and create pictures about their experiences.

Give special time at nap time and bed time (including letting the child sleep with parents).

For school-age children . . .

Give verbal and physical assurance that you and they will be okay.

Help them know where their important adults are at any given time.

Ask what is on their minds and answer their questions honestly.

Make emergency plans so children know safety measures for the future.

Provide guided exposure to the media; try to watch/hear with them.

Begin to explain what motivates people to act in violent ways.

Take action: Send help directly, help them organize relief efforts.

Allow them extra time at bed time (including letting the child sleep with parents).

FIGURE 15-5 A catastrophe such as an earthquake, hurricane, or fire, or a disaster such as war or an act of terrorism is frightening to both adults and children (AACAP, 1999; Davis & Keyser, 2001; Farish, 1995; Greenman, 2001).

and counselors also remind adults to monitor children's media exposure to war. Teachers help children find peaceful resolutions to their everyday conflicts, ensuring that, in their daily school life, war will not break out and take over (see Chapters 7 and 14 for suggestions).

This last suggestion may take several paths. A family child care provider of infants and toddlers may spend extra time giving hugs and helping children share toys. One class of preschoolers may choose a cross-town child care center to exchange drawings and visits with, to increase their knowledge of their city neighbors and of ideas they could create to solve each others' problems. In a first-grade class, children were so concerned that they chose to write letters to the President. ("I don't like it when you make war. My big sister says to use words when I have a problem and you should too.")

What to Do

For the larger issues of war and violence, teachers can look at several courses of action. It is helpful to consider the options teachers have in these situations.

- Talk about and decide on your viewpoint and values with parents and the school board.
- Develop guidelines that address your values and the needs of the children.
- Talk with parents about toys and the role of the media in the development of children's interests and the role of parents in helping children decide and choose what and how to play.
- Investigate peace education and building peaceable classrooms that have conflict resolution teaching as part of the curriculum (see Chapters 7 and 14).

Creating safer environments for children in school will help children cope with violence (Groves & Mazur, 1995). Listening to children's own dilemmas both at school and from home allows teachers to provide opportunities for problem solving and for vehicles for safe self-expression (Carter, 1995). Helping children and their families handle anger is a crucial step toward preventing violence. Take care of yourselves as professionals; teachers need someone to talk to (Farish, 1995), and may need to adjust the curriculum to give everyone more breathing room.

Social Diversity

Facing Reality

America as "melting pot," where all racial and cultural differences are smoothly mixed into one single blend, is a myth, both an unrealistic and unnecessary goal. Moreover, much of America's history can be characterized as **racist**, **classist**, **sexist**, and **ethnocentric** in nature by one group or another. The discrepancy between our ideals of equal opportunity and freedom and the daily reality can be altered only if we recognize the problems and then set specific goals for change.

Today's **demographics** point to a trend of an increasingly diverse society (see Chapter 3). The issue is that attitudes have not yet responded to reality. A University of Chicago survey on racial attitudes found that, although support for racial equality has grown, "negative images of members of other racial and ethnic groups are widespread among whites, and most groups have at least one prejudice against all the other groups" (Armstrong, 1991). Segregation of schools by color is still a reality by virtue of neighborhood configurations and of white families sending

their children to private schools; indeed schools with high populations of African American and/or Latino children almost without exception are also high-poverty schools, which correlates with less-qualified teachers, fewer classroom resources, and higher absenteeism among teachers and students Frankenberg, Lee, & Orfield, 2003).

Moreover, school reform efforts have done little to meet the educational needs of America's demographic profile.

Research shows a strong relationship between education attainment and economic well-being. Children who are provided a comprehensive, high quality education are less likely to be poor and more likely to find employment and receive higher wages than their less educated peers. In addition, we find that children from low-income families are constantly outperformed by their wealthier peers across a broad range of academic measures. Poor children, therefore, often find themselves in a Catch-22 with their economic circumstances denying them access to the escape valve out of a life of poverty—a quality education. (CDF, 2005)

See Figure 15-6 to illustrate this point.

Not Whether, but What Kind. We know that children exhibit an awareness of racial and gender differences by age three (Derman-Sparks, 1989) and are formulating rudimentary concepts about the meaning of those differences in the preschool years. It is logical to conclude that, by the end of the early childhood years, children have consolidated their attitudes about race, ethnicity, gender, and (dis)ability, and are far along the path of **attitude crystallization**. Unless the social environment changes, children will recreate the prejudices of the current adult society. Teachers and families need to look with sensitivity to the meaning of diversity. (See Figure 15-7.)

Multicultural Education

Multicultural education is the system of teaching and learning that includes the contributions of all ethnic and racial groups. In other words, it is a comprehensive educational approach that reflects more than just the dominant culture's perspective, providing all children with a fuller, more balanced truth about themselves, their own history, and culture. This means a responsiveness to the child's origins, habits at home, ways of self-expression.

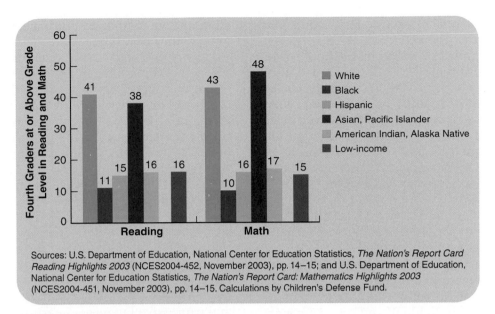

Sources: U.S. Department of Education, National Center for Education Statistics, *The Nation's Report Card Reading Highlights 2003* (NCES2004-452, November 2003), pp. 14–15; and U.S. Department of Education, National Center for Education Statistics, *The Nation's Report Card: Mathematics Highlights 2003* (NCES2004-451, November 2003), pp. 14–15. Calculations by Children's Defense Fund.

FIGURE 15-6 The disparate levels of education in America's diverse cultures confirm that school reforms have not yet met the needs of all children. (Reprinted with permission from Children's Defense Fund, *The State of America's Children 2005*, Chapter 4, Figure 1, Web version (Washington, D.C.: Children's Defense Fund, 2005).)

Diversity and Teacher Attitudes

1. "Teachers need to learn to recognize developmentally equivalent patterns of behavior. Before children come to school, they have all learned many of the same things, such as a primary language and communication styles." Before judging a child as difficult or problematic, assume he or she is normal and look again. Your own vision may be clouded with "cultural myopia."

2. "It is essential not to value some ways of achieving developmental milestones more highly than others." When children find that the way they talk is not understood or appreciated in school, they are apt to become confused or disengaged. Remember, different is not deficient.

3. "Teachers need to begin instruction with interactive styles and content that is familiar to the children. . . . [Teachers] can become more adept at planning and implementing a culturally sensitive curriculum." You may not be fluent in a child's primary language, but you can learn key words and phrases that help a child feel a sense of belonging.

4. "School learning is most likely to occur when family values reinforce school expectations." Parent involvement is more than just a phrase; when parents and teachers are partners in education, children are the winners.

5. "When differences exist between the cultural patterns of the home and community and those of the school, the teacher must deal with those discrepancies directly." Teachers ask questions and create shared understandings between themselves and children, inviting children to be interested in creating a common culture of the classroom.

FIGURE 15-7 There are several guidelines teachers can follow regarding diversity. (Bowman, 1991, with authors' interpretations.)

At higher levels of education there is a great debate about how to deal with diversity. Two views dominate. One is a "separatist" education in which education is taught from a particular viewpoint, be it European, Afro-centrist, or the like. The other is a more traditional, "pluralist" approach in which education stresses the commonalities of varying peoples. Janice E. Hale (1993) offers the idea that "a more culturally appropriate pedagogy would expose African American children to [both] Anglo-centric and Afro-centric literature at each grade level . . . [T]o educate African American children in a culturally appropriate manner, there is a kind of dual educational process that is required."

Further, Hale sees the miseducation of black children as a form of "educational malpractice."

In *Learning While Black* (2001), Hale notes that "academic failure, incarceration and unemployment are outcomes of the public schooling for African American boys." The hidden racism that permeates both private and public schools in the United States must be addressed. What underlies these issues is how we see ourselves as a common culture. When we change the metaphor of "melting pot" to one of "mosaic" or "mixed salad," we encourage a way of thinking that might be termed **cultural pluralism**—the idea that "Yes, we are all one people, but we do not necessarily divest ourselves of our ethnic origins." And that we reform schools to create models that coordinate the efforts of teachers, parents, churches and community volunteers to provide educational excellence for all children. Based on developmental principles, responsive to the individual, and proactive in its embrace of societal realities, a good early childhood program represents the best of multicultural education.

Bilingual Education

The 1980s left unresolved basic questions concerning bilingual education, and the 1990s were an explosive and exploratory time for the issues of language and learning. The goals and purposes of bilingual education remain controversial, for there are still disagreements over how to define bilingualism, how to determine who needs it, and who is to provide the services. Chapter 13 discusses bilingual education in light of language learning and curriculum development. This section highlights the broader issues and implications.

Bilingual education has been part of the American experience since before the Revolutionary War, when school was taught in any one of the more than 18 languages that were spoken by the colonists. Nonetheless, numerous cultures have been suppressed with regularity in the United States. Both Native American and immigrant groups have categorically faced discrimination. Speaking English is only part of bilingual education: At issue are the civil and educational rights of people who speak limited English, the respect or assimilation of their culture, and their participation and acceptance in society.

Changing populations and the influx of immigrants from Asia as well as from the Hispanic nations have brought with them today new challenges of bilingual education. Bilingual programs serve primarily Spanish-speaking students. States that do not have bilingual programs still need to meet the needs of limited English-proficient (LEP) students in schools through other means. In 1998, a California state initiative effectively ended publicly funded bilingual programs, to be replaced by shorter-term, intensive English-immersion programs at the elementary and secondary levels. The number of school-age Spanish-speaking children in the United States increased by 50% between 1980 and 2000, and both elementary and early childhood teaching has been affected.

The School-Age Child. The questions about bilingualism for the school-age child are different from those for the young child. In elementary school, teachers and children are forced to deal with issues beyond those of receptive and expressive language. Learning graphic language (reading and writing), acquiring concepts in other subject areas through listening, and dealing with the more complex social patterns and interpersonal issues are just a few of these issues. Moreover, the age at which children should be taught a second language is highly controversial. Research shows that children can acquire native-like mastery of a second language if they learn to speak the language before the age of five. Others will argue that a child should learn all the fine points of the first language before being exposed to a second one and that this exposure should not occur before the age of six.

Much research is centered on how children achieve second-language competence and performance. We do know that by age five children know most of the sounds and grammatical structure of their native tongue and appear to learn a second language in a similar way. With a bilingual child, the level of competence in both languages may be low while gaining mastery in the second language.

The two government actions that have most influenced the bilingual issue in our time are the passing of the 1968 Bilingual Education Act and the 1974 Lau v. Nichols Supreme Court decision. In 1974, the Supreme Court determined that a lack of instruction in one's first language is a violation of children's civil rights.

Since 1968, Title VII programs (the Elementary and Secondary Education Act, also known as the Bilingual Education Act) addressed the needs of students with limited proficiency in English. State bilingual education laws followed, requiring special instruction for children who lack competence in English.

The result is that children are taught, in public kindergarten and elementary schools, by using both the primary language and English. For instance, children may be taught to read in their primary language first; once they have learned the reading process in their own language, they are then taught to decode in English. Yet bilingual programs are so varied that it is difficult to assess them. Some work to mainstream children into regular classrooms as quickly as possible; others try to maintain the child's native language. A more recent program, the dual or bilingual immersion method, attempts a blending of language instruction by putting both English speakers and those with limited English into classes together and teaching "two-way" bilingual education. By bringing together both groups for language instruction, this method also indicates respect for both languages as assets. It shows promise as a truly multicultural tool for desegregation.

Still, the controversy continues. Another political backlash occurred in the late 1980s against non-English speakers. The U.S. Office of Education claimed that bilingual education programs have not helped children learn English. California voters declared English as the official state language, and in 1998 publicly funded bilingual programs were voted down. Without consensus on the effectiveness and goals of bilingual education, educators must press for continuing research and clarity.

The Young Child. In preschools and child care centers, children are still taught in regular class settings, usually with little extra instruction. This type of instruction is known as the English immersion system. Recent research has generated controversy about what is best for children under age five. In a survey for the National Association for Bilingual Education conducted in 1990, professor of education Lily Wong Fillmore of the University of California, Berkeley, found striking differences between families who participated in English-based programs and those whose children received native-language instruction. Her data indicate that language-minority children in English-speaking schools experience a substantial erosion of their native-language ability and have difficulty communicating with their parents.

The Plight of the Immigrant

Another serious challenge for schools is posed by the educational and socioeconomic needs of immigrant children. Attempting to immerse new children into a "national way" and to teach basic skills needed to succeed in the new country have been central functions of schools throughout history (see Chapter 1). In the United States, there are more than 2.5 million school-age immigrants and at least as many children under five; one in six children in the United States has a foreign-born mother (Children's Defense Fund, 2000). Immigrant enrollment in schools varies among the states and can reach as high as 95% in some schools.

Financial and social supports for legal immigrant children are a critical problem. For instance, the 1996 federal welfare law denied supplemental Social Security income and food stamps to most legal immigrants until they become citizens and prohibited Medicaid and Temporary Assistance for Needy Families (TANF) for five years to immigrants who entered the country after August 1996. Although every state except Alabama has voted to continue TANF to some degree, only a few states are providing aid in some form to families without food stamps. Estimates (Children's Defense Fund, 2000) are that 70% to 75% of the legal immigrants in this country are unaided by food stamps; the actual need is difficult to calculate.

The language barrier is the most immediate problem, followed by that of acceptance of the immigrants' native culture. Further, many newcomers arrive from countries wracked with war, violence, and poverty. These children and families are under tremendous pressures and need help coping with the overwhelming stress and dislocation. Many young children in immigrant families do not have access to health and education services. Key issues are (Takanishi, 2006):

- Children's skills in kindergarten and their achievement at the end of third grade are important predictors of their future life prospects

- Although well-designed early education and after school programs hold promise to reduce ethnic group-related inequalities in children's cognitive skills and social competence, children in immigrant families are less likely to participate in these programs than are children in native-born families.

- Availability and access are important factors: when pre-kindergarten programs are offered in public schools, Hispanic and Asian American children are more likely to participate.

- Family literacy programs are a promising strategy for improving language skills of children in immigrant families, as well as their parents.

The way schools place and monitor immigrant children—both their educational progress and their general well-being—challenges educators and all American citizens to clarify the responsibilities our society has toward its newcomers. Chapter 8 describes the needs of immigrant families.

Inclusive Education

Since the 1970s, recognition of people with disabilities has been paired with public funding for education. The Americans with Disabilities Act (ADA) and its legislative authorization, the Individuals with Disabilities into Education Act (IDEA), are designed "to reasonably accommodate individuals with disabilities in order to integrate them into the program to the extent feasible, given each individual's limitations" (Child Care Law Center, 1994). Key principles are:

- Individuality (understand the limitations and needs of each individual).
- Reasonableness (of the accommodation to the program and the person).
- Integration (of the individual with others).

Accommodating a child with special needs is unreasonable only if it puts an undue burden on a program, would fundamentally alter the nature of the program, or poses a threat to the health or safety of the other children and staff. With these guidelines in mind, children with special needs will do best in the least restrictive environment, as fully included in a program as possible. Chapter 3 describes in detail the implications of ADA and IDEA for early childhood professionals.

Many programs, including all Head Start at the early childhood level, have welcomed children with special needs. All children, regardless of their abilities or disabilities, are more alike than different. Early intervention for children with special needs can minimize the effect of a condition or help such special needs from becoming more serious problems than need be.

Still, many children have special needs that remain undiagnosed. Many others have difficulty finding appropriate placement, particularly in programs for children under age five. Early childhood special education is a relatively new area of our profession. Exemplary programs are those in which:

- Intervention is focused on specific and measurable child goals.
- Services are family-centered.
- Regular monitoring and adjustments of the intervention occur.

- Planning for transitions and changes occurs.
- Multidisciplinary services are provided.

Early childhood educators need support in learning about special needs and in understanding what it means to be inclusive of children with special needs without diminishing program quality for all children or overwhelming and exhausting staff. Programs that are engaged in developmentally appropriate practices already have activities and equipment that provide for a wide range of abilities, a schedule that emphasizes child-initiated play, and a curriculum that merges the children with the teachers' plans. Those teachers who are committed to an anti-bias approach will find that inclusion of children with special needs is another way to honor diversity.

Class Differences

In the 1990s the ethnic gap in academic achievement was either staying the same or widening, depending on grade and subject area. A 1997 report from the Department of Education found that

> schools with the highest proportion of poor children have markedly fewer resources than schools serving affluent students. . . . Schools serving large numbers of poor children have fewer books and supplies and teachers with less training. . . . Many schools are in disrepair, but those in the poorest communities are in the most dire shape. (CDF, 2000)

Although no one likes to talk about it, the class differences cause many children, particularly children of poor and minority families, to get less:

- Less in the way of experienced and well-trained teachers
- Less in the way of a rich and well-balanced curriculum
- Less actual instructional time
- Less in the way of well-equipped and well-stocked laboratories and libraries
- Less of what undoubtedly is most important of all—a belief that they can really learn (Haycock, 1991).

So what can teachers do? First, we will have to deal with the "lesses." All of us know what makes good schools work, and our work on developmentally appropriate practices, though still needing continual refinement, helps us articulate what makes good teaching and improved educational experiences for all children. We will have to join with other community efforts in building support systems so families can thrive and help their children succeed. In speaking out about children's needs and pushing for adequate teaching conditions, we in early childhood education can do our part.

Equal Play and Gender Issues

There is ample research to confirm the widespread occurrence of gender segregation in childhood (American Association of University Women, 1992; Grossman & Grossman, 1994). Sex differences are less apparent in early childhood than the gender-based behavior (see Chapter 4). Although adults may not always directly contribute to biased development, teachers and parents are indirectly responsible for the inequity between the sexes in their children. For instance, in unstructured play situations, the free-play backbone of early education programs and most at-home play, children will choose playmates and play situations that are comfortable to them. They will not, typically, choose those activities with which they have had little or no experience, nor will they ordinarily choose cross-sex playmates (particularly as peer pressure increases with age). Further, boys still get more attention than girls do at most grade levels and in most subject areas (Sadker & Sadker, 1994). This is not always an advantage to boys, as there is increasing concern that early education programs are becoming less compatible with active behavior or less developed fine motor skills. Sexist treatment in the classroom encourages the formation of patterns of power and dominance that occur very early (Maccoby & Jacklin, 1985).

Adults must take an assertive role in recognizing this sexist bias and replacing it with more equitable experiences for all children. Summaries of wide-ranging research (Grossman & Grossman, 1994) indicate that both our homes and schools are "gendered environments" that spell different expectations and conduct for children on the basis of their gender. If we are committed to an anti-bias education and environment (see Chapters 9 to 14), we must attempt to reduce gender-stereotypical behavior.

What are teachers to do? Educators Schlank and Metzger (1997) suggest that these guidelines be followed when trying to teach for change:

- *Begin with yourself.* Just as in other issues of diversity and anti-bias, it all begins with self-awareness and reflection on one's own behavior, responses, and attitudes.

- *What you say and do can make a difference.* Whenever possible, be gender inclusive or neutral, acknowledging positive behaviors and

milestones by describing what you see and avoiding using gender designations (such as "all boys get your jackets," or "all girls go to the snack tables.")

- *Watch your language.* Avoid descriptions of children such as "pretty/handsome" and treat the class as a group ("friends" rather than "boys and girls"); be careful of word choices that reflect gender bias (such as "He is confident/She is full of herself").

- *Establish rules and conduct for cooperation and gender equity.* Everybody may play everywhere with any toy; blocks are not just for boys and the house corner is not for girls only; no child may be kept from playing because of something she or he cannot change—skin color, disability, or gender.

- *Be ready to intervene and support.* If you hear a "No boys allowed," or "Girls can't do that," be ready to intervene in a supportive way, finding out why children think that, and what you think or what the class rule is.

- *Think about how to cope with superheroes and Barbie dolls.* Weapon and doll play can both be viewed in a "developmental versus sociocultural" way.

Expanding children's learning styles is helpful. Girls need more experiences with spatial exploration and gross-motor coordination as well as quality attention from—without dependence on—adults. Boys in particular need experiences in flexibility, nurturance, and learning from modeling.

Eliminating stereotypical relationships is also important. Be sure that all members of a group have the opportunity to participate equally. For instance, try to reduce male dominance of females in mixed-gender situations. Keep a watchful eye in the environment to see that areas do not get labeled "off limits" by one gender, such as the blocks and trikes that become "boy places" or the house corner and art "for girls only." Encourage cross-gender interaction, and use cooperative learning activities. Whereas there is little research about the long-term effects of these strategies, a combination of these techniques has been found effective to increase mixed-gender interactions, helping behavior and friendships (Lockheed & Klein, 1985).

Sexuality

One of the most complicated issues that touches the lives of early childhood educators is sexuality. Although human sexuality is not likely to be among typical early childhood curriculum topics, teachers are increasingly more likely to encounter issues of homosexuality in the following ways: working with gay or lesbian families or co-workers, dealing with aspects of femininity and masculinity in children's sex role identity, and having multicultural children's books about gay families. Some experts estimate that approximately 10% of the children in our classes will grow up to be gay or lesbian adults (Corbett, 1993). Whether or not the estimates are accurate, gay issues are controversial and anxiety-producing for many; it is difficult and risky and often seems easier to ignore the whole issue and conclude that it is an "adult problem."

A number of studies suggest a possible genetic basis for homosexual behavior. "It is difficult, however, to conclusively establish genetic origins for any human behavior, and the study of homosexuality presents some unique problems" (Friemann, O'Hara, & Settel, 1996). Little direct research has been done with young children, and it is likely that, "while a handful may show early indications of seeming 'different' in some way, the vast majority will offer no clue to even the most observant eye" (Corbett, 1993).

If teachers are relinquishing stereotypes about ethnic, ability, and gender, they must also consider avoiding the rejection of a family for its choice of lifestyle or the criticism of a child on the basis of some notion of "femininity" or "masculinity." The homophobia at the root of such biased behavior, either subtle on the part of teachers or overt by other children, can be hurtful and harassing. Friemann et al. (1996) offer steps for teachers to take that will sound familiar because they are similar to those dealing with other forms of bias:

> Teachers should examine their own feelings about homosexuality. . . . [They] must honestly recognize any biases that they may have about children who are stigmatized as sissies [or tomboys], and keep those biases out of the classroom. . . . Second, teachers should immediately handle any instances of students-to-student abuse and harassment, no matter how slight. . . . [Third,] teachers should challenge negative remarks about gay people and other minority groups. . . . Classroom meetings are a good tool to deal with harassment cases. Start with a "stem" phrase for the children to complete, such as "When I am teased it makes me feel . . ." and help children focus on how people feel when they are harassed.

Our attitude ought to be one that no child should feel ashamed about her family, her teachers, or herself.

PROFESSIONALISM

Every day, early childhood professionals open their doors to young children by the millions. As they do, they are influencing the course of our history in the 21st century. Consider this: A child born in 2002 will be a voting adult in 2020, and may live until the end of the century. We are teaching the children of the future!

If you are thinking about working with young children as a career, you may be wondering if early childhood education is a profession worthy of a lifetime commitment as a career. Can a person look forward to a challenging, intellectually stimulating, and rewarding future? To find those answers in today's world, we look at three issues: standards (for children's programs and teacher preparation), teaching for human values, and child advocacy.

Standards

Children's programs. In chapter 2, you read about the rich array of programs offered for children in group care from infancy through age eight. Because they are so diverse, it is often difficult to define and assess the standard of care and education with one set of guidelines. Consider these statistics:

- Thirty-two states do not require prior training to teach in child care centers, and 39 and the District of Columbia do not require training of family child care providers (CDF, 2001).

- A study of child-staff ratios (Snow, Teleki, & Reguero-de-Atiles, 1996) found that fewer states met NAEYC-recommended standards for four-year-olds in 1995 than in 1981.

- Snow et al. (1996) also found that only 18 states met the NAEYC recommendations for group size for infants.

The most comprehensive set of standards for quality education and care in early childhood is known as Developmentally Appropriate Practices (NAEYC, 1999). The National Academy of Early Childhood Programs (2005) reports that more than 9,000 programs are accredited, serving 800,000 children.

We need a core set of standards and an assessment system to evaluate them. Early learning standards (Gronlund, 2006, and Chapter 6) will connect teaching practice and curriculum to state and community guidelines. This will ensure young children receive quality care and will help us to achieve professional status.

Teacher preparation. In Chapter 5 you read about the multiple roles of teachers and the "trilemma" regarding the connections between quality of program, availability for families, and compensation for professionals. The challenge is before all of us—the child care professionals, the parents, the leaders of business and industry, and the legislators on the local, state, and national scene. National efforts called "Worthy Wage Campaign" and "Full Cost of Quality in Early Childhood Education Programs Campaign" are leading the early childhood field to advocacy and in bringing the issues of the child care crisis to national attention. It is a formidable challenge—and a worthy one for all of us as early childhood professionals.

The quality of care in child development centers is linked to the training and education of the staff. Consequently, it is imperative that we attract and recruit to the field of early childhood education individuals who not only are dedicated to working with young children but also are skilled and competent. Many states are working on developing a career lattice and professional development plan for early childhood staff. Consideration must be given to developing a coordinated system that (1) welcomes people into the field from a variety of points; (2) offers clear career pathways with articulated training and credentialing systems, and (3) provides a variety of incentives to stay in the field.

Further, teacher preparation institutions are embarking on a cycle of self-study and articulation of coursework and experience that is offered at both the community college and four-year institutions in the United States. NAEYC's Standards for Programs (1999), (Hyson, 2003) is leading the charge, as do incentive programs such as California's Mentor Teacher Program. We look to continued efforts to articulate and upgrade the standards of care and education in early childhood programs. See Chapter 5 for a description of teacher preparation in the early childhood field.

Teaching for Human Values

The complexities of modern life can complicate the development of values in children. In a world so diverse, it is sometimes difficult to determine what values are "basic." With changing family structures, shifting political and religious viewpoints, and a multitude of cultures to consider, the teacher can, understandably, feel confused and reluctant to "teach" any particular values at all.

Teaching, however, is not a "value-neutral" endeavor. Whenever something is taught, the

A program that responds to diversity and invites individual expression is one that invites acceptance and respect.

choice of what and how to teach it implies the teacher's values. When a teacher prevents a child from hitting another, she states the value of peaceful conflict resolution. When a caregiver puts a crying child into his lap, he shows the value of responsive comforting. When children are taught reading, given free-play choices, asked to sing, they are being given a sense of what is important.

The school of the past could be concerned with simply academic and vocational, leaving the moral and personal responsibilities to the parents. The school of the present and future can not afford that luxury. Look back at Chapter 4, and consider Brazelton and Greenspan's list of the irreducible needs of children in this chapter; this work helps educators identify key values. Professionals talk about what is important to teach.

Ask yourself:

- Why am I teaching? Why young children? Why children at all?
- What made me choose early childhood education as my career?
- What do I stand for? Why?
- How did I come to have my beliefs?
- Do I allow others their beliefs?
- How do I state my values to children? To parents?
- How do I keep my values and integrity while allowing myself to grow and change?

Integrity, honesty, harmony, individuality, self-confidence, and responsibility can all be taught

Programs that offer children opportunities for playful expression are often those that are supportive of teachers' professional growth as well.

Video VIEW PoinT 15-3

"Defining ECE as a profession: Early childhood teachers and caregivers are part of a large and growing body of professionals."

COMPETENCY: Professionalism

AGE GROUP: Preschool

CRITICAL THINKING QUESTIONS:

1. Do you see yourself as a professional? Why or why not?

2. How do the characteristics on the video clip compare with the themes of the text?

in authentic ways to young children. We prepare children to live successfully by embracing the willingness to change while at the same time holding to our beliefs of personal choice, equality, and opportunity.

Early childhood professionals need some guidelines as they decide, each moment, every day, through a year, how to teach. The National Association for the Education of Young Children (NAEYC) has two helpful resources. The first, built from in-depth study of Developmentally Appropriate Practices, is known as the "Mariner's Star." It is depicted in Figure 15-8. The second is the NAEYC Code of Ethics; we have included it as Appendix A. We must be certain that we respect and celebrate the uniqueness of each child and the values of others.

Child Advocacy

Teachers are, by definition, advocates for children. They dedicate themselves to providing a better future for America's children.

With the issues of diversity, distribution of resources, money, and educational reform of such immediate concern, teachers need to understand the forces that affect how these issues are resolved. Teachers will have to educate themselves about the political process. They will need to know the rules and regulations regarding public funding sources. It is important to know how monies are allocated and with whom to work to affect the decisions regarding education. By being acquainted with legislation, teachers can rally support for bills that will help children, families, and schools.

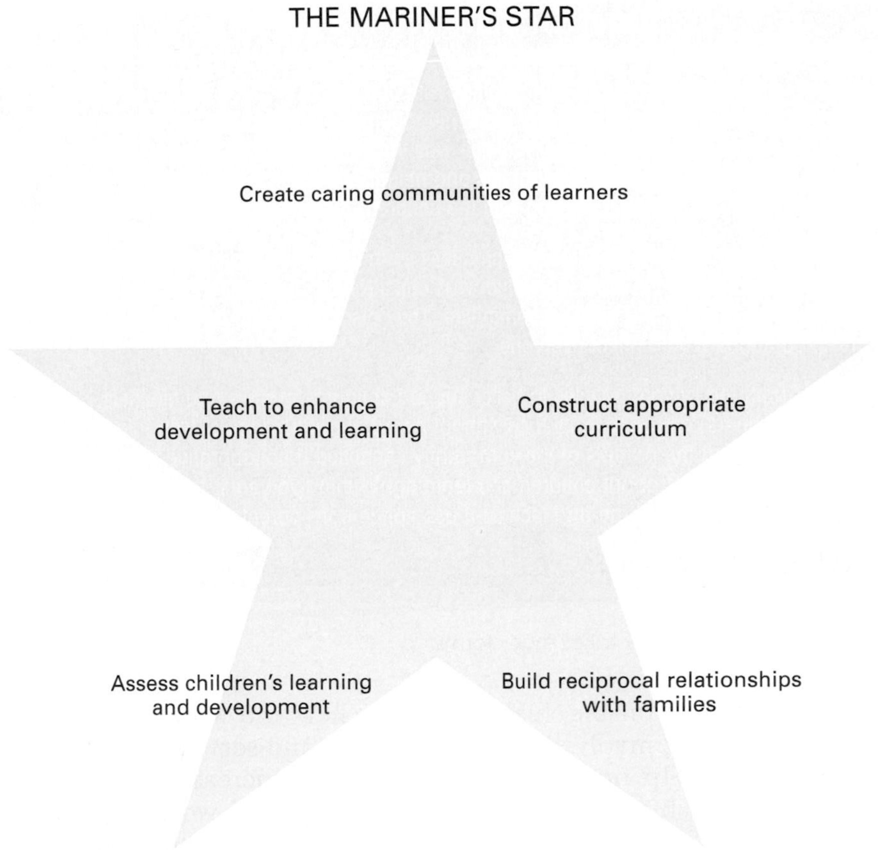

THE MARINER'S STAR

Create caring communities of learners

Teach to enhance development and learning

Construct appropriate curriculum

Assess children's learning and development

Build reciprocal relationships with families

FIGURE 15-8 Five big ideas for effective practice; look up to the star and look within yourself (Hyson, 2000, and NAEYC, 1999).

Teachers have long kept out of the political process. But they have not been immune from its effects. As teachers we must become informed to increase our power in the political and financial arenas of daily life. Just as we encourage children to help themselves, we must support each other in taking the initiative for our own profession's well-being. It was just such a coalition and coordinated effort among many people in child advocacy that secured the passage of the Child Care and Development Block Grants in 1990, the first such legislation to pass Congress in 20 years. Large-scale cooperation increased significantly the political success of that bill on behalf of all children.

Every teacher can become a child advocate. By working for children and children's services, teachers advocate for themselves as well. There are different kinds of advocacy; look at Figure 15-9 and see where you fit in. By finding your voice and keeping focused, you express your commitment and make change for children more likely to be successful. See Figure 15-9 for several ways to engage in advocacy.

"You have chosen to enter the nation's most powerful profession. You will be the caretakers, educators, and teachers of your nation's future: our children" (Edelman, 2000). Jonah Edelman, executive director of Stand for Children, leads a grassroots membership that advocates for children to become a higher priority in our public agencies and our lives. Begun in 1996 by the Children's Defense Fund, it challenges us to become effective advocates. How can you take these steps?

1. Make a personal commitment.
2. Keep informed.
3. Know the process.
4. Express your views.
5. Let others know.
6. Be visible.
7. Show appreciation.
8. Watch the implementation.
9. Build rapport and trust.
10. Educate your legislators.

It seems sometimes as if our society has arranged its priorities to put making a living first,

Different Kinds of Child Advocacy

Personal advocacy: Sharing personal views and philosophies with others.
Example: "Maria was concerned about the safety of the neighborhood playground. While pushing her toddler on the swing, she mentioned to the mother next to her that she was frustrated by the litter in the park including broken glass in the sandbox. The two women agreed to ask other parents and neighbors to come back the next day with trash bags and gloves to pick up litter while taking turns playing with the children" (Robinson & Stark, 2002).

Public policy advocacy: Influencing public policies and practices so that they are more responsive to children.
Example: Frustrated with changes the state legislature was considering, the local child care planning council sent a letter to state legislators and the chair of the funding committee. They also attended a hearing to offer testimony about how the allocation of preschool funds would affect everyone.

Private-sector advocacy: Changing private policies to better support children, families and teachers.
Example: A group of teachers approached its local school board about the lack of technology in the schools. They talked to local businesses and the parents of the community, identified a collaborative committee of all three groups, and began volunteering their expertise about children and learning. Within two years, the school had a list of needs and priorities, has received donations of time and technical assistance from parents, and received a grant for computers in the classrooms.

FIGURE 15-9 Early childhood advocacy takes many forms.

making more money second, and raising children a distant third place. By getting involved, early childhood educators could help our societies make child-friendly choices, which help today's children who will be tomorrow's parents. The

How do adults become advocates to ensure a fulfilling life for children in the 21st century?

teacher who works to ensure high-quality programs and services for children and their families also increases the likelihood of achieving the improved working conditions, professional opportunities, and public recognition that the field of early childhood education so richly deserves. Every day, we open our doors to young children by the millions. As we do, we are influencing the course of our nations in the 21st century. Consider this: A child born in 2007 will be a voting adult by 2025, and may live until the end of the century. We are teaching the children of the future!

Is this profession a worthwhile one? The early years are a special time of life, and those who work with young children might reflect on the following aspects of professionalism:

- *Sense of identity.* Early childhood professionals see themselves as caregivers who strive to educate the whole child, taking into consideration the body, the mind, and the heart and soul (see Chapter 1).

- *Purpose to engage in developmentally appropriate practices (DAP).* Quality care and education calls for blending child development and learning the strengths, interests, and needs of each child, and the social and cultural contexts in which children live (see Chapter 2).

- *Commitment to ethical teaching and to child advocacy.* Being a professional means behaving with a child's best interests in mind, keeping confidentiality when discussing issues in the classroom and about families, upholding a code of ethics, and taking themselves and their work seriously (see Chapter 5 and Appendix A).

● *Participation in the work as a legitimate livelihood.* The people who provide care and education to young children deserve wages and working conditions that are worthy of their efforts.

Ours is a profession that is constantly growing, branching out in many directions and ready to meet emerging challenges in flexible, innovative ways. We have professional organizations to guide us. The National Association for the Education of Young Children (NAEYC) is the largest professional organization. ACEI (Association for Childhood Education International) includes both preschool and elementary school. Children's Defense Fund (CDF) is a lobbying organization begun in 1973 by Marian Wright Edelman to advocate for children, particularly addressing the needs of poor and minority children and those with disabilities. All these efforts have resulted in important improvements in the status of children, and they have begun to outline standards and practices for the people who call themselves early childhood professionals.

SUMMARY

How might we approach the future as we start this new century? By reflecting on our past and looking closely at the present, we are reminded of several important factors that illuminate today's issues:

1. Out of the past, we create a vision of the future. A backward glance along the timeline shows us that today we have a living, viable organism: a growing comprehensive vision of the field of early childhood; a growing definition of what early childhood means; a growing collaboration of early childhood professionals from all walks of life; a growing involvement in the education reform movement; a growing system of early childhood programs to serve the families of the 21st century; and a growing sense of our own effectiveness as advocates.

2. The ultimate goal seems timeless but bears frequent repetition. Our aim is to help all children learn so that they can live full and satisfying lives, to help them develop their talents and capabilities so

What is our vision of the future for these children?

that they are prepared for the challenges and responsibilities of adult life.

3. Today's children are learning in a new century. The growing cultural diversity and global connectedness provides rich opportunities and new challenges from which to learn. Learning about the values and attributes of other cultures through meaningful and accurate experience becomes an imperative agenda for the children, families, and early childhood professionals of the 21st century.

What do You Think?

1. Why do you think child care workers have low salaries? How can you work to change these conditions?

2. Is it possible for child care centers to provide quality programs at the same time they pay fair wages and work benefits? How?

3. What can you say to parents who ask what you teach their child? How can you respond to their insistence on teaching children to read and print before kindergarten?

4. What would you do if you suspected that a child in your center was being seriously neglected or abused?

5. What can you say to help children handle separation and divorce? How will you deal with *both* parents?

6. What does the phrase "It takes a village to raise a child" mean in your program? How could that adage be applied to your community?

7. What can you do to support diversity while building a classroom community of common goals?

8. What do you do when children say "No boys (girls) allowed"? How will you include a new child with little English proficiency into your program? How do you respond when someone is called a "sissy"? Do you fully include children with special needs?

9. How do you think the education reform movement will affect your community? An early childhood program you know or work in?

10. What changes in AIDS statistics and research have occurred since this text was published? What other health issues lie ahead?

11. Select one of the pioneers discussed in this book, and describe how that person had an impact on the reform movements of the times; compare the issue and its resolution with today's reform movement. What issues do you see repeated over time?

KEY TERMS

ethic of social reform

importance of childhood

child abuse

child neglect

accreditation

social capital

racist

classist

sexist

ethnocentric

demographics

attitude crystallization

cultural pluralism

REFERENCES

Ethic of Social Reform

Child Care

Children's Defense Fund. (2005). *The state of America's Children*. Washington, DC: Author.

Costs, Quality and Child Outcomes Study Team. (1995). *Cost, quality and child outcomes in child care centers, executive summary*. Denver: Economics Department, University of Colorado at Denver.

Galinsky, E., Howe, C., Cantos, S., & Schinn, M. (1994). *The study of children in family child care and relative care: Highlight of findings*. New York: Families and Work Institute.

Hofferth, S. (1994). Bringing parents and employers back. In *The implications of new finding for child care policy*. Washington, DC: Urban Institute.

Kagan, S. L., & Neuman, M. J. (1997, September). Highlights of the Quality 2000 Initiative: Not by chance. *Young Children*, pp. 54–62.

Neugebauer, R. (2002, May). Continuing demand projected for child care. *Child care information exchange*, pp. 34–36.

Peisner-Feinberg, E. S., Burchinal, M. R., Clifford, R. M., Culkin, M. L., Howes, C., Kagain, S. L., Yazejian, N., Byler, P., Rustici, J., & Zelazo. J. (1999). *The children of the cost, quality and outcomes study go to school: Technical report*. Chapel Hill: University of North Carolina at Chapel Hill, Frank Porter Graham Child Development Center.

The Children's Foundation. (2001). *Family child care licensing summary data*.

U.S. Census Bureau. (1999, October). *School enrollment in the United States—Social and economic characteristics of students*. Washington, DC: Author.

U.S. Department of Education. (2001). *National household education survey*. Washington, DC: Author.

Whitebook, M., Sakai, L., Gerber, E., & Howes, C. (2001). *Then and now: Changes in child care staffing, 1994–2000*. Washington, DC: Center for the Child Care Workforce.

Education Reform

Committee for Economic Development. (2005). *Preschool for all. Executive Summary*.

Hyson, M.[ed.] (2003). *Preparing early childhood professionals: NAEYC's standards for programs*. Washington, DC: NAEYC.

National Association of State Boards of Education. (1988). *Right from the start*. Alexandria, VA: The report of the NABE Task Force on Early Childhood Education.

U.S. Department of Education. (2001). *The No Child Left Behind Act of 2001*. Executive Summary and Fact Sheet. Washington, DC: United States Department of Education.

The Importance of Childhood

Childhood Stress

Brazelton, T. B., & Greenspan, S. D. (2000, March). The irreducible needs of children. *Young Children*, pp. 6–13.

Child Abuse and Neglect and AIDS

Centers for Disease Control and Prevention. (1999). *AIDS surveillance by race/ethnicity*. Atlanta, GA: Author.

Children's Defense Fund. (2005). *The state of America's Children*. Washington, DC: Author.

Lung, C., & Daro, D. (1996). *Current trends in child abuse reporting and fatalities: The results of the 1995 annual fifty-state survey*. Chicago: National Committee to Prevent Child Abuse.

National Association for the Education of Young Children. (1997, March). *Position statement on the prevention of child abuse in early childhood programs and the responsibilities of early childhood professionals to prevent child abuse*, pp. 42–46. Washington, DC: Author.

U.S. Department of Health and Human Services. (1998). *Child sexual abuse prevention—Tips to parents*. Washington, DC: Author.

U.S. Department of Health and Human Services. (2002). *National Child Abuse and Neglect Data System: Summary of Key Findings from Calendar Year 2000*. Washington, DC: Author.

Wang, C. T., & Daro, D. (1998). *Current trends in child abuse reporting and fatalities: The results of the 1997 annual fifty state survey*. Chicago: National Committee to Prevent Child Abuse.

Poverty

Casey Foundation. (2005). *Kids Count Data Book*, Annie E. Casey Foundation.

Center for Children and Families (2000). *"Growing Up in Poverty" Project*. New York: Teachers College, Columbia University.

Children's Defense Fund. (2000). *The state of America's children: Yearbook 2000*. Washington, DC: Author.

Children's Defense Fund. (2002). *The state children in America's union*. Washington, DC: Author.

National Commission on Children. (1990). *Survey of parents and children*, AFDA Data Set No. 19, www.socio.com.

Family Support

Brazelton, T. B. (1989, February 13). Working parents. *Newsweek*.

Children's Defense Fund. (2002). *The state of children in America's union*. Washington, DC: Author.

Clarke-Stewart, K. A. (1989, January). Single-parent families: How bad for the children? *NEA Today*.

DelCampo, D., & DelCampo, R. (2006). *Taking Sides: Clashing Views in Childhood and Society* (6ed.). Dubuque, IA: McGraw-Hill. "Issue 7: Does Divorce Create Long-Term Negative Effects for Children?"

Elkind, D. (1991, September). The family and education in the postmodern world. *Momentum*.

Wallerstein, J. (2002). *The Unexpected Legacy of Divorce*.

Transmitting Values

Television and Other Media

Carter, B. (1991, May 1). Children's TV, where boys are king. *New York Times*.

Center for Media Literacy. (1993, August). *Beyond blame: Challenging violence in the media: Report from the American Psychological Association's Commission on Violence and Youth in America*.

DelCampo, D. S., & DelCampo R. L. (2006). *Taking Sides: Clashing Views in Childhood and Society* (6th ed.). Dubuque, IA: McGraw-Hill. "Issue 8: Is Television Violence Viewing Harmful for Children?"

Johnson, M. O. (1996, April). Television violence and its effect on children. *Journal of Pediatric Nursing*, 11(2).

Levin, D. (1998). *Remote control children?* Washington, DC: National Association for the Education of Young Children.

Minow, N. (1991, June 19). Worth noting. Address to commemorate 30th anniversary of his "vast wasteland" speech. *Education Week*.

National Association for the Education of Young Children. (1990). *Media violence and children*. Washington, DC: Author.

Nielsen Report on Television. (1989). New York, NY: Nielsen Media Research.

Violence and Disaster

Adults and Children Together Against Violence (ACT). (2002). *Violence prevention for families of young children*. Washington, DC: American Psychological Association.

American Academy for Child and Adolescent Psychiatry (1999, October). Facts for Families: Posttraumatic Stress Disorder, No. 70, www.aacap.org.

Carlsson-Paige, N., & Levin, D. (1987). *The war play dilemma*. New York: Teachers College.

Davis, L., & Keyser, J. (1997). Becoming the parent you want to be. NY: Broadway Books.

Farish, J. M. (1995). *When disaster strikes: Helping young children cope*. Washington, DC: NAEYC.

Greenman, J. (2001). *What happened to the world? Helping children cope in turbulent times*. The Dougy Center: National Center for Grieving Children and Families.

Groves, B. M., & Mazur, S. (1995, March). Shelter from the storm: Using the classroom to help children cope with violence. *Exchange*.

Hoot, J., & Roberson, G. (1994). Creating safer environments for children in the home, school and community. *Childhood Education*. Annual Theme.

Diversity

General

Bowman, B. T. (1991). *Educating language-minority children*. ERIC Digest, University of Illinois.

Multicultural

Armstrong, L. S. (1991, January 16). Racial ethnic prejudice still prevalent, survey finds. *Education Week*.

Children's Defense Fund. (2000). *The state of America's children: Yearbook 2000*. Washington, DC: Author.

Derman-Sparks, L. (1989). *Anti-bias curriculum*. Washington, DC: National Association for the Education of Young Children.

Frankenberg, E., Lee, C., & Orfield, G. (2003, January). *A multiracial society with segregated schools; are we losing the dream?* Cambridge, MA: The Civil Rights Project, Harvard University.

Hale, J. E. (1993). Culturally appropriate pedagogy and the African American child. In A. Gordon & K. B. Browne (Eds.), *Beginnings and beyond* (3rd ed.). Clifton Park, NY: Thomson Delmar Learning.

Hale, J. E. (2001). *Learning while black: Creating educational excellence for African American children*. Baltimore, MD: Johns Hopkins University Press.

Bilingual

Fillmore, L. W. (1991, June 19). A question for early-childhood programs: English first or families first? *Education Week*.

Immigrant

Children's Defense Fund. (2002). *The state of America's children: Leave no child behind*. Washington, DC: Author.

Takanishi, R. (2006). *Leveling the playing field: Supporting immigrant children from birth to eight. The Future of Children*. Princeton, NJ: Brookings Institute.

Inclusion

Child Care Law Center. (1994, November). *The ADA: A new way of thinking*. San Francisco, CA. Cruz, M. personal communication, 2001–02.

Class Differences

Children's Defense Fund. (2000). *The state of America's children: Yearbook 2000*. Washington, DC: Author.

Haycock, K. (1991, March). Reaching for the year 2000. *Childhood Education*.

Gender

American Association of University Women. (1992). *How schools short change girls*. Washington, DC: Author.

Grossman, H., & Grossman, S. H. (1994). *Gender issues in education*. Boston: Allyn & Bacon.

Lockheed, M., & Klein, S. (1985). Sex equity in classroom organization and climate. In S. Klein (Ed.). *Handbook for achieving sex equity through education*. Baltimore: Johns Hopkins Press.

Maccoby, E., & Jacklin, C. N. (1985, April). *Gender segregation in nursery school: Predictors and outcomes*. Paper presented to the National Society for Research in Child Development. Toronto.

Sadker, M., & Sadker, D. (1994). *Failing at fairness: How our schools cheat girls*. New York: Simon & Schuster.

Schlank, C. H., & Metzger, B. (1997). *Together and equal*. Boston, MA: Allyn & Bacon.

Sexuality

Corbett, S. (1993, March). A complicated bias. *Young Children*.

Friemann, B. B., O'Hara, H., & Settel, J. (1996, Fall). What heterosexual teachers need to know about homosexuality. *Childhood Education.*

Professionalism

Brazelton, T. B., & Greenspan, Stanley, I. (2000). *The irreducible needs of children: What every child must have to grow, learn, and flourish.* Cambridge, MA: Perseus Publishing.

Children's Defense Fund. (2001). *The state of America's children: Leave no child behind.* Washington, DC: Author.

Edelman, J. (2000). Take a stand for children, in Gordon & Browne, *Beginnings & Beyond* (5th ed.). Albany, NY: Thomson Delmar Learning.

Gronlund, G. (2006). *Make early learning standards come alive.* St. Paul, MN: Redleaf Press.

Hyson, M. (2000, November). Is it OK to have calendar time? Look up to the star . . . look within yourself. *Young Children, 55*(6).

NAEYC. (1999). *Tools for teaching developmentally appropriate practice—The leading edge in early childhood education* [videos]. Washington, DC: Author.

NAEYC. (2005). *Accreditation criteria and procedures of the National Academy of Early Childhood Programs.* Washington, DC: Author.

Robinson, A., & Stark, D. R. (2002). *Advocates in action: Making a difference for young children.* Washington, DC: NAEYC.

Snow, C. W., Teleki, J. K., & Reguero-de-Atiles, J. T. (1996, September). Child care center licensing standards in the United States: 1981 to 1995. *Young Children,* pp. 36–41.

HELPFUL WEB SITES

Adults & Children Together (ACT) Against Violence	http://www.ACTagainstviolence.org
American Academy of Pediatrics	http://www.aap.org
American Red Cross	http://www.redcross.org/disaster/masters/
Annie E. Casey Foundation/KidsCount	http://www.aecf.org
Center for the Child Care Workforce	http://www.ccw.org
Centers for Disease Control	http://www.cdc.gov
Child Maltreatment	http://www.acf.dhhs.gov
Child Statistics	http://www.childtrends.org
Child Welfare League of America	http://www.cwla.org
Children's Defense Fund	http://www.childrensdefensefund.org
Coping with Disaster	http://www.counselingforloss.com
Developmental Assets	http://www.search-institute.org
Divisions of HIV/AIDS Prevention	http://www.edc.gov/hiv
Educators for Social Responsibility	http://www.esrnational.org
Military Family Resource Center	http://www.mfrc.calib.com
National Association for the Education of Young Children	http://www.naeyc.org
National Center for Children Exposed to Violence	http://www.nccev.org
National Center for HIV, STD and TB Prevention	http://www.edc.gov/nchstp
National Clearinghouse on Child Abuse and Neglect	http://www.calib.com/nccanch
National Indian Child Welfare Association	http://www.nicwa.org
Prevent Child Abuse America	http://www.childabuse.org
Stand for Children	http://www.stand.org
U.S. Census Bureau	http://www.census.gov
U.S. Department of Education	http://www.ed.gov
U.S. Department of Health and Human Services	http://www.dhhs.gov

For more activities and information, visit our Web site at http://www.EarlyChildEd.delmar.com

Appendix A
NAEYC Code of Ethical Conduct

Preamble

NAEYC recognizes that many daily decisions required of those who work with young children are of a moral and ethical nature. The NAEYC Code of Ethical Conduct offers guidelines for responsible behavior and sets forth a common basis for resolving the principal ethical dilemmas encountered in early childhood care and education. The primary focus is on daily practice with children and their families in programs for children from birth through eight years of age, such as infant/toddler programs, preschools, child care centers, family child care homes, kindergartens, and primary classrooms. Many of the provisions also apply to specialists who do not work directly with children, including program administrators, parent and vocational educators, college professors, and child care licensing specialists.

Core Values

Standards of ethical behavior in early childhood care and education are based on commitment to core values that are deeply rooted in the history of our field. We have committed ourselves to

- Appreciating childhood as a unique and valuable stage of the human life cycle
- Basing our work with children on knowledge of child development
- Appreciating and supporting the close ties between the child and family
- Recognizing that children are best understood and supported in the context of family, culture, community, and society
- Respecting the dignity, worth, and uniqueness of each individual (child, family member, and colleague)
- Helping children and adults achieve their full potential in the context of relationships that are based on trust, respect, and positive regard

Conceptual Framework

The Code sets forth a conception of our professional responsibilities in four sections, each addressing an arena of professional relationships: (1) children, (2) families, (3) colleagues, and (4) community and society. Each section includes an introduction to the primary responsibilities of the early childhood practitioner in that arena, a set of ideals pointing in the direction of exemplary professional practice, and a set of principles defining practices that are required, prohibited, and permitted.

The ideals reflect the aspirations of practitioners. **The principles** are intended to guide conduct and assist practitioners in resolving ethical dilemmas encountered in the field. There is not necessarily a corresponding principle for each ideal. Both ideals and principles are intended to direct practitioners to those questions which, when responsibly answered, will provide the basis for conscientious decision-making. While the Code provides specific direction and suggestions for addressing some ethical dilemmas, many others will require the practitioner to combine the guidance of the Code with sound professional judgment.

The ideals and principles in this Code present a shared conception of professional responsibility that affirms our commitment to the core values of our field. The Code publicly acknowledges the responsibilities that we in the field have assumed and in so doing supports ethical behavior in our work. Practitioners who face ethical dilemmas are urged to seek guidance in the applicable parts of this Code and in the spirit that informs the whole.

Ethical Dilemmas Always Exist

Often, "the right answer"—the best ethical course of action to take is not obvious. There may be no readily apparent, positive way to handle a situation. One important value may contradict another. When we are caught "on the horns of a dilemma," it is our professional responsibility to consult with all relevant parties in seeking the most ethical course of action to take.

Section I: Ethical responsibilities to children

Childhood is a unique and valuable stage in the life cycle. Our paramount responsibility is to provide safe, healthy, nurturing, and responsive settings for children. We are committed to support children's development, respect individual differences, help children learn to live and work cooperatively, and promote health, self-awareness, competence, self-worth, and resiliency.

Ideals

I-1.1. To be familiar with the knowledge base of early childhood care and education and to keep current through continuing education and in-service training.

I-1.2. To base program practices upon current knowledge in the field of child development and related disciplines and upon particular knowledge of each child.

I-1.3. To recognize and respect the uniqueness and the potential of each child.

I-1.4. To appreciate the special vulnerability of children.

I-1.5. To create and maintain safe and healthy settings that foster children's social, emotional, intellectual, and physical development and that respect their dignity and their contributions.

I-1.6. To support the right of each child to play and learn in inclusive early childhood programs to the fullest extent consistent with the best interests of all involved. As with adults who are disabled in the larger community, children with disabilities are ideally served in the same settings in which they would participate if they did not have a disability.

I-1.7. To ensure that children with disabilities have access to appropriate and convenient support services and to advocate for the resources necessary to provide the most appropriate settings for all children.

Principles

P-1.1. Above all, we shall not harm children. We shall not participate in practices that are disrespectful, degrading, dangerous, exploitative, intimidating, emotionally damaging, or physically harmful to children. This principle has precedence over all others in this Code.

P-1.2. We shall not participate in practices that discriminate against children by denying benefits, giving special advantages, or excluding them from programs or activities on the basis of their race, ethnicity, religion, sex, national origin, language, ability, or the status, behavior, or beliefs of their parents. (This principle does not apply to programs that have a lawful mandate to provide services to a particular population of children.)

P-1.3. We shall involve all of those with relevant knowledge (including staff and parents) in decisions concerning a child.

P-1.4. For every child we shall implement adaptations in teaching strategies, learning environment, and curricula, consult with the family, and seek recommendations from appropriate specialists to maximize the potential of the child to benefit from the program. If, after these efforts have been made to work with a child and family, the child does not appear to be benefiting from a program, or the child is seriously jeopardizing the ability of other children to benefit from the program, we shall communicate with the family and appropriate specialists to determine the child's current needs; identify the setting and services most suited to meeting these needs; and assist the family in placing the child in an appropriate setting.

P-1.5. We shall be familiar with the symptoms of child abuse, including physical, sexual, verbal, and emotional abuse, and neglect. We shall know and follow state laws and community procedures that protect children against abuse and neglect.

P-1.6. When we have reasonable cause to suspect child abuse or neglect, we shall report it to the appropriate community agency and follow up to ensure that appropriate action has been taken. When appropriate, parents or guardians will be informed that the referral has been made.

P-1.7. When another person tells us of a suspicion that a child is being abused or neglected, we shall assist that person in taking appropriate action to protect the child.

P-1.8. When a child protective agency fails to provide adequate protection for abused or neglected children, we acknowledge a collective ethical responsibility to work toward improvement of these services.

P-1.9. When we become aware of a practice or situation that endangers the health or safety of children, but has not been previously known to do so, we have an ethical responsibility to inform those who can remedy the situation and who can protect children from similar danger.

Section II: Ethical responsibilities to families

Families are of primary importance in children's development. (The term family may include others, besides parents, who are responsibly involved with the child.) Because the family and the early childhood practitioner have a common interest in the child's welfare, we acknowledge a primary responsibility to bring about collaboration between the home and school in ways that enhance the child's development.

Ideals

I-2.1. To develop relationships of mutual trust with families we serve.

I-2.2. To acknowledge and build upon strengths and competencies as we support families in their task of nurturing children.

I-2.3. To respect the dignity of each family and its culture, language, customs, and beliefs.

I-2.4. To respect families' childrearing values and their right to make decisions for their children.

I-2.5. To interpret each child's progress to parents within the framework of a developmental perspective and to help families understand and appreciate the value of developmentally appropriate early childhood practices.

I-2.6. To help family members improve their understanding of their children and to enhance their skills as parents.

I-2.7. To participate in building support networks for families by providing them with opportunities to interact with program staff, other families, community resources, and professional services.

Principles

P-2.1. We shall not deny family members access to their child's classroom or program setting.

P-2.2. We shall inform families of program philosophy, policies, and personnel qualifications, and explain why we teach as we do, which should be in accordance with our ethical responsibilities to children (see Section I).

P-2.3. We shall inform families of, and when appropriate, involve them in, policy decisions.

P-2.4. We shall involve families in significant decisions affecting their child.

P-2.5. We shall inform the family of accidents involving their child, of risks such as exposures to contagious disease that may result in infection, and of occurrences that might result in emotional stress.

P-2.6. To improve the quality of early childhood care and education, we shall cooperate with qualified child development researchers. Families shall be fully informed of any proposed research projects involving their children and shall have the opportunity to give or withhold consent without penalty. We shall not permit or participate in research that could in any way hinder the education, development, or well-being of children.

P-2.7. We shall not engage in or support exploitation of families. We shall not use our relationship with a family for private advantage or personal gain, or enter into relationships with family members that might impair our effectiveness in working with children.

P-2.8. We shall develop written policies for the protection of confidentiality and the disclosure of children's records. These policy documents shall be made available to all program personnel and families. Disclosure of children's records beyond family members, program personnel, and consultants having an obligation of confidentiality shall require familial consent (except in cases of abuse or neglect).

P-2.9. We shall maintain confidentiality and shall respect the family's right to privacy, refraining from disclosure of confidential information and intrusion into family life. However, when we have reason to believe that a child's welfare is at risk, it is permissible to share confidential information with agencies and individuals who may be able to intervene in the child's interest.

P-2.10. In cases where family members are in conflict, we shall work openly, sharing our observations of the child, to help all parties involved make informed decisions. We shall refrain from becoming an advocate for one party.

P-2.11. We shall be familiar with and appropriately use community resources and professional services that support families. After a referral has been made, we shall follow up to ensure that services have been appropriately provided.

Section III: Ethical responsibilities to colleagues

In a caring, cooperative work place, human dignity is respected, professional satisfaction is promoted, and positive relationships are modeled. Based upon our core values, our primary responsibility in this arena is to establish and maintain settings and relationships that support productive work and meet professional needs. The same ideals that apply to children are inherent in our responsibilities to adults.

A. Responsibilities to coworkers

Ideals

I-3A.1. To establish and maintain relationships of respect, trust, and cooperation with coworkers.

I-3A.2. To share resources and information with coworkers.

I-3A.3. To support coworkers in meeting their professional needs and in their professional development.

P-3A.4. To accord coworkers due recognition of professional achievement.

Principles

P-3A.1. When we have concern about the professional behavior of a coworker, we shall first let that person know of our concern, in a way that shows respect for personal dignity and for the diversity to be found among staff members, and then attempt to resolve the matter collegially.

P-3A.2. We shall exercise care in expressing views regarding the personal attributes or professional conduct of coworkers. Statements should be based on firsthand knowledge and relevant to the interests of children and programs.

B. Responsibilities to employers

Ideals

I-3B.1. To assist the program in providing the highest quality of service.

I-3B.2. To do nothing that diminishes the reputation of the program in which we work unless it is violating laws and regulations designed to protect children or the provisions of this Code.

Principles

P-3B.1. When we do not agree with program policies, we shall first attempt to effect change through constructive action within the organization

P-3B.2. We shall speak or act on behalf of an organization only when authorized. We shall take care to acknowledge when we are speaking for the organization and when we are expressing a personal judgment.

P-3B.3. We shall not violate laws or regulations designed to protect children and shall take appropriate action consistent with this Code when aware of such violations.

C. Responsibilities to employees

Ideals

I-3C.1. To promote policies and working conditions that foster mutual respect, competence, well-being, and positive self-esteem in staff members.

I-3C.2. To create a climate of trust and candor that will enable staff to speak and act in the best interests of children, families, and the field of early childhood care and education.

I-3C.3. To strive to secure equitable compensation (salary and benefits) for those who work with or on behalf of young children.

Principles

P-3C.1. In decisions concerning children and programs, we shall appropriately utilize the education, training, experience, and expertise of staff members.

P-3C.2. We shall provide staff members with safe and supportive working conditions that permit them to carry out their responsibilities, timely and nonthreatening evaluation procedures, written grievance procedures, constructive feedback, and opportunities for continuing professional development and advancement.

P-3C.3. We shall develop and maintain comprehensive written personnel policies that define program standards and, when applicable, that specify the extent to which employees are accountable for their conduct outside the work place. These policies shall be given to new staff members and shall be available for review by all staff members.

P-3C.4. Employees who do not meet program standards shall be informed of areas of concern and, when possible, assisted in improving their performance.

P-3C.5. Employees who are dismissed shall be informed of the reasons for their termination. When a dismissal is for cause, justification must be based on evidence of inadequate or inappropriate behavior that is accurately documented, current, and available for the employee to review.

P-3C.6. In making evaluations and recommendations, judgments shall be based on fact and relevant to the interests of children and programs.

P-3C.7. Hiring and promotion shall be based solely on a person's record of accomplishment and ability to carry out the responsibilities of the position.

P-3C.8. In hiring, promotion, and provision of training, we shall not participate in any form of discrimination based on race, ethnicity, religion, gender, national origin, culture, disability, age, or sexual preference. We shall be familiar with and observe laws and regulations that pertain to employment discrimination.

Section IV: Ethical responsibilities to community and society

Early childhood programs operate within a context of an immediate community made up of families and other institutions concerned with children's welfare. Our responsibilities to the community are to provide programs that meet its needs, to cooperate with agencies and professions that share responsibility for children, and to develop needed programs that are not currently available. Because the larger society has a measure of responsibility for the welfare and protection of children, and because of our specialized expertise in child development, we acknowledge an obligation to serve as a voice for children everywhere.

Ideals

I.4.1. To provide the community with high-quality (age and individually appropriate, and culturally and socially sensitive) education/care programs and services.

I-4.2. To promote cooperation among agencies and interdisciplinary collaboration among professions concerned with the welfare of young children, their families, and their teachers.

I-4.3. To work, through education, research, and advocacy, toward an environmentally safe world in which all children receive adequate health care, food, and shelter, are nurtured, and live free from violence.

I-4.4. To work, through education, research, and advocacy, toward a society in which all young children have access to high-quality education/care programs.

I-4.5. To promote knowledge and understanding of young children and their needs. To work toward greater social acknowledgment of children's rights and greater social acceptance of responsibility for their well-being.

I-4.6. To support policies and laws that promote the well-being of children and families, and to oppose those that impair their well-being. To participate in developing policies and laws that are needed, and to cooperate with other individuals and groups in these efforts.

I-4.7. To further the professional development of the field of early childhood care and education and to strengthen its commitment to realizing its core values as reflected in this Code.

Principles

P-4.1.   We shall communicate openly and truthfully about the nature and extent of services that we provide.

P-4.2.   We shall not accept or continue to work in positions for which we are personally unsuited or professionally unqualified. We shall not offer services that we do not have the competence, qualifications, or resources to provide.

P-4.3.   We shall be objective and accurate in reporting the knowledge upon which we base our program practices.

P-4.4.   We shall cooperate with other professionals who work with children and their families.

P-4.5.   We shall not hire or recommend for employment any person whose competence, qualifications, or character makes him or her unsuited for the position.

P-4.6.   We shall report the unethical or incompetent behavior of a colleague to a supervisor when informal resolution is not effective.

P-4.7.   We shall be familiar with laws and regulations that serve to protect the children in our programs.

P-4.8.   We shall not participate in practices which are in violation of laws and regulations that protect the children in our programs.

P-4.9.   When we have evidence that an early childhood program is violating laws or regulations protecting children, we shall report it to persons responsible for the program. If compliance is not accomplished within a reasonable time, we will report the violation to appropriate authorities who can be expected to remedy the situation.

P-4.10.   When we have evidence that an agency or a professional charged with providing services to children, families, or teachers is failing to meet its obligations, we acknowledge a collective ethical responsibility to report the problem to appropriate authorities or to the public.

P-4.11.   When a program violates or requires its employees to violate this Code, it is permissible, after fair assessment of the evidence, to disclose the identity of that program.

Statement of commitment

As an individual who works with young children, I commit myself to furthering the values of early childhood education as they are reflected in the NAEYC Code of Ethical Conduct.

To the best of my ability I will

- Ensure that programs for young children are based on current knowledge of child development and early childhood education.
- Respect and support families in their task of nurturing children.
- Respect colleagues in early childhood education and support them in maintaining the NAEYC Code of Ethical Conduct.
- Serve as an advocate for children, their families, and their teachers in community and society.
- Maintain high standards of professional conduct.
- Recognize how personal values, opinions, and biases can affect professional judgment.
- Be open to new ideas and be willing to learn from the suggestions of others.
- Continue to learn, grow, and contribute as a professional.
- Honor the ideals and principles of the NAEYC Code of Ethical Conduct.

This document is an official position statement of the National Association for the Education of Young Children. This statement may be purchased as a brochure, and the Statement of Commitment is available as a poster suitable for framing. See our catalog for ordering information. © 1998 National Association for the Education of Young Children

Appendix B

NAEYC Position Statement: Responding to Linguistic and Cultural Diversity—Recommendations for Effective Early Childhood Education

Authors' Note: The Position Statement was adopted by NAEYC in November, 1995. The following passage was excerpted by the authors (November 1998) to give readers a sense of the position statement. It is strongly recommended that the Statement be read in its entirety. It is published in the January 1996 edition of Young Children.

INTRODUCTION

The children and families in early childhood programs reflect the ethnic, cultural, and linguistic diversity of the nation. The nation's children all deserve an early childhood education that is responsive to their families, communities, and racial, ethnic, and cultural backgrounds. For young children to develop and learn optimally, the early childhood professional must be prepared to meet their diverse developmental, cultural, linguistic, and educational needs. Early childhood educators face the challenge of how best to respond to those needs. . . .

Linguistic and culturally diverse is an educational term used by the U.S. Department of Education to define children enrolled in educational programs who are either non-English-proficient (NEP) or limited-English-proficient (LEP). Educators use this phrase, linguistically and culturally diverse, to identify children from homes and communities where English is not the primary language of communication. For the purposes of this statement, the phrase will be used in a similar manner. . . .

NAEYC's position. NAEYC's goal is to build support for equal access to high-quality educational programs that recognize and promote all aspects of children's development and learning, establish all children to become competent, successful, and socially responsible adults. . . . For the optimal development and learning of all children, educators must accept the legitimacy of children's home language, respect (hold in high regard) and value (esteem, appreciate) the home culture, and promote and encourage the active involvement and support of all families, including extended and nontraditional family units. . . .

The challenges. Historically, our nation has tended to regard differences, especially language differences, as cultural handicaps rather than cultural resources. "Although most Americans are reluctant to say it publicly, many are anxious about the changing racial and ethnic composition of the country." As the early childhood profession transforms its thinking,

The challenge for early childhood educators is to become more knowledgeable about how to relate to children and families whose linguistic or cultural background is different from their own.

RECOMMENDATIONS FOR A RESPONSIVE LEARNING ENVIRONMENT

The issue of home language and its importance to young children is also relevant for children who speak English but come from different cultural backgrounds, for example, speakers of English who have dialects, such as people from Appalachia or other regions having distinct patterns of speech, speakers of Black English, or second- and third-generation speakers of English who maintain the dominant accent of their heritage language. Although this position statement basically responds to children who are from homes in which English is not the dominant language, the recommendations provided may be helpful when working with children who come from diverse cultural backgrounds, even when they speak only English. The overall goal for early childhood professionals, however, is to provide every child, including children who are linguistically and culturally diverse, with a responsive learning environment. The following recommendations help achieve this goal:

A. Recommendations for working with children

- Recognize that all children are cognitively, linguistically, and emotionally connected to the language and culture of their home.
- Acknowledge that children can demonstrate their knowledge and capabilities in many ways.
- Understand that without comprehensive input, second-language learning can be difficult.

B. Recommendations for working with families

- Actively involve parents and families in the early learning program and setting.

633

- Encourage and assist all parents in becoming knowledgeable about the cognitive value for children of knowing more than one language, and provide them with strategies to support, maintain, and preserve home-language learning.
- Recognize that parents and families must rely on caregivers and educators to honor and support their children in the cultural values and norms of the home.

C. Recommendations for professional preparation

- Provide early childhood educators with professional preparation and development in the areas of culture, language, and diversity.
- Recruit and support early childhood educators who are trained in languages other than English.

D. Recommendations for programs and practice

- Recognize that children can and will acquire the use of English even when their home language is used and respected.

- Support and preserve home language usage.
- Develop and provide alternative and creative strategies for young children's learning.

SUMMARY

Early childhood educators can best help linguistic and culturally diverse children and their families by acknowledging and responding to the importance of the child's home language and culture. Administrative support for bilingualism as a goal is necessary within the educational setting. Educational practices should focus on "school culture" while preserving and respecting the diversity of the home language and culture that each child brings to the early learning setting. Early childhood professionals and families must work together to achieve high-quality care and education for *all* children.

Appendix C
Early Childhood Organizational Resources

ACEI
Association for Childhood Education
    International
17904 Georgia Avenue, Suite 215
Olney, MD 20832-2277
1-800-423-3563
http://www.acci.org

ACT
Action for Children's Television
46 Austin Street
Newtonville, MA 02160

American Academy of Pediatrics
141 Northwest Point Blvd.
Elk Grove Village, IL 60007
1-800-433-9016
http://www.aap.org

AMS
American Montessori Society
175 Fifth Avenue
New York, NY 10010

Canadian Association for Young Children
252 Bloor Street, W, Suite 12-155
Toronto, Ontario M5S 1V5
Canada

CDF
Children's Defense Fund
25 E Street, NW
Washington, DC 20001
1-800-424-2460
http://www.childrensdefense.org

Center for Child Care Workforce
733 15th Street NW, Suite 1037
Washington, DC 20005-2112
202-737-7700
http://www.ccw.org

Child Care Action Campaign
330 Seventh Avenue, 14th Floor
New York, NY 10001-5010
212-239-0138
http://www.childcareaction.org

CLAS
Culturally and Linguistically Appropriate
    Services
Early Childhood Research Institute
51 Gerty Drive
Champaign, IL 61820-7498
http://www.clas.uiuc.edu

Council for Early Childhood Professional
    Recognition
2460 16th Street, NW
Washington, DC 20009-3575
800-424-4310
http://www.cdacouncil.org

CWLA
Child Welfare League of America, Inc.
440 First Street, NW, Suite 310
Washington, DC 20001-2085
202-638-2952
http://www.cwla.org

DEC/CEC
Division for Early Childhood Council for
    Exceptional Children
1380 Lawrence St., Suite 650
Denver CO 80204
303-556-3328
http://www.dec-sped.org

Ecumenical Child Care Network
8765 W. Higgins Rd., Suite 405
Chicago, IL 60631
312-693-4040

Educational (Gender) Equity Concepts
1114 East 32nd Street
New York, NY 10017

Educators for Social Responsibility
23 Garden Street
Cambridge, MA 02138

ERIC/ECE
Educational Clearinghouse on Elementary
   and Early Childhood Education
Children's Research Center
51 Gerty Dr.
Champaign, IL 61820
217-333-1386
http://www.ericeece.org

Families and Work Institute
330 Seventh Avenue, 14th Floor
New York, NY 10001
212-465-2044
http://www.familiesandwork.org

High/Scope Educational Resource Foundation
600 North River Street
Ypsilanti, MI 48197
734-485-2000
http://www.highscope.org

I Am Your Child
P.O. Box 15605
Beverly Hills, CA 90209
310-285-2385
http://www.iamyourchild.org

International Nanny Association
900 Haddon Avenue, Suite 438
Collingswood, NJ 08108
http://www.nanny.org

NAEYC
National Association for the Education
   of Young Children
National Academy of Early Childhood
   Programs
National Institute for Early Childhood
   Professional Development
1509 16th Street, NW
Washington, DC 20036-1426
1-800-424-8777
http://www.naeyc.org/naeyc

National Association for Family Child Care
5202 Pinemont Dr.
Salt Lake City, UT 84123
800-359-3817
http://www.nafcc.org

National Association of Child Care Resource
   and Referral Agencies
1319 F Street, NW, Suite 500
Washington, DC 20004-1106
202-393-5501
http://www.naccrra.org

National Black Child Development Institute
1101 15th Street, NW, Suite 900
Washington, DC 20005
202-833-2220
http://www.nbcdi.org

National Coalition for Campus Children's
   Centers
119 Schindler Education Center
University of Northern Iowa
Cedar Falls, IA 50614
319-273-3113
http://www.campuschildren.org

National Head Start Association
1651 Prince St.
Alexandria, VA 22314
703-739-0875
http://www.nhsa.org

National Institute on Out-Of-School Time
Wellesley College
106 Central Street
Wellesley, MA 02181
781-283-2547
http://www.niost.org

National Latino Children's Institute
320 El Paso Street
San Antonio, TX 78207
210-228-9997
http://www.nlci.org

Office of Head Start
Administration for Children and Families
370 L' Enfant Promenade, S.W.
Washington, DC 20447
http://www.acf.hhs.gov/programs/hsb

OMEP
Organisation Mondiale pour l'Education
   Prescolaire
School of Education
Indiana State University
Terre Haute, IN 47809

Prevent Child Abuse America
200 South Michigan Avenue, 17th Floor
Chicago, IL 60604
312-663-3520
http://www.preventchildabuse.org

Reggio Children USA
1341 G Street, NW, Suite 400
Washington, DC 20005
202-265-9090

SECA
Southern Early Childhood Association
P.O. Box 55930
Little Rock, AR 72215
800-305-7322
http://www.seca50.org

SRCD
Society for Research in Child Development
Univ. of Michigan
505 East Huron, Suite 301
Ann Arbor, MI 48104
734-998-6578
http://www.srcd.org

Stand For Children
1420 Columbia Rd., NW, 3rd Floor
Washington, DC 20009
202-234-0095
http://www.stand.org

WestEd Laboratory for Educational Research
    and Development
Center for Child and Family Studies
180 Harbour Drive, Suite 112
Sausalito, CA 94965

Zero to Three/National Center for Infants,
    Toddlers, and Families
2000 M St., NW, Suite 200
Washington, DC 20036
202-638-1144
http://www.zerotothree.org

Glossary

Aberrant. Deviating from the usual or natural type; abnormal, atypical.

Academic Redshirting. The practice of postponing children's entry into kindergarten in order to allow another year for growth and maturity.

Accommodation. A concept in Piaget's cognitive theory as one of two processes people use to learn and incorporate new information; the person adjusts what is already known to "accommodate" new learning. Children usually will change their way of thinking into a "schema," once they see that their usual ways do not take new information into account; they then will add new thought patterns to handle the new knowledge.

Accountability. The quality or state of being answerable to someone or of being responsible for explaining exact conditions; schools often must give specific account of their actions to a funding agency to assure the group that the funds and operation of the school are being handled properly.

Accreditation. A system of voluntary evaluation for early childhood centers. The goal is to improve the quality of care and education provided for young children. Accreditation is administered by the National Academy, a branch of the National Association for the Education of Young Children.

Active Listening. A child guidance technique of reflecting back to the speaker what the listener thinks has been said.

Activity Centers. Similar to learning centers and interest areas; areas in a classroom or yard that are designed and arranged for various activities to take place. An early childhood setting will offer several centers, or stations, that are based on both children's interests and what the staff hopes for them to learn in class.

Advocate. One who maintains, defends, or pleads the cause of another; in early childhood terms, an advocate is someone who furthers the principles and issues of the field by speaking to others about such issues.

Aesthetics. Sensitivity to what is beautiful; the study of beauty.

After-School Care. Programs designed to care for children after the regular academic school day.

Age-Level Characteristics. Those features of children's development and behavior that are most common among a given age group.

Androgynous. Having to do with either sex; associated with both the male and the female identity, behavior, etc.

Anecdotal Notes. Notes taken in the form of a short and amusing or interesting story about a real incident or person.

Anti-bias. A phrase describing the development of curriculum that emphasizes an inclusive look at people and problems, extending the tenets of multicultural education and pluralism.

Arbitrary. A decision based on individual judgment or on a whim.

Articulation. The manner in which sounds and words are actually spoken.

Asperger Syndrome. A developmental disorder linked to autism and characterized by a lack of social skills, poor concentration, self-absorption, and limited interests.

Assessment. An evaluation or determination of importance, disposition, or state of something or someone, such as in evaluating a child's skills, a teacher's effectiveness, or a classroom environment.

Assimilation. A concept in Piaget's cognitive theory as one of two processes people use to learn and incorporate new information; the person takes new information and puts it together with what is already known in order to "assimilate" the new information intellectually, such as when a toddler shakes a toy magnet first, as with all other toys, in order to get to know this new object. Children usually first try to put new experiences into the "schema," or categories, they already know and use.

Atelierista. A person trained in the arts who acts as a resource and teaches techniques and skills to children in the schools of Reggio Emilia, Italy.

Attachment/Attachment Behaviors. The relational bond that connects a child to another important person; feelings and behaviors of devotion or positive connection.

Attention-Deficit/Hyperactivity Disorder (ADHD). A condition affecting children and adults, making them prone to restlessness, anxiety, short attention spans, and impulsiveness.

Attitude Crystallization. To assume a definite, concrete form in one's attitudes; refers to the formation of a firm set of attitudes and behaviors about others' race, ethnicity, gender, and ability that may be prejudicial and difficult to change.

Authentic Assessment. The quantitative and qualitative study of a child's work, activity, and interactions that focuses on the whole child within the context of family, school, and community. Such assessment occurs in a child's natural settings in which the child is performing real tasks. Viewed as a process rather than an end, authentic assessment includes collecting and organizing information over time, from multiple sources, and using a variety of methods.

Autonomy. The state of being able to exist and operate independently, of being self-sufficient rather than dependent on others.

Baby Biographies. One of the first methods of child study, these narratives were written accounts by parents of what their babies did and said, usually in the form of a diary or log.

Back to Basics. A movement of the 1970s and 1980s prompted by a desire for schools to return to teaching the "basic" skills usually associated with academic learning, such as reading, writing, and arithmetic.

Baseline. A picture of the status of a child, teacher, or environment that serves as the basis for evaluation and later comparison.

Basic Emotions. Those emotions that are present and observable in the newborn or within the first few months of life; they include happiness, interest, surprise, disgust, distress, fear, anger, and sadness.

Basic Needs. Conditions, described by Abraham Maslow and other humanists, that are necessary for growth; these needs, such as physiologic conditions and safety and security, are critical for a person's survival.

Behavior Model. A guidance and behavior technique based on the adult's actions and behavior as an example to follow.

Behavior Swings. Shifts from one behavior to another, usually by a sharp change in what one is doing; e.g., from highly active to motionless or from gregarious to shy.

Behaviorist Theory. A psychological theory developed in the United States in the 20th century, which states that all important aspects of behavior and people are learned and can be modified or changed by varying external conditions.

Bias. A tendency that prevents an unprejudiced consideration of a question, person, or action; a prejudice or favoritism that can affect one's thinking or behavior.

Bicognitive Development. A term coined by Ramirez and Casteneda (see Chapter 4) to describe a set of experiences and environments that promote children's ability to use more than one mode of thinking or linguistic system. Each of us grows up with a preferred cognitive style, such as global or analytic, field dependent or field independent, seeing the parts vs. seeing the whole, as well as a linguistic style. For true cultural democracy to take place, we need to develop a flexibility to switch learning styles or cognitive modes (i.e., develop bicognitive abilities) and have an awareness of and respect for differing cognitive styles.

Bilingualism. The acquisition of two languages during the first years of life; using or being able to use two languages.

Brainstorming. The process of thinking that involves bringing up as many ideas as possible about a subject, person, event, etc.

Building Block Years. The phrase refers to the foundation years of early childhood; namely, the first eight years of life in which the basic skills of life and future learning is set, such as locomotor skills of walking and manipulating, cognitive skills of language/literacy and thinking, and affective skills of social interaction, personal identity, and self-expression.

Cephalocaudal. In the direction from head (cephalic) to toe (caudal, of the tail or hind part of the body), as in how children develop physically.

Cerebral Palsy. A disorder that is the result of damage to a certain part of the brain (motor cortex); CP, as it is commonly called, is a nonprogressive disorder (does not get worse as the child grows older); usually movement dysfunction is paired with some intellectual and perceptual impairment.

Checklist. A modified child study technique that uses a list of items for comparison, such as a "yes/no" checklist for the demonstration of a task.

Child Abuse. Violence in the form of physical maltreatment, abusive language, and sexual harassment or misuse of children.

Child Care Center. A place for care of children for a large portion of their waking day; includes basic caretaking activities of eating, dressing, resting, toileting, as well as playing and learning time.

Child-Centered Approach. The manner of establishing educational experiences that takes into consideration children's ways of perceiving and learning; manner of organizing a classroom, schedule, and teaching methods with an eye toward the child's viewpoint.

Child Neglect. The act or situation of parents' or other adults' inattention to a child's basic health needs of adequate food, clothing, shelter, and health care; child neglect may also include not noticing a child or not paying enough attention in general.

Church-Related Schools. Educational programs affiliated with a church or religious organization; they may have a direct relationship with the church by including religious education, by employing church members as teachers, or by being housed in a church building and using the facilities for a fee.

Classical Conditioning. The most common and basic category of learning in behaviorist theory, involving an association between a stimulus and a response so that a reflex response (eye-blinking, salivating, etc.) occurs *whenever* a neutral and new stimulus is activated (a bell for a light, food, etc.); conditioned-response experiments conforming to the pattern of Pavlov's experiment, sometimes known as "stimulus substitution."

Classification. The ability to group like objects in sets by a specific characteristic.

Classist. A biased or discriminating attitude based on distinctions made between social or economic classes.

Clinical Method. An information-gathering technique, derived from therapy and counseling fields, in which the adult observes and then interacts with the client (in this case, children) by asking questions and posing ideas to the person or group being observed.

Coacting. A situation in which the participants simply act together in a spontaneous way; a goal is not required, as in cooperation, and may be one-on-one rather than in groups; a necessary prerequisite to cooperation is the ability to engage in coactivity.

Cognition. The act or process of knowing, thinking, and perceiving. Cognition involves perceptual, intellectual, and emotional skills that begin as a child makes connections among objects and people and later extends to formulating mental representations.

Cognitive Confusion. State of being unsure or forgetful about what is already known, such as becoming perplexed about things or facts already learned.

Cognitive Theory. The psychological theory developed by Jean Piaget and others; the theory focuses on thought processes and how they change with age and experience; this point of view contrasts with the stimulus-response aspects of behaviorist theory.

Collaborated/Assisted Learning. A type of teaching-learning experience in which a child is helped by another, usually more skilled, person, often an older child or adult; this kind of learning is highly regarded in Vygotsky's theory of child development.

Compensatory Education. Education designed to supply what is thought to be lacking or missing in children's experiences or ordinary environments.

Competency-Based Assessment. Evaluation in which a teacher is judged or rated in comparison with a predetermined set of skills, or competencies, related to the job.

Complex Emotions. Those emotions that emerge in the child after infancy; these include shame, guilt, envy, and pride.

Comprehensive. Inclusive, covering completely, such as a program for children that concerns itself with the physical, intellectual, social, emotional, creative, and health needs of the children.

Concrete. Concerning the immediate experience of actual things or events; specific and particular rather than general or symbolic.

Connected Knowledge. That kind of knowledge and information that is connected to the child in ways that are real and relevant to that individual; also known as meaningful knowledge in Piagetian terms, it is elaborated by Gilligan (see Chapter 4) and others.

Constructivism. A theory of learning, developed from the principles of children's thinking by Piaget and implemented in programs as those in Reggio Emilia, Italy, which states that individuals learn through adaptation. The "constructivist" model of learning posits that children are not passive receptacles into which knowledge is poured but rather are active at making meaning, testing out theories, and trying to make sense of the world and themselves. Knowledge is subjective as each person creates personal meaning out of experiences and integrates new ideas into existing knowledge structures.

Continuing Education. The commitment of teachers to learning new approaches and ideas and to continuing to challenge themselves to higher levels of learning and competence.

Continuum. Something that is continuous; an uninterrupted, ordered sequence.

Core Values. The basic purposes or issues a professional group acknowledges as common concerns to all its members.

Cortisol. Hormone released when the brain perceives a threat or stress.

Cultural Pluralism. A state or society in which members of diverse ethnic, racial, or cultural groups maintain participation in and development of their traditional culture within the common society.

Culturally Appropriate Curriculum. Curriculum that helps children understand the way individual histories, families of origins, and ethnic family cultures make us similar to and yet different from others.

Custodial. Those tasks relating to guardianship of a child's basic needs for food, clothing, and shelter; they include providing for eating, dressing, toileting, resting, and appropriate protection from physical hardships such as weather, danger, etc.

Decoding. Converting from code into ordinary language; in terms of language development, decoding is the process of making sense out of printed letters or words.

Deficiency Needs. In Maslow's theory, those needs without which a person will have insufficient resources to survive.

Demographics. The statistical graphics of a population, especially showing average age, income, etc.

Dendrites. Branches of brain cells that reach out to make connections with other cells.

Development Tasks. Those functions or work to be done by children at a particular point in their development.

Developmental Schedule. Arrangement of a daily plan for children that is based on both individual and group levels of development.

Developmentally Appropriate Practice (DAP). That which is suitable or fitting to the development of the child; refers to those teaching practices that are based on the observation and responsiveness to children as learners with developing abilities who differ from one another by rate of growth and individual differences, rather than of differing amounts of abilities. It also refers to learning experiences that are relevant to and respectful of the social and cultural aspects of the children and their families.

Dialect. A variation of a language, sufficiently different from the original to become a separate entity but not different enough to be considered as a separate language.

Diary Descriptions. A form of observation technique that involves making a comprehensive narrative record of behavior, in diary form.

Disability. A measurable impairment or incapacity that may be moderate to severe. The Individuals with Disabilities Act defines 13 categories that identify specific limitations or challenges, such as hearing, speech, visual, or orthopedic impairments. Individuals who are classified with one or more impairments may be eligible for early intervention and special education classes.

Discipline. Ability to follow an example or to follow rules; the development of self-control or control in general, such as by imposing order on a group. In early childhood terms, discipline means everything adults do and say to influence children's behavior.

Disequilibrium. Loss of balance, or a period of change.

Divergent Thinking. The processes of thought and perception that involve taking a line of thought or action different from what is the norm or common; finding ideas that branch out rather than converge and center on one answer.

Documentation. Keeping written records of events, progress, correspondence, etc.

Down Syndrome. A genetic abnormality that results in mongolism, one of the most common and easily identified forms of mental retardation.

Downshifting. A process by which the brain reacts to perceived threat. The brain/mind learns optimally when appropriately challenged; however, should the person sense a threat or danger (either physical or emotional), the brain will become less flexible and revert to primitive attitudes and procedures (downshift).

Dramatic Play. Also known as imaginative play, this is a common form of spontaneous play in which children use their imagination and fantasy as part of the setting and activity.

Dynamic. Having energy or effective action; a basic skill is one with consequences that will motivate the child, affecting development or stability.

Early Childhood Education. Education in the early years of life; the field of study that deals mainly with the learning and experiences of children from infancy through the primary years (up to approximately eight years of age).

Early Learning Standards. Statements that describe expectations for the learning and development of young children across the domains of: health and physical well-being; social and emotional well-being; approaches to learning; language development and symbol systems; and general knowledge about the world around them (CCSSO, 2005).

Ebonics. Term used to describe "black English" and the center of a controversy in the late 1990s over whether such language is a dialect of standard English or a separate language altogether.

Eclectic. Choosing what appears to be best in various doctrines, methods, styles; comprising elements drawn from various sources.

Ecology of the Family. The concept of viewing the child in the context of his or her impact on the family and the family's impact on the child; stresses the interrelationship of the various family members with one another.

Ecosystems. A community of interacting organisms and their physical environment; a term Bronfenbrenner uses.

Educaring. A concept of teaching as both educating and care giving; coined by Magda Gerber in referring to people working with infants and toddlers.

Egocentric. Self-centered; regarding the self as the center of all things; in Piaget's theory, young children think using themselves as the center of the universe or as the entire universe.

Elaboration. The act of expanding language; developing language by building complex structures from simple ones and adding details.

Emergent Curriculum. A process for curriculum planning that draws on teachers' observations and children's interests. Plans emerge from daily life interests and issues. This approach takes advantage of children's spontaneity and teachers' planning.

Emergent/Early Literacy. The process of building upon prereading skills in a child-centered fashion, so that the ability to read evolves from children's direct experiences.

Emotional Framework. The basic "feeling" structure of a classroom that determines the tone and underlying sensibilities that affect how people feel and behave while in class.

Employer-Sponsored Child Care. Child care supported in some way by the parents' employers. Support may be financial (as an employee benefit or subsidy) or physical (offering on-site care).

Entry Level. The level of development or behavior that a child shows on beginning a program or group experience; usually an observation-based informal assessment after the first few weeks of school.

Environment. All those conditions that affect children's surroundings and the people in them; the physical, interpersonal, and temporal aspects of an early childhood setting.

Environmental. Forces that are not innate or hereditary aspects of development; in early childhood terms, environmental aspects of growth are all those influences of physical conditions, interpersonal relationships, and world experiences that interact with a person to change the way he or she behaves, feels, and lives.

Equilibration. To balance equally; in Piaget's theory, the thinking process by which a person "makes sense" and puts into balance new information with what is already known.

Ethic of Social Reform. The quality of programs and services needed for children under eight and the education reforms that provide it.

Ethics. A theory or system of oral principles and standards; what is "right and wrong"; one's values; the principles of conduct governing both an individual teacher and the teaching profession.

Ethnocentric. Having one's race as a central interest, or regarding one's race or cultural group as superior to others.

Evaluation. A study to determine or set significance or quality.

Event Sampling. An observation technique that involves defining the event to be observed and coding the event to record what is important to remember about it.

Experimental Procedure. An observation technique that gathers information by establishing a hypothesis, controlling the variables that might influence behavior, and testing the hypothesis.

Expressive Language. Those aspects of language development and skill that deal with expression: pronunciation, vocabulary, and grammar, as well as speaking and articulation.

Extended Discourse. Denoting written or spoken communication that goes on for longer than most; in the case of language development, this is meant to be a conversation between child and adult that serves to extend the child's expressive language skills.

Extrinsic. Originating from or on the outside; external, not derived from one's essential nature.

Family Child Care. Care for children in a small, home-like setting; usually six or fewer children in a family residence.

Feedback Loop. In terms of evaluation, *feedback loop* is used to describe the process whereby an evaluator gives information to a teacher, who in turn uses this information to improve teaching skills.

Fine Motor. Having to do with the smaller muscles of the body and the extremities, such as those in the fingers, toes, and face.

Flexibility. Capable of modification or change; willing or easily moved from one idea to another.

Fluency. The ability to produce many ideas; an easy and ready flow of ideas.

Formal Tests. Evaluation instruments that are administered in a conventional, "testlike" atmosphere for use with groups of children and that may or may not be developed commercially.

Four "I"s. The four components (I, Initiative, Independence, and Interaction) of early childhood curriculum for building self-esteem.

Frames of Mind. A theory of intelligence developed by Gardner that refers to intelligence as a host of different skills and abilities.

Full Inclusion. Providing the "least restrictive environment" for children with physical limitations.

Gender Identity. The characteristics determining who or what a person is; in this case, those social and cultural differences around being male and female.

Gender Role. The function or part played by a person according to the social and cultural expectations of being male and female.

Genes. The biological elements that transmit hereditary characteristics.

Gifted Children. Children who have unusually high intelligence, as characterized by: learning to read spontaneously; being able to solve problems and communicate at a level far advanced from their chronological age; excellent memory; extensive vocabulary; and unusual approaches to ideas, tasks, people.

Gross Motor. Having to do with the entire body or the large muscles of the body, such as the legs, arms, and trunk.

Group Times. Those parts of the program in which the whole class or group is together during one activity, such as music, movement, fingerplays, or stories.

Growth Needs. Conditions, as described by Abraham Maslow and other humanists, that are important to a person's well-being; these needs, such as love and belonging, self-esteem and respect for others, playfulness, truth, beauty, etc., while not critical to a person's survival, are necessary for growth.

Holistic. A viewpoint that takes into account several conceptions of a child or situation to form a wider, more rounded description; in early childhood terms, this view includes a child's history, present status, relationships with others, and the interrelationships of development to arrive at a picture of the child; in medicine, this view includes dealing with a person's mental and emotional state, relationships, etc., as well as body signs.

Humanist Theory. The psychological theory of Abraham Maslow and others; it involves principles of motivation and wellness, centering on people's needs, goals, and successes.

Hypothesis. A tentative theory or assumption made to draw inferences or test conclusions; an interpretation of a practical situation that is then taken as the ground for action.

Identity Crisis. A period of uncertainty or confusion in which a person's sense of self becomes insecure.

IEP. An individualized education plan is a process of planning for the education of children with special needs that involves joint efforts of specialists, teachers, and parents.

Importance of Childhood. Children's health and welfare and the changes in family life.

Inadequacy. The state of being or feeling insufficient, of not being or having "enough"; if feeling discouraged, children will display their feelings of inadequacy by misbehaving.

Inclusion. When a child with a disability is a full-time member of a regular classroom with children who are developing normally as well as with children with special needs.

Inclusive. Those aspects of a program that reflect awareness of and sensitivity to a person's culture, home language, religion, gender, and abilities.

Independent. Not controlled or influenced by others; thinking for oneself and autonomous.

Individualized Curriculum. A course of study developed and tailored to meet the needs and interests of an individual, rather than those of a group without regard for the individual child.

Inductive Guidance. A guidance process in which children are held accountable for their actions and are called on to think about the impact of their behavior on others. Reasoning and problem-solving skills are stressed.

Inference. A conclusion reached by reasoning from evidence or after gathering information, whether direct or indirect.

Informal Assessment. Evaluation based on methods and instruments that are not administered formally, as in paper-and-pencil tests, but rather are done while the subjects are at work or play in their natural environments.

Infusion. The integration of multicultural awareness into the current learning environment. It allows for the integration of many diverse perspectives while maintaining the existing curriculum.

Initiative. An introductory step; in early childhood terms, the energy, capacity, and will to begin taking action.

Integrated Curriculum. A set of courses designed to form a whole; coordination of the various areas of study, making for continuous and harmonious learning.

Integrated Day. A school schedule with no prescribed time periods for subject matter, but rather an environment organized around various interest centers among which children choose in organizing their own learning experiences.

Integrated Development. Growth that occurs in a continuous, interrelated manner; a child's progress as a whole, rather than in separate areas.

Intelligence. The cluster of capabilities that involves thinking (see Chapter 13 for details.)

Interaction. Acting on one another, as in the interplay or reciprocal effect of one child upon another.

Interdependence. Dependence on one another, as in the relationship between teachers' experience in the areas of discipline and their competence at knowing and using appropriate language for discipline.

Interdisciplinary Approach. A method of teaching/learning that draws from sources in more than one field of study: e.g., a course in education that uses background from the fields of medicine, psychology, and social work as well as education itself.

Interest Areas. Similar to learning centers and activity areas; one way to design physical space in a classroom or yard, dividing the space into separate centers among which children move about, rather than assigning them desks.

Interpersonal. Relating to, or involving relationships with, other people; those parts of the environment that have to do with the people in a school setting.

Intervention. Entering into a situation between two or more persons or between a person and an object; to interpose oneself into another's affairs, such as when teachers enter into children's interactions when their behavior calls for some action on the part of an adult.

Intrinsic. Belonging to the essential nature of or originating from within a person or body, such as intrinsic motivation, whereby one needs no external reward in order to do something.

Intuition. The direct perception of a fact or truth without any reasoning process; immediate insight.

Invented Spelling. Children's first attempts at spelling words the way they sound to them, based on their current knowledge of letters and sounds. Far from "correct" ("scnd" for second, "grrn" for green, or "relly" for really), invented spelling becomes more conventional over time.

Job Burnout. Exhaustion and stress from one's job, characterized by a wearing down of body and attitude.

Kindergarten. A school or class for children four to six years old; in the United States, kindergarten is either the first year of formal, public school or the year of schooling before first grade.

Kindergartners. (1) A modern term to describe the children who are attending kindergarten programs; (2) a term used in 19th-century America to describe early childhood practitioners who worked in kindergartens patterned after Froebelian models.

Laboratory Schools. Educational settings whose purposes include experimental study; schools for testing and analysis of educational and/or psychological theory and practice, with an opportunity for experimentation, observation, and practice.

Latchkey Children. Children who are left home after school unattended or unsupervised by an adult; children who are responsible after school for themselves and perhaps younger siblings while their parents/guardians are not at home, usually working; such children have a "latchkey" (housekey) to let themselves into an empty home. Also referred to as "self-care."

Laterality. Of or relating to the side, as in children having an awareness of what is situated on, directed toward, or coming from either side of themselves.

Learning Centers. Similar to interest areas and activity areas; hubs or areas in a classroom designed to promote learning; the classroom is arranged in discrete areas for activity, and children move from one area to another rather than stay at an assigned desk or seat.

Learning Styles. A child's preferred method of integrating knowledge and experiences.

Least Restrictive Environment (LRE). Under the Individuals with Disabilities Education Act (IDEA), a child with identified special needs is entitled to a placement into an environment that is most like that of other children in which the child can succeed; this refers to the physical location of the child's learning and how the child will be taught, so the preference is that the child be included in regular education activities as much as possible.

Licensing. The process of fulfilling legal requirements, standards and regulations for operating child care facilities.

Limits. The boundaries of acceptable behavior beyond which actions are considered misbehavior and unacceptable conduct; the absolute controls an adult puts on children's behavior.

Linchpin. Something that serves to hold together the elements of a situation.

Log/Journal. A form of observation technique that involves making a page of notes about children's behavior in a cumulative journal.

Logical Mathematical Knowledge. One of three types of knowledge in Piagetian theory; the component of intelligence that uses thinking derived from logic.

Looping. The practice of keeping a teacher and a group of children in a class together for two or more years.

Mainstreaming. The process of integrating handicapped children into classrooms with the nonhandicapped.

Maturation. The process of growth whereby a body matures regardless of, and relatively independent of, intervention such as exercise, experience, or environment.

Maturation Theory. A set of ideas based on the notion that the sequence of behavior and the emergence of personal characteristics develop more through predetermined growth processes than through learning

and interaction with the environment; the theory of growth and development proposed and supported by Dr. Arnold Gesell and associates.

Meaningful Knowledge. The form of knowing that is learned within the context of what is already known; that knowledge that has meaning because it has particular significance of value to an individual.

Merit Pay. A system for teachers that gives pay bonuses for excellent teaching.

Methode Clinique. A kind of information-gathering technique, first used extensively by Jean Piaget, that involves observing children and asking questions as the situation unfolds. The purpose of this technique is to elicit information about how children are thinking as they behave naturally.

Misbehavior. Improper behavior or conduct.

Miseducation. David Elkind's term describing the end result of contemporary parents rushing their children into formal instruction too early.

Mixed-Age Groups. The practice of placing children of several levels, generally one year apart, into the same classroom. Also referred to as family grouping, heterogeneous grouping, multiage grouping, vertical grouping, and ungraded classes.

Modeling. A part of behavior theory, modeling is a way of learning social behavior that involves observing a model (either real, filmed, or animated) and mimicking its behavior, thus acquiring new behavior.

Multiple Intelligences. A theory of intelligence, proposed by Howard Gardner, that outlines several different kinds of intelligence, rather than the notion of intelligence as measured by standardized testing, such as the IQ (see Frames of Mind).

Myelination. The forming of the myelin sheath, the material in the membrane of certain cells in the brain; the development of the myelination of the brain seems to parallel Piagetian stages of cognitive development.

Narratives. A major observation technique that involves attempting to record nearly everything that happens, in as much detail as possible, as it happens. Narratives include several subtypes such as baby biographies, specimen descriptions, diary descriptions, and logs or journals.

Nature/Nurture Controversy. The argument regarding human development that centers around two opposing viewpoints; *nature* refers to the belief that it is a person's genetic, inherent character that determines development; *nurture* applies to the notion that it is the sum total of experiences and the environment that determine development.

Negative Reinforcement. Response to a behavior that decreases the likelihood that the behavior will recur; for instance, a teacher's glare might stop a child from whispering at group time, and from then on, the anticipation of such an angry look could reinforce not whispering in the future.

Networking. Making connections with others who can further career and professional opportunities.

Nonpunitive. Methods that do not involve or aim at punishment; for instance, letting a child be hungry later when he refuses to eat at snack time is a nonpunitive method of enforcing the need to snack with the group; hunger is a natural and logical consequence of the child's behavior rather than a punishment meted out by the teacher (such as scolding or threatening).

Norm. An average or general standard of development or achievement, usually derived from the average or median of a large group; a pattern or trait taken to be typical of the behavior, skills, or interests of a group.

Objectivity. The quality or state of being able to see what is real and realistic, as distinguished from subjective and personal opinion or bias.

Observational Learning. Any acquired skills or knowledge having to do with interacting with others; in Bandura's Social Learning theory, observational learning occurs when children watch other people directly or in film, etc., and imitate what they have seen in the model.

Open-ended. Activities or statements that allow a variety of responses, as opposed to those that allow only one response; anything organized to allow for variation.

Open School. A style of education, developed in progressive American schools and in the British infant schools, that is organized to encourage freedom of choice and that does not use predetermined roles and structure as the basis of education; an educational setting whose ultimate goal and base for curriculum is the development of the individual child, rather than of programmed academic experiences.

Operant Conditioning. A category of learning in behavior theory that involves a relation between a stimulus and a response. The response is learned, rather than reflexive, and is gradually and carefully developed through reinforcement of the desired behavior as it occurs in response to the stimulus; behavior leading to a reward.

Organic Reading. A system of learning to read, popularized by Sylvia Ashton-Warner, that lets children build their own vocabulary with the words they choose.

Out-of-School Time Care. Programs for school-age children that take place before and after their regular school day.

Parent Cooperative Schools. An educational setting organized by parents for their young children, often with parental control and/or support in the operation of the program itself.

Pedagogista. A person trained in early childhood education who meets weekly with the teachers in the schools of Reggio Emilia, Italy.

Pediatrician. A medical specialist in pediatrics, the branch of medicine dealing with children, their development, care, and diseases.

Peer Interactions. Associations with people of the same age group or with those one considers equals.

Perceptual-Motor Development. The growth of a person's ability to move (motor) and perceive (perceptual) together; perceptual-motor activity involves the body and the mind together, to co-ordinate movement.

Performance-Based Assessment. Evaluation based on observable, specific information on what a teacher actually does (performance while on the job).

Philosophy. Concepts expressing one's fundamental beliefs; in early childhood educational terms, the beliefs, ideas, and attitudes of our profession.

Phobia. A strong, exaggerated, and illogical fear of an object or class of things, people, etc.; one of several reactions children often have to divorce.

Phonemes. Language sounds; the smallest units of meaningful speech; two examples of phonemes are /a/ (as in hat) and /p/ (as in sip).

Phonemic Awareness. Having knowledge or perception of the distinct units of sounds that distinguish one word from another; in English this would include buh [b], puh [p], and sss [s], among others.

Physical Environment. Having to do with equipment and material, room arrangement, the outdoor space, and facilities available.

Physical Knowledge. One of three types of knowledge in Piagetian theory; that knowledge that is learned through external, sensory experiences.

Pluralism. (1) A theory that holds to the notion that there is more than one kind of reality or correct way of perceiving and acting upon the world; (2) a state in which members of diverse ethnic, racial, religious, or social groups participate in their traditional cultures while still belonging to the common society.

Portfolio. An intentional compilation of materials and resources, collected over a period of time that provides evidence for others to review.

Portfolio-based Assessment. An evaluation of a teacher's work using materials, journals, and other resources compiled over a period of time.

Positive Reinforcement. A response to a behavior that increases the likelihood that the behavior will be repeated or increased; for instance, if a child gets attention and praise for crawling, it is likely that the crawling will increase—thus, the attention and praise were positive reinforcers for crawling.

Positive Stress. Refers to an amount of strain or tension that encourages a person to be active and challenged rather than overwhelmed or discouraged.

Power Assertive Discipline. Harsh, punitive discipline methods that rely on children's fear of punishment rather than on the use of reason and understanding. Hitting and spanking are examples of power assertion.

Practice Teaching. The period of "internship" that students experience when working in a classroom with supervision, as opposed to having a role as a regular working staff member.

Precedent. Something done or said that serves as an example or rule to authorize or justify other acts of the same or similar kind; an earlier occurrence of something similar.

Precursor. What precedes and indicates the approach of another; predecessor or forerunner.

Prejudices. Ideas and attitudes that arc already formed about other people, situations, ideas, etc., before hearing or experiencing full or sufficient information; in teaching terms, those attitudes or biases that may be based less on mature thought and reasoning than on incomplete or nonexistent personal experiences.

Prepared Environment. The physical and interpersonal surroundings of an educational setting that are planned and arranged in advance with the group of children in mind.

Prerequisite. Something necessary or essential to carrying out an objective or performing an activity; when early childhood teachers determine what skills children will need in order to successfully engage in an activity, they are clarifying the prerequisites for that activity.

Private (Inner) Speech. The language children use for self-guidance and self-direction, as well as for helping them think about their behavior and plan for action; once known as "egocentric speech," it is used for self-regulation.

Professional. One engaged and participating in a profession and accepting the technical and ethical standards of that profession; in early childhood terms, one who has accumulated methods, course work, and teaching experience with young children along with attitudes of competency, flexibility, and continual learning.

Professional Confidentiality. Spoken, written, or acted on in strict privacy, such as keeping the names of children or schools in confidence when discussing observations.

Professional Organizations. Those associations developed for the purpose of extending knowledge and teaching/learning opportunities in the field of education.

Professionalism. The competence or skill expected of a professional; in early childhood education, this includes a sense of identity, purpose to engage in developmentally appropriate practices, a commitment to ethical teaching and to child advocacy, and participation in the work as a legitimate livelihood.

Project Approach. An in-depth study of a particular subject or theme by one or more children. Exploration of themes and topics over a period of days or weeks. Working in small groups, children are able to accommodate various levels of complexity and understanding to meet the needs of all the children working on the project.

Prosocial. Behaviors that are considered positive and social in nature, such as sharing, inviting, including, and offering help or friendship.

Proximal to Distal. In the direction from the center of the body (proximal) toward the outer part (distal, far from the center), as in the way children's bodies develop.

Psychodynamic Theory. The psychological theory of Dr. Sigmund Freud and others; it asserts that the individual develops a basic personality core in childhood and that responses stem from personality organization and emotional problems as a result of environmental experiences.

Psychometric. Having to do with measurement of mental traits, abilities, and processes; usually a formal assessment using a standardized test.

Psychosocial. Those psychological issues that deal with how people relate to others and the problems that arise on a social level; a modification by Erikson of the psychodynamic theories of Freud with attention to social and environmental problems of life.

Punishment. The act of inflicting a penalty for an offense or behavior.

Racist. Attitudes, behavior, or policies that imply either a hatred or intolerance of other race(s) or involving the idea that one's own race is superior and has the right to rule or dominate others.

Rating Scale. A modified child study technique similar to a checklist that classifies behavior according to grade or rank, such as using the descriptors "always, sometimes, never" to describe the frequency of a certain behavior.

Readiness. The condition of being ready, such as being in the state or stage of development so that the child has the capacity to understand, be taught, or engage in a particular activity.

Receptive Language. Those aspects of language development and skill that deal with the ability to receive messages: listening, understanding, and responding.

Reciprocal. The stage of children's friendship in which friendship is given or felt by each toward the other; a kind of give-and-take or two-way relationship, this is the stage most often seen in the latter part of the early childhood years.

Reinforcement. A procedure, such as reward or punishment, that changes a response to a stimulus; the act of encouraging a behavior to increase in frequency.

Reinforcers. Rewards in response to a specific behavior, thus increasing the likelihood that behavior will recur; reinforcers may be either social (praise) or nonsocial (food) in nature and may or may not be deliberately controlled.

Rote Knowledge. A form of knowing that is learned by routine or habit and without thought of the meaning.

Roughhousing. Rough and disorderly, but playful, behavior.

Routines. Regular procedures; habitual, repeated or regular parts of the school day; in early childhood programs, routines are those parts of the program schedule that remain constant, such as indoor time followed by cleanup and snack, regardless of what activities are being offered within those time slots.

Running Record. The narrative form of recording behavior; this kind of descriptive record of one's observations involves writing down all behavior as it occurs.

Scaffolding. A useful structure to support a child in learning. A child who gets advice or hints to help master an activity is said to have scaffolding learning, a term Vygotsky used.

Schema. A plan, scheme, or framework that helps make an organizational pattern from which to operate; in Piaget's theory, cognitive schemas are used for thinking.

Screening. Evaluations to determine a child's readiness for a particular class, grade, or experience.

Self-Actualization. The set of principles set forth by Abraham Maslow for a person's wellness or ability to be the most that a person can be; the state of being that results from having met all the basic and growth needs.

Self-Awareness. An awareness of one's own personality or individuality; in teaching terms, an ability to understand one's self and assess personal strengths and weaknesses.

Self-Care. A current description for latchkey children (see Latchkey Children).

Self-Concept. A person's view and opinion of self; in young children, the concept of self develops as they interact with the environment (objects, people, etc.); self-concept can be inferred in how children carry themselves, approach situations, use expressive materials such as art, etc.

Self-Correcting. Materials or experiences that are built or arranged so that the person using them can act automatically to correct errors, without needing another person to check or point out mistakes.

Self-Esteem. The value we place on ourselves; how much we like or dislike who we are; self-respect.

Self-Help. The act of helping or providing for oneself without dependence on others; in early childhood terms, activities that a child can do alone, without adult assistance.

Self-Regulation. The term used to describe a child's capacity to plan and guide the self. A disposition or part of the personality (rather than a skill or behavior such as self-control), self-regulation is a way of monitoring one's own activity flexibly over changing circumstances.

Sensorimotor. Relating to or functioning in both sensory and motor aspects of body activity.

Sensory. Having to do with the senses or sensation, as in an awareness of the world as it looks, sounds, feels, smells, tastes.

Separation Process. The act and procedure that occur when parents leave a child at school.

Sequential Learning. Learning based on a method of consecutive steps; an arrangement of concepts or ideas in a succession of related steps so that what is learned results in continuous development.

Seriation. The process of sequencing from beginning to end or in a particular series or succession.

Sex Differences. The biological differences between males and females.

Sex-Role Stereotyping. A standardized mental picture or set of attitudes that represents an oversimplified opinion of people's abilities or behavior according to their sex; overgeneralizing a person's skills or behavior on the basis of an inequitable standard of sex differences.

Sexist. Attitudes or behavior based on the traditional stereotype of sexual roles that includes a devaluation or discrimination based on a person's sex.

Shadow Study. A modified child study technique that profiles an individual at a given moment in time; similar to diary description, the shadow study is a narrative recorded as the behavior happens.

Simultaneous/Successive Acquisition. The two major ways second-language learning occurs. Simultaneous acquisition happens if a child is exposed to two languages from birth. Successive acquisition occurs as a child with one language begins to learn another language.

Social Action. Individual or group behavior that involves interaction with other individuals or groups, especially organized action toward social reform.

Social Capital. The richness and resources that social relationships provide for a child.

Social Cognition. The application of thinking to personal and social behavior; giving meaning to social experience.

Social Competence. The ability to successfully deal with social interactions and problems; the skills and personal knowledge to deal with others.

Social Knowledge. One of three types of knowledge in Piagetian theory; that knowledge that is learned about and from people, such as family and ethnic culture, group behavior, social mores, etc.

Social Learning Theory. A psychological theory developed in the 20th century by Albert Bandura of Stanford University, which states that learning often takes place by observing and modeling others.

Social Mores. Standards of conduct and behavior that are determined by society, as opposed to those established by family or personal preference.

Social Referencing. The process used to gauge one's own response to a situation by relying on another person's emotional reaction, such as a child who looks to a teacher after falling down before crying or getting up.

Social Reform. The ethic of social reform is a major theme in early childhood education and history, and refers to the idea that schooling for young children will lead to social change and improvement.

Social Skills. Strategies children learn to enable them to respond appropriately in many environments.

Socialization. The process of learning the skills, appropriate behaviors, and expectations of being part of a group, particularly society at large.

Sociocentric. Oriented toward or focused on one's social group rather than on oneself.

Sociocultural. Aspects of theory or development that refer to the social and cultural issues; key descriptor of Vygotsky's theory of development.

Sociodramatic Play. At least two children participating in dramatic play or play that involves two basic elements; imitation and make-believe.

Software. The programs used to direct the operation of a computer, as opposed to the physical device on which they are run (known as "hardware").

Spatial. Having to do with the nature of space, as in the awareness of the space around a person's body.

Special-Needs Children. Children whose development and/or behavior require help or intervention beyond the scope of the ordinary classroom or adult interactions.

Specific Development. Area of a person's growth and maturation that can be defined distinctly, such as physical, social, emotional, intellectual, and creative growth.

Specimen Description. A form of narrative observations technique that involves taking on-the-spot notes about a child (the "specimen") to describe behavior.

Spontaneous Play. The unplanned, self-selected activity in which a child freely participates.

Standardized Testing. Formal assessment techniques whose results have been tabulated for many children and thus have predetermined standards, or norms, for evaluating the child being tested.

Stewardship. Responsibility for judicious management of resources; the obligation assumed by an individual or agency to act responsibly in the use of both personal and natural resources.

Stimulus–Response. The kind of psychological learning, first characterized in behavior theory, that makes a connection between a response and a stimulus; that is, the kind of learning that takes place when pairing something that rouses or incites an activity with the activity itself in such a way that the stimulus (such as a bell) will trigger a response (such as salivating).

Stress. The physical and emotional reactions and behaviors that come from having to cope with difficult situations beyond one's capabilities.

Superhero. Those characters who embody a higher nature and powers beyond ordinary human abilities, such as Superman, Wonder Woman, etc.

Support System. A network of people who support each other in their work and advancement.

Surrogate. Substitute, such as a teacher acting in the place of the parent, a school toy taking the place of a blanket from home, a thumb taking the place of a pacifier.

Tabula Rasa. A mind not affected yet by experiences, sensations, and the like. In John Locke's theory, a child was born with this "clean slate" upon which all experiences were written.

Tactile. Perceptible or able to be learned through the sense of touch.

Teaching Objectives. A set of goals teachers set for themselves as they plan activities for children; these goals remind teachers what they will do to help children learn.

Team Teaching. Group-based manner of teaching, where a group composed of people with varying skills, experience, and training teach jointly.

Temporal. Having to do with time and time sequence; in the early childhood setting, refers to scheduling and how time is sequenced and spent, both at home and in school.

Theory. A group of general principles, ideas, or proposed explanations for explaining some kind of phenomenon; in this case, child development.

Time Sampling. A form of observational technique that involves observing certain behavior and settings within a prescribed time frame.

Tourist Approach. A curriculum theme or experience that provides only a superficial look at a culture through differences rather than similarities.

Traditional Nursery School. The core of early childhood educational theory and practice; program designed for children aged two-and-a-half to five years of age, which may be a part- or an all-day program.

Transactional Model. A model of education that describes the interaction of an individual with one or more persons, especially as influenced by their assumed roles. This model implies that the role of parent, child, or teacher has an effect on what and how information is taught and learned.

Transcurricular. Able to be used or applied in a variety of situations or activities.

Transitions. Changes from one state or activity to another; in early childhood terms, transitions are those times of change in the daily schedule (whether planned or not), such as from being with a parent to being alone in school, from playing with one toy to choosing another, from being outside to being inside, etc.

Transmission Model. A model of education describing the transference of information directly from one person to another, such as in the sense of passing on knowledge directly from teacher to child.

Transmitting Values. A major theme in early childhood education and history, helping children learn and accept basic values of the family and community has been one of the reasons for education for centuries.

Trauma. A deeply distressing or disturbing experience.

Unconscious. Not conscious, without awareness, occurring below the level of conscious thought.

Undifferentiated. The stage of children's friendships in which children do not distinguish between "friend" and "person I'm playing with," considered the first stage, usually from infancy into the preschool years.

Unilateral. The stage of children's friendships in which children think of friendship as involving one side only; that is, a one-way situation in that a "friend" is "someone who does what I want him to do," usually spanning the preschool years and into early primary.

Unobtrusive. Being inconspicuous, as in remaining in the background while observing children.

Upward Evaluation. Assessment procedure in which employees evaluate their superiors.

Vicariously. Experienced or realized through the imagination or the participation of another, rather than from doing it oneself, as in learning vicariously about something by listening to a story.

Volatile. Easily aroused; tending to erupt into violent action or explosive speech or behavior.

Webbing. A process through which teachers create a diagram based on a topic or theme. It is a planning tool for curriculum and includes as many resources as teachers can name.

Whole Language. The area of graphic language development that refers to a particular way in which language, particularly reading and writing, is learned; whole language refers to that movement within primary education that emphasizes an integrated and literary-based approach rather than a phonics, decoding-skills approach.

Word Pictures. Descriptions of children that depict, in words, norms of development; in this text, these are age-level charts that describe common behaviors and characteristics, particularly those that have implications for teaching children (in groups, for curriculum planning, with discipline and guidance).

Working Portfolio. A type of child portfolio that is used and added onto regularly, documenting a child's skills and behavior over time. Rather than one that collects only a child's exemplary work or everything a child has done, this type of portfolio attempts to capture key documentation to demonstrate a child's growth.

Zone of Proximal Development. The term in Vygotsky's sociocultural theory that defines which children can learn. Interpersonal and dynamic, the zone refers to the area a child can master (skill, information, etc.) with the assistance of another skilled person; below that, children can learn on their own; above the limit are areas beyond the child's capacity to learn, even with help.

Subject Index

A

Abuse, child, 597–600
Academic redshirting, 77
Accommodation, 143
Accreditation, 597
Accreditation movement, 37
Active listening, 293–294
Active problem solving, 297, 298
Activity centers, 401, 403
Adaptive processes of
    assimilation and
    accommodation, 143, 144
ADHD predominately
    hyperactive-impulsive type
    (ADHD-HI), 117
ADHD predominately inattentive
    type (ADHD-I), 117
Adults, skills learned with,
    551–552
Advocacy, 208–209, 618–621
Affective domain, 526–528
Affiliations, professional, 207
Age-level characteristics, 100
Aggression, role of, 141
Aggressive and disruptive
    behavior, 300–301
AIDS, children and, 600
Ainsworth, Mary, 174
Anti-bias approach, 198
Anti-bias curriculum, 38, 413
Anti-bias environment, 337–339
Applying cognitive theory to
    work with children, 148–149
Art, 574–576
Articulation, 493–494
Asperger syndrome (AS), 117–118
Assessment
    as administrative tool, 258
    authentic, 263–265
    baseline for, 248, 249
    challenges and possible
      pitfalls of, 262
    entry-level, 248, 249
    to monitor progress, 248,
      250–253

observation and, 232–233
    as planning tool, 254–256
    reasons for, 246, 248–262
Assimilation, 143
Associative play, 164
Atelierista, 422
Attachment, role of, 160–163
Attention-deficit/hyperactivity
    disorder (ADHD), 116–117
Attention span, 462
Attitude crystallization, 610
Audiovisual resources, 519–520
Auditory learner, 395
Authentic assessment, 263–265
Authentic inclusion, 389
Automobile safety, 349

B

Baby biographies, 238
Balance, role of, 134
Balancing process of
    equilibrium, 143
Bandura, Albert, 139, 174
Bank Street: Developmental-
    Interaction Model, 420
Bank Street College of
    Education, 27, 57
Basic emotions, 530
Beginning teacher
    guidelines for, 217
    student teacher, 217–219
Behavior, understanding,
    278–279
    active listening, 293–294
    active problem solving,
      297, 298
    aggressive and disruptive
      behavior, 300–301
    behavior model, teacher
      as a, 289
    choices, giving, 295
    cultural factors, 283–285
    culturally appropriate
      guidance, 287
    developmental factors,
      279–280

developmentally appropriate
    guidance, 286–289
discipline, 285, 286
distraction, 297
emotional and social factors,
    282–283
environmental factors, 280–281
factors that affect behavior,
    279–285
guidance, process of, 285
guidance and discipline,
    287–289
guidance strategies, 293–299
"I" messages, 294
ignoring behavior, 293
implications for teaching,
    289–292
individual factors, 281–282
inductive guidance, 292–293
interdependence, 287
natural and logical
    consequences, 297–299
power assertive discipline, 293
punishment, 285, 286
redirecting the activity, 295
reinforcement, positive and
    negative, 294–295
self-discipline, working
    toward, 285–286
setting limits, 295–297
theories, 279
time out, 299
Behavior model, teacher as a, 289
Behaviorist theory, 174
    aggression, role of, 141
    application to work with
      children, 142
    Bandura, Albert, 139
    classical conditioning,
      139–140
    development of, 138
    learning, types of, 139
    modeling, 139, 140–141
    observational learning, 139,
      140–141
    operant conditioning, 139

Name Index